THE MOTLEY BIBLIOGRAPHIES: TWO
Series Editor: John Cavanagh

# UNITED STATES THEATRE

# A BIBLIOGRAPHY
from the beginning to 1990

Robert Silvester

G. K. HALL & CO.
New York

MOTLEY PRESS
Romsey
1993

For

Walter Stump

Published simultaneously in the United States by
G. K. Hall & Co.,
an imprint of Macmillan Publishing Co.,
866 Third Avenue, New York, NY 10022.

ISBN 0-7838-2059-3

©1993 J. P. Cavanagh

Published by Motley Press, PO Box 37, Romsey,
Hampshire SO51 0RD, England

ISBN 0–900281–03–0

Printed by BAS Printers Limited
Typesetting by iO, Hillingdon

# INTRODUCTION

This is the second volume in a series of bibliographies that is planned to encompass the whole of the world's theatrical publication in every culture and in most languages.

These volumes are not isolated works. They are all derived from a common data base, which is continuously corrected and up-dated. At suitable intervals, the appropriate section of the database is off-loaded as the basis for publication in book form. Already on printing, this book will be less comprehensive than the database, as new information is added almost daily. There is no point at which a volume can be said to be complete and probably never will be. However, this is not a reason for delaying a bibliography, which, despite its omissions, is at least an order of magnitude more complete than anything else available, and will be an immediate aid to research. In the case of most countries there is no existing national bibliography in this field, and the series provides the first attempt to provide those areas with a definitive guide to their theatrical literature.

It may be of interest to know that there is currently a file of over a thousand provisional title entries that supplement this present volume. These are for titles not as yet located in physical form, not checked, and hence not listed here. These, together with doubtless many more titles that will surface, and an up-date for the extended time coverage, we hope to include in a second edition after about five years.

It will be realized that we are very anxious to be informed of any corrections, desirable amplifications, or omissions that may be noticed by the users of this volume. Please send them with your comments on such aspects as ease of reference and practicality of classification, so that we may further improve the next edition. We are particularly dependent on readers' reports, since few journals review bibliographies. In any case, most reviewers would probably not have the time nor the occasion to work closely with a bibliography over the period necessary to gain enough experience for evaluation.

Eventually it may be possible to publish in an electronic format, or provide direct access to the database. This depends on the general support received for the series.

JOHN CAVANAGH

# PREFACE

A. *General*

The basic arrangement of the Motley Bibliographies is by culture, not by geography. Consequently this volume on theatre in the United States of America does not cover all kinds of theatrical activity, but is almost entirely devoted to the English cultural tradition. It deals with English language texts, either originating in or translated into English, performed in English by English speaking actors. Additionally, it includes theatre from the Amerindian culture. There is, of course, a rich diversity of other cultural contributions to the history of theatre in the United States: for example, Swedish theatre in Chicago, Yiddish theatre in New York, Chicano theatre in Texas. These will be recorded in the volumes devoted respectively to Scandinavian, Jewish, and Spanish theatre, and other ethnic theatres will be treated similarly.

This is a true bibliography in the sense that it is confined to separate publications: books, pamphlets, and theses. It does not include journal articles.

Titles, except theses, have been physically examined where a copy could be found, and the location is noted. Where this has not been possible, the work has been checked in a library catalogue and the entry marked with an asterisk. No entry has been taken on trust.

Some categories of library material have been omitted: programs and souvenirs of particular productions, unless they contain significant informative or illustrative matter, recordings, slide sets, microforms, and booksellers' catalogues. Periodicals, unless of particular biographical or regional interest, are included only if not recorded in C. J. Stratman: *American theatrical periodicals, 1798-1967: a bibliographical guide (1970)*, or in C. Edwards: *The world guide to performing arts periodicals (1982)*, and will be found in the appropriate sections. A single issue of a normally non-theatrical periodical may be treated as a monograph if its content is substantially theatrical.

Play texts, even when extensively edited, are admitted only if there is important biographical material, substantial production history, or illustrations of productions or scene or costume designs.

Fiction is omitted, except when the text (often by a performer) appears to offer an authentic reproduction of the theatrical conditions and atmosphere of its period. Fictionalized biography is included and, where titles are ambiguous, identified as such.

Each title recorded is, as a general rule, present in the best, normally the latest and most fully revised, edition. Other editions are noted when they contain significant text or illustration not retained in the later edition. Titles are listed chronologically in each classified section, and appear according to the date of the edition cited, not necessarily the date of the first publication which, if different, is noted. Within any one year, listing is in alphabetical order of author, or of the initial word of the title if no author is given.

For books published both in the US and the UK, the UK edition is sometimes the one described. In such cases the US edition is noted and any variations recorded.

Annotation is strictly limited to bibliographical matters; explanations of uninformative title pages, the listing of contents of some collections and anthologies, and other factual information. Value judgments are not offered.

No titles are included that were published after December 1990.

B. *Classification System*

There are three major divisions: A. *Theatre*, B. *Drama*, C. *Music*. Division A emphasizes performance, describing theatres, stage conditions and the lives and work of individuals engaged in production. Division B covers dramatic theory, the history of genres and influences, and the lives and work of dramatists. Although theatre and drama are obviously closely linked, it has been convenient to try to separate them in the classification, referring on the one hand to theatre as the practical expression of drama in performance, and on the other to drama as the literary basis of the theatrical experience. 'Theatre' is used here to cover performing arts dependent on the spoken or sung word, performed live on stage. Dance, mime, circus and puppetry are excluded. Opera, which would have been included by this definition is in fact excluded because it will receive its own subject bibliography later in the series. The only opera titles included are those on the history of opera in a specific state, town, or theatre, since opera and drama have often shared the same theatre. Cinema and television titles are in principle omitted but included if they offer significant theatrical information. Division C is primarily concerned with the musical and the individuals who create and perform it. Musical comedy, which, in view of its now wider basis, we have entitled 'The Musical' as section 17, is intended to be very fully covered. It includes material in this genre in the UK and other countries as well as from the USA, since its development became largely identified with the United States.

Notes on some individual sections, numbered as in the Classification:

1.4 This includes only catalogues of a general nature, whether exhibition, auction or collection. Catalogues devoted to the work of an individual will be listed in the biography sections (8.4, 10.2, 16.2, 17.2), or to a specific theatre or company in 6 or 7.

2.3 Subvention is here covered in general terms. Subvention of specific theatres or plays will be found in the appropriate sections.

4.1 Architecture includes works on cinema buildings if their history or current circumstances involves live entertainment.

4.3 Scene design includes staging, effects and properties. It also extends to dance and opera where such reference is necessary to represent fully the work of particular designers.

4.6 This includes publicity and advertising, contracts and accounting.

4.9 This reflects an increasing interest in the nature, function and influence of the audience.

5.1 This covers works on theatre world-wide, which may make only passing reference to US theatre or even omit it completely, as for example a history of European theatre. The title is included here if it originates in the US, as a reflection of US thinking, and/or forms a record of the influence of other cultures on the American Stage.

5.2 This refers only to US theatre over several historical periods.

5.3-5.6 Titles do not always match parameter dates precisely, but are placed in the group that best reflects their substantive content.

6.1 Covers travelling companies and other inter-regional theatre activities, such as tent theatre.

7. This includes companies, usually not tied to specific theatres, who have achieved distinctive character as touring or occasional groups and/or are the product of distinctive historic events.

8.3 'Tangential' memoirs consist largely of autobiographies and anecdotage by those, often journalists or lawyers, who, while not directly connected with the theatre, were interested enough in it to record their impressions of playgoing and their acquaintance with performers,

8.4 This covers people closely connected with the stage, such as actors, directors, managers, designers and dramatic critics. Sometimes their activities extend to playwriting, in which case their plays are covered here also. Those who were primarily dramatists are listed in 16.2. Where an individual is associated with an event, not itself primarily concerned with the theatre, that has generated a substantial written record, firm selectivity has been applied. An obvious example is J. W. Booth.

9.2 Collected criticism relating to a specific author or work is listed under 16.2.

10 This includes minstrelsy and burlesque, but not specialty acts.

11.1 This covers general works on little theatre and related non-profit theatre movements and activities. Specific theatres and companies will be found under 6.2.

11.2 Although the colleges and universities are among the strongest sources of non-profit theatre, and their work frequently merges with community and summer theatre, it was felt that a separate listing would be helpful.

12.1 and 12.2 In awareness of a bewildering proliferation of educationists' terms, these seek to provide a distinction between dramatic activity by children and theatrical performance for them, while recognizing that the difference is sometimes slight.

13.1 This includes bibliographies of plays that are not included in 1.1, which only covers bibliographies of works on the theatre.

14.1 As with 5.1, this section contains works on world drama, not necessarily including the US, but originating there.

15. This covers adaptations of foreign drama on the US stage and the general influence of other cultures on American drama. It does not include immigrant and other foreign companies or individual performers playing in the US in their own language.

16.2 No attempt is made to cover the work of dramatists in fields other than the drama.

17.2 Where individuals are best remembered for careers outside the theatre, the works recorded are selected for significant theatre coverage. This applies also to 8.4 and 16.2.

18. This includes incidental music and songs in plays, and 'plays-with-music'.

Subject index. This contains the names of persons, places, and subjects mentioned in titles and notes. However, the classified table of contents is itself intended as a basic subject index, and where the information it offers will lead the user to the reference he seeks, such information is not necessarily repeated in the detailed subject index.

Author index. This includes not only the authors and editors of the titles themselves, but also the authors of introductions and contributions.

C. *Bibliographical format*

1. *Authors' names.* These are not necessarily given exactly as they appear on the title-page. The fore-name may be the first, rather than the one used on the title page, to provide easier access to library catalogues in the case of common surnames. Where names have changed through hyphenation or marriage, the tendency has been to follow British Library practice. The names of up to three authors are given individually. Above three, only the first is shown followed by 'et al'. Names are only in [ ] if they are nowhere recorded in the book, not just because they are omitted from the title page. The name is only repeated in the title transcription if its omission would reduce clarity. Personal titles are not shown, and 'Mrs' is included only if there is a possible confusion with the husband. Where the author is not known, the first few words of the title are capitalized to provide a clear beginning to each entry.

2. *Title.* This may be abbreviated, but any deletion is indicated by an ellipsis. Punctuation may be modified for clarity. All information given in a title is given here rather in the notes. If the title is taken from the cover instead of from the title page, it is shown as [cover title], or, if it is taken from a heading on the first page of text, as [drop title]. Series titles are not usually given. Omitted from the transcription are mottoes, references to previous works by the same author, and general descriptions of illustrations. The capitalisation, line arrangement, and typography are not necessarily maintained. Cyrillic titles have been transliterated according to the British Library system.

3. *Collation.* This has been kept as brief as possible, since this is a subject and not an author bibliography. Preliminary pages are given in Roman numerals up to the last such page bearing significant print, whether or not paginated; terminal blank pages are not included. The main text is given as an Arabic numeral, signifying the last page of text. Advertisements are not recorded. If a book is continuously paginated, any use of Roman numerals in the preliminaries is ignored.

4. *Illustrations.* All plates integrally numbered with the text, occupying either a part- or whole-page, are indicated by 'ill. in text'. Plates, *hors texte*, are indicated separately, each leaf of illustration being treated as one plate. If a frontispiece is the only plate, it is shown as 'front.' The use of colour is indicated.

5. *Library code.* This shows the location of the copy described.

| | |
|---|---|
| BP | Birmingham Public Library |
| CB | University of California at Berkeley |
| CSB | University of California at Santa Barbara |
| CSC | University of California at Santa Cruz |
| CSt | Stanford University |
| DFO | Folger Shakespeare Library, Washington DC |
| DL | Library of Congress, Washington DC |
| HW | Winchester Reference Library, Hants |
| L | British Library |
| M | Mottisfont Library |
| MB | Boston Public Library |
| MH | Harvard University Widener Library and Theatre Collection |
| MESM | University of Southern Maine Library |
| O | Oxford University, Bodleian Library |
| P | Private collections |
| SU | University of Southampton, Hartley Library |
| ★ | An asterisk, with or without a library code, indicates that no copy has been seen. A blank space indicates that the entry is a thesis. |

6. *Place of publication*. If the publisher lists several places of business on the title, only the first is shown. Addresses are omitted and the state is not shown unless there is possible ambiguity.

7. *Imprint*. If there is more than one publisher listed on the title, only the first is shown. If two organizations are shown on the imprint, separated by a slash, this means that the first is publishing on behalf of the second. In the case of theses, the publisher is the university, and the type of degree (or the word 'thesis') is given in brackets as part of the imprint.

8. *Date*. Only shown in [ ] if nowhere indicated in the book. The date given is that of the edition described, not necessarily the date of first publication, and is always in Arabic. Dates shown with '?' come before definite dates.

D. *Acknowledgements*

I have many debts of gratitude. Perhaps the greatest is to John Cavanagh, overall editor of the Motley Bibliographies and theatre scholar, whose private collection provided a firm base for this book and whose unique blend of velvet and steel has levered it into existence. Barbara Cavanagh, too, I thank for her unfailing kindness and support. Gwen Hughes has my heartfelt gratitude for a wealth of assistance in tracing and recording and for her limitless diligence and patience. I received the most unstinting and friendly assistance from the many libraries I visited, but would like particularly to thank Jeanne Newlin, Joe Keller and their colleagues in the Harvard Theatre Collection and the staff of the British Library, notably Nina Evans, Michael Maher, and David McGrath. My special thanks must also go to the librarians of the Widener Library at Harvard, Boston Public Library, the Bodleian Library, the University of Southern Maine, the Winchester Reference Library where I was never begrudged valuable space and was treated with the greatest courtesy, King Alfred's College, and the University of Southampton. I am delighted to have an opportunity to thank the many individuals who have given their help; Harriet Baxter in Cambridge, and Walter Stump, Minor Rootes and my other hospitable friends in Maine, made my time in the US a great pleasure. Penny Jowitt, Caroline Silvester and Alison Loftin all took on the thankless work of transcription, and many people supplied me with invaluable information, not least Jane Hallé, James Ellis, Sidney Jowers, and Stephen Archer. Peter Van Peborgh's mastery of the computer made available the capacity of a data base and prevented my destruction of it more than once. My friends in the Hyde Tavern rarely allowed their boredom to show! I thank them for their support as I do all those who have helped me through the long and taxing business of bibliography.

# TABLE OF CONTENTS
# and
# CLASSIFICATION

(References are to title numbers)

INTRODUCTION

PREFACE

**A. THEATRE**
  1. GENERAL REFERENCE
    1.1    Bibliographies      1–67
    1.2    Dictionaries, directories, encyclopedias, glossaries      68–100
    1.3    Iconographies, discographies      101–113
    1.4    Catalogues. Exhibitions and collections      114–165

  2. FEDERAL AND STATE INTERVENTION
    2.1    Legislation      166–171
    2.2    Regulation, censorship and copyright      172–211
    2.3    Economics, subvention and trade unions      212–254

  3. RELIGION
    3.1    Morality      255–323
    3.2    Religion in drama      324–378

  4. THEATRE ARTS
    4.1    Architecture and machinery      379–471
    4.2    Lighting and sound      472–544
    4.3    Stage-design and effects      545–694
    4.4    Costume design      695–733
    4.5    Make-up      734–749
    4.6    Management, administration, and general      750–792
    4.7    Acting      793–1053
    4.8    Directing      1054–1171
    4.9    Audiences      1172–1202

  5. HISTORY
    5.1    International      1203–1263
    5.2    General      1264–1379
    5.3    1665-1850      1380–1425
    5.4    1851-1918      1426–1503
    5.5    1919-1945      1504–1569
    5.6    1946-1990      1570–1657

  6. LOCATION
    6.1    Regions      1658–1700
    6.2    States and towns
        6.2.1    Alabama      1701–1713
        6.2.2    Alaska      1714–1717
        6.2.3    Arizona      1718–1720
        6.2.4    Arkansas      1721–1724

|  |  |  |
|---|---|---|
| 6.2.5 | California | 1725–1818 |
| 6.2.6 | Colorado | 1819–1842 |
| 6.2.7 | Connecticut | 1843–1854 |
| 6.2.8 | Delaware | 1855–1859 |
| 6.2.9 | Florida | 1860–1869 |
| 6.2.10 | Georgia | 1870–1878 |
| 6.2.11 | Hawaii | 1879–1883 |
| 6.2.12 | Idaho | 1884–1885 |
| 6.2.13 | Illinois | 1887-1943 |
| 6.2.14 | Indiana | 1944–1958 |
| 6.2.15 | Iowa | 1959–1972 |
| 6.2.16 | Kansas | 1973–1984 |
| 6.2.17 | Kentucky | 1985–2002 |
| 6.2.18 | Louisiana | 2003–2057 |
| 6.2.19 | Maine | 2058–2061 |
| 6.2.20 | Maryland | 2062–2069 |
| 6.2.21 | Massachusetts | 2070–2146 |
| 6.2.22 | Michigan | 2147–2184 |
| 6.2.23 | Minnesota | 2185–2206 |
| 6.2.24 | Mississippi | 2207–2212 |
| 6.2.25 | Missouri | 2213–2244 |
| 6.2.26 | Montana | 2245-2251 |
| 6.2.27 | Nebraska | 2252–2260 |
| 6.2.28 | Nevada | 2261-2270 |
| 6.2.29 | New Hampshire | 2271 |
| 6.2.30 | New Jersey | 2272–2276 |
| 6.2.31 | New Mexico | 2277–2282 |
| 6.2.32 | New York State | 2283–2297 |
| 6.2.33 | New York City | 2298–2468 |
| 6.2.34 | North Carolina | 2469–2491 |
| 6.2.35 | North Dakota | 2492–2501 |
| 6.2.36 | Ohio | 2502–2553 |
| 6.2.37 | Oklahoma | 2554–2557 |
| 6.2.38 | Oregon | 2558-2567 |
| 6.2.39 | Pennsylvania | 2568–2633 |
| 6.2.40 | Rhode Island | 2634–2636 |
| 6.2.41 | South Carolina | 2637–2648 |
| 6.2.42 | South Dakota | 2649–2655 |
| 6.2.43 | Tennessee | 2656–2672 |
| 6.2.44 | Texas | 2673–2717 |
| 6.2.45 | Utah | 2718–2738 |
| 6.2.47 | Virginia | 2739–2759 |
| 6.2.48 | Washington | 2760–2772 |
| 6.2.49 | Washington DC | 2773–2790 |
| 6.2.50 | West Virginia | 2791–2792 |
| 6.2.51 | Wisconsin | 2793–2808 |
| 6.2.52 | Wyoming | 2809–2811 |
| 6.3 | Other countries | 2812 |

## 7. THEATRE COMPANIES, CLUBS, SOCIETIES     2813–2960

## 8. THEATRICAL BIOGRAPHY
| | | |
|---|---|---|
| 8.1 | Collected notices and biographical dictionaries | 2961–3126 |
| 8.2 | Collections of anecdotes, and satires | 3127–3143 |

|  |  |  |
|---|---|---|
| 8.3 | Tangential | 3144–3258 |
| 8.4 | Individual | 3259–4563 |

### 9. THEATRICAL CRITICISM
| | | |
|---|---|---|
| 9.1 | General and historical | 4654–4615 |
| 9.2 | Collected notices | 4616–4709 |

### 10. REVUE, VAUDEVILLE, AND SHOWBOATS
| | | |
|---|---|---|
| 10.1 | General | 4710–4807 |
| 10.2 | Individual performances | 4808–4887 |

### 11. COMMUNITY THEATRE AND UNIVERSITY THEATRE
| | | |
|---|---|---|
| 11.1 | Community theatre | 4888–4954 |
| 11.2 | University theatre | 4955–5085 |

### 12. THEATRE AND EDUCATION
| | | |
|---|---|---|
| 12.1 | Creative dramatics in schools | 5086–5201 |
| 12.2 | Children's theatre | 5202–5265 |
| 12.3 | Chautauqua and lyceum | 5266–5296 |
| 12.4 | Special forms and therapy | 5297–5313 |
| 12.5 | Theatre as a career | 5414–5340 |

## B. DRAMA
### 13. GENERAL
| | | |
|---|---|---|
| 13.1 | Play lists | 5341–5398 |
| 13.2 | Playwriting and publishing | 5399–5464 |
| 13.3 | Theory and genres | 5465–5578 |

### 14. HISTORY
| | | |
|---|---|---|
| 14.1 | International | 5579–5626 |
| 14.2 | General | 5627–5705 |
| 14.3 | 1665-1850 | 5706–5752 |
| 14.4 | 1851-1918 | 5753–5809 |
| 14.5 | 1919-1945 | 5810–5892 |
| 14.6 | 1946-1990 | 5893–5992 |

### 15. FOREIGN INFLUENCES
5993–6051

### 16. DRAMATIC BIOGRAPHY AND CRITICISM
| | | |
|---|---|---|
| 16.1 | Collected notices and biographical dictionaries | 6052–6143 |
| 16.2 | Individual dramatists | 6144–7201 |

## C. MUSIC
### 17. THE MUSICAL
| | | |
|---|---|---|
| 17.1 | General | 7202–7318 |
| 17.2 | Biographies | 7319–7458 |

### 18. MUSIC IN THEATRE
7459–7464

## D. INDEXES
Subject Index

Author Index

# A. THEATRE
## 1. GENERAL REFERENCE
### 1.1 BIBLIOGRAPHIES

**1** PENCE, JAMES H. The magazine and the drama: an index
pp.xiii, 190     MH
NY: Dunlap Society     1896
250 copies. Reference to 166 US, Canadian and English periodicals.

**2** [BROWN, FRANK C.]. The Drama League of America. A selective list of essays and books about the drama and the theatre exclusive of biography
pp.27     MB
[Boston]: National Publication Department     1912

**3** A CATALOGUE OF THE ALLEN A. BROWN COLLECTION of books relating to the stage in the Public Library of the City of Boston
pp.952     M
Boston: Trustees of the Public Library     1919
Includes 116 pp. of plays, but most entries refer to the stage rather than to the drama. There is no reference to periodicals. Extensively cross-referenced and including the Library's other theatre holdings.

**4** GILDER, ROSAMOND. A theatre library: a bibliography of one hundred books relating to the theatre
pp.xiv, 74     L
NY: Theatre Arts / National Theatre Conference     1932

**5** BAKER, BLANCH M. Dramatic bibliography: an annotated list of books on the history and criticism of the drama and stage and on the allied arts of the theatre
pp.xiv, 320     M
NY: H. W. Wilson     1933

**6** A CATALOGUE OF THE DIVISION OF DRAMA library, University of Washington
pp.vi, 69     M
Seattle: U. of Washington Book Store     1934

**7** MAGRIEL, PAUL D. (Ed.). A bibliography of dancing. A list of books and articles on the dance and related subjects
pp.229; front., ill. in text     M
NY: H.W. Wilson     1936
Includes Amerindian dances (pp.54-58). Fourth cumulated supplement was issued in 1941.

**8** AMBLER, MARY E. Classification system for theatre libraries
Illinois: U. of Chicago (MA)     1939

**9** McDOWELL, JOHN H. et al. A selected bibliography on theatre and the social scene prepared by the committee on research...
pp.60     M
[Minneapolis]: AETA     1946

**10** McDOWELL, JOHN H. et al (Eds). A selected bibliography and critical comment on the art, theory and technique of acting
pp.32     M
Ann Arbor MI: AETA     1948

**11** McDOWELL, JOHN H. & McGAW, CHARLES. A bibliography on speech and drama in American colleges and universities, 1937-1947
    DL★
NY: AETA     1949
*Speech Monograph*, Volume XVI, No. 3, November.

**12** STALLINGS, ROY & MYERS, PAUL. A guide to theatre reading
pp.ix, 138     MH
NY: National Theatre Conference     1949
Foreword by Rosamond Gilder. Narrow range.

**13** BAKER, BLANCH M. Theatre and allied arts: a guide to books dealing with the history, criticism, and technic of the drama and theatre and related arts and crafts
pp.xiv, 536     M
NY: H. W. Wilson     1952

**14** SATTLER, WILLIAM M. et al. A selected list of texts in public address, oral interpretation, theatre, radio and television, speech and hearing therapy, and speech science
pp.97     DL★
Ann Arbor: [U. of Michigan]     [1956?]

**15** WEINGARTEN, JOSEPH A. (Ed.). Modern American playwrights 1918-1945: a bibliography
pp.72; 56     MH★
NY:     1946
Two volumes in one.

**16** MELNITZ, WILLIAM W. (Ed.). Theatre arts publications in the United States 1947-1952: a five year bibliography
pp.xiii, 91     M
[Minneapolis]: AETA     1959

**17** BELKNAP, SARAH Y. Guide to the performing arts 1957
pp.iv, 467     L
NY: Scarecrow P.     1960
Periodical listings world-wide. Volumes for 1958 and 1959 were published in 1961, and one for 1968, edited by Louis A. Rachow and Katherine Hartley, in 1972.

**18** BURROUGHS, ROBERT C. (Ed.). Industrial and technical publications: a bibliography of interest to theatre workers
pp.43     DL★
[Evanston,IL]: AETA     1960

**19** RYAN, PAT M. History of the modern theatre: a selective bibliography
pp.28     M
Tucson: U. of Arizona     1960

**20** MULGRAVE, DOROTHY I.; MARLOR, CLARK S. & BAKER, ELMER E. Bibliography of speech and allied areas, 1950-1960
pp.x, 184     L
Philadelphia: Chilton P.     1962

**21** BROCKETT, OSCAR G.; BECKER, SAMUEL L. & BRYANT, DONALD C. A bibliographical guide to research in speech and dramatic art
pp.viii, 118     M
Glenview,IL: Scott, Foresman     1963

**22** BUSFIELD, ROGER M. (Ed.). Theatre arts publications available in the United States 1953-1957: a five year bibliography
pp.xiii, 188     M
[Evanston,IL]: AETA     1964

**23** CORNYN, STAN. A selective index to *Theatre Magazine*
pp.289     M
NY: Scarecrow P.     1964

*Theatre Magazine*, 1900-1930, (360 issues).

**24** DUKORE, BERNARD F. A bibliography of theatre arts publications in English, 1963
pp.vi, 82     M
Washington DC: AETA     1965

**25** FAXON, FREDERICK W. et al. (Eds). Cumulated dramatic index, 1909-1949
pp.xii, 912; x, 935     L
Boston: G.K.Hall     1965

Two volumes. A consolidation of the 41 annual volumes. A guide to articles and illustrations in American and British periodicals. There are three appendices: 1. Author list of books about the drama (over 6,500 titles); 2. Title list of published play texts (about 24,000); 3. Author list of published play texts (about 20,000 entries).

**26** STRATMAN, CARL J. Bibliography of the American theatre excluding New York
pp.xv, 397     M
Chicago: Loyola U.P.     1965

**27** SANTANIELLO, A.E. Theatre books in print: an annotated guide to the literature of the theatre, the technical arts of the theatre, motion pictures, television and radio
pp.xiii, 509     M
NY: The Drama Bookshop     1966

2nd edtion. First published, NY 1963.

**28** GOHDES, CLARENCE. Literature and theater of the states and regions of the USA
pp.xii, 276     M
Durham NC: Duke U.P.     1967

**29** HUNTER, FREDERICK J. Guide to the theatre and drama collections at the University of Texas
pp.ii, 86; ill. in text     M
Austin TX: U. of Texas HRC     1967

**30** LITTO, FREDRIC M. American dissertations on the drama and the theatre; a bibliography
pp.ix, 519     M
[Kent, OH]: Kent State U.P.     1969

**31** RYAN, PAT M. American drama bibliography: a checklist of publications in English
pp.viii, 240     M
Fort Wayne TX: Public Library     1969

Mostly periodicals but with some book titles.

**32** ARNOTT, JAMES F. & ROBINSON, JOHN W. English theatrical literature, 1559-1900: a bibliography
pp.xxii, 486     M
London: Society for Theatre Research     1970

The close relationship of English with US theatre during the 18th and 19th centuries, involving both artistes and repertoire, renders this a useful guide to early American theatre history.

**33** STRATMAN, CARL J. American theatrical periodicals, 1797-1967: a bibliographical guide
pp.xxii, 133     M
Durham, NC: Duke U.P.     1970

**34** BESTERMAN, THEODORE. Music and drama: a bibliography of bibliographies
pp.xiv, 365     M
Totowa, NJ: Rowman and Littlefield     1971

**35** CATALOG OF MANUSCRIPTS of the Folger Shakespeare Library
pp.vii, 738; 751; 775     L
Boston: G. K. Hall     1971

Three volumes.

**36** HUNTER, FREDERICK J. Drama bibliography: a short-title guide to extended reading in dramatic art for the English-speaking audience and students in theatre
pp.x, 239; front.     L
Boston: G.K.Hall     1971

**37** SCHOOLCRAFT, RALPH N. Performing arts books in print: an annotated bibliography
pp.xiii, 761     DL★
NY: Drama Book Specialists     1973

Books printed before 1971. A supplement lists missed titles and 1971 publications. Continues A. E. Santaniello: *Theatre books in print*, second edition, 1966.

**38** LISTE DES PUBLICATIONS THEATRALES dans le monde
ll.25     M
Paris: ITI     1974

Seven leaves of US entries, including newsletters.

**39** MATTHEWS, WILLIAM. American diaries in manuscript, 1580-1954: a descriptive bibliography
pp.xvi, 176     DL★
Athens: U. of Georgia P.     1974

**40** A SELECTIVE BIBLIOGRAPHY OF CEREMONIES, dances, music and songs of the American Indian from the books in the library of Gregory Javitch with an annotated list of Indian dances
pp.71; ill. in text     M
Montreal: Osiris     1974

280 numbered copies. Dances alphabetically arranged by theme with references to written accounts. For a fuller picture of Amerindian dance ritual, consult the annual reports of the Smithsonian Institution Bureau of American Ethnology.

**41** SPILLER, ROBERT E. et al. Literary history of the United States: history, bibliography
pp.xxvi,1556; xxviii,1466     HW
NY: Macmillan     1974

Two volumes. 4th edition revised, including two supplements.

**42** MATTHEWS, GERALDINE O. et al. Black American writers, 1773-1949: a bibliography and union list
pp.xv, 221     L
Boston: G.K.Hall     1975

**43** ARATA, ESTHER S. More black American playwrights; a bibliography
pp.xiii, 321     O
Metuchen: Scarecrow P.     1976

## 1.1. BIBLIOGRAPHIES

**44** ARATA, ESTHER S. & ROTOLI, NICHOLAS J. Black American playwrights, 1800 to the present: a bibliography
pp.vii, 295     O
Metuchen NJ: Scarecrow P.     1976

**45** FRENCH, WILLIAM P. et al. Afro-American poetry and drama, 1760-1975: a guide to information sources
pp.ix, 493     O
Detroit: Gale Research     1978
Second part comprises Genevieve Fabre, *Afro-American drama, 1850-1975* with author checklist.

**46** WILMETH, DON B. The American stage to World War 1: a guide to information sources
pp.xxi, 269     M
Detroit: Gale Research     1978

**47** LARSON, CARL F.W. American regional theatre history to 1900: a bibliography
pp. xi, 187     M
Metuchen NJ: Scarecrow P.     1979

**48** MERENDA, MARILYN D. & POLICHAK, JAMES W. Speech communication and theatre arts. A classified bibliography of theses and dissertations 1973-1978, with an introduction by Arthur N. Krugh
pp.xiv, 326     L
NY: IFI/Plenum     1979

**49** MOYER, RONALD L. American actors, 1861-1910: an annotated bibliography of books published in the United States in English from 1861 through 1976
pp.xv, 268     M
Troy, NY: Whitston Publishing     1979

**50** PEAVY, CHARLES D. Afro-American literature and culture since World War II, a guide to information sources
pp.xiv, 302     MH
Detroit: Gale Research     1979

**51** ANDERSON, JOHN Q.; GASTON, EDWIN W. & LEE, JAMES W. Southwestern American literature: a bibliography
pp.xiii, 445     L
Chicago: Swallow P.     1980
Includes folk and professional theatre.

**52** MESERVE, WALTER J. American drama to 1900: a guide to information sources
pp.xviii, 254     M
Detroit: Gale Research     1980

**53** WILMETH, DON B. American and English popular entertainment: a guide to information sources
pp.xviii, 465     M
Detroit: Gale Research     1980

**54** LITTLEFIELD, DANIEL & PARINS, JAMES W. A bibliography of native American writers, 1772-1924
pp.xvii, 343     O
Metuchen NJ: Scarecrow P.     1981
A supplement, pp. ix, 339, was published by Scarecrow P. in 1985.

**55** NADEL, IRA B. Jewish writers of North America: a guide to information sources
pp.xix, 493     L
Detroit: Gale Research     1981

Part 4, dramatists.

**56** PERFORMING ARTS BOOKS 1876-1981. Including an international index of current serial publications
pp.xviii, 1656     HW
NY: R.R.Bowker     1981

**57** EDWARDS, CHRISTOPHER. The world guide to performing arts periodicals. With a foreword by Simon Trussler
pp.66     M
London: British Centre of the ITI     1982
Full data on 636 current periodicals.

**58** ELLIOT, PAULA. Performing arts information, 1975-1980. A bibliography of reference works
pp.iv, 41     M
Manhattan: Kansas State U. Libraries     1982

**59** JOHNSON, CLAUDIA D. & JOHNSON, VERNON E. Nineteenth-century theatrical memoirs
pp.xvii, 269     M
Westport: Greenwood P.     1982

**60** WILMETH, DON B. Variety entertainment and outdoor amusements: a reference guide
pp.xiii, 242     M
Westport, CT: Greenwood P.     1982
Outdoor amusements, wild west shows, medicine shows, minstrel shows, variety and vaudeville, burlesque, revue and musical theatre, showboat and tent theatre.

**61** BAILEY, CLAUDIA J. A guide to reference and bibliography for theatre research
pp.xi, 149     M
Columbus: Ohio State Universities Libraries     1983
Second, enlarged edition. First published 1971 under author's maiden name of *Lowe*. About half the entries refer to background reference works applicable to all literary research, and in general the titles tend to complement the present bibliography.

**62** ORTOLANI, BENITO (Ed.). International bibliography of theatre, 1982-
pp.av.400     M
NY: City U., Theatre Research Data Center     1983-
Annual. Continuing. Initiated by the ASTR. Mostly periodical references. Curiously classified, necessitating mammoth indexes, amounting to 80% of the total pages. Choice of entry is arbitrary rather than systematic. Each volume is selected from one year's publications, making reference cumbersome as every volume has to be consulted for any one subject. Usefulness very limited.

**63** BRYAN, GEORGE (Ed.). Stage lives: a bibliography and index to theatrical biographies in English
pp.xvi, 368     M
Westport CT: Greenwood P.     1985

**64** CARPENTER, CHARLES A. Modern drama scholarship and criticism 1966-1980: an international bibliography
pp.xxxv, 587     M
Toronto: U.P.     1986

**65** SALZMAN, JACK (Ed.). American studies; an annotated bibliography 1900-1988
pp.xii, 2058; xi, 1085     L
Cambridge: U.P.     1986-90
In three volumes with a supplement. Includes section on popular culture.

**66** CAVANAGH, JOHN. British theatre: a bibliography 1901 to 1985
pp.510　　　　　　　　　　　　　　　M
Mottisfont: Motley P.　　　　　　　　1989
Many entries are relevant to American theatre history.

**67** GRAY, JOHN. Black theatre and performance: a pan-African bibliography
pp.xvii, 414　　　　　　　　　　　　MH
NY: Greenwood P.　　　　　　　　　1990

## 1.2 DICTIONARIES, DIRECTORIES, ENCYCLOPEDIAS, GLOSSARIES

**68** FISKE, HARRISON G. (Ed.). The New York Mirror annual and directory of the theatrical profession for 1888
pp.x, 208; pl. 6　　　　　　　　　　M
NY: The New York Mirror　　　　　1888

**69** ADAMS, W. DAVENPORT. A dictionary of the drama. A guide to the plays, playwrights, players, and playhouses of the United Kingdom and America, from the earliest times to the present. Vol.1, A-G
pp.viii, 627　　　　　　　　　　　　M
London: Chatto & Windus　　　　　1904
All published. The second volume exists in manuscript draft, and is available through *University Microfilms*.

**70** GILDER, ROSAMOND & FREEDLEY, GEORGE. Theatre collections in libraries and museums: an international handbook
pp.vii, 182　　　　　　　　　　　　M
NY: Theatre Arts/National Theatre Conference　1936

**71** THORNTON, HELEN. Thesaurus of technical stage terms
Denver: U. of Colorado (PhD)　　　1951

**72** HART, JAMES D. The Oxford companion to American literature
pp.viii, 890　　　　　　　　　　　　M
NY: Oxford U. P.　　　　　　　　　1956
Reprinted with corrections 1957. First published 1941.

**73** RAE, KENNETH & SOUTHERN, RICHARD (Eds). An international vocabulary of technical theatre terms
pp.139　　　　　　　　　　　　　　M
Brussels: Elsevier P./ITI　　　　　　1959
American, Dutch, English, French, German, Spanish, Swedish.

**74** SOBEL, BERNARD (Ed.). The new theatre handbook and digest of plays, preface by George Freedley
pp.xv, 749　　　　　　　　　　　　M
NY: Crown Publishing　　　　　　　1959
Second edition, revised. First published 1940. Includes a glossary of theatre terms, bibliography, biographies, and production information.

**75** BOWMAN, WALTER P. & BALL, ROBERT H. (Eds). Theatre language: a dictionary of terms in English of the drama and stage from medieval to modern times
pp.xii, 428　　　　　　　　　　　　M
NY: Theatre Arts Books　　　　　　1961

**76** SHARP, H. S. & SHARP, M. Z. Index to characters in the performing arts Part 1. Non-musical plays. An alphabetical listing of 30,000 characters. [Part II. Operas and musical productions]
pp.1533; ix,1255　　　　　　　　　　L
NY: Scarecrow P.　　　　　　　　1966-69
Three volumes.

**77** MATLAW, MYRON. Modern world drama: an encyclopedia
pp.xxiii, 960; ill.in text　　　　　　　M
London: Secker & Warburg　　　　1972

**78** CUMMING, MARSUE & EPTON, ANLI (Eds). Theatre profiles: an informational handbook of nonprofit professional theatre in the U.S.
pp.various; ill. in text　　　　　　　M
NY: Theatre Communication Group　1973-
Biennial. A guide to fringe theatre. Subsequent editors included Laura Ross and John Istel (1986).

**79** PRIDE, LEO B. (Ed.). International theatre directory: a world directory of the theatre and the performing arts
pp.xxi, 577; ill in text　　　　　　　M
NY: Simon and Schuster　　　　　1973
Lists theatres, with capacities and addresses in every country. Also lists companies, and amateur and community theatres.

**80** PRIMUS, MARK (Ed.). Black theatre: a resource directory
pp.28　　　　　　　　　　　　　　DL★
NY: Black Theatre Alliance　　　　1973

**81** SERGEL, SHERMAN L. The language of show biz: a dictionary
pp.251; ill.　　　　　　　　　　　　DL★
Chicago: Dramatic Publishing　　　1973

**82** COHEN-STRATYNER, BARBARA N. et al (Eds). Performing arts resources. Volume 1-
pp.c.150; some vols ill. in text　　　M
NY: TLA　　　　　　　　　　　　1974-
Annual. Continuing. Edited by Ted Perry (1-3), Mary C. Henderson (4-6), Giannine Cocuzzo (7-11). International. Of US relevance are: Vol 1, (1974), a directory to performing arts resource collections; Vol 2 (1975) includes James E. Fletcher & W. Worth McDougald: *The Peabody collection of the University of Georgia*; Vol 3 (1976) includes Mark Gladstone: *A bibliography of US Government documents pertaining to government support of the arts, 1962-72*; L. Terry Oggel: *A short title guide to the Edwin Booth literary materials at the Players*; Llewellyn H. Hedgbeth: *The Chuck Callahan burlesque collection*; Vol 6 (1980) includes Laraine Correll (Ed.): *Federal Theatre project records at George Mason University*; Dorothy L. Swerdlove: *Research materials of the Federal Theatre project in...the NYPL*; R. Eric Gustafson: *The San Francisco archives for the performing arts*; Vol 8 (1983) is dedicated to stage and costume design and exhibition; Vol 10 (1985) includes Steve Nelson: *Performing arts collection at the Robert F. Wagner labor archives*; Cynthia G. Swank: *Performing arts on Madison Avenue*; Lee R. Nemchek: *The Pasadena Playhouse collection*; William Allison: *The Penn State archives of theatre lighting*; Bruce Whitehead: *Engineering contributions to theatre technology...*; Vol 12, (1987) *Topical bibliographies of the American theatre*, contains: Jonathan Levy & Martha Mahard: *Checklist of early printed children's plays in English*; Noreen Barnes & Laurie J. Wolf: *Nineteenth-century sources on women in nineteenth-century American theatre*; Rosemary L. Cullen: *A checklist of American civil war drama: beginnings to 1900*;

## 1.2. DICTIONARIES, DIRECTORIES, ENCYCLOPEDIAS, GLOSSARIES −100

Geraldine Maschio: *Female impersonators on the American stage, 1820 to 1927...*; Colette A. Hyman: *Workers on stage: an annotated bibliography of labor plays of the 1930s*; Vol 13, (1988), *The Drews and the Barrymores*; Vol 14, (1989), *Performances in periodicals*, includes: Florence C. Smith: *Introducing parlor theatricals to the American home*; Jack W. McCullough: *The theatre as seen through late nineteenth century technical periodicals*; Stephen M. Vallillo: *...a case study of the* New York Clipper *and the* New York Dramatic Mirror; Sara Velez: *Sound recording periodicals*; Maryann Chach: *The New York Review*; Vol 15 (1990), *Arts and access*, includes Liz Fugate: *Theatre companies in the US: an ephemeral collection at the University of Washington drama library*; Victor T. Cardell: *The archive of popular American music: strategies...for management...*; Maryann Chach: *Costume sketches in the Shubert archive*; Nena Couch: *The Theatre Research Institution and its collections within a large institution...*; Sheila Ryan: *'At the Goodman Theatre', an essay on performing arts documentation*.

**83** SIMON, BERNARD (Ed.). Simon's directory of theatrical materials services & information
pp.388  M
NY: Package Publicity Service  1975

Fifth edition. Introduction by Harold Burris-Meyer. First published NY: 1956.

**84** WHALON, MARION K. Performing arts research. A guide to information sources
pp.xl, 280  M
Detroit: Gale Research  1976

A thorough account of background reference titles which largely supplement this bibliography.

**85** SYPHER, F. J. (Ed.). The reader's adviser; a layman's guide to literature. Volume 2, the best in American and British drama and world literature in English translation
pp.774  L
NY: R. R. Bowker  1977

Twelfth edition, revised. First published NY, 1921. Brief bio-bibliographical entries. Volume one deals with fiction, poetry, essays, literary biography, works of reference.

**86** MERIN, JENNIFER & BURDICK, ELIZABETH B. International directory of theatre, dance and folklore festivals
pp.ix, 480  L
Westport CT: Greenwood P./ITI  1979

**87** BRONNER, EDWIN. The encyclopedia of the American theatre 1900-1975
pp.659; ill.in text  M
San Diego: A.S.Barnes  1980

**88** BLACK THEATRE directory
pp.20  ★
Washington DC: J. F. Kennedy Center for the Performing Arts  1981

**89** RACHOW, LOUIS A. (Ed.). Theatre & performing arts collections
pp.viii, 166; ill. in text  M
NY: Haworth P.  1981

Volume 1 No. 1 of *Special Collections* series of thematic journal issues. Historical introduction and guide to Library of Congress, NYPL, *Players* library, Princeton library, U. of Texas library, Wisconsin Center for film and theater research, Metropolitan Toronto library, Boothbay ME theatre museum. Includes list of available theatre and drama awards.

**90** WILMETH, DON B. The language of American popular entertainment: a glossary of argot, slang and terminology
pp.xxi, 306  M
Westport, CT: Greenwood P.  1981

**91** WASSERMAN, STEVEN R. (Ed.). The lively arts information directory
pp.xiii, 846  ★
Detroit: Gale Research  1982

**92** WOLL, ALLEN. Dictionary of the black theatre: Broadway, off-Broadway and selected Harlem theatre
pp.xvi, 359  MH
Westport, CT: Greenwood P.  1983

Includes a chronology of black theatre, and play, film and song indexes.

**93** BORDMAN, GERALD (Ed.). The Oxford companion to American theatre
pp.vi, 734  M
NY: OUP  1984

A *Concise Companion* was published in 1987; pp.viii, 451.

**94** HOCHMAN, SHIRLEY (Ed). McGraw-Hill encyclopedia of world drama
pp.approx.600; ill.in text  L
NY: McGraw-Hill  1984

Five volumes. Second edition. First published 1972.

**95** O'DONNELL, MONICA M. Contemporary theatre, film, and television: a biographical guide
pp.xii,545; xi, 374  L
Detroit: Gale Research  1984-

Two volumes. The successor to *Who's Who in the Theatre*, 1912-81. Published irregularly, each edition dropping some names and adding others, according to degree of celebrity.

**96** EPSTEIN, LAWRENCE (Ed.). A guide to theatre in America
pp.xv, 443  MESME
NY: Macmillan  1985

Comprehensive directory of theatre information, indexed.

**97** TRAPIDO, JOEL et al (Eds). An international dictionary of theatre language
pp.xxxvi, 1032  L
Westport, CT: Greenwood P.  1985

**98** FRICK, JOHN W. & WARD, CARLTON (Eds). Directory of historic American theatres...for the League of Historic American Theatres
pp.xviii, 384; pl.25  M
NY: Greenwood P.  1987

A work partly founded on, and extending, the researches of Gene Chesley, U. of California, Davis, first president of the League of Historic American Theatres. Chesley published lists of theatres between 1975 and 1979; he died in 1981 and in 1983 an updated list was published, completed by Carlton Ward. Chesley's collected data was bequeathed to the Princeton U. Theatre Collection. The 1987 directory supersedes all previous editions.

**99** HANDEL, BEATRICE et al (Eds). Handel's national directory for the performing arts and civic centers
pp.various  MH
Dallas & NY: NDPACC/John Wiley  1988

Two volumes. Fourth edition. First published 1973. Theatres and other performance centres arranged regionally.

**100** SLIDE, ANTHONY; HANSON, PATRICIA K. & HANSON, STEPHEN L. (Eds). Sourcebook for the performing arts; a directory of collections, resources, scholars and critics in theatre, film and television
pp.viii, 227  L
NY: Greenwood P.  1988

## 1.3 ICONOGRAPHIES, DISCOGRAPHIES

**101** CATALOGUE OF ENGRAVED PORTRAITS OF ACTORS of olden time. January 24 to February 14, MCMVII
pp.vi, 46; ill. in text                              M
NY: The Grolier Club                              1907
Introduction signed R.C.

**102** POPE, A. WINTHROP. Theatrical bookplates
pp.[32]; ill.in text                                MB
Kansas City: H. Alfred Fowler                       1914
150 copies. A selective checklist.

**103** HALL, LILLIAN A. Catalogue of dramatic portraits in the theatre collection of the Harvard College library
pp.ix,438; v,427; v,456; v,358                       M
Cambridge,MA: Harvard U.P.                       1930-34
Four volumes. Index and corrigenda in Vol.4

**104** SHIFFLER, HAROLD C. Theatre philatelic [cover title]
pp.103; ill.                                        DL★
Milwaukee,WI: American Topical Association        1969
Catalogue of postage stamps commemorating the theatre.

**105** SMOLIAN, STEVEN. A handbook of film, theater, and television music on record, 1948-1969
pp.64, 64                                           M
NY: Record Undertaker                              1970
Two volumes in one slip case.

**106** PORTRAITS of the American stage 1771-1971: an exhibition in celebration of the inaugural season of the John F. Kennedy Center for the Performing Arts
pp.203; ill. in text, some col.                     MH
Washington DC: Smithsonian Institute P.            1971

**107** RUST, BRIAN & DEBUS, ALLEN G. The complete entertainment discography from the mid-1890s to 1942
pp.iv, 677                                          M
New Rochelle: Arlington House                      1973

**108** HODGINS, GORDON W. The Broadway musical: a complete LP discography
pp.v, 183                                           M
Metuchen NJ: Scarecrow P.                          1980

**109** LIBRARY AND MUSEUM of Performing Arts. Catalogue of the Rodgers and Hammerstein archives of recorded sound
                                                   DL★
Boston: G. K. Hall                                 1981
Fifteen volumes.

**110** HOFFMAN, HERBERT H. Recorded plays; indexes to dramatists, plays and actors
pp.ix, 139                                         DL★
Chicago: American Library Association              1985

**111** LYNCH, RICHARD C. Broadway on record. Directory of New York cast recording of musical shows, 1931-1986
pp.x, 347                                           L
NY: Greenwood P.                                   1987

**112** SEELEY, ROBERT & BUNNETT, REX. London musical shows on record 1889-1989
pp.vi, 457                                          M
Harrow: General Gramophone                         1989
Supersedes Brian Rust & Rex Bunnett: *London musical shows on record 1897-1976*, 1977, but does not have so comprehensive a coverage of individual performers. Complements and partly duplicates Brian Rust: *The complete entertainment discography, 1973*. Covers US transfers.

**113** GÄNZL, KURT. The Blackwell guide to the musical theatre on record
pp.xiv, 547                                         L
Oxford UK: Blackwell                               1990

## 1.4 CATALOGUES. EXHIBITIONS AND COLLECTIONS

**114** CATALOGUE OF A VALUABLE COLLECTION of books on the drama; belonging to Mr T. H. Morrell...comprising biographies...theatrical criticisms...Shakespeare and his works. Also, a collection of rare and valuable dramatic portraits...and a superb original miniature of Madame Malibran...to be sold at auction
pp.31                                               MB
NY: Bangs, Merwin                                  1869

**115** CATALOGUE OF AN EXHIBITION of illustrated bill posters at the rooms of the Grolier Club at 29 East 32d St...
pp.12                                                L
NY: Grolier Club                                   1890
Predominantly French, but includes seven US posters.

**116** CATALOGUE OF THE DRAMATIC LIBRARY of Walter C. Bellows. Dramatic biography, history of the stage, plays, Shakespeariana, criticism, poetry, miscellaneous literature; also playbills, portraits and other engravings to be sold at auction
pp.29                                               MB
NY: Bangs                                          1893

**117** CATALOGUE OF THE EXTENSIVE DRAMATIC COLLECTION of the late James H. Brown, esq. of Malden, Mass. comprising a valuable collection of works relating to the history of the stage in all its branches...to be sold by auction...
pp.v,202; iv,242; 102; front.                       MH
Boston: C. F. Libbie                               1898

**118** A CATALOGUE OF CHOICE AND RARE BOOKS...dramatic and musical literature...
pp.34                                               MB
Boston: P. K. Foley                              [1900?]
Foley's catalogue, no. 10. Drama items #355-567 and #589 to end.

**119** RARE AND FINE BOOKS AND AUTOGRAPHS. The choice private library of Miss Eleanor Barry of the Richard Mansfield company...comprising...books on the drama, including the manuscript journal of Edmund Simpson of the old Park

## 1.4. CATALOGUES. EXHIBITIONS AND COLLECTIONS

Theatre...for sale at auction
pp.110 MB
NY: Anderson Auction [1900?]

**120** CATALOGUE OF A COLLECTION of books, dramatic works, theatre bills, portraits of actors...to be sold at auction
pp.34 MB
NY: Bangs 1901

**121** CATALOGUE OF DRAMATIC BOOKS, first editions of American authors...together with another small dramatic collection [auction catalogue]
pp.86 MB
Boston: C. F. Libbie 1901

**122** CATALOGUE OF THE COLLECTION of dramatic and literary autographs of the late Frederick W. French...to be sold by auction May 2nd & 3rd...
pp.iv,158; pl. 6 (1 folding) M
Boston,: C. F. Libbie 1901

**123** CATALOGUE OF THE COLLECTION 0f prints formed by the late Henry Nebe...for sale at auction
pp.89 MB
NY: John Anderson 1902
Nebe, a professional book-binder, was responsible for many of the extra-illustrated volumes of the period. Most of the pen-and-ink items described are the work of David E. Cronin.

**124** CATALOGUE OF INTERESTING BOOKS from private sources including a small dramatic library together with some portraits and autograph letters. For sale at auction Dec. 29,..
pp.31 MB
NY: Anderson Auction 1903

**125** CATALOGUE of the W. Erasmus Tefft collection of theatrical photographs, bills of the play and autographs
pp.92; ill. in text MH
NY: Alexander P./New York Arts Galleries 1903

**126** CATALOGUE OF THE...LIBRARY of the late Rev. William Rouseville [Rounseville] Alger, including many first editions of American authors, presentation copies, Americana, bibliography, dramatic literature. With his collection of autograph letters. To be sold at auction, May 10th and 11th
pp.123 MB
Boston: C.F.Libbie 1905

**127** CATALOGUE OF THE DRAMATIC COLLECTION of the late Mr George Becks...also a collection of costumes, wigs, etc...to be sold March 1905
pp.68 MB
NY: Merwin-Clayton 1905

**128** CATALOGUE OF THE DRAMATIC COLLECTION of the late Lucius Poole, Esq., of Boston, comprising many rare and interesting books relating to the biography and history of the stage including extra illustrated books...autograph letters...portraits and prints...collections of play bills and theatre programmes
pp.ii, 125 MH
Boston: C. F. Libbie 1905

**129** CATALOGUE OF THE LIBRARY of Mr William J. Le Moyne...drama and dramatic literature; old plays and playbills and other rare dramatic items...
pp.119 MH
NY: Merwin-Clayton 1905

**130** CATALOGUE OF THE REMAINING PORTION of the library of Mr George Becks comprising dramatic biographies, scarce dramatic catalogues and photographs,... and other material relating to the stage which will be sold at auction...Nov 1905
pp.27 MB
NY: Merwin-Clayton 1905

**131** CATALOGUE OF THE BECKS COLLECTION of prompt books in the New York Public Library
pp.49 L
NY: Public Library 1906
Also printed in *NYPL Bulletin*, Feb.,1906, pp. 101-148.

**132** CATALOGUE OF THE VALUABLE DRAMATIC and American historical library of William H. Terry comprising books, manuscripts, prints, etc., relating to the history and biography of the English and American stage...
pp.150;136;43 MH
NY: Anderson Auction 1906

**133** THE DRAMATIC COLLECTION of the late Albert M. Palmer
pp.51 MH
NY: Merwin-Clayton 1906
In three parts. Part three only inspected, containing engravings, prints, ephemera, photographs.

**134** THE LIBRARY of a dramatic author and critic
★
NY: Merwin-Clayton Sales 1906

**135** CATALOGUE OF BOOKS, comprising Americana, dramatic, Dunlap Society publications etc. A choice selection of standard music and a collection of portraits...June 21
pp.28 MB
NY: Anderson Auction 1907

**136** A PARTICULARLY INTERESTING COLLECTION of English and American playbills mainly formed by Augustus Toedteberg (Brooklyn NY)...for sale at auction
pp.31 MB
NY: Anderson Auction 1907

**137** CATALOGUE OF THE LIBRARY, autographs, prints and playbills, including the fine collection of extra-illustrated books of the late Douglas Taylor, president of the Dunlap Society...
pp.232 MH
NY: Anderson Auction 1913

**138** THE ILLUSTRATED CATALOGUE of literature relating to American history and the stage, extra illustrated and finely bound comprising the extensive and valuable collection formed during a period of almost fifty years by the late Charles C. Moreau
Unpaginated; ill. in text; front. MH
NY: American Art Association 1915

**139** MATTHEWS, BRANDER (Ed.). A catalogue of models and of stage sets in the Dramatic Museum of Columbia University
pp.v, 55 M
NY: Dramatic Museum of Columbia U. 1916

Introduction by Matthews, expanded from the foreword he provided for the 1913 catalogue, which this publication supersedes. Sets include *The Garden of Allah*, Century Theatre, NY, 1911; *The Return of Peter Grimm*, Belasco Theatre, NY, 1910; *Leah Kleschna*, Standard Theatre, NY, 1904; *Around the Map*, New Amsterdam Theatre, NY, 1915

**140** BOOKS ON EARLY AMERICAN DRAMA and kindred works collected by Fred. W. Atkinson, Brooklyn, N.Y., to be sold by his order...
pp.ii, 48     M
NY: Anderson Galleries     1925

**141** THE ROBINSON LOCKE DRAMATIC COLLECTION [exhibition catalogue]
pp.44     L
NY:     1925

**142** THE THEATRE IN ART. Drama, motion picture, vaudeville, circus, dance, opera, burlesque. Exhibition by American artists...(second edition...)
pp.[32]; ill. in text     MH
NY: Sidney Ross Gallery     1932
Catalogue of an exhibition for the benefit of the Actors' Fund of America, with an introduction by Oliver M. Sayler.

**143** THE DALLAS PUBLIC LIBRARY presents an exhibit of selected material from the W. E. Hill Theatre Collection on the occasion of the opening of the collection April 28th...
pp.[40]; ill. in text     M
Dallas TX: Public Library     1936

**144** VAN LENNEP, WILLIAM. The Harvard theatre collection
pp.ii, 21; pl. 2     M
Cambridge MA: [Harvard U.P.]     1952
Reprinted from *Harvard Library Bulletin*, VI, 2.

**145** THE AMERICAN THEATRE; an exhibition of the U.S. Information Agency prepared under the direction of the Smithsonian Institution, Washington, D.C.
pp.46     MH
Norwich, UK: Norfolk County Drama Committee 1956
Foreword by W. Nugent Monck, introductory historical survey by Geoffrey Harvey. A version lacking the foreword was also issued.

**146** THE FINE LIBRARY of the late Philip Moeller (New York City) sold by order of Miss Hannah Moeller. Unrestricted public auction...September 10th, 11th [in two parts]
pp.54; 34     M
NY: Swann Galleries     1958

**147** THE GLENN HUGHES DRAMA and imagist poetry collection [exhibition catalogue]
pp.14; MS facsimile in text     L
Austin TX: U. of Texas HRC     1959
Drama items included text of Hughes's play, *Mrs Carlyle*, with related materials.

**148** COLLECTION OF THEATRICAL PORTRAIT DOLLS from the estate of the late Daniel Blum [cover title]
pp.15; ill. in text     M
NY: O. Rundle Gilbert     [1965]
Auction catalogue, September 16, 1965. 751 items, comprising dolls, portraits, illustrated titles and 8 mm. silent films.

**149** KATZ, HERBERT & KATZ, MARJORIE. Museums, USA: a history and guide
pp.x, 395; ill.     DL★
Garden City, NY: Doubleday     1965

**150** PICTORIAL AMERICANA. [Part one] Posters and broadsides: theatrical...circus...etc. [Part two] American trades and trade catalogues
pp.34     M
NY: Swann Galleries     1965
Auction catalogue, February 11, 1965.

**151** THEATRE AND SUBJECT HEADINGS authorized for use in the catalog of the theatre collection [NYPL]
pp.386     DL★
Boston: G. K. Hall     1966
Second edition, enlarged.

**152** THE ALIX JEFFREY PHOTOGRAPHIC ARCHIVE of the off-Broadway theatre 1952-1976 comprising the negatives of production photographs of over 250 plays...
pp.ix, 34; ill. in text     M
NY: Parke-Bernet Galleries     1967

**153** CATALOG of the theatre and drama collections [of New York Public Library]
pp.av. 900     L
Boston: G. K. Hall     1967-
Facsimile index cards. Part I: *Drama collection*, author listing in six volumes; listing by cultural origin in six volumes. Part II: *Theatre collection*, books on the theatre in nine volumes. The title of the second part is misleading because as well as books on theatre (and cinema and other performing arts), it also includes plays in manuscript and typescript, promptbooks, and cinema, radio, and TV scripts. A one-volume supplement to Part I, and a two-volume supplement to Part II were issued in 1973. The first annual, supplementary volume was published in 1976. Part III: *Non-book collection* was published in 30 volumes in 1976.

**154** ILLUSION AND REALITY
    MH★
North Salem NY: Hammond Museum     1967
Exhibition catalogue. 657 English and American prints and playbills.

**155** CORRIGAN, MARIE. Leo Weidenthal. The Weidenthal collection: books and theatrical memorabilia [cover title]
pp.11, inc, wrappers     M
[Cleveland OH]: [Public Library]     1968

**156** CATALOG OF PRINTED BOOKS of the Folger Shakespeare Library, Washington, D.C. Volume 1 [-28]
pp.approx. 700     SU
Boston: G. K. Hall     1970

**157** MAGNIFICENT COSTUMES including ... theatrical costumes from the distinguished firm of Max Berman & Sons...at auction 5-8 June
pp.188; ill. in text     M
Los Angeles: Sotheby, Parke-Bernet     1971

**158** YOUNG, WILLIAM C. American theatrical arts: a guide to manuscripts and special collections in the United States and Canada
pp.ix, 166     M
Chicago: ALS     1971

**159** CATALOG OF PRINTED BOOKS of the Folger Shakespeare Library, Washington, D.C. First Supplement. Volume 1 [-3]
pp. Approx. 700     SU
Boston: G. K. Hall     1976

**160** ROBBINS, JOHN A. et al. American literary manuscripts: a checklist of holdings in academic, historical, and public libraries, museums, and authors' homes in the United States
pp.lv, 387     L
Athens: U. of Georgia P.     1977

**161** BREITMAN, ELLEN. Art and the stage
pp.72; ill. in text     M
Cleveland OH: Cleveland Museum of Art     1981
Catalogue of exhibition, May 22-Aug 16, 1981, illustrating the relationship between the visual and the performing arts.

**162** CATALOG OF PRINTED BOOKS of the Folger Shakespeare Library, Washington, D.C. Second supplement. Volume 1 [-2]
pp. Approx. 700     SU
Boston: G. K. Hall     1981

**163** COHEN-STRATYNER, BARBARA N. & KUEPPERS, BRIGITTE (Eds). Preserving America's performing arts: papers from the conference on preservation management for performing arts collections, April 28-May 1, 1982, Washington, D.C.
pp.ix, 167; ill. in text     M
NY: Theatre Library Association     1985

**164** ELLIS, MORRIS R. A catalog: the Robert L. B. Tobin collection: scene designs: sixteenth through nineteenth centuries
Lubbock: Texas Tech U. (PhD)     1987

**165** LENTHAL, FRANKLYN et al. Boothbay Theatre Museum at unreserved auction...Friday, June 22-Sunday, June 24
Unpaginated; ill. in text     M
Kennebunk ME: Oliver's     1990
Catalogue, with addendum, errata slip and price list, of museum contents. Approx. 1180 items.

## 2. FEDERAL AND STATE INTERVENTION

### 2.1 LEGISLATION

**166** GARDINER, JOHN. Gardiner on the theatre. [On reverse of title]:The speech of John Gardiner, Esquire. Delivered in the [Massachusetts] House of Representatives on Thursday the 26th day of January, 1792; on the subject of the report of the committee appointed to consider the expediency of repealing the law against theatrical exhibitions within this commonwealth
pp.159; pl.1 folding     L
Boston: For the author     1792
An exhortation to repeal 'this unsocial, this illiberal, this rigid, unconstitutional, *blue law*'. A second section of the book is headed 'the letter to the author on the theatre' [as referred to on p. 99] written May 24, 1792. *Evans 24301* records four printings in 1792.

**167** BRACKETT, J. ALBERT. Theatrical law: the legal rights of manager, artist, author, and public in theaters, places of amusement, plays, performances, contracts and regulations
pp.xviii, 503     L
Boston: C. M. Clark     1907

**168** LUDES, FRANCIS J. & GILBERT, HAROLD J. Corpus juris secundum. A complete restatement of the entire American law as developed by all reported cases
pp.xxii, 1205     SU
Brooklyn NY: American Law Book     1954
Theatres and shows, pp. 657-770, 1163-1175. This work is updated by annual cumulative pocket parts, now issued by West Publishing, St Paul MN.

**169** AN ACT to amend the penal law, in relation to unlawful charges for theatre tickets [&] An act to amend the general business law, in relation to providing for the regulation of theatrical financing, requiring accounts thereof and making an appropriation therefor
pp.2, 13     M
NY: State Department of Law     1964

**170** FILIPPO, IVAN J. Landmark litigation in the American theatre
Gainesville: U. of Florida (PhD)     1972

**171** BEIL, NORMAN et al (Eds). The actor's manual: a practical legal guide sponsored by the Beverly Hills Bar Association...
pp.206     DL★
NY: Hawthorn Books     1980
Compiled as a syllabus for the symposium for actors and actresses held in Los Angeles, Nov 11, 1978.

### 2.2 REGULATION, CENSORSHIP AND COPYRIGHT

**172** SOLBERG, THORVALD. International copyright. 1. The revised statutes of the United States relating to copyright, as amended by the Senate Act of May 9, 1888, with proposed alterations. 2. The text of the Senate act, with suggested amendments. 3. Reasons for the changes suggested. Submitted...Oct 24, 1889
pp.21     DL★
Washington DC: McQueen & Wallace     1889

**173** PETITION TO THE SENATE and House of Representatives of the United States, for the amendment of copyright law, relating to the fraudulent production of plays. From the dramatists, theatrical managers and other members of the dramatic profession of the United States
pp.28     MB
[NY]: [American Dramatists Club]     [1891]
The petition was to amend the wording of Section 4,966 of Title 60, Chapter 3 of the Revised Statutes by the addition of the phrase '...or operatic' with a lengthy statement of the penalties to be incurred by transgressors.

**174** AMERICAN DRAMATISTS CLUB LIST. A standard of reference for the protection of dramatic property, no. VI, 1902. A catalogue of plays and operas by

American and foreign authors and composers that have been produced in the United States and that are now in use or have been recently used upon the American stage and that are entitled to protection under state, federal, and international law. Compiled and published by the American Dramatists Club, for the information of managers and owners of theatres, opera houses and halls, and managers of traveling dramatic and operatic companies...
pp.44 MB
NY: American Dramatists Club 1902
First issued 1895.

**175** PUTNAM, GEORGE H. (Ed.). The question of copyright: comprising the text of the copyright law of the United States...[and] a summary of the copyright laws at present in force in the chief countries of the world
pp. DL★
NY: G. P. Putnam's Sons 1904
Third edition, revised and enlarged. First published 1891.

**176** ELIAS, S. P. The law of theater tickets...
pp.v, 48 MH
San Francisco: W. A. Hiester 1905
To ascertain the legal status of the theatre ticket and to extract the law on the subject from the decided cases.

**177** WINCHESTER, THOMAS P. Legal matters of interest to managers of theatres and other places of entertainment
pp.8 DL★
Fort Smith AR: Weldon, William & Lick 1905
Parochial, but wider application can be inferred.

**178** LORD, EVERETT W. Children of the stage
pp.31 MB
NY: [National Child Labor Committee] 1910
'To consider the conditions surrounding stage employment [of children] and to indicate the basis for objection to such employment'.

**179** BOWKER, RICHARD R. Copyright, its history and its law: being a summary of the principles and practice of copyright with special references to the American code of 1909 and the British act of 1911
pp.xxiii, 709 O
Boston: Houghton Mifflin 1912

**180** PUTNAM, GEORGE P. (Ed.). Nonsenseorship...Sundry observations concerning prohibitions, inhibitions and illegalities. Illustrated by Ralph Barton
pp.xiii, 181; pl. 15 O
NY: G. P. Putnam's Sons 1922
Attacks on censorship, including contributions on stage censorship from Heywood Broun and Alexander Woollcott.

**181** McADOO, WILLIAM. When the court takes a recess
pp.xi, 234 DL★
NY: E. P. Dutton 1924
Includes section on the theatre and the law.

**182** DE WOLF, RICHARD C. Outline of copyright law
pp.xxiv, 330 L
Boston: John W. Luce 1925

Introduction by Thorvald Solberg.

**183** CLARK, BARRETT H. Oedipus or Pollyanna, with a note on dramatic censorship
pp.38 M
Seattle: U. of Washington Book Store 1928
Concerning the right of literature and drama to treat 'unpleasant' topics. The note on censorship was first broadcast over WEAF, NYC, in March, 1927.

**184** ERNST, MORRIS L. & SEAGLE, WILLIAM. To the pure...A study of obscenity and the censor
pp.347 L
London UK: Jonathan Cape 1929

**185** BEMAN, LAMAR T. (Ed.). Selected articles on censorship of the theater and moving pictures
pp.385 DL★
NY: H. W. Wilson 1931

**186** HOMBURG, R. Legal rights of performing artists
pp.vii, 184 DL★
NY: Baker, Voorhis 1934
An edited translation, with addendum, by Maurice J. Speiser, of Le droit d'interpretation des acteurs et des artistes executants, Paris: Recueil Sirey, 1930.

**187** MARCHETTI, ROGER. Law of the stage, screen and radio: including authors' literary property and copyright in drama, music, photoplays and radio script...
pp.4476 DL★
San Francisco: Suttonhouse 1936
Updating by subsequent pocket supplements.

**188** WITTENBERG, PHILIP. Protection and marketing of literary property
pp.395 DL★
NY: J. Messner 1937

**189** SOLBERG, THORVALD. Copyright miscellany...concerning the protection of literary and artistic property, with autobiographical sketch
DL★
Boston: J. W. Luce 1939
A collection of 22 papers bound in one volume. 175 copies.

**190** ERNST, MORRIS L. & LINDEY, ALEXANDER. Censor marches on: recent milestones in the administration of the obscenity law in the United States
pp.xiii, 346 L
Garden City NY: Doubleday Doran 1940

**191** HARKEN, ANNE H. & ZIMAND, GERTRUDE. Children in the theatre. A study of children employed on the legitimate stage
pp.95; front. MH
NY: National Child Labor Commission 1941
Based on a study of 65 children, and interviews with 16 former child actors.

**192** HOWELL, HERBERT A. Copyright law: an analysis of the law of the United States governing registration and protection of copyright works, including prints and labels
pp.ix, 302 L
Washington DC: Bureau of National Affairs 1942
Second edition.

**193** REARDON, WILLIAM R. Banned in Boston. A study of theatrical censorship in Boston from 1630 to 1950
Stanford: U. (PhD) 1953

**194** DEISLER, FAITH. A survey of stage censorship in New York, Boston, Chicago and Philadelphia from 1900 to 1950
Washington DC: Catholic U. of America (MA)   1955

**195** NICHOLSON, MARGARET. Manual of copyright practice for writers, publishers, and agents
pp.x, 273   L
NY: Oxford U.P.   1956
New and revised edition. First published 1945. Includes dramas and music-dramas.

**196** CURREY, WILLIAM L. Comstockery. A study in the rise and decline of a watchdog censorship, with attention particularly to reports of the New York Society for the Suppression of Vice, to magazine articles and to news items and editorials in the New York Times, suplementing other standard studies on Comstock and censorship
NY: Columbia U. (PhD)   1957

**197** KERR, WALTER. Criticism and censorship
pp.86   DL★
Milwaukee: Bruce Publishing   1957
Co-sponsored by the National Catholic Educational Association and Trinity College, Washington DC.

**198** PILPEL, HARRIET F. & ZAVIN, THEODORE S. Rights and writers: a handbook of literary and entertainment law
pp.384   L
NY: E. P. Dutton   1960
Includes a discussion of the law of obscenity as interpreted in the Roth case.

**199** SALISBURY, HAROLD E. A survey and analysis of current attitudes toward censorship of legitimate theatre in the United States
Los Angeles: U. of Southern California (PhD)   1961

**200** ERNST, MORRIS L. & SCHWARTZ, ALAN U. Censorship: the search for the obscene
pp.xvi, 288   L
NY: Macmillan   1964

**201** DOLL, JOHN L. The *New York Dramatic Mirror* and the war against play piracy in the United States, 1880-1909
Minnepolis: U. of Minnesota (PhD)   1968

**202** VAUGHN, ROBERT F. A historical study of the House Committee on Un-American Activities' influence on the American theatre
Los Angeles: U. of Southern California (PhD)   1969

**203** BAIN, REGINALD F. The Federal government and theatre: a history of federal involvement in theatre from the end of the Federal Theatre Project in 1939 to the establishment of the National Foundation on the Arts and Humanities in 1965
Minnepolis: U. of Minnesota (PhD)   1971

**204** HILD, STEPHEN G. United States patents pertaining to theatre 1916-1945
Columbia: U. of Missouri (PhD)   1972

**205** JACOBS, MILTON C. Outline of theatre law
pp.xii, 148   DL★
Westport CT: Greenwood P.   1972
First published 1949.

**206** FERRAR, ELEANOR B. The place of law in the commercial theatre
NY: U. (PhD)   1974

**207** EASTMAN, JAMES E. The application of the Occupational Safety and Health Act to contemporary United States theatre
Bowling Green: State U. (PhD)   1977

**208** GOODMAN, PAUL. Creator spirit come ! The literary essays of Paul Goodman
pp.xxii, 284   MH
NY: Free Life   1977
A section on dramatic art and theatre includes an essay on censorship and pornography on the stage. Edited by Taylor Stoehr.

**209** WHITLATCH, MICHAEL D. The House Committee on un-American Activities' entertainment hearings and their effects on performing arts careers
Bowling Green: State U. (PhD)   1977

**210** LAUFE, ABE. The wicked stage: a history of theater censorship and harassment in the United States
pp.xvi, 191; ill. in text   M
NY: Frederick Ungar   1978

**211** BUDKE, TIMOTHY D. Assessing the 'offense of public decency': the advent of censoring particular dramas on the New York stage, 1890-1905
Colombia: U. of Missouri (PhD)   1989

## 2.3 ECONOMICS, SUBVENTION AND TRADE UNIONS

**212** WILLIAMS, J. E. 'Lyceumize the theatre' A suggested remedy for the disease that afflicts the one night stands
pp.[9]   MB
Chicago: The Drama League of America   [19-?]
Reprinted from the Streator IL *Independent Times*. The author was director of the Drama League of America and urges the League's support in providing security for the one night-stand theatres by organizing pre-pledged ticket sales.

**213** LEE, FRANK. Stage secrets and tricks of the trade. Being the confessions of an actor
pp.ii, 119   LU
[?]: For the author   1913
Concerned with economics and the perfidy of agents and managers.

**214** GEMMILL, PAUL F. Collective bargaining by actors: a study of trade-unionism among performers of the English-speaking legitimate stage in America
pp.iii, 108   L
Washington DC: Government Printing Office   1926

**215** ANDERSON, JOHN. Box office
pp.121   M
NY: Jonathan Cape and Harrison Smith   1929

## 2. FEDERAL AND STATE INTERVENTION

An examination of the economics of theatre production.

**216** HARDING, ALFRED. The revolt of the actors
pp.xvii, 575; pl. 8     M
NY: William Morrow     1929
A history of the Actors' Equity Association from its inception in 1913.

**217** BERNHEIM, ALFRED L. & HARDING, SARA et al. The business of the theatre: an economic history of the American theatre prepared on behalf of the Actors' Equity Association
pp.xii, 219     M
NY: Actors' Equity Association     1932
First printed in *Equity Magazine*, 1930-32

**218** BAKER, ROBERT O. The International Alliance of Theatrical Stage Employees & Moving Picture Machine Operators of the United States & Canada
Lawrence: U. of Kansas (PhD)     1933

**219** BROWN, BENJAMIN W. Theatre at the left
pp.ix, 108     M
Providence RI: The Booke Shop     1938
A study of the effect of Russian economy upon the Soviet theatre. Comparison is made with US theatre. Introduction by James H. Shoemaker.

**220** OVERMYER, GRACE. Government and the arts
pp.338     L
NY: W. W. Norton     1939
International in scope. US section includes material on the Federal Theatre Project.

**221** PIETAN, NORMAN. Federal government and the arts
NY: Columbia U. (PhD)     1950

**222** MIDDLETON, GEORGE. The Dramatists Guild. What it is and does...How it happened and why...[cover title]
pp.28     MH
NY: Dramatists Guild of the Authors League of America     1959
Fourth revised version of pamphlet first issued in 1939.

**223** LOWRY, W. M. The Ford Foundation and the theatre
pp.[6]     M
NY: The Ford Foundation     1961
Reprinted from *Equity Magazine*, Volume XLVI, No. 5, May, 1961.

**224** BIRKENHEAD, THOMAS B. Economics of the Broadway theatre
NY: New School for Social Research (Thesis)     1963

**225** CAUBLE, J. R. A study of the International Alliance of Theatrical Stage Employees and Moving Picture Machine Operators of the United States and Canada
Los Angeles: U. of California (MA)     1964

**226** TAUBMAN, JOSEPH (Ed.). Financing a theatrical production...a symposium of the committee on the law of the theatre of the Federal Bar Association of New York, New Jersey and Connecticut...
pp.xxiv, 499     M
NY: Federal Legal Publications     1964

**227** TOFFLER, ALVIN. The cultural consumer: a study of art and affluence in America
pp.vii, 263     MH
NY: St Martin's P.     1964

**228** THE PERFORMING ARTS: Rockefeller Panel report on the future of theatre, dance, music in America: problems and prospects
pp.xiv, 258     M
NY: McGraw-Hill     1965
Topics include financing and sponsorship, federal government's role, university theatre, strategies for encouraging national appreciation of the arts. Permanent theatres and orchestras are listed.

**229** BAUMOL, WILLIAM J. & BOWEN, WILLIAM G. Performing arts - the economic dilemma...a study of problems common to theater, music and dance
pp.xvi, 582     L
Cambridge MA: Massachusetts Institute of Technology     1966

**230** FORD FOUNDATION: support in theatre (1957-1967)
pp.14     DL★
NY: Ford Foundation     1967
Lists fellowships, grants and other awards.

**231** RITTERBUSH, ALICE McC. *Variety's* involvement in Broadway labor-management disputes, 1905-1931
New Orleans: Tulane U. (PhD)     1967

**232** MOORE, THOMAS G. The economics of the American theater
pp.xv,192     M
Durham NC: Duke U. P.     1968

**233** POGGI, JACK. Theater in America: the impact of economic forces, 1870-1967
pp.xx, 328     M
Ithaca NY: Cornell U. P.     1968

**234** GINGRICH, ARNOLD. Business and the arts: an answer to tomorrow
pp.xiii, 145; ill in text     L
NY: Paul S. Eriksson     1969
Foreword by David Rockefeller.

**235** MOSKOW, MICHAEL H. Labor relations in the performing arts: an introductory study
pp.xvi, 218     DL★
[NY]: Associated Council of the Arts     [1969]
Foreword by John T. Dunlop.

**236** ACTORS FUND OF AMERICA (incorporated by the State of New York, June 8, 1882)...annual report
pp.av. 90; ill. in text     L
NY: Offices of the Actors' Fund     1970-77
Seven examples inspected.

**237** CHAGY, GIDEON (Ed.). Business in the arts '70
pp.xi, 176; ill. in text     MH
NY: Paul S. Eriksson     1970

A report sponsored by the Business Committee for the Arts to make available results of the latest research into the economic condition of the arts and the amount and nature of business support and sponsorship.

**238** McLAUGHLIN, ROBERT G. Broadway and Hollywood: a history of economic interaction
Madison: U. of Wisconsin (PhD)   1970

**239** WATTS, JOHN G. Economics of the New York legitimate theatre
NY: Columbia U. (PhD)   1970

**240** PLOTKIN, JOEL A. State Arts Council theater projects: an aspect of America's pluralistic cultural policy
East Lansing: Michigan State U. (PhD)   1971

**241** THE FINANCES OF THE PERFORMING ARTS: Volume 1. A survey of 166 professional non-profit resident theaters, operas, symphonies, ballets and modern dance companies. [Volume 2. A survey of the characteristics and attitudes of audiences for theater, opera, symphony and ballet in 12 US cities]
pp.vi, 116 + tables; v, 117   M
NY: Ford Foundation   1974

**242** GUIDELINES. Fiscal year 1976
pp.16   L
Washington: [National Endowment for the Arts Theatre Program]   1974
An explanation of funding available and methods of making application, aimed at non-profit professional organizations.

**243** KRAWITZ, HERMAN E. & KLEIN, HOWARD K. Royal American symphonic theater; a radical proposal for a subsidized professional theater
pp.xiii, 211   M
NY: Macmillan   1975
Proposes a network of subsidized repertory theatres.

**244** SMITH, GARY L. The International Ladies Garment Workers Union's labor stage, a propagandistic venture
Kent OH: State U. (PhD)   1975

**245** NEELY, MONTY K. The National Endowment for the Arts theatre program: an historical analysis
Detroit: Wayne State U. (PhD)   1976

**246** LaHOUD, JOHN & BOGGS, NANCY. Theater awakening; a report of the Ford Foundation assistance to American drama

pp.ii, 44; ill. in text   M
NY: Ford Foundation   1977

**247** MENSH, ELAINE & MENSH, HARRY. Behind the scenes in two worlds
pp.vi, 342   MH
NY: International   1978
Examines theatre conditions in East Germany and the US against the larger economic and political background.

**248** HANLON, R. BRENDON. A guide to taxes and record keeping: for performers, designers, directors
pp.77   ★
NY: DBS   1980
First published 1978.

**249** MOORE, LOU & KASSAK, NANCY (Eds). Computers and the performing arts: a report on the National Project for the Performing Arts
pp.113; ill.   DL★
NY: Theatre Commercial Group   1980

**250** STANBRIDGE, ALAN. The skin of our teeth: a report on the funding of the contemporary performing arts in the United States [cover title]
pp.ii, 56 (14)   M
London UK: City U.   1982

**251** BAUMOL, HILDA & BAUMOL, WILLIAM J. (Eds). Inflation and the performing arts
pp.xiv, 210   L
NY: U.P.   1984
Record of a conference held at U. of Nevada, Las Vegas, August 6,7, 1981. Sections on large- and small-budget groups, including off-off Broadway and 'far-off Broadway'; performance standards and audience expectation; inflation and the arts. An appendix by William T. White examines the idea of a center for the study of the performing arts.

**252** COPP, KAREN H. The state of the corporate-arts relationship as viewed through the perspective of the non-profit theatre
Columbus: Ohio State U. (PhD)   1988

**253** DEWBERRY, JONATHAN. Black actors unite: the Negro Actors Guild of America, 1937-1982
NY: U. (PhD)   1988

**254** PINEAULT, WALLACE. Industrial theatre: the businessman's Broadway
Bowling Green: State U. (PhD)   1989

# 3. RELIGION

## 3.1 MORALITY

**255** [HALIBURTON, WILLIAM]. Effects of the stage on the manners of a people: and the propriety of encouraging and establishing a virtuous theatre. By a Bostonian...
pp.76; pl. 1 folding   MH
Boston: Young & Etheridge   1792
Urging the construction of a theatre. Written in the year that the New Exhibition Room, later the Broad Alley Theatre, was opened in Boston.

**256** CAREY, MATHEW. Desultory reflections, excited by the recent calamitous fate of John Fullerton. Addressed to those who frequent the theatres, and to the dramatic critics
  DL★
Philadelphia: G. F. Hopkins for the author   1802
Fourth edition. Fullerton's acting was so savagely criticized that he drowned himself on 29 Jan. 1802.

**257** ALEXANDER, A [= Tuke, Ann]. A discourse occasioned by the burning of the theatre in the city of Richmond, Virginia, on the twenty-sixth of December, eighteen hundred and eleven, by which awful calamity a large number of valuable lives were lost. Delivered in...Philadelphia on the eighth day of January, 1812

pp.6-24 MB
Philadelphia: Farrand, Hopkins, Zantzinger 1812
An attack on theatre, using the Richmond disaster as a starting-point. Another edition was published for the author in York, UK the same year under the title *Remarks on the theatre and on the late fire at Richmond, Virginia* (pp.32).

**258** DASHIELL, GEORGE. A sermon occasioned by the burning of the theatre in the city of Richmond, Virginia on the twenty-sixth day of December, 1811. By which disastrous event more than one hundred lives were lost. Delivered in St Peter's church, Baltimore on the twelfth of January, 1812
pp.16 L
Baltimore MD: J. Kingston [1812]

**259** EDWARDS, JOHN. Warning to sinners, or an address to all play-actors, play-hunters, legislators, governors, magistrates, clergy, churchmen, deists, and the world at large
pp.20; ill. in text MH
NY: For the author 1812
At least one variant edition was issued, lacking the first four words of the title and illustrated on the lower wrapper (L).

**260** MILLER, SAMUEL. A sermon, delivered January 19, 1812, at the request of a number of young gentlemen of the city of New York, who had assembled to express their condolence with the inhabitants of Richmond, on the late mournful dispensation of providence in that city
pp.42 MB
NY: Whiting and Watson 1812
Claiming divine disapproval of the theatre, with the Richmond fire as evidence.

**261** WITHERSPOON, JOHN & MILLER, SAMUEL et al. A serious inquiry into the nature and effects of the stage; with the addition of a letter respecting play actors. By the Rev. John Witherspoon, late president of the college at Princeton, New Jersey. Also a sermon, on the burning of the theatre at Richmond...by Samuel Miller. Together with an introductory address by several ministers in New York, etc.
pp.199 MH
NY: Whiting and Watson 1812
Attacks on the stage. Witherspoon's tract was first published in Glasgow, Scotland,1757, before the author came to America. It was reprinted after the Richmond fire. The letter respecting play actors was first published NY, 1793, according to *Arnott and Robinson* (#404).

**262** DWIGHT, TIMOTHY. An essay on the stage: in which arguments in its behalf, and those against it, are considered; and its morality, character, and effects illustrated
pp.166 MH
Middleton CT: [For the author?] 1824
Anti-theatre. Dwight was sometime President of Yale. Doubt has been cast on the ascribed authorship of this work, which was reprinted the same year in London by Sharp, Jones.

**263** HENRY, T. CHARLTON. An inquiry into the consistency of popular amusements with a profession of Christianity
pp.vii, 183 DL*
Charleston SC: Wm. Riley 1825

**264** A DEFENCE OF THE DRAMA, containing Mansel's free thoughts, extracts from the most celebrated writers, and a discourse on the lawfulness & unlawfulness of plays, by the celebrated Father Caffaro, Divinity professor at Paris
pp.iii, 294 MH
NY: George Champley 1826
A brief chapter, 'On Judgments', querying divine disapproval in the recent destruction of theatres by fire, is signed 'D. F.'

**265** AIKEN, SAMUEL C. Theatrical exhibitions, a sermon...published by request
pp.i,19 MB
Cleveland OH: Penniman 1836
Anti-theatre. This copy lacks pp.3-6.

**266** [OTWAY]. The theatre defended. A reply to two discourses...
pp.32 inc. top wrapper MH
Charleston SC: [For the author?] 1838
In response to Thomas Smyth's sermons.

**267** A REVIEW OF THE REV. THOMAS SMYTH's two sermons against theatres by Thespis
pp.20, inc. wrappers MH
Charleston SC: E. C. Councell 1838

**268** SMYTH, THOMAS. The theatre a school of religion, manners and morals! Two discourses, delivered on the opening of the new theatre in Charleston: ...published without request. Second edition
pp.55 inc. top wrapper MH
Charleston SC: Jenkins and Hussey 1838
Anti-theatre.

**269** TURNBULL, ROBERT. The theatre, its influence upon literature, morals, and religion
pp.110 MH
Boston: Gould, Kendall and Lincoln 1839
Second edition, enlarged, of a treatise 'originally delivered as a discourse, when a measure in favor of theatres was pending before the Legislature of Connecticut'. First published Hartford CT: Canfield and Robins, 1837.

**270** AN ADDRESS on the subject of theatrical amusements, from the monthly meeting of friends, held in New-York, to its members
pp.12 MH
NY: Mahlon Day 1840
Urging avoidance of theatrical amusements, as the growth of theatre building increases.

**271** BRAINERD, THOMAS. Influence of theatres; or, the true nature and tendency of theatrical amusements...
pp.36 MH
Philadelphia: Presbyterian Board of Publication [c. 1840]
Anti-theatre tract.

**272** WINCHESTER, S. G. The theatre
pp.239 MH
Philadelphia: William S. Martien 1840

Originally an address before the Belles Lettres Society and the Adelphic Institute, here amplified, offering an anti-theatre argument, with an historical preamble.

**273** HAMILTON, WILLIAM T. A sermon on theatrical entertainments...delivered Mar. 21st, 1841. Published by request
pp.12 MH
Mobile AL: Dade and Thompson 1841
Anti-theatre.

**274** MAY, ROBERT. A voice from Richmond, and other addresses to children and youth...with a brief account of the author. Revised by the committee of publication of the American Sunday School Union
pp.300; pl. 3 MH
Philadelphia: American Sunday School Union 1842
Reference to the Richmond theatre fire (Dec 26, 1811) which the author perceives as a divine punishment.

**275** SAWYER, FREDERIC W. A plea for amusement
pp.iv, 320 DL★
NY: D. Appleton 1847

**276** THOMPSON, JOSEPH P. Theatrical amusements. A discourse on the character and influence of the theatre...published by request
pp.40 MH
NY: Baker and Scribner 1847
Anti-theatre. Provoked by the erection of a new theatre on Broadway adjacent to the Broadway Tabernacle Church.

**277** [JOHNSON, OLIVER]. Amusements: their uses and abuses. Testimony of progressive friends
pp.16 MB
NY: for the author [1856]
A paper originally delivered before the Pennsylvania yearly meeting of Progressive Friends, conceding the acceptability of a reformed and morally sound theatre.

**278** AGNEW, D. HAYES. Theatrical amusements; with some remarks on the Rev. Henry W. Bellows' address before the Dramatic Fund Society, N.Y.
pp.23 MH
Philadelphia: William S. Young (Printer) 1857
Anti-theatre and anti-Bellows. 'The general character of actors is bad'.

**279** BELLOWS, HENRY W. The relation of public amusements to public morality, especially of the theatre to the highest interests of humanity. An address, delivered at the Academy of Music, New York, before the American Dramatic Fund Society for the benefit of the fund
pp.53 MH
NY: C. S. Francis 1857
A defence of the theatre against attacks by the church. A condensed version was published in the *New York Herald* and later that year printed verbatim in London with an introduction by J. B. Buckstone.

**280** CONWAY, M. D. The theater: a discourse delivered in the Unitarian Church, Cincinnati, O., on June 7, 1857
pp.29 MH
Cincinnati: Truman & Spofford 1857
Defence of the theatre as provider of necessary entertainment, if properly conducted.

**281** HALE, EDWARD E. Public amusement for poor and rich: a discourse delivered before the Church of the Unity, Worcester, December 16, 1855 and repeated, by request, before the Worcester Lyceum, January 15, 1857
pp.24 L
Boston: Phillips, Sampson 1857
Cautious approval of a regulated theatre.

**282** THOMASON, D. R. Fashionable amusements; with a review of Rev. Dr. Bellows' lecture on the theatre...
pp.230 MH
NY: M. W. Dodd 1857
It is clear from the preface that this is the third edition, revised, with chapter two, on the theatre, expanded in response to Bellows's *Relation of public amusements...* (q.v.). The author envisages a theatre restricted to scriptural representations and the satirical scourging of vice.

**283** DAVIDGE, WILLIAM. The drama defended. Addressed, with respect, to the public generally, and with commiseration, to Messrs. the Rev. Strickland, T. L. Cuyler, etc., etc., etc. by William Davidge, comedian
pp.22 MH
NY: Samuel French 1859
A retort through the press to anti-theatre sermons in which Davidge was singled out. The wrangle is here described and continued.

**284** BURROWS, J.L. The new Richmond theatre. A discourse, delivered on Sunday, February 8, 1863 in the First Baptist Church
pp.16 MH
Richmond VA: Smith, Bailey 1863
Sermon delivered the day before the opening of the theatre, strongly anti-theatrical in tone.

**285** NEWHALL, FALES H. The theater: a discourse preached at the Bromfield Street M. E. Church, March 15, 1863
pp.27 MB
Boston: J. P. Magee 1863
Anti-theatre. A revised and amplified version of the original sermon.

**286** COWELL, W. An oration in defence of the theatre delivered at M'Vicker's theatre, December 30th, 1865...being her second public reply to the late scandalous strictures on the theatre by the Rev. R. M. Hatfield...
pp.28 MB
Chicago: Rounds & James 1865
The oration was delivered by Anna Cowell.

**287** HATFIELD, ROBERT M. The theater: its character and influence. An address...delivered at the Clark-St. methodist episcopal church of Chicago, Monday evening, December 11, 1865 (reported by James T. Ely...) with an introduction by Rev. C. H. Fowler
pp.40 MB
Chicago: Methodist Book Depository 1866
Anti-theatre.

**288** CLEVELAND, CHARLES. Theatrical amusements: letter to a professing Christian,...from the *Columbian Sentinel*, (Edited by the late Benjamin Russell, Esq.)...
pp.7 MH
Boston: [For the author?] 1868

## 3. RELIGION

Anti-theatre tract, written originally to the author's brother, now intended for the Boston YMCA.

**289** WARE, JNO F. W.   May I go to the theatre? A discourse delivered in Baltimore, before the Society of the Church of the Savior, Sunday evening, Feb'y 5th, 1871
pp.21 MB
Baltimore MD: Sun Book Office [1871]
In defence of the theatre, whose wholesomeness can be assured by a discriminating public.

**290** ANDREWS, CHARLES W. et al.   On the incompatibility of theater-going and dancing with membership in the christian church. An address of the clergy of the convocation of the valley of Virginia, to the people of their respective parishes
pp.31 MB
Philadelphia: Office of Leighton Publications 1872
In two sections, or chapters. 1. the theatre, presented as a 'school of vice'; 2. dancing, a lesser, but no less real, vice.

**291** BUCKLEY, J. M.   Christians and the theater
pp.iii, 156 MH
NY: Nelson & Phillips 1875
An attempt to present a rational, non-inflammatory opposition to theatre-going.

**292** NEWTON, WILLIAM W.   Christianity and popular amusements; or, the church and the theatre. A paper read at the church congress of the protestant episcopal church held in New York, November 1, 1877...
pp.19 MH
Boston: Alfred Mudge 1877
Urges the moral reform of the theatre while conceding its power and energy. An appendix expounds the principles of the New England Theatre Reform Association.

**293** [TRYON, GEORGE W.].   Church and stage
pp.12 MB
[Philadelphia]: [For the author?] [1880]
In defence of the theatre.

**294** JOHNSON, HERRICK.   A plain talk about the theater
pp.83 MB
Chicago: F. H. Revell 1882
Anti-theatre. The first 'plain talk' is followed by 'a plainer talk' which reprints letters questioning the author's central propositions and J. H. McVicker's response to an indictment of the quality of his theatre's entertainment.

**295** PELTZER, OTTO.   The church and the theatre: an argument by 'an outsider'
pp.15 DL★
Chicago: [For the author?] 1882

**296** McVICKER, J. H.   The press, the pulpit and the stage: a lecture delivered at Central Music Hall, Chicago
pp.79; front. MH
Chicago: Western News 1883
In defence of the stage.

**297** LEEDS, JOSIAH W.   The theatre: an essay upon the non-accordancy of stage-plays with the christian profession
pp.85 DL★
Philadelphia: For the author 1884

A Quaker tract. A number of editions were published.

**298** PELTZER, OTTO.   The moralist and the theatre: a series of articles which originally appeared in *Music and Drama*, embracing a brief history of the stage, its relation to the church, its influence, its present condition and needed reform. With a criticism by John Fraser...and a biblical drama entitled *Moses and Pharaoh*
pp.94; ill. DL★
Chicago: Donald Fraser 1887

**299** DALY, CHARLES P.   A consideration of the objections to the stage from the earliest period and the conclusion it warrants, being the concluding part of the Dunlap Society's publication entitled *When was the drama first introduced in America?*
pp. 27 MH
NY: For the author 1896
Brief historical survey, and a conclusion that the character of the actor, and the power of drama to exalt, are discernibly improving and increasing.

**300** SINKS, PERRY W.   Popular amusements and the Christian life
pp.176 MB
NY: Fleming H. Revell 1896
Addresses, including 'The theater from a bible standpoint', urging self-denial and arguing the moral deficiency of contemporary theatre.

**301** BROWN, HENRY.   The impending peril; or, methodism and amusements: a compilation of testimony, rules, speeches, and articles on the amusement question with an article in review
pp.304: front. DL★
Cincinatti: Jennings and Pye 1904

**302** LUMMIS, ELIZA O'B.   The Catholic theatre movement
pp.7, with insert MB
NY: Styles & Cash 1913
Offering a solution to 'the amusement problem' through a morally sound drama organized under the auspices of the Catholic church.

**303** STURGIS, GRANVILLE F.   The influence of the drama
203 MH
NY: Shakespeare P. 1913
Attempt at a rational inquiry into the moral influence of the stage. Includes a list of authors and their plays presented in New York city 'in the last decade'.

**304** EDWARDS, RICHARD H.   Popular amusements
pp.239 DL★
NY: Association P. 1915

**305** EDWARDS, RICHARD H.   Public recreation
pp.157 DL★
NY: Association P. 1915

**306** EDWARDS, RICHARD H.   Christianity and amusements
DL★
NY: Association P. 1915

**307** BROUN, HEYWOOD & LEECH, MARGARET.   Anthony Comstock: roundsman of the Lord
pp.285; pl.14 L
NY: Albert & Charles Boni 1927

**308** STRATON, JOHN R. Fighting the devil in modern Babylon
pp.xiii, 287; front. DL★
Boston: Stratford 1929
Includes an attack on the movies and the theatre.

**309** EASTMAN, FRED. Religion and drama; friends or enemies. Being a brief account of their historical connection and their present relation
pp.19 L
NY: Century 1930

**310** CLARK, BARRETT H. The blush of shame: a few considerations on verbal obscenity in the theatre
pp.16 M
NY: Gotham Book Mart 1932

**311** MATHER, INCREASE. Testimony against several prophane and superstitious customs, now practised by some in New England, the evil whereof is evinced from the Holy Scriptures and from the writings both of ancient and modern divines. Reproduced from 1687 edn. with introduction and notes by William Peden. Bibliographical note by Lawrence Starky
pp.59 L
Chatlottesville: U. of Virginia P. 1953
First published London: 1687. In the preface, written after the main work, Mather refers to 'much discourse now of beginning of Stage-Plays in New-England'.

**312** SHIFFLER, HARROLD C. The opposition of the Presbyterian church in the United States of America to the theatre in America
Iowa City: U. of Iowa (PhD) 1953

**313** BUTLER, IGNATIUS W. The moral problems of the theatre
Washington DC: Catholic U. of America (PhD) 1958

**314** KELLY, MICHAEL F. The reaction of the Catholic church to the commercial theatre in New York City, 1900 to 1958
Iowa City: U. of Iowa (PhD) 1958

**315** KUSSROW, VAN C. On with the show. A study of public arguments in favor of the theatre in America during the eighteenth century
Bloomington: U. of Indiana (PhD) 1959

**316** NORBERG, JANET L. From opposition to appropriation: the resolution of Southern Baptist conflict with dramatic forms, 1802-1962
Iowa City: U. of Iowa (PhD) 1964

**317** LESTRUD, VERNON A. An analysis of the moral attitudes toward the theater of the Pacific states from 1849 to 1899
Eugene: U. od Oregon (PhD) 1965

**318** SALEM, JAMES M. Revolution in manners and morals. The treatment of adultery in American drama between the wars
Baton Rouge: Louisiana State U. (PhD) 1965

**319** MARSH, WILLIAM H. The attitude of the United Presbyterian Church in the USA towards the theatre in America, 1891-1967
Lawrence: U. of Kansas (PhD) 1967

**320** LITTLE, PAUL V. Reactions to the theatre: Virginia, Massachusetts, and Pennsylvania, 1665-1793
Syracuse NY: U. (PhD) 1969

**321** GUNN, DONALD L. Moral censorship of the Los Angeles stage, 1966-1968: two case studies
Los Angeles: U. of California (PhD) 1970

**322** PIKE, MORRIS R. The attitudes of the significant constituencies of the Christian College Consortium toward certain aspects of theatre
Kent OH: State U. (PhD) 1976

**323** GARRETT, KURT L. Actors' strategies for avoiding the anti-theatre movement in America before 1793
Detroit: Wayne State U. (PhD) 1978

## 3.2 RELIGION IN DRAMA

**324** SMITH, JOHN T. The parish theatre: a brief account of its rise, its present condition, and its prospects...
pp.v, 90 M
NY: Longman, Green 1917

**325** THORPE, WILLIAM H. The Mormons and the drama
NY: Columbia U. (MA) 1921

**326** CANDLER, MARTHA [= Cheney, Martha S.]. Drama in religious service
pp.xv, 259; ill. in text, front. DL★
NY: Century 1922

**327** FERRIS, ANITA B. Following the dramatic instinct: an elementary handbook on the use of dramatics in missionary and religious education
pp.vi, 106 DL★
NY: Missionary Education Movement of US and Canada 1922
Emma (Sheridan) Fry's dramatic method adapted to prepare religious/missionary play material for childen.

**328** BATES, ESTHER C. The church play and its production
pp.ix, 303; ill. DL★
Boston: Walter H. Baker 1924

**329** BOYD, CHARLES A. Worship in drama: a manual of methods and materials for young people and their leaders
pp.175 DL★
Philadelphia: Judson P. 1924

**330** WELCH, MILDRED [= Lane, Margaret]. Through the eye-gate into the city of Mansoul: a primer on the principles and the production of religious drama
pp.141; ill. DL★
Louisville KY: Presbyterian Church 1927

**331** ATKINS, ALMA N. Drama goes to church
pp.196; ill. DL★
St Louis MO: Bethany P. 1931

**332** WOOD, WILLIAM C. The dramatic method in religious education

pp.344; ill. in text DL★
NY: Abingdon P. 1931

**333** HILL, RUTH K. Measurable changes in attitude resulting from the use of drama in worship
Chicago: U. (PhD) 1933

**334** MERSAND, JOSEPH. American drama presents the jew: an evaluation of jewish characters in contemporary drama
pp.21 MH
NY: Modern Chapbooks 1939
Reprinted from the *Jewish Outlook*, November, 1938.

**335** EVANS, EDMUND E. An historical study of the drama of the Latter Day Saints
Los Angeles: U. of Southern California (PhD) 1941

**336** EASTMAN, FRED & WILSON, LOUIS. Drama in the church: a manual of religious drama production
pp.xiii, 187; ill. in text L
NY: Samuel French 1942
Revised edition. First published 1933.

**337** EASTMAN, FRED. Christ in the drama: a study of the influence of Christ on the drama of England and America
pp.xv, 174 L
NY: Macmillan 1947

**338** HANSEN, HAROLD I. A history and influence of the Mormon theatre from 1839-1869
Columbus: Ohio State U. (PhD) 1949

**339** BARNARD, FLOY M. Drama in the churches
pp.132; ill. DL★
Nashville TN: Broadman P. 1950

**340** BLOORE, J. S. The Jew in American dramatic literature, 1794-1930
NY: U. (PhD) 1950

**341** GLEDHILL, PRESTON R. Mormon dramatic activities
Madison: U. of Wisconsin (PhD) 1950

**342** SKIDMORE, REX A. Mormon recreation in theory and practice. A study of social change
Philadelphia: U. of Pennsylvania (PhD) 1951

**343** EDYVEAN, ALFRED R. A critical appraisal of American dramas (1935-1949) in the light of the Christian view of man
Evanston: Northwestern U. (PhD) 1952

**344** MOSELEY, JOSEPH E. Using drama in the church
pp.96 DL★
St Louis MO: Bethany P. 1955
Revised edition. First published 1939, under joint authorship with Florence A. Moseley.

**345** ENTERLINE, MILDRED H. Best plays for the church
pp.90 DL★
Philadelphia: Christian Education P. 1959
A new edition.

**346** GEIER, WOODROW A. Images of man in five American dramatists. A theological critique
Nashville TN: Vanderbilt U. (PhD) 1959

**347** JEAN, T. C. G. The function of religious drama and dance in the parish day schools of the episcopal church
Tucson: U. of Arizona (PhD) 1960

**348** BRANDT, ALVIN G. Drama handbook for churches
pp.xii, 176 DL★
NY: Seabury P. 1964

**349** KERR, JAMES S. The key to good church drama
pp.72; ill. DL★
Minneapolis: Augsburg Publishing 1964

**350** MURPHY, D. B. Dramatic portrayals of Christ
Madison: U. of Wisconsin (PhD) 1964

**351** DUBIN, KAREN E. VAN L. A history of the forms of dramatic expression in the adult program of the Riverside Church, 1929-1959
NY: Columbia U. (PhD) 1965

**352** KEEFE, MARY M. The National Catholic Theatre Conference: its aims and its achievements
Evanston: Northwestern U. (PhD) 1965

**353** JOHNSON, ALBERT. Church plays and how to stage them
pp.xviii, 174 DL★
Philadelphia: United Church P. 1966

**354** ROWLEY, THOMAS L. A critical and comparative analysis of Latter-Day Saint drama
Minneapolis: U. of Minnesota (PhD) 1966

**355** REYNOLDS, ROBERT E. The history of four acting companies in California devoted to producing drama-for-the-church
Minneapolis: U. of Minnesota (PhD) 1967

**356** STEWART, GARY L. A rhetorical analysis of Mormon drama
Iowa City: U. of Iowa (PhD) 1967

**357** WHITMAN, CHARLES W. A history of the Hill Cumorah Pageant (1937-1964) and an examination of the dramatic development of the text of *America's Witness for Christ*
Minneapolis: U. of Minnesota (PhD) 1967
According to John Smith the name 'Hill Cumorah' was revealed to him in a vision.

**358** BUCH, ARTHUR T. The bible on Broadway: a source book for ministers, educators, librarians, and general readers
pp.xxi, 175; ill. DL★
Hamden CT: Archon Books 1968

**359** JOHNSON, ALBERT. Best church plays: a bibliography of religious drama
pp.x, 180 L
Philadelphia: Pilgrim P. 1968

**360** KATZ, SUSAN G. Jewish socio-political problems in the American drama: 1920-1962
NY: U. (PhD) 1968

**361** ELLISON, EARL J. God on Broadway
pp.96; ill. in text  MH
Richmond VA: John Knox P.  1971

**362** FERLITA, ERNEST. The theatre of pilgrimage
pp. vii, 172  L
NY: Sheed & Ward  1971

Theological essays, based on play analyses, by a Jesuit. Seeks to define a theatre 'in which man...would free himself of every illusion, but will not close his mind to mystery'.

**363** MARTIN, WILLIAM G. Theological concepts in representative American dramas during the second Great Awakening (ca. 1795-1845)
Madison: U. of Wisconsin (PhD)  1971

**364** VAN ZANTEN, JOHN. Caught in the act: modern drama as prelude to the Gospel
pp.201  DL★
Philadelphia: Westminster P.  1971

Examines the implications for christian faith in a range of contemporary plays.

**365** MONTLEY, PATRICIA A. Judith on Broadway: a comparison of twentieth-century dramatic adaptations of the biblical story of Judith produced on the New York Stage
Minneapolis: U. of Minnesota (PhD)  1975

**366** BODMAN, JAMES E. A survey of religious drama in the United Presbyterian Church, U.S.A, Synod of Southern California
Los Angeles: U. of Southern California (PhD)  1976

**367** WADDY, LAWRENCE. Drama in worship
pp.210  ★
NY: Paulist P.  1978

**368** DITSKY, JOHN. The onstage Christ
 DL★
Totowa NJ: Barnes & Noble  1980

**369** MARSHALL-MARTIN, DAVID. Ecclesiastical dress and vestments of the Roman Catholic church from the eleventh century to the present: a handbook of patterns, construction and vesting procedure for use in the theatre
Tallahassee: Florida State U. (PhD)  1980

**370** HUBBARD, OLIVER F. A critical analysis of selected American dramas (1950-1975) in light of a christian view of man
Kent OH: State U. (PhD)  1981

**371** OGDEN-MALOUF, SUSAN M. American revivalism and temperance drama: evangelical protestant ritual and theatre in Rochester, New York, 1830-1845
Evanston: Northwestern U. (PhD)  1981

**372** BOYDEN, WALTER E. The road to Hill Cumorah
Provo: Brigham Young U. (PhD)  1982

**373** SCHIFF, ELLEN. From stereotype to metaphor: the jew in contemporary drama
pp.xiii, 276; ill. in text  L
Albany: State U. of NY P.  1982

Wide reference to US drama.

**374** COHEN, SARAH B. (Ed.). From Hester Street to Hollywood: the jewish/american stage and screen
pp.ix, 278  M
Bloomington: Indiana U. P.  1983

Nahma Sandrow: *Yiddish theater and American theater*; Mark Slobin: *Some intersections of jews, music and theater*; June Sochen: *Fanny Brice and Sophie Tucker...*; Jules Chametzky: *Elmer Rice, liberation, and the great ethnic question*; R. B. Shuman: *Clifford Odets and the jewish context*; Bonnie Lyons: *Lillian Hellman: first jewish nun on Prytania St*; Enoch Brater: *Ethnics and ethnicity in the plays of Arthur Miller*; Leslie Field: *Paddy Chayefsky's jews and jewish dialogues*; Daniel Walden: *Neil Simon's jewish-style comedies*; Keith Opdahl: *The 'mental comedies' of Saul Bellow*; Sarah B. Cohen: *The jewish folk drama of Isaac Bashevis Singer*; Lawrence L. Lange: *The Americanization of the holocaust on stage and screen*.

**375** EINSEL, ALAN D. Developing faith communication skills of adults through drama
Madison NJ: Drew U. (D.Min.)  1985

**376** WINDERL, RONDA R. New York professional productions depicting the gospel, 1970-1982
NY: U. (PhD)  1985

**377** HARAP, LOUIS. Dramatic encounters: the jewish presence in twentieth century drama, poetry, and humor and the black-jewish literary relationship
pp.xiv, 177  L
NY: Greenwood P.  1987

**378** SHIELDS, SHIRLEE H. History of the general activities committee of the Church of Latter Day Saints
Provo: Brigham Young U. (PhD)  1987

# 4. THEATRE ARTS

## 4.1 ARCHITECTURE AND MACHINERY

**379** TONER, J. M. Notes on the burning of theatres and public halls. Reflections on some of the causes of the great mortality occasionally attending them, with suggestions as to improved security to life. The antiquity of the drama and the introduction of theatres into America, with a chronological list of theatres and other public edifices burned
pp.22  MB
Washington DC: R. O. Polkinhorn, printer  1876

**380** LANSING'S PICTORIAL DIAGRAMS of the leading opera houses, theatres, etc. in the United States
pp.128; ill. in text  MB
Boston: Lansing  1880

Reference to twenty-six states.

**381** GERHARD, WILLIAM P. Theatre fires and panics; their causes and prevention
pp.vii, 175  MH
NY: J. Wiley & Sons  1896

**382** GERHARD, WILLIAM P. Theatres: their safety from fire and panic, their comfort and healthfulness
pp.v, 110  MH
Boston: Bates & Guild  1900

Originally a paper prepared for the Publications of the British Fire Prevention Committee. Many references, both statistical and descriptive, to US theatre buildings. A second edition was published NY: Baker & Taylor, 1915 (not seen).

**383** BIRKMIRE, WILLIAM H.  The planning and construction of American theatres
pp.x, 117; ill. in text, pl. 38  M
NY: John Wiley & Sons  1903
Using NY, Boston and Chicago theatres as examples, and with a substantial appendix, *The New York building law*.

**384** FREEMAN, JOHN R.  On the safeguarding of lives in theaters: being a study from the standpoint of an engineer...an address made at the opening of the annual meeting of the Society [of Mechanical Engineers] in New York City, Dec. 4, 1905
pp.106; ill. in text  M
NY: American Society of Mechanical Engineers  1906
Reprinted from the *Transactions*. A study provoked by the Iroquois Theatre fire, Chicago, 1903.

**385** SUGGESTED ORDINANCE REGULATING the construction and equipment of theatres adopted by the national board of fire underwriters...New York...and the national fire protection association...Boston
pp.24  MH
[NY]:  1913

**386** MELOY, ARTHUR S.  Theatres and picture houses: a practical treatise on the proper planning and construction of such buildings and containing useful suggestions, rules and data for the benefit of architects, prospective owners, etc.
pp.vii, 121; ill. in text, pl. 8  M
NY: Architects Supply & Publishing  1916

**387** KINSILA, EDWARD B.  Modern theatre construction
pp.296; ill. in text  M
NY: Moving Picture World  1917

**388** WAUGH, FRANK A.  Outdoor theatres: the design, construction and use of open-air auditoriums
pp.151; ill. in text, pl. 20  M
Boston: Richard G. Badger  1917

**389** PICHEL, IRVING.  On building a theatre: stage construction and equipment for small theatres, schools and community buildings
pp.78; ill. in text  MH
NY: Theatre Arts  1920

**390** PICHEL, IRVING.  Modern theatres
pp.xi, 102; ill. in text, pl. 15  M
NY: Harcourt, Brace  1925
The principles underlying stage construction, and the relationship of auditorium to stage.

**391** SEXTON, R. W. (Ed.).  American theatres of today: plans, sections, and photographs of exterior and interior details of modern motion picture and legitimate theatres throughout the United States...with a foreword by S. L. Rothafel...
pp.iii, 175; v, 164; ill in text, fronts. 2  M
NY: Architectural Book Publishing  1927-30
Two volumes, the second with the collaboration of B. F. Betts. In each volume explanatory chapters on theatre design precede a substantial section of plates.

**392** URBAN, JOSEPH.  Theatres
pp.32; pl, 48  M
NY: Theatre Arts  1929
Describes and illustrates the Ziegfeld Theatre, the Paramount Theatre, and projects for a metropolitan opera house, a Reinhardt theatre, a Jewish art theatre and a music centre. Limited edition included 200 autographed copies.

**393** SHAND, P. M.  Modern theatres and cinemas
pp.viii, 40; ill. in text. front., pl.39  M
London: B. T. Batsford  1930
Text, photographs and plans. International. Includes New York, Santa Barbara.

**394** THEATRE FIRES
pp.52; ill. in text  M
Boston: National Fire Protection Association  1930
On wrapper, 'a record of eight hundred and sixty-three theatre fires...'. Reprinted from NFPA *Quarterly*, July, 1930. Analyzes typical causes and discusses safety precautions.

**395** PAWLEY, FREDERICK.  Theatre architecture: a brief bibliography
pp.32  M
NY: Theatre Arts/NTC  [1932]

**396** ISAACS, EDITH J. R. (Ed.).  Architecture for the new theatre:...theatre planning, by Lee Simonson: theatre types, by Frederick Pawley:...a community theatre, by William Howard Lescaze:...projects by Norman Bel Geddes...new Russian theatres...new Swedish theatres
pp.125; ill. in text  M
NY: Theatre Arts  1935
Published for the National Theatre Conference.

**397** BARROWS, ALICE & SIMONSON, LEE.  School auditorium as a theater
pp.51; plans/diagrams in text  L
Washington DC: US Dept. of Interior/Office of Education  1939
In two parts: the evolution of the auditorium; and planning the auditorium as a theater.

**398** STRONG, HARRY H.  Stages through the ages
No text; pl.38  M
Toledo OH: Rad-Mar P.  [c. 1945]
A series of full-page architectural drawings with captions, of which 28 are US theatres 1766-1942.

**399** BAKER, PAUL & FREEDLEY, GEORGE (Eds).  Are you going to build a theatre ? A guide to selected authorities on theatre plans and architecture
pp.31  DL*
Cleveland OH: National Theatre Conference  1947

**400** GORELIK, MORDECAI.  New theatres for old
pp.xvii, 553; ill in text, pl. 28  M
London: Dennis Dobson  1947
First published NY: Samuel French, 1940. A history of theatre and stage design.

**401** PAPERS PRESENTED at the eighth Ann Arbor conference. The theatre [cover title]
pp.iii, 63  M
Ann Arbor: U. of Michigan  1950

## 4.1. ARCHITECTURE AND MACHINERY

The focus of the two-day conference was theatre design and planning. Kenneth MacGowan: *Architecture for the audience*; Lee Mitchell: *The stage designer*; Edward C. Cole: *Technical problems of the stage*; Theodore Fuchs: *Planning an installation of stage lighting for the school & college auditorium*; George C. Izenour: *The future of electricity & electronics in the theatre*; Jean Rosenthal: *Notes on new developments in technical equipment*; Joseph Hudnut: *Neon lights and Louis Quinze*; Gerald G. Gentile: *Planning an outdoor theatre*; Abe H. Feder: *The professional theatre: its emotional impact*; Walter H. Stainton: *Multi-purpose theatre*.

**402** ELLEMAN, JOSEPH. Nineteenth century stage machines
Columbus: Ohio State U. (MA)     1951

**403** FREEMAN, SIDNEY L. The form of the non-proscenium theatre, their history and theories
Ithaca: Cornell U. (PhD)     1951

**404** BOYLE, WALTER P. Central and flexible staging: a new theatre in the making...drawings by John H. Jones
pp.vii, 117: ill. in text     M
Berkeley CA: U. of California P.     1956
Preface by Kenneth MacGowan.

**405** BURRIS-MEYER, HAROLD & GOODFRIEND, LEWIS S. Acoustics for the architect
pp.126; ill.     DL★
NY: Reinhold     1957

**406** ALOI, ROBERTO. Architetturi per lo spettacolo con un saggio dell'architetto Agnoldomenico Pica
pp.lxv, 504; ill. in text, some col.     M
Milan: Ulrico Hoepli     1958
With illustrated accounts of a number of American theatres and other performance spaces, including U. of Miami Theatre, MIT, College Station TX, Orange Coast College, Sarah Lawrence, U. of Arkansas Theatre and U. of Oregon Theatre, and the then proposed design by Gropius for Tallahassee. Text in Italian, French, English, German.

**407** [BOWMAN, NED A.]. Suggested readings in theatre architecture revised by Ned A. Bowman [caption title]
pp.various     DL★
Pennsylvania: Pittsburg U./AETA     1960-61
Four pamphlets in one.

**408** FOX, HOWARD L. Principles for designing the high school auditorium
NY: U. (PhD)     1960

**409** OPEN STAGE THEATRE check list
pp.24; ill. in text     MH
NY: [ANTA]     [c. 1960]
Compiled by the Board of Standards and Planning for the Living Theatre, a standing committee of ANTA, to suggest basic minimum standards of physical structure.

**410** DeGAETANI, THOMAS et al. Theatre architecture, or: how does it look from where you're sitting
pp.[16]; ill. in text     M
[NY]:     1961
Reprint from *Journal of the American Institute of Architects*, August, 1961. Includes Eric Pawley: *The role of the architect*; Joel E. Rubin: *Theatre lighting, a new era...*; and *A theatre portfolio* illustrating Stanford Music Centre, the theatre at Western Springs, the Tyrone Guthrie Theatre, and Kent State U.'s music and speech centre.

**411** HRUBY, JOHN F. An original design of an adaptable theatre
Denver: U. (PhD)     1961

**412** BOWMAN, NED A. Contemporary theatre architecture. Two divergent perceptual concepts
Stanford: U. (PhD)     1963

**413** COGSWELL, MARGARET (Ed.). The ideal theatre: eight concepts. An exhibition of designs and models resulting from the Ford Foundation program for theatre design. Prepared and circulated by the American Foundation of Arts
pp.144; ill. in text     M
NY: AFA/October House     1963
Projects include a multi-media complex, an outdoor theatre with movable roof, an open stage theatre, a college drama complex and an urban theatre centre.

**414** EDWARDS, JOHN C. A history of nineteenth century theatre architecture in the United States
Evanston: Northwestern U. (PhD)     1963

**415** GOOCH, DONALD B. (Ed.). Theatre and Main Street
pp.170: ill. in text     M
Ann Arbor: U. of Michigan P.     1963
Papers presented at the twelfth Ann Arbor conference sponsored by the College of Architecture and Design. The emphasis was on the place, future and form of US theatre.

**416** WATSON, THOMAS S. A study of contemporary theatre planning and architectural design for educational theatre
Cleveland: Case Western Reserve U. (PhD)     1964

**417** IRVING, GEORGE W. Methods by which volumes of space are modified in nine flexible theatres
Stanford: U. (PhD)     1965

**418** THE OPEN STAGE. Based on the designs of James Hull Miller [cover title]
pp.71; ill. in text     DL★
Chicago: Hub Electric     1965

**419** RABBY, L. B. An experimental investigation of the effects of theatre acoustics on intelligibility
Lawrence: U. of Kansas (PhD)     1965

**420** SILVERMAN, MAXWELL & BOWMAN, NED A. Contemporary theatre architecture: an illustrated survey. A checklist of publications 1946-1964
Unpaginated; ill. in text     M
NY: Public Library     1965

**421** BLACKWOOD, BYRNE D. The theatres of J. B. McElfratrick and Sons, architects, 1855-1922
Lawrence: U. of Kansas (PhD)     1966

**422** DORST, KENNETH R. A descriptive investigation of the theatrical structures built by Thomas Maguire in the far west
Denver: U. (PhD)     1966

**423** IRON, WILLIAM Z. A study in theatre space
Eugene: U. of Oregon (PhD)     1967

**424** POE, HAROLD W. Critical elements of functional theatre architecture in American colleges and universities
Tallahassee: Florida State U. (PhD)      1967

**425** WILLIS, RICHARD. Fire at the theatre: theatre conflagration in the United States from 1798 to 1950
Evanston: Northwestern U. (PhD)      1967

**426** GROSS, LORRAINE H. The influence of thrust and proscenium stage forms on audience response to a production of *Hamlet*
East Lansing: Michigan State U. (PhD)      1968

**427** JORDAN, CHESTER I. A history of theatre architecture in the Rocky Mountain region to 1900
Laramie: U. of Wyoming (MA)      1968

**428** KOOK, EDWARD F. et al. Porto theatre: a new concept in totally integrated portable theatre design. Created by the KOHM Group, Edward F. Kook, Donald Oenslager, Cyril Harris, Jo Mielziner
pp.25; ill. in text      M
[NY]: The authors/ Ford Foundation      1968
Portable inflatable theatre.

**429** McNAMARA, BROOKS. The American playhouse in the eighteenth century
pp.xix, 174; ill. in text, col. front.      M
Cambridge MA: Harvard U. P.      1969

**430** NAGLER, A. D. & MAYOR, A. HYATT. Architects in the theatre: a checklist [exhibition catalogue]
pp.32; ; ill. in text, pl. 1      M
NY: Grolier Club      1969
Included in the *Gazette* NS, No. 9.

**431** THEATRE CHECK LIST; a guide to the planning and construction of proscenium and open stage theatres. Prepared and published for the American Theatre Planning Board. Inc...with drawings by Ming Cho Lee
pp.71; ill. in text      M
Middletown CT: Wesleyan U.P.      1969

**432** BLEDSOE, JERRY H. The ideal outdoor theatre: criteria and plans for a new design
W. Lafayette: Purdue U. (PhD)      1970

**433** MAYER, MARTIN. Bricks, mortar and the performing arts: report of the twentieth century fund task force on performing arts centers: background paper...
pp.ix, 99; ill. in text      MH
NY: Twentieth Century Fund      1970
Considers motives for building performing arts centres, facilities required, operating and maintenance costs, sources of revenue.

**434** MIELZINER, JO. The shapes of our theatre...edited by C. Ray Smith
pp.160; ill. in text      M
NY: Clarkson N. Potter      1970
History and development of theatre design with comments on modern tendencies. Preface by Brooks Atkinson.

**435** MULLIN, DONALD. The development of the playhouse: a survey of theatre architecture from the renaissance to the present
pp.xvi, 197; ill. in text      M
Berkeley: U. of California P.      1970

**436** WHALEY, FRANK L. An analytical study of production facilities of contemporary professional American repertory companies
Tallahassee: Florida State U. (PhD)      1970

**437** BRIDGEMAN, FRIEDA E. The development of a theatre concept as reflected in the theatrical architecture of Frank Lloyd Wright
Madison: U. of Wisconsin (PhD)      1971

**438** ROBINSON, HORACE W. Architecture for the educational theatre
pp.147; ill.      DL★
Eugene: U. of Oregon P.      1971
Research project (no. 5-8290, contract OE-6-10-025, 1966) pursuant to contract with US Office of Education.

**439** SCHUBERT, HANNELORE. The modern theatre: architecture, stage design, lighting
pp.222; ill. in text      M
NY: Praeger      1971
A translation by J. C. Palmer of *Moderner Theaterbau*, Stuttgart: Karl Kramer. Pp.57-69 describe and illustrate US theatre buildings.

**440** ALOI, ROBERTO. Teatri e auditori
pp.x, 453; ill. in text, some col.      M
Milan: Ulrico Hoepli      1972
A sequel to the monograph of 1958 (q.v.). Includes: Arena Stage, Washington; U. of Illinois Theatre, Urbana; Lincoln Center, NY; Tyrone Guthrie Theatre, Minneapolis. Text in Italian and English.

**441** YOUNG, WILLIAM C. Documents of American theatre history: famous American playhouses Vol. 1, 1716-1899; Vol 2, 1900-1971
pp.xxiii, 327; xiii, 297; pl. 63      M
Chicago: American Library Association      1973

**442** MILLER, JAMES H. Designing small theatres...thirty years of highlights in designing small, arena, flexible, open, proscenium and thrust theatres [cover title]
pp.2-24; ill. in text      M
Downer's Grove IL: Arthur Meriwether      1974

**443** UNITED STATES INSTITUTE FOR THEATRE TECHNOLOGY commission on theatre architecture: theatre orientation package
pp.iii, 87      M
NY: USITT      1974
Comprises a descriptive list of theatres built since 1960, arranged by stage-type and region; a bibliography of theatre planning; and an index to a set of slides illustrating aspects and models of theatre design.

**444** BURRIS-MEYER, HAROLD & COLE, EDWARD C. Theatres and auditoriums
pp.vii, 470; ill. in text      M
NY: Robert E. Krieger      1975
Second edition with supplement. First published NY: Reinhold, 1949. The application of new science to the solution of theatre architectural and acoustic problems, and an assessment of recent forms of theatre building.

**445** FRINK, PETER H. (Ed.). Theatre design 75...a project of the Theatre Architecture Commission
pp.79; ill. in text      M
NY: US Institute of Theatre Technology      1975

## 4.1. ARCHITECTURE AND MACHINERY —468

Thirty-one designs for a range of theatre projects, mostly in US.

**446** McNAMARA, BROOKS; ROJO, JERRY & SCHECHNER, RICHARD. Theatres, spaces, environments: eighteen projects
pp.ix, 181; ill. in text    M
NY: Drama Book Services    1975
Experiments in theatre space carried out in the 1970s in the Performing Garage, NY, and elsewhere.

**447** REINERT, THOMAS D. Contemporary manual rigging systems and their relationship to theatre types
Bowling Green: State U.    1976

**448** IZENOUR, GEORGE C. Theater design. With two essays on the room acoustics of multiple-use by Vern O. Knudsen and Robert B. Newman. Foreword by A. M. Nagler
pp.xxxiii, 631; ill. in text    M
NY: McGraw-Hill    1977
Detailed examination of historical and contemporary practice.

**449** BURTON, CHESTER J. Recycling found spaces in existing structures as theatres and related support areas
Tallahassee: Florida State U. (PhD)    1978

**450** HUFSTETLER, LOREN R. A critical study of fluid powered stage machinery in the United States
Los Angeles: U. of Southern California (PhD)    1978

**451** STARBUCK, JAMES C. American non-collegiate performing arts centers
pp.14    M
Monticello IL: Vance Bibliographies    1978
A listing of articles in periodicals.

**452** STODDARD, RICHARD. Theatre and cinema architecture: a guide to information sources
pp.xi, 367    M
Detroit MI: Gale Research    1978
International. Chaper 14 in Part 2 makes specific reference to US theatre architecture.

**453** STODDARD, ROBERT. Preservation of concert halls, opera houses and movie palaces [drop title]
pp.28 inc. wrappers; ill. in text    M
Washington DC: Preservation P.    1978
Pamphlet prepared for the National Trust for Historic Preservation.

**454** ELDER, ELDON; IMHOF, MARTHA & RYDER, SHARON L. Will it make a theatre. A guide to finding, renovating, financing, bringing up-to-code, the non-traditional peformance space...
pp.ix, 206; ill. in text    M
NY: DBS    1979
Illustrated by Elder. Addenda slip.

**455** FOGELBERG, DONALD D. The impact of the architecture of the Tyrone Guthrie Theatre on the process of play production
Minneapolis: U. of Minnesota (PhD)    1979

**456** GIBBS, DAVID A. The architectural programming of university performing arts centers
Urbana-Champaign: U. of Illinois (PhD)    1980

**457** PILDAS, AVE. Movie palaces...text by Lucinda Smith
pp.128; ill. in text, mostly col.    L
NY: Clarkson N. Potter    1980
Photographic studies. Many of the buildings described began as legitimate theatres. Foreword by King Vidor.

**458** TONER, MARIJO C. Architect and theatre: Ralph Rapson
Minneapolis: U. of Minnesota (PhD)    1980

**459** DUNNING, GLENDA. Theater architecture in California: an annotated bibliography
pp.29    M
Monticello IL: Vance Bibliographies    1981

**460** THEATER FACILITY IMPACT study: theater facilities; guidelines and strategies [by the staff of the Milwaukee Repertory Theatre company, et al]
pp.vi, 139    *
Wisconsin: Centre Arch-Urban    1981
In series *Publications in architecture and urban planning*.

**461** VANCE, MARY. Theatre architecture: a basic bibliography
pp.6    M
Monticello IL: Vance Bibliographies    1981

**462** ATHANASOPULOS, CHRISTOS G. Contemporary theater: evolution and design
pp.xviii, 341; ill. in text    M
NY: John Wiley & Sons    1983
History of theatre design, informed by an architect's perception, with substantial section on contemporary forms and trends.

**463** FORSYTH, MICHAEL. Auditoria: designing for the peforming arts
pp.220; ill. in text, pl.8 col.    M
London: Mitchell    1987
International. Includes accounts of 9 US theatres.

**464** GLERUM, JAY O. Stage rigging handbook
pp.xi, 138; ill. in text    M
Carbondale: Southern Illinois U. P.    1987

**465** HALL, BEN M. The best remaining seats: the golden age of the movie palace. Foreword by Bosley Crowther. New preface by B. Andrew Corsini
pp.x, 262; ill. in text    M
NY: Da Capo P.    1987
Revised edition. First published NY: Bramhall House, 1961. Emphasis on cinema architecture and design. Includes material on live shows.

**466** KAUFMANN, PRESTON J. Skouras-ized for showmanship
pp.44 inc. wrappers; ill. in text    M
Notre Dame IN: Theatre Historical Society    1987
Theatres and movie theatres created for the Skouras Brothers in the 1940s and '50s.

**467** IZENOUR, GEORGE C. Theater technology
pp.xxxi, 553; ill. in text    M
NY: McGraw-Hill    1988
Complements author's *Theater design*.

**468** ZIVANOVIC, JUDITH K. et al (Eds). Opera houses of the midwest
pp.vii, 115; ill. in text    M
[Manhattan]: Mid-American Theatre Conference    1988

Directory to surviving buildings in Iowa, Nebraska and N. and S. Dakota.

**469** CARLSON, MARVIN. Places of performance: the semiotics of theatre architecture
pp.x, 212; ill. in text M
Ithaca NY: Cornell U. P. 1989
Examines cultural, social and political implications of theatre architecture down the years.

**470** GROVE, EDWIN M. Arena theatre: dimensions for the space age
pp.132 ★
Troy NY: Whitson Publishing 1989

**471** PREDDY, JANE. Glamour, glitz and sparkle: the deco theatres of John Eberson
pp.40; ill. in text M
Chicago: Theatre History Society of America 1989

## 4.2 LIGHTING AND SOUND

**472** LUCKIESH, M. Light and shade and their applications
pp.xii, 265; ill. in text M
NY: D. Van Nostrand 1916
With a chapter on light and shade in stagecraft.

**473** LUCKIESH, M. The lighting art: its practice and possibilities
pp.ix, 229; ill. in text M
NY: McGraw-Hill 1917
Chapter on stage lighting.

**474** McCANDLESS, STANLEY R. Glossary of stage lighting [cover title]
pp.16; ill. in text M
NY: Theatre Arts 1926

**475** BAUER, MARY V. The science and art of 'light' painting for the stage: a study of what color does to color
Evanston: Northwestern U. (MA) 1928

**476** FUCHS, THEODORE. Stage lighting
pp.viii, 500; ill. in text M
Boston: Little, Brown 1928

**477** THEATRE LIGHTING past and present
pp.48; ill. ★
Mount Vernon NY: Leonard Electric 1928
The third edition.

**478** DOLCH, CATHERINE. A history of stage lighting to 1880
Ann Arbor: U. of Michigan (MA) 1929

**479** HARTMANN, LOUIS. Theatre lighting: a manual of the stage switchboard. Foreword by David Belasco
pp.xiii, 138; ill. in text M
NY: D. Appleton 1930
Author was chief electrician to David Belasco from 1901.

**480** MELLINGER, M. The evolution of stage lighting in America since 1850
Los Angeles: U. of Southern California (MA) 1930

**481** OSGOOD, CHESTER W. Light as an element of design in the evolution of stage setting in the late 19th century
Ames: Iowa State U. (MA) 1931

**482** POWELL, ALVIN L. & RODGERS, R. Lighting the non-professional stage production
pp.39; ill. DL★
NY: Krieger Publications 1931

**483** FALGE, FRANCIS M. & WEITZ, C. E. Theatre lighting...presenting new ideas and methods in lighting for display, for atmosphere, for decoration, and for utility in places of amusement
pp.60; ill. in text DL★
Cleveland OH: General Electric 1938

**484** WALKER, JOHN A. Stage lighting apparatus in England and America during the nineteenth century
Chapel Hil: U. of North Carolina (MA) 1939

**485** HAMILTON, JOHN L. Stage lighting in American theatres between 1800 and 1850
Minneapolis: U. of Minnesota (MA) 1941

**486** PIERCE, JAMES F. Audience reactions to certain primary colors of light on actors' faces in dramatic scenes
Ames: State U. of Iowa (MA) 1942

**487** BARSNESS, LAWRENCE. The relationship of stage lighting sources and methods to acting style in theatres, 1850 to 1915
Eugene: U. of Oregon (MA) 1950

**488** PETERSON, RITA. Stage lighting methods: eighteenth century American theatre
Madison: U. of Wisconsin (MA) 1950

**489** WEESE, STANLEY. Gas lighting on the English and American stages during the nineteenth century
Urbana: U. of Illinois (MA) 1950

**490** MAHOVLICK, FRANK. Influences of artificial light upon the theatre
Los Angeles: U. of Southern California (PhD) 1951

**491** WATERS, WALTER K. Early uses of electricity for the theatre 1880-1900
Stanford: U. (MA) 1951

**492** ALLISON, WILLIAM H. A graphic survey of stage lighting
New Haven: Yale U. (MFA) 1952

**493** DEWEY, WALTER S. An experimental study of the use of visual arts in teaching of stage lighting
Iowa City: U. of Iowa (PhD) 1952

**494** WALKER, JOHN A. The functions of stage lighting in the changing concepts of the stage
Ithaca: Cornell U. (PhD) 1952

**495** HELD, McDONALD W. A history of stage lighting in the United States in the nineteenth century
Evanston: Northwestern U. (PhD) 1955

## 4.2. LIGHTING AND SOUND

**496** HUNTLEY, STIRLING L. Some emotional reactions of a theatre audience with regard to coloured light
Stanford: U. (PhD) 1956

**497** MURRAY, DONALD L. Experimental design of a stage lighting system using low voltage sealed beam lamps
East Lansing: Michigan State U. (MA) 1956

**498** BOWMAN, WAYNE. Modern theatre lighting
pp.xvii, 228: ill. in text, pl. 3  O
NY: Harper & Bros. 1957
Illustrated by Jean Bowman.

**499** DAVIS, ARIEL R. Lighting the modern stage: a handbook for architects, engineers and drama directors
pp.25; ill. in text  DL★
Salt Lake City: Ariel Davis Manufacturing 1958

**500** McCANDLESS, STANLEY R. A method of lighting the stage. New revised edition
pp.143; ill. in text  M
NY: Theatre Arts Books 1958
Fourth edition, revised. First published 1932 for the National Theatre Conference.

**501** BURRIS-MEYER, HAROLD & MALLORY, VINCENT. Sound in the theatre
pp.95; ill.  DL★
Mineola NY: Radio Magazines 1959
Electronic sound control techniques.

**502** HEMSLEY, GILBERT V. A history of stage lighting in America, 1879-1917
New Haven: Yale U. (MFA) 1960

**503** RUBIN, JOEL E. The technical development of stage lighting apparatus in the United States, 1900-1950
Stanford: U. (PhD) 1960

**504** HARRIS, JUDY. A bibliography of books related to stage lighting
Pittsburgh: Carnegie-Mellon U. (MFA) 1961

**505** HOWARD, JOHN. Stage lighting handbook
ll. 96: ill. in text  L
Los Angeles: State College 1962
Revised edition of handbook first published 1960 as *Practical stage lighting*. Errata slip.

**506** KOOK, EDWARD F. Images in light for the living theatre
pp.1v, 248  M
[NY]: For the author 1963
A study of scenic projection.

**507** LYNCH, EDMUND. An analytical and descriptive study of Louis Hartmann's contribution to modern theatre lighting
Denver: U. (PhD) 1963

**508** GARNESS, JON M. Lighting for the arena stage
New Haven: Yale U. (MFA) 1964

**509** McCANDLESS, STANLEY R. Syllabus of stage lighting
pp.v, 135; ill. in text  M
NY: Drama Book Specialists 1964
Eleventh edition. First published 1931.Chapter on lighting control revised by John Hood.

**510** CARNINE, DENNIS & KAUFMAN, ROGER. Design and construction of an analogue punch card lighting control system
New Haven: Yale U. (MFA) 1965

**511** JOHNSON, RAOUL F. United States and British patents for scenic and lighting devices for the theatre from 1861 to 1915
Urbana: U. of Illinois (PhD) 1966

**512** RUBIN, JOEL E. & WATSON, LELAND H. Theatrical lighting practice
pp.xiv, 142; ill. in text  M
NY: Theatre Arts 1966
First published 1954.

**513** AVERYT, WILLIAM B. Lighting for the arena stage
Austin: U. of Texas (MFA) 1967

**514** HOLLOWAY, C. L. The development of stage lighting equipment 1920-1930
Austin: U. of Texas (MFA) 1967

**515** GOLTRY, THOMAS S. An experimental study of the effect of light intensity on audience perception of character dominance
Madison: U. of Wisconsin (PhD) 1969

**516** SCALES, ROBERT. Stage lighting theory, equipment and practice in the United States from 1900 to 1935
Minneapolis: U. of Minnesota (PhD) 1969

**517** MURRAY, DONALD L. The rise of the American professional lighting designer to 1960
Ann Arbor: U. of Michigan (PhD) 1970

**518** BONGAR, EMMET W. Practical stage lighting
pp.124; ill.  ★
NY: Richards Rosen P. 1971

**519** BEAGLE, T. A. The development of Belasco's lighting techniques
San José: State U. (MA) 1972

**520** BURCH, ROGER B. The design of electrical lighting and control systems in the United States
Urbana: U. of Illinois (PhD) 1972

**521** MARKLEY, DAVID J. The development and design of lighting control systems in American theatre
University Park: Pennsylvania State U. (MA) 1972

**522** WEDWICK, DARYL M. United States and British patents of scenic and illusionistic devices and effects for the theatre, 1916-1970
Bowling Green: State U. (PhD) 1972

**523** CORDRAY, LAURIE A. The development of stage lighting theories and practices in America from the beginnings to 1850
Columbia: U. of Missouri (PhD) 1973

**524** ELECTRICAL DATA on three major theatres: Warner - Hollywood, Calif.; Stanley - Jersey City, N. J.; The Mosque - Richmond, Va
pp.[20]: ill. in text  MH
[Washington DC]: Theatre Historical Society 1973

Originally published by Frank Adam Electric Company.

**525** MINCHER, JOHN. A conceptual approach to stage lighting design: four plays in repertory
Carbondale: Southern Illinois U. (PhD)     1973

**526** WARFEL, WILLIAM B. Handbook of stage lighting graphics
pp.41; ill.     DL★
NY: Drama Book Specialists     1973
Second edition, revised and enlarged.

**527** WEIDNER, R. W. Louis Hartmann: electrician, inventor and stage lighting designer
University Park: Pennsylvania State U. (Thesis)     1973

**528** BELLMAN, WILLARD F. Lighting the stage: art and practice
pp.xv, 480; ill.     DL★
NY: Chandler Publishing     1974
Second edition, enlarged. First published 1967.

**529** WEHLBURG, ALBERT F. Theatre lighting: an illustrated glossary
pp.62; ill. in text     MH
NY: Drama Book Specialists     1975

**530** HOUCHEN, RUSSELL E. Comparative spectrophotometric analysis of representative plastic color media used in stage-lighting
Eugene: U. of Oregon (MA)     1976

**531** HUBBELL, DOUGLAS K. *Scientific American* and its supplement as sources for information about theatre technology
Bloomington: Indiana U. (PhD)     1978

**532** OLSON, RONALD C. Edward F. Kook: link between the theater artist and technician
NY: U. (PhD)     1978

**533** PENZEL, FREDERICK. Theatre lighting before electricity
pp.xii, 180; ill. in text     M
Middletown CT: Wesleyan U. P.     1978

**534** ALVIS, ARTHUR. Applications of laserium technique to performance lighting
NY: Columbia U. (PhD)     1980

**535** CULVER, MAX K. A history of theatre and sound effects devices to 1927
Urbana-Champaign: U. of Illinois (PhD)     1981

**536** HOOD, W. EDMUND. Practical handbook of stage lighting and sound
pp.304     DL★
Blue Ridge Summit PA: Tab Books     1981

**537** UTTERBACK, JAMES. A system to teach stage lighting: photographic transparencies as a visual means for a visual subject.
Carbondale: Southern Illinois U. (PhD)     1981

**538** WARFEL, WILLIAM B. & KLAPPERT, WALTER R. Color science for lighting the stage
pp.xiv, 158; ill. in text; annexed charts     L
New Haven: Yale U. P.     1981

**539** SELLMAN, HUNTON D. & LESSLEY, MERRILL. Essentials of stage lighting
pp.xix, 199; ill in text; pl, 2 col.     MH
NY: Prentice-Hall     1982
Second edition, revised by Lessley. Originally the second section of Selden and Sellman, *Stage scenery and lighting*, NY, 1930. First published separately NY: Appleton, 1972.

**540** PALMER, RICHARD H. The lighting art: the aesthetics of stage lighting design
pp.xvii, 237; ill. iin text, pl. 2 col.     L
Englewood Cliffs NJ: Prentice-Hall     1985

**541** FORT, TIMOTHY W. Incandescence and the birth of modern lighting design
Toronto: U. (PhD)     1989

**542** HAYS, DAVID. Light on the subject: stage lighting for directors and actors - and the rest of us. With an introduction by Peter Brook
pp.vi, 173; ill. in text     M
NY: Limelight Editions     1989

**543** GILLETTE, J. MICHAEL. Designing with light: an introduction to stage lighting
pp.256     ★
Palo Alto CA: Mayfield     1990
Revised edition. First published, 1978.

**544** WATSON, LEE. Lighting design handbook
pp.xxii, 458; ill. in text, pl. 7 col.     M
NY: McGraw Hill     1990

## 4.3 STAGE-DESIGN AND EFFECTS

**545** HOPKINS, ALBERT A. (Ed.). Magic: stage illusions and scientific diversions including trick photography...with an introduction by Henry Ridgely Evans...with four hundred illustrations
pp.xii, 556; ill. in text     M
London: Sampson Low, Marston     1897
American edition published NY: Munn, 1897. Includes section *science in the theatre*, with chapters on stage construction, effects and illusions, cycloramas, aquatic theatre. Based on articles in the *Scientific American*.

**546** FITZKEE, DARIEL. Professional scenery construction
pp.94; ill. in text     DL★
San Francisco: Banner Play Bureau     1903
Edited by Ellen M. Gall.

**547** THE O. L. STORY SCENIC Co. Inc. Catalogue: decorations, stage scenery and supplies. Everything needed on a stage [cover title]
pp.24; ill. in text     M
Boston: O. L. Story Scenic Co.     [1910]

**548** THEATRICAL SCENE PAINTING: a thorough and complete work on how to sketch, paint and install theatrical scenery
pp.177; ill. in text     DL★
Omaha NB: Appleton     1916

**549** GAMBLE, WILLIAM B. Stage scenery: a list of references to illustrations since 1900 in the New York

## 4.3. STAGE-DESIGN AND EFFECTS

Public Library
pp.86 MH
NY: NYPL 1917

Reprinted, with supplement, August 1917, from the Bulletin of the NYPL of April-May 1917. 2125 items with artist and theatre indexes. An earlier, unpublished list is mentioned.

**550** AMERICAN STAGE DESIGNS: an illustrated catalogue of the models, drawings and photographs exhibited at the Bourgeois Galleries in New York...April 5th to 26th, 1919 with articles by Maxwell Armfield, Michael C. Carr, Norman Bel Geddes, C. Raymond Johnson, Robert Edmond Jones, Rollo Peters, Irving Pichel, Herman Rosse, Lee Simonson, J. Blanding Sloan, Joseph Urban, John Wenger, and Kenneth MacGowan
pp.53; ill. in text M
NY: Theatre Arts Magazine 1919

**551** CHENEY, SHELDON. Modern art and the theatre. Being notes on certain approaches to a new art of the stage, with special reference to parallel developments in painting, sculpture, and the other arts
pp.iv, 19 MH
Scarborough on Hudson: The Sleepy Hollow P. 1921

120 copies, printed by the author.

**552** MacGOWAN, KENNETH & JONES, ROBERT EDMOND. Continental stagecraft
pp.xvi, 233; pl. 40, some col. M
NY: Harcourt, Brace 1922

European influence on US design.

**553** SMITH, ANDRE. The scenewright: the making of stage models and settings...illustrated by the author
pp.vii, 135; ill. in text M
NY: Macmillan 1926

**554** ATKINSON, FRANK H. Scene painting and bulletin art
pp.248; ill, in text M
Chicago: Frederick J. Drake 1927

**555** CHENEY, SHELDON. Stage decoration
pp.xxii, 149, pl. 127 M
London: Chapman & Hall 1928

Historical survey but emphasizing practice and theory in the 20th century. Published NY: Day, 1928.

**556** FUERST, WALTER R. & HUME, SAMUEL J. XXth century stage decoration...with an introduction by Adolphe Appia. Volume one: text. [Volume two: the illustrations]
pp.xv, 178, v; ill. in text, pl. 98, some col. M
London: Alfred A. Knopf 1928

Nineteen page index to plates inserted in volume one.

**557** GAMBLE, WILLIAM B. The development of scenic art and stage machinery. A list of references in the New York Public Library
pp.v, 231 M
NY: NYPL 1928

Second edition, revised. First published 1920.

**558** KROWS, ARTHUR E. Equipment for stage production: a manual of scene building. Preface by Barrett H. Clark
pp.xi, 152; ill. in text L
NY: D. Appleton 1928

**559** SELDEN, SAMUEL. Scenery and lighting for school and little theatre stages
pp.64; ill. DL★
Chapel Hill: U. of North Carolina P. 1928

**560** GRAIN, AMELIA. Stage settings for operas
pp.72; ill. in text M
Philadelphia: For the author [1930]

*New Art* catalogue No. 34. The author ran a scenery rental service and the illustrations provide an interesting record of conventional stage design of the period.

**561** SELDEN, SAMUEL & SELLMAN, HUNTON D. Stage scenery and lighting: a handbook for non-professionals
pp.xvii, 398; ill in text, pl. 7 M
NY: F. S. Crofts 1930

In two distinct sections, later issued and reissued separately.

**562** D'AMICO, VICTOR E. Theater art
pp.217;ill. in text, col. front. M
Peoria IL: Manual Arts P. 1931

Handbook of stage design.

**563** HELVENSTON, HAROLD. Scenery: a manual of scene design
pp.xvi, 95; ill. in text; col. front. M
Stanford: U. P. 1931

Author was director of dramatics at Stanford U.

**564** DESIGNS FOR THE THEATRE: settings and costumes [exhibition catalogue]
MH★
Cambridge MA: Harvard Society for
Contemporary Art 1932

**565** SIMONSON, LEE. The stage is set
pp.xvii, 585; ill. in text M
NY: Harcourt, Brace 1932

A history of scene design and the relationship of designer to playwright.

**566** JOSSIC, YVONNE F. (Ed.). Stage and stage settings
ll. 21; pl. 20 MH
Philadelphia: H. C. Perlberg [1933]

Portfolio of plates 'to suggest stage settings and the possibilities of transformation...to assist teacher and student...'

**567** SIMONSON, LEE (Ed.). Theatre art, edited and with an introduction by Lee Simonson. Contributions by Allardyce Nicoll, John Anderson, Paul Alfred Merbach, Oliver M. Sayler, John Mason Brown
pp.68, pl. 37 M
NY: Museum of Modern Art 1934

Exhibition catalogue. Additions and corrections slip.

**568** WEBSTER, GLENN R. & WETZEL, WILLIAM. Scenery simplified: a director's digest of scenery and stage equipment
pp.viii, 167: ill. DL★
Franklin OH: Eldridge Entertainment 1934

**569** HEWITT, BARNARD. Theatre and the graphic arts
Ithaca: Cornell U. (PhD) 1935

**570** JONES, LESLIE A. Painting scenery: a 'handy book' for amateur producers
pp.107; ill. DL★
Boston: Walter H. Baker 1935

**571** VOORHEES, MARIETTA (Ed.). Theatre arts and crafts: a primer of practical aids for producers
pp.50; ill. DL★
San Mateo CA: Drama Teachers Association 1935

**572** BARBER, PHILIP. The scene technician's handbook
pp.32; ill. DL★
New Haven CT: Whitlock 1936

**573** DAMERON, LOUISE (Ed.). Bibliography of stage settings to which is added an index to illustrations of stage settings
ll.48 MH
Baltimore MD: Enoch Pratt Free Library 1936
Lists play titles and designers, with page references.

**574** HEFFNER, HUBERT C.; SELDEN, SAMUEL & SELLMAN, HUNTON D. Modern theatre practice: a handbook for the non-professionals
pp.xviii, 378; ill. in text, pl. 8 M
London: George G. Harrap 1936
First published NY: F. S. Crofts, 1935

**575** HICKS, AMI M. & OGLESBY, CATHARINE. Colour in action
pp.xvi, 259; col front. M
NY: Funk & Wagnalls 1937
With a chapter on application of Hicks's colour theory to the stage.

**576** BURRIS-MEYER, HAROLD & COLE, EDWARD C. Scenery for the theatre: the organisation, processes, materials and techniques used to set the stage...
pp.xiii, 473; ill. in text; col. chart M
Boston: Little, Brown 1938

**577** JONES, LESLIE A. Scenic design and model building: a 'handy book' for amateur producers
pp.108; ill. DL★
Boston: Walter H. Baker 1939

**578** NELMS, HENNING. A primer of stagecraft
pp.xvii, 158; ill. in text L
NY: Dramatists Play Service 1941

**579** STAGES OF THE WORLD
Unpaged; pl. 40 M
NY: Theatre Arts 1941
Theatre Arts prints, series 4. Substantial section on modern US stages. An earlier series, *Arts of the theatre from the days of the Greeks to our own* NY: John Day, 1929 has little US relevance. Note also J. Alan Hammack: *An index to photographs of scene designs in Theatre Arts 1916-1964*, in *TD*, vol 3, nos 1/2 pp.29-59.

**580** DESIGNS FOR THE THEATRE in modern times
MH★
Cambridge MA: Fogg Museum of Art 1942

**581** SIMONSON, LEE. The art of scenic design: a pictorial analysis of stage setting and its relation to theatrical production
pp.174; ill. in text, col. front. M
NY: Duell, Sloan and Pearce 1943

**582** AMBERG, GEORGE. Art in modern ballet
pp.115; pl.64 b/w, 8 col. M
London: Routledge [1946]
Published NY: Pantheon. Scene and costume design from 1909.

**583** FRIEDERICH, WILLARD J. & FRASER, JOHN H. Scenery design for the amateur stage
pp.xvii, 262; ill. DL★
NY: Macmillan 1950

**584** THE HARVARD THEATRE COLLECTION in cooperation with the Fogg Art Museum presents *Three designers for the contemporary theatre. Robert Edmond Jones...Donald Oenslager...Lee Simonson*
pp.[39] M
Cambridge MA: Fogg Art Museum/Harvard U. 1950
Exhibition catalogue Oct. 16-Nov. 25.

**585** PEET, TELFAIR B. A system of portable stage setting and lighting: what it is and what it does, how to make it and how to use it
pp.46; ill. in text DL★
[Auburn?: Alabama Polytechnic 1950

**586** BOWEN, ROY H. A study of arena staging based on audience reaction to the first season of stadium theatre
Columbus: Ohio State U. (PhD) 1951

**587** BRUDER, KARL C. A materials approach to the study of stage design
NY: Columbia Teachers' College (EdD) 1951

**588** ASHWORTH, BRADFORD. Notes on scene painting...edited by Donald Oenslager
pp.ii, 47 M
New Haven CT: Whitlock's 1952
Edited version of Ashworth's notes for talks given to Yale's drama department.

**589** COLE, WENDELL. Scenery on the New York stage, 1900-1920
Stanford: U. (PhD) 1952

**590** DOUTY, JOHN T. Scenic styles in the modern American theatre
Denver: U. (PhD) 1953

**591** PHILIPPI, HERBERT. Stagecraft and scene design
pp.448; ill. DL★
Boston: Houghton Mifflin 1953

**592** LITWACK, SYDNEY Z. Study of projected scenery: history, technology, design
Chapel Hill: U. of North Carolina (MA) 1954

**593** BUTLER, D. E. Projected scenery
Seattle: U. of Washington (Thesis) 1955

**594** GREEN, JOHN H. The development of stage rigging in the United States (1766-1893)
Denver: U. (PhD) 1955

**595** ADIX, VERNON. Theatre scenecraft for the backstage technician and artist
pp.xxi, 309; ill. in text, front. M
Anchorage KY: Children's Theatre P. 1956

## 4.3. STAGE-DESIGN AND EFFECTS

With drawings and photographs of U. of Utah theatre productions.

**596** THE AMERICAN STAGE [exhibition catalogue]
pp.52; ill. in text M
Washington DC: Corcoran Gallery of Art 1957
Designs since 1915.

**597** CORNBERG, SOL & GEBAUER, EMANUEL L. A stage crew handbook...drawings by Jack Forman
pp.xi, 291; ill. in text M
NY: Harper and Brothers 1957
Revised edition. First published 1941.

**598** DAVIS, JED H. The art of scenic design and staging for children's theatre
Minneapolis: U. of Minnesota (PhD) 1958

**599** HAKE, ROBERT. Here's how: a basic stagecraft book
pp.128; ill. DL★
Evanston, IL: Row, Peterson 1958
Revised edition. First published 1947 as ...a guide to economy in stagecraft.

**600** THOMPSON, JAMES R. Twentieth century scene design. Its history and stylistic origins
Minneapolis: U. of Minnesota (PhD) 1958

**601** HAYS, DAVID. Scenery for the theatre
MH★
Middletown CT: Wesleyan U. P. 1959

**602** SMITH, MARJORIE M. Expressionism in twentieth century stage design
Ann Arbor: U. of Michigan (PhD) 1960

**603** JOSAL, WENDELL J. A semiotic approach to the aesthetic problem of the quality of stage design as a spatial and temporal art
Evanston: Northwestern U. (PhD) 1961

**604** LARSON, ORVILLE K. (Ed.). Scene design for stage and screen. Readings on the aesthetics and methodology of scene design for theatre, opera, music comedy, ballet, motion pictures, television, and arena theatre
pp.xviiii, 334 M
Lansing MI: Michigan State U. P. 1961
Contributors include Robert Edmond Jones, Lee Simonson, Norris Houghton, Oliver Smith.

**605** PEET, ALICE L. The history and development of simultaneous scenery in the west from the middle ages to modern United States
Madison: U. of Wisconsin (PhD) 1961

**606** ARNOLD, RICHARD. The new stagecraft: developments in scenery and lighting on the New York stage between 1900 and 1915
Evanston: Northwestern U. (PhD) 1962

**607** TOMPKINS, DOROTHY L. Handbook for theatrical apprentices: a practical guide in all phases of theatre
pp.181 L
NY: Samuel French 1962

**608** NACAROW, DAVID A. Selected sources and a bibliography for a history of scenery to 1660
New Haven: Yale U. (MFA) 1963

**609** ALEXANDER, R. E. Index of patents concerning theatre illusions and appliances
Los Angeles: U. of California (Thesis) 1964

**610** CARNES, EDWIN H. A descriptive study of form and purpose in the surrealist stage-setting
Los Angeles: U. of Southern California (PhD) 1964

**611** MIDDLETON, HERMAN D. The use of the design elements in the stage designs of Robert Edmond Jones and Lee Simonson
Gainsville: U. of Florida (PhD) 1964

**612** PARKER, WILFRED O. Sceno-graphic techniques
pp.vi, 85; ill in text M
Pittsburgh: Carnegie Institute of Technology 1964
Second edition, revised and enlarged. First published 1957.

**613** KALLOP, EDWARD. Summary catalogue of drawings and prints designed for theater in the Cooper Union Museum
ll.18; pl.2 M
NY: Cooper Union 1965
Supplemental list of books illustrated with designs (ll.3) loosely inserted. See also *Chronicle of the Museum of the Cooper Union*, vol. 1, no. 8, *August, 1941*. This issue (pp.40) is devoted to an account of the Museum's holdings in theatre by Rudolf Berliner.

**614** WILFRED, THOMAS. Projected scenery, a technical manual
pp.iii, 59; ill. in text M
NY: Drama Book Shop 1965

**615** BIRTWISTLE, MICHAEL D. Modern developments of the open stage form as seen in the work of James Hull Miller
New Orleans: Tulane U. (PhD) 1966

**616** BOCK, FRED C. Scheme for arena theatre lighting and design in terms of grid spacing, walkway space, and masking by louvres
Columbus: Ohio State U. (PhD) 1966

**617** HIPPELY, E. C. An encyclopedia of American scenographers: 1900-1960
Denver: U. (PhD) 1966

**618** EGAN, JENNY. A system of re-usable furniture, properties, and costumes for the small repertory theatre
NY: U. (PhD) 1967

**619** GILLETTE, A. S. An introduction to scenic design
pp.xi, 210; ill. in text M
NY: Harper & Row 1967

**620** ALBRIGHT, HARRY D.; HALSTEAD, WILLIAM P. & MITCHELL, LEE. Principles of theatre art
pp.xii,547; ill. DL★
Boston: Houghton Mifflin 1968
The second edition. First published 1955.

**621** DINE, JIM. Designs for *A Midsummer Night's Dream*: introduction by Virginia Allen
pp.32; ill. in text, some col. M
NY: Museum of Modern Art 1968

1966 production by San Francisco Actors' Workshop.

**622** HINDERYCKX, LESLIE A. Firearms in the theatre: a comprehensive study of the problem of staging shooting scenes
Evanston: Northwestern U. (PhD)     1968

**623** ANATOMY OF AN ILLUSION: studies in nineteenth-century scene design, Lectures of the fourth international congress on theatre research, Amsterdam, 1965
pp.92; ill. in text     M
Amsterdam: Scheltema & Holkema/IFTR     1969
Includes Thomas F. Marshall: *Charles W. Witham: scenic artist to the nineteenth century American stage*.

**624** BRUDER, KARL C. Properties and dressing the stage
pp.117; ill.     DL★
NY: Richards Rosen P.     1969

**625** KADLEC, ANTHONY L. Descriptive study of scenic styles in the productions of successful serious American drama on the New York stage of the 1920s
East Lansing: Michigan State U. (PhD)     1969

**626** SEAY, DONALD W. Effects of new materials and techniques in stage scenery on the theater director and designer
Minneapolis: U. of Minnesota (PhD)     1969

**627** WELKER, DAVID. Theatrical set design: the basic techniques
pp.xi, 349; ill. in text     M
Boston: Allyn and Bacon     1969

**628** JACKSON, ALLAN S. & ROMAN, LISBETH J. (Eds). An exhibition of theatrical designs and historical materials from the SUNY-Binghamton collections
pp.32, inc, wrappers; ill. in text, some col.     M
Binghamton: U. Art Gallery     1970
Costume and set designs, memorabilia, ephemera, panoramas.

**629** KUEMMERLE, CLYDE V. An investigation of selected contemporary American scene designers
Minneapolis: U. of Minnesota (PhD)     1970

**630** NELMS, HENNING. Scenic design: a guide to the stage
pp.96; ill. in text     M
NY: Stirling Publishing     1970

**631** STELL, W. JOSEPH. Scenery
pp.256: ill. in text     DL★
NY: Richards Rosen P.     1970

**632** YALE THEATRE [cover title]
pp.55,59; ill. in text     M
New Haven: Yale U. P.     1970
Volume 3, No. 1. A double issue on design and film, with articles on Robert Edmond Jones, the theatre designs of Kandinsky and Kokoschka, Will Steven Armstrong, Magic Lantern, and Ming Cho Lee.

**633** STEIN, DONNA M. Thomas Wilfred: Lumia. A retrospective exhibition
pp.102; ill. in text, some col.     M
Washington DC: Corcoran Gallery of Art     1971
Catalogue, April 16-May 30. 'Lumia' was Wilfred's term for kinetic art 'employing form, colour and motion in a dark place' and he developed a number of experimental projection devices including a 'clavilux' which combined light with sound. He had begun his work as early as the 1920s but is perhaps best remembered for his experiments with projected scenery at the Playhouse Theatre of the U. of Washington in Seattle.

**634** BRYSON, NICHOLAS L. Thermoplastic scenery for theatre
Ill. in text     DL★
NY: Drama Book Specialists     1972

**635** BUERKI, F. A. Stagecraft for non-professionals
pp.xii, 131; ill. in text     L
Madison: U. of Wisconsin P.     1972
Third edition of this basic primer. First published 1945.

**636** HODGE, FRANCIS (Ed.). Innovations in stage and theatre design. Papers of the sixth congress, International Federation for Theatre Research, Lincoln Center, New York, NY, October 6-10, 1969
pp.xii, 165; ill. in text     M
NY: ASTR     1972
Includes Donald Oenslager on Robert Edmond Jones, Frederick J. Hunter on Norman Bel Geddes, George C. Izenour on the multi-purpose theatre/concert-hall.

**637** SELDEN, SAMUEL & REZZUTO, TOM. Essentials of stage scenery
pp.xv, 263; ill. in text     MH
NY: Appleton-Century-Crofts     1972
Revised, expanded edition. First published as section of Selden and Sellman, *Stage scenery and lighting...*, NY: 1930

**638** TWENTIETH CENTURY STAGE DESIGN: an exhibition...held in the Houghton Library
pp.23     M
Cambridge MA: Harvard Theatre Collection     1972

**639** WHALEY, FRANK L. A descriptive compendium of selected historical accessories commonly used as stage properties
Tallahassee: Florida State U. (PhD)     1972

**640** LIPSCHUTZ, MARK. Selected 'still' projection apparatus for scenic and effects projection
pp.vii, 229; ill. in text     M
NY: USITT     [1973?]
Lipschutz produced a supplement describing developments in projection; [1976?], pp.46.

**641** COUGHENOUR, KAY L. The contribution of the Robert Bergman scenic design studio to contemporary American scene design
Kent OH: State U. (PhD)     1973

**642** MILLER, JAMES H. Self-supporting scenery for children's theatre...and grown-up's too (a scenic workbook for the open stage)
pp.91; ill. in text     M
Shreveport LA: For the author     1973
Revised edition.

**643** NORDVOLD, ROBERT O. Showcase for the new stagecraft: the scenic designs of the Washington Square Players and the Theatre Guild, 1915-1929
Bloomington: Indiana U. (PhD)     1973

**644** BAY, HOWARD. Stage design
pp.v, 219; ill. in text     M
NY: Drama Book Specialists     1974

Emphasizes 20th c. UK and US stage design. Appendices on stage machinery by William Cruise and on lighting controls by Ralph Holmes.

**645** BURDICK, ELIZABETH B.; HANSEN, PEGGY C. & ZANGER, BRENDA. Contemporary stage design
pp.163; ill. in text, some col.     M
Middletown CT: Wesleyan U. P./ITI     1974
Exhibition catalogue, Lincoln Center, NY, Dec. 16, 1974. Includes, Rosamond Gilder: *Contemporary stage design*; Donald Oenslager: *US stage design, past and present*; Howard Bay: *The designer and the Broadway scene*; Jerry Rojo: *Environmental design*; David Jenkins: *Designing for resident theatres*; Patricia Ziprodt: *Designing costumes*; Boris Aaronson: *Notes on designing musicals*; Charles Elson: *Training the stage designer*; Eldon Elder: *The new international designer*...

**646** COLLOM, JEFFREY R. The role of contemporary scene building houses for Broadway theatre
East Lansing: Michigan State U. (PhD)     1975

**647** PECKTAL, LYNN. Designing and painting for the theatre
pp.iv, 412; ill. in text, pl. 8 col.     M
NY: Holt, Rinehart and Winston     1975

**648** PHILLIPS, JERROLD. The new stage craft in America: a history of the development of scenic design, 1915-1949
NY: U. (PhD)     1975

**649** STELL, WALTER J. An investigation of personality variables as factors affecting responses to theatrical set designs
Bowling Green: State U. (PhD)     1975

**650** AMERICAN BALLET THEATRE: thirty-six years of scenic and costume design 1940-1976 presented by Ballet Theatre Foundation...
pp.[48]; ill. in text     M
[Washington DC]: American Ballet Theatre     1976

**651** BOATRIGHT, JOEL. United States patents for scenic and lighting devices for the theatre from 1876 to 1975
Tallahassee: Florida State U. (PhD)     1976

**652** RUSSELL, DOUGLAS A. Theatrical style: a visual approach to the theatre
pp.ix, 237; ill. in text     M
Stanford CA: Mayfield Publishing     1976
A revision of the author's *Stage costume design: theory, technique and style*, NY, 1973, with a broader application to stage design.

**653** BECK, ROY A. Stagecraft
pp.81; ill.     DL★
Skokie, IL: National Textbooks     1977

**654** BELLMAN, WILLARD F. Scenography and stage technology: an introduction
pp.xv, 625; ill. in text, pl. 4 col.     M
NY: Thomas Y. Crowell     1977

**655** PEVITTS, ROBERT. Annotated bibliography of scene and costume design in the past hundred years
Carbondale: Southern Illinois U, (PhD)     1977

**656** STODDARD, RICHARD. Stage scenery, machinery, and lighting: a guide to information sources
pp.xi, 274     M
Detroit MI: Gale Research     1977
International in scope.

**657** WELKER, DAVID. Stagecraft: a handbook for organization, construction and management
pp.xviii, 423; ill. in text     DL★
Boston: Allyn and Bacon     1977

**658** WOLFE, WELBY B. Materials of the scene; an introduction to technical theatre
pp.ix, 315; ill. in text     L
NY: Harper & Row     1977

**659** BAKER, JAMES W. Elements of stagecraft
pp.xii, 241; ill.     ★
Sherman Oaks CA: Alfred Publishing     1978

**660** KOOK, EDWARD F. The link between the theatre artist and technician
NY: U. (PhD)     1978

**661** MASHBURN, ROBERT R. An aesthetic and method for designing stage furniture
Tallahassee: Florida State U. (PhD)     1978

**662** PALKOVIC, TIMOTHY J. An analysis of five selected drawing systems as scenic design tools for the proscenium, arena, thrust, and open space stages
Minneapolis: U. of Minnesota (PhD)     1979

**663** [ROTHGEB, JOHN R.]. An American collection. Selection from the library of Robert L. B. Tobin, San Antonia, Texas
pp.11; ill in text     M
[San Antonio]: U. of Texas     [1979]
Catalogue. Examples of scene design exhibited in Prague.

**664** TATE, HILARY. A space for magic: stage settings by Richard L. Hay. The work of Oregon Shakespearean Festival's resident theatre and scenic designer...
pp.48; ill. in text     MH
[Ashland OR]: Oregon Shakespearean Festival     1979

**665** McEVOY, OWEN. The new stagecraft: Robert Edmond Jones, Norman Bel Geddes, Lee Simonson
NY: U. (PhD)     1980

**666** RUSSELL, DOUGLAS A. Period style for the theatre
pp.xviii, 461; ill. in text     M
Boston: Alyn and Bacon     1980
An historical survey from the ancient world to the present day.

**667** UNITED STATES INSTITUTE FOR THEATRE TECHNOLOGY. The first biennial exposition 1980 [cover title]
pp.36; ill. in text     M
NY: USITT     1980
Catalogue. Exhibition opened Kansas City, March 12.

**668** ARONSON, ARNOLD. The history and theory of environmental scenography
pp.xiv, 282; ill. in text     M
Ann Arbor MI: UMI Research P.     1981

International in scope. The term 'environmental scenography' was coined by Richard Schechner to describe 'non-frontal' staging; i.e. where the scenography cannot be totally apprehended by a spectator maintaining a single frontal relationship to the performance.

**669** PAYNE, DARWIN R. The scenographic imagination
pp.xxi, 294; ill. in text  M
Carbondale: Southern Illinois U. P.  1981
Revised version of *Design for the stage*, 1974. Introduction to history, principles and practice of scene design.

**670** HELD, R. L. Endless innovations. Frederick Kiesler's theory and scenic design
pp.xvii, 258; ill. in text  MH
Ann Arbor MI: UMI Research P.  1982
Foreword by Lillian Kiesler.

**671** HOWARD, JOHN T. A bibliography of theatre technology. Acoustics and sound, lighting, properties, and scenery
pp.xii, 345  M
Westport CT: Greenwood P.  1982
5719 items, mostly periodical references. International.

**672** UNITED STATES INSTITUTE FOR THEATRE TECHNOLOGY. The second biennial scenography exposition 1982
pp.55; ill. in text  M
NY: USITT  1982
Catalogue of exhibition held in Denver.

**673** BELLMAN, WILLARD F. Scene design, stage lighting, sound, costume & makeup: a scenographic approach
pp.xv, 474; ill. in text, pl. 8 col.  M
NY: Harper & Row  1983
In effect, a second, revised edition of the author's *Scenography and stage technology*, (1977).

**674** HELGESEN, TERRY. Grand drapes, tormentor and teasers
pp.40; ill in text, folding insert  M
Notre Dame IN: Theatre Historical Society  1983
Lavishly illustrated survey of theatre curtaining.

**675** HOW-TO
pp.av, 160; ill. in text  M
NY: Drama Book Publishers  1984, 89
Two volumes offering a selection of articles reprinted from *Theatre Crafts Magazine*.

**676** UNITED STATES INSTITUTE FOR THEATRE TECHNOLOGY. Third biennial scenography exposition
pp.95; ill. in text  M
NY: USITT  1984
Catalogue of exhibition, Orlando FL, April 4-7.

**677** ARNOLD, RICHARD. Scene technology
pp.viii, 343; ill. in text  L
Englewood Cliffs NJ: Prentice Hall  1985

**678** ARONSON, ARNOLD. American set design...foreword by Harold Prince
pp.ix, 182; ill. in text, pl. 4 col.  M
NY: Theatre Communication Group  1985

**679** HOSTETLER, ROBERT D. The American nuclear theatre
Evanston: Northwestern U. (PhD)  1985
Examination of nuclear technology in five productions.

**680** PARKER, WILFRED O.; SMITH, HARVEY K. & CRAIG, WOLF R. Scene design and stage lighting
pp.Ix, 596; ill. in text, pl. 8 col.  M
NY: Holt, Rinehart and Winston  1985
Fifth edition. First published 1963 under authorship of Parker and Smith. A sixth edition (unexamined) was published in 1990.

**681** PAYNE, DARWIN R. Theory and craft of the scenographic model.
pp.xxvii, 163; ill. in text  M
Carbondale: Southern Illinois U. P.  1985
Revision of *Materials and craft of the scenic model*, 1976.

**682** BLUMENTHAL, ARTHUR R. Theater designs in the collection of the Cooper-Hewitt Museum
pp.32; ill. in text  M
Washington DC: Smithsonian Institution  1986

**683** FEINSOD, ARTHUR B. The origins of the minimalist mis-en-scene in the United States
NY: U. (PhD)  1986

**684** UNITED STATES INSTITUTE FOR THEATRE TECHNOLOGY: fourth biennial scenography exposition [Oakland CA]
pp.104; ill. in text  M
NY: USITT  1986

**685** GILLETTE, J. MICHAEL. Theatrical design and publication: an introduction to scene design and construction, lighting, sound, costume, and makeup
pp.xii, 500; ill. in text, pl. 8 col.  M
Mountain View CA: Mayfield Publishing  1987

**686** MAHFOUZ, NAZIH H. Toward an aesthetic of scenography through art and movement-space-time
Evanston: Northwestern U. (PhD)  1987

**687** PINNELL, WILLIAM H. Theatrical scene painting: a lesson guide
pp.ix, 170; ill. in text, some col.  M
Carbondale: Southern Illinois U. P.  1987

**688** SCHRAFT, ROBIN J. An investigation of computer-aided theatrical scenic and lighting design
NY: U. (PhD)  1987

**689** DESIGN EXPOSITION '88: scenery, costumes, and lighting in the performing arts
pp.63; ill. in text, some col.  M
NY: USITT  1988
Fifth biennial collection, Anaheim CA.

**690** JAMES, THURSTON. The prop builder's molding and casting handbook
pp.236; ill.  DL★
White Hall VA: Betterway  1989

**691** LARSON, ORVILLE K. Scene design in the American theatre from 1915 to 1960: a chronicle of the activities of the New Stagecraft designers and their followers with an appraisal of the state of the art and the European influences previous to their appearance
pp.xx, 385; ill. in text, some col.  M
Fayetteville: U. of Arkansas P.  1989

## 4.4. COSTUME DESIGN

**692** LACY, ROBIN T. A biographical dictionary of scenographers 500 B.C. to 1900 A.D.
pp.xxiii, 762; front. M
NY: Greenwood P. 1990

**693** ROSE, RICH. Drafting scenery for theater, film and television
pp.176; ill. DL★
White Hall VA: Betterway 1990

**694** SPORRE, DENNIS J. & BURROUGHS, ROBERT C. Scene design in the theatre
pp.viii, 312 DL★
Englewood Cliffs NJ: Prentice-Hall 1990

## 4.4 COSTUME DESIGN

**695** MacGOWAN, KENNETH & ROSSE, HERMAN. Masks and demons
pp.xiii, 177; ill. in text L
London: Martin Hopkinson 1924
Masks of the world, including brief reference to Amerindian mask rituals.

**696** GRIMBALL, E. B. & WELLS, RHEA. Costuming a play. Inter-theatres arts handbook
pp.133; ill. in text DL★
NY: Century 1925

**697** DABNEY, EDITH & WISE, C.M. A book of dramatic costume
pp.x, 163; ill. in text M
NY: F. S. Crofts 1930

**698** MACKAY, CONSTANCE D. Costumes and scenery for amateurs: a practical working handbook
pp.viii, 257; ill. in text DL★
NY: Henry Holt 1932
New edition, revised. First published 1915.

**699** ROEDIGER, VIRGINIA M. Ceremonial costumes of the Pueblo indians. Their evolution, fabrication, and significance in the prayer-drama
New Haven: Yale U. (PhD) 1937

**700** RICHARDSON, GENEVIEVE. Costuming on the American stage, 1751-1901. A study of the major developments in wardrobe practice and costume style
Urbana: U. of Illinois (PhD) 1953

**701** COSTUME DESIGN FOR THE THEATRE...
pp.20; ill. in text M
Los Angeles: County Museum 1956
Exhibition catalogue. Addenda/corrigenda slip.

**702** ZIRNER, LAURA. Costuming for the modern stage
pp.50; ill. in text M
Urbana: U. of Illinois P. 1957

**703** LANGNER, LAWRENCE. The importance of wearing clothes
pp.xv, 350; ill. in text M
London: Constable 1959
Introduction by James Laver. Chapters on clothes and the performing arts. US edition lacks the errata page.

**704** PATEREK, JOSEPHINE. Costuming for the theatre
pp.x, 150; ; ill. in text CSt
NY: Crown Publishers 1959

**705** WALKUP, FAIRFAX P. Dressing the part: a history of costume for the theatre
pp.x, 423; ill. in text, pl. 16 M
NY: Appleton-Century-Crofts 1959
Revised edition. Foreword by Gilmor Brown.

**706** LORING, JANET. Costuming on the New York stage from 1895-1915 with particular emphasis on Charles Frohman's companies
Ames: State U. of Iowa (PhD) 1960

**707** PATEREK, JOSEPHINE. A survey of costuming on the New York commercial stage, 1914-1934
Minneapolis: U. of Minnesota (PhD) 1962

**708** VOLLAND, VIRGINIA. Designing woman: the art and practice of theatrical costume design
pp.xi, 197 CB
Garden City: Doubleday 1966
Author designed for, e.g., *Two for the Seesaw, A Raisin in the Sun*.

**709** COREY, IRENE. The mask of reality: an approach to design for theatre
x, 124: ill. in text, some col. M
Anchorage KY: Anchorage P. 1968
Use of the mask in stage design, developed by Irene and Orlin Corey during sixteen years' experience in educational theatre.

**710** HARRISON, EELIN S. The rise of the costume designer. A critical history of costume on the New York stage from 1934 to 1950
Baton Rouge: Louisiana State U. (PhD) 1968

**711** PRISK, BERNEICE & BYERS, JACK A. Costuming
pp.108; ill. in text CSB
NY: Richards Rosen P. 1970
Revised edition. First published 1969.

**712** QUITTNER, C. J. The history, iconology and uses of masks in the theatre past and present, with procedures, materials and techniques for modern day use on the stage
Salt Lake City: U. of Utah (PhD) 1970

**713** STOWELL, DONALD. The new costuming in America: the ideas and practices of Robert Edmond Jones, Norman Bel Geddes, Lee Simonson, and Aline Bernstein
Austin: U. of Texas (PhD) 1972

**714** ROWE, GABRIELLE. Structure and thematic function of the face mask in the development of modern theatre
Ann Arbor: U. of Michigan (PhD) 1974

**715** SMITH, C. RAY (Ed). The *Theatre Crafts* book of costume
pp.224; ill. in text M
London: White Lion 1974

First published NY: Rodale P., 1973. Articles reprinted from *Theatre Crafts* journal.

**716** KARDON, JANET. Artists' sets and costumes. Recent collaborations between painters and sculptors, and dance, opera and theater...
pp.iv, 51; ill. in text     M
Philadelphia: College of Art     1977
Exhibition catalogue, October 31-December 17.

**717** FLETCHER, WINONA B. Andrew Jackson Allen, 'internal and external costumer' to the early nineteenth century Americ [*sic*] theatre
Bloomington: Indiana U. (PhD)     1978

**718** KESLER, JACKSON. Theatrical costume: a guide to information sources
pp.x, 308     P
Detroit: Gale     1979
Mostly general costume history and fashion; pp.13-31 deal specifically with costume for the theatre.

**719** KLINE, RUTH F. Domestic servants of the New York and London stages 1880-1920 with an emphasis on costume
Urbana-Champaign: U. of Illinois (PhD)     1980

**720** DRYDEN, DEBORAH M. Fabric painting & dyeing for the theatre
pp.xiv, 176; ; ill. in text, 8 col.     CSC
NY: Drama Book Specialists     1981

**721** EMERY, JOY S. Stage costume techniques...drawings by Jerry R. Emery
pp.xxi, 362; ill. in text, pl. 2 col.     M
Englewood Cliffs NJ: Prentice-Hall     1981

**722** WITSEN, LEO V. Costuming for opera; who wears what and why
pp.xxiii, 232; ill. in text     M
Bloomington: Indiana U. P.     1981

**723** O'DONNOL, SHIRLEY M. American costume 1915-1970: a source book for the stage costumer
pp.xv, 270; ill. in text     L
Bloomington: Indiana U. P.     1982

**724** THOMAS, BEVERLY J. A practical approach to costume design and construction. Volume I, fundamentals and design. [Volume II, construction]
pp.xvii, 236; xi, 322; ill. in text, pl. 2 col.     M
Boston: Allyn and Bacon     1982

**725** INGHAM, ROSEMARY & COVEY, LIZ. Costume designer's handbook: a complete guide for amateur and professional costume designers
pp.viii, 264; ill. in text, pl. 2 col.     L
Englewood Cliffs NJ: Prentice-Hall     1983

**726** PATTON, ELEANOR N. The costuming practices of the Living Theatre, the Open Theatre, and the Performance Group: theory, form, and function
Lawrence: U. of Kansas (PhD)     1984

**727** SMITH, SUSAN V. H. Masks in modern drama
pp.xi, 237, pl. 8     M
Berkeley: U. of California P.     1984
Includes a chronological list of plays involving masking, with early and recent US examples.

**728** WINKELBAUER, STEFANIE M. Wake up and dream ! Costume designs for Broadway musicals 1900-1925 from the theatre collection of the Austrian National Library
pp.60; pl. 18, some col.     M
Vienna: Böhlau     1986

**729** OWEN, BOBBI. Costume design on Broadway: designers and their credits, 1915-1985
pp.xv, 255; pl. 43     M
NY: Greenwood P.     1987

**730** TOBIN, ROBERT L. B. Thespis adorned
pp.40; ill. in text, mostly col.     M
San Antonio TX: McNay Art Museum     1987
Exhibition catalogue. Costume designs, and sculptures and illustrated books displaying costume, from the Tobin Collection.

**731** JAMES, THURSTON. The prop builder's mask-making handbook
pp.203; ill. in text     P
White Hall VA: Betterway     1990

**732** LEWIS, JAC & LEWIS, MIRIAM. Costume: the performing partner. Foreword by Julie Harris
pp.186; ill. in text     CLA
Colorado Springs: Meriwether     1990
The effect of dress on performance; examples from stage, film and TV.

**733** WENTWORTH, BRENDA K. The development of the professional stage costumer in the American theatre
Columbia: U. of Missouri (PhD)     1990

## 4.5 MAKE-UP

**734** FROBISHER, JOSEPH E. Frobisher's make-up book; a complete guide to the art of making-up the face for the stage; including directions for the use of wigs, beards, mustaches, and every variety of artificial hair, etc...With an appendix of hints on acting
pp.444; ill in text     PAST
NY: College of Oratory and Acting     1882

**735** YOUNG, JAMES. Making up...
pp. vi, 179; ill. in text     M
NY: M. Witmark     1905
Illustrated by Edgar Keller.

**736** HOLLAND, CECIL. The art of stage make-up for stage and screen
pp.102; ill.     CSt
Hollywood: Cinematex Publishing     1927

**737** GALL, ELLEN M. & CARTER, LESLIE H. Modern make-up. A practical textbook and guide for student, director, and professional
pp.128; ill. in text, pl. 1 col, folding     DL★
San Francisco: Banner Play Bureau     1928

**738** CHALMERS, HELENA. The art of make-up: for the stage, for the screen, and social use
pp.viii, 167; ill. in text, front.     L
NY: D. Appleton     1930
Second edition. First published 1925.

**739** BAIRD, JOHN F. Make-up: a manual for the use of actors, amateur and professional. Illustrated by Lee Mitchell
pp.xi, 155; ill. in text  M
NY: Samuel French  1931

**740** STRENKOVSKY, SERGE. The art of make-up...edited by Elizabeth S. Taber
pp.xix, 350; ill. in text, col. front.  M
London: Frederick Muller  1937

**741** SCHWERIN, ARTHUR H. Make-up magic: a modern handbook for beginners or advanced students...
pp.106, ill.  DL★
Minneapolis: Northwestern P.  1939
Emphasis on character makeup.

**742** CORSON, RICHARD. Stage makeup
pp.xvi, 354; ill. in text  M
London: Peter Owen  1961
First published NY: Appleton, 1949. An eighth edition was published NY: Prentice Hall, 1990 (not seen).

**743** BOWMAN, NED A. Handbook of technical practice for the performing arts; Ned Bowman's inter-galactic serial shop cookbook
pp.xiv, 180; ill. in text  M
Wilkinsburg: Scenographic Media  1972-
In two sections, *make-up formulas* and *plastics*; corrections sheet issued in 1975.

**744** BUCHMAN, HERMAN. Stage makeup. Demonstration photographs by Susan E. Meyer
pp.192; ill. in text, some col.  M
NY: Watson-Guptill  1972

**745** SMITH, C. RAY (Ed.). The *Theatre Crafts* book of make-up, masks, and wigs
pp.238; ill. in text  M
London: White Lion  1974
First published NY: Rodale P., 1974. Articles reprinted from *Theatre Crafts* journal.

**746** LIZST, RUDOLPH G. The last word in make-up
pp.xviii, 151; pl.23  CSC
NY: Dramatists Play Service  1977
Revised edition.

**747** BAYGAN, LEE. techniques of three-dimensional makeup
pp.183; ill. in text, some col.  L
NY: Watson-Guptill  1982

**748** BAYGAN, LEE. Makeup for theatre, film & television: a step by step photographic guide
pp.xix, 182; ill. in text  CSC
NY: Drama Book Specialists  1989
First published 1982.

**749** COREY, IRENE. The face is a canvas: the design and technique of theatrical make-up
pp.310; ill. in text, some col.  CSC
New Orleans: Anchorage P.  1990
First published 1987 as *The face is a canvas: a complete guide to...*

## 4.6 MANAGEMENT, ADMINISTRATION, AND GENERAL

**750** FYLES, FRANKLIN. The theatre and its people
pp.viii, 259; pl. 19  M
NY: Doubleday, Page  1900
The practicalities and business background of theatre production. Author was drama critic of the *New York Sun*.

**751** THE THEATRICAL CYPHER CODE: adapted especially to the use of everyone connected in any way with the theatrical business
pp.194  DL★
Los Angeles: Theatrical Code Publishing  1905
Telegraph code.

**752** JOHNSON, FREDERICK G. The press-agent's handbook. How to advertise a play, as necessary as the play itself to amateurs, designed for dramatic clubs and other groups of amateur entertainers
pp.68  DL★
Chicago: T. S. Denison  [1916]

**753** THE TRUTH ABOUT THE THEATRE: by one of the best known theatrical men in New York
pp.vii, 111  M
Cincinnati: Stewart & Kidd  1916
Analysis of theatre organization and policy, and the difficulties and pitfalls awaiting the beginner.

**754** BEREZNIAK, LEON A. The theatrical counselor
pp.233; front.  DL★
Chicago: Cooper Syndicate  1923

**755** HINDSELL, OLIVER. Making the little theatre pay. A practical handbook
pp.xii, 122; pl. 16 (1 folding)  M
NY: Samuel French  1925
Dallas Little Theatre used as a model to describe organization and policy.

**756** SANFORD, E. S. Theatre management: a manual of the business of the theatre including full texts of author's and actor's standard contracts. Preface by Charles B. Dillingham
pp.x, 154; ill. in text  L
NY: D. Appleton  1929

**757** STAGE MANAGER'S GUIDE. *The Sunbonnet Girl*, a comic operetta in two acts...by Geoffrey F. Morgan and Frederick G. Johnson...containing full stage business, action on songs, dance-steps, diagrams of the stage and cut of stage-setting...to be used in connection with the regular score
pp.26; ill. in text  L
Cincinnati OH: Willis Music  1929
This and similar guides provide interesting insight into touring company style.

**758** GLUCKMAN, EMANUEL M. General instructions manual for theatre managers
pp.61, vi  DL★
Chicago: Chicago Show Printing  1930
250 copies.

**759** WHORF, RICHARD B. & WHEELER, ROGER. Runnin' the show: a practical handbook
pp.72; ill,  DL★
Boston: W. H. Baker  1930

**760 EUSTIS, MORTON.** B'way, Inc.! The theatre as a business
pp.xi. 356      L
NY: Dodd, Mead      1934

**761 STARCH, DANIEL.** Survey of the *Playbill*...
pp.23      MH
[NY]: [Theatre Program Corporation]      1935
'To determine certain basic factual data with reference to the reading of and the interest in the theatre program on the part of the theatre patrons of New York'.

**762 COLE, EDWARD C.** A stage manager's manual compiled for use at the Yale University theatre [cover title]
pp.26: ill. in text      DL★
New Haven: Yale U. P.      1937

**763 HENDRICKS, BILL L. & WAUGH, HOWARD.** Charles 'Chick' Lewis presents the encyclopedia of exploitation
pp.xxii, 439; ill. in text      DL★
NY: Showman's Trade Review      1937
Reference book for merchandizing entertainment.

**764 WASHBURN, CHARLES.** Press agentry
pp.153      M
NY: National Library P.      1937
Handbook, supplemented with opinions on press agentry from prominent editors.

**765 HALSTEAD, WILLIAM P.** Stage management for the amateur theatre with an index to the standard works on stagecraft and stage lighting
pp.xviii, 265; ill. in text      L
London: George Harrap      1938

**766 BRICKER, HERSCHEL L. (Ed.).** Our theatre today: a composite handbook on the art, craft, and management of the contemporary theatre
pp.xxvii, 427; ill. in text      M
NY: Samuel French      1948
Includes, Barrett H. Clark: *Playwright and theatre*; Arthur Hopkins: *Producer and play*.

**767 PLUMMER, GAIL.** The business of show business
pp.xi, 238; ill. in text      L
NY: Harper & Bros.      1961
A handbook for theatre managers.

**768 CULLMAN, MARGUERITE.** Occupation: angel
pp.256      M
NY: W. W. Norton      1963
Reminiscences of a theatrical backer.

**769 DODRILL, CHARLES W.** Theatre management: selected bibliography
ll.10      DL★
Westerville OH: [AETA]      1966

**770 RUSSELL, RUFUS T.** A study of factors influencing theatre attendance
Iowa City: U. of Iowa (PhD)      1968

**771 FARBER, DONALD C.** Producing on Broadway: a comprehensive guide
pp.xxxviii, 399      L
NY: Drama Book Specialists      1969

**772 LITTLE, STUART W. & CANTOR, ARTHUR.** The playmakers: Broadway from the inside
pp.320; pl. 8      M
NY: Dutton      1970

**773 SPECIMENS OF SHOW PRINTING** being facsimiles in miniature of poster cuts comprising coloured and plain designs
Unpaginated; pl. 142      M
California: Cherokee P.      [c. 1970]
A facsimile of a samples collection, first printed by the *Philadelphia Ledger* c.1870 and now held in the Harvard Theatre Collection.

**774 CIRKER, HAYWARD & CIRKER, BLANCHE** (Eds). The golden age of the poster
pp.vi, 72: ill in text, col.      M
NY: Dover      1971
Seventy European and American posters.

**775 GRUVER, BERT.** The stage-manager's handbook
pp.xxi, 220      M
NY: Drama Book Specialists      1972
First published 1953. Here revised by Frank Hamilton.

**776 CAVANAUGH, JIM.** Organization and management of the nonprofessional theatre, including backstage and front-of-house
pp.176; ill.      DL★
NY: Richards Rosen P.      1973

**777 KOVAR, LINN S.** Strategic marketing: an approach to theatre management
Lawrence: U. of Kansas (PhD)      1976

**778 FARBER, DONALD C.** From option to opening
pp.xiv, 144      M
NY: Drama Book Specialists      1977
Third edition, revised. First published 1968. Business background and financial technicalitles of play production.

**779 DUFFY, SUSAN.** Elmer Bernard Kenyon: an examination of the career of a press agent
Pittsburgh: U. (PhD)      1979

**780 A PICTORIAL SURVEY** of marquees [cover title]
pp.40 inc. wrappers; ill. in text      M
Notre Dame IN: Theatre Historical Society      1980
Heavily pictorial account of theatre publicity signboards.

**781 PYE, MICHAEL.** Moguls. Inside the business of show business
pp.vi, 250; ill. in text      M
London: Temple Smith      1980
Accounts of Jules Stein, W. S. Paley, David Merrick, Peter Guber, Trevor Nunn, Robert Stigwood.

**782 CRAWFORD, ROBERT W. (Ed.).** In art we trust: the board of trustees in the performing arts
pp.xiii, 72      M
Ohio: State U. P.      1981

Published in collaboration with the Foundation for the Extension and Development of the American Professional Theatre (FEDAPT), a national not-for-profit service offering management and technical assistance to professionally oriented theatre and dance companies.

**783** SKAL, DAVID J. (Ed.).  Graphic communications for the performing arts
pp.viii, 152; ill. in text                                M
NT: Theatre Communications Group              1981
Urges effective design in marketing and publicizing the performing arts.

**784** DILKER, BARBARA.  Stage management: forms and formats
pp.x, 177                                                  *
NY: DBS                                                 1982

**785** TELFORD, ROBERT S.  Handbook for theatrical managers: a community theatre system that really works
pp.279; diagrams                                           L
NY: Samuel French                                       1983

**786** WALLACE, WILLIAM J.  An analysis of selected marketing concepts and their application to the non-profit theatre
Minneapolis: U. of Minnesota (PhD)                      1985

**787** STERN, LAURENCE.  Stage management: a guidebook of practical techniques
pp.xviii, 324; ill. in text                               L
Boston: Allyn & Bacon                                   1987
Third edition. First published 1974.

**788** LONDON, TODD.  The artistic home. Discussions with artistic directors of America's institutional theatres...Introduction by Lloyd Richards. Foreword by Peter Zeisler
pp.xv, 92                                                  M
NY: Theatre Communications Group              1988
Report of the TCG's National Artistic Agenda Project, an attempt to articulate motives and principles of the nonprofit professional theatre.

**789** SSUTU, PATRICIA C.  Children's theatre management: financial management and promotion strategies
Lawrence: U. of Kansas (PhD)                            1988

**790** WILSON, KAREN P.  A study of managerial techniques practised by directors of theatre at LORT [League of Resident Theatres] A, B+, B, C, and D theatres in 1987-88
Minneapolis: U. of Minnesota (PhD)                      1988

**791** LOUNSBURY, WARREN & BOULANGER, NORMAN.  Theatre backstage from A to Z
pp.xxvii, 213; ill. in text                               L
Seattle: U. of Washington P.                            1989
Third edition, revised. First published 1967.

**792** LANGLEY, STEPHEN.  Theatre management and production in America: commercial, stock, resident, college and community theatre & presenting organizations
pp.720; ill. in text                                       M
NY: Drama Book Specialists                              1990
Revised edition. First published 1974.

## 4.7 ACTING

**793** BURGH, JAMES.  The art of speaking: containing I. an essay; in which are given rules for expressing properly the principal passions and humors, which occur in reading or public speaking and II, lessons taken from the ancients and moderns...exhibiting a variety of matter for practice...
pp.299                                                   DL*
Philadelphia: R. Aitken                                 1775
The fourth edition. A work issued by many publishing houses in a variety of editions in the closing decades of the century.

**794** THE THESPIAN PRECEPTOR, or, a full display of the scenic art: including ample and easy instructions for treading the stage, using proper action, modulating the voice, and expressing the several dramatic passions...
pp.158                                                     *
Boston: Elam Bliss                                      1810
Seemingly the first edition, making it the first acting manual to be printed in America. UK editions were published London: 1811, 1818.

**795** RUSH, JAMES.  The philosophy of the human voice embracing its physiological history; together with a system of principles; by which criticism in the art of elocution may be rendered intelligible, and instruction, definite and comprehensive. To which is added a brief analysis of song and recitative
pp.499; charts and musical notations in text              L
Philadelphia: J. Crissy, printer                        1845
Third edition, enlarged.

**796** THE ART OF ACTING, or, guide to the stage: in which the dramatic passions are defined, analyzed, and made easy of acquirement
pp.24                                                     MB
NY: Samuel French                                    [1855?]

**797** THE AMATEUR, OR GUIDE TO THE STAGE: containing lessons for theatrical novices...; with all the rudimental information necessary to lead a stranger to the stage, from the novice up to the actor by a Retired Performer
pp.64; front.                                              M
Philadelphia: Fisher & Brother                       [c. 1860]
Interesting insights into nineteenth century stage practice.

**798** REDE, THOMAS L.  The guide to the stage containing clear and ample instructions for obtaining theatrical engagements...with additional information, making it applicable to the American stage...also. a list of the American theatres and copies of their rules and articles of engagement. Edited by Francis C. Wemyss
pp.58                                                      M
NY: Samuel French                                       1864

**799** FROBISHER, JOSEPH E.  A new and practical system of the culture of voice and action...
pp.262                                                   DL*
NY: Ivison Phinney Blakeman                             1867

**800** [WARFORD, AARON A.].  On the stage: or, how to become an actor. With dramas, dialogues,

speeches, burlesques, sketches...songs, and complete instructions as to the duties of the stage manager, prompter, scenic artist...by a prominent stage manager
pp.39, iv　　　　　　　　　　　　　　　　DL★
NY: Tousey & Small　　　　　　　　　　　1878
Reprinted NY: F. Tousey, 1895

**801**　FROBISHER, JOSEPH E.　Acting and oratory: designed for public speakers, teachers, actors, etc.
pp.415; ill. in text　　　　　　　　　　　　M
NY: College of Oratory and Acting　　　　1879

**802**　MURDOCH, JAMES E.　A plea for the spoken language. An essay upon comparative elocution, condensed from lectures delivered throughout the United States
pp.320　　　　　　　　　　　　　　　　　L
Cincinnati OH: Van Antwerp, Bragg　　　1883
Murdoch acknowledges the influence of Dr James Rush. Appended are Dr Barber: *Essay on rhythmus*, 1823; and A. Hill: *An essay on the dramatic passions*, 1779.

**803**　DELSARTE, FRANÇOIS.　The art of oratory: system of Delsarte from the French of M. L'Abbe Delaumosne and Mme Angelique Arnaud (pupils of Delsarte) with an essay on the attributes of reason...
pp.xx, 170; 116; ill. in text　　　　　　　　M
Albany NY: Edgar S. Werner　　　　　　　1884
Second edition. Two books in one. Includes a biographical sketch, the system itself, and a commentary on the system.

**804**　MURDOCH, JAMES E.　Analytic elocution, containing studies, theoretical and practical, of expressive speech
pp.504　　　　　　　　　　　　　　　　　L
Cincinnati OH: Van Antwerp, Bragg　　　1884
Complements the author's *A plea for the spoken language*.

**805**　STEBBINS, GENEVIEVE.　Delsarte system of dramatic expression. Original illustrations
pp.viii, 271; ill. in text, pl. 1 folding　　　MB
NY: Edgar S. Werner　　　　　　　　　　1886

**806**　MORGAN, ANNA.　An hour with Delsarte: a study of expression
pp.ii, 115; pl. 24　　　　　　　　　　　　L
Boston: Lee & Shepard　　　　　　　　　1889
Last chapter is on the stage. Illustrated by Rose M. Sprague and Marian Reynolds.

**807**　PHELPS, HENRY P.　*Hamlet* from the actors' standpoint: its representatives and a comparison of their performances
pp.x, 180; pl. 10　　　　　　　　　　　　M
NY: Edgar S. Werner　　　　　　　　　　1890
Includes accounts of Edwin Booth and Edwin Forrest.

**808**　SANBURN, FREDERICK (Ed.).　A Delsartean scrapbook: health, personality, beauty, house-decoration, dress, etc.
pp.xvi, 250　　　　　　　　　　　　　　L
NY: U.S.Book　　　　　　　　　　　　　1890
Includes chapters on the nature of Delsartism, with reference to Edwin Forrest, art education, natural expression, breath control, and offers an account of a private lesson with Edmund Russell. Preface by Walter Crane.

**809**　ADAMS, FLORENCE A. [= Fowle, Florence].　Gesture and pantomimic action
pp.221; ill.　　　　　　　　　　　　　　DL★
NY: E. S. Werner　　　　　　　　　　　1891
The second edition.

**810**　CURRY, SAMUEL S.　The province of expression: a search for principles underlying adequate methods of developing dramatic and oratoric delivery
pp.461　　　　　　　　　　　　　　　　L
Boston: School of Expression　　　　　　1891

**811**　BISHOP, EMILY M.　Americanized Delsarte culture
pp.202, vi　　　　　　　　　　　　　　　L
Washington DC: For the author　　　　　1892
A course for the author's pupils.

**812**　[DELSARTE, FRANÇOIS].　Delsarte system of oratory containing 1. the complete work of L'Abbe Delaumosne; 2. the complete work of Mme. Angelique Arnaud; 3. All the literary remains of Francois Delsarte (given in his own words); 4. the lecture and lessons given by Mme Marie Geroldy (Delsarte's daughter) in America; 5. articles by Alfred Giraudet, Francis A. Durivage, and Hector Berlioz
pp.xxix, 606; ill. in text, pl 4 (2 folding)　　M
NY: Edgar S. Werner　　　　　　　　　　1892
The fourth edition.

**813**　WARMAN, EDWARD B.　Gestures and attitudes: an exposition of the Delsarte philosophy of expression, practical and theoretical
pp.422; ill. in text, front.　　　　　　　　L
Boston: Lee and Shepard　　　　　　　　1892

**814**　GIRAUDET, A.　Mimique, physionomie et gestes: méthode pratique d'après le système de F. del Sarte pour servir a l'expression des sentiments
pp.128; pl. 34　　　　　　　　　　　　　M
Paris France: Libraires-Imprimeries Reunies　1895
Illustrations by Gaston Le Doux showing expression, posture and gesture.

**815**　NORTHROP, HENRY D.　The Delsarte speaker; or, modern elocution, designed for young folks and amateurs. Containing a practical treatise on the Delsarte system of physical culture
pp.512; ill.　　　　　　　　　　　　　　DL★
Philadelpia: National Publishing　　　　　[1895]

**816**　CURRY, SAMUEL S.　Imagination and dramatic instinct: some practical steps for their development
pp.i, 369　　　　　　　　　　　　　　　L
Boston: [School of] Expression　　　　　1896
Study of vocal expression as 'the direct revelation of the processes of the mind in thinking and feeling'.

**817**　AYRES, ALFRED [= Osmun, Thomas E.].　The essentials of elocution
pp.147　　　　　　　　　　　　　　　　DL★
NY: Funk & Wagnalls　　　　　　　　　1897
New and enlarged edition.

**818**　FOSTER, J. EDGAR.　10 lessons in elocution, (founded on the teachings of Delsarte and Sheridan) by Rev. J. Edgar Foster, M.A. (pupil of Delsarte)[drop title]
pp.64　　　　　　　　　　　　　　　　　L
Washington Co.Durham: Alfred Watson　[1900]

Second impression.

**819** FOSTER, J. EDGAR. Lessons in oratory; its theory and practice
pp.52 L
London: J. F. Spriggs [1900]

**820** [GILLETTE, HENRY C.]. Success on the stage: an encyclopedia of dramatic art containing complete information on every subject connected with the actor's profession...
pp.96; ill. MH★
Chicago: Chicago Manuscript [1903?]

**821** CURRY, SAMUEL S. Browning and the dramatic monologue. Nature and interpretation of an overlooked form of literature
pp.v, 308 L
Boston: School of Expression 1908
A guide to the dramatic rendering of monologues for actors and others, illustrated from Browning.

**822** THE ACTOR'S MANUAL and handbook, containing useful information for amateurs and professionals, with list of plays particularly adapted for amateur production
pp.64 M
Chicago: Chicago Manuscript [1910]

**823** FOSTER, J. EDGAR. The power of dramatic expression: a book for all public speakers
pp.47 L
London: J. F. Spriggs 1911

**824** MACKAY, F. F. The art of acting, embracing the analysis of expression and its application to dramatic literature
pp.296; front. M
NY: For the author 1913

**825** MATTHEWS, BRANDER. On acting
pp.v, 90 M
NY: Charles Scribner's Sons 1914

**826** COIGNE, FRANK B. The art of acting for stage and screen, in 80 lessons
Ill. DL★
NY: [For the author?] 1919

**827** TALLCOTT, ROLLO A. The art of acting and public readings: dramatic interpretation
pp.xxvii, 224, diagrams in text L
Indianapolis: Bobbs-Merrill 1922

**828** STANISLAVSKY, CONSTANTIN. My life in art. Translated from the Russian by J. J. Robbins
pp.xii, 586; pl. 31 M
Boston: Little, Brown 1924
Autobiography. First edition. The fuller Russian edition appeared later.

**829** KJERBUHL-PETERSON, LORENZ. Die Schauspielkunst: Untersuchungen über ihr Wirken und Wesen
pp.217 M
Berlin: Deutsche Verlags-Anstalt 1925
Published Boston: Expression, 1935 as *The psychology of acting*, translated by Sarah T. Barrows.

**830** SMEDLEY, CONSTANCE. Greenleaf Theatre elements. I Action; II Speech; III Production
pp.78;90;85; ill. in text M
London: Samuel French [1925]
Three textbooks for home study 'for the amateur who wishes to acquire professional dexterity'. The Greenleaf Theatre, Smedley's own company, gave lecture recitals and demonstrations, exemplifying these books.

**831** WAYBURN, NED. The art of stage dancing: the story of a beautiful and profitable profession, a manual of stage-craft
pp.383; ill. DL★
NY: Ned Wayburn Studios 1925

**832** YOUNG, STARK. Glamour: essays on the art of the theatre
pp.xii, 208 M
NY: Charles Scribner's Sons 1925
Reprinted reviews and essays on acting and directing.

**833** BOSWORTH, HALLIAM. Technique in dramatic art: a delineation of the art of acting by means of its underlying principles and scientific laws. With technical instruction in the art of play production and public speaking. With a foreword by Oliver Hindsell, director of the Little Theatre, Dallas
pp.xix, 438; ill. in text, pl. 4 M
NY: Macmillan 1926

**834** BOUCICAULT, DION. The art of acting
pp.vi, 63 L
NY: Columbia U. 1926
333 copies. A lecture given at the Lyceum Theatre, London, first printed in the *Era*, 29 July 1882. *Brander Matthews Dramatic Museum Papers in Acting*, series 5, no. 1. Introduction by Otis Skinner.

**835** YOUNG, STARK. Theatre practice
pp.xii, 208; pl.12 M
NY: Charles Scribner's Sons 1926
Influential account of acting and directing, in part revised from articles in *Theatre Arts*.

**836** GOODHUE, MARY L. The cure of stage-fright
pp.64 DL★
Boston: Four Seas 1927

**837** O'NEILL, ROSE M. The science and art of speech & gesture: a comprehensive survey of the laws of gesture and expression, founded on the art and life work of Delsarte, with his exercises. Illustrated with photographs and diagrams
pp.198; ill. in text, pl. 8 M
London: C. W. Daniel 1927

**838** CRAFTON, ALLEN & ROYER, JESSICA. Acting: a book for the beginner
pp.xiii, 318; ill. in text, front. L
NY: F. S. Crofts 1928

**839** CHALMERS, HELENA. Modern acting
pp.ix, 151; ill. in text O
NY: D. Appleton 1930

**840** FLEISCHMAN, EARL E. The theory of speech technique in drama
Ann Arbor: U. of Michigan (PhD) 1930

## 4. THEATRE ARTS

**841** CAMPBELL, WAYNE. Amateur acting and play production...with five original non-royalty one-act plays
pp.xvii, 347; ill. in text, pl. 10   L
NY: Macmillan   1931

**842** BOLESLAVSKY, RICHARD. Acting: the first six lessons
pp.122   O
NY: Theatre Arts   1933
Introduction by Edith J. R. Isaacs. Author was sometime director of the Moscow Art Theatre and, *inter alia*, of the Laboratory theatre. Reissued London: Dennis Dobson, 1949 with a preface by Alec Guinness.

**843** LITTLEFIELD, HAROLD. The actor's roadway, a psychology for the player
pp.75   DL★
Newark NJ: J. James   1934

**844** MACKAY, EDWARD J. & MACKAY, ALICE B. Elementary principles of acting, a textbook for teachers and students, based on *The art of acting* by F. F. Mackay
pp.xvii, 253   L
NY: Samuel French   1934

**845** SELDEN, SAMUEL. A player's handbook the theory and practice of acting
pp.xi, 252; ill. in text, pl.4   MH
NY: F. S. Crofts   1934

**846** COWAN, J. M. Pitch, intensity and rhythmic movements in American dramatic speech
Iowa City: U. of Iowa (PhD)   1935

**847** MATHER, CHARLES C.; SPAULDING, ALICE H. & SKILLEN, MELITA H. Behind the footlights: a book on the technique of dramatics
pp.xii, 495; ill. in text   MH
NY: Silver, Burdett   1935
Textbook for the training actor.

**848** PARK, MARIE. Diagnostic study of development in rehearsal and performance of students in dramatic interpretation
Iowa City: U. of Iowa (PhD)   1935

**849** [RAINES, LESTER (Ed.)]. New Mexico theatre conference proceedings, 1935
ll. 31; ill in text   L
[Las Vegas]: For the editor   1935
Affiliated with the National Theatre Conference. Emphasis on speech.

**850** BRIDGE, WILLIAM H. Actor in the making: a handbook on improvization and other techniques of development
pp.115   DL★
Boston: Expression   1936

**851** CARTMELL, VAN H. A handbook for the amateur actor. Including *George*, a one-act play, with complete stage directions and a running commentary for the director, together with a descriptive glossary of stage terms
pp.xiv, 203; ill. in text   L
Garden City NJ: Doubleday Doran   1936

**852** ROSENSTEIN, SOPHIE; HAYDON, LARRAS & SPARROW, WILBUR. Modern acting; a manual
pp.xiii, 129   L
NY: Samuel French   1936
Derived from work carried out at the U. of Washington Division of Drama and in the professional theatre. Foreword by Glenn Hughes.

**853** EUSTIS, MORTON. Players at work: acting according to actors. With a chapter on the singing actor by Lotte Lehmann
pp.127; pl. 8   M
NY: Theatre Arts   1937
Helen Hayes, Alfred Lunt and Lynn Fontanne, Alla Nazimova, Katharine Cornell, Ina Claire, Burgess Meredith and Fred Astaire.

**854** SHAVER, CLAUDE L. The Delsarte system of expression as seen in the notes of Steele MacKaye
Madison: U. of Wisconsin (PhD)   1937

**855** GOATES, WALLACE A. Pitch change in the voices of actors in rehearsal
Iowa City: U. of Iowa (PhD)   1938

**856** ORMSBEE, HELEN. Backstage with actors from the time of Shakespeare to the present day
pp.xiv, 343; pl. 24   M
NY: Thomas Y. Crowell   1938
An attempt to show how a representative range of performers down the ages approached their craft. Includes Orson Welles, Burgess Meredith.

**857** WATTS, STEPHEN (Ed.). Behind the screen: how films are made
pp.xix, 176; pl. 17   M
London: Arthur Baker   1938
With chapter by Lionel Barrymore on the difference between stage and screen acting.

**858** CROCKER, CHARLOTTE; FIELDS, VICTOR & BROOMALL, WILL. Taking the stage: self-development through dramatic art
pp.viii, 339; ill. in text   MH
NY: Pitman   1939
Reference to acting techniques, monodrama and dialect.

**859** D'ANGELO, ARISTIDE. The actor creates
pp.xii, 96   O
NY: Samuel French   1939
Manual.

**860** ADAMS, MAUDE. The first steps in speaking verse. With an anthology
pp.ix, 358   MH
[?]:   [c. 1940]
160 copies, circulated by Phyllis Robbins. An anthology of pieces to speak, with some annotation. The pagination is erratic.

**861** COLVAN, EZEKIEL B. Face the footlights! A new and practical approach to acting
pp.xv, 318; ill. in text   O
NY: Whittlesey House   1940

**862** DILLON, JOSEPHINE [= Gable, Josephine]. Modern acting: a guide for stage, screen and radio
pp.ix, 313   DL★
NY: Prentice-Hall   1940

**863** LEES, CHARLES L. A primer of acting
pp.xx, 188   DL★
NY: Prentice-Hall   1940

## 4.7. ACTING

**864** WATKINS, DWIGHT E. & KARR, HARRISON M. Stage fright and what to do about it
pp.110; ill. DL★
Boston: Expression 1940

**865** IRVINE, HARRY. The actor's art and job. With forewords by Dorothy Stickney and Howard Lindsay. Prefaced and prompted by Alice White
pp.251; front. M
NY: E. P. Dutton 1942

**866** LEWIS, HARRISON. Lewis' technique of acting
pp.248; ill. DL★
NY: Harrison Lewis Screen and Stage School 1942

**867** MOROSCO, SELMA P.; LOUNSBURY, ALTHEA & assisted by OSCAR. Stage technique made easy
pp.94; ill. DL★
NY: M. S. Mill 1942

**868** CRAFTON, ALLEN & ROYER, JESSICA. The complete acted play from script to final curtain
pp.xiv, 385; ill. in text O
NY: F. S. Crofts 1943

**869** ALBERTI, EVA. A handbook of acting based on the new pantomime. Edited by R. Hyndman
pp.ix, 205 M
NY: Samuel French 1946
A system of training developed at the American Academy of Dramatic Arts, Alberti School of Expression, and Columbia U. Teachers' College.

**870** ALBRIGHT, HARRY D. Working up a part: a manual for the beginning actor
pp.x, 224; ill. DL★
NY: Houghton 1947

**871** DUNN, EMMA. You can do it
pp.xxiv, 190; ill. DL★
Agoura CA: [For the author?] 1947
Speech, acting.

**872** HERMAN, LEWIS H. & HERMAN, MARGUERITE S. American dialects: a manual for actors, directors and writers
pp.xvii, 328; ill in text L
NY: Theatre Arts Books 1947
Phonological description.

**873** SELDEN, SAMUEL. First steps in acting
pp.xiv, 344 L
London: George C. Harrap 1947

**874** A SELECTED BIBLIOGRAPHY and critical comment on the art, theory and technique of acting
pp.32 M
Ann Arbor MI: AETA 1948
290 items organized under history of acting, art and techniques, theatrical and dramatic criticism and commentary, biography, autobiography.

**875** COLE, TOBY & CHINOY, HELEN K. (Eds). Actors on acting: the theories, techniques and practices of great actors of all times as told in their own words...with introductions and biographical notes
pp.xiv, 596 M
NY: Crown 1949
The US section ranges from Edwin Forrest to Howard Lindsay, 23 entries in all.

**876** DOLMAN, JOHN. The art of acting
pp.xxii, 313; pl. 16 M
NY: Harper & Brothers 1949
History and technique of acting, with a glossary of stage terms.

**877** STANISLAVSKY, CONSTANTIN. Building a character
pp.xx, 292 M
NY: Theatre Arts Books 1949
Translated by Elizabeth Reynolds Hapgood. Introduction by Joshua Logan.

**878** MAGARSHACK, DAVID. Stanislavsky and the art of the stage
pp.511; front., pl. 7 M
London: Faber 1950

**879** STANISLAVSKY, CONSTANTIN. An actor prepares
pp.xvi, 295 M
NY: Theatre Arts 1950
First published 1936. Introduction by John Gielgud.

**880** MARLOWE, JOAN & BLAKE, BETTY. The keys to Broadway: an actor's handbook for study and reference
pp.42 DL★
NY: Theatre Information Publications 1951

**881** COGER, LESLIE. A comparison for the oral interpreter of the teaching methods of Curry and Stanislavsky
Evanston: Northwestern U. (PhD) 1952

**882** CHEKHOV, MICHAEL. To the actor: on the technique of acting...drawings by Nicolai Remisoff
pp.xviii, 201 M
NY: Harper & Brothers 1953
Account of his training system, begun at Dartington Hall, Devon, UK and continued in the US. Foreword by Yul Brynner.

**883** WALLACE, KARL R. (Ed.). History of speech education in America: background studies
pp.x, 687: ill. DL★
NY: Appleton-Century-Crofts 1954
Includes history of actor training.

**884** GOODMAN, EDWARD. Make believe: the art of acting...with a foreword by Katharine Cornell
pp.xiv, 242: pl. 4 M
NY: Charles Scribner 1956

**885** STRICKLAND, FRANCIS C. Technique of acting
pp.306; ill. DL★
NY: McGraw-Hill 1956

**886** COLLIER, GAYLAN. A historical survey of six dialects in the American theatre
Denver: U. (PhD) 1957

**887** HETLER, LOUIS. The influence of the Stanislavsky theories of acting on the teaching of acting in the United States
Denver: U. (PhD) 1957

## 4. THEATRE ARTS

**888** CICDUREL, ARON V. Organizational structure, social interaction, and the phenomenal world of the actor. A case study
Ithaca: Cornell U. (PhD)    1958

**889** LEWIS, ROBERT. Method or madness?
pp.xi, 165; pl. 6 inc. folding chart    M
NY: Samuel French    1958
Eight lectures on the acting method developed by and derived from Constantin Stanislavsky, with some account of misconceptions and misunderstandings.

**890** STANISLAVSKY's legacy: comments on an actor's art and life by Constantin Stanislavsky edited and translated by Elizabeth Reynolds Hapgood
pp.157    M
London: Max Reinhardt    1958

**891** PARIS, ROBERT G. How to act
pp.xiii, 178    L
NY: Harper & Brothers    1959

**892** CARTMELL, VAN H. Amateur theater: a guide for actor and director
pp.vi, 220    L
Princeton NJ: D. Van Nostrand    1961

**893** FUNKE, LEWIS & BOOTH, JOHN E. Actors talk about acting. Fourteen interviews with stars of the theatre
pp.viii, 469    M
NY: Random House    1961
Includes Lynn Fontanne, Alfred Lunt, Helen Hayes, Jose Ferrer, Maureen Stapleton, Katharine Cornell, Morris Carnovsky, Shelley Winters, Bert Lahr, Sidney Poitier, Paul Muni, Anne Bancroft.

**894** MAROWITZ, CHARLES. The method as means: an acting survey
pp.174    M
London: Herbert Jenkins    1961

**895** DUERR, EDWIN. The length and depth of acting...with a foreword by A. M. Nagler
pp.xiii, 590    M
NY: Holt, Rinehart & Winston    1962
A history of acting, with bibliography.

**896** KAHAN, STANLEY. Introduction to acting
pp.312; ill.    DL★
NY: Harcourt, Brace & World    1962

**897** A PORTRAIT HISTORY of American acting
Ill. in text    MH★
Austin TX: Hoblitzelle Theatre Arts Library    1962

**898** COGER, LESLIE (Ed.). Studies in readers' theatre
pp.35    DL★
Brooklyn NY: [Scott, Foresman?]    1963

**899** FEST, THORREL B. & COBIN, MARTIN T. Speech and theater
pp.av. 120    DL★
Washington DC: Center for Applied Research in Education    1963-
Annual. From 1965 the publication place was New York.

**900** KEPKE, ALLEN N. A study of changes in perception of character by actors, director and audience using G-methodology
East Lansing: Michigan State U. (PhD)    1963

**901** STANISLAVSKY, CONSTANTIN. Creating a role
pp.ix, 271    M
London: Geoffrey Bles    1963
Translated by Elizabeth Reynolds Hapgood.

**902** WHITE, EDWIN C. & BATTYE, MARGUERITE. Acting and stage movement
pp.182; ill.    DL★
NY: Arc Books    1963

**903** FENAUGHTY, THOMAS J. An approach to a beginning course in the fundamentals of acting for college students
NY: Columbia U. (EdD)    1964

**904** REDFORD, HYRUM E. A study of the image of Stanislavsky in America
Salt Lake City: U. of Utah (PhD)    1964

**905** WHEATLEY, WILLIAM T. Some problems in sustaining a role in acting
NY: U. (PhD)    1964

**906** EDWARDS, CHRISTINE. The Stanislavsky heritage: its contribution to the Russian and American theatre
pp.xxiii, 346, pl. 4    M
NY: U.P.    1965
Foreword by Robert Lewis. Chapters 5-10 are primarily concerned with American acting and stage practice.

**907** HOBGOOD, BURNET M. The theoretical bases of Stanislavsky's system
Ithaca: Cornell U. (PhD)    1965

**908** JAEGAR, WILLIAM. The application of the psycho-analytic theories of Karen Horney to the Stanislavsky system of acting
NY: U. (PhD)    1965

**909** MOORE, SONIA. The Stanislavski system: the professional training of an actor. Revised and enlarged edition of *The Stanislavski Method* digested from the teachings of Konstantin S. Stanislavski
pp.xvi, 112; front.    M
NY: Viking P.    1965
First published 1960. Forewords by John Gielgud and Joshua Logan.

**910** NEEL, CHARLES D. The star's 'golden era': a study of the craft of acting in America, 1850-1870
Ithaca: Cornell U. (PhD)    1965

**911** BLUNT, JERRY. The composite art of acting
pp.xiv, 450; ill. in text    L
NY: Macmillan    1966

**912** EASTY, EDWARD D. On method acting
pp.191    DL★
NY: Allograph P.    1966

**913** MACHLIN, EVANGELINE. Speech for the stage
pp.x, 246; ill. in text    M
NY: Theatre Arts Books    1966

Author was director of speech studies at the Neighborhood Playhouse school and professor of theatre arts at Boston U.

**914** MARSH, FLORENCE. The case against the Stanislavsky 'system' of acting
pp.79 MH
NY: Vantage P. 1966
A survey of Stanislavsky's theory and a questioning of its validity.

**915** MUNK, ERICA. Stanislavski and America: an anthology from the *Tulane Drama Review*
pp.279 MH
NY: Hill and Wang 1966
Reprinted from the 1964 issues of TDR.

**916** REIDENBAUGH, GERALD. The development of an interstructional program in acting: a comparison of the effectiveness of programed instruction with the lecture-demonstration approach to teaching basic acting
Syracuse NY: U. (PhD) 1966

**917** ROCKWOOD, JEROME. The craftsmen of Dionysus: an approach to acting
pp.230; ill. DL★
Glenview IL: Scott, Foresman 1966
Introduction by Burgess Meredith.

**918** ROGERS, CLARK McC. The influence of Dalcroze eurhythmics in the contemporary theatre
Baton Rouge: Louisiana State U. (PhD) 1966

**919** WILSON, GARFF B. A history of American acting
pp.x, 310; pl. 8 M
Bloomington: Indiana U. P. 1966

**920** COGER, LESLIE & WHITE, MELVIN R. Readers theatre handbook: a dramatic approach to literature
pp.259; ill. DL★
Glenview IL: Scott, Foresman 1967
Revised edition.

**921** CONFERENCE ON THE EDUCATION and training of actors
pp.vi, 88 DL★
Minneapolis: U. of Minnesota P. 1967
Conference proceedings, U. of Minnesota, 1965.

**922** KAHAN, STANLEY. An actor's workbook
pp.x, 320 DL★
NY: Harcourt, Brace & World 1967

**923** BENTLEY, MARION J. An examination of the British system of actor training in contrast to actor training in America
Salt Lake City: U. of Utah (PhD) 1968

**924** MOORE, SONIA. Training an actor: the Stanislavski system in class
pp.xxiii, 260; front. DL★
NY: Viking P. 1968
Record of 24 classes comprising 2 years of a 4-year course.

**925** SHAWN, EDWIN C. Every little movement: a book about Francois Delsarte by Ted Shawn [drop title]
pp.127 L
NY: Dance Horizons 1968

Unabridged republication of the second, revised and enlarged edition, 1963. Delsarte's theories and their influence in America, particularly on dance.

**926** STOCK, WILLIAM H. Some psychological and physiological factors affecting excellence in acting
East Lansing: Michigan State U. (PhD) 1968

**927** BEN AVRAM, RACHMAEL. The act and the image
pp.x, 292 DL★
NY: Odyssey P. 1969
Art and craft of acting. Substantial reference to Wilder: *Our Town* and to *Romeo and Juliet*.

**928** PATTISON, SHERON J. An analysis of readers' theatre based on selected theatre theory with special emphasis on characterization
Minneapolis: U. of Minnesota (PhD) 1969

**929** KLEINER, DICK. ESP and actors
pp.ix, 209 DL★
NY: Grosset & Dunlap 1970
Actors and psychical research.

**930** KRILEY, JAMES D. A comparative study of the effects of group training on actors in two theatrical groups
Salt Lake City: U. of Utah (PhD) 1970

**931** PRESS, DAVID R. The acting teaching of Alvina Krause: theory and practice
Pittsburgh: Carnegie-Mellon U. (PhD) 1970

**932** RAWSON, RUTH. Acting
pp.119; ill. DL★
NY: Richards Rosen P. 1970

**933** SCHRECK, EVERETT M. [= Morrill, Richard]. Principles and styles of acting
pp.354; ill. DL★
Reading MA: Addison-Wesley 1970
Includes contributions from William R. McGraw and Faber B. De Chaine. An eclectic approach to actor training.

**934** SMITH, ROBERT W. A study of the relationship between actor-character self concepts in a theatre production
Bowling Green OH: State U. (PhD) 1970

**935** THOMPSON, RAYMOND L. An analysis of the concepts contained within the Stanislavsky system of acting which are most often criticized and misunderstood
Madison: U. of Wisconsin (PhD) 1970

**936** COLE, TOBY (Ed.). Acting: a handbook of the Stanislavski method...introduction by Lee Strasberg
pp.223; ill. in text M
NY: Bonanza Books 1971
Revised edition. A collection of articles and essays by Stanislavsky and other Russian practitioners and theorists.

**937** FARBER, DONALD C. Actor's guide: what you should know about the contracts you sign
pp.134 ★
NY: DBS 1971

**938** HARRIS, JULIE with TARSHIS, BARRY. Julie Harris talks to young actors
pp.192; ill. DL★
NY: Lothrop, Lee & Shepard 1971

**939** KING, NANCY. Theatre movement: the actor and his space
pp.viii, 175; ill. DL★
NY: Drama Book Specialists 1971
Foreword by Brooks McNamara.

**940** KLINE, PETER & MEADOWS, NANCY. Physical movement for the theatre
pp.156; ill. in text MH
NY: Richards Rosen P. 1971

**941** ZALK, MARK. The natural history of a role: a study of the development and significance of an actor's movement behavior in rehearsals
Boulder: U. of Colorado (PhD) 1971

**942** HOBBS, GARY L. The influence of counter-attitudinal acting on the attitudes of actors
Evanston: Northwestern U. (PhD) 1972

**943** BARLOW, WILFRED. The Alexander principle
pp.223; ill. in text, pl. 12 L
London: Victor Gollancz 1973
Illustrated by Gwyneth Cole. With a biographical sketch of F. M. Alexander.

**944** BROWN, RICHARD P. (Ed.). Actor training [by] Richard Schechner [and others] V.1
pp.x, 125 DL★
NY: Drama Book Specialists 1973
Institute for Research in Acting.

**945** HAGEN, UTA with FRANKEL, HASKEL. Respect for acting
pp.ix, 227 M
NY: Macmillan 1973
Reflections and advice on the art of acting.

**946** LESSAC, ARTHUR. The use and training of the human voice: a practical approach to speech and voice dynamics. Preface by Irene Dailey. Illustrated by John Wilson
pp.xix, 297; ill. in text M
NY: Drama Book Specialists 1973
Second edition, with a preface by Alfred G. Brooks. First published 1960.

**947** RAPHAEL, BONNIE N. A descriptive study of the relationship between the demands of specific characterization and functional voice problems in the male actor
East Lansing: Michigan State U. (PhD) 1973

**948** WILSON, JOHN M. A natural philosophy of movement style for theater performers
Madison: U. of Wisconsin (PhD) 1973

**949** PENROD, JAMES. Movement for the performing artist
pp.vii, 180; ill. DL★
Palo Alto CA: National Press Books 1974

**950** GOLDMAN, MICHAEL. The actor's freedom: towards a theory of drama
pp. xi, 180 M
NY: Viking P. 1975

Explores the synthesis of text and performance.

**951** GRANDSTAFF, RUSSELL J. Acting and directing
pp.80; ill. DL★
Skokie IL: National Textbook 1975
New edition (not seen) 1989.

**952** KLEIN, MAXINE. Time space and designs for actors
pp.xviii, 342; ill. in text MH
Boston: Houghton Mifflin 1975
A handbook, 'to cultivate the actor's sense of self'.

**953** PELUSO, JOSEPH L. & VOSBURGH, DAVID. Presenting: acting and directing
pp.ix, 158; ill. DL★
Boston: Houghton Mifflin 1975
Amateur theatre.

**954** PICKERING, JERRY. Readers' theatre
pp.viii, 180; ill. DL★
Encino CA: Dickenson Publishing 1975
Oral interpretation.

**955** RIZZO, RAYMOND. The total actor
pp.xiii, 246; ill. DL★
Indianapolis: Odyssey P. 1975

**956** VAN DYKE, LEON J. A comparative analysis of movement training in eight American theatre schools
Detroit: Wayne State U. (PhD) 1975

**957** CAMPBELL, C. JEAN. An approach to human movement for the stage
Bowling Green: State U. (PhD) 1976

**958** COLE, JOHN R. A collective portrait of the modern professional American actor listed in *Players' Guide*
Kent OH: State U. (PhD) 1976

**959** KATZ, ALBERT M. Stage violence
pp.160; ill. DL★
NY: Richards Rosen P. 1976

**960** NELSON, ROBERT A. An experiment in the application of group training to theatre
Salt Lake City: U. of Utah (PhD) 1976

**961** PLAX, PAMELA M. Guidelines for interpretive performance of four narrative genres: commentator, dramatized narrator, scenic narration, and internal narration
Los Angeles: U. of Southern California (PhD) 1976

**962** RELPH, PATRICIA C. The application of bioenergetic theory and techniques to actor training
Bowling Green: State U. (PhD) 1976

**963** BLUM, RICHARD. The 'method' from Stanislavski to Hollywood: the transition of acting theory from stage to screen
Los Angeles: U. of Southern California (PhD) 1977

**964** GLENN, STANLEY L. The complete actor
pp.xii, 339; ill. in text L
Boston: Allyn and Bacon 1977
Manual, with emphasis on period and Shakespearian style.

**965** HOUSE, SANDRA K. Effectiveness of Chamber theatre compared to acting for the understanding of literature
Tulsa OK: U. (EdD) 1977

## 4.7. ACTING —992

**966** HUNT, GORDON. How to audition: a casting director's guide for actors
pp.vii, 332 *
Westport CT: Dramatic Publishing 1977

**967** MARSHALL, HENRY. Srage swordplay or 'So you want to be Errol Flynn?'. A manual of dramatic armed combat for actors
pp.v, 98 L
[Tarrytown NY]: [Marymount College] 1977

**968** McGAW, CHARLES J. Working a scene: an actor's approach
pp.ix, 209; ill. in text L
NY: Holt, Rinehart & Winston 1977

**969** NEIMAN, JACK. Stanislavski: his acting principles and their significance for the field of oral interpretation
Bowling Green: State U. (PhD) 1977

**970** COHEN, ROBERT. Acting power: an introduction to acting
pp.xiv, 266; ill. in text L
Palo Alta CA: Mayfield Publishing 1978

**971** LESSAC, ARTHUR. Body wisdom: the use and training of the human body
pp.xxvi, 314; ill. in text M
NY: Lessac Research 1978
A methodology of physical training which complements *Use and training of the human voice* (q.v.).

**972** MAROWITZ, CHARLES. The act of being
pp.x, 196; pl. 8 M
London: Secker & Warburg 1978
Discussion of acting and directing with emphasis on post-Stanislavsky techniques.

**973** MOFFITT, DALE E. Stanislavsky and Spolin: synthesis and extension
Pullman: Washington State U. (PhD) 1978

**974** PRICHARD, ROSEMARY F. Goals inherent in the acting theories of Zeami, Stanislavski and Grotowski
Los Angeles: U. of Southern California (PhD) 1978

**975** SHARP, KIM T. Performers' perceptions of auditioning for a theatrical production
Bowling Green: State U. (PhD) 1978

**976** SHURTLEFF, MICHAEL. Audition: everything an actor needs to know to get the part
pp.xiii, 187 *
NY: Walker 1978

**977** BAISCH, JON E. Creating presence: a theory of performance in acting
Ann Arbor: U. of Michigan (PhD) 1979

**978** KALTER, JOANMARIE. Actors on acting: performing in theatre and film today
pp.256; ill. in text M
NY: Sterling Publishing 1979
Eleven interviews. Subjects include Lynn Redgrave, Geraldine Page, Estelle Parsons, Sam Waterston, Bruce Dern.

**979** MARKUS, TOM. The professional actor, from audition to performance
pp.186 *
NY: DBS 1979

**980** McGAW, CHARLES J. Acting is believing: a basic method
pp.vii, 264; ill. in text L
NY: Holt, Rinehart & Winston 1979
Fourth edition, revised, prepared by Gary Blake. First published 1955.

**981** SETO, JUDITH R. (Ed.). The young actor's workbook
pp.xx, 339 *
Garden City: Doubleday 1979

**982** ALBRIGHT, H. & ALBRIGHT, A. Acting: the creative process
pp.xxv, 393; ill. DL*
Belmont CA: Wadsworth Publishing 1980
Third edition. First published Belmont: Dickenson, 1967.

**983** BLUNT, JERRY. More stage dialects
pp.xiii, 140; maps DL*
NY: Harper & Row 1980
Issued with audio tapes.

**984** CAHN, DUDLEY D. An experiment based on a three factor emotion theory of stage fright
Detroit: Wayne State U. (PhD) 1980

**985** CRAWFORD, JERRY L. Acting in person and in style
pp.xix, 460; ill. DL*
Dubuque IA: Wm. C. Brown 1980
Second edition. First published 1976.

**986** FINK, JOEL G. Depersonalization and personalization as factors in a taxonomy of acting
NY: U. (D.A.) 1980

**987** LEWIS, ROBERT. Advice to the players
pp.xvi, 174 DL*
NY: Harper & Row 1980
Foreword by Harold Clurman.

**988** MORGAN, JOYCE V. Stanislavski's encounter with Shakespeare: the evolution of a method
New Haven: Yale U. (PhD) 1980

**989** PETERSON, ERIC E. A semiotic phenomenology of performing
Carbondale: Southern Illinois U. (PhD) 1980

**990** RATLIFF, GERALD L. Learning scenes: basic acting, Aristophanes to Albee
pp.xi, 115; ill. DL*
NY: Richards Rosen P. 1980

**991** SCHREIBER, LESLEY C. Movement training for the actor: laying the foundation in movement principles
Minneapolis: U. of Minnesota (PhD) 1980

**992** FISHER, SEYMOUR & FISHER, RHODA L. Pretend the world is funny and forever: a psychological analysis of comedians, clowns, and actors
pp. xv, 252 L
Hillsdale NJ: Lawrence Erlbaum 1981

**993** GARCIA, ANTONINA C. Using sociodrama for training acting students in audition and interview techniques
New Brunswick NJ: Rutgers State U. (EdD) 1981

**994** GELB, MICHAEL. Body learning: an introduction to the Alexander technique
pp.xiii, 146; ill. in text M
London: Aurum P. 1981
Useful bibliography.

**995** MONOS, JAMES. The use of Stanislavsky principles and techniques in professional actor training in New York City
NY: City U. (PhD) 1981

**996** PHANEUF, CYNTHIA L. Ensemble: a process of actor training
Lubbock: Texas Tech U. (PhD) 1981

**997** STEFANO, JOHN P. The experience of Caliban: a foundation for peace between actors and scholars
Los Angeles: U. of California (PhD) 1981

**998** STRANSKY, JUDITH & STONE, ROBERT B. The Alexander technique: joy in the life of your body
pp.xi, 308; ill. DL★
NY: Beaufort Books 1981

**999** ANDERSON, DEBORAH D. Story theatre: its development, implementation and significance as a theatrical art form and a performance technique
pp.
Minneapolis: U. of Minnesota (PhD) 1982
1968-1980. Enactment and narration techniques. Particularly appropriate to the dramatization of folklore.

**1000** CLARKE, JANIS D. The influence of the Delsartean system of expression on American acting 1871-1970
Pullman: Washington State U. (PhD) 1982

**1001** HARROP, JOHN & EPSTEIN, SABIN R. Acting with style
pp.viii, 292; ill. DL★
Englewood Cliffs NJ: Prentice-Hall 1982
Actor training.

**1002** PLUMMER, RICK J. Revivifying America's historical figures: acting problems in creating a role for one-performer biography-drama
Carbondale: Southern Illinois U. (PhD) 1982

**1003** FRANKLIN, MIRIAM A. Rehearsal: the principles and practice of acting for the stage
pp.xiii, 287; ill. in text MH
NY: Prentice-Hall 1983
Sixth edition, revised. First published 1938.

**1004** MULHOLLAND, MOIRA K. Speech training for actors in twentieth century America: change and continuity
Seattle: U. of Washington (PhD) 1983

**1005** SMITH, WILLIAM F. A method to help determine an appropriate acting style for a modern production of a period play
Columbus: Ohio State U. (PhD) 1983

**1006** TRIPLETT, ROBERT. Stagefright: letting it work for you
pp.vii, 200 DL★
Chicago: Nelson Hall 1983

**1007** BIANCO, PATRICIA S. Analyzing relationships among characters in drama: a combination of precepts from Constantin Stanislavsky's system of acting and Eric Berne's system of transactional analysis
Tallahassee: Florida State U. (PhD) 1984

**1008** CARNOVSKY, MORRIS with SANDER, PETER. The actor's eye...
pp.203, ill. in text M
NY: Performing Arts Journal 1984
On the art of acting. Foreword by John Houseman.

**1009** CUMMINGS-WING, JULIA. Speak for yourself: an integrated method of voice and speech training
pp.257 DL★
Chicago: Nelson Hall 1984

**1010** FLYNN, MEREDITH. The feeling circle, company collaboration, and ritual drama: three conventions developed by the Women's Theater, at the foot of the mountain
Bowling Green OH: State U. (PhD) 1984

**1011** GROETZINGER, RICHARD A. Fantasy and the actor: implications of research on acting theory
Bowling Green: State U. (PhD) 1984

**1012** HERRON, CLIFFORD D. An empirical analysis of actor audition behavior at the Florida theatre conference's 1982 Fall auditions
Tallahassee: Florida State U. (PhD) 1984

**1013** KEDEM, ARI. Acting and directing with the aid of music and sound
Urbana-Champaign: U. of Illinois (PhD) 1984

**1014** KOHANSKY, MENDEL. The disreputable profession: the actor in society
pp.x, 194 M
Westport CT: Greenwod P. 1984
Chapter nine concerns the growth of the acting profession in the US.

**1015** MOLIN, DONALD C. Actor's encyclopedia of dialects
pp.256; ill. in text L
NY: Sterling Publishing 1984
Phonological descriptions. International in scope.

**1016** OGDEN, DUNBAR H. Actor training and audience response: an evaluation of performance techniques taught at Berkeley by Shireen Strooker from the Amsterdam Werktheater
pp.150 DL★
Fresno CA: The Oak House 1984

**1017** ROYCE, ANYA P. Movement and meaning
pp.xviii, 234 DL★
Bloomington: Indiana U. P. 1984

**1018** WORTHEN, WILLIAM B. The idea of an actor: drama and the ethics of performance
pp.ix, 270; ill. in text M
Princeton: U. P. 1984

Examines the ethical ambiguity implicit in the actor's craft. Divided into three periods, Elizabethan/Jacobean, the age of Garrick, and the modern.

**1019** BETHUNE, ROBERT W. The effect of Kabuki training on the western performances of western acting students
Honolulu: U. of Hawaii (PhD) 1985

**1020** Du PREY, DEIRDRE H. (Ed.). Lessons for the professional actor: Michael Chekhov. From a collection of notes transcribed and arranged
pp.165 M
NY: Performing Arts Journal 1985

A record of lectures and exercises presented at Chekhov's studio classes in NY, 1941.

**1021** HEYS, SANDRA (Ed.). Contemporary stage roles for women. A descriptive catalogue
pp.xix, 195 L
Westport CT: Greenwood P. 1985

**1022** ROACH, JOSEPH R. The player's passion: studies in the science of acting
pp.255; ill. in text M
Newark: U. of Delaware P. 1985

An historical approach.

**1023** SUZUKI, TADASHI. The way of acting: the theatre writings of Tadashi Suzuki
pp.x, 158; ill. in text, pl. 4 L
NY: Theatre Communications Group 1985

Translated by J. T. Rimer. Includes a version of the *Clytemnestra*. Suzuki was resident professor at U. of Wisconsin and taught also at the Juilliard School in New York.

**1024** VINEBERG, STEVE E. Method in performance: fifty years of American method acting
Stanford: U. (PhD) 1985

**1025** AARON, STEPHEN. Stage fright. Its role in acting
pp.xx, 156 L
Chicago: U. P. 1986

**1026** BATES, BRIAN. The way of an actor: a new path to knowledge and power
pp.viii, 216 MH
Boston: Shambhala 1986

**1027** DELGADO, RAMON. Acting with both sides of your brain: perspectives on the creative process
pp.xiii, 303; ill. in text L
NY: Holt, Rinehart & Winston 1986

On harmonizing the cognitive and affective brain hemispheres.

**1028** ELLIS, ROGER. An audition handbook for student actors
pp.234 DL★
Chicago: Nelson Hall 1986

**1029** FLESHMAN, BIB (Ed.). Theatrical movement: a bibliographical anthology
pp. xiv, 742 L
Metuchen NJ: Scarecrow P. 1986

Movement, dance, mime. Part 1. Preliminary studies. Part 2. Movement performance in other cultures, including Marcia Herndon: *Native American dance and drama*.

**1030** HENDEL, DOUGLAS B. Actor preference for director behavior
Bowling Green: State U. (PhD) 1986

**1031** LUNDRIGAN, PAUL J. Ensemble: the group approach to performing
Carbondale: Southern Illinois U. (PhD) 1986

**1032** PETERS, STEVEN J. Modern to postmodern acting and directing: an historical perspective
Lubbock: Texas Tech U. (PhD) 1986

**1033** CASSADY, MARSHALL. The book of cuttings for acting and directing
pp.x, 195 ★
Chicago: National Textbooks 1987

**1034** FELNAGLE, RICHARD H. Beginning acting: the illusion of natural behaviour
pp.xiii, 253; ill. in text L
Englewood Cliffs NJ: Prentice-Hall 1987

**1035** FRIEDMAN, MICHAEL B. Advice to the players: acting theory in America, 1923 to 1973
Bloomington: Indiana U. (PhD) 1987

**1036** HILL, HOLLY. Playing Joan: actresses on the challenge of Shaw's *Saint Joan*
pp.xvi, 255; ill. in text M
NY: Theatre Communications Group 1987

Includes Constance Cummings, Uta Hagen, Ellen Geer, Jane Alexander, Lee Grant, Joyce Ebert, Laurie Kennedy.

**1037** SULLIVAN, CLAUDIA N. Movement training for the actor: a twentieth century comparison and analysis
Boulder: U. of Colorado (PhD) 1987

**1038** ADLER, STELLA. On acting
pp.144; ill. ★
NY: Bantam Books 1988

Note also *The technique of acting* (unexamined), Bantam Books, 1990.

**1039** BISHOP, CYNTHIA A. The deconstructed actor: towards a postmodern acting theory
Boulder: U. of Colorado (PhD) 1988

**1040** GORDON, MEL. The Stanislavsky technique: Russia. A workbook for actors
pp.xv, 252 M
NY: Applause 1988

A conflation of the training systems of Constantin Stanislavsky, Vakhtangov, and Michael Chekhov, with an historical survey.

**1041** HALPERIN, ELLEN I. Acting and psychotherapy: applications of kinetic and imaging techniques to actor training, an empirical study
Eugene: U. of Oregon (PhD) 1988

**1042** KUBIAK, ANTHONY J. Phobos and performance: the stages of terror
Milwaukee: U. of Wisconsin (PhD) 1988

**1043** BLUM, RICHARD. Working actors: the craft of television, film, and stage performance...with special thanks to Laurence Frank
pp.x,153; ill. in text L
Boston: Focal P. 1989

Transcribed interviews.

**1044** COLYER, CARLTON. The art of acting: from basic exercises to multi-dimensional performances
pp.224 DL★
Colorado Springs: Meriwether 1989

**1045** EAKER, SHERRY (Ed.). The *Back Stage* handbook for performing artists. The how-to and who-to-contact reference for actors, directors, singers, and dancers
pp.239 M
NY: Back Stage Books 1989

Factual information, including names and addresses, on training, finding work, and a variety of venues, from dinner theatres to cruise liners.

**1046** JOHNSON, NORMAN W. Period movement style and the waltz: a choreo-kinesic model for actor training
Eugene: U. of Oregon (PhD) 1989

**1047** POLSKY, MILTON E. Let's improvise: becoming creative, expressive & spontaneous through drama
pp.xvii, 316; ill. in text L
Lanham: U. P. of America 1989

First published Englewood Cliffs NJ: Prentice-Hall, 1980. Child and student oriented.

**1048** YOUNG, JORDAN R. Acting solo
DL★
Beverly Hills CA: Moonstone P. 1989
History of the one-man show.

**1049** COHEN, ROBERT. Acting in Shakespeare
pp.230 ★
Mountain View CA: Mayfield 1990

**1050** CRAWFORD, RAY S. Music in the acting studio: an approach to actor training
Lubbock: Texas Tech U. (PhD) 1990

**1051** LEIBOWITZ, JUDITH & CONNINGTON, BILL. The Alexander technique
pp.208; ill. DL★
[NY?]: Souvenir P. 1990
Foreword by Kevin Kline.

**1052** SELLERS, BARBARA. Kanriye Fujima: traditional Japanese dance theatre teacher in the United States
Eugene: U. of Oregon (PhD) 1990

**1053** SULLIVAN, CLAUDIA N. The actor moves
pp.165 DL★
Jefferson NC: McFarland 1990

## 4.8 DIRECTING

**1054** KROWS, ARTHUR E. Play production in America
pp.x, 414; ill. in text, pl. 30 M
NY: Henry Holt 1916

**1055** TAYLOR, EMERSON G. Practical stage directing for amateurs: a handbook for amateur managers and actors
pp.194: front. DL★
NY: E. P. Dutton 1916

**1056** STRATTON, CLARENCE. Producing in little theatres
pp.xi, 258; ill. in text, pl. 16 M
NY: Henry Holt 1921

A *vade mecum*, with an appendix listing suitable plays.

**1057** CRAFTON, ALLEN & ROYER, JESSICA. The process of play production: a book for the non-professional theatre worker
pp.x, 314; ill. in text O
NY: F. S. Crofts 1926

**1058** JONES, CHARLES T. & WILSON, DON. Musico-dramatic producing: a manual for the stage and musical director
pp.140; ill. in text MH
Chicago: Gamble 1930

**1059** MITCHELL, ROY. Creative theatre...with seventeen geometrical projections in wood-block by Jocelyn Taylor
pp.xx, 256; ill. in text M
London: Noel Douglas 1930

A visionary account of a 'new' anti-commercial theatre.

**1060** ASHTON, De WITT C. The art of directing plays
pp.119 DL★
Franklin OH: Eldridge Entertainment 1931

**1061** BATES, ESTHER W. How to produce a pageant in honor of George Washington: written for the bicentennial celebration in 1932
pp.30 L
Washington DC: Bicentennial Commission [1931]

**1062** HOPKINS, ARTHUR. How's your second act? Notes on the art of production
pp.ix, 43 M
NY: Samuel French 1931

New edition with introduction by Barrett H. Clark. First published 1918.

**1063** MATHER, CHARLES C. Dramatics technique
pp.175 DL★
Culvewr IN: Citizen P. 1931
Amateur theatre.

**1064** [WHIPS, CLARA E.]. Bobby: an American romance [by Clair Johnson and Sarah G. Clark]: stage directions by Clara E. Whips
pp. av. 40; diagrams in text L
Cincinnati: Willis Music 1932-

Offered here as an example of many such acting editions produced by Clara Whips in the 30s, providing an interesting record of popular touring company stage practice.

**1065** STOUT, ROYAL C. A professional touch, a story of play direction supplying a practical course in dramatics and stage mechanics
pp.71; ill. DL★
Chicago: T. S. Denison 1934
Amateur theatre.

**1066** BROWN, GILMOR & GARWOOD, ALICE. General principles of play direction
pp.ix, 190; ill. in text     O
NY: Samuel French     1936
Brown was director of the Pasadena Community Playhouse.

**1067** LEVERTON, GARRETT H. The production of later nineteenth-century American drama, a basis for teaching
NY: Columbia U. Teachers' College (PhD)     1936

**1068** DRUMMOND, A. M. A manual of play production
pp.78; ill. in text     M
[Ithaca]: For the author     1937
The third, revised edition of *Play production for the country theatre*, first published NY: for the author, 1924. Illustrated with production photographs of Cornell U. Dramatic Club.

**1069** SELDEN, SAMUEL. First principles of play direction
pp.57     DL★
Chapel Hill: U. of North Carolina P./Bureau of Community Drama     1937

**1070** CRAFTON, ALLEN. Play directing
pp.ix, 264; ill.     DL★
NY: Prentice-Hall     1938

**1071** MERSAND, JOSEPH. The rediscovery of the imagination: an evaluation of the new stagecraft of the American drama
pp.17     DL★
Brooklyn NY: [For the author?]     1938

**1072** SCHONBERGER, EMANUEL D. Play production for amateurs
pp.xiii, 241; ill.     DL★
NY: T. Nelson and Sons     1938

**1073** MINTER, GORDON & BROWN, JOSEPH LEE]. Amateur theatrical manual for use in military and naval establishments by personnel of the armed forces, prepared at the suggestion of the Morale Branch, War Department, by the National Theatre Conference
pp.72; ill.     DL★
NY: Citizens Committee for Army & Navy     1941

**1074** SELDEN, SAMUEL. The stage in action...illustrated by Wantell Selden
pp.xvii, 324; ill. in text, pl. 16     M
NY: Appleton-Century-Crofts     1941
An analysis of those factors that contribute to theatrical effectiveness.

**1075** BROWN, BENJAMIN W. Upstage-downstage: directing the play
pp.94; ill. in text     L
Boston: Walter Baker     1946
Illustrated by Leslie Allen Jones. A primer.

**1076** SMITH, MILTON M. Play production for little theatres, schools and colleges
pp.xii, 482; ill. in text, pl. 11 (1 col)     L
NY: Appleton-Century-Crofts     1948

Revised edition. First published 1926 with an introduction by Brander Matthews.

**1077** GASSNER, JOHN & BARBER, PHILIP. Producing the play:...with the new scene technician's handbook by Philip Barber...
pp.xviii, 915; ill. in text     M
NY: Dryden P.     1949
Revised edition. First published 1941. Contributors include Worthington Miner, Lee Strasberg, Harold Clurman, Margaret Webster, Mordecai Gorelik, Abe H. Feder, Earl McGill, Guthrie McClintic.

**1078** VARDAC, A. NICHOLAS. Stage to screen: theatrical method from Garrick to Griffith
pp.xvii, 283; ill. in text, pl. 24     M
Cambridge MA: Harvard U. P.     1949
Extends to US theatre practice, with particular reference to David Belasco and Steele MacKaye.

**1079** McMULLEN, FRANK. Play interpretation and direction: an outline
pp.127     DL★
New Haven: Yale U. P.     1951

**1080** HEWITT, BARNARD; FOSTER, J. F. & WOLLE, MURIEL S. Play production; theory and practice
pp.viii, 488; ill. in text     L
Chicago: J. B. Lippincott     1952
A revised version of Barnard Hewitt: *Art and craft of play production*, 1940.

**1081** NELMS, HENNING. Play production, a handbook for the backstage worker: a guidebook for the student of drama
pp.xviii, 301; ill. in text     MH
NY: Barnes and Noble     1952
First published 1950.

**1082** KLEIN, RUTH. The art and technique of play directing
pp.179; ill.     DL★
NY: Rinehart     1953

**1083** BROCKETT, LENYTH S. Theories of style in stage production
Stanford CA: U. (PhD)     1954

**1084** BAILEY, HOWARD. The ABCs of play producing: a handbook for the non-professional
pp.276; ill.     DL★
NY: D. McKay     1955

**1085** SCHALL, DAVID G. Rehearsal-direction practices and actor-director relationships in the American theatre from the Hallams to Actors' Equity
Urbana: U. of Illinois (PhD)     1956

**1086** SHAFFER, JAMES F. The director, the actor, and the stage
pp.102; ill.     DL★
Portland OR: Allied Publishers     1956

**1087** SELDEN, SAMUEL. Man in his theatre
pp.113     DL★
Chapel Hill: U. of North Carolina P.     1957

**1088** COCHRAN, JAMES P. The development of the professional stage director. A critical historical examination of representative professional directors on the New York stage, 1896-1916
Iowa City: U. of Iowa (PhD)     1958

**1089** COX, CHARLES W. The evolution of the stage director in America
Evanston IL: Northwestern U. (PhD) 1958

**1090** HUTCHINSON, WILLIAM C. A study of the history and methods of production for theatre-in-the-round
Canyon: West Texas State U. (MA) 1958

**1091** JEHLINGER, CHARLES. Charles Jehlinger in rehearsal transcribed by Eleanor Cody Gould
pp.30 MH
NY: AADA 1958
Verbatim notes taken in rehearsal classes at the American Academy of Dramatic Art. No commentary is offered on the notes, which are often laconic.

**1092** YOUNG, JOHN W. Directing the play: from selection to opening night
pp.171 DL★
NY: Harper 1958

**1093** METTEN, CHARLES H. The development in America of theories of directing as found in American writings, 1914-1930
Iowa City: U. of Iowa (PhD) 1960

**1094** ROWE, KENNETH T. A theater in your head
pp.ix, 438, pl. 2 MH
NY: Funk and Wagnalls 1960
Examines the traditional dramatic modes and the roles of director and designer. Includes a detailed analysis and visualization of Theodore Ward's *Our Lan'*, reprinted in full, and excerpts from Elia Kazan's notebooks for his production of *Death of a Salesman*.

**1095** YOUNG, MARGARET M. & YOUNG, JOHN W. How to produce the play: the complete production handbook
pp.95; ill. DL★
Chicago: Dramatic Publishing 1960

**1096** McMULLAN, FRANK. The directorial image: the play and the director
pp.xvi, 249; ill. in text M
Hamden CT: Shoestring P. 1962

**1097** CANFIELD, CURTIS. The craft of play directing...drawings by W. Oren Parker
pp.xi, 349; ill. in text M
NY: Holt, Rinehart and Winston 1963

**1098** CHEKHOV, MICHAEL & LEONARD, CHARLES. To the director and playwright. Compiled and written by Charles Leonard [pseud. of Charles Leonard Appleton]
pp.329; pl. 12 M
NY: Harper and Row 1963
Notes on directing published after Chekhov's death in 1955. A substantial part of the book is occupied by a rehearsal script of Charles Appleton's adaptation of Gogol's *Revisor*.

**1099** GALLAWAY, MARIAN. The director in the theatre
pp.xiii, 386: ill. in text O
NY: Macmillan 1963
Author was sometime director of the Alabama University theatre.

**1100** McMULLEN, FRANK. The director's handbook: an outline for the teacher and student of play interpretation and direction
pp.181 DL★
Hamden CT: Shoe String P. 1964
Revised edition of *Play interpretation and direction* published 1951.

**1101** HANSEN, AL. A primer of happenings & time/space art
pp.xii, 145; ill. in text M
NY: Something Else P. 1965

**1102** KIRBY, MICHAEL. Happenings: an illustrated anthology
pp.288; ill. in text L
NY: E. P. Dutton 1965
Includes working scripts and descriptions of 14 productions by Jim Dine, Red Grooms, Allan Kaprow, Claes Oldenburg and Robert Whitman.

**1103** SEYMOUR, VICTOR. Stage directors' workshop. A descriptive study of the Actors Studio directors unit, 1960-1964
Madison: U. of Wisconsin (PhD) 1965

**1104** KAPROW, ALLAN. Assemblage, environments, & happenings with a selection of scenarios...
pp.343: ill. in text L
NY: Harry N. Abrams 1966
A survey. pp. 210-341 illustrate and annotate happenings.

**1105** LEBEL, JEAN-J. Le happening
pp.89; pl. 12 L
Paris: Denoel 1966
'Tableaux vivants-en-train-de-se-faire.' Includes examples from New York.

**1106** CLAY, JAMES H. & KREMPEL, DANIEL. The theatrical image
pp.xiv, 300; ill. in text L
NY: McGraw-Hill 1967
Examines methods of theatrical realization.

**1107** AUSTELL, JAN. What's in a play?
pp.160; ill. DL★
NY: Harcourt, Brace and World 1968
Production notes on *Our Town*, *Macbeth*, *The Glass Menagerie*.

**1108** GREGORY, WILLIAM A. The director: a guide to modern theatre practice
pp.x, 369 L
NY: Funk & Wagnalls 1968

**1109** KOZELKA, PAUL. Directing
pp.184; ill. DL★
NY: Richards Rosen P. 1968

**1110** BENEDETTI, ROBERT L. Encounter theatre
Evanston: Northwestern U. (PhD) 1970

**1111** EMBLER, JEFFREY. Film applications in legitimate theatre production
Pittsburgh: U. (PhD) 1970

**1112** GROSS, ROGER D. The director's interpretation of the playscript
Eugene: U. of Oregon (PhD) 1970

**1113** JACQUOT, JEAN (Ed.). Les voies de la création théatrâle
pp.various; ill. in text M
Paris: CNRS 1970-90

Seventeen volumes. Detailed examination of *mise en scène*. Vol. 1, 1970 (pp. 347): The Living Theatre, *The Brig; Frankenstein; Antigone; Paradise Now*. The Open Theatre, *The Serpent*. Vol. 1V, 1975 (pp. 427): includes *Death of a Salesman* on Broadway; *The Iceman Cometh* at Le Théâtre de la Commune d'Aubervilliers. Vol. 1X, 1981 (pp. 387): *Profils de l'enseignemont théâtral américain*. Vol. X11, 1984 (pp. 327): Catherine Mounier: *Le monde de Robert Wilson*. Continuing.

**1114** JOHNSON, ALBERT & JOHNSON, BERTHA.   Directing methods
pp.443                                                                                    L
South Brunswick NJ: A. S. Barnes             1970

**1115** SHARP, WILLIAM L.  Language in drama: meanings for the director and the actor
pp.xi, 162                                                                          DL★
Scranton PA: Chandler                                 1970
A structuralist approach to interpretation.

**1116** COOKE, THOMAS P. Directing in three dimensions: principles for staging in open space using three-dimensional form as demonstrated by theatre-in-the-round
Tallahassee: Florida State U. (PhD)          1971

**1117** CULP, RALPH B.  The theatre and its drama: principles and practices
pp.ix, 455                                                                          DL★
Dubuque IA: Wm. C. Brown                      1971
The reader is asked to assume the viewpoint of a range of theatre practitioners.

**1118** HERR, JUDITH L. A philosophy of theatricality: a phenomenological description of the aesthetic structures in the arts of performance
Tallahassee: Florida State U. (PhD)          1971

**1119** HODGE, FRANCIS R.   Play directing: analysis, communication and style
pp.xv, 394; ill. in text                                                       L
Englewood Cliffs NJ: Prentice-Hall             1971

**1120** ALBRIGHT, HARDIE.  Stage direction in transition
pp.xii, 340; ill.                                                                 DL★
Encino CA: Dickenson Publishing                1972

**1121** BRAUN, THOMAS C. The theory of 'aesthetic distance' and the practice of 'audience participation'
Minneapolis: U. of Minnesota (PhD)          1972

**1122** CLURMAN, HAROLD.   On directing
pp.xii, 308, pl. 4                                                                M
NY: Macmillan                                              1972
Wide-ranging general account, followed by 'director's notes' for author's own productions and examples of work scripts.

**1123** COLE, TOBY & CHINOY, HELEN K. (Eds). Directors on directing: a source book of the modern theatre...with an illustrated history of directing by Helen Krich Chinoy
pp.xv, 464; ill. in text                                                       M
London: Peter Owen                                    1973
Revised edition, with a new section on staging Shakespeare. First published 1953 as *Directing the play*.

**1124** DOLMAN, JOHN & KNAUB, RICHARD K. The art of play production
pp.xx, 458; ill. in text                                                        O
NY: Harper & Row                                         1973
Third edition, revised. First published 1928 under single authorship of Dolman.

**1125** GLENN, STANLEY L.   A director prepares
pp.257; ill.                                                                        DL★
Encino CA: Dickenson Publishing                1973

**1126** KEARNS, WILLIAM G.  An examination of materials and methods used in professional and educational readers theatre productions from 1967-8 to 1971-2
Athens: Ohio U. (PhD)                                  1973

**1127** PERDUE, MARGARET F.  The influence of the director on cast and audience perception of the message of a play as measured by paired comparison scaling
University Park: Pennsylvania State U. (PhD)         1973

**1128** PORTER, ROBERT E.  Interaction analysis and the rehearsal process: director-actor influence and response
Ann Arbor: U. of Michigan (PhD)              1973

**1129** SPOLIN, VIOLA.  Improvisation for the theatre: a handbook of teaching and directing techniques
pp.xxv, 395; diagrams in text                                            L
Evanston IL: Northwestern U. P.                 1973

**1130** COHEN, ROBERT & HARROP, JOHN. Creative play direction
pp.xi, 308; ill in text                                                            L
Englewood Cliffs NJ: Prentice-Hall             1974
Historical account of the development of the director, analysis of tasks and methods, and accounts of practising directors.

**1131** HILKER, GORDON.  The audience and you: practical dramatics for the park interpreter
pp.65                                                                                   L
Washington DC: National Park Services     1974
Specially designed for NPS employees, offering techniques to lend greater impact to presentations and talks to visitors.

**1132** KUBICKI, JAN T.  Techniques of group theatre
pp.142; ill.                                                                         DL★
NY: Richards Rosen P.                                   1974

**1133** BLACK, MALCOLM.  First reading to first night; a candid look at stage directing
pp.xiii, 87; ll. [3]; ill. in text                                          DL★
Seattle: U. of Washington P.                          1975

**1134** COLE, DAVID.  Theatrical event: a 'mythos', a vocabulary, a perspective
pp.xii, 177; ill.                                                                 DL★
Middletown CT: Wesleyan U. P.                  1975

**1135** McGEEVER, CHARLES J.  Towards a theory of chamber theatre production; the function of first person
Ann Arbor: U. of Michigan (PhD)              1975

**1136** RUBLE, RONALD M.  Performer descriptions of stressed rehearsal conditions created by an authoritarian and a libertarian directing method
Bowling Green: State U. (PhD)                   1975

**1137** VIGNEAULT, RONALD P. The effects of manipulation of the theatrical communication system upon audience response: an investigation
Bowling Green: State U. (PhD)     1975

**1138** LANGLEY, STEPHEN (Ed.). Producers on producing
pp.ix, 341; ill. in text     M
NY: Drama Book Specialists     1976

Transcribed interviews and other commentaries. Contributors, organized under the theme to which they contributed, are: *Grassroots theatre*: Akila Kouloumbis, Marketa Kimbrell, Vantile Whitfield. *Educational theatre*: Anthony Reid, Norris Houghton, John Houseman. *Resident theatre*: Zelda Fichandler, Adrian Hall, Peter Zeisler. *Off- and off-off-Broadway*: Theodore Mann, Paul Libin, Ellen Stewart. *Broadway theatre*: Alexander H. Cohen, Morton Gottlieb, Warren Caro. *The cultural centers*: Norman Singer, Sir Rudolf Bing, Harvey Lichtenstein. *Government, business and the foundations as producers*: Alvin H. Reiss, G. A. McLellan, Stephen Benedict. *The predominance of the New York theatre: three viewpoints*: James M. Nederlander, Robert Kalfin, Herman E. Krawitz.

**1139** WILLIAMS, ALLEN. Theatre handbook
pp.viii, 214; ill.     DL★
Grambling LA: Louisiana State U. P.     1976

**1140** WILLIS, J. ROBERT (Ed.). The director in a changing theatre: essays on theory and practice, with new plays for performance
pp.viii, 351     DL★
Palo Alto CA: Mayfield     1976

**1141** WOODBURY, LAEL J. Mosaic theatre: the creative use of theatrical constructs
pp.xi, 212; ill. in text     M
Provo UT: Brigham Young U. P.     1976

Challenges the primacy of language in theatrical communication.

**1142** HORNBY, RICHARD. Script into performance: a structuralist view of play production
pp.xi, 215     L
Austin: U. of Texas P.     1977

Intention, 'to develop approaches to the production of classical playscripts that will be valid, imaginative, and powerful'.

**1143** PROSSER, WILLIAM L. American directorial approaches to Shakespeare, 1960-1976
NY: City U. (PhD)     1977

**1144** BERLIN, RICHARD M. Theatrical transactional analysis: a model for the director-actor communication process
Philadelphia: Temple U. (PhD)     1978

**1145** BEATH, ROBERT P. Towards a new focus in script analysis: an evaluation of directorial methods of script analysis published 1960-1977
Salt Lake City: U. of Utah (PhD)     1979

**1146** CROUCH, PAUL H. Patterns in contemporary outdoor historical drama: a guide for directors
Tallahassee: Florida State U. (PhD)     1979

**1147** WELKER, DAVID. Theatrical direction: the basic techniques
pp.xiii, 479; ill. in text     L
Boston: Allyn and Bacon     1979

Second edition, revised. First published 1969.

**1148** DRAKE, EDWINA B. Non-traditional Shakespeare production: an examination of the work of five directors and nine plays performed at the New York and Connecticut Shakespeare festivals
Boulder: U. of Colorado (PhD)     1980

**1149** FURLONG, JAMES (Ed.). The journal of the Society of Stage Directors and Choreographers
pp.various: ill. in text     M
NY: SSDC     1980-

Issued to members only, Summer and Winter. Seven copies seen, 1982-1988. Articles, transcripts, etc., contributed by working professionals.

**1150** WILLS, J. ROBERT. Directing in the theatre: a casebook
pp.vi, 60     L
Metuchen NJ: Scarecrow P.     1980

Instructor's manual, designed to accompany the 'casebook' (i.e. a set of scenarios for exploration in the rehearsal studio).

**1151** BLAU, HERBERT. Take up the bodies: theater at the vanishing point
pp. xxv, 301; ill. in text     M
Urbana: U. of Illinois P.     1982

An exposition of the author's production theory. With photographs of Kraken Group productions.

**1152** ARCHER, STEPHEN M. How theatre happens
pp.304     DL★
NY: Macmillan     1983

The second edition.

**1153** DIETRICH, JOHN E. & DUCKWALL, RALPH W. Play direction
pp.VII, 334; ill in text     L
NY: Prentice-Hall     1983

Second edition, revised. First published 1953 (?) under the single authorship of Dietrich.

**1154** HENNIGAN, SHIRLEE. The woman director in the contemporary professional theatre
Pullman: Washington State U. (PhD)     1983

**1155** MITCHELL, LEE. Staging pre-modern drama. A guide to production problems
pp.xiv, 236     M
Westport CT: Greenwood P.     1983

**1156** BALL, WILLIAM. A sense of direction: some observations on the art of directing
pp.xiv, 182     DL★
NY: Drama Book Publishers     1984

**1157** CONSTANTINIDIS, STRATOS E. The poetics of a theatre industry: a play production model
Iowa City: U. of Iowa (PhD)     1984

**1158** GARDNER, BONNIE M. The emergence of the playwright-director. A new artist in the American theatre, 1960
Kent: State U. (PhD)     1985

**1159** KIRK, JOHN M. The art of directing
pp.xvi, 240     ★
Belmont CA: Wadsworth Publishing     1985

Includes the text of William Saroyan's *Hullo out there*.

**1160** SPOLIN, VIOLA. Theater games for rehearsal: a director's handbook
pp.128 ★
Evanston: Northwestern U. P. 1985

**1161** FINNEY, JAMES R. Aspects and correlates of directors' nonverbal behavior in the rehearsal process
Evanston: Northwestern U. (PhD) 1987

**1162** KIRBY, MICHAEL. A formalist theatre
pp.xix, 159 M
Philadelphia: U. of Pennsylvania P. 1987
Expresses an antisemiotic, structuralist view of performance.

**1163** O'NEILL, R. H. & BORETZ, N. M. The director as artist; play direction today
pp.xix, 347; ill. in text L
NY: Holt, Rinehart and Winston 1987

**1164** BARTOW, ARTHUR. The director's voice: twenty-one interviews
pp.xv, 382 ★
NY: TCG 1988

**1165** COHEN, EDWARD M. Working on a new play: a play development book for actors, directors, designers and playwrights
pp.xxiv, 216 DL★
NY: Prentice-Hall 1988

**1166** ISSACHAROFF, MICHAEL & JONES, ROBIN E. (Eds). Performing arts
pp.vii, 157 L
Philadelphia: U. of Pennsylvania P. 1988
Papers read at an international symposium on theory and practice of performance, U. of Western Ontario, April, 1983, here revised. Includes Anna Whiteside: *Self-referring artifacts*; Keir Elam: *Some problems in the pragmatics of theatre and drama*; Michael Issacharoff: *Stage codes*; Patrick Pavis: *From text to performance*.

**1167** MARSHALL, BRENDA K. A semiotic phenomenology of directing
Carbondale: Southern Illinois U. (PhD) 1988

**1168** WOHL, DAVIS. A study of group phasic development in the theatre rehearsal process
Kent OH: State U. (PhD) 1988

**1169** CATRON, LOUIS E. The director's vision; play direction from analysis to production
pp.xxi, 358; ill. in text L
Mountain View CA: Mayfield Publishing 1989

**1170** DEAN, ALEXANDER & CARRA, LAWRENCE. Fundamentals of play directing
pp.x, 374; ill. in text L
NY: Holt, Rinehart & Winston 1989
Fifth edition, revised by Carra. First published NY: Farrar and Rinehart, 1941.

**1171** LONEY, GLENN. Staging Shakespeare: seminars on productions
pp.xviii, 278 DL★
NY: Garland 1990

## 4.9 AUDIENCES

**1172** HOLLINGWORTH, HARRY L. The psychology of the audience
pp. x, 232 L
NY: American Book 1935
Includes chapters on audience types, securing an audience, holding an audience, the psychology of persuasion, structure of the auditorium, experimentation in audience effects, stage fright.

**1173** MORGAN, WILLIAM. An experimental study and comparison of the responses of men and the responses of women in theatre audiences
Iowa City: U. of Iowa (PhD) 1951

**1174** CLARK, EDWIN L. An experimental study of age as a factor in audience response in the theater
Iowa City: Iowa U. (PhD) 1952

**1175** MOODY, STANLEY E. Experimental study of the concentration of audience interest in ten theatre productions
Iowa City: U. of Iowa (PhD) 1955

**1176** WILLIAMS, KENNETH R. Audience analysis and adaptation. A conceptual clarification
University Park: Pennsylvania State U. (PhD) 1964

**1177** WITT, DANIEL M. A comparative analysis of audience response to realistic and anti-realistic drama when perceived through acting, readers theatre and silent reading
Denver: U. (PhD) 1964

**1178** HAYDEN, DONALD E. (Ed.). His firm estate: essays in honour of Franklin James Eikenberry by former students...
pp.xvi, 78 L
Tulsa: Oklahoma U. P. 1967
Includes Ben G. Henneke: *The American playgoer*, an examination of the developing nature of the theatre audience.

**1179** NEWMAN, CHARLES & HENKIN, WILLIAM A. (Eds). Under 30
pp.vii, 300; ill. in text, pl. 4 L
Bloomington: Indiana U. P. 1969
Anthology of essays on the arts. Includes Leslie Epstein: *Beyond the baroque: the role of the audience in modern theatre*, with particular reference to Ronald Tavel.

**1180** CRANE, JOSHUA. An investigation of cast and audience semantic agreement in Readers' Theatre productions
Columbus: Ohio State U. (PhD) 1971

**1181** LEWY, THOMAS. The role of the audience in modern theatre
NY: U. (PhD) 1971

**1182** CALDWELL, GEORGE R. Quantitative investigation of audience response to theatrical settings
Bowling Green OH: State U. (PhD) 1974

**1183** TRAUTH, SUZANNE M. An investigation of the effects of the director's system of communication on actor inventiveness and the rehearsal atmosphere
Bowling Green: State U. (PhD) 1975

**1184** KWAL, TERI S. An experimental study of sex as a factor influencing audience evaluation of

performance effectiveness and audience comprehension of performance for selected dramatic monologues
NY: U. (PhD) 1976

**1185** DAUBERT, DARLENE M. Distance in the theatre: the aesthetics of audience response
Iowa City: U. of Iowa (PhD) 1981

**1186** FRANTZ, ALICE H. Audience response to interpersonal distance in live and videotaped theatre scenes and its implications for teaching methodology
Gainsville: U. of Florida (PhD) 1981

**1187** MATHESON, DIANA L. The relationship of self perception and audience members' perceptions of stage characters
Bowling Green OH: State U. (PhD) 1981

**1188** BLAU, HERBERT. Blooded thought: occasions of the theatre
pp. 166 M
NY: Performing Arts Journal 1982
An inquiry, influenced by post-structuralist theory, into the nature of performance and audience.

**1189** GOATLEY, CYNTHIA A. The discomfort-relief quotient as an indicator of theatrical genre and dramatic structure
Bowling Green OH: State U. (PhD) 1982

**1190** MILLARD, DAVID E. The nature and origin of the dramatic spectator's knowledge
Seattle: U. of Washington (PhD) 1982

**1191** MOORE, JOHN J. A phenomenological approach to the aesthetic receptivity of a dramatic art work
Buffalo: State U. of New York (PhD) 1982
The application of Roman Ingarden's approach to audiences of three productions of Sam Shepard's *Curse of the Starving Class*.

**1192** SCHULMAN, MARTIN. The application of the exchange theory of social behavior to analysis of theatre audiences: a methodological study
Tallahassee: Florida State U. (PhD) 1983

**1193** WASSERMAN, NINA M. Toward the development of a critically responsive audience: an aesthetic inquiry employing Edward Bullough's theory and criticism of contemporary theatre
NY: U. (PhD) 1983

**1194** CHAIM, DAPHNA B. Distance in the theatre. The aesthetics of audience response
pp. xi, 111 L
Ann Arbor: UMI Research P. 1984
Originally a thesis, under the name Darlene M. Daubert.

**1195** EIFERT, EUNICE R. The fourth wall shattered: a study of the performer-audience relationship in selected full-length monodramas
Minneapolis: U. of Minnesota (PhD) 1984

**1196** TAYLOR, GUY S. Audience emotional response to the dramatic performance as a result of aesthetic imitation: an examination of the catharsis hypothesis
Bowling Green: State U. (PhD) 1985

**1197** DAVIS, KEN. Rehearsing the audience: ways to develop student perceptions of theatre
pp. ix, 73 DL★
Urbana IL: National Council of Teachers of English 1988

**1198** DOLAN, JILL. The feminist spectator as critic
pp.xii, 154; ill. in text MH
Ann Arbor: UMI Research P. 1988

**1199** HOMAN, SIDNEY. The audience as actor and character
DL★
Lewisburg PA: Bucknell U. P. 1989

**1200** BECKERMAN, BERNARD. Theatrical presentation: performance, audience and act. Edited by Gloria Brim Beckerman and William Coco
pp. xi, 212 M
London: Routledge 1990
An elaboration of ideas first expressed in the author's *Dynamics of drama*(1970).

**1201** BENNETT, SUSAN. Theatre audiences: a theory of production and perception
pp.ix, 219 L
NY: Routledge Chapman & Hall 1990
Theatre audience as a social phenomenon.

**1202** BLAU, HERBERT. The audience
pp. x, 414 M
Baltimore: John Hopkins U. P. 1990
A theory of audience character and function in the creative process.

# 5. HISTORY

## 5.1 INTERNATIONAL

**1203** JENNINGS, JOHN J. Theatrical and circus life or, secrets of the stage, green-room and sawdust arena, embracing a history of the theatre from Shakespeare's time to the present day...a complete exposition of the mysteries of the stage...origin and growth of negro minstrelsy...a history of the hippodrome...
pp.608; ill. in text, pl. 8 col. M
Hartford CT: Park 1883
Popular, anecdotal, sprawling. Several editions recorded, including St. Louis: M. S. Barnett, 1882; Brandon VT: Sidney M. Southard, 1884.

**1204** CHENEY, SHELDON. The new movement in the theatre
pp.303; pl. 16 M
NY: Mitchell Kennerley 1914
Essays, many reprinted from *The Theatre* or *The Forum*, on the experimental theatre in the US and Europe.

**1205** CHENEY, SHELDON. The open-air theatre
pp.xv, 188; ill. in text, pl. 39 M
NY: Mitchell Kennerley 1918
History and recent developments.

## 5.1. INTERNATIONAL

**1206** MacGOWAN, KENNETH. The theatre of tomorrow
pp.iii, 308; ill. in text; pl. 40, some col.　L
NY: Boni & Liveright　1921
The new experimental theatre of the early 20th century in Europe and the US. The UK edition, London: T. Fisher Unwin, 1923 has an appendix giving additions and corrections.

**1207** CHENEY, SHELDON. The art theatre: its character as differentiated from the commercial theatre; its ideals and organization; and a record of certain European and American examples...with sixteen new illustrations
pp.ix, 281; ill. in text, pl. 15　M
NY: Alfred A. Knopf　1925
Revised edition. First published 1917 as *The art theatre: a discussion of its ideals, its organization and its promise as a corrective for present evils in the commercial theatre*. With sixteen photographs of productions at the Arts and Crafts Theatre of Detroit. Reference includes Sam Hume's pioneering set designs, the Theatre Guild, the Provincetown Players, the Neighbourhood Playhouse, the Actors' Theatre.

**1208** INTERNATIONAL THEATRE exposition New York 1926 Steinway Building [cover title]
pp.124 inc. wrappers; ill. in text　M
NY: The Little Review　1926
Special theatre number of the *Little Review* on the occasion of an exhibition organized by F. Kiesler and Jane Heap.

**1209** HUGHES, GLENN. The story of the theatre
pp.xiii, 422; pl. 29　M
London: Ernest Benn　1928
Revised edition. World theatre history.

**1210** MILLER, ANNA I. The independent theatre in Europe 1887 to the present
pp.xv, 435　M
NY: Ray Long & Richard R. Smith　1931

**1211** STEVENS, THOMAS W. The theatre: from Athens to Broadway
pp.xii, 264; ill. in text　M
NY: D. Appleton　1932

**1212** DICKINSON, THOMAS H. (Ed.). The theatre in a changing Europe
pp.vi, 492; ill. in text, pl. 16　M
London: Putnam　[1938]

**1213** SCHUBERT, LELAND. The realistic tendency in the theatre
Ithaca: Cornell U. (PhD)　1938

**1214** FULLER, EDMUND. A pageant of the theatre
pp.xii, 270; pl. 12　MH
NY: Thomas Y. Crowell　1941
Popular history.

**1215** O'HARA, FRANK H. & BRO, MARGUERITE H. Invitation to the theatre
pp.xi, 211　DL★
NY: Harper & Brothers　1951
Revised and enlarged edition. First published as *Handbook of drama*, Chicago, Clark, 1938.

**1216** STEPHENSON, JIM B. Chronological chart of theatre history
pp.ii, 57　L
Ann Arbor MI: For the author　1951
Lists persons and places. Excludes Oriental and Asian theatre.

**1217** NAGLER, A. M. Sources of theatrical history
pp.xxiii, 611; ill. in text　M
NY: Theater Annual　1952
A collection of basic documents and other primary material, fifth century BC to the early twentieth century. Includes a section on US theatre ranging from Lewis Hallam to David Belasco. Reissued NY: Dover, 1959, unabridged, as *A source book in theatrical history*.

**1218** ALTMAN, GEORGE; FREUD, RALPH & MacGOWAN, KENNETH et al. Theater pictorial: a history of world theater as recorded in drawings, paintings, engravings, and photographs
Unpaged; ill. in text　M
Berkeley: U. of California P..　1953
516 illustrations. Includes the new stagecraft in America and technological developments in the twentieth century.

**1219** PRIDEAUX, TOM (Ed.). World theatre in pictures from ancient times to modern Broadway
pp.256; ill. in text　M
NY: Greenberg　1953
Photographs from *Life* magazine.

**1220** SAMACHSON, DOROTHY & SAMACHSON, JOSEPH. Let's meet the theatre
pp.255; ill.　DL★
NY: Abelard Schuman　1954
Introduction by John Gassner.

**1221** MacGOWAN, KENNETH & MELNITZ, WILLIAM. The living stage: a history of the world theater...including 50 illustrations by Gerda Becket With
pp.xiii, 543; ill. in text　M
Englewood Cliffs NJ: Prentice-Hall　1955
A condensed version, *Golden ages of the theatre*, was published by Prentice-Hall in 1959 (pp.ix, 166; ill. in text, pl. 6).

**1222** SAMACHSON, DOROTHY & SAMACHSON, JOSEPH. The dramatic story of the theatre
pp.viii, 168; ill. in text　L
London: Abelard-Schuman　1957

**1223** WHITING, FRANK M. An introduction to the theatre
pp.xxi, 369; ill. in text, pl. 32　L
NY: Harper and Brothers　1961
Second edition, revised. A history and a survey of technique and practice.

**1224** ROBERTS, VERA M. On stage: a history of theatre
pp.ix, 534; ill. in text　M
NY: Harper & Row　1962

**1225** CORRIGAN, ROBERT W. (Ed.). Theatre in the twentieth century
pp.320　M
NY: Grove P.　1963
Three sections: *The playwright: vision and method*; *The artist: acting and directing*; *The critic: analysis and appraisal*. Contributors include Arthur Miller, Morris Carnovsky and John Gassner.

**1226** GASSNER, JOHN & ALLEN, RALPH G. Theatre and drama in the making
pp.xvi, 1071; front.　L
Boston: Houghton Mifflin　1964

General history. Part seven presents US theatre, 1800-1930.

**1227** GASSNER, JOHN. Directions in modern theeatre and drama: an expanded edition of *Form and idea in modern theatre*
pp. xvi, 457; pl. 8     L
NY: Holt, Rinehart & Winston    1965
Survey of western theatre development since the mid-nineteenth century. First published in 1956.

**1228** REA, TOM P. A history of the International Theatre Institute
New Orleans: Tulane U. (PhD)    1966

**1229** KERNODLE, GEORGE R. Invitation to the theatre
pp.viii, 677; ill.     DL★
NY: Harcourt, Brace and World    1967

**1230** SAQUET, LABEEBEE J. H. The evolution of the theatre
pp.107     DL★
NY: Carlton P.    1968

**1231** KIRBY, E. T. (Ed.). Total theatre: a critical anthology
pp.xxxi, 280     MH
NY: E. P. Dutton    1969
Collection of extracts and essays ranging from Appia to accounts of contemporary practice.

**1232** DRIVER, TOM F. Romantic quest and modern theory: a history of the modern theatre
pp.xviii, 493     M
NY: Delacorte P.    1970

**1233** BROCKETT, OSCAR G. Perspectives on contemporary theatre
pp.vii, 158     L
Baton Rouge: Louisiana State U. P.    1971

**1234** GEISINGER, MARION. Plays, players and playwrights: an illustrated history of the theatre
pp.767; ill. in text     DL★
NY: Hart    1971

**1235** CHENEY, SHELDON. The theatre: three thousand years of drama, acting and stagecraft...with a new bibliography
pp.xvii, 710; ill. in text     M
NY: David McKay    1972
Revised and reset, illustrated edition. First published 1929.

**1236** FREEDLEY, GEORGE & REEVES, JOHN A. A history of the theatre. Third newly revised edition, with a supplementary section
pp.xvi, 1008; pl. 80     M
NY: Crown Publishers    1972
First published 1941 and here updated.

**1237** SANDROW, NAHMA. Surrealism: theater, art, ideas
pp.xi, 124; pl. 17     L
NY: Harper & Row    1972
Includes the first English translation of Vitrac's *Entrée Libre*.

**1238** WRIGHT, EDWARD A. Understanding today's theatre
pp.viii, 184     MH
Englewood Cliffs NJ: Prentice-Hall    1972

Second edition. First published 1955. Examines acting, writing, directing, technology as an aid to the theatregoer.

**1239** BROCKETT, OSCAR G. & FINDLAY, ROBERT R. Century of innovation: a history of European and American theatre and drama since 1870
pp.xv, 826; ill. in text     M
Englewood Cliffs NJ: Prentice-Hall    1973

**1240** LAHR, JOHN & PRICE, JONATHAN. Life-show: how to see theater in life and life in theater. Designed by Stephanie Tevonian
pp.ix, 204; ill. in text     L
NY: Viking P.    1973
Theatre as a cultural mirror. In collage form, the book seeks to draw attention to the relationship between theatre and human society/experience.

**1241** BROCKETT, OSCAR G. The theatre: an introduction
pp.x, 692; ill. in text     M
NY: Holt, Rinehart and Winston    1974
Third edition, revised and enlarged. First published 1964.

**1242** BURDICK, JACQUES. Theater
pp.192; ill. in text     M
NY: Newsweek Books    1974
General history.

**1243** PICKERING, JERRY V. Theatre: a contemporary introduction
pp.xxxii, 304; ill. in text, pl. 2 col.     M
St Paul MN: West Publishing    1975

**1244** WOODS, ALAN (Ed.). The historiography of theatre history...proceedings of the 1974 Ohio State University theatre history symposium
pp.iv, 42     M
Columbus: Ohio State U. P.    1975
Issued as a supplement to *Theatre Studies* No. 21, 1974-75.

**1245** HOLTON, ORLEY I. Introduction to theatre: a mirror up to nature
pp.vi, 250; ill. in text     L
Englewood Cliffs NJ: Prentice-Hall    1976

**1246** MARRANCA, BONNIE & DASGUPTA, GAUTAM (Eds). Performing arts journal
    ★
NY: PAJ Publications    1976-
3/year.

**1247** CORRIGAN, ROBERT W. The world of the theatre
pp.xiv, 359; ill. in text, some col.     M
Glenview IL: Scott, Foresman    1979

**1248** STUMP, WALTER R. & RUFF, LOREN K. Imitation: the art of the theatre [a history]
pp.viii, 287; ill. in text     M
Winston-Salem NC: Hunter    1979

**1249** WILSON, EDWIN. The theater experience
pp.xiv, 431; ill. in text     L
NY: McGraw-Hill    1980

New and revised edition. First published 1976. A basic introduction to theatre.

**1250** CAMPBELL, PAUL N. Form and the art of theatre
pp.136 ★
Bowling Green: State U. P. 1981

**1251** CORRIGAN, ROBERT W. (Ed.). The making of theatre: from drama to performance
pp.340 DL★
Glenview IL: Scott, Foresman 1981
An anthology of articles on theatre arts

**1252** INNES, CHRISTOPHER D. Holy theatre: ritual and the avant garde
pp.xi, 283; ill. in text L
Cambaridge UK: U. P. 1981
Includes material on Richard Schechner's Performance Group and the Living Theatre.

**1253** CASSADY, MARSHALL & CASSADY, PAT. Theatre: a view of life
pp.xii, 291; ill in text, pl. 4 col. L
NY: Holt, Rinehart and Winston 1982
Eclectic survey of the elements and forms of theatre.

**1254** GLOVER, J. GARRETT. The cubist theatre
pp.xvii, 154; ill. in text M
Ann Arbor MI: UMI Research P. 1983

**1255** WILSON, EDWIN & GOLDFARB, ALVIN. Living theater: an introduction to theater history
pp.xiv, 482; ill. in text MH
NY: McGraw-Hill 1983
A survey, with final section on Asian and black theatre.

**1256** NATALLE, ELIZABETH J. Feminist theatre. A study in persuasion
pp.v11, 155 MH
Metuchen NJ: Scarecrow P. 1985
Development of feminist theatre, sexual politics, woman-identified woman, family roles and relationships, feminist theatre as belief-bolstering persuasion, the woman's movement.

**1257** BROCKETT, OSCAR G. History of the theatre
pp.xiii, 779; ill. in text M
Boston: Allyn and Bacon 1987
Fifth edition. First published 1968.

**1258** CASE, SUE-ELLEN. Feminism and theatre
pp.ix, 149 M
London UK: Macmillan 1988
Examples from US, UK and European theatre.

**1259** CAMERON, KENNETH M. & GILLESPIE, PATTI P. The enjoyment of theatre
pp.vii, 434; ill in text, pl. 4 col. L
NY: Macmillan 1989
The second edition. First published 1980. Analytical and historical introduction for students.

**1260** KERNODLE, GEORGE R. The theatre in history
pp.xiii, 606; ill. in text M
Fayetteville: U. of Arkansas P. 1989

**1261** POSTLEWAIT, THOMAS & McCONACHIE, BRUCE A. (Eds). Interpreting the theatrical past: essays in the historiography of performance
pp.xi, 325; ill. in text M
Iowa City: U. of Iowa P. 1989
Includes R. W. Vince: *Theatre history as an academic discipline*; H. Lindenberger: *Opera as historical drama*; James V. Hatch: *Scholarship and black theatre history*; Thomas Postlewait: *Autobiography and theatre history*; Tracy C. Davis: *Questions for a feminist methodology in theatre history*.

**1262** RITTER, NAOMI. Art as spectacle. Images of the entertainer since Romanticism
pp.360; ill. DL★
Columbia: Missouri U. P. 1989

**1263** CARLSON, MARVIN & SHAFER, YVONNE. The play's the thing: an introduction to theatre
pp.xx, 635 DL★
NY: Longman 1990
Note also Leslie Wade: *Instructor's manual...*, a sister volume, White Plains NY: Longman, 1990.

## 5.2 GENERAL

**1264** DUNLAP, WILLIAM. History of the American theatre and anecdotes of the principal actors. Second edition, improved, incorporating a list of early plays
pp.xii, 412; vi, 387, front. MH
London: Richard Bentley 1833
Two volumes. First published NY: Harper, 1832.

**1265** HUTTON, LAURENCE. Curiosities of the American stage
pp.xv, 347; ill. in text M
London: Osgood, McIlvaine 1891
Essays on native American drama, the stage negro, burlesque, infant phenomena, American Hamlets.

**1266** HYAMS, FRANCES I. A brief history of the American theatre, with especial reference to the eighteenth century, supplemented by collections towards a bibliography before 1900
Cambridge MA: Radcliffe College (PhD) 1916

**1267** HORNBLOW, ARTHUR. A history of theatre in America from its beginnings to the present time
pp.356; 374; pl. 64 M
Philadelphia: J. B. Lippincott 1919
Two volumes.

**1268** HARTLEY, MARSDEN. Adventures in the arts
pp.254 MH
NY: Boni & Liveright 1921
With chapters on American Indian ritual dance, acrobats and vaudeville, John Barrymore.

**1269** MATTHEWS, BRANDER. Playwrights on playmaking and other studies of the stage
pp.xiii, 314 M
NY: Charles Scribner's Sons 1923
Includes chapters, *Mark Twain and the theater*, *Stage humor*, *The 'old comedies'*, *The organization of the theater*. A section, *Memories of actors* includes material on John Brougham, John T. Raymond and Nat C. Goodwin.

**1270** CRAWFORD, MARY C. The romance of the American theatre
pp.xv, 508, pl. 40     M
Boston: Little, Brown     1925
First published 1913.

**1271** KAHN, OTTO H. The American stage: reflections of an amateur
pp.24     M
[Pittsburgh?]: [For the author?]     1925
Text of an address delivered at a conference on the drama in American universities and little theatres, Carnegie Institute of Technology, Pittsburgh, PA, November 27, 1925.

**1272** ISAACS, EDITH J. R. (Ed.). Theatre: essays on the arts of the theatre
pp.xxiii, 341; ill. in text, pl. 32     M
Boston: Little, Brown     1927
Articles reprinted from *Theatre Arts Monthly* and elsewhere, providing 'a formulation of the American theatre idea'.

**1273** YOUNG, STARK. The theatre
pp.182     MH
NY: George H. Wang     1927
Reprinted articles forming an overview of theatre art.

**1274** COAD, ORAL S. & MIMS, E. The American stage
pp.v, 362; ill. in text, col. front.     M
New Haven: Yale U. P.     1929

**1275** VILLARD, LÉONIE. Le théâtre américain
pp.viii, 202
Paris: Boivin     1929

**1276** CLARK, BARRETT H. An hour of American drama
pp.159     M
Philadelphia: J. B. Lippincott     1930
Essays on theatre topics.

**1277** GREGOR, JOSEPH & FÜLÖP-MILLER, RENE. Das amerikanische Theater und Kino: zwei kulturgeschichtliche Abhandlungen
pp.112; pl. 150, some col.     M
Zurich: Amalthea Verlag     1931

**1278** KEPPEL, FREDERICK P. & DUFFUS, ROBERT L. The arts in American life
pp.xi, 227     O
NY: McGraw-Hill     1933
A social survey. Chapter XIII, 'Theatre and cinema'.

**1279** WESTON, PEARL O. Pageantry in the United States
Pittsburgh: Duquesne U. (PhD)     1934

**1280** BRAWLEY, BENJAMIN. The negro genius: a new appraisal of the achievement of the American negro in literature and the fine arts
pp.xiii, 366; pl 16     L
NY: Dodd, Mead     1937
Chapter x: *Drama and the stage, 1916-1936*.

**1281** FOND MEMORIES number of *Stage*
pp.195; ill. in text     M
NY: Stage Publishing     1937
Special issue, August 1937: 'landmarks of the American theatre covering a period of 129 years'.

**1282** ANDERSON, JOHN & FÜLÖP-MILLER, RENE. The American theatre and the motion picture in America
pp.viii, 430; ill. in text, some col., front.     M
NY: Dial P.     1938

**1283** CAUGHEY, MARY B. A history of the settlement house theaters in the United States
Baton Rouge: Louisiana State U. (MA)     1939

**1284** DUNN, ESTHER C. Shakespeare in America
pp.xv, 310; pl. 8     M
NY: Macmillan     1939
An historical survey of Shakespearian production in the US.

**1285** ISAACS, EDITH J. R. The negro in the American theatre
pp.143; ill. in text     M
NY: Theatre Arts     1947

**1286** RITTER, CARL. Amerikanisches Theater vom Rampenlicht zum Scheinwerfer
pp.173; ill. in text     M
Hamburg: J. P. Toth     1949

**1287** HOLLAND, REGINALD. The American theatre as a form of public address
Ithaca: Cornell U. (PhD)     1951

**1288** HUGHES, GLENN. A history of the American theatre 1700-1950
pp.xiii, 562; pl. 9     M
NY: Samuel French     1951

**1289** KNEPLER, HENRY W. Mary Stuart on the stage in England and America
Chicago: U. (PhD)     1951

**1290** MORRIS, LLOYD. Curtain time; the story of the American theatre
pp.xvi, 381; ill. in text     M
NY: Random House     1953
A history from 1820.

**1291** GOLDEN, JOSEPH. The position and character of theatre-in-the-round in the United States
Urbana: U. of Illinois (PhD)     1954

**1292** COGDILL, JOHN C. An analytical study of the American colonial theatre
Denver: U. (PhD)     1955

**1293** SELDES, GILBERT V. The seven lively arts
pp.xi, 306     L
NY: Sagamore P.     1957
Revised edition. First published NY, Harper & Brothers, 1924; here with some omissions in the appendix, a new introduction and some minor additions. Theatre content includes a tribute to Florenz Ziegfeld; *The daemonic in the American theatre*; *A plan for a lyric theatre*.

**1294** ARCHER, LEONARD C. The National Association for the Advancement of Colored People and the American theatre. A study of relationships and influence
Colombus: Ohio State U. (PhD)     1959

**1295** HEWITT, BARNARD. Theatre U.S.A. 1665 to 1957
pp.xi, 528; ill. in text     M
NY: McGraw-Hill     1959

The growth of the professional theatre; a collection of eye-witness accounts with commentary.

**1296** HANDLEY, JOHN G. A history of *Theatre Arts* magazine, 1916-1948
Baton Rouge: Louisiana State U. (PhD)   1960

**1297** DULLES, FOSTER R. America learns to play: a history of popular recreation, 1607-1940
pp.xvii, 441; ill. in text, front., pl. 32   L
Gloucester MA: Peter Smith   1963
New edition. First published 1940. Wide reference to theatre.

**1298** KATTER, NATE E. *Theatre Arts* under the editorship of Edith J. R. Isaacs
Ann Arbor: U. of Michigan (PhD)   1963

**1299** MEERMAN, ROGER L. The *Theatre* magazine. An analysis of its treatment of selected aspects of American theatre
Urbana: U. of Illinois (PhD)   1963

**1300** PASTALOSKY, ROSA. Historia del teatro norteamericano
pp.184   L
Santa Fe, Argentina: Editorial Castellvi   1964

**1301** COULSON, JAMES P. The development of the American National Theatre concept
Lawrence: U. of Kansas (PhD)   1965

**1302** TAUBMAN, HOWARD. The making of the American theatre
pp.402; pl. 22   L
NY: Coward McCann   1965
Foreword by Richard Rodgers.

**1303** DAVIS, JOHN P. (Ed.). The American negro reference book
pp.xxii, 969   L
Englewood Cliffs NJ: Prentice-Hall   1966
Includes Langston Hughes: *The negro and American entertainment*.

**1304** PEROSA, SERGIO. Il teatro nord-americano
pp.vii, 158   L
Milan: Vallardi   1966
General history.

**1305** BROWN, JOHN R. & HARRIS, BERNARD (Eds). American theatre
pp.228   MESM
NY: St Martin's P.   1967
Collected essays including John Gassner on Eugene O'Neill, Eric Mottram on Arthur Miller.

**1306** DOWNER, ALAN S. (Ed.). The American theater
pp.x, 221; ill. in text   M
Washington DC: U. S. Information Agency   1967
Essays on early theatre, Broadway and off-Broadway, and current practice in the 1960s.

**1307** HUGHES, LANGSTON & MELTZER, MILTON. Black magic: a pictorial history of the negro in American entertainment
pp.375; ill. in text   DL★
Englewood Cliffs NJ: Prentice-Hall   1967

**1308** KOSTELANETZ, RICHARD (Ed.). The new American arts
pp.270   L
NY: Collier Books   1967
First published 1965. Kostelanetz writes on the American theatre.

**1309** KOURILSKY, FRANCOISE. Le théâtre aux Etats-Unis
pp.98; pl. 6   M
[Brussels]: Le Renaissance du Livre   1967

**1310** MITCHELL, LOFTEN. Black drama: the story of the American negro in the theatre
pp.vii, 248; ill. in text   M
NY: Hawthorn Books   1967

**1311** HUGHES, LANGSTON & MELTZER, MILTON. A pictorial history of the negro in America. Third revision by C. Eric Lincoln and Milton Meltzer
pp.380; ill. in text   L
NY: Crown Publishers   1968
Section on the arts includes theatre and entertainment.

**1312** SEILHAMER, GEORGE O. History of the American theatre
pp.xxi,376; ix,381; ix,426   M
NY: Blom   1968
First published Philadelphia: Globe Printing House, 1888-91. Here with a new introduction by Norman Philbrick. In three volumes.

**1313** PATTERSON, LINDSAY (Ed.). Anthology of the American negro in the theatre: a critical approach
pp.xiv, 306; ill. in text   MH
NY: Publishers Company   1969
Second edition, revised.

**1314** SMITH, MILO L. The theatrical function of prologues and epilogues in British and American drama
Eugene: U. of Oregon (PhD)   1969

**1315** CAMPBELL, DOUGLAS & DEVLIN, DIANA. Theater
pp.101; ill.   DL★
Minneapolis: Dillon P.   1970
A history, intended for children.

**1316** KOSTELANETZ, RICHARD. The theatre of mixed means: an introduction to happenings, kinetic environments and other mixed-means performances
pp.xix, 313; pl. 4   M
London: Pitman   1970
First published NY: Dial P., 1968.

**1317** NATHAN, GEORGE J. Encyclopaedia of the theatre
pp.xxii, 449   M
Rutherford: Fairleigh Dickinson U. P.   1970
First published 1940, here with additional material and a new preface by Charles Angoff.

**1318** SUMPTER, CLYDE G. Militating for change: the black revolutionary theatre movement in the United States
Lawrence: U. of Kansas (PhD)   1970
Note also the author's *The negro in twentieth century American drama: a bibliography*, TD, vol 3, nos. 1/2, pp. 3-27.

**1319** THE AMERICAN THEATRE: a sum of its parts
pp.xi, 431   M
NY: Samuel French   1971

Transcribed contributions to the symposium, 'American theatre - a cultural process' conducted at the first American College Theatre Festival, Washington DC, 1969. Francis Hodge: *European influences on American theatre, 1700-1969*; Alan S. Downer: *Waiting for O'Neill*; Richard Moody: *American actors and acting before 1900, the making of a tradition*; Alan Hewitt: *Repertory to residuals*; Helen K. Chinoy: *The profession and the art*; Lawrence Carra: *The influence of the director - for good or bad*; Barnard Hewitt: *The producer's many roles*; A. S. Gillette: *American scenography 1716-1969*; Ned A. Bowman: *American theatre architecture...*; Julian Mates: *American musical theatre, beginnings to 1900*; William Green: *Broadway book musicals 1900-1969*; Ralph G. Allen: *Musical theatre 1850-1969*; Elliot Norton: *...American dramatic criticism*; Bernard Beckerman: *The university accepts the theatre...*; James H. Butler: *University theatre begins to come of age, 1925-1969*; Ralph Edmonds: *Black drama in the American theatre, 1700-1970*.

**1320** KAUFMAN, JULIAN. Appreciating the theatre: cues for theatregoers
pp.xv, 336; diagrams in text  MH
NY: McKay  1971
Survey and analysis of theatre form, using US theatre practice as basis.

**1321** ROBERTS, VERA M. The nature of theatre
pp.xi, 500; ill. in text  L
NY: Harper & Row  1971
Introductory survey.

**1322** BROCKETT, OSCAR G. (Ed.). Studies in theatre and drama: essays in honor of Hubert C. Heffner
pp.217; front.  M
The Hague: Mouton  1972
Includes Hubert C. Heffner:*Theatre and drama in liberal education*; Paul Green:*Some notes on music and drama*; Sam Smiley:*Thought as plot in didactic drama*; Norman Philbrick:*...an examination of 'Andre' by William Dunlap*; Richard Moody:*American actors and American plays on the London stage in the nineteenth century*; Walter J. Meserve:*Barney Williams: a genuine American paddy*.

**1323** BUTCHER, MARGARET J. The negro in American culture...based on materials left by Alain Locke
pp.xi, 327  L
NY: Alfred A. Knopf  1972
Second edition. First published 1956. With a chapter, *The negro in American drama*, and a postscript surveying recent developments including theatre.

**1324** DACE, LETITIA & DACE, WALLACE. Modern theatre and drama
pp.200; ill. in text  MH
NY: Richards Rosen P.  1972
General introduction and survey.

**1325** TRAORÉ, BAKORY. The black African theatre and its social function
pp.xvii, 130  L
Ibadan: U. P.  1972
With a chapter, 'black theatre outside Africa' which compares negro-African with American black theatre. Translated, and with a preface by, Dapo Adelugba.

**1326** ARCHER, LEONARD C. Black images in the American theatre: NAACP protest campaigns – stage, screen, radio and television
pp.xi, 351; ill. in text  MESM
NY: Pageant- Poseidon  1973

**1327** WILSON, GARFF B. Three hundred years of American drama and theatre: from *Ye Bear and Ye Cub* to *Hair*
pp.viii, 536; ill. in text  M
Englewood Cliffs NJ: Prentice-Hall  1973

**1328** GOODMAN, GERALD T. The black theatre movement
Philadelphia: U. of Pennsylvania (PhD)  1974

**1329** WEHRUM, VICTORIA. The American theatre
pp.88; ill in text  DL★
NY: Franklin Watts  1974
Brief history intended for children.

**1330** JENKINS, LINDA C. The performances of the native Americans as American theatre: reconnaissance and recommendations
Minneapolis: U. of Minnesota (PhD)  1975

**1331** LION, PAUL D. A critical study of the origins and characteristics of documentary theater of dissent in the United States
Los Angeles: U. of Southern California (PhD)  1975

**1332** SINGLETON, CAROLE W. Black theatre as cultural communication: an educative process
Adelphi: U. of Maryland (PhD)  1975

**1333** WOODS, ALAN (Ed.). Research in theatre history: current projects and new directions. Papers of the 1976 Ohio State University theatre history conference 'Aspects of the American theatre'
pp.45  M
Columbus: Ohio State U. P.  1976
Issued as a supplement to *Theatre Studies* No. 22, 1975-76.

**1334** BLUM, DANIEL & WILLIS, JOHN. A pictorial history of the American theatre 1860-1976 by Daniel Blum, enlarged and revised by John Willis. New, fourth, edition
pp.448; ill. in text  M
NY: Crown Publishers  1977
Foreword by Helen Hayes.

**1335** HORTON, JOEL E. Off-off-Broadway theater: its philosophical foundations
Oxford: U. of Mississippi (PhD)  1977

**1336** KINGSBURY, BARRY M. The use of information retrieval in theatre research
Bowling Green: State U. (PhD)  1977

**1337** BERKHOFER, ROBERT F. The white man's Indian: images of the American Indian from Columbus to the present
pp.xvii, 261; pl. 4  L
NY: Alfred A. Knopf  1978
Makes brief reference to the Indian in literature and popular entertainment.

**1338** LOHNER, EDGAR & HAAS, RUDOLF (Eds). Theater und Drama in Amerika: Aspekt und Interpretationen
pp.394  ★
Berlin: Schmidt  1978

## 5.2. GENERAL

**1339** JACKSON, ESTHER M. & EZELL, JOHN D. Report on the feasibility of establishing an Institute for American Theatre Studies (December 1977-November 1979)
ll.56, [76]     M
Madison: U. of Wisconsin     1979

Appended material comprises sample theatre study material, including the WARF redbook report, *Depression-era theatre: a new view*; *American theatre of the thirties*; *Theatre of Thornton Wilder*.

**1340** KARTER, M. JOSHUA. The dynamic between the individual and the community in selected Native American performances
NY: U. (PhD)     1979

**1341** KOSTELANETZ, RICHARD. Twenties in the sixties: previously uncollected critical essays
pp.328     L
Westport: Greenwood P.     1979

Includes *American theater: performance, not literature*.

**1342** FJELSTER, STAN & ROHLING, PETER (Eds). The American theatre
pp.215     ★
Copenhagen: Gyldendal     1980

**1343** RIPLEY, JOHN. *Julius Caesar* on stage in England and America, 1599-1973
pp.xiii, 370; ill. in text     M
Cambridge UK: U. P.     1980

**1344** MORDDEN, ETHAN. The American theatre
pp.xiv, 365     M
NY: Oxford U. P.     1981

**1345** BARTHOLOMEUSZ, DENNIS. *The Winter's Tale* in performance in England and America, 1611-1976
pp.xv, 279; ill. in text     M
Cambridge UK: U. P.     1982

**1346** GAINES, FREDERICK E. The effect of collective theatre practices on the American playwright
Minneapolis: U. of Minnesota (PhD)     1982

Emphasizes the Group Theatre.

**1347** JOHNSON, HELEN A. Black America on the stage
pp.41; ill. in text     M
Vienna: Österreichisches Theater Museum     1982

Exhibition catalogue, June 17-September 19. Exhibits from the Armstead-Johnson Foundation for Theatre Research, arranged by Don Vlack, covering period 1821-1982.

**1348** PEROSA, SERGIO. Storia del teatro americano
pp.204     ★
Milan: Bompiani     1982

**1349** THATCHER, NEIL G. The fundamental philosophical principles of theatre art
Minneapolis: U. of Minnesota (PhD)     1982

**1350** KOLIN, PHILIP C. (Ed.). Shakespeare in the South: essays on performance
pp.vii, 287; ill. in text     M
Jackson: U. of Mississippi P.     1983

Philip C. Kolin: *S. in the South, an overview*; Arnold Aronson: *S. in Virginia, 1751-1863*; Christopher J. Thaiss: *S. in Maryland, 1752-1860*; Sara Nalley: *S. on the Charleston stage, 1764-1799*; Woodrow L. Holbein: *S. in Charleston, 1806-1860*; Joseph P. Roppolo: *S. in New Orleans, 1817-1865*; Mary D. Toulmin: *S. in Mobile, 1822-1861*; Linwood E. Orange: *S. in Mississippi, 1814-1980*; Waldo F. McNeir: *The reception of S. in Houston, 1839-1980*; Charles B. Lower: *Othello as black on Southern stages, then and now*. Also four essays on Shakespeare Festivals in the South; Larry S. Champion: *S. in North Carolina*; Carol McG. Kay: *The Alabama S. festival*; Earl D. Dackslager: *S. at the Globe of the great Southwest*; Stuart E. Omans & Patricia A. Madden: *S. dull and dusty? Some revolutions in central Florida*.

**1351** LONEY, GLENN. 20th century theatre
pp.xv, 520; ill. in text     M
NY: Facts on File Publications     1983

A record of theatre in North America and the British Isles, 1900-1979, by year, month and day. Two volumes.

**1352** NATALLE, ELIZABETH J. The function of feminist theatre as a rhetorical medium within the women's movement
Tallahassee: Florida State U. (PhD)     1983

**1353** STAGGENBORG, ROBERT G. 'New literary history' and the postmodern paradigm: implications for theatre history
Baton Rouge: Louisiana State U. (PhD)     1983

**1354** CONLIN, KATHLEEN A. Performance documentation: an analysis of written materials [promptbooks, post-scriptive texts]
Ann Arbor: U. of Michigan (PhD)     1984

**1355** REILINGH, MAARTEN A. Paradigm and style in American theatre historiography
Bowling Green: State U. (PhD)     1984

**1356** WOODS, PORTER. Experiencing theatre
pp.viii, 279; ill. in text     L
Englewood Cliffs NJ: Prentice-Hall     1984

Basic introduction.

**1357** BAILEY, CHRISTINE E. From narrative to theatre: living history theatre
NY: City U. (PhD)     1985

**1358** KAPLAN, MIKE (Ed.). Variety presents: the complete book of major U.S. show business awards
pp.x, 564; pl. 20     L
NY: Garland Publishing     1985

Oscar, Emmy, Tony, Grammy and Pulitzer awards, chronologically listed. Nominees and winners indexed.

**1359** WATSON, HARMON S. Not for whites only: ritual and archetypes in negro ensemble company successes
Bowling Green: State U. (PhD)     1985

**1360** BENEDETTI, ROBERT L. Theater at work
pp.xv, 288     DL★
Englewood Cliffs NJ: Prentice-Hall     1986

**1361** FULLERTON, MARY E. Reception and representation: the western vision of native American performance on the Northwest coast
Seattle: U. of Washington (PhD)     1986

**1362** HENDERSON, MARY C. Theater in America: two hundred years of plays, players and productions
pp.328; ill. in text, some col.     M
NY: Harry N. Abrams     1986

Foreword by Joseph Papp.

**1363** MOLETTE, CARLTON & MOLETTE, BARBARA J. Black theatre: premise and presentation
pp.v, 166 MH
Bristol IN: Wyndhan Hall P. 1986

**1364** WEINBERG, MARK S. Performance generation: the history and evolution of collective theatre in America
Minneapolis: U. of Minnesota (PhD) 1986

**1365** COOPER, T. G. & SINGLETON, CAROLA. On stage in America
pp.viii, 119; ill. in text MH
Bristol IA: Wyndham Hall P. 1987
History, general survey and handbook.

**1366** CURTIN, KAIER. 'We can always call them Bulgarians': the emergence of lesbians and gay men on the American stage
pp.342; ill. in test M
Boston: Alyson Publications 1987

**1367** HALSTEAD, JOHN S. Autonomous theater: theory and practice
Salt Lake City: U. of Utah (PhD) 1987

**1368** HILL, ERROL (Ed.). The theater of black Americans: a collection of critical essays. Roots and rituals: the search for identity. The image-makers: plays and playwrights. The presenters: companies of players. The participators: audiences and critics
pp.ix, 363 MH
NY: Applause Books 1987
First published in two volumes, Englewood Cliffs: Prentice-Hall, 1980. James V. Hatch: *Some African influences on the Afro-American theatre*; Shelby Steele: *Notes on ritual in the new black theatre*; Eleanor W. Traylor: *Two Afro-American contributions to dramatic form*; Kimberly W. Benston: *The aesthetic to modern black drama: from 'mimesis' to 'methexis'*; Jim Haskins & Hugh B. Butts: *America's debt to the language of black Americans*; Eileen Southern: *An origin for the negro spiritual*; Robert Farris Thompson: *An aesthetic of the cool: West African dance*; Bernard L. Peterson: *Willis Richardson: pioneer playwright*; Helen A. Johnson: *'Shuffle along': keynote of the Harlem renaissance*; Darwin T. Turner: *Langston Hughes as playwright*; C. W. Bigsby: *Three black playwrights: Loften Mitchell, Ossie Davis, Douglas Turner Ward*; William Cook: *Mom, dad and god: values in black theatre*; Samuel A. Hay: *Structural elements in Ed Bullins' plays*; Michael W. Kaufman: *The delicate world of reprobation: a note on the black revolutionary theatre*; M. Francesca Thompson: *The Lafayette Players, 1915-1932*; Ronald Ross: *The role of blacks in the Federal Theatre, 1935-1939*; Ethel Pitts Walker: *The American negro theatre*; Thomas Dent: *Black theatre in the south: report and reflections*; Ellen Foreman: *The Negro Ensemble Company: a transcendent vision*; Jessica B. Harris: *The National Black Theatre: the sun people of 125th Street*; Larry Neal: *Into nationalism, out of parochialism*; Adam David Miller: *It's a long way to St. Louis: notes on the audience for black drama*; Thomas D. Pawley: *The black theatre audience*; Margaret B. Wilkerson: *Critics, standards and black theatre*; Biodun Jeyifous: *Black critics on black theatre in America*; Eric Bentley: *Must I side with blacks or whites?*; Stanley Kauffman: *Enroute to the future*; Lindsay Patterson: *Black theatre: the search goes on*; chronology of important events.

**1369** TROIANI, ELISA A. The players come to the Americas: the development of the theatrical and dramatic traditions of the United States and Argentina
Toledo OH: U. (PhD) 1987

**1370** AYERS, STEPHEN M. The selection process of the National Endowment for the Arts' theatre program: an historical-critical study
Boulder: U. of Colorado (PhD) 1988

**1371** COHEN, ROBERT. Theatre
pp.xiv, 497; ill. in text, some col., pl. 4 col. L
Mountain View CA: Mayfield Publishing 1988
Second edition, revised. First published 1981. A survey for students. A condensed version was also issued, 1988.

**1372** LEVINE, LAWRENCE W. Highbrow/lowbrow: the emergence of cultural hierarchy in America
pp.xiii, 306; ill. in text L
Cambridge MA: Harvard U. P. 1988
Includes an account of Shakespearian performance on the nineteenth century US stage.

**1373** SANDERS, LESLIE C. The development of black theatre in America: from shadows to selves
pp.xi, 252 M
Baton Rouge: Louisiana State U. P. 1988
Makes particular reference to Willis Richardson, Randolph Edmonds, Langston Hughes, LeRoi Jones (Imamu Amiri Baraka), Ed Bullins.

**1374** CAMERON, N. Developments in British and American political theatre as aesthetic responses to cultural crises in the 20th century
Manchester: U. (M.Phil.) 1989

**1375** GENTILE, JOHN S. Cast of one: one-person shows from the Chautauqua platform to the Broadway stage
pp.xi, 246; ill. in text, pl.26 M
Urbana: U. of Illinois P. 1989

**1376** HENDERSON, MARY C. Broadway ballyhoo: the American theater seen in posters, photographs, magazines, caricatures and programs
pp.184; ill. in text M
NY: Harry N. Abrams 1989

**1377** LAUBIN, REGINALD & LAUBIN, GLADYS. Indian dances of North America: their importance to Indian life
pp.576; ill. some col. ★
Norman: U. of Oklahoma P. 1989

**1378** FERRIS, LESLEY. Acting women: images of women in theatre
pp.xiv, 193 M
Basingstoke UK: Macmillan 1990
Examines, both historically and in terms of contemporary gender studies, the nature and function of women in a male-dominated art-form. Discusses David Belasco's *The Girl of the Golden West*, and Lotta Crabtree.

**1379** SCHOFIELD, MARY A. & MACHESKI, CECILIA (Eds). Curtain calls: British and American women and the theater
pp.iii, 403; ill. DL★
Athens: Ohio U. P. 1990

## 5.3 1665-1850

**1380** [ASTON, ANTHONY]. *The Fool's Opera; or, the Taste of the Age.* Written by Mat Medley. And performed by his company in Oxford, to which is prefix'd a sketch of the author's life. Written by himself
pp.vi, 22; pl. 1          O
London: for T. Payne      1731
In the sketch, the author claims to have written and staged a play in New England.

**1381** WANSEY, HENRY. An excursion to the United States of North America in the summer of 1794...by Henry Wansey, F.A.S., a Wiltshire clothier
pp.xi,270, 14; front., pl. 1 folding     L
Salisbury: J.Easton, printer    1798
The second edition 'with additions'. First published Salisbury: J. G. Van Staphorst, 1796 as *The journal of an excursion...*, with errata slip facing the final page. Reissued as *Henry Wansing and his American journal*, Philadelphia: American Philological Society, 1970, edited by David J. Jeremy. Makes reference to the theatre in New York and Boston.

**1382** GRYPHON, GREGORY (Ed.). The theatrical censor and critical miscellany for 1806-1807
pp.34-192          L
[Philadelphia?]:       [1806]
Periodical. No. III, October 11, 1806 - No.XIII, December 20, 1806. No more seen. Theatrical news of Philadelphia, New York, Boston and Charleston.

**1383** BERNARD, KARL [= Duke of Saxe-Weimar Eisenach]. Travels through North America during the years 1825 and 1826
pp.212, 238         ★
Philadelphia: Carey, Lea & Carey   1828
Two volumes. Brief reference to theatre.

**1384** THE THEATRICAL BUDGET. New series nos. I -VI
pp.192; fronts. 6        MH
NY: Elton/ Elton & Perkins    1828
Drop title: *Elton's theatrical budget, or actor's regalio*. Records London and New York theatres. Continuous pagination.

**1385** [FIELD, JOSEPH M.]. The drama in Pokerville, the bench and bar of Jurytown, and other stories. By Everpoint
pp.200; ill.         DL★
Philadelphia: Getz and Buck    1847
Fiction. Early touring theatre with specific reference to Sol Smith.

**1386** THE PROMPTER'S WHISTLE. A weekly miscellany devoted to public amusements. Edited by the man behind the curtain...August 31 - 28 September, 1850
pp.24; front.         MB
NY: S. French      1850
Four issues.

**1387** WEMYSS, FRANCIS C. Wemyss' chronology of the American stage from 1752 to 1852
pp.191         M
NY: W. Taylor      1852
Lists theatres, managers, performers.

**1388** HACKETT, JAMES H. Notes and comments upon certain plays and actors of Shakespeare, with criticisms and correspondence
pp.354; front.         L
NY: Carleton      1864
The third edition. Accounts of performances on the American stage, 1818-1842. Includes biographical material on the author. The British Library holds two letters written to Hackett in 1863, one from G. C. Verplanck, NY. March 31, thanking him for the dedication of this book; the other from Abraham Lincoln, written August 17, commending Hackett's Falstaff and singling out *Macbeth* as the finest play.

**1389** HUTTON, LAURENCE (Ed.). Opening addresses
pp.xv, 145; front.         M
NY: Dunlap Society      1887
A selection of poetical addresses delivered on the opening or re-opening of playhouses, 1752-1880.

**1390** HUTTON, LAURENCE & CAREY, WILLIAM. Occasional addresses
pp.xvii, 138; ill. in text         M
NY: Dunlap Society      1890
A sequel to *Opening Addresses*.

**1391** DALY, CHARLES P. First theatre in America: when was the drama first introduced in America ? An inquiry...including a list of the objections that have been made to the stage
pp.viii, 115; front., pl. 1 folding     MH
NY: Dunlap Society      1896
Augmented reprint of paper first read before the New York Historical Society, 1863, and published in the *New York Evening Post*. In 1864, Daly published a limited printing in pamphlet form: *When was the drama introduced in America ? An historical inquiry, anterior to Dunlap's History of the American theatre, read ...November 3rd 1863.* Daly added a supplement to the 'list of objections' for the later edition. The argument is for the existence of a playhouse in Nassau Street, N.Y. prior to Hallam's arrival in the US. (An autograph note on the copy of the 1864 pamphlet in the Harvard Theatre Collection, signed Ths. F. Deval (?), claims that the original research for the paper was the signatory's.)

**1392** FORD, PAUL L. Washington and the theatre
pp.vi, 68, 14; ill. in text, pl. 10     M
NY: Dunlap Society      1899
A history of George Washington's visits to the theatre. An appendix comprises a facsimile of William Dunlap's *Darby's Return* (1789).

**1393** WISE, JENNINGS C. Ye kingdome of Accawmacke or the eastern shore of Virginia in the seventeenth century
pp.x, 406         L
Richmond VA: Bell, Book & Stationery   1911
A history. Reference to the performance of *Ye Bare and Ye Cubb*, 1665.

**1394** THE FIRST AMERICAN PLAY-BILL known to be in existence, announcing a performance of *The Orphan* at the theatre in Nassau Street, New York, on Monday evening, March 26th, 1750: given to Harvard College library by the late Evert Jansen Wendell
pp.6; pl. 1         M
Boston MA: Club of Odd Volumes    1920

Facsimile of play-bill, with brief descriptive account, signed 'GPW', suggesting an actual performance date of April 2, 1750 on the basis of a contemporary newspaper advertisement (reproduced).

**1395** WRIGHT, RICHARDSON. Hawkers and walkers in early America: strolling peddlers, preachers, lawyers, doctors, players, amd others, from the beginning to the civil war, with...illustrations from old sources
pp.317; ill. MH★
Philadelphia: J. B. Lippincott 1927

**1396** WRIGHT, RICHARDSON. Revels in Jamaica: plays and players of a century, tumblers and conjurers, musical refugees and solitary showmen, dinners, balls and cockfights, darky mummers and other memories of high times and merry hearts
pp.xv, 378; pl. 24 M
NY: Dodd, Mead 1937

Covering the period 1682-1838, the book offers a detailed survey of English and American visiting companies and performers of theatre and other entertainment, with a substantial section on the Montego Bay season, c.1780-90. It constitutes a major addition to the available information on Jamaican theatre, hitherto described only in Seilhamer's *History of the American stage before the revolution* (1888).

**1397** ROURKE, CONSTANCE. The roots of American culture and other essays...edited, with a preface, by Van W. Brooks
pp.xiii, 305 L
NY: Harcourt, Brace 1942

'The rise of theatricals' includes material on Royall Tyler and his influence on the development of the Yankee character, Susannah Rowson, the elder Booth; *Traditions for a negro literature* makes reference to T. D. Rice, Dan Emmett and minstrelsy.

**1398** BELCHER, FANNIS S. The place of the negro in the evolution of the American theatre, 1767 to 1940
New Haven: Yale U. (PhD) 1945

**1399** GALE, CEDRIC. Shakespeare on the American stage in the eighteenth century
NY: U. (PhD) 1945

**1400** PARROTT, FREDERICK J. The mid-nineteenth century American theatre 1840-1860. A survey of the theatre production, comment, and opinion
Ithaca: Cornell U. (PhD) 1948

**1401** WALSH, CHARLES R. Shakespeare on the colonial stage
NY: Fordham U. (PhD) 1948

**1402** MULDROW, BLANCHE. The American theatre as seen by British travellers, 1790-1861
Madison: U. of Wisconsin (PhD) 1953

**1403** HENNEKE, BEN G. The playgoer in America (1752-1952)
Urbana: U. of Illinois (PhD) 1957

**1404** HODGE, FRANCIS. Yankee theatre: the image of America on the stage, 1825-1850
pp.x, 320; pl. 21 M
Austin: U. of Texas P. 1964

**1405** RANKIN, HUGH F. The theater in colonial America
pp.xvi, 239; ill. in text, pl.2 M
Chapel Hill: U. of N. Carolina P. 1965

**1406** GRIMSTED, DAVID. Melodrama unveiled: American theater and culture 1800-1850
pp.xvi, 285 M
Chicago: U. P. 1968

**1407** McCOSKER, SUSAN. The American Company, 1752-1791, founders of the American theatre
Washington DC: Catholic U. of America (MA) 1968

**1408** HEWITT, BARNARD. History of the theatre fom 1800 to the present
pp.viii, 210: ill. DL★
NY: Random House 1970

**1409** MEINKEN, ERNEST F. American actors in London, 1825-1862: their reception by professional theatre critics
Los Angeles: U. of California (PhD) 1972

**1410** WHEELER, CHARLES R. The stage Irishman on the nineteenth-century American stage
Lawrence: U. of Kansas (PhD) 1973

**1411** NYE, RUSSEL B. Society and culture in Americaa 1830-1860
pp.xv, 432; pl. 8 L
NY: Harper & Row 1974

With section on theatre.

**1412** SHATTUCK, CHARLES H. Shakespeare on the American stage from the Hallams to Edwin Booth
pp.xiv, 170; ill. in text M
Washington DC: Folger Shakespeare Library 1976

**1413** SILVERMAN, KENNETH. A cultural history of the American revolution: painting, music, literature, and the theatre in the colonies and the United States from the *Treaty of Paris* to the *Inauguration of George Washington*, 1763-1789
pp.xix, 699; ill. in text L
NY: Thomas Y. Crowell 1976

**1414** SPRITZ, KENNETH. Theatrical evolution: 1776-1976
pp.120; ill. in text M
NY: Hudson River Museum 1976

Development of the theatre displayed graphically, through a selection of items from US theatre collections.

**1415** BOST, JAMES S. Monarchs of the mimic world: or the American theatre of the eighteenth century through the managers – the men who made it
pp.xx,201; ill in text, front. M
Orono ME: U. of Maine at Orono P. 1977

**1416** SORENSON, GEORGE W. The American actor as political activist from 1800-1865: a mythic process
Columbia: U. of Missouri (PhD) 1977

**1417** ANDERSON, BRENDA J. The North American Indian in theatre and drama from 1605 to 1970
Urbana-Champaign: U. of Illinois (PhD) 1979

**1418** LARSEN, CARL F. Shakespeare's contemporaries on the American stage before the Civil War
Los Angeles: U. of Southern California (PhD) 1980

**1419** BROOKS, MONA R. The development of American theatre management practice between 1830 and 1896
Lubbock: Texas Tech U. (PhD) 1981

**1420** HALTTUNEN, KAREN. Confidence men and painted women: a study of middle-class culture in America, 1830-1870
pp.xviii, 262; ill. in text      L
New Haven: Yale U. P. 1982
With chapter: *Disguises, masks and parlour theatricals*.

**1421** McCONACHIE, BRUCE A. & FRIEDMAN, DANIEL H. (Eds). Theatre for working-class audiences in the United States, 1830-1980
pp.viii, 266      M
Westport: Greenwood P. 1985

**1422** AGNEW, JEAN-CHRISTOPHE. Worlds apart: the market and the theater in Anglo-American thought, 1550-1750
pp.xvi, 262      L
Cambridge: U. P. 1986

Theatre history in a context of economics. Emphasizes English texts and experience but the significance of the US implication is also stressed.

**1423** BURGE, JAMES C. Lines of business: casting practice and policy in the American theatre, 1752-1899
pp.viii, 305      M
NY: Peter Lang 1986
Presents the historical background to 'lines of business' tradition and examines its persistent influence, its decline, the dissolution of the stock system, the low comedian. Appendices concern the roles of Joseph Jefferson, George Holland and James Lewis.

**1424** DURHAM, WELDON B. (Ed.). American theatre companies 1749-1887
pp.ix, 598      M
Westport CT: Greenwood P. 1986
Eighty-one descriptions of stock companies.

**1425** JONES, EUGENE H. Native Americans as shown on the stage, 1753-1916
pp.ix, 209      L
Metuchen NJ: Scarecrow P. 1988

## 5.4 1851-1918

**1426** JEFFERY, JNO. B. (Ed.). Jno B. Jeffery's guide and directory to the opera houses, theatres, public halls, bill posters, etc. of the cities and towns of America
pp. av.350; front.      MH
Chicago: Jno B. Feffery [c. 1878-]
Annual. 'Intended for the use of amusement managers and their agents, lecturers, lessees and proprietors of public halls, theatres and concert rooms, bill posters, hotel proprietors, and the travelling public.' A second revised edition was published in 1879 and an eleventh revised edition in 1890

**1427** MINER, HARRY (Ed.). Harry Miner's American dramatic directory for the season of 1885-'86: a complete directory of the dramatic and operatic professions and a guide to the opera houses, theatres and public halls of America. Together with much other information of value to the amusement profession
pp.338; front.      MH
NY: Armand Wolf 1885

**1428** FULLER, EDWARD. The dramatic year [1887-88]: brief criticisms of important theatrical events in the United States with a brief sketch of the season in London by William Archer
pp.viii, 258      M
London: Sampson Low, Marston 1888

**1429** 'PROSPERO'. An imaginary history of the American theatre from 1890 to 1900
pp.64      MH
NY: [For the author?] 1890
An analysis of the ills, commercial, social and financial, that beset the theatrical profession, and a recommendation of the formation of a theatre guild to remedy matters.

**1430** DALE, ALAN [= Cohen, Alfred J.]. My footlight husband: a story of the stage
pp.203      MH
NY: Cleveland Publishing 1893
Fiction. Catches quite effectively something of theatre conditions and conventions of the time.

**1431** MATTHEWS, BRANDER. Rip Van Winkle goes to the play and other essays on plays and players
pp.vii, 256      M
NY: Charles Scribner's Sons 1894
Includes: *Uncle Sam, exporter of plays*, *The development of scenic devices*, *Memories of actresses*.

**1432** MATTHEWS, BRANDER. Studies of the stage
pp.vii, 214; front.      M
NY: Harper & Brothers 1894
Essay titles include *The dramatic outlook in America* and *The Players*, a description of the club and its premises.

**1433** [FIELD, EDWIN A.]. Through the stage-door: a complete hand-book of the theatre containing original and accurate descriptions of all features connected with the stage of a modern playhouse, including special chapters upon 'the old stage-door', 'the stage-door keeper', 'the stage and its employees', 'supernumaries', 'rules' and regulations', etc, etc. comprising a fund of information never before published and of real practical value to every lady or gentleman desirous of adopting the stage as a profession. With advice upon this subject by the eminent comedian Joseph Jefferson Esq...illustrated expressly for this work...by a stage-door keeper
pp.36; ill. in text      MH
[Boston?]: Printed, McIndoe [for the author?] [1896]

**1434** NIRDLINGER, CHARLES F. Masques and mummers: essays on the theatre of here and now
pp.x, 370      M
NY: De Witt 1899
Articles reprinted from *Illustrated American*, *Criterion*, *Town Topics*, *Empire Magazine*.

**1435** HAPGOOD, NORMAN. The stage in America 1897-1900
pp.ix, 408      M
NY: Macmillan 1901

Reprinted essays and articles.

**1436** STRANG, LEWIS C. Players and plays of the last quarter century: an historical summary of causes and a critical review of conditions as existing in the American theatre at the close of the nineteenth century
pp.325, 335; pl. 66     M
Boston: L. C. Page     1903
Two volumes.

**1437** MANUAL OF THE NATIONAL ART THEATRE Society of New York, incorporated, March, 1904
pp.157; pl. 12     MB
NY: National Art Theatre Society     1904
The Society's primary aim was to see constructed and maintained by private endowment in New York a modern playhouse dedicated to the advancement of American theatre. The manual presents its manifesto supported by a survey of major subsidized theatre in Europe.

**1438** DAVENPORT, ALLEN. Stage affairs in America today. A series of fifteen pamphlets issued weekly on Tuesdays from Jan. 15 to April 23, inclusive [cover title]
pp.av. 10     MH
Boston: [For the author?]     1907
Titles: the playwright; the business manager; actor; stage-manager; theatre orchestra; dramatic critic; vaudeville system; prevailing stock system; star system; repertoire system; one play combination system; dramatic school; acting; Shakespeare; the new theatre.

**1439** DAVENPORT, ALLEN. The theatrical independent movements. The organized theatre. The leadership of Shakespeare.
pp.20; 16; 10     MB
Boston: [For the author]     1907-8
Miscellaneous pamplet series, Nos. 1-3 'to enable the author to elaborate on suggestions contained in *Stage affairs in America today*. Projected titles, 'of no certain date', were: *the society of actor, the order of manager, the office of playwright*.

**1440** EATON, WALTER P. The American stage of to-day
pp.x, 338     M
Boston: Small, Maynard     1908
Based on articles first printed in the *New York Sun*.

**1441** BRISCOE, JOHNSON. The dramatic record and guide for 1912
pp.64     DL★
Brooklyn NY: Guide Publishing     1912

**1442** RUHL, ARTHUR B. Second nights. People and ideas of the theatre today
pp.ix, 374     M
NY: Charles Scribner     1914
With material on Eugene Walter, George M. Cohan, *Some women playwrights*, and *The Great American play*.

**1443** VAN VECHTEN, CARL. Music after the great war, and other studies
pp.168     DL★
NY: G. Schirmer     1915
Section on theatres and stage decoration.

**1444** MATTHEWS, BRANDER. A book about the theater
pp.xii, 334; pl. 26, some col.     M
NY: Charles Scribner's Sons     1916
Essays on a wide range of theatre topics including minstrelsy and the variety theatre.

**1445** PHELPS, WILLIAM L. The twentieth century theatre: observations on the contemporary English and American stage
pp.ix, 147     M
NY: Macmillan     1918
Includes chapters on actors and acting, with material on George Ade, Richard Mansfield, Maude Adams and Louis Calvert; and on dramatic criticism.

**1446** MAYO, MARGARET. Trouping for the troops: fun-making at the front
pp.149; front.     M
NY: George H. Doran     1919

**1447** EVANS, JAMES W. & HARDING, GARDNER L. Entertaining the American army: American stage and lyceum in the world war
pp.xii, 259; ill.     DL★
NY: Association P.     1921

**1448** LEWISOHN, LEWIS. The drama and the stage
pp.vi, 245     M
NY: Harcourt, Brace     1922
Essays reprinted from the *Nation* magazine. In four sections, the third of which is devoted to the US theatre, making particular reference to David Belasco, the Theatre Guild, Arthur Hopkins, Susan Glaspell and the one-act play.

**1449** NATHAN, GEORGE J. Since Ibsen: a statistical historical outline of the popular theatre since 1900
pp.x, 163     M
NY: Alfred A. Knopf     1933

**1450** SCHLESINGER, ARTHUR M. The rise of the city, 1878-1898
pp.xvii, 494; front., pl. 16     L
NY: Macmillan     1933
Volume ten of *A History of American Life*. Includes material on the development of the theatre.

**1451** WAUGH, JENNIE. Das Theater als Spiegel der amerikanischen Demokratie
pp.148; map     L
Berlin: Junker & Dunnhaupt     1934
A history from the mid-nineteenth century to the Federal Works Project.

**1452** LIPPMAN, MONROE. The history of the Theatrical Syndicate. Its effect upon the theatre in America
Ann Arbor: U. of Michigan (PhD)     1937

**1453** HOFFMAN, FREDERICK J.; ALLEN, CHARLES A. & ULRICH, CAROLYN F. Little magazine; a history and a bibliography
pp.xiii, 440; pl 4     L
Princeton: U. P.     1946
Includes theatre and stage periodicals, and offers an evaluation as well as a survey. Bibliography, 1891-1945.

**1454** BIRDOFF, HARRY. The world's greatest hit: *Uncle Tom's Cabin*. Illustrated with old-time playbills, daguerrotypes, vignettes, music-sheets, poems and cartoons
pp.xiv, 440; ill. in text     L
NY: S. F. Vanni     1947

A production history, US and elsewhere,

**1455** MORRIS, LLOYD. Postscript to yesterday: America, the last fifty years
pp.xxvi, 475      L
NY: Random House      1947
Account of social change, with a chapter on the theatre.

**1456** LATCHAN, TRULY T. The Traisdale brothers theatrical companies from 1896 to 1915
Minneapolis: U. of Minnesota (MA)      1948

**1457** FIFE, ILINE. The theatre during the confederacy
Baton Rouge: Louisiana State U. (PhD)      1949

**1458** HURLBUT, GLADYS. Next week East Lynne!
pp.254      M
NY: E. P. Dutton      1950
Stock companies.

**1459** TREADWELL, BILL. 50 years of American comedy
pp.241      MH
NY: Exposition P.      1951
Anecdotal survey.

**1460** DIEROLF, CLAUDE E. The pageant drama and American pageantry, 1905-1952
Philadelphia: U. of Pennsylvania (PhD)      1953

**1461** HOYT, HARLOW R. Town hall tonight
pp.xi, 292; ill. in text      M
Englewood Cliffs NJ: Prentice-Hall      1955
Small-town theatre, 1880-1900.

**1462** FURNAS, JOSEPH C. Goodbye to Uncle Tom
pp.x, 435; ill. in text, pl. 4      O
NY: William Sloane Associates      1956
Primarily an examination of the novel *Uncle Tom's Cabin* and its reputation, set against an account of slavery conditions. A chapter, 'ordeal by footlights', offers a description of dramatizations and performance.

**1463** HYMAN, STANLEY E. (Ed.). The critical performance: an anthology of American and British literary criticism of our century
pp.x, 337      L
NY: Vintage Books      1956
Reprints Constance Rourke: *The rise of theatricals*, concerning early American Indian theme dramas.

**1464** GORDON, GEORGE N. Theatrical movements in the Theatre Arts Magazine from 1916 to 1948
NY: U. (PhD)      1957

**1465** OBEE, HAROLD B. A prompt script study of nineteenth-century legitimate stage versions of Rip Van Winkle
Colombus: Ohio State U. (PhD)      1961

**1466** SWINNEY, DONALD H. Production in the Wallack Theatres, 1852-1888
Bloomington: Indiana U. (PhD)      1961

**1467** CHINOY, HELEN K. The impact of the stage director on American plays, playwrights, and theatres, 1860-1930
NY: Columbia U. (PhD)      1963

**1468** BRADLEY, ROBERT H. Proposals for the reform in the art of the theatre as expressed in general American periodicals, 1865-1915
Urbana: U. of Illinois (PhD)      1964

**1469** HENRY, DONALD R. The American theatre as viewed by 19th century British travellers, 1860-1900
Madison: U. of Wisconsin (PhD)      1964

**1470** OAKS, HAROLD R. An interpretative study of the effects of some upper midwest productions of *Uncle Tom's Cabin* as reflected in local newspapers between 1852 and 1860
Minneapolis: U. of Minnesota (PhD)      1964

**1471** VILLARD, LÉONIE. Panorama du théâtre Américain du renouveau 1915-1962
pp.314, (5)      M
Paris: Seghers      1964

**1472** PALMER, RICHARD H. The outdoor theatre movement in tne United States from 1900 to 1920
Iowa City: U. of Iowa (Thesis)      1965

**1473** TINAPP, A. RICHARD. A historical study of selected American and British directors 1869 to 1890
Evanston: Northwestern U. (PhD)      1966

**1474** BENSON, RICHARD L. Jarrett and Palmer's 1875 production of *Julius Caesar*: a reconstruction
Urbana: U. of Illinois (PhD)      1967

**1475** KESLER, WILLIAM J. The early productions of the Aiken-Howard versions of *Uncle Tom's Cabin*
Austin: U. of Texas (PhD)      1967

**1476** ADAMS, ALLEN J. Peter McCourt Jr. and the silver theatrical circuit 1889-1910: an historical and biographical study
Salt Lake City: U. of Utah (PhD)      1969

**1477** McPHERSON, JAMES M et al. Blacks in America: bibliographical essays
pp.xxii, 430      L
NY: Doubleday      1971
Section 9, part VIII, *Blacks in American culture 1900-1970*, documents a wide range of black theatre.

**1478** DURHAM, WELDON B. An invisible armor: the United States army's liberty theatres, 1917-1919
Iowa City: U. of Iowa (PhD)      1973

**1479** RUDE, JOHN A. Description and analysis of four monthly American theatre magazines 1900-1950
Columbia: U. of Missouri (PhD)      1973

**1480** SEE, EARL E. The political image of American actors, 1865-1920
Columbia: U. of Missouri (PhD)      1974

**1481** WILLIAMS, JAY. Stage left
pp.ix, 278; ill. in text      M
NY: Charles Scribner's Sons      1974
History of the radical theatre in America from 1915.

**1482** TOLL, ROBERT C. On with the show: the first century of show business in America
pp.361; ill. in text      M
NY: Oxford U. P.      1976

General survey of popular theatre in the late nineteenth and early twentieth centuries.

**1483** APPELBAUM, STANLEY (Ed.). Scenes from the 19th. century stage in advertising woodcuts
pp.xvii, 152: ill. in text                                              M
NY: Dover                                                            1977

Introduction, brief captions and some notes.

**1484** GOLDBERG, ROSELEE. Performance: live art 1909 to the present with 174 illustrations
pp.128; ill. in text                                                     M
NY: Harry N. Abrams                                                  1979

Survey from futurism to contemporary performance arts.

**1485** ERENBERG, LEWIS. Steppin' out: New York night life and the transformation of American culture 1890-1930
pp.xix, 291; ill.                                                      DL★
Westport CT: Greenwood P.                                             1981

**1486** BUSS, STEPHEN R. The military theatre: soldier-actor theatricals on the frontier plains
Seattle: Washington State U. (PhD)                                     1982

**1487** CONOLLY, L. W. (Ed.). Theatrical touring and founding in North America
pp.xiv, 245; ill. in text                                               M
Westport CT: Greenwood P.                                             1982

Includes: Alan Woods: ...*the career of Thomas W. Keene*; Douglas McDermott & Robert K. Sarlos: *Founding and touring in America's provincial theatre: Woodland, California, 1902-03*; Mary Brown: *Ambrose Small, a ghost in spite of himself*; Richard Moody: *Theatre USA, 1909-1919: the formative decade*; Helen K. Chinoy: *The chosen ones: the founding of the Group Theatre*; Don B. Wilmeth: *The Margo Jones Theatre*; Ann Saddlemyer: *Thoughts on national drama and the founding of theatres*. Also gives information on the US tours of Ernesto Rossi and Henry Irving.

**1488** TACKEL, MARTIN S. Women and American pageantry: 1908 to 1918
NY: City U. (PhD)                                                     1982

**1489** TOLL, ROBERT C. The entertainment machine: American show business in the twentieth century
pp.xii, 284; ill.                                                      DL★
NY: Oxford U. P.                                                      1982

**1490** AUSTER, ALBERT. Actresses and suffragists: women in the American theater, 1890-1920
pp.ix, 177; pl. 3                                                       M
NY: Praeger                                                          1984

A history, with chapters specifically on Mary Shaw, Lillian Russell, Ethel Barrymore.

**1491** McARTHUR, BENJAMIN. Actors and American culture 1880-1920
pp.xiv, 289; pl. 6                                                      M
Philadelphia: Temple U. P.                                            1984

Theatre organization and the development of the acting profession, seen in a social context.

**1492** GOSSETT, THOMAS F. *Uncle Tom's Cabin* and American culture
                                                                       DL★
Dallas TX: Southern Methodist U. P.                                   1985

**1493** LYNES, RUSSELL. The lively audience: a social history of the visual and performing arts in America 1890-1950
pp.xi, 489; ill. in text                                                L
NY: Harper and Row                                                   1985

Includes chapters, *Showbiz with music, the 'legit' theatre*.

**1494** SALMON, ERIC. Is the theatre still dying?
pp.xv, 294                                                              M
Westport CT: Greenwood P.                                             1985

An evaluation of English-speaking theatre from 1900. Plays, playing, and staging are examined 'for signs of life'.

**1495** SAMUEL, RAPHAEL; MacCOLL, EWAN & COSGROVE, STUART. Theatres on the left, 1880-1935. Workers' theatre movements in Britain and America
pp.xx, 364; ill. in text                                                M
London: Routledge & Kegan Paul                                        1985

Errata slip.

**1496** COOLEY, EDNA H. Women in American theatre, 1850-1879: a study in professional equity
College Park: U. of Maryland (PhD)                                    1986

**1497** PEISS, KATHY. Cheap amusements: working women and leisure in turn-of-the-century New York
                                                                       DL★
Philadelphia: Temple U. P.                                            1986

**1498** DURHAM, WELDON B. (Ed.). American theatre companies 1888-1930
pp.xi, 541                                                              L
NY: Greenwood P.                                                     1987

Seventy descriptions of stock companies and thirty-five accounts of experimental and other groups, listed alphabetically, each followed by a source bibliography.

**1499** SHATTUCK, CHARLES H. Shakespeare on the American stage. Volume 2: from Booth and Barrett to Sothern and Marlowe
pp.339; ill. in text, pl. 2 col.                                        M
Washington DC: Folger Shakespeare Library                             1987

**1500** MAGNUSON, LANDIS K. Circle stock repertoire theatre in America, 1907-1957
Urbana-Champaign: U. of Illinois (PhD)                                1988

**1501** SAMPSON, HENRY T. The ghost walks: a chronological history of blacks in show business, 1865-1910
pp.x, 570; ill. in text                                                 L
Metuchen NJ: Scarecrow P.                                             1988

**1502** FISHER, JUDITH L. & WATT, STEPHEN (Eds). When they weren't doing Shakespeare: essays on nineteenth-century British and American theatre
pp.xxii, 345; ill. in text                                              M
Athens: U. of Georgia P.                                              1989

Includes Bruce A. McConachie: *The theatre of Edwin Forrest*; Myron Matlaw: *James O'Neill's launching of 'Monte Christo'*; Tice L. Miller: *The image of fashionable society in American comedy*.

**1503** GLASSBERG, DAVID. American historical pageantry: the uses of tradition in the early twentieth century
                                                                       DL★
Chapel Hill: U. of N. Carolina P.                                     1990

## 5.5 1919–1945

**1504** GILLESPIE, RICHARD H. A first trip to America
pp.101     M
London: For the author     1920
Account of play-going and encounters with theatre and other show business personalities. Author was sometime chairman of Moss Empires.

**1505** MANTLE, BURNS & SHERWOOD, GARRISON P. (Eds). The best plays: and the year book of the drama in America
pp.various; ill. in text (after 1923)     M
NY: Dodd, Mead     1920-
Annual. Complements George C. D. Odell, *Annals of the New York stage*. Originally under the sole editorship of Mantle. Believing Odell's concluding date to be 1900, the editors sought to complete the chronology by publishing an additional two volumes, *Best plays of 1899-1909* (NY: 1944) and *Best plays of 1909-1919* (NY: 1943), each with 'year book' information. When Odell died with his project uncompleted at the year 1893, in order to fill the gap Sherwood, in collaboration with John Chapman, published a third additional volume, *Best plays of 1894-1899* (NY, 1955), again with 'year book' material, i.e. accounts of playwrights represented and credits of NY productions, indexed. Subsequent editors have been Louis Kronenberger and Henry Hewes. Note also Otis L. Guernsey: *Directory of the American Theatre 1894-1971. Indexed to the complete series of Best Plays...*, NY: Dodd, Mead, 1971. This supersedes Lydia S. Mantle: *Index to the best plays series, 1899-1950*.

**1506** JEWETT, FRANCES H. The repertory theatre idea. Three addresses by Mrs Jewett given before the members of the Frances Jewett Repertory Theatre Club at the meetings of March 3, 1920, March 2, 1921 and January 4, 1922
pp.[14]     MH
Boston: Repertory Theatre Club     1922
'The health of the theatre'; 'The higher aim of the theatre'; 'The power of the spoken word in the theatre'.

**1507** SAYLER, OLIVER M. Our American theatre: important productions on the American stage
pp.xiv, 399; ill. in text     M
NY: Brentano's     1923
Critical survey with appendices on award-winning plays, O'Neill, Washington Square players, the Theatre Guild, little theatres, Robert Edmond Jones and other designers. Illustrated from drawings by Lucie R. Sayler.

**1508** LAWREN, JOSEPH (Ed.). The drama year book 1924
pp.343     L
NY: For the author     1924
Chronology of plays, with credits, both for NY and regionally; listing of actors, with roles; dramatic books of 1923; producers, directors, playwrights, scenic designers.

**1509** LOCKE, ALAIN (Ed.). The new negro: an interpretation
pp.xviii, 452; col. front., pl. 16 col.     L
NY: Albert and Charles Boni     1925
Decorations and portraits by Winold Reiss. An anthology, including Montgomery Gregory: *The drama...*, and Jessie Fauset: *The gift of laughter* [Bert Williams, Paul Robeson].

**1510** MODERWELL, HIRAM K. The theatre of today
pp.338; ill. in text, pl. 32     M
NY: Dodd, Mead     1927
Second edition, enlarged. First published 1914.

**1511** LYND, ROBERT S. & MERRELL, HELEN M. Middletown: a study in contemporary American culture
pp.xi, 550     L
NY: Harcourt, Brace     1929
Sociological study, including reference to attitudes towards theatre and other entertainments. A sequel, *Middletown in transition*, 1937, pp.xviii, 604, makes reference to the appearance of a civic theatre.

**1512** NATHAN, GEORGE J. Monks are monks: a diagnostic scherzo
pp.x, 300     M
NY: Alfred A. Knopf     1929
A novel intended as a comment on contemporary *mores* and the state of the arts.

**1513** SAYLER, OLIVER M. Revolt in the arts: a survey of the creation, distribution and appreciation of art in America...with contributions by thirty-six representative authorities in the several arts
pp.xiv, 351     L
NY: Brentano's     1930
Contributors include David Belasco, Alfred Lunt, Eva Le Gallienne, George P. Baker, Paul Green, Arthur Hopkins, Joseph Urban, George Gershwin, Arthur Hammerstein.

**1514** GEDDES, VIRGIL. Theatre of dreadful nights
pp.22     MH
Brookfield: Brookfield Players     [1933?]
A satirical account of the current theatre, addressed to producers.

**1515** GEDDES, VIRGIL. American theatre. What can be done?
pp.12     MH
Brookfield: Brookfield Players     1933
Pamphlet defining an intellectual crisis in American theatre.

**1516** GEDDES, VIRGIL. Towards revolution in the theatre
pp.15     MH
Brookfield: Brookfield Players     1933
Urging an intelligent drama.

**1517** GEDDES, VIRGIL. Left turn for American drama
pp.48     DL★
Brookfield: Brookfield Players     1934
Urging revolutionary action to reform the theatre.

**1518** BLAKE, BEN. The awakening of the American theatre
pp.62; ill.     DL★
NY: Tomorrow     1935
The development of a 'people's theatre'. Reference to the Laboratory Theatre, the Theatre Union, the Group Theatre.

**1519** HOLMES, MARGARET G. The theatre today
pp.39     DL★
Chapel Hill: U. of N, Carolina P.     1937

**1520** BLOCK, ANITA. The changing world in plays and theatre
pp.xiii, 449     M
Boston: Little, Brown     1939

Chapters on changing sexual standards, conflict within the individual, social conflict, plays against war, the current American theatre and the Federal Theatre.

**1521** HOUGHTON, NORRIS. Advance from Broadway: 19,000 miles of American theatre
pp.xii, 416     M
NY: Harcourt, Brace     1941
An evaluation of nationwide theatre activity.

**1522** LYONS, EUGENE. The red decade: the Stalinist penetration of America
pp.423     L
Indianapolis: Bobbs Merrill     1941
Anti-bolshevist polemic. Chapter 24, 'Revolution comes to Hollywood and Broadway', and other reference to theatre and the entertainment industry throughout.

**1523** STONE, EZRA C. & MELICK, WELDON. Coming, major
pp.267; ill.     DL★
NY: J. B. Lippincott     1944
Army camp shows, particularly at Camp Upton and with reference also to a touring production of Berlin's *This is the army*.

**1524** GILLMORE, MARGALO & COLLINGE, PATRICIA. The B.O.W.S
pp.vii, 173; pl 8     M
NY: Harcourt, Brace     1945
Account of the WW2 touring production of *The Barretts of Wimpole Street* organized by USO with the American Theater Wing.

**1525** OGDEN, AUGUST R. The Dies Committee: a study of the Special House Committee for the investigation of un-American Activities, 1938-1944
pp.vi, 318     L
Washington DC: Catholic U. of America P.     1945
Second, revised edition. Material on the Federal Theatre Project and several references to the acting profession.

**1526** DYCKE, MARJORIE L.P. The living newspaper. A study of the nature of form and its place in modern social drama
pp.
NY: U. (PhD)     1948

**1527** GILDER, ROSAMOND et al (Eds). Theatre Arts anthology: a record and a prophecy
pp.xvi, 687     M
NY: Theatre Arts Books/Robert M MacGregor     1950
Selections, 1916-1948.

**1528** FREEDMAN, ANN C. Development of arena-policies and methods and modifications of stage productions in the United States since 1925
Pittsburgh: U. (MA)     1951

**1529** MALOFF, SAUL. The new theatre movement in America
Iowa City: U. of Iowa (PhD)     1953

**1530** KRAMER, WILLIAM. The Civic Repertory Theatre, 1926-1933
NY: Coluimbia U. (MA)     1955

**1531** CHAPMAN, JOHN. Broadway's best, 1957. The complete record of the theatrical year
pp.329     M
NY: Doubleday     1957

Playbills and synopses, some very substantial, bibliography and obituaries. The only issue.

**1532** BARER, BERTRAM. A rhetorical analysis of the American presentational social theatre of the thirties
Minneapolis: U. of Minnesota (PhD)     1960

**1533** ROBINSON, MARIE J. Revivals on the New York stage, 1930-1950, with a statistical survey of their performances from 1750-1950
Evanston: Northwestern U. (PhD)     1960

**1534** CHURCHILL, ALLEN. The improper Bohemians: a recreation of Greenwich Village in its heyday
pp.343; ill. in text     O
London: Cassell     1961
Published NY: E. P. Dutton, 1959. Includes material on the Provincetown Players and Eugene O'Neill.

**1535** GREENHALL, MARGARET P. et al (Eds). Plays and players; a survey of the modern drama [cover title]
pp.23     DL★
NY: Branch Library Book News     1963
Volume 41, no. 2, December, 1963

**1536** HAZZARD, ROBERT T. The development of selected American stage directors from 1926 to 1960
Minneapolis: U. of Minnesota (PhD)     1963

**1537** HIMELSTEIN, MORGAN Y. Drama was a weapon: the left-wing theatre in New York 1929-1941
pp.xix, 300     M
New Brunswick: Rutgers U. P.     1963
Foreword by John Gassner.

**1538** LEA, FLORENCE B. Repertory theatre in America, 1926-1962
Columbia: U. of Missouri (PhD)     1965

**1539** WOODS, PORTER S. The negro on Broadway. Transition years, 1920-1930
New Haven: Yale (DFA)     1965

**1540** COWLEY, MALCOLM. Think back on us...a contemporary chronicle of the 1930s...edited, with an introduction by Henry Dan Piper
pp.xv, 400     L
Carbondale: Southern Illinois U. P.     1967
Essays and reviews. Includes material on the Federal Theatre Project and the poetic drama of Archibald MacLeish.

**1541** GOLDEN, JOSEPH. The death of Tinker Bell: the American theatre in the 20th century
pp.ix, 181     M
NY: Syracuse U. P.     1967

**1542** GOODMAN, WALTER. The committee: the extraordinary career of the House Committee on un-American Activities.
pp.xix, 564; pl. 8     MH
NY: Farrar, Straus and Giroux     1968
Foreword by Richard H. Rovere. Chapters on the Federal theatre, the Hollywood ten, Broadway and Arthur Miller.

**1543** LEWIS, EMORY. Stages: the fifty-year childhood of the American theatre
pp.xiv, 290     M
Englwood Cliffs NJ: Prentice-Hall     1969

Theatre history 1915-1965.

**1544** AMORY, CLEVELAND & BRADLEE, FREDERICK (Eds). *Vanity Fair*: selections from America's most memorable magazine: a cavalcade of the 1920s and 1930s
pp.327; ill. in text, some col.     O
NY: Viking P.     1970

Includes Dorothy Parker: *The first hundred plays are the hardest*; Stark Young: *David Garrick to John Barrymore*; Mary C. Canfield: *Mrs Fiske...*; picture article on Clifton Webb and a number of *Hall of Fame* biographical sketches with portraits.

**1545** DUFFUS, ROBERT L. The American renaissance
pp.321     DL★
NY: A.M.S. Press     1970

New edition. First published NY: Alfred A. Knopf, 1928. Sections on the theatre, school and college drama, community theatre.

**1546** BENTLEY, ERIC (Ed.). Thirty years of treason: excerpts from hearings before the House Committee on Un-American Activities, 1938-1968
pp. xxviii, 991     O
NY: Viking P.     1971

The committee's investigations as they related to the entertainment industry, from the Federal Theatre Project in 1938 to Joseph Papp's Shakespeare Festival in 1958, with final chapters on hearings in 1966 and 1968. Appendices provide details of committee membership, a translation of Brecht's and Eisler's *Die Massnahme*, and a statement by Paul Robeson.

**1547** JONES, MAY W. A history of the radical theatre in the United States from 1930 to 1970
New Orleans: Tulane U. (PhD)     1971

**1548** TAYLOR, KAREN M. People's theatre in Amerika...documents by the people who do it
pp.xix, 332     MH
NY: Drama Book Specialists     1972

A documented review of *avant-garde* theatre since the 1930s. Preface by John H. Lawson.

**1549** VAUGHN, ROBERT F. Only victims: a study of show business black listing
pp.355     MH
NY: Putnam     1972

Examines the influence of the House Committee on un-American Activities, 1938-58. Introduction by George McGovern.

**1550** KANFER, STEFAN. A journal of the plague years
pp.xi, 306; pl. 4     MH
NY: Atheneum     1973

Account of the blacklisting of writers, performers, directors and other theatre workers that culminated in the McCarthy years.

**1551** MAY, ROBIN. A companion to the theatre. The Anglo-American stage from 1920
pp.304; pl. 8     M
Guildford: Lutterworth P.     1973

An encyclopedia of English-speaking theatre.

**1552** GOLDSTEIN, MALCOLM. The political stage: American drama and theater of the great depression
pp.x, 482; pl. 8     M
NY: Oxford U. P.     1974

**1553** CHMEL, PATRICK J. Sociopolitial activities of American actors, 1920-1940
Columbia: U. of Missouri (PhD)     1975

**1554** CHURCHILL, ALLEN. The theatrical twenties
pp.viii, 326; ill. in text     L
NY: McGraw-Hill     1975

Popular survey.

**1555** FRENCH, WARREN (Ed.). The twenties: fiction, poetry, drama
pp.xvii, 532     DL★
Deland FL: Everett Edwards     1975

Second edition, revised. A survey, one of a series also covering the decades, *Thirties; Forties; Fifties* originally published 1967-71.

**1556** PITTS, ETHEL L. The American negro theatre: 1940-1949
Columbia: U. of Missouri (PhD)     1975

**1557** FRANK, FELICIA N. The magazines *Workers Theatre*, *New Theatre* and *New Theatre and Film* as documents of the American left-wing theatre movement of the nineteen-thirties
NY: City U. (PhD)     1976

**1558** MÜLLER, KURT. Konventionen und Tendenzen der Gesellschaftskritik im expressionistischen amerikanischen Drama der zwanzige Jahre
pp.249     ★
Frankfurt: Lang     1977

**1559** FAWKES, RICHARD. Fighting for a laugh: entertaining British and American forces, 1939-1946
pp.192. ill. in text     M
London: Macdonald and Jane's     1978

Includes material on the USO.

**1560** ISRAEL, MARY C. Film takes over the theatre: an historical study of American resident stock companies from 1920 to 1932
NY: City U. (PhD)     1979

**1561** KAZMARK, MARY E. The portrayal of women in American theatre, 1925-1930
Los Angeles: U. of California (PhD)     1979

**1562** BANKS, ANN (Ed.). First person America
pp.xxv, 287; ill.     DL★
NY: Alfred A. Knopf     1980

Eighty transcribed narratives, originally recorded by members of the Writers' Project of the FWP.

**1563** BONGAS, PAMELA J. The woman's woman on the American stage in the 1930s
Columbia: U. of Missouri-Columbia     1980

**1564** WILSON, EDMUND. The thirties: from notebooks and diaries of the period. Edited and with an introduction by Leon Edel
pp.xxxii, 753; front., pl. 8     L
London: Macmillan     1980

Includes *Notes for Beppo and Beth* (pp.215-225), written for Provincetown. NY: Farrar, Straus and Giroux, 1980.

**1565** ELAM, HARRY J. Theatre for social change. The artistic and social vision in revolutionary theatre in America, 1930-1970
Berkeley: U. of California (PhD)     1984

**1566** AMIARD-CHEVREL, CLAUDINE. L'ouvrier au théâtre
pp.355; ill. in text      M
Louvain: Cahiers Théâtre      1987
Includes Genevieve Fabre: *'Love's Labour Lost', luttes ouvrières et aventures théâtrales* (US, 1911-1939).

**1567** MORROW, LEE A. The Tony Awards Book: four decades of great American theatre
     DL★
NY: Abbeville P.      1987

**1568** FEARNOW, MARK. A grotesque spectacle: American theatre of the Great Depression as cultural history
Bloomington: Indiana U. (PhD)      1990

**1569** SCHMITT, NATALIE C. Actors and onlookers: theater and twentieth-century scientific views of nature
pp.x, 163      DL★
Evanston IL: Northwestern U. P.      1990

## 5.6 1946-1990

**1570** BLUM, DANIEL et al (Eds). Theatre world, season 1944-45 -
pp.av. 250; ill. in text      M
NY: Theatre World      1945–
Yearbook, providing pictorial and statistical record, chronologically listed. Previously *Play Pictorial*. Subsequently published NY: Greenburg, 1950-51; Philadelphia: Chilton P., 1962-63; NY: Crown P. 1968-69, edited by John Willis.

**1571** CROYDEN, MARGARET. Lunatics, lovers and poets. The contemporary experimental theatre
pp.xxvii, 320; pl. 14      M
NY: McGraw-Hill      1947
With chapters on Chaikin's *Open Theatre*, Schechner's Performance Group, The Living Theatre, happenings, and other *avant-garde* work in the US and Europe.

**1572** RITTENOUR, ROBERT G. Four years of army theatre
Ann Arbor: U. of Michigan (MA)      1947

**1573** A REPORT ON AMERICAN THEATRE participation in support of the United Nations and its objectives. Prepared by the American National Theatre and Academy
pp.i, 20; ill. in text      L
Washington DC: US National Commission for UNESCO      [1951]
Cover title: 'Curtain call for '52: international theatre month'. Introduction by Rosamond Gilder. Includes a review of the international theatre month by Elizabeth Birdsall.

**1574** GASSNER, JOHN. The theatre in our times: a survey of the men, materials and movements in the modern theatre
pp.xiv, 609; ill.      DL★
NY: Crown Publishers      1954

**1575** JACK, WILLIAM T. The decline of the American theatre since 1946
Austin: U. of Texas (PhD)      1957

**1576** BANHAM, MARTIN J. Innovations in the American theatre since 1945
Leeds UK: U. (MA)      1962

**1577** [MCDONALD, DONALD]. Stage and screen [cover title]
pp.51      DL★
NY: Fund for the Republic      1962
Transcribed interviews, including Walter Kerr and Stanley Kramer.

**1578** WOLF, DANIEL & FANCHER, EDWIN (Eds). The Village Voice reader: a mixed bag from the Greenwich Village newspaper with line drawings by Muriel Jacobs, Hasse Nordenstrom, Jules Feiffer, Jean Shepherd, Shel Silverstein, Alek Smit
pp.349; ill. in text      MH
Garden City: Doubleday      1962
Includes an article on Arthur Laurents, a review, *Godot on Broadway*, and pieces by Norman Mailer, Julian Beck and Judith Malina, Lorraine Hansberry.

**1579** NORTON, ELLIOT & HIRSCH, SAMUEL. Repertory theatre in America: the problem and the promise. A report based on statements made at the New England Theatre Conference convention at Tufts University, Medford, Mass. October 24
pp.v, 42      M
Medford MA: NETC      1964
Appended are a transcribed address to the conference by Harold Clurman referring to the Lincoln Center Repertory Theatre, and a message from Nina Vance of the Alley Theatre, Houston.

**1580** SAINER, ARTHUR. The sleepwalker and the assassin, a view of the contemporary theatre
pp.127; ill.      DL★
NY: Bridgehead Books      1964
Introduction by Geraldine Lust.

**1581** GARDNER, R. H. The splintered stage: the decline of the American theater
pp.159      M
NY: Macmillan      1965

**1582** PARONE, EDWARD (Ed.). New theatre in America
pp.214      DL★
NY: Dell Publications      1965

**1583** BJORKSTEN, INGMAR. Scenbild USA: en amerikansk teaterhistoria
pp.157; ill. in text      L
Stockholm: Sveriges Radio      1967
Survey of contemporary theatre.

**1584** CRUSE, HAROLD. The crisis of the negro intellectual
pp.iv, 594 (1)      O
NY: Morrow      1967
Includes chapters, *Intellectuals and the theatre of the 1960s* and *The Harlem Black Arts Theater*.

**1585** DOWNER, ALAN S. (Ed.). Conference on theatre research: a report on the Princeton University conference, November 20, 1965 - April 29-30 1966, October 7-8, 1966
pp.233-309      M
Washington DC: AETA      1967

*Educational Theatre Journal* special issue. June, 1967.

**1586** DOWNER, ALAN S. (Ed.). The American theater today
pp.xii, 212 MH
NY: Basic Books 1967
Essays on pre-WW1 drama, post WW2 Broadway and major dramatists, the director, the musical, emerging writers in the mid-60s, off-Broadway and college theatre. Also published as *The American Theater*, Washington DC: Voice of America, 1967. Originally lectures broadcast on the radio.

**1587** GOTTFRIED, MARTIN. A theater divided: the postwar American stage
pp.330 M
Boston: Little, Brown 1967

**1588** FELDMAN, LEE G. A critical analysis of improvisational theatre in the United States from 1955-1968
Denver: U. (PhD) 1968

**1589** GARD, ROBERT E.; BALCH, MARSTON & TEMKIN, PAULINE B. Theater in America. Appraisal and challenge
pp.xvii, 192 M
Madison WI: Dembar Educational for the NTC 1968

**1590** JASWAL, ALICE J. Oral interpretation as a form of professional theatre on the New York stage from 1945 to 1965
East Lansing: Michigan State U. (PhD) 1968

**1591** SCHROEDER, ROBERT J. (Ed.). The new underground theatre
pp.xi, 211 MH
NY: Bantam 1968
Playtexts: Includes Maria Irene Fornes, Jean-Claude Van Itallie, Sam Shepard, Murray Medwick, Grant Duay, Rachelle Owens, Ronald Tavel. Introduction and production histories.

**1592** SLABAUGH, RICHARD G. A new orthodoxy: the history and theory of the modern open stage
Seattle: U. of Washington (PhD) 1968

**1593** GILDER, ROSAMOND et al (Eds). Theatre 1. American theatre 1967-
pp.av. 130; ill. in text M
NY: ITI 1969–
Annual year-book, initially compiled to record the twelfth ITI Congress, June, 1967, published by Charles Scribner for the ITI of the US. Later under the editorship of Martha W. Coigney as *Theatre 2* etc. Contributors include Brooks Atkinson, Clive Barnes, Harold Clurman, John Houseman, Arthur Miller, Harold Prince, Richard Schechner. Illustrators include Al Hirschfeld. Articles in French and English.

**1594** NOVICK, JULIUS. Beyond Broadway: the quest for permanent theatres
pp.xxi, 393; pl. 8 L
NY: Hill and Wang 1969
Second printing with new preface. First published 1968. A national survey of resident professional theatres. Excludes off- and off-off Broadway but includes Joseph Papp's Shakespeare Festival.

**1595** SCHECHNER, RICHARD. Public domain: essays on the theatre
pp.xi, 244 M
NY: Bobbs-Merrill 1969
Topics, many reprinted from *TDR* which Schechner edited during the 60s, include Megan Terry and transformational theatre, pornography, Stanislavsky and his influence, the absurd, happenings, and the environmental and radical theatre of the 60s.

**1596** VAUGHAN, STUART. A possible theatre. The experiences of a pioneer director in America's resident theatre
pp.ix, 257 M
NY: McGraw-Hill 1969
Describes the rise of non-profit professional theatre, with particular reference to the New York Shakespeare Festival, the Phoenix Theatre, N.Y., and the Seattle Repertory Theatre.

**1597** JOTTERAND, FRANCK. Le nouveau théâtre américain
pp.255 M
Paris: Seuil 1970
Concentrates on post WW2 developments, particularly the *avant-garde*,

**1598** NYE, RUSSEL B. The unembarrassed muse: the popular arts in America
pp.x, 497; pl. 20 L
NY: Dial P. 1970
Part two, *The popular theatre*.

**1599** ROCKEY, JAMES R. A study of the term 'convention' as used in major undergraduate theatre books in the United States published between 1945-1970
Iowa City: U. of Iowa (PhD) 1970

**1600** BRUSTEIN, ROBERT. Revolution as theatre: notes on the new radical style
pp.x, 170 O
NY: Liveright 1971

**1601** HEILMEYER, JENS & FRÖHLICH, P. Now: Theater der Erfahrung: Materiel zur neuen amerikanischen Theaterbewegung
pp.317; ill. in text MH
Cologne: M. D. Schauberg 1971
Articles and interviews emphasizing personalities and companies asociated with the experimental theatre movements of the 1960s.

**1602** HINDMAN, JAMES T. Happening theory and methodology: Allan Kaprow, Claes Oldenburg, Ann Halprin: 1959-1967
Athens: U. of Georgia (PhD) 1971

**1603** KIRBY, MICHAEL. Futurist performance: with manifestos and playscripts translated from the Italian by Victoria Nes Kirby
pp.xvi, 335; ill. in text L
NY: E. P. Dutton 1971
Substantially an examination of Italian futurist theatre. Some parallels drawn with US theatre.

**1604** MESHKE, GEORGE L. The rise of neo-expressionism in the American theatre of the post-Kennedy years
Seattle: U. of Washington (PhD) 1971

**1605** SZYDLOWSKI, ROMAN. Anglosaka melpomena
pp.376; pl 16 L
Krakow: Wydnawnictwo Literackie 1971

Post WW2 theatre staging with much US material, including reference to the Living Theatre, La Mama, Richard Schechner.

**1606** SHANDLER, DONALD D. American Shakespeare festival theatres: a sense of occasion
Columbus: Ohio State U. (PhD) 1972

**1607** LESNICK, HENRY (Ed.). Guerilla street theatre
pp.442; ill. DL★
NY: Avon Books 1973

**1608** SCHECHNER, RICHARD. Environmental theatre
pp.xii, 339; ill. in text MH
NY: Hawthorn Books 1973
Derived from the author's experience with the Performance Group.

**1609** SCHEVILL, JAMES (Ed.). Break out! In search of new theatrical environments
pp.xv, 413; ill. DL★
Chicago: Swallow P. 1973
Articles on contemporary theatre.

**1610** WEISMAN, JOHN. Guerrilla theatre: scenarios for revolution
pp.ix, 202; pl. 8 MH
NY: Anchor/Doubleday 1973
A collage of interviews, scripts, photographs, letters and journal entries describing 'a combination of drama, political consciousness, and community action...'

**1611** ZEIGLER, JOSEPH W. Regional theatre; the revolutionary stage
pp.xix, 277; pl. 8 M
Minneapolis: U. of Minnesota P. 1973
Regional theatre in the 1960s and '70s.

**1612** BRECHT, STEFAN. Nuovo teatro Americano 1968-1973
pp.366; ill. in text M
Rome: Butzoni 1974
Essays on the *avant-garde*, some reprinted from *The Drama Review*.

**1613** CORRIGAN, ROBERT W. The theatre in search of a fix
pp.xii, 368 DL★
NY: Dell Publications 1974

**1614** GROSSMAN, SAMUEL L. Trends in the avant-garde theatre of the United States during the 1960s
Minneapolis: U. of Minnesota (PhD) 1974

**1615** KIRBY, MICHAEL. The new theatre: performance documentation
pp.xiv, 239; ill. in text M
NY: U. P. 1974
Descriptions of a range of *avant-garde* productions. Erratum slip.

**1616** MIRALLES, ALBERTO. Nuevos rumbos del teatro
pp.143; ill. DL★
Barcelona: Salvat Editores 1974
Emphasis on new trends in the US theatre.

**1617** SHAPIRO, STEPHEN R. The theme of homosexuality in selected theatrical events produced in the United States between 1969 and 1974
Santa Barbara: U. of California (PhD) 1974

**1618** JOY, JOHN F. 'A joyful plague on all our houses': an inside view of the American theatre before, during and beyond the theatre of the sixties
Pittsburgh: Carnegie-Mellon U. (PhD) 1975
This is also recorded, with a shortened title, for the year 1979.

**1619** LITTLE, STEWART W. After the fact: conflict and consensus, a report on the first American congress of theatre
pp.109 M
NY: Arno 1975
Convened June 2 in Princeton NJ. Brief, 'to identify problems and design practical programs which American theatre can undertake'.

**1620** SAINER, ARTHUR. The radical theatre notebook
pp.xiv, 367; ill. DL★
NY: Discus-Avon 1975
Collection of scripts, dialogues, notes from several experimental theatre *ensembles*.

**1621** SIMON, JOHN. Singularities: essays on the theater 1964-1973
pp.xiv, 239 DL★
NY: Random House 1975

**1622** STEVENSON, ISABELLE (Ed.). The Tony award: a complete listing with a history of the American Theater Wing
pp.138; ill. in text, front. M
NY: Arno P. 1975

**1623** RONEN, DAN. The experimental theater: vocabulary, description, and analysis of the American experimental theater in the sixties
Pittsburgh: Carnegie-Mellon U. (PhD) 1976

**1624** VINCENTINI, CLAUDIO. The American political theatre of the sixties
NY: U. (PhD) 1976

**1625** DACE, WALLACE. Proposal for a national theater
pp.viii, 151; ill. in text M
NY: Richards Rosen P. 1978

**1626** DINI, MASSIMO. Teatro d'avanguardia americanó
pp.239; pl. 8 MH
Florence: Vallecchi 1978
Includes accounts of the Living Theatre, the Bread and Puppet Theatre, Café la Mama, Robert Wilson.

**1627** LOWRY, W. M. (Ed.). The performing arts and American society
pp.vi, 218 MH
Englewood Cliffs NJ: Prentice-Hall 1978
Originally a background reading book for the 53rd American Assembly, 1977, whose topic was *The future of the performing arts*. Includes W. M. Lowry: *The past twenty years*; Julius Novick: *The theatre*; Lincoln Kirstein: *The performing arts and our egregious elite*.

**1628** PASQUIER, MARIE-C. Le theatre américain d'aujourd'hui
pp.261 MH
[Paris]: Presses Universitaires 1978

Material on André Serban, Meredith Monk, Robert Wilson, Richard Foreman, happenings, black theatre, the *avant-garde* groups of the 1960s and '70s.

**1629** COHEN, HILARY U. Ritual and theater: an examination of performance forms in the contemporary American theatre
Ann Arbor: U. of Michigan (PhD)     1980

**1630** LEAVITT, DINAH L. Feminist theatre groups
pp.vi, 153     M
Jefferson: McFarland     1980

**1631** MANCE, WILLIAM R. The color of black theatre: a critical analysis of the black theatre movement of the 1960's and 1970's
Columbia: U. of Missouri (PhD)     1980

**1632** ROUSSELOW, JESSE L. A rhetorical analysis of the movement towards an alternative theatre in the United States 1947-1969
Minneapolis: U, of Minnesota (PhD)     1980

**1633** SITUATIONS CONTEMPORAIRES du théâtre populaire en Amérique
pp.168     M
Rennes: U. de Haute Bretagne     1980

**1634** BERKOWITZ, GERALD M. New Broadways. Theatre across America, 1950-1980
pp.x, 198; ill. in text     O
Totowa NJ: Rowman & Littlefield     1982
American theatre in 1950; Broadway; off-Broadway; off-off- and other alternatives; regional theatre; American theatre in 1980.

**1635** RIESER, JUDITH E. The American avant-garde ensemble theaters of the sixties in their historical and cultural context
Evanston: Northwestern U. (PhD)     1982

**1636** SCHECHNER, RICHARD. The end of humanism: writings on performance
pp.128     M
NY: Performing Arts Journal Publications     1982
Includes chapters: *Decline and fall of the (American) avant-garde*, *The crash of performative circumstances*. *A modernist discourse on postmodernism*.

**1637** SHANK, THEODORE. American alternative theatre
pp.xi, 202; ill. in text     M
London: Macmillan     1982
Non-literary theatre of the 1960s and '70s

**1638** FABRE, GENEVIEVE. Drumbeats, masks and metaphor: contemporary Afro-American theatre
pp.xi, 274; pl. 6     L
Cambridge MA: Harvard U. P.     1983
Translated from the French by Melvin Dixon. First published Paris: 1982 as *Le théâtre noir aux Etats-Unis*.

**1639** ROTH, MOIRA (Ed.). The amazing decade: women and performance art in America 1970-1980
    DL★
Los Angeles: Astro Arts     1983

**1640** SCHECHNER, RICHARD. Performative circumstances from the avant-garde to Ramlila
pp.xii, 337; pl. 8, 1 folding chart.     L
Calcutta: Seagull Books     1983
International in range. Includes material on the Performance Group in India, and the Environmental Theatre and the Performing Garage.

**1641** WE ARE STRONG. A guide to the work of popular theatres across the Americas, volume 1
pp.xv, 244     ★
Mankato MN: Institute for Cultural Policy Studies     1983
1980-83. Work of 63 theatres 'of social relevance'. A publication of *Theatrework* magazine.

**1642** FERNANDEZ, DOREEN G. (Ed.). Contemporary theater arts: Asia and the United States
pp.iv, 79     L
Quezon City: New Day     1984
Derived from a seminar conducted by the US Information Service, Manila. Includes James V. Hatch: *Black theater in the USA*; Nestor U. Torre: *Perceptions of American theater*; Jose Javier Reyes: *Filipino perceptions of American theater*.

**1643** RUBIN, MICHELE McN. The great American pie: theatre as a social force in race relations in contemporary America
Atlanta: Emory U. (PhD)     1984

**1644** WILLIAMS, MANCE. Black theatre in the 1960s and 1970s: a historical-critical analysis of the movement
pp.v, 188     MH
Westport CT: Greenwood P.     1985

**1645** FORTE, JEANIE K. Women in performance art: feminism and postmodernism
Seattle: U. of Washington (PhD)     1986

**1646** SZILASSY, ZOLTAN. American theatre of the 1960s
pp.xiii, 113     MH
Carbondale: Southern Illinois U. P.     1986
First section emphasizes Albee, the second examines radical theatre movements and happenings.

**1647** DOHERTY, MARY L. A ritual analysis of encounter groups and experimental theatre in the sixties
Chicago: U. (PhD)     1987

**1648** GREENE, ALEXIS. Revolutions off off Broadway, 1959-1969: a critical study of changes in structure, character, language, and theme in experimental drama in New York city
NY: City U. (PhD)     1987

**1649** MARINIS, MARCO DE. Il nuovo teatro 1947-1970
pp.ix, 310     M
Milan: Bompiani     1987
Material on the *avant-garde* theatre on and off-Broadway, the Living Theatre, happenings, San Francisco Mime Troupe, the Bread and Puppet Theatre.

**1650** GRAY, SIMON. How's that for telling 'em, fat lady ?
pp.iv, 236     M
London: Faber     1988
An account of the US production of Gray's play *The Common Pursuit*.

**1651** HOUSE, JANE (Ed.). Political theatre today
pp.iii,116     ★
NY: Columbia U.     1988

**1652** JENKINS, RON. Acrobats of the soul: comedy and virtuousity in contemporary American theatre
pp.xx, 179 ★
NY: TCG 1988

**1653** NEWHOUSE, JOHN W. An examination of closed circuit television integrated into avant-garde theatre performance
NY: U. (PhD) 1988

**1654** PARNES, UZI. Pop performance, four seminal influences: the work of Jack Smith, Tom Murrin-the alien comic, Ethyl Eichenberg, and the Split Britches Company
NY: U. (PhD) 1988

**1655** SCHECHNER, RICHARD. Performance theory
pp.xv, 304; ill. in text L
NY: Routledge 1988

A revised and expanded edition. First published NY: DBS, 1977 as *Essays on performance theory*. The semiotics of performance presented in a planned sequence of essays drawing on a wide range of cultures and historical periods.

**1656** VAN ERVEN, EUGENE. Radical people's theatre
pp.xv, 238; ill. in text M
Bloomington: Indiana U. P. 1988
A history of radical popular theatre in Western Europe and the US, focusing on the author's perception of the most resilient groups. Chapter two provides an historical perspective. Chapter three examines the San Francisco Mime Troupe, El Teatro Campesino, and the Bread and Puppet Theatre.

**1657** SAYRE, HENRY M. The object of performance: the American avant-garde since 1970
pp.xvi, 308; ill. in text, pl. 2 col. M
Chicago: U.P. 1989
Examines dance, photography, oral poetry, performance art, earth sculpture and suggests an audience-orientated association.

# 6. LOCATION

## 6.1 REGIONS

**1658** BUNN, ALFRED. Old England and New England, in a series of views taken on the spot
pp.xxi, 313; viii, 328; pl. 2 (1 folding, 1 col.) L
London: Richard Bentley 1853
Two volumes. US edition in one volume, Philadelphia: Hart, 1853.

**1659** DORMON, JAMES H. Theater in the ante-bellum South
pp.xvi, 322; pl. 4 M
Chapel Hill: U. of N. Carolina P. 1867

**1660** THE THEATRICAL GUIDE: route and date book of the New England states, middle states, western states, and provinces
pp.396 MH
Boston: W. B. Johnson 1881
The fifth edition.

**1661** THE DONALDSON GUIDE...[to] all opera-houses in the United States and Canada, together with descriptions of their stages, their seating capacity, and the names of the managers of each...in conjunction with the Showman's Encyclopedia...and the International Professional Register...to which is added the complete code of the Donaldson cypher
pp.418 DL★
Cincinnati OH: W. H. Donaldson 1894

**1662** CAHN, JULIUS. Julius Cahn's official theatrical guide containing information of the leading theatres and attractions in America
pp.750; ill. in text MH; M
NY: Empire Theatre Publication Office 1896-1921
A vital source for booking agents and producers, offering 'definite information concerning theatres, newspapers, hotels and railroads in every city and town of any importance...' Later, the title was extended by the addition '...Canada, Mexico and Cuba'. In 1921 the guide was co-edited by Gus Hill, and subsequently merged with the *Gus Hill theatrical and motion picture guide*.

**1663** GUS HILL'S NATIONAL THEATRICAL directory...1914-1915
pp.686 M
NY: Hill 1914

**1664** HALLOWELL, ALFRED I. Bear ceremonialism in the Northern hemisphere
Philadelphia: U. of Pennsylvania (PhD) 1926

**1665** HINTON, M. M. Southern regional drama, 1918-1933: a study of local and universal aspects of the Southern mountain and farm plays
Northampton MA: Smith College (MA) 1934

**1666** SNOW, CLAUDE S. The drama of the Hopi, Zuni, and Navaho Indians of Southwestern United States
Provo UT: Brigham Young U. (MA) 1934

**1667** CRAIG, HARDIN (Ed.). The Parrott presentation volume
pp.vii, 470; front, M
Princeton: U. P. 1935
Includes George R. Stewart: *The drama in a frontier theater*.

**1668** GARNER, MADELYN L. The early theatre of the Rocky Mountain west
Denver: U. (MA) 1935

**1669** MORSE, WILLIAM N. Contributions to the history of the New England stage in the eighteenth century with special reference to Boston and Portsmouth
Cambridge MA: Harvard U. (PhD) 1936

**1670** ORMAN, GRACE. The straw hat theatre presents
pp.ix, 117 MH
[?]: Printed and published by author 1940
Handbook on summer theatre, with a directory.

**1671** ERNST, ALICE H. The wolf ritual of the Northwest coast
pp.ix, 107; ill. in text, pl. 14 ★
Eugene: U. of Oregon P. 1952

Some of the material first appeared in *Theatre Arts*.

**1672** LANGWORTHY, HELEN. The theater in the frontier cities of Lexington, Kentucky and Cincinatti, Ohio, 1797-1835
Iowa City: U. of Iowa (PhD)      1952

**1673** EFFRAT, JOHN. Blueprint for summer theatre...compiled and edited under the auspices of the American National Theatre and Academy
pp.145; ill. in text      M
NY: John Richard P.      1954
First published NY: 1948. Supplements issued annually.

**1674** SPIER, LESLIE. The sun dance of the plains Indians, its development and diffusion
NY: Columbia U. (PhD)      1959

**1675** BALL, ZACHARY [= Masters, Kelly]. Tent show
pp.186; ill.      DL★
NY: Holiday House      1964

**1676** McKENNON, MARIAN. Tent show
pp.192      M
NY: Exposition P.      1964
Fictionalized reminiscences.

**1677** DAVIS, RONALD L. A history of opera in the American West
pp.xii, 178; pl. 3      L
Englewood Cliffs NJ: Prentice-Hall      1965
Contains much incidental theatre information.

**1678** SNYDER, SHERWOOD. The toby shows
Minneapolis: U. of Minnesota (PhD)      1966

**1679** CADBY, LOUISE K. The history and functioning of the summer theatre in New England
Hempstead NY: Hofstra U. (MA)      1967

**1680** BOCK, FRANK G. A descriptive study of the dramatic function and significance of the clown during Hopi Indian public ceremony
Los Angeles: U. of Southern California (PhD)      1971

**1681** HARRIGAN, W. PATRICK. A history of the Southwest theatre conference
Baton Rouge: Louisiana State U. (PhD)      1971

**1682** SLOUT, WILLIAM L. Theatre in a tent: the development of a provincial entertainment
pp.xi, 153; pl. 13      M
Bowling Green OH: U. P.      1972
Travelling dramatic companies in portable tents and small town fit-ups, c. 1885-1920.

**1683** LEWIS, PHILIP C. Trouping: how the show came to town
pp.xiv, 266; ill. in text      M
NY: Harper & Row      1973
An evocation of the life of a touring player.

**1684** GOODRICH, ANNE. Enjoying the summer theatres of New England
pp.ii, 250; ill. in text      MH
Chester CT: Pequot P.      1974

A guide book.

**1685** KUTRZEBA, JOSEPH S. Artistic guidelines for the establishment of resident theatres in the United States
NY: U. (PhD)      1974

**1686** MICKEL, JERE C. Footlights on the prairie
pp.xii, 226; ill. in text, pl. 4      MH
St Cloud MN: North Star P.      1974
'The story of the repertory tent players in the midwest', c.1915-63.

**1687** WRIGHT, JAMES C. Development of the Black Hills Passion Play in Spearfish, South Dakota and Lake Wales, Florida
Columbus: Ohio State U. (PhD)      1974

**1688** LONEY, GLENN & McKAY, PATRICIA. The Shakespeare complex: a guide to summer festivals and year-round repertory in North America
pp.182; ill.      DL★
NY: Drama Book Specialists      1975

**1689** SCHWARZ, LYLE A. Theatre on the Gold Frontier: a cultural study of five Northwest mining towns, 1860-1870
Pullman: Washington State U. (PhD)      1975
Boise, Helena, Idaho City, Virginia City, Walla Walla.

**1690** DIXON, HAROLD W. Regional theatres profile: decentralized theatre in America. A comparative study and critical analysis of two regional centres: Minneapolis, St Paul and Los Angeles
Minneapolis: U. of Minnesota (PhD)      1976

**1691** BERLOGEA, ILEANA. Teatrul american de azi: calatorie teatrala prin Statele Unite
pp.194      ★
Cluj: Dacia      1978
A survey of theatre centres.

**1692** SANTINO, JACK (Ed.). Festival of American folklife
pp.40, 16 (programme); ill. in text      M
Washington DC: Smithsonian Institute      1981
Includes Glenn Hinson: *Trouping under canvas, the American tent show tradition*.

**1693** SELLER, MAXINE S. (Ed.). Ethnic theatre in the United States
pp.viii. 607; ill. in text      M
Westport CT: Greenwood P.      1983
Nishan Parlakian: *Armenian-American*; Edward G. Smith: *Black*; Vitaut Kipel & Zora Kipel: *Byelorussian-American...*; Clinton M. Hyde: *Danish-American*; Timo R. Riipa & Michael G. Karni: *Finnish-American*; Mathé Allain & Adele C. St Martin: *French theatre in Louisiana*; Christa Carvajal: *German-American*; Thomas Szendrey: *Hungarian-American*; Maureen Murphy: *Irish*; Emelise Aleandri & Maxine S. Seller: *Italian-American*; Alfreds Straumanis: *Latvian-American*; Bronius Vaskelis: *Lithuanian-American*; John W. Brokaw: *Mexican-American*; Jeffrey F. Huntsman: *Native American*; Arthur L. Waldo: *Polish-American*; Rosa Luisa Marquez & Lowell A. Fiet: *Puerto Rican theatre on the mainland*; M. Martina Tybor: *Slovak-American...*; Anne-Charlotte H. Harvey: *Swedish-American...*; Larissa Onyshkevych: *Ukrainian-American...*; David S. Lifson: *Yiddish*. Ethnic theatre in other languages than English is not treated in this bibliography. The various cultures e.g German, Spanish etc., will be discussed in the appropriate volumes of *The Motley Bibliographies* .

**1694** BIRDWELL, CHRISTINE R. Heroines of American midwestern repertoire theatre comedy-dramas (melodrama, tent shows, popular culture)
East Lansing: Michigan State U. (PhD)      1984

**1695** MARTIN, JERRY L. Henry L. Brunk and Brunk's comedians tent repertoire empire of the southwest
pp.vi, 191; ill. in text  L
Bowling Green OH: State U. Popular P.  1984
Includes substantial listing of shows and personnel, 1916-1958.

**1696** KASH, BETTYE C. Outdoor historical dramas in the Eastern United States
Indianapolis: Indiana U. (PhD)  1985

**1697** NORMAN, STANLEY S. A systems analysis of the Southwest Theatre Association: an internship
Lubbock: Texas Tech U. (PhD)  1988

**1698** KOON, HELENE W. How Shakespeare won the West. players and performances in America's Gold Rush, 1849-1865
pp.xiii, 177; pl. 4  M
Jefferson NC: McFarland  1989

**1699** SPRAGUE, KATHLEEN J. The Haverstock family Tent Show
Lubbock: Texas Tech U. (PhD)  1989

**1700** OGDEN, DUNBAR H.; McDERMOTT, DOUGLAS & SARLOS, ROBERT K. (Eds). Theatre west: image and impact
pp.viii, 254; ill. in text  M
Amsterdam: Rodopi  1990
Joanne Lafler: *Seeded in the grove itself: theatrical evolution at the Bohemian Club encampment*; Wendell Cole: *Myth makers and the early years of the Carmel Forest Theatre*; Roberta R. Asahina: *The Salt Lake City theatre, a civilizing agent*; Margaret B. Wilkerson: *The black theatre experience: PASLA*; Douglas McDermott: *An American theatrical everyman, the career of Lambert F. Beatty*; Richard G. Hiatt: *Lady troupers along the Oregon Trail*; Charles E. Lanterbach: *Langrishe and Glenn's 'Black Crook' tour of California, Nevada and Mexico, 1874-1875*; Rosemarie K. Bank: *Frontier melodrama*; Dana S. McDermott: *Western landscape as archetypal dream: the influence of Taos, New Mexico, on Robert Edmond Jones's 'Macbeth'*. Foreword by William Everson.

## 6.2 STATES AND TOWNS
### 6.2.1 ALABAMA

**1701** BAILEY, FRANCES M. A history of the stage in Mobile, Alabama from 1824-1850
Iowa City: U. of Iowa (MA)  1934

**1702** CHILES, RUTH. The Birmingham theatres 1866-1900
Birmingham: Southern College (MA)  1936

**1703** DUGGAR, MARY M. The theatre in Mobile, 1822-1860
Tuscaloosa: U. of Alabama (MA)  1941

**1704** ELLISON, RHODA C. Early Alabama publications: a study in library interests
pp.xv, 213  MH
Tuscaloosa: Alabama U. P.  1947
Some reference to theatre reviews and published plays.

**1705** TURNIPSEED, La M. The ante bellum theatre in Montgomery, Alabama: 1840-1860
Auburn AL: U. (MS)  1948

**1706** BROWN, EDWARD D. A history of theatrical activities at the Mobile Theatre, Mobile, Alabama from 1860-1875
East Lansing: Michigan State U. (MA)  1952

**1707** ADAMS, HENRY V. The Montgomery Theatre 1822-1835
pp.v, 81  M
Tuscaloosa: U. of Alabama P.  1955

A history based on notes left by James R. Rutland.

**1708** GORDON, BARBARA E. Prosperous and preposterous theatres in Alabama 1817-1860
Chapel Hill: U. of North Carolina (MA)  1971

**1709** WALTON, ELSIE M. A history of theatre in Mobile, Alabama 1822-1971
University Park: Pennsylvania State U. (MA)  1971

**1710** HAARBAUER, DON W. A critical history of the non-academic theatre in Birmingham, Alabama
Madison: U. of Wisconsin (PhD)  1973

**1711** GOING, WILLIAM T. Essays in Alabama literature
pp.vii, 176  MH
Tuscaloosa: Alabama U. P.  1975
Includes an essay on Augustus Thomas, comparing *Alabama* with Lillian Hellman's *Little Foxes* and *Another Part of the Forest*.

**1712** WOODRUFF, BOYKIN M. A chronicle of professional dramatic activities at the Mobile theatre under the management of Jacob Tannenbaum from 1844 through 1889
Athens: U. of Georgia (MA)  1975

**1713** VOLZ, JIM. Shakespeare never slept here. The making of a regional theatre. A history of the Alabama Shakespeare festival
pp.x, 171; ill. in text, some col.  M
Atlanta GA: Cherokee Publishing  1986

### 6.2.2 ALASKA

**1714** O'CONNOR, RICHARD. High jinks on the Klondike
pp.284  DL★
NY: Bobbs-Merrill  1954
With material on late nineteenth century Yukon theatre, tenting shows and Uncle Tom companies.

**1715** O'CONNOR, RICHARD. Gold, dice and women
pp.284  L
London: Alvin Redman  [1956]

Includes a chapter on theatre entertainment in the Klondyke of the Gold Rush.

**1716** EVANS, CHAD. Frontier theatre: a history of nineteenth-century theatrical entertainment in the Canadian far west and Alaska
pp.326; front., pl. 20  M
Victoria B.C.: Sono Nis P.  1983

**1717** STEVENS, GARY L. Gold rush theatre in the Alaska-Yukon frontier
Eugene: U. of Oregon (PhD)  1984

## 6.2.3 ARIZONA

**1718** WILLSON, CLAIR E. Mimes and miners. A historical study of the theater in Tombstone
pp.207; ill. in text      M
Tucson: U. of Arizona      1935
*U. of Arizona Fine Arts Bulletin No. 1 (U. of Arizona Bulletin VI, 7, 1/11/35)*

**1719** RYAN, PAT M. Tombstone theatre tonight ! A chronicle of entertainment on the southwest mining frontier
pp.49-76; ill. in text      M
Tucson: Tucson Corral of the Westerners      1966
*The Smoke Signal*, no. 13. Tombstone theatre in the 1880s.

**1720** GIPSON, ROSEMARY P. The history of Tucson theatre before 1906
Tucson: U. of Arizona (MA)      1967

## 6.2.4 ARKANSAS

**1721** WOOTEN, DENHAM L. Annals of the stage in Little Rock. Arkansas 1834-1890
NY: Columbia U. (MA)      1935

**1722** REED, CHARLES E. An historical study of professional dramatic entertainment in Little Rock, Arkansas 1889-1899
Gainsville: U. of Florida (MA)      1949

**1723** TEDFORD, HAROLD. A study of the theatrical entertainments in northwest Arkansas from their beginnings through 1889
Baton Rouge: Louisiana State U. (PhD)      1965

**1724** MENEFEE, LARRY T. Death of a road show town: Little Rock, Arkansas 1899-1921
Denver: U. (PhD)      1977

## 6.2.5 CALIFORNIA

**1725** ORPHEUM CIRCUIT of theatres: brochure published upon the occasion of the dedication of the New Orpheum Theatre, San Francisco, April 19, 1909
pp.44; ill. in text      DL★
]NY]: [Orpheum Theatre and Realty]      1909

**1726** THE ART THEATRE of Hollywood (Incorporated)
pp.4      M
[Hollywood]:      [1924]
Pamphlet publicizing the aims and principles of the proposed theatre and soliciting subscriptions.

**1727** KER, MINETTE A. The history of the theatre in California in the nineteenth century
Berkeley: U. of California (MA)      1924

**1728** BORUM, MAY R. A history of the Pasadena community playhouse
Los Angeles: U. of Southern California (MA)      1929

**1729** BARNETT, MARTHA I. A historical sketch of the professional theatre in the city of Los Angeles to 1911
Los Angeles: U. of Southern California (MA)      1930

**1730** CHESTER, VIOLET L. The history of the theatre in San Francisco from the gold rush to the conflagration
Stanford: U. (MA)      1930

**1731** KAUFFMAN, WILLIAM C. A study of the historical plays and pageants of California
Los Angeles: U. of Southern California (MA)      1931

**1732** NEVILLE, AMELIA R. The fantastic city: memoirs of the social and romantic life of old San Francisco
pp.xiii, 285; front., pl. 31      L
Boston: Houghton Mifflin      1932
Frequent reference to theatre and other entertainments. Edited and revised by Virginia Brastov.

**1733** HARRINGTON, DONAL F. Productions of Shakespeare in San Francisco from 1850 through 1855
NY: Columbia U. (MA)      1933

**1734** BAER, WARREN. *The Duke of Sacramento*; a comedy in four acts reprinted from the rare edition of 1856, to which is added a sketch of the early San Francisco stage, by Jane Bissell Grabhorn, and illustrations by Arvilla Parker
pp.xii, 78; ill. in text      MH
San Francisco: Grabhorn P.      1934
550 copies.

**1735** GREEN, HARRIET L.; CHAPIN, ROBERT F. & MAXWELL, EVERETT C. Book of the Pasadena Community Playhouse
pp.76      NN★
Pasadena CA: Pasadena Playhouse P.      1934

**1736** HINKEL, EDGAR J. (Ed.). Bibliography of Californian fiction, poetry, drama...in three volumes...produced on a Works Progress Administration project [Volume 3, drama]
pp.ii, 306      DL★
Oakland CA: Alameda County Library      [1938?]
Mimeographed. A companion work, *Criticism of California literature...* was completed and issued in 1940 in similar format, three volumes continuously paged with the third volume on drama.

**1737** SAN FRANCISCO THEATRE research: history of the San Francisco theatre
pp.various; ill. in text      MH
San Francisco: Writers' Project of the WPA      1938-42
Twenty volumes, mimeographed. A series of monographs: 'the theatre and its people in San Francisco from 1849 to the present day.' l. Introduction; Stephen Massett, singer, writer, showman; Joseph A. Rowe, pioneer circus manager. 2. Tom Maguire; Dr David G. (Yankee) Robinson; M. B. Leavitt. 3. The Stars; the Bakers; the Chapmans. 4. Junius Brutus Booth, the elder; Junius Brutus Booth Jr; Edwin Booth. 5. Lola Montez; Adah Isaacs Menken; Mrs Judah. 6. Lotta Crabtree; John McCullough. 7. Opera in S.F. part one. 8. part two. 9. The French theatre in S.F.; the German theatre in S. F. 10. The Italian theatre in S. F. 11. Edwin Forrest; Catherine Sinclair. 12. Little theatres [by Alan Harrison]. 13. Minstrelsy. 14. History of burlesque [by Ettore Rella]. 15. Theatre buildings, 1849-61. 16. Famous playhouses, 1861-75. 17. Famous playhouses, 1861-1906. 18 & 19, not seen. 20. James O'Neill. The series was suspended, the given reason

being 'the present emphasis placed on works furthering the war effort' (letter from W. R. Lawson, administrator, August 1942).

**1738** WALKER, FRANKLIN D.  San Francisco's literary frontier
pp.xiii, 400, xxv; pl. 16  MH
NY: Alfred A. Knopf  1939
Includes material on Ada Clare, Adah Isaacs Menken.

**1739** BULLETIN OF THE DRAMATISTS' ALLIANCE: competitions and assembly 1941
DL★
Stanford CA: U.P.  1941–
Annual. Titles of subsequent issues vary.

**1740** JACOBSON, PAULINE.  City of the golden 'fifties
pp.xvii, 290  L
Berkeley: U. of California P.  1941
Impressions of old San Francisco. Chapters on Stephen Massett, Lola Montez, Adah Isaacs Menken, Edwin Booth, Matilda Heron, Tom Maguire, minstrelsy, the playhouses. Edited by Harold S. Small.

**1741** MacMINN, GEORGE R.  The theater of the golden era in California
pp.529; pl. 35  M
Caldwell, ID: Caxton Printers  1941
Gold Rush period, 1850-60.

**1742** MASON, RAYMOND M.  An historical study of the little theatre movement in the city of San Diego, California
Los Angeles: U. of Southern California (MA)  1942

**1743** TYLER, PAMELA F.  The Los Angeles Theatre 1840-1900
Los Angeles: U. of Southern California (MA)  1942

**1744** DICKSON, SAMUEL.  San Francisco in your home
pp.viii, 262; ill. in text, tinted  O
Stanford CA: U. P.  1947
Chapters on Adah Isaacs Menken, Edwin Booth, Lotta Crabtree, minstrelsy, David Belasco.

**1745** EARNEST, SUE W.  An historical study of the growth of the theatre in Southern California 1848-1894
Los Angeles: U. of Southern California (PhD)  1947

**1746** ANDERSON, EARL.  The San Francisco opera company. The first twenty-five years
Seattle: U. of Washington (MA)  1948

**1747** GAGEY, EDMOND M.  The San Francisco stage: a history, based on annals compiled by the research department of the San Francisco Federal Theatre
pp.xv, 264; pl. 8  M
NY: Columbia U. P.  1950

**1748** TRULSSON, BERTON E.  A historical study of the theatre of the Mother-Lode during the gold rush period
Stockton CA: U. of the Pacific (MA)  1950

**1749** FENTON, FRANK L. (Ed.).  Pioneer western playbills
DL★
San Francisco: Book Club of California  1951

Boxed set of facsimiles with commentary. Includes the opening of the California Theatre, 1869; Adah Isaacs Menken's *Mazeppa* at Maguire's Opera House, San Francisco, 1863; Baldwin's Theatre, Virginia City NV; Lotta Crabtree in *Little Nell and the Marchioness*.

**1750** JOHNSON, HAROLD E.  A survey of theatre organization as practised by a select group of community theatres in the Los Angeles area
Los Angeles: U. of Southern California (MA)  1951

**1751** JONES, IDWAL.  Ark of empire: San Francisco's Montgomerie Block. Illustrated by A. J. Camille
pp.253; ill. in text  MH
Garden City: Doubleday  1951
With theatrical associations.

**1752** McCURDY, EVELYN M.  The history of the Adelphi Theatre, San Francisco, California 1850-1858
Stanford: U. (MA)  1952

**1753** FENTON, FRANK L.  The San Francisco theatre 1849-1859
Stanford: U. (PhD)  1953

**1754** JUMONVILLE, MARY L.  The history and philosophy of the Pasedena Community Playhouse
Ann Arbor: U. of Michigan (MA)  1953

**1755** STOCK, MORGAN E.  The Carmel theatre from 1910-1935
Stanford: U. (MA)  1953

**1756** GRIFFITHS, PHILIP R.  A history of the Emerson Minstrels on the San Francisco stage 1870-1889
Stanford: U. (MA)  1954

**1757** HUME, CHARLES V.  The Sacramento theatre 1849-1885
Stanford: U. (PhD)  1955

**1758** SCHMIDT, INGE.  Stanford's developing theatre, 1905-1920
Stanford: U. (MA)  1955

**1759** ABRAMS, DOLORES.  A history of Palo Alto community theatre, 1931-1936
Stanford: U. (MA)  1956

**1760** LEECING, WALDEN A.  The Santa Ana community players (1920-1927)
Stanford: U. (MA)  1956

**1761** REPORT TO THE COUNTY of Los Angeles on a new auditorium and music center
pp.101; ill. in text, some col.  DL★
Cambridge MA: Arthur D. Little  1956
A feasibility study.

**1762** ZELVER, LESLIE H.  Non-investment theatre in San Francisco, 1914-1954
Los Angeles: U. of California (MA)  1956

**1763** BAZARINI, RON.  The organization and management of the actors' workshop of the San Francisco Drama Guild Incorporated
Stanford: U. (MA)  1957

**1764** DICKSON, SAMUEL.  Tales of San Francisco comprising *San Francisco is your home*, *San Francisco kaleidoscope* and *The streets of San Francisco*
pp.viii, 711  M
Stanford: U. P.  1957

Three books in one, originally published separately. Late 19th-early 20th century, with theatre reference throughout.

**1765** DONNELLY, JOHN E. The old Globe Theater in San Diego, California: an historical survey of its origin and development
Los Angeles: U. of California (MA)     1957

**1766** WILSON, ADRIAN. Printing for the theater
pp.v, 57; ill. in text, interleafed material     MH
San Francisco: [For the author?]     1957
Wilson, self-described as 'printer to the Interplayers', describes his work with this San Francisco drama group and incidentally evokes their style and attitude. 250 copies.

**1767** THUNEN, FRANCES H. The Sacramento Civic Theatre: a study of its origins, development, and functions as a community service
Berkeley: U. of California (MA)     1959

**1768** BLOOMFIELD, ARTHUR J. The San Francisco opera, 1923-1961
pp.xi, 251; pl 16     L
NY: Appleton-Century-Crofts     1961

**1769** DEUEL, PAULINE B. Mexican serenade: the story of the Mexican players and the Padua Hills theatre...photographs by Irene Welch Garner
pp.xv, 80; ill. in text     M
Claremont CA: Padua Institute     1961

**1770** KRUMM, WALTER C. The San Francisco stage 1969-1879
Stanford: U. (PhD)     1961

**1771** ECKLEY, DON M. The world's longest run: a descriptive and analytical study of the Los Angeles theater mart's twenty-six years of continuous production of *The Drunkard* and its musical companion *The Wayward Way*
Los Angeles: U. of California (MA)     1962

**1772** BETTENDORF, FRANK B. Dramatic activities of the Humboldt Bay area 1880 to 1912
Los Angeles: U. of California (MA)     1963

**1773** BOWER, HOMER T. San Francisco Opera Company scene design, 1932-1955
Stanford: U. (PhD)     1963

**1774** WENTE, WILLIAM C. The Oakland Theatre 1890-1915
Stanford: U. (PhD)     1965

**1775** SHOUP, GAIL L. The Pasadena Community Playhouse: its origins and history from 1917 to 1942
Los Angeles: U. of California (PhD)     1967

**1776** THUNEN, FRANCES H. A historical study of The Circle, The Player's Ring, and The Player's Ring Gallery Theatres in Hollywood from 1945 to 1966
Los Angeles: U. of Southern California (PhD)     1967

**1777** BURGESS, FRANK G. Behind the scenes: glimpses of fin-de-siècle San Francisco
pp.128; ill. in text     O
San Francisco: Book Club of California     1968

**1778** McCRARY, MARGARET M. The Alcazar and the President Theatre in San Francisco under the management of Henry Duffy, 1924-26
Stanford: U. (MA)     1968

**1779** NOLD, BENJAMIN M. History of the theatre in Stockton, California, 1880-1892
Salt Lake City: U. of Utah (PhD)     1968

**1780** LANE, MORGAN J. Commercial theatre in San Diego with special emphasis 1892-1917
San Diego: State U. (MA)     1969

**1781** LARIMER, MICHAEL W. Theatre in the San Joaquin Valley: a pilot study of theatrical activities 1870-1900
Fresno: California State U. (MA)     1969

**1782** SMITH, TALLANT. The history of the theatre in Santa Barbara 1767-1894
Santa Barbara: U. of California (MA)     1969

**1783** AUSBURN, LYNNE J. Highlights of the theatre of the West: its beginnings and its development on the mining frontiers of California and Nevada
Tulsa: U. (MA)     1970

**1784** CONN, ARTHUR L. The history of the Loring Opera House, Riverside, California
Los Angeles: U. of California (MA)     1970

**1785** GAER, JOSEPH (Ed.). The theatre of the gold rush decade in San Francisco
pp.iv, 101     M
NY: Burt Franklin     1970
Reprint of first edition (1935). Originally an abstract from SERA project, California library research project 5. Alphabetical listing of titles, with date and theatre, of plays, extravaganzas, ballets and pantomimes, opera, and minstrel shows, with author index.

**1786** KIRSCHMAN, MARVIN. A historical study of the Belasco Theatre in Los Angeles and the forces that shaped its history
Los Angeles: U. of Southern California (PhD)     1970

**1787** SMITH, LARRY A. The history of the Barton Opera House, Fresno, California 1890-1914
Fresno: California State U. (MA)     1970

**1788** WILBUR, CHERYL R. A phoenix comes to rest: the history of the Los Angeles Shrine Civic Theatre Auditorium, 1920-1965
Los Angeles: U. of California (PhD)     1970

**1789** EGAN, FRANK. Minstrelsy in San Francisco 1848-1870
Sacramento: California State U. (MA)     1971

**1790** KAUFMAN, EDWARD K. A history of the development of professional theatrical activity in Los Angeles 1880-1895
Los Angeles: U. of Southern California (Thesis)     1972

**1791** McELHANEY, JOHN S. The professional theatre in San Francisco 1880-1889
Stanford: U. (PhD)     1972

**1792** WADE, JERE D. The San Francisco stage 1859-1869
Eugene: U. of Oregon (PhD)     1972

**1793** WALKER, PHILLIP N. A history of theatrical activity in Fresno, California from its beginnings in 1872 to the opening of the White Theatre in 1914
Los Angeles: U. of Southern California (PhD)     1972

**1794** WILKERSON, MARGARET B. Black theatres in the San Francisco Bay area and in the Los Angeles area: a report and analysis
Berkeley: U. of California (PhD) 1972

**1795** WOODS, ALAN L. The interaction of Los Angeles theatre and society between 1895 and 1906: a case study
Los Angeles: U. of Southern California (PhD) 1972

**1796** BOKAR, CAMILLE N. An historical study of the legitimate theatre in Los Angeles, 1920-1929, and its relation to the national theatrical scene
Los Angeles: U. of Southern California (PhD) 1973

**1797** EMMES, DAVID M. South Coast repertory, 1963-1972: a case study
Los Angeles: U. of Southern California (PhD) 1973

**1798** HELGESEN, TERRY. The Hollywood Pantages
pp.[24]; ill. in text M
Washington DC: Theatre Historical Society 1973
A photographic record of the theatre restored in the 1960s.

**1799** ESSER, GRACE D. Madame Impressario: a personal chronicle of an epoch. Foreword by Merle Armitage
pp.iv,230; ill. in text M
Yucca Valley CA: Manzanita P. 1974
Memoirs of Grace Denton, founder of the Musical Academy of the West in Santa Barbara.

**1800** STARK, SAM (Ed.). Early California theatres
pp.various; ill. in text MH
San Francisco: Book Club of California 1974
A boxed set of folders, comprising an introduction and ten brief monographs. Theatres are: Nevada Theatre; American Theatre, San Francisco; Woodland Opera House; Eagle Theatre, Sacramento; Stockton Theatre; Fallon House, Columbia; Maguire's Opera House, San Francisco; Grand Opera House, San Francisco; First Theatre, Monterey; and Merced Theatre, Los Angeles.

**1801** WEBSTER, MARY V. The San Francisco stage: a daily calendar of performances 1849-1859
Northridge: California State U. (MA) 1974

**1802** MONSON, WILLIAM N. Frontier theatre town: an historical study of some paratheatrical activities in Visalia, California 1852 to 1889
Eugene: U. of Oregon (PhD) 1976

**1803** RATHER, LOIS. Bonanza theater
pp.114 DL★
Oaklands CA: Rather P. 1977
150 numbered copies.

**1804** JENCKS, LANCE H. The San Francisco Mime Troupe in its social context
Davis: U. of California (PhD) 1978

**1805** MANN, MARY & TATAR, RAY (Eds). The Los Angeles theatre book - a comprehensive handbook for playgoers...with articles by Ron Pennington of *The Hollywood Reporter*, Gil Laurence of *The California Arts Council*, Estelle Busch and Cyndi Turtledove of *The Los Angeles Theatre Alliance*
pp.iv, 188; ill. in text MH
Los Angeles: Ariel Publications 1978
In effect, a directory.

**1806** NARDONE, DIANE C. The history of the San Quentin drama workshop
NY: U. (PhD) 1978

**1807** THIS, JAMES L. The old Globe Theatre and Carter Center stage, San Diego: an analytical and historical study
Los Angeles: U. of Southern California (PhD) 1978

**1808** SACKS, BENJAMIN. Carson Mansion and Ingomar Theatre. Cultural adventures in California
pp.xvi, 165; ill. in text M
Fresno CA: Valley 1979
Historical and architectural account of the Ingomar Theatre, Eureka CA.

**1809** SHEFFEY-STINSON, SANDI. The history of theatre productions at the Los Angeles Inner City Cultural Center: 1965-1976
Kent OH: State U. (PhD) 1979

**1810** DORAN, PHILIP C. From the company theatre to the provisional theatre, Los Angeles, 1967-1979: a contemporary search for aesthetic balance
Los Angeles: U. of Southern California (PhD) 1980

**1811** HUBER, ROBERT C. The Merced Theatre of Los Angeles: an analysis of its management and architecture, 1870-1879
Los Angeles: U. of Southern California (PhD) 1980

**1812** DEVINE, PHILIP P. The relationship between the leadership effectiveness of theatre administrators and the organizational effectiveness of non-profit professional theatre organizations in the San Francisco Bay area
San Francisco: U. (EdD) 1981

**1813** STONE, SUSANNAH H. The Oakland Paramount
pp.94; ill. in text, some col. M
Berkeley CA: Lancaster-Miller 1981
Art-deco theatre and movie house built in 1925.

**1814** PIPER, JUDITH A. Visual theatre, San Francisco Bay area, 1975-1984. Creating exceptional realities
Davis: U. of California (PhD) 1985

**1815** GERSH, ELLYN M. The Mark Taper Forum [Los Angeles], 1967-1982: a critical assessment
Los Angeles: U. of California (PhD) 1986

**1816** WEINER, SYDELL S. South Coast repertory theatre; growth and development, 1973-1985
NY: U. (PhD) 1986

**1817** HORNER, JOHN. The San Francisco Passion Play of 1879
Santa Barbara: U. of California (PhD) 1989

**1818** SHANK, THEODORE. California performance. Volume 1. San Francisco Bay area: interviews and essays...
pp.297; ill. in text M
Pomona CA: Pomona College Theatre Dept./Claremont Colleges 1989
An issue of the annual *Mime Journal*. Includes a survey of experimental theatre and transcribed interviews.

## 6.2.6 COLORADO

**1819** GRIFFIN, EVELYN. Early theatres and theatrical events in Denver
Denver: U. (MA) 1923

**1820** HOLLINGSWORTH, MARY C. A history of the theatre of Denver, Colorado
Los Angeles: U. of Southern California (MA) 1933

**1821** DEGITZ, DOROTHY M. History of the Tabor Opera House, Leadville, Colorado from 1879 to 1905
Gunnison: Western State College of Colorado (MA) 1935

**1822** PERRIGO, LYNN. A social history of Central City, Colorado, 1859-1900
Boulder: U. of Colorado (PhD) 1936
Includes chapters on theatre and opera.

**1823** NICHOLS, DEAN G. Pioneer theatres of Denver, Colorado
Ann Arbor: U. of Michigan (PhD) 1938

**1824** CROWLEY, ELMER S. History of the Tabor Grand Opera House, Denver, Colorado 1881-1891
Denver: U. (MA) 1940

**1825** BELL, WILLIAM C. A history of the Denver theatre during the post-pioneer period (1881-1901)
Evanston: Northwestern U. (PhD) 1941

**1826** SCHOBERLIN, MELVIN. From candles to footlights: a biography of the Pike's Peak Theatre, 1859-1876
pp.xviii, 322; pl. 20  L
Denver: Fred A. Rosenstock 1941
Preface by Barrett H. Clark. Also lists Colorado theatres, with locations and opening dates.

**1827** STEINHARDT, GERTRUDE M. Dramatic episodes in the history of the Denver Tabor Grand Opera House
Denver: U. (MA) 1941

**1828** WINTERS, EARLE. A history of theatrical activities in Denver, 1901 to 1921
Denver: U. (PhD) 1957

**1829** GERN, JESSE W. Colorado mountain theatre: a history of theatre at Central City 1859-1885
Columbus: Ohio State U. (PhD) 1960

**1830** LEVY, EDWIN L. Elitch's Gardens, Denver, Colorado: a history of the oldest summer theatre in the United States
NY: Columbia U. Teachers' College (PhD) 1960

**1831** HENSLEY, MICHAEL. A history of the theatre in Leadville, Colorado from its beginning to 1900
Laramie: U. of Wyoming (MA) 1963

**1832** DECHAINE, FABER B. Colorado mountain theatre. A history of theatrical festivals of Central City, Colorado, from 1932 to 1960
Minneapolis: U. of Minnesota (PhD) 1964

**1833** KLAIBER, ROGER C. A historical study of theatre in Georgetown, Colorado 1867-1892
Boulder: U. of Colorado (MA) 1964

**1834** RIKER, KITTIE B. Theatrical activity in Aspen, Colorado from 1881 to 1893
Boulder: U. of Colorado (MA) 1964

**1835** SHAW, BERTHA L. History of the Wheeler Opera, Aspen, Colorado 1889-1894
Gunnison CO: Western State College (MA) 1965

**1836** ADAMS, ALLEN J. A historical study of the legitimate theatre in Cripple Creek, Colorado 1897-1907
De Kalb: Northern Illinois U. (MA) 1967

**1837** JONES, KENNETH L. The theatrical history of Greeley, Colorado 1870-1908
Fenver: U. (PhD) 1967

**1838** DRAPER, BENJAMIN P. Colorado theatres 1859-1869
Denver: U. (PhD) 1969

**1839** HATCHER, E. MARTIN. A history of the theatre in Gunnison, Colorado and Salida, Colorado
Denver: U. (PhD) 1969

**1840** FURMAN, EVELYN E. The Tabor Opera House: a captivating history
pp.188; ill.  DL★
Leadville CO: [For the author?]  [1972?]

**1841** BARNES, JACK D. Simeon Nash Nye, pioneer Colorado theatre manager 1882-1914
Denver: U. (PhD) 1972

**1842** DONEGAN, BILLIE D. An historical analysis of theatre audiences in Cripple Creek, Colorado from 1897-1907
Fort Collins: Colorado State U. (MA) 1972

## 6.2.7 CONNECTICUT

**1843** JOHNSON, FRANCES H. Musical memories of Hartford drawn from records, public and private
pp.313; ill.  DL★
Hartford: Witkower's  [1931]

**1844** HARMON, CHARLOTTE & TAYLOR, ROSEMARY. Broadway in a barn...Illustrated by Sam Norkin
pp.ix, 242; ill. in text  MH
NY: Thomas Y. Crowell  1957
Summer stock in Connecticut.

**1845** HOUSEMAN, JOHN & LANDAU, JACK. The American Shakespeare festival: the birth of a theatre
pp.96; ill. in text  M
NY: Simon and Schuster  1959
History of the theatre at Stratford CT from its inception in 1950 through the fourth repertory season in 1958.

**1846** WOODMAN, WILLIAM E. The third Stratford: a history of the American Shakespeare Festival, 1950-1958
NY: Columbia U. (MA)  1959

**1847** JOHNSON, FOSTER M.  The Royal Little Lincoln Theatre
pp.xi, 115; ill.　　　　　　　　　　　　　　DL★
Meriden CT: Bayberry Hill P.　　　　　　　1962

**1848** BUXTON, AMITY L.  Audiences and audience reactions at the American Shakespeare Festival Theatre, Stratford, Connecticut. Summer repertory, 1957
NY: Columbia U. (PhD)　　　　　　　　　1963

**1849** GOURD, E. W.  A study of the Henry Opera House, Rochville, Connecticut
Athens: Ohio U. (MFA)　　　　　　　　　1964

**1850** BLOOM, ARTHUR W.  The history of the theatre in New Haven, Connecticut before 1860
New Haven: Yale U. (PhD)　　　　　　　　1966

**1851** COOTE, ALBERT W.  Four vintage decades: the performing arts in Hartford (1930-1970)
pp.xvi, 378; ill. in text　　　　　　　　　　M
Hartford CT: Huntington　　　　　　　　　1970

**1852** MOSES, WILLIAM A.  Critical response to the costuming styles for Shakespearean productions at the American Shakespeare Festival Theatre, 1955-1976
Kent OH: State U. (PhD)　　　　　　　　1977

**1853** HERKO, MARK S.  A history of the Godspeed Opera House and its contribution to the American musical theatre
Denver: U. (PhD)　　　　　　　　　　　　1983

**1854** COOPER, ROBERTA K.  American Shakespeare Theatre: Stratford, 1955-85
pp.353; ill. in text　　　　　　　　　　　　M
Washington DC: Folger Books　　　　　　1986
Lists productions, with credits, prompt-books and scripts.

## 6.2.8 DELAWARE

**1855** CHANCE, THOMAS E.  A history of theatre in Delaware
Newark: U. of Delaware (BA)　　　　　　1952

**1856** NEESON, JACK M.  The devil in Delaware: a study of theatre in Newcastle County
Cleveland OH: Case Western Reserve U. (PhD)　1959

**1857** BOND, ROGER B.  Wilmington's Masonic Temple and Grand Opera House
Newark: U. of Delaware (MA)　　　　　　1969

**1858** YOUNG, TONI.  The grand experience: a drama in five acts containing a description of Wilmington's Grand Opera House and Masonic Temple, a Victorian building in the second empire style and a history of the many parts it has played in the Delaware community for more than a century
pp.206; ill. in text　　　　　　　　　　　　M
NY: American Life Foundation　　　　　　1976

**1859** STODDARD, ROBERT.  A grand strategy: the scenario for saving the Grand Opera House, Wilmington, Delaware
pp.iv, 40; ill. in text　　　　　　　　　　　M
Washington DC: Preservation P.　　　　　1978

## 6.2.9 FLORIDA

**1860** NOT USED

**1861** BAGLEY, RUSSELL E.  An historical study of theatrical entertainment in Pensacola, Florida 1882-1892
Gainesville: U. of Florida (MA)　　　　　1949

**1862** PARRAMORE, ANNIE E.  An historical study of theatrical presentations at the Jacksonville (Florida) Opera House: 1883-1887
Gainsville: U. of Florida (MA)　　　　　　1954

**1862A** WEST, WILLIAM R.  An historical study of professional theatre activities in Tallahassee, Florida from January 1874 to November 1893
Tallahassee: Florida State U. (MS)　　　　1854

**1863** GILBERT, CREIGHTON.  The Asolo Theatre [cover title]
pp.[46] inc. wrappers; ill. in text　　　　　MH
Sarasota FL: Ringling Museum of Art　　1959
'The only eighteenth century Venetian theatre in America'. Removed from Asolo and re-erected in Florida in 1958.

**1864** ESTES, MAXIE C.  A century of theatre activity in the capital city of Florida: a historical study of theatrical entertainment in Tallahassee Florida from 1857 to 1957
Tallahassee: Florida State U. (PhD)　　　1962

**1865** MILTON, PAULA.  A study of the development of theatre in Greater Miami until 1935
Coral Gables: U. of Miami (MA)　　　　1962

**1866** RYDER, RICHARD D.  A comparative study of selected theatre buildings in South Florida completed between 1951 and 1961
Coral Gables: U. of Miami (MA)　　　　1962

**1867** McDANIEL, HENRY A.  A history of drama in recreation from 1964-1974 in five Florida municipal recreation programs: Tallahassee, Hollywood, Delroy Beach, Dunedin, and Sarasota
Tallahassee: Florida State U. (PhD)　　　1980

**1868** ELLIS, LESLIE E.  The early history of a University-related, regional theatre: a study of the Asolo Theatre, the Asolo theatre festival and the Asolo state theatre through 1966
Tallahassee: Florida State U. (PhD)　　　1982

**1869** McKENNON, JOE.  Rape of an estate
pp.80; ill. in text　　　　　　　　　　　　M
[Sarasota?]: For the author　　　　　　　1986
On the alleged mis-management of the Ringling estate and the Asolo Theatre.

## 6.2.10 GEORGIA

**1870** HESTER, WYOLINE.  The Savannah stage
Auburn AL: U. (MA)　　　　　　　　　　1930

**1871** LANGLEY, WILLIAM O.  The theatre in Columbus, Georgia 1828-1878
Auburn AL: U. (MS)　　　　　　　　　　1937

**1872** SPARKS, ANDREW.  A history of the theatre in Savannah 1800-1836
Athens: U. of Georgia (MA)　　　　　　　1940

## 6.2. STATES AND TOWNS   −1895

**1873** BRAGG, LILLIAN C. & GODLEY, MARGARET W.  Stories of old Savannah: first series...with a special article on the Savannah theater, by Charles Coburn
pp.35,(5)   DL★
[Savannah?]: [For the authors?]   1948

**1874** PATRICK, J. MAX.   Savannah's pioneer theater from its origins to 1810
pp.viii, 94   M
Athens: U. of Georgia P.   1953
Indexes stage performances and performers from 1781.

**1875** KNIGHT, VIRGINIA D.   The New Opera House of Athens, Georgia 1887-1932
Athens: U. of Georgia (MFA)   1970

**1876** OVERSTREET, ROBERT L.   The history of the Savannah theatre 1865-1906
Baton Rouge: Louisiana State U. (PhD)   1970

**1877** GREEN, ELVERA M.   Theatre and other entertainments in Savannah, Georgia, from 1810-1865
Iowa City: U. of Iowa (PhD)   1971

**1878** McCALL, JOHN C.   Atlanta Fox album: mecca at Peachtree Street
pp.32; ill. in text   DL★
Atlanta GA: For the author   1975
The Atlanta Fox Theatre.

### 6.2.11 HAWAII

**1879** FROWE, MARGARET M.   The history of the theatre during the reign of King Kalakaua 1874-1891
Honolulu: U. of Hawaii (MA)   1937

**1880** BROWN, THELMA.   A history of the theatre in Honolulu during the reign of Kamehameha V 1863-1872
Honolulu: U. of Hawaii (MA)   1942

**1881** BRENEMAN, LUCILLE N.   A history of the theatre in Honolulu during the second world war (1941-1946)
Honolulu: U. of Hawaii (MA)   1949

**1882** TOPHAM, HELEN A.   A history of the theatre in Honolulu 1891-1900
Honolulu: U. of Hawaii (MA)   1950

**1883** SCOTT, KATHLEEN S.   The professional legitimate theatre in Honolulu, 1900-1910
Honolulu: U. of Hawaii (MA)   1953

### 6.2.12 IDAHO

**1884** EGGERS, ROBERT F.   A history of theatre in Boise, Idaho from 1863 to 1963
Eugene: U. of Oregon (MA)   1963

**1885** AVERETT, RICHARD A.   History of the Auditorium Theatre in Pocatello, Idaho from 1893-1939
Pocatello: Idaho State U. (MA)   1970

### 6.2.13 ILLINOIS

**1887** WALKER, WILLIAM S.   The Chicago stage: containing sketches of the prominent members of the local amusement profession, for the season of 1870-71
pp.i, 15-61 [incomplete?]   MH
Chicago: Harton & Leonard   1871
Reprinted from the *Chicago Sunday Times*.

**1888** PHOTOGRAPHIC DIAGRAMS, descriptions and location of the theaters and halls of Chicago
pp.[27]; diagrams   MH
[Chicago?]: J. H. Hunter   1875
Hooley's, Academy, Farwell Hall, McVicker's, Grand Opera House, Great Adelphi, McCormick Hall. Seating details and a facetious commentary.

**1889** McVICKER, J. H.   The theatre, its early days in Chicago: a paper read before the Chicago Historical Society, February 10. 1884
pp.88   M
Chicago: Knight & Leonard   1884

**1890** THE AUDITORIUM
pp.32; ill. in text   MH
Chicago: [Orcutt?]   [1890]
Short history of the conception and construction of the Auditorium building in Chicago, with plans and photographs.

**1891** McVICKER'S OBSERVANDA demonstrated: containing a graphic historical sketch of McVicker's theatre from its inception to the present date
pp.[32]; ill. in text   MB
Chicago: W. J. Jefferson P.   1891
Unusually well illustrated with drawings and photographs.

**1892** GLOVER, LYMAN B.   The story of a theatre
pp.129; ill. in text   M
Chicago: Lakeside P.   [c. 1899]
History of Hooley's, later Powers's Theatre, with notes on other Chicago theatres.

**1893** THE ILLINOIS THEATRE...souvenir programme, dedicatory performance. Charles Frohman presents Julia Marlowe in *Barbara Frietchie*...Chicago, Ill. Oct 15th. 1900
pp.45; ill. in text   MH
Chicago: Rand, McNally   1900
Includes Charles E. Nixon: *Epitome of Chicago's theatrical history* and an illustrated account of the planning, design and construction of the theatre.

**1894** [FREIBERGER, EDWARD et al].   Iroquois Theatre souvenir program. Dedicatory performance November 23, 1903. Opening attraction Klaw and Erlanger's *Mr Blue Beard*
pp.93; ill. in text   MH
Chicago: Thomas J. Noonan   [1903]
Includes an illustrated description of the theatre by Charles E. Nixon, and an article by Edward Freiberger: *From Sauganash to Iroquois*, (Chicago theatre 1833-1902).

**1895** EVERETT, MARSHALL.   The great Chicago theater disaster:...the complete story told by the survivors, presenting a vivid picture, both by pen and camera, of one of the greatest fire horrors of modern times...
pp.384; ill. in text   M
[Chicago]: Publishers Union of America   1904
The Iroquois Theatre was destroyed on December 30, 1903, by a fire which began during a performance of *Mr Bluebeard*. This volume was also issued as: *Lest we forget. Chicago's awful theater horror*...,[Chicago]: Memorial Publishing, 1904, with an introduction by Bishop Fallows but unattributed to an author.

**1896** NORTHROP, HENRY D. World's greatest calamities, the Baltimore fire and the Chicago theatre horror
pp.474; ill. DL★
Philadelphia: National Publishing [1904]

**1897** GELATT, RICHARD H. Gelatt's Chicago theatrical directory and route book: a business directory of Chicago theatrical enterprises and all local and foreign amusements represented in this city
pp.64 DL★
Chicago: R. H. Gelatt [c. 1912]

**1898** RICE, WALLACE. Illinois centennial plays: suggestions for giving six little plays for Illinois children
pp.14 DL★
Springfield: Illinois Centennial Commission 1918
To accompany Rice's book of plays.

**1899** NORTON, ALBERT J. Chicago theatre: a poem
pp.[8] DL★
Chicago: Ye Cloister Print Shop 1922

**1900** WOODS, ROBERT A & KENNEDY, ALBERT J. The settlement horizon: a national estimate
pp.vi, 399 DL★
NY: Russell Sage Foundation 1922
Makes reference to the Hull House settlement, Chicago, and the Hull House Players.

**1901** WILT, JAMES N. The history of the Chicago theatre from 1847 to 1857
Chicago: U. (PhD) 1923

**1902** BERGSTROM, LOIS M. The history of the McVicker's Theatre 1857-1861
Chicago: U. (MA) 1930

**1903** MOORE, EDWARD C. Forty years of opera in Chicago
pp.vi, 430; pl. 32 MH
NY: Horace Liveright 1930
Beginning with Gounod's *Romeo and Juliet* at the Auditorium, 1889. Much incidental theatre information.

**1904** LIMPUS, ROBERT M. Theatres, plays and theatrical criticism in Chicago in 1908
Chicago: U. (MA) 1931

**1905** STURTEVANT, CATHERINE. A study of the dramatic productions of two decades in Chicago: 1847-1857, and 1897-1907
Chicago: U. (PhD) 1931

**1906** JOHNSON, GENEVIEVE G. A history of the Chicago theatre October 21 1871-1872
Chicago: U. (MA) 1932

**1907** VAN KIRK, GORDON. The beginnings of the theatre in Chicago, 1837-1839
Evanston IL: Northwestern U. (MA) 1934

**1908** BERGFALD, MILBURN J. Productions of Shakespeare in Chicago 1836-1857
Evanston: Northwestern U. (MA) 1936

**1908A** BULLIET, CLARENCE J. How grand opera came to Chicago
pp.46 DL★
[Chicago?]: For the author [194-?]

**1909** STORIES FROM THE STAGE in Chicago compiled by workers of the writers program of the Work Projects Administration in the state of Illinois...
pp.iv, 65; ill. in text MB
[Chicago]: Board of Education 1941
Fictionalized episodes in the history of Chicago theatre intended as 'a happy means of introducing schoolchildren to...the American actor...'

**1910** DAY, MYRLE. The history of the theatre of Chicago
Chapel Hill: U. of North Carolina (MA) 1942

**1911** THORSON, LILLIAN T. A record of the first year of McVicker's Theater, November 7 1857-November 7 1858
Ann Arbor: U. of Michigan (MA) 1946

**1912** TUCKER, LAURENCE E. The Passion Play in Bloomington, Illinois
Iowa City: U. of Iowa (PhD) 1951

**1913** HIGHLANDER, JAMES L. An historical study of the New Theatre and the Robertson Players of Chicago
Urbana: U. of Illinois (MA) 1952

**1914** YONICK, CORA J. A history of the theatre in Springfield, Illinois from 1855 to 1876
Laramie: U. of Wyoming (MA) 1952

**1915** DONAHOE, NED. Theatres in central Illinois 1850-1900
Urbana: U. of Illinois (PhD) 1953

**1916** CRAIG, WILLIAM S. The dramatic activity of certain Indian tribes of Illinois
Urbana: U. of Illinois (MA) 1957

**1917** SHERMAN, ROBERT L. Chicago stage: its records and achievements. Volume one gives a complete record of all entertainment and, substantially, the cast of every play presented in Chicago, on its first production in the city from the beginning of theatricals in 1834 down to the last before the fire of 1871
pp.x, 792; ill. in text MH
Chicago: For the author 1957

**1918** SOZEN, JOYCE L. Annals of the Opera House in Beardstown, Illinois, from 1872-1900
Urbana: U. of Illinois (MA) 1957

**1919** LUDWIG, JAY F. McVicker's Theatre 1857-1896
Urbana: U. of Illinois (PhD) 1958

**1920** GRANDGEORGE, WILLIAM N. The Prairie Playhouse of Galesburg, Illinois, 1915-1917
Urbana: U. of Illinois (MA) 1960

**1921** DRYDEN, WILMA J. Chicago theatre as reflected in the newspapers, 1900 through 1904
Urbana-Champaign: U. of Illinois (PhD) 1961

**1922** BRADLEY, LAWRENCE. A atudy of the relationship of Louis Sullivan's architectural theory to his designs for the Chicago Auditoriom
San José: State College (MA) 1962

**1923** CORVEY, LANE. The birth of a theatre: the Goodman Memorial Theatre
Chicago: Goodman School of Drama (MA) 1963

**1924** DREXLER, RALPH D. A history of the theatre in Bloomington, Illinois from its beginning to 1873
Normal: Illinois State U. (MA) 1963

**1925** REED, CAROLE F. A history of the Grand Opera House in Peoria, Illinois
Normal: Illinois State U. (MS) 1963

**1926** FARRELL, ROBERT D. The Illinois Theatre Company 1837-1840
Urbana: U. of Illinois (MA) 1964

**1927** WRIGHT, JAMES W. The Chicago Auditorium Theatre: 1866-1966
East Lansing: Michigan State U. (MA) 1966

**1928** OMAN, RICHARD J. Chicago theatre 1837-1847: reflections of an emerging metropolis
Gainsville: U. of Florida (MA) 1970

**1929** OTT, PAMELA W. A comparative study of drama, art, music and dance in Highland, Illinois
Carbondale: Southern Illinois U. (MS) 1971

**1930** MARINE, DON. A history of professional stage theatricals in Peoria, Illinois before the Civil War
New Orleans: Tulane U. (PhD) 1972

**1931** NEWELL, JAMES S. The development and growth of the Kenneth Sawyer Goodman Memorial Theatre and school of drama, Chicago, Illinois, 1925-1971
Detroit: Wayne State U. (PhD) 1973

**1932** BENSON, WILBUR T. A history of the Chicago Auditorium
Madison: U. of Wisconsin (PhD) 1974

**1933** COOPER, ALLEN R. Colonel Wood's Museum: a study in the development of the early Chicago stage
Chicago: Roosevelt U. (MA) 1974

**1934** DENSON, WILBUR T. A history of the Chicago Auditorium
Madison: U. of Wisconsin (PhD) 1974

**1935** WILSON, ROBERT. A history of professional theatre in Bloomington, Illinois from 1874 through 1896
Normal: Illinois State U. (MS) 1976

**1936** THE PARADISE THEATRE, Crawford near Washington. Chicago, Illinois. Architect John Eberson. Opened: September 14, 1928
pp.40 inc. wrappers; ill. in text  M
San Francisco: Theatre Historical Society [1977]

**1937** CZECHOWSKI, JAN. Theatrical trends and production techniques of the art and commercial theatres of Chicago 1900-1920
Ann Arbor: U. of Michigan (PhD) 1978

**1938** MILLER, PETER R. et al (Eds). Chicago theatre...a sixtieth anniversary salute...
pp.53 inc. wrappers; ill. in text  M
San Francisco: Theatre Historical Society 1981

**1939** RIALTO THEATRE [cover title]
pp.12, inc. wrappers; ill. in text  M
New Berlin WI: Conrad Schmitt Studios [1981]
The theatre, in Joliet, was restored and reopened in 1981.

**1940** EGYPTIAN THEATRE [cover title]
pp.8 inc. wrappers; ill. in text  M
New Berlin: Conrad Schmitt Studios [1982]
Dekalb, IL. Issued for the reopening of the restored theatre, that had closed in 1977.

**1941** MURPHY, BREN A. Rhetorical strategies of Chicago regional theaters in the 1970s: a case study of audience development
Evanston: Northwestern U. (PhD) 1984

**1942** SWEET, JEFFREY. Something wonderful right away: an oral history of the Second City and the Compass Players
 DL★
NY: Limelight 1987
First published 1978.

**1943** THE NEW REGAL Theatre [cover title]
pp.6, folded; ill. in text  M
New Berlin WI: Conrad Schmitt Studios [1990]
Chicago theatre, formerly the Avalon, opened 1927, restored 1985.

## 6.2.14 INDIANA

**1944** GOOCH, D. H. A history of the stage in Indianapolis from 1875 to 1890
Iowa City: U. of Iowa (MA) 1932

**1945** CHREIST, FREDERICK M. The history of the professional theatre in South Bend, Indiana
Evanston: Northwestern U. (MA) 1937

**1946** THORNBURG, OPAL. Their exits and their entrances: the story of Richmond civic theatre
pp.144; ill.  DL★
Richmond IN: Graphic P. 1959

**1947** SULLIVAN, WILLIAM G. English's Opera House: a paper read before the Indianapolis literary club March 5, 1951
pp.333-378; ill. in text  MH
Indianapolis: Indiana Historical Society 1960

**1948** BROCK, RICHARD B. A study of the Greencastle, Indiana Opera House 1875-1912
Greencastle IN: De Pauw U. (MA) 1963

**1949** WEINFELD, SAMUEL L. A survey of early theatrical activity at New Harmony, Indiana
Bloomington: Indiana U. (MA) 1964

**1950** SCHAUB, OWEN W. A history of the Grand Opera House stock company of Indianapolis, 1898 to 1900
Bloomington: Indiana U. (MA) 1968

**1951** SCHLUESSER, DOUGLAS. Evansville's early major theatres from 1868 to 1915
Bloomington: Indiana U. (MA) 1968

**1952** TOLAN, ROBERT W. A history of the legitimate professional theatre in Ft. Wayne, Indiana from 1854-1884
West Lafayette: Purdue U. (PhD) 1968

**1953** LAMBERT, MARLENE K. The Terre Haute Opera House from 1869 until 1874
Terre Haute: Indiana State U. (MA)     1972

**1954** STEPHENSON, ROBERT R. The premier season of Wysor's Gand Opera House 1892-1893
Terre Haute: Indiana State U. (MA)     1972

**1955** HANNERS, JOHN. Early entertainments in Terre Haute, Indiana 1819-1865
Terre Haute: Indiana State U. (MA)     1973

**1956** SLATTERY, KENNETH M. A history of theatrical activity in Fort Wayne, Indiana, with emphasis on the professional theatre
Kent OH: State U. (PhD)     1973

**1957** GIGLIO, MARY E. The Terre Haute Grand Opera House 1897-1898
Terre Haute: Indiana State U. (MA)     1974

**1958** MONTILLA, ROBERT B. The history of the Lafayette theatre, 1825-29
Bloomington: Indiana U. (PhD)     1975

## 6.2.15 IOWA

**1959** HURLEY, GEORGE O. Pageantry for Iowa communities
pp.48     DL★
Iowa City: State Historical Society     1923

**1960** LEWISON, AGNES O. A theatrical history of Des Moines, Iowa, 1846-1890
Iowa City: U. of Iowa (MA)     1931

**1961** WILLSON, LORETTA L. A survey of dramatic productions on the legitimate stage in Sioux City, Iowa, 1870-1919
Evanston: Northwestern U. (MA)     1936

**1962** SCHICK, JOSEPH. The early theater in Eastern Iowa: cultural beginnings and the rise of the theater in Davenport and Eastern Iowa, 1836-1863
pp.ix, 384     M
Chicago: U. P.     1939

**1963** BRYANT, RUTH M. Development of commercial recreation in Des Moines
Iowa City: U. of Iowa (MA)     1942
Makes reference to the Princess Stock Company 1909-1928.

**1964** FAY, BARBARA C. The theatre in south-eastern Iowa 1864-1880
Iowa City: U. of Iowa (MA)     1947

**1965** HOOPER, JAMES M. The history of a representative dramatic stock company: the Princess Stock Company of Des Moines, Iowa, 1909-1929
Seattle: U. of Washington (MA)     1948

**1966** HILL, RAYMOND S. A history of the Princess Theatre of Des Moines, Iowa
Iowa City: U. of Iowa (MA)     1949

**1967** HAMILTON, ROBERT T. A history of theatre in Keokuk, Iowa from 1875 to 1900
Ann Arbor: U. of Michigan (MA)     1954

**1968** BEARD, BILL L. The history of community theatre in Cedar Rapids, Iowa
Iowa City: U. of Iowa (MA)     1959

**1969** LANE, MILDRED R. A history of the Des Moines community playhouse
Iowa City: U. of Iowa (MA)     1959

**1970** FUNK, NANCY L. Professional theatrical activity in Iowa from 1890=1895
Iowa City: U. of Iowa (MA)     1966

**1971** ALLEN, REYNOLDS K. Nineteenth century theater structures in Iowa and Nebraska 1857-1900: a classification of selected general utility halls, opera halls and opera houses as described in local papers and histories
Tallahassee: Florida State U. (PhD)     1981

**1972** ARGELANDER, RONALD J. The Iowa Theater Lab, 1970-1975: the development of an improvisational-based, non-verbal theatre
NY: U. (PhD)     1984

## 6.2.16 KANSAS

**1973** PECK, PHOEBE. The theatre in Kansas City
Kansas City: U. of Missouri (MA)     1940

**1974** MELTZER, GEORGE. Social life and entertainment on the frontiers of Kansas 1854-1890
Wichita: State U. (MA)     1941

**1975** MATHER, PATRICIA A. The theatrical history of Wichita, Kansas, 1872-19120
Lawrence: U. of Kansas (MA)     1950

**1976** BLASINGAME, D. M. An analysis of the rehearsal and production problems of a community theatre in Colby, Kansas
Lawrence: U. of Kansas (MA)     1960

**1977** ROSSI, ALFRED A. A case study of an experiment in community theatre in West Kansas: 'Project Colby'
Lawrence: U. of Kansas (MA)     1960

**1978** BIRNER, MONA. A chronological record of theatrical activities in Lawrence, Kansas, between 1879 and 1911 as reported in the Lawrence newspapers
Lawrence: U. of Kansas (MA)     1962

**1979** KEMMERLING, JAMES. A history of the Whitley Opera House in Emporia, Kansas: 1881-1913
Emporia: State U. (MS)     1967

**1980** DOYEN, PEGGY J. The history of the theater 1878-1925 in Concordia, Kansas
Manhattan: Kansas State U. (MA)     1969

**1981** FOWLER, LARRY. History of the Stevens Opera House, Garden City, Kansas 1886-1929
Emporia KS: State U. (MS)     1969

**1982** JONASON, MARVIN G. A history of the Junction City Opera House in Junction City, Kansas, 1880-1919
Emporia KS: State U. (MS) 1970

**1983** GEROUX, CHARLES L. The history of theatres and related theatrical activity in Dubuque, Iowa, 1837-1877
Detroit: Wayne State U. (PhD) 1973

**1984** WORKMAN, THELMA. The best in Kansas: a history of the Brown Grand Theatre and its restoration, Concordia, Kansas, 1980 [cover title]
pp.32; ill. in text M
Concordia KS: For the author 1980

## 6.2.17 KENTUCKY

**1985** DIETZ, MARY M. The history of the theater in Louisville
Louisville KY: U. (MA) 1921

**1986** CLAY, LUCILLE N. The Lexington theatre from 1800 to 1840
Lexington: U. of Kentucky (MA) 1930

**1987** MEEK, BERYL. A record of the stage in Lexington, Kentucky 1799-1850
Iowa City: U. of Iowa (MA) 1930

**1988** JONES, JANE E. History of the stage in Louisville, Kentucky from its beginning to 1855
Iowa City: U. of Iowa (MA) 1932

**1989** CLARKE, MITCHELL. A history of the early theatre in Kentucky
Bowling Green: Western Kentucky U. (MA) 1936

**1990** KAREM, FRED J. The little theatre movement in Louisville
Louisville KY: U. (MA) 1938

**1991** WEISERT, JOHN J. Last night at Macauley's: a checklist, 1873-1925
pp.vi, 218 MH
Louisville KY: U. 1950
Macauley's theatre was destroyed by fire in 1925.

**1992** HILL, WEST T. A study of the Macauley Theatre in Louisville, Kentucky
Iowa City: U. of Iowa (PhD) 1954

**1993** WEISERT, JOHN J. A large and fashionable audience: a checklist of performances at the Louisville Theatre 1846 to 1866
pp.vi, 223 DL★
Louisville KY: For the author 1955

**1994** ARNOLD, JOHN C. A history of the Lexington theatre from 1887 to 1900
Lexington: U. of Kentucky (PhD) 1956

**1995** CRUM, MABEL I. The history of the Lexington Theatre from the beginning to 1860
Lexington: U. of Kentucky (PhD) 1956

**1996** WEISERT, JOHN J. The curtain rose: a checklist of performances at Samuel Drake's City Theatre and other theatres at Louisville from the beginning to 1843
pp.183 DL★
Louisville KY: For the author 1958

**1997** WEISERT, JOHN J. Mozart Hall, 1851 to 1866: a checklist of attractions of a minor theatre of Louisville, Kentucky, known variously as Mozart Hall, Wood's Theatre, or the Academy of Music
pp.82 DL★
Louisville KY: For the author 1962

**1998** COLEMAN, J. WINSTON. Kentucky rarities: a check list of one hundred and thirty-five fugitive books and pamphlets relating to the Bluegrass State and its people
pp.34; front. MH
Lexington KY: Winburn P. 1970
Includes reference to steamboats.

**1999** HILL, WEST T. The theatre in early Kentucky 1790-1820
pp.xiii, 205; pl. 9 M
Louisville: Kentucky U. P. 1971

**2000** TALBOTT, DAVID S. An ATL [Actors Theatre of Louisville] portfolio
pp.ii, 76; ill. in text, some col. DL★
Louisville KY: Studio Gallery 1972
Photographs.

**2001** COMBS, DON W. A history of Macauley's Theatre, Louisville, Kentucky, 1873-1925
Urbana-Champaign: U. of Illinois (PhD) 1977

**2002** SGROI, CAROL T. The Louisville Children's theatre: a history
Carbondale: U. of Illinois (PhD) 1979

## 6.2.18 LOUISIANA

**2003** GAISFORD, JOHN. The drama in New Orleans
pp.55 MH
New Orleans LA: J. B. Steel 1849
Lists and describes theatre buildings and offers anecdotal reminiscence of performers, professional and amateur, and repertoires.

**2004** SOUVENIR of the Odeon Stock Co. season 1904-5
ll. 24, inc. wrappers; ill. in text MH
[St Louis]: Odeon Amusement Co. [1905]

Portraits and brief biographies, interiors, plans, and a short history of the company.

**2005** GAFFORD, LUCILLE. Material condtions in the theatres of New Orleans before the Civil War
Chicago: U. (MA) 1925

**2006** MORROW, MARGUERITE H. A history of the English stage in New Orleans from 1817-1837
Iowa City: U. of Iowa (MA) 1926

**2007** PERKINS, J. A. Dramatic productions in New Orleans from 1817 to 1861
Baton Rouge: Louisiana State U. (MA) 1929

**2008** TURNER, VIVIAN D. The stage in New Orleans, Louisiana, after 1837
Iowa City: U. of Iowa (MA)  1929

**2009** O'POOL, E.S. Commercialized amusements in New Orleans
New Orleans: Tulane U. (MA)  1930

**2010** GAFFORD, LUCILLE. A history of the St Charles Theatre in New Orleans, 1835-1843
pp.(ii), 38  MH
Chicago: U. P.  1932
With particular reference to James H. Caldwell.

**2011** KENT, EVELYN E. A plan for statewide dramatic activities in Louisiana
Madison: U. of Wisconsin (PhM)  1933

**2012** BRADSHER, EVIOLA. The transfer of Louisiana from France to Spain in Louisiana drama
Baton Rouge: Luoiiana State U. (MS)  1935

**2013** LYLE, BEVERLY B. A detailed study of the New Orleans theatre from 1800-1825
Baton Rouge: Louisiana State U. (MA)  1935

**2014** WESTBROOK, VIRGINIA. Old New Orleans and the opera
pp.28  *
New Orleans: [For the author?]  1935

**2015** BENDER, LORELLE C. The French Opera House of New Orleans 1859-1890
Baton Rouge: Louisiana State U. (MA)  1940

**2016** HANLEY, KATHRYN T. The amateur theater in New Orleans before 1835
New Orleans: Tulane U. (MA)  1940

**2017** WARD, WILLIE P. English and American plays in New Orleans 1840-1850
Austin: U. of Texas (MA)  1940

**2018** VARNADO, ALBAN F. A history of theatrical activity in Baton Rouge, Louisiana 1819-1900
Baton Rouge: Louisiana State U. (MA)  1947

**2019** HAMILTON, MARY L. The Lyceum in New Orleans 1840-1860
Baton Rouge: Louisiana State U. (MA)  1948

**2020** ROPPOLO, JOSEPH P. A history of the English language theatre in New Orleans, 1845 to 1861
New Orleans: Tulane U. (PhD)  1950

**2021** BRADFORD, CLINTON W. The non-professional theater in Louisiana: a survey of organized and miscellaneous theatrical activities from the beginnings to 1900
Baton Rouge: Louisiana State U. (PhD)  1951

**2022** BRIAN, GEORGE. A history of theatrical activities in Baton Rouge from 1900 to 1923
Baton Rouge: Louisiana State U. (MA)  1951

**2023** DIAMOND, GLADYS. A history of the community theatre in Monroe, Louisiana
Baton Rouge: Louisiana State U. (MA)  1951

**2024** GRAY, WALLACE A. The professional theatre in Alexandria, Louisiana 1822-1920
Baton Rouge: Louisiana State U. (MA)  1951

**2025** HEIDT, PATSY R. The history of the theatre in Lake Charles, Louisiana, from 1920 to 1950
Baton Rouge: Louisiana State U. (MA)  1951

**2026** LINDSEY, HENRY C. The history of the theatre in Shreveport, Louisiana to 1900
Baton Rouge: Louisiana State U. (MA)  1951

**2027** KENDALL, JOHN S. The golden age of the New Orleans theatre
pp.xii, 624; pl. 7  M
Baton Rouge: Louisiana State U. P.  1952

**2028** ROSS, FRANCES G. The contemporary little theatres of Southwest Louisiana: Crowley, Opelousas, Lafayette, New Iberia, Jennings and Eunice
Baton Rouge: Louisiana State U. (MA)  1952

**2029** TEAGUE, ORAN B. The professional theater in rural Louisiana
Baton Rouge: Luoiiana State U. (MA)  1952

**2030** DOUGHERTY, EDWARD B. Presentational entertainments in Opelousas, Louisiana, from 1886 through 1890
Baton Rouge: Louisiana State U. (MA)  1953

**2031** HAMMACK, JAMES A. Pope's Theatre and St. Louis theatrical history, 1879-1895
Iowa City: U. of Iowa (PhD)  1954

**2032** PRIMEAUX, BEVERLY. Annals of the theatre in Lafayette, Louisiana, 1920-1940
Oxford: U. of Mississippi (MA)  1955

**2033** BROWN, EDWARD D. A history of the Shreveport little theatre 1922 to 1958
Denver: U. (PhD)  1959

**2034** KLING, ESTHER L. The New Orleans Academy of Music theatre, 1853-1861
Baton Rouge: Louisiana State U. (MA)  1960

**2035** MAYS, DAVID D. The Group Theatre of New Orleans. A history
New Orleans: Tulane U. (MA)  1960

**2036** HEAD, SADIE F. E. A historical study of the Tuland and Crescent Theatres of New Orleans, Louisiana, 1897-1937
Baton Rouge: Louisiana State U. (PhD)  1963

**2037** LEGARDEUR, RENE J. The first New Orleans theatre, 1792-1803
pp.viii, 58  M
New Orleans: Leeward Books  1963
Outline history of French and Spanish theatre in New Orleans, using contemporary evidence. Originally printed in *Comptes rendus de l'Athenée Louisianais, La Nouvelle-Orléans*, March, 1954 as *Les Premières années du théâtre à la Nouvelle-Orléans*.

**2038** HARRISON, SHIRLEY M. The Grand Opera House (third Varieties Theatre): a history and analysis. New Orleans, Louisiana, 1871-1906
Baton Rouge: Louisiana State U. (PhD)  1964

**2039** REYNOLDS, INA C. A history of the New Orleans Academy of Music theatre, 1861-1869
Baton Rouge: Louisiana State U. (MA)  1964

**2040** BOYD, THEODORE E. A history of the New Orleans Academy of Music Theatre 1869-1880
Baton Rouge: Louisiana State U. (Thesis) 1965

**2041** BRIAN, GEORGE. The history of the non-professional theatre in Louisiana from 1900 to 1925
Baton Rouge: Louisiana State U. (PhD) 1965

**2042** O'NEAL, AARON B. History of the St Charles Theatre of New Orleans 1880-1888
Baton Rouge: Louisiana State U. (MA) 1965

**2043** ROSS, ALLAN S. The New Orleans Academy of Music theatre, 1880-1887
Baton Rouge: Louisiana State U. (MA) 1965

**2044** KAYMAN, ELEANOR K. Leisure time activities in New Orleans 1855-1863
New Orleans: Tulane U. (MA) 1966

**2045** LAWLOR, JO A. History of the St Charles Theatre of New Orleans 1888-1899
Baton Rouge: Louisiana State U. (MA) 1966

**2046** BARELLO, RUDOLPH V. A history of the New Orleans Academy of Music Theatre 1887-1893
New Orleans: Louisiana State U. 1967

**2047** SMITHER, NELLE. A history of the English theatre at New Orleans 1806-1842
pp.iv, 406, front. M
NY: Blom 1967
A portion printed in *Louisiana Historical Quarterly*,28, January-April, 1945; here in full with the addition of a playlist.

**2048** RODEN, SALLY A. History of the St Charles Theatre of New Orleans under the management of David Bidwell 1880-1888
Denton: North Texas State U. (MA) 1969

**2049** CHAPMAN, FREDERICK L. A history of Le Petit Théâtre du Vieux Carré
New Orleans: Tulane U. (PhD) 1970

**2050** HARGETT, SHEILA. A daybook and a history of the St Charles Theatre 1864-1968 [New Orleans]
Baton Rouge: Louisiana State U. (MA) 1971

**2051** BERRY, MELVIN H. A history of theatre in New Orleans from 1925 to 1935
Baton Rouge: Louisiana State U. (PhD) 1973

**2052** MELEBECK, CLAUDE B. A history of the first and second Varieties Theatres of New Orleans, 1849-1870
Baton Rouge: Louisiana State U. (PhD) 1973

**2053** O'BRIEN, ROSARY H. The New Orleans carnival organizations: theatre of prestige
Los Angeles: U. of California (PhD) 1973

**2054** DE METZ, OUIDA K. The uses of dance in the English language theatres of New Orleans prior to the civil war, 1806-1861
Tallahassee: Florida State U. (PhD) 1975

**2055** CRUISE, BOYD & HARTON, MERLE. Signor Faranta's iron theatre
pp.xi, 144; ill. in text M
New Orleans: Historic New Orleans Collection 1982
Biography of Frederick William Stempel, 1846-1924, showman and contortionist, and the theatre he founded in New Orleans.

**2056** KEY, NANCY M. A narrative history of Lake Charles Little Theatre, Lake Charles, Louisiana, 1927-1982
NY: U. (PhD) 1987

**2057** THOMPSON, PAULA J. A history and day-book of the English language theatre in New Orleans during the Civil War
Baton Rouge: Louisiana State U. (PhD) 1988

## 6.2.19 MAINE

**2058** MORELAND, JAMES. A history of the theatre in Portland, 1794-1850
Orono: U. of Maine (MA) 1934

**2059** THURSTON, FREDERICK C. Annals of the stage in Bangor, Maine, 1882-1900
Orono: U. of Maine (MA) 1940

**2060** MEINECKE, CHARLOTTE D. Annals of the drama in Bangor, Maine, 1834-1882
Orono: U. of Maine (MA) 1941

**2061** OBLAK, JOHN B. Broadway in Maine: a history of the Lakewood Theatre
Lawrence: U. of Kansas (PhD) 1971

## 6.2.20 MARYLAND

**2062** WALLIS, SEVERN T. Address by S. T. Wallis, Esq. Delivered at the Academy of Music in Baltimore, April 10th, 1875 on behalf of the Lee Memorial Association [cover title]
pp.12. DL★
Baltimore: [For the association?] 1875

**2063** SCHARF, J. THOMAS. History of Baltimore city & county from the earliest period to the present day: including biographical sketches of their representative men
pp.947; ill. in text, pl. 103, map L
Philadelphia: Louis H. Everts 1881
Contains much theatre history and biography.

**2064** SHAFFER, VIRGINIA M. The theater in Baltimore from its beginnings to 1786
Baltimore: The John Hopkins U. (MA) 1926

**2065** KUEMMERLE, CLYDE V. A history of Ford's Grand Opera House, Baltimore, from its origin in 1871 to its demise on 1964
Baltimore: U. of Maryland (MA) 1965

**2066** KOENIG, LINDA L. A history of the Vagabond Players, Baltimore, Maryland, 1916-1978
Bowling Green: State U. (PhD) 1978

**2067** RITCHEY, DAVID (Ed.). A guide to the Baltimore stage in the eighteenth century: a history and day book calendar
pp.x, 342 M
Westport CT: Greenwood P. 1982

**2068** KOENIG, LINDA L. The Vagabonds: America's oldest little theatre
pp.166; ill. in text M
Rutherford: Fairleigh Dickinson U. P. 1983
Baltimore's little theatre, founded in 1916.

**2069** CARNEY, BENJAMIN F. The Baltimore theatre project, 1971-1983. Towards a people's theatre
Columbia: U. of Missouri (PhD) 1985

## 6.2.21 MASSACHUSETTS

**2070** [HALE, DAVID]. Letters on the new theatre
pp.16 MH
[Boston]: [For the author?] [1827]
Opposition, on moral grounds, to the erection of the Tremont Theatre, Boston MA.

**2071** THE DRAMATIC MIRROR, containing critical remarks upon the theatrical performances of every night, in the city of Boston, - with bills of the play
pp.various MH
[Boston]: [Benjamin H. Ives ?] 1829-
Issued daily. Thirty-four issues examined, between Tuesday September 14 and Thursday December 10 1829.

**2072** PELBY, WILLIAM. Letters on the Tremont Theatre, respectfully addressed to the primitive subscribers, its friends and patrons...
pp.44 MH
Boston: P. of John H. Eastburn 1830
An appeal to the public by the author who had been removed from the management of the Tremont Theatre. Offers a lively picture of theatre squabbling. The preface, attributed to 'a friend of the author' seems likely to have been written by Pelby himself.

**2073** SAYINGS AND DOINGS at the Tremont House in the year 1832 extracted from the note book of Costard Sly, solicitor and short-hand writer, of London, and edited by Dr Zachary Philemon Vangrifter
pp.268 L
Boston: Allen and Tickner 1833
Two volumes. Much theatre reference, including the Tremont Theatre and its artistes, written as a series of 'conversations'.

**2074** CATALOGUE of the paintings, marble and plaster statuary and engravings, comprised in the collection of the Boston Museum and Gallery of Fine Arts...together with a descriptive sketch of the institution and its collection
pp.24 MB
Boston: Tuttle & Dennett 1844

**2075** CONSTITUTION AND BY-LAWS of the Boston Museum Dramatic Fund Association. Established at Boston, state of Massachusetts, April 6th, 1847
pp.8 MH
Boston: William Marden, printer 1847

**2076** TOM POP'S first visit to the Boston Museum, with his grandfather, giving an account of what he saw, and what he thought...
pp.24; ill. in text MH
Boston: 'Printed for the publisher' 1848
Mostly concerned with museum exhibits, but has engraving of the building and, on the wrappers, a puff for the theatrical entertainment available.

**2077** CATALOGUE of the paintings, portraits, marble and water color drawings, in the collection of the Boston Museum, Tremont, near Court Street, Boston, together with a descriptive sketch of the institution
pp.36 MH
Boston: William Marden 1849

**2078** [FORD, TOM]. A peep behind the curtain, by a supernumary
pp.91; pl. 2 MH
Boston: Redding 1850
Cover title: *Theatrical reminiscences...by a Boston supernumary.*

**2079** CLAPP, WILLIAM W. A record of the Boston stage
pp.xiii, 479 MH
Boston: James Munroe 1853
Reprinted from the *Boston Evening Gazette*, of which the author was editor. Period, c.1750-1853. Clapp later made an index for his own use, but allowed his secretary, Charles E. Wingate to take a copy. In 1860 Wingate duplicated his copy for Harvard library, (headed *An index to the history of the Boston stage*), stating that only three copies existed. In 1965, a separate index, compiled by Carol Blitgen, was published in the Fall number of *Theatre Documentation*.

**2080** [FAIRBANKS, CHARLES B.]. Aguecheek
pp.336; pictorial title MB
Boston: Shepard, Clark and Brown 1859
Largely reprinted material from the Boston *Saturday Evening Gazette* including a chapter on Boston's 'Theatre Alley'.

**2081** BY-LAWS of the proprietors of the Boston Theatre: with a list of stockholders
pp.16 M
Boston: J. H. Eastburn's P. 1860

**2082** THE DIAGRAM: containing plans of theatres and other places of amusement in Boston, being revised and corrected to the present time by authority of the different managers
pp.76; ill. in text MB
Boston: A. C. Tuttle & Jas. A. T. Bird 1869
Illustrations of exteriors and brief written descriptions.

**2083** [CAHILL, THOMAS H.]. The auditorium, containing the plan of seats in all the theatres and public halls in Boston carefully corrected and revised to the present time
pp.46; ill. in text MB
Boston: T. H. Cahill 1875

**2084** THE THEATRES and public halls of Boston [seating plans]
pp.48; ill. in text MB
Boston: Lansing 1879

**2085** BOSTON MUSEUM, established 1841, present structure erected 1846, remodeled 1868, 1872 and 1876, and the auditorium entirely rebuilt 1880. An interesting retrospect and an account of the latest alterations and improvements. Issued for season of 1880-1881. Mr R. M. Field, manager
pp.40; ill. in text MH
[Boston]: [For the theatre] [1880]
Similar, though less elaborate, booklets had been issued in e.g. 1872, 1873, 1875.

**2086** PICTORIAL DIAGRAMS of Boston, New York and Philadelphia
pp.36; ill. in text MB
Boston: Chas. A. Smith 1880
Elaborately engraved plates showing in perspective the seating of every prominent theatre in the three cities. Also a two-page directory to Boston fire-alarm telegraph.

**2087** [CASHIN, CHARLES M.]. Charles M. Cashin's amusement guide with theatre diagrams. Published weekly and issued gratuitously to the patrons of Cashin's theatre ticket office, Young's hotel, Boston...
pp.av. 24; ill. in text MB
[Boston]: Cashin's [c. 1883]

Issue examined was for week ending April 25, 1883.

**2088** HISTORICAL REVIEW of the Boston Bijou Theatre with the original casts of all the operas that have been produced at the Bijou, and with photographs illustrative of the various scenes in them. Presented to the patrons of the Bijou Theatre, April 21st 1884...
pp.[68]; ill. in text  MB
Boston: Edward O. Skelton  [1884]

**2089** WINGATE, CHARLES E. The playgoer's year-book for 1888. Story of the stage the past year with especial reference to Boston...Narrative of the plots of all the new plays and operas, histories of each work, analyses of the plays and the acting, comments of many authors and actors on their own pieces, full casts of characters of the principal performances, complete record of the theatrical year in Boston, lists of theatre officials, biographical sketches and portraits of actors and actresses, with illustrations of plays
pp.87; ill. in text, pl.12  M
Boston: Stage Company  [1888]

**2090** PAINE, NATHANIEL. The drama in Worcester
pp.7  MH
Worcester MA: [For the author?]  [c. 1889]

'Reprinted from *The History of Worcester County*'.

**2091** CATALOGUE...the Gaiety Musée and Bijou Theatre
pp.34; ill. in text  M
Boston: B. F. Keith  [c. 1892]

203 items, paintings, sculptures and curiosities, and brief descriptive and historical notes on the theatres.

**2092** FRENCH, CHARLES E. A year of opera at the Castle Square Theatre, from May, '95 to May 6, '96. Containing portraits and sketches of the principal singers, and a record of the casts of characters of the various operas produced...
pp.150; ill. in text  MH
Bostob: C. E. French  1896

Includes a description of the theatre, with plans.

**2093** KNUDSON, GRACE P. Castle Square Theatre stock company, Boston. Art souvenir published by permission and with the aid of the leading members of the company
pp.16; ill. in text  DL★
Boston: Brown  [1899?]

**2094** DRAKE, SAMUEL A. Old landmarks & historic personages of Boston
pp.xviii, 484; ill. in text, pl. 15  L
Boston: Little, Brown  1900

New and revised edition. First published 1872. Reference to Junius Brutus Booth, and the Tremont, Boston, Federal Street, Board Alley and Haymarket theatres.

**2095** A SOUVENIR of the ninth season Bowdoin Square Theatre, Boston, Mass
Unpaged; ill. in text  MH
Boston: Boston Co-P.  [1900]

Title headed '1892-1900'. History, repertoire, royalties paid, staff names, policy statements. Many photographs.

**2096** CAMBRIDGE SOCIAL DRAMATIC CLUB 1891-1903. Fiftieth performance given in Brattle Hall, February fourteenth, MDCCCCIII
pp.36 inc. wrappers  MH
Cambridge MA: For the Club  1903

Souvenir program of *The Merry Wives of Windsor*, providing a chronological listing of productions and casts together with a brief history of the club.

**2097** [FRENCH, CHARLES E. (Ed.)]. Six years of drama at the Castle Square Theatre with portraits of the members of the the company and complete programs of all plays produced. May 3, 1897-May 3, 1903
pp.406; ill. in text  M
Boston: Charles Elwell French  1903

**2098** SOUVENIR programme. Boston Museum. Final week, May 25th to 30th, prior to its demolition. Sixty-second and last season, 1902-1903 [cover title]
pp.64; ill. in text  MH
Boston: S. A. Lincoln  1903

Programme of *Mrs Dane's Defence* (Henry Arthur Jones) presented by Frohman's Empire Theatre company, together with a history of the theatre, a chronological list of celebrated performers and a selection of productions. Tipped into the Harvard copy are the lines written by Dexter Smith and spoken by Margaret Anglin at the final performance, June 1, 1903.

**2099** BOSTON THEATRES & halls with historical notes past & present. Chronology of principal dramatic & musical events. Diagrams...Issued by John R. Heard, Hotel Touraine
pp.[32]; ill. in text  M
Boston: Winthrop B. Jones  1907

Detailed descriptions of eighteen extant theatres and nineteen former ones, and brief reference to 11 others.

**2100** TOMPKINS, EUGENE & KILBY, QUINCY. The history of the Boston Theatre, 1864-1901
pp.xvi, 551; ill. in text  M
Boston: Houghton Mifflin  1908

Authors were respectively Manager (1878-1901) and Treasurer (1886-1901).

**2101** CRAWFORD, MARY C. (Ed.). Old Boston days and ways: from the dawn of the revolution until the town became a city
pp.xv, 463; ill. in text, pl. 24  MH
Boston: Little, Brown  1909

Includes essays, *When Faneuil was a playhouse* and *Early Boston theatres and their stars*.

**2102** JACKSON, FRANK H. Monograph of the Boston Opera House
ll. [36]; ill. in text  MH
Boston: W. A. Butterfield  1909

Description of building, management, seasons, artistes, seating.

**2103** THE AMUSEMENT SITUATION in the city of Boston based on a study of the theatres for ten weeks from November 28, 1909, to February 5, 1910...
pp.35  MH
[Boston]: [Twentieth Century Club]  [1910]

Analyses the entertainment provided by theatres and moving pictures and examines problems of censorship in the light of the authorities' impotence in this matter under the 1908 Act governing theatre licensing.

**2104** CRAWFORD, MARY C. (Ed.). Romantic days in old Boston
pp.xix, 411; pl. 32  L
Boston: Little, Brown  1910

Includes essay, *The old Boston theatres and their stars*.

**2105** BALL, WILLIAM T. The old Federal Street Theatre
pp.41-92; pl. 2     MB
Boston: Old State House     1911
Bostonian Society *Publications*, 8, 1911. A paper read before the Society, June 11, 1889.

**2106** CRAWFORD, MARY C. Social life in old New England
pp.xiii, 515; front., pl. 32     L
Boston: Little, Brown     1914
Makes reference to theatre and quasi-theatrical entertainments.

**2107** EXHIBITION. Prints, playbills, advertisements, and autograph letters to illustrate the history of the Boston stage from 1791 to 1825 from the collection of Mr Robert Gould Shaw
pp.41     M
Boston: Club of Odd Volumes     1914
Catalogue of 185 items.

**2108** CLAPP, JOHN B. Boston Museum: a history
Unpaged; 108 sheets; ill. in text     MH
Boston: [For the author?]     1915
Final proof sheets of unpublished work, with illustratory materials, mounted by Herbert I. Jackson of Boston.

**2109** EXHIBITION OF PRINTS and playbills to illustrate the histroy of the Boston stage (1825 to 1850). From the collection of Mr. Robert Gould Shaw
pp.101     M
Boston: Club of Odd Volumes     1915
Catalogue of 263 items.

**2110** RYAN, KATE. Old Boston Museum days
pp.xii, 264; pl. 16     M
Boston: Little, Brown     1915

**2111** FISHER, WILLIAM A. Notes on music in old Boston
pp.xvi, 100; ill.     DL★
Boston: Oliver Ditson     1918

**2112** BRAZIER, MARIAN H. Stage and screen
pp.130; front., pl. 38     MH
Boston: For the author     1920
Impressions of players 1870-1920, and a sketch of the Boston Museum and its stock company.

**2113** THE CENTER of things
pp.[24] inc. wrappers; ill. in text     MH
Boston: Daniels Printing     1920
An account of Benjamin Franklin Keith's theatre in Boston.

**2114** DEUTSCH, HELEN & HANAU, STELLA. The Provincetown, a story of the theatre
pp.xvi, 313; ill. in text, pl. 17     M
NY: Farrar & Rhinehart     1931
Introduction by Kenneth MacGowan. Detailed history, 1915-29.

**2115** HERLIHY, ELISABETH M. (Ed.). Fifty years of Boston: a memorial volume issued in commemoration of the tercentary of 1930...
pp.xx, 799; front., ill. in text     MH
Boston: Boston Tercentenary Committee     1932

Includes Charles H. Grandgent: *The stage in Boston in the last fifty years*...

**2116** BONAWITZ, DOROTHY M. The history of the Boston stage from the beginnings to 1810
University Park: Pennsylvania State U. (PhD)     1936

**2117** CLARK, WALTER L. Leaves from an artists's memory
pp.vi, 270; front.     DL★
Camden NJ: Printed by Hadden Craftsmen     1937
Chapter 29: *The Berkshire Playhouse*.

**2118** McGLINCHEE, CLAIRE. The first decade of the Boston Museum
pp.370; pl. 11     M
Boston: Bruce Humphries     1940
This wrappered edition has a substantial appendix listing entertainments, with credits, 1841-1851, not present in the hard-cover edition issued in the same year.

**2119** MICHAEL, MARY R. A history of the professional theatre in Boston from the beginning to 1816
Cambridge MA: Radcliffe College (PhD)     1942

**2120** VORSE, MARY M. Time and the town: a Provincetown chronicle
pp.372     MH
NY: Dial P.     1942
Theatre material includes reference to Susan Glaspell.

**2121** MAMMEN, EDWARD W. The old stock company school of acting: a study of the Boston Museum
pp.89; ill. in text     M
Boston: Trustees of the Public Library     1945

**2122** HUGHES, ELINOR. Passing through to Broadway
pp.354     MH
Boston: Waverly House     1948
Reminiscence and criticism of the Boston stage, 1936-47. An appendix provides an analysis of each season.

**2123** HARRIGAN, RITA K. The Academy of Music
Northampton MA: Smith College (MA)     1949
Makes reference to the Northampton Players, 1912-1919.

**2124** WOODRUFF, JOHN R. The theatrical venture in Boston, as exemplified by the first seasons of the Howard Athenaeum
Ithaca: Cornell U. (PhD)     1949

**2125** STONE, P. M. Boston's theatre district south of Boylston Street
pp.31     MH
Cambridge MA: [For the author]     1957
Typescript.

**2126** STONE, P. M. Boston dramatic stock companies
pp.27     MH
Cambridge MA: [For the author]     [c. 1957]
Typescript.

**2127** FLUHARTY, GEORGE W. Drama activities in the Elizabeth Peabody House in Boston - a history and evaluation
NY: U. (PhD)     1958

**2128** KILE, SARA A. John B. Wright's staging at the National Theatre, Boston, 1836 to 1853
Columbus: Ohio State U. (MA)     1959

## 6.2. STATES AND TOWNS

**2129** THE CHARLES PLAYBOOK. A project of Playhouse Boston, inc.
pp.av. 24   MH
Boston: Charles Playhouse   1960-63
Volumes 1 and 2 contain articles of regional and general theatre interest. Volume 3 is sketchy, from financial problems following the disastrous theatre fire that season.

**2130** STONE, P. M. John Craig Players with Mary Young and their outline history of the famous Castle Square Theatre, Boston, Massachusetts, as prepared by P. M. Stone for Mary Young
pp.32; ill. in text   MH
[Boston]: For the author   1960

**2131** THE THEATER automatique [drop title]
pp.[10]; ill. in text   M
[NY]: [*Architectural Forum*]   1960
Reprint describing the recently completed Loeb Drama Centre in Harvard, Cambridge MA (now the American Repertory Theatre).

**2132** SARLOS, ROBERT K. The Provincetown Players: experiments in style
New Haven: Yale U. (PhD)   1965

**2133** VILHAUER, WILLIAM W. A history and evaluation of the Provincetown Players
Iowa City: U. of Iowa (PhD)   1965

**2134** 10th ANNIVERSARY Charles Playhouse, Boston [cover title]
pp.[44]; ill. in text   M
[Boston]: [For the Playhouse]   [1966]

**2135** LAWSON, EVELYN. Theatre on Cape Cod
pp.vii, 71; pl. 8   MH
Yarmouth Port MA: Parnassus Imprints   1969
Legend on title, ...*the cradle of summer theater...1915...until now*.

**2136** STODDARD, ROGER E. A guide to *Spencer's Boston Theatre*, 1855-1862
pp.(ii), 45-98; ill. in text   M
Worcester MA: American Antiquarian Society   1969
Reprinted from the *Proceedings*, April 1969. William Vaughan Spencer, (1831-1870), was a publisher of plays; his 'Theatre' was a play series.

**2137** TAPER, BERNARD. The arts in Boston
pp.xi, 170; ill. in text   L
Cambridge MA: Harvard U. P.   1970
Social and economic characteristics of the visual and performing arts in Boston, and possible measures to enhance them.

**2138** TOSCAN, RICHARD E. The organization and operation of the Federal Street Theatre from 1793 to 1806
Urbana-Champaign: U. of Illinois (PhD)   1970

**2139** McENTIRE, ROBERT M. Establishing theater in a provincial New England city: Springfield, Massachusetts, 1820-1900
Medford MA: Tufts U. (PhD)   1971

**2140** STODDARD, RICHARD. The architecture and technology of Boston theatres 1794-1854
New Haven: Yale U. (PhD)   1971

**2141** NORTON, ELLIOT. Broadway down East: an informal account of the plays, players and playhouses of Boston from puritan times to the present
pp.x,156; ill. in text   M
Boston: Public Library   1978

**2142** SANKUS, PATRICIA H. Theatrical entertainments and other amusements in Salem, Massachusetts from the colonial period through the year 1830
Medford MA: Tufts U. (PhD)   1981

**2143** BOSTON CONVENTION July 1983, Theatre Historical Society, Paul Chavanne, chairman
pp.[17]; ill. in text, pl. 18   MH
[Boston]: [Theatre Historical Association]   [1983]
Includes Joseph S. Chifre on the Boston movie industry; Samuel Sayward on the Keith Memorial Theatre; J. Paul Chavane: *Victorian theatres of the South end*.

**2144** SHEA, ANN M. Community pageants in Massachusetts 1908-1932
NY: U. (PhD)   1984

**2145** SNOW, STEPHEN E. Theatre of the pilgrims: documentation and analysis of a 'living history' performance in Plymouth, Massachusetts
NY: U. (PhD)   1987

**2146** KRUH, DAVID. Always something doing: a history of Boston's infamous Scollay Square
pp.xiv, 162; ill. in text   M
Boston: Faber and Faber   1990
Emphasizes entertainments.

### 6.2.22 MICHIGAN

**2147** BURTON, CLARENCE M. The Hyde House and the Garrick Theatre on Griswold Street, Detroit
pp.17   ★
Detroit: For the author   1929

**2148** BRINK, ALICE M. The drama of Detroit from its inception to 1870. With a chronological catalog of plays presented in Detroit theatres from 1840 to 1869
Detroit: Wayne State U. (MA)   1937

**2149** McDAVITT, ELAINE E. A history of the theatre in Detroit, Michigan from its beginnings to 1862
Ann Arbor: U. of Michigan (PhD)   1946

**2150** EGAN, JAQUELINE E. A suggested guide to Summer theatre organization based on the experience of the Lerawee players in Adrian, Michigan...1948
Washington DC: Catholic U. of America (MA)   1949

**2151** BEHRINGER, CLARA M. A history of the theatre in Ann Arbor, Michigan, from its beginnings to 1904
Ann Arbor: U. of Michigan (PhD)   1950

**2152** GOODALE, JANE M. An analysis of the history, organization, financing, and operation of the community theatres in Michigan
East Lansing: Michigan State U. (MA)   1950

**2153** RYAN, JAMES. The Lake Michigan Playhouse: a report on its inception, organization, development and achievements
Kent OH: State U. (MA)   1950

**2154** BROOMFIELD, WILLIAM C. A history of the Arts and Crafts Theatre of Detroit, Michigan
Ann Arbor: U. of Michigan (MA) 1951

**2155** SHERIDAN, CHARLES H. The history of Music Hall Opera House, Flint, Michigan, 1883-1893
Detroit: Wayne State U. (MA) 1951

**2156** STEPHENSON, JIM B. History of the legitimate theatre in Ann Arbor, Michigan, from its beginnings to 1904
Ann Arbor: U. of Michigan (PhD) 1951

**2157** BROWNLEE, MARY A. Non-professional theatre in Detroit from 1920 to November, 1953
Detroit: Wayne State U. (MA) 1954

**2158** SPEAR, RICHARD D. The theatre in Detroit 1885-1895, as revealed by the dramatic criticism of George P. Goodale
Detroit MI: Wayne State U. (MA) 1954

**2159** OAS, MABEL W. A history of the legitimate drama in the Copper country of Michigan from 1900 to 1910 with special study of the Calumet Theatre
East Lansing: Michigan State U. (MA) 1955

**2160** BLAKE, PETER H. A descriptive study of the Flint Community Players
East Lansing: Michigan State U. (MA) 1956

**2161** RYDAHL, EUGENE E. A history of the legitimate theatre in East Saginaw, Michigan, from 1860-1884
Iowa City: U. of Iowa (PhD) 1958

**2162** PETERSON, WILLIAM A. A history of the professional theatre of Detroit, Michigan, September 13, 1875 to July 3, 1886
Tallahassee: Florida State U. (PhD) 1959

**2163** SHANOWER, DONALD T. A comparative and descriptive study of three Opera Houses in Southern Michigan 1880-1900
Ann Arbor: U. of Michigan (PhD) 1959

**2164** LEWANDOWSKI, RAYMOND J. A survey of legitimate theatre in Bay City, Michigan
East Lansing: Michigan State U. (MA) 1962

**2165** WEDGE, MARGARET B. The history of the Majestic Theatre, Port Huron, Michigan, 1906-1917
Detroit: Wayne State U. (MA) 1962

**2166** RIDGE, PATRICIA. A history of the Cheboygan Opera House, Cheboygan, Michigan, from 1891 to 1920
East Lansing: Michigan State U. (MA) 1963

**2167** WILSON, JACK A. A history of the Belding Opera House, Belding, Michigan, from 1899-1915
East Lansing: Michigan State U. (MA) 1965

**2168** GORE, JOHN H. A history of platform and stage in Bay City, Michigan, in the nineteenth century
Detroit: Wayne State U. (PhD) 1966

**2169** RODGERS, JAMES W. The history of the Garrick Theatre, Detroit, Michigan: 1909-1928
Detroit: Wayne State U. (PhD) 1967

**2170** KLUSSEN, ROBERT D. The tent-repertoire theatre: a rural American institute
East Lansing: Michigan State U. (PhD) 1970

Exemplified by The Rosier Players of Jackson, Michigan.

**2171** HAINES, PEGGY A. The history of the City Opera House, Traverse City, Michigan, from 1891 until July of 1897
Ypsilanti: Eastern Michigan U. (MA) 1971

**2172** RUDICK, LAWRENCE W. The Detroit theatre comes of age, 1862-1875
Stanford: U. (PhD) 1971

**2173** STERN, ROBERT I. Three Michigan pageants and how they grew
East Lansing: Michigan State U. (PhD) 1971

**2174** TUTOR, RICHARD M. The history of the Detroit Opera House 1869-1897
Detroit: Wayne State U. (PhD) 1972

**2175** ALDRIDGE, HENRY B. Live musical and theatrical presentations in Detroit moving pictures theatres: 1896-1930
Ann Arbor: U. of Michigan (PhD) 1973

**2176** HEZLEP, WILLIAM E. A history of the Detroit Opera House 1898-1931
Detroit: Wayne State U. (PhD) 1973

**2177** STILLWELL, JANET E. A descriptive study of the Kalamazoo civic players, 1929-1968
Ann Arbor: U. of Michigan (PhD) 1973

**2178** MORRISON, ANDREW C. Opera house, nickel show, and palace: an illustrated inventory of theater buildings in the Detroit area
pp.[36]; ill. in text                                         M
Dearborn MI: Greenfield Village Museum      1974
Dates, locations, architects when known, seating capacity and, where appropriate, brief descriptive and historical notes.

**2179** HARBIN, SHIRLEY M. Detroit Recreation Department theatre 1963-1976
Detroit: Wayne State U. (PhD) 1977

**2180** CLEVINGER, DONNA L. Jackson, Michigan: crossroads of theatrical activity in Southern lower Michigan from its beginnings to 1930
Ann Arbor: U. of Michigan (PhD) 1980

**2181** AN INVITATION to participate in the exciting re-creation of the most renowned theatre in history: Shakespeare's Globe Playhouse
pp.[20] inc. wrappers; ill. in col. in text                M
[Detroit MI]: [Wayne State U.]                    [1980]
Prospectus for the building of a reconstructed 'Globe' at Wayne State University, illustrated by C. Walter Hodges, chairman of the advisory committee.

**2182** HODGES, C. WALTER; SCHOENBAUM, S. & LEONE, L. (Eds). The third Globe. Symposium for the reconstruction of the Globe Playhouse, Wayne State University, 1979
pp.267; ill. in text                                          M
Detroit: Wayne State U. 1981

**2183** KONOW, GARY G. The establishment of theatrical activity in a remote settlement: Grand Rapids, Michigan 1827 to 1862
Ann Arbor: U. of Michigan (PhD) 1985

**2184** KLAUTSCH, RICHARD J. An historical analysis of the Clarence B. Hilberry Repertory Theatre, Detroit, Michigan, 1963-1973
Detroit: Wayne State U. (PhD) 1988

## 6.2.23 MINNESOTA

**2185** ANDERSON, EVELYN C. A history of the theatre in St Peter, Minnesota. from its beginning to 1930
Minneapolis: U. of Minnesota (MA) 1946

**2186** WOODS, DONALD Z. A history of the theatre in Minneapolis, Minnesota, from its beginnings to 1883
Minneapolis: U. of Minnesota (PhD) 1950

**2187** HEMMING, MARY R. The history of the Grand Opera House of St Paul, Minnesota from 1883-1889
Washington DC: Catholic U. of America (MA) 1951

**2188** GROSSMAN, A. M. The professional legitimate theatre in Minneapolis from 1890 to 1910
Minneapolis: U. of Minnesota (PhD) 1957

**2189** SHERMAN, JOHN K. Music and theater in Minnesota history
pp.ii, 63: ill. in text  M
Minneapolis: U. of Minnesota P. 1958

**2190** ANDRUS, THOMAS O. A history of the legitimate theatre in St Paul, Minnesota, from 1918 to 1939
Minneapolis: U. of Minnesota (PhD) 1961

**2191** MURPHY, MOLLY. Winona Little Theatre, 1925-1948
pp.23; ill.  DL★
Winona MN: County Historical Society 1961

**2192** GUTHRIE, TYRONE. A new theatre
pp.189; pl. 10  M
NY: McGraw-Hill 1964
The founding of the Minnesota Theatre Company and the Tyrone Guthrie Theatre in Minneapolis.

**2193** METIZER, FRED W. The Duluth Playhouse: a case study in community theatre structure, policy, and practice
Columbus: Ohio State U. (PhD) 1966

**2194** HATFIELD, DOUGLAS P. A history of amateur theatre in St. Paul, Minneapolis and their suburbs 1929-May, 1963
Minneapolis: U. of Minnesota (PhD) 1968

**2195** MORISON, BRADLEY G. & FLIEHR, KAY. In search of an audience: how an audience was found for the Tyrone Guthrie Theatre
pp.xix, 230; ill. in text  M
NY: Pitman 1968
Audience development policies and strategies for the Minnesota Theatre Company, 1959-1966. Foreword by Tyrone Guthrie.

**2196** ROSSI, ALFRED. Minneapolis rehearsals: Tyrone Guthrie directs *Hamlet*
pp.xix; ll.152; pp.89, pl. 10  M
Berkeley: U. of California P. 1970
Includes facsimile of promptscript.

**2197** ELZEY, JOHN M. Professional legitimate theatre in Saint Paul, Minnesota, from 1890-1918
Minneapolis: U. of Minnesota (PhD) 1972

**2198** McDONOUGH, PATRICK D. A comparative descriptive study of management planning practices in the Tyrone Guthrie Theater and the Milwaukee Repertory Theater
Minneapolis: U. of Minnesota (PhD) 1972

**2199** PUFALL, MICHAEL E. A history of the Old Log Theater in Greenwood, Minnesota 1940-1970
Minneapolis: U. of Minnesota (PhD) 1974

**2200** FRANCIS, MARK S. The Mankato Opera House: music on the frontier 1872-1885
Mankato MN: State U. (MM) 1975

**2201** WALLACE, JAMES D. Set design at the Guthrie Theatre in its first ten years
Minneapolis: U. of Minnesota (PhD) 1975

**2202** FOREMAN, LARRY M. A history of the Lyceum Theatre, Duluth, Minnesota, from 1891-1901
Boulder: U. of Colorado (PhD) 1977

**2203** BUNDICK, THERESA J. Costume design at the Guthrie Theatre in its first ten years
Minneapolis: U. of Minnesota (PhD) 1979

**2204** HILL, LAWRENCE J. A history of variety-vaudeville in Minneapolis, Minnesota, from its beginning to 1900
Minneapolis: U. of Minnesota (PhD) 1979

**2205** POPULAR ENTERTAINMENT 1895-1929: the twin city scenic collection
pp.112; ill. in text, some col.  M
Minneapolis: U. of Minnesota Art Museum 1987
Exhibition catalogue April 5-June 14. Includes George Lipsitz: *Theatre space as total space: the Twin City scenic collection*; John R. Rothgeb: *The fugitive art*; C. Lance Brockman: *The age of scenic art: the nineteenth century* and *The twin city scenic studio, a chronology 1896-1980*; Forrest A. Newlin: *The scenic backdrop-some comments on the influences of 'modernism'*; and Lawrence J. Hill: *Late nineteenth century popular and theatrical events in Minneapolis and St Paul: a microcosm*....

**2206** WHITING, FRANK M. Minnesota theatre: from Old Fort Snelling to the Guthrie
pp.xiv, 231; ill. in text  M
[Minneapolis]: Pogo P. 1988
History, 1821-1988.

## 6.2.24 MISSISSIPPI

**2207** FREE, JOSEPH M. The theatre of Southwestern Mississippi to 1840
Iowa City: U. of Iowa (PhD) 1941

**2208** STEVENS, KATHERINE B. Theatrical entertainment in Jackson, Mississippi, 1890-1900
Lafayette: U. of Mississippi (MA) 1951

**2209** McKEE, EDNA H. History of theatrical entertainment in Jackson, Mississippi, from August 1839 to April 1860
Tallahassee: Florida State U. (MS) 1959

**2210** NICHOLSON, RETHA J. The little theatre movement in Mississippi
Hattiesburg: Mississippi Southern College (MA) 1961

**2211** HAMIL, LINDA V. A study of theatrical activity in Natchez, Mississippi from 1800-1840
Oxford: U. of Mississippi (MA) 1976

**2212** KEETON, GUY H. The theatre in Mississippi; from 1840 to 1870
Baton Rouge: Louisiana State U. (PhD) 1979

## 6.2.25 MISSOURI

**2213** BLACKBURN, MARGARET. The stage in St Louis, Missouri after 1850
Iowa City: U. of Iowa (MA) 1927

**2214** A BRIEF HISTORY of Thespian Hall, Boonville, Missouri
pp.16; ill. in text M
[Boonville]: Preservation Committee 1937
Claimed to be the oldest surviving theatre building west of the Alleghenies. Threatened with destruction by Fox-Midwest to make way for a movie palace.

**2215** WILKINSON, ALFRED O. The St. Louis dramatic seasons of 1850 and 1851
St. Louis: Washington U. (MA) 1938

**2216** RIETZ, LOUIS J. History of the theatre of Kansas City, Missouri, from the beginnings until 1900
Iowa City: U. of Iowa (PhD) 1939

**2217** CARSON, WILLIAM G. St Louis goes to the opera 1837-1941
pp.44; ill. DL★
St Louis: Missouri Historical Society 1946

**2218** CARSON, WILLIAM G. Managers in distress: the St Louis stage, 1840-1844
pp.xv, 329; pl. 9, inc. 2 folding M
St Louis: Historical Documents Foundation 1949

**2219** HESSE, RICHARD M. Aspects of the early St Louis stage
St Louis MO: Washington U. (MA) 1950

**2220** WRIGHT, DARLENE VAN B. Survey of little theatre activities in Kansas City, Missouri
Lawrence: U. of Kansas (MA) 1952

**2221** MARSH, WILLIAM S. The Saint Louis municipal Opera: a history of the background and first quarter century
Saint Louis: U. (MA) 1953

**2221A** WILKINSON, COLLEEN M. A history of theatre in St. Louis, 1865-1866
Waco TX: Baylor U. (MA) 1954

**2222** MELTON, ELSTON J. The first hundred years. With a chapter on movies and home talents, by Opal Hollomon Melton
pp.56; ill. DL★
Boonville MO: Missourian Publications 1957
Material on Thespian Hall MO.

**2223** JOHNSON, THEODORE C. A history of the first Olympic Theatre of St. Louis, Missouri, from 1866-1879
Iowa City: U. of Iowa (PhD) 1958

**2224** BOWEN, ELBERT R. Theatrical entertainments in rural Missouri before the civil war
pp.xiii, 141 M
Columbia: U. of Missouri P. 1959

**2225** HAYES, LAURICE M. A history of the Auditorium Stock Company at the Auditorium Theatre, Kansas City, Missouri
Lawrence: U. of Kansas (MA) 1961

**2226** JONES, MARTHA H. Show business in the Bootheel: a history of the performing arts in Cape Girardeau, Missouri, 1868-1963
Carbondale: Southern Illinois U. (MS) 1963

**2227** MACKAY, ALICE. A history of the Coates Opera House, Kansas City, 1870-1901
Warrensburg: Central Missouri State U. (MA) 1963

**2228** THOMPSON, ISABEL C. Amateur theatricals in St. Louis, Missouri, 1875-1890
Iowa City: U. of Iowa (PhD) 1964

**2229** WEST, WILLIAM F. The legitimate theatre in rural Missouri from the beginning of the civil war through 1872
Columbia: U. of Missouri (PhD) 1964

**2230** CARSON, WILLIAM G. The theatre on the frontier: the early years of the St Louis stage
pp.xxi, 361; pl. 16 M
NY: Blom 1965
Second edition with new introduction by author. First published 1932.

**2231** GRISVARD, LARRY E. The final years: the Ludlow and Smith theatrical firm in St Louis, 1845-1851
Columbus: Ohio State U. (PhD) 1965

**2232** TAYLOR, W. ELLARD. A survey of selected professional theatre buildings, Kansas City, Missouri, 1870-1902
Warrensburg: Central Missouri State U. (MA) 1968

**2233** CLIFFORD, CHARLES V. St Louis' fabulous Municipal Theatre: fifty years of summer musicals
pp.xi, 191; ill DL★
Louisiana MO: Midland Graphic Arts 1970

**2234** LAMPE, MICHAEL. Legitimate theatre in Springfield, Missouri: 1840 to 1900
Springfield: Southwest Missouri State U. (MA) 1970

**2235** KARASZ, LAWRENCE J. A history of legitimate theatre in St. Joseph, Missouri, 1865-1900
Springfield: Southwest Missouri State U. (MA) 1972

**2236** SWANSON, ALICE H. A history of Thespian Hall in Boonville, Missouri: 1855-1914
Memphis TN: State U. (MA) 1972

**2237** MERRILL, PATRICIA. A history of the Tootle Opera House, St. Joseph, Missouri
Kansas City: U. of Missouri (MA) 1973

**2238** CALLAHAN, JOHN M. A history of the second Olympic Theatre of Saint-Louis, Missouri, 1882-1916
Kent OH: State U. (PhD) 1974

**2239** WEST, SUSAN K. Thespian Hall, Boonville, Missouri: a sense of heritage, 1839-1976
Columbia: U. of Missouri (PhD) 1978

**2240** THE MIDLAND THEATRE, Kansas City, MO. Thomas W. Lamb architect. Opened: October 28, 1927. Introduction by John K. Kiesendahl...
pp.40; ill. in text M
Notre Dame: Theatre Historical Society 1979

## 6.2. STATES AND TOWNS

**2241** MAHER, DENNIS M. The theatre in St. Louis, 1875-1900
Madison: U. of Wisconsin (PhD) 1981

**2242** BAGLEY, MARY. The front row: Missouri's grand theatres
pp.176; ill. in text, some col. M
St Louis: Gateway 1984
Also includes showboats, opera houses, outdoor theatres, some sixty items in all.

**2243** GILMORE, ROBERT K. Ozark baptizings, hangings, and other diversions: theatrical folkways of rural Missouri, 1885-1910
pp.xxix, 264; front., ill. in text L
Norman: U. of Oklahoma P. 1984
Includes local dramatic productions and other entertainments. Foreword by Robert Flanders.

**2244** STRAUSS, MARY & NAYLOR, DAVID et al. Fox Theatre, St Louis: the fabulous Fox...
pp.64 inc. wrappers; ill. in text M
St Louis MO: Fox Associates 1985
History and description from the opening in 1927.

### 6.2.26 MONTANA

**2245** PORTER, ESTHER. A compilation of materials for a study of the early theatres of Montana (1864-1880)
Missoula: U. of Montana (MA) 1938

**2246** POWER, ESTHER P. The theatre in Montana
Missoula: U. of Montana (MA) 1939

**2247** NOT USED

**2248** BROWN, FIRMAN H. A history of theatre in Montana
Madison: U. of Wisconsin (PhD) 1963

**2249** NOT USED

**2250** JACOBSEN, BRUCE C. A historical study of the Bozeman, Montana Opera House
Minneapolis: U. of Minnesota (PhD) 1969
Period 1890-1920.

**2251** MILLER, FREDERICK K. The history of a Montana summer theater
pp.228; ill. in text, pl. 14 M
[Billings MT]: For the author 1989
The Pioneer Playhouse, Billings MT.

### 6.2.27 NEBRASKA

**2252** TICHY, CHARLES A. The first seventy years of legitimate theatre in Omaha, Nebraska
NY: U. (PhD) 1099

**2253** LANGDON, HARRY. A history of the Omaha Community Playhouse (1924-1955)
Lincoln: U. of Nebrsaka (MA) 1955

**2254** WALTON, JAMES H. A history of the professional theatre at 'The Oliver' in Lincoln, Nebraska (1897-1918)
Lincoln: U. of Nebraska (MA) 1956

**2255** GNUSE, WILLIAM J. The Lincoln community theatre 1947-1960
Lincoln: U. of Nebraska (MA) 1960

**2256** GOSSAGE, FOREST D. A history of the Funke Opera House in Lincoln, Nebraska, 1884-1907
Lincoln: U. of Nebraska (MA) 1961

**2257** FANDERS, REUBEN. History of the Boyd Theatre in Omaha, Nebraska
Omaha: U. of Nebraska (MA) 1963

**2258** NELSON, ROBERT M. A history of the Omaha playhouse from 1924 to 1963
Denver: U. (PhD) 1964

**2259** BABNICH, JUDITH M. A consciousness raising theate in America: the history of the Omaha Magic Theatre from 1969 to 1980
Los Angeles: U. of California (PhD) 1981

**2260** SORENSON, JOHN. Our show houses: the history of movie theaters in Grand Island, Nebraska
pp.iv, 65; ill. in text, pl. 22 M
Grand Island NB: Hall County Historical Soc. 1990
Includes material on stage shows.

### 6.2.28 NEVADA

**2261** SEMENZA, EDWIN S. The history of the professional theatre in the state of Nevada
Los Angeles: U. of Southern California (MA) 1934

**2262** JOSEPH, ROGER. Little theatre movement in Reno, Nevada
Los Angeles: U. of Southern California (MA) 1947

**2263** MILLER, WILLIAM C. An historical study of theatrical entertainment in Virginia City, Nevada; or Bonanza and Borasca theatres on the Comstock (1860-1875)
Los Angeles: U. of Southern California (PhD) 1947

**2264** CRAWFORD, ROBERT A. History and description of Piper's Opera House, Virginia City, Nevada
Los Angeles: U. of California (MA) 1950

**2265** HILLYER, KATHARINE & BEST, KATHARINE. The amazing story of Piper's Opera House in Virginia City, Nevada...
pp.23; ill. DL★
Virginia City: Enterprise P. 1953

**2266** BEST, KATHARINE & HILLYER, KATHARINE. Las Vegas: playtown USA
pp.xii, 178 L
NY: David McKay 1955
Foreword by Lucius Beebe. Chapter on show business.

**2267** LYMAN, GEORGE D. The saga of the Comstock lode: boom days in Virginia City, with an introduction by the Honorable Richard L. Neuberger, U.S. Senator from Oregon
pp.407; pl. 2 L
NY: Charles Scribner's Sons 1957
A new edition, indexed. First published NY, 1934. Includes reference to Adah Isaacs Menken's *Mazeppa* and McGuire's Opera House in Washoe.

## 6. LOCATION

**2268** WATSON, MARGARET G. Silver theatre: amusements on the mining frontier in early Nevada, 1850 to 1864
pp.387; ill. in text     M
Glendale CA: Arthur H. Clark     1964

**2269** ERICSON, ROBERT E. Touring entertainment in Nevada during the peak years of the mining boom, 1876-1878
Eugene: U. of Oregon (PhD)     1970

**2270** SOLDO, BETTY L. The feminine favorites of the Virginia City stage: 1865-1880
Fullerton: California State U. (MA)     1975

### 6.2.29 NEW HAMPSHIRE

**2271** HEWITT, DAVID D. A history of the theater in Manchester NH
Hanover NH: Dartmouth College (Thesis)     1948

### 6.2.30 NEW JERSEY

**2272** MORLEY, CHRISTOPHER. Seacoast of Bohemia
pp.xiii, 68; front., ill. in text     M
NY: Doubleday, Doran     1929
An account of the Old Rialto Theatre, Hoboken NJ, formerly Wareings, and The Empire.

**2273** BORGERS, EDWARD W. A history of dramatic production in Princeton, New Jersey
NY: U. (PhD)     1950

**2274** MOORE, LESTER L. Outside Broadway: a history of the professional theater in Newark, New Jersey from the beginning to 1867
pp.182     M
Metuchen NJ: Scarecrow P.     1970

**2275** MARTIN, CONSTANCE B. Atlantic City as a tryout town
Urbana-Champaign: U. of Illinois (PhD)     1973

**2276** COSTIGAN, DANIEL M. Encore for a worthy performer: illustrated biography of the 'Old Rahway', enduring survivor of the great theatre race
pp.vi, 50; ill. in text     M
Rahway NJ: Rahway Landmarks     1984
The Rahway Theatre opened in October, 1928.

### 6.2.31 NEW MEXICO

**2277** HEWETT, EDGAR L. A proposed Indian theater in Santa Fe
pp.12     DL★
Santa Fe NM: Archaeological Institute of America     1925
From the papers of the School of American Research of the AIE.

**2278** MUNRO, EDWIN C. The nativity plays of New Mexico
Albuquerque: U. of New Mexico (MA)     1940

**2279** VINEYARD, HAZEL. Trails of the trouper: a historical study of the theater in New Mexico from 1880 to 1910
Albuquerque: U. of New Mexico (MA)     1942

**2280** McCROSSAN, JOSEPHINE M. The role of the church and the folk in the development of the early drama in New Mexico
Philadelphia: U. of Pennsylvania (PhD)     1945

**2281** GARTNER, DAVID. A detailed history of the theatre in Santa Fe, New Mexico, 1847-1881, containing in addition an outline of the theatrical activities in this city from 1881-1891
Seattle: U. of Washington (MA)     1951

**2282** O'CONNOR, KATHRYN K. Theatre in the cow country
pp.127     M
South Bend IN: Creative Service/LittleTheatre     1966
History of Albuquerque Little Theatre

### 6.2.32 NEW YORK STATE

**2283** PHELPS, HENRY P. Players of a century: a record of the Albany stage. Including notices of prominent actors who have appeared in America
pp.x, 13-424     M
Albany NY: Joseph McDonough     1880
For the most part, articles reprinted from the Sunday edition of the *Albany Argus* in 1879, covering the period from 1745. 250 initialled copies. A "second edition", unlimited but not reset, was issued later in 1880 with four additional corrections on p. 413 and a frontispiece of Edwin Forrest. Addenda were issued in 1889.

**2284** HILL, RICHMOND C. A thespian temple: a brief history of the Academy of Music and review of the dramatic events of over fifty years in the city of Buffalo NY with illustrations of theaters, actors and old play bills. Also a biographical sketch...of the talented and popular comedian S. Russell
pp.36; ill. in text     MH
Buffalo NY: Courier, printers     1893

**2285** ELWOOD, GEORGE M. Some earlier public amusements at Rochester
pp.62     DL★
Rochester NY: Democrat and Chronicle     1894

**2286** BITZ, NELLIE E. A half-century of theatre in early Rochester
NY: Syracuse U. (MA)     1941

**2287** KOHLER, KATHARINE. The state of the drama in the Rochester Lyceum Theatre, 1912, 1913, 1914
Syracuse NY: U. (MA)     1941

**2288** NIEDECK, ARTHUR E. A sketch of the theatres of Ithaca, 1842-1942
Ithaca: Cornell U. (MA)     1942

**2289** STRONG, EVE E. The theatre in Buffalo, New York
Ann Arbor: U. of Michigan (MA)  1943

**2290** SINNETT, ALICE R. A selective survey of the Syracuse theatre, 1823-1915
Syracuse NY: U. (MA)  1952

**2291** McKELVEY, BLAKE. Rochester: the quest for quality, 1890-1925
pp.xv, 432; front., pl. 12  L
Cambridge MA: Harvard U. P.  1956
Includes reference to Lyceum Players and other theatre information.

**2292** RICKERT, ALFRED E. A history of the theatre in Oswego, New York, from its beginning to 1875
Denver: U. (PhD)  1967

**2293** LEONARD, JAMES M. The letters of William Duffy, Albany Theatre manager, 1830-1835
Ithaca: Cornell U. (PhD)  1971

**2294** BROWN, WILLIAM L. A history of the Leland Opera House, Albany, New York, under the management of John W. Albaugh, 1873-1881
Albany: State U. of New York (MA)  1972

**2295** KELLERHOUSE, MURIEL A. The Green Street Theatre, Albany, New York, under the management of John Bernard, 1813-1816
Bloomington: Indiana U. (PhD)  1973

**2296** SMITH, ARDIS & SMITH, KATHRYN. Theater in early Buffalo
pp.16; ill.  DL★
Buffalo NY: Buffalo and Erie County Hist. Soc.  1975

**2297** HRKACH, JOHN. Theatrical activity and other popular entertainment along the turnpikes of New York State from the end of the American revolution to the beginning of the Civil War
NY: City U. (PhD)  1990

## 6.2.33 NEW YORK CITY

**2298** BARNUM'S AMERICAN Museum illustrated
pp.32; ill. in text  MH
NY: [Van Norden & Frank Leslie?]  1850
Includes an account of the theatre use of the Lecture Room and the moral tone of the entertainments there provided.

**2299** FOSTER, GEORGE G. Celio; or, New York above ground and underground
pp.144  L
NY: Dewitt & Davenport  [1850]
Novel of theatre life.

**2300** FOSTER, GEORGE G. New York by gas-light: with here and there a streak of sunshine
pp.127  L
NY: Dewitt & Davenport  1850
Chapter X: *Theaters and public amusements* includes material on Charlotte Cushman.

**2301** NORTHALL, WILLIAM K. Before and behind the curtain; or, fifteen years' observations among the theatres of New York
pp.229  M
NY: W. F. Burgess  1851
Includes material on the Wallacks, Edwin Forrest and the Astor Place riot, George Holland, and William E. Burton.

**2302** FRANCIS, JOHN W. Old New York or, reminiscences of the past sixty years, being an enlarged and revised edition of the anniversary discourse delivered before the New York Historical Society (Nov. 17, 1857)
pp.384  L
NY: Charles Rose  1858
Includes description of early theatre and opera entertainment.

**2303** IRELAND, JOSEPH N. Records of the New York stage, from 1750 to 1860...in two volumes
pp.iv, 663; ii, 746  M
NY: T. H. Morrell  1866-67
An amplified version of of a work first published under the pseudonym 'H. N. D.': *Fifty years of a play-goer's journal; or, annals of the New York stage from A.D. 1798 to A.D. 1848....* NY: French, 1860 (3 vols).

**2304** BOOTH'S THEATRE behind the scenes
pp.16; ill. in text  MH
NY: Henry L. Hinton  1872
Detailed description, with engravings of stage facilities and machinery.

**2305** McCABE, JAMES D. Lights and shadows of New York life: or, sights and sensations of the great city. A work descriptive of the city of New York in all its various phases...
pp.850; ill. in text, col.  L
Philadelphia: National Publishing  1872
Includes chapters on Broadway and its theatres, metropolitan amusements with descriptions of principal theatres and variety houses, Harry Hills, the Bowery. Illustrations include Booth's Theatre, the Grand Opera House, the old Bowery Theatre. Reissued Philadelphia: Douglass Brothers, in 1882 as *New York by sunlight and gaslight...* with a slightly different layout.

**2306** [MORRISSEY, STARR]. Diagrams of the theatres of New York [cover title]
pp.36  DL★
NY: Morrissey  1874

**2307** HUTTON, LAURENCE. Plays and players
pp.ix, 276  M
NY: Hurd and Houghton  1875
The New York stage, c.1850-1870.

**2308** BROOKLYN THEATRE fire. Memorial services held at the Academy of Music, Hooley's Opera House and Park Theatre, Brooklyn, Dec. 10, 1876, together with proceedings of the common council relative to the burial of the dead
pp.72  MH
Brooklyn: Daily Times Print  1876

**2309** THE FIRE in the Brooklyn Theatre, (Tuesday, 11:15 p.m., December 5, 1876). Special report of the Fire Marshal...Official list of those who lost their lives by the accident...Evidence taken by Fire Marshal Keady as to the cause of the fire
pp.70  MH
Brooklyn NY: Daily Times Print  1876

**2310** FULL ACCOUNT of the burning of the Brooklyn Theatre, Brooklyn, N.Y., Tuesday evening, Dec 5, 1876 with illustrations
pp.16; ill. in text　　　　　　　　　　　　MH
NY: National Police Gazette　　　　　　[1876]

**2311** THE HOLOCAUST at the Brooklyn theatre. With interment and memorial services, and official list of the dead and missing
pp.32　　　　　　　　　　　　　　　　　MB
Brooklyn NY: Daily Argus Office　　　　　1876

**2312** UNION SQUARE Theatre. Souvenir of the one hundredth performance of *Rose Michel*, Monday evening, Feb 28, 1876
pp.104; ill. in text　　　　　　　　　　　　MH
NY: For the theatre　　　　　　　　　　　1876

With illustrations of scenes, portraits of performers and production histories and credits of Blum/Mackaye: *Rose Michel*; Feuillet/Boucicault: *Led Astray*; D'Ennery/Jackson: *Two Orphans*.

**2313** A THRILLING personal experience! Brooklyn's horror. Wholesale holocaust at the Brooklyn, New York, Theatre, on the night of December 5th, 1876. Three hundred men, women and children buried in the blazing ruins! Origin, progress and devastation of the fire. The tragedy in the galleries - a wedge of death - into a pit of fire - harrowing scenes and incidents - affecting and exciting stories of survivors - two actors among the victims - the ghastly array of the disfigured dead -heartrending scenes in identifying the remains - complete list of victims - burial of the dead
pp.62; ill. in text　　　　　　　　　　　　MH
Philadelphia: Barclay　　　　　　　　　　1877

**2314** DIAGRAMS of the leading New York theatres compliments of T. J. McBride arcade news room 71, Broadway M.E.R.R.
pp.40; ill. in text　　　　　　　　　　　　MB
NY: T. J. McBride　　　　　　　　　　　1879

**2315** REPORT of the executive committee of the Brooklyn Theatre fire relief association. Presented, March 25, 1879
pp.8　　　　　　　　　　　　　　　　　MH
[NY]: [For the Association]　　　　　　　[1879]

Report of the final meeting of the committee.

**2316** INTERIOR VIEWS (with seats numbered): New York and Brooklyn theatres
pp.32; ill. in text　　　　　　　　　　　　MB
NY: Lansing　　　　　　　　　　　　　　1880

**2317** MACKEEVER, SAMUEL A. Glimpses of Gotham and city characters by Samuel A. Mackeever, the American Charles Dickens
pp.72; portrait in title　　　　　　　　　　MH
NY: National Police Gazette　　　　　　　1880

**2318** NEW YORK city theatrical and amusement record... a record of every theatre, and its work, in the city of New York, during the year...together with the management of each house as it existed December 1st of that year
pp.av. 8　　　　　　　　　　　　　　　MH
NY: New York Star　　　　　　　　　　1880-

Issued annually as part of the *New York Star* almanac. Five issues examined, 1880-1884.

**2319** VENTILATION OF the Madison Square Theatre
pp.24; ill. in text　　　　　　　　　　　　MH
NY: Madison Square Theatre　　　　　　1880

A pamphlet comprising an introduction and two reprinted articles; James Hogg: *On the ventilation of public buildings* reprinted from *Scientific American*, October 16, 1880 and emphasizing the Madison Square Theatre, and Walter G. Elliot: *Ventilation of the Madison Square Theatre* reprinted from *Sanitary Engineer*, October 15, 1880.

**2320** ILLUSTRATED DESCRIPTION of Wallack's: Broadway and 30th street. Mr Lester Wallack, proprietor and manager
pp.32; ill. in text　　　　　　　　　　　　MH
NY: Russell Bros, printers　　　　　　　[1882]

**2321** CATALOGUE of the Eden Musée, 55 West 23rd St
pp.16; ill. in text　　　　　　　　　　　　MB
NY: Rich. G. Hollaman　　　　　　　　　1884

The complex included a music hall, or winter garden. Among the exhibits were tableaux, some of eminent performers including Mary Anderson and Fanny Davenport. Later, the catalogue was issued monthly.

**2322** HARRISON, GABRIEL. A history of the progress of the drama, music and the fine arts in the city of Brooklyn
pp.64　　　　　　　　　　　　　　　　　MH
Brooklyn NY: W. W. Munsell　　　　　　1884

100 copies. Reprinted from H. R. Stiles, *Illustrated History of King's County*, Munsell, 1884.

**2323** DAYTON, ABRAM C. Last days of knickerbocker life in New York
pp.xxxi, 386; pl.20　　　　　　　　　　　L
NY: G. P. Putnam's Sons　　　　　　　　1897

Second edition, enlarged. Includes chapters on the theatre. Illustrations include views of the Apollo Rooms, the Park Theatre and Niblo's Garden. First published without illustrations NY: Harlan, 1882.

**2324** OPERA IN ENGLISH by the Castle Square Opera Company
pp.158; ill. in text　　　　　　　　　　　　M
NY: American Theatre　　　　　　　　　1899

Issued for the 500th performance on 16 October. Playbills for all productions.

**2325** PATTERSON, ADA & BATEMAN, VICTORY. By the stage door
pp.xi, 217　　　　　　　　　　　　　　MB
NY: Grafton P.　　　　　　　　　　　　1902

Fiction. Stories of the New York stage. An introduction by Annie C. Adams vouches for the underlying authenticity.

**2326** BARNAY, LUDWIG. Erinnerungen
pp.viii, 378; pl. 6　　　　　　　　　　　　M
Berlin: E. Fleischel　　　　　　　　　　　1903

In two volumes. Vol. 2 makes reference to the Germania Theatre.

**2327** BROWN, T. ALLSTON. A history of the New York stage
pp.xii, 523; x, 652; ix, 671　　　　　　　　M
NY: Dodd, Mead　　　　　　　　　　　1903

Three volumes. 358 copies. First published in parts in the *New York Clipper*, c.1888-1893

**2328** THE NEW THEATRE, New York
pp.48; ill. in text, pl. 13 some col.     M
[NY]: [For the theatre]     1909

Issued for the dedication of the theatre on the afternoon of November 6, 1909, two days before its official opening, it provides plans and photographs of the theatre, and lists and illustrates the company. Loosely inserted is a programme and a list of founders. A condensed (16pp) brochure was also issued.

**2329** DAVIS, MICHAEL M. The exploitation of pleasure. A study of commercial recreations in New York City
pp.61     DL★
NY: Dept. of Child Hygiene     1911

**2330** JENKINS, STEPHEN. The greatest street in the world: the story of Broadway, old and new, from the Bowling Green to Albany
pp.xxii, 509; ill. in text, pl. 6 folding     L
NY: G. P. Putnam's Sons     1911

Substantial theatre reference.

**2331** DIMMICK, RUTH C. Our theatre of today and yesterday
pp.97, x; ill. in text, pl. 11     M
NY: H. K. Fly     1913

New York theatre from its origins up to 1913.

**2332** WASHINGTON SQUARE plays...with an introduction by Walter P. Eaton. Preface by Edward Goodman, director of the Washington Square Players
pp.xx, 121     MH
Garden City: Doubleday, Page     1916

Important prefatory material. Plays are Lewis Beach: *The Clod*; Alice Gerstenberg: *Overtones*; Philip Moeller: *Eugenically Speaking*; Edward Goodman: *Helena's Husband*.

**2333** *BILLBOARD* INDEX of the New York legitimate stage
pp.various     DL★
NY: Billboard     1921-
Annual

**2334** MACADAM, GEORGE. The little church around the corner
pp.x, 347: ill.     DL★
NY: G. P. Putnam's Sons     1925

Anecdotal history of the Church of the Transfiguration, 1 East 29th St. NY, c.1850-1923. Includes material on the controversial funeral of George Holland which initiated the church's theatrical associations.

**2335** STEINBERG, MOLLIE B. (Ed.). The Civic Repertory Theatre magazine
pp.various     DL★
NY: Civic Repertory Theatre     [1926-1932?]

Eight numbers a year.

**2336** DUNNIE, PHILIP & ABBOTT, GEORGE. Broadway: a novel...the story of the play
pp.251     L
London: Readers Library Publishing     [c. 1926]

Revealing of its period.

**2337** ODELL, GEORGE C. Annals of the New York stage
pp.av. 750; pl. av. 40     M
NY: Columbia U. P.     1927-49

Fifteen volumes. Comprehensively illustrated with photographs of players. These are numerous, but not indexed. In 1963 the ASTR (NY) published *Index to the portraits...transcribed from the file in the theatre collection at Princeton University*, pp. iv, 179.

**2338** MORLEY, CHRISTOPHER; THROCKMORTON, CLEON & NASH, OGDEN. Born in a beer garden or, she troupes to conquer: sundry ejaculations...and certain of the Hoboken acts with a commentary on them by Earnest Elmo Calkins
pp.121; ill. in text     L
NY: Foundry P.     1930

In part reprinted from the *Saturday Evening Post* and *Theatre Magazine*. Describes the revival of 19th century popular dramas at the Old Rialto and Lyric theatres.

**2339** ATKINSON, BROOKS East of the Hudson
pp.vi, 217     O
NY: Alfred A. Knopf     1931

Manhattan and surrounding district. Chapters on theatre and other entertainments. 200 numbered copies.

**2340** STEINBERG, MOLLIE B. The history of the Fourteenth Street Theatre
pp.105; ill. in text, pl. 9     M
NY: Dial P.     1931

Built 1866, derelict in 1901 and reopened by Eva Le Gallienne as the Civic Repertory Theatre in 1926. Widespread reference to performers, including Edwin Forrest, Laura Keene, Edwin Booth, Fanny Davenport, Clara Morris.

**2341** TOWNE, CHARLES H. This New York of mine
pp.xiii, 290; ill. in text, front.     L
NY: Cosmopolitan Book     1931

Much incidental theatre interest.

**2342** VAN WYCK, FREDERICK. Recollections of an old New Yorker
pp.xvi, 421; ill. in text     MH
NY: Liveright     1932

Chapter 9, *Theatrical memories*.

**2343** OPERA CAVALCADE: the story of the Metropolitan
pp.68; ill. in text     M
NY: Metropolitan Opera Guild     1938

**2344** JOHNSON, JAMES W. Black Manhattan
pp.xvii, 329     DL★
NY: Alfred A. Knopf     1940

Revised edition. First published 1930. Harlem from colonial days to 1940. Substantial section on theatre and other entertainments.

**2345** BOARDMAN, ABIGAIL C. A study of revivals of plays in the New York City (Broadway) theatres from 1925 to 1940
Madison: U. of Wisconsin (PhD)     1944

**2346** WHITE, NATALIE E. Shakespeare on the New York stage, 1891-1941
New Haven: Yale U. (PhD)     1946

**2347** BOYD, ALICE K. The interchange of plays between London and New York, 1910-1939: a study in relative audience response
pp.xii, 125     M
NY: King's Crown P.     1948

Focuses on commercial/critical success and failure and attempts to identify causes.

**2348** MOREHOUSE, WARD. Matinee tomorrow. Fifty years of our theater
pp.xii, 340; pl. 22 M
NY: Whittlesey House 1949
A history of the New York stage.

**2349** SELTSAM, WILLIAM H. (Ed.). Metropolitan Opera annals: a chronicle of artists and performances
pp.xvi, 751 (6); ill. in text M
NY: H. W. Wilson/ Metropolitan Opera 1949

**2350** NAGLE, URBAN. Behind the masque
pp.vii, 309 M
NY: McMullen Books 1951
Account of the Blackfriars' Guild, a Roman Catholic little theatre off-Broadway.

**2351** BENARDETE, DORIS F. The Neighborhood Playhouse in Grand Street
DL★
NY: [For the author?] 1952
Abridged thesis.

**2352** JENNINGS, JOHN. A history of the New Theatre, New York, 1909-1911
Stanford: U. (PhD) 1952

**2353** LEWIS, STANLEY T. The New York theatre. Its background and architectural development, 1750-1853
Columbus: Ohio State U. (PhD) 1954

**2354** KANIN, GARSON. Do re mi
pp.89; ill. DL★
Boston: Little, Brown 1955
'The book of the Broadway Story'. Illustrated by Al Hirschfeld. Not to be confused with the musical of the same title.

**2355** TURNER, DARWIN T. Techniques of and critical reactions towards American nonrepresentational drama on New York professional stages, 1920-1930
Chicago: U. (PhD) 1956

**2356** OLIVER, GEORGE B. Changing patterns of spectacle on the New York stage (1850-1890)
University Park: Pennsylvania State U. (PhD) 1957

**2357** CORDELL, RICHARD A. & MATSON, LOWELL (Eds). The off Broadway theatre
pp.xxvi, 481 L
NY: Random House 1959
Playtexts, but with substantial introduction.

**2358** CROWLEY, ALICE L. The Neighbourhood Playhouse: leaves from a theatre scrapbook
pp.xxiv, 264; pl. 8 M
NY: Theatre Arts 1959

**2359** JONES, CECIL D. The policies and practices of Wallack's Theatre, 1852-1888
Urbana: U. of Illinois (PhD) 1959

**2360** MINOR, CHARLES H. Preferred seats: a current list of seating diagrams for theatres and arenas in and around New York, together with other useful information
pp.95; ill. DL★
NY: Arco Publishing 1959

**2361** RAFFANIELLO, WILLIAM F. The image of New York City in modern drama. Materials for an adult education course stressing the interpretation of literary symbols
NY: Columbia U. Teachers' College (EdD) 1959

**2362** LINCOLN CENTER for the performing arts
pp.4; ill. in text M
[NY]: [Lincoln Center] 1961
Leaflet illustrating the model for the Center. Issued in May.

**2363** WHARTON, JOHN F. Crisis in the free world theatre...from material compiled by O. Glenn Saxon: a statement of the League of New York Theatres
pp.24 DL★
NY: League of New York Theatres 1961
The League, a major force in inter-Union negotiations, has, since 1973, added 'and producers' to its title.

**2364** CHURCHILL, ALLEN. The Great White Way. A re-creation of Broadway's golden era of theatrical entertainment
pp.vii, 310; pl. 4 L
NY: E. P. Dutton 1962
Popular history, 1900-1920.

**2365** KLEE, BRUCE B. An analysis of the production schedules in professional theatres in New York City from 1750 to 1950
Columbia: Ohio State U. (PhD) 1962

**2366** PHILHARMONIC HALL at Lincoln Center: a description
pp.[16] inc. wrappers; ill. in text M
NY: Lincoln Center for the Performing Arts [c. 1962]

**2367** PORTER, JACK. A history of the Phoenix Theatre, New York City, 1953 to 1961
Denver: U. (PhD) 1962

**2368** PRICE, JULIA S. The off-Broadway theater
pp.xv, 279: ill. in text, front. M
Metuchen NJ: Scarecrow P. 1962

**2369** COWAN, ROBERT A. Off-Broadway. A history, 1915-1962
West Lafayette IN: Purdue U. (PhD) 1963

**2370** SAVO, JIMMY. I bow to the stones; memories of a New York childhood. Introduction by George Freedley
pp.144; ill. DL★
NY: Howard Frisch 1963

**2371** HOBBS, ROBERT L. Off-Broadway. The early years, 1944-1952
Evanston: Northwestern U. (PhD) 1964

**2372** LINCOLN CENTER for the performing arts
pp.125; ill. in text L
NY: Lincoln Center 1964

**2373** HENSLEY, JACK A. A history of the theatre section of the *New York Times* as a record of the New York commercial theatre 1920-1950
Madison: U. of Wisconsin (PhD) 1965

**2374** THE LIBRARY and museum of the performing arts at Lincoln Center
pp.52, 3; ill. in text, some col. M
NY: Public Library [1965]

## 6.2. STATES AND TOWNS

**2375** RAOUL, ROSINE. The library and museum of the performing arts at Lincoln Centre
pp.52; ill., some col. DL★
NY: NYPL 1965

**2376** WHITE, JEAN W. Shaw on the New York stage
NY: U. (PhD) 1965

**2377** BARAL, ROBERT. Turn west on twenty-third: a toast to New York's old Chelsea
pp.128; ill. DL★
NY: Fleet 1966
Reference to theatres.

**2378** KOLODIN, IRVING. The Metropolitan Opera 1883-1966: a candid history
pp.xxi, 762, xlvii; pl. 22 M
NY: Alfred A. Knopf 1966
Third edition, enlarged. First published Oxford: U.P, 1936, as *The Metropolitan Opera, 1883-1935*. A second revised edition, NY: Knopf, 1953, *The story of the Metropolitan Opera 1883-1950...*, makes no mention of its predecessor apart from a copyright date.

**2379** LAUFE, ABE. Anatomy of a hit: long-run plays on Broadway from 1900 to the present day
pp.351; ill. in text M
NY: Hawthorn Books 1966

**2380** LINCOLN CENTER [cover title]
pp.24; ill. in text, col. M
NY: Lincoln Center [c. 1966]

**2381** ROBERTS, KENNETH H. The Lincoln Center Repertory Theatre, 1958-1965
Columbus: Ohio State U. (PhD) 1966

**2382** JACOBS, SUSAN. On stage. The making of a Broadway play
pp.xiii, 114; ill. in text MH
NY: Alfred A. Knopf [1967?]
Production history of Mary Mercier: *Johnny No-Trump* (Fall, 1967).

**2383** HAILEY, ROBERT C. Broadway on war: 1933-1941
Cleveland OH: Case Western Reserve U. (PhD) 1967

**2384** KRAWITZ, HERMAN E. An introduction to the Metropolitan Opera House, Lincoln Center Plaza: the official guide book...
pp.66; ill. in text DL★
NY: Saturday Review 1967

**2385** CLARKE, NORMAN. The mighty Hippodrome
pp.144; ill. in text, pl. 2 col. M
Cranbury NJ: A. S. Barnes 1968

**2386** CROGHAN, LELAND A. New York burlesque: 1840-1870. A study in theatrical self-criticism
NY: U. (PhD) 1968
Literary burlesque on the New York stage.

**2387** EATON, QUAINTANCE. The miracle of the Met: an informal history of the Metropolitan Opera 1883-1967
pp.xv, 490; pl 8 M
Westport CT: Greenwood P. 1968

**2388** LEITER, SAMUEL L. The legitimate theatre in Brooklyn, 1861-1898
NY: U. (PhD) 1968

**2389** BRIGGS, JOHN. Requiem for a yellow brick brewery: a history of the Metropolitan Opera
pp.xxii, 359; ill. in text M
Boston: Little, Brown 1969

**2390** FALK, ROBERT F. A critical analysis of the history and development of the Association of Producing Artists (APA) and the Phoenix Theatre (APA-PHOENIX) 1960-1969
Detroit: Wayne State U. (PhD) 1969

**2391** GOLDMAN, WILLIAM. The season: a candid look at Broadway
pp.xii, 432; ill. in text M
NY: Harcourt, Brace & World 1969

**2392** O'CONNEL, MARY B. The Circle in the Square Theatre and Theodore Mann's additional productions: 1950-1967
NY: U. (PhD) 1969

**2393** SELBY, DAVID L. A history of the American Place Theatre 1963-1968
Carbondale: Southern Illinois U. (PhD) 1969

**2394** SPITZER, MARIAN. The Palace
pp.xviii, 268; pl. 8 M
NY: Atheneum 1969
History and description of the Palace Theatre, New York, opened as a variety house in 1913. Introduction by Brooks Atkinson.

**2395** ATKINSON, BROOKS Broadway scrapbook. Illustrated by Hirschfeld
pp.x, 312; ill. in text M
Westport CT: Greenwood P. 1970
Articles reprinted from the *New York Times* and *Sunday Echo*. First published NY, Theatre Arts, 1947.

**2396** BENSON, RAY. The Broadway theater: a problem of stasis
Los Angeles: U. of California (PhD) 1970

**2397** BROUN, DANIEL. The production: a novel of the Broadway theater
pp.x, 369 O
London: Cassell 1970
Published NY: Dial P. Describes a production from first script to first night.

**2398** [NORKIN, SAM]. Theatre drawings: exhibition...Amsterdam Gallery, Library and Museum of the Performing Arts, at Lincoln Center, New York...
pp.64; ill. in text MH
NY: Museum of the Performing Arts [c. 1970]
Booklet of 61 drawings, reproduced from the *New York Sunday Times* and elsewhere, caricaturing mainly New York theatre productions.

**2399** ATKINSON, BROOKS Broadway
pp.ix, 484; ill. in text M
London: Cassell 1971
History of mid-town Manhattan theatre, 1900-1970.

**2400** GREENBERGER, HOWARD. The off-Broadway experience
pp.xiii, 207; ill. in text M
Englewood Cliffs NJ: Prentice-Hall 1971

Brief history from the Washington Square Players to the present, followed by interviews with directors and actors.

**2401** HUGGINS, NATHAN I.   Harlem renaissance
pp.xiii, 343                                                               L
NY: Oxford U. P.                                                      1971
Chapter 6, *White/black faces - black masks* is on theatre and show business.

**2402** MARTIN, RALPH G.   Lincoln Center for the performing arts
pp.192; ill. in text, pl. 16 col.                                   M
Englewood Cliffs NJ: Prentice-Hall                            1971

**2403** SCHIFFMAN, JACK.   Uptown: the story of Harlem's Apollo Theatre
pp.xii, 210; pl. 8                                                    M
NY: Cowles                                                             1971

**2404** BONTEMPS, ARNA (Ed.).   The Harlem renaissance remembered: essays edited with a memoir...
pp.ix, 310; pl. 4                                                     O
NY: Dodd, Mead                                                     1972
Harlem in the 1930s. Includes material on Langston Hughes, Wallace Thurman, Theophilus Lewis, and theatre in Harlem.

**2405** LITTLE, STUART W.   Off-Broadway: the prophetic theater
pp.323; pl. 12                                                         M
NY: Coward, McCann & Geoghegan                        1972
History and survey with chronological list of award-winners and including material on the Living Theatre, Joseph Papp, off-off-Broadway and regional theatre.

**2406** POLAND, ALBERT & MAILMAN, BRUCE (Eds).   The off, off off Broadway book: the plays, people, theatre
pp.lxii, 546                                                            MH
Indianapolis: Bobbs-Merrill                                      1972
Playtexts, but includes a checklist of productions at 17 off-Broadway theatres, and helpful bibliographies.

**2407** STASIO, MARILYN (Ed.).   Broadway's beautiful losers
pp.xxii, 425; ill. in text                                           MH
NY: Delacorte P.                                                     1972
Texts, with comments, of five plays that failed on Broadway, examining background and cause. Playwrights: Hugh Wheeler, S. J. Perelman, Saul Bellow, Jack Richardson, Mary Mercier.

**2408** THOMPSON, MARY F.   The Lafayette Players: 1915-1932
Ann Arbor: U. of Michigan (PhD)                            1972
History of the Lafayette Stock Company, Harlem NY.

**2409** BRUMM, BEVERLY M.   A survey of professional acting schools in New York City: 1870-1970
NY: U. (PhD)                                                         1973

**2410** HENDERSON, MARY C.   The city and the theatre: New York playhouses from Bowling Green to Times Square
pp.xvii, 323; ill. in text                                            M
Clifton NJ: James T. White                                     1973

**2411** WANK, EUGENE M.   The Washington Square Players: experiment towards professionalism
Euigene: U. of Oregon (PhD)                                 1973

**2412** RUBIN, STEPHEN E.   The new Met in profile
pp.xxx, 202; ill. in text                                             M
NY: Macmillan                                                       1974

**2413** DALRYMPLE, JEAN.   From the last row
pp.ix, 301; pl. 12                                                    M
Clifton NJ: James T. White                                     1975
A history of the New York City Center of Music and Drama, 1943-68.

**2414** MILLER, MICHAEL.   Loew's Paradise: Grand Concourse, the Bronx, New York City...foreword by: Drew Eberson
pp.[28]; ill. in text                                                   M
[Notre Dame IN]: Theatre Historical Society            1975
A photographic record of the Paradise Theatre converted into twin cinemas, 1973

**2415** WELLER, JANET H.   Barnumism and Broadway
Madison: U. of Wisconsin (PhD)                             1975

**2416** APPELBAUM, STANLEY (Ed.).   The New York stage: famous productions in photographs. 148 photos, 1883-1939, from the theatre and music collection of the museum of the city of New York
pp.vi, 154; ill in text                                                 M
NY: Dover Publications                                            1976

**2417** CARNEY, SARALEIGH.   The Repertory Theatre of Lincoln Center: aesthetics and economics, 1960-1973
NY: City U. (PhD)                                                  1976

**2418** GREEN, G. E.   The Art Theatre movement in New York City, 1909-1932: a study of the history and ideology of ten theatres
Lancaster UK: U. (PhD)                                           1976

**2419** TIMES SQUARE Paramount
pp.44 inc. wrappers; ill. in text                                 M
Alameda CA: Theatre Historical Society                 1976

**2420** BRECHT, STEFAN.   The original theatre of the city of New York. From the mid-60s to the mid-70s. Book 1: the theatre of visions: Robert Wilson. [Book 2: queer theatre]
pp.441; 178; ill in text                                               M
Frankfurt/Main: Suhrkamp                                        1978
Two volumes.

**2421** GARRETT, THOMAS M.   A history of pleasure gardens in New York City, 1700–1865
NY: U. (PhD)                                                          1978

**2422** HUGHES, CATHARINE (Ed.).   New York theatre annual 1976-77. Volume 1-
pp.v, 149; ill. in text                                                 MH
Detroit: Gale Reseach                                            1978-79
Record of season, with full credits, a description of each play, photographic illustrations and a selection of reviews. Also *New York theatre annual 1977-78* (pp.vii, 183). Later incorporated in *American theatre annual 1978-1979* (pp.viii, 280), Detroit: 1980 (M).

**2423** THE NEW AMSTERDAM Theatre Forty-second street, New York City. Opened: October 26, 1903. Architects: Herts and Tallant
pp.44 inc. wrappers; ill. in text                                 M
Alameda CA: Theatre Historical Society                 1978

**2424** FEHL, FRED; STOTT, WILLIAM & STOTT, JANE. On Broadway. Performance photographs and text
pp.xxxv, 419; ill. in text　　　　　　　　　　M
London: Thames & Hudson　　　　　　　1979
First published Austin: U. of Texas P., 1978.

**2425** FRANCISCO, CHARLES. The Radio City Music Hall. An affectionate history of the world's greatest theater
pp.vii, 136; ill. in text, pl. 32 col.　　　　　M
NY: E. P. Dutton　　　　　　　　　　　　1979

**2426** MONROE, JOHN G. A record of the black theatre in New York City 1920-1929
Austin: U. of Texas (PhD)　　　　　　　1980

**2427** BAUTISTA, MICHAEL P. Ten years of stage design at the Met (1966-1976)
Lubbock: Texas Tech U. (PhD)　　　　　1981

**2428** LEWIS, DAVID L. When Harlem was in vogue
pp.xiv, 381, pl. 16　　　　　　　　　　　DL★
NY: Alfred A. Knopf　　　　　　　　　　1981

**2429** MOSEDALE, JOHN. The men who invented Broadway: Damon Runyon, Walter Winchell and their world
pp.321; ill.　　　　　　　　　　　　　　DL★
NY: R. Marek　　　　　　　　　　　　　1981

**2430** ANDERSON, JERVIS. This was Harlem: a cultural portrait
pp.x, 389; ill.　　　　　　　　　　　　　DL★
NY: Farrar, Straus, Giroux　　　　　　　1982

**2431** BLAIR, JOHN P. Productions at Niblo's Garden Theatre, 1849-1862
Athens: U. of Georgia (PhD)　　　　　　1982

**2432** JUSTESEN, JOEL L. A history of the initial stagings of new productions at the New York City Opera, 1966-1975
NY: City U. (PhD)　　　　　　　　　　　1982

**2433** KNAPP, MARGARET M. A historical study of the legitimate playhouses on West Forty-second Street between Seventh and Eighth Avenues in New York City
NY: City U. (PhD)　　　　　　　　　　　1982

**2434** MORRISON, A. CRAIG & WHEELER, LUCY P. et al. Fox Theatre, Brooklyn, New York...featuring the complete text of the special report made by the Historic American Building survey unit of the United States Department of the Interior
pp.52, inc. wrappers; ill. in text　　　　　M
[San Francisco]: Theatre Historical Society　1982

**2435** BAUM, MARLYN V. The Brooklyn Academy of Music: a case study of the rebirth of an urban cultural center
NY: City U. (PhD)　　　　　　　　　　　1983

**2436** BROADWAY THEATRE district; a preservation, development and management plan
pp.51; pl. 58　　　　　　　　　　　　　M
NY: Save the Theatres Inc.　　　　　　　1983

**2437** FEHL, FRED. Stars of the New York stage 1940-1967 in performance photographs
pp.iv, 122; front., ill. in text　　　　　　M
NY: Dover　　　　　　　　　　　　　　1983

**2438** MAYER, MARTIN. The Met. One hundred years of grand opera
pp.368; ill. in text, some col.　　　　　　M
London: Thames and Hudson　　　　　　1983

**2439** McCULLOUGH, JACK W. Living pictures of the New York stage
pp.ix, 202; ill. in text　　　　　　　　　O
Ann Arbor: UMI Research P.　　　　　1983
Tableaux vivants.

**2440** BOTTO, LOUIS. At this theatre: an informal history of New York's legitimate theatres
pp.xi, 260; ill. in text, some col.　　　　M
NY: Dodd, Mead　　　　　　　　　　　1984

**2441** GARVEY, SHEILA H. 'Not for profit': the history of the Circle in the Square
NY: U. (PhD)　　　　　　　　　　　　1984

**2442** PLACES PLEASE; Broadway's historic theates with commentary by Broadway's playwrights, actors and critics
pp.v, 108; ill. in text　　　　　　　　　M
NY: Vincent Astor Gallery　　　　　　　1984
Exhibition catalogue, 1984 in conjunction with Save the Theatres Inc. Illustrations accompanied by brief personal reminiscences.

**2443** POWELL, MATHEW D. The Blackfriars Guild of New York, 1940-1972. An experiment in Catholic theatre
Madison: U. of Wisconsin (PhD)　　　　1984

**2444** STUBS: the seating plan guide
pp.95; plans　　　　　　　　　　　　　M
NY: Patricia and Ronald S. Lee　　　　1984
The seating plan guide for New York theatres, music halls and sports stadia...expanded edition including major off-Broadway theatres. Vol. 36, no. 1. (Selected as an example). Regional versions also issued.

**2445** FOX, TED. Showtime at the Apollo
pp.xiii, 322; ill. in text　　　　　　　　M
NY: Quartet　　　　　　　　　　　　　1985
First published NY: Holt, Rinehart and Winston, 1983. A history of the Apollo Theatre, Harlem, founded in 1934 as a home for black popular musical entertainment.

**2446** FRICK, JOHN W. New York's first theatrical center: the Rialto at Union Square
pp.xi, 209; ill. in text　　　　　　　　　M
Ann Arbor: UMI Research P.　　　　　1985

**2447** JACOBSON, ROBERT. Magnificence onstage at the Met: twenty great opera productions
pp.256; ill. in text, some col.　　　　　　M
London: Thames and Hudson　　　　　　1985
Erratum slip.

**2448** JOHNSON, STEPHEN B. The roof gardens of Broadway theatres, 1883-1942
pp.xii, 241; ill. in text　　　　　　　　　MH
Ann Arbor: UMI Research P.　　　　　1985

Description of performance spaces and history of the entertainments they housed.

**2449** LEITER, SAMUEL & HILL, HOLLY (Eds). The encyclopedia of the New York stage, 1920-1930. In two vols...
pp.xxiii; xv; 1332     M
Westport CT: Greenwood P.     1985
Another volume covering the period 1930-1940 (pp.1344) was published in 1989 (unexamined).

**2450** THE NEW YORK theatrical sourcebook 1985-86
pp.600     DL★
NY: Broadway P.     1985
For the Association of Theatrical Artists and Craftspeople.

**2451** WHARTON, ROBERT T. The working dynamics of the Ridiculous Theatre Company. An analysis of Charles Ludlam's relationship with his ensemble from 1964 through 1981
Tallahassee: Florida State U. (PhD)     1985

**2452** CHAMPINE, GEMMA E. Troy Music Hall: America's premier acoustical treasure
Albany: State U. of NY (PhD)     1986

**2453** JASPER, LAWRENCE G. A critical history of the Artists' Theatre of New York
Lawrence: U. of Kansas (PhD)     1986

**2454** LEITER, SAMUEL L. Ten seasons. New York theatre in the seventies
pp.xiii, 245     L
NY: Greenwood P.     1986
New plays, revivals, playhouses, actors, directors, critics. Chronological tables categorizing under a range of thematic and other characteristic features.

**2455** NUNNARI, IRENE W. Major productions of *The School for Scandal* on the twentieth-century New York stage
NY: U. (PhD)     1986

**2456** PEREIRA, JOHN W. A history of the Manhattan Theatre Club
NY: City U. (PhD)     1986

**2457** WHEELER, DAVID M. Perceptions of money and wealth on gilded age stages: a study of four long run productions in New York City
Eugene: U. of Oregon (PhD)     1986

**2458** CONDEE, WILLIAM F. The interaction of theatre space and performance in contemporary New York playhouses
NY: Colombia U. (PhD)     1987

**2459** GUERNSEY, OTIS L. Curtain times: the New York theater 1965-1987...photographs by Martha Swope, drawings by Hirschfeld...
pp.viii, 615; ill. in text     M
NY: Applause     1987

Essentially a digest of the season summaries first printed in the *Best Plays...* series.

**2460** RINEAR, DAVID L. The Temple of Momus. Mitchell's Olympic Theatre
pp.vi, 235; ill. in text     M
Metuchen NJ: Scarecrow P.     1987
William Mitchell was manager of the Olympic Theatre NY, 1839-1850.

**2461** ZVONCHENKO, WALTER. A historical study of the relation of theatre and broadcasting to land use in Midtown Manhattan in the years 1925 through 1928
NY: City U. (PhD)     1987

**2462** BACKALENICK, IRENE. East side story: ten years with the Jewish Repertory Theatre
pp.xiii, 197; ill. in text     M
Lanham MD: U. P. of America     1988
Introductory chapters on the history of jewish theatre and the JRT. Main section records the period 1975-85.

**2463** FITZGERALD, GERALD (Ed.). Annals of the Metropolitan Opera: the complete chronicle of performances and artists. Chronology [tables] 1883-1985
pp.xxv, 1000; xiv, 313; ill. in text     L
Boston: G. K. Hall/Opera Guild     1989
Two volumes.

**2464** GROSS, BRENDA. Poets and painters in the theatre: a critical study of the New York Artists' Theatre
NY: City U. (PhD)     1989

**2465** HISTORICAL PHOTOGRAPHS from The Old Met: a book of postcards
pp.iii; pl.30     M
San Francisco: Pomegranate Art Books     1989

**2466** RYZUK, MARY S. The Circle Repertory Company: the first fifteen years
pp.xv, 312, (1); ill. in text     M
Ames: Iowa State U. P.     1989
Founded 1969 by Marshall W. Mason, Lanford Wilson, Robert Thirkield and Tanya Berezin.

**2467** HARRISON-PEPPER, SALLY. Drawing a circle in the Square: street performing in New York City's Washington Square
    ★
Jackson: U. P. of Mississippi     1990

**2468** PARISI, BARBARA. The history of Brooklyn's three major performing arts institutions: the Brooklyn Academy of Music, Brooklyn Center for the Performing Arts at Brooklyn College, St Ann's Center for Restoration and the Arts, Inc.
NY: U. (PhD)     1990

## 6.2.34 NORTH CAROLINA

**2469** [BURR, JAMES G.]. The Thalian Association of Wilmington, N.C., with sketches of many of its members by a member of the association
pp.52     MH
Wilmington NC: J. A. Engelhard     1871

Referred to, and in part reprinted, in James Sprunt: *Chronicles of the Cape Fear River*, Raleigh NC, 1916.

**2470** CAROLINA FOLK PLAYS with an introduction on folk-play making by Frederick H. Koch. Illustrated from photographs of the original productions of the plays

pp.xxxi, 160; ill. in text, front., pl. 5     MH
NY: Henry Holt     1922

**2471** KOCH, FREDERICK H. (Ed.). Carolina folk-plays...with an introduction on making a folk theatre...iluustrated from photographs of the original productions of the plays
pp.xxxiv, 173; ill. in text, pl. 8     MH
NY: Henry Holt     1924

The British Library has a collection of several hundred clippings, programs, flysheets and newsletters, many illustrated, relating to the Carolina Playmakers Theatre for the period 1934-1950, providing an unusually full record.

**2472** RENSHAW, EDYTH. Recent indigenous drama of North Carolina
Dallas: Southern Methodist U. (MA)     1928

**2473** KOCH, FREDERICK H. A log-cabin theatre
pp.4, pl. 1     L
[Chapel Hill]: [Carolina Playmakers]     1932

*Carolina Playbook*, September, 1932, comprising an article describing an enterprise by the community of Ebenezer Neighborhood. Circulated at the National Theatre Conference, New York, 1932.

**2474** KOCH, FREDERICK H. (Ed.). The Carolina Play-book of the Carolina Playmakers and the Carolina Dramatic Association
pp.various     MB
Chapel Hill: Carolina Play-Makers     1934-36

12 issues examined, between March 1934-December 1936. Irregular publication of magazine.

**2475** [KOCH, FREDERICK H (Ed.) ?]. The Carolina Stage. A supplement to *The Carolina Play-Book*
pp.average 12     L
Chapel Hill: Carolina Dramatic Association     1936-44
Vols. 1-9?, March, 1936 - December, 1944.

**2476** A CENTURY of culture: an historical pageant and masque commemorating the centennial of public education in North Carolina...under the direction of Frederick H. Koch
pp.xx, 86; pl. 2     L
[Durham NC]: NC Educational Association     1937
Illustrated with scenes from the production. Foreword by Koch.

**2477** KOCH, FREDERICK H. Drama in the South: the Carolina Playmakers coming of age [drop title]
pp.14     L
Chapel Hill: Carolina Playmakers     1940
Address delivered in the Playmakers Theatre at Chapel Hill on April 5, 1940, commemorating the foundation of the Playmakers in 1918-19.

**2478** THE REPERTORY TOURING COMPANY of the Carolina Playmakers, Frederick H. Koch, founder and director, presenting plays of the South [cover title]
pp.[12] inc. wrappers; ill. in text     L
Chapel Hill: U. of N. Carolina     [1940]

Souvenir program. Includes appreciation of Koch by Archibald Henderson, a brief biographical sketch of Paul Green and a selection of reviews.

**2479** SANDMEL, FRANCES F. The conception and the creation: a critical evaluation of the work of the Carolina Playmakers
Chapel Hill: U. of North Carolina (MA)     1941

**2480** HENDERSON, ARCHIBALD (Ed.). Pioneering a people's theatre
pp.viii, 104; ill. in text     M
Chapel Hill: U. of N. Carolina P.     1945

Reminiscences and descriptions of the Carolina Playmakers theatre, founded by Frederick H. Koch.

**2481** SPECK, FRANK G.; BROOM, LEONARD with LONG, WILL W. Cherokee dance and drama
pp.xv, 106; ill. in text, pl. 12     M
Berkeley: U. of California P.     1951

Based on observations in N. Carolina, 1913-1944, interviews with Will West Long, and printed sources, 1714-1949.

**2482** WILLIAMS, ANNE St C. Theatre promotion in North Carolina
Chapel Hill: U. of North Carolina (MA)     1952

**2483** SPENCE, GEORGE. A historical study of the Raleigh little theatre, 1936-1959
Tallahassee: Florida State U. (MA)     1960

**2484** LOMINAC, HARRY G. The Carolina Dramatic Association, a history, 1922 to 1962
Chapel Hill: U. of North Carolina (MA)     1962

**2485** McDOWELL, SARA-JEAN. The history of the Carolina Playmakers. 1918-1950
Chapel Hill: U. of North Carolina (MA)     1962

**2486** POWELL, WILLIAM S. Paradise preserved
ix, 259; ill.pp.     DL*
Chapel Hill: U. of N. Carolina P.     1965

History of the Roanoke Island Historical Association and related organizations. Includes an account of Paul Green: *The Lost Colony*.

**2487** BARBER, RUPERT T. A history of the theatre in Charlotte, North Carolina, from 1873-1902
Baton Rouge: Louisiana State U. (PhD)     1970

**2488** REINES, PHILIP. A cultural history of the city of Winston-Salem, North Carolina: 1766-1966
Denver: U. (PhD)     1970

**2489** SPEARMAN, WALTER & SELDEN, SAMUEL. The Carolina Playmakers: the first fifty years
pp.xiv, 178; ill. in text     M
Chapel Hill: U. of N. Carolina P.     1970

**2490** DALTON, DONALD B. The history of the theatre in Asheville, North Carolina. 1832-1972
Chapel Hill: U. of North Carolina (MA)     1972

**2491** EPPERSON, JAMES R. The combination touring company and its influence on the theatre in Salisbury, Rowan County, North Carolina
Tallahassee: Florida State U. (PhD)     1977

## 6.2.35 NORTH DAKOTA

**2492** KOCH, FREDERICK H. & BECKER, ALBERT J.]. The Dakota Playmakers: I. An historical sketch [by] Frederick Henry Koch. II The construction of the play-stage [by] Albert John Becker
pp.14-30; ill. in text, pl. 2     L
[Grand Forks]: [U. of North Dakota]     1918

Reprinted from the *Quarterly Journal*, Vol. IX, No. 1, October, 1918.

**2493** ARVOLD, ALFRED G. The Little Country Theatre
pp.xi, 220; pl. 24     M
NY: Macmillan     1922

The founding, development and work of the Little Country Theatre in Fargo, ND.

2494 BIGELOW, EDWIN L. A record of the professional theatre activity in Fargo, North Dakota from 1899 through 1903
Fargo: North Dakota State U. (MS)　　　1955

2495 BROWNING, RICHARD J. A record of the professional theatre activity in Fargo, Dakota Territory from 1880 through 1888
Fargo: North Dakota State U. (MS)　　　1958

2496 PROBSTFIELD, EVELYN. A record of the professional theatre activity in Fargo, North Dakota, from 1904 through 1913
Fargo: North Dakota State U. (MS)　　　1958

2497 WALDERA, JEAN. A record of the professional theatre activity in Fargo, North Dakota from 1914 through 1920
Fargo: North Dakota Agricultural College (MS)　1959

Now the State U. of Agriculture and Applied Science.

2498 MILLER, DALE. A record of the theatrical activity in Bismarck, Dakota Territory from January 1873 to June 1886
Fargo: North Dakota State U. (MA)　　　1960

2499 ASP, BJORNE M. A record of the professional theatre activity in Fargo, North Dakota, 1921-1960
Fargo: North Dakota State U. (MS)　　　1961

2500 ADAIR, ALAN H. History of the Metropolitan Theatre in Grand Forks, North Dakota, under independent management, 1890-1897
Grand Forks: U. of North Dakota (MA)　　1970

2501 TOMASEK, PAUL. The Metropolitan Opera House of Grand Forks, N.D.
Grand Forks: U. of North Dakota (BA)　　1971

## 6.2.36 OHIO

2502 PHISTER, MONTGOMERIE (Ed.). Official hand-book of the dramatic festival held in the Music Hall, Cincinnati April 30-May 5, 1883
pp.74; ill. in text　　　　　　　　　　　　MH
Cininnati: H. C. Hall　　　　　　　　　　1883
Includes theatre plans and illustration, and biographical sketches of the principals, John McCullough, Lawrence Barrett, Mary Anderson, W. H. Daly, Mlle Rhéa, Clara Morris, James E. Murdoch, Nat C. Goodwin.

2503 BELL, ARCHIE. A little journey to B. F. Keith Palace, Cleveland
pp.i,46　　　　　　　　　　　　　　　　MH
[Cleveland?]: [For the author?]　　　　[c. 1895]
Description of the interior of the Palace Theatre at the corner of Euclid Avenue and East 17th Street, built for E. F. Albee, president of the Keith circuit.

2504 [MARTIN, FRANK J.]. Stage lights: Will Shakespeare and Bill Ide at the show, by the Plain Dealer dramatic man
pp.96; ill.　　　　　　　　　　　　　　DL★
Cleveland OH: Ward & Shaw　　　　　　1900

2505 HARVEY, E. T. Recollections of a scene painter
pp.64　　　　　　　　　　　　　　　LBTA
Cincinnati OH: For the author　　　　　1916
Letters reprinted from the *Cincinnati Commercial Tribune*, mostly about Wood's Theatre.

2506 LANGWORTHY, HELEN. The theatre in the lower valley of the Ohio, 1797-1860
Iowa City: U. of Iowa (MA)　　　　　　1926

2507 WEIDENTHAL, LEO. From Dis's wagon, a sentimental survey of a poets' corner...the Shakespeare garden of Cleveland
pp.70; ill.　　　　　　　　　　　　　　DL★
Cleveland: For the author　　　　　　　1926
Describes the creation of the memorial garden. Includes reference to Julia Marlowe, David Belasco, Ethel Barrymore, Richard Mansfield, Mary Anderson.

2508 THOMPSON, FLORENCE L. The theatre in Cincinatti, Ohio, 1860-1883
Iowa City: U. of Iowa (MA)　　　　　　1928

2509 EYSSEN, D. C. The theatre in Ohio, 1800-1890
Delaware OH: Delaware Wesleyan U. (MA)　1934

2510 HARRIS, GERALDINE. A history of the theatre in Ohio, 1815-1880
Columbus: Ohio State U. (MA)　　　　　1937

2511 HERBST, DOROTHY M. A history of the Cleveland Play House from its origin to September, 1936
Evanston: Northwestern U. (MA)　　　　1937

2512 MERRICK, MARY L. A history of the theatre of Zanesville, Ohio, between the years of 1831 and 1866
Columbus: Ohio State U. (MA)　　　　　1941

2513 WILSON, BERTHA A. A history of the theatre in Youngstown, Ohio
Ann Arbor: U. of Michigan (MA)　　　　1945

2514 MIESLE, FRANK L. A history of the Opera House of Fremont, Ohio, from 1890 to 1900
Bowling Green OH: State U. (MA)　　　1948

2515 SHANOWER, DONALD T. A survey of theatre activities in High Schools, colleges, and little theatres in the state of Ohio
Kent OH: State U. (MA)　　　　　　　　1949

2516 ALLMAN, WILLIAM A. An investigation of a successful civic theatre as exemplified by the Cleveland Playhouse
Athens: Ohio U. (MA)　　　　　　　　1951

2517 BURNS, MARY W. The little theatre movement in Cleveland, 1920-1930
Washington DC: Catholic U. of America (MA)　1952

2518 DALVA, HARRY O. A study of Karamu: a predominantly negro, interracial community theatre
Athens: Ohio U. (MA)　　　　　　　　1952

2519 UTZ, KATHRYN E. Columbus, Ohio, theatre seasons 1840-41 to 1960-61
Columbus: Ohio State U. (PhD)　　　　1952

2520 FREBAULT, HUBERT J. Professional theatre in Athens, Ohio, since 1897
Athens: Ohio U. (MA)　　　　　　　　1953

## 6.2. STATES AND TOWNS

**2521** PFENDLER, ROBERT C. A study of the Players' Guild of Canton, Ohio: a typical local nonprofessional theatre group
Athens: Ohio U. (MA) 1953

**2522** DUNLAP, JAMES F. Queen City stages: professional dramatic activity in Cincinnati, 1837-1861
Columbus: Ohio State U. (PhD) 1954

**2523** STOLZENBACH, NORMA F. The history of the theatre in Toledo, Ohio, from its beginnings until 1893
Ann Arbor: U. of Michigan (PhD) 1954

**2524** REVETT, MARION S. A minstrel town
pp.xvi, 335; ill. DL★
NY: Pageant P. 1955
Entertainment in Toledo OH, c.1840-1900.

**2525** SCHESVENTER, ROBERT R. A study of Lancaster, Ohio, to determine its suitability for a community theatre
Athens: Ohio U. (MFA) 1955

**2526** FASNAUGH, CHARLES W. A study of the history and organizatuion of the Toledo Repertoire Company, Inc., from June, 1933, through June, 1943
Bowling Green: State U. (MA) 1956

**2527** SIENA, MARCIA A. The history of the Great Southern Theatre, Columbus, Ohio
Columbus: Ohio State U. (MA) 1957

**2528** COLE, MARION. Theatrical and musical entertainment in early Cleveland
Cleveland: Case Western Reserve U. (MA) 1958

**2529** ROBERTS, KENNETH H. The history and development of the Denison summer theatre
Columbus: Ohio State U. (MA) 1958

**2530** KEPKE, ALLEN N. A history of the Players Club of Columbus, Ohio, 1923-1959
Columbus: Ohio State U. (MA) 1959

**2531** BROWN, IRVING M. Cleveland theatre in the twenties
Columbus: Ohio State U. (PhD) 1961

**2532** FRANKLIN, WILLIAM G. A study of community theatres in Ohio
Bowling Green: State U. (MA) 1961

**2533** SILVER, REUBEN. A history of the Karamu Theatre of Karamu House, 1915-1960
Columbus: Ohio State U. (PhD) 1961

**2534** ANDERSON, MALCOLM C. History of the Youngstown playhouse
Kent OH: State U. (MA) 1962

**2535** HODGSON, SANDRA K. A historical study of the Hartman Stock Company, Columbus, Ohio, 1926-29
Bowling Green OH: State U. (MA) 1962

**2536** BURBICK, WILLIAM G. Columbus, Ohio theatre from the beginning of the civil war to 1875
Columbus: Ohio State U. (PhD) 1963

**2536A** GRANDSTAFF, RUSSELL J. A history of the professional theatre in Cincinnati, Ohio, 1861-1886
Ann Arbor: U. of Michigan (PhD) 1963

**2537** DIX, WILLIAM S. The theatre in Cleveland, Ohio, 1854-1875
Illinois: U. of Chicago (PhD) 1964

**2538** FLORY, JULIA M. The Cleveland Playhouse: how it began
pp.xv, 136; ill. in text M
Cleveland: P. of Western Reserve U. 1965

**2539** CLARK, WILLIAM B. A history of the Cleveland Play House, 1936-1958
New Orleans: Tulane U. (PhD) 1968

**2540** DORRELL, ROBERT E. A history of the early Hartman Theatre: 1911-1921
Columbus: Ohio State U. (PhD) 1968

**2541** EZEKIEL, MARGARET U. The history of the theatre in Cleveland: 1875-1885
Cleveland: Case Western Reserve U. (PhD) 1968

**2542** GRIFFITH, MAX E. The Delaware, Ohio, City Opera House and its nineteenth century activities
Columbus: Ohio State U. (MA) 1968

**2543** NICHOLS, KENNETH L. In order of appearance: Akron's theatres, 1840-1940
Akron OH: U. (MA) 1968

**2544** BOUSLIMAN, CHARLES W. The Mabel Tainter Memorial Theatre: a pictorial case study of a late nineteenth-century American playhouse
Columbus: Ohio State U. (PhD) 1969

**2545** JOYCE, ROBERT S. History of the Armbruster Scenic Studios of Columbus, Ohio
Columbus: Ohio State U. (PhD) 1970

**2546** CASSADY, MARSHALL. The history of the professional theatre in Salem, Ohio, 1847-1894
Kent OH: State U. (PhD) 1972

**2547** STEENROD, SPENCER. A history of Stuart's Opera House, Nelsonville, Ohio [1879-1924]
Athens: Ohio U. (MA) 1973

**2548** LADWIG, RONALD V. A history of public entertainment in Ada, Ohio: 1850-1920
Bowling Green OH: State U. (PhD) 1978

**2549** SHERIDAN, PHIL. Those wonderful old downtown theaters [Columbus]
pp.100 inc, wrappers; ill. in text M
Columbus OH: For the author 1978

**2550** BELL, CHARLES H. An Ohio repertoire-tent show family: the Kinsey Komedy Kompany and the Madge Kinsey Players, 1881-1951
Bowling Green: State U. (PhD) 1979

**2551** CASTRONOVO, FRANK A. The Youngstown Playhouse: a history, 1927-1979
Kent OH: State U. (PhD) 1980

**2552** SHERIDAN, PHIL. More about those wonderful downtown theaters [Columbus]
pp.144; ill. in text M
Columbus OH: For the author 1984

**2553** BLAUGHER, KURT C. The community theatre in Northwestern Ohio, 1932-1984
Evanston: Northwestern U. (PhD) 1985

## 6.2.37 OKLAHOMA

**2554** GOBER, RUTH B. The professional theatre in Oklahoma City, 1889-1941
Evanston: Northwestern U. (MA)     1941

**2555** BRANDES, K. K. Theatrical activities in Oklahoma City from 1889 to 1964
Norman: U. of Oklahoma (MFA)     1964

**2556** ALEXANDER, DARREL E. A history of the Mummers Theatre, Oklahoma City, Oklahoma, 1949-1972
Baton Rouge: Louisiana State U. (PhD)     1974

**2557** LEWANDOWSKI, RAYMOND J. The formation, rise, and decline of the Tulsa Little Theatre as reflected in its changing philosophy of organization and management
Ann Arbor: U. of Michigan (PhD)     1976

## 6.2.38 OREGON

**2558** FOSTER, WILLIAM T. Vaudeville and motion picture shows: a study of theatres in Portland, Oregon...
pp.63     DL★
[Portland]: Reed College     1914

**2559** AKIN, H. F. The little theatre movement in Portland, Oregon
Portland: Reed College (Thesis)     1933

**2560** DEVIN, RONALD B. The history of the theatre in Enterprise, Oregon, 1901-1920
Eugene: U. of Oregon (MS)     1961

**2561** ERNST, ALICE H. Trouping in the Oregon country: a history of frontier theatre
pp.xx, 197; ill. in text     M
Portland: Oregon Historical Society     1961

**2562** SCHILLING, LESTER L. The history of the theatre in Portland, Oregon, 1846-1959
Madison: U. of Wisconsin (PhD)     1961

**2563** LARSON, PATRICIA M. A study of the museum theatre in the United States including an analysis of the Museum Theatre in Portland, Oregon
Eugene: U. of Oregon (MA)     1964

**2564** OYLER, VERNE W. The festival story: a history of the Oregon Shakespearean Festival
Los Angeles: U. of California (PhD)     1970

**2565** HIATT, RICHARD G. A history of theatrical activity on the Oregon Trail: (Boise, Idaho to The Dalles, Oregon: 1880-1910)
Provo UT: Brigham Young U. (PhD)     1974

**2566** BOWMER, ANGUS L. As I remember, Adam: an autobiography of a festival
pp.272; ill.     DL★
Ashland: Oregon Shakespeare Festival     1975

**2567** MATSON, CECIL. Seven nights - three matinees: seventy years of dramatic stock in Portland, Oregon, 1863-1933
pp.112; ill. in text     L
[Portland?]: For the author     1980

## 6.2.39 PENNSYLVANIA

**2568** BOWMAN, NED A. Notes on resources for theatre research in Pittsburgh
ll. [7]     L
[Pittsburgh]: Pennsylvania Library Association     [19-?]
Prepared for the *Library Journal*.

**2569** WALN, ROBERT. The Hermit in America on a visit to Philadelphia: containing some account of the beaux and belles...of that famous city
    DL★
Philadelphia: M. Thomas     1819-21
Series 1 and 2. Two volumes in one. Some reference to theatres.

**2570** THE REJECTED ADDRESSES, presented for the cup offered for the best address, on the opening of the New Theatre, Philadelphia. To which is prefixed, the prize address
pp.viii, 107     MH
Philadelphia: H. C. Carey & I. Lea     1823
In verse. The prize address was by Charles Sprague. The New Theatre was destroyed by fire, April 2, 1820 and the new building opened in 1823. An auction catalogue description mentions a folding view of the theatre interior, lacking in the copy examined.

**2571** A REVISED AND AMENDED schedule of fundamental rules, regulations, and by-laws of the Association of Stockholders in the New Theatre in Philadelphia
pp.12     MH
[Philadelphia]: [For the proprietors?]     [1837]
The earlier *Resolutions and articles...* had been issued in 1799.

**2572** GRAYDON, ALEXANDER. Memoirs of his own time with reminiscences of the men and events of the revolution...Edited by John Stockton Littell
pp.504     L
Philadelphia: Lindsay & Blakiston     1846
First published Harrisburg PA: John Wyeth, 1811 as *Memoirs of a life, chiefly passed in Pennsylvania, within the last sixty years, with occasional remarks on the general occurrences, character and spirit of that eventful period.* Includes a brief, apologetic account of the theatre, with particular reference to David Douglass, Lewis Hallam and the Old American company.

**2573** CHARTER AND PROSPECTUS of the Opera House or American Academy of Music
pp.16     MB
Philadelphia: Crissy & Markley, Printers     1852

**2574** DURANG, CHARLES. The Philadelphia stage; 1749-1821; 1822-1830; 1831-1855. Partly compiled from the papers of his father, the late John Durang: with notes by the editors
Unpaged     MH
Philadelphia: Sunday Dispatch     1854-60
Published serially, May 7, 1854; June 29, 1856; July 8, 1860.

**2575** HISTORY AND DESCRIPTION of the Opera House, or American Academy of Music in Philadelphia. Designed and constructed by N. Le Brun and G. Runce...Corner Stone laid on the 26th of July, 1855. Building completed and opened on the 26th of January, 1857
pp.20; engraving of theatre on title     MH
Philadelphia: G. Andre     1857

## 6.2. STATES AND TOWNS

**2576** RUNGE, G. Das Neue Opernhaus (Academy of Music) in Philadelphia
pp.6, pl. 8    M
Berlin: Ernst & Korn    1882
Detailed description, with interior and exterior plans.

**2577** ARMSTRONG, W. G. A record of the opera in Philadelphia
pp.274    MB
Philadelphia: Porter & Coates    1884
A chronological listing of performers, c.1796-1883 with much incidental commentary. Addenda include an account of the building of the American Academy of Music.

**2578** [CANTLIN, JOHN R. et al]. Security. Letters from John R. Cantlin chief engineer of the Philadelphia fire department. C. John Hexamer, expert and surveyor of the association of fire underwriters. William McDevitt, inspector of the fire patrol
pp.8    MB
[Philadelphia]: [Academy of Music?]    [1885]
Concerning improvements in fire precaution at the Philadelphia Academy of Music. Title headed: *everyone should read this pamphlet*.

**2579** STAGELAND. A journal of Philadelphia theatrical information [cover title]
pp.av. 16; ill. in text    MH
Philadelphia: W. Chandler Stewart    1890
Ten copies, September 1 - November 3, 1890. All published. (Harvard lacks vol. 1, no. 5). Subsequently, it was planned to amalgamate with the *Philadelphia Music Journal*.

**2580** YOUNG, JOHN R. (Ed.). Memorial history of the city of Philadelphia from its first settlement to the year 1895. Vol II Special and biographical
pp.xii, 484; front., ill. in text, pl. 64    L
NY: NY History Company    1898
The second volume has material by George O. Seilhamer on theatre and other entertainments, and dramatists.

**2581** THE GARRICK THEATRE erected 1901 in Philadelphia
pp.[24]; ill. in text    MH
[Philadelphia]: [For the theatre?]    [1901]
Brochure issued on the occasion of the opening and including a programme for the inaugural production, *Beaucaire*, with Richard Mansfield. With biographical notes on Mansfield and the manager, Frank Howe Jr.

**2582** MISHLER, JOHN D. Mishler's memoirs: many mistakes, merely mentioned
pp.191; ill.    DL★
[Reading PA]: P. of Pengelly    [1907]
Reference to theatre in Reading.

**2583** BOUCHER, JOHN N. (Ed.). A century and a half of Pittsburgh and her people
pp.various    DL★
NY: Lewis Publishing    1908
In four volumes. Chapter 32 deals with early theatres and players.

**2584** BREDE, CHARLES F. The German drama in English on the Philadelphia stage from 1794 to 1830 preceded by a general account of the theatre in Philadelphia from 1749 to 1796
pp.x, 295    L
Philadelphia: American Germanica P.    1918

**2585** FLETCHER, EDWARD G. History of the Pittsburgh stage to 1855
Cambridge MA: Harvard U. (PhD)    1931

**2586** JAMES, REESE D. Old Drury of Philadelphia: a history of the Philadelphia stage 1800-1835 including the diary or daily account book of William Burke Wood, co-manager with William Farren of the Chestnut Street Theatre, familiarly known as Old Drury
pp.xv, 694; front., pl. 1    M
Philadelphia: U. of Pennsylvania P.    1932

**2587** POTTS, EDGAR L. The history of the Philadelphia theater, 1890-1900
Philadelphia: U. of Pennsylvania (PhD)    1932

**2588** WILSON, ARTHUR H. History of the Philadelphia theatre, 1835-1855
pp.xi, 724    M
Philadelphia: U. of Pennsylvania P.    1935

**2589** CODER, WILLIAM D. A history of the Philadelphia theater, 1856 to 1878
Philadelphia: U. of Pennsylvania (PhD)    1936

**2590** HANEY, JOHN L. Shakespeare's Philadelphia: an address delivered to City History Society of Philadelphia, November 28 1934
pp.(ii) 41-73; front.    L
Philadelphia: City History Society    1936
Effectively, a history of Shakespeare production in Philadelphia. In *Philadelphia History*, vol 4, no 3, 1936.

**2591** BALDWIN, LELAND D. Pittsburgh: the story of a city
pp.xv, 387; ill. in text, maps    L
Pittsburgh: U. P.    1937
Includes a brief anecdotal history of theatres.

**2592** MECONNAHEY, JOSEPH H. The history of the Philadelphia theater from 1900-1910
Philadelphia: U. of Pennsylvania (PhD)    1937

**2593** LOWRIE, JAMES A. A history of the Pittsburgh stage (1861-1891)
Pittsburgh: U. (PhD)    1943

**2594** MARSHALL, THOMAS F. A history of the Philadelphia theatre, 1878-1890: [an essential portion of] a dissertation in English
pp.ii, 54    MH
Philadelphia: U. of Pennsylvania P.    1943
Includes a day-book, 1878-9 and a checklist of plays, 1878-1890.

**2595** GLASE, PAUL E. Annals of the Reading theatre, (Reading PA), 1791-1948 edited by Milton W. Hamilton
pp.[64]; ill. in text    MH
Reading: [For the author]    1948
Printed originally in the *Historical Review of Berks County* between 1946 and 1949.

**2596** FERGUSON, WILLIAM C. A history of the Savoy company
pp.vii, 135; ill.    DL★
Philadelphia: Savoy Company    1950

New edition. First published as *Savoy annals: a history of the Savoy company, 1901-1940*, Philadelphia, 1941. Founded by Alfred R. Allen to perform Gilbert & Sullivan.

**2597** QUIGLEY, BERNARD J. First seasons in Philadelphia: a study of the Philadelphia stage, 1682-1767
Washington DC: Catholic U. of America (MA)    1951

**2598** STINE, RICHARD D. The Philadelphia theater, 1682-1829: its growth as a cultural institution
Philadelphia: U. of Pennsylvania (PhD)    1951

**2599** KOONTZ, JOHN G. A history of the theater in Johnstown, Pennsylvania, 1890-1900
Pittsburgh: U. (MA)    1952

**2600** McKENZIE, RUTH H. Organization, production, and management of the Chestnut Street Theatre, Philadelphia, from 1791 to 1820
Stanford: U. (PhD)    1952

**2601** JOHNSON, RUTH P. A study of the Hedgerow Repertory Theatre
Athens: Ohio U. (MA)    1953
Founded 1923 by Jasper Deeter in Moylan PA.

**2602** WENTZ, JOHN C. The Hedgerow Theatre: an historical study
Philadelphia: U. of Pennsylvania (PhD)    1954

**2603** JAMES, REESE D. Cradle of culture 1800-1810: the Philadelphia stage
pp.156; pl. 4    M
Philadelphia: U. of Pennsylvania P.    1957
An account of the Chestnut Street Theatre.

**2604** SCHAEFFER, MORTON H. A survey of the little theatre in Philadelphia and its Pennsylvanian suburbs
Philadelphia: Temple U. (MA)    1957

**2605** GARDNER, DOROTHEA B. History of the Nixon Theatre, Pittsburgh, Pennsylvania
Pittsburgh: U. (PhD)    1959

**2606** MOORE, M. MARGUERITE. The history of the Pittsburgh Playhouse
Washington DC: Catholic U. of America (MA)    1959

**2607** SHOEMAKER, ALFRED L. Christmas in Pennsylvania: a folk-cultural study
pp.116; ill.    DL★
Kutztown PA: Pennsylvania Folklife Society    1959
Includes material on mummers.

**2608** BRACKIN, EDWARD G. A history of theatrical production at the Hedgerow Theater
NY: Columbia U. (MA)    1960

**2609** SHOEMAKER, ALFRED L. Eastertide in Pennsylvania: a folk-cultural study
pp.96; ill.    DL★
Kutztown PA: Pennsylvania Folklife Society    1960
Includes material on mummers.

**2610** THE FULTON OPERA HOUSE historic landmark theater...
Folding sheet; ill. in text    M
Lancaster PA: For the theatre    [1961]

A summer season hand-out with programme details and an historical sketch of the theatre.

**2611** BRIDENBAUGH, CARL & BRIDENBAUGH, JESSICA. Rebels and gentlemen: Philadelphia in the age of Franklin
pp.xix, 393; pl. 8    O
NY: Oxford U. P.    1962
Chapter V, *The arts move westward*, has material on the theatre.

**2612** BEEGLE, JOANNE P. A history of Kaier's Grand Opera House [Mahoney City, 1885-1913]
University Park: Pennsylvania State U. (MA)    1964

**2613** HELPS, MARY. The Walnut Street Theatre
Philadelphia: Drexel U. (MLS)    1966

**2614** WOLCOTT, JOHN R. English influences on American acting practice: a case study of the Chestnut Street Theatre, Philadelphia, 1794-1820
Columbus: Ohio State U. (PhD)    1967

**2615** ENGEL, BERNARD B. Chronicles of the Meadville stage: 1800-1899
Pittsburgh: U. (PhD)    1968

**2616** POLLOCK, THOMAS C. The Philadelphia theatre in the eighteenth century together with the *day book* of the same period
pp.xviii, 445; front.    M
NY: Greenwood P.    1968
Reprint. First published U. of Pennsylvania, 1933.

**2617** COPELAND, BOB H. The oil circuit: a history of professional theatre in the oil region of Northwestern Pennsylvania from 1859 to 1900
Denver: U. (PhD)    1969

**2618** WEBB, DOROTHY L. The early history of the Arch Street Theatre, 1828-1834
Bloomington: Indiana U. (PhD)    1970

**2619** KEAN, MANUEL. The Walnut Street Theatre: Philadelphia's new center for the performimg arts
pp.[28] inc. wrappers; ill. in text    M
Philadelphia: For the theatre    1971
For the re-opening. A history of the theatre from 1809.

**2620** MARSH, JOHN L. The Grandin Opera House, or theatre on the kerosene circuit, 1872-1904...with photographs...by Frank B. Acklin
pp.iv, 50; ill. in text    M
Warren PA: Warren County Historical Society    1973
Titusville and other theatres.

**2621** NASSIF, SHAKEEB J. A history of the Pittsburgh Playhouse school of the theatre: 1934 to 1969
Denver: U. (PhD)    1973

**2622** PEEBLES, SHEILA E. A history of the Pittsburgh stage, 1891-1896
Kent OH: State U. (MA)    1973

**2623** GREINER, TYLER L. A history of professional entertainment at the Fulton Opera House in Lancaster, Pennsylvania, 1852-1930
University Park: Pennsylvania State U. (MA)    1977

**2624** KELLEY, PAUL B. Portrait of a playhouse: the 'Troc' of Philadelphia, 1870-1978
NY: U. (PhD)    1982

**2625** CROSSETT, DAVID A. One-night stand: a history of live and recorded entertainment in Warren, Pennsylvania, from 1795 to the present
NY: U. (PhD) 1983

**2626** PUTNAM, CHASE & TRANTER, CHARLES R. Library Theatre, Warren, Pennsylvania, 1885-1983
pp.22 inc. wrappers; ill. in text  M
Warren PA: Library Theatre 1983

**2627** FIELDER, MARI K. Theatre and community in early twentieth-century Philadelphia: the Mae Desmond Players, 1917-1932
Los Angeles: U. of California (PhD) 1986

**2628** GLAZER, IRVIN R. The Earle Theatre, Philadelphia, Penna. Hoffman and Henon, architects: opened, March 24, 1924
pp.40; ill. in text  M
Notre Dame: Theatre Historical Society 1986

**2629** GLAZER, IRVIN R. Philadelphia theatres, A-Z. A comprehensive descriptive record of 813 theatres constructed since 1724
pp.255; ill.  DL★
Westport CT: Greenwood P. 1986

**2630** HENKE, JAMES S. From public house to opera house: a history of theatrical structures in Lancaster, Pennsylvania
Ann Arbor: U. of Michigan (PhD) 1987

**2631** STEPANIAN, LAURIE A. Harry Davis, theatrical entrepreneur, Pittsburgh, Pennsylvania, 1892-1927
Colombia: U. of Missouri (PhD) 1987

**2632** DAVIS, SUSAN. Parades and power: street theatre in nineteenth-century Philadelphia
pp.xiii, 325; ill. in text  M
Berkeley: U. of California P. 1988
First published Philadelphia: Temple U. P., 1986.

**2633** STEPANIAN, LAURIE A. Harry Davis: theatrical entrepreneur, Pittsburgh, Pennsylvania, 1893-1927
Columbia: U. of Missouri (PhD) 1988

## 6.2.40 RHODE ISLAND

**2634** BLAKE, CHARLES. An historical account of the Providence stage, being a paper read before the Rhode Island Historical Society, October 25th, 1860, with additions
pp.297  M
Providence: George H. Whitnew 1868
200 copies.

**2635** WILLARD, GEORGE O. History of the Providence stage 1762-1891 including sketches of many prominent actors who have appeared in America
pp.iii, 298  M
Providence: Rhode Island News 1891
Incorporates Charles Blake: *An historical account of the Providence stage...,1868.*

**2636** THE FIRST twenty-five years: being a chronicle of the history, aspirations, and accomplishments of the Players from 1909 to 1934
pp.28; ill.  DL★
Providence RI: For the Players 1935
Not to be confused with the Players, NY.

## 6.2.41 SOUTH CAROLINA

**2637** A SUCCINCT ACCOUNT of the disturbance which occurred at the Charleston theatre, on the evening of the 12th of March, 1817. With the addresses to the public, by Mr Holman, the manager, and Mr Caldwell
pp.39  ★
Charleston SC: A. E. Miller 1817
Partly reprinted from local newspapers.

**2638** WILLIS, EOLA. The Charleston stage in the XVIII century, with social settings of the time
pp.xv, 483; pl. 12  M
Columbia SC: State Company 1924
Derived substantially from the South Carolina *Gazette*, 1732-1800.

**2639** BASS, ROBERT D. The plays and playwrights of South Carolina
Columbia: U. of South Carolina (MA) 1927

**2640** HOOLE, W. S. The ante-bellum Charleston theatre
pp.xx, 230; pl. 4  M
Tuscaloosa: U. of Alabama P. 1946

**2641** STURCKEN, FRANCIS. A study of the Footlight Players, Charleston, S.C. from 1931 to 1952 as a case history in community theatre
Washington DC: Catholic U. of America (MA) 1953

**2642** ROBINSON, EMMETT. A guide to the Dock Street Theatre and brief résumé of the theatres in Charleston, S.C., from 1730
pp.14; ill.  DL★
Charleston SC: The Footlight Players 1963

**2643** CURTIS, MARY J. The early Charleston stage: 1703-1798
Bloomington: Indiana U. (PhD) 1968

**2644** ST JOHN, JAMES I. Belles lettres in colonial Charleston: a study of its poetry and drama
Columbia: U. of South Carolina (MA) 1969

**2645** COX, JAMES R. The history of the Newberry, South Carolina, Opera House, 1880-1973
Columbia: U. of South Carolina (MA) 1974

**2646** STEPHENSON, NAN L. The Charleston theatre management of Joseph George Holman, 1815 to 1817
Baton Rouge: Louisiana State U. (MA) 1976

**2647** WATSON, CHARLES S. Antebellum Charleston dramatists
pp.xv, 183; ill. in text  M
Tuscaloosa: U. of Alabama P. 1976

**2648** SODDERS, RICHARD P. The theatre management of Alexandre Placide in Charleston, 1794-1812
Baton Rouge: Louisiana State U. (PhD) 1983

## 6.2.42 SOUTH DAKOTA

**2649** BENNETT, ESTELLINE. Old Deadwood days
pp.xiii, 319; pl. 8      O
NY: Charles Scribner's Sons      1928
Chapter 1V refers to theatre, with photograph of the Gem Variety Theater and Dance Hall.

**2650** HARNISH, FRANK J. The history of the Black Hills Playhouse and school of the theatre, 1946, 1947, and 1958
Vermillion: U. of South Dakota (MA)      1949

**2651** STINE, LAWRENCE C. A history of theatre and theatrical activities in Deadwood, South Dakota, 1876-90
Ames: Iowa State U. (PhD)      1962

**2652** SWITZER, THEODORE R. A history of theatre and theatrical activities in Brookings, South Dakota from 1879 through 1898
Brookings: South Dakota State U. (MS)      1962

**2653** FARRELL, KENNETH L. A history of the Matthews Opera House and repertory theatre in Spearfish, South Dakota. from 1888 to 1930
Eugene: U. of Oregon (MS)      1963

**2654** PERRIN, GERRY A. A history of the theatrical and community activities in the early Dell Rapids, South Dakota, Opera House
Brookings: South Dakota State U. (MA)      1970

**2655** KOCH, JOHN C. Yankton Theatre (trading posts to opera house...1865-1900)
Vermillion: U. of South Dakota (MA)      1971

## 6.2.43 TENNESSEE

**2656** DAVENPORT, F. GARVIN. Cultural life in Nashville on the eve of the civil war
pp.xiii, 232; front.      L
Chapel Hill: U. of N. Carolina P.      1841
Chapters V-VII refer to theatre and other amusements.

**2657** WEIR, JAMES. Lonz Powers or, the regulators. A romance of Kentucky founded on facts
pp.xi, 364; 319      L
Philadelphia: Lippincott, Grambo      1850
Two volumes. Reference to Nashville theatre.

**2658** STEVENS, EVA C. The history of the theatre in Nashville Tennessee, 1871-1875
Nashville: Vanderbilt U. (MA)      1934

**2659** CHISMAN, MARGARET S. Literature and the drama in Memphis, Tennessee, to 1860
Durham NC: Duke U. (MA)      1942

**2660** JONES, MARION P. Some notes for a history of the Chattanooga theater, 1877-1888
Durham NC: Duke U. (MA)      1942

**2661** BAIN, HELEN P. A history of the community theatre in Nashville
Ann Arbor: U. of Michigan (MA)      1950

**2662** LUTTRELL, WANDA M. The theatre of Memphis, Tennessee from 1829 to 1860
Baton Rouge: Louisiana State U. (MA)      1951

**2663** POWELL, CAROLYN. The Lyceum Theater of Memphis, Tennessee, 1890-1900
Oxford: U. of Mississippi (MA)      1951

**2664** HUNT, DOUGLAS L. The Nashville theatre, 1830-1840
pp.89      MH
Birmingham AL: Birmingham Southern College      1955
Expanded version of work first issued in *B.S.C. bulletin*, May, 1935.

**2665** MAIDEN, LEWIS S. A chronicle of the theater in Nashville, Tennessee, 1876-1900
Nashville: Vanderbilt U. (PhD)      1955

**2666** BRISTOW, EUGENE K. 'Look out for Saturday night': a social history of professional variety theater in Memphis, Tennessee, 1859-1880
Iowa City: U. of Iowa (PhD)      1956

**2667** RITTER, CHARLES C. The theatre in Memphis, Tennessee, from its beginnings to 1859
Iowa City: U. of Iowa (PhD)      1956

**2668** FAULKNER, SELDON. The New Memphis Theater of Memphis, Tennessee, from 1859 to 1880
Iowa City: U. of Iowa (PhD)      1957

**2669** HENDERSON, JERRY E. A history of the Ryman Auditorium in Nashville, Tennessee, 1892-1920
Baton Rouge: Louisiana State U. (MA)      1961

**2670** STERLING, WALLACE S. The Front St. Theater of Memphis: the emergence of a resident professional theater in the mid-South
Carbondale: Southern Illinois U. (PhD)      1966

**2671** MAIDEN, LEWIS S. Highlights of the Nashville theater, 1876-1890
pp.xi, 202      L
NY: Vantage P.      1979

**2672** ORPHEUM, [cover title]
pp.8 inc. wrappers; ill. in text      M
New Berlin WI: Conrad Schmitt Studios      [1984]
Orpheum Theatre, Memphis TN, designed in 1928, restored 1984.

## 6.2.44 TEXAS

**2673** HOLDEN, WILLIAM C. Frontier problems and movements in West Texas, 1846-1900
Austin: U. of Texas (PhD)      1927
Chapter nine comprises a study of amusements.

**2674** TEMPLE, LAURA. The Dallas little theatre: a history (1920-1927)
Dallas: Southern Methodist U. (MA)      1927

**2675** HERVEY, HUBERT C. A history of the little theater of Texas: emphasizing the Dallas Little Theater as representative
Austin: U. of Texas (MA)      1930

**2676** BARTON, HENRY W. A history of the Dallas opera house
Abilene TX: Hardin College (MA) 1935

**2677** FLETCHER, EDWARD G. The beginnings of the professional theatre in Texas
pp.55 MH
Austin: U. of Texas [1936]
*Bulletin* 3621, June 1, 1936. Period 1838-40.

**2678** KENNEDY, LUCILE B. A history of the Dallas Opera House (a record of the plays and their reception, with a day book for seasons 1911-1912 through 1921
Dallas: Southern Methodist U. (MA) 1940

**2679** ACKER, LULU M. The Little Theatre movement in Texas
Texarkana: East Texas State College (MA) 1942

**2680** CARROW, CATHERINE I. The amusements of Texas from 1880-1890
Austin: U. of Texas (MA) 1943

**2681** LINSKIE, MARGARET. The history of the Little Theatre of Dallas and its influence in the Southwest
Washington DC: Catholic U. of America (MA) 1944

**2682** STONE, DELZA H. Drama in San Antonio, 1889-1894
San Antonio TX: St. Mary's U. (MA) 1944

**2683** PHELPS, LAVERNE P. History of the little theatre movement in Amarillo, Texas, from 1888 to 1946
Canyon: West Texas State College (MA) 1946

**2684** PLASTERS, WARREN H. A history of amusements in Fort Worth from the beginning to 1879
Fort Worth: Texas Christian U. (MA) 1947

**2685** LANE, DORIS A. A history of the Fort Worth theatre from 1880-1888
Fort Worth: Texas Christian U. (MA) 1948

**2686** BROWN, BETTY J. A history of the little theatre movement in Plainview, Texas, from 1924-1949
Canyon: West Texas State College (MA) 1949

**2687** CHESTNUT, GLENN F. The drama in San Antonio, Texas as from 1884 to 1889
San Antonio: St Mary's U. (MA) 1949

**2688** SHANNON, HALLIE D. The theater in Fort Worth from 1892 to 1896
Fort Worth: Texas Christian U. (MA) 1950

**2689** STEPHENS, ANN B. Survey of the little theatre movement in Texas colleges and communities
Fort Worth: Texas Christian U. (MA) 1950

**2690** WALSH, ALICE W. The theater in Fort Worth from 1896 to 1900
Fort Worth: Texas Christian U. (MA) 1952

**2691** YOCUM, JACK H. A history of the theatre in Houston, 1836-1954
Madison: U. of Wisconsin (PhD) 1955

**2692** DAVIS, JACKSON. The history of professional theatre in Dallas, Texas, 1920-1930
Baton Rouge: Louisiana State U. (PhD) 1962

**2693** GALLEGLY, JOSEPH. Footlights on the border: the Galveston and Houston stage before 1900
pp.262; pl. 14 M
The Hague: Mouton 1962

**2694** REEVES, ANN. Nineteenth century theatre in North-east Texas
Austin: U. Texas (MFA) 1962

**2695** ALMARAZ, FELIX D. Standing room only: a history of the San Antonia Little Theatre, 1912-1962
San Antonio: St Mary's U. (MA) [1964?]

**2696** BRADY, DONALD V. The theatre in early El Paso [cover title]
pp.39; pl. 2 M
El Paso: Texas Western College P. 1966

**2697** HAMMACK, HENRY E. A history of the Dallas Little Theatre, 1920-1943
New Orleans: Tulane U. (PhD) 1966

**2698** TRESER, ROBERT M. Houston's Alley Theatre
New Orleans: Tulane U. (PhD) 1966

**2699** KING, CLYDE R. A history of the theater in Texas, 1722-1900
Waco TX: Baylor U. (PhD) 1967

**2700** PRICE, JOYCE D. A history of the King Opera House in Greenville. Texas
Commerce: East Texas State U. (MA) 1967

**2701** MYLER, CHARLES B. History of the English-speaking theatre in San Antonio before 1900
Austin: U. of Texas (PhD) 1968

**2702** BRADEN, EDWINA C. A history of theatre in Corsicana, Texas, 1875 to 1915
Texarkana: East Texas State U. (MS) 1969

**2703** GALLEGLY, JOSEPH. From Alamo Plaza to Jack Harris's saloon: O. Henry and the southwest he knew
pp.213; pl. 10 O
The Hague: Mouton 1970
Includes substantial accounts of the theatre.

**2704** HARDIN, WYLIE A. A history of theatre in Terrell, Texas, from 1890 through 1910
Commerce: East Texas State U. (MS) 1971

**2705** MEGARITY, SHIRLEY A. The theatre in Fort Worth, 1870-1899
Denton: Texas Woman's U. (MA) 1971

**2706** CARROLL, VERNON H. An analysis of theatrical criticisms of plays presented in the Grand Opera House, San Antonio, Texas, 1886-1896, excluding operettas and variety shows
Georgetown TX: Southwestern State U. (MA) 1972

**2707** CLARK, LINDA K. A theater history of Texarkana from 1876 through 1924
Texarkana: East Texas State U. (MS) 1972

**2708** MARDER, CARL J. A history of the development and growth of the Dallas Theater Center
Lawrence: U. of Kansas (PhD) 1972

**2709** RICKER, SUZANNE D. Harley Sadler and his own company
Lubbock: Texas Tech U. (MA) 1973

2710 GROVES, WILLIAM McD. A history of the professional theatre in Marshall, Texas, from 1877 to 1915
Nacogdoches TX: Austin State U. (MA)     1976

2711 SHANK, PHILLIP J. A history of the early variety theatres and legitimate theatres in Waco, Texas, from the beginnings to 1928
Waco: Baylor U. (MA)     1977

2712 MANRY, JOE E. A history of theatre in Austin, Texas, 1839-1905: from minstrels to moving pictures
Austin: U. of Texas (PhD)     1979

2713 THE PEROT THEATRE [cover title]
pp.4 inc. wrappers; ill. in text     M
New Berlin WI: Conrad Schmitt Studios     [1980]
The Perot Theatre, earlier the Saenger, and the Paramount, closed in 1977, restored 1979.

2714 ASHBY, CLIFFORD & MAY, SUZANNE D. Trouping through Texas: Harley Sadler and his tent show
pp.vi, 188; ill. in text     M
Bowling Green OH: U. Popular P.     1982

2715 MAJESTIC THEATRE, Dallas, Texas [cover title]
pp.8, inc. wrappers; ill. in text     M
New Berlin WI: Conrad Schmitt Studios     [1983?]
The restored theatre reopened in January 1983.

2716 BLAIN, LYNDA C. The Shakespeare festival at Dallas: an internship report
Lubbock: Tesas Tech U. (PhD)     1988

2717 STANLEY, NINA J. Nina Vance: founder and artistic director of Houston's Alley Theatre, 1947 to 1980
Bloomington: Indiana U. (PhD)     1990

## 6.2.45 UTAH

2718 LINDSAY, JOHN. The Mormons and the theatre: or, the history of theatricals in Utah, with reminiscences and comments, humorous and critical
pp.178; front.     MH
Salt Lake City UT: [For the author?]     1905
1847-1904. Author had acted with the Salt Lake City stock company.

2719 WHITNEY, HORACE G. The drama in Utah; the story of the Salt Lake Theatre
pp.48; ill. in text     MH
[Salt Lake City]: Deseret News     1915
Reprinted from *Improvement Era* 18.

2720 PYPER, GEORGE D. The romance of an old playhouse
pp.342; ill. in text, pl. 43     M
Salt Lake City UT: Seagull P.     1928
Account of the theatre built by Brigham Young in 1862.

2721 HENDERSON, MYRTLE E. A history of the theatre in Salt Lake City from 1850 to 1870
pp.161     DL★
Evanston IL: [For the author?]     1934

2722 MITCHELL, ALBERT O. Dramatics in Southern Utah - Parawan, Cedar City, Beaver, St George - from 1850 to the coming of the moving pctures
Salt Lake City: U. of Utah (MA)     1935

2723 BROWNING, BETH. History of drama in Ogden
Provo: Brigham Young U. (MA)     1947

2724 MULDER, WILLIAM. Music, drama and the societies of Utah's Nordic language Press
Salt Lake City: U. of Utah (MA)     1947

2725 MARGETTS, WINIFRED S. A study of the Salt Lake City actor from 1850 to 1869
Salt Lake City: U. of Utah (MA)     1948

2726 JONES, JOHN A. The role of the sun dance in Northern Ute acculturation
NY: Columbia U. (PhD)     1950

2727 FERGUSON, BURNETT B. History of the drama in Provo, Utah, 1853-1897
Provo: Brigham Young U, (MA)     1952

2728 JOHNSON, RUE C. A history of the drama in Corinne and Brigham City, Utah, 1855-1905
Provo: Brigham Young U. (MA)     1954

2729 MONSON, LELAND H. Shakespeare in Utah (1847-1900)
Salt Lake City: U. of Utah (PhD)     1956

2730 MAUGHAN, ILA M. Pioneer theatre in the desert
pp.xii, 172; ill.     DL★
Salt Lake City: Deseret P.     1961
Survey of theatrical entertainment given under the auspices of the Church of Jesus Christ of Latter-day Saints in Salt Lake City, 1852-1869. With much material on the Deseret Dramatic Association, 1852-1869.

2731 OAKS, HAROLD R. An evaluation of the beginnings, purposes, and influence of drama in Ogden from 1840 to 1900
Provo: Brigham Young U. (MA)     1962

2732 ROYLANCE, AARON A. The Salt Lake Theatre as an organizational unit
Salt Lake City: U. of Utah (PhD)     1963
Period, 1850-1928.

2733 BREWER, COURTNEY H. A history of drama in Logan, Utah, and neighbouring communities to 1925
Provo: Brigham Young U. (PhD)     1972

2734 TODD, THERALD F. The operation of the Salt Lake theatre 1862-1875
Eugene: U. of Oregon (PhD)     1973

2735 EGYPTIAN THEATER [cover title]
pp.[20] inc. wrappers; ill. in text     M
Notre Dame: Theatre Historical Society     1974
Facsimile of souvenir of the opening of the Egyptian Theatre, Ogden, UT, 1924, issued with *Marquee*, VI: 4.

2736 ASAHINA, ROBERTA R. Brigham Young and the Salt Lake theatre, 1862-1877
Medford MA: Tufts U. (PhD)     1980

2737 SCANLON, LEE E. Buffalo Bill in a boiled shirt: the Salt Lake theatre, 1869-1874
Provo: Brigham Young U. (PhD)     1980

2738 PETRIE, DAVID T. The Sundance Institute: the first four years
Provo: Brigham Young U. (PhD)     1987

## 6.2.47 VIRGINIA

**2739** CALAMITY AT RICHMOND, being a narrative of the affecting circumstances attending the awful conlagration of the theatre, in the city of Richmond, on the night of Thursday, the 26th of December, 1811. By which, more than seventy of its valuable citizens suddenly lost their lives, and many others were greatly injured and maimed. Collected from various letters, publications, and official reports and accompanied with a preface, containing appropriate reflections, calculated to awaken the attention of the public to the frequency of the destruction of theatrical edifices
pp.i, 56; front. MH
Philadelphia: John F. Watson 1812
Also a New York edition, printed by Langin & Thompson, 1812, (pp. 60). Reprint (not seen) by Darton & Harvey, 1812.

**2740** A COLLECTION of facts and statements, relative to the fatal event, which occurred at the theatre, in Richmond, on the 26th December, 1811. Principally extracted from the *Enquirer*
pp.39 MH
Richmond VA: John O'Lynch 1812

**2741** NARRATIVE and report of the causes and circumstances of the deplorable conflagration at Richmond (Virginia) from letters and authentic documents. Printed for the public, January 12th, 1812
pp.72 MH
[Richmond]: [?] 1812

**2742** PARTICULAR ACCOUNT of the dreadful fire at Richmond, December 26, 1811 which destroyed the Theatre and the house adjoining, and in which more than sixty persons were either burnt to death, or destroyed in attempting to make their escape. To which is added some observations on theatrical performances and an essay from the *Virginia Argus*, proving profaneness inconsistent with politeness
pp.48 L
Baltimore: For J. Kingston 1812

**2743** MORDECAI, SAMUEL. Richmond in by-gone days: being reminiscences of an old citizen
pp.359 L
Richmond VA: West & Johnson 1860
Second edition, revised. First published 1856. Includes chapters on 'places of amusement'

**2744** SHOCKLEY, MARTIN S. A history of theatre in Richmond, Virginia, 1810-1838
Chapel Hill: U. of North Carolina (PhD) 1938

**2745** LAND, ROBERT H. The theatre in colonial Virginia
Charlottesville: U. of Virginia (PhD) 1942

**2746** HADLEY, RICHARD H. The theatre in Lynchburg, Virginia, from its beginnings to the outbreak of the civil war
Ann Arbor: U. of Michigan (PhD) 1947

**2747** SIMPSON, MARY P. The Williamsburg theatre 1716-1774
Washington DC: Catholic U. of America (MA) 1948

**2748** SHERMAN, SUSANNE K. Post-revolutionary theatre in Virginia. 1784-1810
Williamsburg: College of William and Mary (MA) 1950

**2749** ELLIOTT, ESTELLE C. Barter Theatre of Virginia Inc...a study of its development and its accomplishments in terms of its announced aims and objectives
Charlottesville: U. of Virginia (MA) 1953

**2750** ANDREWS, JACK E. Community Theatre in Virginia: a summary of activity and methods, 1953-1954
Charlottesville: U. of Virginia (MA) 1954

**2751** DAVIS, RICHARD B. Intellectual life in Jefferson's Virginia 1790-1830
pp.xvi, 507; front. O
Chapel Hill: U. of N. Carolina P. 1964
Includes a chapter, *Plays and the theatre*.

**2752** FULLER, CHARLES F. Kunkel and company at the Marshall Theatre, Richmond, Virginia, 1856-1861
Athens: Ohio U. (MFA) 1968

**2753** HUNT, ALTHEA (Ed.). The William and Mary Theatre: a chronicle
pp.xvi, 231; ill. DL★
Richmond VA: Dietz P. 1968

**2754** WILLIAMS, ANNE St C. Robert Porterfield's Barter Theatre of Abingdon, Virginia: the state theatre of Virginia
Urbana-Champaign: U. of Illinois (PhD) 1969

**2755** WADDELL, RICHARD E. Theatre in Charlottesville, 1886-1912: the Levy Opera House and the Jefferson Auditorium
Charlottesville: U. of Virginia (MA) 1972

**2756** GRAY, VIRGINIA P. A history of the Kanawha Players of Charleston, West Virginia, from 1922 to 1972
Bowling Green: State U. (PhD) 1973

**2757** NIELSEN, MARK S. A study of the Hallam Company's premier production in Williamsburg, *The Merchant of Venice* [1752]
Chapel Hill: U. of North Carolina (MA) 1974

**2758** JORDAN, CHESTER I. A study of the economic development of the Barter Theatre of Virginia, Incorporated, 1933-1973
Bowling Green: State U. (PhD) 1975

**2759** SHOCKLEY, MARTIN S. The Richmond stage, 1784-1812
pp.ix, 451; ill. in text, col. front. M
Charlottesville: U. P. of Virginia 1977

## 6.2.48 WASHINGTON

**2760** GRANT, HOWARD F. & GRANT, ETHEL A. (Eds). Story of Seattle's early theaters
pp.47; ill. in text. maps DL★
Seattle: U. of Washington Book Store 1934
Foreword by Glenn Hughes.

**2761** LADD, JAMES W. Survey of the legitimate theatre in Seattle since 1856
Pullman: State College of Washington (MA) 1937

**2762** ELLIOTT, EUGENE C. A history of variety-vaudeville in Seattle from the beginning to 1914
pp.ix, 84; pl. 8  L
Seattle: U. of Washington P. 1944

**2763** ROHRER, MARY K. The history of Seattle stock companies from their beginnings to 1934
pp.xiii, 76; pl.6  L
Seattle: U. of Washington P. 1945

**2764** NELSON, EDWIN L. A history of road shows in Seattle, from their beginnings to 1914
Seattle: U. of Washington (MA) 1947

**2765** HUGHES, GLENN. The Penthouse Theatre: its history and technique
pp.xii, 71; pl. 7  M
Seattle: U. of Washington P. 1958
Second edition, revised, listing productions 1932-58. First published NY, French, 1942.

**2766** ELBERSON, STANLEY D. The history of the Tacoma little theatre, 1918-1932
Salt Lake City: U. of Utah (MA) 1962

**2767** COYNE, BERNARD A. A history of Arena stage, Washington DC
New Orleans: Tulane U. (PhD) 1964

**2768** REAMS, DANNY I. Spokane theatre, 1880 to 1892
Pullman: Washington State U. (MA) 1970

**2769** KALEZ, JAY J. Saga of a western town... Spokane; a collection of factual incidents and anecdotes...
pp.136  DL★
Spokane, WA: Lawton Printing 1972
Makes reference to the Shirley Stock company 1898-1912.

**2770** WASSERMAN, BRUCE M. Early theatre in Spokane, Washington, 1889-1902
Pullman: Washington State U. (PhD) 1975

**2771** JOHNSON, EVAMARII A. A production history of the Seattle Federal Theatre Project negro repertory theatre company: 1935-1939
Seattle: U. of Washington (PhD) 1981

**2772** THE 5th AVENUE Theatre of Seattle
pp.44; ill. in text  M
Notre Dame: Theatre Historical Society/Fifth Avenue Theatre 1984
Opened September 1926, mixing live shows with movies. Closed 1978 and re-opened, renovated and re-equipped, as a Performing Arts Center in 1980.

## 6.2.49 WASHINGTON DC

**2773** HUNTER, ALEXANDER & POLKINHORN, J. H. New National Theater, Washington, D. C. A record of fifty years...Illustrated by J. Ellsworth Clark
pp.101; ill. in text, pl. 1  MH
Washington DC: R. O. Polkinhorn & Son 1885
A souvenir of the re-opening in 1885. Original theatre completed in 1835 and destroyed by fire in February 1885.

**2774** KENNEDY, MARY A. The theatre movement in Washington 1800-1835
Washington DC: Catholic U. of America (MA) 1933

**2775** BRENNER, WALTER C. The Ford Theatre Lincoln assassination playbills, a study
pp.16; ill.  DL★
Philadelphia: For the author 1937

**2776** DUPLER, DOROTHY. A study of the dramatic activity in the social agencies of Washington DC
Washington DC: Catholic U. of America (MA) 1943

**2777** ATKINSON, GEORGE & KIRALY, VICTOR. – a great curtain falls. Designed and produced under the creative direction of A. Eugene Hawes
pp.68; ill. in text, front.  M
NY: Strand P. 1950
History of the National Theatre, Washington DC, opened December 7, 1835. Introduction by John Golden.

**2778** SULLIVAN, LEO E. The closing of the theater in Washington, 1948
Washington DC: Catholic U. of America (MA) 1950

**2779** THE FOLGER SHAKESPEARE LIBRARY: a research institution dedicated to the advancement of literary and historical scholarship
pp.16; ill.in text  M
[Washington]: Trustees of Amherst College 1951

**2780** RYAN, OWEN E. Arena Stage, Washington DC, an investigation
New Haven: Yale U. (MFA) 1962

**2781** OLSZEWSKI, GEORGE J. Restoration of Ford's Theatre Washington D.C.
pp.xvii, 138; ill. in text  M
Washington DC: Department of the Interior 1963
A report forming a basis for the restoration of the theatre to its condition on the night of the assassination of President Lincoln.

**2782** McCLURE, STANLEY W. Ford's Theatre and the house where Lincoln died
pp.iv, 43; ill. in text  M
Washington DC: Department of the Interior 1969
Revised edition of the National Park Service Historical Handbook 3. Provides an account of the assassination and subsequent events, with an illustrated description of the locations involved.

**2783** JOHN F. KENNEDY CENTER for the Performing Arts Washington DC
pp.[20] inc. wrappers; ill. in text  M
[Washington DC]: Friends of the Center [1971]

**2784** THEATRE at Ford's [cover title]
pp.[16] inc. wrappers; ill. in text  M
[Washington DC]: Ford's Theatre Society [1971]
Brochure for the season 1970-71.

**2785** MORRISON, ANDREW C. Theatres of Washington: an illustrated historical list
pp.[38] inc. wrappers; ill. in text  M
Washington DC: Theatre Historical Society 1972

**2786** MEERMAN, ROGER & BOYER, ROBERT. The National Theatre in Washington: buildings and audiences, 1835-1972 [cover title]
pp.190-242; ill. in text  MH
[Washington DC]: [Columbia Historical Society] 1973
Reprinted from the Society *Records*, 1971-2.

**2787** GILL, BRENDAN. John F. Kennedy Center for the performing arts
pp.160; ill. in text  M
NY: Harry N. Abrams 1981

**2788** LEE, DOUGLAS B.; MEERMAN, ROGER & MURPHY, DONN B. Stage for a nation: the National Theatre – 150 years. Foreword by Harry Teter, with a preface by Helen Hayes
pp.143; ill. in text                                        M
Lanham MD: U. P. of America                  1985

**2789** GARNER, NATHAN C. The Washington [DC] Theater Club: the management of a resident professional theater
Ann Arbor: U. of Michigan (PhD)              1986

**2790** BECKER, RALPH E. Miracle on the Potomac: the Kennedy Center from the beginning
pp.xiii, 217                                              DL★
Silver Spring MD: Bartleby P.                  1990

## 6.2.50 WEST VIRGINIA

**2791** JONES, ROBIN A. A history of the professional legitimate theatre in Huntington from 1871 to 1928
Huntington WV: Marshall U. (MA)            1957

**2792** RADOW, RHODA K. A history of the Burlew Opera House, Charleston, West Virginia from 1891-1920
Huntington WV: Marshall U. (MA)            1964

## 6.2.51 WISCONSIN

**2793** McDAVITT, ELAINE E. A history of the theatre in Milwaukee, Wisconsin, from its beginnings to 1865
Evanston: Northwestern U. (MA)              1936

**2794** YOUNGERMAN, HENRY C. Theatrical activities: Madison, Wisconsin, 1836-1907
Madison: U. of Wisconsin (PhD)                1940

**2795** NUERNBERG, EVELYN A. A study of rural drama in Wisconsin
Madison: U. of Wisconsin (MA)                 1942

**2796** EDDY, JUNIUS. The Wisconsin idea theatre: a program in state-wide drama
Madison: U. of Wisconsin (MS)                 1949

**2797** ALEXANDER, B. SHIRLEY. A critical history of 4-H Club drama in Wisconsin
Madison: U. of Wisconsin (M.S.)               1950

**2798** MITCHELL, JAMES W. Tri-county rural theatre project in Winnebago, Waupaca, and Waushara Counties
Madison: U. of Wisconsin (MS)                 1950

**2799** WARFIELD, JACK W. A history and evaluation of the Wisconsin Players of Milwaukee
Salt Lake City: U. of Utah (PhD)               1953

**2800** ABRAHAMSON, KENNETH Z. A history and eveluation of the Sheboygan (Wisconsin) community theatre
Madison: U. of Wisconsin (M.S.)               1954

**2801** TRIPP, LLOYD M. Racine (Wisconsin) summer theatre, history and management, 1951-1952-1953
Madison: U. of Wisconsin (MS)                 1954

**2802** O'SHEA, JOSEPH J. A history of the English-speaking professional stage in Milwaukee, Wisconsin, 1842-1876
Evanston: Northwestern U. (PhD)             1964

**2803** HEAGLE, LAWRENCE. The cessation of professional theatre at the Mabel Tainter Theatre, Menomonie, Wisconsin: a historical-cultural analysis
Eau Claire: U. of Wisconsin (MS)              1968

**2804** MADSEN, JOHN A. A history of theatre from March 25, 1857 to October 2, 1900 in Whitewater
Whitewater: U. of Wisconsin (MST)          1971

**2805** SIEFKAS, JAMES M. A history of theatre in La Crosse, Wisconsin, from its beginning to 1900
Columbia: U. of Missouri (PhD)                 1972

**2806** WOLFERT, WAYNE R. Theatre in Eau Claire, Wisconsin: a history of the Grand Opera House (1883-1930)
Madison: U. of Wisconsin (PhD)                1972

**2807** OLLERMAN, FREDERICK H. The Milwaukee Repertory Theatre: publicity and promotion
Ann Arbor: U. of Michigan (PhD)              1978

**2808** MYERS, DENYS P. & NAYLOR, DAVID (Eds). The Al Ringling Theatre, Baraboo, Wisconsin 1915-1990
pp.25; ill. in text                                         M
Chicago: Theatre Historical Society          1990
Researched originally for the Historic American Building survey unit of the Department of the Interior and here re-edited.

## 6.2.52 WYOMING

**2809** BELL, WILLIAM C. A history of the theatrical activities of Cheyenne, Wyoming
Evanston: Northwestern U. (MA)              1935

**2810** KAISER, LOUIS H. A theatrical history of Laramie, Wyoming, 1868-1880
Laramie: U. of Wyoming (MA)                   1950

**2811** BOUSTKEON, LINDY. History of the Laramie theatre, (1881-1890)
Laramie: U. of Wyoming (MA)                   1961

## 6.3 OTHER COUNTRIES

**2812** SOUCEK, CAROL B. The use of theater in United States government international relations abroad
Los Angeles: U. of Southern California (PhD)   1976

# 7. THEATRE COMPANIES, CLUBS, SOCIETIES

## Actor's Workshop

**2813** FOWLER, KEITH F. The history of the Actor's Workshop
New Haven: Yale U. (PhD)     1968

## Actors Equity Association

**2814** FAULKENDER, ROBERT E. Historical development and basic policies of the Actors Equity Association
Pittsburgh: U. (PhD)     1954

**2815** ROCKWOOD, JEROME. The cultural activities of the Actors' Equity Association: the first fifty years, 1913-1963
NY: U. (PhD)     1965

**2816** STOYLE, JUDITH. Economic and demographic characteristics of Actors' Equity Association membership
pp.43     DL★
[NY?]: Actors' Equity Association     1970

## Actors Protective Union

**2817** ACTORS PROTECTIVE UNION [cover title]
pp.8     MB
Philadelphia: Sherman (printer)     [1866]
A statement and defence of the Union's aims, and articles of association.

## Actors Studio

**2818** GARFIELD, DAVID. A player's place: the story of the Actors Studio
pp.xii, 308; pl. 12     M
NY: Macmillan     1980

**2819** HIRSCH, FOSTER. A method to their madness: the history of the Actors Studio
pp.367; ill. in text     M
NY: W. W. Norton     1984

## Actors' Fund of America

**2820** SOUVENIR programme of the Actors' Fund Fair, Madison Square Garden, May 2d - 7th 1892
pp.212; ill. in text     M
NY: [Actors' Fund]     1892

**2821** SOUVENIR. Actors' Fund Fair 1910 [cover title]
pp.[6]     MH
NY: [Actors' Fund]     [1910]
Includes reprint of Robert G. Ingersoll: *Children of the stage*, the text of an address first delivered at an Actors' Fund Benefit, Fifth Avenue Theatre, NY, 1899.

**2822** SIMON, LOUIS M. A history of the Actors' Fund of America with special contributions by Ruth Gordon, Nedda Harrigan Logan, Cornelia O. Skinner, and Jean Loggie
pp.xiv, 274; ill. in text     M
NY: Theatre Arts Books     1972
Founded in 1882.

## Actors' Laboratory Theatre

**2823** SALVI, DELIA N. The history of the Actors' Laboratory, Inc
Los Angeles: U. of California (PhD)     1968

## Amateur Comedy Club

**2824** LIST OF MEMBERS of the Amateur Comedy Club...
pp.various     MH
[NY]: [The Amateur Comedy Club]     1884-
Twenty-two volumes examined, to season 1916-17. Club founded in 1884. The list includes membership, past members, by-laws, performances.

## American Conservatory Theatre

**2825** WILK, JOHN R. The creation of an ensemble: the first years of the American Conservatory Theatre
pp.xiii, 183     DL★
Carbondale: Southern Illinois U. P.     1986

## American Dramatic Fund Association

**2826** AMERICAN DRAMATIC FUND ASSOCIATION incorporated April 10, 1848...open alike to every actor and actress in the United States without restriction from age, or length of service in any particular theatre, town or city
pp.various     MH
NY: [ADFA]     1856-87
Annual reports, initially substantial (e.g. pp.63), later brief, with membership lists. The secretary wrote in 1887, 'we are sadly in need of new blood, but I fear we shall never get it, judging by the terrible apathy of our professional brethren, and their utter neglect of providing for incapacity and old age.' The fund was superseded by the Actors' Fund of America, first incorporated in 1882.

## American Dramatists Club

**2827** PLAN and scope for reorganization of the Dramatist's [sic] Club approved January 17, 1909 [cover title]
pp.11     MH
[NY?]: [For the club?]     [1909]
Possibly the *American Dramatists Club* that in 1891 replaced the *American Dramatic Authors Society* and which itself became the *Society of American Dramatists and Composers* before developing into the *Dramatists Guild*.

## American Laboratory Theatre

**2828** WILLIS, R. A. The American Laboratory Theatre: 1923-1930
Iowa City: U. of Iowa (PhD)     1968

## American National Theatre and Academy

**2829** MONTANO, SEVERINO M. The administrative history of the American National Theatre and Academy
Washington DC: The American U. (PhD)     1949

**2830** JOHN, MARY W. ANTA. The American National Theatre and Academy, its first quarter century
NY: U. (PhD)     1965

## American Place Theatre

**2831** WEGNER, PAMELA S. The women's project of the American Place Theatre: 1978-1979
Minneapolis: U. of Minnesota (PhD)     1987

## American Repertory Theatre

**2832** McCLAVE, NANCY. The American Repertory Theatre, Inc. A case study
Kent OH: State U. (PhD)     1982

## Black Theatre Alliance

**2833** THE BLACK THEATRE ALLIANCE touring brochure
pp.ii, 24 (2); ill. in text     M
NY: Black Theatre Alliance

Foreword by Hazel Bryant. Lists BTA theatre and dance companies.

**2834** WILSON, ROBERT J. The Black Theatre Alliance: a history of its founding members
NY: U. (PhD)     1974

## Bohemian Club

**2835** GARNETT, PORTER. The Bohemian jinks: a treatise
pp.xviii, 137; pl. 24, map     M
San Francisco: Bohemian Club     1908

A history. Describes the development of the so-called grove play, an annual *al fresco* club production.

**2836** GARNETT, PORTER. The Green Knight, a vision...the ninth Grove play of the Bohemian Club of San Francisco as produced by the author...on...the twelfth night of August, nineteen hundred & eleven
pp.xxviii, 62; ill. in text, pp. 2 (1 folding)     M
San Francisco: For the Club     1911

Text, with substantial introduction. Photograph and sketch map of the Grove play site.

## Bread and Puppet Theatre

**2837** KOURILSKY, FRANCOISE. Le Bread and Puppet Theatre
pp.278; pl. 14     M
Lausanne: La Cité Editeur     1971

**2838** HAMILTON, ROBERT C. The Bread and Puppet Theatre of Peter Schuman: history and analysis
Bloomington: Indiana U. (PhD)     1978

**2839** BOLTON, RANDY. Peter Schuman's creative method used in making plays with the Bread and Puppet Theatre
Tallahassee: Florida State U. (PhD)     1981

**2840** SELLI, SERGIO. Il teatro dei sogni materializzati: storia e mito del Bread and Puppet Theatre. Con un contributo fotografico di Maurizio Buscarini
pp.108; ill. in text, pl. 7     M
Florence: Usher     1986

**2841** BRECHT, STEFAN. Peter Schuman's Bread and Puppet Theatre
pp.viii, 782; v. 813; ill. in text. pl.48     M
London: Methuen     1988

Two volumes in the series *The original theatre of New York...*

## Drama League of America

**2842** BEST, A. STARR. The Drama League of America: its inception, purposes, wonderful growth and future
pp.[17], ill. in text     MB
NY: Doubleday, Page/ *The Drama*     [1914]

**2843** BOGARD, MORRIS R. The Drama League of America. A history and critical analysis of its activities and achievements
Urbana: U. of Illinois (PhD)     1962

## Dunlap Society

**2844** THE DUNLAP SOCIETY [cover title]
pp.7     MH
NY: [Dunlap Society]     1885

A prospectus.

**2845** BIENNIAL reports of the treasurer and secretary of the Dunlap Society
pp.51; ill. in text     M
NY: Dunlap Society     1888

## Federal Theatre

**2846** [DE ROHAN, PIERRE (Ed.)]. Federal theatre
pp.[av. 30]; ill. in text     MH
NY: WPA     1935-37

Bulletin issued for all workers on Federal Theatre projects throughout America by the Bureau of Research and Publication. Volume 1, nos 1-6. Volume 2, nos 1-5, November, 1935-June, 1937.

**2847** DE ROHAN, PIERRE. Federal Theatre. First Federal summer theatre - a report
pp.36; ill. in text     MH
NY: Works Progress Administration     [1937]

A detailed account of the development of the living newspaper production, *One third of a nation*, at the summer theatre, Vassar Experimental theatre, Poughkeepsie, NY

**2848** WHITMAN, WILLSON. Bread and circuses: a study of Federal Theatre
pp.viii, 191     M
NY: Oxford U. P.     1937

**2849** ZIMMERMAN, LELAND L. The Federal Theatre. An evaluation and comparison with foreign national theatres
Madison: U. of Wisconsin (PhD)     1955

**2850** McDERMOTT, DOUGLAS. The Living Newspaper as a dramatic form
Iowa City: U. of Iowa (PhD)     1964

**2851** BILLINGS, ALAN G. Design in the Works Progress Administration's Federal Theatre Project (1935 to 1939)
Urbana: U. of Illinois (PhD)     1967

**2852** HAMMOUDA, ABDUL-AZIZ A-S. The Living Newspaper: a study in sources and form
Ithaca: Cornell U. (PhD)     1967

**2853** MATHEWS, JANE D. The Federal Theatre, 1935-1939: plays, relief, and politics
pp.xii, 342; pl. 4     M
Princeton: U. P.     1967

A history, documenting the Project's struggle with officialdom.

**2854** McDONALD, WILLIAM F. Federal relief administration and the arts: the origins and administrative history of the arts projects of the Works Progress Administration
pp.xiv, 869     L
Colombus: Ohio State U. P.     1969

Chapters 20-23 chronicle the Federal Theatre Project.

**2855** MARDIS, ROBERT F. Federal Theatre Project in Florida
Gainsville: U. of Florida (PhD)     1971

**2856** ADUBATO, ROBERT A.  A history of the WPA's negro theatre project in New York City, 1935-1939
NY: U. (PhD)                                                                            1978

**2857** KORN, MARJORIE S.  *It Can't Happen Here*: Federal Theatre's bold adventure
Columbia: U. of Missouri (PhD)                                       1978

**2858** O'CONNOR, JOHN & BROWN, LORRAINE.  Free, adult, uncensored: the living history of the Federal Theatre Project.  Foreword by John Houseman
pp.xii, 228; ill. in text, some col.                                          M
Washington DC: New Republic Books                             1978

**2859** KREIZENBECK, ALAN D.  The theatre nobody knows: forgotten productions of the Federal Theatre Project, 1935-1939
NY: U. (PhD)                                                                            1979

**2860** CRAIG, E. QUITA.  Black drama of the Federal Theatre era: beyond the formal horizons
pp.x, 239; pl. 3                                                                         O
Amherst: U. of Massachusetts P.                                       1980
Introduction by James V. Hatch.

**2861** SALTZMAN, JARED.  Design and technology of the Federal Theatre Project
NY: U. (PhD)                                                                            1980

**2862** KOCH, JOHN C.  The Federal Theatre project, region IV - a structural and historical analysis of how it functioned and what it accomplished
Lincoln: U. of Nebraska (PhD)                                          1981

**2863** ROSS, THEOPHIL W.  Conflicting concepts of the Federal Theatre Project: a critical history
Columbia: U. of Missouri (PhD)                                       1981

**2864** BUTTITTA, TONY & WITHAM, BARRY.  Uncle Sam presents: a memoir of the Federal Theatre 1935-1939 with drawings by Don Freeman
pp.xv, 249; ill. in text                                                            M
Philadelphia: U. of Pennsylvania P.                                   1982

**2865** KAHN, DAVID M.  The Federal Theatre Project in San Francisco. A history of an indigenous theatre
Berkeley: U. of California (PhD)                                        1984

**2866** WILLIAMS, ELWOOD P.  An examination of protagonists in selected Federal Theatre Project plays as a reflection of New Deal society and politics
Kent OH: State U. (PhD)                                                    1984

**2867** HEARD, DOREEN B.  A production history of the New York City children's theatre unit of the Federal Theatre Project
Tallahassee: Florida State U. (PhD)                                  1986

**2868** THE FEDERAL THEATRE Project: a catalog-calendar of productions compiled by the staff of the Fenwick Library, George Mason University
pp.xvii, 349                                                                             L
NY: Greenwood P.                                                             1986
With a geographical index. Introduction by Lorraine A. Brown.

**2869** THE FEDERAL THEATRE PROJECT collection: a register of the Library of Congress collection of U.S. Work Project Administration records on deposit at George Mason University
pp.vi, 320; ill. in text                                                           MH
Washington DC: Library of Congress                              1987
Lists playreaders' reports, playscripts, living newspapers, and other productions

**2870** FRIEDMAN, MARTIN E.  Federal Theatre Project Shakespearean productions: a study of presentational and organizational techniques
Ann Arbor: U. of Michigan (PhD)                                    1987

**2871** SOCEANU, MARION.  Das Federal Theatre Project und seine Dramen über amerikanische Geschichte
pp.iii, 372; folding chart                                                     MH
Frankfurt: Peter Lang                                                          1987

**2872** HIGHSAW, CAROL A.  A theatre of action: the Living Newspapers of the Federal Theatre Project
Princeton: U. (PhD)                                                            1988

**2873** LAWRENCE, HAPPY J.  The state-wide tours of the Florida Federal Theatre Project, October, 1937-June, 1939: a description and evaluation of the two seasons on the road for the 'people's popular theatre'
Tallahassee: Florida State U. (PhD)                                  1988

**2874** GILL, GLENDA E.  White grease paint on black performers: a study of the Federal Theatre 1935-1939
pp.xvi, 207                                                                          DL*
NY: Peter Lang                                                                    1989

**2875** KAZACOFF, GEORGE.  Dangerous theatre: the Federal Theatre Project as a forum for new plays
pp.viii, 369; ill. in text                                                         MH
NY: Peter Lang                                                                    1989
A history of the project and an examination of the plays it subsidized and their reception.

### Free Southern Theatre

**2876** DENT, THOMAS; SCHECHNER, RICHARD & MOSES, GILBERT (Eds).  The free southern theater by the Free Southern Theatre: a documentary of the south's radical black theater, with journals, letters, poetry, essays and a play written by those who built it
pp.xvi, 233; ill. in text, pl. 12                                                M
Indianapolis: Bobbs-Merrill                                                1969

**2877** TRIPP, ELLEN L.  Free Southern Theatre: there is always a message
Greensboro: U. of North Carolina (PhD)                         1986
Mississippi, Louisiana. Reference to civil rights.

**2878** KENNEY, JANET R.  The Free Southern Theatre: the relationship between mission and management
Eugene: U. of Oregon (PhD)                                             1987

### Grand Union

**2879** RAMSAY, MARGARET H.  Grand Union (1970-1976), an improvisational performance group
NY: U. (PhD)                                                                            1986

### Green Room Club

**2880** ARTICLES of incorporation, constitution by-laws and house rules, with list of officers and members of the Green Room Club, 139 West 74th Street, New York City
pp.63                                                                                     MH
NY: Green Room Club                                                       1904

## 7. THEATRE COMPANIES, CLUBS, SOCIETIES

### Group Theatre

**2881** GASPER, RAYMOND D. A study of the Group Theatre and its contribution to theatrical production in America
Columbus: Ohio State U. (PhD) 1955

**2882** CAPRIOLE, ETTORE. Il Group Theatre di New York
pp.115; pl. 8 M
Bologna: Cappelli 1960

**2883** SPAULDING, THELMA C. The Group Theatre as it reflected selected contemporary problems
NY: U. (PhD) 1961

**2884** WOLFE, DONALD H. The significance of the Group Theatre
Ithaca: Cornell U. (PhD) 1968

**2885** RICHMOND, NEAL(Ed.). The Group Theatre 1933-1941: an exhibition of photographs...by Alfredo Valente
pp.[31]; ill. in text M
NY: Queen's College, Paul Klapper Library 1969

**2886** CLURMAN, HAROLD. The fervent years: the story of the Group Theatre and the thirties.
pp.ix, 329; ill. CSt
NY: Harcourt Brace Jovanovich [1975]
A reprint of the first edition, NY: Alfred A. Knopf, 1945 but with the foreword and epilogue from the second edition, NY: Hill and Wang, 1957, and a new afterword by the author.

### La Mama

**2887** GRESS, ELSA (Ed.?). Boxiganga. Teater som livsform til minde om Ruth Landhoff York
pp.143; pl. 8 L
Copenhagen: Spectator 1968
The La Mama troupe and their film, *Boxiganga*. In Danish, followed by an English translation: *Boxiganga, theatre as a way of life. To the memory of Ruth Landhoff Yorck [sic]*. Introductory note by Elsa Gress.

**2888** TERRY, MEGAN. Approaching Simone
pp.141; pl. 1 MH★
Old Westbury NY: Feminist P. 1973
Text of play produced first at Boston U., later by La Mama experimental theatre, February 1970. Introduction by Phyllis J. Wagner.

**2889** GAGNON, PAULINE D. The development and achievement of La Mama under the artistic direction of Ellen Stewart
Ann Arbor: U. of Michigan (PhD) 1987

### Lambs

**2890** THE LAMBS. Certificate of incorporation, constitution, by-laws and rules, officers, members and committees. Club house 26 West Thirty-first New York City
pp.117 MH
NY: [The Lambs Club] 1895

**2891** ANNALS of The Lambs: London and New York
pp.86 M
NY: [The Lambs Club] 1899
The London bohemian Club (1869-79) and the NY Club (1874-99) that it inspired. Errata slip.

### Living Theatre

**2892** GOTTLIEB, SAUL. The Living Theatre in exile
pp.[102]; ill. in text M
[Amsterdam]: Mickery Books 1966
Cover title, *The Living Theatre in Europe*. After their brush with the IRS in 1963, the troupe toured Europe where they played *The Brig*, and developed a new version of *Frankenstein, Mysteries and smaller pieces* and *The Maids*, all here described and illustrated.

**2893** BILLETER, ERIKA. The Living Theatre: Paradise Now
pp.141; ill. in text M
Berne: Benteli 1968
Photographs by Dolf Preisig. From the German, *Living Theatre, Paradise Now: ein Bericht in wort und bild*.

**2894** BROWN, KENNETH H. The Brig: a concept for theatre or film. With an essay on the Living Theatre by Julian Beck, and director's notes by Judith Malina
pp.vii, 107; stage plan MH
NY: Hill and Wang 1969
The acting version used by the Living Theatre. Includes a list of Living Theatre productions.

**2895** LEBEL, JEAN-J. Entretiens avec le Living Theatre
pp.382; pl. 16 L
Paris: Pierre Belfond 1969
Detailed account and history, using interviews, scenarios, extracts from the journals of Beck and Malina, poems and letters.

**2896** THE LIVING THEATRE
pp.149; ill. in text M
New Haven: Yale U. School of Drama 1969
Special issue, Vol. 2, No. 2, of *Yale theatre*, Spring, 1969. Contributors include Julian Beck, Steve Ben Israel, Eric Bentley, Larry Bercowitz, Robert Brustein, Joseph Chaikin, and Judith Malina.

**2897** SMITH, MICHAEL. Theatre trip...[autobiography]
pp.xvii, 178; ill. in text M
Indianapolis: Bobbs-Merrill 1969
Introductions by Judith Malina and Julian Beck.

**2898** WRIGHT, JACK B. The Living Theatre: alive and committed
Lawrence: U. of Kansas (PhD) 1969
A history.

**2899** BINER, PIERRE. Le Living Theatre. Histoire sans légende (2nd éd, mise à jour et augm. de la documentation relative à *Paradise Now*)
pp.280; ill. DL★
Lausanne: La Cité-Éditeur 1970
First published 1968. Published NY: Horizon, 1972.

**2900** NEFF, RENFREU. The Living Theatre, USA
pp.x, 254; pl. 12 M
Indianapolis: Bobbs-Merrill 1970

Travelogue of the 1968-69 tour. Photographs by Gianfranco Mantegna.

**2901** ROSTAGNO, ALDO; BECK, JULIAN & MALINA, JUDITH. We, the Living Theatre, a pictorial documentation by Gianfranco Mantegna of the life and pilgrimage of the Living Theatre in Europe and in the U.S. ...introduced by a panel discussion on *theatre as revolution* co-ordinated by Aldo Rostagno with the participation of Julian Beck and Judith Malina
pp.240; ill. in text  M
NY: Ballantine Books  1970

**2902** SWIFT, ELLIOTT C. The Living Theatre
NY: U. (PhD)  1970

**2903** BARTOLUCCI, GIUSEPPE. The Living Theatre: (dall' organismo-microstruttura allo rivendicazione dell'utopia). Saggio di scrittura scenica come movimento-azione
pp.185  DL★
Rome: Nuova Sinistra  [1971?]

**2904** MALINA, JUDITH & BECK, JULIAN. Paradise Now: a collective creation of the Living Theatre, written down by Judith Malina and Julian Beck
pp.vi, 154; ill. in text  L
NY: Random House  1971
Written down more than a year (or 50 performances) after the première in Avignon, July 24, 1968. With a chronology of performances. Photographs by Gianfranco Mantegna.

**2905** SILVESTRO, CARLO. The living book of the Living Theatre
Unpaged; ill. in text  M
Cologne: Dumont Schauberg  1971
Foreword in German by Wilhelm Unger. A photographic record, with text and captions in English.

**2906** BECK, JULIAN. The life of the theatre: the relation of the artist to the struggle of the people
unpaged; front.  M
San Francisco: City Lights  1972
Reflections, articles and jottings on the theatre.

**2907** MALINA, JUDITH. The enormous despair
pp.iv, 249  M
NY: Random House  1972
A log of the Living Theatre, 1968-69.

**2908** WILSON, TIMOTHY. House of the angels
pp.351; front., pl.6  L
London: Michael Joseph  1973
With reference to the Living Theatre. An account of William Berger and Carl Lobravico, with Berger's prison diary after his arrest and imprisonment in Italy on a drugs charge.

**2909** NICELY, TOM. Adam and his work: a bibliography of sources by and about Paul Goodman (1911-1972)
pp.xxvi, 336; front.  MH
Metuchen NJ: Scarecrow P.  1979
Foreword by Burton Weiss. Includes material on the Living Theatre.

**2910** PERKINS, ULRICA B. Visceral politics: the Living Theatre in America
Davis: U. of California (PhD)  1982

**2911** MALINA, JUDITH. The diaries of Judith Malina: 1947-1957
pp.ix, 485; pl. 7  L
NY: Grove P.  1984

## Lotos Club

**2912** ELDERKIN, JOHN. A brief history of the Lotos Club
pp.166; pl. 5  M
NY: Lotos Club  1895
Founded 1870 for a membership of a literary and artistic leaning, the NY club, housed since 1947 in a former Vanderbilt residence, has hosted the Lambs since they relinquished their own clubhouse. Many theatrical associations.

**2913** [ELDERKIN, JOHN]. The Lotos Club of New York City [drop title]
pp.[7]; pl.12  M
NY: For the Club  [c. 1909]
Describes the club-house on 57th Street.

## Manhattan Project

**2914** ARBUS, DOON (Ed.). *Alice in Wonderland*: the forming of a company and the making of a play
pp.xii, 175: ill. in text  M
NY: Merlin House  1973
An account, derived from recorded interviews, of the formation of the Manhattan Project company. Photographs by Richard Avedon.

## Masterworks Laboratory Theatre

**2915** SIGEL, DAVID L. The Masterworks Laboratory Theatre : historical and critical study
NY: City U. (PhD)  1982
1965-1980. Dedicated to non-contemporary drama, produced in accordance with the Stanislavsky system, under Walt Witcover.

## Mercury Theatre

**2916** NOURYEH, ANDREA J. The Mercury Theatre: a history
NY: U. (PhD)  1987

## National Theatre Conference

**2917** BALIO, TINO & NORVELLE, LEE. The history of the National Theatre Conference
pp.v, 119  M
NY: NTC and Theatre Arts Books  1968
The NTC archive, from which this book is substantially derived, is housed in the Lilly Library of Indiana University.

## Negro Ensemble Company

**2918** HILL, EDWARD S. A thematic study of selected plays produced by the Negro Ensemble Company
Bowling Green: State U. (PhD)  1975

## Open Theatre

**2919** PASOLLI, ROBERT. A book on the Open Theatre
pp.xv, 127; pl. 8  MH
Indianapolis: Bobbs-Merrill  1970
An account of Joseph Chaikin's Open Theatre providing a history, a description and a definition of the underlying philosophy.

**2920** MALPEDE, KAREN et al. Three works by the Open Theatre
pp.191: ill in text  M
NY: Drama Book Specialists  1974

Introduction and description with some examples of text. Includes contribution by Joseph Chaikin, and Alex Gildzen: *The Open Theatre: a beginning bibliography*. The pieces are, *Terminal*, dialogue for *The Mutation Show, Nightwalk*. Photographs by Mary Ellen Mark, Inge Morath, Max Waldman, drawings by Mary Frank.

**2921** BLUMENTHAL, EILEEN.   The Open Theatre
New Haven: Yale U. (PhD)                                     1977

**2922** HENDRIX, ERLENE C.   The presence of the actor as kinetic melody: a study of Joseph Chaikin's Open Theatre through the philosophy of Maurice Merleau-Ponty
Columbia: U. of Missouri (PhD)                               1977

## Performance Group

**2923** SCHECHNER, RICHARD (Ed.).   Dionysus in 69: the Performance Group
unpaged; ill. in text                                         M
NY: Farrar, Straus & Giroux                                1969
Detailed photographic record of production derived from *The Bacchae*.

**2924** SHEPHARD, WILLIAM H.   Group dynamics and the evolution of creative choice in the Performance Group's New York production of *Dionysus in 69*
Tallahassee: Florida State U. (PhD)                          1984

**2925** LICHTI, ESTHER S.   Richard Schechner and the Performance Group: a study of acting technique and methodology
Lubbock: Texas Tech U. (PhD)                                1986

## Players Club

**2926** CONSTITUTION of the Players
pp.22                                                         M
NY: [Players Club]                                          1888

**2927** [PARSONS, T. W.].   Address to the assembly at the opening of the Players' Club in New York
pp.2                                                         MB
[NY]: [Players Club]                                      [1888]
In the Boston Public Library copy the last line has been altered by hand.

**2928** THE PLAYERS
pp.various                                                   MH
NY: [Players Club]                                         1889-
The reports, at first annual, later intermittent, began as a statement of the constitution and a list of rules and members of the Club at 16, Gramercy Park, NY, but grew more elaborate, printing memorial and presidential addresses, theatre and club news, and obituaries. The size grew from an initial 40 pages to an average of over 100 between 1889 and 1917. Items of particular interest include:1894, Thomas Jefferson's tribute to Edwin Booth; 1896, Bishop Potter's address; 1897, Stephen H. Olin's address; 1898, Judge Henry E. Howland's address; 1899, E. C. Stedman's address; 1903, Judge Edward Patterson's address; 1905, obituaries for Wilson Barrett and Joseph Jefferson; 1906, Francis Wilson's address, obituary for Henry Irving; 1907, obituaries for Stanford White, J. L. Toole; 1908, obituary for Richard Mansfield; 1909, F. F. Mackay's address, obituary for Bronson Howard; 1910, Brander Matthews's address, obituaries for Clyde Fitch, Samuel Langhorn Clemens. This year and subsequently, Edwin Booth's initial speech of dedication (1888) was reprinted; 1911, Judge Daly's address; 1912, Otis Skinner's address; 1913, Howard Kyle's address; 1915, Evert Janson Wendell's address; 1916, obituaries for Salvini, Lewis Waller; 1917, Guy Nichols's address; 1925-28 (three years in one), Otis Skinner's memorial address on John Drew and programmes for Club play productions, a practice inaugurated in 1922, using initially a Broadway house, more recently the Club's own small stage.

**2929** BAMBURG, WILLIAM C (Ed.).   Catalogue of part of the art treasures owned by the Players
pp.47                                                        DL★
NY: The Players                                            1906

**2930** DAY, ROY (Ed.).   Catalogue of the paintings and the art treasures of the Players
pp.xi, 112                                                    M
NY: [For the Players]                                      1925
921 items.

**2931** MERWIN, SAMUEL.   My favorite club
pp.30; ill. in text                                           M
NY: [For the author?]                                      1933
Affectionate description of the Players Club, reprinted from *Delta Kappa Epsilon Quarterly*.

**2932** PHILLIPS, JOHN S.   The Players: occasional pieces
pp.vii, 32                                                    M
[NY]: [The Players]                                        1936
Reprints four addresses: *Our inheritance*, the Founder's Night address, December 31, 1931; *The club spirit*, 1924; *A gentle Phillipsic*, 1924; and *The jealous gods*, 1936.

**2933** LANIER, HENRY W. (Ed.).   The Players' book: a half-century of fact, feeling, fun and folklore
pp.380; ill. in text, col. front.                             M
NY: The Players                                            1938
A compilation of light-hearted articles, mostly reminisce. Includes list of officers and members.

**2934** OETTAL, WALTER.   Walter's sketch book of the Players...
pp.xi, 131; pl. 5                                            MH
[NY]: [The Players]                                       [1943]
Author was the major-domo of the Players Club. Foreword by Booth Tarkington. Correction slip.

**2935** STEWART, GEORGE W.   The Players after 75 years
pp.267; ill. in text                                          M
NY: The Players                                            1968
Reminiscences, 1938-63.

**2936** [THE PLAYERS CLUB REVIVALS, 1922-1940]
pp.8 inc. wrappers                                            M
NY: New York Times                                        1972
Facsimile reviews and cast lists of the 15 productions.

**2937** HOOKS, EUGENE J.   The Players: Edwin Booth's legacy to American theatre
Columbia: U. of Missouri (PhD)                            1973

## Playwrights' Producing Company

**2938** BASSETT, CLYDE H.   The Playwrights' Producing Company Inc., 1938-1960
Madison: U. of Wisconsin (PhD)                             1965

**2939** GORDON, ALBERT C. A critical study of the history and development of the Playwrights' Producing Company
New Orleans: Tulane U. (PhD)     1965

**2940** FRENCH, ALICE M. The dramaturgy of the Playwrights' Company
Columbia: U. of Missouri (PhD)     1974

**2941** WHARTON, JOHN F. Life among the playwrights; being mostly the story of the Playwrights' Producing Company, Inc.
pp.ix, 336; ill. in text     M
NY: Quadrangle     1974
PPC founded in 1938 out of writers' disaffection with the Theatre Guild.

### Princeton Triangle Club

**2942** MARSDEN, DONALD. The long kickline: a history of the Princeton Triangle Club
pp. xvi, 348; ill.     DL★
Princeton: The Triangle Club     1968
Foreword by Joshua Logan.

### Prolet Buehne

**2943** FRIEDMAN, DANIEL H. The Prolet Buehne: America's first agit-prop theatre
Madison: U. of Wisconsin (PhD)     1979

**2944** BRADBY, DAVID; JAMES, LOUIS & SHARRATT, BERNARD (Eds). Performance and politics in popular drama. Aspects of popular entertainment in theatre, film and television, 1800-1976
pp.xii, 331; ill. in text     M
Cambridge: U. P.     1980
Includes Stuart Cosgrove: *Prolet Buehne: agit-prop in America.*

### San Francisco Mime Troupe

**2945** DAVIS, R. G. The San Francisco Mime Troupe: the first ten years
pp.220; ill. in text     M
Palo Alto CA: Ramparts P.     1975

**2946** EDELSON, MARY E. The San Francisco Mime Troupe as radical theatre
Madison: U. of Wisconsin (PhD)     1975

**2947** BY POPULAR DEMAND: plays and other works by the San Francisco Mime Troupe
pp.ii, 302; ill. in text     M
San Francisco: Mime Troupe     1980
Scripts, photographs, production credits.

### Society of Stage Directors and Choreographers

**2948** COLLEY, THOMAS. An historical study of the Society of Stage Directors and Choreographers through 1973
Detroit: Wayne State U. (PhD)     1974
Founded 1959.

### Theatre Guild

**2949** THEATRE GUILD souvenir programme [cover title]
pp.[20]; ill.     M
NY: National Program Publishers/Theatre Guild     [1928]
Brief history of the Guild by Hiram Motherwell, followed by details of the company, and earlier season repertoires.

**2950** EATON, WALTER P. The Theatre Guild: the first ten years. With articles by the directors
pp.xiv, 299; pl. 16     M
NY: Brentano's     1929

**2951** THE HISTORY of the Theatre Guild: the first fifteen years 1919-1934
pp.46; ill.     DL★
NY: Artcraft Litho and Printing     [1934]

**2952** LANGNER, LAWRENCE. George Bernard Shaw and the lunatic
pp.xi, 303; front.     M
London: Hutchinson     1964
A personal account of the Theatre Guild's productions of Shaw's plays on Broadway.

**2953** NADEL, NORMAN; LANGNER, LAWRENCE & MARSHALL, A. A pictorial history of the Theatre Guild
pp.viii, 312; ill. in text     M
NY: Crown Publishers     1969

**2954** WALDAU, ROY S. Vintage years of the Theatre Guild, 1928-1939
pp.xiv, 519; ill. in text     M
Cleveland OH: Case Western Reserve U. P.     1972

### Theatre of All Possibilities

**2955** TAMBIMUTTO. Theater of All Possibilities
pp.79; ill. in text     M
London: Editions Poetry London     1980
The experimental theatre company founded in San Francisco in 1967 as an actors' ensemble, later to tour Europe, Asia, Australia and America.

### Theatre of Arts and Letters

**2956** THEATRE OF ARTS and Letters
pp.54     MB
NY: [Theatre of Arts and Letters]     1893
Certificate of incorporation, by-laws, list of members. Incorporated November 25, 1892.

### Theatre Union

**2957** WEISSTUCH, MARK. The Theatre Union: a history, 1933-1937
NY: City U. (PhD)     1978

**2958** WINSTEN, LYNNE R. The Theatre Union: a history
Berkeley: U. of California (PhD)     1978

### United Scenic Artists Union

**2959** HABECKER, THOMAS J. History of the United Scenic Artists Union
Urbana-Champaign: U. of Illinois (PhD)     1974

### Wooster Group

**2960** SAVRAN, DAVID. Breaking the rules: the Wooster Group
pp.xvii, 238; ill. in text     L
NY: Theatre Communications Group     1988
Record and evocation in form of a collage of critiques, photographs, interviews and description.

# 8. THEATRICAL BIOGRAPHY

## 8.1 COLLECTED NOTICES AND BIOGRAPHICAL DICTIONARIES

**2961** STEPHENS, HENRY L. The comic natural history of the human race
pp.viii, 216; ill. DL★
Philadelphia: S. Robinson 1851

Caricatures in colour. Includes Frank Chanfrau, Edwin Forrest, Mary Taylor, William E. Burton, T. D. Rice, E. Seguin, Kate Horn.

**2962** [ROSENBERG, G. C.]. You have heard of them, by Q
pp.353 L
NY: Redfield 1854

Biographical sketches. Includes Charlotte Cushman, Lola Montez.

**2963** SHAKESPEARE, WILLIAM. The complete works...and a life...by Charles Knight. Illustrated with...steel engravings, chiefly portraits in character of celebrated American actors, drawn from life, expressly for this edition
pp.liv, 1725; ill. MB★
NY: Martin, Johnson 1855-59

Three volumes. Titles dated 1853, plates 1855-59. An adaptation of the Tallis Shakespeare, London: 1850, with engravings of American performers replacing the English ones.

**2964** ACTORS as they are: a series of sketches of the most eminent performers now on stage
pp.85 MB
NY: O. A. Roorbach 1856

Thirty-four brief biographical/critical sketches.

**2965** BROWN, T. ALLSTON. History of the American stage containing biographical sketches of nearly every member of the profession that has appeared on the American stage from 1753 to 1870
pp.421; ill. in text, front. M
NY: Dick & Fitzgerald 1870

First published in parts in the *New York Clipper*, c.1857-61, together with what the author called 'the history proper of the theatres'. Despite its title, this is purely a biographical dictionary, and very useful since nothing else serves this function in this period.

**2966** BOOTH'S THEATRE portrait gallery with a description of stage and scenery. Illustrated.
pl. 8 MH
NY: Henry L. Hinton 1873

The 'description of stage and scenery' appears to refer to a separate volume, *Booth's theatre behind the scenes* (q.v.) with which this is bound.

**2967** DUYCKINCK, EVERT A. Portrait gallery of eminent men and women of Europe and America embracing [*inter alia*]...drama..., with biographies
pp.640; 638; pl. 119 L
NY: Johnson, Wilson 1873

Two volumes: volume two includes Edwin Booth, Charlotte Cushman.

**2968** STONE, HENRY D. Personal recollections of the drama or theatrical reminiscences, embracing sketches of prominent actors and actresses, their chief characteristics. original anecdotes of them, and incidents connected therewith
pp.xii, 316: ill. in text, pl. 3 M
Albany NY: Charles Van Benthuysen 1873

An index is contained in *Theatre Documentation* 3: 1 and 2, Fall 1970-Spring 1971, compiled by Carl H. Marder.

**2969** MURDOCH, JAMES E. The stage: or recollections of actors and acting from an experience of fifty years. A series of dramatic sketches
pp.510; front. M
Philadelphia: J. M. Stoddart 1880

**2970** SEILHAMER, GEORGE O. An interviewer's album: comprising a series of chats with eminent players and playwrights...embellished with fine portraits never engraved...
pp.128; pl. 16 MH
NY: Alvin Perry 1881-82

Sixteen parts, continuously paginated, each devoted to one subject, with portrait. Issued separately. The subjects are: Mme Achille; Mlle Augusta; Mary Ann Horton, Cornelius Mathews, Herr Cline, Charles R. Thorne, Henry C. Timm, John Bannard, Anne Seguin, Alexina Fisher Baker, Fitz William Rosier; Edmond S. Conner; Benjamin A. Baker; Anna Bishop, Thomas H. Haddaway; Alexander Allan. No more published.

**2971** TRUMBLE, ALFRED. Footlight favorites. A collection of popular American and European actresses in the various roles in which they have become famous. With biographical sketches compiled by a well-known author and journalist expressly for this work
pp.64; pl 29 M
NY: National Police Gazette 1881

A publication characteristic of the *Police Gazette* which, the title notwithstanding, heavily emphasizes ladies from the burlesque houses and the variety stage.

**2972** MORRIS, MOWBRAY. Essays in theatrical criticism
iii,226 M
London: Remington 1882

Includes chapter, *American plays and players*. Corrigenda slip.

**2973** TRUMBLE, ALFRED. Great artists of the American stage: a portrait gallery of the leading actors and actresses of America with critical biographies...
pp.73; pl. 29 MH
NY: Richard K. Fox 1882

Thirty brief sketches of the best known performers of the day, with engraved portraits derived from photographs.

**2974** CARROLL, HOWARD. Twelve Americans: their lives and times
pp.xii, 473; ill. DL★
NY: Harper & Brothers 1883

Includes essays on John Gilbert and Joseph Jefferson.

**2975** MATTHEWS, BRANDER & HUTTON, LAURENCE. Actors and actresses of Great Britain and the United States
pp.av. 300 M
NY: Cassell 1886

Five volumes, from the age of Garrick to the 1880s. Vol. 3: Charlotte Cushman, Edward Loomis Davenport, Anna Cora Mowatt, Matilda Heron, John McCullough, Adelaide Neilson; in Vol. 4: John Howard Payne, J. W. Wallack, Mary Ann Duff, Junius Brutus Booth, Henry Placide, J. H. Hackett, William E. Burton; in Vol. 5: Mary Anderson, Edwin Booth, John S. Clarke, Mr and Mrs Florence, Joseph Jefferson, Clara Morris, John T. Raymond, J. L. Wallack.

**2976** REIGNOLDS-WINSLOW, CATHERINE M. Yesterdays with actors
pp.201; ill. in text, pl. 6     M
Boston: Cupples & Hurd     1887
Charlotte Cushman, Edwin Forrest, John Brougham, Laura Keene, Agnes Robertson, E. A. Sothern, Benedict De Bar, Matilda Heron, J. H. Hackett, Mrs John Wood, James E. Murdoch, Mrs Lauder, and essays on the Boston Museum.

**2977** BUNNER, H. C. et al. A portfolio of players with a packet of notes thereon
pp.89; pl. 22     M
NY: J. W. Bouton     1888
110 copies. Includes William Winter: *Our stage - past and present*, and brief biographical sketches, with portraits, of Ada Rehan, James Lewis, Mrs G. H. Gilbert, John Drew and Charles Fisher.

**2978** STEPHENS, ROBERT N. Queens of the drama: portraits designed and etched on copper by F. L. Kirkpatrick and C. A. Worrall. Biographies by Robert N. Stephens
pp.[16]; pl. 8     MH
Troy NY: Nims and Knight     1889
Includes Julia Marlowe, Fanny Davenport, Ada Rehan and Mary Anderson.

**2979** WINTER, WILLIAM. Brief Chronicles
pp.xiv, 339; ill. in text     M
NY: Dunlap Society     1889
In effect, a biographical dictionary of the American stage.

**2980** ABBE, CHARLES S. Our great actors: portraits of celebrated actors in their most distinguished roles reproduced from paintings in color...
unpaged; pl. 6     M
Boston: Estes and Lauriat     1890
Portfolio. Includes Edwin Booth as Richelieu, Lawrence Barrett as Count Lanciotto, Joseph Jefferson as Bob Acres.

**2981** DALE, ALAN [= Cohen, Alfred J.]. Familiar chats with the queens of the stage
pp.399; pl. 28     M
NY: G. W. Dillingham     1890
Lillian Russell, Mrs Brown Potter, Rose Coghlan, Fanny Davenport, Lotta Crabtree, Helena Modjeska, Isabelle Urquhart, Sadie Martinot. Georgia Cayvan, Agnes Booth, Minnie Palmer, Emma Juch, Marie Jansen, Marie Wainright, Louise Beaudet, Pauline Hall, Marion Manola, Effie Ellsler, Mrs D. P. Bowers, Ada Rehan, Georgia Drew Barrymore, Gertie Homan, Lilly Post, Clara Morris, Rosina Vokes, Nellie McHenry.

**2982** WINTER, WILLAM. Shadows of the stage
pp.387; 367; 351     M
NY: Macmillan     1892-95
Three volumes, comprising *Series i - iii*. Essays, mainly about actors. Includes (repeated subjects not noted) i: Adelaide Neilson, Edwin Booth, Joseph Jefferson, W. J. Florence, John McCullough, Charlotte Cushman, Lawrence Barrett, Richard Mansfield, Charles Fisher, Mrs G. H. Gilbert, James Lewis. ii: Mary Ann Duff, William Wheatley, John E. Owens, Jean Davenport Lander, Clara Morris, John T. Raymond, Helena Modjeska. iii: Augustin Daly, Charles Gayler; *Representative American plays*.

**2983** WILLARD, FRANCES & LIVERMORE, MARY E, (Eds). A woman of the century: fourteen hundred-seventy biographical sketches accompanied by portraits of leading American women in all walks of life
pp. iii, 812; ill. in text     MH
NY: Charles Wells Moulton     1893
Includes many stage performers.

**2984** THE AMERICAN stage
ll.144; ill. in text     MH
Chicago: Hunt & Wall     1894
Photographs of theatre personalities with brief biographical captions.

**2985** BRERETON, AUSTIN et al. Gallery of players from the *Illustrated American* (with 22 full pictures and over 100 portraits in character)
unpaged. Av. 50; ill. in text     MB
NY: Illustrated American Publishing     1894-9
Quarterly. Eleven numbers. Subsequent editors were Charles F. Nirdlinger, Marwell Hall, Henry Austin who introduced biographical sketches, and Arthur Hoeber. In the last issues, the parenthetical wording became *(...with flashlight reproductions of scenes in plays, and many portraits)*.

**2986** BURROUGHS, MARIE. The Marie Burroughs art portfolio of stage celebrities: a collection of photographs of the leaders of dramatic and lyric art
Unpaginated; ill. in text     M
Chicago: A. N. Marquis     1894
280 portraits with brief biographical captions, first issued in 14 parts of 20 portraits each.

**2987** [TOWNSEND, MARGARET]. Theatrical sketches: here and there with prominent actors by Margaret
pp.217; pl. 7     M
NY: Merriam     1894
Includes reference to Lester Wallack, Edwin Booth, Louis James, Maurice Barrymore, Mrs Brown Potter, the Vokes family, Kyrle Bellew, Richard Mansfield, James Morrissey.

**2988** PAUL, HOWARD & GEBBIE, GEORGE (Eds). The stage and its stars past and present: a gallery of dramatic illustration and critical biographies of distinguished English and American actors from the time of Shakespeare till today
pp.xii, 104; 112; 112; ill. in text, pl. 112     M
Philadelphia: Gebbie     [1895]
Three volumes.

**2989** WINGATE, CHARLES E. Shakespeare's heroines on the stage
pp.ix, 255; pl. 53     M
NY: Thomas Y. Crowell     1895
Illustrations include Mary Anderson, Helena Modjeska, Mrs George Barrett, Julia Marlowe, Ada Rehan, Charlotte Cushman.

**2990** McKAY, FREDERICK E. & WINGATE, CHARLES E. (Eds). Famous American actors of to-day...
pp.viii, 399; pl. 41     M
NY: Thomas Y. Crowell     1896

Forty-one brief biographical and critical sketches by different contributors, each illustrated. 'Today' signifies 'the decade just closing'.

**2991** WINGATE, CHARLES E. Shakespeare's heroes on the stage
pp.x, 348; pl. 30      M
NY: Thomas Y. Crowell      1896
Illustrations include Edwin Booth, Edwin Forrest, John McCullough, Richard Mansfield.

**2992** SHIPMAN, LOUIS E. & GLADDING, W. J. A group of theatrical caricatures, being twelve plates by W. J. Gladding with an introduction and biographical sketches by Louis Evan Shipman
pp.viii, 78; pl. 12      MH
NY: Dunlap Society      1897
260 copies. John Brougham; Lester Wallack; Edwin Forrest; Edwin Booth; W. J. Florence; John E. Owens; Frank Chanfrau; George L. Fox; Charles White and Dan Bryant; William Wheatley; and Tony Pastor.

**2993** CLAPP, JOHN B. & EDGETT, EDWIN F. Players of the present
pp.vi, 423; pl. 28, facs. letter      M
NY: Dunlap Society      1899-91
In three parts, continuously paginated. Brief biographies. 265 copies.

**2994** STRANG, LEWIS C. Famous actresses of the day in America
pp.360; pl. 25      M
Boston: L. C. Page      1899
Maude Adams, Julia Marlowe, Sarah Cowell Lemoyne, Minnie Maddern Fiske, Ida Conquest, Blanche Walsh, Annie Russell, Isabel Irving, Maxine Elliott, Ada Rehan, Virginia Harned, Viola Allen, Corona Riccardo, Mary Mannering, Julia Arthur, May Irwin, Effie Shannon, Mrs Leslie Carter, Mary Shaw, Olga Nethersole, Lillian Lawrence, Blanche Bates, Elsie De Wolfe, Rose Coghlan, Margaret Anglin, Fay Davis, Odette Tyler, Marie Burroughs, Kathryn Kidder, Helena Modjeska, May Robson.

**2995** BROWN, JOHN H. (Ed.). Lamb's biographical dictionary of the United States
pp.av.650; ill.in text, pl.71      L
Boston: Federal Book Company      1900-03
Seven volumes. Good coverage of players of the time.

**2996** BYRON'S GALLERY of plays and players
pl. 21      MH
[NY]:      [1900]
Forty photographic studies of play-scenes portraying, inter alia, Kyrle Bellew, Mrs Fiske, William Gillette as Sherlock Holmes, Ethel Barrymore, Julia Marlowe, Maude Adams.

**2997** KELLY, FRANK M. Well known players in caricature (with autographs)
pl. 32      MB
NY: [?]      1900
Includes John Drew, Julia Marlowe, Richard Mansfield, Dan Daly.

**2998** ROBINS, EDWARD. Twelve great actors
pp.xiv, 474; pl. 23      M
NY: G. P. Putnam's Sons      1900
Includes Junius Brutus Booth, Edwin Forrest, William E. Burton, J. L. Wallack.

**2999** ROBINS, EDWARD. Twelve great actresses
pp.x, 446; pl. 20      M
NY: G. P. Putnam's Sons      1900
Includes Charlotte Cushman.

**3000** STRANG, LEWIS C. Famous actors of the day in America
pp.354; pl. 25      M
Boston: L. C. Page      1900
Joseph Jefferson, James A. Herne, Richard Mansfield, E. M. Holland, E. H. Sothern, John Drew, William Faversham, John B. Mason, Nat C. Goodwin, James O'Neill, William H. Crane, Wilton Lackaye, William Gillette, Henry Miller, James K. Hackett, Henry Jewett, Stuart Robson, Melbourne MacDowell, Sol Smith Russell, Otis Skinner, J. E. Dodson, Robert B. Mantell, Roland Reed, Joseph Haworth, Herbert Kelcey.

**3001** THE ILLUSTRATED AMERICAN stage
ll.85      M
NY: R. H. Russell      1901
Souvenir programs and other memorabilia originally issued as separate parts. No text. Subjects include Maude Adams in *L'Aiglon* (1901); Mary Mannering as Janice Meredith (1900); John Drew as Richard Carvell (1900); Annie Russell in *A Royal Family* (1900); William Gillette in *Sherlock Holmes* (1900); Julia Marlowe in *When Knighthood was in Flower* (1901); Olga Nethersole, a souvenir; Maude Adams in *The Little Minister* (1899); Leo Trevor: *Brother Officers* (1900).

**3002** KEESE, WILLIAM L. A group of comedians
pp.vii, 91; pl. 6      M
NY: Dunlap Society      1901
Short biographies of Henry Placide, William Rufus Blake, John Brougham, George Holland, Charles Fisher.

**3003** STORMS, A. D. The players blue book
pp.304; ill. in text      M
Worcester MA: Sutherland & Storms      1901
Brief biographies of the best-known players of the day, with photographs.

**3004** MATHEWS, R. G. Men and women merely players: some drawings...
pp.[8]; ill. in text, pl. 16      M
Montreal: Renaissance P.      [1902?]
Includes Clara Lipmann, Mrs Brown Potter, Lillian Nordica, David Bispham, Harry Kellar.

**3005** HAMM, MARGHERITA A. Eminent actors in their homes: personal descriptions and interviews
pp.xii, 336; pl. 20      M
NY: James Pott      1902
Edward H. Sothern, Richard Mansfield, Marie Bates, Elsie De Wolfe, Minnie Maddern Fiske, Annie O'Neill, Edward Harrigan, Annie Ward Tiffany, May Robson, David Warfield, Viola Allen, Francis Wilson, Julia Marlowe, Annie Russell, Amelia Bingham, Burr McIntosh, Chauncey Olcott, James K. Hackett, Robert Edeson, Joseph Jefferson, Otis Skinner, William H. Crane, Nat C. Goodwin,

**3006** STRANG, LEWIS C. Famous actors of the day in America. Second series
pp.343; pl. 25      M
Boston: L. C. Page      1902

E. H. Sothern, John Drew, Nat C. Goodwin, John B. Mason, Fritz Williams, William Gillette, Edwin Arden, Richard Mansfield, William Faversham, Stuart Robson, James O'Neill, James A. Herne, Maclyn Arbuckle, William H. Crane, Henry Miller, John Blair, Henry Jewett, Louis Mann, Charles J. Richman. Unlike the first volume, essays tend to focus on particular performances or tendencies.

**3007** STRANG, LEWIS C. Famous actresses of the day in America. Second series
pp.340; pl. 25     M
Boston: L. C. Page     1902

Julia Marlowe, Henrietta Crosman, Mary Shaw, Maude Adams, Amelia Bingham, Ida Conquest, Phoebe Davies, Mrs Fiske, Hilda Spong, Annie Russell, Valerie Bergere, Mary Mannering, Mrs Leslie Carter, Anna Held, Sarah Cowell Lemoyne, Mary Sanders, Ada Rehan, Elizabeth Tyree, Grace George, Margaret Anglin, Viola Allen, Maxine Elliott.

**3008** STRANG, LEWIS C. Players and plays of the last quarter century...
pp.325; 335; pl.66     M
Boston: L. C. Page     1902

Two volumes: *The theatre of yesterday*; *The theatre of today*. Volume 1 includes material on Edwin Forrest and Charlotte Cushman, Edwin Booth, a group of actors comprising John Gilbert, John E. Owens, Joseph Jefferson and W. J. Florence, and William Warren. In Volume 2 a section, *Playwriting in America* is followed by accounts of Bronson Howard, William Gillette, James A. Herne, Clyde Fitch, Augustus Thomas, Clara Morris, Minnie Maddern Fiske and Henrietta Crosman.

**3009** WHITTON, JOSEPH. Wags of the stage
pp.xi, 264; ill. in text     MH
Philadelphia: George H. Rigby     1902

Biographical sketches of theatre folk, emphasizing and illustrating their wit. Includes Charles Barras, Junius Brutus Booth, John Brougham, John Drew, W. J. Florence, Edwin Forrest, Samuel Hemple, E. H. Sothern and, most substantially, William Wheatley.

**3010** ROWLANDS, WALTER. Among the great masters of the drama: scenes in the lives of famous actors
pp.xiii, 233; pl. 32     MH
Boston: Dana Estes     1903

Thirty-three brief sketches with portraits. Includes Mary Anderson, Lawrence Barrett, Edwin Booth, Charlotte Cushman, Edwin Forrest, Joseph Jefferson, John McCullough, William Warren.

**3011** FAMOUS PLAYERS of today. Autograph edition.
pp.[36]; ill. in text     MH
NY: G. A. Melbourne     1904

Annual? Brief biographies, each with portrait. This edition includes Maude Adams, David Warfield, Minnie Maddern Fiske, Tyrone Power, Rose Coghlan.

**3012** KOBBÉ, GUSTAV. Famous actresses and their homes
pp.x, 243; ill. in text, front.     M
Boston: Little, Brown     1905

Includes Maude Adams, Viola Allen, Margaret Anglin, Ethel Barrymore, Mrs Leslie Carter, Maxine Elliott, Virginia Harned, Mary Mannering, Julia Marlowe, Annie Russell. First published 1903, bound with *Famous actors...*.

**3013** KOBBÉ, GUSTAV. Famous actors and their homes
pp.x, 222; ill. in text, front.     M
Boston: Little, Brown     1905

Includes John Drew, William Gillette, Richard Mansfield, Francis Wilson.

**3014** BROWNE, WALTER & AUSTIN, F. A. (Eds). Who's who on the stage...
pp.232; ill. in text     M
NY: Walter Browne     1906

The first edition. A second edition was published by Browne in 1908, co-edited by E. de Roy Koch.

**3015** MOSES, MONTROSE J. Famous actor-families in America
pp.viii, 341; pl. 40     M
NY: Crowell     1906

Booths, Jeffersons, Sotherns, Boucicaults, Hacketts, Drews & Barrymores, Wallacks, Davenports, Hollands, Powers.

**3016** BRISCOE, JOHNSON. The actors' birthday book: an authoritative insight into the lives of the men and women of the stage born between January 1 and December 31
pp.285; 296; 288; ill. in text     M
NY: Moffat, Yard     1907-09

Potted biographies. Series 1-3, three volumes. No more published.

**3017** THE AMERICAN stage today: biographies and photographs of one hundred leading actors and actresses with an introduction by William Winter
unpaged; ill. in text     M
NY: P. F. Collier & Son     1910

**3018** WINTER, WILLIAM. Shakespeare on the stage. First series [second, third series]
pp.564; xxx, 664; 538; pl. 93     M
NY: Moffat, Yard     1911-16

Three volumes. Essays on the interpretations of both UK and US actors.

**3019** PARKER, JOHN (Ed.). Who's who in the theatre. A biographical record of the contemporary stage
pp.xx, 760     M
London: Isaac Pitman     1912

Published until 1981 in 17 editions, as follows: 1912-1st; 1914-2nd; 1916-3rd; 1922-4th; 1925-5th; 1930-6th; 1933-7th; 1936-8th; 1939-9th; 1947-10th; 1952-11th; all edited by John Parker. 1957-12th; edited by John Parker Jr. 1961-13th; 1967-14th; edited by Freda Gaye. 1972-15th; 1977-16th; edited by Ian Herbert. 1981-17th; edited by Ian Herbert, two volumes, published by Gale Research, Detroit, who also reprinted the first 16 editions in four volumes. Gale replaced the title in 1984 with *Contemporary Theatre, Film and Television: a biographical guide* (q.v.), with emphasis away from UK and towards US.

**3020** HICHENS, HAL (Ed.). American actors and actresses of today, particularly those favorite to Cleveland, with lists of their principal appearances
pp.100; ill. in text     DL★
Cleveland OH: Cleveland Plain Dealer     1913

**3021** WINTER, WILLIAM. The wallet of time, containing personal, biographical, and critical reminiscence of the American theatre
pp.xxvi, 668; xiv, 680; pl. 66     M
NY: Moffat, Yard     1913

## 8.1. COLLECTED NOTICES AND BIOGRAPHICAL DICTIONARIES —3037

Two volumes. 1250 copies. Includes 1: George Holland, Mary Ann Duff, James H. Hackett, Edwin Forrest, George W. Jamieson, John Brougham, John Gilbert, Charlotte Cushman, William Wheatley, Bogumil Dawison, Emma Waller, Mrs Gilbert, John E. Owens, Mrs Lander, William J. Florence, John McCullough, John S. Clarke, John Raymond, Lawrence Barrett, James Lewis, Augustin Daly, Helena Modjeska, Charles Coghlan, Adelaide Neilson, Clara Morris. 2: E. H. Sothern and Julia Marlowe; Ada Rehan; David Warfield; Frank Worthing; Maude Adams; Blanche Bates; Mrs Fiske; Olga Nethersole; Mrs Leslie Carter; Augustus Thomas; and final chapters headed *Ibsenites and Ibsenism*, *American actors abroad, and how they 'fail' there*, and *The theatre and the pulpit*.

**3022** HINES, DIXIE & HANNAFORD, HARRY P. (Eds). Who's who in music and drama: an encyclopedia of biography of notable men and women in music and the drama
pp.560; pl,15 L
NY: H.P.Hannaford 1914

All published. Includes cast lists, 1910-13, for grand opera in New York, Chicago, Boston and Philadelphia.

**3023** IZARD, FORREST. Heroines of the modern stage
pp.xiii, 390; pl. 10 M
NY: Sturgis & Walton 1915

Includes Helena Modjeska, Ada Rehan, Mrs Fiske, Julia Marlowe, Maude Adams.

**3024** EATON, WALTER P. Plays and players: leaves from a critic's scrapbook
pp.xvi, 424; pl. 10 M
Cincinnati: Stewart & Kidd 1916

Subjects include Maude Adams, George M. Cohan, David Warfield, Ames's Little Theatre.

**3025** WINTER, WILLIAM. Vagrant memories: being further recollections of other days
pp.525; pl. 33 M
London: Hodder & Stoughton 1916

Chapters on William Warren, Laura Keene and Matilda Heron; Lester Wallack; J. W. Wallack the younger, Mark Smith, Edwin Adams and Henry J. Montague; Edwin Booth; Augustin Daly; Edward H. Sothern and Julia Marlowe.

**3026** FRUEH, ALFRED J. Stage folk: a book of caricatures...
pp.1; pl 37, some col. M
NY: Lieber & Lewis 1922

Portfolio. US subjects are: Annette Kellerman, Leo Dietrichstein, Julia Marlowe, William Faversham, Lillian Russell, James T. Powers, William Gillette, Robert Edeson, William Courtenay, Ethel Barrymore, John Drew, Bert Williams, Maude Adams, William Collier, George M. CVohan, Alla Nazimova, Frances Starr, Wilton Lackaye, Arnold Daly, Jacob Ben Ami, Leon Errol, Otis Skinner, Mrs Fiske, Nat Goodwin, Francis Wilson, De Wolf Hopper, Marie Dressler, Barney Bernard, David Warfield, Marie Bates, Joe Weber, Lou Fields, Mary Nash, Raymond Hitchcock.

**3027** ILES, GEORGE (Ed.). Autobiography
pp.various; ill. in text DL★
Garden City NY: Doubleday, Page 1922

Four volumes in two. Vol. 4, 'actors'. Revised edition. First published in 1908 as *Little masterpieces of autobiography* in six volumes with Vol. 6 on actors. A further revision in 1926 reduced material relevant to this bibliography.

**3028** STEVENS, ASHTON. Actorviews: intimate portraits...with drawings by Gene Markey
pp.xiv, 324; ill. in text M
Chicago: Covici-McGee 1923

210 copies.

**3029** EATON, WALTER P. The actor's heritage. Scenes from the theatre of yesterday and the day before
pp.viii, 294; pl. 33 M
Boston: Atlantic Monthly P. 1924

UK and US performers. Includes material on Weber and Fields, William Everett, and the frontier.

**3030** ACTORS DIRECTORY AND STAGE MANUAL
Ill. DL★
NY: Philrose, 1925

Volume one, number one.

**3031** COVARRUBIAS, MIGUEL. The Prince of Wales and other famous Americans
unpaged; pl. 66, col. front. M
NY: Alfred A. Knopf 1925

Caricatures, many of them depicting stage personalities.

**3032** YOUNG, ROLAND. Actors and others...with an introduction by Ashton Stevens
pp.92; ill. in text M
Chicago: Pascal Covici 1925

550 copies. Caricatures. Includes Ethel Barrymore, John Drew, Walter Hampden, Otis Skinner.

**3033** SKOLSKY, SIDNEY. Times Square tintypes: being typewriter caricatures of those who made their names along the not so straight and narrow path of Broadway
pp.xvi, 291; ill. in text L
NY: Ives Washburn 1930

Brief impressions of 49 Broadway actors, producers, song-writers, critics - and Shakespeare. Illustrations by Gard.

**3034** BEAMAN, FRED J. Pearls from past programs
pp.96 DL★
Boston: Christopher Publishing 1931

Accounts of performers, c. 1870-90.

**3035** BROXAM, PEARL B. Glimpses of stage folk: an outline for study clubs based on autobiographies of theatre people
pp.48 DL★
Iowa City: U. of Iowa P. 1933

Brief biobibliographies of John Barrymore, Marie Dressler, John Drew, Joseph Jefferson, Otis Skinner, Francis Wilson.

**3036** THE PICTUREGOER'S WHO'S WHO and encyclopedia of the screen today
pp.608; ill. in text M
London: Odhams P. 1933

Biographical sketches with details of stage experience.

**3037** WINCHESTER, CLARENCE (Ed.). The world film encyclopedia: a universal screen guide fully illustrated with art plates of stars, players, studios, scenes, theatres and maps
pp.512; front., pl. 31 M
London: Amalgamated P. 1933

Biographical entries with details of stage experience.

**3038** BROWN, JOHN M.  Letters from greenroom ghosts
pp.207　　　　　　　　　　　　　　　　　M
NY: Viking P.　　　　　　　　　　　　　1934
The fancied communication of dead to living performers. Includes chapters on Ina Claire and Katharine Cornell.

**3039** BODEEN, DeWITT.  Ladies of the footlights
pp.133; ill in text　　　　　　　　　　　　M
Pasadena CA: Playhouse Association　　　1937
Twenty brief accounts of actresses who appeared on the west coast during the nineteenth and early twentieth centuries,

**3040** BATCHELLER, JOSEPH D.  A comparative study of the contributions of Steele MacKaye and David Belasco to the American theatre
Minneapolis: U. of Minnesota (MA)　　　1938

**3041** BLOCK, MAXINE (Ed.).  Current biography year book: who's news and why
pp.916; ill. in text　　　　　　　　　　　　L
NY: H. W. Wilson　　　　　　　　　　　1940-
Annual. Most volumes make reference to stage performers. After the first edition, the sub-title was dropped and the editorship passed to Charles Moritz.

**3042** HARRIMAN, MARGARET C.  Take them up tenderly: a collection of profiles
pp.xiii, 266; pl. 1 folding　　　　　　　　　M
NY: Alfred A. Knopf　　　　　　　　　　1944
With the exception of a piece on Oscar Hammerstein II, the profiles are reprinted from *New Yorker*: Gilbert Miller, Max Gordon, Moss Hart, Lillian Hellman, Helen Hayes, Cole Porter, Rodgers and Hart, Oscar Hammerstein II, John Frederics, Leland Hayward, Fanny Holtzmann, Mary Pickford, The De Marcos.

**3043** MARKS, EDWARD B.  They all had glamour: from the Swedish Nightingale to the Naked Lady
pp.xix, 448; front., ill. in text　　　　　　　M
NY: Julian Messner　　　　　　　　　　　1944
Includes chapters on *The Black Crook*; Kiralfy brothers; travelling entertainers; George Washington Lafayette Fox; Lola Montez; Adah Isaacs Menken. Part 3 lists, *inter alia*, New York critics, actor families, early minstrel songs.

**3044** COLLINS, LESLIE M.  A song, a dance, and a play – an interpretative study of three American artists
Cleveland: Case Western Reserve U. (PhD)　1945
Black performers.

**3045** ROSS, PAUL L. (Ed.).  Players' guide: Actors' Equity Association's pictorial directory of legitimate theatre people for distribution in entertainment production circles
pp.345; ill. in text　　　　　　　　　　　　M
NY: Actors' Equity Association　　　　　　1948
Founded 1944. This edition includes the second edition of *The Specialty Guide*, a supplement intended to cover the musical theatre.

**3046** HECHT, KEN (Ed).  Who's who in show business
pp.171; ill.　　　　　　　　　　　　　　DL★
NY: Who's Who in Show Business　　　　1950
Volume one. On cover: *Preview Edition*.

**3047** SHERMAN, ROBERT L.  Actors and authors, with composers and managers who helped make them famous. A chronological record and brief biography of theatrical celebrities from 1750 to 1950
pp.v, 433　　　　　　　　　　　　　　　MH
Chicago: For the author　　　　　　　　　1951
Several hundred entries, mostly of performers who have appeared on the stage of an American theatre or dramatists whose work has been staged in American theatres.

**3048** ZOLOTOW, MICHAEL.  No people like show people
pp.xii, 305　　　　　　　　　　　　　　　L
NY: Random House　　　　　　　　　　[1951]
Articles, in part reprinted from periodicals. Accounts of Tallulah Bankhead, Jimmy Durante, Oscar Levant, Jack Benny, Frank Fay, Jed Harris, Fred Allen, Ethel Merman. Introduction by Brooks Atkinson.

**3049** BLUM, DANIEL.  Great stars of the American stage: a pictorial record
pp.151; ill. in text　　　　　　　　　　　　DL★
NY: Greenberg　　　　　　　　　　　　　1952
One hundred and fifty biographical sketches, c.1880-1952, each illustrated with several photographs.

**3050** BAKELESS, KATHARINE L.  In the big time: career stories of American entertainers...illustrated from photographs
pp.ix, 208; pl. 8　　　　　　　　　　　　　L
Philadelphia: J. B. Lippincott　　　　　　　1953
Includes Katharine Cornell, James Stewart, Fred Astaire, John Mulholland, Bing Crosby.

**3051** ZOLOTOW, MAURICE.  It takes all kinds: some actors and eccentrics
pp.xiii, 266; ill. in text　　　　　　　　　　M
London: W. H. Allen　　　　　　　　　　1953
Subjects include Tallulah Bankhead, Jimmy Durante, Jack Benny, Oscar Levant.

**3052** WINFORD, EDGAR C.  Femme mimics
pp.164; ill.　　　　　　　　　　　　　　DL★
Dallas TX: Winford　　　　　　　　　　　1954
An account of female impersonators.

**3053** FORD, GEORGE D.  These were actors: a story of the Chapmans and the Drakes
pp.314; ill. in text, pl. 6　　　　　　　　　M
NY: Library Publishers　　　　　　　　　　1955
Linked theatre families of the nineteenth century, originating in England.

**3054** STEVENS, DAVID H.(Ed.).  Ten talents in the American theatre
pp.x, 299　　　　　　　　　　　　　　　M
Norman: U. of Oklahoma P.　　　　　　　1957
Essays by Robert E. Gard, Paul Baker, Alan Schneider, Margo Jones, Frederick McConnell, Barclay Leathem, Gilmor Brown, Leslie Cheek, George C. Izenour, Paul Green

**3055** OPPENHEIMER, GEORGE (Ed.).  The passionate playgoer: a personal scrapbook
pp.xv, 623; pl. 8　　　　　　　　　　　　M
NY: Viking P.　　　　　　　　　　　　　1958

## 8.1. COLLECTED NOTICES AND BIOGRAPHICAL DICTIONARIES   –3076

An anthology. Includes Ethel Barrymore: *A memory*; Robert E. Sherwood: *The Lunts*; Ruth Gordon: *Those years after 'Years Ago'*; Alexander Woollcott: *Miss Kitty takes the road*; and Tallulah Bankhead: *It's not 'the road', it's detours*.

**3056** HIRSCHFELD, AL.   The American theatre as seen by Hirschfeld
Unpaged; ill. in text                                    M
NY: George Braziller                                  1961

Caricatures, c.1925-1960. Foreword by Brooks Atkinson.

**3057** JESSEL, GEORGE.   Elegy in Manhattan...foreword by Ben Hecht
pp.xv, 198; ill. in text                                 M
NY: Holt, Rinehart and Winston                   1961

Jessel evokes deceased Broadway celebrities by having them 'speak' their own memories in blank verse.

**3058** MARINACCI, BARBARA.   Leading ladies: a gallery of famous actresses
pp.xiii, 396; pl. 8                                      M
NY: Dodd, Mead                                         1961

Subjects include Charlotte Cushman, Minnie Maddern Fiske, Ethel Barrymore, Laurette Taylor.

**3059** WAGNER, FREDERICK & BRADY, BARBARA.   Famous American actors and actresses
pp.160; ill. in text                                     M
NY: Dodd, Mead                                         1961

Brief biographies for young readers, from Edwin Forrest to Julie Harris.

**3060** ROSS, LILLIAN & ROSS, HELEN.   The player: a profile of an art
pp.461; ill. in text                                     M
NY: Simon & Schuster                                1962

Accounts of 55 performers, derived from interviews. Some reprinted from *New Yorker*.

**3061** WAGENKNECHT, EDWARD.   Seven daughters of the theatre
pp.x, 234; pl. 8                                         M
Norman: U. of Oklahoma P.                         1964

Includes Julia Marlowe, Mary Garden, Marilyn Monroe.

**3062** NEWQUIST, ROY.   Showcase. Introduction by Brooks Atkinson. Illustrations by Irma Selz
pp.412; ill. in text                                     M
NY: William Morrow                                  1966

Theatre and show business celebrities. Includes Helen Hayes.

**3063** WAGENKNECHT, EDWARD.   Merely players
pp.xiv, 270: pl. 8                                       M
Norman: U. of Oklahoma P.                         1966

Includes Edwin Forrest, Edwin Booth, Thomas Jefferson, Richard Mansfield.

**3064** GARD, ROBERT E. & SEMMES, DAVID.   America's players
pp.viii, 152; ill. in text                                M
NY: Seaburt P.                                            1967

Historically ordered, emphasizing the nineteenth and early twentieth centuries. Intended for young readers.

**3065** WEISSBERGER, L. ARNOLD.   Close-up: a collection of photographs
pp.[64]; ill. in text                                     M
NY: Arno P.                                                1967

Informal studies of stage and literary celebrities.

**3066** BUELL, WILLIAM A.   The Hamlets of the theatre
pp.175; ill.                                               DL★
NY: Astor-Honor                                       1968

A new edition ? Includes accounts of performances by Edwin Forrest, Edwin Booth, Walter Hampden, John Barrymore.

**3067** DAVIS, DAVID F.   The Hamlets of Edwin Booth, John Barrymore, and Christopher Plummer: a comparative analysis of interpretation, performance, and staging
Detroit: Wayne State U. (PhD)                    1968

**3068** KNEPLER, HENRY W.   The gilded stage: the years of the great international actresses
pp.ix, 308; pl. 12                                       M
London: Constable                                    1968

Includes the appearances in the US of Duse, Bernhardt, Ristori, Rachel.

**3069** WILDE, LARRY.   The great comedians talk about comedy
pp.382; ill. in text                                     MH
NY: Citadel P.                                           1968

Sixteen interviews, with portraits, from Woody Allen to Ed. Wynn.

**3070** REED, REX.   Do you sleep in the nude ?
pp.xii, 275                                                L
London: W. H. Allen                                 1969

Published NY: New American Libary, 1968. Interviews, from the *New York Times*, with actors and directors.

**3071** CAHN, WILLIAM.   A pictorial history of the great comedians
pp.224; ill. in text                                     M
NY: Grosset & Dunlap                               1970

Second edition, revised. First published NY: Bramhall House, 1957 as *The Laugh Makers*, with an introduction by Harold Lloyd.

**3072** FROST, DAVID P.   The Americans
pp.250                                                     O
NY: Stein and Day                                    1970

Interviews. Includes Helen Hayes, Tennessee Williams, Orson Welles.

**3073** THOMPSON, MARION S.   Stars of the New York stage 1870-1970
pp.[38]; ill. in text                                    M
NY: Museum of the City of New York       1970

**3074** ANDREW, RICHARD H.   Augustin Daly's big four: John Drew, Ada Rehan, James Lewis and Mrs G. H. Gilbert
Urbana-Champaign: U. of Illinois (PhD)    1971

**3075** CLARKE, SHAREEN M.   The child stars of the far West: 1849-1865
San José: State U. (MA)                             1971

**3076** DONOHUE, JOSEPH W. (Ed.).   The theatrical manager in England and America: player of a dangerous game
pp.xii, 216; ill. in text, pl. 6                       M
Princeton: U. O.                                         1971

With essays on Edwin Booth and Stephen Price.

**3077** FABIAN, MONROE H. Portraits of the American stage 1771-1971
pp.203; ill. in text, pl. 1 (col)      M
Washington DC: Smithsonian Institute P.      1971
Exhibition catalogue on occasion of the inaugural season of the J. F. Kennedy Center for the Performing Arts. Each portrait is preceded by a brief biographical sketch.

**3078** JAMES, EDWARD T.; JAMES, JANET W. & BAYER, PAUL S. (Eds). Notable American women 1607-1950; a biographical dictionary
pp.i, 686; v, 659; v, 729      L
Cambridge MA: Belknap P of Harvard U.      1971
Three volumes. Includes brief accounts of some 100 American actresses and theatre managers, indexed in Vol. 3. See also the companion volume for the modern period edited by Barbara Sicherman, et al., 1980.

**3079** SHAW, DALE. Titans of the American stage: Edwin Forrest, the Booths, the O'Neills
pp.160; ill. in text      MH
Philadelphia: Westminster P.      1971

**3080** CARROLL, DAVID. The matinee idols
pp.160; ill. in text      O
NY: Arbor House      1972
Brief comments with photographs. Seventeen sketches of theatre personalities, from Edmund Kean to William Faversham.

**3081** FRUEH, ALFRED J. Frueh on the theatre: theatrical cartoons 1906-1962, compiled, with an introduction, by Maxwell Silverman and with a preface by Brendan Gill
pp.xvii, 108; ill. in text      M
NY: Public Library      1972

**3082** RUDISILL, AMANDA. The contributions of Eva Le Gallienne, Margaret Webster, Margo Jones, and Joan Littlewood to the establishment of repertory theatre in the United States and Great Britain
Evanston: Northwestern U. (PhD)      1972

**3083** ABDUL, RAOUL. Famous black entertainers of today...illustrated with photographs
pp.159; pl. 4      MH
NY: Dodd, Mead      1974
For children. Brief interviews with some twenty entertainers.

**3084** GREBANIER, BERNARD. Then came each actor on his ass. Shakespearean actors great and otherwise...
pp.xiii, 626; pl. 16      M
NY: David McKay      1975

**3085** PROBST, LEONARD. Off-camera: levelling about themselves
pp.268; ill.      DL*
NY: Stein and Day      1975
Transcribed interviews with mainly movie personalities. Subjects include Al Pacino, Paul Newman, George C. Scott, Zero Mostel, Gwen Verdon.

**3086** RUSH, THERESA G. Black American writers past and present: a biographical and bibliographical dictionary
pp.865; ill.      DL*
Metuchen, NJ: Scarecrow P.      1975
Two volumes.

**3087** YOUNG, WILLIAM C. Famous actors and actresses on the American stage: documents of American theater history
pp.xxi, xi, 1298; ill. in text      L
NY: R. R. Bowker      1975
Two volumes. 224 biographical and critical treatments.

**3088** FISHER, JOHN. Call them irreplaceable. Drawings by Hirschfeld
pp.224; ill. in text      M
NY: Stein and Day      1976
Sketches of popular entertainers. Includes Bob Hope, Bing Crosby, Danny Kaye, Jack Benny.

**3089** GEMME, LEILA B. The new breed of performer
pp.189; ill. in text      MH
NY: Washington Square P.      1976
Biographical and critical sketches. Includes Liza Minnelli, Shirley Maclaine, George C. Scott, Bette Midler, Jane Fonda, Barbra Streisand, Marlon Brando.

**3090** RIGDON, WALTER (Ed.). Notable names in the American theatre
pp.xi, 1250      L
Clinton NJ: James T. White      1976
Foreword by Paul Myers. Second, revised edition of *The biographical encyclopaedia and who's who of the American theatre*, (NY: James H. Heineman, 1966), edited by Walter Rigdon with an introduction by George Freedley.

**3091** HIRSCHFELD, AL. The entertainers as seen by Hirschfeld
pl. 38      M
London: Elm Tree/ Hamish Hamilton      1977
Caricatures. Foreword by S. J. Perelman.

**3092** PAGE, JAMES A. Selected black American authors: an illustrated bio-bibliography
pp.xv, 398      MH
Boston: G.K.Hall      1977

**3093** MAPP, EDWARD. Directory of blacks in the performing arts
pp.xv, 428      MH
Metuchen NJ: Scarecrow P.      1978
The first edition. A second, revised edition was published in 1990.

**3094** BERG, AUBREY. Collaborators: Arthur Hopkins, Robert Edmond Jones and the Barrymores
Urbana-Champaign: U. of Illinois (PhD)      1979

**3095** OHRINGER, FREDERICK. A portrait of the theatre...with introduction by Joseph Papp
pp.197; ill. in text      M
Toronto: Merritt      1979
A collection of photographs of some 120 theatre people with brief notes and an appendix of short biographies.

**3096** WEARING, J. P. American and British theatrical biography: a directory
pp.1007      M
Metuchen NJ: Scarecrow P.      1979

# 8.1. COLLECTED NOTICES AND BIOGRAPHICAL DICTIONARIES

Lists some 50,000 names, with dates, and references to biographical information in 222 source books. Refers mainly to actors, but includes some playwrights.

**3097** BOGLE, DONALD. Brown sugar: eighty years of America's black female superstars...
pp.208; ill. in text     MH
NY: Harmony Books     1980

**3098** FABIAN, MONROE H. On stage: 200 years of great theatrical personalities
pp.224; ill. in text, some col.     M
NY: Mayflower Books     1980
Portraits with biographical notes.

**3099** PERRY, JEB H. *Variety* obits: an index to obituaries in *Variety* 1905-1978
pp.x, 311     MH
Metuchen NJ: Scarecrow P.     1980
Covers issues December 16, 1905 through June 21, 1978.

**3100** SICHERMAN, BARBARA & GREEN, CAROL H. et al (Eds). Notable American women: the modern period. A biographical dictionary
pp.xxiv, 773; pl. 8     L
Cambridge MA: Belknap P.     1980
Companion volume to Edward T. James et al: *Notable American Women 1707-1950*. Includes entries under 'entertainment' and 'theatre'.

**3101** GILL, GLENDA E. Six black performers in relation to the Federal Theatre
Iowa City: U. of Iowa (PhD)     1981

**3102** MATSON, KATINKA. Short lives: portraits of writers, painters, poets, actors, musicians and performers in pursuit of death
pp.xiii, 362; ill. in text     L
London: Picador     1981
Rather morbidly linked biographical sketches. Includes Lenny Bruce, Montgomery Clift, Stephen Crane, James Dean, Judy Garland, Marilyn Monroe.

**3103** McNEIL, BARBARA & HERBERT, MIRANDA C. (Eds). Performing arts biography master index; a consolidated index to over 270,000 biographical sketches of persons living and dead as they appear in over 100 of the principal biographical dictionaries devoted to the performing arts
pp.xxiv, 701     DL★
Detroit: Gale Research     1981
Second edition. This revises and replaces Dennis La Beau: *Theatre, film and TV biographies master index*, 1979.

**3104** TUMBLESON, TREVA R. Three female Hamlets: Charlotte Cushman, Sarah Bernhardt, and Eva Le Gallienne
Eugene: U. of Oregon (PhD)     1981

**3105** KAPLAN, MIKE (Ed.). *Variety* who's who in show business
pp.v, 330     L
NY: Garland Publishing     1982

**3106** LONG, LINDA S. The art of Beatrice Herford, Cissie Loftus, and Dorothy Sands within the tradition of solo performance
Austin: U. of Texas (PhD)     1982

**3107** APPELBAUM, STANLEY (Ed.). Great actors and actresses of the American stage in historic photographs: 332 portraits from 1850 to 1950
pp.vi, 136; ill. in text     M
NY: Dover     1983

**3108** ARCHER, STEPHEN M. American actors and actresses: a guide to information sources
pp.xxii, 710     M
Detroit: Gale Research     1983

**3109** MACARTHUR, CHARLOTTE W. Portraitists in performance: four women originals
Pittsburgh: U. (PhD)     1983
US artistes are Ruth Draper, Angna Enters.

**3110** MULLIN, DONALD (Ed.). Victorian actors and actresses in review: a dictionary of contemporary views of representative British and American actors and actresses, 1837-1901
pp.xxxvi, 571; ill. in text     M
Westport CT: Greenwood P.     1983

**3111** CHANDLER, CHARLOTTE. The ultimate seduction
pp.xi, 370     L
NY: Doubleday     1984
Enounters with celebrities, often in the form of conversations. Includes Mae West, Henry Fonda, Tennessee Williams.

**3112** FREEDLAND, MICHAEL. So let's hear the applause
pp.x, 262; ill. in text     O
Totawa NJ: Vallentine Mitchell     1984
Brief appreciations of some twenty popular entertainers.

**3113** GREEN, STANLEY. The great clowns of Broadway
pp.xi, 247; pl. 19     M
NY: Oxford U. P.     1984
Includes Fanny Brice, Bobby Clark,Joe Cook, Jimmy Durante, W. C. Fields, Willie Howard, Bert Lahr, Victor Moore, Ed. Wynn.

**3114** HILL, ERROL. Shakespeare in sable: a history of black Shakespearean actors
pp.xxviii, 218; ill. in text     M
Amherst: U. of Massachusetts P.     1984
Foreword by John Houseman.

**3115** JOHNSON, CLAUDIA D. American actress: perspective on the nineteenth century
pp.ix, 202; ill. in text     M
Chicago: Nelson-Hall     1984
Includes Mary Ann Duff, Charlotte Cushman, Anna Cora Mowatt, Laura Keene, Adah Isaacs Menken, Lotta Crabtree.

**3116** HALLQUIST, TERYL W. The makings of a classical actress in the modern twentieth-century western theatre: a comparative study
Ann Arbor: U. of Michigan (PhD)     1985
Frances Hyland, Martha Henry, Rosemary Harris, Zoe Caldwell, Irene Worth.

**3117** HENDERSON, KATHY. First stage: profiles of the new American actors
pp.159     DL★
NY: Quill     1985

**3118** MORLEY, SHERIDAN. The great stage stars. Distinguished theatrical careers of the past and present
pp.x, 425; pl. 20     M
London: Angus & Robertson     1986

**3119** CHINOY, HELEN K. & JENKINS, LINDA W. (Eds). Women in American theatre: careers, images, movements. An illustrated anthology and sourcebook
pp.xiii, 444     M
NY: Theatre Communications Group     1987
Second edition, enlarged. First published NY: Crown, 1981.

**3120** UNTERBRINK, MARY. Funny women: American comediennes, 1860-1985
pp. xvi, 276: ill. in text     M
Jefferson NC: McFarland     1987

**3121** PETERSON, BERNARD L. Contemporary black American playwrights and their plays. A biographical directory and dramatic index
pp.608     DL★
NY: Greenwood P.     1988

**3122** JONES, ROY. Artists in camera: a gallery of star portraits...Introduction by Sir Alec Guinness, text by Michael Owen...
pp.167; ill. in text     M
London: Prion     1989

US subjects include James Stewart, Meryl Streep, Stephen Sondheim, Mickey Rooney, Ginger Rogers, Gregory Peck, Liza Minnelli, Arthur Miller, Walter Matthau, Jack Lemon, Danny Kaye, Dustin Hoffman, Lauren Bacall.

**3123** MORGAN, KATHLEEN A. Of stars and standards: actress-managers of Philadelphia and New York, 1855-1880
Urbana-Champaign: U. of Illinois (PhD)     1989

**3124** ROBINSON, ALICE M.; ROBERTS, VERA M. & BARRANGER, MILLY S. (Eds). Notable women in the American theatre: a biographical dictionary
pp.xvii, 993     MH
NY: Greenwood P.     1989
Appendices list by date of birth and by profession.

**3125** TANNER, JO. Black women performers on the New York stage, 1890-1927
NY: City U. (PhD)     1989

**3126** TURNER, MARY M. Forgotten leading ladies of the American theatre: lives of eight female players, playwrights, directors, managers and activists of the eighteenth, nineteenth and early twentieth centuries
pp.xii, 170; ill. in text     M
Jefferson NC: McFarland     1990
Susannah Rowson, Anna Cora Mowatt, Sophia Turner, Charlotte Cushman, Laura Keene, Mrs John Drew, Fanny Kemble, Minnie Maddern Fiske.

## 8.2 COLLECTIONS OF ANECDOTES, AND SATIRES

**3127** THE GALAXY OF WIT: or laughing philosopher, being a collection of choice anecdotes, many of which originated in or about *The Literary Emporium*
pp.108;108; pl. 11     L
Boston: Printer J. H. A. Frost     1830
Two volumes in one. The plates, etchings by D. C. Johnston, provide portraits of early US actors: William Francis, J. W. Wallack Sr., William Pelby, William Warren Sr., Charles Burke, Thomas Hilson, John Barnes, George H. Andrews, Francis Blisset, Thomas Abthorpe Cooper, Edwin Forrest.

**3128** RITCHIE, ANNA C. [= Mowatt, Anna C.]. Reviewers reviewed: a satire
pp.72     DL★
NY: For the author     1837

**3129** GREEN ROOM YARNS
pp.64; ill.     DL★
NY: J. Haney     1876
Anecdotes of nineteenth century theatre notables.

**3130** HALL, 'BIFF' [= Hall, William T.]. The Turnover Club. Tales told at the meetings of the Turnover Club, about actors and actresses...
pp.234     MH
Chicago: Rand, McNally     1890
Anecdotes. Subjects include Nat C. Goodwin, William H. Crane, Edwin Booth, John McCullough.

**3131** MORGAN, JOHN DE. In lighter vein, a collection of anecdotes, witty sayings, bon mots, bright repartees, eccentricities and reminiscences of well known men and women who are or who have been prominent in the public eye...
pp.164; col. front.     DL★
San Francisco: P. Elder     1907

**3132** COLLIER, WILLIAM. A book of etiquette entitled 'Don't do that'...for sale by no newsdealers. Vol 1, Scriblers sons [sic]
pp.59; pl. 38     MH
NY: Dana T. Bennett     1909
Facetious compilation of 'don'ts' for actors, playwrights, audiences, illustrated with photographs of performers and scenes.

**3133** TRACY, VIRGINIA. Merely players: stories of stage life
pp.ix, 336     L
NY: Century     1909
Fiction, reprinted from periodicals. Convincingly detailed evocations of late nineteenth-early twentieth century stage life.

**3134** NATHAN, GEORGE J. Bottoms up: an application of the slapstick to satire
pp.73     MB
NY: Philip Goodman     1917
Short parodies and/or satires of aspects of theatre and show business.

**3135** LEACOCK, STEPHEN B. Over the footlights
pp.vi, 279     L
London: The Bodley Head     1923
Includes affectionate parodies of nineteenth century American melodrama, the 'modern' drama, the historic drama and the Russian drama.

**3136** LEVY, NEWMAN. Theatre guyed
pp.xiii, 89; ill. in text     M
NY: Alfred A. Knopf     1933
Humorous verses on theatre topics. Illustrated by Rea Irvin.

**3137** ADAMS, JOEY. From gags to riches
pp.336; ill.     DL★
NY: F. Fell     1946
'Alibiography'; illustrated with 80 cartoons by Dave Breger and others.

**3138** ADAMS, JOEY & TOBIAS, HENRY. The Borscht belt
pp.vii, 224; pl. 12     MH
NY: Bobbs-Merrill     1959

Anecdotes of summer resort entertainment.

**3139** WYNDHAM, DONALD (Ed.). Acting, acting, acting
pp.211     DL★
[NY?]: Watts     1963

Stories about would-be actors, intended for children.

**3140** DOLBIER, MAURICE. All wrong on the night. A comedy of theatrical errors
pp.86; ill.     DL★
NY: Walker     1966

**3141** KANIN, GARSON. Cast of characters: stories of Broadway and Hollywood
pp.437     DL★
NY: Atheneum     1969

**3142** HAY, PETER. Theatre anecdotes
pp.xiii, 392     M
NY: Oxford U. P.     1987

**3143** HAY, PETER. Broadway anecdotes
pp.xvi, 395     M
NY: Oxford U. P.     1989

## 8.3 TANGENTIAL

**3144** PRIEST, WILLIAM. Travels in the United States of America commencing in the year 1793 and ending in 1797 with the author's journals of his two voyages across the Atlantic by William Priest... late of the theatres Philadelphia, Baltimore and Boston
pp.ix, 214; front.     L
London: J. Johnson     1802

Includes wide-spread reference to theatre.

**3145** PARKER, JOHN R. A musical biography; or sketches of the lives and writings of eminent musical characters interspersed with an epitome of interesting musical matter
pp.250     L
Boston: Stone & Favell     1825

Some incidental theatre interest includes reference to Miss Broadhurst and Mrs Oldmixon.

**3146** TROLLOPE, FRANCES. Domestic manners of the Americans
pp.xi, 304; vii, 303; pl.24     L
London: Whitaker, Treacher     1832

Two volumes.

**3147** COX, WILLIAM. Crayon sketches by An Amateur. Edited by Theodore S. Fay
pp.x, 240; ii, 246     L
NY: Conner and Cooke     1833

Two volumes. Much theatre material, in part reprinted from the *New York Mirror* where they appeared under the initial 'C'. Of US interest are John Barnes and the Park Theatre, other NY theatres, Clara Fisher, Mr and Mrs Thomas Hilson, Thomas Barry and J. Woodhull, Peter Richings, Mrs Sarah Wheatley, Henry Placide, John Barnes.

**3148** A BIOGRAPHICAL SKETCH of Jane Sloman, the celebrated pianiste
pp.23     L
Boston: Dutton & Wentworth     1841

Up to her US début at Niblo's Theatre with a lively account of her reception.

**3149** TASISTRO, LOUIS F. Random shots and southern breezes, containing critical remarks on the southern states and Southern institutions, with semi-serious observations on men and manners...in two volumes
pp.274; 230     MH
NY: Harper and Brothers     1842

Sporadic reference to theatre *passim*.

**3150** [ROBB, JOHN S.]. Streaks of squatter life and far-West scenes: a series of humorous sketches descriptive of incidents and character in the wild west to which are added other miscellaneous pieces. By Solitaire
pp.187; pl. 8     L
Philadelphia: Carey and Hart     1847

Quasi-fictional memoirs. Includes reference to Danforth Marble and Sol Smith.

**3151** KENNEDY, JOHN P. Memoirs of the life of William Wirt, attorney-general of the United States...a new and revised edition
pp.368; 391; front.     L
Philadelphia: Lea & Blanchard     1850

Two volumes in one. Theatre reference includes the Richmond fire, and a record of Wirt's early efforts at dramatic composition which drew from Judge Dabney Carr an interesting reflection on the drama and its possible effect on reputation.

**3152** ROSENBERG, CHARLES G. Jenny Lind in America
pp.226; front.     L
NY: Stringer and Townsend     1851

Tour arranged by P. T. Barnum. Much incidental theatre reference and a strong impression of nineteenth century touring conditions.

**3153** BADEAU, ADAM. The vagabond
pp.368     M
NY: Rudd & Carleton     1859

Theatre interest extends to a discussion of matinées, and material on the Booth family, American playwrights, Edwin Forrest, Charlotte Cushman and Henry W. Bellows.

**3154** [DOW, LORENZO]. History of Cosmopolite: or, the writings of Rev Lorenzo Dow containing his experience and travels in Europe and America, up to near his fiftieth year. Also his polemic writings. To which is added the *Journey of Life* by Peggy Dow revised and corrected with notes
pp.720; pl. 2     O
Philadelphia: Jas. B. Smith     1859

Memoirs of an itinerant preacher, including details of camp meetings and early frontier and New England life.

**3155** FATHER KEMP and his old folks: a history of the 'Old Folks' concerts, comprising an autobiography of the author and sketches of many humorous scenes and incidents which have transpired in a concert-giving

experience of twelve years in England and America
pp.254; front.                                          MH
Boston: For the author                                  1868
Makes some reference to New York theatre management practice.

**3156** KEELER, RALPH. Vagabond adventures [autobiography]
pp.274                                                  MH
Boston: Fields, Osgood                                  1870
Includes reminiscence of showboat life.

**3157** JONES, JOSEPH S. Life of Jefferson S. Batkins, member from Cranberry Centre, written by himself assisted by the author of the *Silver Spoon*
pp.496; front.                                          L
Boston: Loring                                          1871
Pickwickesque 'memoirs' set in New England including reference to the Boston Museum, and William Warren.

**3158** LEATHES, EDMUND. An actor abroad or gossip dramatic, narrative and descriptive from the recollections of an actor in Australia, New Zealand, the Sandwich Islands, California, Nevada, Central America, and New York
pp.x, 317                                               L
London: Hurst and Blackett                              1880
Includes account of working with John Brougham in Virginia City, and other frontier theatre experience.

**3159** EDWARDS, HENRY. A mingled yarn: sketches on various subjects by Henry Edwards comedian
pp.157                                                  MH
NY: G. P. Putnam's Sons                                 1883
Includes accounts of Edwin Adams and William Barry, and a chapter, *the church and the stage*.

**3160** MASON, RUFUS O. Sketches and impressions, musical, theatrical and social (1799-1895) including a sketch of the Philharmonic Society of New York. From the after-dinner talk of Thomas Goodwin, music librarian
pp.x, 294                                               M
NY: G. P. Putnam's Sons                                 1887
Chapters XVIII-XXIX are concerned with American theatre and music, with material on, *inter alia*, the Park Theatre, William Niblo, Edwin Forrest, Charlotte Cushman, 'Yankee' Hill, T. D. Rice.

**3161** FISKE, MARY H. The giddy gusher papers. Edited by Harrison G. Fiske
pp.viii, 238                                            MH
NY: New York Dramatic Mirror                            1889
Reprinted sketches, some of theatre interest.

**3162** WILDER, MARSHALL P. The people I've smiled with: recollections of a merry little life
pp.xii, 268; pl. 2                                      M
NY: Cassell                                             1889

**3163** CHILDS, GEORGE W. Recollections
pp.404; front.                                          DL★
Philadelphia: J. B. Lippincott                          1890

**3164** HASWELL, CHARLES H. Reminiscences of an octogenarian of the city of New York (1816 to 1860)
pp.xiii, 581; front., ill. in text                      L
NY: Harper & Brothers                                   1897
Much theatre reference, e.g., the Bowery Theatre, the National Theatre fire, Junius Brutus Booth.

**3165** RYAN, THOMAS. Recollections of an old musician
pp.xvi, 274; front., pl. 45                             L
NY: E. P. Dutton                                        1899
Includes reference to Junius Brutus Booth, John Brougham and other stage memories.

**3166** HOWE, JULIA W. Reminiscences 1819-1899...with portraits and other illustrations
pp.vi, 465; front., pl. 24 inc. 1 folding               L
Boston: Houghton Mifflin                                1900
Theatre reference includes Edwin Booth, Charlotte Cushman.

**3167** POND, J. B. Eccentricities of genius. Memories of famous men and women of the platform and stage
pp.xxvi, 564; ill. in text, pl. 24                      M
London: Chatto & Windus                                 1901
First published NY: G. W. Dillingham, 1900. Includes accounts of Joseph Jefferson, William Winter, Charlotte Cushman.

**3168** HORTON, WILLIAM E. About stage folks, by Judge Horton
pp.160; pl. 16                                          M
Detroit: Free Press Printing                            1902

**3169** KEESE, WILLIAM L. The Siamese twins, and other poems
pp.115                                                  DL★
NY: E. W. Dayton                                        1902
Includes a section, *Dramatic portraits*

**3170** HORTON, WILLIAM E. Driftwood of the stage, by Judge Horton
pp.383; pl. 19                                          M
Detroit: Winn & Hammond                                 1904

**3171** WILDER, MARSHALL P. The sunny side of the street
pp.359; ill.                                            MB★
NY: Funk & Wagnalls                                     1905
With anecdotes of actors.

**3172** THE SEAMY SIDE: a story of the true condition of things theatrical by one who has spent twenty years among them
pp.312; front.                                          L
Boston: Percy Ives                                      1906
Fictionalized and moralistic stage biography claimed to be a true representation. Apparently written by an actress, in condemnation of the theatre.

**3173** GRAU, ROBERT. Forty years observation of music and the drama...profusely illustrated from photographs and prints
pp.xxviii, 370; ill. in text, pl. 60                    MH
NY: Broadway Publishing                                 1909
Reminiscences c. 1860-1909, with widespread reference to performers.

**3174** GRAU, ROBERT. The business man in the amusement world: a volume of progress in the field of the theatre
pp.xiii, 362; pl. 42                                    M
NY: Broadway Publishing                                 1910

A second book of reminiscences, somewhat misleadingly titled.

**3175** MORRISSEY, JAMES W. Noted men and women...containing the humor, wit, sentiment, and diplomacy in the social, artistic, and business lives of the people herein set forth
pp.262; ill.     DL★
NY: Klebold P.     1910

Includes material on Rose Coghlan, Joseph Jefferson, Owen Fawcett and Richard Mansfield

**3176** GRAU, ROBERT. The stage in the twentieth century
pp.xxvii, 360; pl. 63 inc. 1 col.     M
NY: Broadway Publishing     1912

A third book of reminiscences, restricted to US theatre.

**3177** BANGS, JOHN K. From pillar to post: leaves from a lecturer's notebook
pp.xii, 338; ill. in text     MB
NY: Century     1916

Memoirs of a professional lecturer, with incidental theatre reference.

**3178** PICKETT, LASALLE C. [= Pickett, Mrs General George E.]. Across my path. Memories of people I have known
pp.ix, 148; pl. 11     MB
NY: Brentano's     1916

Includes reference to Charlotte Cushman, Laura Keene, Anna Cora Mowatt

**3179** VAN VECHTEN, CARL. The merry-go-round
pp.343     DL★
NY: Alfred A. Knopf     1918

Includes *Impressions in the theater, Margaret Anglin produces 'As you like it'*, and material on Avery Hopwood and Philip Moeller.

**3180** ALDRICH, Mrs THOMAS B. [= Woodman, Lilian]. Crowding memories...
pp.ix, 295; pl. 21     O
Boston: Houghton Mifflin     1920

Includes material on John Wilkes Booth, Edwin Booth and his wife (née Mary McVicker), with other theatrical reminiscence.

**3181** FORD, JAMES L. Forty-odd years in the literary shop
pp.ix, 362; pl. 31     O
NY: E. P. Dutton     1921

Reminiscence, with anecdotal reference to theatre.

**3182** MENCKEN, H. L. Prejudices [series 1-6]
pp.various     L
London: Jonathan Cape     1921-27

Collected articles, essays and occasional writings. Volume 1 has reference to George Ade and J. G. Nathan and an article, *Sex on the stage*. Volume 3 includes *Reflections on the drama*.

**3183** HOWE, M[ARK] A. DeW. Memories of a hostess: a chronicle of eminent friendships, drawn chiefly from the diaries of Mrs James T. Fields
pp.ix, 312; ill. in text, front., pl. 27     L
Boston: Atlantic Monthly P.     1922

Includes material on Edwin Booth, Joseph Jefferson, Charlotte Cushman, William Warren.

**3184** PHELPS, WILLIAM L. As I like it
pp.xv, 236; xvii, 282; xvii, 309     MH
NY: Charles Scribner's Sons     1923-26

Three volumes. Reprinted articles from *Scribner's* in the form of monthly chronicles. Wide range of topics, with frequent reference to theatre and drama.

**3185** MINNIGERODE, MEADE. The fabulous forties, 1840-1850: a presentation of private life
pp.xvi, 345; front., pl. 15     L
NY: G. P. Putnam's Sons     1924

Satirical account. Includes reference to Fanny Elssler and to popular entertainments.

**3186** OVERTON, GRANT. Cargoes for crusoes
pp.416; pl. 9     L
NY: D. Appleton     1924

Essays on books and writers. Chapter 14 amounts to a survey of play collections.

**3187** CLARKE, JOSEPH I. My life and memories
pp.xvii, 404; pl. 8     L
NY: Dodd, Mead     1925

Irish journalist and editor. Includes wide reference to stage performers of the late nineteenth – early twentieth centuries.

**3188** MAYNE, ETHEL C. Enchanters of men
pp.x, 358; ill.     DL★
NY: G. P. Putnam's Sons     1925

First published London: Methuen, 1909. Includes accounts of Lola Montez and Adah Isaacs Menken.

**3189** HASTINGS, GEORGE E. The life and works of Francis Hopkinson
pp.ix, 517; pl. 7, front.     L
Chicago: U. P.     1926

Reference to the Douglass company. Hopkinson, politician, writer and musician, was a signer of the Declaration of Independence; his *Seven songs* (1788) was the first book of music published by an American composer.

**3190** SERGEANT, ELIZABETH S. Fire under the Andes, a group of North American portraits
pp.ix, 331; front., pl. 13     L
NY: Alfred A. Knopf     1927

Subjects include Paul Robeson, Pauline Lord, Robert Edmond Jones and Eugene O'Neill.

**3191** KELLY, ETHEL K. Twelve milestones: being the peregrinations of Ethel Knight Kelly
pp.xiii, 240; front., pl. 11     L
NY: Brentano's     1929

Early chapters deal with stage experience, with material on Augustin Daly, Richard Mansfield, Booth Tarkington.

**3192** MORGAN-POWELL, S. Memories that live
pp.x, 282     M
Toronto: Macmillan     1929

Includes reference to E. H. Sothern, Julia Marlowe and Margaret Anglin.

**3193** HAPGOOD, NORMAN. The changing years: reminiscences...
pp.x, 321; pl. 10, front.     L
NY: Farrar & Rinehart     1930

Author was drama critic and sometime editor of *Collier's* and *Harper's Weekly*. Chapter XI: 'the charm of the theatre'.

**3194** GARLAND, HAMLIN. Companions on the trail: a literary garland. Decorations by Constance Garland
pp.vii, 539; front.     L
NY: Macmillan     1931

Theatre references include Helena Modjeska, the Players Club, Chicago Theatre Society, Clyde Fitch.

**3195** GARLAND, HAMLIN. Roadside meetings...decorations by Constance Garland
pp.ix, 474; ill. in text      O
London: John Lane      1931
Published NY: Macmillan, 1930. Reminiscences, 1884-1899, including reference to Edwin Booth and James Herne.

**3196** HART, JEROME A. In our second century. From an editor's note-book
pp.454; front.      L
San Francisco: Pioneer P.      1931
Journalist's memoirs. Chapter XX, *Old-time shows*, makes brief reference to many stage performers of the late nineteenth century.

**3197** GARLAND, HAMLIN. My friendly contemporaries: a literary log
pp.xvii, 544; front.      O
NY: Macmillan      1932
Includes reference to William Gillette, Edward H. Sothern, Zona Gale.

**3198** CARROLL, RENEE. In your hat
pp.287; ill.      DL★
NY: Macaulay      1933
With caricatures by Gard.

**3199** MERRILL, FLORA. Flush of Wimpole Street and Broadway. Illustrated by Edwina
pp.120; ill.      DL★
NY: R. M. McBride      1933
Stage career of the cocker spaniel who first appeared in *The Barretts of Wimpole Street* with Katharine Cornell in 1930. Quasi-autobiography!

**3200** LAWRENCE, RITA. Amateurs and actors of the 19th-20th centuries (American, English, Italian)
pp.270; ill. in text      M
Menton: For the author      1936
Reminiscence, with much material on the Amateur Players of New York and Mrs Brown Potter.

**3201** HAWTHORNE, EDITH G. (Ed.). Memoirs of Julius Hawthorne
pp.ix, 299; front.      L
NY: Macmillan      1938
Makes reference to, *inter alia*, Edwin Booth and Charlotte Cushman.

**3202** MOREHOUSE, WARD. Forty-five minutes past eight
pp.vii, 267      M
NY: Dial P.      1939
Author wrote the *Broadway after dark* column for the *Sun* from 1926 to 1939.

**3203** WAGNER, CHARLES L. Seeing stars
pp.ix, 403; pl. 8      M
NY: G. P. Putnam's Sons      1940
Widely allusive to stage performers and personalities. In four parts, *Chautauqua and Lyceum*, *Concert*, *Theatre*, and *Return to concert*.

**3204** COCROFT, THODA. Great names and how they are made
pp.270; pl. 8      M
Chicago: Dartnell P.      1941
Reminiscences of a former press-agent.

**3205** WOOLF, S. J. Here am I
pp.x, 374; pl. 17      M
NY: Random House      1941
Autobiography. Author worked as an artist for the *New York Times*.

**3206** PETROVA, OLGA. Butter with my bread
pp.371; front.      L
Indianapolis: Bobbs-Merrill      1942
Reminiscences, including vaudeville and musical comedy.

**3207** LEE, AMY. A critic's notebook
pp.334; ill.      DL★
Boston: Manthorne & Burach      1943
Includes reference to little theatre and children's theatre, and an account of Eva Le Gallienne.

**3208** TOWNE, CHARLES H. So far, so good
pp.x, 245; ill. in text      MH
NY: Julian Messner      1945
Reminiscences. Theatre references include Mrs Fiske, Clarence Day, Tony Pastor and early Broadway shows.

**3209** FLAGG, JAMES M. ...Roses and buckshot
pp.224      DL★
NY: G. P. Putnam's Sons      1946
Autobiography. Author was a friend of John Barrymore.

**3210** FRIEDE, DONALD. The mechanical angel: his adventures and enterprises in the glittering 1920s
pp.xi, 247, ix      M
NY: Alfred A. Knopf      1948

**3211** HURLSTONE, KATHARINE (Ed.). William Hurlstone musician: memories and records by his friends
pp.118; ill.      DL★
London: Cary      1949
William Yeates Hurlstone (1876-1906). Incidental theatre interest.

**3212** TAYLOR, ROBERT L. The running pianist
pp.340      DL★
NY: Doubleday      1950
Includes a biographical sketch of Bobby Clark.

**3213** DENT, ALAN. My dear America...
pp.176; front.      L
London: Arthur Barker      1954
A journal of UK theatre critic's visit to America in the fall of 1953.

**3214** FOWLER, GENE. Minutes of the last meeting
pp.vii, 277      M
NY: Viking P.      1954
Reminiscences of a theatre coterie, including John Barrymore, John Decker and W. C. Fields, centred on an account of the eccentric Sadakichi Hartman.

**3215** LOGAN, HERSCHEL C. Buckskin and satin: the life of Texas Jack (C. B. Omohundro) indian fighter, plainsman, cowboy, hunter, guide, and actor, and his wife Mlle Morlacchi, première danseuse in satin slippers
pp.218; ill.      DL★
Harrisburg PA: Stackpole      1954

Foreword by Paul I. Wellman.

**3216** ZUKOR, ADOLPH with KRAMER, DALE. The public is never wrong; the autobiography
pp.vii, 223; pl. 6    L
London: Cassell    1954

Includes early experience in the live entertainment industry.

**3217** KEMPTON, MURRAY. Part of our time: some ruins and monuments of the thirties
pp.ix, 334    MH
NY: Simon and Schuster    1955

Includes accounts of workers' theatre, John Howard Lawson, Paul Robeson.

**3218** GRANLUND, NILS T.; FEDER, SID & HANCOCK, RALPH. Blondes, brunettes and bullets
pp.vii, 300    MH
NY: David McKay    1957

**3219** MANEY, RICHARD. Fanfare: the confessions of a press agent
pp.viii, 374; pl. 4    M
NY: Harper & Brothers    1957

**3220** PREMINGER, MARION M. All I want is everything [autobiography]
pp.viii, 328; pl. 8    M
NY: Funk and Wagnall    1957

**3221** GIBBS, WOLLCOTT. More in sorrow
pp.xii, 308    MH
NY: Henry Holt    1958

Includes a memorial essay on Robert Benchley but otherwise of only marginal theatre interest.

**3222** LOGGINS, VERNON. Where the world ends: the life of Louis Moreau Gottschalk
pp.xii, 261; ill.    DL★
Baton Rouge: Louisiana State U. P.    1958

Includes a chapter on Ada Clare.

**3223** D'ESSEN, LORRAIN. Kangaroos in the kitchen: the story of animal talent scouts
pp.306; ill.    DL★
NY: David McKay    1959

Account of the D'Essen Organization, supplier of trained animals to the entertainment industry.

**3224** GENE FOWLER 1890-1960: recollections by his friends on the occasion of the publication of his last book *Skyline*
pp.29; portrait on title    L
NY: Viking P.    1960

**3225** GUNDELFINGER, GEORGE F. GFG – theatric'ly: an autobiographical review...of Freedley and Reeves' *A History of the Theatre*...
pp.xii, 152; pl. 20    M
NY: Pageant P.    1960

Eccentric, seemingly random, reflections on the theatre.

**3226** HACKETT, NORMAN H. Come my boys
pp.420; ill.    DL★
NY: Hackett Memorial Publication Fund    1960

Autobiography. Theatre references include Louis James, Frederick Warde, Julia Marlowe, James O'Neill, Katharine Cornell.

**3227** MOORE, LILLIAN. The Duport mystery
pp.104    L
NY: Dance Perspectives    1960

An account of the dancer Pierre L. Duport and his self-styled 'son' Louis Duport, with a wealth of information on theatre in Philadelphia, Charleston and elsewhere. Includes also material on Alexander Reinagle and Alexandre Placide and suggests (p. 60) a possible unfinished MS on the Placides by Eola Willis.

**3228** PARRY, ALBERT. Garrets and pretenders: a history of bohemianism in America
pp.xxvii, 422; pl. 8    L
NY: Dover    1960

New edition with additional chapter, *Enter Beatniks*. First published NY: Covici-Friede, 1933. Theatre reference includes Ada Clare, Henry Clapp, George Cram Cook, Mabel Dodge and John Reed.

**3229** FOWLER, GENE. Skyline: a reporter's reminiscence of the 1920s
pp.v, 314    L
NY: Viking P.    1961

Includes substantial reference to Damon Runyon. The final chapter was issued separately by Viking P. in 1961, as a tribute after Fowler's death.

**3230** FOWLER, WILL. The young man fron Denver
pp.310; pl. 8    MH
Garden City NY: Doubleday    1962

Biography of Gene Fowler. Includes material on his friend, John Barrymore.

**3231** HANFF, HELENE. Under foot in show business
pp.188; ill.    DL★
NY: Harper and Row    1962

**3232** ENDREY, EUGENE. Beg, borrow and squeal
pp.293    DL★
NY: Pageant P.    1963

Actor's reminiscences, including reference to Hungarian artists in the US.

**3233** MAXWELL, ELSA. The celebrity circus
pp.180; pl. 8    M
London: W. H. Allen    1964

**3234** GRUEN, JOHN. The new Bohemia: the combine generation. Photos by Fred. W. McDarrah
pp.180; ill.    DL★
NY: Shorecrest    1966

**3235** GRUEN, JOHN. The party's over now: reminiscences of the fifties, new York's artists, writers, musicians, and their friends
pp.v, 282; pl. 16    L
NY: Viking P.    1967

Jack Gelber, Edward Albee and other theatre references.

**3236** WALLACE, DAVID H. John Rogers, the people's sculptor
pp.xv, 326; ill.    DL★
Middletown CT: Wesleyan U. P.    1967

Includes a catalogue of Rogers's work, with seven theatrical sculptures, illustrated.

**3237** DRENNAN, ROBERT E. (Ed.). The Algonquin wits
pp.176; ill. in text    L
NY: Citadel P.    1968

Examples of the wit of, *inter alia*, Robert Benchley, Heywood Broun, George S. Kaufman, Alexander Woollcott.

**3238** MARETZEK, MAX. Crochets and quavers & sharps and flats: revelations of an opera manager in America
pp.xxxv, 346; 94; front., ill. in text     M
NY: Dover     1968
Two volumes in one. First published separately, NY: Samuel French, 1855, 1890, here with new introduction by Charles Hayman. Partly in the form of letters, with a wealth of nineteenth century theatre reference, including performers, performances, buildings and incidents. Author managed Astor Place Opera House for a period from 1849.

**3239** GRAHAME, SHIRLEY. Scratch an actor: confessions of a Hollywood columnist
pp.268     DL★
NY: Morrow     1969

**3240** HALLOWELL, JOHN. The truth game
pp.253     MH
NY: Simon and Schuster     1969
Reminiscences include reference to Broadway and Hollywood Boulevard, with a final piece on Andy Warhol.

**3241** VIERTEL, SALKA. The kindness of strangers [autobiography]
pp.vii, 338; front     M
NY: Holt, Rinehart & Winston     1969
Author was married to the director Berthold Viertel. After WW1 she settled in Hollywood where she associated with many of the leading writers of the time.

**3242** LAMPARSKI, RICHARD. Whatever became of...?
pp.various; ill. in text     L
NY: Crown Publishers     [1970?-75]
Series 1-5. Popular biographical sketches including many stage personalities and other entertainers.

**3243** RUBIN, JERRY. Do it ! Scenarios of the revolution. Introduction by Eldridge Cleaver. Designed by Quentin Fiore. Yipped by Jim Retherford. Zapped by Nancy Kurshan
pp.256: ill. in text     L
NY: Simon & Schuster     1970
A yippie manifesto, with a chapter, 'Revolution is theatre-in-the-streets'.

**3244** KRAFT, HY. On my way to the theater
pp.vii, 216; ill. in text     M
NY: Macmillan     1971
Edited by Eleanor Friede. Includes substantial reference to Theodore Dreiser.

**3245** RUBIN, JERRY. We are everywhere. Written in Cook county jail
pp.256; ill. in text     L
NY: Harper & Row     1971
An account of the author's trial for federal conspiracy and subsequent imprisonment. Complements *Do it !*....

**3246** GRADY, BILLY. The Irish peacock: the confessions of a legendary talent agent
pp.288; ill.     DL★
New Rochelle: Arlington House     1972

**3247** HAPGOOD, HUTCHINS. A Victorian in the modern world
pp.xxiii, 604; pl. 16     L
Seattle: U. of Washington P.     1972
New edition with introduction by Robert A. Skotheim. First published NY: Harcourt, Brace, 1939. Material on Susan Glaspell and the New York theatre of the 1890s.

**3248** CRONIN, JAMES E.(Ed.). The diary of Elihu Hubbard Smith
pp.xvi, 481; front.     O
Philadelphia: American Philosophical Society     1973
Author was a physician and theatre enthusiast. Diary entries include material on William Dunlap and many other references to actors and theatre-going including Mrs Merry, the Hallams, and John Hodgkinson.

**3249** PERRELLA, ROBERT. They call me the showbiz priest [autobiography]
pp.287; ill.     DL★
NY: Trident P.     1973

**3250** COHEN, MICKY. Mickey Cohen: in my own words. The underworld biography...as told to Nugent Peer
pp.264; ill. in text, pl. 8     DL★
Englewood Cliffs NJ: Prentice-Hall     [1975]
Includes encounters with show business personalities.

**3251** DRUTMAN, IRVING. Good company: a memoir, mostly theatrical
pp.xi, 274; ill. in text     M
Boston: Little, Brown     1976
Largely relating to the period 1930-40.

**3252** HAYWARD, BROOKE. Haywire
pp.ix, 325; ill. in text     M
NY: Alfred A. Knopf     1977
A memoir. Author was daughter of actress Margaret Sullavan and Leland Hayward.

**3253** SABINSON, HARVEY. Darling, you were wonderful
pp.xviii, 205     DL★
Chicago: H. Regnery     1977
Memoirs of a press agent.

**3254** SMITH, HARRY A. The life and legend of Gene Fowler
pp.320;ill. in text     L
NY: William Morrow     1977
Includes material on John and Lionel Barrymore and many other theatre personalities.

**3255** LEVINE, SAMUEL P. Ham - kosher style !
pp.vi, 119     L
Canoga Park CA: For the author     1979
Anecdotal biography of bit-part actor 'Phil Arnold'.

**3256** DODY, SANDFORD. Giving up the ghost: a writer's life among the stars
pp.334     L
NY: M. Evans     1980
Memoirs of a ghost writer including material on Mrs John Barrymore, Helen Hayes, Katharine Hepburn, Elsa Lanchester.

**3257** BIER, JESSA. The rise and fall of American humor
pp.xiii, 527     L
NY: Holt Rinehart and Winston     1981
Reprint, with the addition of an 'afterword', of 1968 publication. Reference to entertainers *passim*.

**3258** WILSON, EARL. Hot times: true tales of Hollywood and Broadway by the dean of show business columnists
pp.xi, 260; pl. 8     MH
Chicago: Contemporary Books     1984

## 8.4 INDIVIDUAL

### Abbey, Henry E.
### (1846-1896)
### Theatre manager

**3259** COLLINS, JOHN D. Henry E. Abbey, Akron impressario
Akron OH: U. (MA)     1960

**3260** HOSSALA, RICHARD J. Henry E. Abbey, commercial manager: a study of producing management in the theatre of the late nineteenth century (1870-1900)
Kent OH: State U. (PhD)     1972

### Adams, Maude
### [Kiskadden, Maude]
### (1872-1953)
### Actress

**3261** MAUDE ADAMS acting edition of *Romeo and Juliet*...published with the authorization of Charles Frohman
pp.110; pl. 13     M
NY: R. H. Russell     1899
Illustrated with scenes from her production, opposite William Faversham's Romeo, which opened May 8, 1899 at the Empire Theatre, NY.

**3262** DAVIES, ACTON. Maude Adams
pp.vi, 110; pl. 21     M
NY: Frederick A. Stopes     1901

**3263** PATTERSON, ADA. Maude Adams, a biography
pp.ii, 109; pl. 23     M
NY: Meyer Bros.     1907
Refer.to *The life story of Maude Adams and her mother* published in sections in the *Green Book Magazine*, June - November, 1914, attributed to Annie Kiskadden and Verne H. Porter.

**3264** ROBBINS, PHYLLIS. Maude Adams: an intimate portrait
pp.vii, 308; pl. 8     M
NY: G. P. Putnam's Sons     1956

**3265** ROBBINS, PHYLLIS. The young Maude Adams
pp.163; ill.     DL★
Francestown NH: Marshall Jones     1959
Biography, emphasizing pre-1890s.

**3266** KUEHNL, EILEEN K. Maude Adams, an American idol: true womanhood triumphant in the late 19th and early 20th century theatre
Madison: U. of Wisconsin (PhD)     1984

### Addams, Jane
### (1860-1935)
### Social reformer

**3267** ADDAMS, JANE. Twenty years at Hull House: with autobiographical notes
pp.xvii, 462; ill. in text, pl. 12     L
NY: Macmillan     1910
Includes reference to theatre at Hull House, chapter XVI.

**3268** ADDAMS, JANE. The second twenty years at Hull House September 1909 to September 1929. With a record of a growing world consciousness
pp. xv, 413; ill. in text     L
NY: Mcmillan     1930
Chaper XI: *The play instinct and the arts*.

**3269** TIMS, MARGARET. Jane Addams of Hull House 1860-1935: a centenary study
pp.166; front.     L
London: Allen & Unwin     1961

### Adler, Dankmar
### (1844-1900)

**3270** MORRISON, HUGH. Louis Sullivan, prophet of modern architecture
pp.xxi, 391; ill.     DL★
NY: Museum of Modern Art/W. W. Norton     1935
Includes a biographical sketch of Dankmar Adler.

**3271** GRIMSLEY, CHARLES E. A study of the contributions of Dankmar Adler to the theater building practice of the late nineteenth century
Evanston: Northwestern U. (PhD)     1984

**3272** GREGERSEN, CHARLES E. Dankmar Adler: his theatres and auditoriums...with a biography of Dankmar Adler prepared in collaboration with Joan W. Saltzstein, assisted by Susan Wolfson
pp.xvi, 215; ill. in text     M
Athens GA: Swallow P./Ohio U. P.     1990

### Adler, Stella
### (1902-1992)
### Actress, director

**3273** ROTTE, JOANNA-H. The principles of acting according to Stella Adler
NY: City U. (PhD)     1983

### Aherne, Brian
### [Aherne, De Lacy]
### (1902-1986)
### Actor

**3274** AHERNE, BRIAN. A proper job [autobiography]
pp.xi, 355; pl. 16     M
Boston: Houghton Mifflin     1969

### Allen Fred
### [Sullivan, John Florence]
### (1894-1956)
### Comedian

**3275** ALLEN, FRED. Treadmill to oblivion
pp.vii, 240; ill. in text     MESM
Boston: Little, Brown     1954
Reminiscences, largely concerned with radio drama. Drawings by Al Hirschfeld.

**3276** ALLEN, FRED. Much ado about me [autobiography]
pp.xv, 380; pl. 4     M
Boston: Little, Brown     1956

### Allen, Viola
### (1867-1948)
### Actress

**3277** PLOTNICKI, RITA. The evolution of a star: the career of Viola Allen, 1882-1918
NY: City U. (PhD)     1979

### Amend, Karle O.
### (1889-1944)
### Designer

**3278** BEHIND THE SCENES: the theatre art of Karle O. Amend [exhibition]
pp.7 M
NY: Public Library at Lincoln Center 1982

### Ames, Winthrop
### (1870-1937)
### Producer, director

**3279** MACARTHUR, DAVID E. A study of the theatrical career of Winthrop Ames from 1904 to 1929
Columbus: Ohio State U. (PhD) 1962

### Anderson de Navarro, Mary
### (1859-1940)
### Actress

**3280** FARRAR, J. MAURICE. Mary Anderson. The story of her life and professional career
pp.x, 86; front. M
London: David Bogue 1884

**3281** [WILLIAMS, HENRY L.]. The stage life of Mary Anderson. With tragic and comic recitations from a repertoire of this favourite actress
pp.16; portrait on title P
London: George Vickers [1884]

**3282** THE WINTER'S TALE: a comedy in five acts...as managed by Miss Mary Anderson, with illustrations by Edwin John Ellis and Joseph Anderson, and selection from the incidental music by Andrew Levey
pp.i, 57; ill. in text, pl.5 M
London: Field & Tuer 1888
Mary Anderson as both Hermione and Perdita, with J. Forbes-Robertson as Leontes.

**3283** ANDERSON, MARY. Girlhood of an actress
pp.ii, 105 L
London: Osgood, McIlvaine 1895

**3284** ANDERSON, MARY. A few memories
pp.viii, 267; pl. 6 M
London: Osgood, McIlvaine 1896
The earlier chapters reprint *Girlhood of an actress*. Published NY: Harper, 1896.

**3285** ANDERSON DE NAVARRO, MARY. A few more memories
pp.286; pl. 15 M
London: Hutchinson 1936

**3286** SAWYER, RAYMOND C. The Shakespearean acting of Mary Anderson, 1884-1889
Urbana: U. of Illinois (PhD) 1975

### Anglin, Margaret
### (1876-1958)
### Actress

**3287** JOHNSON, GORDON. The Greek productions of Margaret Anglin
Cleveland OH: Case Western Reserve U. (PhD) 1971

**3288** LE VAY, JOHN. Margaret Anglin: a stage life
pp.326; ill. in text M
Toronto: Simon & Pierre 1989

### Anisfeld, Boris
### (1879-1973)
### Designer

**3289** BRINTON, CHRISTIAN. The Boris Anisfeld exhibition with introduction and catalogue of the paintings...
pp.[48]; pl. 33 M
NY: Redfield-Kendrick-Odell 1918

**3290** EXHIBITION of paintings and drawings by Boris Anisfeld [cover title]
pp.8 inc. wrappers M
Boston: Boston Art Club [1924]
Foreword by Raymond Henniker-Heaton.

**3291** FLINT, JANET A. Boris Anisfeld: twenty years of designs for the theater
pp.35; ill. in text M
Wasington DC: Smithsonian Institution P. 1971

**3292** BORIS ANISFELD 1879-1973
pp.24; ill. in text M
Storrs CT: William Benton Museum of Art 1979

### Armitage, Merle
### (1893-1975)
### Manager

**3293** ARMITAGE, MERLE. Accent on America [autobiography]
pp.403; front., ill. in text MH
NY: E. Weyhe 1944

**3294** ARMITAGE, MERLE. Accent on life. Foreword by John Charles Thomas
pp.xv, 386; pl. 12 L
Ames: Iowa State U. P. 1964

### Arnold, Edward
### (1890-1956)
### Actor

**3295** ARNOLD, EDWARD. Lorenzo goes to Hollywood [autobiography]
pp.282; pl. 13 L
NY: Liveright 1940

### Aronson, Boris
### (1900-1980)
### Designer

**3296** GEORGE, WALDEMAR (Ed.). Boris Aronson et l'art du théâtre
pp.iii, 19; pl. 32, some col. M
Paris: Editions des Chroniques du Jour 1928
315 copies.

**3297** RICH, FRANK with ARONSON, LISA. The theatre art of Boris Aronson
pp.xi, 323; ill. in text, some col. M
NY: Alfred A. Knopf 1987

**3298** RICH, FRANK (Ed.). Boris Aronson: stage design as visual metaphor [exhibition catalogue]
pp.24; ill. in text, some col. M
Katonah NY: Katonah Gallery 1989
Transferred to Harvard 1990.

## Aronson, Rudolph
### (1856?-1920)
### Producer, entrepreneur

**3299** ARONSON, RUDOLPH. Theatrical and musical memories
pp.xiv, 283; pl. 39     M
NY: McBride, Nast     1913
Conceived and built the Casino Theatre (1882) as a home for musical productions.

## Ashley, Elizabeth
### (1939-)
### Actress

**3300** ASHLEY, ELIZABETH with FIRESTONE, ROSS. Actress: postcards from the road [autobiography]
pp.ii, 252; ill. in text     M
NY: M. Evans     1978

## Atkinson, Justin Brooks
### (1894-1984)
### Critic

**3301** McNEELY, JERRY C. The criticism and reviewing of Brooks Atkinson
Madison: U. of Wisconsin (PhD)     1955

## Ayers, Lemuel
### (1915-1955)
### Designer

**3302** NEWLIN, FORREST A. The New York stage designs of Lemuel Ayers
Lincoln: U. of Nebraska (PhD)     1979

## Bacall, Lauren
### (1924-)
### Actress

**3303** BACALL. LAUREN. By myself [autobiography]
pp.vi, 377; pl. 16     O
NY: Alfred A. Knopf     1979
Includes early theatre experience.

## Bacon, Frank
### (1864-1922)
### Actor, playwright

**3304** GLYER, RICHARD T. Frank Bacon and his work in the theatres of the west (1880-1910)
Stanford: U. (MA)     1941

## Bailey, Pearl
### [Bailey, Mae]
### (1918-)
### Singer, actress

**3305** BAILEY, PEARL. The raw pearl
pp.xv, 206; pl. 6     MESM
NY: Harcourt, Brace & World     1968
Autobiography derived from taped conversations, edited by Wendell Shakelford and Hiram Haydn.

**3306** BAILEY, PEARL. Talking to myself [autobiography]
pp.xiv, 233     L
NY: Harcourt Brace Jovanovich     1971

**3307** BAILEY, PEARL. Hurry up, America, & spit
pp.106     DL★
NY: Harcourt Brace Jovanovich     1976

## Baker, George L.
### (1868-1941)
### Manager

**3308** WATERS, WALTER K. George L. Baker and the Baker stock company
Stanford: U. (PhD)     1964

## Baker, George Pierce
### (1866-1935)
### Teacher, author

**3309** TRYON, VIRGINIA V. The '47 workshop: its history and significance
Los Angeles: U. of Southern California (MA)     1932

**3310** BROWN, JOHN M. et al (Eds). George Pierce Baker: a memorial
pp.45     ★
NY: Dramatists' Play Service     1939

**3311** SMITH, ELDEN T. George Pierce Baker: a critical study of his influence as a teacher of theatre arts
Cleveland: Case Western Reserve U. (PhD)     1947

**3312** KINNE, WISNER P. George Pierce Baker and the American theatre
pp.xv, 348; pl. 5     M
Cambridge MA: Harvard U. P.     1954
From the '47 workshop' at Harvard to the Yale Drama School.

**3313** HINKEL, CECIL E. An analysis and evaluation of the 47 workshop of George Pierce Baker
Columbus: Ohio State U. (PhD)     1960

## Ball, Lucille
### (1911-1989)
### Actress

**3314** GREGORY, JAMES. The Lucille Ball story
pp.210     ★
NY: New American Library     1974

**3315** ANDREWS, BART & WATSON, THOMAS J. Loving Lucy. Foreword by Gale Gordon
pp.226; ill. in text     L
NY: St Martin's P.     1980

## Ball, William
### (1931-)
### Director, actor

**3316** EATMAN, RODNEY H. In search of directorial style: a study of the productions of William Ball at the American Conservatory, San Francisco, 1965-1976
Ann Arbor: U. of Michigan (PhD)     1983

## Ballard, Lucinda
### (1908-)
### Costume designer

**3317** [NEWLIN, JEANNE et al]. Dressing Broadway: costume designs of Lucinda Ballard. Checklist of the exhibition
pp.iv, 28; ill. in text     M
Cambridge MA: Harvard Theatre Collection     1987

Biographical introduction and a brief article, *The Costume Designer*, by Ballard. A set of slides intended to accompany the catalogue was not, in the event, issued.

## Bandmann, Daniel
### [Bandmann, Edward]
### (1840-1905)
### Actor

3318   BANDMANN, DANIEL E.   An actor's tour: or seventy thousand miles with Shakespeare
pp.xviii, 305; front.                            M
Boston: Cupples, Upham                    1885
An account of his tour of Australasia. Edited by E. Gisby.

## Bankhead, Tallulah
### (1903-1968)
### Actress

3319   BANKHEAD, TALLULAH.   Tallulah: my autobiography
pp.xiii, 335; pl. 13, (1 col.)                   M
NY: Harper & Brothers                       1952

3320   BRIAN, DENNIS.   Tallulah, darling: a biography of Tallulah Bankhead
pp.xi, 292; pl. 6                                  O
NY: Pyramid                                       1972

3321   ISRAEL, LEE.   Miss Tallulah Bankhead
pp.384; pl. 8                                       M
London: W. H. Allen                            1972

3322   GILL, BRENDAN.   Tallulah
pp.287; ill. in text                                M
London: Michael Joseph                       1973
A pictorial biography. NY: Holt, Rinehart and Winston, 1972.

3323   TUNNEY, KIERAN.   Tallulah: darling of the gods
pp.228; pl. 4                                       M
NY: E. P. Dutton                                  1973

3324   CAMPBELL, SANDY.   B: twenty-nine letters from Coconut Grove
pp.64; ill. in text                                  M
Verona: For the author                        1974
Letters by the author to Donald Windham in 1956, with reference to Tallulah Bankhead and a production of *Streetcar Named Desire* which had a warm-up in Florida during January and February, 1956.

3325   RAWLS, EUGENIE.   Tallulah: a memory. Edited by James Hatcher [cover title]
pp.97 inc. top wrapper; ill. in text         MH
Birmingham: U. of Alabama                 1979
Author acted with Bankhead in *The Little Foxes*, National Theatre, 1939, and includes some letters.

## Barnabee, Henry Clay
### (1833-1917)
### Actor, singer

3326   BARNABEE, HENRY C.   Reminiscences of Henry Clay Barnabee being an attempt to account for his life, with some excuses for his professional career. Edited by George Leon Varney
pp.x, 461; pl. 12                                   M
Boston: Chapple                                  1913

## Barrett, Lawrence Patrick
### (1838-1891)
### Actor

3327   WINTER, WILLIAM.   Essay upon the great play entitled *Harebell; or, the man o' Airlie*, produced originally at Booth's Theatre, New York by Mr Lawrence Barrett where it ran several weeks successfully
pp.12                                                 MB
[Philadelphia?]: [Ledger Steampower Printing]   [c. 1871]
Wrapper and 2nd title read '...the dramatic sensation of London 1868 and acted with equal success in America'. The play was by W,. G. Wills. Nicoll gives only the sub-title.

3328   VERBATIM REPORT of the reception to Lawrence Barrett, by Wilson Barrett. Langham Hotel, London, England, April 2nd, 1884
pp.20                                                 MB
[London]: Clement-Smith, printer         [1884]
Prior to Barrett's London début at the Lyceum Theatre. Speakers included Charles Dickens, J. L. Toole, Carl Rosa.

3329   BARRON, ELWYN A.   Lawrence Barrett: a professional sketch
pp.98; ill. in text                                MH
Chicago: Knight & Leonard                 1889
Emphasizes the period 1856-89.

3330   BAILEY, MARK.   Lawrence Barrett, 1838-1891
Ann Arbor: U. of Michigan (PhD)         1942

3331   MILLER, JAMES R.   Lawrence Barrett on the New York stage
Medford MA: Tufts U. (PhD)                1972

## Barrymore family

### Barrymore, Maurice
### [Blythe, Herbert]
### (1849-1905) Actor
### Barrymore, Lionel
### (1878-1954) Actor
### Barrymore, Ethel
### (1879-1959) Actress
### Barrymore, John
### (1882-1942) Actor
### Barrymore, Diana
### (1921-1960) Actress

3332   ALPERT, HORACE.   The Barrymores
pp.xviii, 398; pl. 16                             M
NY: Dial P.                                         1964

3333   BARRYMORE, JOHN.   Confessions of an actor [autobiography]
pp.[128]; pl. 32                                   MH
Indianapolis: Bobbs-Merrill                  1926

3334   BARRYMORE, JOHN.   We three: Ethel–Lionel–John
pp.[156]; ill. in text                              L
Akron OH: Saalfield                            1935

3335   STRANGE, MICHAEL [=Oelrichs, Blanche]. Who tells me true [autobiography]
pp.xv, 396; pl. 8                                  M
NY: Charles Scribner                           1940

Author, John Barrymore's second wife, wrote *Clair de Lune* for Ethel Barrymore.

**3336** POWER-WATERS, ALMA. John Barrymore: the legend and the man
pp.xiv, 282; pl. 16     M
NY: Julian Messner     1941
Foreword by Brooks Atkinson.

**3337** FOWLER, GENE. Good night, sweet prince: the life and times of John Barrymore
pp.447; pl 8     M
London: Hammond, Hammond     1949

**3338** BARRYMORE, LIONEL with SHIFF, CAMERON. We Barrymores
pp.viii, 244; pl. 8     M
NY: Appleton Century Croft     1951

**3339** BARRYMORE, ETHEL. Memories: an autobiography
pp.x, 310; pl. 17     M
NY: Harper & Brothers     1955

**3340** BARRYMORE, DIANA with GEROLD, FRANK. Too much, too soon [autobiography]
pp.303; pl. 6     M
London: Frederick Muller     1957

**3341** BARRYMORE, ELAINE with DODY, SANDFORD. All my sins remembered [autobiography]
pp.ix, 274; pl. 4     M
NY: Appleton-Century     1964
Author was John Barrymore's fourth wife.

**3342** NEWMAN, SHIRLEE P. Ethel Barrymore, girl actress
pp.200; col. ill.     DL★
Indianapolis: Bobbs Merrill     1966
Intended for children.

**3343** OTIS, JOHN F. The Barrymore Hamlet, 1922-1924
Urbana: U. of Illinois (PhD)     1966

**3344** KANIN, GARSON. Hollywood: stars and starlets, tycoons and flesh-peddlers, frauds and geniuses, hopefuls and has-beens, great lovers and sex symbols
pp.vii, 393     MH
NY: Viking P.     1967
Mostly movie reminiscences, but with recollections of John Barrymore at the end of his career.

**3345** BERGER, SPENCER M. Opening night introduction to the tribute to John Barrymore at Dryden Theatre, Rochester NY May 6-June 2, 1969
pp.v, 30     M
NY: [Dryden Theatre?]     [1969]

**3346** CARD, JAMES. The films of John Barrymore as shown in the Dryden Theatre tribute series May-June 1969
pp.[30]; ill. in text     M
Rochester NY: George Eastman House     [1969]
Includes a filmography, 1914-1941, compiled by Spencer M. Berger

**3347** FOX, MARY V. Ethel Barrymore: a portrait
pp.133     DL★
Chicago: Reliiy and Lee     1970

Biography intended for children.

**3348** KOBLER, JOHN. Damned in paradise: the life of John Barrymore
pp.xiv, 418; pl. 8     M
NY: Atheneum     1977

**3349** KOTSILIBAS-DAVIS, JAMES. Great times, good times: the odyssey of Maurice Barrymore
pp.xiii, 538; pl. 16     M
NY: Doubleday     1977

**3350** KOTSILIBAS-DAVIS, JAMES. The Barrymores: the royal family in Hollywood
pp.viii, 376; ill. in text     M
NY: Crown     1981

**3351** PETERS, MARGOT. The house of Barrymore
pp.xi, 642; pl.24     M
NY: Alfred A, Knopf     1990
Biography of Ethel, Lionel and John Barrymore.

### Barton, Lucy Adelaide
### (1891-1979)
### Costume designer

**3352** LUCY BARTON: the Texas years: an exhibition of costume designs...
pp.20; ill. in text     M
Austin: U. of Texas P.     1965

### Bateman, Kate
### (1842-1917)
### Actress

**3353** BADAL, ROBERT S. Kate and Ellen Bateman: a study in precocity
Evanston: Northwestern U. (PhD)     1971

### Bay, Howard
### (1912-1986)
### Scene designer

**3354** DAVIS, JERRY L. Howard Bay, scene designer
Lawrence: U. of Kansas (PhD)     1967

### Becks, George
### (1835-1904)
### Actor

**3355** LEONARD, WILLIAM F. The professional career of George Becks in the American theatre of the nineteenth century
Columbus: Ohio State U. (PhD)     1969

### Bel Geddes, Norman
### [Geddes, Norman Melancton]
### (1893-1958)
### Stage designer

**3356** BEL GEDDES, NORMAN. Project for a theatrical presentation of the Divine Comedy of Dante Alighieri
pp.22; pl. 32     M
NY: Theatre Arts     1924
Foreword by Max Reinhardt, photographs by Francis Bruguière.

**3357** WELLER, BETTY H. Norman Bel Geddes: designer, director, stage architect
Iowa City: U. of Iowa (PhD)     1959

**3358** BEL GEDDES, NORMAN & KELLEY, W. Miracle in the evening: an autobiography
pp.352  M
NY: Doubleday  1960

**3359** WORKS, BERNHARD R. Norman Bel Geddes, man of ideas
Madison: U. of Wisconsin (PhD)  1965

**3360** MECHAM, E. J. Norman Bel Geddes, artistic lighting designer
Austin: U. of Texas (MFA)  1966

**3361** DRESER, JAMES W. The theatrical contributions of Norman Bel Geddes
Evanston: Northwestern U. (PhD)  1967

**3362** BOGUSCH, GEORGE. Unity in the new stagecraft: productions designed and directed by Norman Bel Geddes
Bloomington: Indiana U. (PhD)  1968

**3363** HUNTER, FREDERICK J. Norman Bel Geddes: the renaissance man of the American theatre
pp.15; pl. 6  M
Austin: U. of Texas  1969
Text of an address given before the IFTR meeting of October 6, 1969 at Lincoln Center, NY.

**3364** HUNTER, FREDERICK J. (Ed.). Catalog of the Norman Bel Geddes theatre collection, Humanities Research Center, University of Texas at Austin
pp.vi, 333; front.  M
Boston: G. K. Hall  1973

### Belafonte, Harry
### (1924?-)
### Actor

**3365** SHAW, ARNOLD. Belafonte: an unauthorized biography
pp.xiv, 338; pl. 8  L
Philadelphia: Chilton  1960

### Belasco, David
### (1859-1931)
### Dramatist, producer, director

**3366** FORD, JAMES L. The story of Du Barry
pp.14, ix, 288; ill. in text, pl. 6  M
NY: Frederick A. Stokes  1902
Souvenir of the opening of the Belasco Theatre, September 29, 1902. Ssigned limited edition. In addition to programme credits, contents include a fictionalized version of Du Barry's life as dramatized by David Belasco, and illustrations of the theatre interior, with production scenes.

**3367** FIRST NIGHT at David Belasco's Stuyvesant Theatre
pp.[31]; ill. in text  M
[NY]: [For the theatre]  1907
Illustrated description of the theatre with the programme of the inaugural production, A grand army man by Belasco, Pauline Phelps and Marion Short.

**3368** WINTER, WILLIAM. The life of David Belasco
pp.xxxiii, 530; xvii, 563; pl. 123  M
NY: Moffat, Yard  1918
In two volumes.

**3369** BELASCO, DAVID. The theatre through its stage door
pp.xvii, 246; pl. 24  M
NY: Harper & Brothers  1919
Articles, edited by Louis V. Defoe. Belasco's memoirs had been serialised in *Hearst's* magazine, March 1914-December 1915, as *My life story*.

**3370** A SOUVENIR of Shakespeare's *The Merchant of Venice* as presented by David Belasco at the Lyceum Theatre, New York, December 21, 1922
pp.173; ill. in text  DL★
NY: For the author  1923

**3371** PLAYS produced under the stage direction of David Belasco, illustrated...by William F. Kurze
pp.47; ill. in text  M
NY: [For David Belasco?]  1925

**3372** BATCHELLER, JOSEPH D. David Belasco
Minneapolis: U. of Minnesota (PhD)  1942

**3373** TIMBERLAKE, CRAIG. The life and work of David Belasco: the Bishop of Broadway.
pp.xix, 491; ill. in text  M
NY: Library Publisher  1954
Includes a chronology of New York productions and illustrations of production scenes.

**3374** FORDE, GLADYS I. David Belasco: an evaluation of the man and his contributions to American theatre history
Cleveland: Case Western Reserve U. (PhD)  1955

**3375** KLEINFIELD, H. L. The theatrical career of David Belasco
Cambridge MA: Harvard U. (PhD)  1956

**3376** MODISETT, NOAH F. A historical study of the stage directing theory and practice of David Belasco
Los Angeles: U. of Southern Caloifornia (PhD)  1963

**3377** EVANS, BETTY E. The nature of Belasco's use of music in representative productions
Eugene: U. of Oregon (PhD)  1965

**3378** MARKER, LISE-LONE. David Belasco: naturalism in the American theatre
pp.xiv, 249; pl. 4  M
Princeton NJ: U. P.  1975

### Belasco, Frederick
### (1862-1920)
### Producer, manager

**3379** SCHULTZ, JACQUELINE A. The life and career of Frederick Belasco (1862-1920)
Long Beach: California State U. (MA)  1980

### Bellamy, Ralph
### (1904-1992)
### Actor

**3380** BELLAMY, RALPH. When the smoke hit the fan [autobiography]
pp.ix, 276; pl. 16  L
Garden City NY: Doubleday  1979

## Benchley, Robert Charles
### (1889-1945)
### Critic, humorist, actor

**3381** ROSMOND, BABETTE. Robert Benchley: his life and good times
pp.ii, 240; pl. 12     MH
Garden City: Doubleday     1970

**3382** GOLDSTEIN, RICHARD M. The dramatic criticism of Robert Charles Benchley
Ann Arbor: U. of Michigan (PhD)     1980

## Bennett, Joan
### (1911-1990)
### Actress

**3383** BENNETT, JOAN & KIBBEE, LOIS. The Bennett playbill
pp.xv, 332; pl. 8     M
NY: Holt, Rinehart and Winston     1970

An account of the Morrison-Wood-Bennett theatrical family. Joan Bennett was the daughter of Richard Bennett (1873-1944), a successful Broadway actor.

## Bentley, Eric Russell
### (1916-)
### Critic

**3384** BENTLEY, ERIC. In search of theatre
pp.xxiii, 411, ix; ill. in text, pl. 12     O
London: Denis Dobson     1954

Autobiographical. Includes accounts of NY production of Bertolt Brecht's *Galileo* and of the author's work in Westport and Cambridge MA.

**3385** CUNNINGHAM, DONALD H. Eric Bentley's dramatic criticism: background and theory
Gainsville: U. of Florida (PhD)     1981

## Bentley, Walter Edmund
### (1864-1962)
### Actor, priest

**3386** BURGGRAAFF, WINFIELD. Walter Edmund Bentley: actor, priest, missioner, 1864-1962. Founder of the Actors' Church Alliance
pp.32; ill. in text     MH
[NY?]: For Mrs M.A.F.Bentley     [c. 1963]

## Berg, Gertrude E.
### (1899-1966)
### Actress

**3387** BERG, GERTRUDE with BERG, CHERNEY. Molly and me
pp.x, 278     O
NY: McGraw-Hill     1961

Cover title: *Memoirs of Gertrude Berg*.

## Berman, Eugene
### (1899-1972)
### Designer

**3388** EUGENE BERMAN: catalogue of the retrospective exhibition of his paintings, drawings, illustrations and designs
pp.68; ill. in text, some col.     MH*
Boston: Institute of Modern Art     1941

**3389** [AMBERG, GEORGE]. The theatre of Eugene Berman
pp.32; ill. in text, some col.     M
NY: Museum of Modern Art     1947

Costume and set designs.

**3390** LEVY, JULIEN (Ed.). Eugene Berman
pp.xv, 80; ill. in text, col. front.     DL*
NY: American Studio Books     1947

**3391** EXHIBITION OF DESIGNS for the theatre by Eugene Berman [catalogue]
    MH*
Austin: U. of Texas     1960

**3392** PAINTINGS BY EUGENE BERMAN 1958-1959 and twenty-five small paintings and sketches in mixed media...
pp.[12]; ill. in text     M
[London]: Lefevre Gallery     1960

**3393** EUGENE BERMAN: ballet, opera and theatre designs. Forum Gallery...October 5th to October 22nd
pp.[8]; ill. in text     M
NY: Harkness House for Ballet Arts     1966

**3394** [BARR-SHARRAR, BERYL]. Eugene Berman et al. Artistes en exil, 1939-1946. USA exposition du 16 Mai au 6 Juin 1968
pp.55; ill.     DL*
Paris: American Center for Students and Artists     1968

**3395** EUGENE BERMAN: recent paintings
    MH*
NY: Lafcarda Gallery     1969

**3396** THE GRAPHIC WORK of Eugene Berman
pp.xviii, 332; ill.     DL*
NY: C. N. Potter     1971

**3397** BERMAN
pp.[16]; ill. in text     M
Florence: Galleria Santacroce     1972

Exhibition catalogue, 5-21 December.

**3398** EUGENE BERMAN: drawings for the stage
    *
NY: Whitney     1989

Exhibition catalogue: stage and costume designs, 1937-1972.

## Bernard, John
### (1756-1828)
### Actor, manager

**3399** BERNARD, JOHN. Retrospections of the stage by the late John Bernard manager of the American theatres and formerly secretary to the Beef-Steak Club
pp.xii, 235; vii, 215     M
Boston: Carter and Hendee     1832

Two volumes in one. Edited by William Bayle Bernard. Irish and English stage experience prior to his departure for the US in 1797.

**3400** BERNARD, JOHN. Retrospections of America 1797-1811 edited from the manuscript by Mrs Bayle Bernard with an introduction, notes and index by Laurence Hutton and Brander Matthews
pp.xv, 380; pl.10     M
NY: Harper & Brother     1887

Derived from the unpublished biography and from material in *Tallis's Magazine* and *Manhattan Magazine*.

3401   EAST, NAPOLEON B.   John Bernard, actor-manager 1756-1828
Lawrence: U. of Kansas (PhD)     1970

### Bernstein, Aline
### [Frankau, Aline]
### (1881-1955)
### Designer

3402   BERNSTEIN, ALINE.   An actor's daughter [autobiography]
pp.ix, 228     M
NY: Alfred A. Knopf     1941
Daughter of actor Joseph Frankau.

3403   BARTON, MIKE A.   Aline Bernstein: a history and evaluation
Bloomington: Indiana U. (PhD)     1971

3404   KLEIN, CAROLE.   Aline [biography]
pp.xiii, 352; pl. 4     M
NY: Harper & Row     1979

3405   STUTMAN, SUZANNE (Ed.).   My other loneliness. Letters of Thomas Wolfe and Aline Bernstein [1925-36]
pp.xxv, 390; ill. in text     MH
Chapel Hill: U. of North Carolina P.     1983

### Bickford, Charles
### (1892-1967)
### Actor

3406   BICKFORD, CHARLES.   Bulls, balls, bicycles and actors [autobiography]
pp.viii, 336     MH
NY: Paul S. Eriksson     1965

### Blinn, Holbrook
### (1872-1928)
### Actor

3407   HIRSEN, RONALD B.   The stage career of Holbrook Blinn
Urbana-Champaign: U. of Illinois (PhD)     1975

### Bloom, Sol
### (1870-1949)
### Actor, songwriter

3408   BLOOM, SOL.   The autobiography of Sol Bloom
pp.v, 345; front.     O
NY: G. P.Putnam's Sons     1948
Parts one and two comprise memoirs of the theatre in San Francisco, Chicago and New York.

### Bloomgarden, Kermit
### (1904-1976)
### Producer

3409   DOHERTY, LYNN.   The art of producing: the life and work of Kermit Bloomgarten
NY: City U. (PhD)     1989

### Blumenthal, George
### (1863-1943)
### Producer, actor

3410   BLUMENTHAL, GEORGE with MENKIN, ARTHUR H.   My sixty years in show business: a chronicle of the American theatre 1874-1934
pp.xiv, 336; pl. 16     M
NY: Frederick C. Osberg     1936

### Boleslavsky, Richard
### (1889-1937)
### Director

3411   HARDY, MICHAEL C.   The theatre art of Richard Boleslavsky
Ann Arbor: U. of Michigan (PhD)     1971

3412   ROBERTS, J. W.   Richard Boleslavsky: his life and work in the theatre
pp.x, 288; ill. in text     MH
Ann Arbor MI: UMI Research P.     1981

### Bonstelle, Jessie
### [Bonstelle-Stuart, Laura Justine]
### (1872-1932)
### Producer, director

3413   DEAM, WILLIAM L.   A biographical study of Laura Justine Bonstelle-Stuart, together with an evaluation of her own contribution to the modern theatrical world
Ann Arbor: U. of Michigan (PhD)     1954
Managed the Detroit Civic Theatre.

### Booth, Edwin Thomas
### (1833-1893)
### Actor

3414   HAMLET, as performed by Edwin Booth
pp.vi, 40; ill. in text     MH
Ny: Baker & Goodwin, printers     1866
The text, together with a translation of Georg Gottfried Gervinus's essay on *Hamlet* and an appendix surveying performances, including also J. B. Booth's.

3415   HENNESSY, W. J.   Mr Edwin Booth in his various dramatic characters from life by W. J. Hennessy
pp.51; ll. 13; pl. 12     M
Boston: Jas. R. Osgood     1872
Cover title: *Edwin Booth in twelve dramatic characters...the engraving by W. J. Linton, The biographical sketch by William Winter.* The plates depict Booth as Hamlet, Richelieu, Othello, Bertuccio, Richard III, Brutus, Lear, Shylock, Macbeth, Benedick, Don Caesar de Bazan, Claude Melnotte.

3416   BLUMENTHAL, OSCAR.   Theatralische Eindrücke
pp.iii, 351     M
Berlin: Hofmann     1885
Text in German. Includes a chapter on Edwin Booth.

3417   DALY, AUGUSTIN & PALMER, A. M. (Eds.)].   Excerpts from the many good words uttered in honor of Edwin Booth at the supper given on Saturday night, March 30, 1889 by Augustin Daly and A. M. Palmer
pp.23     MH
NY: For the Players     1889
Comprises *a narrative of the event* reprinted from the *New York Times*, April 1, 1889; a letter from George William Curtis; a salute from Constant Coquelin; the transcribed address by Stephen H. Olin; and a tribute by William Winter

3418   HUTTON, LAURENCE.   Edwin Booth
pp.iii, 59; front., pl. 6     L
NY: Harper & Brothers     1893

## 8.4. INDIVIDUAL

**3419** MEMORIAL CELEBRATION of the sixtieth anniversary of the birth of Edwin Booth held in Madison Square Garden concert hall
pp.60; front     M
NY: Gillis for the Players Club     1893

Includes the text of addresses by Joseph Jefferson, Parke Godwin, reprinted in his *Commemorative Addresses*, NY: 1895, and Henry Irving; an elegy read by George E. Woodberry; and a tribute from Tommaso Salvini in Italian with the translation read by Henry Miller.

**3420** GROSSMAN, EDWINA B. Edwin Booth: recollections by his daughter...and letters to her and to his friends
pp.viii, 292; ill. in text, pl. 9     M
NY: Century     1894

**3421** WINTER, WILLIAM. Life and art of Edwin Booth. New edition, revised
pp.437; front.     M
NY: Macmillan     1894

First published 1893. This edition includes additional letters and notes that captions to two illustrations in the earlier edition were inaccurate.

**3422** WINTER, WILLIAM (Ed.). The Shakespearean plays of Edwin Booth. The miscellaneous plays of Edwin Booth
pp.various; fronts. 3     M
Philadelphia: Penn     1899

Three volumes. Acting copies, with notes by Winter.

**3423** COPELAND, CHARLES T. Edwin Booth
pp.xvii, 159; front.     M
Boston: Small, Maynard     1901

**3424** STEDMAN, EDMUND C. Genius and other essays
pp.vi, 288     L
NY: Moffat, Yard     1911

Includes an essay on Edwin Booth, evaluating his acting with particular reference to his Hamlet and Richelieu.

**3425** BENEDICT, E. C. Address...at the Players Club on Founder's Night...
pp.19     MH
[NY]: [The Players Club]     1917

Effectively, personal recollections of Edwin Booth. Appended is a printing of a letter to Benedict from Robert Lincoln, recalling his rescue by Booth from a dangerous predicament on a rail depot.

**3426** KYLE, HOWARD. The history of the Edwin Booth memorial, April 2nd, 1906 to November 13th, 1918 prepared by Howard Kyle and approved by the executive committee
pp.63; pl. 7     MH
NY: Corlies, Macy     [1918]

Description of the creation of the memorial statue in Gramercy Park, with photographs, and transcription of speeches made at the dedication.

**3427** ABBOTT, LYMAN [= Brown, Ira V.]. Silhouettes of my contemporaries...
pp.xi, 361; front.     L
NY: Doubleday, Page     1922

Includes an essay on Edwin Booth.

**3428** FURNESS, HORACE H. The letters of Horace Howard Furness, edited by H. H. F. J
pp.xxxv, 351; vii, 296; pl. 7     O
Boston: Houghton Mifflin     1922

Two volumes. Includes two letters to Edwin Booth, one describing Booth's Othello.

**3429** MAHONEY, ELLA V. Sketches of Tudor Hall and the Booth family
pp.59; ill.     DL★
Belair MD: Tudor Hall     1925

Author was a resident of Tudor Hall, once the Booth family estate, which she describes as well as offering biographical sketches of the Booths.

**3430** BRADFORD, GAMALIEL. As God made them: portraits of some nineteenth-century Americans
pp.xi, 295; pl. 8     L
Boston: Houghton Mifflin     1929

Includes an essay, with portrait, on Edwin Booth, emphasizing his personality rather than his acting ability.

**3431** GOODALE, KATHERINE [= Molony, Kitty]. Behind the scenes with Edwin Booth
pp.xiv, 328; pl. 12     M
Boston: Houghton Mifflin     1931

Author toured with Booth. Foreword by Minnie Maddern Fiske.

**3432** LOCKRIDGE, RICHARD. Darling of misfortune: Edwin Booth 1833-1893
pp.xi, 358; pl. 8     M
NY: Century     1932

**3433** ROYLE, EDWIN M. Edwin Booth as I knew him
pp.36; front.     M
NY: The Players     1933

**3434** SKINNER, OTIS. The last tragedian: Booth tells his own story...with illustrations
pp.xii, 213; pl. 11     M
NY: Dodd, Mead     1939

Biography largely derived from Booth's letters.

**3435** RUGGLES, ELEANOR. Prince of players; Edwin Booth
pp.xii, 401; pl.5     M
NY: W. W. Norton     1953

**3436** POWER-WATERS, ALMA. The story of the young Edwin Booth
pp.192; ill.     DL★
NY: E. P. Dutton     1955

Intended for children. Foreword by Eva Le Gallienne.

**3437** BECK, MARTHA R. A comparative study of the prompt copies of Hamlet used by Garrick, Booth and Irving
Ann Arbor: U. of Michigan (PhD)     1956

**3438** HONAKER, GERALD L. Edwin Booth, producer: a study of four productions at Booth's Theatre. *Romeo and Juliet*, *Hamlet*, *Richelieu*, and *Julius Caesar*
Bloomington: Indiana U. (PhD)     1969

**3439** KIMMEL, STANLEY. The mad Booths of Maryland: second revised and enlarged edition
pp.vi, 418; ill. in text; pl. 27     M
NY: Dover     1969

First published Indianapolis: Bobbs-Merrill, 1940.

**3440** OGGEL, LYNWOOD T. Edwin Booth and America's concept of Shakespearean tragedy
Madison: U. of Wisconsin (PhD)     1969

**3441** SHATTUCK, CHARLES H. The Hamlet of Edwin Booth
pp.xxvii, 321; pl. 11     M
Urbana: U. of Illinois P.     1969

**3442** ZACEK, DENNIS C. Acting techniques of Edwin Booth
Evanston: Northwestern U. (PhD)     1969

**3443** MORAY, JOHN S. Booth's Richelieu reviewed. This remarkable critical and historical essay on Edwin Booth's representation of Bulwer's great play originally appeared in *The Season* of January 14, 1871
pp.ii, 14     MH
NY: Saxton Torrey/ *Season* P.     1971
A blistering attack on Booth's acting, direction and, with few exceptions, his company.

**3444** WATERMEIER, DANIEL J. (Ed.). Between actor and critic: selected letters of Edwin Booth and William Winter
pp.ix, 329; pl. 6     M
Princeton: U. P.     1971

**3445** SOLIDAY, JOHN C. The 'Joint Stars' tours of Edwin Booth and Lawrence Barrett
Minneapolis: U. of Minnesota (PhD)     1974

**3446** COMMERET, LORRAINE M. Edwin Booth's German tour, 1883
Urbana-Champaign: U. of Illinois (PhD)     1980

**3447** LeCASSE, DONALD E. Edwin Booth: theatre manager
East Lansing: Michigan State U. (PhD)     1980

**3448** OGGEL, L. TERRY (Ed.). The letters and notebooks of Mary Devlin Booth
pp.xxxiv, 166; front., pl.2     L
NY: Greenwood P.     1987

**3449** WATERMEIER, DANIEL J. (Ed.). Edwin Booth's performances: the Mary Isabella Stone commentaries...with a foreword by Charles H. Shattuck
pp.xx, 220; ill. in text     M
Ann Arbor MI: UMI Research P.     1990
Stone's commentaries, in the Harvard Theatre Collection, substantial on Booth's Hamlet, less so on his Othello and Iago, and sketchy on his Lear, provide analysis and evaluation of the actor's approach and achievement.

### Booth, John Wilkes
### (1839-1865)
### Actor

**3450** DEVERE, PAUL. The flight of J. Wilkes Booth
pp.8     MH
NY: [For the author?]     [19-?]

**3451** HACO, DION. John Wilkes Booth, the assassinator of President Lincoln
pp.(ii), 16-102     MH
NY: T. R. Dawley     1865

Popularized account of the assassination.

**3452** POORE, BEN P. (Ed.). The conspiracy trial for the murder of the president and the attempt to overthrow the government by the assassination of its principal officers
pp.552     DL★
Boston: J. E. Tilton     1865

**3453** TOWNSEND, GEORGE A. The life, crime, and capture of John Wilkes Booth, with a full sketch of the conspiracy of which he was the leader, and the pursuit, trial, and execution of his accomplices
pp.iv, 79; ill.     DL★
NY: Dick & Fitzgerald     1865
An enlarged reissue. First published NY earlier in the same year. Comprises articles first written for the New York *World*.

**3454** THE ASSASSINATION of Abraham Lincoln and the attempted assassination of W. H. Seward
pp.xxxiv, 717; front.     MH
Washington DC: Government Printing Office     1866
Issued by the U. S. Department of State.

**3455** THE GREAT CONSPIRACY. A book of absorbing interest! Startling developments. Eminent persons implicated. Full secret of the assassination plot. John H. Surratt and his mother with biographical sketches of Junius Brutus Booth and John Wilkes Booth and the life & extraordinary adventures of John H. Surratt, the conspirator
pp.(3), 20-201; pl. 15     L
Philadelphia: Barclay     1866

**3456** HACO, DION (Ed.). The private journal and diary of John H. Surratt, the conspirator
pp.ii, 104     L
NY: Frederic A. Brady     1866
Includes references to John Wilkes Booth.

**3457** HARRIS, T. M. Assassination of Lincoln: a history of the great conspiracy. Trial of the conspirators by a military commission and a review of the trial of John H. Surratt
pp.419; front., pl. 9     L
Boston: American Citizen     1892

**3458** JONES, THOMAS A. J. Wilkes Booth: an account of his sojourn in Southern Maryland after the assassination of Abraham Lincoln, his passage across the Potomac, and his death in Virginia by...the only living man who can tell the story
pp.126; ill. in text     MH
Chicago: Laird & Lee     1893
The author claims to have offered assistance to the fugitive Booth for which he was imprisoned.

**3459** BATES, FINIS L. The escape and suicide of John Wilkes Booth, or the first true account of Lincoln's assassination, containing a complete confession by Booth many years after the crime, giving in full detail the plans, plot and intrigue of the conspirators, and the treachery of Andrew Johnson, then Vice-President of the United States, written for the correction of history
pp.viii, 309; pl. 16     MH
Memphis TN: Historical Publishing     1907

Advances the theory that J. W. Booth assumed the aliases, first John St Helen to whom the author was attorney in the 1870s, later David E. George, and in the latter identity took his own life in 1903. An unconvincing thesis.

**3460** BABCOCK, MRS BERNIE. Booth and the spirit of Lincoln: a story of a living dead man
pp.320 DL★
Philadelphia: J. B. Lippincott 1925

**3461** HART, F. W. The assassination of the President
pp.8 MH
[California]: [For the author] 1926
Off-print of the final chapter of Col. Hart's book, *Abraham Lincoln the great commoner, the sublime emancipator.*

**3462** WILSON, FRANCIS. John Wilkes Booth: fact and fiction of Lincoln's assassination
pp.xv, 322; ill. DL★
Boston: Houghton Mifflin 1929

**3463** FERGUSON, W. J. I saw Booth shoot Lincoln
pp.v, 63; pl. 8 MH
Boston: Houghton Mifflin 1930
Author was call-boy at Ford's Theatre. He played in *Our American Cousin* and was in the wings at the moment of the assassination.

**3464** FORRESTER, IZOLA. This one mad act: the unknown story of John Wilkes Booth and his family
pp.xii, 500; pl. 16 M
Boston: Hale, Cushman 1937

**3465** CLARKE, ASIA B. The unlocked book: a memoir of John Wilkes Booth by his sister...with a foreword by Eleanor Farjeon
pp.199; front., pl 15 M
London: Faber 1938
Addenda provide family letters and brief memoirs by other acquaintances, including Surrat.

**3466** STERN, PHILIP VAN D. The man who killed Lincoln: the story of John Wilkes Booth and his part in the assassination
pp.vii, 408; pl. 5 M
NY: LGA 1939

**3467** BRYAN, GEORGE S. The great American myth
pp.xii, 436; ill. in text, pl. 12 L
NY: Carrick & Evans 1940
An attempt to de-mythologize Lincoln's assassination and the fate of John Wilkes Booth.

**3468** MILLER, ERNEST C. John Wilkes Booth, oilman: a previously unknown part of the assassin's life now told from newly discovered material
pp.78; pl. 4 L
NY: Exposition P. 1947
An account of Booth's involvement, c. 1864, with 'The Dramatic Oil Company', Franklin, Venango Co., PA, based substantially on notes left by Louis J. Mackey.

**3469** BISHOP, JIM. The day Lincoln was shot: with illustrations selected and arranged by Stefan Lorant
pp.vi, 264; pl. 4, 1 folding map O
London: Weidenfeld and Nicholson 1955

A detailed reconstruction.

**3470** GRAY, CLAYTON. Conspiracy in Canada
pp.145; ill. in text MH
Montreal: L'Atelier P. 1957
Events involving John Wilkes Booth in Canada, prior to the assassination of Lincoln.

**3471** REUTER, WILLIAM L. The king can do no wrong
Unpaginated MH
NY: Pageant P. 1958
The capture of John Wilkes Booth, mainly in the words of Col. E. J. Conger, derived from an unpublished stenographed transcript.

**3472** ROSCOE, THEODORE. The web of conspiracy: the complete story of the men who murdered Abraham Lincoln
pp.xv, 562; pl. 24 MH
Englewood Cliffs NJ: Prentice-Hall 1959

**3473** BORRESON, RALPH. When Lincoln died
pp.231; ill. in text MH
Ny: Appleton-Century 1965

**3474** FOWLER, ROBERT H. Album of the Lincoln murder: illustrating how it was planned, committed and avenged
pp.64; ill. in text MH
Harrisburg PA: Historical Times 1965

**3475** COTTRELL, JOHN. Anatomy of an assassination
pp.260; front., ill. in text MH
NY: Funk & Wagnalls 1966

**3476** COLEMAN, JOHN W. Assassination of President Lincoln and the capture of John Wilkes Booth
pp.10; front. DL★
Lexington: For the author 1969
Text of speech before the Chevy Chase Coffee Club, Lexington, Fenruary 10, 1969.

**3477** JORDAN, JAN. Dim the flaring lamps: a novel of the life of John Wilkes Booth
pp.vi, 282 DL★
Englewood Cliffs NJ: Prentice-Hall 1972
Claims to be based on research into actual events.

**3478** NASH, JAY R. Bloodletters and bad men
pp.640; ill. DL★
NY: M. Evans 1973
Includes material on John Wilkes Booth.

**3479** LEONARDI, DELL. The reincarnation of John Wilkes Booth: a case study in hypnotic regression
pp.180 DL★
Old Greenwich CT: Devin-Adair 1975

**3480** WEICHMAN, LOUIS J. A true history of the assassination and of the conspiracy of 1865 edited by Floyd E. Risvold
pp.xxxii, 492, xvi; pl. 8 MH
NY: Alfred A. Knopf 1975

**3481** STARKEY, LARRY. Wilkes Booth came to Washington
pp.xiii, 209; map L
NY: Random House 1976

Reconstruction of the Lincoln assassination.

**3482** GUTMAN, RICHARD J. & GUTMAN, KELLIE O. John Wilkes Booth himself
pp.88; ill. in text M
Dover DE: Hired Hand P. 1979

A study of the known photographs of J. W. Booth.

**3483** WITHERS, NAN W. The acting style and career of John Wilkes Booth
Madison: U. of Wisconsin (PhD) 1980

**3484** BOOTH, JOHN N. Booths in history: their roots and lives, encounters and achievements
pp.xii, 231; ill. in text O
Los Alamitos CA: Ridgeway P. 1982

**3485** SAMPLES, GORDON. Lust for fame: the stage career of John Wilkes Booth
pp.xiv, 238; ill. in text M
Jefferson NC: McFarlane 1982

**3486** RECK, W. EMERSON. Abraham Lincoln: his last 24 hours
pp.vii, 232; ill. in text L
Jefferson: McFarland 1987

A reconstruction. Includes a substantial bibliography.

**3487** KINCAID, ARTHUR (Ed.). John Wilkes Booth, actor: the proceedings of a conference weekend in Bel Air, Maryland, May 1988
pp.viii, 73 M
North Leigh, Oxon: For the editor 1989

Includes Louis A. Rachow: *Promptbooks as historical resources for theatre study of the 1860s*; Don B. Wilmeth: *The American theatre in transition*; Gayle Harris: *John Ford's theatre*.

### Booth, Junius Brutus, Jr.
### (1821-1883)
### Actor-manager

**3488** HOLMES, SUSAN C. Junius Brutus Booth, Jr.: a pioneer actor-manager of the California stage
San Jose CA: State U. (MA) 1971

### Booth, Junius Brutus
### (1796-1852)
### Actor

**3489** MEMOIRS OF JUNIUS BRUTUS BOOTH, from his birth to the present time; with an appendix, containing original letters...and copious extracts from the journal kept by Mr. Booth during his theatrical tour on the continent
pp. 80; front. L
London: Chapple, Miller, Rowden & E. Wilson 1817

There are no pages numbered 33-36 and 45-48.

**3490** MEMOIRS OF THE LIFE OF Mr BOOTH, containing a true statement of all the circumstances attending his engagements at the rival theatres, with a few remarks upon his conduct, by an old actor
pp.27 MB
[London]: T. Keys [1817]

**3491** MIDLESEX TO WIT. James Salter...maketh oath...
bs MH
London: E. Macleish, printer [1817]

Affidavit sworn 25 February in Booth's defence after his failure to appear with Edmund Kean at Drury Lane on 22 February, from which occasion stem all the 1817 pamphlets.

**3492** Mr BOOTH. Covent Garden Theatre. Monday Feb. 24
bs DFO
London: E. Macleish (printer) [1817]

Justifies the proprietors of Covent Garden in the dispute with Drury Lane, over the employment of Booth.

**3493** Mr BOOTH. The sub-committee of Drury Lane Theatre, consisting of five gentlemen...
bs MH
London: E. Macleish, printer [1817]

With a copy of a letter from Thomas Harris to Douglas Kinnaird, a member of the sub-committee, 27 February.

**3494** Mr BOOTH. Theatre Royal, Drury-Lane
bs DFo
London: Lowndes, printer 1817

Dated 27 February 1817.

**3495** Mr BOOTH's appeal to the public
bs DFO
London: E. Maclesh, printer 1817

**3496** MR. BOOTH. Covent Garden Theatre. Monday Feb. 24
bs DFO
London: E. Macleish (printer) [1817]

Justifies the proprietors of Covent Garden in their dispute with Drury Lane, over the employment of Booth.

**3497** ORIGINAL MEMOIR and portrait of Mr. Booth. Presented, gratis, to the purchasers of *Bell's Original Weekly Dispatch* [issue of 9 March]
bs; ill. in text MH
[London]: Hay & Turner, printers 1817

**3498** THEATRE ROYAL, COVENT GARDEN. Mr. Booth
bs DFO
London: E. Macleish, printer [1817]

Justification of Covent Garden proprietors.

**3499** THEATRICAL SQUABBLES, or a Booth in Covent Garden
bs; ill. in text MH
London: Jno. Green [1817]

A street ballad.

**3500** TO MR. JUNIUS BRUTUS BOOTH from a lover of truth
bs DFo
[London]: 1817

**3501** THE ACTOR: or, a peep behind the curtain: being passages in the lives of Booth and some of his contemporaries
pp.xi, 180 M
NY: W. H. Graham 1846

**3502** [CLARKE, ASIA B.]. Booth memorials. Passages, incidents, and anecdotes in the life of Junius Brutus Booth (the elder) by his daughter
pp.184; front. M
NY: Carleton 1866

## 8.4. INDIVIDUAL

**3503** GOULD, THOMAS R. The tragedian; an essay on the histrionic genius of Junius Brutus Booth
pp.v, 190; front.                                                     M
NY: Hurd & Houghton                                              1868

**3504** SEILHAMER, GEORGE O. Junius Brutus Booth; the player and his people. Introductory...in twelve parts - Part 1
pp.i. 40; front.                                                    MH
NY: Alvin Perry                                                      1881

No more published. A lengthy statement on the title page announced the intention to create 'a picture of the epoch...rather than a biography of the tragedian...'

**3505** CLARKE, ASIA B. The elder and the younger Booth
pp.vii, 194; pl. 7 (1 folding)                                       M
Boston: James R. Osgood                                           1882

**3506** SKINNER, OTIS. Mad folk of the theatre: ten studies in temperament
pp.297; pl. 12                                                       M
Indianapolis: Bobbs-Merrill                                       1928

A chapter on Junius Brutus Booth.

**3507** MATTHEWS, BRANDER (Ed.). Papers on acting
pp.viii, 312                                                         M
NY: Hill & Wang                                                    1958

Preface by Henry W. Wells. Includes the first printing of Edwin Booth: *Edmund Kean and Junius Brutus Booth*.

**3508** ROMAN, LISBETH J. The acting style and career of Junius Brutus Booth
Urbana-Champaign: U. of Illinois (PhD)              1968

### Bowman, Laura
### (1881-1957)
### Actress

**3509** ANTOINE, LE ROI. Achievement: the life of Laura Bowman
pp.439; pl. 4                                                       MH
NY: Pageant P.                                                      1961

A commemoration 'of the negro in the theatre', written in first person as though autobiography.

### Brady, Alice
### (1892-1939)
### Actress

**3510** LANG, WILLIAM A. The career of Alice Brady, stage and screen actress
Urbaba-Champaign: U. of Illinois (PhD)              1971

### Brady, William Aloysius
### (1863-1950)
### Producer

**3511** BRADY, WILLIAM A. The fighting man
pp.v, 227; pl. 17                                                    L
Indianapolis: Bobbs-Merrill                                       1916

Includes information on the author's early theatre experience.

**3512** BRADY, WILLIAM A. Showman [autobiography]
pp.ii, 278; pl. 8                                                    M
NY: E. P. Dutton                                                   1937

**3513** WILKER, LAWRENCE J. The theatrical business practices of William A. Brady
Urbana-Champaign: U. of Illinois (PhD)              1973

**3514** HAGLER, NEVIS E. William A. Brady: theatre entrepreneur
Gainsville: U. of Florida (PhD)                           1975

### Bragdon, Claude
### (1866-1946)
### Designer

**3515** BRAGDON, CLAUDE. Merely players
pp.xv, 216; pl. 8                                                    M
NY: Alfred A. Knopf                                               1929

Includes essays on the one-night stand, and clowns and clowning.

**3516** BRAGDON, CLAUDE. The frozen fountain: being essays on architecture, and the art of design in space
pp.ix, 125; ill. in text                                             L
NY: Alfred A. Knopf                                               1932

Illustrations include examples of author's designs for Walter Hampden's *Othello*, *Cyrano*.

**3517** BRAGDON, CLAUDE. The secret springs: an autobiography
pp.vii, 368, vi; pl. 8                                               M
London: Andrew Dakers                                          1938

**3518** SIEGFRIED, DAVID A. Claude Bragdon. Artist-in-the-theatre
Urbana-Champaign: U. of Illinois (PhD)              1979

### Brando, Marlon
### (1924-)
### Actor

**3519** CAREY, GARY. Brando !
pp.vii, 278; pl. 11                                                 MH
NY: Pocket Books                                                 1973

**3520** MORELLA, JOE & EPSTEIN, EDWARD Z. Brando: the unauthorized biography
pp.248; ill. in text                                                MB
NY: Crown                                                              1973

**3521** OFFER, RON. Brando
pp.xv, 222; pl. 11                                                 MB
Chicago: Henry Regnery                                        1973

**3522** THOMAS, BOB. Brando: portrait of the rebel as an artist
pp.x, 296; pl. 8                                                     O
NY: W. H. Allen                                                    1973

**3523** SHIPMAN, DAVID. Brando
pp.127; ill. in text                                                MB
London: Macmillan                                                1974

**3524** FIORE, CARLO. The Brando I knew: the untold story of Brando's private life
pp.207; pl. 16                                                       O
London: Hart Davis                                                1975

**3525** HIGHAM, CHARLES. Brando: the unauthorised biography
pp.413; pl. 8                                                        L
NY: Sidgwick and Jackson                                      1987

## Broun, Heywood Campbell
## (1888-1939)
## Critic

**3526** LEWIS, JOHN L. et al. Heywood Broun as he seemed to us
pp.48; front. MH
NY: Random House 1940

Printed for the Newspaper Guild of New York. A stenographic record of the Heywood Broun Memorial meeting, February 12, 1940. Biography and tributes. Contributors include Edward G. Robinson, Edward McNamara, Edna Ferber.

**3527** BROUN, HEYWOOD. Collected edition of Heywood Broun
pp.xxx, 561 MH
NY: Harcourt, Brace 1941

Author was dramatic editor of *Vanity Fair* and subsequently of the *New York World*, and a columnist for the *New York World Telegram*. The collected writings, 1908-39, contain many essays and articles on theatre topics.

**3528** KRAMER, DALE. Heywood Broun: a biographical portrait
pp.xi, 316; front., pl. 4 L
NY: A. A. Wyn 1949

**3529** BROUN, HEYWOOD. A studied madness [autobiography]
pp.vi, 298 DL★
Garden City: Doubleday 1965

## Brown, Gilmor
## (1887?-1960)
## Manager

**3530** GREEN, HARRIET L. Gilmor Brown, portrait of a man - and an idea
pp.[21]; ill. in text, front. M
Pasadena CA: Burns Printing 1933

Founder of the Pasadena Community Playhouse.

**3531** ALTENBERG, ROGER M. A historical study of Gilmor Brown's Fairoaks Playbox, 1924-1927
Los Angeles: U. of Southern California (PhD) 1964

## Brown, Joe E.
## [Brown, Joseph Evans]
## (1892-1973)
## Comedian

**3532** BROWN, JOE E. & HANCOCK, RALPH. Laughter is a wonderful thing [autobiography]
pp.viii, 312; pl. 24 MH
NY: A. S. Barnes 1956

## Brown, John Mason
## (1900-1969)
## Critic

**3533** BROWN, JOHN M. Insides out: being the saga of a drama critic who attended his own opening
pp.128; ill. in text M
London: Herbert Jenkins [1942]

Autobiography, humorously recounting experience of a surgical operation. Illustrations by Hirschfeld.

**3534** STEVENS, GEORGE. Speak for yourself, John. The life of John Mason Brown, with some of his letters and many of his opinions
pp.xv, 308; ill. in text M
NY: Viking P. 1974

**3535** MYUNG, INN S. A dramatic and theatrical criticism of John Mason Brown
Ann Arbor: U. of Michigan (PhD) 1988

## Browne, Maurice
## (1881-1955)
## Producer, manager

**3536** BROWNE, MAURICE. Road from Delavan
pp.39 M
London: Cyril Edwards 1947

An autobiographical poem, 1912-1942. Browne deemed it a more revealing autobiography than *Too late to lament*, and notes that it sold only four copies.

**3537** BROWNE, MAURICE. Too late to lament. An autobiography
pp.403; front. M
London: Victor Gollancz 1955

**3538** DUKORE, BERNARD F. Maurice Browne and the Chicago little theatre
Urbana: U. of Illinois (PhD) 1957

**3539** CHOPCIAN, KENDRA A. An analysis of Maurice Browne's directing theories and practices with the Chicago Little Theatre
Ann Arbor: U. of Michigan (PhD) 1989

## Brustein, Robert Sanford
## (1927-)
## Critic, artistic director

**3540** BRUSTEIN, ROBERT. Making scenes: a personal history of the turbulent years at Yale 1966-1979
pp.ix, 342; pl. 8 M
NY: Random House 1981

Author founded Yale Repertory Theatre; in 1980 left Yale for Harvard.

## Brynner, Yul
## (1915?-1985)
## Actor

**3541** BRYNNER, ROCK. Yul: the man who would be king. A memoir
pp.xiii, 263; front., pl. 12 L
London: Collins 1989

## Burke, Billie
## [Ziegfeld, Mrs Flo]
## (1885-1970)
## Actress

**3542** BURKE, BILLIE with SHIPP, CAMERON. With a feather on my nose. With a foreword by Ivor Novello [autobiography]
pp.x, 261; pl. 20 M
NY: Appleton Century 1949

**3543** BURKE, BILLIE with SHIPP, CAMERON. With powder on my nose [autobiography]
pp.249; ill. in text M
NY: Coward McCann 1959

### Burke, Joseph
### (1818-1902)
### Actor, musician

**3544** MEMOIR OF MASTER BURKE the Irish Roscius who is now playing with distinguished success, at the Tremont Theatre, in this city
pp.8     MH
Boston: 1831     1831

Reprinted from the *Dramatic Magazine* and the *London Atlas*. Also contains a reprint of a sketch of Burke written by Sheridan Knowles, c. 1818.

### Burton, Philip
### (1905-)
### Actor, director

**3545** BURTON, PHILIP. Early doors: my life and the theatre. With a preface by Agnes de Mille [autobiography]
pp.xv, 238; front., pl. 12     M
NY: Dial P.     1969

### Burton, William Evans
### (1804-1860)
### Actor

**3546** CATALOGUE, of the theatrical and miscellaneous library of the late William E. Burton, the distinguished comedian comprising an immense assemblage of books relating to the stage...
pp.viii, 463; front.     M
NY: J. Sabin     1860

**3547** KEESE, WILLIAM L. William E. Burton, actor, author and manager: a sketch of his career with recollections of his performances
pp.xi, 230; pl. 7     M
NY: G. P. Putnam's Sons     1885

**3548** KEESE, WILLIAM L. William E. Burton, a sketch of his life other than that of actor, with glimpses of his home life, and extracts from his theatrical journal
pp.x, 56; ill. in text     M
NY: Dunlap Society     1891

**3549** JOHNSON, RUE C. The theatrical career of William E. Burton
Bloomington: Indiana U. (PhD)     1967

### Caldwell, James H.
### (1793-1863)
### Manager, actor

**3550** HOSTETLER, PAUL S. James H. Caldwell, theatre manager
Baton Rouge: Louisiana State U. (PhD)     1964
New Orleans theatres.

### Calhoun, Eleanor Hulda
### (1862-1957)
### Actress

**3551** LAZAROVIC-HREBELIANOVIC, PRINCESS [= Calhoun, Eleanor]. Pleasures and palaces [autobiography]
pp.x,360; pl. 25     L
NY: Century     1915

### Cantor, Eddie
### [Itzkowitz, Isidore]
### (1892-1964)
### Comedian

**3552** CANTOR, EDDIE. Caught short ! A saga of wailing Wall Street
pp.45; ill     DL★
NY: Simon and Schuster     1929
Humorous reminiscence.

**3553** CANTOR, EDDIE. Between the acts
pp.xii     DL★
NY: Simon and Schuster     1930

**3554** CANTOR, EDDIE & FREEDMAN, DAVID. Your next president
pp.52; ill.     DL★
NY: R. Long & R. R. Smith     1930

### Carnovsky, Morris
### (1897-)
### Actor

**3555** BERKSON, MICHAEL A. Morris Carnovsky: actor and teacher
Urbana-Champaign: U. of Illinois (PhD)     1975

### Carter, Mrs Leslie
### [Dudley, Caroline Louise]
### (1862-1937)
### Actress

**3556** MRS LESLIE CARTER as Zaza: with a history of her stage career, and the successful production of the play
ll.8     ★
NY: [For the theatre]     1899

**3557** MRS LESLIE CARTER in David Belasco's *Du Barry* with portraits of Mrs Carter by John Cecil Clay together with [a] portrait of David Belasco and numerous engravings...
pp.59; ill. in text     MH
NY: Frederick A. Stopes     1902

Readers are also referred to the autobiographical *Portrait of a lady with red hair...* published in sections in *Liberty* magazine between January and March, 1927. (Unexamined).

**3558** HARPER, CHARLES H. Mrs Leslie Carter: her life and acting career
Lincoln: U. of Nebraska (PhD)     1978

### Cassidy, Claudia
### (1905?-)
### Critic

**3559** SULLIVAN, GERALD E. Claudia Cassidy and American theatre criticism
Minneapolis: U. of Minnesota (PhD)     1968

**3560** CASEY, J. C. Theatrical revision of Claudia Cassidy
College Park: U. of Maryland (PhD)     1988

### Cather, Willa Sibert
### (1876-1947)
### Novelist, critic

**3561** SLOTE, BERNICE (Ed.). The kingdom of art: Willa Cather's first principles and critical statements 1893-1896
pp.xiv, 489; pl. 4     L
Lincoln: U. of Nebraska P.     1966

Introduction and a selection of critical writings including a section on the drama, and other articles commenting on actors and entertainers, e.g. Richard Mansfield, Nat C. Goodwin.

**3562** HARPER, CHARLES H. The dramatic criticism of Willa Cather from 1893 to 1900
Lincoln: U. of Nebraska (MA)      1967

### Chaikin, Joseph
### (1935-)
### Director

**3563** CHAIKIN, JOSEPH. The presence of the actor
pp.xiii, 162; ill. in text      MH
NY: Atheneum      1972
Autobiography with substantial reference to the Open Theatre.

**3564** BLUMENTHAL, EILEEN. Joseph Chaikin. Exploring at the boundaries of theater
pp.xvi, 261; ill. in text      P
Cambridge: U. P.      1984

**3565** HERMAN, RICHARD J. Joseph Chaikin: thematic investigations of life and death
Lubbock: Texas Tech U. (PhD)      1986

### Chamberlain, Richard
### (1935-)
### Actor

**3566** SIEGEL, BARBARA & SIEGEL, SCOTT. Richard Chamberlain: an actor's life
pp.x, 174; pl. 4      L
Sevenoaks, Kent: New English Library      1989
Includes stage work in US and UK.

### Chapman, Caroline
### (1818-1876)
### Actress

**3567** ROGERS, VIRGINIA M. Caroline Chapman, American actress: her contributions to the San Francisco stage
Stanford: U. (MA)      1940

### Charles, James S.
### (1808-1865)
### Actor

**3568** PARSONS, BILLY D. The contributions of James S. Charles to the professional and non-professional theatre in Louisiana
Baton Rouge: Louisiana State U. (MA)      1958

### Chase, Ilka
### (1905-1978)
### Actress

**3569** CHASE, ILKA. Past imperfect [autobiography]
pp.ix, 278      M
NY: Doubleday, Doran      1942

**3570** CHASE, ILKA. Free admission [memoirs]
pp.272      L
London: W. H. Allen      [1948]
Published Garden City: Doubleday.

**3571** CHASE, ILKA. The Carthagenian rose, with drawings by Mircea Vasiliu
pp.430; ill. in text      L
London: W. H. Allen      1962

First published Garden City: Doubleday, 1961. Travels around the world.

### Chekhov, Michael Alexandrovitch
### (1891-1955)
### Director

**3572** KINDELAN, NANCY A. The theatre of inspiration: an analysis of the acting theories of Michael Chekhov
Madison: U. of Wisconsin (PhD)      1977

**3573** BLACK, LENDLEY C. Mikhail Chekhov as actor, director, and teacher
pp.xiv, 116      M
Ann Arbor: UMI Research P.      1987
In part derived from taped lectures to Hollywood Society of Film Actors, 1955.

### Cheney, Sheldon Warren
### (1886-1980)
### Editor, writer

**3574** HOPPER, ARTHUR B. Sheldon Cheney: spokesman for the new movement in the American theatre, 1914-1929
Bloomington: Indiana U. (PhD)      1969

### Clapp, Henry Austin
### (1841-1904)
### Critic, writer

**3575** CLAPP, HENRY A. Reminiscences of a dramatic critic with an essay on the art of Henry Irving
pp.ix, 241; pl. 6      M
Boston: Houghton, Mifflin      1902
Includes material on the Boston Museum, minstrelsy, Edwin Booth.

**3576** MORRIS, WILLIAM C. The theatrical writings of Henry Austin Clapp
Urbana-Champaign: U. of Illinois (PhD)      1973

### Clark, Marguerite
### (1887-1940)
### Actress

**3577** NUNN, CURTIS. Marguerite Clark: America's darling of Broadway and the silent screen
pp.viii, 189; ill. in text      M
Fort Worth: Texas Christian U.P.      1981

### Clarke, John Sleeper
### (1833-1893)
### Actor

**3578** SKETCH of the life of Mr John S. Clarke, comedian
pp.8; caricature portrait on wrapper      MB
[London]: Printed by J. W. Last      [1872]
John Wilkes. Booth's brother-in-law, Clarke managed the Walnut Street Theatre in Philadelphia. Later settled in London and became manager of the Charing Cross Theatre.

**3579** STUART, WILLIAM. Sketches and reminiscences of John S. Clarke, comedian, with the journalistic and public opinions of America and Great Britain
pp.24      MH
NY: [For the author?]      1881

Reprinted from *Lippincott's* 28, November, 1881.

**3580** A BIOGRAPHICAL SKETCH of Mr. John S. Clarke
pp.4    M
London: W. S. Johnson, printer    1882

### Clift, Montgomery
### (1920-1966)
### Actor

**3581** BOSWORTH, PATRICIA. Montgomery Clift
pp.xi, 433; pl. 16    L
NY: Bantam    1979
First published NY: Harcourt Brace Jovanovich, 1978. Biography. An appendix provides a theatre chronology.

### Clurman, Harold Edgar
### (1901-1980)
### Director, critic

**3582** BLAKELY, DON. Harold Clurman as theatrical director and critic: his philosophic, artistic, and critical theories
Detroit: Wayne State U. (PhD)    1968

**3583** CLURMAN, HAROLD. All people are famous: (instead of an autobiography)
pp.xvi, 327    M
NY: Harcourt Brace Jovanovich    1974

**3584** SWEET, BRUCE. The invisible director: the stage direction of Harold Clurman as witnessed by actors, stage managers, producers, playwrights and critics from three representative productions
NY: U. (PhD)    1981

### Coburn, Charles Douville
### (1877-1961)
### Actor

**3585** FREEMAN, BENJAMIN P. The stage career of Charles D. Coburn
New Orleans: Tulane U. (PhD)    1970

### Conried, Heinrich
### (1855-1909)
### Director, producer

**3586** MOSES, MONTROSE J. The life of Henry Conried
pp.xvii, 367; pl. 18    M
NY: Thomas Y. Crowell    1916
An important figure in late nineteenth century New York German theatre and later director of the Metropolitan Opera House.

### Cook, George Cram
### (1873-1924)
### Director, dramatist

**3587** GLASPELL, SUSAN (Ed.). Greek coins. Poems by George Cram Cook, with memorabilia by Floyd Dell, Edna Kenton and Susan Glaspell
pp.142; front    O
NY: Doran    1925
Includes recollection of the Wharf theatre in Provincetown and an account of Cook's last days in Greece.

**3588** GLASPELL, SUSAN. The road to the temple
pp.xii, 364    L
London: Ernest Benn    1928
First published NY: Stokes, 1926. The story of George Cram Cook by his wife.

**3589** SARLOS, ROBERT K. Jig Cook and The Provincetown players: theatre in ferment
pp.xii, 265; ill. in text    M
Amherst: U. of Massachusetts P.    1982

### Cooper, Thomas Abthorpe
### (1776-1849)
### Actor, manager

**3590** IRELAND, JOSEPH N. A memoir of the professional life of Thomas Abthorpe Cooper
pp.xiii, 102; ill. in text    M
NY: Dunlap Society    1888

**3591** ARANT, F. FAIRLIE. A biography of the actor Thomas Abthorpe Cooper
Minneapolis: U. of Minnesota (PhD)    1971

### Corbin, John
### (1870-1959)
### Critic

**3592** CLARK, DAVIS M. John Corbin: dramatic critic
Lincoln: U. of Nebraska (PhD)    1976

### Cornell, Katharine
### (1893-1974)
### Actress

**3593** MALVERN, GLADYS. Curtain going up! The story of Katharine Cornell. With a foreword by Katharine Cornell
pp.xi, 244    M
NY: Julian Messner    1943
Biography in form of a novel.

**3594** KATHARINE CORNELL: a gallery of stage portraits
pp.[20] inc. wrappers    M
NY: Printed by Artcraft    [c. 1930]
Captioned photographic portraits.

**3595** CORNELL, KATHARINE with SEDGWICK, RUTH W. I wanted to be an actress [autobiography]
pp.xviii, 361;.pl. 17    M
NY: Random House    1939

**3596** MOSS, LYNDA. An historical study of Katharine Cornell as an actress-producer: 1931-1960
Los Angeles: U. of Southern California (PhD)    1972

**3597** MOSEL, TAD & MACY, GERTRUDE. Leading lady: the world and theatre of Katharine Cornell...with a foreword by Martha Graham
pp.x, 534; ill. in text    M
Boston: Little, Brown    1978

### Corsaro, Frank
### (1924-)
### Director

**3598** CORSARO, FRANK. Maverick: a director's personal experience in opera and theater
pp.xvi, 318    M
NY: Vanguard P.    1978
Preface by Julius Rudel. Foreword by Lee Strasberg.

### Cosgrave, Luke
### [Maccosggain, Sean]
### (1862-1949)
### Actor

**3599** COSGRAVE, LUKE. Theater tonight
pp.245; pl. 8      M
Hollywood: House-Warven      1952
Travelling theatre in the American West in the early 20th century.

### Cotten, Joseph Cheshire
### (1905-)
### Actor

**3600** COTTEN, JOSEPH. Vanity will get you somewhere [autobiography]
vii, 235; pl. 16p.      MH
San Francisco: Mercury House      1987

### Count Joannes
### [né Jones, George]
### (1810-1879)
### Actor

**3601** MEMOIR OF GEORGE JONES, Esq., the American tragedian
     MB
[Stratford?]:      [1836]
Initialled 'L.C' at end. Issued when Jones was in Stratford/Avon to address the Royal Shaksperian Club, April 23, 1836.

### Cowell, Joe
### [Witchett, Joseph Hawkins]
### (1792-1863)
### Actor

**3602** COWELL, JOE. Thirty years passed among the players in England and America: interspersed with anecdotes and reminiscences of a variety of persons, directly or indirectly connected with the drama during the theatrical life of Joe Cowell, comedian. Written by himself
pp.103      M
NY: Harper & Brothers      1844
Part I - England. Part II - America. Continuously paginated but each part with discrete chapter sequence, i-xix, i-xxi respectively.

### Cox, Wallace
### (1924-1973)
### Actor

**3603** COX, WALLACE. My life as a small boy [autobiography]
pp.128; ill.      DL★
NY: Simon and Schuster      1961
Illustrated by the author.

### Crabtree, Lotta
### [Crabtree, Charlotte Mignon]
### (1847-1924)
### Actress

**3604** ROURKE, CONSTANCE. Troupers of the Gold Coast or the rise of Lotta Crabtree
pp.xvii, 262; pl. 11      M
NY: Harcourt, Brace      1928

**3605** BATES, HELEN M. Lotta's last season
pp.viii, 306; pl. 4      M
Brattleboro VT: For the author      1940
Effectively two books in one. The author played leads in Lotta Crabtree's company during her last season. Part two is titled *Shreds and patches: episodes of the stage of a bygone era* and comprises reminiscences.

**3606** JACKSON, PHYLLIS W. Golden footlights: the merry-making career of Lotta Crabtree
pp.310      ★
NY: Holiday House      1949
Fictionalized biography.

**3607** DEMPSEY, DAVID & BALDWIN, RAYMOND P. The triumphs and trials of Lotta Crabtree
pp.viii, 343; pl. 4      M
NY: William Morrow      1968

### Crafton, Allen
### (1890-1966)
### Director, playwright

**3608** GAFFNEY, PAUL J. Allen Crafton: American theatre pioneer
Laurence: U. of Kansas (PhD)      1979

### Crawford, Cheryl
### (1902-1986)
### Producer, director

**3609** CRAWFORD, CHERYL. One naked individual: my fifty years in the theatre
pp.xi, 275; pl. 8      M
Indianapolis: Bobbs-Merrill      1977
Author was co-founder of the Group Theatre and the Actors Studio, founder of the American Repertory Theatre, and Joint-General Director of ANTA play series.

**3610** CALDWELL, CAROLYN E. Cheryl Crawford: her contributions to the development of twentieth century American theatre
Ann Arbor: U. of Michigan (PhD)      1987

### Crisp, William Henry
### (1791-1861)
### Actor, manager

**3611** YEOMANS, GORDON A. The contributions of William Henry Crisp to the southern ante-bellum theatre [1850-1860]
Baton Rouge: Louisiana State U. (PhD)      1952

**3612** LEWIS, JIM G. The southern core of William Henry Crisp: actor-manager, 1844-1871
Austin: U. of Texas (PhD)      1981

### Cukor, George
### (1899-1983)
### Director

**3613** LAMBERT, GAVIN. On Cukor
pp.ix, 276; ill. in text      L
NY: G. P..Putnam's Sons      1972
Transcribed interviews, recorded in 1970.

### Cushman, Charlotte Saunders
### (1816-1876)
### Actress

**3614** CUSHMAN, HENRY W. A historical and biographical genealogy of the Cushmans: the descendants of Robert Cushman, the puritan, from the year 1617 to 1855

pp.666; front., pl. 30 L
Boston: Little, Brown 1855
pp.497-511 are devoted to Charlotte Cushman and include an engraved portrait.

**3615**  MISS CHARLOTTE CUSHMAN
bs. MH
Boston: Boston Daily Advertiser 1871
Tribute, dated Dec 6, issued as a supplement, December 9, 1871.

**3616**  WALKER, MRS D. Reminiscences of the life of the world-renowned Charlotte Cushman, compiled from various records by...her chosen medium: together with some of her spirit experiences, expressions of regret, etc. Dedicated to the world
pp.96; pl. 2 MB
Boston: William T. Penny 1876

**3617**  STEBBINS, EMMA (Ed.). Charlotte Cushman: her letters and memories of her life
pp.ix, 308; pl. 3 M
Boston: Houghton, Osgood 1878

**3618**  CLEMENT, CLARA E. Charlotte Cushman
pp.ix, 193; pl. 7 M
London: David Bogue [1882]
US edition published Boston: James R. Osgood, 1882, with author's name as Clara E. Waters.

**3619**  BARRETT, LAWRENCE. Charlotte Cushman, a lecture: with an appendix containing a letter from Joseph N. Ireland
pp.vi, 44; ill. in text M
NY: Dunlap Society 1889

**3620**  PRICE, WILLIAM T. A life of Charlotte Cushman
pp.v, 180, (xviii); front. MH
NT: Brentano's 1894

**3621**  CARR, CARMELIA (Ed.). Harriet Hosmer, letters and memories
pp.xiii, 377; front., pl. 30 L
London: John Lane, The Bodley Head 1913
Published NY: Moffat, Yard, 1913. Hosmer, the sculptress, was a close friend of Charlotte Cushman and makes frequent reference to her.

**3622**  YEATER, JAMES W. Charlotte Cushman, American actress
Urbana: U. of Illinois (PhD) 1959

**3623**  LEACH, JOSEPH. Bright particular star: the life and times of Charlotte Cushman
pp.xvi, 453; pl. 4 M
New Haven CT: Yale U. P. 1970

**3624**  MERRILL, LISA. Charlotte Cushman. American actress in the vanguard of new roles for women
NY: U. (PhD) 1985

### Dale, Alan
### [Cohen, Alfred J.]
### (1861-1928
### Critic

**3625**  OWEN, BRUCE B. The criticism of Alan Dale
Lawrence: U. of Kansas (PhD) 1966

### Dalrymple, Jean
### (1910-)
### Producer, director

**3626**  DALRYMPLE, JEAN. September child: the story of Jean Dalrymple by herself
pp.xvi, 318; pl. 8 M
NY: Dodd, Mead 1963
Author was director of New York City Center's light opera and drama companies.

### Daly, John Augustin
### (1838-1899)
### Manager, poducer, dramatist

**3627**  A CATALOGUE of rare books, original drawings...extra illustrated works and other interesting literary material chiefly from the library of the late Augustin Daly with many interesting and valuable additions from other sources...
pp.68 MH
NY: Geo D. Smith 1900
Includes some theatrical items. Smith, the bookseller, deprecates the quality of the auction catalogue (compiler, J. O. Wright).

**3628**  CATALOGUE of the valuable literary and art property gathered by the late Augustin Daly...
pp.xi, 381 MH
NY: American Art Association 1900
Part II, books. Includes a full description of the sumptuous extra illustrated *Records of the New York Stage* (Ireland, Joseph N. and Hagan, J. S. G.) created for Daly by A. Toedtberg. This auction catalogue was also issued by J. O. Wright in bound 4to, amplified by a price list.

**3629**  THE AUGUSTIN DALY collection of portraits of eminent men and women of the stage
pp.28; ill. in text MH
NY: Anderson Galleries 1912
Sale catalogue. 70 items.

**3630**  DALY, JOSEPH F. The life of Augustin Daly
pp.xi, 672; pl. 16 M
NY: Macmillan 1917

**3631**  FELHEIM, MARVIN. The theater of Augustin Daly: an account of the late nineteenth century American stage
pp.xv, 329; pl. 2 M
Cambridge MA: Harvard U. P. 1956

**3632**  MICHALAK, MARION V. The management of Augustin Daly's stock company 1869-1899
Bloomington: Indiana U. (PhD) 1961

**3633**  CUTLER, JEAN V. Realism in Augustin Daly's productions of contemporary plays
Urbana-Champaign: U. of Illinois (PhD) 1963

**3634**  GEORGES, CORWIN A. Augustin Daly's Shakespearean productions
Columbus: Ohio State U. (PhD) 1972

**3635**  ASERMELY, ALBERT A. Daly's initial decade in the American theatre, 1860-1869
NY: City U. (PhD) 1973

**3636**  VENTIMIGLIA, PETER J. The William Winter/Augustin Daly Shakespeare productions, 1885-1895
NY: Fordham U. (PhD) 1973

### Daly, John Augustin
(1838-1899)
Manager, producer, dramatist

**3637** [DITHMAR, EDWARD A.]. Memories of Daly's theatres with passing recollections of others including a record of plays and actors at the Fifth Avenue Theatre and Daly's Theatre 1869-95
pp.143: ill. in text     MB
[NY]: For the author     1896

Revised and enlarged version of Dithmar's *Memories of one theatre, with passing recollections of many others* which reached proof stage in the early 1890s but was not itself published. A final chapter on Augustin Daly is by John T. Smith.

### Daly, Peter C. Arnold
(1875-1927)
Actor, producer

**3638** GOLDSMITH, BERTHOLD H. Arnold Daly
pp.57     DL★
NY: James T. White     1927

**3639** PIERCE, GLENN Q. Arnold Daly's productions of plays by Bernard Shaw
Urbana: U. of Illinois (PhD)     1961

**3640** REED, RONALD M. The nature of the scenic practices in Daly's New York productions 1869-1899
Eugene: U. of Oregon (PhD)     1968

### Dandridge. Dorothy
(1922-1965)
Actress

**3641** MILLS, EARL. Dorothy Dandridge: a portrait in black
pp.248; ill.     DL★
Los Angeles: Holloway House     1970

### Davenport, Edward Loomis
(1815-1877)
Actor
### Davenport, Fanny
(1826-1891)
Actress

**3642** EDGETT, EDWIN F. Edward Loomis Davenport, a biography
pp.x, 145; pl. 10     MH
NY: Dunlap Society     1901

Based on a manuscript discovered among the papers of the late Fanny Davenport, though not by her. 265 copies.

**3643** REID, NORMAN M. Edward Loomis Davenport. A study in acting versatility
Ann Arbor: U. of Michigan (PhD)     1941

**3644** WHITLATCH, R. C. Fanny Davenport: actress and manager
Urbana: U. of Illinois (PhD)     1962

### Davidge, William Pleater
(1814-1888)
Actor

**3645** DAVIDGE, WILLIAM. Footlight flashes [autobiography]
pp.xii, 274; ill. in text     M
NY: American News     1866

### Davis, Bette
(1908-1989)
Actress

**3646** NOBLE, PETER. Bette Davis: a biography
pp.231; ill. in text     L
London: Skelton Robinson     [1948]

**3647** DAVIS, BETTE. The lonely life: an autobiography
pp.256; pl. 16     L
London: Macdonald     1962

**3648** VERMILYE, JERRY. Bette Davis
pp.159; ill.     DL★
NY: Pyramid     1973

### Day, Charles H.
(1842?-1907)
Showman

**3649** DAY, CHARLES H. Show life illustrated: its humors, adventure and romance
pp.31; ill.     DL★
NY: S. Booth     1873

### De Angelis, Thomas Jefferson
(1859-1933)
Actor

**3650** DE ANGELIS, JEFFERSON & HARLOW, ALVIN F. A vagabond trouper
pp.v, 325; pl. 11     M
NY: Harcourt Brace     1931

### De Bar, Benedict
(1812?-1877)
Actor-manager

**3651** HERBSTRUTH, GRANT M. Benedict De Bar and the Grand Opera House at St Louis, Missouri, from 1855 to 1879
Iowa City: U. of Iowa (PhD)     1954

**3652** NUGENT, BEATRICE. Benedict De Bar's management of the St Charles Theatre in New Orleans, Louisiana, 1853-1861
Baton Rouge: Louisiana State U. (MA)     1967

### De Mille, Cecil Blount
(1881-1959)
Director, producer

**3653** DeMILLE, CECIL B. The autobiography
pp.viii, 432; pl. 24     M
London: W. H. Allen     1960

Edited by Donald Hayne.

**3654** HIGHAM, CHARLES. Cecil B. De Mille
pp.xiv, 335; ill. in text     M
London: W. H. Allen     1974

First published NY: 1973.

**3655** EDWARDS, ANNE. The De Milles: an American family. Photographic editor Louise Kerz
pp.248; ill. in text     M
London: Collins     1988

Biography embracing Henry, William, Cecil B., Katherine and Agnes.

### De Wolfe, Elsie
### (1865-1950)
### Actress

3656  DE WOLFE, ELSIE.  After all [autobiography]
pp.x,253; pl.14  O
London: Heinemann  1935
Published NY: Harper.

3657  BEMELMANS. LUDWIG.  To the one I love the best
pp.223; pl. 2  O
London: Hamish Hamilton  1955
NY: Viking P.

### Dean, Julia
### (1830-1868)
### Actress

3658  MARGETTS, RALPH E.  A study of the theatrical career of Julia Dean Hayne
Salt Lake City: U. of Utah (PhD)  1959

### Deland, Lorin
### Manager

3659  DELAND, MARGARET.  Golden yesterdays [autobiography]
pp.v, 351  L
NY: Harper & Brothers  1941
Includes substantial account of Lorin Deland, sometime manager of the Castle Square Theatre, Boston and founder of the Wage-earners Theatre League.

### Dell, Floyd
### (1887-1969)

3660  DELL, FLOYD.  Homecoming; an autobiography
pp.xi, 368  O
NY: Kennikat P.  1969
Reissue. First published NY: Farrar, 1938.

### Derwent, Clarence
### (1884-1959)
### Actor

3661  DERWENT, CLARENCE.  The Derwent story: my first fifty years in the theatre in England and America
pp.ix, 304; pl. 16  M
NY: Henry Schuman  1953

### Dickinson, Anna Elizabeth
### (1842-1932)
### Actress

3662  CHESTER, GIRAUD.  Embattled maiden: the life of Anna Dickinson
pp.xi, 307; ill.  DL★
NY: G. P. Putnam's Sons  1951

### Dithmar, Edward Augustus
### (1854-1917)
### Critic

3663  LOUDON, GEORGE W.  The theatre criticism of Edward A. Dithmar: New York Times drama critic, 1884-1901
Lincoln: U. of Nebraska-Lincoln (PhD)  1981

### Doyle, Mary
### Actress

3664  DOYLE, MARY.  Life was like that [autobiography]
pp.vii, 256; pl. 8  M
Boston: Houghton Mifflin  1936

### Drake, Frances Ann
### [Denny, Mary Frances]
### (1797-1875)
### Actress, manager

3665  SWAIN, JAMES W.  Mrs Alexander Drake: a biographical study
New Orleans: Tulane U. (PhD)  1970
Proposes her as the first indigenous woman theatre manager and ranking actress.

### Draper, Ruth
### (1884-1956)
### Solo actress

3666  ZABEL, MORTON D. (Ed.).  The art of Ruth Draper: her dramas and characters. With a memoir
pp.viii, 396; pl. 17  M
London: Oxford U. P.  1960

3667  WARREN, NEILLA (Ed.).  The letters of Ruth Draper 1920-1956: a self-portrait of a great actress. Foreword by John Gielgud
pp.xxii, 362  M
London: Hamish Hamilton  1979

### Dressler, Marie
### [Koerber, Leila Marie]
### (1869-1934)
### Actress

3668  DRESSLER, MARIE.  The eminent American comedienne Marie Dressler in the life story of an ugly duckling, an autobiographical fragment in several parts illustrated with many pleasing scenes from former triumphs and from private life...
pp.xi, 234; ill. in text, pl. 29  L
London: Hutchinson  [1925]
Published NY: McBride, 1924.

3669  DRESSLER, MARIE & HARRINGTON, MILDRED.  My own story
pp.256; pl. 8  M
London: Hurst & Blackett  1935
Foreword by Will Rogers.

3670  RAIDER, ROBERTA.  A descriptive study of the acting of Marie Dressler
Ann Arbor: U. of Michigan (PhD)  1970

### Drew, John
### (1853-1927)
### Actor

3671  DITHMAR, EDWARD A.  John Drew
pp.vi, 137; pl. 25  M
NY: Frederick A. Stokes  1900

3672  DREW, JOHN.  My years on the stage. With a foreword by Booth Tarkington
pp.xii, 242; ill. in text, pl. 42  M
NY: E. P. Dutton  1922

**3673** WOOD, PEGGY. A splendid gypsy: John Drew
pp.64 M
NY: E. P. Dutton 1928
A record of Drew's last grand tour of the US with A. W. Pinero's *Trelawny of the Wells* in 1927.

### Drew, Mrs John
### [Lane, Louisa]
### (1820-1897)
### Actress

**3674** [DREW, MRS JOHN]. Autobiographical sketch of Mrs John Drew with an introduction by her son John Drew with biographical notes by Douglas Taylor
pp.xiv, 200; ill. in text M
NY: Charles Scribner's Sons 1899

**3675** STOLP, DOROTHY E. Mrs John Drew, American actress-manageress, 1820-1897
Baton Rouge: Louisiana State U. (PhD) 1953

**3676** BARNES, NOREEN. 'Actress of all work': a survey of the performing career of Louisa Lane Drew
Medford: Tufts U. (PhD) 1986

### Drew, Philip Yale
### (1880-1940)
### Actor

**3677** WHITTINGTON-EGAN, RICHARD. The ordeal of Philip Yale Drew: a real life murder melodrama in three acts
pp.360; ill. in text, pl. 8 M
London: George G. Harrap 1972
Drew, obscurely related to actor John Drew, was tried for murder in 1929 and acquitted.

### Duff, Mrs John
### [Mary Ann (or Marianna) Dyke]
### (1794-1857)
### Actress

**3678** IRELAND, JOSEPH N. Mrs Duff
pp.xiii, 188; pl.6 M
Boston: James R. Osgood 1882

**3679** LANDAU, PENNY M. The career of Mary Ann Duff, the American Siddons 1810-1839
Bowling Green OH: State U. (PhD) 1979

### Duffy, Henry 'Terry'
### (1890-1961)
### Producer

**3680** MOURING, MURIEL A. Henry 'Terry' Duffy, the west coast's leading producer
Los Angeles: U. of California (MA) 1969

### Durang, John
### (1768-1822)
### Actor

**3681** SHETTEL, JAMES W. A York boy of 1776. John Durang in diary tells of life here before and during [the] American Revolution
pp.[7] L
[York PA]: For the author [1945]
Reprinted articles from *York, Pa., Dispatch* February 22, March 13, 1945.

**3682** DOWNER, ALAN S. (Ed.). The memoir of John Durang, American actor 1785-1816
pp.xix, 176; pl.5 some col. M
Pittsburgh: U. P./ASTR 1966

### Eagels, Jeanne
### (1894-1929)
### Actress

**3683** DOHERTY, EDWARD. Rain girl: the tragic story of Jeanne Eagels
pp.313; pl. 7 MH
Philadelphia: Macrae, Smith 1930
Title derived from her performance as Sadie Thompson in *Rain* (1922).

### Eaton, Walter Prichard
### (1878-1957)
### Critic, scholar

**3684** MYERS, NORMAN J. The theatre criticism of Walter Prichard Eaton, 1905-1930
Urbana: U. of Ilinois (PhD) 1963

**3685** STEPHENSON, CLARENCE E. The theater criticism of Walter Prichard Eaton
Ann Arbor: U. of Michigan (PhD) 1963

### Elkins, Hillard
### (1929-)
### Producer

**3686** DAVIS, CHRISTOPHER. The producer
pp.xi, 321; pl. 8 M
NY: Harper & Row [1972]
A detailed portrait from his production of *Oh, Calcutta* to the musical *The Rothschilds*.

### Elliott, Maxine
### (1868-1940)
### Actress

**3687** FORBES-ROBERTSON, DIANA. Maxine
pp.xii,266, pl. 14 M
London: Hamish Hamilton 1964
US title, *My Aunt Maxine*. By her niece.

### Ellsler, John Adam
### (1821?-1903)
### Actor-manager

**3688** [WESTON, EFFIE E. (Ed.)]. The stage memories of John A. Ellsler...
pp.xi, 159; front. O
Cleveland OH: The Rowfant Club 1950
Edited by Ellsler's daughter. 182 copies.

### Enters, Angna
### (1907-1989)
### Dancer, mime, dramatist

**3689** ENTERS, ANGNA. First person plural [autobiography]
pp.386; ill. in text, front., pl. 9 L
NY: Stackpole Sons 1937

**3690** ENTERS, ANGNA. Silly girl, a portrait of personal remembrance. Illustrated by the author
pp.xi, 322; ill. in text, col. front, pl. 4 L
Cambridge MA: Houghton Mifflin 1944

**3691** COCUZZA, GINNINE. The theatre of Angna Enters, American dance-mime
NY: U. (PhD) 1987

### Evans, Maurice
### (1901-1989)
### Actor

**3692** MAURICE EVANS's G.I. production of *Hamlet*. Acting edition with a preface by Maurice Evans. Designer's sketches by Frederick Stover
pp.191; ill. in text, pl. 16 MH
Garden City NY: Doubleday 1947
Substantial explanatory introduction. Illustrations include production photographs.

**3693** EVANS, MAURICE. All this and Evans too! A memoir
pp.x, 331; pl. 10 M
Columbia: U. of S. Carolina P. 1987

### Eytinge, Rose
### (1835-1811)
### Actress

**3694** EYTINGE, ROSE. The memories of Rose Eytinge: being recollections and observations of men, women, and manners, during half a century
pp.xiii, 311; pl. 8 M
NY: Frederick A. Stokes 1905

### Fairbanks Jr., Douglas
### (1909-)
### Actor

**3695** CONNELL, BRIAN. Knight errant: a biography of Douglas Fairbanks Jr
pp.288; pl. 12 O
London: Hodder and Stoughton 1955

**3696** FAIRBANKS, DOUGLAS. The salad days [autobiography]
pp.ix, 412; ill. in text M
NY: Doubleday 1988

### Fairbanks, Douglas
### [Ulman, Douglas]
### (1883-1939)
### Actor

**3697** HANCOCK, R. & FAIRBANKS, LETITIA. Douglas Fairbanks: the fourth musketeer
pp.260; pl. 9 M
London: Peter Davis 1953

**3698** SCHICKEL, RICHARD. His picture in the papers: a speculation on celebrity in America. Based on the life of Douglas Fairbanks, Sr.
pp.ix, 171; front., pl. 12 M
NY: Charterhouse 1973
Part biography, part examination of the phenomenon of stardom.

### Farrar, C. A.

**3699** [FARRAR, C. A. J.]. Amateur and professional stage life; or, the adventures of Billy Shakespoke before and behind the curtain. By one who has been there
pp.266; ill. in text M
Jamaica Plain MA: Jamaica Publishing 1882
Quasi-fictional autobiography.

### Faversham, William
### (1868-1940)
### Actor

**3700** FAVERSHAM, WILLIAM. The theatre as a power: an address given...in the Chicago University extension course of the lectures on the drama
pp.[ii, 14] MH
[Chicago]: [For the author?] [1911]
Urging theatre as an educative force, and advocating the creation of a statue to honour Edwin Booth as Irving had been honoured in England.

### Fay, Francis Anthony (Frank)
### (1897-1961)
### Actor, monologuist

**3701** FAY, FRANK. How to be poor. Illustrated by James M. Flagg
pp.xi, 172; ill. in text L
NY: Prentice-Hall 1945
Memoirs of the celebrated monologuist who, the previous year, had created the role of Elwood P. Dowd in Mary Chase's *Harvey*.

### Fennell, James
### (1766-1816)
### Actor

**3702** FENNELL, JAMES. An apology for the life of James Fennell. Written by himself [autobiography]
pp.510; front. M
Philadelphia: Moses Thomas 1814

**3703** POTTS, NORMAN B. The acting career of James Fennell in America
Bloomington: Indiana U. (PhD) 1969

### Ferguson, Francis
### (1904-1986)
### Critic

**3704** LEONARD, BOB F. Practice and theory: an analysis of the dramatic criticism of Francis Ferguson
Lawrence: U. of Kansas (PhD) 1970

### Field, Joseph M.
### (1810-1856)
### Actor, playwright

**3705** HEIDGER, JOHN M. Family ties: a biography of the Fields on the frontier stage
Columbia: U. of Missouri (PhD) 1988

### Field, Kate
### (1835-1896)
### Author, actress

**3706** WHITING, LILIAN. Kate Field, a record
pp.xii, 610; pl. 6, some col. M
Boston: Little, Brown 1899
Daughter of actor-manager Joseph M. Field.

### Fields, W. C.
### [Dukenfield, William Claude]
### (1879-1946)
### Comedian

**3707** TAYLOR, ROBERT L. W. C. Fields, his follies and fortunes
pp.vii, 283; pl. 8 M
London: Cassell 1950

**3708** EVERSON, WILLIAM K. The art of W. C. Fields
pp.xii, 232; ill. in text  O
London: Allen and Unwin  1968
Almost wholly concerned with movies.

**3709** FIELDS, W. C. Fields for president. Commentary and photographic selection by Michael M. Taylor
pp.xxiii, 163; ill. in text  L
London: Peter Owen  1971
Humorous pieces. First published 1940.

**3710** FIELDS, W. C. W. C. Fields by himself. His intended autobiography. Commentary by Ronald J. Fields
pp.xiv, 510; pl. 42 (1 col.)  O
London: W. H. Allen  1974
Comprises hitherto unpublished letters, notes, scripts and articles.

**3711** MONTI, CARLOTTA with RICE, CY. W. C. Fields and me
pp.xi, 227; pl. 8  O
London: Michael Joseph  1974
First published NY: Prentice-Hall, 1971.

**3712** GEHRING, WES D. W. C. Fields: a bio-bibliography
pp.xv, 233; ill. in text  MH
Westport CT: Greenwod P.  1984

### Finn, Henry James
### (1785-1840)
### Actor

**3713** MYERS, CLARENCE F. A descriptive biography of Henry James Finn: 19th century actor, manager, playwright
Ann Arbor: U. of Michigan (PhD)  1977

### Fiske, Harrison Grey
### (1861-1942)
### Editor, producer, playwright

**3714** ROTEN, PAUL. The contribution of Harrison Grey Fiske to the American theatre as editor of the *New York Dramatic Mirror*
Ann Arbor: U. of Michigan (PhD)  1963

**3715** WEBB, J. EDGAR. Harrison Grey Fiske's management of the Manhattan Theatre, 1901-1906
Bloomington: Indiana U. (PhD)  1971

### Fiske, Minnie Maddern
### [Davy, Mary (or Marie) Augusta]
### (1865-1932)
### Actress

**3716** THE TALENTED YOUNG ACTRESS Minnie Maddern in an entirely new comedy, entitled *Fogg's Ferry* written by Chas. E. Callahan [cover title]
pp.8; portrait on wrapper  MH
Detroit: Free Press Theatrical Printing House  1882
Brief biographical note, advertising performance at Park Theatre, New York, with press reviews.

**3717** GRIFFITH, FRANK C. Mrs Fiske
pp.146; front., pl. 9  M
NY: Neale Publishing  1912

Author was sometime acting manager for Mrs Langtry, later for Mrs Fiske.

**3718** WOOLLCOTT, ALEXANDER. Mrs Fiske: her views on actors, acting, and the problems of production recorded by Alexander Woollcott
pp.vi, 229; ill. in text, col. front.  M
NY: Century  1917

**3719** BINNS, ARCHIE & KOOKEN, OLIVE. Mrs Fiske and the American theatre
pp.x, 436; pl. 17  M
NY: Crown  1955

**3720** MINNIE MADDERN FISKE: a register of her papers in the Library of Congress
pp.iv, 16  MH
Washington DC: Library of Congress  1962
Period 1884-1932.

**3721** NEILL, ELIZABETH. The art of Minnie Maddern Fiske: a study in early realistic acting
Medford MA: Tufts U. (PhD)  1969

**3722** DONKIN, ELLEN. Mrs Fiske's 1897 *Tess of the D'Urbevilles*. A structural analysis of the 1897-1898 production
Seattle: U. of Washington (PhD)  1982

**3723** MESSANO-CIESLA, MARY A. Minnie Maddern Fiske: her battle with the Theatrical Syndicate
NY: U. (PhD)  1982

**3724** DWERLKOTTE, CAROLYN R. The directorial aesthetic of America's first woman director: Mrs Fiske
Berkeley: U. of California (PhD)  1990

### Flanagan, Hallie
### [Ferguson, Hallie]
### (1890-1969)
### Teacher, author

**3725** FLANAGAN, HALLIE. Shifting scenes of the modern European theatre
pp.viii, 280; pl. 14  M
London: George G. Harrap  1929
A record of a year spent visiting European theatres.

**3726** FLANAGAN, HALLIE. Summary of Federal Theatre activities to September, 1938. A report to Mr Harry L. Hopkins, administrator, works progress administration by Hallie Flanagan, director, Federal Theatre Project
ll. 11  MH
[NY]: WPA  [1938]

**3727** FLANAGAN, HALLIE. What was Federal Theatre?
pp.23  M
Washington DC: American Council on Public Affairs  [1939?]
Account of the political background to the Woodrum Committee's recommendation that led to the ending of the Federal Theatre Project.

**3728** FLANAGAN, HALLIE. Arena: the history of the Federal Theatre
pp.ix, 475; pl. 8  M
NY: Duell, Sloan and Pearce  1940

**3729** FLANAGAN, HALLIE. Dynamo [autobiography]
pp.x, 176; pl. 8     M
NY: Duell, Sloan and Pearce     1943

Much about the author's work at Vassar Experimental Theatre, 1925-1942. Re-prints a third part, in prose, to *Sweeney Agonistes*, provided by T. S. Eliot for a projected production at Vassar.

**3730** RIDGE, PATRICIA. The contributions of Hallie Flanagan to the American theatre
Boulder: U. of Colorado (PhD)     1971

**3731** MENDOZA, BARBARA M. Hallie Flanagan: her role in American theatre, 1924-1935
NY: U. (PhD)     1976

**3732** SWISS, CHERYL D. Hallie Flanagan and the Federal Theatre Project: an experiment in form
Madison: U. of Wisconsin (PhD)     1982

**3733** BENTLEY, JOANNE. Hallie Flanagan: a life in the American theatre
pp.xviii, 436; pl. 6     M
NY: Alfred A. Knopf     1988

### Fletcher, Tom
### (1873-1954)
### Actor

**3734** FLETCHER, TOM. The Tom Fletcher story. 100 years of the negro in show business [autobiography]
pp.xxii, 350; ill. in text     L
NY: Da Capo P.     1984

New edition, revised, with new introduction and index by Thomas L. Riis. First published NY: Burdge, 1954.

### Fonda, Henry Jaynes and his family
### (1905-1982)
### Actor

**3735** SPRINGER, JOHN. The Fondas: the films and careers of Henry, Jane and Peter Fonda
pp.viii, 279; ill. in text     MH
NY: Citadel P.     1970

With a section *The Fondas of the theatre* and contributions from Joshua Logan, Robert Ryan and John Steinbeck.

**3736** FONDA, HENRY. Fonda: my life as told to Howard Teichmann
pp.xii, 372; pl. 16     M
London: W. H. Allen     1982

**3737** GOLDSTEIN, NORM. Henry Fonda, his life and work
pp.124; ill. in text     M
London: Michael Joseph     1982

### Ford, John Thompson
### (1829-1894)
### Manager

**3738** SOLLERS, JOHN F. The theatrical career of John T. Ford
Stanford: U. (PhD)     1963

### Forrest, Edwin
### (1806-1872)
### Actor

**3739** BIOGRAPHY of Edwin Forrest: the distinguished American tragedian: embellished with a full-length portrait of this celebrated national actor in the character of Corwin, drawn and engraved by W. Harvey Ellis
pp.16, pl. 1     MH
Philadelphia: Turner and Fisher     1835

The biographical sketch is initialled 'E. T. W.'

**3740** FORREST, EDWIN. Oration delivered at the Democratic Republican celebration of the sixty-second anniversary of the independence of the United States, in the city of New York, fourth July, 1838...published by request of the Democratic Republican committee
pp.24     MH
NY: Jared W. Bell     1838

**3741** [RANNEY, R. H. ?]. Account of the terrific and fatal riot at the New-York Astor Place Opera House on the night of May 10th, 1849: with the quarrels of Forrest and Macready, including all the causes which led to that awful tragedy! Wherein an infuriated mob was quelled by the public authorities and military, with its mournful termination in the sudden death or mutilation of more than fifty citizens, with full and authentic particulars
pp.32; pl. 1     M
NY: H. M. Ranney     1849

**3742** A REJOINDER to *the replies from England, etc., to certain statements circulated in this country respecting Mr. Macready*. Together with an impartial history and review of the lamentable occurrences at the Astor Place Opera House on the 10th of May, 1849. By an American Citizen
pp.119; riot pictured on upper wrapper     MB
NY: Stringer & Townsend     1849

**3743** THE REPLIES from England, etc., to certain statements circulated in this country respecting Mr. Macready
pp.21     L
NY: Stringer & Townsend     1849

**3744** A REPLY to the pamphlet entitled *Remarks on the Law of Divorce in Pennsylvania connected with the application of Edwin Forrest for a divorce*
pp.7     MH
Philadelphia: [For the author?]     1850

Dated April 11.

**3745** TESTIMONY in the Forrest divorce case
pp.34     MH
Philadelphia: For the District Court     1850

Correspondence and depositions. Issued by Clerk's Office of the District Court of the U. S. for the eastern district of Pennsylvania.

**3746** THE FORREST DIVORCE SUIT - report of the trial of Catharine N. Forrest vs Edwin Forrest for divorce held in the superior court of New York, Dec 1851 before Chief Justice Oakley and a special jury. Reported by the law reporter of the *New York Herald*
pp.185; ill. in text     MB
NY: [New York Herald]     1851

**3747** THE FORREST DIVORCE case [drop title]
pp.36     MH
[NY]:     [1851]

Harvard copy lacks wrappers.

**3748** THE FORREST DIVORCE case. Catharine N. Forrest against Edwin Forrest fully and correctly reported by the reporter of the *National Police Gazette*: with opening and concluding arguments of counsel, charge of the court letters from Mr and Mrs Forrest, and other persons of standing and influence, together with the Consuelo letter, and other interesting details, leading to this controversy [cover title]
pp.110; portraits on wrappers    MH
NY: Stringer & Townsend    1852

**3749** THE FORREST DIVORCE CASE. Catharine Norton Forrest vs Edwin Forrest before the Superior Court of New York, Chief Justice Oakley presiding. Case tried in December, 1851, and January, 1852
pp.106    MH
Boston: [For the court?]    1852

**3750** THE FORREST DIVORCE case. Superior court of the City and County of New York Chief Justice Oakley, presiding
pp.112    MH
[NY]: [For the court?]    [1852]

**3751** REPORT OF THE FORREST DIVORCE case, containing the full and unabridged testimony of all the witnesses, the affidavits and depositions, together with the Consuelo and Forney letters. This edition is published under the direct supervision of the law reporter of the *New York Herald*, and is the only one containing the suppressed testimony
pp.185; portrait on title    MH
NY: Dewitt and Davenport    1852

**3752** REVIEW of the Forrest divorce, containing some remarkable disclosures of the secret doings of the jury. By an old lawyer
pp.31    L
NY: Stringer and Townsend    1852

**3753** CASE OF CATHARINE N. FORREST, plaintiff against Edwin Forrest, defendant, containing the record in the Superior Court of the city of New York, for the opinions in that court, the statement and points for each party in the court of appeals and the judgment of the latter court. In two volumes
pp.viii, 1415    MH
NY: [For the court?]    1863

**3754** SABIN, JOSEPH (Ed.). Catalogue of the library of Edwin Forrest
pp.iv, 188    MB
Philadelphia: Collins    1863

**3755** COURT OF APPEAL of the state of New York. Catharine N. Forrest plaintiff and respondent, against Edwin Forrest, defendant and appellant. Opinion of court of appeals [cover title]
pp.16    MH
NY: Wm. C. Bryant, printers    1864

**3756** REES, JAMES. The life of Edwin Forrest. With reminiscences and personal recollections. By James Rees (Colley Cibber)
pp.17-524; front.    M
Philadelphia: T. B. Peterson    1874

**3757** HOUSE RULES of the Edwin Forrest home
pp.10    MH
Philadelphia: [For the Home]    [c. 1876]

**3758** ALGER, WILLIAM. Life of Edwin Forrest the American tragedian
pp.864; pl. 14    M
Philadelphia: J. B. Lippincott    1877
Two volumes. 100 copies. Probably written by Horatio Alger, Jr. See Gary Scharnhorst: *A note on the authorship of Alger's 'Life of Edwin Forrest'*, Theatre Studies, no. 23, 1976/77.

**3759** BARRETT, LAWRENCE. Edwin Forrest
pp.ix, 171; pl. 7    M
London: David Bogue    [1881]

**3760** HARRISON, GABRIEL. Edwin Forrest: the actor and the man. Critical and reminiscent.
pp.210; pl. ii    M
Brooklyn NY: Brooklyn Eagle Book Printing    1889
200 copies.

**3761** PRICE, WILLIAM T. A life of William Charles Macready
pp.iii, 201, xii: front.    MH
NY: Brentano's    1894
Author claims 'distinctively an American estimate of...an English actor.' Chapter VI offers an account of Edwin Forrest and the Astor Place riot.

**3762** NEWTON, A. EDWARD. Edwin Forrest and his noble creation
pp.11; ill. in text    MH
Philadelphia: Edwin Forrest Home    1928
Forrest left a fund to establish and maintain a home for the support of actors and actresses 'decayed by age or disabled by infirmity', initially at Springbrook PA, later in Parkside Avenue in Philadelphia.

**3763** MOSES, MONTROSE J. The fabulous Forrest: the record of an American actor
pp.xxi, 369; pl. 16    M
Boston: Little, Brown    1929

**3764** MOODY, RICHARD. The Astor Place riot
pp.xii, 243; ill. in text, front.    M
Bloomington: Indiana U. P.    1958

**3765** MOODY, RICHARD. Edwin Forrest: first star of the American stage
pp.xii, 416, xi (2); pl. 12    M
NY: Alfred A. Knopf    1960

**3766** GREEN, RICHARD L. The Shakespearean acting of Edwin Forrest
Urbana-Champaign: U. of Illinois (PhD)    1968

**3767** REYNOLDS, DONALD M.; BRENNAN, JANE N. & BARRY, MARY D. Fonthill castle; paradigm of Hudson-River gothic
pp.32; ill. in text    MH
Riverdale NY: College of Mount Saint Vincent    1976
A history and description of the house built by Edwin Forrest and completed in 1852. It was acquired by the Academy of S. Vincent in 1856. Includes much incidental information about Forrest.

### Forrest, Sam
### (1870-1944)
### Director

**3768** FORREST, SAM. Variety of miscellanea
pp.ix, 100; ill.    DL★
NY: [For the author]    1939
Reminiscences.

### Foy, Eddie
### (1854-1928)
### Actor, comedian

**3769** FOY, EDDIE with HARLOW, ALVIN F. Clowning through life [autobiography]
pp.v, 331; pl. 22    M
NY: E. P. Dutton    1928

### Francis, Arlene
### (1908-)
### Actress

**3770** FRANCIS, ARLENE & ROME, FLORENCE. Arlene Francis: a memoir
pp.204; ill. in text, front.    L
NY: Simon & Schuster    1978

### Frederick, Pauline
### (1885-1938)
### Actress

**3771** LIBBY, CHARLES T. The Libby family in America 1602-1881
pp.628; ill.    DL★
Portland ME: For the author    1882

The Libbys were ancestors of Pauline Frederick.

**3772** ELWOOD, MURIEL. Pauline Frederick: on and off the stage
pp.225; ill.    DL★
Chicago: A. Kroch    1940

### Frohman, Charles
### (1860-1915)
### Producer

**3773** MARCOSSON, ISAAC F. & FROHMAN, DANIEL. Charles Frohman: manager and man. With an appreciation by James M. Barrie
pp.xv, 440; pl. 33    M
London: John Lane    1916

**3774** STIVER, HARRY E. Charles Frohman and the Empire Theatre stock company
Urbana: U. of Illinois (PhD)    1960

### Frohman, Daniel
### (1851-1940)
### Producer, manager

**3775** FROHMAN, DANIEL. Memories of a manager: reminiscences of the old Lyceum and of some players of the last quarter century
pp.xvii, 235; pl. 33    M
London: Heinemann    1911

Reprinted from the *Saturday Evening Post*.

**3776** FROHMAN, DANIEL. Daniel Frohman presents. An autobiography
pp.xv, 397; ill. in text    M
NY: Claude Kendall & Willoughby Sharp    1935

**3777** FROHMAN, DANIEL. Encore [autobiography]
pp.xvi, 295; pl. 20    M
NY: Lee Furman    1937

**3778** HIGHLANDER, JAMES L. Daniel Frohman and the Lyceum Theatre
Urbana: U. of Illinois (PhD)    1960

### Fuller, Loie
### (1863-1928)
### Actress, dancer

**3779** FULLER, LOIE. Fifteen years of a dancer's life with some account of her distinguished friends
pp.288; front., ill. in text    L
London: Herbert Jenkins    1913

Published Paris: Felix Juven, 1908 as *Quinxe ans de ma vie* with a foreword by Anatole France.

**3780** HOLLOWAY, ELIZABETH R. Loie Fuller, the great white lily: a study of the contribution of Loie Fuller to the development of stage lighting
New Haven: Yale U. (MFA)    1966

**3781** LOIE FULLER: magician of light. A loan exhibition... Organized by Margaret Haile Harris
pp.95; ill. in text    M
Richmond: Virginia Museum    1979

**3782** SOMMER, SALLY. Loie Fuller: from the theater of popular entertainment to the Parisian avant-garde
NY: U. (PhD)    1979

### Gable, Clark
### (1901-1962)
### Actor

**3783** McBRIDE, MARY M. The life story of Clark Gable: the child, the trouper, the screen sensation
pp.61; ill.    DL★
NY: Star Library    1932

**3784** GARCEAU, JEAN & COCKE, INEZ. Dear Mr G –
pp.255    L
London: New English Library    1961

Biography of Clark Gable. Published Boston: Little, Brown, 1961.

**3785** SAMUELS, CHARLES. The king of Hollywood
pp.222; pl. 6    L
London: W. H. Allen    1962

NY: Howard McCann. Biography of Clark Gable with much early theatre experience.

### Gabor, Eva
### (1925-)
### Actress

**3786** GABOR, EVA. Orchids and salami [autobiography]
pp.219; front.    L
London: W. H. Allen    1954

### Gaige, Crosby
### [Gaige, Roscoe Conkling]
### (1882-1949)
### Producer, director

**3787** GAIGE, CROSBY. Footlights and highlights [autobiography]
pp.320    M
NY: E. P. Dutton    1948

### Garfield, John
### [Garfinkel, Jules]
### (1913-1952)
### Actor

**3788** SWINDELL, LARRY. Body and soul: the story of John Garfield
pp.288; pl. 12     DL★
NY: Morrow     1975

### Gargan, William
### (1905-1979)
### Actor

**3789** GARGAN, WILLIAM. Why me? An autobiography
pp.311; pl. 8     MH
NY: Doubleday     1969

### Gassner, John Waldhorn
### (1903-1967)
### Critic, writer

**3790** CRAIN, WILLIAM H. (Ed.). Some personal notes and manuscripts of John Gassner. A checklist of the holographic materials in the John Gassner collection of dramatic criticism
pp.(iii), 23; portrait on wrapper     M
Austin: Hoblitzelle Library, U. of Texas     1968

### Geer, Will
### (1902?-1978)
### Actor

**3791** NORTON, SALLY O. A historical study of the actor Will Geer, his life and work in the context of twentieth-century American social, political, and theatrical history
Los Angeles: U. of Southern California (PhD)     1981

### Gest, Morris
### (1881-1942)
### Producer

**3792** PYROS, JOHN A. Morris Gest, producer-impresario in the American theatre
NY: U. (PhD)     1973

### Gibbs, Oliver Wolcott
### (1902-1958)
### Critic

**3793** BLOOM, GILBERT L. An analysis of the dramatic criticism of Wolcott Gibbs as it appeared in the *New Yorker* 1933-1958
NY: U. (PhD)     1970

### Gilbert, John
### [Gibbs, John]
### (1810-1889)
### Actor

**3794** WINTER, WILLIAM. Sketch of the life of John Gilbert, together with extracts from his letters and souvenirs of his career
pp.viii, 55; ill. in text     M
NY: Dunlap Society     1890

### Gilbert, Mrs George Henry
### [née Hartley, Ann]
### (1821-1904)
### Actress

**3795** MARTIN, CHARLOTTE M. (Ed.). The stage reminiscences of Mrs Gilbert
pp.xvi, 248; ill. in text     M
NY: Charles Scribner's Sons     1901

### Gilder, Rosamond
### (1891-1986)
### Critic, writer

**3796** DODGE, CAROLINE. Rosamund Gilder and the theatre
Urbana-Champaign: U. of Illinois (PhD)     1974

### Gilfert, Charles
### (1787-1829)
### Manager

**3797** STEPHENSON, NAN L. The Charleston [NC] theatre management of Charles Gilfert, 1817 to 1822
Lincoln: U. of Nebraska (PhD)     1988

### Gillette, William
### (1855-1937)
### Actor

**3798** WILLIAM GILLETTE in *Sherlock Holmes* as produced at the Garrick Theatre, New York. Published with the authority of Mr Charles Frohman
Unpaginated. Title, pl. 8     M
NY: R. H. Russell     1900

**3799** HOOKER, EDWARD. The descendants of Rev. Thomas Hooker, Hartford, Connecticut, 1856-1908...edited by Margaret Huntingdon Hooker
pp.xxxvi, 558     DL★
Rochester NY: [For the editor]     1909
An account of William Gillette's ancestry.

**3800** GILLETTE, WILLIAM. The illusion of the first time in acting...with an introduction by George Arliss
pp.v, 58     M
NY: Dramatic Museum of Columbia U.     1915
No. 1 in the series 'papers on acting', edited by Brander Matthews. Originally an address given before the fifth joint-session of the American Academy of Arts and Letters and the National Institute of Arts and Letters, Chicago, Nov. 14, 1913. A gloss on the text is provided by Matthews.

**3801** HAMILTON, CLAYTON & FOX, BEAVOIS (Eds). Letters of salutation and felicitation received by William Gillette on the ocasion of his farewell to the stage in *Sherlock Holmes* [cover title]
ll.[62]     MH
NY: [George Tyler]     [1930]
61 letters from a wide range of theatrical and other celebrities, including Sir Arthur Conan Doyle.

**3802** BURTON, GUTHRIE. Three parts scotch: an informal autobiography
pp.288     MH
Indianapolis: Bobbs-Merrill     1946
Includes material on William Gillette.

**3803** SHERK, H. DENIS. William Gillette: his life and works
University Park: Pennsylvania State U. (PhD)     1961

Published under the same title, Bloomington IN: Gaslight, 1983 (not seen).

**3804** COOK, DORIS E. Sherlock Holmes and much more, or some of the facts about William Gillette
pp.viii, 112; ill. in text      M
Hartford: Connecticut Historical Society    1970

**3805** THE CURTAIN IS UP on the William Gillette exhibit…honoring the famous actor-playwright who was born at Nook Farm, Hartford, Connecticut
pp.24; ill. in text      ★
Hartford CT: Stowe-Day Foundation    1970

**3806** SCHUTTLER, GEORGE W. William Gillette, actor and playwright
Urbana-Champaign: U. of Illinois    1976

**3807** MALEC, ANDREW. Molding the image. William Gillette as Sherlock Holmes: an exhibit illustrative of the profound impact of the American actor on past and present conceptions of Sherlock Holmes from the Mary Kahler & Philip S. Hench Collection
pp.[16]; ill. in text      M
Minneapolis: U. of Minnesota    1983
Errata slip facing title.

## Gillmore, Margalo
## (1897-1986)
### Actress

**3808** GILLMORE, MARGALO. Four flights up [autobiography]
pp.xii, 171; ill.      DL★
Boston: Houghton Mifflin    1964
Decorations by R. D. Rice. Author's father, Frank Gillmore, was founder of Actors' Equity.

## Gish, Lillian
## (1899?-1993)
### Actress

**3809** FRASHER, JAMES E. (Ed.). Lillian and Dorothy Gish
pp.vii, 312; ill. in text      L
London: Macmillan    1973
Published NY: Charles Scribner's Sons, 1973. A pictorial biography. Edited by James E. Frasher.

**3810** WAGENKNECHT, EDWARD. Lillian Gish: an interpretation
pp.27; front.      MH
Seattle: U. of Washington Bookstore    1927

**3811** PAINE, ALBERT B. Life and Lillian Gish
pp.xv, 303; front., pl. 16      L
NY: Macmillan    1933
Refers to the early stage experience of the Gish sisters and to Lillian Gish's work with Jed Harris and Max Reinhardt.

**3812** GISH, LILLIAN with PINCHOT, ANN. Lillian Gish: the movies, Mr Griffith and me
pp.xiii, 388; pl. 31      L
Englewood Cliffs NJ: Prentice-Hall    1969
Chapters 1-4 describe the early stage experience of the Gish sisters as children.

## Gleason, Jackie
## (1916-1987)
### Comedian

**3813** BISHOP, JAMES A. The golden ham: a candid biography of Jackie Gleason
pp.298      DL★
NY: Simon and Schuster    1956

## Golden, John
## (1874-1955)
### Producer

**3814** GOLDEN, JOHN & SHORE, VIOLA B. Stage-struck John Golden
pp.xvii, 324; pl. 25      M
NY: Samuel French    1930
Memoirs, originally serialised in *Saturday Evening Post* as *Cleaning Up*.

**3815** RYAN, PATRICIA C. John Golden: American theatrical producer
NY: U. (PhD)    1971

## Goodman, Philip
## (1885-1940)
### Producer

**3816** GOODMAN, PHILIP. Franklin Street
pp.277      DL★
NY: Alfred A. Knopf    1942
Reminiscences of childhood.

## Goodwin, George K.
## (1830-1882)
### Actor, manager

**3817** [GOODWIN, GEORGE K.]. Reminiscence of George K. Goodwin 1849-1881
pp.i, 87; front.      MH
[Philadelphia]: [For the author?]    [1881]
Initially a journal of author's early travels, then a somewhat random set of reminiscences. Goodwin, after a travelling showman's career, became lessee and manager of the New Chestnut Street Opera House, Philadelphia.

## Goodwin, Nat
## [Goodwin, Nathanial Carl]
## (1857-1919)
### Actor

**3818** GOODWIN, NAT C. Nat Goodwin's book [autobiography]
pp.366; pl. 48      M
Boston: Richard G. Badger    1914

**3819** COX, KENNETH D. Nat Goodwin: a theatrical biography
Lincoln: U. of Nebraska-Lincoln (PhD)    1976

## Gordon, Max
## [Salpeter, Mechel]
## (1892-1978)
### Producer

**3820** GORDON, MAX with FUNKE, LEWIS. Max Gordon presents [autobiography]
pp.vi, 314; pl. 8      M
NY: Bernard Geis Associates    1963

### Gordon, Ruth
### [Jones, Ruth]
### (1896-1985)
### Actress

**3821** GORDON, RUTH. Myself among others [autobiography]
pp.vi, 389     M
NY: Atheneum     1971

**3822** GORDON, RUTH. My side [autobiography]
pp.vi, 502; pl. 12     M
NY: Harper & Row     1976

**3823** GORDON, RUTH. Ruth Gordon, an open book [autobiography]
pp.xi, 395     MH
NY: Doubleday     1980

### Gorelik, Mordecai
### (1899-1992)
### Designer

**3824** PALMER, JAMES C. Mordecai Gorelik's theory of the theatre
Carbondale: Southern Illinois U. (PhD)     1966

### Greene, John
### (1795-1866)

**3825** DURANG, CHARLES. The theatrical rambles of Mr and Mrs John Greene...edited by William L. Slout
pp.142     M
San Bernardino CA: Borgo P.     1987

Weekly articles first printed in the New York *Clipper*, February to October, 1865, based on the unpublished memoirs of Mrs Greene who, with her husband, acted with stock companies in Philadelphia and elsewhere.

### Greenwall, Henry
### (183?-1913)
### Manager

**3826** BEACH, CLAUDIA A. Henry Greenwall: theatre manager
Lubbock: Texas Tech U. (PhD)     1986

### Gregory, Paul
### (1920-)
### Director

**3827** JOHNSON, JAMES L. The art of Paul Gregory: an examination of Gregory's historic, aesthetic and pedagogic contributions to interpretation and the theatre
Los Angeles: U. of Southern California (PhD)     1981

### Gregory, Richard C.
### Actor

**3828** GREGORY, DICK & LIPSYTE, ROBERT. Nigger: an autobiography
pp.224; pl. 4     L
NY: E. P. Dutton     1964

### Hackett, James Henry
### (1800-1871)
### Actor, manager

**3829** SOMMERS, JOHN J. James H. Hackett: the profile of a player
Iowa City: U. of Iowa (PhD)     1966

### Hagen, Uta
### (1919-)
### Actress

**3830** SPECTOR, SUSAN J. Uta Hagen: the early years, 1919-1951
NY: U. (PhD)     1982

**3831** HAGEN, UTA. Sources: a memoir. With drawings by the author
pp.135; ill. in text, pl. 6     M
NY: Performing Arts Journal Publications     1983

### Hall, Adrian
### (1910-)
### Director

**3832** WOODS, JEANNE. The theatre of Adrian Hall
NY: City U. (PhD)     1989

### Hamblin, Thomas Sowerby
### (1800-1853)
### Actor, manager

**3833** [CLARKE, M[ARY]]. A concise history of the life and amours of Thomas S. Hamblin late manager of the Bowery Theatre as communicated by his legal wife, Mrs Elizabeth Hamblin, to Mrs M. Clarke...
pp.40     MB
Philadelphia: 45 Arcade     [c. 1837]

A counterblast to a eulogy by Hamblin's mistress Louisa Medina (Mrs Thornton) printed in *The Lady's Companion* of June, 1837.

### Hammond, Percy
### (1873-1936)
### Critic

**3834** ADAMS, FRANKLIN P. et al. Percy Hammond - a symposium in tribute
pp.xviii, 69; front.     MH
NY: Doubleday     1936

Hammond was drama critic for the *New York Herald Tribune*, 1921-36. Among those paying tribute are Brooks Atkinson, John M. Brown, Burns Mantle, George J. Nathan, G. S. Seldes, Walter Winchell.

### Hampden, Walter
### [Dougherty, Walter]
### (1879-1955)
### Actor, manager

**3835** LAURENT, EUGENE M. Walter Hampden: actor manager
Urbana-Champaign: U. of Illinois (PhD)     1969

**3836** PAROLA, GENE J. Walter Hampden's career as actor-manager
Bloomington: Indiana U. (PhD)     1970

### Harris, Jed
### [Horowitz, Jacob]
### (1900-1979)
### Director, producer

**3837** HARRIS, JED. Watchman, what of the night?
pp.ix, 154     M
NY: Doubleday     1963

Reminiscences, with much emphasis on author's productions, *The Heiress* and *Our Town*.

**3838** BURROUGHS, PATRICIA. The theatrical career of Jed Harris in New York, 1925-1956
Baton Rouge: Louisiana State U. (PhD)     1978

**3839** HARRIS, JED. A dance on the high wire: recollections of a time and a temperament
pp.iii, 188; pl. 2     M
NY: Crown     1979

**3840** GOTTFRIED, MARTIN. Jed Harris, the curse of genius
pp.vii, 280; pl. 4     MH
Boston: Little, Brown     1984

### Harrison, Richard Berry
### (1864-1935)
### Actor

**3841** DANIEL, WALTER C. *De Lawd*:Richard B. Harrison and *The Green Pastures*
pp.ix, 180; ill. in text     L
NY: Greenwood P.     1986
A production history.

### Hart, William S.
### (1870-1946)
### Actor

**3842** HART, WILLIAM S. My life east and west [autobiography]
pp.viii, 363; col. front., pl. 24     L
Boston: Houghton Mifflin     1929
With account of early theatre experience including a memoir of Modjeska.

### Haskin, Byron
### Director

**3843** ADAMSON, J. Byron Haskin interviewed.
pp.vii, 314; pl. 6     O
Metuchen NJ: Scarecrow P.     1984
A theatre oral history sponsored by the Directors Guild of America. Reference to early San Francisco theatre experience.

### Havoc, June
### (1916-)
### Actress

**3844** HAVOC, JUNE. Early Havoc [autobiography]
pp.276; pl. 3     M
London: Hutchinson     1960

**3845** HAVOC, JUNE. More Havoc [autobiography]
pp.ix, 277; pl. 8     M
NY: Harper & Row     1980

### Hayes, Helen
### [Brown, Helen]
### (1900-1993)
### Actress

**3846** BROWN, CATHERINE H. Letters to Mary
pp.xi, 343; pl. 15     M
NY: Random House     1940
A biography of Helen Hayes by her mother, in the form of letters to her granddaughter. Foreword by Charles MacArthur.

**3847** THE AMERICAN NATIONAL THEATRE and Academy West and the Antans present the 1976 national artist award to Miss Helen Hayes at a gala premiere performance of *A Chorus Line* at the Shubert Theatre...July 6
unpaged; ill. in text     MH
Los Angeles: ANTA West     1976
Souvenir program, copiously illustrated and with tributes from many theatrical celebrities. Includes a (not wholly accurate) chronology of her career.

**3848** ROBBINS, JHAN. Front page marriage
pp.224; pl. 8     M
NY: G. P. Putnam's Sons     1982
Biographical account of Helen Hayes and Charles MacArthur.

**3849** HAYES, HELEN with FUNKE, LEWIS. A gift of joy [autobiography]
pp.254; pl. 8     M
NY: M. Evans     1965

**3850** HAYES, HELEN with DODY, SANDFORD. On reflection: an autobiography
pp.253; pl. 8     M
NY: M. Evans     1968

**3851** HAYES, HELEN & LOOS, ANITA. Twice over lightly: New York then and now
pp.vii, 343; pl. 4     M
NY: Harcourt Brace Jovanovich     1972

**3852** HAYES, HELEN with HATCH, KATHERINE. My life in three acts [autobiography]
pp.v, 266; pl. 8     M
San Diego: Harcourt Brace Jovanovich     1990

### Hayes, Peter Lind
### (1915-)
### Actor

**3853** HAYES, PETER L. & HEALY, MARY. Twenty-five minutes from Broadway. Illustrated by Aliki [autobiography]
pp.ix, 149; ill. in text     M
NY: Duell, Sloan & Pearce     1961

### Hayward, Leland
### (1902-1971)
### Producer

**3854** PRESENTING LELAND HAYWARD [cover title]
[8] inc. wrappers; ill. in text     M
NY: [Public Library]     1974
Produced for the Leland Hayward Exhibition at the Vincent Astor Gallery.

**3855** BERMAN, SONIA. The crossing, Adano to Catonsville: Leland Hayward's producing career
NY: Colombia U. (PhD)     1980

### Head, Edith
### [Ihnen, Edith]
### (1898?-1981)
### Designer

**3856** HEAD, EDITH & ARDMORE, JANE K. The dress doctor [memoirs]
pp.240; ill. in text, pl.4     CSC
Boston: Little, Brown     1959

### Helburn, Theresa
### (1887-1959)
### Producer

3857 HELBURN, THERESA. A wayward quest
pp.viii, 344; pl. 2   M
Boston: Little, Brown   1960
Author was executive director of the Theatre Guild.

### Hellinger, Mark
### (1903-1947)
### Actor, dramatist

3858 BISHOP, JIM. The Mark Hellinger story: a biography of Broadway and Hollywood
pp.xv, 367; pl. 4   MH
NY: Appleton-Century-Croft   1952

### Hepburn, Katharine Houghton
### (1907-)
### Actress

3859 MARILL, ALVIN H. Katharine Hepburn
pp.160; ill. in text   L
NY: Galahad Books   1973

3860 HIGHAM, CHARLES. Kate: the life of Katharine Hepburn
pp.xix, 244; pl. 6   M
London: W. H. Allen   1975

3861 CAREY, GARY. Katharine Hepburn
pp.vii, 284; pl. 6   O
London: Robson   1983

3862 MORLEY, SHERIDAN. Katharine Hepburn: a celebration...
pp.192; ill. in text   M
London: Pavilion   1984

3863 EDWARDS, ANNE. Katharine Hepburn: a biography
395; pl. 8   M
London: Hodder and Stoughton   1986

3864 ANDERSEN, CHRISTOPHER. Young Kate
pp.254; pl. 8   M
London: Macmillan   1988

3865 BRYSON, JOHN. The private world of Katharine Hepburn
pp.176; ill. in text, col   L
Boston: Little, Brown   1990
Foreword by Katharine Hepburn. A photographic biography, with a section, On the boards.

### Heron, Matilda Agnes
### (1830-1877)
### Actress

3866 HUMBLE, ALBERTA L. Matilda Heron, American actress
Urbana: U. of Illinois (PhD)   1959

### Heston, Charlton
### (1921?-)
### Actor

3867 HESTON, CHARLTON with ALPERT, HOLLIS. The actor's life: journals 1956-76
pp.xvii, 482; ill. in text, pl. 6   M
London: Allen Lane   1979

Published in US, NY: E. P. Dutton, 1978.

### Hill, George Handel 'Yankee'
### (1809-1849)
### Actor

3868 NORTHALL, WILLIAM K. Life and recollections of Yankee Hill: together with anecdotes and incidents of his travels...
pp.vii, 303; ill. in text   MH
NY: For Mrs Cordelia Hill by W. F. Burgess   1850

3869 [HILL, GEORGE H.]. Scenes from the life of an actor...by a celebrated comedian [autobiography]
pp.246; pl. 6   M
NY: Garrett   1853

### Hirschfeld, Albert
### (1903-)
### Caricaturist

3870 HIRSCHFELD, AL. Show business is no business
pp.ix, 142; ill. in text   M
NY: Smon and Schuster   1951
Profusely illustrated, light-hearted account of the genesis of a Broadway show.

3871 HIRSCHFELD, AL. The world of Hirschfeld...introduction by Lloyd Goodrich
pp.233; ill. in text   M
NY: Harry N. Abrams   [1970]
Theatre caricatures, 1925-1968.

### Hodgdon, Sam K.
### (1853-1922)
### Actor, manager

3872 HODGDON, SAM K. Town hall tonight. or show life on the cross roads. The personal reminiscences of the author's ten years' experience as a performer in the small towns of America
pp.93   DL★
Boston: [For the author?]   1891

### Hodgkinson, John
### [Meadowcroft, John]
### (1767-1805)
### Actor

3873 HODGKINSON, JOHN. A narrative of his connection with the Old American Company, from the fifth September, 1792, to the thirty-first of March, 1797...
pp.29   MH
NY: Printed by J. Oram   1797
Account of the managerial squabble involving Hodgkinson, the Hallams and William Dunlap. The final unpaged leaf contains the author's sworn statement of the veracity of his account.

3874 SKETCH of the life of the late Mr Hodgkinson
pp.302-345   MB
[Philadelphia]: [The Mirror of Taste?]   [c. 1810]
A hand-written note in the Boston Library copy states the piece to have been extracted from the Mirror of Taste, a Philadelphia journal.

3875 HARBIN, BILLY J. The career of John Hodgkinson in the American theatre
Bloomington: Indiana U. (PhD)   1970

## 8.4. INDIVIDUAL

### Hoffman, Dustin
### (1937-)
### Actor

3876 AGAN, PATRICK. Hoffman vs. Hoffman. The actor and the man
pp.x, 166; pl. 8 L
Sevenoaks, Kent: New English Library 1987
First published London: Robert Hale, 1986.

### Holbrook, Harold Rowe
### (1925-)
### Actor

3877 HOLBROOK, HAL. Mark Twain tonight! An actor's portrait. Selections from Mark Twain edited, adapted and arranged with a prologue
pp.xiii, 272; pl. 4 L
NY: Ives Washburn 1959
Genesis of the author's one-man show, together with the completed script.

3878 JACKSON, NORMAN L. An analysis of Hal Holbrook's development and performance of the role of Mark Twain
Provo: Brigham Young U. (PhD) 1981

### Holland, George
### (1791-1870)
### Actor

3879 [MORRELL, THOMAS H.]. Holland Memorial. Sketch of the life of George Holland, the veteran comedian, with dramatic reminiscences, anecdotes, etc.
pp.i, 124; ill. in text, pl. 2 M
NY: For the author 1871
Includes a chapter: *The little church around the corner*, the Church of the Transfiguration at 1 East 29th Street, NY, where Holland's funeral service took place after he was refused rites by Sabine of the nearby Episcopal church. Also provides a detailed account of the Holland Testimonial. 250 copies.

3880 MOSS, THEODORE & MAGONIGLE, J. H. Report of the Holland benefit
pp.27 MB
NY: Thitchener & Glastaeter 1871
The George Holland Testimonial was organized by William Winter and comprised 19 different presentations throughout the nation's major cities. Some $13,000 net was raised for Holland's widow.

### Holland, Joseph Jefferson
### (1860-1926)
### Actor

3881 SKINNER, OTIS. Joseph Jefferson Holland: a tribute by Otis Skinner delivered at the funeral service in the Church of the Transfiguration, New York, September 28, 1926
pp.[10] MH
NY: For the author 1926

### Holliday, Judy
### [Tuvim, Judith]
### (1922-1965)
### Actress

3882 CAREY, GARY. Judy Holliday: an intimate life story
xii, 271; pl. 4p. O
London: Robson 1983

### Holman, Libby
### [Holtzman, Elizabeth]
### (1906-1971)
### Singer

3883 BRADSHAW, JOHN. Dreams that money can buy: the tragic life of Libby Holman
pp.431; pl. 8 M
NY: William Morrow 1985

### Holzer, Adela
### Producer

3884 HOLZER, ADELA. If at first... [autobiography]
pp.214; pl. 4 L
NY: Stein and Day 1977
Author invested financially in *Hair* and later became a producer of e.g. Schisgal's *All over the Town* and McNally's *The Ritz*.

### Hope, Bob
### [Hope, Leslie Townes]
### (1903-)
### Comedian

3885 HOPE, BOB. I never left home
pp.144; ill. in text L
London: Bernards 1946
Entertaining the forces in WW2. Illustrated by Carl Rose.

3886 HOPE, BOB. This is on me [autobiography]
pp.239; pl. 9 M
London: Frederick Muller 1954

3887 HOPE, BOB. I owe Russia $1200
pp.191; pl. 8 L
London: Robert Hale 1963
Includes trouping experience with MATS during the 1950s

3888 HOPE, BOB. Five women I love: Bob Hope's Vietnam story
pp.189; pl. 8 L
London: Robert Hale 1967

3889 MORELLA, JOE; EPSTEIN, EDWARD Z. & CLARK, ELEANOR. The amazing careers of Bob Hope: from gags to riches
pp.256; ill. in text O
London: W. H. Allen 1973

3890 FAITH, WILLIAM R. Bob Hope and the popular oracle in American humor
Los Angeles: U. of Southern California (PhD) 1976

3891 TRESCOTT, PAMELA. Bob Hope: a comic life
pp.188; pl.4 M
London: W.H. Allen 1987

### Hopkins, Arthur Melancthon
### (1878-1950)
### Producer

3892 HOPKINS, ARTHUR. To a lonely boy [memoirs]
pp.iii, 250 M
NY: Doubleday, Doran 1937

3893 HOPKINS, ARTHUR. Reference point
pp.xi, 135 M
NY: Samuel French 1948

On acting and directing. Based on papers read to Fordham U.

3894  HANSEN, DELMAR J.  The directing theory and practice of Arthur Hopkins
Iowa City: U. of Iowa (PhD)  1961

3895  HALVERSON, BRUCE A.  Arthur Hopkins: a theatrical biography
Seattle: U. of Washington (PhD)  1971

### Houseman, John
### [Haussmann, Jacques]
### (1902-1988)
### Actor, director, producer

3896  HOUSEMAN, JOHN.  Run-through: a memoir
pp.507; pl.16  M
London: Allen Lane, The Penguin P.  1973
First published NY: Simon and Schuster, 1972.

3897  HOUSEMAN, JOHN.  Front and centre
pp.512; pl. 24  M
NY: Simon and Schuster  1979
A second book of memoirs.

3898  SPEERS, SUSAN D.  An evaluative examination of the development and achievement of the acting [American Repertory] company under the artistic direction of John Houseman
Santa Barbara: U. of California (PhD)  1982

3899  HOUSEMAN, JOHN.  Final dress
pp.559; pl. 16  M
NY: Simon and Schuster  1983
A third book of memoirs.

3900  HOUSEMAN, JOHN.  Unfinished business
pp.x, 498; pl. 10  M
London: Chatto and Windus  1986
A condensation of the author's three preceding books of memoirs, with an update.

### Hoyt, Harlowe Randall
### (1882-1971)
### Critic

3901  WINGET, JACK B.  Harlowe Randall Hoyt: renaissance man of the theatre 1882-1971. A historical study
Kent OH: State U. (PhD)  1983

### Hubbard, Elbert
### (1856-1915)
### Actor

3902  HUBBARD, ELBERT.  In the spot-light: personal experiences...on the American stage
pp.135; front., ill. in text  M
East Aurora NY: The Roycrofters  1917
Reminiscences of vaudeville and theatre life in NY state, c. 1900.

### Hull, Josephine
### [Sherwood, Josephine]
### (1886-1957)
### Actress

3903  CARSON, WILLIAM G.  Dear Josephine: the theatrical career of Josephine Hull
pp.xii, 313; pl. 6  M
Norman: U. of Oklahoma P.  1963

### Hume, Samuel J.
### Designer

3904  BOLIN, JOHN S.  Samuel Hume: artist and exponent of American art theatre
Ann Arbor: U. of Michigan (PhD)  1969

### Huneker, James Gibbons
### (1857-1921)
### Critic

3905  SCHWAB, ARNOLD T.  James Gibbons Huneker, critic of the seven arts
pp.xv, 384; front., pl. 4  L
Stanford MA: U. P.  1963
Includes reference to his theatre criticism and his views on drama.

3906  WARD, ROYAL A.  The theatrical and dramatic criticism of James Gibbons Huneker
Ann Arbor: U. of Michigan (PhD)  1984

### Huneker, James Gibbons
### (1857-1921)
### Critic

3907  HUNEKER, JAMES G.  Steeplejack [autobiography]
pp.ix, 320; vii, 327, pl. 25  M
NY: Charles Scribner's Sons  1920
Two volumes. Huneker's *Iconoclasts*, 1905, had drawn America's attention towards the emerging European drama and his autobiography contains much theatre reference, including Edwin Booth, the Drews, Richard Mansfield.

### Hunter, Ruth
### (1902-1976)
### Actress

3908  HUNTER, RUTH.  ...Come back on Tuesday [memoirs]
pp.265  DL★
NY: Charles Scribner's Sons  1945

3909  HUNTER, RUTH.  Barefoot girl on Broadway: the story of the original Ellie May of *Tobacco Road*
pp.115  DL★
NY: Exposition P.  1965
Autobiography. Foreword by Carl Sandford.

### Hurok, Sol
### (1888-1974)
### Impresario

3910  HUROK, S. with GOODE, RUTH.  Impresario: a memoir
pp.272; pl. 16  M
London: Macdonald  1947

### Huston, Walter
### [Houghston, Walter]
### (1884-1950)
### Actor

3911  BAILEY, LEON E.  The acting career of Walter Huston
Urbana-Chanpaign: U. of Illinois (PhD)  1973

3912  GROBEL, LAWRENCE.  The Hustons
DL★
NY: Charles Scribner's Sons  1989

## Hutton, Laurence
## (1943-1904)
## Critic

**3913** MOORE, ISABEL. Talks in a library with Laurence Hutton
pp.xvii, 458; pl. 58   M
NY: G. P. Putnam's Soms   1905

## Isaacs, Edith Juliet Rich
## (1878-1956)
## Critic, editor

**3914** TABOR, CATHERINE-A. Edith Juliet Rich Isaacs: an examination of her theories and influence on the American theatre
Madison: U. of Wisconsin (PhD)   1984

## Jackson, Anne
## (1926-)
## Actress

**3915** JACKSON, ANNE. Early stages [autobiography]
pp.viii, 212   M
Boston: Little, Brown   1979

## James, William
## (1938-)
## Actor

**3916** TEBBE, MARGARET M. Contributions of William James to speech and theatre
Bloomington: Indiana U. (PhD)   1962

## Janauschek, Fannie
## [Janauschek, Francesca Romana Magdalena]
## (1830-1904)
## Actress

**3917** CORTEZ, JERRY V. Fanny Janauschek: America's last queen of tragedy
Urbana-Champaign: U. of Illinois (PhD)   1973

## Jefferson, Joseph
## (1825-1905)
## Actor

**3918** JEFFERSON, JOSEPH. The autobiography of Joseph Jefferson
pp.xv, 501; pl. 77   M
NY: Century   1890
Re-published under this title in an edition by Alan S. Downer, Harvard U. P.,1964 (pp.xxv, 361). Also a 're-discovered' edition, under the title '*Rip Van Winkle*: the autobiography of Joseph Jefferson' was published London: Reinhardt & Evans, 1949, with a foreword by Eleanor Farjeon (pp. xxxii, 375).

**3919** WINTER, WILLIAM. The life and art of Joseph Jefferson together with some account of his ancestry and of the Jefferson family of actors
pp.xv, 319; pl. 16   M
NY: Macmillan   1894
A revised and enlarged edition of work first published NY: 1881 as *The Jeffersons*.

**3920** RIP VAN WINKLE as played by Joseph Jefferson. Now for the first time published
pp.199; ill. in text, pl. 12   MH
NY: Dodd, Mead   1895
Acting copy of text with brief setting descriptions before each act. Illustrated with scenes from the production, and paintings by Jefferson. Introduction by Jefferson. 100 copies of proof edition.

**3921** DOLE, NATHAN H. Joseph Jefferson at home
pp.110; ill. in text, front.   M
Boston: Estes & Lauriat   1898

**3922** WILSON, FRANCIS. Joseph Jefferson: reminiscences of a fellow player
pp.xii, 354; front., pl. 32   M
NY: Charles Scribner's Sons   1906
A signed edition was also issued, restricted to 160 copies, with an embellished title and seven additional plates.

**3923** JEFFERSON, EUGENIE P. Intimate recollections of Joseph Jefferson
pp.xiv, 366; pl. 70   M
NY: Dodd, Mead   1909
Written by Jefferson's daughter.

**3924** BRADFORD, GAMALIEL. American portraits, 1875-1900
pp.xvii. 249; pl. 8   O
Boston: Houghton Mifflin   1922
Includes an account, with portrait, of Joseph Jefferson.

**3925** FARJEON, ELEANOR. Portrait of a family
pp.528; pl.13   O
NY: Frederick A. Stokes   1936
Published London: Gollancz, 1935 as *Nursery in the nineties*. Reprinted London: Oxford U.P., 1960 with a postscript 1959 of five pages. Includes material on Joseph Jefferson, the author's grandfather.

**3926** McKENZIE, DOUGLAS C. The acting of Joseph Jefferson III
Eugene: U. of Oregon (PhD)   1973

## Jessel, George Albert
## (1898-1981)
## Actor, comedian, producer

**3927** JESSEL, GEORGE. So help me. The autobiography...with a foreword by William Saroyan
pp.xx, 240; pl. 9   M
NY: Random House   1943

**3928** JESSEL, GEORGE. 'Hello, Momma'...the never to be forgotten, never to be heard again phone conversation between Georgie and his momma...and other monologues and essays. Foreword by Eddie Cantor. Illustrated by Carl Rose
pp.155; ill. in text   M
Cleveland OH: World Publishing   1946

**3929** JESSEL, GEORGE. This way, miss. With a foreword by William Saroyan
pp.xvii, 229; pl. 4   M
NY: Henry Holt   1955
Memoirs. Chapter 28 devoted to John Barrymore.

**3930** JESSEL, GEORGE. Jessel, anyone?
pp.xi, 179; ill. in text   L
Englewood Cliffs NJ: Prentice-Hall   1960
Foreword by Jack Benny.

**3931** JESSEL, GEORGE with AUSTIN, JOHN. The world I lived in [autobiography]
pp.ix, 213; pl 12   MH
Chicago: Henry Regnery   1975

## Jones, James Earl
### (1931-)
### Actor

**3932** SETRAKIAN, EDWARD. The acting of James Earl Jones
NY: U. (PhD) 1976

## Jones, Margo
### (1913-1955)
### Manager, director

**3933** JONES, MARGO. Theatre-in-the-round
pp.xi, 244; pl. 8 M
NY: Holt, Rinehart & Winston 1951
A description of the theatre and a log of the author's productions at Theatre '47, which changed its name every year, in Dallas TX.

**3934** WILMETH, DON B. A history of the Margo Jones theatre
Urbana: U. of Illinois (PhD) 1964

**3935** LARSEN, JUNE B. Margo Jones: a life in the theatre
NY: City U. (PhD) 1982

**3936** SHEEHY, HELEN. Margo: the life and theatre of Margo Jones
pp.vii, 316; pl. 16 M
Dallas TX: Southern Methodist U. P. 1989

## Jones, Robert Edmond
### (1887-1954)
### Designer, producer, director

**3937** EXHIBITION OF STAGE MODELS and designs by Robert Edmond Jones [cover title]
pp.[17]; ill. in text M
NY: Bourgeois Galleries 1920
Catalogue. Includes an essay by Percy Mackaye: *Robert Edmond Jones: a comment on his work in the theatre.*

**3938** JONES, ROBERT EDMOND. Drawings for the theatre
pp.16; ill. in text, pl. 35 M
NY: Theatre Arts 1925
600 signed copies. Introduction by Arthur Hopkins. Reprinted NY: Theatre Arts Books, 1970 with new biographical introduction by Donald Oenslager.

**3939** CONNELLY, MARC. The Green Pastures...with illustrations by Robert Edmond Jones
pp.xvii, 141; ill. in text M
NY: Farrar & Rinehart 1930
Jones designed the original production and, while not actual scene designs, many of the illustrations give a theatrical impression.

**3940** JONES, ROBERT EDMOND. The dramatic imagination: reflections and speculations on the art of the theatre
pp.157 M
NY: Duell, Sloan and Pearce 1941
Reprinted essays from *Yale Review, Theatre Arts,* and *Encyclopaedia Britannica* on aspects of theatre and stage design. Reprinted NY: Theatre Arts Books, 1967 with an introduction by John M. Brown.

**3941** BLACK, EUGENE. Robert Edmond Jones: poetic artist of the new stagecraft
Madison: U. of Wisconsin (PhD) 1956

**3942** PENDLETON, RALPH (Ed.). The theatre of Robert Edmond Jones...with a chronology...With contributions by John M. Brown, Mary Hall Furber, Kenneth MacGowan, Jo Mielziner, Donald Oenslager, Lee Simonson, Stark Young
pp.xiii, 198; ill. in text. pl. col 3 M
Middletown: Wesleyan U. P. 1958
250 copies. A trade edition lacks the coloured plates, issued as a supplement to the limited edition.

**3943** HICKS, LEE R. Robert Edmond Jones: stage director
Boulder: U. of Colorado (PhD) 1969

**3944** WALDO, PAUL R. Production concepts exemplified in selected presentations directed by Robert Edmond Jones
Eugene: U. of Oregon (PhD) 1970

**3945** MILLER, THOMAS C. Robert Edmond Jones and the modern movement: a study of related elements in art, architecture, and theatre
Boulder: U. of Colorado (PhD) 1977

**3946** McDERMOTT, DANA S. A theatre of dreams: Robert Edmond Jones' theatrical vision and creative process
Berkeley: U. of California (PhD) 1979

**3947** ROBBINS, KATHLEEN M. The poetics of symbolism: Robert Edmond Jones and the stage-costume
Bloomington: Indiana U. (PhD) 1980

## Joyce, Peggy Hopkins
### [Upton, Margaret]
### (1893-1957)
### Entertainer

**3948** JOYCE, PEGGY H. Men, marriage and me
pp.viii, 279 M
London: Geoffrey Bles 1930

## Kahn, Otto H.
### (1867-1934)
### Impresario, philanthropist

**3949** KAHN, OTTO H. Of many things: being reflections and impressions on international affairs, domestic reflections and the arts
pp.437 L
NY: Boni and Liveright 1926
Kahn helped found the New Theatre (1909). The first section of his memoirs contains two transcribed addresses, on the Theatre Guild and on the American stage.

**3950** ANDERSON, JOYCE M. Otto H. Kahn: an analysis of his theatrical philanthropy in the New York City area from 1909 to 1934
Kent OH: State U. (PhD) 1983

**3951** MATZ, MARY J. The many lives of Otto Kahn
pp.xi, 166; pl. 15 M
London: Robson 1984

## Kane, Whitford
### (1881-1956)
### Actor

**3952** KANE, WHITFORD. Are we all met?
pp.294; ill. in text, pl. 40 M
London: Elkin Mathews & Marrot 1931

Memoirs. Includes material on the Theatre Guild, the Goodman Theatre Company, the Equity strike of 1919 and reference to, *inter alia*, John Barrymore, David Belasco, Ben Iden Payne. Preface by St. John Ervine.

### Karloff, Boris
### (1887-1969)
### Actor

3953   UNDERWOOD, PETER.   Horror man: the life of Boris Karloff
pp.238; pl. 7                                                MH
London: Leslie Frewin                                      1972

In US, Drake, 1972 as *Karloff: the life...*

### Kauffman, Stanley
### (1916-)
### Critic

3954   KAUFFMAN, STANLEY.   Albums of early life
pp.ix, 229                                                    L
New Haven CT: Tickner & Fields                             1980

Reminiscences. Section two has substantial reference to theatre experience.

3955   CARDULLO, BERT (Ed.).   Before his eyes. Essays in honor of Stanley Kauffman
pp.x, 185; ill. in text                                       M
Lanham MD: U. P. of America                                1986

Includes Michael Berlin: *The Broadway 'Salesman'*; Gautam Dasgupta: *Squat: nature theatre of New York*; Robert James: *'Southern Theatre Chronicle'*.

### Kaye, Danny
### [Kominsky, David Daniel]
### (1913-1987)
### Comedian

3956   RICHARDS, DICK.   The life story of Danny Kaye
pp.70; ill.                                                 DL★
London: Convoy                                             1949

3957   SINGER, KURT.   The Danny Kaye saga
pp.206; front., pl. 8                                         L
London: Robert Hale                                        1957

### Kazan, Elia
### (1909-)
### Director

3958   TAILLEUR, ROGER.   Elia Kazan: présentation par Roger Tailleur. Panorama critique. Témoignages. Filmographie. Théatrographie. Bibliographie. Documents iconographiques
pp.219; ill. in text                                          L
Paris: Seghers                                             1971

New edition. First published 1967.

3959   CIMENT, MICHAEL (Ed.).   Kazan on Kazan
pp.199; ill. in text                                          O
London: Secker and Warburg                                 1973

Chronologically arranged interviews. Includes account of early theatre experience.

3960   KAZAN, ELIA.   On what makes a director
pp.22                                                         M
NY: Directors Guild of America                             1973

A talk given at the conclusion of a retrospective of Kazan's films at Wesleyan University, Middletown, CT in 1973. Primarily concerned with film directing, but mentions theatre experience and parallels.

3961   SCHUENEMAN, WARREN W.   Elia Kazan: director
Minneapolis: U. of Minnesota (PhD)                         1974

3962   RICCI, FREDERICK.   An analysis of the directing techniques of Elia Kazan in theatre and film as illustrated in *A Streetcar named Desire*
NY: Columbia U. Teachers' College (EdD)                    1975

3963   CLARK, LEROY W.   The directing practices and principles of Elia Kazan
Kent OH: State U. (PhD)                                    1976

3964   PAULY, THOMAS H.   An American odyssey: Elia Kazan and American culture
pp.viii, 282; ill. in text                                    M
Philadelphia: Temple U. P.                                 1983

3965   JONES, DAVID.   Great directors at work. Stanislavsky, Brecht, Kazan, Brook
pp.x, 289; ill. in text                                       M
Los Angeles: U. of California P.                           1986

3966   CIMENT, MICHAEL (Ed.).   An American odyssey: Elia Kazan
pp.237; ill. in text                                          L
London: Bloomsbury                                         1988

Translated from the French, *Une Odyssée Américaine*, Paris, Calman Lévy, 1987. A heavily illustrated collection of interviews, articles, letters and speeches given by Kazan. Introduction, *Elia Kazan at the cross roads* translated by Sally Sampson. Section three specifically on the theatre.

3967   KAZAN, ELIA.   Elia Kazan: a life
pp.v, 851; ill. in text                                       M
London: Andre Deutsch                                      1988

First published NY: Alfred A. Knopf.

### Keene, Laura
### (1826?-1873)
### Actress, manageress

3968   CREAHAN, JOHN.   The life of Laura Keene, actress, artist, manager and scholar. Together with some interesting reminiscences of her daughters
pp.254; pl. 14                                                M
Philadelphia: Rodgers                                      1897

3969   TAYLOR, DOROTHY J.   Laura Keene in America
New Orleans: Tulane U. (PhD)                               1966

### Keene, Thomas Wallace
### [Eagleson, Thomas R.]
### (1840-1898)
### Actor, manager

3970   BOOKS, LETTERS AND PORTRAITS: the library of the late Thomas W. Keene (tragedian) with some additions from other sources, for sale at auction, October...1904
pp.59                                                        MB
NY: Anderson Auction                                       1904

757 items, predominantly stage literature.

### Kellerd, John E.
### (1863-1929)
### Actor

**3971** FROST, JONATHAN B. The greatest Hamlet...involving a new and unique interpretation of the drama, Hamlet...and an appreciative review of Hamlet as presented by John E. Kellerd and his capable company
ll.[36]; ill. in text  MB
[Atlanta GA]: [For the author]  [1915?]
Adulatory account of the performance and interpretation, with production photographs. In 1912, Kellerd gave 102 consecutive performances of *Hamlet* in New York, thus surpassing Edwin Booth's achievement of 100 performances in 1864-65.

### Kerr, Walter Francis
### (1913-)
### Critic

**3972** ORAM, ROBERT E. The popular theatre and Broadway: recommendations for survival by Walter Kerr
Detroit: Wayne State U. (PhD)  1974

**3973** BLADEL, RODERICK. Walter Kerr: an analysis of his criticism
pp.v, 210; ill. in text  M
Metuchen NJ: Scarecrow P.  1976

**3974** KIMES, WILLIAM H. Walter Kerr: the critic as theorist. A study of aesthetic, theatrical, and dramatic principles
Madison: U. of Wisconsin (PhD)  1976

### Kiralfy, Bolossy
### (1847-1932)
### Producer

**3975** BARKER, BARBARA M. Bolossy Kiralfy, creator of great musical spectacles
pp.xxxiv, 286; ill. in text  M
Ann Arbor: UMI Research P.  1988

### Kiralfy, Imre
### (1849?-1919)
### Producer

**3976** GREGORY, B. E. The spectacle plays and exhibitions of Imre Kiralfy, 1887-1894
Manchester: U. (PhD)  1988
Includes reference to NY, Staten Island, Cincinnati.

### Koch, Frederick Henry
### (1877-1944)
### Teacher, designer, playwright

**3977** SELDEN, SAMUEL & SPHANGOS, MARY T. Frederick Henry Koch: pioneer playmaker. A brief biography...with notes by Jonathan Daniels and others
pp.viii, 92; ill.  DL*
Chapel Hill: U. of N. Carolina P.  1954

**3978** HAGAN, JOHN P. Frederick Henry Koch and the American folk drama
Bloomington: Indiana U. (PhD)  1969

### Krone, Charles S.
### Actor

**3979** KRONE, CHARLES A. Recollections of an old actor...(read at a meeting of the [Missouri Historical] Society, 20 October, 1905 and subsequently)
pp. various; pl. 8  MB
St Louis: Missouri Society  1906
Printed in the Society Collections: Vols II, III and IV in nine instalments. Reminiscences of the old Bates Theatre in St Louis, and other early theatrical experiences in the South.

### Kronenberger, Louis
### (1904-1980)
### Critic, editor

**3980** KRONENBERGER, LOUIS. No whippings, no gold watches: the saga of a writer and his job [autobiography]
pp.ix, 309  MH
NY: Little, Brown  1970
Drama critic, teacher. Edited *Best Plays* series, 1952-1961. Adapted Anouilh's *Colombe* (1954) for Broadway.

### Krutch, Joseph Wood
### (1893-1970)
### Critic

**3981** GREEN, GORDON C. An analytical study of the dramatic criticism of Joseph Wood Krutch as published in *The Nation*, 1924-1952
Los Angeles: U. of Southern California (PhD)  1959

**3982** KRUTCH, JOSEPH W. More lives than one [autobiography]
pp.v, 378  MH
NY: William Sloane Associates  1962

**3983** GREEN, JOSEPH G. Joseph Wood Krutch, critic of the drama
Bloomington: Indiana U. (PhD)  1965

**3984** PRIZEMAN, HERBERT H. Joseph Wood Krutch and the human image in modern American drama
New Orleans: Tulane U. (PhD)  1969

**3985** FIET, LOWELL A. Joseph Wood Krutch: humanist critic of the drama
Madison: U. of Wisconsin (PhD)  1973

### Lahr, Bert
### [Lahreim, Irving]
### (1895-1967)
### Comedian, actor

**3986** LAHR, JOHN. Notes on a cowardly lion: the biography of Bert Lahr
pp.xv, 394; pl. 16  M
London: Penguin P.  1970
First published NY: Alfred A. Knopf, 1969.

### Landis, Jessie Royce
### [Medbury, Jessie Royce]
### (1904-1972)
### Actress

**3987** LANDIS, JESSIE R. So you won't be so pretty (but you'll know more) [autobiography]
pp.256; pl. 11  M
London: W.H. Allen  1954

### Langner, Lawrence
### (1890-1962)
### Producer

**3988** LANGNER, LAWRENCE. The magic curtain: the story of a life in two fields, theatre and invention, by the founder of the Theatre Guild
pp.xiii, 498; pl. 31  M
NY: E. P. Dutton  1951

## 8.4. INDIVIDUAL

**3989** LAWRENCE LANGNER May 30, 1890-December 26, 1962: a memorial tribute at the ANTA Theatre, New York City, January 10, 1963 [cover title]
pp.(i), 30; front. M
[NY]: [For ANTA?] [1963]
Text of tributes and messages, including the eulogy delivered by S. N. Behrman at the funeral service, December 30, 1962.

### Larkin, Peter
### (1926-)
### Designer

**3990** WEAVER, ARDEN W. A look at the stage designs of Peter Larkin through a system of critical analysis
Lubbock: Texas Tech U. (PhD) 1982

### Latrobe, Benjamin Henry
### (1764-1820)
### Architect

**3991** WOLLOCK, ABE. Benjamin Henry Latrobe's activities in the American theatre (1797-1808)
Urbana: U. of Illinois (PhD) 1962
Designed a projected theatre for Richmond VA.

### Le Gallienne, Eva
### (1899-)
### Actress

**3992** LE GALLIENNE, EVA. At 33 [autobiography]
pp.viii, 262; pl. 12 M
NY: Longmans, Green 1940
First published 1934.

**3993** LE GALLIENNE, EVA. With a quiet heart: an autobiography
pp.viii, 311; pl. 8 M
NY: Viking P. 1953
The author is at pains to establish that this is 'not a continuation' of her earlier At 33.

**3994** COOPER, PAUL R. Eva Le Gallienne's Civic Repertory Theatre
Urbana: U. of Illinois (PhD) 1967

**3995** NOT USED

**3996** SCHANKE, ROBERT A. Eva Le Gallienne: a bio-bibliography
pp.xi, 208; ill. in text MH
Westport CT: Greenwood P. 1989

### Le Noire, Rosetta
### (1911-)
### Actress, singer

**3997** NORFLETT, LINDA K. The theatre career of Rosetta Le Noire
NY: U. (PhD) 1983

### Leavitt, Michael Bennett
### (1843-1935)
### Manager

**3998** LEAVITT, M. B. Fifty years in theatrical management
pp.xxv, 735; pl. 110 M
NY: Broadway Publishing 1912

### Leiber, Fritz
### (1883-1949)
### Actor, director

**3999** DIERS, HERMAN H. Fritz Leiber, actor and producer of Shakespeare
Urbana-Champaign: U. of Illinois (PhD) 1965

### Leman, Walter M.
### (1810-1890)
### Actor

**4000** LEMAN, WALTER M. Memories of an old actor
xv, 406; front. M
San Francisco: A. Roman 1886

### Leslie, Amy
### [Buck, Lillie]
### (1860-1939)
### Critic

**4001** LESLIE, AMY. Some players: personal sketches
pp.vii, 624; pl. 45 inc. 10 facsimile letters M
Chicago: Herbert S. Stone 1899
Performed as Lillie West. After retiring, became drama critic for the Chicago *Daily News* for 40 years. 175 copies.

### Leslie, Elsie
### [Lyde, Elsie]
### (1881-1966)
### Actress

**4002** DOUGLASS, JANE (Ed.). Trustable & preshus friends
pp.95; ill. in text L
NY: Harcourt Brace Jovanovich 1977
The career of Elsie Leslie. Foreword by Julie Harris.

### Lewis, Robert
### (1909-)
### Actor, director, teacher

**4003** REYNOLDS, STEVEN C. The theatre art of Robert Lewis: an analysis and evaluation
Ann Arbor: U. of Michigan (PhD) 1981

**4004** LEWIS, ROBERT. Slings and arrows: theater in my life
pp.369; ill. in text M
NY: Stein and Day 1984
Autobiography-cum-diary. Author worked for the Group Theatre and at the Actors Studio before becoming Chair of the acting and directing departments at Yale School of Drama and later Chair of Drama at Rice, Houston.

### Lewisohn, Ludwig
### (1885-1955)
### Critic, scholar

**4005** OKIN, LESLIE. The dramatic criticism of Ludwig Lewisohn: a critical study
NY: U. (PhD) 1977

### Lissim, Simon
### (1900-)
### Designer

**4006** TESSIER, ANDRÉ. Simon Lissim
pp.57; ill. in text, some col. M
Paris: Le Trident 1928

**4007** COGNIAT, RAYMOND.  Simon Lissim
pp.118; ill. in text, some col.      M
Paris: Editions du Cygne      1933
Preface by Paul Léon.

**4008** SIMON LISSIM: fourteen plates with a text by George Freedley
pp.54; ill. in text      M
NY: James Hendrickson      1949
280 copies, signed by Lissim.

**4009** SIMON LISSIM interviewed by Raymond Lister with an introduction by Yvon Bizardel
pp.23; pl. 7      M
Cambridge UK: Golden Head P.      1962

**4010** DREAMS IN THE THEATRE: designs of Simon Lissim [cover title]
pp.40; ill. in text      M
NY: Public Library & Readex Books      1976
Three essays and a checklist of designs exhibited at the Vincent Astor Gallery, NYPL at Lincoln Center.

**4011** THE WORLD OF SIMON LISSIM: 90 designs for the theatre [cover title]
pp.[16]; ill. in text      M
Washington DC: International Exhibitions Foundation      1979
Catalogue of travelling exhibition. Introduction by Elaine Evans Dee.

### Livingstone, Belle
### [Graham, Isabel]
### (1875-1957)
### Cabaret owner

**4012** LIVINGSTONE, BELLE.  Belle of Bohemia: the memoirs
pp.318; pl. 10      M
London: John Hamilton      1927

**4013** LIVINGSTONE, BELLE.  Belle out of order
pp.vii, 291; front.      M
London: Heinemann      1960
First published NY: Henry Holt, 1959. A second book of memoirs.

### Logan, Joshua Lockwood
### (1908-1988)
### Director, producer

**4014** BOROFF, PHIL D.  Joshua Logan's directorial approach to the theatre and motion pictures: an historical analysis
Carbondale: Southern Illinois U. (PhD)      1976

**4015** LOGAN, JOSHUA.  Josh: my up and down, in and out life [autobiography]
pp.vii, 408; ill. in text      M
London: W. H. Allen      1977

**4016** LOGAN, JOSHUA.  Movie stars, real people, and me
pp.xv, 368; ill. in text      L
NY: Delacorte P.      1978

### Logan, Olive
### [Sykes, Olive]
### (1839?-1909)
### Actress, playwright

**4017** LOGAN, OLIVE.  Apropos of women and theatres with a paper or two on Parisian topics
pp.240      M
NY: Carleton      1869
An example of early feminism. Largely reprinted material includes chapters *The drunken drama, The leg business, Nudity in theatres, The green room*. Author was one of three daughters of Cornelius A. Logan, dramatist and actor, and defender of the stage against religious attack.

**4018** LOGAN, OLIVE.  Before the footlights and behind the scenes: a book about 'the show business' in all its branches from puppet shows to grand opera: from mountebanks to menageries: from learned pigs to lecturers: from burlesque blonds to actors and actresses: with some observations and reflection (original and reflected) on morality and immorality in amusements: thus exhibiting the 'show world' as seen from within, through the eyes of the present lecturer and author
pp.612; ill. in text, pl. 34      M
Philadelphia: Parmelee      1870
Somewhat eccentric autobiography with wide reference to performers c.1840-1870. The numbered list of plates bears no relation to their actual order. The work was reissued in 1871, Philadelphia, New-World Publishing, with the first chapter omitted and with fewer plates, under the title, *The mimic world and public exhibitions. Their history, their morals, and effects.*

**4019** WILLS, J. ROBERT.  The riddle of Olive Logan: a biographical profile
Cleveland: Case Western Reserve U. (PhD)      1970

### Long, Mary Elitch
### (1850?-1936)
### Theatre owner, manager

**4020** DIER, CAROLINE L.  The lady of the Gardens: Mary Elitch Long
pp.xii, 139; pl. 80      M
Los Angeles: Saturday Night Publishing      1932
Biography of the co-founder of Elitch's summer theatre and gardens, Denver CO.

### Loos, Anita
### (1893-1981)
### Actress, writer

**4021** LOOS, ANITA.  A girl like I [autobiography]
pp.x, 275; pl. 16      M
NY: Viking P.      1966

**4022** CAREY, GARY.  Anita Loos: a biography
pp.xv, 331; ill. in text      M
London: Bloomsbury      1988

### Losey, Joseph
### (1909-1984)
### Director

**4023** MILNE, TOM.  Losey on Losey
pp.192; ill. in text      M
London: Secker & Warburg/ BFI      1967
Mostly concerning the movies, but with a chapter on Losey's production of Brecht's *Galileo*.

### Ludlow, Noah Miller
### (1795-1886)
### Manager, producer, actor

**4024** LUDLOW, NOAH M.  Dramatic life as I found it: a record of personal experience: with an account of

the rise and progress of the drama in the West and South, with anecdotes and biographical sketches of the principal actors and actresses who have at times appeared upon the stage in the Mississippi Valley
pp.xlvii, 779 M
NY: Blom 1966
First published St Louis: 1880. Here reproduced in facsimile, indexed and with a new introduction by Francis Hodge.

## Lunt, Alfred David
## (1892-1980)
## Actor
## Fontanne, Lynn
## [Fontanne, Lillie Louise]
## (1887-1983)
## Actress

4025 ZOLOTOW, MAURICE. Stagestruck: Alfred Lunt and Lynn Fontanne
pp.x, 278; pl. 8 M
London: Heinemann 1965

4026 HANNUM, CHARLES R. A study of Alfred Lunt's approach to the role
Detroit: Wayne State U. (PhD) 1974

4027 BROWN, JARED. The fabulous Lunts: a biography of Alfred Lunt and Lynn Fontanne. Foreword by Helen Hayes.
pp.xviii, 525; pl. 9 M
NY: Atheneum 1988

4028 FREEDLEY, GEORGE. The Lunts...an illustrated study of their work, with a list of their appearances on stage and screen
pp.134; front., ill. in text M
London: Rockliffe 1957

## MacGowan, Kenneth
## (1888-1963)
## Producer, critic, writer

4029 MacGOWAN, KENNETH. William Andrews Clark Memorial Library. The welcoming address by Kenneth MacGowan. Founder's Day celebration, Los Angeles, June 1, 1952
pp.7 L
Los Angeles: U. of California 1952

4030 BLOM, THOMAS A. Kenneth MacGowan and the aesthetic paradigm for the new stagecraft in America
Ann Arbor: U. of Michigan (PhD) 1987

## MacKaye, Steele
## (1842-1894)
## Director, manager, playwright

4031 MACKAYE, PERCY. Epoch: the life of Steele MacKaye, genius of the theatre, in relation to his times and contemporaries
pp.xlvii, 489; cxxvi, 483; ill. in text, pl. 52 M
NY: Boni and Liveright 1927
Two volumes. Written by subject's son.

4032 VORENBERG, WILLIAM. Steele MacKaye's ideas and theories as incorporated in the Lyceum Theatre
Stanford: U. (Thesis) 1949

4033 CURRY, WADE C. Steele MacKaye, producer and director
Urbana: U. of Illinois (PhD) 1958

4034 MARIENTHAL, HAROLD S. A historical study of the New York Lyceum Theatre under the management of Steele MacKaye, 1884-1885
Los Angeles: U. of Southern California (PhD) 1965

4035 HANNON, DANIEL L. The MacKaye Spectatorium: a reconstruction and analysis of a theatrical spectacle planned for the World's Columbian Exposition of 1893 with a history of the producing organizations
New Orleans: Tulane U. (PhD) 1970
A failed project, through insolvency. Steele MacKaye died soon after a model of the project had been contstructed.

4036 GUTHRIE, FAVID G. The innovations of Steele MacKaye in scenic design and practice as contributions to the American theatre
NY: U. (PhD) 1974

4037 WOODARD, DEBRA J. The plays of Steele MacKaye: the beginning of a movement towards realism
Evanston: Northwestern U. (PhD) 1981

## Macready, Mrs
## (1829-1873)
## Actress

4038 MEMOIR OF MRS MACREADY with opinions of the press in the cities where she has performed
pp.132 M
NY: [For the author?] 1859
Errata slip.

## Maeder, Clara Fisher
## [née Fisher, Clara]
## (1811-1898)
## Actress

4039 A SKETCH of the life of Miss Clara Fisher the lilliputian actress, of the theatres-royal, Drury Lane, and Covent Garden
pp.24; front. MH
Glasgow: William Tait printer 1820
The third edition.

4040 TAYLOR, DOUGLAS (Ed.). Autobiography of Clara Fisher Maeder
pp.xlviii, 138 MH
NY: Dunlap Society 1897
260 copies.

## Mamoulian, Rouben
## (1897-1987)
## Director

4041 MILNE, TOM. Rouben Mamoulian
pp.176; ill. in text L
Bloomington: Indiana U. P. 1969
Includes reference to the Theatre Guild, the American Opera Company and musicals of the 1940s.

4042 BECVAR, WILLIAM J. The stage and film career of Rouben Mamoulian
Lawrence: U. of Kansas (PhD) 1975

4043 OBERSTEIN, BENNETT T. The Broadway directing career of Rouben Mamoulian
Bloomington: Indiana U. (PhD) 1977

4044 SPERGEL, MARK. Rouben Mamoulian: reinventing reality - his art and life
NY: City U. (PhD) 1990

### Mansfield, Richard
### (1854-1907)
### Actor

4045 ROSTAND, EDMOND. Cyrano de Bergerac...translated from the French by Gladys Thomas and Mary F. Guillemard with illustrations from stage scenes and character pictures of Richard Mansfield and Margaret Anglin
pp.250; pl. 8 M
NY: G. W. Dillingham 1898
The translation is the one used by Arnold Daly in his production at the Chestnut Street Opera House, Philadelphia, with Ada Rehan and Charles Richman. The illustrations are derived from Mansfield's production at the Garden Theatre, NY. Both productions opened on October 3, 1898. Daly's failed.

4046 THE MANSFIELD CALENDAR, with pictures of Richard Mansfield's favorite characters, a few quotations and some good wishes
pp.[24]; ill. in text MH
[NY?: [?] 1900
Monthly calendars with facing studies of Mansfield in role, including a striking double exposure depicting Jekyll and Hyde. Harvard copy lacks December.

4047 WILSTACH, PAUL. Richard Mansfield: the man and the actor
pp.xx, 500; pl. 49 M
London: Chapman & Hall 1908
First published NY: Charles Scribner's Sons, 1908.

4048 WINTER, WILLIAM. Life and art of Richard Mansfield with selections from his letters
pp.361; 353; pl. 76 M
NY: Moffat, Yard 1910
In two volumes.

4049 THE CONTENTS of 'The Grange' New London, Conn. the residence of the late Richard Mansfield...sold by order of Mrs Richard Mansfield (Beatrice Cameron)...
pp.iv, 70; ill. in text, front. M
NY: Anderson Galleries 1926
Auction catalogue May 7-8, 1926.

4050 BURR, DAVID H. Richard Mansfield: a re-evaluation of his artistic career
Ann Arbor: U. of Michigan (PhD) 1972

4051 BIBEE, JACK L. The acting of Richard Mansfield
Urbana-Champaign: U. of Illinois (PhD) 1974

4052 PINKSTON, CLAUDE A. Richard Mansfield's Shakespearean productions
Los Angeles: U. of California (PhD) 1980

### Mantell, Robert Bruce
### (1854-1928)
### Actor

4053 BULLIET, CLARENCE J. Robert Mantell's romance [biography]
pp.vii, 256; pl. 12 MH
Boston: John W. Luce 1918

4054 FAVORINI, ATTILIO A. The last tragedian. Robert B. Mantell and the American theatre
New Haven: Yale U. (PhD) 1969

### Mar, Helen

4055 MAR, HELEN. May I tell you a story [memoirs]
pp.156; front. M
London: J & J Bennett 1912

### Marble, Danforth
### (1810-1849)
### Actor

4056 [KELLEY, JONATHAN F.]. Dan. Marble: a biographical sketch of that famous and diverting humorist, with reminiscences, comicalities, anecdotes, etc., etc. By Falconbridge
pp.xvi, 235; pl. 6 MH
NY: Dewitt & Davenport 1851

4057 DOBKIN, WILLIAM E. The theatrical career of Danforth Marble: stage Yankee
Bloomington: Indiana U. (PhD) 1970

### Marbury, Elisabeth
### (1856-1933)
### Agent

4058 MARBURY, ELISABETH. My crystal ball: reminiscences
pp.320; pl. 12 M
London: Hurst and Blackett 1924
Author was a celebrated authors' agent, possibly the first to negotiate a percentage of box-office receipts for her clients.

### March, Fredric
### [Bickel, Frederick McIntyre]
### (1897-1975)
### Actor

4059 BURROWS, MICHAEL B. Charles Laughton and Fredric March
pp.41; ill. in text O
St Austell UK: Primestyle 1969

4060 QUIRK, LAWRENCE J. The films of Fredric March
pp.255; ill DL★
NY: Citadel P. 1971
Includes biographical sketch.

### Markham, Pauline
### (1847-1919)
### Actress

4061 [MARKHAM, PAULINE]. Life of Pauline Markham. Written by herself
pp.31; front. MH
NY: For the author 1871
An account of her début with Lydia Thompson at Wood's Museum in New York and her subsequent success in America.

### Marlowe, Julia
### [Frost, Sarah Frances]
### (1866-1950)
### Actress

4062 BARRY, JOHN D. Julia Marlowe
pp.iv, 87; pl. 16 M
Boston: Richard G. Badger 1899

4063 BRERETON, AUSTIN. The house of Sothern, and Miss Julia Marlowe
pp.23; pl. 8 M
London: [For the author?] 1907

Brief career sketches published on the occasion of their English debut in April 1907.

4064 SYMONS, ARTHUR. Plays acting and music: a book of theory
xii, 322pp. M
London,: Archibald Constable 1909

Includes the essay: *Great acting in English* (pp. 182-199), first published privately in 1907, which reviews the acting of Julia Marlowe and Edward H. Sothern on their visit to London.

4065 RUSSELL, CHARLES E. Julia Marlowe: her life and art
pp.xxvii, 582; ill. in text, pl. 24 M
NY: D. Appleton 1926

4066 LITERATURE relating to the theatre...property of Mrs Julia Marlowe Sothern (et al)
★
NY: Parke-Bernet Galleries 1942

4067 SOTHERN, EDWARD H. & DOWNEY, FAIRFAX (Ed.). Julia Marlowe's story
pp.xiii, 237; pl. 4 M
NY: Rinehart 1954

Biography written, as if in the first person, by the actress's second husband and later edited.

4068 OVINGTON, ADELAIDE. The star that didn't twinkle
pp.145; ill. DL★
NY: Vantage P. 1961

Biography of Julia Marlowe.

4069 MITCHELL, SALLIE. The early career of Julia Marlowe: the making of a star
Urbana-Champaign: U. of Illinois (PhD) 1977

## Massett, Stephen
### (1818?-1898)
### Singer, entertainer

4070 BIOGRAPHICAL SKETCH, words of the songs, ballads, etc., of the composer and vocalist, Mr Stephen Massett, *Jeems Pipes, of Pipesville*, with opinions of the press on his entertainments in England, California, Oregon, Australia, the Sandwich Isles, and the East Indies. By C. J. P.
pp.52; portrait on title MH
NY: [Wm Hall & Sons?] 1858

English-born entertainer who toured a one-man show of readings and songs.

4071 MASSETT, STEPHEN C. 'Drifting about,' or what 'Jeems of Pipesville' saw-and-did. An autobiography...with many comic illustrations by Mullen
pp.371; ill. in text M
NY: Carleton 1863

## Matthau, Walter
### (1920-)
### Actor

4072 HUNTER, ALLAN. Walter Matthau
pp.208; ill. DL★
NY: St Martin's P. 1984

## Matthews, James Brander
### (1852-1929)
### Teacher, writer, playwright

4073 MATTHEWS, BRANDER. [Pamphlet comprising letters from Matthews to William Moy Thomas and others]
pp.[6] M
NY: [For the author] [1884]

Denying a charge by H. P. Stephens that Matthews's play *Margery's Lovers* had plagiarized Stephens's play *Hearts*.

4074 MATTHEWS, BRANDER. These many years: recollections of a New Yorker [autobiography]
pp.ix, 463 M
NY: Charles Scribner's Sons 1917

4075 BENDER, JACK E. The theatre of Brander Matthews
Ann Arbor: U. of Michigan (PhD) 1954

4076 WEYANT, GEORGE W. A critical study of Brander Matthews's dramatic theory
Los Angeles: U. of Southern California (PhD) 1965

## Mayo, Frank
### (1839-1896)
### Actor

4077 FIKE, DUANE J. Frank Mayo: actor, playwright, and manager
Lincoln: U. of Nebraska (PhD) 1980

## McClintic, Guthrie
### (1893-1961)
### Director, producer

4078 McCLINTIC, GUTHRIE. Me and Kit
pp.ix, 341; pl. 8 M
Boston: Little, Brown 1955

Reminiscences of author and his wife, Katharine Cornell.

4079 TILLINGHAST, JOHN K. Guthrie McClintic, director
Bloomington: Indiana U. (PhD) 1964

## McCullough, John Edward
### (1832-1885)
### Actor

4080 [EDWARDS, MARY]. Address delivered by Henry Edwards at St George Hall, Philadelphia, November 12th, 1885. Obsequies of McCullough
bs. MH
[Philadelphia]: [For Mrs Edwards?] [1885]

4081 IN MEMORY of John McCullough
pp.66; pl. 2 M
NY: DeVinne P. 1889

Contributors include William Winter who provided a biographical sketch and tribute, Steele MacKaye, Henry Williams, William F. Johnson. Also a list of subscribers to the McCullough monument in Mount Maria cemetery.

4082 CLARK, SUSIE C. John McCullough as man, actor and spirit
pp.368; pl. 8 M
NY: Broadway Publishing 1914

First published Boston: Murray and Emery, 1905.

4083 WOODRUFF, BRUCE E. 'Genial' John McCullough: actor and manager
Lincoln: U. of Nebraska (PhD) 1984

### Meade, Edwards Hoag
### (1863-1914)
### Actor

4084 MEADE, EDWARDS H. Doubling back: autobiography of an actor serio-comical...containing plain anecdotes of the stage, how I became an actor and the result, stories while barnstorming and some original verse...
pp.180; ill. in text, pl. 10 M
[Chicago?]: For the author 1916

### Menken, Adah Isaacs
### [Adah Bertha Theodore]
### (1835-1869)
### Actress

4085 THEATRE de la Gaité. *Les Pirates de la Savane.* Notice biographique sur Miss Adah Isaacs Menken, artiste Américaine. Deuxième edition
pp.14 MH
Paris: [For the theatre?] 1867
On the occasion of her Paris début; a brief notice of acclaim, referring to her American successes and, inevitably, to *Mazeppa*.

4086 BARCLAY, GEORGE L. (Ed.). The life and remarkable career of Adah Isaacs Menken, the celebrated actress. An account of her career as a danseuse, an actress, an authoress, a poetess, a sculptor, an editress, as a captain of the *Dayton Life Guard*, as the wife of the pugilist John C. Heenan, and of 'Orpheus Kerr'...edited by G. Lippard Barclay, comedian
pp.63; ill. in text, front. MB
Philadelphia: Barclay 1868
pp.55-63 are devoted to sketches of performers: William Warren, Jennie Gourlay, James Pilgrim, Lizzie Cooper, C. W. Tayleure, Dollie Bidwell and William Wallace.

4087 MENKEN, ADAH I. Infelicia [verses]
pp.v, 141; ill. in text, pl. 2 M
London: For the author 1868

4088 JAMES, ED (Ed.). Biography of Adah Isaacs Menken. With selections from *Infelicia*
pp.24; ill. in text MH
NY: For the editor [1881]

4089 SWINBURNE, ALGERNON C. Adah Isaacs Menken: a fragment of autobiography
pp.x, 2; pl. 2 L
London: For the author 1917
Introduction signed 'XYZ' offers a brief sketch of Menken's life and association with Swinburne. The 'fragment' comprises three letters from Swinburne and one from Julian Field, augmented by photographs of Swinburne and Menken, and a facsimile of a dedication to her by him. It is possible that the material was edited by Clement Shorter.

4090 NORTHCOTT, RICHARD. Adah Isaacs Menken. An illustrated biography
pp.53; ill. in text L
London: The Press Printers 1921

4091 WYNDHAM, HORACE. Victorian sensations
pp.288; pl. 24 L
London: Jarrolds 1933

Chapter 5: *Poetry and passion* is an essay on Adah Isaacs Menken with pl. 6.

4092 FALK, BERNARD. The naked lady, or storm over Adah: a biography of Adah Isaacs Menken
pp.306; ill. in text, pl. 33 M
London: Hutchinson 1934

4093 LESSER, ALLEN. Weave a wreath of laurel: the lives of four Jewish contributors to American civilization
pp.x, 75; ill. in text DL★
NY: Crown P. 1938
Includes a study of Adah Isaacs Menken.

4094 FLEISCHER, NAT. Reckless lady: the life story of Adah Isaacs Menken
pp.36; ill. in text L
[NY]: For the author 1941
A biographical sketch. Author was editor of *The Ring* magazine.

4095 LESSER, ALLEN. Enchanting rebel: (the secret of Adah Isaacs Menken)
pp.284; pl. 4 M
NY: Beechhurst P. 1947

4096 EDWARDS, SAMUEL. Queen of the Plaza: a biography of Adah Isaacs Menken
pp.ix, 307 M
London: Alvin Redman 1965
First published NY: Funk & Wagnalls, 1964 under the authorship of Paul Lewis, [N. B. Gerson], and here under a second pseudonym. Fictionalized, unreliable.

4097 MANKOWITZ, WOLF. Mazeppa: the lives, loves and legends of Adah Isaacs Menken. A biographical quest
pp.vi, 270; ill. in text M
London: Blond & Briggs 1982

### Merrill, John
### (1875-1956)
### Actor, educationist

4098 MERRILL, JOHN. Son of Salem: the autobiography of John Merrill
xi, 202; pl. 8 MH
NY: Vantage P. 1953
Author worked at the Francis W. Parker school, Chicago.

### Merry, Mrs Anne Brunton
### (1769?-1808)
### Actress

4099 DOTY, GRESDNA A. The career of Mrs Anne Brunton Merry in the American theatre
pp.xiii, 170; ill. in text, pl. 4 M
Baton Rouge: Louisiana State U. P. 1971

### Metcalfe, James Stetson
### (1858-1927)
### Critic

4100 DOXTATOR, ROBERT L. James Stetson Metcalfe's signed criticism of the legitimate theatre in New York City, 1888-1927
Lincoln: U. of Nebraska (PhD) 1985

## 8.4. INDIVIDUAL

### Mielziner, Jo
### (1901-1976)
### Designer

**4101** EXHIBITION of stage models and designs by Jo Mielziner [catalogue]
NY: International Galleries    MH★    1932

**4102** MIELZINER, JO. Designing for the theatre: a memoir and a portfolio
pp.x, 243; ill. in text, some col.    M
NY: Atheneum    1965

**4103** SMITH, HARRY W. Mielziner and Williams, a concept of style
New Orleans: Tulane U. (PhD)    1965

**4104** WEISS, DAVID W. Jo Mielziner's contribution to the American theatre
Bloomington: Indiana U. (PhD)    1965

**4105** JO MIELZINER theatrical designer: selected works 1928-1960 from the collection of Jules Fisher
pp.29; ill. in text    M
Pittsburgh PA: Carnegie-Mellon U.    1983

### Miller, James
### [Wilmot, Fred]
### (1867?-1917)
### Actor

**4106** STEWART, WALTER P. The dramatic career of James Miller
Austin: U. of Texas (PhD)    1939

### Miller, John Henry
### (1860-1926)
### Actor

**4107** MORSE, FRANK P. Backstage with Henry Miller. With an introduction by George M. Cohan
pp.288; pl. 6    M
NY: E. P. Dutton    1938

### Miner, Worthington
### (1900-1982)
### Director

**4108** SCHAFFNER, FRANKLIN J. Worthington Miner interviewed by Franklin J. Schaffner
pp.ix, 296; front., pl. 8    O
Metuchen NJ: Scarecrow P.    1988
Wide reference to NY theatre of the 1930s.

### Ming Cho Lee
### (1930-)
### Designer

**4109** FLATEN, DAVID. Ming Cho Lee, designer
Berkeley: U. of California (PhD)    1978

### Minnelli, Vincente
### (1903-1986)
### Director, designer

**4110** MINNELLI, VINCENTE with ARCE, HECTOR. I remember it well [autobiography]
pp.xvi, 391; pl. 32    MH
NY: Doubleday    1974
Foreword by Alan Jay Lerner.

### Modjeska, Helena
### (1840-1909)
### Actress

**4111** ALTEMUS, JAMESON T. Helena Modjeska
pp.217; front.    DL★
NY: J. S. Ogilvie    1883

**4112** COLLINS, MABEL. The story of Helena Modjeska (Madame Chlapowska)
pp.iii, 296    M
London: W. H. Allen    1883

**4113** MODJESKA, HELENA. Memories and impressions: an autobiography
pp.ix, 571; ill. in text, pl. 16    M
NY: Macmillan    1910

**4114** SIEDLECKI, FRANCISZEK. Helena Modrzejewska
pp.173; pl. 20    L
Warsaw: Nakladem Zwiazku    1927
Biography. Copyrighted 1917, epilogue dated 1927.

**4115** [GAWLIK, JAN P.]. Helena Modrzejewska na scenie krakowskiego
pp.44, xi; pl. 68    L
Cracow: Wydawnictwo Literackie    1956
Brief introduction. Mostly photographic studies of Modjeska in role.

**4116** GRONOWICZ, ANTONI. Modjeska; her life and loves
pp.254; pl. 8    M
NY: Thomas Yoseloff    1956

**4117** STRAUS, STEFAN. Bibliografia zrodel do historii teatru w Polsce...
pp.xi, 495    M
Wroclaw: Wydawnictwo Polskiej Akademii    1957
Errata slip. Extensive reference to Helena Modjeska. See also *Pamietnik Teatralany* Rok.viii, Zeszyt 4 (32), Warsaw, 1957, an issue devoted to her.

**4118** GOT, JERZY & SCZUBLEWSKI, JOZEF. Helena Modrzejewska
pp.xi, 257; pl. 16    M
Warsaw: Panstwowy Instytut Wydawniczy    1958
Biography, repertoire, itinerary, including US tour, and selected notices. Errata slip facing table of contents.

**4119** SZCZUBLEWSKI, JOZEF. Helena Modrzejewska
pp.149; pl. 16    L
Warsaw: Panstwowy Instytut Wydawniczy    1959

**4120** TERLECKI, TYMAN. Pani Heleni: opowiesc biograficzna o Modrzejewskiej
pp.282; pl. 8    L
London: Katolickiego Osrodka Wydawniczego    [1962]

**4121** COLEMAN, ARTHUR P. & COLEMAN, MARION M. Wanderers twain, Modjeska and Sienkiewicz: a view from California
pp.xiii; 110; ill. in text    M
Cheshire CT: Cherry Hill Boks    1964

Makes particular reference to the planned Utopian community at Anaheim CA.

**4122** COLEMAN, MARION M. American debut: source materials on the first appearance of the Polish actress Helena Modjeska on the American stage including letters and dispatches by Henryk Sienkiewicz
pp.40; ill. in text M
Cheshire CT: Cherry Hill Books 1965

Début at California Theatre, San Francisco, August 20, 1877 as Adrienne Lecouvreur.

**4123** GOT, JERZY & SZCZUBLEWSKI, JOZEF (Eds). Korespondencja Heleny Modrzejewskiej i Karola Chlapowskiego: Tom Pierswszy (1859-1880) [Tom Drugi (1881-1909)]
pp.525, 111; 495, i; pl. 25, inserted genealogy L
Warsaw: Instytut Wydawniczy 1965

Includes letters written during her US sojourn.

**4124** COLEMAN, MARION M. [Ed.]. Letters to Emilia: a record of a friendship. Seven letters of Helena Modjeska to a friend back home. Translated by Michael Kwapiszewski
pp.39; ill. in text M
Cheshire CT: Cherry Hill Books 1967

**4125** COLEMAN, MARION M. Fair Rosalind: the American career of Helena Modjeska
pp.xii, 1019; pl. 8 M
Cheshire CT: Cherry Hill Books 1969

Biography, 1840-1909, with alphabetical and chronological lists of plays presented by her, and a chronological list of her appearances.

**4126** KOSBERG, MILTON L. The Polish colony of California 1876-1914
pp.80; ill. in text L
San Francisco: R & E Associates 1971

Includes much material on Modjeska.

**4127** KYDRYNSKI, JULIUSZ. Gwiazda dwoch kontynentow
pp.229; pl. 8 L
Warsaw: Instytut Wydawniczy nasza Ksiegarnia 1973

**4128** SZCZUBLEWSKI, JOZEF. Zywot Modrzejewskieij
pp.725; pl. 13 M
Warsaw: Panstowy Instytut Wydawniczy 1975

### Moeller, Philip
### (1880-1958)
### Producer, director

**4129** WILEY, DAVID W. Philip Moeller of the Theatre Guild: an historical and critical study
Bloomington: Indiana U. (PhD) 1973

**4130** KISER, EDMOND L. The 'inspirational' system of Philip Moeller, Theatre Guild director
Detroit: Wayne State U. (PhD) 1981

### Monk, Meredith

**4131** QUADRI, FRANCO (Ed.). Il tempo e gli ambienti di Meredith Monk con il testo parlato di *Quarry*
pp.71; ill. in text L
Venice: Edizione de la Biennale di Venezia 1976

Comprises the title essay by Quadri; R. Baker: *Cronaca in molti paessagi*; an interview with Brooks McNamara, *Una scenografia di citta*; Germano Celant: *Un teatro composito*; an interview by Philippe du Vignol, *Uno spazio a due dimensioni*; an interview by 'La danza e l'avanguardia'; a transcribed debate involving Monk, Donaggio, Messinis, Ranconi; and Monk: *Quarry*.

### Montalban, Ricardo
### (1920-)
### Actor

**4132** MONTALBAN, RICARDO & THOMAS, BOB. Reflections: a life in two worlds [autobiography]
pp.164; pl. 8 L
Garden City NY: Doubleday 1980

Includes an account of the acclaimed touring production of Shaw's *Don Juan in Hell* in which the author played the Don.

### Montez, Lola
### [Gilbert, Marie Dolores Eliza Rosanna]
### (1818?-1861)
### Actress

**4133** LOLA MONTEZ: or, a reply to the *Private History & Memoirs* of that celebrated lady recently published, by the Marquis Papon, formerly secretary to the King of Bavaria, and for a period the professed friend and attendant of the Countess of Landsfeld
pp.72; front. MH
NY: [For the author?] 1851

Concerning an alleged relationship betweeen Montez and the King of Bavaria.

**4134** MONTEZ, LOLA. Arts of beauty
pp.vii, 123; front. L
London: James Blackwood [1858]

How to be and remain beautiful. Also hints to gentlemen on the art of fascinating.

**4135** MONTEZ, LOLA. Lectures of Lola Montez (Countess of Landsfeld). Including her autobiography
pp.292; front. M
NY: Rudd & Carleton 1858

The first two chapters comprise an 'autobiography' in the form of an address, the speaker referring to herself throughout in the third person.

**4136** [HAWKS, FRANCIS L.]. The story of a penitent: Lola Montez, by F.L.H.
pp.46 L
NY: Protestant Episcopal Society 1867

A brief biographical sketch, together with fragments from her diary of 1859, presented as evangelical homily. F.L.H. (Francis L. Hawks DD) supplied an initialled statement of his attendance on Montez in her last days, dated 1861. The biography is unattributed but plainly not Hawks's. The work was entered by H. Dyer DD and may have been his.

**4137** MIRECOURT, EUGENE DE. Lola Montez
pp.62; front. L
Paris: Librairie des Contemporains 1871

Biography. The third edition.

**4138** D'AUVERGNE, EDMUND B. Lola Montez, an adventuress of the 'forties. Illustrated
pp.xi, 375; pl. 7 MH
London: T. Werner Laurie [1909]

**4139** LINDBLOM, ERNST. Svenska teaterminnen fran Chicago. Anteckningar och anekdoter...med fjorton teaterportrait
pp.192; ill. in text  L
Stockholm: C. L. Gullbergs  1916
Includes material on Lola Montez.

**4140** WYNDHAM, HORACE. Feminine frailty
pp.352; ill.  DL★
London: Benn  1929
Includes material on Lola Montez.

**4141** WYNDHAM, HORACE. The magnificent Montez. From courtesan to convert
pp.288; pl. 12  M
London: Hutchinson  1935

**4142** AUGUSTIN-THIERRY, A. Lola Montez, favorite royale
pp.220  DL★
Paris: B. Grasset  1936

**4143** GOLDBERG, ISAAC. Queen of hearts. The passionate pilgrimage of Lola Montez
pp.308; front.  DL★
NY: John Day  [1936]

**4144** LEWIS, OSCAR. Lola Montez: the mid-Victorian bad girl in California
pp.69; ill.  DL★
San Francisco: Colt P.  [1938]
Woodcuts by Mallette Dean. 750 copies.

**4145** BARTON, MARGARET & SITWELL, OSBERT (Eds). Sober truth: a collection of nineteenth-century episodes, fantastic, grotesque and mysterious
pp. 234; pl. 8  M
London: Macdonald  1944
First published London: Duckworth, 1930. Includes a chapter on Lola Montez.

**4146** HOLDREDGE, HELEN. The woman in black. The life of Lola Montez
pp.309; ill.  DL★
NY: G. P. Putnam's Sons  1955

**4147** FOLEY, DORIS. Lola Montez and the newspapers. The divine eccentric
pp.228; ill. in text  MH
Los Angeles: Westernlore P.  1969
Biography emphasizing her Pacific Coast appearances, derived substantially from Californian newspapers, 1853-1861.

**4148** AVEDISIAN, LOUISE J. Lola Montez in California (1853-1856)
Los Angeles: U. of California (MA)  1971

**4149** DARLING, AMANDA. Lola Montez
pp.240; front.  L
NY: Stein & Day  1972

**4150** ROSS, ISHBEL. The uncrowned queen: life of Lola Montez
pp.xv, 349; pl. 6  L
NY: Harper & Row  1972

**4151** BRADFIELD, RAYMOND A. Lola Montez and Castlemaine: some early theatrical history
pp.[64] inc. wrappers; ill. in text  MH
Vaughan (Victoria): [For the author?]  [1980?]

## Moorehead, Agnes
### (1906-1974)
### Actress

**4152** SHERK, WARREN. Agnes Moorehead: a very private person
pp.x, 137; ill. in text  L
Philadelphia: Dorrance  1976

## Morehouse, Ward
### (1899-1966)
### Critic

**4153** MOREHOUSE, WARD. Just the other day: from Yellow Pines to Broadway [autobiography]
pp.v, 240  M
NY: McGraw-Hill  1953

**4154** CHRISTOVICH, DAVID P. The dramatic criticism of Ward Morehouse
Athens: U. of Georgia (PhD)  1980

## Morgan, Mona
### Actress

**4155** MORGAN, MONA with CRUIKSHANK, ALFRED B. 'Hamlet the Dane!' An explanation of the true character of Hamlet and the meaning of the play, told for the first time by a player...
pp.54  DL★
Philadelphia: Patterson & White  1936
Author played Ophelia to Walter Hampden's Hamlet.

## Morley, Christopher Darlington
### (1890-1957)
### Journalist, essayist

**4156** MORLEY, CHRISTOPHER. Shakespeare and Hawaii
pp.xi, 96  M
NY: Doubleday, Doran  1933
Lectures given at the U. of Hawaii.

**4157** AN EXHIBITION of CDM [Christopher Morley]...December 1961-February 1962
pp.48; ill. in text  L
Austin: U. of Texas  1962
Catalogue of books, papers, letters, chronologically arranged, 1890-1957, including several items of theatre interest.

## Morosco, Oliver
### [Mitchell, Oliver]
### (1876-1945)
### Manager, producer

**4158** MOROSCO, HELEN M. & DUGGER, LEONARD P. Life of Oliver Morosco: the oracle of Broadway, written from his own notes and comments
pp. iv, 391; pl. 27  M
Caldwell ID: Caxton printers  1944

**4159** SORRELLS, ROY W. The Los Angeles theatre activities of Oliver Morosco
Long Beach: California State U. (MA)  1966
The Morosco Theatre stock company, 1913-1922.

**4160** SCHOEN, LEONARD. A historical study of Oliver Morosco's long run premiere productions in Los Angeles, 1905-1922
Los Angeles: U. of Southern California (PhD)  1971
With reference to the Burbank Stock Company.

## Morris, Clara
### (1848-1925)
### Actress

**4161** MORRIS, CLARA. Life on the stage: my personal experiences and recollections
pp.xv, 399; front. M
London: Isbister 1902
First published NY: McClure, Phillips, 1901.

**4162** MORRIS, CLARA. Stage confidences: talks about players and play acting
pp.316; pl. 16 M
Boston: Lothrop Publishing 1902

**4163** MORRIS, CLARA. The life of a star
pp.ix, 363 M
NY: McClure, Phillips 1906

**4164** HOWARD, MILDRED L. The acting of Clara Morris
Urbana: U. of Illinois (PhD) 1957

## Morris, Felix
### (1850-1900)
### Actor

**4165** MORRIS, FELIX. Reminiscences
pp.176; pl. 4 M
NY: International Telegram 1892
Medical student turned actor who toured in US and UK.

## Morrison, Hobe
### (1904-)
### Critic

**4166** KANDEL, GERALD A. Hobe Morrison and the theatre of Broadway
NY: City U. (PhD) 1978

## Moses, Montrose Jonas
### (1978-1934)
### Critic, scholar

**4167** GRABISH, RICHARD F. Montrose Jonas Moses: critic of American drama
Kent OH: State U. (PhD) 1979

## Mostel, Zero
### (1915-1977)
### Actor

**4168** MOSTEL, ZERO. Zero, by Mostel
pp.[97]; ill. in text MH
NY: Horizon P. 1965
Brief autobiographical introduction in interview form and photographic studies by Max Waldman of Mostel in role.

**4169** MENDOZA, GEORGE. Sesame Street book of opposites with Zero Mostel
pp.[46]; ill. some col. DL★
NY: Platt and Munk 1974
For children. Includes photographs of Mostel by Sheldon Secunda.

**4170** MOSTEL, KATE & GILFORD, MADELINE. 170 years of show business
pp.xi, 175; pl 16 M
NY: Random House 1978

## Mowatt, Anna Cora
### [Ogden, Anna Cora]
### (1819-1870)
### Actress

**4171** MOWATT, ANNA CORA. Autobiography of an actress; or, eight years on the stage
pp.448; front. M
Boston: Ticknor, Reed, & Fields 1854

**4172** RITCHIE, ANNA C. [= Mowatt, Anna C.]. Mimic life; or, before and behind the curtain: a series of narratives
pp.xiv, 408; front. M
Boston: Ticknor & Fields 1856
Fictionalized episodes from Anna Cora Mowatt's theatre experience.

**4173** BLESI, MARIUS. The life and letters of Anna Cora Mowatt
Charlottesville: U. of Virginia (PhD) 1938

**4174** BARNES, ERIC W. The lady of fashion: the life and theatre of Anna Cora Mowatt
pp.xi, 308; pl. 6 M
NY: Charles Scribner's Sons 1954

**4175** SCHOOLEY, BILL J. Anna Cora Mowatt: public reader
Baton Rouge: Louisiana State U. (MA) 1980

## Muni, Paul
### [Weisenfreund, Frederich]
### (1895-1967)
### Actor

**4176** FARBERMAN, BORIS. Paul Muni
pp.46; ill. in text L
Buenos Aires: Congreso Judio Mundial 1970
Biography. Text in Spanish.

**4177** GERLACH, MICHAEL C. The acting of Paul Muni
Ann Arbor: U. of Michigan (PhD) 1971

**4178** LAWRENCE, JEROME. Actor: the life and times of Paul Muni
pp.380; ill. in text M
London: W. H. Allen 1975
First published NY: G. P. Putnam's Sons, 1974.

## Murdoch, James Edward
### (1811?-1893)
### Actor

**4179** BOWYER, FRANCES E. James E. Murdoch, the elocutionist
Boulder: U. of Colorado (MA) 1952

**4180** EDGE, TURNER W. James E. Murdoch, American actor
Urbana-Champaign: U. of Illinois (PhD) 1964

**4181** KIRKLAND, AUDREY S. The elocutional theory and practice of James Edward Murdoch
Detroit MI: Wayne State U. (PhD) 1964

## Murray, Ken
### [Dancourt, Kenneth]
### (1903-1988)
### Comedian

4182 MURRAY, KEN. Life on a pogo stick: autobiography of a comedian
pp.180; ill DL★
Philadelphia: John C. Winston 1960

### Nathan, George Jean
### (1882-1958)
### Critic

4183 GOLDBERG, ISAAC. George Jean Nathan: a critical study
pp.64; ill. in text M
Girard KS: Haldeman-Julius 1925

4184 NATHAN, GEORGE J. The autobiography of an attitude
pp.vii, 292 M
NY: Alfred A. Knopf 1925

Includes chapter, *Attitude towards the drama*.

4185 GOLDBERG, ISAAC. The theatre of George Jean Nathan
pp.xi, 269; pl. 9 M
NY: Simon and Schuster 1926

4186 KOZLENKO, VLADIMIR. The quintessence of Nathanism
pp.53; front M
NY: Vrest Orton 1930

Critical appreciation of George Jean Nathan.

4187 FRICK, CONSTANCE. The dramatic criticism of George Jean Nathan
pp.xiii, 165; front. M
Ithaca NY: Yale U. P. 1943

4188 ANGOFF, CHARLES (Ed.). The world of George Jean Nathan
pp.xxxii, 489 M
NY: Alfred A. Knopf 1952

An anthology, including articles on the theatre.

4189 RUDIN, SEYMOUR. George Jean Nathan. A study of his criticism
Ithaca: Cornell U. (PhD) 1953

4190 HOOD, DONALD F. A study of George Jean Nathan's views on acting
Tallahassee: Florida State U. (PhD) 1970

4191 RUFFINO, ARTHUR S. A cumulative index to the books of George Jean Nathan
Carbondale: Southern Illinois U. (PhD) 1971

### Nazimova, Alla
### (1879-1945)
### Actress

4192 McKERROW, MARGARET. A descriptive study of the acting of Alla Nazimova
Ann Arbor: U. of Michigan (PhD) 1974

### Neal, Patricia
### (1926-)
### Actress

4193 FARRELL, BARRY. Pat and Roald
pp.v, 243; pl. 8 M
NY: Random House 1969

An account of Patricia Neal's fight for health after a massive series of strokes in 1965, and the part played in her recovery by her husband Roald Dahl.

4194 NEAL, PATRICIA & DE NEUF, RICHARD. As I am: an autobiography
pp.384; pl. 16 MH
NY: Simon and Schuster 1988

### Neill, James F.
### (1860-1931)
### Actor, manager

4195 ZUCCHERO, WILLIAM H. The contributions of James F. Neill to the development of the modern American theatrical stock Company
Columbus: Ohio State U. (PhD) 1964

### Nellé, Anthony
### [Nellé, Zdislaw Antoni]
### (1894-1977)
### Dancer, choreographer, designer

4196 SHIRE, SANFORD (Ed.). Nellé
pp.128; ill. in text, many col. M
NY: Rizzoli 1981

Nellé came to the US in 1921 with Pavlova and remained to make his career there as a scenic designer for stage and screen.

### Nesbit, Evelyn
### (1884-1967)
### Actress

4197 NESBIT, EVELYN. The untold story
pp.288 M
London: John Long 1934

Autobiography, purporting to reveal the facts of the notorious Harry Thaw/Stanford White murder case. The author made her theatre début in *Floradora* at the Casino Theatre in 1901.

4198 MOONEY, MICHAEL. Evelyn Nesbit and Stanford White. Love and death in the gilded age
pp.320; ill. DL★
NY: Morrow 1976

### Nethersole, Olga Isabel
### (1866-1951)
### Actress

4199 REILLY, JOY H. From wicked woman of the stage to new woman. The career of Olga Nethersole (1870-1951), actress-manager, suffragist, health pioneer
Columbus: Ohio State U. (PhD) 1984

### Nobles, Milton
### (18470-1924)
### Actor, manager, dramatist

4200 NOBLES, MILTON. Shop talk. Stage stories, anecdotes of the theatre, reminiscences, dialogues and character sketches...
pp.205; front., ill. in text M
Milwaukee: For the author [1889]

### Norton, William Elliot
### (1903-)
### Critic

4201 HADLEY, CHARLES O. Elliot Norton: dramatic critic in the tryout system
Athens: U. of Georgia (PhD) 1973

### Nugent, John C.
### (1868-1947)
### Actor, playwright

**4202** NUGENT, JOHN C. It's a *great* life [autobiography]
pp.331; pl. 6     MH
NY: Dial P.     1940

Father of Elliott Nugent. Vaudeville and theatrical touring in the small towns of the West. Reprints a selection of articles written by the author for *Variety*.

### O'Brien, Pat
### (1899-1983)
### Actor

**4203** O'BRIEN, PAT. The wind at my back: the life and times of Pat O'Brien by himself
pp.331; pl. 8     M
NY: Doubleday     1964

### O'Neill, James
### (1847-1920)
### Actor

**4204** FISHER, LAWRENCE F. A descriptive study of the acting of James O'Neill
Ann Arbor: U. of Michigan (PhD)     1969

### Oenslager, Donald Mitchell
### (1902-1975)
### Designer

**4205** OENSLAGER, DONALD. Scenery then and now
pp.265; ill in text, col. front.     M
NY: W. W. Norton     1936

Collection of scene design projects, many of which were realized.

**4206** DONALD OENSLAGER stage designer and teacher: a retrospective exhibition
pp.49; ill. in text     M
Detroit: Institute of Arts     1956

Catalogue of exhibition which subsequently toured until January, 1958. Foreword by Guthrie McClintic.

**4207** THEATER DRAWINGS from the Donald Oenslager collection
pp.48; ill. in text     M
Minneapolis: Minneapolis Institute of Arts     1963

*Institute Bulletin*, vol. 52, March, 1963, comprising a catalogue of historic scene designs.

**4208** FOUR CENTURIES OF THEATER DESIGN: drawings from the Donald Oenslager collection with an essay by A. Hyatt Mayor, *the Italian sources of European stage design*...
pp.[52]; ill in text     M
Princeton: Yale U. Art Gallery     1964

Loan exhibition catalogue, October 15-November 8, 1964. A slightly condensed version of the Minneapolis Institute of Arts exhibition of the previous year, sharing much of the contents.

**4209** OENSLAGER COLLECTION. Changing concepts in scenic design
Ill. in text     MH★
[?]: Finch College Museum of Art     1971

**4210** TOLLINI, FREDERICK P. The fine art of variation in the scene designs of Donald Mitchell Oenslager
New Haven: Yale U. (PhD)     1971

**4211** OENSLAGER, DONALD. Four centuries of scenic invention: drawings from the collection of Donald Oenslager. Introduction and catalogue...
pp.187; ill. in text     M
Washington DC: Int. Exhibitions Foundation     1974

Not to be confused with Oenslager's *Stage design: four centuries of scenic invention*, which it precedes but some passages from which it anticipates.

**4212** OENSLAGER, DONALD. Stage design: four centuries of scenic invention. Illustrated with drawings for the theatre from [the author's] collection
pp.303; ill. in text     M
NY: Viking P.     1975

**4213** OENSLAGER, DONALD. The theatre of Donald Oenslager
pp.xv, 176; ill. in text, pl. 8 col.     M
Middletown CT: Wesleyan U. P.     1978

Autobiography, with checklists of projects and productions.

### Olcott, Chauncey
### (1860?-1932)
### Actor, singer

**4214** OLCOTT, RITA. Song in his heart
pp.304; pl. 10     MH
NY: House of Field     1939

Biography of Chauncey Olcott.

### Olney, Julian
### Manager

**4215** OLNEY, JULIAN. Beyond Broadway [memoirs]
pp.xii, 255; ill. in text     M
Ardmore PA: Dorrance     1979

### Olsen, Moroni
### (1884?-1954)
### Actor, director

**4216** WILSON, CRAE J. The acting and directing career of Moroni Olsen
Provo: Brigham Young U. (PhD)     1981

### Owens, John Edmond
### (1823-1886)
### Actor

**4217** OWENS, MRS JOHN E. Memories of the professional and social life of John E. Owens. By his wife
pp.vii, 292; pl. 22     M
Baltimore: John Murphy     1892

**4218** BOGAR, THOMAS A. The theatrical career of John E. Owens (1823-1886)
Baton Rouge: Louisiana State U. (PhD)     1982

### Packer, Tina
### Director

**4219** EPSTEIN, HELEN. The companies she keeps: Tina Packer builds a theatre
pp.126; ill. in text     MH
Cambridge MA: Plunkett Lane P.     1985

English-born Packer founded the Shakespeare Company in Berkshire MA, and also directed the Boston Shakespeare Company.

### Paine, Robert Treat
### (1773-1811)
### Critic

**4220** HALEY, WHITNEY W. Robert Treat Paine Jr., and early theatrical criticism in Boston
Medford MA: Tufts U. (MA)     1958

**4221** PUKNAT, E. M. & PUKNAT, S. B. An American critic and a German vogue: the theatrical pioneering of Robert Treat Paine
pp.203-289     M
Boston: Colonial Society of Massachusetts     1966
Offprint of *Transactions*, Vol. 43. Makes particular reference to Paine's response to the vogue for August von Kotzebue.

### Palmer, Albert Marshall
### (1838?-1905)
### Producer, manager

**4222** RYAN, PATRICK M. Albert Marshall Palmer, producer. A study of management, dramaturgy, and stagecraft in the American theatre, 1872 to 1896
New Haven: Yale U. (PhD)     1959

### Papp, Joseph
### [Papirofsky, Joseph]
### (1921-1992)
### Director, producer

**4223** FAUST, RICHARD & KADUSHIN, CHARLES. Shakespeare in the neighborhood: audience reaction to *A Midsummer-night's Dream* as performed by Joseph Papp for the Delacorte Mobile Theater. A report...
pp.73; ill.     DL★
NY: Twentieth Century Fund     1965
Prepared for the Bureau of Applied Social Research of Columbia University.

**4224** PAPP, JOSEPH with CORNELL, TED. William Shakespeare's 'naked' *Hamlet*: a production handbook
pp.187; pl. 4     M
London: Macmillan     1969
Detailed account, with text, of Papp's New York Shakespeare Festival public theatre production of 1968.

**4225** HASHIMOTO, YOKO. Joseph Papp and New York Shakespeare Festival
Ann Arbor: U. of Michigan (PhD)     1972

**4226** LITTLE, STEWART W. Enter Joseph Papp: in search of a new American theater
pp.320     M
NY: Coward, McCann & Geoghegan     1974
An account of Papp and the New York Shakespeare Festival.

**4227** CARO, ROBERT A. The power broker: Robert Moses and the fall of New York
pp.xl, 1280; ill. in text, pl.21 inc.1 folding     L
NY: Vintage Books     1975
First published NY, Alfred A. Knopf, 1974. Includes material on Joseph Papp and the political background to the Central Park Shakespeare season.

**4228** KING, CHRISTINE E. & COVEN, BRENDA. Joseph Papp and the New York Shakespeare Festival: an annotated bibliography
pp.xxxii, 369     L
NY: Garland Publishing     1988
References to articles in newspapers and periodicals.

### Parker, Dorothy
### [Rothschild, Dorothy]
### (1893-1967)
### Critic, wit, playwright

**4229** KEATS, JOHN C. You might as well live [biography]
pp.319; front.     L
NY: Simon & Schuster     1970

### Parker, Henry Taylor
### (1867-1934)
### Critic

**4230** CANNING, BEVERLY E. Henry Taylor Parker, drama critic
Ann Arbor: U. of Michigan (PhD)     1960

### Payne, Ben Iden
### (1881-1976)
### Director, teacher

**4231** PAYNE, BEN IDEN. A life in a wooden O: memoirs of the theatre
pp.xvii, 204; ill. in text     M
New Haven CT: Yale U. P.     1977
English born actor/director and father of Rosalind Iden. Director of Stratford 1935-1943. Taught theatre at Carnegie Institute of Technology

**4232** RUCKER, PATRICK C. Ben Iden Payne and the development of the modified Elizabethan stage
Lubbock: Texas Tech U. (PhD)     1982

### Payne, John Howard
### (1791-1852)
### Actor, playwright, lyricist

**4233** PAYNE, JOHN H. (Ed.). Thespian Mirror: a periodical publication comprising a collection of dramatic biography, theatrical criticism, miscellaneous literature, poetry, etc., etc...
pp.iv, 120; front.     MH
NY: For the editor.     1806
Volume 1, Nos. 1-14, Dec. 28, 1805-May 31, 1806. No more published. All but the last number have section, *the American stage*. Errata slip facing table of contents.

**4234** MEMOIRS OF JOHN HOWARD PAYNE, the American Roscius: with criticisms of his acting, in the various theatres of America, England and Ireland. Compiled from authentic documents
pp.iii, 131; front.     L
London: printed for John Miller     1815
Reprinted articles, press notices and addresses. Reference to appearances in Providence RI, New York, Baltimore, Philadelphia, Norfolk VA, Petersburg VA, London, Dublin, Cork.

**4235** FAY, THEODORE S. A sketch of the life of John Howard Payne as published in the Boston *Evening Gazette*, compressed, (with additions bringing it forward to a later period). By one of the editors of the New York *Mirror*: now first printed in a separate form. With

an appendix containing selections of poetry and further illustrations
pp.27; ill. DL★
Boston: W. W. Clapp 1833

**4236** BRAINARD, CHARLES H. John Howard Payne: a biographical sketch of the author of *Home, Sweet Home* with a narrative of the removal of his remains from Tunis to Washington
pp.xi, 144; pl. 8 M
Washington DC: George A. Coolidge 1885

**4237** HARRISON, GABRIEL. John Howard Payne, dramatist, poet, actor and author of *Home, Sweet Home*. His life and writings
pp.404; ill. in text, pl. 2 M
Philadelphia: J. B. Lippincott 1885
Revised, enlarged second edition. First issued as *The life and writings of John Howard Payne...*, Albany NY: Munsell, 1875.

**4238** WEGELIN, OSCAR. The writings of John Howard Payne
MH★
Greenwood CT: Literary Collector P. [c. 1905]
Reprinted from the *Literary Collector*, March, 1905.

**4239** [SHELLEY, MARY W.]. The romance of Mary W. Shelley, John Howard Payne and Washington Irving. Annotated by H. H. Harper
pp.101; front., ill. in text, pl. 1 L
Boston: Bibliophile Society 1907
Correspondence suggesting Payne's unrequited affection for Mrs Shelley and her use of him as a go-between with Irving. Two title pages with a note from the treasurer explaining the inadequacy of the original engraving. A drop title has the words 'with remarks by F. B. Sanborn'. Printed for members only.

**4240** HANSON, WILLIS T. The early life of John Howard Payne with contemporary letters heretofore unpublished
pp.226; pl. 5 M
Boston: Bibliophile Society 1913
483 copies. Payne's life up to 1813. Reprints nos.1, 13, 14 of Payne's magazine, *The Thespian Mirror*.

**4241** CHILES, ROSA P. John Howard Payne: American poet, actor, playwright, consul and the author of *Home, Sweet Home*.
pp.ii, 89; front. M
Washington DC: Columbia Historical Society 1930

**4242** FOREMAN, GRANT (Ed.). Indian justice: a Cherokee murder trial at Tahlequah in 1840 as reported by John Howard Payne
pp.xiii, 132; front. L
Oklahoma City: Harlow Publishing 1934
Includes introductory biographical sketch of Payne. The description of the proceedings is informed with Payne's sense of the dramatic.

**4243** TRINKA, ZENA I. Home, sweet home
pp.168 DL★
NY: International Book Publishers 1942
John Howard Payne's trip to and experience in North Africa. Peripheral theatre interest.

**4244** BLAKELY, SIDNEY H. John Howard Payne, dramatic craftsman
Chapel Hill: U. of North Carolina (PhD) 1947

**4245** OVERMYER, GRACE. America's first Hamlet
pp.439; front. M
NY: U. P. 1957
Biography of John Howard Payne.

**4246** BAILLOU, CLEMENS DE. John Howard Payne to his countrymen
pp.v, 61 L
Athens: U. of Georgia P. 1961
Reprinted documents written by Payne after 1828, when gold was discovered in Cherokee territory in Georgia. One recounts his abduction from Tennessee and imprisonment by the Georgia Guard; the other is titled *The Cherokee nation: to the people of the U. States*. Foreword by W. P. Kellam.

### Payton, Corse
### (1867-1934)
### Actor

**4247** ANDREWS, GERTRUDE. The romance of a western boy: the story of Corse Payton...illustrated by J. Arthur Day
pp.121; ill. in text, pl. 7 MH
Brooklyn NY: Andrews P. 1901
Biography of barnstormer, later actor-manager and, in 1900, founder of Payton Theatre stock company.

### Pemberton, Brock
### (1885-1950)
### Producer

**4248** HILL, CHARLES R. The Pemberton technique: a study of Brock Pemberton's activities in the American theatre, 1920-1950
Lawrence: U. of Kansas (PhD) 1971

### Phelps, William Lyon
### (1865-1943)
### Critic

**4249** PHELPS, WILLIAM L. William Lyon Phelps yearbook
pp.ix, 453 L
NY: Macmillan 1935
Selection of articles from periodicals arranged as brief daily entries. Intermittent reference to theatre,

**4250** PHELPS, WILLIAM L. Autobiography with letters
pp.xxiii, 986; pl. 17 M
NY: Oxford U. P. 1939

### Pickford, Mary
### [Smith, Gladys]
### (1893-1979)
### Actress

**4251** WINDELER, ROBERT. Sweetheart: the story of Mary Pickford
pp.x, 226;.pl. 17 M
London: W. H. Allen 1973

### Picon, Molly
### (1898-)
### Actress

**4252** PICON, MOLLY with ROSENBERG, ETH C. So laugh a little [autobiography]
pp.175 DL★
NY: Julian Messner 1962

## 8.4. INDIVIDUAL

**4253** PICON, MOLLY with GRILLO, JEAN B. Molly! An autobiography
pp.319; pl. 8     MH
NY: Simon and Schuster     1980
Preface by Helen Hayes.

### Piot, René
### Designer

**4254** SCHAB, FREDERICK G. René Piot: landscape painter, theater designer. Retrospective exhibition...
pp.ii, 42; ill. in text     M
NY: William H. Schwab Gallery     1976

### Placide, Henry
### (1799-1870)
### Actor

**4255** KAOUGH, JOSEPH B. Henry Placide, American comedian
Lawrence: U. of Kansas (PhD)     1970

### Placide, Jane
### (1804-1835)
### Actress

**4256** BURROUGHS, PATRICIA. The career of Jane Placide in New Orleans
Baton Rouge: Louisiana State U. (MA)     1970

### Poe, Edgar Allan
### (1809-1849)
### Author, critic

**4257** QUINN, ARTHUR H. Edgar Allan Poe: a critical biography
pp.xvii, 804; front., ill. in text, pl. 17     L
NY: D. Appleton-Century     1941
Includes material on his actor-parents, listing parts played, on his theatre criticism, and on dramatizations of his fiction.

**4258** FAGIN, NATHAN B. The histrionic Mr Poe
pp.xiii, 289; ill. in text     O
Baltimore: John Hopkins P.     1949
An examination of theatre and theatricality in his work and life.

**4259** LUBELL, ALBERT J. Edgar Allan Poe, critic and reviewer
NY: U. (PhD)     1951

**4260** REILLY, JOHN E. Poe in imaginative literature. A study of American drama, fiction, and poetry devoted to Edgar Allen Poe or his works
Charlottesville: U. of Virginia (PhD)     1965

**4261** JACOBS, ROBERT D. Poe, journalist and critic
pp.xiii, 464     L
Baton Rouge: Louisiana State U. P.     1969
Analyses Edgar Allan Poe's dramatic principles with reference to his theatre criticism.

**4262** KETTERER, DAVID. Edgar Allan Poe: life, work and criticism
pp.51     ★
Fredericton NB: York P.     1989

### Poe, Eliza
### (1787-1811)
### Actress

**4263** SMITH, GEDDETH. The brief career of Eliza Poe
pp.174     M
Rutherford: Fairleigh Dickinson U. P.     1988
Actress mother of E. A. Poe.

### Poitier, Sidney
### (1924-)
### Actor

**4264** HOFFMAN, WILLIAM. Sidney
pp.175; ill.     DL★
NY: Lyle Stuart     1971

**4265** POITIER, SIDNEY. This life [autobiography]
pp.vii, 374; pl. 12     M
London: Hodder & Stoughton     1980

### Power, Frederick Tyrone
### (1869-1931)
### Actor

**4266** WINTER, WILLIAM. Tyrone Power
pp.192; pl. 21     M
NY: Moffat, Yard     1913
Grandson of the first Tyrone Power.

### Power, Tyrone
### (1797-1851)
### Actor

**4267** POWER, TYRONE. Impressions of America during the years 1833, 1834, and 1835...in two volumes
pp.xv, 440; vi, 408; pl. 2     M
London: Richard Bentley     1836
Author was lost at sea in the sinking of the *President* when returning to England after a third tour of America in 1841.

### Power, Tyrone
### (1913-1958)
### Actor

**4268** ARCE, HECTOR. The secret life of Tyrone Power
pp.312     ★
NY: William Morrow     1979
Biography, with material on his father.

**4269** GUILES, FRED L. Tyrone Power; the last idol
pp.xvii, 389; pl. 32     M
NY: Doubleday     1979
Biography of the great grandson of the eldest Power, best remembered as a movie star.

### Price, Vincent
### (1911-)
### Actor

**4270** PRICE, VINCENT. I like what I know: a visual autobiography
pp.313; ill.     DL★
Garden City: Doubleday     1959

### Prince, Harold Smith
### (1928-)
### Director, producer

**4271** PRINCE, HAL. Contradictions: notes on twenty-six years in the theatre
pp.xi, 242; pl. 4     M
NY: Dodd, Mead     1974

### Quinn, Elizabeth
#### Actress

**4272** QUINN, ELIZABETH & OWEN, MICHAEL. Listen to me. The story of Elizabeth Quinn
pp.xii, 208; pl. 4   M
London: Michael Joseph   1984

### Quinn, Germain
#### (1866-)
#### Actor

**4273** QUINN, GERMAIN. Fifty years back stage: being the life story of a theatrical stage mechanic
pp.204; ill. in text   M
Minneapolis: Stage Publishing   1926

### Quintero, José Benjamin
#### (1924-)
#### Director

**4274** QUINTERO, JOSÉ. If you don't dance they beat you [autobiography]
pp.viii, 296   M
Boston: Little, Brown   1974
Author directed *Long Day's Journey into Night* on Broadway, and founded the Circle in the Square.

**4275** COOK, DAVID B. José Quintero: the Circle in the Square years, 1950-1963
Lawrence: U. of Kansas (PhD)   1981

### Rabb, Ellis
#### (1930-)
#### Actor, director

**4276** LAMING, DOROTHY W. Ellis Rabb: a man of repertory
Columbus: Ohio State U. (PhD)   1972

### Ranous, Dora Knowlton
#### Writer, actress

**4277** [RANOUS, DORA]. Diary of a débutante: being passages from the journal of a member of Augustin Daly's famous company of players
pp.v, 249; pl. 16   M
NY: Duffield   1910
Period 1879-80.

**4278** JOHNSON, ROSSITER. Dora Knowlton Ranous, author, editor, translator. A simple record of a noble life
pp.36; ill.   DL★
NY: Publishers Printing   1916
100 copies.

### Rascoe, Burton
#### (1892-1957)
#### Critic

**4279** HENSLEY, DONALD M. Burton Rascoe
pp.162   L
NY: Twayne   1970

### Rathbone, Basil
#### (1892-1967)
#### Actor

**4280** RATHBONE, BASIL. In and out of character [autobiography]
pp.278; ill.   ★
Garden City NY: Doubleday   1962

**4281** DRUXMAN, MICHAEL B. Basil Rathbone. His life and his films
pp.359; ill. in text   L
NY: A. S. Barnes   1975

### Raymond, John T.
### [O'Brien, John T.]
#### (1836-1887)
#### Actor

**4282** SOUVENIR of the representative American comedian John T. Raymond, in his last & greatest success, the political satire in (4) acts by David D. Lloyd Esq., entitled *For Congress*
ll.8; pl. 8   MB
[Boston]: [For the author]   [1884]

### Reed, Joseph V.
#### (1902-1973)
#### Producer

**4283** REED, JOSEPH V. The curtain falls [autobiography]
pp.282; ill. in text, pl. 7   M
NY: Harcourt, Brace   1935

### Rehan, Ada
### [née Crehan, Ada]
#### (1860-1916)
#### Actress

**4284** LYNCH, ARTHUR. Human documents. Character sketches of representative men and women of the time
pp.xi, 304   L
London: Bertram Dobell   1896
With a chapter on Ada Rehan.

**4285** WINTER, WILLIAM. Ada Rehan a study...new edition revised and enlarged
pp.211; front., pl. 24   M
NY: For Augustin Daly   1898
First published 1891 (113 copies), sub-titled *A daughter of comedy* and in a much shorter form.

**4286** MacGHEE, MILDRED M. The acting of Ada Rehan [drop title]
pp.32   L
Canton MO: Culver-Stockton College   1927
Whole issue of the *Culver-Stockton quarterly journal* Vol. 3 No. 1 January, 1927.

**4287** HENDRICKS-WENCK, AILEEN A. Ada Rehan: American actress (1856-1916)
Baton Rouge: Louisiana State U. (PhD)   1988

### Rhys, Charles Horton
### ['Morton Price']
#### (1824-1876)
#### Amateur actor, theatre lessee

**4288** RHYS, HORTON. Theatrical trip for a wager! Through Canada and the United States. By Captain Horton Rhys, ('Morton Price')
pp.111, 140; pl. 5   M
London: For the author   1861

## Rivers, Joan
## (1935?-)
## Entertainer

**4289** RIVERS, JOAN. Enter talking [autobiography]
pp.ix, 394; pl. 12    MH
London: W. H. Allan    1986

## Robeson, Paul
## (1898-1976)
## Singer, actor

**4290** ROBESON, ESLANDA G. Paul Robeson, negro
pp.153; pl. 16    M
London: Gollancz    1930

**4291** GRAHAM, SHIRLEY. Paul Robeson: citizen of the world
pp.viii, 264; pl. 1    MH
NY: Messner    1946
Biography. Foreword by Carl Van Doren.

**4292** GOROKHOV, V. Robeson
pp.358; front.    L
Moscow: Sovetsky Pisatel    1952
Biography. Text in Russian.

**4293** ROBESON, PAUL. Here I stand
pp.128    MH
NY: Othello Associates    1958
A declaration of rights and principles.

**4294** SETON, MARIE. Paul Robeson. With a foreword by Sir Arthur Bryant
pp.254; front.    M
London: Dennis Dobson    1958

**4295** HOYT, EDWIN P. Paul Robeson
pp.ix, 228    M
London: Cassell    1967

**4296** SCHLOSSER, ANATOL I. Paul Robeson: his career in the theatre, in motion pictures, and on the concert stage
NY: U. (PhD)    1969

**4297** WRIGHT, CHARLES H. Robeson; labor's forgotten champion
pp.vii, 171; ill. in text    L
Detroit: Balamp    1975
Account of his activities as a labor activist. An appendix transcribes part of his Peace Arch speech of May, 1952.

**4298** BROWN, LLOYD L. Paul Robeson rediscovered
pp.23    DL★
NY: American Institute for Marxist Studies    1976
Transcript of an address delivered at the National Conference on Paul Robeson, Purdue U., April 1976.

**4299** FONER, PHILIP S. (Ed.). Paul Robeson speaks: writings, speeches, interviews 1918-1974...with introduction and notes...
pp.xvi, 624; ill. in text    M
London: Quartet Books    1978

**4300** PAUL ROBESON, April 9. 1989 - January 23, 1976
   DL★
Berlin: Academy of Arts of G. D. R.    1978
Exhibition catalogue.

**4301** NAZEL, JOSEPH. Paul Robeson: biography of a proud man
pp.216    L
Los Angeles: Holloway House    1980

**4302** ROBESON, SUSAN. The whole world in his hands: a pictorial biography of Paul Robeson
pp.254; ill. in text    DL★
Secaucus NJ: Citadel P.    1981

**4303** DAVIS, LENWOOD G. A Paul Robeson research guide: a selected annotated bibliography
pp.xxv, 879; front.    L
Westport CT: Greenwood P.    1982

**4304** EXTON, M. A. Paul Robeson and South Wales: a partial guide to a man's beliefs
Exeter: U. (MA)    1984

**4305** PAUL ROBESON- citizen of the world. An exhibition by J. D. Douglas 21 March - 25 April 1987 [cover title]
bs; ill. in text    M
London: Borough of Camden Arts Department    1987
Presented at Swiss Cottage Library, London NW3.

**4306** RAMDIN, RON. Paul Robeson
pp.223; pl. 2    M
London: Peter Owen    1987

**4307** DUBERMAN, MARTIN B. Paul Robeson
pp.xi, 804; pl. 24    M
London: Bodley Head    1989

## Robinson, David
## (1868-1913?)
## Manager, writer, actor

**4308** MERING, YOLLA. The San Francisco theatrical career of Dr. D. G. Robinson
Long Beach: California State U. (MA)    1977

## Robinson, Edward G.
## [Goldenberg, Emanuel]
## (1893-1973)
## Actor

**4309** ROBINSON, EDWARD G. & SPIGELGLASS, LEONARD. All my yesterdays: an autobiography
pp.vii, 344; pl. 16    L
London: W. H. Allen    1974
Early stage experience included work with the Theatre Guild.

## Robson, Eleanor Elise
## [Belmont, Eleanor]
## (1879-1979)
## Actress

**4310** SOME IMPARTIAL excerpts from the various reviews by the critics in those cities visited having special reference to Miss Robson's signal triumph which by general acclaim was accounted the most pronounced since that of the greatest of all modern Juliets, Adelaide Neilson
pp.[31]; ill. in text    M
[NY?]: [For Liebler and Co.?]    1903

*The author accepted a wager that he could not earn £500 in twelve months as an actor. He won the bet, later became lessee of Sadler's Wells Theatre (1862).*

Eleanor Robson played Juliet to the Romeo of Kyrle Bellew in Liebler and Company's (Theodore Liebler and George C. Tyler) Spring tour.

**4311** BELMONT, ELEANOR R. The fabric of memory
pp.vii, 311; pl. 8     M
NY: Farrar, Straus and Cudahy     1957
Reminiscences. Founder of the Metropolitan Opera Guild and a star of the New York stage.

### Robson, Stuart
### [Stuart, Henry Robson]
### (1836-1903)
### Crane, William Henry
### (1845-1928)
### Comic actors

**4312** SHAKESPEARE'S *Comedy of Errors* produced by Robson and Crane under the direction of Joseph Brooks: arranged for the stage and illustrated by Alfred Thompson, M.A.
pp.[16]; ill. in text     MB
[Detroit]: Detroit Free P.     [1885]
A revival of the 1878 production. A description of the production and the historical research behind it.

**4313** CRANE, WILLIAM H. Footprints and echoes [autobiography]
pp.xi, 232; pl. 13     M
NY: E. P. Dutton     1927

**4314** MORGAN, JOHN B. The partnership of Stuart Robson and William H. Crane: American comedians
Urbana-Champaign: U. of Illinois (PhD)     1983

### Rockwell, Kitty
### [Rockwell, Kathleen Eloisa]
### (1876-1957)
### Actress

**4315** LUCIA, ELLIS. Klondike Kate: the life and legend of Kitty Rockwell
pp.xi, 305; pl. 4     L
NY: Hastings House     1962

### Rogers, Will
### [Rogers, William Penn Adair]
### (1879-1935)
### Cowboy humorist/entertainer

**4316** BEATTY, JEROME. The story of Will Rogers
pp.[156]; ill. in text     L
Akron OH: Saalfield     1935

**4317** HITCH, ARTHUR M. (Ed.). Will Rogers, cadet: a record of his two years as a cadet at the Kemper Military School, Boonville, Missouri:...compiled from letters from his fellow cadets and interviews with them and from school records
pp.23; ill.     DL★
Boonville MO: Kemper Military School     1935

**4318** LAIT, JACK. Our Will Rogers
pp.ix, 117; ill.     DL★
NY: Greenberg     1935

**4319** O'BRIEN, P. J. Will Rogers: ambassador of good will. With an appreciation by Lowell Thomas
pp.256; pl. 8     M
London: Hutchinson     [1935]

**4320** LAIT, JACK (Ed.). Will Rogers' wit and wisdom
pp.xix, 124; ill. in text, front.     L
NY: Stokes     1936
Pictorial edition. Anecdotes, brief quotations.

**4321** MILSTEN, DAVID R. An appreciation of Will Rogers
pp.xxi, 258; front., pl. 12     L
San Antonio TX: Naylor     1936
Introduction by Tom Mix.

**4322** PAYNE, WILLIAM H. & LYONS, JAKE G. (Eds). Folks say of Will Rogers: a memorial anecdotage. Auspices the Oklahoma Society of Washington D.C.
pp.xv, 224; front.     L
NY: G. P. Putnam's Sons     1936

**4323** KEITH, HAROLD. Boys' life of Will Rogers
pp.ix, 271; ill.     DL★
NY: Thomas Crowell     [1937]

**4324** TRENT, SPI M. My cousin Will Rogers by...his cousin, boyhood playmate and lifelong friend
pp.x, 266; ill. in text     MH
NY: G. P. Putnam's Sons     1938

**4325** ACCEPTANCE of the statue of Will Rogers presented by the state of Oklahoma. Proceedings in the Congress and in the Rotunda, United States Capitol
pp.80; front.     L
Washington DC: Government Printing Office     1939
76th Congress 1st Session. House document 571. Brief biographies of Rogers and the sculptor Jo Davidson, together with a record and transcription of the proceedings.

**4326** ROWLAND, LLOYD W. Will Rogers. Illustrated by Paul E. Corrubia
ll.[18]; ill. in text     L
Tulsa OK: For the illustrator     1940
Lithographed part-illuminated hand-prints interspersed with elaborate pencil sketches. Text attempts 'to interpret the mind of Will Rogers in terms of his origins and to use him as a standard for judging contemporary American life.'

**4327** ROGERS, BETTY B. Will Rogers: his wife's story
pp.312; front., pl. 7     L
Indianapolis: Bobbs-Merrill     1941

**4328** DAY, DONALD (Ed.). The autobiography of Will Rogers, selected and edited ...with a foreword by Bill and Jim Rogers
pp.xix, 410; front.     M
Boston: Houghton Mifflin     [1949]

**4329** CROY, HOMER. Our Will Rogers
pp.xii, 377     M
NY: Duell, Sloan & Pearce     1953

**4330** DAY, DONALD. Will Rogers: a biography
pp.xiii, 370; ill.     DL★
NY: David Mackay     1962

**4331** McSPADDEN, MAURICE. The public speaking of Will Rogers
Tucson: U. of Arizona (PhD)     1972

**4332** KETCHUM, RICHARD M. *Will Rogers, his life and times*...in cooperation with the Will Rogers Memorial Commission and staff of the Will Rogers Memorial, Claremore, Oklahoma
pp.415; ill. in text     MH
NY: American Heritage Publishing     1973

**4333** [ROGERS, WILL]. *Will Rogers' daily telegrams*. James M. Smallwood, editor
pp.various; fronts., ill. in text     MH
Stillwater OK: Oklahoma State U. P.     1978-79
Four volumes spanning 1926-1935. No. III of a series, *The writings of Will Rogers* which also includes I *Books of Will Rogers*; II *Convention articles of...*; IV *Weekly articles of...*; V *Worst story I've heard today*. Other titles to be announced.

**4334** GIBSON, ARRELL M. (Ed.). *Will Rogers: a centennial tribute*
pp.vii, 150; ill. in text     MH
Oklahoma City: Oklahoma Historical Society     1979
Ten essays, including James Smallwood: *A centennial review of his career*.

**4335** ROLLINS, PETER C. *Will Rogers: a bio-bibliography*
pp.xiii, 282; ill. in text     L
Westport CT: Greenwood P.     1984

### Rose, Billy
### [Rosenberg, William Samuel]
### (1899-1966)
### Producer, manager, lyricist

**4336** ROSE, BILLY. *Wine, women and words*, Illustrated by Salvador Dali
vii, 295; ill. in text     M
NY: Simon and Schuster     1948
Reminiscences.

**4337** CONRAD, EARL. *Billy Rose: Manhattan primitive*
pp.xvi, 272; pl. 4     M
Cleveland OH: World Publishing     1968

**4338** GOTTLIEB, POLLY R. *The nine lives of Billy Rose*
pp.290; ill. in text     M
NY: Crown     1968

**4339** NELSON, STEPHEN. *Only a paper moon: the theatre of Billy Rose*
pp. xiv, 169; ill. in text     L
Ann Arbor: UMI Research P.     1987

### Rosenthal, Jean
### (1912-1969)
### Lighting designer

**4340** ROSENTHAL, JEAN & WERTENBAKER, LAEL. *The magic of light: the craft and career of Jean Rosenthal, pioneer in lighting for the modern stage*...illustrations by Marion Kinsella
pp.xi, 256; ill. in text     M
Boston: Little, Brown/Theatre Arts     1972

**4341** SESAK, MARY M. *The lighting designs of Jean Rosenthal*
Columbus: Ohio State U. (PhD)     1976

### Ross, Frederick G.
### (1858-1942)
### Actor

**4342** ROSS, FREDERICK G. *The actor from Point Arena: excerpts taken from the Memories of an old theatrical man by Frederick G. Ross*. Edited with a commentary by Travis Bogard
pp.iv, 38; pl. 5     M
[Berkeley]: U. of California     1977
From a typescript in the Frederick G. Ross collection in the Bancroft Library.

### Roth, Lillian
### (1910-1980)
### Singer, actress

**4343** ROTH, LILLIAN; with CONNOLLY, MIKE & FRANK, GERALD. *I'll cry tomorrow* [autobiography]
pp.296; front; pl. 1     L
London: Arthur Barker     1955
Published NY: Fell, 1954.

**4344** ROTH, LILLIAN. *Beyond my worth* [autobiography]
pp.227; front., pl. 4     L
London: Arthur Barker     1959
Published NY: Fell, 1958.

### Rowson, Susannah Haswell
### (1762-1824)
### Actress, writer

**4345** COBBETT, WILLIAM. *A kick for a bite. or review upon review*
Unpaged     O*
Philadelphia: T. Bradford     1795
Reference to Susannah Rowson, questioning her patriotism.

**4346** SPARGO, JOHN. *Anthony Haswell, printer-patriot-ballader: a biographical study with a selection of his ballads and an annotated bibliographical list of his imprints*
pp.xv, 293; front., pl. 34     L
Rutland VT: Tuttle     1925
Makes reference to Susannah Rowson, the subject's daughter. 300 copies.

**4347** VAIL, ROBERT W. G. *Susannah Haswell Rowson...a bibliographical study*
pp.43-116; front.     MH*
Worcester MA: American Antiquarian Society     1933
Includes a list of roles, 1794-97 and an annotated bibliography. First published in the *Proceedings* n.s. 2, April 20 - October 19, 1932.

**4348** WEIL, DOROTHY. *In defence of women: Susannah Rowson (1762-1824)*
pp.204; ill.     DL*
University Park: Pennsylvania State U. P.     1976

### Runyon, Alfred Damon
### (1884-1946)
### Author, columnist

**4349** WEINER, ED. *The Damon Runyon story*
pp.xiv, 258     L
NY: Longman's, Green     1948

**4350** HOYT, EDWIN P. *A gentleman of Broadway*
pp.xi, 369; pl 4     M
Boston: Little, Brown     1964

### Russell, Rosalind
### (1912-1976)
### Actress

**4351** RUSSELL, ROSALIND & CHASE, CHRIS. Life is a banquet! [autobiography]
pp.xxii, 260; pl. 16          L
London: W. H. Allen          1978
First published NY: Random House, 1977. Early stage experience included the Theatre Guild.

### Russell, Sol Smith
### (1848-1902)
### Comic actor

**4352** BAZALDUA, CHARLES. 'Going to the people': the career of Sol Smith Russell
Columbia: U. of Missouri (PhD)          1976

### Sargent, Epes Winthrop
### (1872-1938)
### Critic

**4353** PRATT, JUDITH S. The vaudeville criticism of Epes Winthrop Sargent, 1896-1910
Lincoln: U. of Nebraska (PhD)          1985

### Sarony, Napoleon,
### (1821-1896)
### Photographer

**4354** BASSHAM, BEN L. The theatrical photographs of Napoleon Sarony
pp.ix, 122; ill. in text          M
Kent OH: Kent State U. P.          1978

### Schaffner, Neil E.
### (1892-1969)
### Actor, manager

**4355** CLARK, LARRY D. Toby shows: a form of American popular theatre
Urbana: U. of Illinois (PhD)          1963

**4356** SCHAFFNER, NEIL & JOHNSON, VANCE. The fabulous toby and me
pp.xii, 212; pl. 8          M
Englewood Cliffs NJ: Prentice Hall          1968
Founder of the Schaffner Players which toured from the 1920s to the 1960s.

**4357** KITTLE, RUSSELL D. Toby and Susie: the show-business success story of Neil and Caroline Schaffner
Columbus: Ohio State U. (PhD)          1969

**4358** LANGFORD, MARTHA F. The tent repertoire theatre of Neil and Caroline Schaffner: a case in tent repertoire theatre as communication
Boulder: U. of Colorado          1978

### Schneider, Alan
### (1917-1984)
### Director

**4359** HAWKINS, JOHN A. A critical biography of Alan Schneider
Medford MA: Tufts U. (PhD)          1978

**4360** SCHNEIDER, ALAN. Entrances: an American director's journey. Preface by Edward Albee
xv, 416; pl. 13          MH
NY: Viking P.          1986
Autobiography, published posthumously. Author, responsible for directing *Who's Afraid of Virginia Woolf?*, *Tiny Alice* and many other important premières, was killed in a London road accident.

### Sears, Zelda
### [Paldi, Zelda]
### (1873-1935)
### Actress, playwright

**4361** BETTISWORTH, DENNY. The life and career of Zelda Sears
Athens: U. of Georgia (PhD)          1974

### Seldes, Marian
### (1928-)
### Actress

**4362** SELDES, MARIAN. The bright lights; a theatre life [autobiography]
pp.vii, 280; ill. in text          MH
Boston: Houghton Mifflin          1978

### Selznick, Irene M.
### (1910-)
### Producer

**4363** SELZNICK, IRENE M. A private view [autobiography]
pp.384; pl. 16          M
London: Weidenfeld & Nicolson          1983
Daughter of Louis B. Mayer; married David O. Selznick. Productions included *A Streetcar named Desire*.

### Seymour, William Gorman
### (1855-1933)
### Director, actor

**4364** MILLER, RALPH E. William Seymour, American director, 1855-1933
Detroit: Wayne State U. (PhD)          1973

### Sharaff, Irene
### (1908-)
### Costume designer

**4365** SHARAFF, IRENE. Broadway and Hollywood: costumes designed by Irene Sharaff [autobiography]
pp.136; ill. in text, some col.          L
NY: Van Nostrand Reinhold          1976

**4366** GRAUCH, ARLENE E. A comparison of four stage and motion picture productions designed by Irene Sharaff
Ann Arbor: U. of Michigan (PhD)          1988

### Shaw, Mary
### (1860-1929)
### Actress, lecturer

**4367** IRVING, JOHN D. Mary Shaw, actress, suffragist, activist
NY: Columbia U. (PhD)          1978

### Sherin, Edwin
### (1930?-)
### Director

**4368** BEAN, LISA K. The theatrical career and directing strategies of Edwin Sherin
Provo: Brigham Young U. (PhD)          1989

### Shubert, Lee
### (1873?-1953)
### Shubert, Samuel
### (1876?-1905)
### Shubert, Jacob J.
### (1878?-1963)
### [nés Szemanski]

**4369** STAGG, JERRY. The brothers Shubert
pp.xii, 433; ill. in text     M
NY: Random House     1968

**4370** THE PASSING SHOW: newsletter of the Shubert Archive
pp. av. 14; ill. in text     M
NY: The Shubert Archive     1977-
Bi-annual. Edited by Brooks McNamara.

**4371** McNAMARA, BROOKS. The Shuberts of Broadway: a history drawn from the collections of the Shubert Archive
pp.xxvi, 230; ill. in text     M
NY: Oxford U. P.     1990

### Shumlin, Herman
### (1898-1979)
### Director, producer

**4372** BLAKE, GARY. Herman Shumlin: the development of a director
NY: City U. (PhD)     1873

### Sillman, Leonard Dexter
### (1908-1982)
### Producer

**4373** SILLMAN, LEONARD D. Here lies Leonard Sillman straightened out at last: an autobiography
pp.404; pl. 16     L
NY: Citadel P.     1959
Author produced the revues *New Faces* between 1934 and 1968, seven in all.

### Silvers, Phil
### [Silver, Philip]
### (1911-1985)
### Comic actor

**4374** SILVERS, PHIL & SAFFRON, ROBERT. The man who was Bilko: the autobiography of Phil Silvers
pp.ix, 276; pl. 12     M
London: W. H. Allen     1974
Published Englewood Cliffs: Prentice-Hall, 1973, as *This laugh is on me: the Phil Silvers story*.

### Sime, Silverman
### (1873-1933)
### Founder of "Variety"

**4375** STODDART, DAYTON. Lord Broadway: Variety's Sime
pp.x, 385; ill. in text, pl. 2 inc 1 folding     M
NY: Wilfred Funk     1941

### Simonson, Lee
### (1888-1967)
### Designer

**4376** SIMONSON, LEE. Part of a lifetime: drawings and designs, 1919-1940
pp.xxi, 100; pl. 41, some col.     M
NY: Duell, Sloan & Pearce     1943

**4377** YORK, ZACK L. Lee Simonson, artist-craftsman of the theatre
Madison: U. of Wisconsin (PhD)     1950

### Simpson, Edmund Shaw
### (1784-1848)
### Manager, actor

**4378** LITTO, FREDRIC M. Edward Simpson of the Park Theatre, New York, 1809-1848
Bloomington: Indiana U. (PhD)     1969

### Skinner, Cornelia Otis
### (1901-1979)
### Actress, playwright, author

**4379** SKINNER, CORNELIA O. Our hearts were young and gay
pp.vii, 247; ill. in text     L
London: Constable     1944
First published NY: Dodd, Mead, 1939. A light-hearted account of travels in Europe. Illustrated by Alajalov.

**4380** SKINNER, CORNELIA O. Family circle [autobiography]
pp.ix, 310; pl. 4     M
Boston: Houghton Mifflin     1948
A UK edition, London: Constable, 1950, has different illustrations.

**4381** SKINNER, CORNELIA O. That's me all over: Cornelia Otis Skinner's first omnibus
pp.vii, 312; ill. in text     L
London: Constable     1949
First published NY, Dodd, Mead, 1948. Collected humorous articles, some with theatre themes.

**4382** SKINNER, CORNELIA O. Nuts in May
pp.188; ill. in text     L
London: Constable     1951
First published NY: Dodd, Mead, 1942. Humorous sketches, some concerning the stage. Illustrated by Alajalov.

**4383** LOGANBILL, BRUCE. Cornelia Otis Skinner and her art form of monologue-drama
East Lansing: Michigan State U. (PhD)     1961

### Skinner, Otis
### (1858-1942)
### Actor

**4384** SKINNER, OTIS. The actor's ethical viewpoint. An address given by Otis Skinner in the Chicago University course of lectures on the drama, January 21st, 1908
pp.14     MH
[Chicago?]: [U. of Chicago?]     1908

**4385** SKINNER, OTIS. Footlights and spotlights: recollections of my life on the stage
pp.xiii, 367; col front., pl 32     M
Indianapolis: Bobbs-Merrill     1924
First published NY: Blue Ribbon Books, 1923 and serialized that year in *Ladies Home Journal*.

**4386** CORBIN, GERMAINE. The acting of Otis Skinner
Urbana-Champaign: U. of Illinois (PhD)     1971

### Slezak, Walter
(1902-1983)
Actor

**4387** SLEZAK, WALTER. What time's the next swan ? (as told to Smith Corona Model 88 E) [autobiography]
pp.xi, 227; pl. 8    L
Garden City: Doubleday    1962

### Smith, Oliver Lemuel
(1918-)
Designer

**4388** MIKOTOWICZ, THOMAS J. Oliver Smith: an American scenographer
NY: U. (PhD)    1985

### Smith, Russell
(1812-1896)
Designer

**4389** LEWIS, VIRGINIA E. Russell Smith, romantic realist [biography]
pp.xix, 348; ill.    DL★
Pittsburgh: U. P.    1956

### Smith, Solomon Franklin
(1801-1869)
Actor-manager

**4390** SMITH, SOL. The theatrical apprenticeship and anecdotal recollections of Sol. Smith, comedian, attorney-at-law. etc., etc.; comprising a sketch of the first seven years of his professional life; together with some sketches of adventure in after years
pp.216; pl. 8    MH
Philadelphia: Carey & Hart    1846
A first book of reminiscences. Theatre experience in the West, Cincinnati, Pittsburgh, Philadelphia, New York, Syracuse, Lewiston, Kentucky. Includes a chapter on the early days of Edwin Forrest. Period 1815-1833.

**4391** SMITH, SOL. The theatrical journeywork and anecdotal recollections of Sol. Smith, comedian, attorney-at-law, etc., etc.; comprising a sketch of the second seven years of his professional life; together with sketches of adventures in after years. With a portrait of the author
pp.254; front.    MH
Philadelphia: T. B. Peterson    1854
Experience mostly in the South. Includes a sketch of George Holland and two letters defending the stage.

**4392** CRAIG, WILLIAM S. The theatrical management of Sol Smith: organization, operations, methods and techniques
Urbana-Champaign: U. of Illinois (PhD)    1964

**4393** SMITH, SOL. Theatrical management in the West and South for thirty years. New edition with an introduction and index by Arthur Thomas Tees
pp.xx, 294; ill. in text    M
NY: Blom    1968
Facsimile reprint with additions. Originally published NY: Harper, 1868 as *Theatrical management...interspersed with anecdotal sketches: autobiographically give by Sol. Smith, retired actor...*

### Sobel, Bernard
(1887-1964)
Critic, press agent

**4394** SOBEL, BERNARD. Broadway heartbeat: memoirs of a press agent
pp.352    MH
NY: Hermitage House    1953

### Sobotka, Ruth
(1925-)
Dancer, actress, designer

**4395** [SOBOTKA, WALTER (Ed.)]. Ruth Sobotka [cover title]
pp.80; ill. in text    L
NY: For the editor    [1967]
A commemorative biographical compilation. Vienna born, she emigrated to US in 1938, danced with Balanchine's company, designed for ballet, acted off-Broadway and with the Seattle Repertory company.

### Sothern, Edward Hugh
(1859-1933)
Actor

**4396** SOTHERN, EDWARD H. The melancholy tale of 'me': my remembrances
pp.xvi, 409; ill. in text, pl. 49    M
NY: Charles Scribner's Sons    1916
The UK edition, London: 1917, has the title and sub-title in reverse order.

**4397** SOTHERN, EDWARD H. Matter for a May morning: poems fond and foolish
pp.194    DL★
NY: [For the author]    1929
200 copies.

**4398** SOGLIUZZO, A. Edward Sothern and Julia Marlowe
Bloomington: Indiana U. (PhD)    1967

### Stapleton, Lois Maureen
(1925-)
Actress

**4399** ROPSEN, ESTHER M. Maureen Stapleton, American actress
Tucson: U. of Arizona (PhD)    1983

### Stark, Sarah Kirby
Actress

**4400** WHITEHEAD, MARJORIE. Sarah Kirby Stark: California's pioneer actress-manager
Sacramento: California State U. (MA)    1972

### Stevens, Thomas Wood
(1880-1942)
Producer

**4401** FELDMAN, DONNA R. An historical study of Thomas Wood Stevens' Globe Theatre company
Iowa City: U. of Iowa (PhD)    1953

**4402** TEAGUE, ANNA D. Thomas Wood Stevens' contribution to American art theatre with emphasis on the Kenneth Sawyer Goodman Memorial Theatre, 1922-30
Baton Rouge: Louisiana State U. (PhD)    1973

**4403** RAMBIN, WILLIAM R. Thomas Wood Stevens: American pageant master
Baton Rouge: Louisiana State U. (PhD)    1977

### Stickney, Dorothy
### (1900-)
### Actress

**4404** STICKNEY, DOROTHY. Openings and closings [autobiography]
pp.vii, 201; pl. 12   M
NY: Doubleday   1979

### Stoddart, James Henry
### (1827-1907)
### Actor

**4405** STODDART, JAMES H. Recollections of a player
pp.xxi, 255; pl. 37   M
NY: Cenrury   1902

Played in comedy at Wallack's and Laura Keene's, but later specialized in villains.

### Stone, Fred
### [Stone, Val Fred Andrew]
### (1873-1959)
### Actor

**4406** STONE, FRED. Rolling stone [autobiography]
pp.vii, 246; front., pl. 7   L
NY: Whittlesey House/ McGraw-Hill   1945

Partnered Dave Montgomery in many musical comedies in the first two decades of this century. Later a star in his own right through the thirties.

### Strasberg, Lee
### [Strassberg, Israel]
### (1901-1982)
### Director, actor

**4407** SCHARFENBERG, JEAN. Lee Strasberg, teacher
Madison: U. of Wisconsin (PhD)   1963

**4408** HETHMON, ROBERT H. (Ed.). Strasberg at the Actors Studio. Tape-recorded sessions
pp.xiv, 428; pl. 6   M
London: Jonathan Cape   1966

**4409** ADAMS, CINDY. Lee Strasberg: the imperfect genius of the Actors Studio
pp.v, 398; pl. 12   L
Garden City NY: Doubleday   1980

**4410** STRASBERG, SUSAN. Bittersweet [autobiography]
pp.285; pl. 16   MH
NY: G. P. Putnam's Sons   1980

Includes material on Lee Strasberg, the author's father.

**4411** STRASBERG, LEE. A dream of passion: the development of the method. Edited by Evangeline Morphos
pp.xvii, 203, pl. 8   M
London: Bloomsbury   1987

### Streep, Meryl
### [Streep, Mary Louise]
### (1949-)
### Actress

**4412** MAYCHICK, DIANA. Meryl Streep: the reluctant superstar
pp.xi, 166; pl. 8   M
London: Robson   1984

### Streisand, Barbra
### (1942-)
### Actress, singer

**4413** ZEC, DONALD & FOWLES, ANTHONY. Barbra: a biography of Barbra Streisand
pp.253; ill. in text   M
London: New English Library   1981

### Taylor, Justus H.
### (1834-1894)
### Actor

**4414** TAYLOR, JUSTUS H. Joe Taylor, barnstormer: his travels, troubles and triumphs during fifty years in footlight flashes...with illustrations by Ripley [autobiography]
pp.v, 248; pl. 25   M
NY: William R. Jenkins   1913

### Taylor, Laurette
### [Cooney, Laurette]
### (1884-1946)
### Actress

**4415** TAYLOR, LAURETTE. 'The greatest of these –': a diary with portraits of the patriotic all-star tour of *Out There*
pp.61; pl. 19   M
NY: George H. Doran   1918

The piece by J. Hartley Manners, glorifying the Red-Cross nurse, toured the nation in 1918 to raise funds for the Red Cross Society. The company included Taylor, George M. Cohan, H. B. Warner and George Arliss.

**4416** COURTNEY, MARGUERITE. Laurette. Introduction by Samuel H. Adams
pp.xiii, 433; pl. 4   MH
NY: Rinehart   1955

Biography of Laurette Taylor by her daughter. Includes reference to Tennessee Williams. Reissued NY: Atheneum, 1968 with an introduction by Brooks Atkinson.

### Taylor, Oliver
### (1862-1923)
### Actor, manager

**4417** PEYROUSE, JOHN C. Oliver Taylor: a pioneer regional theatre man in Southern Appalachia 1862-1923
Lincoln: U. of Nebraska (PhD)   1979

### Tellegen, Lou
### [van Dammeler, Isidor L. B.]
### (1881-1934)
### Actor

**4418** TELLEGEN, LOU. Women have been kind: the memoirs of Lou Tellegen
pp.288; front., pl. 22   M
London: Jarrolds   1932

First published Vanguard P., 1931. Born in Holland, author, sometimes billed Lou-Tellegen, acted in US with Alla Nazimova, Geraldine Farrar; toured with Sarah Bernhardt on her US début.

### Ter Arutunian, Rouben
### (1920-1992)
### Designer

4419 TER-ARUTUNIAN, ROUBEN. In search of design
pp.[52] inc. wrappers; ill. in text     M
NY: Dance Perspectives     1966
*Dance Perspectives* 28, Winter, 1966. Ter-Arutunian designed for, *inter alia*, the American Shakespeare Festival, 1956-, New York City Opera, 1952-.

### Thompson, Denman
### (1833-1911)
### Actor, playwright

4420 BRADY, JAMES J. Life of Denman Thompson (Joshua Whitcomb)
pp.83; ill. in text     MH
NY: E. A. McFarland & Alex Comstock     1888
A biographical sketch, followed by an appraisal of the character Joshua Whitcomb created by or for Thompson and developed by him in his play *The Old Homestead* and subsequently.

4421 WALSH, WILLIAM H. Historical and personal reminiscences of Denman Thompson the grand old man of the dramatic profession [drop title]
pp.[28] including wrappers; ill. in text     M
[?]: [For the author?]     [c. 1910]
Cover title: *Souvenir booklet of Denman Thompson*.

4422 LEACH, SHELTON B. Denman Thompson and his production of *The Old Homestead*: their place in the evolution of New England rural drama
NY: U. (PhD)     1974

### Thompson, Woodman
### (1899-1955)
### Designer

4423 LEITNER, PAUL. The scene designs of J. Woodman Thompson
Lincoln: U. of Nebraska (PhD)     1990

### Thorne, Charles Robert
### (1814?-1893)
### Actor

4424 MEMOIRS of Charles R. Thorne by himself. Old times – theatres and professionals
pp.various     MB
NY: Dramatic Times     [187?]
Printed in the New York *Dramatic Times* and discontinued after 28 chapters. Not published elsewhere. Charles Robert Thorne Jr. (1840-83) became a prominent leading man in the 1870s but died prematurely.

### Throckmorton, Cleon
### (1897-1965)
### Designer

4425 PAPARONE, JOSEPH C. Cleon Throckmorton: his career as a scene designer in New York
Bloomington: Indiana U. (PhD)     1977

### Todd, Michael
### [Goldbogen, Avrom]
### (1907-1858)
### Producer

4426 COHN, ART. The nine lives of Mike Todd
pp.304; pl. 4     L
London: Hutchinson     1959

### Towse, John Rankin
### (1854-1933)
### Critic

4427 TOWSE, JOHN R. Sixty years of the theatre: an old critic's memoirs
pp.xvi, 464; pl. 40     M
NY: Funk & Wagnalls     1916
Author was drama critic for the New York *Evening Post* for over fifty years until his retirement in 1927.

4428 MILLER, TICE L. The theatre criticism of John Ranken Towse
Urbana-Champaign: U. of Illinois (PhD)     1968

### Tracy, Spencer
### (1900-1967)
### Actor

4429 SWINDELL, LARRY. Spencer Tracy: a biography
pp.xii, 319; pl. 16     L
London: W. H. Allen     1970
First published NY: World, 1969. Chapter 2, *The theater years*.

4430 KANIN, GARSON. Tracy and Hepburn: an intimate memoir
pp.x, 307     M
NY: Viking P.     1971

### Truax, Sarah
### (1877-1958)
### Actress

4431 TRUAX, SARAH. A woman of parts: memories of a life on the stage [autobiography]
pp.viii, 247; pl. 8     M
NY: Longmans, Green     1949
Foreword by Guthrie McClintic.

### Trumble, Alfred
### Actor

4432 [TRUMBLE, ALFRED]. Secrets of the stage; or, playhouse mysteries unveiled. By an old actor
pp.69; pl. 17     MH
NY: Richard K. Fox     1881
Sketches of back-stage work and life.

### Tucker, Lorenzo
### (1907-1986)
### Actor

4433 GRUPENHOFF, David G. The black Valentino: the stage and screen career of Lorenzo Tucker
pp.xi, 188     ★
Metuchen NJ: Scarecrow P.     1988

### Tyler, George Crouse
### (1867-1946)
### Producer

4434 TYLER, GEORGE C. with FURNAS, J. C. Whatever goes up – : the hazardous fortunes of a natural born gambler. With a word of introduction by Booth Tarkington [autobiography]
pp.317; pl. 16     M
Indianapolis: Bobbs-Merrill     1934

4435 SHEREN, PAUL. To G. C. – the best from G. C. Edward Gordon Craig designs *Macbeth* for George Crouse Tyler
Princeton: U. (MA)     1967

**4436** WORKMAN, JOHN P. The George C. Tyler star revivals, 1924 to 1928
Urbana-Champaign: U. of Illinois (PhD) 1968

**4437** HARRIS, KENNETH. George C. Tyler and the Liebler Company: a study of the American theatrical producer at work, 1897-1914
Iowa City: U. of Iowa (PhD) 1974

### Tyler, Priscilla Cooper
### (1816-1889)
### Actress

**4438** COLEMAN, ELIZABETH T. Priscilla Cooper Tyler and the American scene
pp.xiii, 203; pl. 5     M
Tuscaloosa: U. of Alabama P. 1955
Biography of daughter of Thomas Abthorpe Cooper, later daughter-in-law to President John Tyler.

### Urban, Joseph
### (1872-1933)
### Stage designer

**4439** MARKS, SAMUEL M. 'Settings by Joseph Urban'...an evaluation of his stagecraft
Madison: U. of Wisconsin (PhD) 1955

**4440** ILKO, DONALD W. Joseph Urban: the relation of design and architecture in his work
Cleveland OH: Case Western Reserve U. (PhD) 1968

### Vandenhoff, George
### (1813-1885)
### Actor

**4441** VANDENHOFF, GEORGE. Leaves from an actor's notebook: with reminiscences and chit-chat of the green-room and the stage, in England and America
pp.vi, 347     M
NY: D. Appleton 1860
Published London: J. C. Hotten, as *Dramatic reminiscences: or, actors and actresses in England and America*.

**4442** SCHOOLEY, BILL J. George Vandenhoff, nineteenth century elocutionist in America
Baton Rouge: Louisiana State U. (PhD) 1984

### Vincent Mrs J. R.
### [Farley, Mary Ann]
### (1818-1887)
### Actress

**4443** APRIL, 1835. FIFTIETH ANNIVERSARY of the first appearance on the stage of Mrs J. R. Vincent, Boston's favorite actress. Fifty years of an actress's life
pp.28; front.     MH
NY: For Augustin Daly 1885

**4444** RICHARDSON, JAMES B. Mrs James R. Vincent: a memorial address delivered at a meeting of the managers of the Vincent Memorial Hospital April 9, 1911
pp.ii, 39; front.     MB
[Boston]: The Vincent Club 1911
Reminiscence of Mrs Vincent who, with her husband, became particularly associated with the Boston Museum.

### Waite, James R.
### (d.1913)
### Manager

**4445** WAITE, J. RICHARD. James R. Waite: pioneer of 'the ten - twenty - thirty' repertory
Lubbock: Texas Tech U. (PhD) 1979

### Walker, Stuart
### (1884-1941)
### Manager, director

**4446** JACKSON, RICHARD S. Stuart Walker and company: Broadway in the Middle West
West Lafayette: Purdue U. (MS) 1958

### Wallack, James William
### (1794-1864)
### Actor

**4447** [MORRELL, THOMAS H.]. Sketch of the life of James William Wallack (Senior), late actor and manager
pp.62; portrait on title     M
NY: For the author 1865

### Wallack, John Johnson Lester
### (1819-1888)
### Actor

**4448** [LOMAS, JOHN]. A report of the very singular and interesting divorce case Wallack vs Wallack recently decided by his Honour the Vice-Chancellor, in the court of Chancery, New York, with introductory remarks by John Lomas
pp.19     MH
NY: By the proprietor 1834
Lester Wallack sued for divorce on grounds of his wife's alleged adultery with the actor John Povey.

**4449** WALLACK, LESTER. Memories of fifty years. With an introduction by Laurence Hutton
pp.xiv, 190; pl. 74     M
NY: Charles Scribner's Sons 1889
One plate is unindexed. 500 copies. A UK edition, London: 1889, has fewer illustrations.

### Walton, Lester
### (1882-1965)
### Critic

**4450** YOUNG, ARTEE F. Lester Walton: black theatre critic
Ann Arbor: U. of Michigan (PhD) 1980

### Ward, Artemus
### [Brown, Charles Farrar]
### (1834-1867)
### Journalist, lecturer, showman

**4451** HINGSTON, EDWARD P. The genial showman: being the reminiscences of the life of Artemus Ward and pictures of a showman's career in the western world. New illustrated edition complete in one volume
pp.x, 519; pl. 20 (1 col.)     L
London: John Camden Hotten [1871]
First published 1870 in two volumes, each with a coloured frontispiece but otherwise unillustrated.

### Ward, Douglas Turner
### (1930-)
### Actor, director, playwright

**4452** REED, CLIFFORD A. A critical overview of selected work and accomplishments of Douglas Turner

Ward and their impact on American theatre arts
Detroit: Wayne State U. (PhD)  1987

### Warde, Frederick
### (1851-1935)
### Actor

**4453** WARDE, FREDERICK. The fools of Shakespeare: an interpretation of their wit, wisdom and personalities
pp.ix, 214; pl. 8  MH
NY: McBride, Nast  1913
Analysis based on author's own performances and his observation of other actors.

**4454** WARDE, FREDERICK. Fifty years of make-believe [autobiography]
pp.314; pl. 32  M
Los Angeles: Times-Mirror P.  1923

### Warfield, David
### [Wollfeld/Wohlfelt, David]
### (1866-1951)
### Actor

**4455** WARFIELD, DAVID & HAMM, MARGHERITA A.  Ghetto silhouettes
pp.viii, 189; pl. 5  M
NY: James Pott  1902
Sketches of life in New York's East Side by an actor celebrated for his jewish roles, with photographs of him in character.

**4456** COOK, GARY D.  David Warfield: a theatrical biography
Lincoln: U. of Nebraska-Lincoln (PhD)  1975

### Warren, William
### (1767-1832)
### Actor, manager

**4457** THE WARREN FAMILY. Issued for private distribution only
pp.17  MH
NY: [For William Warren Jr.?]  1893
A biographical sketch of William Warren Sr. and his wives and family, especially William Warren the younger. It seems clear that the material is reprinted from a periodical.

**4458** PRITNER, CALVIN L.  William Warren Sr.'s management of the Chestnut Street Theatre Company
Urbana: U. of Illinois (PhD)  1964

### Warren, William [Jr.]
### (1812-1888)
### Actor

**4459** OCTOBER 1832. Fiftieth anniversary of the first appearance on the stage of William Warren, Boston's favorite comedian. Fifty years of an actor's life
pp.51; front.  MH
[Boston]: James Daly  1882
Biographical sketch derived from an article written by W. W. Ball for the *Daily Evening Traveller*, together with reviews of the anniversary performances at the Boston Museum, *Heir at Law* and *School for Scandal*, given October 28.

**4460** [BALL, WILLIAM T.]. Life and memoirs of William Warren, Boston's favorite comedian. With a full account of his golden jubilee. Fifty years of an actor's life
pp.70; pl. 6  M
[Boston]: James Daly  [c. 1888]

The account changes tense after 52 pages and the tribute to Warren in his prime gives way to a description of his funeral, and to obituaries.

**4461** McCONNELL, MARGARET E. William Warren II: the Boston comedian
Bloomington: Indiana U. (PhD)  1963

**4462** GOLDEN, EDWIN J.  Funny man in the snake shop: the art of William Warren Jr., leading actor at the Boston Museum
Medford MA: Tufts U. (PhD)  1973

### Waters, Ethel
### (1900?-1977)
### Actress, singer

**4463** WATERS, ETHEL & SAMUELS, CHARLES. His eye is on the sparrow: an autobiography...
pp.260; pl. 5  M
London: W. H. Allen  1951

**4464** WATERS, ETHEL. To me it's wonderful [autobiography]
pp.ix, 162; pl. 8  MH
NY: Harper & Row  1972
Introduction by Eugenia Price and Joyce Blackburn.

### Watkins, Harry
### (1830?-1894)
### Actor

**4465** SKINNER, MAUD & SKINNER, OTIS (Eds). One man in his time: the adventures of H. Watkins, strolling player 1845-1863, from his journal...
pp.xvii, 258; pl. 8  M
Philadelphia: U. of Pennsylvania P.  1938
Watkins, an actor and dramatist of modest achievement, maintained a lively, latterly an aggrieved journal, 1845-1863.

### Watts, Richard
### (1898-1981)
### Critic

**4466** SCHOENBERGER, MARK A.  The dramatic criticism of Richard Watts, Jr.
New Orleans: Tulane U. (PhD)  1978

### Webster, Margaret
### (1905-1972)
### Actress, director

**4467** WEBSTER, MARGARET. Shakespeare without tears. With an introduction by John M. Brown
pp.xii, 319  BP
NY: McGraw-Hill  1942

**4468** WEBSTER, MARGARET. Shakespeare today. Introduction by M. R. Ridley
pp.319  M
London: J. M. Dent  1957
On her productions.

**4469** SILVERMAN, ELY.  Margaret Webster's theory and practice of Shakespearean production in the United States (1937-1953)
NY: U. (PhD)  1969

**4470** WEBSTER, MARGARET. The same only different: five generations of a great theatrical family
pp.xviii, 395, xiv; pl. 12  M
London: Gollancz  1969

Biography of the Webster/Witty family.

**4471** WEBSTER, MARGARET. Don't put your daughter on the stage [autobiography]
pp.xix, 379, xi; pl. 8   M
NY: Alfred A. Knopf   1972

**4472** WORSLEY, RONALD. Margaret Webster: a study of her contributions to the American theatre
Detroit: Wayne State U. (PhD)   1972

**4473** CARROLL, JANET. A promptbook study of Margaret Webster's production of *Othello*
Baton Rouge: Louisiana State U. (PhD)   1977

**4474** SONG, OAK. A promptbook study of Margaret Webster's production of *Macbeth*
Eugene: U. of Oregon (PhD)   1982

## Welles, George Orson
### (1915-1990)
### Actor, director

**4475** FOWLER, ROY A. Orson Welles
pp.100; pl. 10   M
London: Pendulum Publications   1946

**4476** NOBLE, PETER. The fabulous Orson Welles
pp.276; pl. 16   M
London: Hutchinson   1956

**4477** TURGEON, THOMAS S. The 'super artist' of the classical revival: a study of the productions of Orson Welles and Tyrone Guthrie, 1936-1939
New Haven: Yale U. (PhD)   1967

**4478** McBRIDE, JOSEPH. Orson Welles
pp.192; ill. in text   M
London: Secker and Warburg/ BFI   1972
Substantially Welles's movies, but some broader biographical material.

**4479** FRANCE, RICHARD. The theatre of Orson Welles
pp.212; ill. in text   M
Lewisburg PA: Bucknell U. P.   1977
Period 1931-40.

**4480** BAZIN, ANDRE. Orson Welles: a critical view. Foreword by François Truffaut. Translated from the French by Jonathan Rosenbaum
pp.v, 138; ill. in text   M
London: Elm Tree Books   1978

**4481** NAREMORE, JAMES. The magic world of Orson Welles
pp.viii, 339; ill. in text   L
NY: Oxford U. P.   1978

**4482** LEAMING, BARBARA. Orson Welles: a biography
pp.xiii, 562; pl. 8   M
NY: Viking P.   1985

**4483** HIGHAM, CHARLES. Orson Welles: the rise and fall of an American genius
pp.xii, 377; pl. 9   M
London: New English Library   1986

First published NY: St Martin's P., 1985.

**4484** TAYLOR, JOHN R. Orson Welles, a celebration...picture research by the Kobal collection
pp.176; ill. in text   M
London: Pavilion/ Michael Joseph   1986

**4485** BRADY, FRANK. Citizen Welles: a biography of Orson Welles
pp.xv, 655; pl. 8   M
NY: Charles Scribner's Sons   1989

**4486** FRANCE, RICHARD (Ed.). Orson Welles on Shakespeare: The W.P.A. and Mercury Theatre playscripts
pp.xv, 297; pl. 9   M
NY: Greenwood P.   1990
Texts of *Macbeth*, *Julius Caesar* and the *Five Kings* with substantial introduction and prefatory notes.

**4487** WOOD, BRET. Orson Welles: a bio-bibliography
pp.384   DL★
NY: Greenwood P.   1990

## Wemyss, Francis Courtney
### (1797-1859)
### Actor, manager

**4488** WEMYSS, FRANCIS C. Twenty-six years of the life of an actor and manager, interspersed with sketches, anecdotes and opinions of the professional merits of the most celebrated actors and actresses of the day
pp.402   MH
NY: Burgess, Stringer   1847
Published Glasgow: Griffin, 1848.

## Wenger, John
### (1891-1976)
### Designer

**4489** FORNARO, CARLO DE. John Wenger
pp.24; pl. 51   M
NY: Joseph Lawton   1925

## West, Mae
### (1892-1980)
### Actress

**4490** WEST, MAE. Goodness had nothing to do with it [autobiography]
pp.xiii, 271; pl. 8   L
Englewood Cliffs NJ: Prentice-Hall   1959

**4491** WEST, MAE. On sex, health and ESP
pp.vi, 237; pl. 6   MH
London: W. H. Allen   1975
Appended is a substantial biographical portrait edited by David Ray Johnson.

**4492** CASHIN, FERGUS. Mae West: a biography
pp.197   L
London: Star Books   1982
First published in UK, W. H. Allen, 1981.

**4493** EELLS, GEORGE & MUSGROVE, STANLEY. Mae West
pp.351; pl. 8   O
London: Robson Books   1984

**4494** HELFER, RICHARD. Mae West on the stage: themes and persons
NY: City U. (PhD)   1990

### Wheatley, William
### (1816-1876)
### Actor, manager

**4495** DAY, SUSAN S. Productions at Niblo's Garden Theatre, 1862-1868, during the management of William Wheatley
Eugene: U. of Oregon (PhD)      1972

### Wheeler, Andrew Carpenter
### (1835-1903)
### Critic

**4496** WRIGHT, THOMAS K. The theatre criticism of Andrew Carpenter Wheeler
Urbana-Champaign: UI. of Illinois (PhD)      1971
Wheeler wrote for the *World* and other publications under the *nom de plume* 'Nym Crinkle'.

### Whiffen, Mrs Thomas
### [née Galton, Blanche]
### (1845-1936)
### Actress

**4497** WHIFFEN, MRS THOMAS. Keeping off the shelf...with many illustrations by Bernard J. Rosenmeyer and Walter Jack Duncan [autobiography]
pp.viii, 203; ill. in text, pl. 15      M
NY: E. P. Dutton      1928

### White, Miles Edgren
### (1914?-)
### Costume designer

**4498** HOLCOMB, RICHARD. New stagecraft principles applied to two musical comedy costume designs of Miles White
Lubbock: Texas Tech U. (PhD)      1986

### Wignell, Thomas
### (1753-1803)
### Actor, manager

**4499** DELARUE, ALLISON. The chevalier Henry Wikoff: impresario, 1840
pp.60; ill.      DL★
Princeton: U. P. for the author      1968

**4500** HERR, JOHN H. Thomas Wignell and the Chestnut Street Theatre
East Lansing: Michigan State U. (PhD)      1969

### Wikoff, Henry
### (1811-1884)
### Impresario. journalist

**4501** WIKOFF, HENRY. The reminiscences of an idler
pp.xii, 596; front.      DL★
NY: Fords, Howard & Hulbert      1880
Includes material on Edwin Forrest.

**4502** CROW, DUNCAN. Henry Wikoff the American chevalier
pp.236; pl. 5      M
London: Macgibbon & Kee      1963
Biography. Wikoff was an adventurer, a friend of Edwin Forrest and later an associate of Henry Irving, who based 'Digby Grant' on him.

### Wilk, Max
### (1920-)
### Actor

**4503** WILK, MAX. Every day's a matinee: memoirs scribbled on a dressing room door
pp.288; ill. in text      M
NY: W. W. Norton      1975

### Wilson, Francis
### (1854-1935)
### Actor

**4504** GUNN, ARCHIE. Impressions of Francis Wilson's new comic opera *Half a King*. Direction of A. H. Canby. Adapted from the French by Harry Bache Smith. Music by Ludwig Englander
pp.[16]; ill. in text      MB
NY: J. Ottmann      [1896]
Brief synopsis, and fifteen drawings of the production. Adapted from *Le Roi S'Amuse*.

**4505** WILSON, FRANCIS. Recollections of a player [autobiography]
pp.xi, 81; pl. 32. some col.      MH
NY: DeVinne P.      1897
Errata slip. 120 copies.

**4506** [WILSON, FRANCIS]. Address to graduates of American Academy of Dramatic Arts...Empire Theater, March 19, 1907
pp.8      MB
[NY?]: [For the author?]      [1907]
A plea for good elocution, lack of affectation and true humility.

**4507** WILSON, FRANCIS. Francis Wilson's life of himself, with illustrations
pp.xi, 463; pl. 49      M
Boston: Houghton Mifflin      1924
The celebtrated comedian was also president of Actors Equity from 1913 until his retirement from the stage in 1921.

**4508** [WILSON, FRANCIS]. Rare books, autographs, manuscripts comprising the library collected by the late Francis Wilson, actor-bibliophile
     ★
NY: G. A. Baker      1940

### Wilson, George W.
### (1849-1931)
### Actor

**4509** COBURN, FRANK W. Life of the popular comedian George W. Wilson as originally published by the *Opera Glass*, Boston, Mass.
pp.4; portrait on title      MB
[Boston]: [For the author?]      [c. 1896]
Omits the illustrations that accompanied the original article.

### Wilson, Margery
### (1898-1986)
### Actress

**4510** WILSON, MARGERY. I found my way: an autobiography
pp.296; ill.      DL★
Philadelphia: J. B. Lippincott      1956
Author was leading lady to William S. Hart.

## Wilson, Robert
## (1941-)
## Designer, director

**4511** GALIZIA, LUIZ R. Robert Wilson's creative processes: whole works of art for the contemporary American theatre
Berkeley: U. of California (PhD)      1980

**4512** ROBERT WILSON. The theater of images. Second edition. The Contemporary Arts Center, Cincinnati. The Byrd Hoffman Foundation, N. Y.
pp.157; ill. in text      M
NY: Harper & Row      1984

Originally published in conjunction with an exhibition, *Robert Wilson - from a Theater of Images*, Cincinnati, 1980, of which a catalogue is included. With four articles describing and evaluating Wilson's designs, together with a brief biographical note.

**4513** SHYER, LAURENCE. Robert Wilson and his collaborators
pp.xxii, 347; ill. in text      L
NY: TCG      1989

An account derived in part from interviews with the collaborators. Foreword by Robert Brustein.

## Winter, William
## (1836-1917)
## Critic

**4514** WINTER, WILLIAM. The press and the stage: an oration...delivered before the Goethe Society, at the Brunswick Hotel, New York, January 28, 1889
pp.62      M
NY: Lockwood & Coombes      1889

A reply to an attack on the critical press by Dion Boucicault. 250 copies.

**4515** WINTER, WILLIAM. The actor and other speeches chiefly on theatrical subjects and occasions
pp.x, 80; ill. in text      M
NY: Dunlap Society      1891

**4516** WINTER, WILLIAM. A wreath of laurel, being speeches on dramatic and kindred occasions
pp.xvii, 149; pl. 5      MH
NY: Dunlap Society      1898

Includes a tribute to Joseph Jefferson and essays, *The stage and its apostles* and *Intellectual standard*. 260 copies.

**4517** WINTER, WILLIAM. Other days: being chronicles and memories of the stage
pp.389; pl. 17      M
NY: Moffat, Yard      1908

With chapters on: A royal line, Joseph Jefferson, John Brougham, Charlotte Cushman, John McCullough, Lawrence Barrett, Adelaide Neilson, Stage conditions-past and present; and notes on Mrs Marshall, and William Dunlap.

**4518** WINTER, WILLIAM. Old friends: being literary recollections of other days
pp.407; pl. 21      M
NY: Moffat, Yard      1914

Includes chapters on Ada Cavendish, Charles Dickens, Wilkie Collins, Artemus Ward. Otherwise a non-theatrical volume.

**4519** THE WILLIAM WINTER testimonial. Century Theatre, Tuesday afternoon, March fourteenth 1916
pp.[34]; ill. in text      MB
NY: [Brentano's]      1916

Running title: *Reproduction of original manuscript presented to Mr Winter*. Signatories are headed by Woodrow Wilson and include a formidable number of celebrities, within and without the theatre.

**4520** [WINTER, JEFFERSON]. In the matter of William Winter and the New York Tribune as to the facts/truth *versus* falsehood...The *New York Tribune* having chosen to revive the scandal of its treatment of the late William Winter, falsify the facts as to his retirement from that journal, defame him as the victim of a 'passionate anti-semitic obsession', and then having refused to publish a letter defending him, the record of the facts is published in this form by his son, Jefferson Winter
pp.23      MH
NY: For the author      1918

Winter retired as drama critic for the *New York Tribune* in 1909.

**4521** [WINTER, WILLIAM]. The library of the late William Winter sold by order of his son Jefferson Winter...at auction Friday...April 28
pp.45      M
NY: Walpole Galleries      1922

The dispersal of Winter's library was a protracted affair, with the final session as late as 1927. In 1932 there was a further sale, by the firm of J. C. Morgenthau of New York, of books, letters, dramatic portraits, etc, including busts of Walter Scott and Henry Irving, from the estates of Winter and J. M. Andreini.

**4522** McGRAW, CHARLES J. An analysis of the theatrical criticism of William Winter
Ann Arbor: U. of Michigan (PhD)      1940

**4523** BROOKS, VAN W. The world of Washington Irving
pp.ix, 387      O
NY: E. P. Dutton      1944

Includes a chapter on William Winter.

**4524** LUDWIG, RICHARD M. A critical biography of William Winter
Cambridge MA: Harvard U. (PhD)      1950

**4525** RUBENSTEIN, GILBERT M. The Shakespearean criticism of William Winter. An analysis
Bloomington: Indiana U. (PhD)      1951

## Winters, Shelley
## (1923?-)
## Actress

**4526** WINTERS, SHELLEY. Shelley, also known as Shirley
pp.511; pl. 24      MH
NY: William Morrow      1890

Stage experience includes work with Lee Strasberg at the Actors Studio.

## Wood, Audrey
## Agent

**4527** WOOD, AUDREY with WILK, MAX. Represented by Audrey Wood
pp.340      *
Garden City: Doubleday      1981

### Wood, Joseph
(1801-1890)
### Wood, Mrs Joseph
[née Paton, Mary Ann]
[1802-1863]
### Singing actors

**4528** MEMOIR OF MR AND MRS WOOD containing an authentic account of the principal events in the lives of these celebrated vocalists: including the marriage of Miss Paton, to Lord William Lennox; and the causes which led to their divorce: her subsequent marriage to Joseph Wood, and a full statement of the popular disturbance at the Park Theatre, New York
pp.36; portrait on first title MH
NY: Turner & Fisher 1840

The furore at the Park Theatre occurred in May 1836, occasioned by articles in the press reporting Wood's alleged lack of gallantry to a Mrs Conduit in arrangements for her benefit performance.

### Wood, Peggy
(1892-1978)
### Actress

**4529** WOOD, PEGGY. Actors - and people: both sides of the footlights [autobiography]
pp.vii, 178; pl. 6 M
NY: D. Appleton 1930

**4530** WOOD, PEGGY. Star-wagon
pp.311 DL★
NY: Farrar & Rinehart 1936

**4531** WOOD, PEGGY. How young you look: memoirs of a middle-sized actress
ix, 277; pl. 8 M
NY: Farrar & Rinehart 1941

**4532** WOOD, PEGGY. Arts and flowers [autobiography]
pp.189; pl. 8 M
NY: William Morrow 1963

**4533** SIMON, BARBARA. Twentieth century American performing arts as viewed through the career of Peggy Wood
NY: U. (PhD) 1981

### Wood, William Burke
(1779-1861)
### Actor, manager

**4534** WOOD, WILLIAM B. Personal recollections of the stage embracing notices of actors, authors and auditors during a period of forty years
pp.477; front. M
Philadelphia: Henry Carey Baird 1855

Wood was director of theatres in, *inter alia*, Philadelphia, Baltimore, Washington DC and Alexandria VA. An index, compiled by Alfred H. Sanka is printed in *Theatre Documentation*, 1:2, Spring 1969.

### Woollcott, Alexander
(1887-1943)
### Critic

**4535** WOOLLCOTT, ALEXANDER. While Rome burns
pp.viii, 328 DL★
NY: Viking P. 1934

Includes reminiscence.

**4536** PHILISTINA. Alec the great: an account of the curious life and extraordinary opinions of the late Alexander Woollcott: with special emphasis on an affair of the heart, known only to three survivors, of whom the humblest signs herself Philistina
pp.253 DL★
NY: Avalon P. 1943

**4537** KAUFMAN, BEATRICE & HENNESSEY, JOSEPH (Eds). Letters of Alexander Woollcott
pp.xxiv, 410; pl. 2 M
NY: Garden City Publishing 1944

Introductory biographical sketch.

**4538** ADAMS, SAMUEL H. Alexander Woollcott: his life and his world
pp.388; pl. 8 M
London: Hamish Hamilton 1946

**4539** HOYT, EDWIN P. Alexander Woollcott: the man who came to dinner. A biography
pp.vii, 357; front., ill. in text L
NY: Abelard-Schuman 1968

**4540** TEICHMANN, HOWARD. Smart Aleck: the wit, world and life of Alexander Woollcott
pp.334; pl. 9 M
NY: William Morrow 1976

**4541** BURNS, MORRIS U. The dramatic criticism of Alexander Woollcott
pp.v, 286 M
Metuchen NJ: Scarecrow P. 1980

### Wynn, Keenan
(1916-1986)
### Actor

**4542** WYNN, KEENAN & BROUGH, JAMES. Ed. Wynn's son [autobiography]
pp.237;pl. 8 MH
Garden City: Doubleday 1959

### Young, Stark
(1881-1963)
### Critic, author, playwright

**4543** YOUNG, STARK. The pavilion of people and times remembered, of stories and places [autobiography]
pp.viii, 194 M
NY: Charles Scribner's Sons 1951

**4544** THURMAN, BEDFORD. Stark Young. A bibliography of his writings with a selective index to his criticism of the arts
Ithaca: Cornell U. (PhD) 1954

**4545** LUMIANSKI, ROBERT M. Stark Young and his dramatic criticism
East Lansing: Michigan State U. (PhD) 1955

**4546** LINK, JAMES O. The central premise in Stark Young's theories of art and criticism
Ithaca: Cornell U. (PhD) 1963

**4547** MILLER, JOHN M. Stark Young's principles of theatre art
New Orleans: Tulane U. (PhD) 1963

## 9.1. GENERAL AND HISTORICAL

**4548** DREXLER, MALCOLM B. Stark Young's ideas on theatre practice
Urbana-Champaign: U. of Illinois (PhD) 1964

**4549** PILKINGTON, JOHN. Stark Young: a life in the arts. Letters 1900-1962
pp.xxxi, vii, 1454 M
Baton Rouge: Louisiana State U. P. 1975
Two volumes, continuously paginated.

**4550** PILKINGTON, JOHN. Stark Young
pp.xii, 164; ill. in text M
Boston: Twayne 1985

### Yurka, Blanche
### (1887-1974)
### Actress

**4551** YURKA, BLANCHE. Dear audience: a guide to the enjoyment of theatre. Drawings by Rafaello Busoni
pp.vii, 167; ill. in text M
Englewood Cliffs NJ: Prentice-Hall 1959

**4552** YURKA, BLANCHE. Bohemian girl: Blanche Yurkas's theatrical life
pp.xii, 306; col. front., pl. 16 M
Athens: Ohio U. P. 1970
Afterword by Brooks Atkinson.

### Ziegfeld, Florenz
### (1867-1932)
### Manager, producer

**4553** CANTOR, EDDIE & FREEDMAN, DAVID. Ziegfeld, the great glorifier
pp.166; front., pl. 30 L
NY: Alfred H. King 1934
Account of Florenz Ziegfeld with many photographs of the celebrated showgirls by Alfred Cheney Johnston.

**4554** JOHNSTON, ALVA. The great Goldwyn
pp.99; pl. 4 L
NY: Random House 1937
Makes reference to Florenz Ziegfeld.

**4555** FARNSWORTH, MARJORIE. The Ziegfeld follies...with an introduction by Billie Burke Ziegfeld
pp.194; ill. in text M
London: Peter Davies 1956

**4556** ZIEGFELD, PATRICIA. The Ziegfelds' girl: confessions of an abnormally happy childhood [autobiography]
pp.ix, 210; pl. 6 M
Boston: Little, Brown 1964

**4557** BADRIG, ROBERT. Florenz Ziegfeld, twentieth century showman
pp.27 DL★
Charlotteville NY: SamHar P. 1972

**4558** HIGHAM, CHARLES. Ziegfeld
pp.ix, 245; pl. 16 M
NY: W. H.Allen 1972

**4559** PHILLIPS, JULIEN. Stars of the Ziegfeld Follies
pp.79; ill. DL★
Minneapolis: Lerner 1972
Brief history with biographies of notable entertainers. Intended for children.

**4560** ZIEGFELD, a special exhibition...
ll.3 M
NY: Museum of the City of New York 1973
Press release comprising brief chronology of Ziegfeld's shows, heralding an exhibition to open June 5.

**4561** MASCHIO, GERALDINE. The Ziegfeld Follies: form, content, and significance of an American revue
Madison: U. of Wisconsin (PhD) 1981

**4562** STONE, ROSALINE B. The Ziegfeld Follies: a study of theatrical opulence from 1907 to 1931
Denver: U. (PhD) 1985

**4563** CARTER, RANDOLPH. Ziegfeld: the time of his life
pp.160; ill. in text, some col. M
London: Bernard P. 1988
Revised edition. First published London: Elek, 1974 as *The world of Flo Ziegfeld*, here with additional illustrations. A feature of the book is the well illustrated record of the designs of Joseph Urban.

# 9. THEATRICAL CRITICISM

## 9.1 GENERAL AND HISTORICAL

**4564** CAFFIN, CHARLES H. The appreciation of the drama
pp.ix, 280; ill. DL★
NY: Baker & Taylor 1908

**4565** QUINLAN, MICHAEL A. Poetic justice in the drama: the history of an ethical principle in literary criticism
pp.vi, 236 DL★
Notre Dame IN: U. P. 1912

**4566** BURTON, RICHARD. How to see a play
pp. xi, 217 MB
NY: Macmillan 1914
To sharpen the discrimination and appreciation of the untutored play-goer.

**4567** SMITH, SAMUEL S. The craft of the critic
pp.xiii, 401 L
NY: Thomas Y. Crowell 1931
Part II, 'play reviewing' comprises essays: *The theatrical v. the dramatic, The play as picture, Modern decor, Acting, The theatrical review, The gayer arts* [vaudeville, jazz, musical comedy, revue], *Comic opera, Comedy, Melodrama, Modern tragedy, The art of dramatic criticism.*

**4568** SPINGARN, JOEL E. Creative criticism and other essays
pp.ix, 221 L
NY: Harcourt Brace 1931
New and enlarged edition. First published NY: Holt, 1917, here with four additional essays and a new appendix. Includes an essay on dramatic criticism and the theatre.

## 9. THEATRICAL CRITICISM

**4569** MOSES, MONTROSE J. & BROWN, JOHN M. (Eds). The American drama as seen by its critics 1752-1934
pp.391 M
NY: W. W. Norton 1934
An anthology of critical reviews.

**4570** BLYMER, LOUISE A. Journalistic dramatic criticism. A survey of theatre reviews in New York, 1857-1927
Baton Rouge: Louisiana State U. 1939

**4571** FALK, ROBERT P. Representative American criticism of Shakespeare, 1830-1885
Madison: U. of Wisconsin (PhD) 1939

**4572** WESTFALL, ALFRED van R. American Shakespearean criticism
pp.xii, 305 M
NY: H. W. Wilson 1939

**4573** BROWN, LAURENCE R. Frontier dramatic criticism, St.Louis 1835-1839
Madison: U. of Wisconsin (MS) 1949

**4574** WALTERS, WALTER H. Representative trends in American theatrical criticism from 1900-1940
Cleveland: Case Western Reserve U. (PhD) 1950

**4575** WEST, L. EDNA. Contemporary Broadway criticism
Madison: U. of Wisconsin (PhD) 1952

**4576** PEDIGO, FRANCES M. Critical opinions of poetry, drama, and fiction in the *Christian Examiner*, 1824-1869
Chapel Hill: U. of North Caroline (PhD) 1953

**4577** HUNTER, FREDERICK J. Clayton Hamilton and the technical mode in American dramatic criticism
Stanford: U. (PhD) 1954

**4578** GREGORIC, MICHAEL T. Principles and practice in modern dramatic criticism
Ithaca: Cornell U. (PhD) 1962

**4579** KIRK, JOHN W. Dramatism and the theatre. An application of Kenneth Burke's critical methods to the analysis of two plays
Gainsville: U. of Florida (PhD) 1962

**4580** ROBERTSON, WILLIAM J. Dramatic criticism and reviewing in Chicago, 1920-1930
Madison: U. of Wisconsin (PhD) 1964

**4581** FRIEDMAN, SIDNEY J. Critical standards and assumptions in New York daily newspapers' theatre reviews 1955-1956
Iowa City: U. of Iowa (PhD) 1966

**4582** O'LEARY, RONALD T. The Broadway reviewers, 1950 to 1960
Madison: U. of Wisconsin (PhD) 1966

**4583** ANGOTTI, VINCENT L. American dramatic criticism, 1800-1820
Lawrence: U. of Kansas (PhD) 1967

**4584** PALMER, HELEN H. & DYSON, JANE A. (Eds). American drama criticism. Interpretations, 1890-1965 inclusive, of American drama since the first play produced in America
pp.vi, 239 MH
Hamden CT: Shoe String P. 1967
Substantially, reviews from commercial periodicals. A supplement was issued in 1970 and a revised version and supplement under the editorship of Floyd E. Eddleman in 1979 & 1984.

**4585** FALK, ARMAND E. Theatrical criticism in the *New York Evening Post*, 1807-1830
East Lansing: Michigan State U. (PhD) 1969

**4586** WRIGHT, EDWARD A. & DOWNS, LENTHIEL H. A primer for playgoers
pp.xiii, 335; ill. DL★
Englewood Cliffs NJ: Prentice-Hall 1969
Second edition, revised and enlarged. First published 1958.

**4587** ROTHMAN, JOHN. The origin and development of dramatic criticism in the *New York Times*, 1851-1880
pp.ix, 96 DL★
NY: Arno P. 1970

**4588** DALEY, ELIZABETH M. A structural-functional approach to dramatic criticism
Madison: U. of Wisconsin (PhD) 1971

**4589** LUCAS, THOMAS E. Elder Olson
pp.198 L
NY: Twayne 1972
Includes Chapter 2: *A theory of the drama*; chapter 5: *Practical criticism: the drama*.

**4590** MEINKEN, ERNEST F. American actors in London, 1825-1861: their reception by professional theatre critics
Los Angeles: U. of California (PhD) 1972

**4591** NEARMAN, MARK J. Theatre criticism and the phenomenon of theatre
Seattle: U. of Washington (PhD) 1972

**4592** ROTH, EMALOU. Immanent form: toward a dramatic/theatrical criticism
Lawrence: U. of Kansas (PhD) 1972

**4593** BELLINGHIERE, JOSEPH J. A methodology for a content analysis of theatre critics' reviews
Tallahassee: Florida State U. (PhD) 1973

**4594** THE NEW YORK TIMES directory of the theatre. Introduction by Clive Barnes
pp.[113], 51, 1009; ill. in text M
NY: Arno P. 1973
The *New York Times* reprinted every theatre review and news story from 1920 to 1970 in eight volumes, with an additional two volumes of appendix and index. These last two volumes are here reprinted in one volume. Lists productions (21,000) by play title, and identifies every participant.

**4595** WALLACE, RAYMOND V. Theatre critics for daily New York newspapers, 1960-1970
Kent OH: State U. (PhD) 1973

**4596** STATHAM, CHARLES M. The application of prevailing principles of elocution to theatrical criticism of American acting, 1815-1840
Madison: U. of Wisconsin (MA) 1974

**4597** DALEY, MARY P. Journalistic criticism of theatre in eighteenth century America
Cleveland: Case Western Reserve U. (PhD) 1976

## 9.2. COLLECTED NOTICES

**4598** ENGEL, LEHMAN. The critics
pp.xix, 332   M
NY: Macmillan   1976
An examination of the responsibility and the power of the theatre reviewers.

**4599** OGUNBIYI, YEMI. New black playwrights in America (1960-1975); essays in theatrical criticism
NY: U. (PhD)   1976

**4600** SAMPLES, GORDON. How to locate reviews of plays and films
pp.x, 114   L
Metuchen NJ: Scarecrow P.   1976

**4601** BURATTI, DAVID. *The Spirit of the Times*: its theatrical criticism and theories as a reflection of cultural attitudes
Bloomington: Indiana U. (PhD)   1977

**4602** STANLEY, WILLIAM T. Broadway in the West End. An index of reviews of American theatre in London, 1950-1975
pp.xxxii, 206   L
Westport: Greenwood P.   1978
Listed under name of playwright. Appendix provides information on long-running shows in London and New York.

**4603** EDDLEMAN, FLOYD E. (Ed.). American drama criticism: interpretations, 1890-1977
pp.viii, 488   L
Hamden CT: Shoe String P.   1979
The second edition. First published 1976. An updating of Helen H. Palmer and Jane Dyson: *American drama criticism...* (q.v.). A source book, indexing and where necessary describing critics, adapted authors and works, books and journals, play titles and playwrights. A supplement (pp.vii, 255) was issued in 1984.

**4604** SALVAGGIO, ODETTE C. American dramatic criticism, 1830-1860
Tallahassee: Florida State U. (PhD)   1979

**4605** STRAUS, TODD T. Toward a theatrical criticism
Berkeley: U. of California (PhD)   1980

**4606** LEWIS, WILLIAM R. A semiotic model for theatre criticism
Carbondale: Southern Illinois U. (PhD)   1981

**4607** MILLER, TICE L. Bohemians and critics: American theatre criticism in the nineteenth century
pp.x, 190   M
Metuchen NJ: Scarecrow P.   1981
Examines the critics Henry Austin Clapp, Edward G. P. Williams, William Winter, Stephen Ryder Fiske and Andrew Carpenter Wheeler (Nym Crinkle).

**4608** WASHINGTON, RHONNIE L. The relationship between the white critic and the black theatre from 1959-1969
Ann Arbor: U. of Michigan (PhD)   1983

**4609** MARKS, PATRICIA. American literary and drama reviews: an index to late nineteenth century periodicals
pp.xviii, 313   MH
Boston: G. K. Hall   1984

**4610** SALEM, JAMES M. A guide to critical reviews. Part 1 American drama 1909- [ Part 2 The musical, 1909-]
pp.av 650   L
Metuchen NJ: Scarecrow P.   1984 -
Two volumes. Several updates have been issued.

**4611** MEISTER, CHARLES W. Dramatic criticism: a history
pp.vii, 318   L
Jefferson NC: McFarland   1985
Includes chapters on US theatre criticism before and after 1920.

**4612** BERTIN, Michael (Ed.). The play and its critic. Essays for Eric Bentley
pp. xxvii, 349   M
Lanham MD: U. P. of America   1986
Includes Robert Brustein: *Repertory memories*; Ruby Cohn: *Exits from 'No Exit'*; Arthur Franz: *Sam Shepard, iconographer of the depths*; Gordon Strogoff: *Eric Bentley on acting*.

**4613** YANOSKY, SABRINA K. A theatrical-critical approach to *Hamlet*'s women for actors and critics
Berkeley: U. of California (PhD)   1987

**4614** ANDERSON, DAVID J. Theatre criticism: a minor art with a major problem
Columbus: Ohio State U. (PhD)   1988

**4615** PALMER, RICHARD H. The critics' canon: standards of theatre reviewing in America
pp.xiii, 183   L
NY: Greenwood P.   1988

## 9.2 COLLECTED NOTICES

**4616** [EWING, ROBERT W.]. The drama, by Jacques
pp.184, 4   MB
[Philadelphia]: [Ash & Mason?]   [1825]
Weekly theatre reviews, each headed 'Philadelphia' and printed originally in the *United States Gazette*, here reprinted and continuously paginated with some editorial annotation.

**4617** *NEW YORK TIMES* theatre reviews
pp.various; ill. in text   DL★
NY: New York Times   1870-
Collected reviews, initially in six volumes covering the period 1870-1919 with index, updated biennially.

**4618** AYRES, ALFRED [= Osmun, Thomas E.]. Acting and actors - elocution and elocutionists. A book about theater folk and theater art...with preface by Harrison G. Fiske, introduction by Edgar S. Werner, prologue by James A. Waldron
pp.287; ill. in text, pl. 5   MH
NY: D. Appleton   1894
Reviews of contemporary performances by distinguished artists from an elocutionary viewpoint, largely reprinted from *Werner's Magazine* and the *Dramatic Mirror*.

**4619** SYLE, LOUIS D. Essays in dramatic criticism: with impressions of some modern plays
pp.xi,161   L
NY: William R. Jenkins   1898

Articles on the endowed theatre and the future of the drama, reprinted from the San Francisco *Examiner*. Includes an observation on the actor's art, and reviews of *Rip Van Winkle* and James A. Herne's *Shore Acres*.

**4620** CLAPP, JOHN B. & EDGETT, EDWIN F. Plays of the present
pp.331; pl. 34 M
NY: Dunlap Society 1902
Reviews. 250 copies.

**4621** TALL, BROUGHTON [= Tall, Stanley B.]. Papers from a critic's note-book
pp.68 DL★
[Baltimore]: For the author 1913

**4622** NATHAN, GEORGE J. Another book on the theatre
pp.xvi, 358 M
NY: B. W. Huebsch 1915

**4623** NATHAN, GEORGE J. Mr George Jean Nathan presents
pp.310 M
NY: Alfred A. Knopf 1917

**4624** NATHAN, GEORGE J. The popular theatre
pp.236 M
NY: Alfred A. Knopf 1918
Second edition 1923 (not seen).

**4625** NATHAN, GEORGE J. Comedians all
pp.267 M
NY: Alfred A. Knopf 1919
'A book of contradictory criticism'. Includes material on David Belasco, George M. Cohan.

**4626** HAMILTON, CLAYTON. Seen on the stage
pp. x, 270 M
NY: Henry Holt 1920
Articles reprinted from *Vogue* and *The Bookman*, intended as a suffix to the author's *The theory of the theater*.

**4627** WHITMAN, WALT. The gathering of the forces: editorials, essays, literary and dramatic reviews and other material written by Walt Whitman as editor of the Brooklyn *Daily Eagle* in 1846 and 1847, edited by Cleveland Rodgers
pp.lxiii, 272; 386; ill. DL★
NY: G. P. Putnam's Sons 1920
Two volumes. Includes accounts of Charlotte Cushman and Edwin Forrest.

**4628** NATHAN, GEORGE J. The theatre, the drama, the girls
pp.361 M
NY: Alfred A. Knopf 1921

**4629** NATHAN, GEORGE J. The critic and the drama
pp.x, 152 M
London: John Lane The Bodley Head [1923]
First published NY: Alfred A. Knopf, 1922.

**4630** NATHAN, GEORGE J. The world in falseface
pp.xxix, 326 M
NY: Alfred A. Knopf 1923

**4631** WOOLLCOTT, ALEXANDER. Shouts and murmurs: echoes of a thousand and one first nights
pp.ix, 264 M
London: Leonard Parsons 1923

**4632** YOUNG, STARK. The flower in drama
pp.ix, 162 M
NY: Charles Scribner's Sons 1923
Collected essays on acting in general, and on individual performances, from the *New Republic* & *Theatre Arts Magazine*.

**4633** NATHAN, GEORGE J. Materia critica
pp.vi, 242 M
NY: Alfred A. Knopf 1924

**4634** WOOLLCOTT, ALEXANDER. Enchanted aisles
pp.viii, 260 M
NY: G. P. Putnam's Sons 1924

**4635** NATHAN, GEORGE J. The house of Satan
pp.viii, 295 M
NY: Alfred A. Knopf 1926

**4636** CANFIELD, MARY C. Grotesques and other reflections
pp.vii, 238 L
NY: Harper & Brothers 1927

**4637** HAMMOND, PERCY. But – is it art
pp.vi, 186 M
NY: Doubleday, Page 1927
Lighthearted theatre reviews.

**4638** NATHAN, GEORGE J. Art of the night
pp.x, 296 M
NY: Akfred A. Knopf 1928

**4639** WOOLLCOTT, ALEXANDER. Going to pieces
pp.x, 256 MH
NY: G. P. Putnam's Sons 1928
Includes material on the Marx Brothers, Carlotta LeClerq, Ruth Draper.

**4640** BROWN, JOHN M. Upstage: the American theatre in performance
pp.xii, 276 M
NY: W. W. Norton 1930

**4641** NATHAN, GEORGE J. Testament of a critic
pp.viii, 257 M
NY: Alfred A. Knopf 1931

**4642** NATHAN, GEORGE J. The intimate notebooks of George Jean Nathan
pp.vi, 326 M
NY: Alfred A. Knopf 1932

**4643** FIRKINS, OSCAR W. Selected essays
pp.ix, 298 O
Minneapolis: U. of Minnesota P. 1933
Includes essays: *Action in drama*, *Source of pleasure in familiar plays*.

**4644** NATHAN, GEORGE J. Passing judgments
pp.xii, 271 M
NY: Alfred A. Knopf 1935

**4645** BROWN, JOHN M. The art of playgoing
pp.204 DL★
NY: W. W. Norton 1936

## 9.2. COLLECTED NOTICES

**4646** NATHAN, GEORGE J. The theatre of the moment: a journalistic commentary
pp.xiv, 310 M
NY: Alfred A. Knopf 1936

**4647** BROWN, JOHN M. Two on the aisle: ten years of the American theatre in performance
pp.321 M
NY: W. W. Norton 1938
Reviews reprinted from the *New York Evening Post*.

**4648** NATHAN, GEORGE J. The morning after the first night
pp.ix, 282 M
NY: Alfred A. Knopf 1938

**4649** BROWN, JOHN M. Broadway in review
pp.295 MH
NY: W. W. Norton 1940

**4650** HAMMOND, PERCY. This atom in the audience. A digest of reviews and comments
pp.xvi, 275 M
NY: J. C. Hammond 1940
Reprinted articles from the *Chicago Tribune* and the *New York Herald Tribune*.

**4651** NEW YORK THEATRE critics' reviews
pp.various M
NY: Critics Theatre Reviews/Proscenium 1940-
Reproduced in facsimile. Irregular, 18-20/yr. Cumulative indexes issued for 1940-1960, 1961-1972, 1973-1986.

**4652** NATHAN, GEORGE J. The theatre book of the year 1942-1943 [-1953-1954]: a record and an interpretation
pp.various M
NY: Alfred A. Knopf 1943-54
Eleven annual volumes.

**4653** NATHAN, GEORGE J. The entertainment of a nation or three sheets in the wind
pp.x, 290 M
NY: Alfred A. Knopf 1943

**4654** WOOLLCOTT, ALEXANDER. Long, long ago
pp.vii, 280 M
NY: Viking P. 1943

**4655** BROWN, JOHN M. Seeing things
pp.viii, 341 M
London: Hamish Hamilton [1946]
Articles reprinted from the *Saturday Review of Literature*.

**4656** BROWN, JOHN M. Seeing more things
pp.ix, 347 M
London: Hamish Hamilton 1948
Articles reprinted from the *Saturday Review of Literature*.

**4657** YOUNG, STARK. Immortal shadows: a book of dramatic criticism
pp.x, 290 M
NY: Charles Scribner's Sons 1948

**4658** GAVER, JACK. Curtain calls
pp.ix, 310 M
NY: Dodd, Mead 1949

Broadway reflections, mostly of the 1940s.

**4659** BROWN, JOHN M. Still seeing things
pp.ix, 335 M
London: Hamish Hamilton 1951
Articles reprinted from the *Saturday Review of Literature*.

**4660** BROWN, JOHN M. As they appear
pp.viii, 258 M
London: Hamish Hamilton 1953
Articles reprinted from the *Saturday Review*.

**4661** NATHAN, GEORGE J. The theatre in the fifties
pp.v, 306 M
NY: Alfred A. Knopf 1953

**4662** BENTLEY, ERIC. The dramatic event: an American chronicle
pp.285 M
NY: Horizon P. 1954

**4663** BENTLEY, ERIC. What is theatre? A query in chronicle form
pp. x, 273 M
London: Dennis Dobson 1957
First published in US in 1956. Collected criticism.

**4664** CLURMAN, HAROLD. Lies like truth: theatre reviews and essays
pp.ix, 300 M
NY: Macmillan 1958

**4665** McDERMOTT, WILLIAM F. Best of McDermott. Selected writings. Foreword by John M. Brown
pp.281 L
Cleveland OH: World Publishing 1959
Drama critic and columnist for the *Cleveland Plain Dealer*.

**4666** NATHAN, GEORGE J. The magic mirror: selected writings on the theatre, edited, together with an introduction by Thomas Q. Curtis
pp.xviii, 278; front. M
NY: Alfred A. Knopf 1960

**4667** HURRELL, JOHN D. Two modern American tragedies: reviews and criticisms of *Death of a Salesman* and *A Streetcar named Desire*
pp.xx, 153 L
NY: Charles Scribner's Sons 1961
Contributors include: George J. Nathan, Harold Clurman, Robert Edmond Jones, Signi L. Falk, Kenneth Tynan, Eric Bentley, Joseph W. Krutch, W. David Sievers.

**4668** DUPREY, RICHARD A. Just off the aisle: the ramblings of a Catholic critic
pp.209 DL★
Westminster MD: Newman P. 1962

**4669** KERR, WALTER. The decline of pleasure
pp.319 M
NY: Simon and Schuster 1962

**4670** ATKINSON, BROOKS Tuesdays & Fridays
pp.xii, 275 M
NY: Random House 1963

Articles, some theatrical, reprinted from the *New York Times*. Introduction by Samuel N. Behrman.

**4671** BROWN, JOHN M.  Dramatis personae: a retrospective show
pp.xii, 563　　　　　　　　　　　　　　　　　　M
NY: Viking P.　　　　　　　　　　　　　　　　1963
Articles reprinted from the *Saturday Review* and *Esquire*.

**4672** KERR, WALTER.  Pieces at eight
pp.vii, 245　　　　　　　　　　　　　　　　　　M
London: Max Reinhardt　　　　　　　　　　　　1963
Reviews of Broadway and off-Broadway theatre, 1957-1962.

**4673** KERR, WALTER.  The theater in spite of itself
pp.319　　　　　　　　　　　　　　　　　　　　M
NY: Simon & Schuster　　　　　　　　　　　　　1963

**4674** McCARTHY, MARY.  Mary McCarthy's theatre chronicles 1937-1962
pp.xxi, 248　　　　　　　　　　　　　　　　　MH
NY: Noonday P.　　　　　　　　　　　　　　[1963]
An updating of *Sights and Spectacles 1937-1958*, NY: Farrar Straus and Cudahy, 1956. Articles reprinted in revised form largely from the *Partisan Review*.

**4675** SIMON, JOHN.  Acid test
pp.288　　　　　　　　　　　　　　　　　　　DL★
NY: Stein & Day　　　　　　　　　　　　　　　1963
Literary, film and play reviews, including the Broadway seasons 1960-62. Introduction by Dwight MacDonald.

**4676** DOWNER, ALAN S. (Ed.).  American drama and its critics: a collection of critical essays
pp.xxi, 258　　　　　　　　　　　　　　　　　　M
Chicago: U. P.　　　　　　　　　　　　　　　　1965
James A. Herne: *Art for truth's sake in drama* (1897); William Dean Howells: *Some new American plays* (1904); Walter P. Eaton: *Our infant industry* (1908); James G. Huneker: *David Belasco* (1921); Robert Benchley: *The musical theater* (1921-36); Stark Young: *The apron string in our theater* (1922); George J. Nathan: *Eugene O'Neill* (1924-29); H. T. Parker: *'Green Grow the Lilacs'; 'Hotel Universe'* (1930); John H. Lawson: *The law of conflict* (1935); Malcolm Goldstein: *Clifford Odets and the found generation* (1965); Vincent Wall: *Maxwell Anderson, the last anarchist* (1941); Francis Fergusson: *James's idea of dramatic form* (1943); Eric Bentley: *The American drama, 1944-1954* (1954); Arthur Ganz: *The desperate morality of the plays of Tennessee Williams* (1962); Henry Popkin: *Arthur Miller, the strange encounter* (1960); Tom F. Driver: *What's the matter with Edward Albee?* (1964); Robert Brustein: *Why American plays are not literature*.

**4677** ATKINSON, BROOKS  Brief chronicles
pp.255　　　　　　　　　　　　　　　　　　　MH
NY: Coward McCann　　　　　　　　　　　　　1966
Pieces written after the author's retirement as drama critic for the *New York Yimes*. Marginal theatre reference.

**4678** BRUSTEIN, ROBERT.  Seasons of discontent: dramatic opinions 1959-1965
pp.322　　　　　　　　　　　　　　　　　　　　M
London: Cape　　　　　　　　　　　　　　　　1966

**4679** CLURMAN, HAROLD.  The naked image: observations on the modern theatre
pp.viii, 312　　　　　　　　　　　　　　　　　　M
NY: Macmillan　　　　　　　　　　　　　　　　1966

**4680** COLEMAN, ARTHUR & TYLER, GARY R.  Drama criticism, volume one. A checklist of interpretation since 1940 of English and American plays
pp.457; 446　　　　　　　　　　　　　　　　　　O
Denver / Chicago: Alan Swallow / Swallow P. 1966-71
Lists criticism in books and periodicals 1940-1964. Second volume deals with classical and European plays.

**4681** GAVER, JACK.  Season in season out 1965-1966
pp.xv, 223　　　　　　　　　　　　　　　　　　M
NY: Hawthorn Books　　　　　　　　　　　　　1966
Review of the Broadway season.

**4682** SONTAG, SUSAN.  Against interpretation, and other essays
pp.xii, 304　　　　　　　　　　　　　　　　　　L
NY: Farrar, Straus & Giroux　　　　　　　　　　1966
Reprinted articles and reviews. Includes *Going to the theatre...* which, in part, examines Arthur Miller's *After the Fall*, James Baldwin's *Blues for Mister Charlie* and LeRoi Jones's *Dutchman*.

**4683** GASSNER, JOHN.  Dramatic soundings: evaluations and retractions culled from 30 years of dramatic criticism. Introduction and posthumous editing by Glenn Loney
pp.xx, 716; front.　　　　　　　　　　　　　　　M
NY: Crown　　　　　　　　　　　　　　　　　1968

**4684** GOTTFRIED, MARTIN.  Opening nights: theater criticism of the sixties
pp.384　　　　　　　　　　　　　　　　　　　　M
NY: G. P. Putnam's Sons　　　　　　　　　　　1969
Reviews reprinted from *Women's Wear Weekly* and *Vogue*.

**4685** KERR, WALTER.  Thirty plays hath November: pain and pleasure in the contemporary theater
pp.343　　　　　　　　　　　　　　　　　　　　M
NY: Simon and Schuster　　　　　　　　　　　1969

**4686** BRUSTEIN, ROBERT.  The third theatre
pp.xx, 294　　　　　　　　　　　　　　　　　　M
London: Cape　　　　　　　　　　　　　　　　1970
First published NY: Alfred A. Knopf, 1969. Reprinted articles, 1957-68.

**4687** GILMAN, RICHARD.  The confusion of realms
pp.xi, 272　　　　　　　　　　　　　　　　　　M
NY: Random House　　　　　　　　　　　　　1970
Includes essays on Garson's *Macbird*, and the Living Theatre, and notes on 'the true and only crisis of the theater', from the author's course on playwriting at Yale.

**4688** GILMAN, RICHARD.  Common and uncommon masks: writings on theatre 1961-70
pp.xxiii, 321　　　　　　　　　　　　　　　　　M
NY: Random House　　　　　　　　　　　　　1971
Collected reviews from, e.g., *Commonweal*, *Newsweek*, *New Republic*.

**4689** KERR, WALTER.  God on the gymnasium floor
pp.320　　　　　　　　　　　　　　　　　　　　M
NY: Simon and Schuster　　　　　　　　　　　1971

**4690** SHEED, WILFRED.  The morning after: selected essays and reviews
pp.xx, 304　　　　　　　　　　　　　　　　　　L
NY: Farrar, Straus & Giroux　　　　　　　　　　1971

Part III comprises reprinted reviews, including material on Eugene O'Neill, Arthur Miller, Edward Albee, Tennessee Williams, and the Living Theatre.

**4691** WALDMAN, MAX. Waldman on theatre
pp.185; ill. DL★
Garden City: Doubleday 1971

Includes accounts of Richard Schechner's *Dionysus in '69* and Living Theatre's *Paradise Now*. Introduction by Clive Barnes, preface by Peter Bunnell.

**4692** BENTLEY, ERIC. Theatre of war: comments on 32 occasions...
pp. xiv, 428 M
London: Eyre Methuen 1972

Collected criticism written during the 1960s.

**4693** LAHR, JOHN. Acting out America
pp.203 M
Harmondsworth UK: Pelican 1972

Expanded reprint of *Up against the fourth wall* (NY: Grove P., 1970). Articles on the theatre reprinted from the *Evergreen Review* and *London Magazine*.

**4694** ATKINSON, BROOKS & HIRSCHFELD, ALBERT. The lively years: 1920-1973
pp.viii, 312; ill. in text MH
NY: Association P. 1973

Critical appreciation of plays in performance. Reissued NY: Da Capo P., 198?, with a new introduction by Walter Kerr.

**4695** BECKERMAN, BERNARD & SIEGMAN, HOWARD (Eds). On stage: selected theater reviews from the *New York Times*, 1920-1970
pp.xxix, 560; ill. DL★
NY: Quadrangle 1973

**4696** LAHR, JOHN. Astonish me: adventures in contemporary theatre
pp.272; ill. DL★
NY: Viking P. 1973

**4697** CLURMAN, HAROLD. The divine pastime
pp.xiii, 321 M
NY: Macmillan 1974

**4698** SIMON, JOHN. Uneasy stages: a chronicle of the New York theater, 1963-1973
pp.xv, 491 M
NY: Random House 1975

Reviews, revised, from *New York* magazine, *Commonweal* and the *Hudson Review*.

**4699** KAUFFMAN, STANLEY. Persons of the drama: theater criticism and comment
pp.x, 397 M
NY: Harper & Row 1976

**4700** COMTOIS, M. E. & MILLER, LYNN F. (Eds). Contemporary American theater critics. A directory and anthology of their works
pp.xxxviii,979 O
Metuchen NJ: Scarecrow P. 1977

**4701** KERR, WALTER. Journey to the center of the theater
pp.x, 332 M
NY: Alfred A. Knopf 1979

Substantially, reviews of Broadway theatre of the 1970s.

**4702** BRUSTEIN, ROBERT. Critical moments: reflections on theatre and society, 1973-1979
pp.xx, 232 DL★
NY: Random House 1980

**4703** HUNEKER, JAMES G. Americans in the arts 1890-1920. Critiques edited by Arnold T. Schwab
pp.lxix, 673; ill. in text M
NY: AMS P. 1985

Reviews and other criticism reprinted from periodicals. Substantial section on drama (pp.175-314) arranged under playwrights, performers, critics, topics.

**4704** SLIDE, ANTHONY (Ed.). Selected theatre criticism. Volume 1: 1900-1919; [Volume 2: 1920-1930; Volume 3: 1931-1950]
pp.ix, 383; ix, 270; viii, 289 M
Metuchen NJ: Scarecrow P. 1985-86

Productions listed alphabetically by title, with theatre and opening date. Reviews reprinted in their entirety.

**4705** McNAMARA, BROOKS; DOLAN, JILL & BROCKETT, OSCAR G. (Eds). *The Drama Review*. Thirty years of commentary on the avant-garde
pp.xiii, 371 L
Ann Arbor: UMI Research P. 1986

**4706** NIGHTINGALE, BENEDICT. Fifth row center. A critic's year on and off Broadway
v, 346 M
London: Andre Deutsch 1987

First published NY: Times Books, 1986. A diary of UK critic's guest period with the *New York Times*.

**4707** ROGOFF, GORDON. Theatre is not safe: theatre criticism 1962-1986
pp.310 L
Evanston IL: Northwestern U. P. 1987

Essays and reviews, many reprinted from *Village Voice*.

**4708** HILL, ANTHONY D. J. A. Jackson's page in *Billboard*: a voice for black performance during the Harlem Renaissance between 1920-1925
NY: U. (PhD) 1988

**4709** BRUSTEIN, ROBERT. Who needs theatre: dramatic opinions
pp.xv, 234 M
London: Faber 1989

First published NY: Atlantic Monthly P,. 1987. Essays and reviews, 1980-86.

# 10. REVUE, VAUDEVILLE, AND SHOWBOATS

## 10.1 GENERAL

**4710** TRYON, JOHN. The old clown's history in three periods. Introducing graphic sketches of show life in its multifarious phases. On the route, under the canvas, in the hotels, and at the roadside caravansaries, with characteristics of distinguished showmen. Embellished with numerous engravings

pp.242; pl. 5     MH
NY: Torrey Brothers     1872

**4711** JAMES, ED. The amateur negro minstrel's guide, containing full instructions for everything appertaining to the business. With specimen programmes, stump speeches, end men's gags, etc., etc., illustrated with characters, scenes and portraits
pp.[52] inc. wrappers; ill. in text     MH
NY: Ed. James     1873

**4712** DAY, CHARLES H. Fun in black, or sketches of minstrel life with the origin of minstrelsy by Col. T. Allston Brown, giving a history of ethiopian minstrelsy from 1799
pp.70; ill. in text     MH
NY: Robert M. de Witt     1874

**4713** AMERICA. Official libretto Haverly's minstrels [cover title]
pp.32; ill. in text     L
Providence RI: Farmer, Livermore     [1881]
Drop title: *Haverly's American United Mastodon Minstrels*. Prepared as a program for a performance at Her Majesty,s Theatre, London. A synopsis of the bill, with illustrations of John H. Haverly's theatres in New York and Chicago, portraits of Haverly and William Foote, and a brief biographical sketch of Haverly.

**4714** SIMOND, IKE. Old Slack's reminiscences and pocket history of the coloured profession from 1865 to 1891 by Ike Simond, banjo comique
pp.33     MH
Chicago: [For the author?]     [c. 1891]
An edited version was published Bowling Green OH: State U. Popular P., 1974 with substantial commentary by the editors, Robert C. Toll and Francis L. Utley.

**4715** DUMONT, FRANK. The Witmark amateur minstrel guide and burnt cork encyclopedia
pp.vii, 149,19; ill. in text     M
Chicago: M. Witmark & Sons     1899
A final section described as a 'directory' is devoted to the advertisement of minstrel songs and accessories.

**4716** HAVERLY, JACK. Negro minstrels: a complete guide to negro minstrelsy
pp.129     DL★
Chicago: Frederick J. Drake     [1902]

**4717** GOLDEN, GEORGE F. My lady vaudeville and her white rats
pp.199; ill.     DL★
NY: Broadway Publishing     1909
Published under the auspices of the White Rats of America. An account of the attempt to create a Union for vaudeville performers, modelled on the UK 'Water Rats'.

**4718** HARTT, ROLLIN L. The people at play: excursions in the humor and philosophy of popular amusements, with illustrations drawn by the author from prints and photographs
pp.316; ill. in text     DL★
Boston MA: Houghton Mifflin     1909
Includes material on burlesque and melodrama.

**4719** RICE, EDWARD L. 1000 men of minstrelsy and 1 woman...
pp.20     M
NY: [For the author?]     1909
A who's who of minstrelsy, listing given names, nicknames, partnerships, dates.

**4720** [LeFEVRE, JOHN J.]. LeFevre's 'international' railway fare, vaudeville guide & date book
pp.ii, 150     DL★
NY: LeFevre     1910
The fifth edition.

**4721** RICE, EDWARD L. Monarchs of minstrelsy, from 'Daddy' Rice to date
pp.xviii, 366; ill. in text     M
NY: Kenny Publishing     1911

**4722** CLARK, SAMUEL S. Sam S. Clark's burlesque guide and route book, 1913/14
Ill.     DL★
NY: J. A. Cantor     1913
The first edition.

**4723** CAFFIN, CAROLINE & DE ZAYAS, MARIUS. Vaudeville. The book by Caroline Caffin, the pictures by Marius de Zayas
pp.iv, 231; pl. 49     M
NY: Mitchell Kennerley     1914
Includes a chapter on the incursion of legitimate theatre into vaudeville with the introduction of plays and sketches.

**4724** CRESSY, WILL M. Continuous vaudeville
pp.181; ill.     DL★
Boston: Richard H. Badger     1914

**4725** PAGE, BRETT. Writing for vaudeville with nine complete examples of various vaudeville forms by Richard H. Davis, Aaron Hoffman, Allan Woolf, Taylor Granville, Louis Weslyn, Arthur Denvir and James Madison
pp.xvii, 639; diagrams in text     M
Springfield MA: Home Correspondence School     1915

**4726** RENTON, EDWARD. The vaudeville theatre: building, operation. management
pp.308     M
NY: Gotham P.     1918

**4727** LLOYD, HERBERT. Vaudeville trails thru the West, 'by one who knows'
pp.320; ill.     DL★
Chicago: [For the author]     [1919]

**4728** McNALLY, WILLIAM. Mack's vaudeville guide
pp.47; diagrams in text     DL★
NY: W. McNally     1920

**4729** BRANEN, JEFF & JOHNSON, FREDERICK G. How to stage a minstrel show: a manual for the amateur burnt cork director
pp.65; ill.     DL★
Chicago: T. S. Denison     1921

**4730** HARE, WALTER B. The minstrel encyclopedia
pp.222     M
Boston: Walter H. Baker     1926

Revised and enlarged edition. Substantially script and synopsis material, but with section 'how to produce a minstrel show'.

**4731** PAGE, WILL A. Behind the curtains of the Broadway Beauty Trust...including several letters by Bernard Shaw
pp.viii, 227; pl. 34          M
NY: A, & H. Margolin          1926
An account of the Broadway girlie revue as developed by Ziegfeld and others.

**4732** SHAYNE, EDDIE. Down front on the aisle
pp.60; ill.          DL★
Denver CO: Parkway          1929
Quasi-interview, providing an account of vaudeville and its antecedents.

**4733** STEWARD, JULIAN H. The clown in native North America
Los Angeles: U. of California (PhD)          1929

**4734** WITTKE, CARL. Tambo and Bones. A history of the American minstrel show
pp.ix, 269          MH
Durham NC: Duke U. P.          1930

**4735** SOBEL, BERNARD. Burleycue: an underground history of burlesque days.
pp.xiv, 284; ill. in text          M
NY: Farrar & Rinehart          1931

**4736** BRYANT, BILLY. Children of ol' man river: the life and times of a show-boat trouper
pp.xiv, 303; pl. 17, (1 folding)          MH
NY: Lee Furman          1936

**4737** KNOX, ROSE B. Footlights afloat. Illustrated E. P. Couse
pp.xiii, 300; ill. in text          L
Garden City NY: Doubleday, Doran          1937
Novel of showboat life, loosely based on the recollections of Callie French, and her husband who captained the showboat *French's New Sensation*.

**4738** WITMARK, ISIDORE & GOLDBERG, ISAAC. The story of the House of Witmark: from ragtime to swingtime
pp.xvii, 480; ill.          DL★
NY: Lee Furman          1939

**4739** BURMAN, BEN L. Big river to cross: Mississippi life today. Drawings by Alice Caddy
pp.294; ill. in text          O
NY: John Day          1940
Includes an account of showboat entertainment in the 1930s.

**4740** GILBERT, DOUGLAS. American vaudeville: its life and times
pp.x, 427; ill. in text          M
NY: McGraw-Hill          1940
A history, 1880-1930.

**4741** WILSON, EARL. Let 'em eat cheesecake. Introduction by Arthur Godfrey
pp.xviii, 302; ill.          DL★
Garden City NY: Doubleday          1949

**4742** GRAHAM, PHILIP. Showboats: the history of an American institution
pp.x, 224; pl. 12          M
Austin: U. of Texas P.          1951

**4743** GREEN, ABEL & LAURIE, JOSEPH. Show biz: from vaude to video
pp.xxiii, 613          M
NY: Henry Holt          1951

**4744** DAVIDSON, FRANK C. The rise, development, decline and influence of the American minstrel show
NY: U. (PhD)          1952

**4745** GREEN, ABEL (Ed.). The spice of variety
pp.ix, 277          L
NY: Henry Holt          1952
Articles reprinted from *Variety*.

**4746** LAURIE, JOSEPH. Vaudeville: from the honky-tonks to the Palace
xiii, 561          M
NY: Henry Holt          1953
A history, with examples. Foreword by Gene Fowler.

**4747** CROWTHER, BOSLEY. The lion's share: the story of an entertainment empire
pp.320; pl. 8          M
NY: E.P. Dutton          1957
History of M.G.M. studios. Early chapters deal with Marcus Loew and vaudeville theatres, the basis of his film empire.

**4748** ADAMS, JOEY. It takes one to know one: the Joey Adams do-it-yourself laugh kit
pp.219; ill. in text          L
NY: G. P. Putnam's Sons          1959
A light-hearted examination of techniques and exponents of stand-up comedy, with a brief autobiographical sketch.

**4749** BARBER, ROWLAND. The night they raided Minsky's: a fanciful expedition to the Lost Atlantis of show business
pp.vii, 352; ill. in text          M
NY: Simon and Schuster          1960
The burlesque show.

**4750** CALVIN, JUDITH S. A history of the showboat theatre on the Northern rivers
University Park: Pennsylvania State U. (MA)          1960

**4751** PECK, IRA & SPRINGER, JOHN et al (Eds). This was show business
pp.76 inc. wrappers; ill. in text          M
London: Strato Publications          [c. 1960]
'50 glorious years of entertainment history'. Popular photo-essays on US show business, including vaudeville, musical comedy, burlesque, the legitimate stage.

**4752** SOBEL, BERNARD. A pictorial history of vaudeville. Foreword by George Jessel
pp.224; ill. in text          M
NY: Citadel P.          1961
First published NY: Putnam, 1956 without the foreword.

**4753** BARAL, ROBERT. Revue: the great Broadway period...introduction by Robert J. Landry
pp.296; ill. in text          M
NY: Fleet          1962

An appendix provides a chronological listing of casts and other credits. An earlier edition in the same year, *Revue: a reprise of the great Broadway period*, lacked an index and had an introduction by Abel Green.

**4754** ADAMS, JOEY. On the road for Uncle Sam
pp.viii, 311; pl.8 M
NY: Bernard Geis Associates 1963
Touring vaudeville troupe in Asia and India, 1961-2.

**4755** DISTLER, PAUL A. The rise and fall of the racial comics in American vaudeville
New Orleans: Tulane U. (PhD) 1963

**4756** PRICE, WILLARD. The amazing Mississippi
pp.ix, 188; pl. 24 L
NY: John Day 1963
Includes material on showboat entertainment in early 1960s.

**4757** BURTON, JACK. In memoriam...old-time show biz, with headstones for the minstrels, the grand op'ry house, the road show, the one-night stand, the big top, burlesque and vaudeville, and a few tears for the Great White Way that used-to-be
pp.102 DL★
NY: Vantage P. 1965

**4758** McCORMICK, WALTER J. An historical study of showboat theatre on the Missouri river
Warrensburg: Central Missouri State U. (MA) 1965

**4759** McLEAN, ALBERT F. American vaudeville as ritual
pp.xvii, 250; pl. 8 L
[Lexington]: U. of Kentucky P. 1965
Relates vaudeville to social and 'psychic' forces at work in American history.

**4760** PATTERSON, PERRY W. A critical study of jazz-vaudeville drama (1923-1934) in the United States
Denver: U. (PhD) 1965

**4761** HAYWOOD, CHARLES. Negro minstrelsy and Shakespearean burlesque
pp.[16] M
Hatboro PA: Folklore Associates 1966
A reprint from *Folklore & society: essays in honor of B. A. Botkin*. Minstrel parodies and the acting style associated with them.

**4762** ZEIDMAN, IRVING. The American burlesque show
pp.272; ill. in text M
NY: Hawthorn 1967
A history from 1866.

**4763** CORIO, ANNE with DIMONA, JOSEPH. This was burlesque
pp.207; ill. in text L
NY: Madison Square P. 1968

**4764** HARRITY, RICHARD. The world famous Harrity family
pp.160; pl. 6 M
NY: Trident P. 1968
Reminiscence of early days in vaudeville.

**4765** LOCKE, ALAIN. The negro and his music
pp.v, 142 L
Port Washington NY: Kennikat P. 1968

First published by the Association of Negro Folk Education, 1936. Includes chapters on minstrelsy and musical comedy.

**4766** SNYDER, FREDERICK E. American vaudeville theatre in a package: (the origins of mass entertainment)
New Haven: Yale U. (PhD) 1970

**4767** MAIN STREET STUDIO: an exhibition of photographs of famous vaudeville entertainers by Orval Hixon
MH★
Lawrence: U. of Kansas 1971

**4768** MATTFELD, JULIUS. Variety music cavalcade: musical-historical review, 1620-1969
pp.xxii, 766 L
NY: Prentice-Hall 1971
Third edition of chronological checklist of US popular music, with brief historical sketches of each period. First published 1952, revised 1964.

**4769** WILSON, EARL. Show business nobody knows
pp.xviii, 428; pl. 16 MH
Chicago: Cowles 1971
Somewhat ambiguous examination of moral license in popular show business.

**4770** BARRETT, RAINA. First your money, then your clothes: my life and *Oh ! Calcutta !*
pp.166 DL★
NY: Morrow 1973

**4771** DiMEGLIO, JOHN E. Vaudeville U.S.A.
pp.v, 259; pl. 7 M
Bowling Green OH: State U. Popular P. 1973

**4772** ROANE, ANDREA T. The showboat as a theatrical institution in New Orleans, 1831-1940
New Orleans: U. (MA) 1973

**4773** SAMUELS, CHARLES & SAMUELS, LOUISE. Once upon a stage: the merry world of vaudeville
pp.ix, 278; pl. 8 M
NY: Dodd, Mead 1974

**4774** TOLL, ROBERT C. Blacking up: the minstrel show in nineteenth-century America
pp.x, 310; ill. in text M
NY: Oxford U. P. 1974

**4775** WILSON, EARL. Show business laid bare
pp.336; pl. 8 MH
NY: G. P. Putnam's Sons 1974

**4776** GILVARY, PATRICK S. The floating theatre: an analysis of the major factors of showboat theatre in the United States
Columbus: Ohio State U. (PhD) 1975

**4777** KEEGAN, MARCIA. We can still hear them clapping
pp.159; ill. in text MH
NY: Avon Books 1975
'Performers from vaudeville's golden age, still living in Times Square, recall their past glory.' Photographic record with text.

**4778** PASKMAN, DAILEY & [SPAETH, SIGMUND]. 'Gentlemen, be seated!': a parade of the American minstrels
pp.xvi, 253; ill. in text L
NY: Clarkson N. Potter 1976

Revised edition. First published Garden City: Doubleday, Doran, 1928 with subtitle *parade of the old-time minstrels*. Foreword by Daniel Frohman.

**4779** SMITH, BILL. The vaudevillians
pp.ix, 278; ill. in text  MH
NY: Macmillan  1976

A collection of memoirs by former entertainers, derived from interviews.

**4780** FLINT, RICHARD W. Step right up ! Amusement for all: show business at the turn of the century [cover title] [exhibition]
pp.[20] inc. wrappers; ill. in text  M
Rochester: Strong Museum  1977

**4781** CSIDA, JOSEPH & CSIDA, JUNE B. American entertainment: a unique history of popular show business...with a special remembrance of *Billboard*'s founder, W. H. Donaldson, by his grandson, Roger S. Littleford
pp.448; ill. in text  M
NY: Billboard/ Watson-Guptill  1978

In effect a scrapbook of articles, reviews and illustrations from *Billboard*, arranged in five historical sections 1700-1977, with a final section on musical entertainment.

**4782** ENGLE, GARY D. This grotesque essence: plays from the American minstrel stage
pp.xxxi, 200; pl. 6  L
Baton Rouge: Louisiana State U. P.  1978

Introductory essay: *American minstrelsy and democratic art*, followed by a selection of afterpieces, each with a brief commentary.

**4783** INGE, M. THOMAS (Ed.). Handbook of American popular culture
pp.x, 558; x, 423; x,404  L
Westport CT: Greenwood P.  1978-81

Three volumes. Includes Don B. Wilmeth: *Circus and outdoor entertainment* and *Stage entertainment*. The latter offers a survey of vaudeville and other popular theatre forms. Material on stage entertainments and musicals in Vol. 1.

**4784** LEAVITT, PENELOPE M. Spalding and Rogers floating palace, 1852-1860
Pullman: Washington State U. (PhD)  1978

**4785** REED, DUANE E. A history of showboats on the western rivers
East Lansing: Michigan State U. (PhD)  1978

**4786** SWORTZELL, LOWELL. Here come the clowns: a cavalcade of comedy from antiquity to the present
pp.viii, 245; ill. in text  L
NY: Viking P.  1978

Illustrated by C. Walter Hodges. Includes a chapter, *Clowns in the living theatre*.

**4787** FRANKLIN, JOE. Joe Franklin's encyclopedia of comedians
pp.349; ill. in text  M
Secaucus NJ: Citadel P.  1979

**4788** MATLAW, MYRON (Ed.). American popular entertainment: papers and proceedings of the conference on the history of American popular entertainment
pp.xiv, 338; ill. in text  M
Westport CT: Greenwood P.  1979

Conference held at Lincoln Center, NY, November, 1977.

**4789** SAMPSON, HENRY T. Blacks in blackface: a source book on early black minstrel shows
pp.x, 552; ill. in text  L
Metuchen NJ: Scarecrow P.  1980

Historical survey, with listing of producers, theatres, show synopses, biographies.

**4790** CAMPBELL, PATRICIA J. Passing the hat: street performers in America
pp.vi, 260; ill.  DL★
NY: Delacorte P.  1981

**4791** CONNORS, TIMOTHY D. American vaudeville managers: their organization and influence
Lawrence: U. of Kansas (PhD)  1981

**4792** LAFORSE, MARTIN W. & DRAKE, JAMES A. Popular culture and American life; selected topics in the study of American popular culture
pp.xiii, 257  L
Chicago: Nelson-Hall  1981

Part four on American vaudeville.

**4793** SLIDE, ANTHONY. The vaudevillians: a dictionary of vaudeville performers
pp.xv, 173; ill. in text  MH
Westport CT: Arlington House  1981

**4794** PLOTKINS, MARILYN J. Irving Berlin, George Gershwin, Cole Porter and the spectacular revue: the theatrical context of revue songs from 1910 to 1937
Medford: Tufts U. (PhD)  1982

**4795** STAPLES, SHIRLEY. Male-female comedy teams in American vaudeville, 1865-1932
pp.vii, 328  L
Ann Arbor: UMI Research P.  1984

**4796** BERGER, PHIL. The last laugh; the world of stand-up comics
  DL★
NY: Limelight Editions  1985

**4797** BORDMAN, GERALD. American musical revue: from *The Passing Show* to *Sugar Babies*
pp.vii, 184; pl. 8  M
NY: Oxford U. P.  1985

**4798** FELLOM, MARTIE. The skirt dance: a dance fad of the 1890s
NY: U. (PhD)  1985

Includes material on variety halls.

**4799** GOTTFRIED, MARTIN. In person: the great entertainers
pp.264; ill. in text, some col.  M
NY: Harry N. Abrams  1985

Profusely illustrated account of a wide range of paopular stage entertainers from early vaudeville and burlesque to the present.

**4800** STEIN, CHARLES W. (Ed.). American vaudeville as seen by its contemporaries
pp.xviii, 395; ill. in text  M
NY: Da Capo P.  1985

## 10. REVUE, VAUDEVILLE, AND SHOWBOATS

First published NY: Alfred A. Knopf, 1984, here with the author's corrections. A collection of reminiscences, appreciations and commentaries.

**4801** LEONARD, WILLIAM T. Masquerade in black
pp.xii, 431; ill. in text      L
Metuchen NJ: Scarecrow P.      1986
A history of white entertainers in blackface.

**4802** LESLIE, PETER. A hard act to follow: a music hall review. Introduction by Pearl Bailey
pp.256; ill. in text      M
NY: Paddington P.      1987
International.

**4803** SINGER, STANFORD P. Vaudeville west: to Los Angeles and the final stages of vaudeville
Los Angeles: U. of California (PhD)      1987

**4804** HIRSCH, JOHN. Glorifying the American showgirl: a history of revue costume in the United States from 1866 to the present
NY: U. (PhD)      1988

**4805** SLIDE, ANTHONY (Ed.). Selected vaudeville criticism
pp.x, 308      L
Metuchen NJ: Scarecrow P.      1988
Critical reviews of entertainers and some general critical articles, together with a reprinting of Grace La Rue: *My vaudeville years (1937)*.

**4806** HEBERT, CHAUTEL. Le burlesque Québecois et Américain. Textes inédits
pp.xvi, 335      M
Quebec: P. de l'Université Laval      1989
An examination of the *genre*, comparing the Quebecois with the American repertoire, and the influence of the latter on the former.

**4807** SNYDER, ROBERT W. The voice of the city: vaudeville and popular culture in New York
pp.220; ill.      DL★
NY: Oxford U. P.      1990

## 10.2 INDIVIDUAL PERFORMANCES

### Allen, Steve
### (1921-)
### Comedian

**4808** ALLEN, STEVE. Mark it and strike it: an autobiography
pp.xi, 432; pl.4      L
NY: Holt, Rinehart and Winston      1960
Includes memories of early vaudeville experience.

### Anderson, John Murray
### (1886-1954)
### Director

**4809** GRESSLER, THOMAS H. John Murray Anderson: director of revues
Kent OH: State U. (PhD)      1973

### Baker, Josephine
### (1906-1975)
### Dancer, singer

**4810** SAUVAGE, MARCEL (Ed.). Les mémoires de Josephine Baker recueillis et adaptés...avec 30 dessins inédit de Paul Colin
pp.187; ill. in text      M
Paris: Kra      1927

**4811** BAKER, JOSEPHINE & BOUILLON, JO. Josephine
pp.xiii, 302; front., pl. 8      M
London: W. H. Allen      1978
Translated from the French by Mariana Fitzpatrick.

**4812** HANEY, LYNN. Naked at the feast; a biography of Josephine Baker
pp.xiii, 338; ill. in text      M
London: Robson      1981

**4813** HAMMOND, BRYAN (Ed.). Josephine Baker
pp.xvi, 304; ill. in text, some col.      P
London: Cape      1988
Theatrical biography by Patrick O'Connor. Foreword by Elizabeth Welch.

**4814** ROSE, PHYLLIS. Josephine Baker in her time
pp.352; ill.      ★
NY: Doubleday      1989
Also NY: Random, 1990 as *Jazz Cleopatra*.

### Benny, Jack
### (1894-1974)
### Comedian

**4815** BENNY, JACK & BENNY, JOAN. Sunday nights at seven: the Jack Benny story
pp.302; ill.      DL★
NY: Warner      1990

### Bruce, Lenny
### (1926-1966)
### Comedian

**4816** BRUCE, LENNY. How to talk dirty and influence people. An autobiography
pp.206; pl 4      O
London: Peter Owen      1966

**4817** COHEN, JOHN (Ed.). The essential Lenny Bruce
pp.263      O
NY: Open Gate      1967
Bruce's stage material transcribed and arranged loosely under topic. Includes *Performing and the art of comedy*.

**4818** BRUCE, KITTY. The almost unpublished Lenny Bruce
     DL★
Philadelphia: Running P.      1984

### Burns, George
### (1896-)
### Comedian, actor

**4819** BURNS, GEORGE & with LINDSAY, CYNTHIA H. I love her, that's why ! Prologue by Jack Benny
pp.213; pl. 4      M
London: W. H. Allen      1956

Autobiography of George Burns and Gracie Allen

**4820** BURNS, GEORGE. Living it up, or they still love me in Altoona ! [autobiography]
pp.251; ill. in text, pl. 8     M
London: W. H. Allen     1977

**4821** BURNS, GEORGE. The third time around [autobiography]
pp.219; pl. 16     L
NY: G. P. Putnam's Sons     1980

**4822** BURNS, GEORGE. Gracie: a love story
pp.319; pl. 24     M
London: Hodder & Stoughton     1989

### Cantor, Eddie
### [Itzkowitz, Isidore]
### (1892-1964)
### Comedian

**4823** CANTOR, EDDIE. My life is in your hands...as told to David Freeman
pp.xiv, 300; pl. 16     O
NY: Harper & Brothers     1928
Foreword by Will Rogers. Includes memories of the Ziegfeld Follies.

**4824** CANTOR, EDDIE & OSTROFF, MANNING. *The life and times of Eddie Cantor*: a dramatic composition
pp.[26]     L
NY: For the authors     1947
Autobiographical fragment in comic-sketch form.

**4825** CANTOR, EDDIE & with ARDMORE, JANE K. Take my life [autobiography]
pp.288; ill.     DL★
Garden City NY: Doubleday     1957
With wide reference to fellow artistes.

**4826** CANTOR, EDDIE. The way I see it [autobiography]
pp.ix, 204     M
Englewood Cliffs: Prentice-Hall     1959
Edited by Phyllis Rosenteur.

**4827** CANTOR, EDDIE. As I remember them
pp.v, 144; ill. in text     MH
NY: Duell, Sloan and Pearce     1963

### Carroll, Earl
### (1893?-1948)
### Producer

**4828** MURRAY, KEN. The body merchant: the story of Earl Carroll
pp.xiii, 243; ill.     DL★
Pasadena CA: W. Ritchie P.     1976

### Davis, Sammy
### (1925-1992)
### Actor, singer

**4829** DAVIS, SAMMY; BOYAR, JANE & BOYAR, BURT. Yes I can: the story of Sammy Davis Jr.
pp.viii, 612; pl.8     O
London: Cassell     1965

Published NY: Farrar, Straus & Giroux.

### Dillon, William A.
### (1877-1966)
### Variety entertainer

**4830** DILLON, WILLIAM A. Life doubles in brass [autobiography]
pp. 239 inc. music; pl. 17     M
Ithaca NY: House of Nollid     1944

### Durante, Jimmy
### [Durante, James Francis]
### 1893-1980
### Comedian

**4831** FOWLER, GENE. Schnozzola: the story of Jimmy Durante
pp.vii, 261; pl. 8     M
NY: Viking P.     1951

**4832** CAHN, WILLIAM. Good night, Mrs Calabash: the secret of Jimmy Durante
pp.191; ill.     DL★
NY: Duell, Sloan & Pearce     1963

**4833** ADLER, IRENE. I remember Jimmy: the life and times of Jimmy Durante
pp.189; ill.     DL★
Westport CT: Arlington House     1980

### Emmett, Dan
### [Emmett, Daniel Decatur]
### (1815-1904)
### Minstrel, composer

**4834** NATHAN, HANS. Dan Emmett and the rise of early negro minstrelsy
pp.xiv, 496; ill. in text     L
Norman: U. of Oklahoma P.     1962
A second, revised printing was issued in 1977 (not seen).

### Faye, Joey
### [Palladino, Joseph Antony]
### (1910-)
### Comedian

**4835** LESSER, JOSEPH L. Top banana Joey Faye: the evolution of a burlesque comedian
NY: U. (PhD)     1987

### Fox, George Washington Lafayette
### (1825-1877)
### Pantomimist, actor

**4836** DRAPER, WALTER H. George L. Fox, comedian, in pantomime and travesty
Urbana: U. of Illinois (PhD)     1958

**4837** SENELICK, LAURENCE. The age and stage of George L. Fox
pp.xvii, 286; ill. in text     M
Hanover MA: U. P. of New England     1988

### Hart, Bob
### [Sutherland, James M.]
### (1832-1888)
### Minstrel, actor

**4838** SUTHERLAND, J. M. From stage to pulpit: life of 'Senator' Bob Hart, 28 years an actor and minstrel
pp.48; portrait on wrapper     MH
NY: C. S. Hamilton     [1883]

### Horne, Lena
### 1917-
### Singer

**4839** HASKINS, JAMES & BENSON, KATHLEEN. Lena: a personal and professional biography of Lena Horne
pp.226; pl. 8 M
NY: Stein & Day 1984

### Janis, Elsie
### [Bierbower, Elsie]
### (1889-1956)
### Vaudeville entertainer

**4840** JANIS, ELSIE. The big show: my six months with the American Expeditionary Force
pp.xii, 227; pl. 8 M
NY: Cosmopolitan Book 1919

**4841** JANIS, ELSIE. So far, so good ! An autobiography
pp.287; pl. 15 M
London: John Long 1933
First published NY: E. P. Dutton, 1932.

**4842** MORROW, LEE A. Elsie Janis: a compensatory biography
Evanston: Northwestern U. (PhD) 1988

### Keaton, Buster
### (1896-1966)
### Actor

**4843** BLESH, RUDI. Keaton
pp.xii, 395; ill. in text M
London: Secker & Warburg 1967
First published NY: Macmillan, 1966. Biography, with substantial reference to early vaudeville experience.

**4844** KEATON, BUSTER & with SAMUELS, CHARLES. My wonderful world of slapstick [autobiography]
pp.282; pl. 8 L
London: Allen & Unwin 1967
First published NY, Doubleday, 1960. Includes his early experience in vaudeville.

**4845** ROBINSON, DAVID. Buster Keaton
pp.199; ill. in text L
Bloomington: Indiana U. P. 1969
Biography. Includes his early vaudeville experience.

### Keith, Benjamin Franklin
### (1846-1914)
### Manager

**4846** A TRIBUTE to Benjamin Franklin Keith 'father of modern vaudeville'. Ceremonies attending the laying of the cornerstone, Keith Memorial Theatre, Boston, Massachusetts, August 25th, 1927
pp.[39]; ill. in text MH
Boston: [For the theatre?] 1927

### Kelly, Walter C.
### (1873-1939)
### Vaudeville entertainer

**4847** KELLY, WALTER C. Of me I sing...an informal autobiography
pp.x, 246; pl. 4 MH
NY: Dial P. 1953
Creator of the celebrated comic character 'the Virginia Judge'. Foreword by George Ade.

### Langdon, Harry
### (1884-1944)
### Comedian

**4848** RHEUBAN, JOYCE. Harry Langdon: the comedian as metteur-en-scène
pp.244; ill. in text M
Rutherford: Fairleigh Dickinson U. P. 1983
Includes his early vaudeville experience.

### Lee, Gypsy Rose
### [Hovick, Rose Louise]
### (1913-1970)
### Striptease artist, actress, writer

**4849** LEE, GYPSY R. Gypsy: a memoir [autobiography]
pp.iv, 337; front., pl. 20 MH
NY: Harper & Brothers 1957

### Leonard, Eddie
### [Tooney, Lemuel Gordon]
### (1875-1941)
### Minstrel, actor

**4850** LEONARD, EDDIE. What a life I'm telling you
pp.xv (17), 240: ill. DL★
NY: For the author 1934
Perhaps the last of the old-time minstrels. Composed *Ida, sweet as apple cider*.

### Lewis, Joe E.
### (1902-1971)
### singer, entertainer

**4851** COHN, ART. Joker is wild; the story of Joe E. Lewis
pp.ix, 368; front., pl. 6 L
London: Bernard Harrison 1958
First published NY: Random House, 1955.

### Madison, Kitty

**4852** HARVEY, JOEL. American burlesque as reflected through the career of Kitty Madison
Tallahassee: Florida State U. (PhD) 1980

### Marx Brothers
### Chico [Leonard]
### (1887?-1961)
### Harpo [Adolph]
### (1888?-1964)
### Groucho [Julius]
### (1890?-1977)
### Gummo [Milton]
### (1895?-1977)
### Zeppo [Herbert]
### (1901?-1979)
### Comedians

**4853** CRICHTON, KYRLE. The Marx brothers
pp.vi, 326; pl. 8 M
London: Heinemann 1951

## 10.2. INDIVIDUAL PERFORMANCES

Published in US, Garden City: Doubleday, 1950.

**4854** MARX, ARTHUR. Groucho
pp.254; pl. 11     L
London: Victor Gollancz     1954
Published NY: Simon and Schuster, 1954. Also NY: Popular Books, 1960, as *Life with Groucho* (unillustrated).

**4855** MARX, GROUCHO. Groucho and me [autobiography]
pp.256; pl. 8     L
London: Victor Gollancz     1959
Published NY: Bernard Geiss Associates, 1959.

**4856** MARX, HARPO & with BARBER, ROWLAND. Harpo speaks !
pp.475; ill. in text, pl. 8     M
London: Victor Gollancz     1961
Illustrated by Susan Marx. With substantial account of early stage work.

**4857** MARX, GROUCHO. The Groucho letters: letters from and to Groucho Marx
pp.319     L
London: Michael Joseph     1967
Includes section *Broadway and Hollywood*.

**4858** GARDNER, MARTIN A. The Marx Brothers
NY: U. (PhD)     1969

**4859** ADAMSON, JOE. Groucho, Harpo, Chico – and sometimes Zeppo. A history of the Marx brothers and a satire on the rest of the world
pp.464; ill. in text     L
NY: Simon & Schuster     1973

**4860** MARX, ARTHUR. Son of Groucho
pp.xiii, 357; pl. 4     L
London: Peter Owen     1973

**4861** MARX, GROUCHO & ANOBILE, RICHARD J. The Marx Brothers scrapbook
pp.256; ill. in text     L
NY: Dorion House     1974
Interviews with Groucho Marx and some fellow comedians. Substantial reference to live performance.

**4862** MARX, GROUCHO & with ARCE, HECTOR. The secret word is Groucho
pp.217; pl. p     L
NY: G. P. Putnam's Sons     1976
Mostly concerned with TV, but some reference to early theatre experience.

**4863** MARX, GROUCHO. The Grouchophile: an illustrated life
pp.xvi, 384; ill.     ★
Indianapolis: Bobbs-Merrill     1976
Introduction by Hector Arce.

**4864** GEHRING, WES D. The Marx brothers: a bio-bibliography
pp.277; ill.     DL★
NY: Greenwood P.     1987

### McKinley, Myrtle
### (1885-?)
### Entertainer

**4865** YOUNG, MIRIAM. Mother wore tights
pp.255; ill.     DL★
NY: Whittesley House     1944

Author's mother, Myrtle McKinley, was the youngest of the Floradora girls.

### Mills, Steve
### (1895-1988)
### Entertainer

**4866** CONNER, PATRICIA S. Steve Mills and the twentieth century American burlesque show. A backstage history and a perspective
Urbana-Champaign: U. of Illinois (PhD)     1979

### Minsky, Morton
### (1902-1987)
### Burlesque owner

**4867** MINSKY, MORTON & MACHLIN, MILT. Minsky's burlesque
pp.v, 312; pl. 9     M
NY: Arbor House     1986
Morton Minsky was the last survivor of the four brothers who founded the celebrated chain of burlesque houses.

### Pantages, Alexander
### (186?-1936)
### Vaudeville impresario

**4868** TARRACH, DEAN A. Alexander Pantages: the Seattle Pantages and his vaudeville circuit
Seattle: U. of Washington (MA)     1973
Period 1897-1940.

### Pastor, Tony
### (1837-1908)
### Vaudeville entertainer, actor

**4869** ZELLERS, PARKER. Tony Pastor, dean of the vaudeville stage
pp.xix, 155; ill. in text,, pl. 4     M
Ypsilanti: E. Michigan U. P.     1971

### Proctor, Frederick Francis
### (1851-1929)
### Vaudeville and theatre manager

**4870** MARSTON, WILLIAM M. & FELLER, JOHN H. F. F. Proctor, vaudeville pioneer
pp.191; pl. 32     M
NY: Richard R. Smith     1943

### Rice, Dan
### (1823-1900)
### Clown

**4871** SKETCHES from the life of Dan Rice, the Shakspearian jester & original clown. With illustrations by Darley and others
pp.93,14; ill. in text     MB
Albany NY: Edward James     1849
An appendix advertises Rice's 'odd equestrian establishment'.

**4872** BROWN, MARIA W. The life of Dan Rice
pp.ix, 501; pl. 22     MH
Long Branch NJ: For the author     1901
Drop title: *Reminiscences of Dan Rice*.

**4873** KUNZOG, JOHN C. The one-horse show: the life and times of Dan Rice, circus jester and philanthropist. A chronicle of early circus days
pp.xiv, 434; ill. in text     MH
Jamestown NY: For the author     1962

Includes account of his early theatre experience.

**4874** GILLETTE, DON C. He made Lincoln laugh. The story of Dan Rice
pp.170; ill. in text  MB
NY: Exposition P.  1967

**4875** BISHOP, GEORGE V. The world of clowns
pp.xii, 184; ill.  DL★
Los Angeles: Brooke House  1976
Includes material on Dan Rice.

**4876** TOWSON, JOHN H. Clowns
pp.xiii, 400; ill. in text, col. pl. 8  M
NY: Hawthorn Books  1976
Includes material on Dan Rice.

**4877** ENGDAHL, ERIC L. A biographic and critical study of the life and works of Dan Rice: American circus clown
Los Angeles: U. of California (PhD)  1990

### Richman, Harry
### [Reichman, Harry]
### (1895-1972)
### Singer

**4878** RICHMAN, HARRY & with GEHMAN, RICHARD. A hell of a life
pp.pp. xiii, 242; pl. 4  MH
NY: Duell, Sloan & Pearce  1966
Anecdotal autobiography of a Broadway revue singer and entertainer.

### Rodgers, Jimmy
### Singing entertainer

**4879** RODGERS, MRS J. My husband, Jimmy Rodgers
pp.(ii), 264; pl. 4  MH
Nashville TE: Tubb  1935
Biography of the vaudeville performer popularly known as 'the singing brakeman'.

### Rubin, Benny

**4880** RUBIN, BENNY. Come backstage with me [memoirs]
pp.218; pl. 16  M
Bowling Green OH: U. Popular P.  [1972]

### Sanford, Samuel S.
### (1821-1905)
### Minstrel

**4881** BAINES, JIMMY D. Samuel S. Sanford and negro minstrelsy
Tulane: U. (PhD)  1967

Founder of the Sanford Minstrels, 1853.

### Sherwood, Robert Edmund
### (1856-1946)
### Clown

**4882** SHERWOOD, ROBERT E. Here we are again: recollections of an old circus clown
pp.293; pl. 11  M
Indianapolis: Bobbs Merrill  1926
Chapter eleven is concerned with the legitimate theatre.

### Sothern, Georgia
### (1920-1981)
### Dancer

**4883** SOTHERN, GEORGIA. My life in burlesque
pp.351; ill.  DL★
NY: New American Library  1972

### Thompson, Lydia
### (1836-1908)
### Burlesque entertainer

**4884** MOSES, MARILYN. Lydia Thompson and the 'British Blondes' in the United States
Eugene: U. of Oregon (PhD)  1978

### Webb, Margot
### Dancer

**4885** DIXON-STOWELL, BRENDA M. Dancing in the dark: the life and times of Margot Webb in Aframerican vaudeville of the swing era
NY: U. (PhD)  1981

### Williams, Bert
### [Williams, Egbert Austin]
### (1876?-1922)
### Comedian

**4886** ROWLAND, MABEL (Ed.). Bert Williams, son of laughter: a symposium of tribute to the man and to his work, by his friends and associates with a preface by David Belasco
pp.xix, 218; pl. 12  MH
NY: The English Crafters  1923
Contributors include W. C. Fields, Heywood Broun, Rennold Wolf, E. F. Albee, George M. Cohan.

**4887** CHARTERS, ANN. Nobody: the story of Bert Williams
pp.157; ill. in text  M
London: Macmillan  1970

# 11. COMMUNITY THEATRE AND UNIVERSITY THEATRE

## 11.1 COMMUNITY THEATRE

**4888** DE WITTS'S HOW TO MANAGE amateur theatricals, showing the easiest way for arranging drawing room performances; and giving plain directions for making scenery, getting up dresses, giving out parts, making up the face, and properly adopting wigs, mustaches and beards
pp.64; pl. 6  MB
NY: De Witt  1880

**4889** BATES, ESTHER W. Pageants and pageantry
pp.vii, 294; ill.  DL★
Boston: Ginn  1912
With a substantial introduction by William Orr.

**4890** MACKAYE, PERCY. The civic theatre in relation to the redemption of leisure: a book of suggestions
pp.308  MH
NY: Mitchell Kennerley  1912

## 11.1. COMMUNITY THEATRE

Seeks to define, prescribe for, describe amd illustrate by example the civic theatre, with chapters on children's theatre, pageants and university theatre.

**4891** MACKAY, CONSTANCE D. Plays of the pioneers: a book of historical pageant plays...illustrated from photographs of historical pageants
pp.175; front., pl. 7   L
NY: Harper & Brothers   1915

Includes chapters on costuming the plays and outdoor pageant and play production, with suggestions for music.

**4892** BEEGLE, MARY P. & CRAWFORD, JACK R. Community drama and pageantry
pp.ix, 370; pl. 12   L
New Haven: Yale U. P.   1916

A survey of the techniques of writing and staging, based on courses taught at Dartmouth College summer school.

**4893** KOCH, FREDERICK H. Toward the municipal theater
pp.121   DL★
[Grand Forks ND]: [U. of N. Dakota P.]   [1916]

Reprinted from the *Quarterly Journal* of the U. of N. Dakota, Vol. VI, No. 2, January 1916.

**4894** MACKAYE, PERCY. Caliban by the yellow sands
pp.xxxii, 223; pl. 8   M
Garden City NY: Doubleday, Page   1916

A community masque of the art of the theatre devised and written to commemorate the tercentenary of the death of Shakespeare. Illustrations by Joseph Urban and Robert Edmond Jones, together with ground plans and other guides to staging. Introduction by the author.

**4895** ROCKWELL, ETHEL T. (Ed.). Historical pageantry: a treatise and a bibliography
pp.19   DL★
[Madison]: State Historical Society   1916

**4896** BURLEIGH, LOUISE. The community theatre in theory and practice...
pp.xxxvii. 188; pl. 8   MB
Boston: Little, Brown   1917

Prefatory letter from Percy Mackaye. An account of the developing little theatre movement, with a directory.

**4897** DICKINSON, THOMAS H. The insurgent theatre
pp.251   M
NY: B. W. Huebsch   1917

The development of the little theatre movement in the early years of this century.

**4898** MACKAY, CONSTANCE D. The little theatre in the United States
pp.viii, 277; pl. 17   M
NY: Henry Holt   1917

**4899** MACKAYE, PERCY. Community drama, its motive and method of neighborliness. An interpretation...
pp.xiv, 65   MH
Boston: Houghton Mifflin   1917

Substantially, the text of an address given before the American Civic Association in Washington DC in 1916. An appendix reprints reviews of the 1916 New York pageant, *Caliban...* to which the author refers in his address.

**4900** MACKAY, CONSTANCE D. Patriotic drama in your town: a manual of suggestions
pp.ix, 135   MH
NY: Henry Holt   1919

On the importance of community drama 'especially as an aid to Americanization'.

**4901** RAINWATER, CLARENCE E. The play movement in the United States. A study of community recreation
Chicago: U. (PhD)   1921

**4902** DAYTON, HELENA S. & BARRATT, LOUISE B. The book of entertainments and theatricals
pp.xv, 298; ill.   DL★
NY: Robert M. McBride   1923

A handbook of organization and techniques for the amateur theatre.

**4903** DE GOVEIA, CLARENCE J. Community playhouse: a manual on its organization and maintenance
pp.165; ill. in text   DL★
NY: Huebsch   1923

**4904** BATES, ESTHER W. The art of producing pageants
pp.268; ill.   DL★
Boston: Walter H. Baker   1925

**4905** DEAN, ALEXANDER. Little theatre organization and mamagement for community, university and school including a history of the amateur in drama...preface by Walter P. Eaton
pp.xiii, 333; chart   M
NY: D. Appleton   1926

**4906** SHAY, FRANK. The practical theatre: a manual for little theatres, community players, amateur dramatic clubs and other independent producing groups
pp.xii, 144; ill. in text, pl. 2   M
NY: D. Appleton   1926

**4907** STRATTON, CLARENCE. Theatron: an illustrated record...
pp.xvi, 303; ill. in text   M
NY: Henry Holt   1928

Regional, repertory, little, community and college theatres, alleging their superiority to the debased commercial theatre.

**4908** MacGOWAN, KENNETH. Footlights across America: towards a national theater
pp.xviii, 398; ill. in text, pl. 16   L
NY: Harcourt, Brace   1929

A survey and history of the little theatre movement, university theatre, and such Broadway theatre as is relevant to the sub-title, estimating the extent, nature and significance of the American non-commercial theatre.

**4909** ROCKWELL, ETHEL T. A study course in American one-act plays...a program for women's clubs
pp.48   DL★
Chapel Hill: North Carolina U. P.   1929

Revised edition of an outline for individual and group study first published in 1924.

**4910** KOCH, FREDERICK H. Making a regional drama
pp.8   L
[NY]: [National Theatre Conference]   1932

## 11. COMMUNITY THEATRE AND UNIVERSITY THEATRE

Text of an address delivered before the American Library Association, New Orleans, LA, April 26, 1932. Reprinted from the ALA *Bulletin*.

**4911** ASHTON, DE WITT C. (Ed.). Ashton's list of little theatres and little theatre groups; revised by Phil. York
ll.60 ★
NY: Lindner 1933

**4912** PERRY, CLARENCE A. The work of the little theatres: the groups they include, the plays they produce, their tournaments, and the handbooks they use
pp.228 M
NY: Russell Sage Foundation 1933

**4913** ISAACS, EDITH J. R. The American theatre in social and educational life: a survey of its needs and opportunities
pp. 55; map. DL★
NY: National Theatre Conference [1934?]

**4914** SIMON, S. SYLVAN. Camp theatricals: making your camp entertainments more effective
pp.vii, 146; ill. in text M
NY: Samuel French 1934

**4915** KOCH, FREDERICK H. et al. Play producing for school and little theatre stages
pp.90; ill. in text, pl. 4 M
Chapel Hill: U. of N. Carolina P. 1935

**4916** CARTER, JEAN & OGDEN, JESS. Everyman's drama: a study of the non-commercial theatre in the United States
pp.xiii, 136 L
NY: American Association for Adult Education 1938
Based on observations in 27 states.

**4917** COMMUNITY THEATERS: a reference study...
pp.30; ill. in text M
NY: F. W. Dodge 1939
Reprinted from the 'building types' section of *Architectural Record*. Organized under sections: 'bases for design', 'time-saver standards data' and 'case studies'.

**4918** McCLEERY, ALBERT & GLICK, CARL. Curtains going up
pp.xi, 407; pl. 30 M
NY: Pitman 1939
Community theatre, nationwide.

**4919** SELDEN, SAMUEL (Ed.). Organizing a community theatre
pp.128 MH
NY: Theatre Arts Books 1945
Papers from the National Theatre Conference, 1945.

**4920** PEARSON, TALBOT. Encores on Main Street: successful community theatre leadership
pp.xii, 175; ill. in text M
Pittsburgh PA: Carnegie Institute P. 1948
Includes a list of plays produced by Dallas Little Theatre, 1920-1943.

**4921** SPER, FELIX. From native roots: a panorama of our regional drama
pp.341; pl. 11 M
Caldwell ID: Caxton 1948

A study of 14 regions, surveying growth of local drama from early pageants and similar productions to later plays identifying themselves with their locality.

**4922** RAMEY, HOWARD L. The community theatre: equipping the stage
New Haven: Yale U. (MFA) 1950

**4923** THE EDUCATIONAL THEATRE in adult education
pp. 44 DL★
Washington DC: National Education Association 1951
Robert E. Gard: *The university and adult education in theatre*; K. Jurgen: *Extending a university theatre*; L. E. Brown: *The theatre in an urban community*; Junius Eddy: *Creativity in a small community*; M. Rife: *Drama for community recreation*; T. E. Poag: *The negro theatre and adult education*.

**4924** MANNING, FERDINAND L. The community theatres of the South-west
New Haven: Yale U. (MFA) 1951

**4925** SCHOELL. EDWIN R. A quantitative analysis of the contributions of the community theatre to the development of the drama
Denver: U. (PhD) 1951

**4926** MARSH, DOROTHY D. A descriptive study of the social psychological function of a community theatre as exemplified by the Downers Grove Civic Theatre [CA]
Los Angeles: U. of Southern California (MA) 1953

**4927** SELDEN, SAMUEL. Producing America's outdoor dramas
pp.44; ill. in text MH
Chapel Hill: U. of North Carolina P. 1954

**4928** GARD, ROBERT E. Grassroots theatre. A search for regional arts in America
pp.xiii, 263 M
Madison: U. of Wisconsin P. 1955

**4929** YOUNG, JOHN W. The community theatre and how it works
pp.xi, 166 L
NY: Harper & Brothers 1957

**4930** GARD, ROBERT E. & BURLEY, GERTRUDE S. Community theatre: idea and achievement
pp.x, 182 L
NY: Duell, Sloan & Pearce 1959
Transcribed conversations with leaders in the Little Theatre movement, with directory of theatres.

**4931** RAPPEL, WILLIAM J. & WINNIE, JOHN R. Community theatre handbook
pp.77 DL★
Iowa City: Institute of Public Affairs, State U. 1961

**4932** FREE, WILLIAM & LOWER, CHARLES B. History into drama: a source book on symphonic drama, including the complete text of Paul Green's *The Lost Colony*
pp.xii, 243; ill. DL★
NY: Odyssey P. 1963

**4933** CONFERENCE NOTES from the first playwrights conference May 8, 9, 1964
pp. 97; front.　　　　　　　　　　　　　　MH
Chapel Hill: U. of North Carolina　　　　1964
Arranged by the Institute of Outdoor Drama, director Mark R. Summer, moderator John Gassner. The theme was *a challenge to the American playwright* and the subject, outdoor drama planning and presentation.

**4934** McCALMON, GEORGE & MOE, CHRISTIAN. Creating historical drama: a guide for the community and the interested individual
pp.xvi, 393; ill.　　　　　　　　　　　　　DL★
Carbondale: Southern Illinois U. P.　　　1965

**4935** SUMNER, MARK R. Planning for an outdoor historical drama
pp.26　　　　　　　　　　　　　　　　　　DL★
Chapel Hill: U. of N. Carolina　　　　　1965

**4936** BIDDULPH, HELEN R. & MAILER, JULIA H. Bibliography of books, pamphlets and magazines relating to community theatre
pp.21　　　　　　　　　　　　　　　　　　DL★
Washington DC: AETA　　　　　　　　1966

**4937** WARYE, RICHARD J. A descriptive study of community theatres in the metropolitan areas of the United States
Columbus: Ohio State U. (PhD)　　　　1966

**4938** SUMNER, MARK R. An investigation of existing outdoor drama techniques and a determination of methods to improve training
ll. 126; ill　　　　　　　　　　　　　　　　DL★
Chapel Hill: U. of N. Carolina　　　　　1967

**4939** HAVENS, JOHN F. Description of community theatres in the United States
pp.v, 164　　　　　　　　　　　　　　　　DL★
Washington DC: Department of Health　1968

**4940** SUMNER, MARK R. A survey of outdoor drama techniques
pp.vii, 64; ill.　　　　　　　　　　　　　　DL★
NY: ANTA　　　　　　　　　　　　　1968

**4941** SUMNER, MARK R. A selected bibliography on outdoor drama
ll. 11　　　　　　　　　　　　　　　　　　DL★
Chapel Hill: U. of N. Carolina　　　　　1968
Revised issue. First published 1965.

**4942** YOUNG, JOHN W. Community theatre: a manual for success
pp.155　　　　　　　　　　　　　　　　　MH
NY: Samuel French　　　　　　　　　1971

**4943** ROBERTSON, COSBY W. The theatre as a vehicle for community action
Tallahassee: Florida State U. (PhD)　　1972

**4944** FRÖHLICH, P. Das nicht-kommerzielle amerikanische Theater
pp.vii, 236　　　　　　　　　　　　　　　M
Rheinfelden: Schäuble　　　　　　　　1974
Material on the little theatre movement, left-wing theatre, off- and off-off Broadway.

**4945** WALLER, ADRIAN. Theatre on a shoestring
pp.158; ill.　　　　　　　　　　　　　　　DL★
Totowa NJ: Littlefield, Adams　　　　　1975
Amateur theatre organization.

**4946** KAMINSKY, LAURA J. (Ed.). Nonprofit repertory theatre in North America, 1958-1975: a bibliography and indexes to the playbill collection of the Theatre Communication Group
pp.ix, 268　　　　　　　　　　　　　　　L
Westport CT: Greenwood P.　　　　　1977
Listed by city. Playbills indexed under title, author, director, translator, adapter, composer/lyricist/musical-director, theatre.

**4947** BRADBY, DAVID & McCORMICK, JOHN. People's theatre
pp.179; pl. 8　　　　　　　　　　　　　　M
Totowa NJ: Rowman & Littlefield　　1978
Survey of European and US radical and community theatre.

**4948** KLEIN, MAXINE. Theatre for the 98%
pp.iv, 170; ill. in text　　　　　　　　　　MH
Boston: South End P.　　　　　　　　1978
Urging, and prescribing for, a people's theatre.

**4949** McCASLIN, NELLIE. Shows on a shoestring: an easy guide to amateur productions
pp.ix, 118　　　　　　　　　　　　　　　★
NY: McKay　　　　　　　　　　　　1979

**4950** CUMMINS, DOUGLAS M. Management by objectives in community theatre: an internship report
Lubbock: Texas Tech U. (PhD)　　　　1980

**4951** JENKINS, ROBERT F. A description of working principles and procedures employed by selected peoples' theatres in the United States
Tallahassee: Florida State U. (PhD)　　1980

**4952** LYNCH, TWINK. Rationale and text for a correspondence course in volunteer and staff development for community theatre
Lawrence: U. of Kansas (PhD)　　　　1981

**4953** ALLENSWORTH, CARL; ALLENSWORTH, DOROTHY & RAWSON, CLAYTON. The complete play production handbook for schools, colleges, little theatres, community theatres, summer stock – for anyone staging a play
pp.xiii, 384; ill. in text　　　　　　　　　M
NY: Harper & Row　　　　　　　　　1982
Revised edition. First published 1973.

**4954** PREVOTS, NAIMA. American pageantry
　　　　　　　　　　　　　　　　　　　DL★
Ann Arbor: UMI Research P.　　　　1990

## 11.2 UNIVERSITY THEATRE

**4955** CATALOGUE of the officers and members of the Hasty Pudding Club in Harvard College
pp.94, ill. in text　　　　　　　　　　　　MH
Boston: Rockwell & Collins (printers)　1867

**4956** NORMAN, HENRY. An account of the Harvard Greek play
pp.x, 129; ill. in text, pl. 15 MH
Boston: James R. Osgood 1882

Preparation and performance of Sophocles's *Oedipus Tyrannus* at the Sanders Theatre, Harvard University, May 15, 1881. According to Professor W. W. Goodwin, the first performance in the US of a Greek play. The illustrations of the cast are interesting early examples of photography under electric light.

**4957** TYLER, HENRY M. A Greek play and its presentation
pp.64; ill. in text, pl. 3 M
Northampton MA: [Smith College] 1891

Production of Sophocles's *Elektra* at Smith College in 1889.

**4958** ...AN ACCOUNT of the presentation of the *Antigone* of Sophocles at the Leland Stanford Junior University, April seventeenth and nineteenth, nineteen hundred and two
pp.70; ill. in text DL*
San Francisco: Paul Elder 1903

Contains, in addition to programme material, H. W. Rolfe: *The Antigone at Stanford University*; A. T. Murray: *Antigone, a dramatic study*; H. R. Fairclough: *The choral side of Antigone*.

**4959** PROCEEDINGS of the conference on the drama in American universities and little theatres held at the Carnegie Institute of Technology, Pittsburg, Pennsylvania, November twenty-seventh and twenty-eighth, MDCCCCXXV
pp.180 M
Pittsburgh: Carnegie Institute [1925]

Contributors included Otto H. Kahn, Richard Boleslavsky, George P. Baker, Ben Iden Payne, Walter P. Eaton.

**4960** [DODD, LEE W.]. A prologue for the opening of the University theatre at Yale University
pp.[12] MH
New Haven: Yale U. P. 1927

Verses written and read by Lee Wilson Dodd at the request of George Pierce Baker. 40 copies, for private circulation.

**4961** SEYMOUR, GEORGE D. A letter dated New Haven, July 11, 1774, from James Hillhouse to his Yale classmate, Nathan Hale, now for the first time printed. Together with an account of the first plays produced by Yale undergraduates, and many digressions
pp.[46] MH*
New Haven: [For the author?] 1930

Reprinted from *New Haven*.

**4962** AN ILLUSTRATED history of the Hasty Pudding Club with a directory of members...1771-1935
Unpaginated; ill. in text M
Cambridge MA: Hasty Pudding Club 1933

First published in 1897 with an introduction by J. T. Wheelwright and pl. 11. Revised and updated in 1899. Includes an historical sketch, posters, playbills and credits for the annual productions.

**4963** KRETZMANN, ALBERT J. The universities, colleges, and the theatre
NY: U. (PhD) 1933

**4964** DOYLE, MARY P. A study of play selection in women's colleges
pp.vii, 75 L
NY: Columbia U. Teachers College 1935

Examines plays presented 'in the light of the educational advantages proposed for the theatre arts in the liberal arts college'.

**4965** MAYER, HAROLD F. Materials for a history of dramatics in Saint Louis University from 1818 to 1900
Saint Louis: U. (MA) 1938

**4966** PLUGGÉ, DOMIS E. History of Greek play production in American colleges and universities from 1881 to 1936
NY: Columbia U. Teachers' College (PhD) 1938

**4967** SCHLOSSMACHER, STEPHAN. Das deutsche Drama in amerikanischen College - und Universitäts - Theater
pp.xi, 194; pl. 35 M
Emsdetten: H. & J. Lechte 1938

**4968** REINER, AILEEN. Contributions of the University of North Carolina to the American drama (1918-1935)
Columbus: Ohio State U. (MA) 1941

**4969** CHENOWETH, EUGENE C. An investigation of the training and occupations of Bachelor of Arts graduates in speech and dramatic art, State University of Iowa, 1931-40
Ames: State U. of Iowa (PhD) 1942

**4970** WELSCH, JAMES D. A peoposed reorganization of the Department of Speech and Dramatic Arts at Coe College, Cedar Rapids, Iowa
Denver: U. of Colorado (PhD) 1944

**4971** ROBINSON, MARION P. College theatres of tomorrow
Madison: U. of Wisconsin (PhD) 1945

**4972** BUTT, WILLIAM G. A history of dramatic activities at Michigan State College to 1937
East Lansing: Michigan State College (MA) 1947

**4973** WALKER, PHILLIP N. A history of dramatics at the University of Washington from the beginning to June, 1919
Seattle: U. of Washington (MA) 1947

**4974** COLLINS, BETTY J. History of dramatic art at the University of South Dakota from 1882-1947
Vermillion: U. of South Dakota (MA) 1948

**4975** ENGAR, KEITH M. History of dramatics at the University of Utah from beginning until June, 1919
Salt Lake City: U. of Utah (MFA) 1948

**4976** DRAKE, FRANCIS. A study of the personality traits of students interested in acting
Minneapolis: U. of Minnesota (PhD) 1949

**4977** GEE, ROBERT F. A history of the theatre at the University of Minnesota from its beginnings to 1937
Minneapolis: U. of Minnesota (MA) 1949

**4978** HOMRIGHOUS, MARY E. A history of non-professional theatrical production at the University of Illinois from its beginning to 1923
Urbana: U. of Illinois (MA) 1949

**4979** ABBOTT, BILLY M. History of the dramatic activity of Southern Methodist University (1815-1942)
Dallas TX: Southern Methodist U. (MA) 1951

## 11.2. UNIVERSITY THEATRE

**4980** BACH, EARL C. The status of dramatic education in Roman Catholic colleges and universities in the United States
Denver: U. (EdD) 1951

**4981** BUSH, JOAN D. The history of dramatic activities at Central Michigan College of Education from 1892 to 1950
East Lansing: Michigan State U. (PhD) 1951

**4982** COPE, GARRETT L. History of the origin and development of theatre arts at Indiana University
Bloomington: Indiana U. (MA) 1951

**4983** DAVEE, PAUL W. Definitions of the philosophy underlying the recognition and teaching of theatre as a fine art in the liberal arts and graduate curricula at the State University of Iowa
Iowa City: U. of Iowa (Ed.D) 1951

**4984** HOUGHTON, NORRIS. But not forgotten: the adventure of the University Players
pp.346; pl. 8 M
NY: William Sloane 1951
The University Players Guild and their summer stock company on Cape Cod.

**4985** MACDONALD, ROBERT J. The 1948 Kent State University showboat: the record of an experiment
Kent OH: State U. (MA) 1951

**4986** ROACH, HELEN P. History of speech education at Columbia College, 1754-1940
NY: Columbia U. Teachers' College (EdD) 1951

**4987** SHAY, THOMAS M. The University of Kansas Laboratory Theatre
Lawrence: U. of Kansas (MA) 1951

**4988** BRAZEE, ANNIE L. A history of the theatre at Stanford University (1891-1906)
Stanford: U. (MA) 1952

**4989** HAMAR, CLIFFORD E. The rise of drama and theatre in the American college curriculum, 1900-1920
Stanford: U. (PhD) 1952

**4990** STIVER, HARRY E. A history of the theatre of the University of Nebraska, 1900-1950
Lincoln: U. of Nebraska (MA) 1952

**4991** FLINT, MARTHA M. Dramatic art at Harvard University during the nineteenth century
NY: Columbia U. (MA) 1953

**4992** WAGNER, HILDA S. A history of forms of dramatic expression in Mount Holyoke College 1873-1950
NY: Columbia U. Teachers' College (PhD) 1953

**4993** ACKER, WILL. History of the theatrical activities at Lou Morris College, Jacksonville, Texas, from September, 1873 to September, 1942
Dallas: Southern Methodist U. (MA) 1954

**4994** DAMON, RUTH A. A study of the origin and rise of curricular instruction in dramatics in the colleges and universities of the United States, 1900-1925
NY: U. (EdD) 1954

**4995** ELLIS, ELIZABETH. A history of play production at the University of Michigan from 1928-1953
Ann Arbor: U. of Michigan (MA) 1954

**4996** HOAK, EUGENE Q. Some basic specific problems of staging the play in the college and university theatre
Columbus: Ohio State U. (PhD) 1954

**4997** SEXSON, KEITH D. Touring theater at the University of Washington
Seattle: U. of Washington (MA) 1954

**4998** CLARK, JOHN L. Dramatic activity in colleges and universities of the United States prior to 1905
Stanford: U. (PhD) 1955

**4999** STEVENS, HAROLD K. A survey of drama curriculums, programs and facilities in Washington colleges and high schools
Denver: U. (PhD) 1955

**5000** HARTON, HELEN L. An historical, analytical and interpretative study of educational theatre programs in Michigan Protestant church-related liberal arts colleges
Evanston: Northwestern U. (PhD) 1956

**5001** MAXWELL, BERNICE J. An historical study of the non-professional theatrical activities at the University of Georgia from 1785 through 1955
Athens: U. of Georgia (MFA) 1956

**5002** WEAR, ELIZABETH. The method of work at the Baylor theater with a critical analysis of the production of *Othello*
Waco TX: Baylor U. (MA) 1956

**5003** CLITHERO, EDITH P. History of dramatic activity at DePauw University
Greencastle IN: DePauw U. (MA) 1957

**5004** DOWELL, GEORGE. *Heritage*. The Smith College anniversary play - a project in communication arts through educational theatre
NY: Columbia U. (EdD) 1957

**5005** ROBINSON, GILES F. A historical study of dramatic activities at the University of Southern California
Los Angeles: U. of Southern California (MA) 1957

**5006** SCHILLING, KATHERINE T. The history of dramatic art at Dakota Wesleyan University, 1885-1956
Vermillion: U. of South Dakota (MA) 1957

**5007** BORCHARDT, DONALD D. The history of the theater at the University of Minnesota
Minneapolis: U. of Minnesota (MA) 1958

**5008** BRISCOE, ADELAIDE M. A history of theatre at Ohio University (1920-1957)
Athens: U. of Ohio (MA) 1959

**5009** HULSOPPLE, BILL G. The development of a graduate achievement test in theatre
Columbus: Ohio State U. (PhD) 1959

**5010** LEES, SONDRA. A history of dramatics at the University of Utah from September 1919
Salt Lake City: U. of Utah (MFA) 1959

## 11. COMMUNITY THEATRE AND UNIVERSITY THEATRE

**5011** MAGRUDER, HENRY P. The role of dramatic literature in integral courses in state universities and land grant colleges
Denver: U. (EdD) 1959

**5012** MAHON, THOMAS A. A history of St. Louis University theatre
St. Louis: U. (MA) 1959

**5013** SANDLE, FLOYD L. A history of the development of the educational theatre in the negro colleges and universities, 1911-1959
Baton Rouge: Louisiana State U. (PhD) 1959

**5014** YARCHO, YVONNE V. The Stanford University Theatre: from the dramatic council to the division of speech and drama, 1934-1940
Stanford: U. (MA) 1959

**5015** REYNOLDS, ELWIN C. A practical approach to theatrical business management in the college and university theatre
Madison: U. of Wisconsin (PhD) 1961

**5016** MORRISON, JACK S. Four hundred new students in theatre arts. An experimental study of those who dropped out and those who received the B.A. degree of UCLA
Los Angeles: U. of Southern California (EdD) 1962

**5017** OLAUSON, CLARENCE R. Dramatic activities at the Brigham Young University from the earliest beginnings to the present, 1849-1961
Salt Lake City: U. of Utah (MFA) 1962

**5018** WHITE, IRLE E. The development of educational theatre at the university level as exemplified by the dramatic activity at the University of Oregon, 1876-1962
Eugene: U. of Oregon (MS) 1962

**5019** CLINGER, MORRIS M. A history of theater in Mormon colleges and universities
Minneapolis: U. of Minnesota (PhD) 1963

**5020** FUTURES in American theatre. A series of lectures presented to commemorate the twenty-fifth anniversary of the department of drama and the dedication of its new building season of 1962-1963
pp.65 M
Austin: U. of Texas P. 1963
Contains: Paul Green: *Some credo notes for theatre workers*; Jo Mielziner: *The future of theatre architecture*; John Gassner: *The dramatic critic looks at the contemporary theatre*; Samuel Selden: *Future directions of educational theatre*; Alan Schneider: *The director and the theatre in transition*.

**5021** KARL HOBLITZELLE and the university: a dedication of benefactions from the Hoblitzelle Foundation of Dallas to the University of Texas
pp.23; pl. 4 L
Austin: U. of Texas, Karl Hoblitzelle Library 1963
Record of the ceremony. Includes address by Frederick J. Hunter: *The value of a theatre arts library*.

**5022** BALDWIN, JOHN J. A study of student attenders and non-attenders at the University theatre, Michigan State University, 1963-64
East Lansing: Michigan State U. (PhD) 1964

**5023** BRADY, WILLIAM H. A history of theatre at Ohio University (1804 to 1920)
Athens: U. of Ohio (MFA) 1964

**5024** ENGLAND, THEORA C. An investigation of the educational theatre programs in the liberal arts colleges sponsored by the Reformed Church in America
Minneapolis: U. of Minnesota (PhD) 1964

**5025** McBRIDE, DONALD M. The design and equipment specifications of a theatre building for the University of Mississippi
Denver: U. (PhD) 1964

**5026** 50 YEARS of curricular theatre at the University of Michigan
pp.32; ill. in text M
Ann Arbor: U. of Michigan [1965]
Illustrated chronological record of productions, 1915-1965.

**5027** CAMPBELL, KENNETH. A descriptive history of the origins, development and theoretical bases of theatrical production at the speech and drama department of the Catholic University of America, 1937-1957
Denver: U. (PhD) 1965

**5028** DODRILL, CHARLES W. History of speech and theatre at Otterbein College, 1847-195 [Westerville OH]
Columbus: Ohio State U. (PhD) 1965

**5029** PEVEY, WAYNE. A history of the Department of Drama [the University of Texas]
Austin: U. of Texas 1965

**5030** RABB, NORMAN S. et al. Theater and the university: the dedication of the Nate B. and Frances Spingold Theatre Arts Centre
Unpaginated; ill. in text M
Waltham MA: Brandeis U. P. 1965
Includes a detailed account of the theatre, with photographs.

**5031** SLOTT, MELVIN M. Summer theatre in American colleges and universities: a directory
Columbus: Ohio State U. (PhD) 1965

**5032** BAROQUE OPERA at Smith College, 1926-1931. Record of a pioneer venture in music. Monteverdi and Handel operas as performed under the direction of Werner Josten
pp.x, 187; ill. in text M
NY: Smith College 1966

**5033** BROWN, JAMES L. Theatre at Southern Illinois University 1893-1966: a history
Carbondale: Southern Illinois U. (MS) 1966

**5034** TALAROWSKI, JOSEPH. Institute for Advanced Studies in the Theatre Arts: a study of its themes and practice
Denver: U. (PhD) 1966

**5035** WARNER, FRANK L. A history of the Tulane University theatre, 1937-1967
New Orleans: Tulane U. (PhD) 1967

**5036** WESTHAFER, STEVEN J. A history of drama at East Texas State University, 1889-1967
Commerce: East Texas State U. (MS) 1967

## 11.2. UNIVERSITY THEATRE

**5037** JACKSON, ALLAN S. et al (Eds). Theatre seminar
pp.various; ill. in text     M
Binghamton: Dept. of Theater, SUNY     1968-
Periodical publication of student papers on theatre topics.

**5038** KENWORTHY, O. FRANKLIN. A study of non-student educational theatre attenders in selected heartland colleges and universities
East Lansing: Michigan State U. (PhD)     1968

**5039** LONDRÉ, FELICIA H. A guide to the production of plays in foreign languages in American colleges and universities
Madison: U. of Wisconsin (PhD)     1968

**5040** MOLETTE, CARLTON W. Concepts about theatre: a survey of some college students in the Florida counties of Broward, Dade and Palm Beach comparing those who have had a theatre and drama appreciation course with those who have not
Tallahassee: Florida State U. (PhD)     1968

**5041** CARPENTER, BARBARA L. A history of theatre at Illinois State Normal University 1857-1959
Normal: Illinois State U. (MA)     1969

**5042** KRANNERT CENTER for the performing arts [cover title]
pp.[20] inc. covers; ill. in text     M
Urbana: U. of Illinois     1969
Published for the dedication, April 19-20.

**5043** LEMMERMAN, HAROLD B. Exploring the arts of the theatre: a proposed course for art majors utilizing experimental theatre techniques
NY: Columbia U. Teachers' College (PhD)     1969

**5044** DYE, OTTIS D. An analysis of the role of the business manager in the college or university theatre
Tallahassee: Florida State U. (PhD)     1970

**5045** PERLETT, ROBERT. A survey of reforms in theatre arts programs at selected New Jersey colleges and universities 1945 to 1969
NY: U. (PhD)     1970

**5046** BRACEWELL, JOHN L. A study of the problems of establishing training for the South specialist in college and university theatre departments
Tallahassee: Florida State U. (PhD)     1971

**5047** KLAR, LAWRENCE R. Affiliations between selected universities and professional theatre companies
Tallahassee: Florida State U. (PhD)     1971

**5048** MARTIN, JAMES L. A history of the Van Cliburn Auditorium, a small theater with a multiform stage constructed as a portion of the Applied Arts Building at Kilgore College, Kilgore, Texas
Los Angeles: U. of California (PhD)     1971

**5049** MORGAN, FLOYD T. Thespis in academia
pp.ii, 34     DL*
Logan: Utah State U. P.     1971

**5050** STRUCK, JAMES A. The history of theatre at Eastern Michigan University, 1849 to 1859
Ypsilanti: Eastern Michigan U. (MA)     1971

**5051** ARNDT, XAVIA D. A history of theatre at South Dakota State University, 1892 through Summer, 1972
Brookings: South Dakota State U. (MA)     1972

**5052** BEER, ARTHUR J. A descriptive study of courses in play direction at ten American universities
Detroit: Wayne State U. (PhD)     1972

**5053** SWISS, CHERYL D. A history of theatre at Muskingum College [New Concord OH]
Columbus: Ohio State U. (MA)     1972

**5054** HOVAR, LINN. Application of digital computing machinery to theatre arts education
Lawrence: U. of Kansas (PhD)     1973

**5055** KERN, JUDY B. A model for a speech and drama program for an upper-division college: Tyler State College
Denton: North Texas State U. (PhD)     1973

**5056** MEYER, ARTHUR C. A survey of speech programs in community colleges
Columbia: U, of Missouri (PhD)     1973

**5057** MOSS, ARNOLD. The professional actor as performing guest artist in theatre productions of American colleges and universities
NY: U. (PhD)     1973

**5058** CAMERON, KENNETH M. & HOFFMAN, THEODORE J. C. A guide to theatre study
pp.vii, 439; ill. in text     L
NY: Macmillan     1974
A basic primer for theatre non-majors. First published as *The Theatrical Response*, 1969

**5059** CHAPEL, ROBERT C. The University of Michigan professional theatre program, 1961-1973
Ann Arbor: U. of Michigan (PhD)     1974

**5060** FINSEL, TAMARA J. The history of the theatre at the University of Arkansas from 1893 to the summer of 1973
Fayetteville: U. of Arkansas (MA)     1974

**5061** LANPHIER, DAVID N. A history of the American College Theatre Festival: 1963-1973
Tallahassee: Florida State U. (PhD)     1974

**5062** DIRECTORY of American college theatre
pp.av. 60     M
East Lansing MI: ATA     1976
Earlier editions published by AETA. First published 1960.

**5063** KANTER, DAVID R. The academy approach to the teaching of acting in a liberal arts university setting: an examination of the history, philosophy and practical results for students of the Meadow Brook Academy at Oakland University from its inception to date
Minneapolis: U. of Minnesota (PhD)     1976

**5064** STEADMAN, DANIEL L. A performing arts center in the community college
Greeley: U. of Northern Colorado (DA)     1976

**5065** CARPENTER, DANA. A study of the selected ethnic theatrical experience incorporated in the theatre programs of American colleges and universities
Manhattan: Kansas State U. (PhD)     1977

**5066** CERMELE, DOMINICK J. An investigation of the effect of theatre study on the occupations and personal lives of certain Minnesota Bachelor graduates
Minneapolis: U. of Minnesota (PhD)     1977

**5067** FLOWERS, H. D. Educational theatre at forty predominantly black colleges and universities in the United States
Carbondale: Southern Illinois U. (PhD)     1977

**5068** GARRETT, MICHAEL D. A study of department chairmen of selected college and university theatre programs: their perceived problems and prospects
Tallahassee: Florida State U. (PhD)     1977

**5069** THIEDE, RICHARD W. A descriptive study of the course introduction to theatre in American colleges and universities
Columbia: U. of Missouri (PhD)     1977

**5070** KOEP, JEFFERY P. Profile of a college touring company: a study of the Commedians [sic] of Washington State University as touring company and actor training program
Pullman: Washington State U. (PhD)     1978

**5071** PHILLIPS, JERRY S. An analysis of theatre programs and activities with community-services orientations in selected public two-year colleges
Commerce: East Texas State U. (EdD)     1978

**5072** BERNHARD, RANDALL L. Contemporary musical theatre: history and development in the major colleges and universities of Utah
Provo: Brigham Young U. (PhD)     1979

**5073** TADIE, NANCY B. A history of drama at Gallaudet College [Washington DC]
NY: U. (PhD)     1979

**5074** GELTNER, FRANK J. Standards and accreditation for theatre arts programs in American higher education: a history and analysis
Eugene: U. of Oregon (PhD)     1980

**5075** MARSHALL, ALEXANDER C. Representative directors, black theatre productions, and practices at historically black colleges and universities
Bowling Green: State U. (PhD)     1980

**5076** DILWEG, JOAN K. A history of drama: Idaho State University 1901-1960
Provo: Brigham Young U. (PhD)     1981

**5077** BENNETT, MARILYN D. The Glenn Hughes years, 1927-1962: University of Washington School of Drama
Seattle: U. of Washington (PhD)     1982

**5078** LEWIS, JUDITH A. The selection process of dramatic literature for production at Southern Baptist colleges and universities
Oxford: U. of Mississippi (PhD)     1983

**5079** WARDRIP, MARK A. A western portal of culture. The Hearst Greek Theatre of the University of California, 1903-1984
Berkeley: U. of California (PhD)     1984

**5080** CROWE, RACHAEL M. Musical theatre in higher education: a survey and an analysis of course and degree programs offered in colleges and universities in the United States
Tallahassee: Florida State U. (PhD)     1985

**5081** BANK, ROSEMARIE K. & NICHOLS, HAROLD J. (Eds). Status of theatre research 1984: a project of the commission on theatre research of the American Theatre Association
pp.vi, 59     M
Lanham MD: U. P. of America     1986
Includes a substantial analysis of theatre research funding by the Guggenheim Foundation and the National Endowment for the Humanities, 1979-83.

**5082** EDGECOMBE, DAVID P. Educational programs of four North American Shakespeare festivals: Stratford Shakespeare festival<<, the New Jersey Shakespeare festival, the Folger Shakespeare festival, and the Oregon Shakespearean festival
Kent OH: State U. (PhD)     1986

**5083** FLEMING, CAROL A. Promoting university/college theatre in rural areas: program analysis and consumer oriented planning
Lubbock: Texas Tech U. (PhD)     1986

**5084** SEAY, DONALD W. Sponsored project funding; the development of the Center for the Advancement of Professional Theatre Training and Applied Research at Texas Tech University
Lubbock: Texas Tech U. (PhD)     1987

**5085** HOBGOOD, BURNET M. (Ed.). Master teachers of theatre: observations on teaching theatre by nine American masters
pp.ix, 212     MH
Carbondale: Southern Illinois U. P.     1988
Bernard Beckerman on dramatic literature; Oscar G. Brockett on theatre history; C. Baird on theatrical interpretation; Robert L. Benedetti on acting; J. Walker on stage movement; C. Weber on directing; Howard Bay on design; W. Smith on theatre in the secondary school; Agnes Haaga on child drama.

# 12. THEATRE AND EDUCATION

## 12.1 CREATIVE DRAMATICS IN SCHOOLS

**5086** HOBBS, MABEL F. Children's playground theatre
ill.     DL★
NY: National Recreation Association     [193-?]

**5087** CHUBB, PERCIVAL et al. Festivals and plays in schools and elsewhere [a symposium]
pp.xxi, 402; ill.     DL★
NY: Harper & Brothers     1912

**5088** CRAIG, ANNA A. The dramatic festival. A consideration of the lyrical method as a factor in preparatory education...with a foreword by Percival Chubb and an introduction by Peter W. Dykema...
pp.xxix, 363     MB
NY: G. P. Putnam's Sons     1912

## 12.1. CREATIVE DRAMATICS IN SCHOOLS — 5112

Urging the value of play, and of drama as a synthesis of the arts and literature.

**5089** FRY, EMMA S. Educational dramatics: a book on the educational player method
pp.69 DL★
NY: L. A. Noble 1917
Revised and elarged edition. First published NY: Moffat, Yard, 1913. Author was director of the NY Educational Children's Theatre Center, 1903-1909, and originated the educational player method.

**5090** THE OUT-DOOR PLAYERS
pp.12; ill. in text MH
[Peterborough NH]: [For the Outdoor Players] 1924
Brochure for the summer school camp in Peterborough NH, specializing in dramatic activities. Director, Marie Ware Laughton.

**5091** RUSSELL, MARY M. Drama as a factor in social education
pp. 140 L
NY: George H. Doran 1924
Pays substantial attention to educational dramatics.

**5092** MITCHELL, ROY. The school theatre: a handbook of theory and practice
viii, 104; ill. in text M
NY: Brentano's 1925

**5093** OVERTON, GRACE. Drama in education: theory and practice
xiii, 289; front., ill. in text L
NY: Century 1926
Intended for teachers in training.

**5094** MERRILL, JOHN & FLEMING, MARTHA. Play-making and plays: the dramatic impulse and its educative use in the elementary and secondary school
xix, 579; ill. in text L
NY: Macmillan 1930

**5095** SMITH, MILTON M. The equipment of the school theatre
NY: Columbia U. Teachers College (PhD) 1930

**5096** WARD, WINIFRED. Creative dramatics for the upper grades and junior high schools
pp. xiv, 304; ill. DL★
NY: D. Appleton 1930

**5097** HUME, SAMUEL J. & FOSTER, LOIS M. Theater and school. With appendices by Isabel McReynolds Gray and Tempe E. Allison and twenty-five line drawings by Mary Elizabeth Plehn
pp.viii, 417; ill. in text. pl. 15 MH
NY: Samuel French 1932

**5098** SIMON, HENRY W. The reading of Shakespeare in American schools and colleges: an historical survey
NY: Columbia U. (PhD) 1932

**5099** DAUBER, MAX. Dramatic productions in the foreign language work at the New York City high schools
NY: U. (EdD) 1933

**5100** EVANS, DINA R. Changes in social behavior and emotional attitudes of High School students participating in dramatic art in the high school of Cleveland Heights, Ohio
Iowa City: U. of Iowa (PhD) 1933

**5101** HOBBS, MABEL F. Play production made easy
pp. 71 DL★
NY: National Recreation Association 1933

**5102** ADOLPHE, JULES W. Dramatics in the High School. A survey, an analysis and a discussion of some of the major problems
NY: U. (Ed.D) 1934

**5103** WELSH, HELEN C. (Ed.). The school theater, a bibliography [cover title]
pp. 7 DL★
Albany NY: Philip Schuyler High School 1935

**5104** KRAMER, MAGDALENE E. Dramatic tournaments in the secondary schools
NY: Columbia U Teachers' College (PhD) 1936

**5105** WINBIGLER, HUGH D. The teaching of dramatic art in 103 Iowa high schools
Iowa City: U. of Iowa (DEd) 1938

**5106** BRADFORD, ARTHUR L. The direction of educational dramatics in the high school
Nashville: George Peabody College (D.Ed) 1939

**5107** CLINE, JAY J. Directing dramatics in high school: a handbook of suggestions
pp. 135; ill. DL★
Minneapolis: Northwestern P. 1944

**5108** WARD, WINIFRED. Playmaking with children, from the kindergarten to high school
pp. xiv, 312; ill. DL★
NY: Appleton-Century 1947
Practical guide to improvised drama.

**5109** SMITH, HARVEY. Dramatic production in the private secondary schools of Connecticut
New Haven: Yale U. (MFA) 1948

**5110** EDUCATIONAL THEATRE JOURNAL vol 1, no 1 - vol 30, no 4
Washington DC: AETA 1949-1978
Continued as *Theatre Journal*, now published Baltimore MD: John Hopkins U. P. (1979-). Quarterly. Special issues included Clifford E. Hamar: *American theatre history, a geographical index*, December, 1949; Alan S. Downer: *Conference on theatre research*, July, 1967, a report on the 1965-66 Princeton conference; Travis Bogard (Ed.): *International conference of theatre education and development* August, 1968, a report on the Washington DC conference, June, 1967. A ten-year index, 1949-1958, was issued in 1959.

**5111** KARSCHNER, DONALD W. Trends in teaching dramatic literature in American high schools 1900-1945
Stanford: U. (EdD) 1949

**5112** TURBYFILL, SUBERT. My Panama Canal theatre adventure: the story of fifteen years of drama at the Panama Canal
pp. 146; pl. 10 M
Philadelphia: Dorrance 1949

Development of theatre/drama activity in Balboa H. S. and Canal Zone Junior College.

**5113** BURGER, ISABEL B. Creative play acting: learning through drama
pp. xv, 199; ill. DL★
NY: A. S. Barnes 1950

**5114** FISHER, CAROLINE E. & ROBERTSON, HAZEL G. Children and the theatre
pp.xv, 235; ill. in text L
Stanford: U. P. 1950
Revised edition. First published 1940. A system of child drama derived from eight years' experimentation at the Palo Alto theatre. Appendix by Edith W. Ramstad.

**5115** DURLAND, FRANCES C. Creative dramatics for children: a practical manual for teachers and leaders
pp. 181 DL★
Yellow Spring OH: Antioch P. 1952

**5116** LEASE, RUTH & SIKS, GERALDINE B. Creative dramatics in home, school, and community
pp.xix, 306; front. L
NY: Harper & Brothers 1952

**5117** BLANK, EARL. The effectiveness of creative dramatics in developing voice, vocabulary and personality in the primary grades
Denver: U. (PhD) 1953

**5118** GOULD, HAROLD V. Functions of dramatic activity in American schools. colleges, and universities in the twentieth century
Ithaca: Cornell U. (PhD) 1953

**5119** WINSHIP, FRANK L. The development of educational theatre in Texas
Austin: U. of Texas (EdD) 1953

**5120** WINSHIP, LOREN. The development of educational dramatics with status in Texas secondary schools
pp.61 DL★
Austin: U. of Texas P. 1953

**5121** LANE, LE ROI. Children should be heard: a complete textbook in speech and dramatics for grammar-achool and junior high pupils
pp. 230 DL★
NY: Children's Drama Guild 1954

**5122** CITRON, S. J. (Ed.). Dramatics the year round
pp. 543; ill. DL★
NY: United Synagogue Commission of Jewish Education 1956
Includes dramatic ceremonial services of Jewish content for schools, community centers and summer camps.

**5123** POPOVICH, JAMES E. A study of significant contributions to the development of creative dramatics in American education
Evanston: Northwestern U. (PhD) 1956

**5124** SPONSLER, W. R. A manual for high school and college theatrical administration
ll. 65; ill. DL★
Hollywood: American Legitimate Theatre Service 1956
Loose-leaf format.

**5125** SIMOS, JACK. Social growth through play production
pp. 192 DL★
NY: Association P. 1957
Case-illustrated account of drama's contribution to personality development in teenagers and young adults.

**5126** BLANCHARD, DAGNY. Creative dramatics in the elementary classroom
NY: U. (EdD) 1958

**5127** OSBORNE, KARIN. A survey of the speech and theatre program at the University of Minnesota High School
Minneapolis: U. of Minnesota U. (PhD) 1958

**5128** OMMANNEY, KATHERINE A. The stage and the school
xiv, 530; ill. in text L
NY: McGraw-Hill 1960
A course in high school drama. Revised edition with material on Stanislavski, epic theatre, theatre in the round. First published 1932.

**5129** SIKS, GERALDINE B. & DUNNINGTON, HAZEL B. (Eds). Children's theatre and creative dramatics
pp. xv, 277; front., ill. in text L
Seattle: U. of Washington P. 1961
Symposium, under auspices of AETA, examining methods and potential, research in the field, basic principles and practices.

**5130** LEECH, ROBERT M. Education through theatre for children
Austin: U. of Texas (EdD) 1963

**5131** A SUGGESTED OUTLINE for a course of study in theatre arts: secondary school level
DL★
[Eugene OR]: AETA 1963
Report of a committee of the secondary school theatre conference of AETA presented August 21, 1962 at Eugene.

**5132** ZINSMASTER, W. M. Exploring the contribution of the art of creative dramatics in the social studies in the third grade
NY: Columbia U. (EdD) 1963

**5133** ABRAMS, DOLORES (Ed.). Theatre in the junior college
pp. iv, 58 DL★
Washington DC: AETA 1964

**5134** ELKIND, SAMUEL. High school drama as self-discovery
NY: Columbia U. (EdD) 1964

**5135** MILLER, FRED R. A history of the development of the theatre programs of selected Texas junior colleges
Austin: U. of Texas (EdD) 1964

**5136** CROSSCUP, RICHARD. Children and dramatics
pp. xii, 271 DL★
NY: Charles Scribner's Sons 1966

**5137** MERSAND, JOSEPH. Index to plays with suggestions for teaching
pp.114 L
NY: Scarecrow P. 1966

One-act and longer plays appropriate for use in schools with suggested ancillary reading to aid the teacher.

**5138** HENKEL, DONALD D. Assessment of effects of an acting experience upon participants in a public recreation department children's dramatics program
Urbana-Champaign: U. of Illinois (PhD) 1967

**5139** KARIOTH, EMIL J. Creative dramatics as an aid in developing creative thinking abilities
Minneapolis: U. of Minnesota (PhD) 1967

**5140** BOGARD, TRAVIS (Ed.). International conference on theatre education and development: a report on the conference sponsored by AETA, State Department, Washington D.C. June 14-18, 1967
pp.xi, 249-362 M
Washington DC: AETA 1968
Special issue of *Educational Theatre Journal*, August, 1968. Includes Vera M. Roberts: *Theatre education in the United States*.

**5141** BYERS, RUTH. Creating theatre: from idea through performance with children and teens
pp.xiv, 225; ill. in text MH
San Antonio: Trinity U. P. 1968

**5142** JOHNSON, ALBERT & JOHNSON, BERTHA. Drama for classroom and stage
pp.569 L
South Brunswick: A. S. Barnes 1969

**5143** LAYNE, WILLIAM J. The effect of curricular dramatics on children's acting skill
Evanston: Northwestern U. (PhD) 1969

**5144** PELUSO, JOSEPH L. A survey of the status of theatre in United States high schools
pp. 95; diagrams in text M
Washington DC: US Dept. of Health 1970

**5145** PRITNER, CALVIN L. & ARCHER, STEPHEN. Secondary school theatre bibliography: a selected and annotated bibliography for the secondary school theatre teacher and student
pp. 38 DL★
[Washington DC]: AETA 1970
First published 1968.

**5146** REARDON, WILLIAM R. & PAWLEY, THOMAS D. (Eds). The black teacher and the dramatic arts: a dialogue, bibliography, and anthology
pp. xviii, 487; front., ill. in text L
Westport CT: Negro Universities P. 1970

**5147** CHEIFETZ, DAN. Theater in my head
pp. 178; ill. DL★
Boston: Little, Brown 1971
The author directed a theatre workshop for disadvantaged children in NYC and describes his improvisational work.

**5148** CONRAD, EDNA & VAN DYKE, MARY. History on the stage: children make plays from historical novels
pp.128; ill. in text P
NY: Van Nostrand Reinhold 1971

**5149** HARDY, CAMILLE C. The contributions of Samuel Selden to educational theatre
Ann Arbor: U. of Michigan (PhD) 1971

**5150** JEFFREYS, HARVEY E. The necessary role of the college and the university in the development of the secondary school drama program in Florida: a survey and analysis of the needs of the Florida secondary schools, and an examination of the role of the college and university in the drama program of secondary schools in selected states
Tallahassee: Florida State U. (PhD) 1971

**5151** KLOCK, MARY E. Writings in creative dramatics concerned with children of elementary school age (pre-school through sixth grade): an annotated bibliography from 1890 through 1970
Denver: U. (PhD) 1971

**5152** PIERINI, MARY P. Creative dramatics: a guide for educators
pp. 166; ill. DL★
NY: Herder & Herder 1971

**5153** PIRO, RICHARD. Black fiddler
pp. xii, 242; ill. DL★
NY: Morrow 1971
Account of a Brooklyn H. S. production of *Fiddler on the Roof* by black and Puerto Rican students.

**5154** WRIGHT, LIN. The effects of creative drama on person perception
Minneapolis: U. of Minnesota (PhD) 1971

**5155** BLACKIE, PAMELA; BULLOUGH, BESS & NASH, DORIS. Drama
pp.63; ill. in text O
Basingstoke: Macmillan 1972
Part of an Anglo-American primary school project.

**5156** KUNESH, GREGORY D. A descriptive analysis of curricular theatre in Missouri public high schools
Columbia: U. of Missouri (PhD) 1972

**5157** SPRINGMAN, JAY K. A survey of the status of dramatic arts in Nebraska secondary schools, 1970-71
Lincoln: U. of Nebraska (EdD) 1972

**5158** WILLIAMS, ALLEN. Sheppard Randolph Edmonds: his contribution to black educational theatre
Bloomington: Indiana U. (PhD) 1972

**5159** CONNER, LAURENCE M. An investigation of the effects of selected educational dramatics techniques on general cognitive abilities
Carbondale: Southern Illinois U. (PhD) 1973

**5160** NELSON, KENT E. A survey of dramatic activity in Michigan junior and community colleges
Detroit: Wayne State U. (PhD) 1973

**5161** WEHLBURG, ALBERT F. An analytical survey of the staging facilities and dramatic arts production problems in the Florida senior high schools
Gainsville: U. of Florida (EdD) 1973

**5162** DUKE, CHARLES R. Creative dramatics and English teaching
pp. x, 180 DL★
Urbana IL: National Council of Teachers of English 1974

**5163** HAWLEY, CHARLES R. The status of curricular and co-curricular theatre in Arkansas high schools
Kent OH: State U. (PhD) 1974

**5164** YOUNG, BARRIE J.  Theatre-arts experiences of Arizona high school students and teachers
Tucson: U. of Arizona (EdD) 1974

**5165** FORDYCE, RACHEL.  Children's theatre and creative dramatics: an annotated bibliography of critical works
pp. viii, 275 DL★
Boston: G. K. Hall 1975

**5166** KLOCK, MARY E.  Creative drama; a selected and annotated bibliography
pp. vi, 26 L
[Washington DC]: Children's Theatre Association 1975

**5167** RICHEY, MICHAEL M.  An analysis of educational theatre's role in playwright development
Tallahassee: Florida State U. (PhD) 1975

**5168** JONES, CHARLES V.  Educational theatre: form and facility for the secondary school
Seattle: U. of Washington (EdD) 1976

**5169** LEVITT, BRUCE.  The historical and practical evolution of Viola Spolin's theatre games
Ann Arbor: U. of Michigan (PhD) 1976

**5170** RAINS, DALE O.  A study of educational theater programs in ten selected small liberal arts colleges in South Carolina
Baton Rouge: Louisiana State U. (PhD) 1976

**5171** WESTERFIELD, WILLIAM A.  A model program of creative dramatic training for children: a formulation based upon investigation of the historical/critical evolution of creative dramatics in America integrated with the theories of English child drama
Detroit: Wayne State U. (PhD) 1976

**5172** HELFERT, CHARLES J.  The identification and analysis of theatre competencies needed by high school theatre teachers in Texas
Madison: U. of Wisconsin (PhD) 1977

**5173** MURPHY, JAMES R.  An examination of the status of theatre arts as taught in the public secondary schools of New Jersey
NY: Columbia U. Teachers' College (EdD) 1977

**5174** SMITH, JOE E.  Educational theatre philosophy: its major principles
Columbia: U. of Missouri (PhD) 1977

**5175** MALKIN, MICHAEL R.  Training the young actor
pp.128; ill. in text L
South Brunswick: A. S. Barnes 1979
Child drama.

**5176** TABBERT, JONATHAN C.  A study of a selected secondary school theatre arts program
Grand Forks: U. of North Dakota (Ed.D) 1979

**5177** TIFT, THOMAS N.  Theatre education in the Illinois public community college system, 1967-77: a comprehensive study
Urbana-Champaign: U. of Illinois (PhD) 1979

**5178** BURKE, JOHN J.  The effect of creative dramatics on the attitudes and reading abilities of seventh grade students
East Lansing: Michigan State U. (PhD) 1980

**5179** DE HART, STANLEY C.  A study of the administrative evaluation of the condition of the Florida secondary school drama curriculum as compared to the curriculums of art, band, chorus, and music
Tallahassee: Florida State U. (PhD) 1980

**5180** DOMEY, RICHARD L.  Theatre arts in the schools: a pragmatic defense
Pullman: Washington State U. (PhD) 1980

**5181** FERTIK, MARIAN I.  The use of literature and library resources in creative dramatics
Urbana-Champaign: U. of Illinois (PhD) 1980

**5182** KLINE, PETER.  Diary of a play production
pp. xiv, 145; ill. DL★
NY: Richards Rosen P. 1980
An account of a High School production of *Romeo and Juliet*.

**5183** LEAF, LINAYA L.  The identification and classification of educational objectives for creative dramatics when it is done with handicapped children and youth in the United States
Eugene: U. of Oregon (PhD) 1980

**5184** SOLOMON, THEODORE O'B.  Theoretical foundations and curriculum guide for creative drama K-3
Carbondale: Southern Illinois U. (PhD) 1980

**5185** KENNEDY, CAROL J.  Child drama: a selected and annotated bibliography 1974-1979: a project of the Theatre Department, Arizona State University
pp. iv, 51 L
Washington DC: CTAA/ATA 1981

**5186** McCALL, ELLEN M.  Creative dramatics, plus creative dramatics/parental intervention: strategies for developing moral reasoning skills in pre-adolescents in a church school setting – an experimental study
Provo: Brigham Young U. (PhD) 1981

**5187** McCASLIN, NELLIE (Ed.).  Children and drama
pp.xxx, 249; ill. in text L
NY: Longman 1981
Includes Geraldine B. Siks: *Drama in education - a changing scene*; Margaret Jendyck: *Creative drama, improvisation-theatre*; Virginia Tanner: *Thoughts on a creative process*; Agnes Haaga: *Reflections on a spring day*; Ann M. Shaw: *Co-respondents: the child & the drama*; Eliza F. Kelly: *Curriculum drama*; Joanne H. Kraus: *Dramatizing history*; Grace Stanistreet: *'Acting' and children*; Moses Goldberg: *The theatre: a side view*; Lowell Swortzell: *Smoking chimneys*; Aurand Harris: *Plees make more*; Nancy King: *From literature to drama to life*.

**5188** LANDY, ROBERT J.  Handbook of educational drama and theatre
pp. xiv, 282; ill. in text L
Westport CT: Greenwood P. 1982

**5189** BECK, ROY A. et al.  Play production today!
pp.x, 309 DL★
Skokie IL: National Textbook 1983

One of several manuals intended for teachers, including *Play production in the High School*, revised 1976 and *Stagecraft...*, 1984.

**5190** COOPER, JANET L. A study of the effects of pre-performance materials on the child's ability to respond to theatrical performance
Athens: U. of Georgia (PhD)     1983

**5191** FOSTER, ROBERT B. A history of the American Educational Theatre Association: the formative years
Eugene: U. of Oregon (PhD)     1983

**5192** ROSENBLATT, BERNARD A. A theory for curriculum for theatre education at the elementary grades
Columbia: U. of Missouri (PhD)     1983

**5193** McCASLIN, NELLIE. Creative drama in the classroom
xxiv, 423; ill. in text     L
NY: Longman     1984
Fourth edition. First published 1968.

**5194** MOTTER, CHARLOTTE K. Theatre in high school: planning, teaching, directing
pp.xiii, 187; ill. in text     L
Lanham MD: U. P. of America     1984
First published Englewood Cliffs, Prentice-Hall, 1970.

**5195** SALAZAR, LAURA G. The emergence of children's theatre and drama, 1900 to 1910
Ann Arbor: U. of Michigan (PhD)     1984

**5196** TANNER, FRAN A. Readers' theatre: a cumulative approach to theory and creative activities for use in secondary schools
Provo: Brigham Young U. (PhD)     1984

**5197** DAVIS, JED H. (Ed.). Theatre education: mandate for tomorrow
    DL★
New Orleans: Anchorage P.     1985

**5198** DIETMEYER, CATOL W. A survey of secondary school theatre teacher certification standards and practices in the United States and the District of Columbia: 1984-1985
Madison: U. of Wisconsin (PhD)     1985

**5199** SPOLIN, VIOLA. Theatre games for the classroom
    DL★
Evanston IL: Northwestern U. P.     1986
Accompanied with a file of 210 cards of 'games'.

**5200** ROSENBERG, HELANE S. & PINCIOTTI, PATRICIA et al. Creative drama and imagination: transforming ideas into action
pp. xviii, 350; ill. in text     L
NY: Holt, Rinehart & Winston     1987

**5201** KELLER, BETTY. Improvisations in creative drama: a program of workshops and dramatic sketches for students
pp. 192     DL★
Colorado Springs: Meriwether P.     1988

## 12.2 CHILDREN'S THEATRE

**5202** HERTS, ALICE M. [=HENIGER, ALICE M.]. Children's educational theatre
pp.xiii, 151; front., pl. 15     L
NY: Harper & Brothers     1911
Author was founder and co-director of the first New York Children's Educational Theatre, whose work she describes. Chapter XIV comprises the bulk of an address first delivered by James J. Walsh: *The drama in its relation to education*.

**5203** MACKAY, CONSTANCE D. How to produce children's plays
pp.151     DL★
NY: Henry Holt     1915
Articles reprinted from periodicals.

**5204** MACKAY, CONSTANCE D. Children's theatre and plays
xiii, 265; front., pl. 11     L
NY: Appleton     1927
International in scope. Surveys methods and source materials.

**5205** HYATT, AEOLA L. (Ed.). Index to children's plays
pp. ix, 214     L
Chicago: American Library Association     1931
Third edition, revised. Based on Alice I. Hazeltine: *Plays for children* (revised edition, 1921).

**5206** WAGER, WILLIS. Stage manager's guide. *Ride 'em, cowboy!* an operetta for boys' voices. Book and lyrics by Beatrice H. McNeil
pp.36; pl, 2     L
NY: G. Schirmer     1939
Description and explanation of roles, costume, makeup, stage settings, properties, sound effects, action on songs and dances, stage business and stage pictures, with production photographs. Comprises interesting record of high school play practice of the period.

**5207** WARD, WINIFRED. Theatre for children
pp. xv, 335; ill.     DL★
NY: Appleton-Century     1939
History of children's theatre and advice on how to organize one.

**5208** MERSAND, JOSEPH. The play's the thing: how to appreciate and enjoy the drama
pp.39     MH
NY: Modern Drama Chapbooks     1941
Intended for high school and college students.

**5209** MEEK, BERYL. The establishment of a children's theatre in a teacher training institution
NY: U. (EdD)     1942

**5210** GILLETTE, ARNOLD S. Planning and equipping the educational theatre
pp. 31; diagrams in text     DL★
Cincinnati: National Thespian Society     [1945]

**5211** CHILDREN'S THEATRE manual: a guide for the organization and operation of a non-profit community children's theatre, compiled by the Seattle Junior Programs, Inc.
pp.56     DL★
Chicago: Children's Theatre P.     1951

## 12. THEATRE AND EDUCATION

**5212** GRAHAM, PHILIP B. An introductory study of evaluation of plays for children's theatre in the United States
Salt Lake City: U. of Utah (PhD)    1952

**5213** SMITH, ROSE M. Plans for organizing and managing children's theatre in Oklahoma City...
Ann Arbor: U. of Michigan (MA)    1952

**5214** GROSS, EDWIN A. & GROSS, NATHALIE. Teen theatre: a guide to play production and six royalty-free plays
pp.ix, 245; ill. in text    L
NY: McGraw Hill    1953
Foreword by Margaret C. Scroggin.

**5215** JONES, CHARLES A. An evaluation of the educational significance of the children's theatre of Evanston
Evanston: Northwestern U. (PhD)    1953

**5216** CHORPENNING, CHARLOTTE B. Twenty-one years with children's theatre
pp.xiii, 112; ill. in text, front.    M
[Chicago]: Children's Theatre P.    1954

**5217** KASE, CHARLES R. Children's theatre comes of age: for school, college and community theatres
pp.32; front.    L
NY: Samuel French    1956
A brief history, with notes on practice and principles.

**5218** HERGET, PATSY J. A history and evaluation of the children's theatre of Cedar Rapids
Iowa City: U. of Iowa (PhD)    1957

**5219** WATTRON, FRANK J. A descriptive study of the most popular high school plays in the United States produced by members of the Thespian Society, 1938-1954
Los Angeles: U. of Southern California (PhD)    1957

**5220** MEYER, JEANETTE R. The history and organization of the Racine Children's Theatre
Madison: U. of Wisconsin (MA)    1958

**5221** EEK, NATHANIEL S. Attitudes towards playgoing in a selected contemporary educational theatre audience
Columbus: Ohio State U. (PhD)    1960

**5222** BATCHELLER, DAVID R. The status of the technical director in American educational theatre
Columbus: Ohio State U. (PhD)    1961

**5223** FORKERT, OTTO M. Children's theatre that captures its audience
pp. 158; ill.    DL★
Chicago: Coach House P.    1962
A documentary and pictorial account of a production of *Tom Sawyer* at the Goodman Memorial Theatre, Chicago. Includes also illustrations of children's theatre productions by Charlotte B. Chorpenning and her colleagues.

**5224** HACKETT, JOAN. A study of the educational theatre tours sponsored by the President's special international program for cultural presentations, 1957-1960
Detroit: Wayne State U. (PhD)    1964

**5225** KINGSLEY, WILLIAM H. Happy endings, poetic justice, simplified and softened characterization in plays for children in the United Sates
Pittsburgh: U. (PhD)    1964

**5226** WENSTROM, DAVID D. An experiment in children's drama
Salt Lake City: U. of Utah (PhD)    1964

**5227** DAVIS, JED H. Prospectus for research in children's theatre
ll. 7    DL★
Lawrence: U. of Kansas P.    1965
Reprinted from the *Educational Theatre Journal*.

**5228** WAGNER, JEARNINE & BAKER, KITTY. A place for ideas: our theatre
pp. 208; ill.    DL★
San Antonio: Principia P. of Trinity U.    1965
Children's theatre.

**5229** LATSHAW, GEORGE T. AJLA children's theatre manual
pp. x, 61; ill.    DL★
NY: Association of the Junior Leagues of America    1966

**5230** CAPBERN, A. MARTIAL. The drama publicist: a discussion and presentation of procedures and methods for publicizing educational theatre
pp.xvi, 119; ill. in text    O
NY: Pageant P.    1968

**5231** DAVIS, JED H. & HERSH, SALLY S. (Eds). A directory of children's theatres in the United States
pp. 205    DL★
Washington DC: AETA    1968

**5232** HOWARD, VERNON. The complete book of children's theatre
pp. 544; ill.    DL★
Garden City NY: Doubleday    1969
A manual for beginners.

**5233** JOHNSON, RICHARD C. Producing plays for children
pp. 154; ill.    DL★
NY: Richards Rosen P.    1971

**5234** McCASLIN, NELLIE. Theatre for children in the United States: a history
pp.xvi, 317; pl. 16    MH
Norman: U. of Oklahoma P.    1971

**5235** BOGEN, MEL. The magic of children's theatre
pp. 72; ill.    DL★
Tucson AR: Omen P.    1972
Illustrated by children of Schweitzer School, Tucson, aged 5 through 9.

**5236** CLIFFORD, JOHN. Educational theatre management
pp. 236; ill.    DL★
Skokie IL: National Text Book    1972

**5237** KREIDER, BARBARA. Index to children's plays in collections
pp.138    L
Metuchen NJ: Scarecrow P.    1972
New books published in US, 1965-69 culled from 25 collections. Author, title, subject, cast analysis.

**5238** CHICOREL, MARIETTA (Ed.). Chicorel Index Series, Volume 9. Chicorel theater index to plays for young people in periodicals, anthologies and collections
pp.490     L
NY: Chicorel Library Publishing     1974

**5239** GOLDBERG, MOSES. Children's theatre: a philosophy and a method
pp. xii, 228; ill.     DL★
Englewood Cliffs NJ: Prentice-Hall     1974

**5240** JENNINGS, COLEMAN A. The dramatic contributions of Aurand Harris to children's theatre in the United States
NY: U. (EdD)     1974

**5241** CORNELISON, GAYLE L. Death and childhood: attitudes and approaches to society, children's literature and children's theatre and drama
Lawrence: U. of Kansas (PhD)     1975

**5242** MASHIACH, SELLINA. Allegory in children's theatre and drama
Lawrence: U. of Kansas (PhD)     1975

**5243** REGAN, FREDERICK S. The history of the International Children's Theatre Association from its founding to 1975
Minneapolis: U. of Minnesota (PhD)     1975

**5244** VAN TASSEL, WESLEY. Children's theatre: a selected and annotated bibliography
pp. 31     L
[NY]: Children's Theatre Association of America     1975

**5245** GAMBLE, MICHAEL W. Clara Tree Major children's theatre, 1923-1954
NY: U. (PhD)     1976

**5246** FULLER, MICHAEL W. Make a circle with your head: the 'playing' of children's theater. An avant-garde approach
Los Angeles: U. of Southern California (PhD)     1978

**5247** RUBIN, JANET E. The literary and theatrical contributions of Charlotte B. Chorpenning to children's theatre
Columbus: Ohio State U. (PhD)     1978

**5248** BEDARD, ROGER L. The life and work of Charlotte B. Chorpenning
Lawrence: U. of Kansas (PhD)     1979

**5249** COPLEY, DEANA K. Creating and directing a musical play for children's theatre, *Fabulous Aesop*
Greeley: U. of Northern Colorado (Ed.D)     1980

**5250** RODMAN, ELLEN R. Edith King and Dorothy Coit and the King-Coit school and children's theatre
NY: U. (PhD)     1980

**5251** SUCKE, GREER W. Participation plays for young audiences: problems in theory, writing, and performance
NY: U. (PhD)     1980

**5252** ABOOKIRI, NOEREENA. Children's theatre activities at Karamu House in Cleveland, Ohio 1915-1975
NY: U. (PhD)     1982

**5253** DAVIS, JED H. & EVANS, MARY J. Theatre, children and youth
pp.xii, 362; ill.     ★
New Orleans: Anchorage P.     1982
Supersedes Jed H. Davis et al: *Children's theatre, play production*, NY: Harper, 1960.

**5254** HICKS, JOHN V. The history of the Children's Theatre Company and School of Minneapolis 1961-1981
Madison: U. of Wisconsin (PhD)     1982

**5255** HECHT, STUART J. Hull-House Theatre: an analytical and evaluative history
Evanston: Northwestern U. (PhD)     1983
Hull-House children's theatre, Chicago IL.

**5256** PARCHEM, GEORGA L. The Paper Bag Players [NY]. A theatre for children, 1958-1982: development, creative process, and principles
Columbus: Ohio State U. (PhD)     1983

**5257** GREMORE, CONSTANCE F. Characteristics of stage adaptations of works of children's literature
Minneapolis: U. of Minnesota (PhD)     1984

**5258** BEGER, LOIS L. John Donahue and the Children's Theatre Company and School of Minneapolis, 1961-1978
Tallahassee: Florida State U. (PhD)     1985

**5259** BELLVILLE, CHERYL W. Theater magic: behind the scenes at a children's theater
pp. 48     DL★
Minneapolis: Carolrhoda Books     1986

**5260** DRAKEFORD, VERE N. Play wishes manifested in children's theatre
NY: U. (PhD)     1986

**5261** WILLENBRINK, ROBERT H. Analysis of plays for young audiences: an approach
Bowling Green: State U. (PhD)     1986

**5262** HUBERMAN, CARYN & WETZEL, JO ANNE. Onstage/backstage
pp. 56     DL★
Minneapolis: Carolrhoda Books     1987
Children's theatre.

**5263** McCASLIN, NELLIE. Historical guide to children's theatre in America
xvii, 348; pl. 8     L
NY: Greenwood P.     1987
Foreword by Jed H. Davis.

**5264** BEDARD, ROGER L. & TOLCH, C. J. (Eds). Spotlight on the child. Studies in the history of American children's theatre
pp.ix, 203     L
Westport CT: Greenwood P.     1989
Jonathan Levy: *Dramatic dialogues of Charles Stearns*; Laura G. Salazar: *Theatre for young audiences in New York City, 1900-1910*; Roger L. Bedard: *Junior league children's theatre*; Ellen R. Rodman: *King-Coit school and children's theatre*; Noereena Abookiri & Jennifer S. McNair: *Children's theatre activities at Karamu House 1915-1975*; Roger L. Bedard: *Charlotte B. Chorpenning, playwright and teacher*; Doreen B. Heard: *Children's theatre in the Federal Theatre Project*; Charles E. Combs: *Winifred Ward*; Katherine Krzys: *Sara Spencer*; Joan V. Hicks: *Children's theatre company and school*; Rachel Fordyce: *Aurand Harris*.

**5265** SWORTZELL, LOWELL (Ed.). International guide to children's theatre and educational theatre: a historical and geographical source book
pp. li, 448; ill. in text, pl. 5     L
NY: Greenwood P.     1990
Nellie McCaslin contributes the section on the US (pp. 333-346).

## 12. THEATRE AND EDUCATION

### 12.3 CHAUTAUQUA AND LYCEUM

**5266** VINCENT, JOHN H. The Chautauqua movement
pp. ix, 308 DL★
Boston: Chautauqua P. 1886
With an introduction by President Lewis Miller.

**5267** VINCENT, JOHN R. Chautauqua: a popular university
pp. 13 DL★
[Plainfield NJ]: [For the author?] 1887
Reprinted from *Contemporary Review*, May, 1887.

**5268** ORCHARD, HUGH A. Fifty years of Chautauqua: its beginnings, its development, its message and its life
pp. 313; ill. DL★
Cedar Rapids IA: Torch P. 1923

**5269** HORNER, CHARLES F. The life of James Redpath and the development of the modern lyceum
pp. ix, 302; front., pl. 7 L
NY: Barse & Hopkins 1926

**5270** TOZIER, ROY B. A short life-history of the Chautauqua
Iowa City: U. of Iowa (PhD) 1932

**5271** BESTOR, ARTHUR E. Chautauqua publications: an historical and bibliographical guide
pp.iv, 67; front. O
Chautauqua NY: Chautauqua P. 1934

**5272** RICHMOND, REBECCA. Chautauqua in brief
pp. 46; ill. DL★
Yonkers NY: For the author 1934

**5273** MacLAREN, GAY. Morally we roll along
xii, 308; pl. 12 M
Boston: Little, Brown 1938
Experience as a travelling player in Chautauqua. Errata slip.

**5274** RICHMOND, REBECCA. Chautauqua summer
pp. 166; ill. DL★
NY: The Little Print 1938

**5275** SCOTT, MARION. Chautauqua caravan
pp. v, 310; front., pl. 15 L
NY: D. Appleton-Century 1939
Reminiscences of a performer.

**5276** RICHMOND, REBECCA. Chautauqua, an American place
pp. ix, 180; ill. DL
NY: Duell, Sloane & Pearce 1943
A history, with emphasis on the original Chautauqua.

**5277** CASE, VICTORIA & CASE, ROBERT O. We called it culture: the story of Chautauqua
pp.x, 272 DL★
Garden City NY: Doubleday 1948

**5278** PHILLIPS, HAZEL. The Chautauqua in American life
Evanston: Northwestern U. (MA) 1948

**5279** GRAHAM, DONALD L. Circuit Chautauqua, a middle western institution
Iowa City: U. of Iowa (PhD) 1953

**5280** MARTIN, ROBERT C. The early lyceum, 1826-1845
Evanston: Northwestern U.(PhD) 1953

**5281** HORNER, CHARLES F. Strike the tents: the story of the Chautauqua
pp.204 DL★
Philadelphia: Dorrance 1954

**5282** SMOOT, JAMES S. Platform theater. Theatrical elements of the Lyceum-Chautauqua
Ann Arbor: U. of Michigan (PhD) 1954

**5283** BODE, CARL. The American lyceum, town meeting of the mind
pp.xiii, 275; ill. in text O
NY: Oxford U. P. 1956
A history.

**5284** HADLEY, DOROTHY S. Oral interpretation at the Chautauqua institution and the Chautauqua school of expression, 1874-1900
Evanston: Northwestern U. (PhD) 1956

**5285** HARRISON, HARRY P. & DETZER, KARL. Culture under canvas: the story of tent Chautauqua
pp.xxviii, 287; ill. in text, pl. 8 L
NY: Hastings House 1958
Period 1904-1932. Author was manager of Redpath Chautauqua.

**5286** REYNOLDS, NYDIA J. A historical study of the oral interpretation activities of the circuit Chautauqua, 1904-1932
Los Angeles: U. of Southern California (PhD) 1960

**5287** GOULD, JOSEPH E. The Chautauqua movement: an episode in the continuing American revolution
pp.xiv, 108, pl. 8 L
NY: State U. P. 1961
A history, 1874-1932, emphasizing the educational aspects of the movement.

**5288** EUBANKS, MARJORIE H. The Redpath Lyceum bureau from 1868 to 1901
Ann Arbor: U. of Michigan (PhD) 1968

**5289** JENSON, JOHN R. A history of Lakeside, Ohio, with particular emphasis on the Chautauqua activities as they existed within the religious, cultural, and health framework there
Bowling Green OH: State U. (PhD) 1970

**5290** MORRISON, THEODORE. Chautauqua: a center for education, religion, and the arts in America
pp.viii, 351; ill. in text L
Chicago: U. P. 1974
History of the first 100 years.

**5291** FRANCK, TIMOTHY D. An historical descriptive study of Rutherford Birchard Hayes and the Chautauqua
Bowling Green: State U. (PhD) 1975

**5292** HANSCOM, WARREN D. Pioneers in greasepaint
pp. vi, 115; pl. 37 M
Bradenton FL: Collins 1975

Reminiscences of Chautauqua.

**5293** HEDGES, R. ALAN. Actors under canvas: a study of the theatre of the circuit Chautauqua, 1910-1933
Columbus: Ohio State U. (PhD) 1976

**5294** TAPIA, J. E. Circuit Chautauqua's promotional visions: a study of program brochures, circa 1904 to 1932
Tucson: U. of Arizona (PhD) 1978

**5295** MANDERSON, M. SANDRA. The Redpath Bureau, an American critic: decision making and programming methods for circuit Chautauquas, circa 1912 to 1920
Iowa City: U. of Iowa (PhD) 1981

**5296** SELF, LOIS S. Agrarian Chautauqua: the lecture system of the Southern Farmers Alliance movement
Madison: U. of Wisconsin (PhD) 1981

## 12.4 SPECIAL FORMS AND THERAPY

**5297** FRIEDMAN, ARTHUR B. A descriptive study of the American Educational Theater Association – veterans administration program for neuropsychiatric patients of the Veterans Hospital, Los Angeles, California, 1950-1953
Los Angeles: U. of Southern California (PhD) 1955

**5298** DODD, DOROTHY V. Children's theatre for the deaf: a guide to production
NY: U. (PhD) 1970

**5299** POWERS, HELEN. Signs of silence. Bernard Bragg and the National Theatre of the Deaf
pp. xiv, 176; ill.    DL★
NY: Dodd, Mead 1972

**5300** GRAY, PAULA G. Dramatics for the elderly: a guide for residential care settings and senior centers
pp. 59    DL★
NY: Teachers College P. 1974

**5301** MONAGHAN, THERESE A. Releasing playfulness in the adult through creative drama
NY: Columbia U. Teachers' College (EdD) 1976

**5302** COFFMAN, VICTORIA M. Creative drama and the elderly: the use of reminiscence and role-playing with nursing home residents
Eugene: U. of Oregon (PhD) 1979

**5303** BATCHELOR, RONALD. Creative dramatics and theater arts among socially and emotionally handicapped inner-city adolescents: a description and analysis of a drama project
NY: Columbia U. Teachers' College (EdD) 1981

**5304** DEL VECCHIO, ANN. Modifying creative drama for senior adult participants: the theories and methods of selected practitioners
Minneapolis: U. of Minnesota (PhD) 1981

**5305** HART, STEVEN E. The family: a theatre company working with prison inmates and ex-inmates
NY: City U. (PhD) 1981

**5306** ZIF, YAEL L. Theater and therapy: an interpersonal study
Boston: U. School of Ed. (EdD) 1981

**5307** McGOVERN, CATHERINE B. Psychodrama: its theatrical origins
Vermillion: U. of South Dakota (EdD) 1983

**5308** GREENBLATT, FRED S. Drama with the elderly...
    DL★
Springfield IL: C. C. Thomas 1985

**5309** CURRY, RICHARD J. A practical philosophy of theatre education for the disabled
NY: U. (PhD) 1986

**5310** GAY, ELISABETH F. Gert Schattner's drama sessions for short-term in-patients. A videotape and report of the methods of a founder of drama therapy in the United States
NY: U. (PhD) 1986

**5311** ANDREWS, RUSALYN H. Deaf theatre performance: an Aristotelean approach
Carbondale: Southern Illinois U. (PhD) 1988

**5312** BLOOMQUIST, JANE McC. Directing and designing for physically disabled actors in educational theatre
Evanston: Northwestern U. (PhD) 1988

**5313** BALDWIN, STEPHEN C. A history of the National Theatre of the Deaf from 1959 to 1989
Austin: U. of Texas (PhD) 1989

## 12.5 THEATRE AS A CAREER

**5314** HUBERT, PHILIP G. The stage as a career: a sketch of the actor's life; its requirements, hardships, and rewards. The qualifications and training essential to success – expert opinions from famous actors...disappointments and pitfalls – the actor and society...how to begin – dramatic schools and teachers – contracts and salaries
pp. vii, 192    M
NY: G. P. Putnam's Sons 1900
'Famous actors' include Lawrence Barrett, Joseph Jefferson and Maggie Mitchell.

**5315** THE ALVIENE SCHOOLS, dramatic and expressive arts
pp. various    DL★
NY: P. of C. S. Nathan 1910-
Catalogues and brochures of the Alviene United Stage-training Schools, Inc. Examples seen from 1910, 1915, 1917, 1918. In 1918 the institution offered additionally *photoplay and expressive arts...* and *dance arts*

**5316** [HORNMANN, OTTO]. You can be an actor or actress: complete instructions how to begin in show business...also a list of the principal American theatres, their managers, agents, rules, regulations etc.
pp. 56; ill.    DL★
NY: Stage Supply Studio 1913

## 12. THEATRE AND EDUCATION

**5317** HORNBLOW, ARTHUR. Training for the stage: some hints for those about to choose the player's career...with a foreword by Mr David Belasco
pp. 193; pl. 8   M
Philadelphia: J. B. Lippincott   1916

**5318** FRAZER, FRED. The stage, radio and talkies, and how to get there
pp. 60; ill. in text   DL★
San Francisco: Korsmeier & Clark   1930

**5319** TRAUBE, SHEPARD. So you want to go into the theatre? A 'manual'
pp. xix, 258   MH
Boston: Little, Brown   1936
Foreword by Barrett H. Clark.

**5320** CAREERS in the theatre
pp.[24]; ill. in text   M
Chicago: Institute for Research   1939

**5321** CASS, CARL B. Occupational opportunities in the New York theatre
Madison: U. of Wisconsin (PhD)   1946

**5322** DENIS, PAUL. Your career in show business
pp. 240; ill.   DL★
NY: E. P. Dutton   1948

**5323** VREELAND, FRANK. Opportunities in acting, stage, screen, radio and television
pp. 128   DL★
NY: Vocational Guidance Manuals   1951

**5324** HARMON, CHARLOTTE. How to break into the theatre
pp. 127   DL★
NY: Dial P.   1961

**5325** SAVAN, BRUCE. Your career in the theatre
pp. 238   M
NY: Doubleday   1961
*Vade mecum* for theatre aspirants.

**5326** HIRSCHFELD, BURT. Stage struck. Your career in theatre
pp. 191; ill.   DL★
NY: J. Messner   1963

**5327** ORBEN, ROBERT. If you have to be a comic
pp. 57   DL★
NY: Orben Publications   1963

**5328** THE NEIGHBORHOOD PLAYHOUSE school of the theatre
p. 20; ill. in text   M
NY: [Neighborhood Playhouse]   [1968]

**5329** DALRYMPLE, JEAN. Careers and opportunities in the theatre
pp. 256; ill.   DL★
NY: E. P. Dutton   1969

**5330** JOELS, MERRILL E. How to get into show business
pp. 157; ill.   DL★
NY: Hastings House   1969
Second edition, revised. First published 1955 as *Acting is a business*.

**5331** ENGEL, LEHMAN. Getting started in the theater
pp.x, 228   M
NY: Collier Macmillan   1973

**5332** BABCOCK, DENNIS. Careers in the theater
pp. 36; ill.   DL★
Minneapolis: Lerner   1975

**5333** MOORE, DICK. Opportunities in acting careers
pp. 138; ill.   DL★
Louisville KY: Vocational Guidance Manuals   1975
First published 1963.

**5334** THE NATIONAL DIRECTORY for the performing arts; educational
pp. 821   DL★
Dallas TX: Handel   1975
A guide to major schools and other institutions offering a training in the performing arts.

**5335** MATSON, KATINKA. The working actor: a guide to the profession
pp. xii, 177   L
NY: Viking P.   1976

**5336** NAHAS, REBECCA. Your acting career: how to break into and survive in the theatre
pp. xi, 148; maps.   DL★
NY: Crown Publishers   1976

**5337** DEZSERAN, CATHERINE A. The development of the audition as a method of selecting actors for the professional theatre
Minneapolis: U. of Minnesota (PhD)   1977

**5338** WAACK, WILLIAM L. Careers and career education in the performing arts: an annotated bibliography
pp. iii, 57   DL★
[NY?]: The American Theatre Association   [1981?]

**5339** GREENBERG, JAN W. Theater careers: a comprehensive guide to non-acting careers in the theater
pp. 216   DL★
NY: Holt, Rinehart and Winston   1983

**5340** COHEN, ROBERT. Acting professionally: raw facts about careers in acting
pp.xiii, 122   L
NY: Barnes & Noble   1985
Third edition. First published NY, National P., 1972.

# B. DRAMA
## 13. GENERAL
### 13.1 PLAY LISTS

**5341** INDEX to American poetry and plays in the collection of C. Fiske Harris
pp. 171     MH
Providence RI: For the author     1874

4129 items listed under author, title, place of origin, date and size. 'Anything in the form of dialogue or of verse has been treated as a play or a poem.'

**5342** CATALOGUE of the dramas and dramatic poems contained in the Public Library...
pp. 192     MB
Cincinnati: Public Library     1879

**5343** BOSTON CATALOGUE of plays [drop title]
pp. various     MH
Boston: Walter H. Baker     [1900?]

Cover title: *Descriptive catalogue of plays and elocutionary works for public and private representation*. Regional distributors in Clyde [TX?] and Chicago issued editions with minor variations in content.

**5344** RODEN, ROBERT F. Later American plays 1831-1900; being a compilation of the titles of plays by American authors published and performed in America since 1831
pp.iii, 132     MH
NY: Dunlap Society     1900

A selection, rather than a complete record. 265 copies.

**5345** WEGELIN, OSCAR. Early American plays 1714-1830. Being a compilation of the titles of plays by American authors, published and performed in America previous to 1830...edited with an introduction by John Malone
pp.xxvii, 113     MH
NY: Dunlap Society     1900

265 copies. A second edition of 200 copies (pp.94) was issued in 1905.

**5346** THE CATALOGUE of the American Play Co. with original casts.
pp. v, 221 (8)     MH
NY: American Play Co.     1908

**5347** [HASKELL, DANIEL C.]. A list of American dramas in the New York Public Library
pp. 63     L
NY: Public Library     1916

Reprinted, with additions, from the *Bulletin* of October, 1915.

**5348** KAPLAN, SAMUEL (Ed.). Actable one-act plays
pp.15     L
Chicago: Public Library     1916

**5349** PARSONS, HENRY S. (Ed.). Dramatic compositions copyrighted in the United States, 1870 to 1916
pp.3546     M
Washington DC: Government Printing Office     1918

Two volumes. For later lists of copyright drama, see Henriette Mertz: *Copyright bibliography*, Library of Congress, 1950; also *Catalogue of copyright entries, third series, part 3-4: drama and works prepared for oral delivery*, vol. 1, no. 1, Jan/June 1947.

**5350** SHAY, FRANK (Ed.). One thousand and one plays for the little theatre
pp.94     DL★
Cincinnati: Stewart Kidd     1923

Revised and enlarged edition of *Plays and books of the little theatre*, 1910.

**5351** LOGASA, HANNAH & VER NOOY, WINIFRED (Eds). Index to one-act plays
pp.327     L
Boston: F. W. Faxon     1924

One-act plays written in or translated into English and published since 1900. Supplements issued in 1932, 1941, 1950 (with addition to title: *...for stage and radio*), 1958 (with addition to title: *...for stage, radio, and television*)

**5352** DRURY, FRANCIS K. View points in modern drama: an arrangement of plays according to their essential interest
pp. 119     DL★
Chicago: American Library Association     1925

**5353** SHAY, FRANK (Ed.). A guide to longer plays: a list of 1500 plays for little theatres, professional and stock companies, art theatres, schools, amateurs and readers
pp.131     DL★
NY: D. Appleton     1925

**5354** THE BOOKSHELF of Brander Matthews
pp. xii, 114     M
NY: Columbia U. P.     1931

A list of books presented by Matthews to Columbia University Library.

**5355** HILL, FRANK P. (Ed.). American plays printed 1714-1830: a bibliographical record
pp. xii, 152; pl. 2     M
NY: Stanford U. P.     1934

Corrigenda and addenda, by Roger E. Stoddard, in *Papers of the Bibliographical Society of America*, Vol. 65, 1971.

**5356** SMITH, MILTON. Guide to play selection: a descriptive index of full-length and short plays for production by schools, colleges and little theaters
pp.ix, 174; ill. in text     L
NY: D. Appleton-Century     1934

**5357** COE, KATHRYN C. & CORDELL, WILLIAM H. The Pulitzer Prize plays, 1918-1934
pp. xii, 856     L
NY: Random House     1935

Introduction by William L. Phelps. Prints the winning plays with the exception of *The Old Maid* (1934/5) by Zoe Atkins who refused permission to publish.

**5358** FIRKINS, INA T. (Ed.). Index to plays 1800-1926 [with] a supplement
pp.ix, 307; ix, 140     O
NY: H. W. Wilson     1935

The index was first published in 1927. The supplement was issued in 1935, and the two bound in a single volume. Lists available editions of plays by nineteenth and twentieth century authors, arranged under author, and under title and subject. See also *Play Index*.

**5359** HALLINE, ALAN G.   American plays, selected and edited with critical introductions and bibliographies
pp. vii, 787                                                                                L
NY: American Book                                                                 1935

Includes chronological tables. Material on Royall Tyler: *The Contrast*; William Dunlap: *Andre*; James K. Paulding: *The Bucktails*; J. N. Barker: *Superstition*; Robert Montgomery Bird: *The Gladiator*; N. P. Willis: *Bianca Visconti*; Anna Cora Mowatt: *Fashion*; George Henry Boker: *Francesca da Rimini*; Augustin Daly: *Horizon*; Joaquin Miller: *The Danites in the Sierras*; Bronson Howard: *The Henrietta*; Langdon Mitchell: *The New York Idea*; Philip Moeller: *Madame Sand*; Philip Barry: *You and I*; Owen Davis: *Icebound*; Eugene O'Neill: *The Great God Brown*; Paul Green: *The Field God*.

**5360** CARMICHAEL, HERBERT K.   The best representative short plays in the United States, 1900-1940
Minneapolis: U. of Minnesota (PhD)                                   1943

**5361** SHERMAN, ROBERT L.   Drama cyclopedia: a bibliography of plays and players
pp.i, 612; portrait on title                                                         MH
Chicago: For the author                                                         1944

An attempt, not wholly successful, to record every full-length play and opera in English produced professionally in the US between 1750 and 1944, giving author, title, city and year of first performance, together with some cast details. Undocumented. Also a brief history of the American theatre until the nineteenth century.

**5362** EARLY AMERICAN drama: from the Herbert C. Ely memorial collection...Dec 31, 1947
pp. 4                                                                                        L
Ann Arbor: U. William L. Clements Library                          1947

Library bulletin 51, comprising a list of playtexts.

**5363** IRELAND, NORMA O.   An index to monologs and dialogs
pp. xxiii, 127                                                                           MH
Boston: F. W. Faxon                                                              1949

Revised and enlarged. First published 1939 under the joint editorship of Norma and David Ireland. A supplement (pp.160) was issued in 1959.

**5364** CHORBA, ALBERT VON (Ed.).   Check list of American drama published in the English colonies of North America and the United States through 1865 in the possession of the library, with an introduction by Arthur H. Quinn
ll. x, 92                                                                                     MH
Philadelphia: U. of Pennsylvania Library                             1951

592 items, including variant editions, listed by author with chronologically arranged index.

**5365** PLAY INDEX
pp.various                                                                            DL★
NY: H. W. Wilson                                                                1953-

Started with Ina T. Firkins: *Index to plays...* (q.v.). 1949-1952, edited by Dorothy H. West & Dorothy M. Peake; 1953-1960, edited by E. A. Fidell and Dorothy M. Peake; 1961-67; 1968-1972; 1973-77; 1978-1982, edited by Juliette Yaakov; 1983-87. Continuing.

**5366** GAVER, JACK (Ed.).   Critics choice: New York Drama Critics' Circle prize plays 1935-55
pp. 661                                                                                    L
NY: Hawthorn Books                                                          1955

Sixteen texts, each preceded by a context-setting and briefly descriptive introduction. A 14 page foreword provides an account of the formation and development of the Critics' Circle.

**5367** IRELAND, NORMA O.   An index to skits and stunts
pp. xxix, 348                                                                          MH
Boston: F. W. Faxon                                                              1958

Single titles grouped thematically. Collections under author, title and subject.

**5368** LOVELL, JOHN (Ed.).   Digests of great American plays: complete summaries of more than 100 plays from the beginning to the present
pp.452                                                                                   DL★
NY: Crowell                                                                         1961

**5369** BERGQUIST, G. WILLIAM.   Three centuries of English and American plays: a check list. England:1500-1850, United States:1714-1830
pp.xii, 281; ill. in text                                                              M
NY: Hafner                                                                            1963

Compiled to serve as an index to the Readex Microprint edition of collected plays. Lists approx. 5500 titles. Reviewed with corrections in *RECTR*, vol.3, May 1964.

**5370** [BIEBER, ALBERT A].   The Albert A. Bieber collection of American plays, poetry and songsters
pp.v, 103; pl. 6                                                                        O
NY: Cooper Square                                                              1963

**5371** 1765-1964 TWO HUNDRED YEARS of American plays. An exhibition arranged to celebrate the bicentennial of the publication of Thomas Godfrey's *The Prince of Parthia*
pp.[51]                                                                                    M
Providence RI: Brown U. P.                                                  1965

**5372** IRELAND, NORMA O.   Index to full-length plays 1944 to 1964
pp. xxxii, 296                                                                          L
Boston: F. W. Faxon                                                              1965

A continuation of Ruth G. Thomson: *Index...1926-1944* (1946). Selected coverage of plays published in English.

**5373** MOODY, RICHARD.   Dramas from the American theatre, 1762-1909
pp.xv, 873; pl. 10                                                                   MH
Cleveland OH: World Publishing                                        1966

27 examples of early drama, each with a useful introduction.

**5374** TOOHEY, JOHN L.   A history of the Pulitzer Prize plays
pp.viii, 344; ill. in text                                                              L
NY: Citadel P.                                                                       1967

1916-1967. Each play described, with illustrations of production, and a summary of critical response.

**5375** CHICOREL, MARIETTA (Ed.).   Chicorel theatre index to plays, in anthologies, periodicals, discs and tapes
pp. xv, 573; xv, 502; xiii, 466                                                    L
NY: Chicorel Library                                                          1970-72

Three volumes.

**5376** HATCH, JAMES V.   Black image on the American stage: a bibliography of plays and musicals, 1770-1970
pp.xiii, 162                                                                               L
NY: Drama Book Specialists                                               1970

Criteria for entry: 1. at least one black character; 2. black authorship; 3. black theme; 4. written or produced in America.

**5377** PATTERSON, CHARLOTTE A. (Ed.). Plays in periodicals: an index to English language scripts in twentieth century journals
pp.xi, 24     L
Boston: G. K. Hall     1970

4000 plays from 97 periodicals, 1900-1968, cross-indexed by title, author, cast analysis, and periodical. Errata slip.

**5378** BONIN, JANE F. Prize-winning American drama: a bibliographical and descriptive guide
pp.xii, 222     MH
Metuchen NJ: Scarecrow P.     1973

Each play summarized and given a brief critical and historical gloss. 1917-1971.

**5379** CHICOREL, MARIETTA (Ed.). Chicorel theatre index to plays in periodicals
pp. 500     L
NY: Chicorel Library     1973

Index Series, Vol. 8. Supplements previous volumes in this series.

**5380** DUBOIS, WILLIAM R. English and American stage productions: an annotated checklist of prompt books 1800-1900 from the Nisbet-Snyder Drama Collection, Northwestern University Libraries
pp.xiv, 524     M
Boston: G.K.Hall     1973

Prompt books is a misnomer. Few of the 2025 titles listed are in that category.

**5381** SAMPLES, GORDON. The drama scholar's index to plays and filmscripts. A guide to plays and filmscripts in selected anthologies, series and periodicals
pp.xii, 448; x, 695     L
Metuchen NJ: Scarecrow P.     1974

Two volumes, indexed. International in scope.

**5382** BONIN, JANE F. Major themes in prize-winning American drama
pp.xvii, 188     MB
Metuchen NJ: Scarecrow P.     1975

A listing, with brief analytical descriptions and commentary. Categories are: women and marriage; work and material rewards; war and physical violence; politics; religion. Preface by Paul T. Nolan.

**5383** STODDARD, ROGER E. A catalogue of the dramatic imprints of David and Thomas Longworth, 1802-1821
pp.ii, 317-398; ill. in text     M
Worcester MA: American Antiquarian Society     1975

Reprinted from the *AAS proceedings* October, 1974.

**5384** HATCH, JAMES V. & OMANII, ABDULLAH (Eds). Black playwrights,1823-1977: an annotated bibliography of plays
pp.xxi, 319     L
NY: R.R.Bowker     1977

**5385** HIXON, DON L. & HENNESSEE, DON A. Nineteenth-century American drama: a finding guide
pp. xi, 579     M
Metuchen NJ: Scarecrow P.     1977

Initially a finding guide to the Readex Corporation's microprint collection, *American plays 1831-1900*, here given wider publication.

**5386** ERHARD, THOMAS A. 900 American plays: a synopsis history of American drama
pp.xxii, 106     ★
NY: Richards Rosen P.     1978

**5387** SALEM, JAMES M. Drury's guide to best plays
pp.v, 421     L
Metuchen NJ: Scarecrow P.     1978

The third edition. International in scope. Dramatists listed alphabetically. Indexes include subject, cast analysis, prize plays, recommended plays under various categories. Started as Francis K. Drury: *Some of the best dramas*, NY: 1917 (pp.24). A fourth edition was published in 1987 (not seen).

**5388** KELLER, DEAN H. Index to plays in periodicals
pp.824     DL★
Metuchen NJ: Scarecrow P.     1979

Revised edition. First published 1971. A supplement, 1977-1987, was published in 1990 (not seen).

**5389** HELBING, TERRY (Ed.). Gay theatre alliance: directory of gay plays
pp. 122     MH
NY: John Hopkins P.     1980

Lists titles alphabetically with brief synopses. Two appendices: *Lost plays* and *Gay theatre companies*.

**5390** LEONARD, WILLIAM T. Theatre: stage to screen to television. Vol 1 A-L. [Vol 2 M-Z]
pp.vii, 1804     M
Metuchen NJ: Scarecrow P.     1981

Two volumes. Plays listed by title, with a synopsis of each and full credits, stage history in several countries, critical comments, and screen, ballet and TV adaptations.

**5391** HARRIS, RICHARD H. Modern drama in England and America, 1950-1970: a guide to information sources
pp.xii, 606     M
Detroit: Gale Research     1982

**5392** KING, KIMBALL. Ten modern American playwrights: an annotated bibliography
pp.xv, 251     L
NY: Garland P.     1982

Edward Albee, Imamu Amiri Baraka, Ed Bullins, Jack Gelber, Arthur Kopit, David Mamet, David Rabe, Sam Shepard, Neil Simon, Lanford Wilson.

**5393** LEONARD, WILLIAM T. Broadway bound: plays that died aborning
pp.x, 618     M
Metuchen NJ: Scarecrow P.     1983

**5394** MALPEDE, KAREN. Women in theatre: compassion and hope.
pp.xviii; pl. 1     MH
NY: Drama Book Publishers     1983

Texts, with introductions, and a final section on feminist plays and performances. Writers are: Eva Le Gallienne, Angna Enters, Emma Goldman, Susan Glaspell, Lorraine Hansberry, Hallie Flanagan, Judith Malina, Barbara Ann Teer.

**5395** STODDARD, ROGER E. United States dramatic copyrights, 1790-1830: a provisional catalogue
pp.231-254     M
[Cambridge MA]: [Goethe Institute of
Boston/Houghton Library]     [1983]

Offprint from *Essays in honor of James Edward Walsh*.

**5396** ENSER, A. G. Filmed books and plays: a list of books and plays from which films have been made, 1928-83
pp. xiii, 705      O
Aldershot UK: Gower      1985
Revised edition. First published London: Deutsch, 1968.

**5397** LEONARD, WILLIAM T. Once was enough
pp.xvii, 282      L
Metuchen NJ: Scarecrow P.      1986

A detailed listing of plays that folded after a single performance, with synopses and reviews.

**5398** CONNOR, BILLY M. & MOCHEDLOVER, HELENE G. Index to plays in collections: an author and title index to plays appearing in collections published between 1900 and 1985
pp. xi, 564      L
Metuchen NJ: Scarecrow P.      1988
Seventh edition, revised and enlarged, of John H. Ottemiller's *Index to plays in collections...*

## 13.2 PLAYWRITING AND PUBLISHING

**5399** HILLHOUSE, JAMES A. An oration pronounced at New-Haven before the Phi Beta Kappa, September 12, 1826 on some of the considerations which should influence an epic or a tragic writer, in the choice of an era
pp. 32      L
New-Haven: A. H. Maltby      1826

**5400** HENNEQUIN, ALFRED. The art of playwriting: being a practical treatise on the elements of dramatic construction intended for the playwright, the student, and the dramatic critic
pp.xxiii, 187      M
Boston: Houghton Mifflin      1890

**5401** PRICE, WILLIAM T. The technique of the drama
pp.vii, 287      MH
NY: Brentano's      1892
'To state such obvious and accepted principles as underlie the drama...'

**5402** PRICE, WILLIAM T. The analysis of play construction by W. T. Price, author of *The technique of the drama*
pp.vi, 415 (3)      MB
NY: W. T. Price      1908

**5403** MATTHEWS, BRANDER. A study of the drama
pp.x, 320; pl. 10      M
Boston: Houghton Mifflin      1910
A study of dramatic technique.

**5404** MARBLE, THOMAS L. How to appreciate the drama: an elementary treatise on dramatic art
pp.285; front.      DL★
NY: Hinds, Noble & Eldredge      1914
Substantially, analysis of play construction.

**5405** ANDREWS, CHARLTON. The technique of playwriting
pp.xxix, 269      DL★
Springfield MA: Home Correspondence School      1915

**5406** CANNON, FANNY. Writing and selling a play: practical suggestions for the beginner
pp.vi, 321; diagrams      DL★
NY: Henry Holt      1915

**5407** HAMILTON, CLAYTON. Problems of the playwright
pp. xv, 339      M
London: Allen & Unwin      1917

**5408** BAKER, GEORGE P. Dramatic technique
pp. vii, 531      M
Boston: Houghton Mifflin      1919

Play construction. Developed from course notes for lectures delivered before the Lowell Institute in 1913 and intended for the novice playwright.

**5409** CANNON, FANNY. Do's and don'ts for the playwright: a manual for the writer of plays for amateurs
pp.65      DL★
Chicago: T. S. Denison      [1922]

**5410** MALEVINSKY, MOSES L. The science of playwriting...with an introduction by Ossie Davis
pp.xi, 356; folding chart      M
NY: Brentano's      1925

**5411** WALTER, EUGENE. How to write a play: a practical handbook for students
pp.[361]      DL★
NY: Eugene Walter Corporation      1925

**5412** SWAN, MARK E. How you can write plays
pp.v, 254      L
NY: Samuel French      1927

**5413** THE ART OF PLAYWRITING: lectures delivered at the University of Pennsylvania on the Mask and Wig Foundation
pp. 134      L
Philadelphia: U. of Pennsylvania P.      1928
Jesse Lynch Williams: *Writing and playwriting*; Langdon Mitchell: *Substance and art in the drama*; Lord Dunsany: *The carving of the ivory*; Gilbert Emery: *A play is presented*; Rachel Crothers: *The construction of a play*. Foreword by Arthur H. Quinn

**5414** KROWS, ARTHUR E. Playwriting for profit...illustrated with 20 workshop pages provided...by well known dramatists and producers
pp.xix, 549; ill. in text      M
NY: Longmans, Green      1928

**5415** DREW, ELIZABETH A. Discovering drama
pp. 252      M
London: Cape      1937
First published NY: W. W. Norton. A plea for the acknowledgment of the dramatic text as an essential element in theatre.

**5416** MERSAND, JOSEPH. When ladies write plays: an evaluation of their contribution to the American drama
pp.25      DL★
NY: Modern Chapbooks      1937

**5417** KOZLENKO, WILLIAM (Ed.). The one-act play today: a discussion of the technique, scope and history of the contemporary short drama
pp.vii, 324      M
NY: Harcourt, Brace      1938

Contributors include Glenn Hughes, Barrett H. Clark, John Gassner.

**5418** HOWARD, LOUIS & CRISWELL, JERON. How your play can crash Broadway: the authoritative handbook for a successful playwriting career: the 36 authentic plots streamlined for your convenience
pp.134; pl. 4 MH
NY: Howard and Criswell 1939
Introduction by Barrett H. Clark.

**5419** ROWE, KENNETH T. Write that play
pp.418; diagrams DL★
NY: Funk & Wagnalls 1939

**5420** KRAMER, SIDNEY. A history of Stone & Kimball and Herbert S. Stone and Co with a bibliography of their publications
pp.xxii, 379; ill. DL★
Chicago: Norman W. Forgue 1940

**5421** POLTI, GEORG. The thirty-six dramatic situations. Translated by Lucille Ray
pp.181 M
Boston: The Writer 1940
One of a series of US editions, from 1916, of the French classic (Paris: *Mercure de Framce*, 1895), the playwright's guide to the 36 plots into which all plays are said to fit.

**5422** CENTENO, AUGUSTO (Ed.). Intent of the artist
pp.v, 162; pl. 4 O
Princeton: U. P. 1941
Symposium. Includes Thornton Wilder: *Some thoughts on playwriting*.

**5423** SHAFTEL, GEORGE A. Dynamics of drama: fundamentals of writing craftsmanship
pp.287 DL★
St Louis MO: Comfort P. 1942
The second edition, revised. First published 1941.

**5424** SHULL, LEO. Playwriting for Broadway
pp.xi, 122 DL★
Tuckahoe NY: Gramatan Publishing 1945

**5425** SELDEN, SAMUEL. An introduction to playwriting
pp.vi, 120 MH
NY: F. S. Crofts 1946

**5426** FINCH, ROBERT. How to write a play
pp.xiii, 172 DL★
NY: Greenberg 1948
Advice on construction and marketing.

**5427** HOARE, JOHN E. The psychology of playwriting: audience, writer, play
pp.xv, 211 DL★
NY: Dramatists Play Service 1949

**5428** RAPHAELSON, SAMSON. The human nature of playwriting
pp.ix, 267 MH
NY: Macmillan 1949
Record of a playwriting class at the University of Illinois, 1948.

**5429** EGRI, LAJOS. Art of dramatic writing: its basis in the creative interpretation of human motives. With an introduction by Gilbert Miller
pp.xxii, 294 M
London: Pitman 1950

A revised and updated version of the author's *How to write a play...*, NY: Simon & Schuster, 1942.

**5430** GALLAWAY, MARIAN. Constructing a play...with a foreword by Tennessee Williams
pp.xxi, 380 MH
NY: Prentice-Hall 1950
A cautiously supportive introduction by Williams.

**5431** HOGAN, ROBERT. The influence of the well-made play upon American playwriting
Cleveland OH: Case Western Reserve U. (PhD) 1950

**5432** MacGOWAN, KENNETH. A primer of playwriting
pp.ix, 210 M
NY: Random House 1951
Examples from and reference to contemporary dramatists including Eugene O'Neill, Arthur Miller, Lillian Hellman.

**5433** TARG, WILLIAM. A reader for writers
pp.322 DL★
NY: Hermitage House 1951

**5434** VAN DRUTEN, JOHN. Playwright at work
pp.vii, 210; front. M
NY: Harper 1953
On the craftmanship of the playwright. The UK edition, London: Hamish Hamilton, 1953, has an added preface.

**5435** HALLAUER, JOHN W. Some problems of dramatization
Columbus: Ohio State U. (PhD) 1954

**5436** SCHEYER, BETTY. So you want to be a playwright: big headaches in the little theatre
pp. 61 DL★
NY: Exposition P. 1954

**5437** KERR, WALTER. How not to write a play
pp.viii, 244 M
London: Max Reinhardt 1956
An examination of the dwindling popularity of the NY theatre in the fifties, here attributed largely to the playwrights.

**5438** JASSPE, ARTHUR. Critical theory and playwriting practice of contemporary American playwrights. A study of the relationship of critical theory to playwriting practice as evidenced in the prize winning plays of contemporary playwrights during the years 1920 to 1940
NY: U. (PhD) 1958

**5439** HOHENBERG, JOHN (Ed.). The Pulitzer Prize story: news stories, editorials, cartoons, and pictures from the Pulitzer Prize Collection at Columbia University
pp.xxii, 375; front., ill. in text, pl. 8 L
NY: Columbia U. P. 1959
Lists drama awards, 1917-1958.

**5440** LAWSON, JOHN H. Theory and technique of playwriting
pp. 313 M
NY: Hill & Wang 1960

First published NY: G. P. Putnam, 1936. Here with a substantial introduction commenting on post WW2 theatre.

**5441** LORD, WILLIAM J. How authors make a living: an analysis of free-lance writers' incomes, 1953-1957
pp. xxii, 318 L
NY: Scarecrow P. 1962
Chapter V: *Playwrights*.

**5442** TINSLEY, JAMES R. A study of the techniques of modern American farce
Philadelphia: U. of Pennsylvania (PhD) 1962

**5443** BADER, A. L. (Ed.). To the young writer
pp. vii, 196 MESM
Ann Arbor: U. of Michigan P. 1964
Advice and encouragement for writers. Includes essays by Saul Bellow, Archibald MacLeish, Arthur Miller, John Gassner.

**5444** WEALES, GERALD C. A play and its parts
pp.165 DL*
NY: Basic Books 1964
Instruction in playwriting.

**5445** LITCHFIELD, HOPE P. & STODDARD, ROGER E. A. D. Ames, first dramatic publisher in the west. With a guide to the publications of A. D. Ames and Ames' Publishing Co. of Clyde, Ohio, 1870-1917
pp.[62]; pl. 3 MH
Providence RI: Brown U. P. 1966
Reprinted from *Books at Brown*, Vol XXI, 1966. Brief introduction, but substantially a printing of *Ames' Series of Standard and Minor Drama* catalogue, with details of other of his catalogues. Indexed.

**5446** HULL, RAYMOND. Profitable playwriting
pp. vi, 257 DL*
NY: Funk & Wagnalls 1969

**5447** LANGNER, LAWRENCE. The play's the thing
pp.258 M
NY: G. P. Putnam's Sons 1969
Informal analysis of play construction and classification with examples from the period 1920-1960. Derived in part from lectures on playwriting for theatre and TV delivered at Westport CT during 1958.

**5448** BURMAN, HOWARD V. A history and evaluation of the New Dramatists Committee
Columbus: Ohio State U. (PhD) 1970

**5449** KLINE, PETER. Playwriting
pp.186 DL*
NY: Richards Rosen P. 1970

**5450** FROST, WARREN L. Novel into play: an examination and illustration of techniques used in the adaptation of selected American novels for stage performance
Minneapolis: U. of Minnesota (PhD) 1971

**5451** SMILEY, SAM. Playwriting: the structure of action
pp.xiv, 315 DL*
Englewood Cliffs NJ: Prentice-Hall 1971

**5452** STODDARD, ROGER E. Notes on American play publishing, 1765-1865
pp.(ii), 161-190 M
Worcester MA: American Antiquarian Society 1971
Reprinted from the *Proceedings*, April, 1971.

**5453** MABLEY, EDWARD. Dramatic construction: an outline of basic principles...
pp.xiv, 430 M
Philadelphia: Chilton 1972

**5454** BURACK, A. S. (Ed.). Writer's handbook
pp. x, 819 O
Boston: Writer 1973
Includes essays on playwriting and marketing.

**5455** HUBENKA, LLOYD J. & GARCIA, R. The design of drama: an introduction
pp.x, 564 DL*
NY: McKay 1973

**5456** HOHENBERG, JOHN. The Pulitzer prizes: a history of the awards in books, drama, music, and journalism, based on the private files over six decades
pp.vii, 434; front. L
NY: Columbia U. P. 1974

**5457** GREBANIER, BERNARD. Playwriting: how to write for the theatre
pp.xiii, 386 *
NY: Harper & Row 1979

**5458** DRAMATIST'S BIBLE
*
Chicago: St James P. 1980-
Annual. Script needs and submission rules for theatres in US, UK and Canada.

**5459** EARLEY, MICHAEL. Information for playwrights
pp.99 *
NY: TCG 1980

**5460** DRAMATIST'S SOURCEBOOK
NY: TCG 1982-
Annual. Opportunities for playwrights, translators, composers, lyricists, librettists.

**5461** MASON, LOUISE C. The fight to be an American woman and a playwright: a critical history from 1773 to the present
Berkeley: U. of California (PhD) 1983

**5462** CATRON, LOUIS E. Writing, producing and selling your play: the complete guide for the beginning and advanced playwright
pp. xv, 272 DL*
Englewood Cliffs NJ: Prentice-Hall 1984

**5463** LAUREL, BRENDA K. Toward the design of a computer-based interactive fantasy system
Columbus: Ohio State U. (PhD) 1986
Includes possible use in playwriting.

**5464** BANKS, CAROL P. Playwriting for different age levels
NY: U. (PhD) 1988

## 13.3 THEORY AND GENRES

**5465** NOT USED

**5466** WOODBRIDGE, ELISABETH. The drama: its law and its technique
pp.xvi, 181 MH
Boston: Lamson, Wolffe 1898

**5467** HUNT, ELIZABETH R. The play of today. Studies in play structure for the student and the theatre-goer
pp. 238 L
NY: Dodd, Mead 1924
Second edition, revised. First published 1913.

**5468** KAUCHER, DOROTHY J. Modern dramatic structure
pp.183 L
Columbia: U. of Missouri P. 1928
Includes a chapter on Eugene O'Neill.

**5469** CARPENTER, BRUCE. Way of the drama: a study of dramatic forms and moods
pp. xv, 263 L
NY: Prentice-Hall 1929
Basic analysis of *genres* precedes brief accounts of Theatre guilds, the little theatre movement, stage censorship and morality.

**5470** McDERMOTT, JOHN F. & TAFT, KENDALL B. (Eds). Sex in the arts: a symposium
pp.xviii, 328 L
NY: Harper & Brothers 1932
Includes an introductory essay by Floyd Dell; Elmer Rice: *Modern drama*; June E. Downey: *The arts of entertainment*.

**5471** ROSS, ROBERT T. Studies in the psychology of the theater
pp.125-190; diagrams in text M
Bloomington IN: Principia P. [1938]
Reprinted from the *Psychological Record* 1938, 2.

**5472** ANDERSON, MAXWELL. The essence of tragedy and other footnotes and papers
pp. vii, 53 M
Washington DC: Anderson House 1939

**5473** HAMILTON, CLAYTON. The theory of theatre and other principles of dramatic criticism. Consolidated edition including *The theory of theatre, Studies in stagecraft, Problems of the playwright, Seen on the stage*...with a foreword by Burns Mantle
pp. xviii, 481 M
NY: Henry Holt 1939
Abridged, omitting chapters 'whose pertinence appeared to have been diminished by the passage of the years.' The author originally described the works as 'a minor contribution to an instant need'; i.e. the critical addressing of the 'new' drama. The title piece was first published NY: Holt, 1910 (pp.v, 240).

**5474** DAWSON, MARY E. The idea of tragedy in modern American theatre
Iowa City: U.of Iowa (PhD) 1944

**5475** THOMPSON, ALAN R. The anatomy of drama
pp.xxv, 417 L
Berkeley: U. of California P. 1946
Second edition revised and with additional preface. First published 1942.

**5476** BENTLEY, ERIC. The modern theatre: a study of the dramatists and the drama
pp. xxv, 290 M
London: Robert Hale 1948
First published NY: Reynal & Hitchcock, 1946 as *The playwright as thinker*. The UK edition has an additional foreword explaining the change of title and declaring the work 'a general discussion of drama since about 1800...'

**5477** THOMPSON, ALAN R. The dry mock: a study of irony in drama
pp.ix, 278 L
Berkeley: U. of California P. 1948

**5478** COOK, ALBERT. The dark voyage and the golden mean: a philosophy of comedy
pp.188 DL★
Cambridge MA: Harvard U. P. 1949

**5479** FERGUSSON, FRANCIS. The idea of a theater: a study of ten plays. The art of drama in a changing perspective
pp. xiii, 240 M
Princeton: U. P. 1949
Plays are all drawn from the mainstream European tradition.

**5480** ROSENHEIM, RICHARD. The eternal drama: a comprehensive treatise of the syngenetic history of humanity, dramatics, and theatre
pp.xiii, 303; pl. 8 L
NY: Philosophical Library 1952
Chapter XVIII examines US drama and theatre.

**5481** MYERS, HENRY A. Tragedy: a view of life
pp.viii, 210 L
Ithaca NY: Cornell U. P. 1956
Tragedy seen as 'a form of art and as a pattern of moral values'. A philosophical inquiry. Exemplification includes reference to Eugene O'Neill

**5482** KNUTSON, WAYNE. A definition of modern tragedy
Denver: U. (PhD) 1957

**5483** McCOLLUM, WILLIAM G. Tragedy
pp.vi, 254 DL★
NY: Macmillan 1957

**5484** SHARPE, ROBERT B. Irony in the drama: an essay on impersonation, shock, and catharsis
pp.xv, 222 L
Chapel Hill: U. of North Carolina P. 1959
Chapters on modern trends make reference to US writers, particularly Eugene O'Neill, Arthur Miller and Tennessee Williams.

**5485** DUSENBURY, WINIFRED L. The theme of loneliness in modern American drama
pp. vi, 231 L
Gainsville: U. of Florida P. 1960
Widely allusive. Headings: personal failure; homelessness; unhappy family; failure of love affair; socio-economic forces; the South; the material v. the spiritual; the lonely hero.

**5486** LEVIN, RICHARD L. Tragedy: plays, theory and criticism
pp.217 DL★
NY: Harcourt, Brace & World 1960

**5487** RAPHAEL, D. D. The paradox of tragedy: the Mahlon Powell lectures, 19159
pp.112   L
London: Allen & Unwin   1960
First published Bloomington: Indiana U. P. A philosophical inquiry, 'why does tragedy please ?', together with an account of aspects of the philosophical drama.

**5488** SEDERHOLM, FREDERICK L. The development of theories of dramatic comedy in America through 1830
Ames: Iowa State U. (PhD)   1961

**5489** STEINER, GEORGE. The death of tragedy
pp.viii, 355, xii   L
London: Faber   1961
First published NY: Knopf, 1961. International in scope.

**5490** BARNET, SYLVAN; BERMAN, MORTON & BURTO, WILLIAM. Aspects of the drama: a handbook
pp. x, 270; front.   O
Boston: Little, Brown   1962
Collected essays examining basic issues, together with a dictionary of dramatic terms. Includes Arthur Miller: *Tragedy and the common man*; Mary McCarthy: *The American realist playwrights*.

**5491** BENSTON, ALICE N. Theatricality in contemporary drama
Atlanta: Emory U. (PhD)   1962

**5492** ABEL, LIONEL. Metatheatre: a new view of dramatic form
pp.xi, 146   M
NY: Hill and Wang   1963
Loosely linked essays, leading towrds a definition of 'metatheatre' as a projection of human consciousness, replacing classical and traditional versions and definitions of tragedy. A final section forms an appendix and questions the validity of 'absurd' as a term to define a form of contemporary drama.

**5493** JOHNSON, ALBERT. Drama: technique and philosophy
pp.282; ill.   DL★
Valley Forge: Judson P.   1963

**5494** CLARK, BARRETT H. [Ed.]. European theories of the drama with a supplement on the American drama. An anthology of dramatic theory and criticism from Aristotle to the present day, in a series of selected texts, with commentaries, biographies and bibliographies...newly revised by Henry Popkin
pp. xiv, 628   M
NY: Crown P.   1965
First published Cincinnati: Stewart & Kidd, 1918.

**5495** WEISSMAN, PHILIP. Creativity in the theatre: a psychoanalytic study
pp.xi, 275   MH
NY: Basic Books   1965
Historically arranged. The final section proposes and examines a crisis in creativity in the modern theatre.

**5496** BENTLEY, ERIC. The life of the drama
pp.x,371   M
London: Methuen   1966
Analyses aspects and genres of dramatic form.

**5497** GUTHKE, KARL S. Modern tragicomedy: an investigation into the nature of the genre
pp.xviii, 204   L
NY: Random House   1966

**5498** MENDELSOHN, HAROLD A. Mass entertainment
pp.203   DL★
New Haven CT: Yale U. P.   1966

**5499** ALTSHULER, THELMA & JANARO, RICHARD P. Responses to drama: an introduction to plays and movies
pp.xii, 351; ill.   DL★
Boston: Houghton Mifflin   1967

**5500** KERR, WALTER. Tragedy and comedy
pp.350   M
NY: Simon and Schuster   1967
A critical investigation into cause and effect.

**5501** BENTLEY, ERIC. The theatre of commitment and other essays on drama in our society
pp.xiv, 241   M
London: Methuen   1968
Includes *The American drama - 1944-1954* and *The pro and con of political theatre*.

**5502** BENTLEY, ERIC (Ed.). The theory of the modern stage: an introduction to modern theatre and drama
pp.493   M
London: Penguin   1968
An anthology, selected from outstanding theorists and practitioners.

**5503** JAMES, SIDNEY. Transactional analysis in drama criticism
New Orleans: Tulane U. (PhD)   1968

**5504** SAUNDERS, WALTER E. The English-speaking game-drama
Evanston: Northwestern U. (PhD)   1969

**5505** SELDEN, SAMUEL. Theatre double game
pp.xi, 123   L
Chapel Hill: U. of North Carolina P.   1969
An examination of the nature of the play and its audience.

**5506** SHANK, THEODORE. The art of dramatic art
pp.xiii, 206; ill. in text   M
Belmont CA: Dickenson   1969
A theory of drama as 'a single, unique fine art.' Foreword by Martin Esslin.

**5507** BARRY, JACKSON G. Dramatic structure: the shaping of experience
pp. x, 261   M
Berkeley: U. of California P.   1970
Towards a general theory of dramatic form from structural analysis.

**5508** BECKERMAN, BERNARD. Dynamics of drama: theory and method of analysis
pp.xii, 263, viii   L
NY: Alfred A. Knopf   1970

**5509** VAN LAAN, THOMAS F. The idiom of drama
pp. xiv, 374   M
Ithaca: Cornell U. P.   1970

## 13.3. THEORY AND GENRES

Schematic theory of dramatic structure.

**5510** SCHOLES, ROBERT & KLAUS, CARL H. Elements of drama
pp.vii, 78    M
NY: Oxford U. P.    1971
Introductory study of the drama in both a literary and a theatrical context. A recognition that the drama is written to be staged.

**5511** STATES, BERT O. Irony and drama: a poetics
pp.xix, 243    L
Ithaca NY: Cornell U.    1971
Examines the play as 'an embodiment of ironic tension' offering a complement to the traditional approach through *genre*.

**5512** SZELISKI, JOHN VON. Tragedy and fear: why modern tragic drama fails
pp.x, 257    MH
Chapel Hill: U. of North Carolina P.    1971
Makes particular reference to US drama.

**5513** WEILAND, RICHARD J. The changing concepts of dramatic action and their relationship to theatrical form
Minneapolis: U. of Minnesota (PhD)    1971

**5514** ANN-AYYA GAUDA, HENNUR H. Dramatic poetry, from medieval to modern times. A philosophic enquiry into the nature of poetic drama in England, Ireland, and the United States of America
pp.xiv, 406    L
Madras: Macmillan    1972
Includes chapters on US romantic period and on the twentieth century in which the author identifies US dramatists as 'progressives' or 'experimenters'.

**5515** BURNS, ELIZABETH. Theatricality: a study of convention in the theatre and in social life
pp. vii, 246    L
NY: Harper & Roe    1972
Sociological study, examing the notion that the stage provides an analogy with real life.

**5516** HARRISON, PAUL C. The drama of Nommo
pp. xxiv, 245    MH
NY: Grove P.    1972
An attempt to identify an African aesthetic within the American experience.

**5517** BEACHAM, RICHARD C. Theatre of fact: a study of plays dramatizing contemporaneous events
Madison: U. of Wisconsin (PhD)    1973

**5518** BERMEL, ALBERT. Contradictory characters: an interpretation of the modern theatre
pp. xiv, 298    L
NY: E. P. Dutton    1973
Includes *The poet as solipsist* and *The family as villain*, examining Eugene O'Neill's *Long Day's Journey into Night*; also material on LeRoi Jones's *Dutchman*.

**5519** BURNS, ELIZABETH & BURNS, TOM (Eds). Sociology of literature and drama...selected readings
pp. 506    O
Harmondsworth UK: Penguin    1973

**5520** SOMERS, JOHN W. The sources and aesthetics of modern drama
Colombia: U. of Missouri (PhD)    1973

**5521** DUKORE, BERNARD F. Dramatic theory and criticism: Greeks to Grotowski
pp.xv, 1003    L
NY: Holt, Rinehart & Winston    1974
Anthology, with section on nineteenth and twentieth century US drama.

**5522** VOGEL, DAN. The three masks of American tragedy
pp.xiv, 180    DL★
Baton Rouge: Louisiana State U. P.    1974

**5523** LINDENBERGER, HERBERT S. Historical drama: the relation of literature and reality
pp.xiv, 194    DL★
Chicago: U. P.    1975

**5524** LYMAN, STANFORD M. & SCOTT, MARVIN B. The drama of social reality
pp.xi, 180    L
NY: Oxford U. P.    1975
Sociopsychological concepts of 'dramatism' derived from an examination of a group of Shakespeare's plays, formalized and particularized in a series of studies.

**5525** McCLOUD, GEORGE E. Plot as a staging determinant for Chamber theatre
Ann Arbor: U. of Michigan (PhD)    1975

**5526** PARTIN, BRUCE L. The horror play: its transition from the epic to the dramatic mode
Columbus: Ohio State U. (PhD)    1976

**5527** SCHECHNER, RICHARD & SCHUMAN, MADY (Eds). Ritual, play and performance
pp.xviii, 230    DL★
NY: Seabury P.    1976
J. V. Lawick-Goodall: *The rain-dance play*; J. Huizinga: *Nature and significance of play as a cultural phenomenon*; G. A. Bateson: *A theory of play and fantasy*; C. Levi-Strauss: *The science of the concrete - ritual and performance in everyday life*; E. Goffman: *Performances*; J. Grotowski: *The theatre's new testament*; Richard Schechner: *From ritual to theater and back*.

**5528** GOETSCH, PAUL. Bauformen des modernen englischen und amerikanischen Dramas
pp. ix, 231    L
Darmstadt: Wissenschaftliche Buchgsellschaft    1977
An analysis of conventions of speech, space and time in the different *genres* of drama.

**5529** RAJNATH (Ed.). Twentieth century American criticism: interdisciplinary approaches
pp.xv, 302    L
New Delhi: Arnold-Heinemann    1977
Includes Narindar S. Pradhan: *Modern American theories of drama and sociological thought*; Rupin Desai: *Approaches to Shakespeare in twentieth century America*.

**5530** DUMAIS, ALFRED. An analysis of the dramaturgical use of history in the writing of two full length plays about Mary Todd Lincoln
NY: U. (PhD)    1978

**5531** ROLAND, ALAN (Ed.). Psychoanalysis, creativity, and literature: a French-American inquiry
pp.ix, 368    L
NY: Columbia U. P.    1978

Includes a reprint of Margaret Brenman-Gibson: *The creation of plays: with a specimen analysis* which makes substantial reference to Clifford Odets's *Rocket to the Moon*.

**5532** GALYEAN, JOHN G. An approach to playscript interpretation based on the poetic theories of John Crowe Ransom
Bowling Green: State U. (PhD)     1979

**5533** BERNSTEIN, SAMUEL J. The strands entwined: a new direction in American drama
pp. xv, 171     O
Boston: Northeastern U. P.     1980
An overview and a summary. Material on David Rabe, John Guare, Ed Bullins, Robert Anderson and Edward Albee.

**5534** GEORGE, KATHLEEN. Rhythm in drama
pp. xi, 194     L
Pittsburgh: U. P.     1980
An examination of the effect on emotion and perception of structural rhythms.

**5535** GUTTING, JOHN G. Toward a structuralist poetic of the drama
Columbus: Ohio State U. (PhD)     1980

**5536** TURNER, DENNIS G. A demonstration of changing theatrical genre to communicate an intensification of the original theme
San Diego: United States International U. (PhD)     1980

**5537** ZINDER, DAVID G. The surrealist connection: an approach to a surrealist aesthetic of theatre
pp.vii, 163     L
Ann Arbor: UMI Research P.     1980

**5538** BERLIN, NORMAND. The secret cause: a discussion of tragedy
pp. xi, 189     L
Amherst: U. of Massachusetts P.     1981
Includes a critical examination of Arthur Miller: *Death of a Salesman* and Eugene O'Neill: *Desire Under the Elms*.

**5539** BROWNSTEIN, OSCAR L. & DAUBERT, DARLENE M. Analytical sourcebook of concepts in dramatic theory
pp. xxi, 560     O
Westport CT: Greenwood P.     1981
Arranged as a dictionary of key words from *action* to *wonder*, with related sources presented chronologically.

**5540** GANZ, ARTHUR. Realms of the self. Variations on a theme in modern drama
pp. zvi, 240     L
NY: U. P.     1981
Chapter three includes material on Tennessee Williams and Arthur Miller.

**5541** HATLEN, THEODORE. Orientation to the theater
pp. xv, 361; ill. in text     M
Englewood Cliffs NJ: Prentice-Hall     1981
Third edition. First published NY: Appleton-Century-Crofts, 1962. Study of dramatic and theatrical structure, their techniques and forms, intended for college students. Fourth edition, 1989 (not seen).

**5542** KAGAN-MOORE, PATRICK. The world of the play: a method of playscript analysis
Columbus: Ohio State U. (PhD)     1982

**5543** NICHOLSON. DAVID B. The fairy-tale in modern drama
NY: City U. (PhD)     1982

**5544** TURNER, VICTOR. Celebration: studies in festivity and ritual
pp.320; ill.     DL★
Washington DC: Smithsonian Institute P.     1982

**5545** TURNER, VICTOR. From ritual to theatre: the human seriousness of play
pp.127     ★
NY: PAJ Publications     1982

**5546** WILCOX, ROBERT H. The poetry of realistic drama
Madison: U. of Wisconsin (PhD)     1982
Emphasis on US drama.

**5547** WILSHIRE, BRUCE. Role playing and identity: the limits of theatre as metaphor
pp.xvii, 301     L
Bloomington: Indiana U. P.     1982

**5548** ARAI, ANUAR M. The journeying souls: the verbal and visual quest in metaphysical theatre and film
Los Angeles: U. of Southern California (PhD)     1983

**5549** KAMERMAN, JACK B. & MARTORELLA, ROSEANNE et al. Performers and performances: the social organization of artistic work
pp. xiv, 303: ill. in text     L
NY: Praeger     1983
Introduction by Joseph Bensman: *The phenomenology and sociology of the performing arts*. Includes Karen Gaylord: *Theatrical performances: structure and process, tradition and revolt*.

**5550** STEVENSON, MARK P. Moral and social schizophrenia: a view of the bourgeoisie in naturalistic drama
Pittsburgh: U. (PhD)     1983

**5551** ABEL, SAMUEL D. Susanne Langer and the rhythm of dramatic action
Bloomington: Indiana U. (PhD)     1984

**5552** CARLSON, MARVIN. Theories of the theatre: a historical and critical survey, from the Greeks to the present
pp. 529     M
Ithaca: Cornell U. P.     1984
Concluding chapters on the twentieth century include reference to US theorists and practitioners.

**5553** MACALOON, JOHN J. (Ed.). Rite, drama, festival, spectacle: rehearsals towards a theory of cultural performances
    DL★
Philadelphia: Institute for the Study of Human Issues     1984

**5554** ZACHARY, SAMUEL J. An analysis of deaf issues and their social setting as dramatized by representative playscripts
Bowling Green: State U. (PhD)     1984

**5555** CARTER, KATHRYN E. A phenomenology of feminist theatre and criticism
Carbondale: Southern Illinois U. (PhD)     1985

**5556** LEVINE, IRA A. Left-wing dramatic theory in the American theatre
pp.xvi, 233; ill. in text  L
Ann Arbor MI: UMI Research P.  1985

**5557** ROD, DAVID K. Kenneth Burke and Susanne Langer: dramatic theorists
Lawrence: U. of Kansas (PhD)  1985

**5558** SCHECHNER, RICHARD. Between theater and anthropology
pp.xiv, 342  DL★
Philadelphia: U. of Pennsylvania P.  1985

**5559** SCHECHTER, JOEL. Durov's pig: clowns, politics and theatre
 DL★
NY: Theatre Communications Group  1985

**5560** STATES, BERT O. Great reckonings in little rooms. On the phenomenology of the theater
pp.xi, 213  L
Berkeley: California U. P.  1985

**5561** TAYLOR, ROGAN P. The death and resurrection show
pp.224; ill. in text  M
London: Anthony Blond  1985
Popular entertainment examined in a framework of religio-mystical experience.

**5562** WILSON, GLENN. The psychology of the performing arts
pp.viii, 180  L
London: Croom Helm  1985

**5563** ADAMS, HAZARD & SEARLE, LEROY. Critical theory since 1965
pp.x, 891  DL★
Tallahassee: U. P. of Florida  1986

**5564** GRUBER, WILLIAM E. Comic theaters: studies in performance and audience response
pp. ix, 198  L
Athens: U. of Georgia P.  1986
'A sequence of essays with a common theme', emphasizing reaction to the comic figur (sic).

**5565** HORNBY, RICHARD. Drama, metadrama, and perception
pp.189  DL★
Lewisburg PA: Bucknell U. P.  1986

**5566** McKENNA, SUZANNE. 'Getting out': the impact of female consciousness on dramaturgy
Salt Lake City: U. of Utah (PhD)  1986

**5566A** MURRAY, JOEL K. Deconstructive playscript interpretation: a creative and critical analysis
Bowling Green: State U. (PhD)  1986

**5567** TURNER, VICTOR. The anthropology of performance.
pp.185; ill. in text  M
NY: Performing Arts Journal  1986
A study of the social function of spectacle and ritual, and other examinations of the interplay of event, spectacle, audience and culture. Foreword by Richard Schechner.

**5568** BENTLEY, ERIC. Thinking about the playwright: comments from four decades
pp. x, 364  M
Evanston IL: Northwestern U. P.  1987
Repeats virtually no material from his work in print in 1987. Complements, and advances from, *The Playwright as Thinker* (1946).

**5569** BRUCH, DEBRA L. A method of affective analysis for the drama
Columbia: U. of Missouri (PhD)  1987

**5570** LEVIN, HARRY. Playboys and killjoys. An essay on the theory and practice of comedy
pp.ix, 214  L
NY: Oxford U. P.  1987

**5571** SZONDI, PETER. Theory of the modern drama. A critical edition, edited and translated by Michael Hays. Foreword by Jochen Schulte-Sasse
pp.xviii, 128  M
Cambridge: Polity P.  1987
First published Frankfurt: Suhrkamp, 1956 as *Theorie des modernen Dramas*. US edition, Minneapolis: U. of Minnesota P., 1987.

**5572** ABBOTT, ANTHONY. The vital lie: reality and illusion in modern drama
pp.272  DL★
Tuscaloosa: U. of Alabama P.  1988

**5573** PRESSIER, TERRA D. Transformative comedy: an emerging genre
Eugene: U. of Oregon (PhD)  1988

**5574** GARNER, STANTON B. The absent voice. Narrative comprehension in the theatre
 DL★
Urbana: U. of Illinois P.  1989

**5575** KASE-POLISINI, JUDITH (Ed.). Drama as a meaning-maker
pp.xiv, 247  L
Lanham MD: U. P. of America  1989
Papers from the fifth (of five) regional symposia on creative drama sponsored by ACTA, held at Rutger's University, August 14-16, 1986. The recurrent phrase 'ludic-lucid' suggests the overall semantic emphasis.

**5576** ALTER, JEAN. A sociosemiotic theory of theatre
pp.281  ★
Phildadelphia: Pennsylvania U. P.  1990

**5577** CARLSON, MARVIN. Theatre semiotics: signs of life
 DL★
Bloomington: Indiana U. P.  1990

**5578** CASE, SUE-ELLEN. Performing feminisms: feminist critical theory and theatre
pp.320  DL★
Baltimore: John Hopkins U. P.  1990

# 14. HISTORY

## 14.1 INTERNATIONAL

**5579** HALE, EDWARD E. Dramatists of today: Rostand, Hauptmann, Sudermann, Pinero, Phillips, Maeterlinck. Being an informal discussion of their significant work
pp.v, 284; pl. 7     M
NY: Henry Holt     1911
Sixth edition, revised and enlarged.

**5580** ANDREWS, CHARLTON. The drama today
pp.236     M
Philadelphia: J. B. Lippincott     1913
Chapter, 'the Americans', offers a survey from Thomas Godfrey to Edward Knoblauch.

**5581** HENDERSON, ARCHIBALD. The changing drama: contributions and tendencies
pp.xvi, 321     M
NY: Henry Holt     1914
Includes material on the Drama League of America.

**5582** HUNEKER, JAMES G. Iconoclasts: a book of dramatists
pp.vii, 430     M
NY: Charles Scribner     1917
European.

**5583** GOLDBERG, ISAAC. The drama of transition: native and exotic playcraft
pp.487     M
Cincinnati: Stewart Kidd     1922
An appraisal of post WW1 drama, with chapters on Yiddish drama, and US drama with particular reference to Eugene O'Neill and Susan Glaspell.

**5584** HENDERSON, ARCHIBALD. European dramatists
pp.vii, 479; pl. 8     M
NY: D. Appleton     1924
Enlarged edition. First published 1913. Survey, from Strindberg to Galsworthy.

**5585** MILLER, NELLIE B. Living drama: historical development and modern movements visualised. A drama of the drama
pp.xxi, 437     L
NY: Century     1924
A history of the drama in *quasi*-play form, organized into prologue, episode, act, etc. 'Act five' concerns the emergent American drama, introducing William Vaughn Moody, Augustus Thomas, Percy MacKaye, Eugene O'Neill, Susan Glaspell.

**5586** CLARK, BARRETT H. A study of the modern drama: a handbook for the study and appreciation of the best plays, European, English, and American, of the last half century
pp.xi, 527     M
NY: D. Appleton     1925
Section on US drama considers work by Bronson Howard, Augustus Thomas, Clyde Fitch, Percy MacKaye, Eugene Walter, Edward Sheldon, George M. Cohan, Booth Tarkington, Eugene O'Neill.

**5587** CLARK, BARRETT H. The modern drama
pp.26     DL*
Chicago: American Library Association     1927

**5588** KRAFT, IRMA. Plays, players, playhouses: international drama of today...with forewords by Eva Le Gallienne and George Arliss
pp.xix, 263; ill. in text, front., pl. 15     M
NY: George Dobsevage     1928
Survey of European and US drama. Includes material on the Provincetown Playhouse, negro drama, the American Laboratory Theatre, civic repertory theatre.

**5589** STUART, DONALD C. Development of dramatic art
pp.x, 679     M
NY: Appleton     1928

**5590** EATON, WALTER P. The drama in English
pp.xv, 365     O
NY: Charles Scribner's Sons     1930
International. US material includes post Civil War drama, David Belasco, Clyde Fitch, William Vaughn Moody, Paul Green, Eugene O'Neill.

**5591** MILLETT, FRED B. & BENTLEY, GERALD E. The art of the drama
pp.viii, 253     M
NY: Appleton-Century-Crofts     1935
History, modes and techniques.

**5592** GASSNER, JOHN. Masters of the drama
pp.xvii, 804     M
NY: Random House     1940
International historical survey. Chapters 29 and 30 deal with US drama from O'Neill onwards.

**5593** CLARK, BARRETT H. & FREEDLEY, GEORGE (Eds). A history of modern drama
pp.xiii, 832     M
NY: D. Appleton-Century     1947
International in scope. Chapter XIII deals with US drama.

**5594** LAMM, MARTIN. Modern drama
pp.xx, 359     L
Oxford: Blackwell     1952
Translated by Karin Elliott.

**5595** FERGUSSON, FRANCIS. The human image in dramatic lierature
pp. xxi, 217     M
NY: Doubleday Anchor     1957
Essays. Includes substantial reference to US drama, and in particular to Thornton Wilder, in the section, *The modern theater*.

**5596** LEONARD, DYMPHNA. Mary Stuart. The historical figure in English and American drama
NY: U. (PhD)     1964

**5597** BRUSTEIN, ROBERT. The theatre of revolt
pp.ix, 435     M
London: Methuen     1965
An approach to the modern drama, from Ibsen to Genet.

**5598** WELLWARTH, GEORGE. The theatre of protest and paradox: developments in the avant-garde drama
pp.xvii, 315     M
London: Macgibbon & Kee     1965

## 14.1. INTERNATIONAL

Post WW2 drama in Europe, Britain and the US.

**5599** DECKER, PHILIP H. The use of classic myth in twentieth-century English and American drama, 1900-1960. A study of selected plays
Evanston: Northwestern U. (PhD) 1966

**5600** BALEANU, ANDREI. Teatrul furiei si al violentei: privire asupra dramaturgiei americane si engleze (1956-1966)
pp.295 DL★
Bucharest: Pentru Literatura Universala 1967

**5601** FREEDMAN, MORRIS. The moral impulse: modern drama from Ibsen to the present
pp.vii, 136 DL★
Carbondale: Southern Illinois U. P. 1967

**5602** RAHILL, FRANK. The world of melodrama
pp.xviii, 334 M
University Park: Pennsylvania State U. P. 1967
A history of the *genre* in France, UK, US.

**5603** HEILMAN, ROBERT B. Tragedy and melodrama: versions of experience
pp.xiii, 326 L
Seattle: U. of Washington P. 1968

**5604** BELLI, ANGELA. Ancient Greek myths and modern drama: a study in continuity
pp.x, 201 DL★
NY: U. P. 1969
Includes reference to Tennessee Williams: *Orpheus Descending*.

**5605** COHN, RUBY. Currents in contemporary drama
pp.xi, 276 L
Bloomington: Indiana U. P. 1969
Survey of post WW2 theatre movements in Europe and the US.

**5606** DUKORE, BERNARD F. & GEROULD, DANIEL C. Avant-garde drama: major plays and documents post world war I
pp.xiv, 588 DL★
NY: Bantam 1969
Includes essays by Kenneth MacGowan and Robert Edmond Jones, and the text, with introduction, of E. E. Cummings's *Him*.

**5607** GASSNER, JOHN & QUINN, EDWARD. The reader's encyclopedia of world drama
pp.xiii, 1030; ill. in text M
London: Methuen 1970
Published NY: Thomas Y. Crowell.

**5608** ANDERSON, MICHAEL et al. Crowell's handbook of contemporary drama
pp.vi, 505 L
NY: Thomas Y. Crowell 1971

**5609** HOUGHTON, NORRIS. The exploding stage: an introduction to twentieth century drama
pp.xv, 269 L
NY: Weybright & Tolley 1971
European and US drama.

**5610** KIENZLE, SIEGFRIED. Modern world theatre: a guide to production in Europe and the United States since 1945
pp.v, 509 M
NY: Ungar 1971

A translation by Alexander and Elizabeth Henderson of *Modernes Welttheater...*, Stuttgart: Kroner, 1966. Over 700 works alphabetically listed by writer and providing summary of plot, critique, translator's name, premiere information and publishing details.

**5611** LEWIS, ALLAN. The contemporary theatre: the significant playwrights of our time...with a foreword by John Gassner
pp.ix, 374 MH
NY: Crown 1971
Revised edition. First published 1962.

**5612** BOOKS ABROAD: an international literary quarterly.
Ill. in text M
Oklahoma: U. P. 1972
Volume 46 No. 3, Summer 1972. Major section, *The impact of the theater of the absurd on world drama*.

**5613** MASON, GREGORY H. Documentary drama: a study of the form
Madison: U. of Wisconsin (PhD) 1972

**5614** RAINES, ROBERT A. (Ed.). Modern drama and social change
pp.xi, 339 L
Englewood Cliffs NJ: Prentice-Hall 1972
Playtexts with introductions, notes and other editorial matter. Includes Eugene O'Neill: *The Hairy Ape*.

**5615** HEILMAN, ROBERT B. The iceman, the arsonist and the troubled agent. Tragedy and melodrama on the modern stage
pp.xviii, 357 L
London: Allen & Unwin 1973

**5616** GILMAN, RICHARD. The making of modern drama. A study of Büchner, Ibsen, Strindberg, Chekhov, Pirandello, Brecht, Beckett, Handke
pp.xii, 292 L
NY: Farrar, Straus & Giroux 1974
Re-published NY: Da Capo P. with new introduction by the author.

**5617** MATTHEWS, J. H. Theatre in dada and surrealism
pp.xiii, 286 L
Syracuse NY: U. P. 1974

**5618** EDWARDS, FLORA M. The theater of the black diaspora: a comparative study of black drama in Brazil, Cuba and the United States
NY: U. (PhD) 1975

**5619** PROCTOR, GEORGE L. An introduction to British and American drama
pp.207; ill. DL★
Berlin: Cornelson-Velhagen & Klasing 1975

**5620** WHITE, KENNETH S. Savage comedy since King Ubu: a tangent to 'the absurd'
pp.ii, 94 L
Washington DC: U. P. of America 1977
Includes reference to Edward Albee.

**5621** SZANTO, GEORGE H. Theater and propaganda
pp.x, 226 L
Austin: U. of Texas P. 1978

Wide range of allusion and example, stretching from the Wakefield Cycle to Jack Gelber.

**5622** HARTIGAN, KARELISA V. (Ed.). The University of Florida Department of Classics Comparative Drama conference papers
pp. various  M
Lanham MD: U. P. of America  1980–

Each volume under a general title, e.g. I 'To hold a mirror to nature: dramatic images and reflections' (1982); II 'All the world: drama past and present'(1982); III 'From pen to performance' (1983) which includes William P. French: *Maryat Lee's Ecotheatre: an indigenous American theatre*; IV 'Legacy of Thespis' (1984); VII 'From the Bard to Broadway' (1987) which includes Nicholas F. Radel: *What's the meaning of this Corn Tilden!: mimesis in Sam Shepard's 'Buried Child'*. IX 'Text and presentation' (1989).

**5623** SIMARD, RODNEY. Postmodern drama
pp.xvi, 163; ill. in text  MH
Lanham MD: U. P. of America  1984

Includes chapter on Sam Shepard and David Rabe.

**5624** QUIGLEY, AUSTIN E. The modern stage and other worlds
pp.xvi, 320  M
NY: Methuen  1985

Part one establishes a critical framework. Part two examines a selection of UK and European plays, from Ibsen to Beckett.

**5625** DAHL, MARY K. Political violence in drama: classical models, contemporary variations
pp.161  DL★
Ann Arbor: UMI Research P.  1987

**5626** FINNEY, GAIL. Women in modern drama: Freud, feminism, and European theater at the turn of the century
pp.xi, 234  L
Ithaca NY: Cornell U. P.  1989

## 14.2 GENERAL

**5627** [JEWETT, I. A.]. Prize essay. A brief history and defence of the drama
pp.69  MB
[Cincinnati OH]: [Caldwell?]  [1832]

The $111 prize winning essay, together with the runner-up, author unnamed but from New Orleans, *An outline of the history and a vindication of the drama*. The competition was sponsored by the manager of the American Theatre and the prize awarded in Cincinnati. There were seven entries.

**5628** GARLAND, HAMLIN. Crumbling idols: twelve essays on art dealing chiefly with literature, painting and the drama
pp.ix, 192  L
Chicago: Stone and Kimball  1894

Essay 7: *The drift of the drama*; 8: *The influence of Ibsen*.

**5629** MATTHEWS, BRANDER. Books and play-books: essays on literature and the drama
pp.vii, 250  M
London: Osgood, McIlvaine  1895

Includes *The dramatization of novels*, *The evolution of copyright*; *On certain parallelisms between the ancient and the modern drama* (individually published for the author the previous year); *The whole duty of critics*.

**5630** BATES, ALFRED (Ed. in chief). American drama
pp.ii, 336; x, 344; ill. in text, pl. 3, 3  MH
London: Stuart and Stanley  1903

Volumes xix and xx in a twenty volume series, *The Drama*. Each offers a substantial historical survey followed by representative texts. Indexed in Vol. xx.

**5631** FRANK, WALDO D. Salvos: an informal book about books and plays
pp.286  L
NY: Boni & Liveright  1924

Reprinted essays, some on theatre topics.

**5632** JONES, HENRY B. The death song of the 'noble savage', a study of the idealization of the American indian
Chicago: U. (PhD)  1924

**5633** GREEN, ELIZABETH L. The negro in contemporary American literature: an outline for individual and group study
pp.94  L
Chapel Hill: U. of N. Carolina P.  1928

Part II, drama: *The negro's contribution to the art of the theatre*; *Drama for negro actors*; *Negro plays of Eugene O'Neill*; *Paul Green*.

**5634** ROCKWELL, ETHEL T. American life as represented in native one-act plays
pp.66  DL★
Madison: U. of Wisconsin P.  1931

**5635** RUSSELL, JASON A. The Indian in American literature
Ithaca: Cornell U. (PhD)  1932

**5636** HALLINE, ALAN G. Main currents of thought in American drama
Madison: U. of Wisconsin (PhD)  1935

**5637** LOGAN, RHEA D. Drama and the machine
Columbus: Ohio State U. (PhD)  1935

**5638** SAVAGE, GEORGE M. Regionalism in American drama
Seattle: U. of Washington (PhD)  1935

**5639** BROWN, STERLING A. Negro poetry and drama
pp.200  DL★
Washington DC: Associates in Negro Folk Education  1937

**5640** CLARK, BARRETT H. 'Lost' plays of the American theater
pp. [12]  L
[NY?]: [For the author]  [1937]

Reprinted, in part, from the *New York Times*. Essentially, a description of Clark's research into forgotten and vanished plays and his projected publication of such plays under the aegis of the *Authors League* and the *Dramatists Guild*, together with a request for information from an interested public.

**5641** LAWSON, HILDA H. The negro in American drama
Urbana: U. of Illinois (PhD)  1939

**5642** BOND, FREDERICK W. The negro and the drama. The direct and indirect contribution which the American negro has made to drama and the legitimate stage, with the underlying condition responsible
pp.x, 213 L
Washington DC: Associated Publishers 1940

**5643** STUDIES IN SPEECH and drama in honor of Alexander M. Drummond
pp.viii, 472; front. O
Ithaca NY: Cornell U. P. 1944
Includes Harry D. Albright on musical drama; Edwin Duerr on Constantin Stanislavsky, Barnard Hewitt on stage scenery, J. W. Curvin on the stage yankee, Walter H. Stainton on color music.

**5644** PEMBROOK, CARRIE D. Negro drama through the ages
NY: U. (PhD) 1946

**5645** MANGUM, VALERIE B. American attitudes towards war as reflected in American drama, 1773-1946
Austin: U. of Texas (PhD) 1947

**5646** THOMPSON, DAVID W. The rise of realism in American drama and the theatre
Ithaca: Cornell U. (PhD) 1947

**5647** LINNEHAN, EDWARD. We wear the mask. Life and character of the negro in American drama
Philadelphia: U. of Pennsylvania (PhD) 1949

**5648** PETTIT, PAUL B. The important American dramatic types to 1900. A study of the yankee, negro, indian, and frontiersman
Ithaca: Cornell U. (PhD) 1949

**5649** DAVIS, BLANCHE E. The hero in American drama, 1787-1900: a critical appraisal of American dramas through a consideration of the hero
NY: Columbia U. (PhD) 1950

**5650** MOWRY, VERA L. Satire in American drama
Pittsburgh: U. (PhD) 1950

**5651** OWENSBY, EDWARD. The theatre of social protest in the United States: studies of seven important plays representative of the four principal themes for protest
Mexico DF: Universidad Nacional Autónoma (Thesis) 1951

**5652** QUINN, ARTHUR H. (Ed.). The literature of the American people: an historical and critical summary
pp.xix, 1172 L
NY: Appleton-Century-Crofts 1951
In four sections. Includes Arthur H. Quinn: *Revolt and celebration in the drama*; Clarence Gohdes: *Amusements on the stage* [in the later 19th c.]; G. F. Whicher: *Vitalizers of the drama* [in the 20th c.].

**5653** TILLSON, M. W. The frontiersman in American drama. An analytical study of the characters and plays reflecting the phenomenon of westward expansion
Denver: U. of Colorado (PhD) 1951

**5654** QUINN, JAMES J. The Jonathan character in the American drama
NY: Columbia U. (PhD) 1954

**5655** COOPER, CHARLES W. Preface to drama: an introduction to dramatic literature and theater art
pp. 773 MH
NY: Ronald P. 1955
Textbook for undergraduates. Brief analytical discussion of a range of printed playtexts, including Howard Lindsay & Russel Crouse: *Life with Father*; Arthur Miller: *The Crucible*; Tennessee Williams: *The Glass Menagerie*.

**5656** GLENN, STANLEY L. Ludicrous characterization in American comedy from the beginning until the civil war
Stanford: U. (PhD) 1955

**5657** MOODY, RICHARD. America takes the stage: romanticism in American drama and theatre, 1750-1900
pp.xi, 322; pl. 9 M
Bloomington: Indiana U. P. 1955

**5658** ROACH, JOSH P. A study of some unpublished American melodramas
Denver: U. (PhD) 1955

**5659** SIEVERS, W. DAVID. Freud on Broadway: a history of psychoanalysis and the American drama
pp.479 L
NY: Hermitage House 1955

**5660** BOSSONE, RICHARD M. The educational significance of certain major works in twentieth century American fiction and drama
Los Angeles: U.of Southern California (EdD) 1958

**5661** MOE, CHRISTIAN. From history to drama. A study of the influence of the pageant, the outdoor epic drama and the historical play upon the dramatization of three American historical figures
Ithaca: Cornell U. (PhD) 1958

**5662** KUHLKE, WILLIAM. 'They too sing America': the new negro as portrayed by negro playwrights
Lawrence: U. of Kansas (PhD) 1959

**5663** PRYOR, WILLIAM D. An examination of the southern milieu in representative plays by southern dramatists 1923-56
Tallahassee: Florida State U. (PhD) 1959

**5664** RUSSELL, HELEN. Social comment as depicted in the plays of American women dramatists
Denver: U. (PhD) 1959

**5665** FRENZ, HORST & CLÜVER, CLAUS VON (Eds). Amerikanische dramaturgie
pp.177 DL★
Hamburg: Rowohlt 1962

**5666** ANIKST, ALEKSANDR A. & BOYADZHEV, G. 6. Rasskazov ob amerikansko teatre
pp.148; pl. 8 L
Moscow: Iskusstvo 1963

**5667** CROW, PORTER J. The teacher as a character in American drama
Denton: North Texas State U. (EdD) 1963

**5668** KERNAN, ALVIN B. Character and conflict: an introduction to drama
pp.757 DL★
NY: Harcourt, Brace & World 1963

**5669** CORRIGAN, ROBERT W. & ROSENBERG, JAMES L. (Eds). The contexts and craft of drama
pp. x, 416 MH
San Francisco: Chandler 1964

**5670** LANGLEY, STEPHEN G. Three puritanical stage figures in the American drama
Urbana-Champaign: U. of Illinois (PhD) 1965

**5671** MARCHAND, WILLIAM M. The changing role of the medical doctor in selected plays in American drama
Minneapolis: U. of Minnesota (PhD) 1965

**5672** MARCUSON, LEWIS R. The Irish, the Italians, and the Jews: a study of three nationality groups as portrayed in American drama between 1820 and 1960
Denver: U. (PhD) 1965

**5673** MESERVE, WALTER J. An outline history of American drama
pp.xiv, 378 MH
Totowa NJ: Littlefield, Adams 1965

**5674** GILLIAM, THEODORE E. The negro image in representative American dramas
New Orleans: Tulane U. (PhD) 1967

**5675** BULLINS, ED (Ed.). Black theatre
pp.180 DL★
NY: U. P. 1968
Special issue of the *Drama Review*, XII, 4, Summer 1968.

**5676** BAKER, DONALD G. Shakespeare and the American west
Adams: State College (MA) 1969

**5677** BIGSBY, C. W. (Ed.). The black American writer. Volume 2, poetry and drama
pp.253 DL★
Deland FL: Everett Edwards 1969
The second of two volumes.

**5678** HERRON, IMA H. The small town in American drama
pp.xxiii, 564; pl. 12 M
Dallas TX: Southern Methodist U. P. 1969

**5679** LONG, EUGENE H. American drama from its beginning to the present
pp.xi, 78 L
NY: Appleton-Century-Crofts 1970
Selective guide to major resources, published in the twentieth century, for the study of the US drama.

**5680** COHN, RUBY. Dialogue in American drama
pp.vii, 340 O
Bloomington: Indiana U. P. 1971
Specific reference to Eugene O'Neill, Arthur Miller, Tennessee Williams, and chapters also on playwrights better known for fiction or poetry.

**5681** DUKORE, BERNARD F. (Ed.). Documents for drama and revolution
pp.255; map DL★
NY: Holt Rinehart & Winston 1971
Anthology of documents intended to supplement Dukore's collection of plays : *Drama and Revolution*.

**5682** FREEDMAN, MORRIS. American drama in social context
pp.xv, 143 L
Carbondale: Southern Illionois U. P. 1971
With material on Eugene O'Neill, Arthur Miller, musical drama, and chapters: *Violence in American theatre* and *Towards an American tragedy*. Preface by Harry T. Moore.

**5683** HARTMAN, JOHN G. The development of American social comedy from 1787 to 1936
pp.151 MH
NY: Octagon 1971

**5684** ITSCHERT, HANS (Ed.). Das amerikanische Drama von den Anfangen bis zur Gegenwart
pp.xiv, 449 MH
Darmstadt: Wissenschaftliche Buchgesellschaft 1972
International essays reprinted in original languages. Includes sections on eighteenth and nineteenth century Yankee theatre, twentieth century US theatre including O'Neill, Wilder, Williams, Miller, Albee.

**5685** MILLS, KATHERINE B. American live drama in the year 2000: A Delphi study
Santa Barbara: U. of California (PhD) 1972

**5686** THOMAS, MARJORIE. An overview of Miss Anne: white women as seen by black playwrights
Tallahassee: Florida State U. (PhD) 1973

**5687** DOLKEY, MATTHEW. Follies in fashion: the afterpiece in the American theatre
NY: U. (PhD) 1974

**5688** HARRISON, PAUL C. (Ed.). Kuntu drama: plays of the African continuum...preface by Oliver Jackson
pp.xv, 352 MH
NY: Grove P. 1974
Playtexts, with brief introductions. Editorial essay: *Black theater in search of a source*.

**5689** ANDERSON, BO. Svart drama från slavtid till ghettorevolt
pp.221; ill. in text MH
Stockholm: Forum 1975

**5690** JEYIFOUS, BIODUN. Theatre and drama and the black physical and cultural presence in America: essays in interpretation
NY: U. (PhD) 1975

**5691** STEVENSON, ROBERT L. The image of the white man as projected in the published plays of black Americans, 1847-1973
Bloomington: Indiana U. (PhD) 1976

**5692** BOGARD, TRAVIS; MOODY, RICHARD & MESERVE, WALTER J. (Eds). American drama [in the series *Revels History of Drama in English*]
pp.xlxii, 324; pl. 12 M
London: Macmillan 1977

**5693** PRINCE, JANE E. Treatment of female characters in selected tent show dramas
Lubbock: Texas Tech U. (MA) 1977

**5694** SAROTTE, GEORGES-M. Like a brother, like a lover: male homosexuality in the American novel and theater from Herman Melville to James Baldwin.
pp.xvii, 339 MH
Garden City: Anchor P./Doubleday 1978

Translated by Richard Miller. First published Paris: Flammarion. Includes material on Tennessee Williams, William Inge, Edward Albee.

**5695** TYLER, MOSES C. A history of American literature 1607-1765
pp.xx, 293; xi, 330   MH
NY: G. P. Putnam's Sons   1979-81
Two volumes.

**5696** GEROULD, DANIEL C. (Ed.). Melodrama
pp.xiv, 282; ill. in text   M
NY: NY Literary Forum   1980
Essays, with some reprinted documents and playtexts, most notably *The Forest of Bondy; or, the dog of Montargis*. Contributions include Michael Kirby: *Melodrama manifesto of structuralism*; Stephen Sondheim on *Sweeney Todd*; and James Leverett on the resurgence of melodrama in the work of e.g. Sam Shepard and Richard Foreman.

**5697** VORLICKY, ROBERT H. America's power plays: the traditional hero in male cast drama
Madison: U. of Wisconsin (PhD)   1981

**5698** BIGSBY, C. W. A critical introduction to twentieth century American drama, 1900-1940
pp.ix, 342; viii, 355; x, 485; ill. in text   O
Cambridge: U. P.   1982
Three volumes. 1. Provincetown; Eugene O'Neill; Theatre Guild, Group Theatre and Clifford Odets; left-wing theatre; FTP and Living Newspaper; black drama; Thornton Wilder; Lillian Hellman. 2. Tennessee Williams, Arthur Miller and Edward Albee. 3. Beyond Broadway; performance theatre - the Living Theatre, the Open Theatre, the Performance Group; theatre of images - art, theatre and the real, Robert Wilson, Richard Foreman, Lee Breuer; the playwright - Sam Shepard, David Mamet; theatre of commitment - San Francisco Mime Troupe, El Teatro Campesino, American Indian theatre, black theatre, gay theatre, women's theatre.

**5699** BENES, PETER (Ed.). American speech: 1600 to the present
  DL★
Boston: U. P.   [1985]

Section IV: *Linguistic studies of popular literature and drama.*

**5700** SIEBALD, MANFRED & IMMEL, HORST (Eds). Amerikanisierung des Dramas und Dramatisierung Amerikas: Studien ehren von Hans Helmcke
pp.281   MH
Frankfurt: Peter Lang   1985
Includes general accounts of seventeenth and eighteenth century US drama, the plays of James A. Herne, *Uncle Tom's Cabin*, *Arsenic and Old Lace*, *Ecstacy of Rita Joe*, and the work of Eugene O'Neill, Thomas Wolfe, Edward Albee, LeRoi Jones, Loften Mitchell.

**5701** ELLIOT, EMORY (Ed.). Columbia literary history of the United States
  DL★
NY: Columbia U.P.   1988
Includes essays on drama by Claudia D. Johnson and Ruby Cohn.

**5702** GUSTAFSON, ANTOINETTE McC. The image of the West in American popular performance
NY: U. (PhD)   1988

**5703** HOROWITZ, SUSAN N. Funny women: a study of female comedic personae
NY: City U. (PhD)   1988

**5704** PROEHL, GEOFFREY S. Coming home again: American family drama and the figure of the prodigal
Stanford: U. (PhD)   1988

**5705** EUBA, FEMI. Archetypes, imprecators and victims of fate: origins and developments of satire in black drama
pp. xiv, 199; ill. in text   L
NY: Greenwood P.   1989
An inquiry into Yoruba origins and archetypes. A section, *The new world expression* refers to LeRoi Jones, Langston Hughes and Lorraine Hansberry.

## 14.3 1665-1850

**5706** FORD, PAUL L. Some notes towards an essay on the beginnings of American dramatic literature, 1606-1789...25 copies printed as manuscript for suggestion and revision...
ll. 29   MH
NY: [For the author]   1893

**5707** MENEELY, JOHN H. A study of American drama prior to 1801
NY: U. (PhD)   1911

**5708** ELLIS, HAROLD M. Joseph Dennie and his circle: a study in American literature from 1792 to 1812
pp.285; front.   O
Austin: U. of Texas P.   1915
*Bulletin*, July 1915. Theatre references include material on Royall Tyler.

**5709** REED, PERLEY I. The realistic presentation of American characters in native American plays prior to eighteen-seventy
Columbus: Ohio State U. (PhD)   1916

**5710** COLBY, ELBRIDGE. Early American comedy
pp.11   M
NY: Public Library   1919
Reprinted from the *Bulletin*, July, 1919. Comprises a survey, 1801-1860.

**5711** VINING, ROSCOE H. Early American drama considered as historical material
Boston: U. (PhD)   1922

**5712** SCHOENBERGER, HAROLD W. American adaptations of French plays on the New York and Philadelphia stages from 1793-1833
Philadelphia: U. of Pennsylvania (PhD)   1924

**5713** LESCARBOT, MARC. Neptune's theatre: the first existing play written and produced in North America
pp.14; pl. 2   L
NY: Samuel French   1927
A translation by Edna B. Holman of *Le Théâtre de Neptune en la Nouvelle-France*, verses for a pageant to celebrate the return to Acadia of Jean de Biencourt in 1606. Text and annotations. Introductory note on provenance, photographs of the site of the first performance in Port Royal, Acadia, and Champlain's plan

of Port Royal. A commemoration had taken pace at Annapolis Royal, on August 2, 1926.

**5714** WARE, RALPH H. American adaptations of French plays on the New York and Philadelphia stages from 1834 to the civil war
pp.138 DL★
Philadelphia: Westbrook 1930

**5715** MAYORGA, MARGARET G. A short history of the American drama: commentaries on plays prior to 1920. With illustrations and bibliographies
pp.xxi, 472; pl. 16 MH
NY: Dodd, Mead 1932

**5716** KEISER, ALBERT. The Indian in American literature
pp.vii, 312 L
NY: Oxford U. P. 1933
Chapter eight concerns plays featuring the stage Indian, 1766-1911.

**5717** LEES, CHARLES L. An introductory study of the American people of the eighteenth century through drama and theatrical theory
Madison: U. of Wisconsin (PhD) 1934

**5718** COLES, ELIZABETH E. Aspects of pre-Civil War historical drama
Hayes KS: Fort Hayes State U. (MS) 1939

**5719** QUINN, ARTHUR H. A history of American drama from the beginning to the civil war
pp.xvii, 530 M
NY: Appleton-Century-Crofts 1943
Second edition, revised. First published 1923.

**5720** VON TORNOW, GEORGIANA J. The heroine in American drama and theatre down to the civil war, and her relation to 'life' in the novels of the times
Ithaca: Cornell U. (PhD) 1945

**5721** SKINNER, DONALD T. The civil war as a subject for American drama
Evanston: Northwestern U. (PhD) 1949

**5722** NETTLETON, GEORGE H. Sheridan's introduction to the American stage
pp.163-182 L
NY: MLA of America 1950
Reprinted from *PMLA* LXV, 2, March 1950. Period 1777-1783, with reference extended to include Goldsmith.

**5723** CULP, RALPH B. Drama and theatre as a source of colonial American attitudes towards independence, 1748-1776
Ithaca: Cornell U. (PhD) 1951

**5724** ELFENBEIN, JOSEF A. American drama, 1782-1812, as an index to social change
NY: U. (PhD) 1951

**5725** NARY, BRUCE L. A study of major Lincoln dramas in relationship to selected Lincoln biographies
Ann Arbor: U. of Michigan (PhD) 1956

**5726** TURNER, WILLIS L. City low-life on the American stage to 1900
Urbana: U. of Illinois (PhD) 1956

**5727** LOWN, CHARLES R. Business and the businessman in American drama prior to the civil war
Stanford: U. (PhD) 1957

**5728** REARDON, JOHN D. Verse drama in America from 1765 to the Civil War. The end of a tradition
Lawrence: U. of Kansas (PhD) 1957

**5729** SMITH, IRVINE N. American plays and playwrights of the nineteenth century
Denver: U. (PhD) 1959

**5730** SITTON, FRED. The Indian play in America, 1750-1900
Evanston: Northwestern U. (PhD) 1962

**5731** COLLINS, JOHN D. American drama in antislavery agitation, 1792-1861
Iowa City: Iowa U. (PhD) 1963

**5732** ROBINSON, ALICE J. The developing ideas of individual freedom and national unity as reflected in American plays and theatre, 1722-1819
Stanford: U. (PhD) 1965

**5733** GALLAGHER, KENT G. The foreigner in early American drama: a study in attitudes
pp.206 L
The Hague: Mouton 1966

**5734** McGRAW, REX T. The role of villain in civil war melodrama
Bloomington: Indiana U. (PhD) 1966

**5735** KLEIN, RALPH A. The American military heroes and heroines of the Revolutionary War, the War of 1812, and the Civil War: an analysis of character based on representative American plays written between the years of 1774 and 1907
Denver: U. (PhD) 1967

**5736** LAUGHLIN, H. T. *The Disappointment* [Andrew Barton, 1767] and *The Wheel of Fortune* [St George Tucker, 1797]: two amateur playwrights' use of local and national events in early American plays
Carbondale: Southern Illinous U. (PhD) 1970
Annotated texts, evaluation and theatre history.

**5737** MARCHIAFAVA, BRUCE T. The influence of patriotism in the American drama and theatre, 1773-1830
Evanston: Northwestern U. (PhD) 1970

**5738** PAGEL, CAROL A. A history and analysis of representative American dramatizations from American novels, 1800-1960
Denver: U. (PhD) 1970

**5739** SCHERTING, JOHN A. Partisan drama and the American stage, 1783-1807
Detroit: Washington State U. (PhD) 1970

**5740** SCHULTZ, CHARLES A. The Yankee figure in early American theatre prior to 1820
Bowling Green OH: State U. (PhD) 1970

**5741** HAVENS, DANIEL F. The Columbian muse of comedy: the development of a native tradition in early American social comedy 1787-1845
pp.vii, 181 L
Carbondale: Southern Illinois U. P. 1973

**5742** ANDERSON, MARILYN J. The image of the American Indian in American drama: from 1766 to 1845
Minneapolis: U. of Minnesota (PhD) 1974

**5743** LITTLE, THOMAS J. An examination of poetic justice in three selected types of nineteenth-century melodrama: the Indian play, the temperance play, and the Civil War play
Bowling Green: State U. (PhD) 1974

**5744** GRAFF, STEPHEN J. The evolution of the American military spy play from the beginning to 1900
NY: U. (PhD) 1976

**5745** TALIAFERRO, JAMES. The propagandist role of women in selected American plays from 1736 to 1860
NY: U. (PhD) 1976

**5746** MESERVE, WALTER J. An emerging entertainment. The drama of the American people to 1828
pp.x, 342 M
Bloomington: Indiana U. P. 1977

**5747** McCONACHIE, BRUCE A. Economic values in popular American melodramas, 1815-1860
Madison: U. of Wisconsin (PhD) 1978

**5748** GROSE, BURL D. Here come the Indians: an historical study of the representations of the Native American upon the North American stage, 1808-1969
Columbia: U. of Missouri (PhD) 1979

**5749** PASTERNACK, ARON L. The development of popular American stage comedy from the beginning to 1900
Medford MA: Tufts U. (PhD) 1980

**5750** MARSHALL, ERIC R. Playwriting contests and Jacksonian democracy, 1829-1841
Los Angeles: U. of Southern California (PhD) 1983
A history of the contests popularized by Edwin Forrest.

**5751** ROBINSON, KAY M. The depiction of the cowboy in selected nineteenth-century American popular drama
East Lansing: Michigan State U. (PhD) 1983

**5752** MESERVE, WALTER J. Heralds of promise: the drama of the American people during the age of Jackson, 1829-1849
pp.xiii, 269; ill. in text MH
NY: Greenwood P. 1986

## 14.4 1851-1918

**5753** BURTON, RICHARD. The new American drama
pp.viii, 277 M
NY: Thomas Y. Crowell 1913

**5754** HAMILTON, CLAYTON. Studies in stagecraft
pp. ix, 298 M
London: Grant Richard 1914
First published NY: Holt. Current practice and trends and their possible influence on the development of drama and theatre.

**5755** CLARK, BARRETT H. The British and American drama of today. Outlines for their study...
pp.xiii, 315 M
NY: Henry Holt 1915

**5756** DICKINSON, THOMAS H. The case of American drama
pp.xi, 223 M
Boston: Houghton Mifflin 1915
'A study of the forces that may, in the fullness of time, bring forth an American theatre of a form that will be appropriate to the event.'

**5757** MATTHEWS, BRANDER. The principles of playmaking and other discussions of the drama
pp.vii, 306 M
NY: Charles Scribner's Sons 1919
Includes a chapter, *Memories of Edwin Booth*.

**5758** PLESSOW, GUSTAV L. Das amerikanische Kurzschauspiel zwischen 1910 und 1930
pp.x111, 269; pl. 2 L
Halle: Max Niemeyer 1933

**5759** GELLER, JAMES J. Grandfather's follies
pp.219; ill. in text M
NY: Macaulay 1934

Affectionate account of popular drama at the turn of the nineteenth century.

**5760** QUINN, ARTHUR H. A history of the American drama from the civil war to the present day
pp.xxv, 296; i, 432; pl. 33 M
NY: Appleton-Century-Crofts 1936
Revised edition. First published 1927. Two volumes in one.

**5761** KOSTER, DONALD N. The theme of divorce in American drama, 1871-1939
Philadelphia: U. of Pennsylvania (Thesis) 1942

**5762** ANDREWS, MARY L. Modern poetic drama in America (1900-1942)
NY: U. (PhD) 1943

**5763** BUCKS, DOROTHY S. The American drama of ideas from 1890 to 1929
Evanston: Northwestern U. (PhD) 1944

**5764** DUSENBURY, DELWIN B. A study of comedy in the American theatre represented in the productions of native comedy in New York City from 1900 to 1920
Minneapolis: U. of Minnesota (PhD) 1947

**5765** GOFF, LEWIN A. The popular priced melodrama in America, 1890-1910, with its origins and development to 1890
Cleveland: Case Western Reserve U. (PhD) 1948

**5766** JOHNSON, ALBERT E. American dramatizations of American literary materials from 1850 to 1900
Ithaca: Cornell U. (PhD) 1948

**5767** BANK, ROSEMARIE K. Rhetorical, dramatic, theatrical and social contexts of selected American frontier plays 1871 to 1906
Seattle: U. of Washington (MA) 1949

**5768** HARPER, ROBERT D. Economic and political attitudes in American drama, 1865-1900
Chicago: U. (PhD) 1950

**5769** NARDIN, JAMES T. A study in popular American farce, 1865-1914
Chicago: U. (PhD) 1950

**5770** DOWNER, ALAN S. Fifty years of American drama 1900-1950
pp.ix, 158 M
Chicago: Henry Regnery 1951

**5771** SIEVERS, WIEDER D. An analysis of the influence of Freudian psychology on American drama, 1909-1939
Los Angeles: U. of Southern California (PhD) 1952

**5772** HAMILTON, STANLEY K. Theatre people as depicted by the playwright
Salt Lake City: U. of Utah (PhD) 1952
Broadway, 1900-1950.

**5773** SMITH, ROSS D. A survey of native American serious drama from 1900 to 1918
Salt Lake City: U. of Utah (PhD) 1952

**5774** WALSH, FREDERICK G. Outdoor commemorative drama in the United States, 1900-1950
Cleveland: Case Western Reserve U. (PhD) 1952

**5775** HYDE, STUART W. The representation of the West in American drama from 1849 to 1917
Stanford: U. (PhD) 1954

**5776** LONEY, GLENN. Dramatizations of American novels, 1900-1917
Stanford: U. (PhD) 1954

**5777** WELSH, WILLARD. The characterization of the male protagonist in serious American drama from 1867 to 1920
Stanford: U. (PhD) 1954

**5778** FIFTY YEARS of American drama
pp.4 L
Princeton: University Library 1955
Leaflet to accompany exhibition.

**5779** SMALL, GEORGE A. American dramatic comedy, 1900-1950. A study of reflected climate of opinion in changing historical perspective
Philadelphia: U. of Pennsylvania (PhD) 1956

**5780** FISCH, MORTIMER L. The politician on the American stage from 1870-1915
NY: U. (PhD) 1959

**5781** HABERMAN, LEROY D. American farce on Broadway, 1914-1950
Stanford: U. (PhD) 1959

**5782** RISLEY, HERBERT J. The reception of American drama in America and in England, 1900-1915. A comparative study with emphasis on the reactions of English critics
Bloomington: Indiana U. (PhD) 1959

**5783** DELL, ROBERT. The representation of the European immigrant on the New York stage (1880-1914)
NY: U. (PhD) 1960

**5784** NANNES, CASPAR H. Politics in the American drama: Broadway plays 1890-1959
pp.xv, 256 MH
Washington DC: Catholic U. of America P. 1960
The dramatic depiction of politicians and political society.

**5785** LOGAN, WINFORD B. An investigation of the theme of the negation of life in American drama from World War II to 1958
Columbus: Ohio State U. (PhD) 1961

**5786** WISMER, LAWRENCE H. Changing concepts of death in American drama, 1885-1960
Stanford: U. (PhD) 1963

**5787** SHERMAN, ALFONSO. The diversity of treatment of the negro character in American drama prior to 1860
Bloomington: Indiana U. (PhD) 1964

**5788** MESERVE, WALTER J. (Ed.). Discussions of modern American drama
pp.x, 150 L
Boston: D. C. Heath 1966
Introduction by John Corbin. Arthur H. Quinn on Eugene O'Neill; Walter J. Meserve on Sidney Howard and the social drama of the '20s; Lionel Trilling on Eugene O'Neill; Harold Clurman on the drama of the '30s; Donna Gerstenberger on verse drama, 1916-39; Edith J. R. Isaacs on Lillian Hellman; Travis Bogard on Thornton Wilder; Joseph W. Krutch on post war drama; Laurence Kitchin on the influence of American drama; Robert Brustein: *Why American plays are not literature*; E. W. Parks on O'Neill; Tom F. Driver on Arthur Miller; Mary McCarthy on American realist playwrights; James A. Herne: *Art for truth's sake*; Owen Davis: *Why I quit writing melodrama*; Eugene O'Neill on *The Great God Brown*; Maxwell Anderson on tragedy; Tennessee Williams: the foreword to *Camino Real*; Arthur Miller: the introduction to the collected plays; Edward Albee on absurd theatre.

**5789** SCHAFFER, PAULINE W. The position of women in society as reflected in serious American drama from 1890-1928
Stanford: U. (PhD) 1966

**5790** ADELMAN, IRVING & DWORKIN, RITA. Modern drama: a checklist of critical literature on 20th century plays
pp.xvii, 370 DL★
Metuchen NJ: Scarecrow P. 1967

**5791** HARDWICK, MARY R. The nature of the negro hero in serious American drama 1910-1964
East Lansing: Michigan State U. (PhD) 1967

**5792** NOLAN, PAUL T. (Ed.). Provincial drama in America, 1870-1916: a casebook of primary materials
pp.234 M
Metuchen NJ: Scarecrow P. 1967

**5793** ESTRIN, MARK W. Dramatizations of American fiction: Hawthorne and Melville on stage and screen
NY: U. (PhD) 1968

**5794** COX, PAUL R. The characterization of the American Indian in American Indian plays 1800-1860, as a reflection of the American romantic movement
NY: U. (PhD) 1970

**5795** NASH, ROSE L. Characterization of blacks in the theatre of the sixties
New York NY: Yeshiva U. (PhD)   1970

**5796** LOUDIN, JOANNE M. The changing role of the comic heroine in American drama from 1900 to 1940
Seattle: U. of Washington (PhD)   1974

**5797** APTER, ANDREW W. Popular American drama as an expression of American society, 1900-1910
Bloomington: Indiana U. (PhD)   1976

**5798** LABORDE, CHARLES B. Form and formula in detective drama: a structural study of selected twentieth century mystery plays
Columbus: Ohio State U. (PhD)   1976

**5799** SALT, GARY M. Cultural nationalism as idealogy in American drama from 1900 to 1920
Stanford: U. (PhD)   1976

**5800** McDONALD, ROBERT A. The popular drama of repertoire, 1880-1914: a formula approach
East Lansing: Michigan State U. (PhD)   1978

**5801** PAM, DOROTHY S. Exploitation, independence and solidarity: the changing role of American working women as reflected in the working-girl melodrama, 1870-1910
NY: U. (PhD)   1980

**5802** LUTER, GARY S. Sexual reform on the American stage in the progressive era, 1900-1915
Gainsville: U. of Florida (PhD)   1981

**5803** HILL, LYNN S. Heroes, heroines and villains in English and American melodrama: 1859-1900
NY: City U. (PhD)   1982

**5804** GEROULD, DANIEL C. (Ed.). American melodrama
pp. 247   M
NY: Performing Arts Journal Books   1983
Four texts with a substantial introduction : *The Americanization of melodrama*.

**5805** BARLOW, JUDITH E. Plays by American women 1900-1930
pp.xxxiii, 261   DL*
NY: Applause   1985
Revised edition. First published NY: Avon, 1981.

**5806** McLENNAN, KATHLEEN A. American domestic drama 1870 to 1910: individualism and the crisis of community
Madison: U. of Wisconsin (PhD)   1985

**5807** FRIEDL, BETTINA (Ed.). On to victory: propaganda plays of the woman suffrage movement
pp.xi, 378; ill. in text   M
Boston: Northeastern U. P.   1987
Reprints twenty plays of the period 1856-1917. Introduction, critical account and bibliography.

**5808** GOLDMAN, EMMA. The social significance of modern drama
pp. xvi, 174   M
NY: Applause   1987
New preface by Erica Munk. New introduction by Harry G. Carlson. Reissue of work first published Boston: Badger, 1914. The author acknowledges the inadequacy of the American drama to furnish material for her inquiry, but detects the beginnings of improvement.

**5809** MURPHY, BRENDA. American realism and American drama, 1880-1940
pp.xiv, 232; ill. in text   M
Cambridge: U. P.   1987

## 14.5   1919-1945

**5810** BOURDET, EDOUARD. *The Captive*...translated from the French by Arthur Hornblow. Introduction by Brooks Atkinson
pp.xi, 255; pl 5   M
NY: Brentano's   1923
The text of the controversial *La Prisonnière* which opened at the Empire NY on September 26 with a cast including Helen Hayes and Basil Rathbone. Production photographs.

**5811** WILLOUGHBY, PEARL V. The achievements of modern dramaturgy, British and American
Charlottesville: U. of Virginia (PhD)   1923

**5812** HAMILTON, CLAYTON. Conversations on contemporary drama...a series of nine lectures delivered Earl Hall, at Columbia University from February 11 to April 7, 1924
pp.xiii, 218   M
NY: Macmillan   1924

**5813** DICKINSON, THOMAS H. Playwrights of the new American theatre
pp.vii, 331   M
NY: Macmillan   1925
Survey ranging from MacKaye to O'Neill.

**5814** DICKINSON, THOMAS H. An outline of contemporary drama
pp.ix, 299   L
Boston: Houghton Mifflin   1927

**5815** BROWN, JOHN M. The modern theate in revolt
pp.xiii, 89   M
NY: W. W. Norton   1929
A study of naturalistic and post-naturalistic movements in the drama, based on lectures given under the auspices of the People's Institute.

**5816** GEDDES, VIRGIL. Beyond tragedy: footnotes on the drama
pp.iii, 33   MH
Seattle: U. of Washington Bookstore   1930
A deprecation of thesis drama.

**5817** JONES, JEAN B. Sociological problems in recent drama
Iowa City: U. of Iowa (PhD)   1931

**5818** SKINNER, RICHARD D. Our changing theatre
pp.327; front., pl. 7   L
NY: Dial P.   1931

Developments in US drama and theatre, with chapters establishing the European and British context. Particular reference to Eugene O'Neill, Sidney Howard, George Kelly. Chapters on the actor's art and on developments in scene design.

**5819** MERSAND, JOSEPH. A decade of biographical plays, 1928-1938: how the contemporary drama presents famous personalities
pp.44 MH
NY: Modern Chapbooks 1939

**5820** O'HARA, FRANK H. Today in American drama
pp.ix, 278 M
Chicago: U. P. 1939
A survey, arranged under tragedy, comedy, melodrama, didactic drama.

**5821** WITTLER, CLARENCE J. Some social trends in WPA drama
pp.vii, 125 MH
Washington DC: Catholic U. of America P. 1939

**5822** MERSAND, JOSEPH. The drama of social significance, 1930-1940 [cover title]
pp.20 MH
NY: [Modern Chapbooks] 1940

**5823** FOSTER, JACOB F. The development of social criticism in the Broadway theatre during the iner-war period, 1919-1939
NY: U. (PhD) 1943

**5824** MARTIN, BOYD. Modern American drama and stage
pp.126; pl. 15 M
London: Pilot P. 1943
Illustrations include caricatures by George Joseph. Author was director of the Louisville KY Playhouse.

**5825** MERSAND, JOSEPH. American drama goes to war: five essays on the contribution of plays to the war effort
pp.43 MH
NY: Modern Chapbooks 1943

**5826** CRAIN, HAROLD C. Characterization in the plays of modern dramatists. Techniques and practices
Iowa City: U. of Iowa (PhD) 1947

**5827** GAGEY, EDMOND M. Revolution in American drama
pp.ix, 315 M
NY: Columbia U. P. 1947
A survey of developments in the serious drama, 1912-1946.

**5828** GOULD, ARTHUR J. The idea of tragedy in modern American drama
Ann Arbor: U. of Michigan (PhD) 1948

**5829** MOORE, KEMPER M. The theater as it reflects the problems of the South: a study of the American theatre from 1919 to 1947 insofar as it has reflected the social and economic problems of the Southeastern region of the United States
Ann Arbor: U. of Michigan (PhD) 1950

**5830** HRUBY, NORBERT J. Successful American plays. 1919-1929. Patterns and their implications
Chicago: Loyola U. (PhD) 1951

**5831** ENGAR, KEITH M. Political satire in selected American plays of the twentieth century
Minneapolis: U. of Minnesota (PhD) 1952

**5832** COBIN, MARTIN T. A standard of serious American dramaturgy, 1920-1945
Madison: U. of Wisconsin (PhD) 1953

**5833** JOSEPH, BARBARA A. Patterns for modern American comedy since 1923
Cleveland OH: Case Western Reserve U. (PhD) 1953

**5834** KRUTCH, JOSEPH W. 'Modernism' in modern drama
pp.xiii, 138 MH
Ithaca NY: Cornell U. P. 1953
Derived from the Messenger lectures, Cornell, 1952. Includes material on Arthur Miller, Maxwell Anderson, Tennessee Williams.

**5835** McGREW, JULIA H. Character and tragedy in eight family sagas
Bryn Mawr: College (PhD) 1954

**5836** MODISETTE, ELDON L. Changing political thought in the American drama, 1919-1951
Minneapolis: U. of Minnesota (PhD) 1954

**5837** McCORMICK, ROBERT A. A study of original American fantasy presented on the New York stage from 1920-1950
Denver: U. (PhD) 1955

**5838** KRUTCH, JOSEPH W. The American drama since 1918: an informal history
pp.xii, 344 M
London: Thames & Hudson 1957
Revised edition, updated by additional chapter. First published NY: Random House, 1939.

**5839** SPRINGER, ROLAND A. Problems of higher education on the Broadway drama. A critical analysis of Broadway plays of 1920-1950, in order to discover their handling of the problems of higher education
NY: U. (PhD) 1957

**5840** WILEY, CHARLES. A study of the American woman as she is presented in the American drama of the 1920s
Albuquerque: U. of New Mexico (PhD) 1957

**5841** HIMELSTEIN, MORGAN Y. Social drama and the communist party in America, 1929-1941
NY: Columbia U. (PhD) 1958

**5842** NAPIECINSKI, THOMAS H. The dramatization of the American serious novel, 1925-1952
Madison: U. of Wisconsin (PhD) 1959

**5843** BAHOU, VICTOR S. The political drama in America since 1930
Syracuse: U. (PhD) 1960

**5844** ELLISTON, STEPHEN F. Dramatic and narrative art: studies of dramatizations on the New York stage, 1919-1958
Urbana: U. of Illinois (PhD) 1960

**5845** KETELS, ARTHUR O. The American drama of the twenties. A critical evaluation
Evanston: Northwestern U. (PhD) 1960

**5846** SMALLEY, WEBSTER L. The characterization of the male protagonist in serious American drama from 1920 to 1940
Stanford: U. (PhD)     1960

**5847** MILLER, JORDAN Y. American dramatic literature: ten modern plays in historical perspective
pp.xiv, 641;ill. in text     L
NY: McGraw-Hill     1961

Introductory section, *The backgrounds of modern American drama*, followed by playtexts, each with its introductory essay: Lillian Hellman: *The Little Foxes*; Tennessee Williams: *Camino Real*; Dubose Heyward: *Porgy*; W. W. Haines: *Command Decision*; S. N. Behrman: *Biography*; James Thurber & Elliott Nugent: *The Male Animal*; Carson McCullers: *The Member of the Wedding*; Mary C. Chase: *Harvey*; Eugene O'Neill: *Desire under the Elms*; Arthur Miller: *The Crucible*.

**5848** MANFULL, HELEN A. The new realism (a study of American dramatic realism from 1918-1929)
Minneapolis: U. of Minnesota (PhD)     1962

**5849** MIRANNE, JOSEPH J. An investigation of the nature of short story adaptation in dramatic presentation for the Broadway theater from 1930 to 1960
NY: U. (PhD)     1962

**5850** GOBRECHT, ELEANOR A. A descriptive study of the value commitments of the principal characters in four recent American plays: *Picnic, Cat on a Hot Tin Roof, Long Day's Journey into Night* and *Look Homeward, Angel*
Los Angeles: U. of Southern California (PhD)     1963

**5851** KNOX, GEORGE A. & STAHL, HERBERT M. Dos Passos and 'the Revolting Playwrights'
pp.230; pl. 6     L
Upsala: Lundequistska Bokhandeln     1964

An account of the New Playwrights' Theatre in New York 1927-29, involving John Dos Passos, John Howard Lawson, Em Jo Basshe, Michael Gold, Francis Edward Faragoh.

**5852** RABKIN, GERALD. Drama and commitment: politics in the American theatre of the thirties
pp.vii, 322     L
Bloomington: Indiana U. P.     1964

Includes material on the Group Theatre, Theatre Union, the Federal Theatre Project, John Howard Lawson, Clifford Odets, S. N. Behrman, Maxwell Anderson.

**5853** DENNING, DENIS. The theme of poverty as expressed in plays by six Depression playwrights
Lawrence: U. of Kansas (PhD)     1965

**5854** HICKLIN, FANNIE E. The American negro playwrights, 1920 to 1964
Madison: U. of Wisconsin (PhD)     1965

**5855** HOFFMAN, FRED J. The twenties: American writing in the postwar decade
pp.516     L
NY: Free P.     1965

Second edition, revised. First published 1955.

**5856** KAUFMAN, ALVIN S. Attitudes and adjustments of the soldier to war and the military as revealed in the American drama, 1940-1960
Stanford: U. (PhD)     1965

**5857** BRÜNING, EBERHARD. Das amerikanische Drama der dreissiger Jahre
pp.406     O
Berlin: Rütter & Loening     1966

**5858** WEISMAN, MARTHA. A study of anti-war plays produced in the New York professional theatre from World War 1 to World War 2
NY: Columbia U. Teachers' College (PhD)     1966

**5859** BARTOLUCCI, GIUSEPPE. America hurrah ! Per un teatro di metafora
pp.132; ill.     DL★
Genoa: Teatro Stabile     1968

Twentieth century US theatre.

**5860** STEINER, DAVID E. The American military: theme and figure in New York stage plays from 1919-1941
Eugene: U. of Oregon (PhD)     1968

**5861** ZAPELL, ALICE L. The effects of the political climate in the United States on the treatment of political subjects in the American theatre from 1920 to 1940
Eugene: U. of Oregon (PhD)     1968

**5862** ABRAMSON, DORIS E. Negro playwrights in the American theatre 1925-1959
pp.xc, 335     M
NY: Columbia U. P.     1969

**5863** DICKINSON, HUGH. Myth on the modern stage
pp.vii, 359; front.     L
Urbana: U. of Illinois P.     1969

Includes chapters on Robinson Jeffers, Eugene O'Neill, Tennessee Williams.

**5864** PORTER, THOMAS E. Myth and modern American drama
pp.285     L
Detroit: Wayne State U. P.     1969

**5865** GILROY, M. N. The political character in Broadway plays from 1929-1969
NY: U. (PhD)     1970

**5866** BURKE, WILLIAM M. American playwrights' treatment of war, 1914-1949
Philadelphia: U. of Pennsylvania (PhD)     1971

**5867** HINDMAN, ANNE A. The myth of the western frontier in American dance and drama:1930-1943
Athens: U. of Georgia (PhD)     1971

**5868** SMILEY, SAM. The drama of attack: didactic plays of the American depression
pp.xii, 236     MESM
Columbia: U. of Missouri P.     1972

**5869** VALGEMAE, MARDI. Accelerated grimace: expressionism in the American drama of the 1920s...with a preface by Henry T. Moore
pp.xiv, 145     M
Carbondale: Southern Illinois U. P.     1972

Material on George C. Cook, Eugene O'Neill, Elmer Rice, John Howard Lawson, the Provincetown players, the New Playwrights' Theatre.

**5870** KIESBY, SUZANNE B. A structural analysis of American war plays 1935-1948
Columbia: U. of Missouri (PhD)     1973

**5871** ZAHLWER, WILLIAM P. The husband and wife relationship in American drama from 1919 to 1939
Kent OH: State U. (PhD) 1973

**5872** JONES, ALFRED H. Roosevelt's image brokers: poets, playwrights, and the use of the Lincoln symbol
pp.ix, 134 L
Port Washington NY: Kennikat P. 1974
Includes material on Robert E. Sherwood's *Abe Lincoln in Illinois*.

**5873** MORGAN, ROBERT L. The American president on the New York stage 1919-1973
Urbana-Champaign: U. of Illinois (PhD) 1975

**5874** SAKALAUSKAS, WILLIAM B. The Third Reich on Broadway: the portrayal of the Nazi character on Broadway by American playwrights from 1933 to 1970
East Lansing: Michigan State U. (PhD) 1975

**5875** WEBER, ALFRED & NEUWEILER, SIEGFRIED (Eds). Amerikanisches drama und theater im. 20. Jahrhundert
pp.363 L
Gottingen: Vandenhoeck & Ruprecht 1975
Essays in German, each with a brief summary in English. Peter Bauland: *Expressionism in modern American drama*; Paul G. Buchloh: *Die Bedeutung aussersprachlicher Mittel in modernen Amerikanischen Theater*; Gerhard Hoffman: *Eugene O'Neill*; Robert Brainerd Pearsall: *Anderson's 'Winterset'*; Joseph C. Schopp: *Wilder's 'Our Town'*; Joseph K. Davis: *Tennessee Williams and the south*; William Heyen, Hartmut Grandel: *Death of a Salesman*; Siegfried Neuweiler: *Lowell's 'The Old Glory'*; Allen Guttmann: *Lorraine Hansberry*; Glen Burns: *Le Roi Jones*; Paul Goetsch: *Edward Albee*; Ruby Cohn: *'Macbeth' off Broadway*; Herbert Grabes: *Jean-Claude Van Itallie's 'America Hurrah'*.

**5876** ZASTROW, SYLVIA. The structure of selected plays by American women playwrights: 1920-1970
Evanston: Northwestern U. (PhD) 1975

**5877** STEPHENS, JUDITH L. The central female characters in the Pulitzer Prize plays, 1918-1949
Kent OH: State U. (PhD) 1977

**5878** LIEBERMAN, JOSEPH A. The emergence of lesbians and gay men as characters in plays produced on the American stage from 1922 to 1954
NY: City U. (PhD) 1981

**5879** OLAUSON, JUDITH. The American woman playwright: a view of criticism and characterization
pp.ix, 182 MH
Troy NY: Whitston 1981
1930-1970 divided into decades, each treating a group of playwrights.

**5880** COSGROVE, STUART. The Living Newspaper: history, production and form
Hull UK: U. (PhD) 1982

**5881** EISENHOUR, JERRY D. Audience, stage, and milieu: long-running Broadway plays in social and historical perspective 1920-1949
Columbia: U. od Missouri (PhD) 1982

**5882** GREENFIELD, THOMAS A. Work and the work ethic in American drama, 1920-1970
pp.x, 187 DL★
Columbia: U. of Missouri P. 1982

**5883** AUSLANDER, PHILIP. The pop sensibility in theatre: plays by the poets of the New York school
Ithaca: Cornell U. (PhD) 1983
Reference to Ashbery, Kock, O'Hara, Schuyler.

**5884** DUKORE, BERNARD F. American dramatists 1918-1945 excluding O'Neill
pp.xiv, 191; pl. 4 M
London: Macmillan 1984

**5885** ZINGALE, JEANNE W. The disabled as taboo: an examination of physically disabled characters in twentieth-century plays produced in New York City
Kent OH: State U. (PhD) 1984

**5886** AUSTIN, ADDELL O. Pioneering black-authored dramas, 1924-1927
East Lansing: Michigan State U. (PhD) 1986

**5887** COSTOPOULOS, JOHN. Homosexuality on the New York Stage: its critical reception, 1926 to 1968
NY: U. (PhD) 1986

**5888** REYNOLDS, R. C. Stage left: the development of the American social drama of the thirties
pp.xxx, 175 M
Troy NY: Whitston 1986

**5889** ADLER, THOMAS. Mirror on the stage: the Pulitzer plays as an approach to American drama
pp.xv, 171 MH
Lafayette IN: Purdue U. P. 1987

**5890** FRIEDL, BETTINA (Ed.). On to victory: propaganda plays of the woman suffrage movement
pp.xi, 375; ill. in text HKA
Boston: Northeastern U. P. 1987
Substantial introduction.

**5891** COUNTS, MICHAEL L. Coming home: the soldier's return in twentieth century American drama
pp.x, 224 ★
NY: Peter Lang 1988

**5892** SCHROEDER, PATRICIA R. The presence of the past in modern American drama
pp. 148 ★
Rutherford: Fairleigh Dickinson U. P. 1989

## 14.6 1946-1990

**5893** McILRATH, PATRICIA A. Typification in the characterization of contemporary American drama. With an analysis of stereotype
Stanford: U. (PhD) 1951

**5894** BASSAGE, HAROLD E. The moral price of freedom. Problems of personal freedom reflected in modern American drama
NY: Columbia U. (PhD) 1952

**5895** FOWLER, FRANK C. Modern American dramatization
NY: Columbia U. (PhD) 1953

**5896** LE THÉÂTRE CONTEMPORAIN en Grande-Bretagne et aux États-Unis [cover title]
pp.190 M
Paris: Librairie Didier 1957

A complete issue of *Etudes Anglaises*, année 10, no. 4. Includes: Léonie Villard: *Introduction à une étude du théâtre Américain d'aujourd'hui*; S. Fleche-Salgues: *Trois pièces récentes d'Eugene O'Neill*; C. Arnavon *La vogue de Thornton Wilder*; Roger Asselineau: *Tennessee Williams ou la nostalgie de la pureté*.

**5897** DONOGHUE, DENIS. The third voice: modern British and American verse drama
pp.vi, 286 M
London: Oxford U. P. 1959

First published Princeton NJ: U. P., 1959. Includes material on E. E. Cummings, Wallace Stevens, Archibald MacLeish, Richard Eberhart.

**5898** CAHALAN, THOMAS L. & DOYLE, PAUL A. Modern American drama
pp.169 DL★
Boston: Student Outlines 1960

**5899** GASSNER, JOHN. Theatre at the crossroads: plays and playwrights of the mid-century American stage
pp.xxi, 327 M
NY: Holt, Rinehart and Winston 1960

An assessment of post-WW2 theatre from the vantage point of Broadway and off-Broadway stage production.

**5900** DOWNER, ALAN S. Recent American drama
pp.46 M
Minneapolis: U. of Minnesota P. 1961

**5901** McCARTHY, MARY. On the contrary: articles of belief, 1946-1961
pp.vii, 312; ill. in text L
NY: Farrar, Straus and Giroux 1961

Includes: *Naming names: the Arthur Miller case*, *The American realist playwrights*.

**5902** BROUSSARD, LOUIS. American drama. Contemporary allegory from Eugene O'Neill to Tennessee Williams
pp.ix, 145; pl. 4 L
Norman: U. of Oklahoma P. 1962

On the influence of expressionism, urging the thesis that the 'drama of despair', deriving from Europe, dominates twentieth century American serious theatre.

**5903** LABRENZ, ERNEST T. A critical analysis of the negative attitudes in plays exclusive of musical comedies which won the Pulitzer Prize between 1948-1957
Stanford: U. (PhD) 1962

**5904** WEALES, GERALD. American drama since world war II
pp.ix, 246 M
NY: Harcourt, Brace & World 1962

**5905** VON SZELISKI, JOHN J. Pessimism and the tragic vision. A study of tragedy in the modern American theatre
Minneapolis: U. of Minnesota (PhD) 1963

**5906** FREEDMAN, MORRIS (Ed.). Essays in the modern drama
pp.x, 374 DL★
Boston: Heath 1964

**5907** THURMAN, WILLIAM R. Anxiety in modern American drama
Athens: U. of Georgia (PhD) 1964

**5908** BOGARD, TRAVIS & OLIVER, WILLIAM I. (Eds). Modern drama: essays in criticism
pp.vi, 393 M
NY: Oxford U. P. 1965

Contributions include Arthur Miller: *The family in modern drama*; John H. Raleigh: Eugene O'Neill; the editor: Thornton Wilder; John Gassner: Tennessee Williams.

**5909** EYSSELINCK, WALTER. The theatricalization of modern American drama
New Haven: Yale U. (DFA) 1965

**5910** LEATHERS, DALE G. A desriptive study of revolutionary reaction of the 1960s: the rhetoric of salvation
Minneapolis: U. of Minnesota (PhD) 1965

**5911** LEWIS, ALLAN. American plays and playwrights of the contemporary theatre
pp.272 MH
NY: Crown 1965

Surveys the major playwrights and looks also at off-Broadway, the musical, topical revue, and discernible trends.

**5912** LITTLEJOHN, DAVID. Black on white: a critical survey of writing by American negroes
pp.180 DL★
NY: Grossman 1966

Includes a section on playwrights.

**5913** PHILLIPS, ELIZABETH C. & ROGERS, DAVID. Modern American drama
pp.125 DL★
NY: Monarch P. 1966

**5914** RAHV, PHILIP (Ed.). Modern occasions...
pp.x, 369 L
NY: Farrar, Straus and Giroux 1966

A selection of hitherto unpublished writings in English. Includes Robert Brustein: *The new American playwrights*.

**5915** BIGSBY, C. W. Confrontation and commitment. A study of contemporary American drama 1959-66
pp.xix, 187 L
London: Macgibbon & Kee 1967

Chapters on Eugene O'Neill, Arthur Miller, the Living Theatre, Edward Albee, the new surrealism, James Baldwin, Leroi Jones, Lorraine Hansberry.

**5916** FLOYD, VIRGINIA. An analytical study of the role of *hubris* in the spiritual environment of American drama from 1945-1961
Evanston: Northwestern U. (PhD) 1967

**5917** KERNAN, ALVIN B. (Ed.). The modern American theater: a collection of critical essays
pp.viii, 183 M
Englewood Cliffs NJ: Prentice-Hall 1967

Contains: an editorial essay, *Attempted dance: a discussion of the modern drama*; Ken Tynan: *American blues: the plays of Arthur Miller*; Tyrone Guthrie: *The world of Thornton Wilder*; Travis Bogard: *The comedy of Thornton Wilder*; Robert Brustein: *The men-taming women of William Inge: The dark at the top of the stairs*; Lee Boxandall: *The theatre of Edward Albee*; Tom F. Driver: *What's the matter with Edward Albee?*; Francis Fergusson: *Broadway*; the editor: *Off Broadway*; Elenore Lester: *The pass-the-hat theater circuit*; Allan Kaprow: *Happenings in the New York scene*; Gordon Rogoff: *The juggernaut of production*; Richard Gilman: *The drama is coming now*; Edward Albee: *Which theater is the absurd one?*; and a chronology of important plays.

**5918** COUCH, WILLIAM (Ed.). New black playwrights
pp.xxiii, 256 L
Baton Rouge: Louisiana U. P. 1968

Playtexts, with substantial introduction. Authors include Douglas Turner Ward, Adrienne Kennedy, Carter Harrison, Ed Bullins, William W. Mackey.

**5919** TAYLOR, WILLIAM E. (Ed.). Modern American drama: essays in criticism
pp.v, 200 MH
Deland FL: Everett Edwards 1968

Chapters on Eugene O'Neill, Clifford Odets, Maxwell Anderson, Tennessee Williams, Arthur Miller, Edward Albee, verse playwrights, novelists as playwrights, off-Broadway plays, comedy of manners.

**5920** GAYLE, ADDISON (Ed.). Black expressions: essays by and about black Americans in the arts
pp.xx, 394 MH
NY: Weybright and Talley 1969

Includes essays by Alain Locke, Montgomery Gregory, Toni Cade, Ed Bullins, K. William Kgositsite, Loften Mitchell, Jessie Fauset.

**5921** HUFFINGTON, DALE D. Post-existential thought in American *avant-garde* drama
Minneapolis: U. of Minnesota (PhD) 1969

**5922** LOWENTHAL, LAWRENCE D. The absurd in recent American drama
NY: U. (PhD) 1969

**5923** SCHALL, CELIA M. The treatment of selected themes in recent American dramas about Negroes: 1959-1967
Lawrence: U. of Kansas (PhD) 1969

Lorraine Hansberry: *Raisin in the Sun*; LeRoi Jones: *Dutchman*; Howard Sackler: *Great White Hope*.

**5924** WEALES, GERALD. The jumping-off place: American drama in the 1960s
pp.xiii, 306 M
London: Macmillan 1969

**5925** AARON, JULES C. The audience in the mirror: the role of game-ritual in contemporary theatre
NY: U. (PhD) 1970

**5926** CORNISH, ROGER N. The decline of the leader: recent English and American historical plays
Minneapolis: U. of Minnesota (PhD) 1970

Includes reference to Arthur Miller: *The Crucible. After the Fall*; Paddy Chayefsky: *The Passion of Josef D.*: Barbara Garson: *MacBird*.

**5927** MADDEN, DAVID (Ed.). American dreams, American nightmares
pp.xlii, 229 L
Carbondale: Southern Illinois P. 1970

Includes: Chester E. Eisinger: *Focus on...'Death of a Salesman', the wrong dreams*; Robert B. Heilman: *The dream metaphor, some ramifications*; Frederick I. Carpenter: *Focus on 'The Iceman Cometh'. The iceman hath come*. Preface by Harry T. Moore.

**5928** RAMA MURTHY, V. American expressionistic drama; containing analyses of three outstanding American plays: O'Neill: *The Hairy Ape*; Williams: *The Glass Menagerie*; Miller: *Death of a Salesman*.
pp.ix, 102 L
Delhi: Doaba House 1970

**5929** CALHOUN, JOHN T. The American comedy: social perspectives since World War II
Boulder: U. of Colorado (PhD) 1971

**5930** GAYLE, ADDISON (Ed.). The black aesthetic
pp.xxiv, 432 O
Garden City: Doubleday 1971

Section four, *Drama*, comprises essays on the theatre by Alain Locke, Larry Neal, Loften Mitchell, Donald Milner, Clayton Riley.

**5931** HAYS, PETER L. The limping hero: grotesques in literature
pp.vii, 248; ill. in text L
NY: U. P. 1971

Widely allusive to Tennessee Williams and Edward Albee.

**5932** RANG, JACK C. Concepts of love in American plays on Broadway, 1950-1965
Evanston: Northwestern U. (PhD) 1971

**5933** HOLDEN, DAVID F. An analytical index to *Modern Drama*, volumes 1-X111, May 1958-February 1971
pp.vi, 218 L
Toronto: *Modern Drama* 1972

**5934** KESSELY, URS. The domineering woman in twentieth century American drama [cover title]
pp.11 L
[Heerbrugg]: For the author 1972

Concentrates on Edward Albee and Arthur Kopit.

**5935** KIDD, T. J. Social alienation in modern American drama
Cambridge: U. (PhD) 1972

**5936** WILLIAMS, SHERLEY A. Give birth to brightness: a thematic study in neo-black literature
pp.252 MH
NY: Dial P. 1972

Includes a chapter on James Baldwin: *Blues for Mister Charlie*, and material on Le Roi Jones and Ernest Games.

**5937** HIRSCH, ROBIN M. Patterns of ritual in the drama and certain avant-garde American dramatists
University Park: Pennsylvania State U. (PhD) 1973

**5938** HUGHES, CATHARINE. Plays, politics and polemics
pp.xvii, 194 MH
NY: Drama Book Specialists 1973

On the contemporary political stage.

**5939** GOETSCH, PAUL (Ed.). Das amerikanische Drama
pp.380     MH
Düsseldorf: Bagel     1974
Interpretations. Eugene O'Neill: *Mourning becomes Electra*, *The Iceman Cometh*; Elmer Rice: *The Adding Machine*; Maxwell Anderson: *Winterset*; Clifford Odets: *Golden Boy*; Thornton Wilder: *The Skin of our Teeth*; Tennessee Williams: *Streetcar named Desire*; Arthur Miller: *Death of a Salesman*, *The Price*; Lillian Hellman: *Autumn Garden*; Jack Gelber: *The Apple*; Edward Albee: *Who's Afraid of Virginia Woolf*; Charles Gordone: *No Place to be Somebody*.

**5940** GUERNSEY, OTIS L. (Ed.). Playwrights, lyricists, composers on theater......The inside story of a decade of theater in articles and comments by its authors, selected from their own publication, the *Dramatists Guild Quarterly*. Drawings by Tom Funk
pp.xii, 435; ill. in text     M
NY: Dodd, Mead     1974

**5941** STARR, JACK D. Manifestations of 'sexuality' on the American stage as illustrated by selected plays from 1960-1969
Minneapolis: U. of Minnesota (PhD)     1974

**5942** TEDESCO, JOHN L. The white image as second 'persona' in black drama, 1955-1970
Iowa City: U. of Iowa (PhD)     1974

**5943** TOUCHET, GENE R. American drama and the emergence of social homophilia, 1952-1972
Gainsville: U. of Florida (PhD)     1974

**5944** BRUSTEIN, ROBERT. The culture watch: essays on theatre and society, 1969-1974
pp.xv, 197, vii     DL★
NY: Alfred A. Knopf     1975

**5945** GOURAN, PATRICK D. Broadway comedy of the 1960s
Boulder: U. of Colorado (PhD)     1975

**5946** LOEFFLER, DONALD L. An analysis of the treatment of the homosexual character in dramas produced in the New York theatre from 1950 to 1968: with a new preface
pp.xiv, 201     MH
NY: Arno P.     1975

**5947** SANDERS, JOSEPH E. Modern American war plays
Los Angeles: U. of California (PhD)     1975

**5948** WINNER, CAROLE A. A study of American dramatic productions dealing with the war in Vietnam
Denver: U. (PhD)     1975

**5949** ANDREWS, W. D. American black activist drama of the 1960s
Belfast: Queen's College (PhD)     1976

**5950** GRABES, HERBERT (Ed.). Das amerikanische Drama der Gegenwart
pp.224     MH
Kronberg: Athenaum     1976

Articles on Arthur Miller, Edward Albee, Arthur Kopit, *Hair*, off- and off-off Broadway, Jack Gelber, Barbara Garson, Lanford Wilson, Jean-Claude Van Itallie, Lorraine Hansberry, James Baldwin, LeRoi Jones, Ed Bullins.

**5951** MILLER, JEANNE-MARIE A. Dramas by black American playwrights produced on the New York professional stage (from *The Chip Woman's Fortune* to *Five on the Black Hand Side*)
Washington DC: Howard U. (PhD)     1976

**5952** SHAFER, GEORGE W. Rhetorical dramaturgy of anti Vietnam war drama
Kent OH: State U. (PhD)     1976

**5953** BRÜNING, EBERHARD; KÖHLER, KLAUS & SCHELLER, BERNHARD. Studien zum amerikanischen Drama nach dem zweiten Weltkrieg
pp.328     ★
Berlin: Rütten & Loening     1977

**5954** FRIEDMAN, SHARON. Feminist concerns in the works of four twentieth century American women dramatists: Susan Glaspell, Rachel Crothers, Lillian Hellman, and Lorraine Hansberry
NY: U. (PhD)     1977

**5955** MATERASSI, MARIO. Il ponte sullo Harlem River: saggi e note sulla cultura e la letteratura afroamericana di oggi
pp.166     MH
Rome: Bulzoni     1977
Includes reference to James Baldwin, Imamu Amiri Baraka, with reprinted reviews.

**5956** COHEN, SARAH B. (Ed.). Comic relief: humor in contemporary American literature
pp.xi, 339     L
Urbana: U. of Illinois P.     1978
Includes Charles H. Nichols: *Comic modes in black America* (with some reference to Imamu Amiri Baraka); Ruby Cohn: *Camp, cruelty, colloquialism* [aspects of humour in the contemporary US theatre].

**5957** PRADHAN, NARINDAR S. Modern American drama: a study in myth and tradition
pp.138     L
New Delhi: Arnold-Heinemann     1978

**5958** SCANLAN, TOM. Family drama and American dreams
pp.xi, 236     MESM
Westport CT: Greenwod P.     1978
Emphasizing the work of Eugene O'Neill, Arthur Miller, Tennessee Williams.

**5959** PHILLIPS, J. M. Modern American prize-winning plays (1965-1975): structural analysis and criticism
Baton Rouge: Louisiana State U. (PhD)     1979

**5960** BIGSBY, C. W. The second black renaissance
pp.xi, 333     O
Westport CT: Greenwood P.     1980
Includes section: *Black drama: the public voice*.

**5961** GONSHER, DEBRA. Stereotypes of women in contemporary American drama, 1958-1978
NY: City U. (PhD)     1980

**5962** PEVITTS, BEVERLEY B. Feminist thematic trends in plays written by women for the American theatre: 1900-1979
Carbondale: Southern Illinois U. (PhD)     1980

**5963** PAUL, JOHN S. The theatrical setting as environment in twelve plays of the modern American theatre
Madison: U. of Wisconsin (PhD) 1981

**5964** METCALF, WILLIAM A. A search for the causes of violence in selected plays of David Rabe and Sam Shepard compared to the patterns of violence found in Rollo May's *Power and Innocence: a search for the sources of violence*
Minneapolis: U. of Minnesota (PhD) 1982

**5965** OLSZEWSKI, JOSEPH F. American theater in the sixties and seventies: the non-Broadway stage and its playwrights
St Louis MO: U. (PhD) 1982

**5966** SCHÄFER, JÜRGEN. Geschichte des amerikanischen Dramas im 20-Jahrhundert
pp.206 MH
Stuttgart: W. Kohlammer 1982

**5967** TURNER, S. H. REGINA. Images of black women in the plays of black female playwrights 1950-1975
Bowling Green: State U. (PhD) 1982

**5968** UMLAS, RODNEY J. Loneliness as motive, theme, and strategy in American theatre of the 1960s
NY: Columbia U. (PhD) 1982

**5969** HAZZARD-PIANKHI, MAISHA L. Black love on stage: a profile of courtship and marriage relationships in selected Broadway shows by black dramatists 1959-1979, and an original play
Bowling Green OH: State U. (PhD) 1983

**5970** JACKMAN, MICHAEL C. Toward a new theater of cruelty
Buffalo: State U. of NY (PhD) 1983

**5971** NEIHEISER, THOMAS N. Heroes and fools: characterizations in holocaust drama
Salt Lake City: U. of Utah (PhD) 1983

**5972** HAYES, DONALD. An analysis of dramatic themes used by selected black-American playwrights from 1950 to 1976 with a backgrounder: the state of the art of contemporary black theatre and playwriting
Detroit: Wayne State U. (PhD) 1984

**5973** KEYSSAR, HELENE. Feminist theatre. An introduction to plays of contemporary British and American women
pp.xvi, 223; pl. 4 M
London: Macmillan 1984

**5974** POWELL, L. LAURENCE. The male homosexual character as portrayed in six selected plays from the American theatre, 1968-1978
Bowling Green: State U. (PhD) 1984

**5975** ROBBINS, LEONARD H. Madness in modern drama
Binghamton: State U. of NY (PhD) 1984

**5976** DAVIS, RONALD O. A rhetorical study of four critically acclaimed black dramatic plays produced on and off-Broadway between 1969 and 1981
Tallahassee: Florida State U. (PhD) 1985

**5977** RESTON, JAMES (Ed.). Coming to terms: American plays and the Viet-Nam war
pp.xi, 312 MH
NY: Theatre Communications Group 1985
Playtexts. Substantial and helpful introduction.

**5978** KIM, YUN-CHEOL. A critical examination of individual, familial, and social destructiveness in selected Pulitzer plays, 1969-1984
Provo: Brigham Young U. (PhD) 1986

**5979** KOLIN, PHILIP C. & KULLMAN, COLBY H. et al (Eds). Studies in American drama 1945 - present
pp.various; ill. in text L
Columbus: Ohio State U. P. 1986-1990
Five volumes. 1. Anne Paolucci: *Albee & the restructuring of the modern stage*; Gilbert Debusscher: *New light on the genesis of 'Sweet Bird of Youth'*; N. Canaday: *...the plays of Ed Bullins*; S. R. Centola : *After the Fall*; Matthew Roudané: *An interview with David Mamet*; D. Grunes :*Tiny Alice*; J. M. Davis & J. Coleman: *A bibliography of David Mamet*. 2. Gerald Weales: *Clifford Odets*; June Schlueter :*Megan Terry*; Don B. Wilmeth: *An interview with Romulus Linney*; J. Diguentani: *An interview with Albert Innaurato*; R. Erben: *Women and other men in Shepard's plays*; W. W. Demostes: *Charles Fuller and 'A Soldier's Play'*; P. Egan: *A Ronald Ribman bibliography*. 3. David Rabe: *Oddo's Response* [playtext]; C. W. Bigsby: *Drama and the critic*; Laura Morrow *Beth Henley and Marsha Norman*; Priscilla S. McKinney: *Jung's 'anima' in Arthur Miller's plays*; Jeane Leure: *Edward Albee*; T. Bonner: *A photo essay on Tennessee Williams*; Jackson R. Bryer: *An interview with Robert Anderson*; Susan H. Smith: *An interview with Charles Gordone*; Alexis Greene: *An interview with Jean-Claude Van Itallie*; Irmgarde H. Wolfe: *A Norma Marsh bibliography*. 4. Megan Terry: *Anybody is as their land...*; J. Timpane: *Ntozake Shange*; Lurana D. O'Malley: *Maria Irene Fornés women's work*; Jean Gagen: *Beth Henley and Chekhov*; J. Dillon: *Photo essay on Alice Childress's 'Wedding Band'*; Elin Diamond: *An interview with Adrienne Kennedy*; Judith E. Barlow: *An interview with Tina Howe*; Felicia H. Londré: *An interview with Megan Terry*; Vivian M. Patraka: *An interview with Joan Schenkar*; Nancy Klementowski & Sonja Kuftinec: *An interview with Constance Congdon*; Philip C. Kolin: *An Emily Mann bibliography*. 5. Laura Chandler: *William Inge's 'The Love Death'* (which is also given its first publication here); Gary Konas: *Tennessee Williams and Lanford Wilson*; N. A. Lester: *An interview with Ntozake Shange*; J. C. Wolter: *David Mamet in German speaking countries*.

**5980** BLAU, HERBERT. The eye of prey: subversions of the postmodern
pp. xxxvii, 213 M
Bloomington: Indiana U. P. 1987
Substantially, an examination of post 1960s drama. Essays include: *Comedy since the absurd*; *The American dream in American gothic: the plays of Sam Shepard and Adrienne Kennedy*; *Universals of performance: or, amortizing play*.

**5981** HERMAN, WILLIAM. Understanding contemporary American drama
pp.xiii, 271 MH
Columbia: U. of South Carolina P. 1987
General introduction. Includes essays on: Sam Shepard, David Rabe, David Mamet, Ed Bullins.

**5982** AUSTIN, GAYLE. Feminist theory and post-war American drama
NY: City U. (PhD) 1988

**5983** COSGROVE, JAMES D. The rebel in modern drama
Princeton: U. (PhD) 1988

**5984** DEMASTES, WILLIAM W. Beyond naturalism: a new realism in American theatre
pp.xii, 174; ill. in text            L
NY: Greenwood P.            1988

General background, and chapters on David Rabe, David Mamet, Sam Shepard, Charles Fuller, Beth Henley, Marsha Norman.

**5985** FENN, JEFFREY W. Culture under stress: American drama and the Vietnam war
Vancouver: U. of British Columbia (PhD)      1988

**5986** GEIS, DEBORAH R. Mythmaking and story-telling: the monologue in contemporary American drama
Ann Arbor: U. of Michigan (PhD)          1988

**5987** MALKIN, JEANETTE R. Verbal violence in modern drama: a study of language as aggression
NY: U. (PhD)             1988

**5988** HART, LYNDA (Ed.). Making a spectacle: feminist essays on contemporary women's theatre
pp.vii, 347; ill. in text            M
Ann Arbor: U. of Michigan P.         1989

Vivian M. Patraka: *Mass culture and metaphors of menace in Joan Schenkar's plays*; Nancy Backes: *Body art: hunger and satiation in the plays of Tina Howe*; Margaret B. Wilkerson: *Music as metaphor: new plays of black women*; Gayle Austin: *The madwoman in the spotlight: plays of Maria Irene Fornés*; Mary K. Deshazer: *Rejecting necrophilia: Ntozake Shange and the warrior revisioned*; Susan Carlson: *Revisionary endings: Pam Gems's 'Aunt Mary' and 'Camille'*; Jonnie Guerra: *Beth Henley: female quest and the family play tradition*; Lynda Hart: *'They don't even look like maids anymore': Wendy Kesselman's 'My Sister in this House'*; Jenny S. Spencer: *Marsha Norman's 'She-tragedies'*; Jan Breslauer & Helene Keyssar: *Making magic public: Megan Terry's travelling family circus*; Stephanie Arnold: *Dissolving the half shadows: Japanese American women playwrights*; Anita Plath Helle: *Re-presenting women writers onstage: a retrospective to the present*; Yolanda Broyles González: *Toward a re-vision of Chicano theatre history: the women of El Teatro Campesino*; Janelle Reinelt: *Micheline Wandor: artist and ideologue*; Elin Diamond: *(In)visible bodies in Churchill's theater*; Sue-Ellen Case: *Toward a butch-femme aesthetic*; Rosemary Curb: *Mirrors moving beyond frames: Sandra Shotlander's 'Framework' and 'Blind Salome'*; Jill Dolan: *Bending gender to fit the canon: the politics of production*.

**5989** SCHLUETER, JUNE (Ed.). Feminist readings of modern American drama
pp.249            MH
Rutherford: Fairleigh Dickinson U. P.      1989

Thirteen essays examining issues of gender in the work of Eugene O'Neill, Arthur Miller, Tennessee Williams, Edward Albee, Sam Shepard.

**5990** BENNETT, BENJAMIN. Theater as problem: modern drama and its place in literature
pp.272            *
Ithaca: Cornell U. P.           1990

**5991** GERSON, LYDIA. The influence of the post-World War II era on the American political theatre, 1968-72
NY: City U. (PhD)           1990

**5992** SCHLUETER, JUNE (Ed.). Modern American drama: the female canon
pp.308            DL*
Rutherford NJ: Fairleigh Dickinson U. P.    1990

## 15. FOREIGN INFLUENCES

**5993** PARRY, ELLWOOD C. Friedrich Schiller in America: a contribution to the literature of the poet's centenary, 1905
pp.116            L
Philadelphia: American Germanica P.      1905

Reprinted from *German American Annals*, III; comprises a bibliography of books and pamphlets bearing on the life and works of Schiller published in the US to the end of 1859, including foreign books with US imprint, preceded by a chronological commentary on the items listed. Includes stage adaptations.

**5994** BAKER, LOUIS C. The German drama in English on the New York stage to 1830
pp.vii, 168            O
Philadelphia: U. P.           1917

**5995** HUDSON, VIRGINIA O. Charles Dickens and the American theatre
Chicago: U. (PhD)           1926

**5996** THORNDIKE, ASHLEY. Shakespeare in America
pp.22            L
London: Oxford U. P./British Academy     1927

'The influence of Shakespeare on some aspects of American schooling and culture'.

**5997** LEUCHS, FRITZ A. The early German theatre in New York 1840-1872
pp.xxi, 298            M
NY: Colombia U. P.           1928

Chapter 2 includes a section, *German drama in English...*; Chapter 7, *Principal points of contact between the German- and the English-language stages of New York during the middle of the nineteenth century*.

**5998** ANDERSON, ANNETTE. Ibsen in America
Iowa City: Iowa U. (PhD)         1931

**5999** NAESETH, HENRIETTE C. Sardou on the American stage
Chicago: U. (PhD)           1931

**6000** PAULSON, ARTHUR C. The Norwegian-American reaction to Ibsen and Björnson, 1850-1900
Iowa City: U. of Iowa (PhD)        1933

**6001** NEEDLE, HAROLD F. The plays of August von Kotzebue on the New York and Philadelphia stages
University Park: Pennsylvania State College (MA)            1934

**6002** BLACKBURN, CLARA B. Influences on American expressionistic drama
Columbus: Ohio State U. (PhD)      1938

**6003** HEBRON, MARY D. Sir Walter Scott in New Orleans 1833-1850
New Orleans: Tulane U. (MA)       1940

**6004** MASON, HAMILTON. French plays in New York: a list of plays, 1899-1939
pp.ix, 442 M
NY: Columbia U. P. 1940

**6005** RAPP, ESTHER J. Strindberg's reception in England and America
Boulder: U. of Colorado (PhD) 1940

**6006** BILGRAY, RUTH. The foreign plays popular in the United States, 1870-1900
Chicago: U. (PhD) 1941

**6007** WALDO, LEWIS P. The French drama in America in the eighteenth century and its influence on the American drama of that period, 1701-1800
pp.xvii, 269; pl. 7 M
Baltimore MD: John Hopkins P. 1942

**6008** LEFEVRE, CARL A. Gogol's first century in England and America (1841-1941)
Minneapolis: U. of Minnesota (PhD) 1944

**6009** GERGELY, EMRO J. Hungarian drama in New York: American adaptations 1908-1940
pp.ix, 197 M
Philadelphia: U. P. 1947

**6010** MEISTER, CHARLES W. English and American criticism of Chekov
Madison: U. of Wisconsin (PhD) 1949

**6011** CAPPEL, EDITH. The reception of Gerhart Hauptmann in the United States
NY: Columbia U. (PhD) 1952

**6012** GREER, LOUISE. Browning and America
pp.xiv, 355 ★
Chapel Hill: U. of North Carolina P. 1952
Performances in the US of Browning's plays.

**6013** SHOEMAKER, ROBERT W. Russian drama on the New York stage from the beginning to 1920
Philadelphia: U. of Pennsylvania (PhD) 1952

**6014** HAUGEN, RALPH H. American drama critics' reactions to productions of August Strindberg
Minneapolis: U. of Minnesota (PhD) 1959

**6015** LYMAN, KENNETH C. Critical reaction to Irish drama on the New York stage, 1900-1958
Madison: U. of Wisconsin (PhD) 1960

**6016** STEENE, KERSTIN B. The American drama and the Swedish theater, 1920-1958
Seattle: U. of Washington (PhD) 1960

**6017** BURKHARD, ARTHUR. Franz Grillparzer in England and America
pp.84; pl. 10 L
Vienna: Bergland 1961
Includes an annotated bibliography, a list of performances and an account of the English translations.

**6018** LAZENBY, WALTER S. Stage versions of Dickens's novels in America to 1900
Bloomington: Indiana U. (PhD) 1962

**6019** ROSWELL, MAY M. Bertolt Brecht's plays in America
Adelphi: U. of Maryland (PhD) 1962

**6020** THUNE, ENSOF Z. Main currents of Ibsen interpretation in England and America
Seattle: U. of Washington (PhD) 1962

**6021** BERTRAM-COX, JEAN DE S. Molière in New York. A comparison of productions of Le Malade Imaginaire and Le Bourgeois Gentilhomme on the New York stage, 1860-1961, with those by actors of the Comedie Française, 1951-1959
Stanford: U. (PhD) 1963

**6022** ARCHER, STEPHEN M. Visiting French repertory companies in New York, 1900 to March, 1964
Urbana: U. of Illinois (PhD) 1964

**6023** BENTLEY, ERIC (Ed.). The storm over The Deputy
pp.254 DL★
NY: Grove P. 1964
Thirty critical responses to Rolf Hochuth's controversial play.

**6024** RAVIV, ZEEV. The production of Chekov's plays on the American professional stage
New Haven: Yale U. (PhD) 1964

**6025** LIFSON, DAVID S. The Yiddish theatre in America
pp.659; ill. in text L
NY: Thomas Yoseloff 1965
A detailed history with which is interwoven much reference to mainstream and fringe New York and regional US theatre history.

**6026** McCARTHY, THOMAS J. American premiere reception of selected contemporary French plays produced on the New York stage, 1946-1960
Los Angeles: U. of Southern California (PhD) 1965

**6027** COLEMAN, MARION M. Mazeppa, Polish and American: a translation of Slowacki's Mazeppa, together with a brief survey of Mazeppa in the United States
pp.viii, 73; pl. 8 M
Cheshire CT: Cherry Hill Books 1966

**6028** EVANS, THOMAS G. Piscator in the American theatre: New York, 1939-1951
Madison: U. of Wisconsin (PhD) 1967

**6029** MURPHY, RUBY A. Ibsen's Hedda Gabler on the New York stage
Urbana-Champaign: U. of Illinois (PhD) 1967

**6030** BAULAND, PETER. The hooded eagle: modern German drama on the New York stage
pp.xv, 299 M
Syracuse NY: U. P. 1968

**6031** BIRDMAN, JEROME M. Professional productions of Luigi Pirandello's plays in New York City
Urbana: U. of Illinois (PhD) 1969

**6032** WEINGARTEN, AARON. Chekhov and the American director
NY: City U. (PhD) 1971

**6033** DE VRIES, JENNY B. Kotzebue on the American stage, 1798-1840
Charlottesville: U. of Virginia (PhD) 1972

**6034** MILLER, KARINA L. The popular acceptance of German drama on the New York stage after World War II:1945-1965
Nashville: Vanderbilt U. (PhD)     1973

**6035** SOLLER, LARRY S. Critical reaction to productions of Henrik Ibsen's *A Doll's House* on the New York stage
Athens: U. of Georgia (PhD)     1973

**6036** TAYLOR, ROBIN. Elements of German expressionism in American drama, 1920-1940
NY: U. (PhD)     1973

**6037** AYSOM, RICHARD H. Parade: cubism as theatre
Ann Arbor: U. of Michigan (PhD)     1974

**6038** KAES, ANTON. Expressionismus in Amerika: rezeption und innovation
pp.ix, 162     DL★
Tübingen: Niemeyer     1975

**6039** CAMPBELL, JOHNSTONE. American culture and the art of Bertolt Brecht: a succession of dawns
Stanford: U. (PhD)     1976

**6040** FUHRICH-LEISLER, EDDA & PROSSNITZ, GISELA. Max Reinhardt in Amerika
pp.iv, 458; ill. in text, pl. 20     M
Salzburg: Otto Müller     1976

**6041** TAMMANY, JANE F. Henrik Ibsen's theatre aesthetics and dramatic arts as a reflection of Kierkegaardian consciousness–its significance for modern dramatic interpretation and the American theatre
Madison: U. of Wisconsin (PhD)     1979

**6042** FENNEMA, DAVIS H. Tommaso Salvini in America: 1873-1893
Bloomington: Indiana U. (PhD)     1980

**6043** ECKARD, BONNIE J. *Camille* in America
Denver: U. (PhD)     1982

**6044** KIRFEL-LENK, THEA. Erwin Piscator im Exil in den USA, 1939-1951
pp.270; pl. 16     M
Berlin: Henschel Verlag     1984

**6045** FLYNN, JOYCE A. Ethnicity after sea-change. The Irish dramatic tradition in nineteenth century American drama
Cambridge MA: Harvard U. (PhD)     1985

**6046** PENDER, THOMAS M. Initial critical response to the plays of Jean Anouilh on the New York stage
Athens: U. of Georgia (PhD)     1986

**6047** ROGERS, PRISCILLA S. Greek tragedy in the New York theatre: a history and interpretation
Ann Arbor: U. of Michigan (PhD)     1986

**6048** EDWARDS, PAUL A. 'Putting on the Greeks': Euripidean tragedy and the twentieth century American theatre
Boulder: U. of Colorado (PhD)     1987

**6049** SMITH, R. J. The influence and effect of German expressionist drama on theatrical practice in Britain and the United States between the wars, 1910-1940
London: U. Royal Holloway College (PhD)     1987
The Provincetown Players, the Washington Square Players and the Theatre Guild.

**6050** SCHANKE, R. A. Ibsen in America: a century of change
pp.xix, 322; pl. 11     L
Metuchen NJ: Scarecrow P.     1988
A history of Ibsen on the US stage, with a selection of comments by actresses, including Minnie Maddern Fiske, Nance O'Neil, Ethel Barrymore, Blanche Yurka, Julie Harris, Jane Fonda.

**6051** BRISTOL, MICHAEL D. Shakespeare's America, America's Shakespeare
pp.ix, 237     L
London: Routledge     1990
Explores the place of Shakespeare in America's cultural history.

# 16. DRAMATIC BIOGRAPHY AND CRITICISM

## 16.1 COLLECTED NOTICES AND BIOGRAPHICAL DICTIONARIES

**6052** REES, JAMES. The dramatic authors of America
pp.144     L
Philadelphia: G. B. Zieber     1845
Arranged alphabetically as a sequence of accounts of individuals or regions. An appendix provides a chronological list of theatres destroyed by fire or other accident.

**6053** WILSON, JAMES G. & FISKE, JOHN (Eds). Appletons' cyclopaedia of American biography
pp.various; ill. in text, pl.73     HW
NY: D. Appleton     1888-1901
Seven volumes including supplement. Indexed in volumes 6 & 7. Later editions omitted many of the original entries.

**6054** PHELPS, WILLIAM L. Essays on modern dramatists
pp.ix, 278     M
NY: Macmillan     1921
With a chapter on Clyde Fitch.

**6055** OVERTON, GRANT. American nights' entertainment
pp.414; pl. 10     L
NY: D. Appleton     1923
Essays on writers. Includes reference to Zona Gale, Booth Tarkington, Christopher Morley.

**6056** BOYNTON, PERCY H. Some contemporary Americans: the personal equation in literature
pp.ix, 289     L
Chicago: U. P.     1924
Includes material on Booth Tarkington, Theodore Dreiser, and emerging forms of theatre.

**6057** MOSES, MONTROSE J. The American dramatist
pp.xviii, 474; ill. in text, pl. 2     M
Boston: Little, Brown     1925

Second edition, revised. First published 1911. A history, founded in accounts of the major playwrights.

**6058** SHERMAN, STUART. Critical woodcuts...illustrated with portraits engraved on wood by Bertrand Zadig
pp.xv, 348; front., ill. in text                                L
NY: Charles Scribner's Sons                                  1926
Includes pen portraits of Floyd Dell and Don Marquis that include reference to their dramatic writing.

**6059** MANTLE, BURNS. American playwrights of today
pp.xi, 324; pl.6                                            M
NY: Dodd, Mead                                              1929

**6060** FLEXNER, ELEANOR. American playwrights: 1918-1938. The theatre retreats from reality. With a preface by John Gassner
pp.xx, 332                                                  L
NY: Simon & Schuster                                        1938
Sidney Howard, S. N. Behrman, Maxwell Anderson, Eugene O'Neill, George S. Kaufman, George Kelly, Rachel Crothers, Philip Barry, Robert E. Sherwood, Clifford Odets, John Howard Lawson. The book was reprinted NY: Books for Libraries, 1969 with a new preface by the author.

**6061** MANTLE, BURNS. Contemporary American playwrights
pp.x, 357                                                   M
NY: Dodd, Mead                                              1938

**6062** MILLETT, FRED B. Contemporary American authors: a critical survey and 219 bio-bibliographies
pp.xiii, 716                                                L
NY: Harcourt, Brace                                         1940

**6063** MERSAND, JOSEPH. The American drama 1930-1940. Essays on playwrights and plays
pp.184                                                      MH
NY: Modern Chapbooks                                        1941
Essays reprinted from the *Players Magazine*. Subjects are George S. Kaufman, Elmer Rice, Clare Boothe, Clifford Odets. Also includes a survey of plays in performance. In effect, a collection of material published separately in individual 'chapbooks' with some amplification.

**6064** STANFORD WRITERS 1891-1941: a book of reprints from undergaduate periodicals, showing the work of men, now eminent in American letters, written while they were students at Stanford University...
ll.v, 118, xxv                                              L
Stanford CA: Dramatists' Alliance                           1941
Includes Maxwell Anderson, Glenn Hughes, John Steinbeck. Index of writers 1891-1941. 300 copies.

**6065** SLOCHOWER, HARRY. No voice is wholly lost: writers and thinkers in war and peace
pp.324                                                      L
London: Dennis Dobson                                       1946
Includes material on Eugene O'Neill and Clifford Odets.

**6066** CLARK, BARRETT H. Intimate portraits, being recollections of Maxim Gorky, John Galsworthy, Edward Sheldon, George Moore, Sidney Howard and others
pp.xiv,232                                                  MH
NY: Dramatists Play Service                                 1951

**6067** FISHER, WILLIAM J. Trends in postdepression American drama. A study of the works of William Saroyan, Tennessee Williams, Irwin Shaw, Arthur Miller
NY: U. (PhD)                                                1952

**6068** TODD, HAROLD J. America's actor-playwrights of the nineteenth century
Ithaca: Cornell U. (PhD)                                    1956

**6069** FERGUSON, PHYLLIS. Women dramatists in the American theatre 1901-1940
Pittsburgh: U. (PhD)                                        1957

**6070** BANDER, ROBERT G. Playwrights of the modern American theatre from O'Neill to Inge
pp.285                                                      DL★
Milan: Scuola Interpreti                                  [1958]

**6071** COLE, TOBY (Ed.). Playwrights on playwriting: the meaning and making of modern drama from Ibsen to Ionesco...Introduction by John Gassner
pp.xx, 299                                                  M
London: McGibbon & Kee                                      1960
Includes Eugene O'Neill, Thornton Wilder, Tennessee Williams, Arthur Miller.

**6072** AARON, DANIEL. Writers of the left
pp.xxv, 460                                                 O
Oxford: U. P.                                               1961
Published NY: Harcourt, Brace. Revised edition with new preface. Wide-ranging survey, including the drama.

**6073** DUBLER, WALTER. O'Neill, Wilder and Albee. The use of fantasy in modern American drama
Cambridge MA: Harvard U. (PhD)                              1962

**6074** HUNNINGHER, BENJAMIN. Kruistocht op Broadway: Eugene O'Neill, Maxwell Anderson, Thornton Wilder, Tennessee Williams, Arthur Miller
pp.160                                                      DL★
The Hague: B. Bakker                                        1963

**6075** SHELDON, NEIL. Social commentary in the plays of Clifford Odets and Arthur Miller
NY: U. (PhD)                                                1963

**6076** CALVERY, CATHERINE A. Illusion in modern American drama. A study of selected plays by Arthur Miller, Tennessee Williams, and Eugene O'Neill
New Orleans: Tulane U. (PhD)                                1964

**6077** COWLEY, MALCOLM (Ed.). After the genteel tradition; American writers since 1910
pp.270                                                      L
NY: W. W. Norton                                            1964
Revised and expanded edition. First published 1937, here updated and with a new foreword by the editor. Includes Lionel Trilling on Eugene O'Neill.

**6078** DAWSON, WILLIAM M. The female characters of August Strindberg, Eugene O'Neill, and Tennessee Williams
Madison: U. of Wisconsin (PhD)                              1964

**6079** FRENZ, HORST (Ed.). American playwrights on drama
pp.xv, 174                                                  MH
NY: Hill & Wang                                             1965

## 16.1. COLLECTED NOTICES AND BIOGRAPHICAL DICTIONARIES  –6097

Contributors include Eugene O'Neill, Maxwell Anderson, John Howard Lawson, Thornton Wilder, Archibald MacLeish, Robinson Jeffers, Tennessee Williams, Arthur Miller, William Inge, Elmer Rice, Lorraine Hansberry, Edward Albee, Paul Green.

**6080** GOULD, JEAN. Modern American playwrights...
pp.xiii, 302; pl. 8     MH
NY: Dodd, Mead     1966
Elmer Rice, Susan Glaspell, Eugene O'Neill, Philip Barry, Robert E. Sherwood, Maxwell Anderson, Sam and Bella Spewack, Howard Lindsay, Russel Crouse, George S. Kaufman, Moss Hart, Elliott Nugent, James Thurber, Lillian Hellman, Clifford Odets, Thornton Wilder, Tennessee Williams, Arthur Miller, Edward Albee, William Inge.

**6081** COY, JAVIER & COY, JUAN J. Teatro norteamericano actual: Miller, Inge, Albee
pp.xix, 282; pl. 2     L
Madrid: Prensa Espa"nola     1967
Preface by Enrique Llovet.

**6082** DOMMERGUES, PIERRE. Les U. S. A. à la recherche de leur identité: rencontres avec 40 écrivains américains
pp.486     O
Paris: Grasset     1967
Includes chapters: *Le théatre entre deux aliénations* and *Le problème blanc*, discussing, inter alia, Arthur Miller, Tennessee Williams, Jack Gelber, Kenneth Brown, LeRoi Jones, Jack Richardson, Murray Schisgal, Edward Albee, Langston Hughes, James Baldwin.

**6083** WAGER, WALTER (Ed.). The playwrights speak...with an introduction by Harold Clurman
pp.xxx, 290     M
NY: Delacorte P.     1967
Includes recorded interviews with Arthur Miller, Edward Albee, William Inge, Tennessee Williams.

**6084** WHO WAS WHO IN AMERICA: historical volume 1607-1896. A component volume of *Who's Who in American History*
pp.689     HW
Chicago: Marquis - Who's Who     1967
Six further volumes were published: 1897-1942; 1943-1950; 1951-1960; 1961-1968; 1969-1973; 1974-1976. The last two volumes carried the addition to the title *with world notables* and included indexes to the series.

**6085** WRITERS at work: the *Paris Review* interviews, third series, conducted by Alfred Kazin
pp.xv, 368; ill. in text     M
London: Secker & Warburg     1967
Subjects include Lillian Hellman, Arthur Miller, Edward Albee.

**6086** JUNEJA, M. M. Vision and form in the drama of Tennessee Williams and Arthur Miller
Leicester: U. (PhD)     1968

**6087** MARGOLIES, EDWARD. Native sons: a critical study of twentieth century negro American writers
pp.209     L
Philadelphia: J. B. Lippincott     1968

Chapter on LeRoi Jones and material on Langston Hughes, James Baldwin, Countee Cullen.

**6088** MILLER, JOSEPH W. Modern playwrights at work. Volume 1
pp.xvii, 576; pl. 2     L
NY: Samuel French     1968
Includes accounts of Eugene O'Neill and Arthur Miller. No more published.

**6089** BRODIN, PIERRE. Vingt-cinq Américains, littérature & littérateurs américains des années 1960
pp.263     O
Paris: Debresse     1969
Includes material on Edward Albee, Le Roi Jones, James Purdy.

**6090** BRYER, JACKSON R. Fifteen modern American authors: a survey of research and criticism
pp.xvi, 493     O
Durham NC: Duke U.P.     1969
Includes John H. Raleigh: *Eugene O'Neill*.

**6091** RUBIN, LOUIS D.(Ed.). A bibliographical guide to the study of southern literature...with an appendix containing sixty-eight additional writers of the colonial south by J. A. Leo Lemay
pp.xxiv, 351     L
Baton Rouge: Louisiana Stae U.P.     1969
Inc. Charles S. Watson: *Eighteenth and nineteenth century drama* and Kimball King: *Twentieth century southern drama*.

**6092** GIBSON, DONALD B. Five black writers: essays on Wright, Ellison, Baldwin, Hughes, and LeRoi Jones
pp.xviii, 310     O
NY: U. P.     1970

**6093** HALEY, ELSIE G. The black revolutionary theatre: Leroi Jones, Ed Bullins, and minor playwrights
Denver: U. (PhD)     1971

**6094** McCRINDLE, JOSEPH F. (Ed.). Behind the scenes: theatre and film reviews from the *Transatlantic Review*...with an introduction by Jean-Claude Van Itallie
pp.x, 341     M
London: Pitman     1971
Includes interviews with Arthur Kopit, William Inge, Harold Clurman, Edward Albee, Alan Schneider, Gore Vidal.

**6095** BIDDLE, STEPHEN P. American avant-garde playwrights of the late sixties
Lawrence: U. of Kansas (PhD)     1972

**6096** BREED, PAUL F. & SNIDERMAN, FLORENCE M. Dramatic criticism index: a bibliography of commentaries on playwrights from Ibsen to the avant-garde
pp.ix, 1022     O
Detroit: Gale Research     1972
12,000 entries. Reference to plays pre-1900 is made only if there is record of recent performance.

**6097** RILEY, CAROLYN (Ed.). Contemporary literary criticism: excerpts from criticism of the works of today's novelists, poets, playwrights, and other creative writers
pp.various     L
Detroit: Gale Research     1973-

Forty volumes examined, together with sixteen accumulative indexes.

**6098** WAGNER, JEAN. Black poets of the United States from Paul Laurence Dunbar to Langston Hughes
pp.xxiii, 561 L
Urbana: U. of Illinois P. 1973

Important biographical material, including Countee Cullen.

**6099** UNGER, LEONARD (Ed.). American writers: a collection of literary biographies
pp.av. 600 HW
NY: Charles Scribner 1974-81

Four volumes with two two-volume supplements. Included are: 1. Edward Albee, E. E. Cummings, Sherwood Anderson. 2. William Dean Howells, Carson McCullers. 3. Archibald MacLeish, H. L. Mencken, Edna St. Vincent Millay, Arthur Miller, Eugene O'Neill. 4. Gertrude Stein, Robert Penn Warren, Thornton Wilder, Tennessee Williams. S1.1. James Baldwin, Lillian Hellman, Langston Hughes. S1.2. James Thurber. S2.1. Imamu Amiri Baraka. S2.2. Robinson Jeffers, Clifford Odets, Kurt Vonnegut.

**6100** MITCHELL, LOFTEN. Voices of the black theatre
pp.xii, 238; ill. in text M
Clifton: James T. White 1975

Studies of Ruby Dee, Abram Hill, Eddie Hunter, Paul Robeson, Dick Campbell, Vinette Carroll, Frederick O'Neal, Regina M. Andrews. The substantial introductory essay is in effect a condensed version of the author's *Black Drama*.

**6101** SAPOZNIK, RAN. The one-act plays of Thornton Wilder, William Saroyan and Edward Albee
Lawrence: U. of Kansas (PhD) 1975

**6102** HUGHES, CATHARINE. American playwrights 1945-75
pp.vi, 114 L
London: Pitman 1976

Brief accounts of Tennessee Williams, Arthur Miller, William Inge, Edward Albee, Neil Simon, Sam Shepard, David Rabe, and the so-called 'newer voices', Arthur Kopit, Lanford Wilson, Jason Miller, Jean-Claude Van Itallie.

**6103** NELSON-CAVE, W. Representative women playwrights of America: 1756-1964
Birmingham: U. (PhD) 1976

**6104** BOEKER, THOMAS W. Two playwrights of the San Francisco renaissance: Lawrence Ferlinghetti and Michael McClure
Athens: U. of Georgia (PhD) 1978

**6105** INGE, M. THOMAS et al. Black American writers. Bibliographical essays
DL★
NY: St Martin's P. 1978

Two volumes. Volume 2 includes essays on James Baldwin and Imamu Amiri Baraka.

**6106** BROWN, JANET. Feminist drama: definition & critical analysis
pp.v, 161 O
Metuchen NJ: Scarecrow P. 1979

Chapters on Alice Childress, Rosalyn Drexler, Tina Howe, David Rabe, Ntozake Shange, and a section analysing several plays by feminist groups.

**6107** CHOUDHURI, A. D. The face of illusion in American drama
pp.vii, 148 MH
Atlantic Highlands NJ: Humanities P. 1979

Essys on Elmer Rice, Clifford Odets, Eugene O'Neill, Arthur Miller, Tennessee Williams, Edward Albee.

**6108** HEIGL, OTTO et al. Von James Baldwin zum Free Southern Theatre: Positionen schwartzamerikanisches Dramatik im soziokulturellen Kontext der USA
pp.iv, 223 MH
Bremen: Übersee-Museum 1979

Unattributed essays on James Baldwin, Imamu Amiri Baraka, Ed Bullins, Ben Caldwell, John O'Neal. German text with brief summary in English.

**6109** MAINIERO, LISA (Ed.). American women writers: a critical reference guide from colonial times to the present
DL★
NY: Frederick Ungar 1980-83

Four volumes.

**6110** MILLER, FRANK M. A generic comparison of the comedies of Philip Barry and S. N. Behrman
Columbus: Ohio State U. (PhD) 1980

**6111** BOCK, HEDWIG & WERTHEIM, ALBERT V. (Eds). Essays on contemporary American drama
pp.ii, 302 O
Munich: Max Hueber 1981

Includes chapters on Tennessee Williams, Arthur Miller, Edward Albee, Arthur Kopit, Ronald Ribman, Lorraine Hansberry, Imamu Amiri Baraka, Ed Bullins, Sam Shepard, David Rabe, David Mamet, Lanford Wilson, black drama, women playwrights, and Mexican-American drama.

**6112** COHN, RUBY. New American dramatists 1960-1980
pp.ix, 182 M
London: Macmillan 1981

Subjects include Neil Simon, Arthur Kopit, Terence McNally, Lanford Wilson, David Rabe, David Mamet, John Guare, Jack Gelber, Jean-Claude Van Itallie, Jack Gelber, Megan Terry, Julian Beck, Imamu Amiri Baraka, Ed Bullins, Adrienne Kennedy, Lee Breuer, Sam Shepard. A second edition, illustrated, updated to 1990 was published in 1991 (not seen).

**6113** DICTIONARY OF AMERICAN BIOGRAPHY vols I - X, supplements 1 - 8 and complete index guide
Various HW
NY: Charles Scribner's Sons 1981-88

**6114** KAYE, PHYLLIS J. (Ed.). National playwrights directory
pp.ix, 507; ill. DL★
Waterford, CT: Eugene O'Neill Theater Centre/Gale, 1981

Second edition.

**6115** KEYSSAR, HELENE. The curtain and the veil: strategies in black drama
pp.xvi, 302; ill. in text MH
NY: Franklin 1981

## 16.1. COLLECTED NOTICES AND BIOGRAPHICAL DICTIONARIES  –6134

Chapters on Willis Richardson, Langston Hughes, Theodore Ward, Lorraine Hansberry, Imamu Amiri Baraka, and Ed Bullins.

**6116** MacNICHOLAS, JOHN (Ed.). Twentieth-century American dramatists. Foreword by John Houseman
pp.xiii, 345; vii, 475; ill. in text    L
Detroit: Gale Research    1981

Two volumes. Bio-bibliographical descriptions. Part two includes essays: Stanley V. Longman: *New forces at work in the American theatre: 1915-1925*; Randolph Goodman: *The Theatre Guild*; Vera M. Roberts: *Off Broadway and off-off-Broadway*; Albert J. Harris: *Actors theatre of Louisville*; Inge Kut: *American Conservatory Theatre*; Robert Klein & Susan Davis: *Arena stage*; Donna Northouse: *The Dallas Theatre Center*. Leon M. Aufdemberge: *The Goodman Theatre*; William A. Mould: *The Guthrie Theatre*; Katharine M. Morsberger: *The Mark Taper Forum*; George H. Jensen: *Off-Loop theatres*; Howard Siegman: *Eugene O'Neill Memorial Theatre Center*.

**6117** MARRANCA, BONNIE & DASGUPTA, GAUTAM. American playwrights: a critical survey 1
pp.x, 238    MH
NY: Drama Book Specialists    1981

Includes Arthur Kopit, Lanford Wilson, Jean-Claude Van Itallie, Imamu Amiri Baraka, Jack Gelber.

**6118** VAUGHN, JACK A. Early American dramatists from the beginnings to 1900...
pp.v, 200; ill. in text    MH
NY: Frederick Ungar    1981

Includes accounts of John Howard Payne, Anna Cora Mowatt, James A. Herne, Augustin Daly, David Belasco.

**6119** AUERBACH, DORIS. Sam Shepard, Arthur Kopit, and the off-Broadway theater
pp.xiv, 145    M
Boston: Twayne    1982

**6120** COVEN, BRENDA. American women dramatists of the twentieth century: a bibliography
pp.v, 237    MH
Metuchen NJ: Scarecrow P.    1982

133 dramatists listed alphabetically, with dates, play-titles, biographical information and selected reviews.

**6121** EHRLICH, EUGENE & CARRUTH, GORTON. The Oxford illustrated literary guide to the United States
pp.xvi, 464; ill. in text    M
NY: OUP    1982

**6122** LAHR, JOHN. Automatic vaudeville
pp.x, 241; front.    M
London: Heinemann    1984

Essays, revised and reprinted from periodicals. Includes accounts of Stephen Sondheim, Sam Shepard, Eugene O'Neill.

**6123** MARRANCA, BONNIE. Theatre writings
pp.205; ill. in text    MH
NY: Performing Arts Journal    1984

Includes accounts of Sam Shepard, Lillian Hellman, Richard Foreman, Robert Wilson.

**6124** PEOPLES, FRANK F. Dance and play, quest and union: language strategies beyond post-modernism in four American playwrights
Evanston: Northwestern U. (PhD)    1984

Jean-Claude Van Itallie, Paul Goodman, Jackson Maclow, Robert Patrick.

**6125** STEIN, RITA & RICKERT, FRIEDHELM (Ed.). Major modern dramatists
pp.xv, 570    L
NY: Frederick Ungar    1984

Selected critical reviews. US playwrights are Edward Albee, Lillian Hellman, Arthur Miller, Clifford Odets, Eugene O'Neill, Thornton Wilder, Tennessee Williams.

**6126** DAVIS, THADIOUS M. & HARRIS, TRUDIER (Eds). Afro-American writers after 1955: dramatists and prose writers... [Before the Harlem renaissance... From the Harlem renaissance to 1940]
pp.xv, 390; xv, 386; xv, 369; ill. in text    L
Detroit: Gale Research    1985-87

Three volumes.

**6127** CAPASSO, MADDALENA R. Teatro Americano contemporaneo
pp.212; ill. in text    M
Milan: Nuovi Autori    1986

Essays on and/or interviews with Lanford Wilson, Elizabeth Le Compte, Bonnie Maranca, Richard Foreman, John Vaccaro, Lee Breuer, Robert Wilson, Sam Shepard.

**6128** FISCHER-SEIDEL, THERESE. Mythenparodie im modernen englischen und amerikanischen Drama. Tradition und Kommunikation bei Tennessee Williams, Edward Albee, Samuel Beckett and Harold Pinter
pp.216    M
Heidelberg: Carl Winter    1986

**6129** LONG, DEBORAH M. The existential quest: family and form in selected American plays
Eugene: U. of Oregon (PhD)    1986

Examines the work of Eugene O'Neill, Arthur Miller, Tennessee Williams.

**6130** BETSKO, KATHLEEN & KOENIG, RACHAEL (Eds). Interviews with contemporary women playwrights
pp.480    DL★
NY: Beech Tree Books    1987

**6131** KIRKPATRICK, D.L. (Ed.). Reference guide to American literature
pp.xviii, 816    L
Chicago: St James P.    1987

Second edition. Introductions by Lewis Leary and Warren French. Brief bio-bibliographies, each accompanied by a signed critical essay on a characteristic work.

**6132** MIDYETT, JUDITH A. The comedy of equitable resolution: S. N. Behrman and Philip Barry
Athens: U. of Georgia (PhD)    1987

**6133** HARRIOTT, ESTHER. American voices: five contemporary playwrights in essays and interviews
pp.xv, 189    L
Jefferson City NC: McFarland    1988

Sam Shepard, Lanford Wilson, David Mamet, Charles Fuller, Marsha Norman.

**6134** KIRKPATRICK, D. L. (Ed.). Contemporary dramatists
pp.xx, 785    M
Chicago: St James P.    1988

Fourth edition, with a preface by Ruby Cohn. Brief biographical accounts of dramatists and librettists writing in English. First published 1973, (edited by James Vinson).

**6135** O'ROURKE, JOYCE W. New female playwrights in the American theatre, 1973-83: a critical analysis of thought in selected plays
Baton Rouge: Louisiana State U. (PhD)     1988

**6136** SAVRAN, DAVID. In their own words: contemporary American playwrights
pp.xv, 320; ill. in text     L
NY: Theatre Communications Group     1988
Transcribed interviews with Lee Breuer, Christopher Durang, Richard Foreman, Maria Irene Fornes, Charles Fuller, John Guare, Joan Holden, David Hwang, David Mamet, Emily Mann, Richard Nelson, Marsha Norman, David Rabe, Wallace Shawn, Stephen Sondheim, Megan Terry, Luis Valdez, Michael Weller, August Wilson, Lanford Wilson.

**6137** AUSLANDER, PHILIP. The New York school poets as playwrights: O'Hara, Ashbery, Koch, Schuyler and the visual arts
pp.xi, 234     DL★
NY: Peter Lang     1989

**6138** BRATER, ENOCH (Ed.). Feminine focus: the new women playwrights
pp.xvi, 283     MH
NY: Oxford U. P.     1989
Contributors: Katharine Worth, A. E. Quigley, Ruby Cohn, Elin Diamond, R. C. Lamont, J. L. Savona, S. A. Willis, Sue-Ellen Case, L. Ben-Zvi, W. B. Worthon, T. Murray, Deborah R. Geis, Helene Keyssar, Judith E. Barlow, L. Kane.

**6139** KOLIN, PHILIP C. (Ed.). American playwrights since 1945: a guide to scholarship, criticism and performance
pp.610     DL★
NY: Greenwod P.     1989

**6140** BROWN-GUILLORY, ELIZABETH. Their place on the stage: black women playwrights in America
pp.xiv, 163     L
NY: Greenwood P.     1990
Foreword by Margaret Walker Alexander. Afterword by Gloria T. Hull. Emphasis on the work of Alice Childress, Lorraine Hansberry, Ntozake Shange.

**6141** CHAMPAGNE, LENORA (Ed.). Out from under: texts by women performance artists
pp.185     ★
NY: Theatre Communications Group     1990

**6142** PETERSON, BERNARD L. Early black American playwrights and dramatic writers: a bibliographical dictionary and catalog of plays, films and broadcasting scripts
pp.xxviii, 298     DL★
NY: Greenwood P.     1990

**6143** SCOTT, FREDA. Five African-American playwrights on Broadway, 1923-29
NY: City U. (PhD)     1990

## 16.2 INDIVIDUAL DRAMATISTS

### Abbott, George
### [Abbott, Francis]
### (1887-?)

**6144** ABBOTT, GEORGE. 'Mister Abbott' [autobiography]
pp.vii, 280     M
NY: Random House     1963

**6145** MACCLENNAN, ROBERT W. The comedy of George Abbott
Bowling Green: State U. (PhD)     1975

**6146** HESS, DEAN W. A critical analysis of the musical theatre productions of George Abbott
Los Angeles: U. of Southern California (PhD)     1976

### Ade, George
### (1866-1944)

**6147** MASSON, THOMAS. Our American humorists
pp.xxi, 448     L
NY: Moffat, Yard     1922
Chapter on George Ade but scant reference to plays.

**6148** KELLY, FRED C. George Ade: warmhearted satirist
pp.282; pl. 12     L
Indianapolis: Bobbs-Merrill     1947

**6149** RUSSO, DOROTHY R. Bibliography of George Ade, 1866-1944
pp.xv, 314; pl. 12     L
Indianapolis: Indiana Historical Society     1947

**6150** NORDHUS, PHILIP B. George Ade. A critical study
Iowa City: U. of Iowa (PhD)     1958

**6151** COYLE, LEE. George Ade
pp.159     L
NY: Twayne     1964

**6152** TOBIN, TERENCE (Ed.). Letters of George Ade
pp.xi, 251; ill. in text, front.     MH
West Lafayette IN: Purdue U. P.     1973

### Albee, Edward
### (1928-)

**6153** DEBUSSCHER, GILBERT. Edward Albee: tradition and renewal
pp.viii, 94     MH
Brussels: Center for American Studies     1967

**6154** BRAEM, HELMUT M. Edward Albee
pp.157; ill. in text     MH
Velber bei Hanover: Friedrich     1968
Critical study. Text in German.

**6155** VOS, NELVIN. Eugene Ionesco and Edward Albee: a critical essay
pp.48     MH
Grand Rapids MI: W. B. Eerdmans     1968

**6156** BIGSBY, C. W. Albee
pp.vi, 120     O
Edinburgh: Oliver & Boyd     1969

## 16.2. INDIVIDUAL DRAMATISTS

**6157** COHN, RUBY. Edward Albee
pp.48      L
Minneapolis: Minnesota U. P.      1969

**6158** ENGLISH, EMMA J. Edward Albee: theory, theme, technique
Tallahassee: Florida State U. (PhD)      1969

**6159** LANGDON, HARRY M. A critical study of *Tiny Alice* by Edward Albee focusing on commanding image and ritual form
Iowa City: U. of Iowa (PhD)      1969

**6160** QUETZ, JÖRGEN. Symbolische und allegorische in der Dramatik Edward Albees: Untersuchung zu *The Zoo Story*, *Who's Afraid of Virginia Woolf?* und *Tiny Alice*
Frankfurt: U. (PhD)      1969

**6161** RUTENBERG, MICHAEL E. Edward Albee: playwright in protest
pp.vii, 280      L
NY: DBS      1969
Includes two interviews with Albee.

**6162** KERJAN, LILIANE. Edward Albee
pp.192; pl. 4      L
Paris: Seghers      1971

**6163** SHELTON, LEWIS E. Alan Schneider's direction of four plays by Edward Albee: a study in form
Madison: U. of Wisconsin (PhD)      1971

**6164** WINCHELL, CEDRIC R. An analysis of the symbology in the earlier plays by Edward Albee
Los Angeles: U. of California (PhD)      1971

**6165** PAOLUCCI, ANNE. From tension to tonic: the plays of Edward Albee. With a preface by Harry T. Moore
pp.xv, 143      MESM
Carbondale: Southern Illinois U. P.      1972

**6166** STEINER, DONALD L. August Strindberg and Edward Albee: the dance of death
Salt Lake City: U. of Utah (PhD)      1972

**6167** STEPHENS, SUZANNE S. The dual influence: a dramaturgical study of the plays of Edward Albee and the specific dramatic forms and themes which influence him
Coral Gables: U. of Miami (PhD)      1972

**6168** AMACHER, RICHARD & RULE, MARGARET. Edward Albee at home and abroad: a bibliography
pp.v, 95      O
NY: AMS P.      1973

**6169** BERGER, JERE S. The rites of Albee
Pittsburgh: Carnegie-Mellon U. (PhD)      1973

**6170** BREDE, REGINE. Die Darstellung des Kommunikationsproblems in der Dramatik Albees
Kiel: U. (Thesis)      1974

**6171** WESTERMAN, SUSAN. Die Krise der Familie bei Edward Albee
Heidelburg: Ruprecht-Karl U. (PhD)      1974

**6172** BIGSBY, C. W. Edward Albee: a collection of critical essays
pp.xii, 180      O
Englewood Cliffs NJ: Prentice-Hall      1975
Contributors are: Gerald Weales, Martin Esslin, Rose A. Zimbaido, Gilbert Debusscher, Richard Shechner, Harold Clurman, Diana Trilling, Michael E. Rutenberg, Henry Hewes, Philip Roth, Abraham N. Franzblau, R. S. Stewart, C. W. Bigsby, Robert Brustein, Anne Paolucci.

**6173** COY, JAVIER & COY, JUAN J. La anarquía y el orden: una clave interpretativa de la literatura norteamericana
pp.vii, 187      L
Madrid: J. P. Turanzas      1976
Includes a substantial account of the work of Edward Albee.

**6174** PREUSS, R. Die Einsamkeit als Grunderfahrung des Menschen. Untersuchung des Menschenbildes in den Dramen Edward Albees
Freiburg: Albert-Ludwigs U. (D.Phil.)      1976

**6175** HIRSCH, FOSTER. Who's afraid of Edward Albee
pp.142      ★
Berkeley: Creative Arts Books      1978

**6176** STENZ, ANITA M. Edward Albee: the poet of loss
pp.xi, 146      MH
The Hague: Mouton      1978

**6177** SCHLUETER, JUNE. Metafictional characters in modern drama
     MH★
NY: Columbia U. P.      1979
Includes a chapter on Edward Albee: *Albee's Martha and George*.

**6178** WARE, ROBERT G. Edward Albee's early plays: a dramaturgical study
Stanford: U. (PhD)      1979

**6179** FUENTE, PATRICIA De La et al. Edward Albee: planned wilderness: interview, essays and bibliography
pp.131      ★
Edinburg TX: Pan American U.      1980

**6180** GREEN, CHARLES L. Edward Albee: an annotated bibliography 1968-1977
pp.xv, 150      MH
NY: AMS P.      1980

**6181** TREIB, MANFRED. August Strindberg und Edward Albee: eine vergleichende Analyse moderner Ehedramen (mit einem Exkurs über Friedrich Dürrenmatts...Strindberg)
pp.186      L
Frankfurt: Peter Lang      1980
Compares *Who's Afraid of Virginia Woolf* with *Dance of Death*.

**6182** HARRIS, ANDREW B. Storytelling in the plays of Edward Albee
NY: Columbia U. (PhD)      1981

**6183** AMACHER, RICHARD. Edward Albee:
pp.xiv, 219; front.      L
Boston: Twayne      1982

Second edition, revised. First published 1969.

**6184** WASSERMAN, JULIAN N. (Ed.). Edward Albee: an interview and essays
pp.xiii, 158     MH
Houston TX: U. of St Thomas     1983

**6185** RUPOLO-HORHAGER, DANA J. The plays of Edward Albee 1959-1980: experiments in dramatic form
Madison: U. of Wisconsin (PhD)     1984

**6186** MILLS, KATHLEEN. A transactional analysis on *Tiny Alice*: an alternative for the study of problematic scripts
Tallahassee: Florida State U. (PhD)     1985

**6187** SOLOMON, RAKESH H. Albee on stage: the playwright as director
Davis: U. of California (PhD)     1986

**6188** TYCE, RICHARD. Edward Albee: a bibliography
pp.viii, 212     M
Metuchen NJ: Scarecrow P.     1986

**6189** GIANTVALLEY, S. Edward Albee: a reference guide
pp.xxiv, 459     MH
Boston: G. K. Hall     1987

**6190** McCARTHY, GERRY. Edward Albee
pp.xi, 168; pl. 2     L
Basingstoke: Macmillan     1987

**6191** ROUDANÉ, MATTHEW. Understanding Edward Albee
pp.xiii, 221     MH
Columbia: U. of S. Carolina P.     1987

**6192** KOLIN, PHILIP C. (Ed.). Conversations with Edward Albee
    DL★
Jackson: U. P. of Mississippi     1988

**6193** MAYBERRY, BOB. Theatre of discord. Dissonance in Beckett, Albee, and Pinter
pp.96     DL★
Cranbury NJ: Fairleigh Dickinson U. P.     1989

**6194** ROUDANÉ, MATTHEW. Who's afraid of Virginia Woolf? Necessary fictions, terrifying realities
pp.xv, 125; ill. in text     MH
Boston: Twayne     1990

### Anderson, James Maxwell (1888-1959)

**6195** CLARK, BARRETT H. Maxwell Anderson: the man and his plays
pp.32; front,     M
NY: Samuel French     1933
Biographical essay with checklist of first productions.

**6196** BLANCHARD, FRED C. The place of Maxwell Anderson in the American theatre
NY: U. (PhD)     1939

**6197** MITCHELL, ALBERT O. A study of irony in the plays of Maxwell Anderson
Madison: U. of Wisconsin (PhD)     1939

**6198** ANDERSON, MAXWELL. Off Broadway. Essays about the theatre
pp.xi, 91     M
NY: William Sloane Associates     1947
Reprinted essays, prefaces, addresses on a range of topics including poetry in the theatre, the role of the critic, the essence of tragedy.

**6199** COX, MARTHA. Maxwell Anderson and his critics
Fayetteville: U. of Arkansas (PhD)     1955

**6200** FOOTE, RONALD C. The verse dramas of Maxwell Anderson in the modern theatre
New Orleans: Tulane U. (PhD)     1956

**6201** BAILEY, MABEL D. Maxwell Anderson: the playwright as prophet
pp.200     M
NY: Abelard-Schuman     1957
A study of Anderson's dramatic theory.

**6202** COX, MARTHA. Maxwell Anderson bibliography
pp.vi, 117     L
Charlottesville VA: U. of Virginia     1958

**6203** BUCHANAN, RANDALL J. Maxwell Anderson's rules for playwriting and their application to his plays
Baton Rouge: Louisiana State U. (PhD)     1964

**6204** WEINMAN, RICHARD J. The 'core of belief' of Maxwell Anderson and the structure of his tragedies
Bloomington: Indiana U. (PhD)     1965

**6205** GILBERT, ROBERT L. The thirties verse tragedies of Maxwell Anderson
Seattle: U. of Washington (PhD)     1966

**6206** LEE, HENRY G. The use of history in the historical plays of Maxwell Anderson
New Orleans: Tulane U. (PhD)     1967

**6207** AVERY, LAURENCE G. (Ed.). A catalogue of the Maxwell Anderson collection at the University of Texas
pp.iv, 175; pl. 9     M
Austin: U. of Texas P.     1968

**6208** ANDERSON, MAXWELL. Notes on a dream
pp.48; front.     O
Austin: U. of Texas HRC     1971
Poems. 750 copies.

**6209** KLINK, WILLIAM. Maxwell Anderson and S. N. Behrman: a reference guide
pp.xii, 103     DL★
Boston: G. K. Hall     1971
An updating to 1982-3 is provided by Klink in *Resources for American Literary Study*, 12 (Autumn), 1982, pp.195-214.

**6210** BOUGHTON, DONALD J. The Broadway plays of Maxwell Anderson
Santa Barbara: U. of California (PhD)     1975

**6211** SHIVERS, ALFRED S. Maxwell Anderson
pp.176; front.     L
Boston: Twayne     1976

**6212** WILLIAMS, RICHARD A. A critical study of religious ideas in five plays of Maxwell Anderson
Urbana-Champaign: U. of Illinois (PhD)     1976

**6213** AVERY, LAURENCE G. (Ed.). Dramatist in America: letters of Maxwell Anderson, 1912-1958
pp.lxxxiii, 367; ill. in text     M
Chapel Hill: U. of N. Carolina P.     1977

**6214** MAXWELL ANDERSON: designs from the premiere productions [exhibition catalogue]
pp.32; ill.in text,some col.     M
Grand Forks ND: North Dakota Museum of Art     1983

**6215** SHIVERS, ALFRED S. The life of Maxwell Anderson
pp.xx, 397; ill. in text, pl. 6     MH
NY: Stein & Day     1983

**6216** SHIVERS, ALFRED S. Maxwell Anderson: an annotated bibliography of primary and secondary works
pp.xi, 287     MH
Metuchen NJ: Scarecrow P.     1985

**6217** ARTHUR, KAY. A guide to the films of Maxwell Anderson [cover title]
pp.20; ill. in text     M
Stamford CT: Ferguson Library     1988

**6218** MAXWELL ANDERSON (1888-1959) and the Playwrights' Producing Company
pp.20; ill. in text     M
Rockland Co. NY: Historical Society     1988

### Anderson, Robert Woodruff
### (1917-)

**6219** AYERS, DAVID H. The apprenticeship of Robert Anderson
Columbus: Ohio State U. (PhD)     1969

**6220** WILKINS, JEANNE. Robert Anderson's women: their ritual role
Columbus: Ohio State U. (PhD)     1976

**6221** ADLER, THOMAS. Robert Anderson
pp.184     MH★
Boston: Twayne     1978

### Anderson, Sherwood
### (1876-1941)

**6222** SCHEVILL, JAMES. Sherwood Anderson, his life and work
pp.xvi, 360; front., pl. 7     L
Denver CO: U. P.     1951

**6223** WEBER, BROM. Sherwood Anderson
pp.48     O
Minneapolis: U. of Minnesota P.     1964

**6224** ANDERSON, SHERWOOD. Memoirs. Newly edited from the original manuscripts by Ray L. White
pp.xxxix, 579; pl. 9     L
Chapel Hill: U. of N. Carolina P.     1969
A revised and edited version of the volume published NY: Harcourt, Brace, 1942.

**6225** WHITE, RAY L. (Ed.). Sherwood Anderson/ Gertrude Stein: correspondence and personal essays
pp.vii, 130     L
Chapel Hill: U. of N. Carolina P.     1972

**6226** MODLIN, CHARLES E. (Ed.). Sherwood Anderson's love letters to Eleanor Copenhaver Anderson
pp.xxi, 338; front., pl. 8     L
Athens: U. of Georgia P.     1989

### Ardrey, Robert
### (1908-

**6227** RODNEY, PETER M. Robert Ardrey: a biography and critical analysis
Cleveland: Case Western Reserve U. (PhD)     1980

### Austin, Mary Hunter
### (1868-1934)

**6228** PEARCE, T. M. Mary Hunter Austin
pp.158     L
NY: Twayne     1965

### Baldwin, James
### [Baldwin, Joseph Burkette]
### (1918-1987)

**6229** ECKMAN, FERN M. The furious passage of James Baldwin
pp.256     O
London: Michael Joseph     1968
Biography. First published NY: Evans, 1966.

**6230** MACEBUH, STANLEY. James Baldwin; a critical study
pp.ix, 194     L
NY: Third P.     1973

**6231** KINNAMON, KENNETH (Ed.). James Baldwin: a collection of critical essays
pp.xiii, 169     L
Englewood Cliffs: Prentice-Hall     1974

**6232** BRUCK, PETER. Von der 'Store Front Church' zum 'American Dream': James Baldwin und der amerikanische Rassenkonflikt
pp.vi, 147     L
Amsterdam: B. R. Grüner     1975

**6233** AYCK, THOMAS. ...gegen die US-Gesellschaft: Gespräche mit Henry Miller & James Baldwin
pp.92     L
Hamburg: Tsumas Dialoge     1977

**6234** O'DANIEL, THERMAN B. (Ed.). James Baldwin: a critical evaluation
pp.xiii, 273     MH
Washington DC: Howard U. P.     1977
Includes section: *Baldwin as playwright*, with essays by Carlton W. Molette, Darwin T. Turner on the dilemma of the black dramatist; W. E. Turpin on *Blues for Mister Charlie*.

**6235** PRATT, LOUIS H. James Baldwin
pp.157     MH★
Boston: Twayne     1978

**6236** STANDLEY, FRED L. & STANDLEY, NANCY V. James Baldwin: a reference guide
pp.xv, 310     L
Boston: G. K. Hall     1980

**6237** SYLVANDER, CAROLYN W. James Baldwin
pp.ix, 181     MH
NY: Frederick Ungar     1980

## 16. DRAMATIC BIOGRAPHY AND CRITICISM

6238  BLOM, HAROLD (Ed.).  James Baldwin
pp.viii, 164                                       MH★
NY: Chelsea House                                  1986

6239  CHAMETZKY, JULES (Ed.). Proceedings of a conference at the University of Massachusetts at Amherst April 22-23, 1988...Black writers define the struggle. [A tribute to James Baldwin]
pp.viii, 83; ill. in text                           L
Amherst MA: Massachusetts U. P.                    1989

6240  STANDLEY, FRED L. & PRATT, LOUIS H. (Eds).  Conversations with James Baldwin
pp.xiii, 297; front.                               MH
Jackson: U. P. of Mississippi                      1989

6241  TROUPE, QUINCY (Ed.).  James Baldwin: the legacy
pp.270; pl. 8                                      MH
NY: Simon & Schuster                               1989
A tribute, comprising contributions from a range of colleagues and friends, together with examples of his writings.

### Baraka, Imamu Amiri
### [Jones, LeRoi]
### (1934-)

6242  EMANUEL, JAMES A. & GROSS, THEODORE L. (Eds). Dark symphony: negro literature in America
pp.xviii, 604                                      DL★
NY: Free P.                                        1968
Includes material on Imamu Amiri Baraka.

6243  DACE, LETITIA; BAKER, JOHN & DIPPOLD, DIANE. LeRoi Jones: a checklist of works by and about him
pp.196                                              O
London: Nether P.                                  1971

6244  MEZU, S. OKECHUKWU (Ed.). Modern black literature
pp.176                                              L
Buffalo NY: Black Academy P.                       1971
Includes John Lindberg on Le Roi Jones's *Dutchman* and *The Slave*.

6245  REED, ROLAND L.  Form and meaning in some plays by Imamu Amiri Baraka (Leroi Jones)
Lincoln: U. of Nebraska (PhD)                      1972

6246  RICARD. ALAIN.  Théatre et nationalisme: Wole Soyinka et Le Roi Jones
pp.235                                             MH
Paris: Présence Africane                           1972
An edition in English was published Nigeria, Ile-Ife: U. of Ife P., 1983.

6247  HAGNELL, VIVEKA. Läs och teater upplevelser Joe Hill: Smä ting till noje och uppbyggelse, Rättegången mot Le Roi Jones Földjdsckrift till Viveka Hagnells avhandling Att läsa litteratur och att se teater
ll.iv, 163, viii; diagrams in text                  L
Lund: U. Institute for the Dramatic Arts           1973
A comparison of the subjective experience of performance and written text. Swedish text with summary in English.

6248  HUDSON, THEODORE F.  From Le Roi Jones to Amiri Baraka: the literary works
pp.xiii, 222                                        L
Durham NY: Duke U. P.                              1973

6249  BENSTON, KIMBERLY W.  Baraka: the renegade and the mask
pp.xxi, 290                                         O
New Haven: Yale U. P.                              1976

6250  BENSTON, KIMBERLY W. (Ed.).  Imamu A. Baraka: a collection of critical essays
pp.xi, 195                                          O
Englewood Cliffs: Prentice-Hall                    1978
John Lindberg: *Dutchman* and *The Slave*; Robert L. Toner: *The Toilet*; Owen E. Brady : *Great Goodness of Life*; Charles D. Peavy :*Madheart*; Kimberley Benston : *Slaveship*.

6251  SOLLORS, WERNER.  Amiri Baraka/Le Roi Jones: the quest for a 'populist modernism'
pp.xii, 338; pl. 4                                MESM
NY: Columbia U. P.                                 1978

6252  RICHARDS, SANDRA L.  Sweet meat from Leroi: the dramatic world of Amiri Baraka
Stanford: U. (PhD)                                 1979

6253  BROWN, LLOYD W.  Amiri Baraka
pp.180                                              L
Boston: Twayne                                     1980

6254  FISHER, EDWARD J.  Radical black thought in the dramatic work of Amiri Baraka
Santa Barbara: U. of California (PhD)              1980

6255  DUVAL, ELAINE I.  Theatre and the double: revolutionary consciousness in Baraka and Artaud
Knoxville: U. of Tennessee (PhD)                   1988

### Barker, James Nelson
### (1784-1858)

6256  MUSSER, PAUL H. James Nelson Barker, 1784-1858 with a reprint of his comedy *Tears and Smiles*
pp.v, 230                                           L
Philadelphia: U. of Pennsylvania P.                1929
Biography. The bibliography refers to an anonymous biographical sketch, typescript: *A combined account of General John Barker and Major J. N. Barker* [1858] in the Keys Collection, Baltimore.

6257  KUHN, JOHN G.  J. N. Barker's play of ideas in 1812 and 1824: or how he got scot free
Philadelphia: U. of Pennsylvania (PhD)             1969
*Marmian* and *Superstition; or, the Tragic Father*

6258  PENNELL, JANE. James Nelson Barker: nineteenth-century American dramatist
Saint Louis: U. (PhD)                              1973

### Barnes, Djuna
### (1892-1982)

6259  SCOTT, JAMES B.  Djuna Barnes
pp.152; front.                                      L
Boston: Twayne                                     1876

6260  GILDZEN, ALEX (Ed.).  A festschrift for Djuna Barnes on her 80th birthday
pp.[18]; front.                                     O
Kent OH: Kent State U.                             1972
Includes tributes from Joseph Chaikin and Richard Eberhart.

6261  MESSERLI, DOUGLAS. Djuna Barnes: a bibliography
pp.xx, 131; ill. in text                            O
[NY?]: David Lewis                                 1975

6262 CLARK, SUSAN F. Djuna Barnes and the American theatre
Medford MA: Tufts U. (PhD)     1989

## Barry, Philip
## (1896-1949)

6263 HAMM, GERALD. The dramas of Philip Barry: a dissertation in American civilization
Philadelphia: U. of Pennsylvania (PhD)     1946

6264 FELDHAUS, EUGENE C. A treatment of moral and psychological values in the plays of Philip Barry
Jamaica NY: St John's U. (PhD)     1958

6265 MAYS, DAVID D. The theme of responsibility in the plays of Philip Barry
New Orleans: Tulane U. (PhD)     1963

6266 ROPPOLO, JOSEPH P. Philip Barry
pp.158     MH
NY: Twayne     1965

6267 GILD, DAVID C. An historical and critical study of the serious plays of Philip Barry
New Haven: Yale U. (PhD)     1968

6268 FENTON, ELAINE R. Philip Barry and his critics
NY: U. (PhD)     1970

6269 GAINES, ROBERT A. The dramatic universe of Philip Barry
Bloomington: Indiana U. (PhD)     1972

## Behrman, Samuel Nathaniel
## (1893-1973)

6270 BEHRMAN, SAMUEL N. The Worcester account
pp.175     O
London: Hamish Hamilton     1954

Reminiscences of early life, largely reprinted from the *New Yorker*.

6271 LEVIN, MILTON. S. N. Behrman. The operation and dilemmas of the comic spirit
Ann Arbor: U. of Michigan (PhD)     1958

6272 HENIFORD, LEWIS W. S. N. Behrman as a social dramatist
Stanford: U. (PhD)     1964

6273 BEHRMAN, SAMUEL N. The suspended drawing room
pp.253     L
London: Hamish Hamilton     1966

Reprinted essays and articles, including essay on Robert E. Sherwood.

6274 HICKENLOOPER, GEORGE. The comedy of illumination in S. N. Behrman
New Haven: Yale U. (PhD)     1966

6275 BEHRMAN, SAMUEL N. People in a diary: a memoir
pp.xii, 338; ill. in text     MESM
Boston: Little, Brown     1972

Autobiography, largely reprinted from the *New Yorker*. UK title: *Tribulations and laughter...*

6276 KESSELY, URS. S. N. Behrman's Komödien: Spiel und Konflikt. Untersuchungen zu einem Gattungsbegriff und zum Verhältnis der Geschlechter
pp.155; ill. in text, pl. 1     MH
Berne: Herbert Lang     1972

6277 ASHER, DON. The eminent yachtsman and the whorehouse piano player
pp.256     MH
NY: Coward, McCann & Geoghegan     1973

Account of author's father's relationship with S. N. Behrman. Provides background material for Behrman's *The Cold Wind and the Warm* (1958).

6278 BAXTER, MARILYN. Modern woman as heroine in representative plays by S. N. Behrman
Madison: U. of Wisconsin (PhD)     1973

6279 REED, KENNETH T. S. N. Behrman
pp.151; ill. in text     MH
Boston: Twayne     1975

6280 SHEA, MAUREEN A. The playwriting technique of S. N. Behrman: the Theatre Guild years, 1927-1938
Columbus: Ohio State U. (PhD)     1977

6281 JORGE, ROBERT R. A delicate giant: S. N. Behrman and the theatrical compromise (an investigation into his last three produced plays)
Minneapolis: U. of Minnesota (PhD)     1979

## Bellow, Saul
## (1915-)

6282 ROVIT, EARL. Saul Bellow
pp.46     L
Minneapolis: U. of Minnesota P.     1967

6283 CLAYTON, JOHN J. Saul Bellow: in defense of man
pp.xi, 273     O
Bloomington: Indiana U. P.     1968

6284 DUTTON, ROBERT R. Saul Bellow
pp.177     O
Boston: Twayne     1971

6285 SCHEER-SCHÄZLER, BRIGITTE. Saul Bellow
pp.x, 150     L
NY: Frederick Ungar     1972

6286 ROVIT, EARL (Ed.). Saul Bellow: a collection of critical essays
pp.ix, 176     L
Englewood Cliffs: Prentice-Hall     1975

Includes Irving Malin: *Bummy's analysis*, a discussion of *The Last Analysis*.

6287 NAULT, MARIANNE. Saul Bellow: his works and his critics, an annotated international bibliography
pp.xxi, 191     MH
NY: Garland P.     1977

6288 NOREEN, ROBERT G. Saul Bellow: a reference guide
pp.xiii, 169     L
Boston: G. K. Hall     1978

Includes a guide to reviews, critiques and studies of *The Last Analysis*.

### Bird, Robert Montgomery
### (1806-1854)

6289  FOUST, CLEMENT E.  The life and dramatic works of Robert Montgomery Bird
pp.xv, 725; front.                         MH
NY: Knickerbocker P.                1919

6290  BIRD, ROBERT M.  The city looking glass. A Philadelphia comedy, in five acts...edited, with an introduction by Arthur H. Quinn
pp.xii, 139                                  MH
NY: Pynson for the Colophon          1933
A useful biographical introduction. 465 copies.

6291  BIRD, MARY M.  Life of Robert Montgomery Bird written by his wife...edited [by E. C. S. Thompson] from her manuscripts...with selections from Bird's correspondence
pp.viii, 130; front.                          P
Philadelphia: U. Library                1945
Reprinted from the U. of Pennsylvania Library *Chronicle*.

6292  WILLIAMS, STANLEY T.  The Spanish background of American literature
                                           DL★
New Haven: Yale U. P.                 1955
Two volumes. Includes material on Robert Montgomery Bird: *Oraloosa* and *The Broker of Bogota*.

6293  DAHL, CURTIS.  Robert Montgomery Bird
pp.144                                        MH
New York: Twayne                    1963

6294  HARRIS, RICHARD A.  The major dramas of Robert Montgomery Bird: a critical analysis of their structure and development
Bloomington: Indiana U. (PhD)       1966

### Bodenheim, Maxwell
### (1892-1954)

6295  DE VOE, E. T.  'A soul in gaudy tatters': a critical biography of Maxwell Bodenheim
University Park: Pennsylvania State U. (PhD)    1957

6296  MOORE, JACK B.  Maxwell Bodenheim
pp.193                                         L
NY: Twayne                               1970

### Boesing, Martha

6297  GREELEY, LYNNE.  Spirals from the matrix. The feminist plays of Martha Boesing, an analysis
College Park: U. of Maryland         1987
Minnesota dramatist.

### Boker, George Henry
### (1823-1890)

6298  BRADLEY, EDWARD S.  George Henry Boker: poet and patriot
pp.xi, 362; pl. 15                       O
Philadelphia: U. of Pennsylvania P.     1927

6299  SMITH, PETER M.  A study of the sociological and cultural milieu of George Henry Boker and the critical responses to the nineteenth-century productions of his plays
Denver: U. (PhD)                    1971

### Boucicault, Dion
### (1820-1890)

6300  WALSH, TOWNSEND.  The career of Dion Boucicault
pp.xviii, 224; pl.9                    M
NY: Dunlap Society               1915

6301  ANDERSON, JESSE M.  Dion Boucicault. Man of the theatre
Chicago: U. (PhD)                 1926

6302  CHESTERTON, G. K.  Avowals and denials. A book of essays
pp.vi, 218                            L
London: Methuen                  1934
Includes an essay: *On a melodrama [The Streets of London]*.

6303  FOLLAND, HAROLD.  The plays of Dion Boucicault
Cambridge MA: Harvard U. (PhD)     1940

6304  TOLSON, JULIUS H.  Dion Boucicault
Philadelphia: U. of Pennsylvania (PhD)    1951

6305  ORR, LYNN E.  Dion Boucicault and the nineteenth-century theatre
Baton Rouge: Louisiana State U. (PhD)   1953

6306  ROHRIG, GLADYS M.  An analysis of certain acting editions and promptbooks of plays by Dion Boucicault
Columbus: Ohio State U. (PhD)      1956

6307  HUNTER, JACK W.  *The Corsican Brothers*. Its history, and technical problems related to the production of the play
Columbus: Ohio State U. (PhD)      1963

6308  AN EXHIBITION of books, prints and manuscripts relating to Dion Boucicault [drop title]
bs                                              P
Dublin: Public Library                 1967

6309  HARRISON, ALLIE C.  The dramatic theories of Dion Boucicault. A study of statements on dramaturgy in his published essays
Lawrence: U. of Kansas (PhD)        1967

6310  STEELE, WILLIAM P.  The character of melodrama. An examination through Dion Boucicault's *The Poor of New York*, including the text of the play. With a foreword by James S. Bost
pp.vi, 111; ill. in text                M
Orono: U. of Maine P.                1968

6311  HOGAN, ROBERT.  Dion Boucicault
pp.146                                       M
NY: Twayne                               1969

6312  FAWKES, RICHARD.  Dion Boucicault
pp.xviii, 274; pl.8                    M
London: Quartet Books               1979
Foreword by Donald Sinden.

6313  MOLIN, SVEN E. & GOODEFELLOWE, ROBIN.  Dion Boucicault, the Shaughraun. A documentary life, letters and selected works. Part one: the early years [Part two: up and down in Paris and London]
pp.108, 88; ill. in text, front.           M
Newark, Del.: Proscenium P.       1979, 1982

In *George Spelvin's Theatre book*, II, 1; IV, 2. Part one also published separately.

**6314** ELLIOTT, ROBERT F. Shadow of *The Shaughraun*. Reflections on the stage Irishman tradition in plays by Boucicault, Shaw, Synge amd O'Casey
Ithaca: Cornell U. (PhD) 1983

**6315** WARREN, LISA C. Boucicault and melodrama on stage. The evidence from nineteenth century advertising illustrations for staging, blocking and costuming
Athens: U. of Georgia (PhD) 1984

### Brackenridge, Hugh Henry
### (1748-1816)

**6316** HEARTMAN, CHARLES F. A bibliography of the writings of Hugh Henry Brackenridge prior to 1825 with a portrait and facsimiles of title pages
pp.37; front., ill. in text, pl. 2 L
NY: For the compiler 1917

**6317** GLASRUD, CLARENCE A. The life and writings of Hugh H. Brackenridge
Cambridge MA: Harvard U. (PhD) 1929

**6318** NEWLIN, CLAUDE M. The life and writings of Hugh Henry Brackenridge
pp.vii, 328 L
Princeton: U. P. 1932

**6319** HARDER, DANIEL. Hugh Henry Brackenridge
pp.159 L
NY: Twayne 1967
With brief reference to the plays.

### Brann, William Cooper
### (1855-1898)

**6320** FLETCHER, EDWARD G. & HART, JACK L. Brann, the playwright: with the text of his English society drama, *That American Woman*
pp.68 MH
Austin: U. of Texas 1941
Includes a biographical sketch of Brann.

### Brougham, John
### (1810-1880)
### Actor, playwright

**6321** WINTER, WILLIAM (Ed.). Life, stories and poems of John Brougham comprising I, his autobiography–a fragment: II, a supplementary memoir: III, sketch of his club life; IV, selections from his miscellaneous writings
pp.461; pl. 9 (1 folding) L
Boston: James R. Osgood 1881
A sketch of club life is supplied by Noah Brooks.

**6322** HAWES, DAVID S. John Brougham as American playwright and man of the theatre
Stanford: U. (PhD) 1953

**6323** RYAN, PAT M. John Brougham, the gentle satirist. A critique, with a handlist and census
pp.22 M
NY: Public Library 1959

Reprinted from the *Bulletin*, Vol. 63, December. Includes a checklist of the plays.

### Brown, William Wells

**6324** FARRISON, WILLIAM E. William Wells Brown: author and reformer
pp.xii, 482; pl. 1 O
Chicago: U. P. 1969
Critical biography. *Experience: or how to give a Northern man a backbone* and *The Escape: or, a leap for freedom*, discussed in chapters eighteen and nineteen.

### Buchwald, Art
### (1925-)

**6325** BUCHWALD, ART. Counting sheep. The log and the complete play *Sheep on the Runway*
pp.219; pl. 2 M
NY: G. P. Putnam's Sons [1970]

### Bullins, Ed
### (1935-)

**6326** WOLFE, ELTON C. An analysis of the language in five plays by Ed Bullins
Stanford: U. (PhD) 1977

### Burk, John Daly
### (1775?-1808)

**6327** CAMPBELL, CHARLES (Ed.). Some materials to serve for a brief memoir of John Daly Burk, author of *A History of Virginia*, with a sketch of the life and character of his only child, Judge John Junius Burk
pp.123 L
Albany NY: Joel Munsell 1868
Burk wrote a number of plays for the Thespian Society of Petersburg, and also acted.

**6328** WYATT, EDWARD A. John Daly Burk: patriot-playwright-historian
pp.32 MH
Charlottesville VA: Historical Publishing 1936

**6329** SHULIM, JOSEPH I. John Daly Burk: Irish revolutionist and American patriot
pp.60 L
Philadelphia: American Philosophical Society 1964
Reprint from *Transactions*, new series, vol. 54, pt.6

### Campbell, Bartley Thomas
### (1843-1888)

**6330** CLAEREN, WAYNE H. Bartley Campbell: playwright of the gilded age
Pittsburgh: U. (PhD) 1975

### Capote, Truman
### (1924-1984)

**6331** NANCE, WILLIAM L. The worlds of Truman Capote
pp.256 L
NY: Stein & Day 1970
Includes a brief account of the plays and of the *Porgy and Bess* tour.

### Chase, Mary Coyle
### (1907-1981)

**6332** BERGER, MAURICE A. Mary Coyle Chase: her battlefield of illusion
Denver: U. (PhD) 1970

## Chayefsky, Paddy
## (1923-1981)

**6333** CLUM, JOHN M. Paddy Chayefsky
pp.149; ill. in text  O
Boston: Twayne  1976

## Connelly, Marcus Cook
## (1890-1981)

**6334** CONNELLY, MARC. Voices offstage: a book of memories [autobiography]
pp.ix, 258; pl. 8  M
NY: Holt, Rinehart & Winston  1968

**6335** NOLAN, PAUL T. Marc Connelly
pp.175  L
NY: Twayne  1969

## Crawford, Jack C.

**6336** NOLAN, PAUL T. Three plays by J. W. (Capt. Jack) Crawford: an experiment in myth-making
pp.285; front.  L
The Hague: Mouton  1966

With a substantial essay on J. W. Crawford, an associate of William F. Cody, who combined frontier scouting with verse and playwriting. Addendum facing final page.

## Crothers, Rachel
## (1878-1958)

**6337** ABRAHAMSON, IRVING. The career of Rachel Crothers in the American drama
Chicago: U. (PhD)  1956

**6338** WILLIAMS, MERRELL. The changing role of the woman as represented in selected plays by Rachel Crothers: 1899-1937
Denver: U. (PhD)  1971

**6339** GOTTLIEB, LOIS C. Rachel Crothers
pp.170  MH★
Boston: Twayne  1979

**6340** KAPLAN, ZOE. Woman in focus in major plays and productions of Rachel Crothers
NY: City U. (PhD)  1979

## Cullen, Countee
## (1903-1946)

**6341** FERGUSON, BLANCHE E. Countee Cullen and the negro renaissance
pp.ix, 213; ill.  DL★
NY: Dodd, Mead  1966

## Cummings, Edward Estlin
## 1894-1962

**6342** FRIEDMAN, NORMAN. e. e. cummings: the growth of a writer...preface by Harry T. Moore
pp.xi, 193  L
Carbondale: Southern Illinois U. P.  1964

**6343** NORMAN, CHARLES. E. E. Cummings: the magic-maker
pp.ix, 246  L
NY: Duell, Sloan and Pearce  1964

Second edition revised. First published 1958.

**6344** FRIEDMAN, NORMAN (Ed.). E. E. Cummings: a collection of critical essays
pp.vi, 185  L
Englewood Cliffs NJ: Prentice-Hall  1972

Includes Robert E. Maurer: E. E. Cummings's 'Him'.

**6345** DUMAS, BETHANY K. E. E. Cummings: a remembrance of miracles
pp.157  O
London: Vision P.  1974

Published NY: Barnes & Noble. Chapter five addresses the drama.

**6346** BRADLEY, MARK J. E. E. Cummings's Him: an annotation with analysis and production history
Minneapolis: U. of Minnesota (PhD)  1984

## Davis, Ossie
## (1917-)

**6347** WASHINGTON, VON H. An evaluation of the play Purlie Victorious and its impact on the American theatrical scene
Detroit: Wayne State U. (PhD)  1979

Produced Cort Theatre, NY, September 28, 1961.

## Davis, Owen
## (1874-1856)

**6348** DAVIS, OWEN. I'd like to do it again
pp.viii, 233; pl. 13  M
NY: Farrar & Rinehart  1931

Reminiscence. Author was first president of the Dramatists Guild and Pulitzer Prize winner with Icebound (1923).

**6349** DAVIS, OWEN. My first fifty years in the theatre: the plays, the players, the theatrical managers and the theatre itself as one man saw them in the fifty years between 1897 and 1947
pp.157  M
Boston: Walter H. Baker  1950

**6350** WITHAM, BARRY B. The dramaturgy of Owen Davis
Columbus: Ohio State U. (PhD)  1968

**6351** WANN, JACK K. The career of Owen Davis (1874-1956) in the American theatre
Baton Rouge: Louisiana State U. (PhD)  1978

**6352** BARTO, DAN. Owen Davis: from melodrama to realism
NY: U. (PhD)  1987

## Davis, Richard Harding
## (1864-1916)

**6353** DAVIS, RICHARD H. Farces. The Director, The Galloper, Miss Civilization. Illustrated by photographs of the actors and scenes in the plays
pp.viii, 332; pl.18  M
NY: Charles Scribner's Sons  1906

**6354** DOWNEY, FAIRFAX. Richard Harding Davis; his day [biography]
pp.xi, 322; ill. in text, pl. 16  O
NY: Charles Scribner's Sons  1933

## Dazey, Charles Turner
## (1855-1938)

**6355** DAZEY, CHARLES T. The first book appearance of...*In Old Kentucky*. Foreword by Barrett H. Clark. Introduction by the author. A historical note and an all-star cast of players depicted...by Paul McPharlin
pp.147: ill. in text   M
Detroit: Fine Book Circle   1937

1000 copies, including 350 autographed. Play first presented in 1893.

## Deering, Nathaniel
## (1791-1881)

**6356** CHAPLIN, LEOLA B. The life and works of Nathaniel Deering, 1791-1881 with the texts of Deering's plays *Carabasset* and *The Clairvoyants*.
pp.244; front., ill. in text   L
Orono ME: U. of Maine P.   1934

Printed in *Maine Bulletin*, XXXVII, 1, August 1934.

## Dos Passos, John
## (1896-1970)

**6357** BERNARDIN, CHARLES W. The development of John Dos Passos
Madison: U. of Wisconsin (PhD)   1949

**6358** DOS PASSOS, JOHN R. Most likely to succeed [autobiography]
pp.285   O
London: Robert Hale   1955

Published NY: Prentice-Hall, 1954.

## Dreiser, Theodore
## (1871-1945)

**6359** BIDDLE, EDMUND R. The plays of Theodore Dreiser
Philadelphia: U. of Pennsylvania (PhD)   1965

**6360** SALZMAN, JACK (Ed.). Theodore Dreiser: the critical reception
pp.xxxvii, 741   DL★
NY: D. Lewis   1972

Includes a section on the plays, reprinting reviews.

**6361** PIZER, DONALD; DOWELL, RICHARD W. & RUSCH, FREDERIC E. Theodore Dreiser: a primary and secondary bibliography
pp.x, 515   L
Boston: G. K. Hall   1975

## Dunlap, William
## (1766-1839)
## Playwright, manager

**6362** DUNLAP, WILLIAM. Memoirs of a water drinker
pp.208, 220   L
NY: Saunders and Otley   1837

Two volumes. Fiction, with strong documentary theatre background. Includes reference to G. F. Cooke.

**6363** DUNLAP, WILLIAM. The Father, or American shandyism, a comedy...with an introduction by Thomas J. McKee
pp.xii, 68; front.   MH
NY: Dunlap Society   1887

Includes a chronology of Dunlap's plays. 175 copies.

**6364** WEGELIN, OSCAR. William Dunlap and his writings, reprinted from *The Literary Collection* January, 1904
pp.i, 8   MH
NY: For the author   1904

125 copies. Lists published and unpublished works, and portraits.

**6365** MARBLE, ANNIE R. Heralds of American literature: a group of patriot writers of the revolutionary and national periods
pp. ix, 383; front., pl. 10   L
Chicago: U. P.   1907

Chapter VII: *William Dunlap: the beginnings of drama.*

**6366** WOOLSEY, THEODORE S. William Dunlap painter and critic: the American Vasari
pp.32   L
[New Haven]: Yale U.   1914

Reprinted from the *Yale Review*, July, 1914. A brief biographical sketch precedes a listing of Dunlap's paintings.

**6367** WEGELIN, OSCAR (Ed.). A bibliographical checklist of the plays and miscellaneous writings of William Dunlap (1766-1839)
ll.26   MH
NY: Charles F. Heartman   1916

**6368** COAD, ORAL S. Willian Dunlap: a study of his life and works and of his place in contemporary culture
pp.ix, 314; pl. 5   M
NY: Dunlap Society   1917

**6369** DUNLAP, WILLIAM. Diary of William Dunlap (1766-1839): the memoirs of a dramatist, theatrical manager, painter, critic, novelist, and historian
pp.xxvii; xiii; xiii, 964; pl. 37   M
NY: Historical Society   1930-32

Three volumes, comprising LXII-LXIV of the John Watts De Peyser Publication Fund Series.

**6370** McGINNIS, WILLIAM C. William Dunlap
pp.35; ill.   DL★
Perth Amboy NJ: City of Perth Amboy   1956

**6371** CANARY, ROBERT H. William Dunlap
pp.162   M
NY: Twayne   1970

**6372** GRINCHUK, ROBERT A. The plays of William Dunlap. A study of dramatic failure and the shift in popular taste, 1795-1805
Minneapolis: U. of Minnesota (PhD)   1972

**6373** GATES, ROBERT A. William Dunlap's managership of the Park Theatre, New York (1798-1805)
NY: U. (PhD)   1978

## Eberhart, Richard
## (1904-)

**6374** ENGEL, BERNARD F. Richard Eberhart
pp.184   L
NY: Twayne   1971

**6375** ROACHE, JOEL. Richard Eberhart: the progress of an American poet
pp.xxix, 299; pl. 4   L
NY: Oxford U. P.   1971

Critical biography. Includes his involvement in a 'poets' theatre' in Massachusetts.

### Faulkner, William
### (1897-1962)

**6376** IZARD, BARBARA & HIERONYMUS, CLARA. *Requiem for a Nun*: on stage and off
pp.xii, 331; ill. in text, pl. 9      M
Nashville TE: Aurora      1970

The background and production history of William Faulkner's only dramatic work.

### Ferber, Edna
### (1887-1968)

**6377** FERBER, EDNA. A peculiar treasure [autobiography]
pp.xi,398; pl. 16      M
NY: Doubleday, Doran      1939

Includes an account of the author's collaboration with George S. Kaufman, and of the genesis of *Showboat*.

**6378** KREUGER, MILES. *Show Boat*: the story of a classic American musical
pp.x, 246; ill. in text      M
NY: Oxford U. P.      1977

A stage and movie history.

**6379** GILBERT, JULIE G. Ferber, a biography
pp.ix, 445; pl. 16      MH
Garden City: Doubleday      1978

**6380** SHOWBOAT
pp.136 inc. wrappers; ill. in text      P
Hayes, UK: EMI Records      1988

Booklet issued to accompany the boxed LP recording, comprising: Miles Kreuger: *Some words about 'Show Boat'*; John McGlinn (orchestra director and conductor): *Notes on 'Show Boat*; 'Goldie' Stanton Clough, secretary to Florenz Ziegfeld, recalls the original production...; *The story*; Libretto. An appendix prints all variants, together with previously unused or deleted material.

### Firkins, Oscar W.
### (1864-1932)

**6381** FIRKINS, OSCAR W. Memoirs and letters...
pp.vii, 312; front.      L
Minneapolis: U. of Minnesota P.      1934

Edited with a preface by Ina T. Firkins. Memoir by Netta W. Wilson. Brief biographical introduction by Richard Burton, a former student.

### Fitch, William Clyde
### (1865-1909)

**6382** BELL, ARCHIE. The Clyde Fitch I knew
pp.v, 121; pl. 6      M
NY: Broadway      1909

**6383** MOSES, MONTROSE J. & GERSON, VIRGINIA (Eds). Clyde Fitch and his letters
pp.xx, 406; pl. 28      M
Boston: Little, Brown      1924

**6384** MASTERS, ROBERT W. Clyde Fitch. A playwright of his time
Evanston: Northwestern U. (PhD)      1942

**6385** MURRAY, JAMES J. The contribution of Clyde Fitch to the American theatre
Boston: U. (PhD)      1942

**6386** HELLIE, THOMAS L. Clyde Fitch, playwright of New York's leisure class
Columbia: U. of Missouri-Columbia (PhD)      1985

### Fitzgerald, Francis Scott
### (1896-1940)

**6387** BRUCCOLI, MATTHEW J. & ATKINSON, JENNIFER M. As ever, Scott Fitzgerald: letters between F. Scott Fitzgerald and his literary agent Harold Ober, 1919-1940
pp.xxii, 441; pl. 8      O
Philadelphia: J. B. Lippincott      1972

Foreword by Scottie Fitzgerald Smith.

**6388** EBLE, KENNETH E. F. Scott Fitzgerald
pp.191      O
Bologna: La Steb      1972

Makes reference to *The Vegetable*. Text in Italian. English version published Boston: G. K. Hall, 1977.

**6389** FITZGERALD, F. SCOTT. *The Vegetable: or, from president to postman*. New edition with unpublished scenes and corrections and an introduction by Charles Scribner
pp.xx, 184      MH
NY: Charles Scribner's Sons      1976

**6390** MARGOLIES, ALAN (Ed.). F. Scott Fitzgerald's St Paul plays 1911-1914
pp.vii, 166; pl. 4      O
Princeton: U. Library      1978

### Flagg, James Montgomery

**6391** MEYER, SUSAN E. James Montgomery Flagg
pp.208; ill. in text, some col.      L
NY: Watson-Guptill      1974

Artist, illustrator and, in his early years, playwright and actor. A close friend of John Barrymore.

### Forbes, James
### (1871-1938)

**6392** GROVER, CHARLES A. James Forbes: his works and his career in the American theatre
Davis: U. of California (PhD)      1976

### Foreman, Richard
### (1937-)

**6393** FALK, FLORENCE A. The aperspective theatre of Richard Foreman
New Brunswick NJ: Rutgers State U. (PhD)      1975

**6394** FOREMAN, RICHARD. Plays and manifestos edited and with an introduction by Kate Davey
pp.xvii, 299; ill. in text      MH
NY: U. P.      1976

Includes *Angelface, Total Recall, Ontological- Hysteric manifesto I, II, III*. Production photographs.

**6395** DAVY, KATE. Richard Foreman and the ontological-hysteric theatre
pp.xii, 253; ill. in text      O
Ann Arbor: U. of Michigan Research P.      1981

**6396** FOREMAN, RICHARD. Reverberation machines. The later plays and essays
pp.245; ill.      DL★
Barrytown NY: Station Hill P.      1985

### Frank, Waldo David
### (1889-?)
### Writer

**6397** MUNSON, GORHAM B. Waldo Frank: a study
pp.95; col. front.  L
NY: Boni & Liveright  1923

Includes a bibliography and a selection of critical opinions of his work.

**6398** CARTER, PAUL J. Waldo Frank
pp.191  L
NY: Twayne  1967

Frank wrote ten plays, of which only one, *New Year's Eve* was published (NY: Scribner's, 1929) and was given a try-out by the Group Theatre, who dropped it.

### Franken, Rose
### [Lewin, Rose]
### (1895-1988)

**6399** FRANKEN, ROSE. When all is said and done [autobiography]
pp.431; pl. 9  L
London: W. H. Allen  1962

### Frederic, Harold
### (1856-1898)

**6400** WOODWARD, ROBERT H. Harold Frederic. A study of his novels, short stories, and plays
Bloomington: Indiana U. (PhD)  1957

### Friedman, Bruce Jay
### (1930-)

**6401** SCHULZ, MAX F. Bruce Jay Friedman
pp.164  L
NY: Twayne  1974

*Scuba Duba*, New Theatre, 1967 was the novelist's only successful play.

### Gale, Zona
### (1874-1938)

**6402** GALE, ZONA. Portage, Wisconsin and other essays
pp.ix, 214; pl. 2  O
NY: Alfred A. Knopf  1928

Includes brief reference to Chautauqua.

**6403** DERLMUTH, AUGUST. Still small voice: the biography of Zona Gale
pp.xi, 319; pl. 8  O
NY: D. Appleton-Century  1940

Best known as a novelist but also a successful playwright, receiving the Pulitzer prize for her dramatization of her novella, *Miss Lulu Bett* (1920).

### Gibson, William
### (1914-)

**6404** GIBSON, WILLIAM. The Seesaw log: a chronicle of the stage production, with the text of *Two for the Seesaw*.
pp.ix, 275  M
NY: Alfred A. Knopf  1959

**6405** GIBSON, WILLIAM. A mass for the dead
pp.ix, 432  MH
NY: Atheneum  1968

Evocative autobiographical articles, and some verses.

### Gilroy, Frank D.
### (1925-)

**6406** GILROY, FRANK. About those roses: or how not to do a play and succeed: and the text of *The Subject was Roses*...
pp.vii, 211; pl. 3  MH
NY: Random House  1965

Production log. The author's unpublished play, which was awarded the Pulitzer Prize and the New York Drama Critics Circle award, opened on Broadway, the Royale Theatre, May 25, 1964, with Martin Sheen playing the son.

### Glaspell, Susan
### (1882-1948)

**6407** WATERMAN, ARTHUR. Susan Glaspell
pp.144  MH
NY: Twayne  1966

**6408** NOE, MARCIA. A critical biography of Susan Glaspell
Iowa City: U. of Iowa  1976

**6409** BACH, GERHARD. Susan Glaspell und die Provincetown Players: die Anfänge des modernen amerikanischen Dramas und Theaters
pp.245  M
Frankfurt: Peter Lang  1979

**6410** GLASPELL, SUSAN. Plays. Edited with an introduction by C. W. E. Bigsby
pp.vii, 161; front.  L
Cambridge: U. P.  1987

A substantial introduction. Additional textual annotation by Christine Dymkowski.

### Godfrey, Thomas
### (1736-1763)

**6411** GODFREY, THOMAS. Prince of Parthia: edited with introduction historical, biographical and critical by Archibald Henderson
pp.xiii, 189; front., pl. 15  L
Boston: Little, Brown  1917

580 copies. Play first performed by Lewis Hallam, David Douglass and the American company, April 23, 1767 in the New Theatre, Pennsylvania.

### Gold, Michael
### (1893-1967)

**6412** BROGNA, JOHN J. Michael Gold: critic and playwright
Athens: U. of Georgia (PhD)  1982

### Green, Paul
### (1894-1981)

**6413** CLARK, BARRETT H. An introduction to the plays of Paul Green
pp.12 inc. wrappers  M
NY: Robert M. McBride  1926

Reprinted from Paul Green: *Lonesome Road*, NY: McBride, 1926.

**6414** CLARK, BARRETT H. Paul Green
pp.36; front.  M
NY: Robert M. McBride  1928

A critical survey with a chronological list of the writings including first play-production dates.

**6415** GREEN, PAUL. The hawthorn tree: some papers and letters on life and the theatre
pp.xi, 157      MH
Chapel Hill: U. of N. Carolina P.      1943

**6416** GREEN, PAUL. Forever growing: some notes on a credo for teachers
pp.iii, 342      MH
Chapel Hill: U. of N. Carolina P.      1945

**6417** OWENS, HENRY G. The social thought and criticism of Paul Green
NY: U. (PhD)      1946

**6418** ADAMS, AGATHA B. Paul Green of Chapel Hill. Edited by Richard Walser
     DL★
Chapel Hill: U. of N. Carolina P.      1951

**6419** GREEN, PAUL. Dramatic heritage
pp.xi, 177      MH
NY: Samuel French      1953
Articles on drama/theatre, many reprinted from periodicals and from the author's *The Hawthorn Tree*.

**6420** GREEN, PAUL. Drama and the weather: some notes and papers on life and the theatre
pp.220      DL★
NY: Samuel French      1958

**6421** HETHMON, ROBERT H. (Ed.). An interview with Paul Green... Comments on the Group Theatre and other things
pp.57      DL★
[Chapel Hill]: [U. of N. Carolina?]      [1961]

**6422** GREEN, PAUL. Plough and furrow: some essays and papers on life and the theatre
pp.ix, 165      L
NY: Samuel French      1963
Includes *With the Group Theatre, a remembrance* (pp.42-56).

**6423** STAROBA, FRANK J. Symphonic outdoor drama. A study of form in the plays of Paul Green
New Haven: Yale U. (PhD)      1964

**6424** GREEN, PAUL. Home to my valley [autobiography]
pp.xii, 140; ill. in text      MH
Chapel Hill: U. of N. Carolina P.      1970
The early years.

**6425** KENNY, VINCENT S. Paul Green
pp.xv, 170      L
NY: Twayne      1971

**6426** CLIFFORD, JOHN. Problems in staging the outdoor symphonic dramas of Paul Green
NY: U. (PhD)      1972

**6427** EADY, FRED A. Paul Green: folk dramatist, social critic
East Lansing: Michigan State U. (PhD)      1974

**6428** ALDRIDGE, ROBERT E. Heraclitian idealism in the plays of Paul Green
Madison: U. of Wisconsin (PhD)      1979

### Greene, Clay Meredith
### (1850-1933)

**6429** JAMES, WILLIAM R. Clay Meredith Greene (1850-1933): a case study of an American journeyman playwright
Iowa City: U. of Iowa (PhD)      1969

### Hansberry, Lorraine
### (1930-1965)

**6430** NEMIROFF, ROBERT (Ed.). To be young, gifted and black. Lorraine Hansberry in her own words adapted by Robert Nemiroff with original drawings and art by Miss Hansberry and an introduction by James Baldwin
pp.xxii; ill. in text      L
Englewood Cliffs NJ: Prentice-Hall      1969
Reminiscences, autobiographical fragments, letters, texts.

**6431** HANSBERRY, LORRAINE. Les Blancs: the collected last plays...edited, with critical backgrounds, by Robert Nemiroff
pp.ix, 372      L
NY: Random House      1972
Includes a 'postscript' to *Les Blancs*. Introduction by Julius Lester.

**6432** CHENEY, ANN. Lorraine Hansberry
pp.xviii, 174; front.      L
Boston: Twayne      1984

**6433** WOOD, DEBORAH-JEAN. The plays of Lorraine Hansberry: studies in dramatic form
Madison: U. of Wisconsin (PhD)      1985

**6434** MARRE, DIANE K. Traditions and departures: Lorraine Hansberry and black Americans in theatre
Berkeley: U. of California (PhD)      1987

### Harby, Isaac
### (1788-1828)

**6435** PINCKNEY, HENRY L. & MOISE, ABRAHAM (Eds.).]. A selection from the miscellaneous writings of the late Isaac Harby Esq., arranged and published...for the benefit of his family: to which is prefixed a memoir of his life...
pp.40, 287      L
Charleston: Pinckney & Moise      1829
Includes Harby's play *Alberti* and his essay: *Defense of the drama* together with other drama criticism. The memoir offers a commentary on the plays. Errata on *verso* of p. 287.

**6436** MOÏSE, LUSIUS C. Biography of Isaac Harby with an account of the Reformed Society of Israelites of Charleston S.C. 1824-1833
pp.xiii, 145; ill. in text, front.      L
[Columbia SC]: [For the author]      1931

### Harper, Henry H.

**6437** HARPER, HENRY H. Experiences of a playwright
pp.30      M
Cedar Rapids: Torch P. for the author      1942
An account of bringing the author's only play to the stage.

### Harrigan, Edward
### (1845-1911)

**6438** KAHN, E. J. The merry partners: the age and stage of Harrigan and Hart
pp.xv, 303; pl. 16      M
NY: Random House      1955

Tony Hart [Anthony J. Cannon] (1855-1891), a celebrated performer in his own time, is today remembered largely as the acting partner of Ned Harrigan and leading performer in Harrigan's plays.

**6439** BURNS, WARREN T.  The plays of Edward Harrigan: the theatre of intercultural communication
University Park: Pennsylvania State U. (PhD)     1969

**6440** MOODY, RICHARD.  Ned Harrigan: from Corlear's Hook to Herald Square
pp.x, 282; pl. 40     M
Chicago: Nelson Hall     1980

**6441** KOGER, ALICIA K.  A critical analysis of Edward Harrigan's comedy
Ann Arbor: U. of Michigan (PhD)     1984

### Hart, Moss
### (1904-1961)

**6442** HART, MOSS.  Act one: an autobiography
pp.vii, 445     M
NY: Random House     1959

**6443** MASON, RICHARD F.  Moss Hart's plays. The persistence of a formula
Madison: U. of Wisconsin (PhD)     1964

**6444** FARMER, PATRICK A.  Moss Hart: American playwright/director
Kent OH: State U. (PhD)     1980

### Hawkes, John
### (1925-)

**6445** BUSCH, FREDERICK M.  Hawkes: a guide to his fictions
pp.xxiii, 192     O
Syracuse NY: U. P.     1973

**6446** KUEHL, JOHN.  John Hawkes and the craft of conflict
pp.xii, 195     MH
New Brunswick NJ: Rutgers U. P.     1975

Critical study with some reference to the plays and the San Francisco actors workshop.

**6447** HRYCIW, CAROL A.  John Hawkes: an annotated bibliography with four introductions by John Hawkes
pp.vi, 199     DL★
Metuchen NJ: Scarecrow P.     1977

**6448** HRYCIW-WING, CAROL A.  John Hawkes: a research guide
pp.xxi, 396     MH
NY: Garland     1986

### Hecht, Ben
### (1894-1964)

**6449** HANSEN, HARRY.  Midwest portraits: a book of memories and friendships
pp.v, 357     L
NY: Harcourt, Brace     1923

With a chapter on Ben Hecht.

**6450** HECHT, BEN.  A child of the century [autobiography]
pp.633; pl. 12     L
NY: Signet     1954

**6451** HECHT, BEN.  Gaily, gaily
pp.ix, 227     L
NY: Doubleday     1963

Memoirs of Chicago experience, including theatre.

**6452** HECHT, BEN.  Letters from Bohemia
pp.192     L
London: Hammond     1965

Reminiscences including chapters on Gene Fowler, Sherwood Anderson, H. L. Mencken, Charles MacArthur, Maxwell Bodenheim.

**6453** FETHERLING, DOUG.  The five lives of Ben Hecht
pp.vii, 228; front.     M
[Toronto]: Lester & Orpen     1977

### Hellmann, Lillian
### (1905-1984)

**6454** BROCKINGTON, JOHN.  A critical analysis of the plays of Lillian Hellman
New Haven: Yale U. (PhD)     1962

**6455** KELLER, A. J.  Form and content in the plays of Lillian Hellman: a structural analysis
Stanford: U. (PhD)     1965

**6456** HALLER, CHARLES D.  The concepts of moral failure in the eight original plays of Lillian Hellman
New Orleans: Tulane U. (PhD)     1967

**6457** TRIESCH, MANFRED (Ed.).  The Lillian Hellman collection at the University of Texas
pp.167; ill. in text     L
Austin: U. of Texas/HRC     1967

Descriptive catalogue. Includes multiple drafts of the plays.

**6458** WHITESIDES, GLENN.  Lillian Hellman: a biographical and critical study
Tallahassee: Florida State U. (PhD)     1968

**6459** ACKLEY, MEREDITH.  The plays of Lillian Hellman
Philadelphia: U. of Pennsylvania (PhD)     1969

**6460** ADLER, JACOB H.  Lillian Hellman
pp.ii, 44     DL★
Austin TX: Steck, Vaughn     1969

**6461** HELLMAN, LILLIAN.  Unfinished woman: a memoir
pp.v, 280; pl. 4     M
Boston: Little, Brown     1969

**6462** LARIMER, CYNTHIA.  A study of the female characters in the eight plays of Lillian Hellman
Weat Lafayette: Purdue U. (PhD)     1970

**6463** ANGERMEIER, CAROL.  Moral and social protest in the plays of Lillian Hellman
Austin: U. of Texas (PhD)     1971

**6464** JOHNSON, ANNETTE.  A study of recurrent character types in the plays of Lillian Hellman
Amherst: U. of Massachusetts (PhD)     1971

**6465** BLITGEN, CAROL.  The overlooked Hellman
Berkeley: U. of California (PhD)     1972

**6466** MOODY, RICHARD. Lillian Hellman, playwright [biography]
pp.xv, 372; ill. in text L
NY: Pegasus 1972

**6467** HELLMAN, LILLIAN. Pentimento. A book of portraits [autobiography]
pp.viii, 297 M
Boston: Little, Brown 1973
Reminiscence of former acquaintances, including Dashiell Hammett.

**6468** HOLMIN, LORENA R. The dramatic works of Lillian Hellman
pp.178 L
Upsala: Almqvist & Wiksell 1973

**6469** CARLSON, EUGENE T. Lillian Hellman's plays as a reflection of the Southern mind
Los Angeles: U. of Southern California (PhD) 1975

**6470** HELLMAN, LILLIAN. Scoundrel time. Introduction by James Cameron. Commentary by Garry Wills
pp.172; pl. 6 M
London: Macmillan 1976
First published Boston: Little, Brown, 1976. An account of the author's experience of the McCarthy-dominated 1950s.

**6471** McPHERSON, MICHAEL L. Lillian Hellman and her critics
Denver: U. (PhD) 1976

**6472** PATRAKA, VIVIAN M. Lillian Hellman, dramatist of the second sex
Ann Arbor: U. of Michigan (PhD) 1977

**6473** FALK, DORIS V. Lillian Hellman
pp.ix, 180 MH
NY: Frederick Ungar 1978

**6474** BILLS, STEVEN H. Lillian Hellman: an annotated bibliography
pp.228 *
NY: Garland 1979

**6475** LEDERER, KATHERINE. Lillian Hellman
pp.159; front. DL*
Boston: Twayne 1979

**6476** ESTRIN, MARK W. Lillian Hellman plays, films, memoirs: a reference guide
pp.xvi, 378 MH
Boston: G. K. Hall 1980

**6477** RIORDAN, MARY M. Lillian Hellman: a bibliography, 1926-1978
pp.xxxiv, 210; front. MH
Metuchen NJ: Scarecrow P. 1980
2pp. addenda.

**6478** BECK-HORN, DEBRAH A. Types of love in selected plays of Lillian Hellman
Denton: North Texas State U. (PhD) 1983

**6479** SHAVER, SARA H. Feminist criticism as role analysis for the interpreter: women in Lillian Hellman's major plays
Tucson: U. of Arizona (PhD) 1984

**6480** BRYER, JACKSON R. (Ed.). Conversations with Lillian Hellman
pp.xxvi, 298 DL*
Jackson: U. P. of Mississippi 1986

**6481** WRIGHT, WILLIAM. Lillian Hellman: the image, the woman
pp.507; pl. 8 MH
NY: Simon & Schuster 1986

**6482** FEIBELMAN, PETER. Lilly: reminiscences of Lillian Hellman
pp.364; pl.16 L
London: Chatto & Windus 1988
Published NY: William Morrow.

**6483** ROLLYSON, CARL. Lillian Hellman: her legend and her legacy
pp.640; ill. DL*
NY: St Martin's P. 1988

**6484** ESTRIN, MARK W. (Ed.). Critical essays on Lillian Hellman
pp.275 DL*
Boston: G. K. Hall 1989

**6485** NOT USED

**6486** NEWMAN, ROBERT P. The cold war romance of Lillian Hellman and John Melby
pp.xv, 375; ill. in text MH
Chapel Hill: U. of N. Carolina P. 1989
Melby, of the State Department, ran foul of McCarthy and the UAAC and was fired, partly because of his involvement with Hellman. Letters, transcripts of evidence, and FBI documents combine to make clear the chain of events.

**6487** TOWNS, SAUNDRA. Lillian Hellman
pp.112 DL*
NY: Chelsea House 1989

### Hemingway, Ernest Miller
### (1899-1961)

**6488** STEPHENS, ROBERT O. (Ed.). Ernest Hemingway: the critical reception
pp.xl, 502 DL*
NY: Burt Franklin 1977

**6489** FELLNER, HARRIET. Hemingway as playwright: *The Fifth Column*
pp.ix, 123 MH
Ann Arbor: UMI Research P. 1986
Synopsis, analysis and an account of the play's reception.

### Herne, James A.
### [Ahearn, James]
### (1839-1901)

**6490** HATLEN, THEODORE. The development of James A. Herne as an exponent of realism in American drama
Stanford: U. (PhD) 1950

**6491** EDWARDS, HERBERT J. & HERNE, JULIA A. James A. Herne: the rise of realism in the American drama
pp.vi, 182 L
Orono: U. of Maine P. 1964

Based on Julia Herne's unpublished biography of her father. Includes material on David Belasco and John Drew.

**6492** SARACENI, EUGENE A. Character and milieu. James A. Herne's development as an actor-manager
Pittsburgh: U. (PhD)     1971

**6493** PERRY, JOHN. James A. Herne, the American Ibsen
pp.x, 343; pl. 12     M
Chicago: Nelson-Hall     1978

**6494** JONES, BETTY J. James A. Herne: the rise of American stage realism
Madison: U. of Wisconsin (PhD)     1983

### Heyward, DuBose
### (1885-1940)

**6495** CAPOTE, TRUMAN. The muses are heard: an account of the *Porgy and Bess* visit to Leningrad
pp.182     O
NY: Random House     1956
The Russian première, presented by the first US company to visit the Soviet Union. Published London: Heinemann, 1957.

**6496** DURHAM, FRANK. Dubose Heyward: the man who wrote *Porgy*
pp.xv, 152; ill. in text, pl. 4     L
Port Washington NY: Kennikat P.     1965
First published Columbia: U. of S. Carolina P., 1954.

**6497** ALPERT, HOLLIS. The life and times of Porgy and Bess: the story of an American classic
    DL★
NY: Alfred A. Knopf     1990

### Hillhouse, James A.
### (1789-1841)

**6498** HAZELRIGG, CHARLES T. American literary pioneer: a biographical study of James A. Hillhouse
pp.226; ill.     DL★
NY: Bookman Associates     1953

### Hopwood, Avery
### (1882-1928)

**6499** SHARRAR, JACK F. Avery Hopwood: his life and plays
pp.xii, 291; ill. in text, front.     L
Jefferson NC: McFarland     1989

### Howard, Bronson C.
### (1842-1908)

**6500** IN MEMORIAM Bronson Howard, 1842-1908, founder and president of the American Dramatists Club. Addresses delivered at the memorial meeting, October 18, 1908, at the Lyceum Theatre, New York. With a brief biography and other appreciations and records of his dramatic works, including a list of his plays with the original casts
pp.130; pl. 7     MB
NY: Marion P./American Dramatists Club     1910
Includes an appreciation by Brander Matthews, a brief biography by Harry P. Mawson, and the text of two addresses by Howard, *Autobiography of a play* (1886) and *Trash on the stage* (n.d.).

**6501** HOWARD, BRONSON. The autobiography of a play...with an introduction by Augustus Thomas
pp.v, 53     MH
NY: Dramatic Museum of Columbia U.     1914
The genesis of *The Banker's Daughter*. Originally the text of an address read before the Shakspere Club of Harvard U. in 1886.

**6502** FRERER, LLOYD A. Bronson Howard: dean of American dramatists
Iowa City: U. of Iowa (PhD)     1971

### Howard, Sidney
### (1891-1939)

**6503** COSTY, JAMES O. A critical evaluation of selected plays of Sidney Howard
Denver: U. (PhD)     1955

**6504** HOUSMAN, ALFRED L. The working methods of Sidney Howard
Iowa City: U. of Iowa (PhD)     1956

**6505** SCOTT, CHARLES E. Sidney Howard, American playwright
New Haven: Yale U. (PhD)     1963

**6506** WHITE, SIDNEY H. Sidney Howard
pp.178; front.     MH
Boston: Twayne     1977

### Howells, William Dean
### (1837-1920)

**6507** COOKE, DELMAR G. William Dean Howells: a critical study
pp.vii, 279     O
London: Stanley Paul     [1922?]

**6508** FIRKINS, OSCAR W. William Dean Howells: a study
pp.ix, 356; front.     O
Cambridge MA: Harvard U. P.     1924

**6509** HOWELLS, EDITH (Ed.). Life in letters of William Dean Howells
pp.xiii, 429; xi, 426; pl.13     L
NY: Doubleday Doran     1928
Two volumes.

**6510** GIBSON, W. M. & ARMS, GEORGE. A bibliography of William Dean Howells
pp.182; front.     O
NY: Public Library     1948

**6511** MESERVE, WALTER J. William Dean Howells and the drama
Seattle: U. of Washington (PhD)     1952

**6512** BALLINGER, RICHARD H. A calendar of the William Dean Howells collection in the library of Harvard University
Cambridge MA: Harvard U. (PhD)     1953

**6513** CARTER, EVERETT. Howells and the age of realism
pp.307     O
Philadelphia: J. B. Lippincott     1954

**6514** CADY, EDWIN H. The road to realism: the early years 1837-1885 of William Dean Howells
pp.xi, 283     O
Syracuse NY: U. P.     1956

**6515** CADY, EDWIN H. The realist at war: the mature years, 1885-1920, of William Dean Howells
pp.xi, 299 O
Syracuse NY: U. P. 1958

**6516** BENNETT, GEORGE N. William Dean Howells: the development of a novelist
pp.xvii, 220; pl. 2 O
Norman: U. of Oklahoma P. 1959
Includes reference to theatre in chapter two.

**6517** BROOKS, VAN W. Howells: his life and work
pp.ix, 296; front. O
London: J. M. Dent 1959

**6518** HOUGH, ROBERT L. The quiet rebel: William Dean Howells as social commentator
pp.ix, 137 L
Lincoln: U. of Nebraska P. 1959

**6519** HOWELLS, WILLIAM DEAN. The complete plays
pp.xxxv, 649 L
NY: U. P. 1960
Edited, with an introduction and brief critical essays, by Walter J. Meserve. Includes an annotated bibliography.

**6520** CADY, EDWIN H. & FRAZIER, DAVID L. (Eds). The war of the critics over William D. Howells
pp.xii, 244 O
Evanston IL: Row, Peterson 1962
Anthology of critical views, 1860-1960. Brief reference by George Bernard Shaw to Howells's excursion into the theatre.

**6521** KIRK, CLARA M. & KIRK, RUDOLPH. William Dean Howells
pp.223 L
New Haven: College and U. P./Twayne 1962
Revised edition. First published NY: American Book, 1950.

**6522** DUBE, ANTHONY. William Dean Howells's theory and practice of drama
Lubbock: Texas Tech U. (PhD) 1967

**6523** GIBSON, WILLIAM H. William Dean Howells
pp.48 O
Minneapolis: U. of Minnesota P. 1967

**6524** WAGENKNECHT, EDWARD. William Dean Howells, the friendly eye
pp.x, 340; front. DL★
NY: Oxford U. P. 1969

**6525** BRENNI, VITA J. (Ed.). William Dean Howells: a bibliography
pp.212 O
Metuchen NJ: Scarecrow P. 1973

**6526** CADY, EDWIN H. (Ed.). William Dean Howells as critic
pp.xvi, 493 O
London: Routledge & Kegan Paul 1973.
Includes drama criticism.

**6527** EICHELBERGER, CLAYTON L. Published comment on William Dean Howells through 1920: a research bibliography
pp.xii, 330 O
Boston: G. K. Hall 1976

**6528** CADY, EDWIN H. & CADY, NORMA W. (Eds). Critical essays on William Dean Howells, 1866-1920
pp.xxxii, 267 O
Boston: G. K. Hall 1983

## Hoyt, Charles Hale
## (1860-1900)

**6529** HUNT, DOUGLAS L. The life and work of Charles H. Hoyt
pp.40 L
Birmingham AL: Southern College 1946
Summary of a PhD thesis, presented Vanderbilt U. 1942, here reprinted in the college *Bulletin*, Vol XXXIX, No 1, January 1946.

**6530** SWORTZELL, NANCY F. The satire of Charles Hoyt. A critical study
New Haven: Yale U. (PhD) 1964

**6531** JONES, LEO M. The structure of the farces of Charles H. Hoyt
Bloomington: Indiana U. (PhD) 1973

## Hughes, Langston
## (1902-1967)

**6532** HUGHES, LANGSTON. The big sea: an autobiography
pp.xi, 335 L
NY: Alfred A. Knopf 1940

**6533** HUGHES, LANGSTON. I wonder as I wander: an autobiographical journey
pp.ix, 405 L
NY: Hill & Wang 1964
First published 1956. Describes the author's travels in Cuba, Russia, Spain, Japan as well as in the US.

**6534** EMANUEL, JAMES A. Langston Hughes
pp.192 L
NY: Twayne 1967

**6535** MELTZER, MILTON. Langston Hughes: a biography
pp.xiii, 281 MH
NY: Thomas Y. Crowell 1968

**6536** MYERS, ELISABETH. Langston Hughes: poet of his people
pp.144; ill. DL★
Champaign IL: Garrard 1970
Intended for children.

**6537** COLEMAN, EDWIN L. Langston Hughes: an American dramatist
Eugene: U. of Oregon (PhD) 1971

**6538** O'DANIEL, THERMAN B. (Ed.). Langston Hughes, black genius: a critical evaluation
pp.x, 245; front. L
NY: William Morrow 1971
Includes Darwin T. Turner: *Langston Hughes as playwright*.

**6539** ROLLINS, CHARLEMAE. Black troubadour; Langston Hughes
pp.143; ill. DL★
Chicago: Rand McNally 1971

Intended for children.

**6540** DICKINSON, DONALD C. A biobibliography of Langston Hughes, 1902-1967
pp.xiv, 273; front.   O
Hamden CT: Shoe String P.   1972
Second, enlarged edition. First published 1967.

**6541** RITTER, S. A. The propagandist craft of Langston Hughes
Canterbury: U. of Kent (MA)   1977

**6542** MILLER, R. BAXTER. Langston Hughes and Gwendolyn Brooks: a reference guide
pp.xxxiii, 149   MH
Boston: G. K. Hall   1978
Biographical introduction.

**6543** NICHOLS, CHARLES (Ed.). Arna Bontemps – Langston Hughes letters, 1925-1967
pp.ix, 529; front.   MH
NY: Dodd, Mead   1980

**6544** BERRY, FAITH. Langston Hughes
pp.xv, 376   O
Westport CT: Lawrence Hill   1983

**6545** RAMPERSAD, ARNOLD. The life of Langston Hughes. Vol 1: 1902-1941. I, too, sing America. [Vol 2: 1941-1967. I dream a world]
pp.ix, 468; ix, 512; pl. 32   MH
NY: Oxford U. P.   1986-88

## Hunter, Robert
## (1680-1743)

**6546** DAVIS, PETER A. The writing of *Androborus*: an historical study and annotation of America's earliest extant play
Los Angeles: U. of Southern California (PhD)   1981
The play, by Robert Hunter is the earliest known American printed play, published 1714.

## Inge, William Motter
## (1913-1973)

**6547** CLARKSON, PHILIP B. The evolution from conception to production of the dramas of William Inge
Stanford: U. (PhD)   1963

**6548** LOCKWOOD, PATTON. The plays of William Motter Inge, 1948-1960
East Lansing: Michigan State U. (PhD)   1963

**6549** EPOLITO, JOSEPH M. A study of character in selected plays of William Inge: *Come back, little Sheba, The Dark at the Top of the Stairs, A Loss of Roses, Natural Affection*
Columbus: Ohio State U. (PhD)   1974

**6550** FISCHLI, RONALD D. The evolution of William Inge's dramatic technique and vision during his bout with the American commercial theatre
Columbia: U. of Missouri (PhD)   1981

**6551** McCLURE, ARTHUR F. William Inge: a bibliography
pp.xxxi, 93   DL★
NY: Garland   1982

**6552** ROSS, RALPH F. A life of William Inge: the strains of triumph
pp.xviii, 315; ill. in text   L
Lawrence: U. P. of Kansas   1989

**6553** SHUMAN, R. B. William Inge
pp.xiii, 170   L
Boston: Twayne   1989
Second edition, revised. First published 1965.

**6554** VOSS, RALPH F. A life of William Inge: the strains of triumph
pp.xviii, 318; ill.   DL★
Lawrence: U. of Kansas P.   1989

**6555** LANGE, JANE W. William Inge: a reassessment
Berkeley: U. of California (PhD)   1990

## Irving, Washington
## (1783-1859)

**6556** IRVING, PIERRE M. (Ed.). Life and letters of Washington Irving
pp.xii, 387; x, 406; viii, 413; vii,347; front.   L
London: Richard Bentley   1862-64
Four volumes. Published NY: G. P. Putnam.

**6557** IRVING, PIERRE M. (Ed.). Biographies and miscellanies of Washington Irving...
pp.487; front.   L
Philadelphia: J. B. Lippincott   1873
Includes *Letters of Jonathan Oldstyle, Gent.*, pungent comments on the theatre of the day originally contributed to the New York *Morning Chronicle*, 1802.

**6558** IRVING, WASHINGTON. Rip Van Winkle...edited with an introduction, together with theatrical history by S. J. Adair Fitzgerald.
pp.203; pl. 6   M
London: Greening   1900
Her Majesty's Theatre edition for the H. B. Tree production. Reprinted in 1911 for Cyril Maude's production at the Playhouse.

## Jeffers, Robinson
## (1887-1962)

**6559** POWELL, LAWRENCE C. Robinson Jeffers: the man and his work, A foreword by Robinson Jeffers. Decorations by Rockwell Kent
pp.xx, 215; front.   L
Los Angeles: Primavera P.   1934

**6560** BREEN, ROBERT S. Symbolic action in oral interpretation of Robinson Jeffers
Evanston: Northwestern U. (PhD)   1950

**6561** STEPHENS, GEORGE D. The narrative and dramatic poetry of Robinson Jeffers. A critical study
Los Angeles: U. of Southern California (PhD)   1953

**6562** CARPENTER, FREDERICK I. Robinson Jeffers
pp.159   L
NY: Twayne   1962

**6563** BENNETT, MELBA B. The stone mason of Far House: the life and work of Robinson Jeffers
pp.xvi, 264; pl. 8   O
Los Angeles: Ward Ritchie P.   1966

**6564** JEFFERS, ROBINSON. The selected letters...1897-1962. Edited by Ann N. Ridgeway. Foreword by Mark Van Doren
pp.xx, 407; ill. in text                         L
Baltimore: John Hopkins U. P.             1968

**6565** COFFIN, ARTHUR B. Robinson Jeffers: poet of inhumanism
pp.xxiv, 300                                     O
Madison: U. of Wisconsin P.               1971
Critical study, including reference to Jeffers's *Medea* and *The Cretan Woman*.

**6566** VARDAMIS, ALEX A. The critical reputation of Robinson Jeffers: a bibliographical study
pp.x, 317                                         O
Hamden CT: Archon                        1972

**6567** BROPHY, ROBERT J. Robinson Jeffers: myth, ritual, and symbol in his narrative poems
pp.xviii, 321; front., ill. in text              O
Cleveland OH: Case Western Reserve U. P.   1973
Critical study, with attempt to reveal the basic dramatic structure.

**6568** NOLTE, WILLIAM H. Rock and hawk: Robinson Jeffers and the romantic agony
pp.ix, 212                                   MH
Athens: U. of Georgia P.                   1978

### Jones, Preston
### (1936-1979)

**6569** SEWELL, BETTE B. The plays of Preston Jones: background and analysis
Los Angeles: U. of California (PhD)        1984

### Kaufman, George Simon
### (1889-1961)

**6570** LEMBKE, RUSSELL W. The esthetic values of dissonance in the plays of George S. Kaufman and his collaborators
Iowa City: U. of Iowa (PhD)                1946

**6571** TEICHMANN, HOWARD. George S. Kaufman: an intimate portrait
pp.xv, 372; pl. 8                            M
London: Angus & Robertson              1973
Published NY: Atheneum, 1972.

**6572** MEREDITH, SCOTT. George S. Kaufman and his friends
xvii, 723; pl. 24                             M
NY: Doubleday                             1974

**6573** MOHAN, ROBERTA N. George S. Kaufman, librettist
Kent OH: State U. (PhD)                   1976

**6574** GOLDSTEIN, MALCOLM. George S. Kaufman: his life, his theater
pp.xiii, 503; pl. 8                           M
NY: Oxford U. P.                            1979

**6575** OLIVER, DONALD (Ed.). By George: a Kaufman collection
pp.xvii, 264; pl. 2                          L
London: Angus & Robertson              1980
Published NY: St Martin's P., 1979. An anthology. Foreword by Dick Cavett. UK edition has an introduction by Sheridan Morley.

**6576** MASON, JEFFREY D. George S. Kaufman, farceur
Berkeley: U. of California (PhD)            1983

**6577** MASON, JEFFREY D. Wisecracks: the farces of George S. Kaufman
pp.xi, 98                                     DL★
Ann Arbor: UMI Research P.             1988

**6578** POLLACK, RHODA G. George S. Kaufman
Boston: Twayne                     DL★
                                          1988

### Kelly, George Edward
### (1887-1974)

**6579** WILLS, ARTHUR. George Kelly. A critical study of his plays
Lawrence: U. of Kansas (PhD)             1959

**6580** HENDERSON, PETER W. A re-evaluation of the major works of George Kelly
Los Angeles: U. of Southern California (PhD)   1972

**6581** TANNEY, MICHAEL J. An analysis of the plays of George Kelly
New Orleans: Tulane U. (PhD)           1973

**6582** HIRSCH, FOSTER. George Kelly
pp.138; front.                            L
Boston: Twayne                        1975

### Kennedy, Adrienne
### (1931-)

**6583** KENNEDY, ADRIENNE. People who led to my plays
pp.viii, 130; ill. in text                   M
NY: Alfred A. Knopf                     1987
A scrapbook-style memoir, evoking author's girlhood and the influences on her playwriting.

### Kennedy, Charles Rann
### (1871-1950)
### Playwright, actor

**6584** STOLL, DONALD R. The dramaturgy of propaganda: Charles Rann Kennedy (1871-1950)
Bloomington: Indiana U. (PhD)          1982

### Kerr, Jean
### (1923-)

**6585** KERR, JEAN. Please don't eat the daisies [memoirs]
pp.xix, 138                               L
London: Heinemann                     1958
Lighthearted autobiographical sketches, some theatrical. First published NY: Doubleday, 1957.

**6586** KERR, JEAN. The snake has all the lines
pp.150                                      L
Garden Cty NY: Doubleday              1960
Second volume of autobiography.

### Kingsley, Sidney
### [Kirschner, Sidney]
### (1906-)

**6587** CLARK, SIDNEY M. A critical analysis of eight selected plays of Sidney Kingsley
NY: City U. (PhD)                         1976

## Kopit, Arthur Lee
## (1937-)

**6588** KOPIT, ARTHUR. Indians: a play
pp.114 DL★
NY: Bantam 1971
Includes a dialogue between Kopit and John Lahr, edited by Anthea Lahr.

## Kreymborg, Alfred
## (1883-1966)

**6589** KREYMBORG, ALFRED. Troubadour: an autobiography
pp.415 L
NY: Boni & Liveright 1925
Author had his early plays performed by the Provincetown Players but failed to make an impact on the commercial theatre.

**6590** WEIST, ELIZABETH M. Alfred Kreymborg in the art theater
Ann Arbor: U. of Michigan (PhD) 1965

## Kummer, Clare R.
## [née Beecher, Clare Rodman]
## (1873?-1958)

**6591** FINIZIO, V. L. Clare Kummer: an analysis of her plays and musicals
Iowa City: U. of Iowa (PhD) 1965

## Lawson, John Howard
## (1894-1977)

**6592** LAWSON, JOHN H. Processional
pp.xiii, 218; front. MH
NY: Thomas Seltzer 1925
Text of play, preceded by substantial account of author's dramatic theory and intent.

**6593** BROWN, RICHARD P. John Howard Lawson as an activist playwright 1923-1927
New Orleans: Tulane U. (PhD) 1964

**6594** McCREATH, HARRISON W. A rhetorical analysis of the plays of John Howard Lawson
Stanford: U. (PhD) 1965

**6595** GARDNER, ROBERT M. International rag: the theatrical career of John Howard Lawson
Berkeley: U. of California (PhD) 1978

**6596** BLOCH, BEVERLE R. John Howard Lawson's *Processional*: modernism in American theatre in the twenties
Denver: U. (PhD) 1988

## Lennox, Charlotte
## (1720-1804)

**6597** SMALL, MIRIAM. The life and literary relations of Charlotte Lennox
New Haven: Yale U. (PhD) 1925

## Lindsay, Howard
## (1889-1968)
## Crouse, Russel
## (1893-1966)

**6598** OSCAR SERLIN PRESENTS *Life with Father* made into a play [cover title]
pp.[20] including wrappers; ill. in text M
[NY]: [For the Empire Theatre?] [1942?]
Souvenir booklet with scenes from the production and re-printed articles from periodicals, notably a biographical sketch of Serlin by Jack Gould and an obituary of Clarence Day.

**6599** WYNN [pseud.]. Chronology of *Life with Father*
bs. M
[NY]: [Bijou Theatre] [1946]
Illustrated sheet providing details of cast changes in NY and touring productions since its opening in 1939 of the Lindsay and Crouse play based on Clarence Day's *New Yorker* articles.

**6600** SKINNER, CORNELIA O. Life with Lindsay & Crouse
pp.xiv, 242; ill. in text, pl. 8 M
Boston: Houghton Mifflin 1976
Foreword by Brooks Atkinson.

**6601** THE BIOGRAPHY OF A HIT: *Life with Father* exhibition sponsored by the...Museum of the City of New York [cover title]
pp.[12]; ill. in text M
NY Playbill for the Empire Theatre [1980]

## London, Jack
## [London, John Griffith]
## (1876-1916)

**6602** LONDON, JACK. Daughters of the rich. With a chronological bibliography of Jack London's plays compiled by James E. Sisson
pp.[40]; front. M
Oakland: Holmes Book 1971

## Longfellow, Henry Wadsworth
## (1807-1882)

**6603** SILBIGER, JOSEF. Henry Wadsworth Longfellow als Dramatiker
Vienna: U. (Thesis) 1911

**6604** CROSBY, ROBERT L. Longfellow as a dramatist
Bloomington: Indiana U. (PhD) 1958

## Lowell, Robert Traill Spence
## (1917-1977)

**6605** COOPER, PHILIP. The autobiographical myth of Robert Lowell
pp.ix, 170 O
Chapel Hill: U. of N. Carolina P. 1970

**6606** LONDON, MICHAEL & BOYERS, ROBERT (Eds). Robert Lowell: a portrait of the artist in his time
pp.ix, 340; front. L
NY: David Lewis 1970
Includes Robert Brustein on *The Old Glory*, and a detailed checklist of writings compiled by J. Mazzaro.

**6607** MARTIN, JAY. Robert Lowell
pp.48 L
Minneapolis: U. of Minnesota P. 1970

**6608** MAZZARO, J. (Ed.). Profile of Robert Lowell
pp.viii, 104 MH
Columbus OH: Merrill 1971
Includes reference to drama in articles by Richard Gilman, Michael Billington, D. S. Carne-Ross, and, fleetingly, V. S. Naipaul.

**6609** CRICK, J. F. Robert Lowell
pp.vii, 166 O
Edinburgh: Oliver & Boyd 1974

Chapter four refers to *Phèdre* and the other plays.

**6610** BOWLES, JAMES B. A strategic analysis of Robert Lowell's *The Old Glory*
Iowa City: U. of Iowa (PhD)     1976

### Luce, Clare Boothe
### (1903-1987)

**6611** HENLE, FAY. Au Clare de Luce: portrait of a luminous lady
pp.vii, 205     MH
NY: S. Daye     1943
Biography. Chapter 6: *The stage*.

**6612** SHADEGG, STEPHEN. Clare Boothe Luce: a biography
pp. 313; pl. 8     M
London: Leslie Frewin     1973

**6613** SHEED, WILFRED. Clare Boothe Luce
pp.viii, 183; pl.16     L
London: Weidenfeld & Nicolson     1982
Published NY: E. P. Dutton.

### MacArthur, Charles
### (1895-1956)

**6614** HECHT, BEN. Charlie: the improbable life and times of Charles MacArthur
pp.xii, 242; pl. 6     M
NY: Harper & Brothers     1957
MacArthur, writer husband of Helen Hayes, was co-author with Hecht of, inter alia, *The Front Page*.

**6615** IRVINE, JOHN C. An analysis of character delineation in selected playscripts of Charles MacArthur and his collaborators
Tallahassee: Florida State U. (PhD)     1976

### MacKaye, Percy
### (1875-1956)

**6616** MACKAYE, PERCY. The playhouse and the play: and other addresses concerning the theatre and democracy in America
pp.xii, 210     M
NY: Macmillan     1909
In addition to the title piece, contents include *Some questions before the curtain* on the importance of the theatre, the drama of democracy, the dramatist as citizen, and self-expression and the American drama.

**6617** MACKAYE, PERCY. A substitute for war, with an introduction by Irving Fisher and with a prefatory letter by the Right Hon Viscount Bryce...and Norman Angell
pp.55     L
NY: Macmillan     1915
A plea for pageantry and the moralizing effect of art and theatre in democratic life. The title piece was first printed in the *North America Review*, May, 1915. An appendix, publicizing the Life Extension Institute of New York, provides an account, written by Luther Ely Smith, of the St Louis Pageant of 1914.

**6618** PERCY MACKAYE: a sketch of his life with [a] bibliography of his works
pp.12; portrait on title     L
Cambridge MA: [Harvard College]     1922
Reprinted from the Twenty-fifth Anniversary Report of the Class of 1897.

**6619** DOGGETT, FRANK A. Dipped in sky: a study of Percy MacKaye's *Kentucky Mountain Cycle*
pp.v, 41     MH
London: Longman     1930

**6620** GROVER, EDWIN O. (Ed.). Annals of an era: Percy MacKaye and the MacKaye family 1826-1932. A record of biography and history in commentaries and bibliography...comprising records chiefly included in the MacKaye Collection at the Dartmouth College library. Prefatory note Gamaliel Bradford
pp.lxxviii, 534; front.     M
Washington DC: Pioneer P./Dartmouth College     1932

**6621** MACKAYE, PERCY. My dear lady, arise - Songs and sonnets in remembrance of Marion Morse MacKaye (Mrs Percy MacKaye). With wood-block design by Gordon Craig
pp.xvi, 272; ill. in text, pl. 6     M
NY: Macmillan     1940

**6622** BLACK, GEORGE W. The plays of Percy MacKaye
Athens: U. of Georgia (PhD)     1971

### MacLeish, Archibald
### (1892-1982)

**6623** MIZENER, ARTHUR. A catalogue of the first editions of Archibald MacLeish prepared for an exhibition of his works held in the Yale University Library
pp.30     L
New Haven: Yale U.     1938

**6624** CARRINGTON, RICHARD H. Archibald MacLeish. A study of his prosody for the oral interpreter
Madison: U. of Wisconsin (PhD)     1964

**6625** DOYLE, ESTHER M. The nature of verse in drama with special reference to *J. B.*, a play in verse by Archibald MacLeish
Evanston: Northwestern U. (PhD)     1964

**6626** FALK, SIGNI L. Archibald MacLeish
pp.189     L
NY: Twayne     1965

**6627** SMITH, GROVER. Archibald MacLeish
pp.48     L
Minneapolis: U. of Minnesota P.     1971

**6628** MULLALY, EDWARD J. Archibald MacLeish: a checklist
pp.xiv, 95     L
Kent OH: Kent State U. P.     1973

**6629** SEMONELLA, JOAN L. The poetic theatre of Archibald MacLeish: a search for meaning
Los Angeles: U. of California (PhD)     1984

### Mailer, Norman
### (1923-)

**6630** MAILER, NORMAN. Existential errands
pp.xv, 365     L
Boston: Little, Brown     1972

Includes chapter, *The playwright as critic*, and a fragment from *Vietnam*, a play.

**6631** POIRIER, RICHARD. Mailer
pp.174 DL★
London: Fontana 1972

**6632** ADAMS, LAURA (Ed.). Norman Mailer: a comprehensive bibliography
pp.xix, 131 O
Metuchen NJ: Scarecrow P. 1974

Includes reviews and articles on plays and filmscripts. Introduction by R. F. Lucid.

**6633** ADAMS, LAURA (Ed.). Will the real Norman Mailer please stand up ?
pp.viii, 274 O
Port Washington NY: Kennikat P. 1974

A collection of essays and articles. Includes Gerald Weales: *The Park in the Playhouse*, a review of *The Deer Park*.

**6634** ADAMS, LAURA. Existential battles: the growth of Norman Mailer
pp.ix, 192 O
Athens: Ohio U. P. 1976

Includes brief account of *The Deer Park*.

### Maltz, Albert
### (1908-1985)

**6635** SALZMAN, JACK. Albert Maltz
pp.160 L
Boston: Twayne 1978

### Mamet, David
### (1947-)

**6636** BIGSBY, C. W. David Mamet
pp.142 MH
London: Methuen 1985

**6637** MAMET, DAVID. Writing in restaurants
pp.xiv, 160 MH
NY: Viking P. 1986

Articles, essays, many on theatre.

**6638** CARROLL, DENNIS. David Mamet
pp.xii, 171; pl. 4 L
Basingstoke: Macmillan 1987

First published NY: St Martin's P.

**6639** MAMET, DAVID. Some freaks
pp.xi, 180 MH
NY: Viking P. 1989

Occasional writings, some on theatre topics.

**6640** BLONDELL, JOHN. Myth and anti-myth in the plays of David Mamet
Santa Barbara: U. of California (PhD) 1990

**6641** DEAN, ANNE. David Mamet: language as dramatic action
pp.248 DL★
Cranbury NJ: Fairleigh Dickinson U. P. 1990

### Maxwell, William Bulloch
### (1787-1814)

**6642** MAXWELL, WILLIAM B. The mysterious father: a tragedy in five acts, 1807...edited with an introduction by Gerald Kahan
pp.xx, 57; pl. 1 M
Athens: U. of Georgia P. 1965

The introduction provides a biographical account, and a Maxwell genealogy. An edited version of the only known copy, with contemporaneous criticism.

### McClure, Michael
### (1932-)

**6643** KING, WILLIAM R. Finding the shape of freedom: an introduction to the plays of Michael McClure
Los Angeles: U. of California (PhD) 1984

### McCullers, Carson Smith
### (1917-1967)

**6644** SMITH, SIMEON M. Carson McCullers. A critical introduction
Philadelphia: U. of Pennsylvania (PhD) 1964

**6645** EVANS, OLIVER. Carson McCullers: her life and work
pp.220; pl. 3 O
London: Peter Owen 1965

**6646** CARR, VIRGINIA S. The lonely hunter: a biography of Carson McCullers
pp.xxii, 600; pl. 24 O
Garden City NY: Doubleday 1975

**6647** McDOWELL, MARGARET B. Carson McCullers
pp.158; front. MH
Boston: Twayne 1980

**6648** CARR, VIRGINIA S. Understanding Carson McCullers
pp.xii,181 ★
Columbia: U. of South Carolina P. 1990

### McHenry, James
### (1785-1845)

**6649** BLANC, ROBERT E. James McHenry (1785-1845), playwright and novelist
Philadelphia: U. of Pennsylvania (PhD) 1939

### McCutcheon, George Barr
### (1866-1928)

**6650** LAZARUS, ARNOLD L. & JONES, VICTOR H. Beyond Graustark: George Barr McCutcheon, playwright discovered
pp.xvi, 187; front. L
Port Washington NY: Kennikat P. 1981

### McNally, Terrence
### (1939-)

**6651** JANKE, ROBERT H. Terence McNally: contemporary American playwright
NY: Columbia U. (PhD) 1974

### Mencken, Henry Louis
### (1880-1956)

**6652** ROSCOE, BURTON et al. H. L. Mencken. Fanfare by Burton Roscoe. The American Critic by Vincent O'Sullivan. Bibliography by F. C. Henderson.
pp.32; front., pl. 3 L
NY: Alfred A. Knopf 1920

**6653** FREY, CARROLL. A bibliography of the writings of H. L. Mencken
pp.iii, 70; front., ill. in text    L
Philadelphia: Centaur Book Shop    1924
85 large paper copies.

**6654** WAGNER, PHILIP. H. L. Mencken
pp.48    L
Minneapolis: U. of Minnesota P.    1966

**6655** BODE, CARL. Mencken [biography]
pp.ix, 452; pl. 12    O
Carbondale: Southern Illinois U. P.    1969

### Middleton, George
### (1880-1967)

**6656** MIDDLETON, GEORGE. These things are mine: the autobiography of a journeyman playwright
pp.xv, 448; pl. 12    M
NY: Macmillan    1947
Founder of the Dramatists Guild.

### Millay, Edna St. Vincent
### (1892-1950)

**6657** PATTON, JOHN. Edna St. Vincent Millay as a verse dramatist.
Boulder: U. of Colorado (PhD)    1963

**6658** BRITTIN, NORMAN A. Edna St. Vincent Millay
pp.192    L
NY: Twayne    1967
Makes reference to Provincetown Players.

**6659** GRAY, JAMES. Edna St. Vincent Millay
pp.48    L
Minneapolis: U. of Minnesota P.    1967

**6660** GOULD, JEAN. The poet and her book: a biography of Edna St. Vincent Millay
pp.xii, 308; pl. 8    L
NY: Dodd, Mead    1969

**6661** NIERMAN, JUDITH. Edna St. Vincent Millay: a reference guide
pp.xiii, 191    L
Boston: G. K. Hall    1977

### Miller, Arthur
### (1915-)

**6662** HITCHENS, GORDON. Attention must be paid: a study of social values in four plays by Arthur Miller
NY: Columbia U. (PhD)    1962
*All My Sons. A Memory of Two Mondays, The Crucible, Death of a Salesman.*

**6663** JOHNSON, VERNON E. Dramatic influences in the development of Arthur Miller's concept of social tragedy
Nashville: George Peabody College (PhD)    1962

**6664** GOODE, JAMES. The story of *The Misfits*
pp.331; ill.    DL★
Indianapolis: Bobbs-Merrill    1963

**6665** HOGAN, ROBERT. Arthur Miller
pp.48    O
Minneapolis: U. of Minnesota P.    1964

**6666** JOHNSON, ROBERT G. A general semantic analysis of three of Arthur Miller's plays. *Death of a Salesman, The Crucible,* and *All My Sons*
Denver: U. (PhD)    1964

**6667** NELSON, BENJAMIN. Review notes and study guide to the major plays of Arthur Miller
pp.96    DL★
NY: Monarch P.    1964

**6668** HUFTEL, SHEILA. Arthur Miller: the burning glass
pp.256; pl. 6    L
NY: Citadel P.    1965
Critical biography. Foreword by J. C. Trewin

**6669** MARTIN, ROBERT A. The major plays and critical thought of Arthur Miller to the *Collected Plays*
Ann Arbor: U. of Michigan (PhD)    1965

**6670** LÜBBREN, RAINER. Arthur Miller
pp.155; ill. in text    MH
Velber bei Hanover: Friedrich    1966

**6671** PITT, D. K. Tragic perspectives, with particular reference to plays by Bernard Shaw and Arthur Miller
Liverpool: U. (MA)    1966

**6672** MOSS, LEONARD. Arthur Miller
pp.160    MH
NY: Twayne    1967

**6673** MURRAY, EDWARD. Arthur Miller: dramatist
pp.xi, 186    MH
NY: Frederick Ungar    1967

**6674** WEALES, GERALD (Ed.). Arthur Miller's *Death of a Salesman*: text and criticism
pp.xxii, 426    DL★
NY: Viking P.    1967

**6675** WEST, CONSTANCE C. The use of persuasion in selected plays of Arthur Miller
Minneapolis: U. of Minnesota (PhD)    1968

**6676** CORRIGAN, ROBERT W. (Ed.). Arthur Miller: a collection of critical essays
pp.ix, 176    O
Englewood Cliffs NJ: Prentice-Hall    1969
Reprinted essays by: Eric Mottram, Tom F. Driver, Raymond William, M. W. Steinberg, Brian Parker, Robert Warshow, Herbert Blau, Gerald Weales, Harold Clurman.

**6677** EVANS, RICHARD I. Psychology and Arthur Miller
pp.xvii, 136    L
NY: E. P. Dutton    1969
Transcriptions of a conversation between the author and Miller, in which the playwright expresses his views of the development of characterization and his understanding of formal psychological concepts of personality.

**6678** MORATH, INGE & MILLER, ARTHUR. In Russia
pp.240; ill. in text    L
London: Secker & Warburg    1969

## 16.2. INDIVIDUAL DRAMATISTS

Photographic and textual record of their experience of Russia. Theatre reference includes Miller's attendance at a production of *View from the Bridge*.

**6679** NELSON, BENJAMIN. Arthur Miller: portrait of a playwright
pp.336; front — L
NY: Peter Owen — 1970
Published NY: McKay.

**6680** RÖSSLE, WOLFGANG. Die soziale Wirklichkeit in Arthur Millers *Death of a Salesman*
pp.129 — MH
Freiburg: U. P. — 1970

**6681** WHITE, SIDNEY H. The Merrill guide to Arthur Miller
pp.47 — DL★
Columbus OH: C. E. Merrill — 1970

**6682** CHUNG, F. K. Man and society in Arthur Miller's works – a study of themes and structure
Leeds: U. (M.Phil.) — 1971

**6683** WEALES, GERALD (Ed.). Arthur Miller, *The Crucible*: text and criticism
pp.xx, 484 — MH★
NY: Viking P. — 1971

**6684** FERRES, JOHN H. (Ed.). Twentieth century interpretations of *The Crucible*: a collection of critical essays
pp.vi, 122 — DL★
Englewood Cliffs NJ: Prentice-Hall — 1972
G. L. Kittredge: *Witchcraft & the puritans*; E. Latham: *The meaning of McCarthyism*; John Gassner: *'The Crucible' as event & play*; R. Hayes: *Hysteria and ideology in...*; Walter Kerr: *A problem playwright*; Leonard Moss: *A 'social' play*; Edward Murray: *Dramatic technique in...*; Dennis Welland: *The devil in Salem*; Herbert Blau: *No play is deeper than its witches*; P. Curtis: *Setting, language and the force of evil in...*; Henry Popkin: *Historical analogy and...*; P. G. Hill: *...a structural view*; Eric Mottram: *J. P. Sartre's 'Les Sorcières de Salem'*; Robert Hogan: *Action & theme in...*; M. W. Steinberg: *Arthur Miller and the idea of modern tragedy*; Gerald Weales: *Arthur Miller, man and his image*; Sheila Huftel: *Subjectivism & self-awareness*; Arthur Ganz: *The silence of Arthur Miller*; Arthur Miller: *A private meeting of John & Abigail*.

**6685** HAYMAN, RONALD. Arthur Miller
pp.vii, 141; ill. in text — L
NY: Frederick Ungar — 1972
Critical study prefaced by transcribed interview with Miller conducted in 1969.

**6686** SWANSON, ALAN M. *Death of a Salesman* in Swedish: an essay in the theory of stage translation
Chicago: U. (PhD) — 1973

**6687** ZURCHER, CARL D. An analysis of selected American criticism of the plays of Arthur Miller in the light of his own commentary on drama
West Lafayette: Purdue U. (PhD) — 1973

**6688** FELDMAN, JACK. The plays of Arthur Miller: theory and practice
Madison: U. of Wisconsin (PhD) — 1975

**6689** HAYASHI, TETSUMARO. An index to Arthur Miller criticism
pp.xiv, 151 — DL★
Metuchen NJ: Scarecrow P. — 1976
Second edition, revised. First published as *Arthur Miller criticism, 1930-1967*.

**6690** CELADA, A. RODRIGUEZ. The conception of tragedy and the dramatic practice of Arthur Miller and Antonio Buero Vallejo, with special reference to six of their plays
Manchester: U. (MA) — 1977

**6691** GOLD, RONALD L. A comparative analysis of Arthur Miller's *Death of a Salesman* by means of dramatic criticism and the Sereno and Bodaken trans-per model
Los Angeles: U. of Southern California (PhD) — 1977

**6692** DOOLING, A. J. Development in the play structures, characterisations, and themes in the plays of Arthur Miller
Exeter UK: U. (MA) — 1978

**6693** MARTIN, ROBERT A. (Ed.). The theater essays of Arthur Miller
pp.xliv, 401 — L
Harmondsworth: Penguin — 1978
Published NY: Viking P., 1978. Foreword by Arthur Miller.

**6694** FERRES, JOHN H. Arthur Miller: a reference guide
pp.xvi, 225 — O
Boston: G. K. Hall — 1979

**6695** MARTINE, JAMES J. (Ed.). Critical essays on Arthur Miller
pp.211 — ★
Boston: G. K. Hall — 1979

**6696** CARSON, NEIL. Arthur Miller
pp.ix, 167 — L
London: Macmillan — 1982
Published NY: Grove P.

**6697** MARTIN, ROBERT A. Arthur Miller: new perspectives
pp.x, 223 — ★
Englewood Cliffs: Prentice-Hall — 1982

**6698** KOON, HELENE W. (Ed.). Twentieth century interpretations of *Death of a Salesman*. A collection of critical essays
pp.vii, 115 — L
Englewood Cliffs: Prentice-Hall — 1983

**6699** MILLER, ARTHUR. *Salesman* in Beijing
pp.xii, 254; ill. in text — M
London: Methuen — 1984
Diary account of the author's direction of his play *Death of a Salesman*, its first presentation in China.

**6700** WELLAND, DENNIS. Miller the playwright
pp.186; pl.4 — M
London: Methuen — 1985
Third edition, revised and expanded. First published 1979.

**6701** SCHLUETER, JUNE & FLANAGAN, JAMES K. Arthur Miller
pp.xix, 171 — MH
NY: Frederick Ungar — 1987
Critical study, up to and including *Archbishop's Ceiling*

**6702** BIGSBY, C. W. (Ed.). File on Miller
pp.80 — M
London: Methuen — 1988

**6703** BIGSBY, C. W. (Ed.). Arthur Miller and company: Arthur Miller talks about his work in the company of actors, designers, directors, reviewers and writers
pp.xv, 224; pl. 4 L
London: Methuen/Arthur Miller Centre 1990

**6704** MILLER, ARTHUR. Timebends: a life
pp.v, 614; pl. 16 L
London: Minerva 1990
First published London: Methuen, 1987.

### Miller, Joaquin
### [Miller, Cincinnatus Hiner]
### (1837-1913)

**6705** PETERSON, MARTIN S. Joaquin Miller, his life and works
Lincoln: U. of Nebraska (PhD) 1932

**6706** PHILLIPS, LEVI D. Arthur McKee Rankin's touring production of Joaquin Miller's *The Danites*
Davis: U. of California (PhD) 1981

### Mitchell, Langdon Elwyn
### (1862-1935)

**6707** PRICE, DAVID M. Langdon Mitchell, the man and his plays
NY: City U. (PhD) 1978

### Mitchell, Loften
### (1919-)

**6708** MURRAY, CLARENCE. Loften Mitchell: description of social themes in selected plays on black America
Bowling Green: State U. (PhD) 1988

### Mizner, Wilson
### (1876-1933)

**6709** JOHNSTON, ALVA. The incredible Mizners
pp.271; pl. 2 L
London: Hart-Davis 1953
Biography of Addison and Wilson Mizner.

### Moody, William Vaughn
### (1869-1910)

**6710** MASON, DANIEL G. (Ed.). Some letters of William Vaughn Moody
pp.xxviii, 171; front. L
Boston: Houghton Mifflin 1913
Includes reference to *The Great Divide*.

**6711** HENRY, DAVID D. William Vaughn Moody: a study
pp.i, 276 L
Boston: Bruce Humphries 1934
Chapters IV-VI examine the plays.

**6712** MOODY, WILLIAM V. Letters to Harriet. Edited and with an introduction and conclusion by Percy MacKaye
pp.x, 457; front. L
Boston: Houghton Mifflin 1935
Letters from Moody to Harriet Converse Tilden 1901-09. Much emphasis on the stage and its performers, providing probably the fullest available picture of Moody's involvement with the New York theatre. Errata slip.

**6713** DILWORTH, MARY L. William Vaughn Moody and the movement for poetic drama in America
Urbana: U. of Illinois (PhD) 1942?
Includes reference to Percy MacKaye, Ridgely Torrence, Edwin Arlington Robinson, Josephine Preston Peabody.

**6714** DUNBAR, OLIVIA H. A house in Chicago
pp.viii, 288; front. O
Chicago: U. P. 1945

**6715** DAVIS, CHARLES T. The poetic drama of Moody, Robinson, Torrence, and MacKaye 1894-1909
pp.i, 17 L
NY: U. P. 1958
Abridged thesis (1951) restricted almost wholly to an account of William Vaughn Moody.

**6716** LICHTENSTEIN, HYMAN. William Vaughn Moody. A poet on the eve of the American renaissance
NY: Columbia U. (PhD) 1959

**6717** HALPERN, MARTIN. William Vaughn Moody
pp.208 L
NY: Twayne 1964

**6718** BROWN, MAURICE F. Estranging dawn: the life and works of William Vaughn Moody
pp.xiii, 321; pl. 8 L
Carbondale: Southern Illinois U. P. 1973
Chapter ten: *Nurslings of American drama*. Chapter eleven: 'The Great Divide'.

**6719** NORTON, SUZANNE F. William Vaughn Moody: conflict and character in the New World
Madison: U. of Wisconsin (PhD) 1974

**6720** KOLDENHOVEN, JAMES J. A structuralist approach to the realistic drama of William Vaughn Moody
Minneapolis: U. of Minnesota (PhD) 1986

### Morse, Salmi
### (1826?-1884)

**6721** NIELSEN, ALAN. Salmi Morse's Passion, 1879-83: the history and consequences of a theatrical obsession
NY: City U. (PhD) 1989

### Munford, Robert
### (1730?-1784)

**6722** LYNN, KENNETH S. Mark Twain and southwestern humor
pp.xi, 300; pl. 4 L
Boston: Little, Brown 1959
Includes material on Robert Munford.

**6723** BAINE, RODNEY M. Robert Munford, America's first comic dramatist
pp.ix, 132 M
Athens: U. of Georgia P. 1967

### Noah, Mordecai Manuel
### (1785-1851)

**6724** NOAH, MORDECAI M. Gleanings from a gathered harvest
pp.216 L
NY: Charles Wells 1845

Belles lettres. Republished NY: Long & Brothers, 1847 and Baltimore: publisher unknown, 1897, as *A literary biography of Mordecai Manuel Noah*, with an introduction by G. A. Kohut.

**6725** WOLF, SIMON. Mordecai Manuel Noah: a biographical sketch
pp.49; front. DL★
Philadelphia: Levytype 1897

**6726** MAKOVER, ABRAHAM B. Mordecai M. Noah...his life and work from the jewish viewpoint
pp.96; ill. DL★
NY: Bloch 1917

**6727** GOLDBERG, ISAAC. Major Noah: American-jewish pioneer
pp.xvii, 316; front., pl. 3 L
NY: Alfred A. Knopf 1937
First published Philadelphia: Jewish Publication Society of America, 1936.

## Nugent, Elliott John (1899-1980)

**6728** NUGENT, ELLIOTT. Events leading up to the comedy: an autobiography
pp.xiv, 304; pl. 5 M
NY: Trident P. 1965

## O'Brien, Fitz-James (1828-1862)

**6729** WOLLE, FRANCIS. Fitz-James O'Brien: a literary Bohemian of the eighteen-fifties
pp.xii, 309; front., ill. in text L
Boulder: U. of Colorado P. 1944

## O'Hara, John Henry (1905-1970)

**6730** GREBSTEIN, SHELDON N. John O'Hara
pp.175 MH
NY: Twayne 1966

**6731** WALCUTT, CHARLES C. John O'Hara
pp.48 L
Minneapolis: U. of Minnesota P. 1969

**6732** BRUCCOLI, MATTHEW J. (Ed.). John O'Hara: a check-list
pp.xxi, 136; ill. in text O
NY: Random House 1972
Includes a previously unpublished transcription of a speech given by O'Hara at a Foyles luncheon, May, 1967.

**6733** BRUCCOLI, MATTHEW J. The O'Hara concern: a biography of John O'Hara
pp.xxix, 417; ill. in text O
NY: Random House 1975

## O'Neill, Eugene Gladstone (1888-1953)

**6734** SUTTON, GRAHAM. Some contemporary dramatists
pp.213 M
London: Leonard Parsons 1924
British and European except for Eugene O'Neill.

**6735** SHIPLEY, JOSEPH. The art of Eugene O'Neill
pp.(i), 34 MH
Seattle: U. of Washington Book Store 1928

**6736** WEISS, ELISABETH. Die Dramen Eugene O'Neill
Vienna: U. (Thesis) 1928

**6737** MICKLE, ALAN D. Six plays of Eugene O'Neill: critical studies
pp.166 L
London: Jonathan Cape 1929
Published NY, Liveright. *Anna Christie, The Hairy Ape, The Great God Brown, The Fountain, Marco Millions, Strange Interlude*. Appreciations by the Australian author, rather than critiques.

**6738** LIEBERMAN, HERMAN. Eugene O'Neill: American dramatist [title translated]
pp.162 DL★
NY: 1930
Text in Yiddish.

**6739** GEORGES LEWYS, PLAINTIFF, against Eugene O'Neill, Boni & Liveright, Inc., Horace Liveright, Inc., and Theatre Guild Inc. defendant
pp 4, ll.3-91; pp.42 DL★
[NY]: [For the court] [1931?]
An alleged infringement of copyright of the plaintiff's [Nom de plume – Gladys Adelina Lewis] book *The Temple of Pallas Athenae* by *Strange Interlude*. Typescript followed by pp.42 printed opinion of the court.

**6740** SANBORN, RALPH & CLARK, BARRETT H. A bibliography of the works of Eugene O'Neill together with the collected poems of Eugene O'Neill
pp.xiv, 171; ill. in text, pl. 8 M
NY: Random House 1931

**6741** GEDDES, VIRGIL. The melodramadness of Eugene O'Neill
pp.48 MH
Brookfield CT: Brookfield Players 1934
A harsh examination.

**6742** SKINNER, RICHARD. Eugene O'Neill; a poet's quest...with a correct chronology of the O'Neill plays as furnished by Eugene O'Neill
pp.xiv, 242 L
NY: Longmans, Green 1935

**6743** KOISCHWITZ, OTTO. O'Neill
pp.150 L
Berlin: Junker & Dünnhaupt 1938
Text in German.

**6744** MIRLAS, LEON. El teatro de O'Neill: estudio de su personalidad y sus obras
pp.198 MH
San José: Editorial Sudamericana 1938

**6745** HAHN, VERA T. The plays of Eugene O'Neill. A psychological analysis
Baton Rouge: Louisiana State U. (PhD) 1939

**6746** CLARK, BARRETT H. Eugene O'Neill: the man and his plays
pp.191 O
NY: Dover 1947
Third edition, revised. First published NY: 1929, without the sub-title, and first revised in 1933.

**6747** HERNDON, GENEVA. American criticism of Eugene O'Neill, 1917-1948
Evanston: Northwestern U. (PhD) 1949

**6748** PARAJÓN, MARIA. El teatro de O'Neill
pp.134     DL★
Havana: Orígenes     1952

**6749** ENGEL, EDWIN A. The haunted heroes of Eugene O'Neill
pp.x, 310     O
Cambridge MA: Harvard U. P.     1953

**6750** ENGEL, EDWIN A. Recurrent themes in the drama of Eugene O'Neill
Ann Arbor: U. of Michigan (PhD)     1953

**6751** FOX, JOSEF. Probability in the plays of Eugene O'Neill
NY: U. (PhD)     1953

**6752** CARPENTER, FREDERICK I. American literature and the drama
pp.vii, 220     L
NY: Philosophical Library     1955
Includes chapter: *The romantic tragedy of Eugene O'Neill* defining the American 'dream' as the ideal democracy.

**6753** GALLADA, ROBERT A. Eugene O'Neill at the Provincetown playhouse
NY: Columbia U. (MA)     1955

**6754** ITKIN, BELLA. The patterns of verbal imagery as found in ten major works of O'Neill
Cleveland OH: Case Western Reserve U. (PhD)     1955

**6755** MULLER, HERBERT J. The spirit of tragedy
pp.xiv, 335, viii     MH
NY: Alfred A. Knopf     1956
Includes a chapter on Eugene O'Neill.

**6756** OLSON, ESTHER J. An analysis of the Nietzchean elements in the plays of Eugene O'Neill
Minneapolis: U. of Minnesota (PhD)     1956

**6757** ZERAFFA, MICHEL. Eugene O'Neill: dramaturge
pp.157; pl. 8     MH
Paris: L'Arche     1956

**6758** ADAMS, WILLIAM J. The dramatic structure of the plays of Eugene O'Neill
Stanford: U. (PhD)     1957

**6759** BOULTON, AGNES. Part of a long story
pp.303     O
Garden City: Doubleday     1958
Biography of Eugene O'Neill. UK edition (London: Peter Davis), has the sub-title: *...Eugene O'Neill as a young man in love.*

**6760** GIEROW, KARL R. Introduktioner till Eugene O'Neills dramatik
pp.47; front.     L
Stockholm: Sveriges Radio     1958

**6761** BOWEN, CROSWELL with O'NEILL, SHANE. The curse of the misbegotten: a tale of the house of O'Neill
pp.xix, 384, 2; pl. 5     M
NY: McGraw-Hill     1959

**6762** ELROD, JAMES F. The structure of O'Neill's serious drama
Bloomington: Indiana U. (PhD)     1959

**6763** MIRLAS, LEON. O'Neill y el teatro contempoáneo
pp.212     MH
Buenos Aires: Editorial Sudamericano     1960
Second edition, revised. First published 1950.

**6764** ARBENZ, MARY H. The plays of Eugene O'Neill as presented by the Theatre Guild
Urbana: U. of Illinois (PhD)     1961

**6765** CARGILL, OSCAR; FAGIN, N.B. & FISHER, W.J. O'Neill and his plays: a survey of his life and works
pp.xi, 528     L
NY: U. P.     1961

**6766** CARGILL, OSCAR et al. O'Neill and his plays: four decades of criticism
pp.xi,528     O
NY: U.P.     1961

**6767** WINCHESTER, OTIS W. A rhetorical analysis of Eugene O'Neill's *Strange Interlude*
Norman: U. of Oklahoma (PhD)     1961

**6768** WINTHER, SOPHUS K. Eugene O'Neill: a critical study
pp.ix, 319     MH
NY: Russell & Russell     1961
Second edition, enlarged. First published NY: 1934.

**6769** ALEXANDER, DORIS. The tempering of Eugene O'Neill
pp.xvii, 301; pl. 4     L
NY: Harcourt, Brace & World     1962
Biography, emphasizing the early years.

**6770** BROWN, R. M. An analysis of conflict in the plays of August Strindberg and Eugene O'Neill
Bristol: U. (MA)     1962

**6771** FICCA, JOHN. Eugene O'Neill's critical reputation in America
Iowa City: U. of Iowa (PhD)     1962

**6772** COOK, THOMAS E. Eugene O'Neill's use of dramatic imagery, 1920-1930. A study of six plays
New Orleans: Tulane U. (PhD)     1963

**6773** LEECH, CLIFFORD. Eugene O'Neill
pp.vi, 120     L
Edinburgh: Oliver & Boyd     1963
Published NY: Grove P.

**6774** BERNSTEIN, SAMUEL J. Eugene O'Neill, theatre artist. A description of and commentary upon the craftsmanship of four plays by Eugene O'Neill
Waltham MA: Brandeis U. (PhD)     1964

**6775** FISKINN, ABRAM M. Eugene O'Neill. A study of a developing creed through the medium of drama
Minneapolis: U. of Minnesota (PhD)     1964

**6776** GASSNER, JOHN (Ed.). O'Neill: a collection of critical essays
pp.ix, 180     O
Englewood Cliffs NJ: Prentice-Hall     1964

Contributors: John H. Raleigh, Hugo von Hofmannsthal, Eugene M. Wraith, John H. Lawson, Richard Hayes, Edgar F. Racey, Travis Bogard, Cyrus Day, Stark Young, Eric Bentley, Helen Muchnic, Tom F. Driver, Robert F. Whitman, John Gassner.

**6777** BRAEM, HELMUT M. Eugene O'Neill
pp.150; ill. in text                    MH
Velber bei Hanover: Friedrich           1965
Critical study. Text in German.

**6778** FITCH, POLLY M. The language of the last three major plays of Eugene O'Neill
Stanford: U. (PhD)                      1965

**6779** GASSNER, JOHN. Eugene O'Neill
pp.48                                   O
Minneapolis: U. of Minnesota P.         1965

**6780** LEE, ROBERT C. Eugene O'Neill. A grapple with a ghost
Madison: U. of Michigan (PhD)           1965

**6781** MILLER, JORDAN Y. (Ed.). Playwright's progress: O'Neill and the critics
pp.184                                  DL★
Chicago: Scott Foresman                 1965

**6782** RAGHAVACHARYULU, DHUPATY V. Eugene O'Neill: a study
pp.xv, 232                              MH
Bombay: Popular Prakashan               1965
2 pp. errata.

**6783** RALEIGH, JOHN H. The plays of Eugene O'Neill with a preface by Harry T. Moore
pp.xvi. 304                             L
Carbondale: Southern Illinois U. P.     1965

**6784** RAY, HELEN H. The relation between man and man in the plays of Eugene O'Neill
Lawrence: U. of Kansas (PhD)            1965

**6785** SCHENKER, UELI. Eugene O'Neills Spätwerk
pp.161                                  MH
Zürich: Juris                           1965

**6786** THE EUGENE O'NEILL Memorial Theater Foundation
pp.[44]; ill.                           DL★
Waterford CT: Eugene O'Neill Foundation [1966?]

**6787** COOLIDGE, OLIVIA. Eugene O'Neill
pp.223; front.                          DL★
NY: Charles Scribner's Sons             1966

**6788** STEIN, DANIEL A. O'Neill and the philosophers: a study of the Nietzschean and other philosophic influences on Eugene O'Neill
New Haven: Yale U. (PhD)                1966

**6789** VUNOVICH, NANCY. The women in the plays of Eugene O'Neill
Lawrence: U. of Kansas (PhD)            1966

**6790** LINK, FRANZ H. Eugene O'Neill und die Wiedergeburt der Tragödie aus dem Unbewussten
pp.iii, 64                              L
Frankfurt: Athenäum                     1967

**6791** WHITAKER, D. Themes and techniques in the plays of Eugene O'Neill during the period 1921-1931
London: U. Royal Holloway College (M.Phil.)  1967

**6792** DORN, KNUT. Die Erlösungsthematik bei Eugene O'Neill: eine Analyse der Strukturen im Spätwerk
pp.136                                  O
Heidelberg: Carl Winter                 1968

**6793** FOWLER, S. The search for expression: Eugene O'Neill's development of dramatic techniques
Keele: U. (MA)                          1968

**6794** LONG, CHESTER C. The role of nemesis in the structure of selected plays by Eugene O'Neill
pp.231                                  O
The Hague: Mouton                       1968

**6795** RALEIGH, JOHN H. Twentieth century interpretations of *The Iceman Cometh*: a collection of critical essays...
pp.ix, 117                              M
Englewood Cliffs NJ: Prentice-Hall      1968

**6796** TIUSANEN, TIMO. O'Neill's scenic images
pp.xiii, 388; pl. 4                     L
Princeton: U. P.                        1968

**6797** HALFMANN, ULRICH. 'Unreal realism': O'Neills dramatisches Werk im Spiegel seiner szenischen Kunst
pp.191                                  L
Berne: Francke                          1969

**6798** LEVIN, M. H. Three plays by Eugene O'Neill: the philosophical roots of a tragic vision, with special reference to *Desire Under the Elms, Mourning becomes Electra* and *The Iceman Cometh*.
Oxford: U. (B.Litt.)                    1969

**6799** REAVER, JOSEPH R. (Ed.). An O'Neill concordance
pp.vii, 1846                            L
Detroit: Gale Research                  1969
Three volumes.

**6800** RIACH, D. C. Eugene O'Neill and the Irish-American mind
Edinburgh: U. (M.Litt.)                 1969

**6801** ROBERTSON, RODERICK. The friendship of Eugene O'Neill and George Jean Nathan
Madison: U. of Wisconsin (PhD)          1969

**6802** SHEAFFER, LOUIS. O'Neill: son and playwright
pp.xx, 543; ill. in text                M
London: J. M. Dent                      1969
Published Boston: Little, Brown, 1968. Biography.

**6803** TÖRNQVIST, EGIL. A drama of souls: studies in O'Neill's super-naturalistic technique
pp.284                                  L
New Haven: Yale U. P.                   1969
First published, in Swedish, Uppsala: Almqvist & Wiksell, 1968.

**6804** TRIESCH, GISELA. Die Motive in *Thirst and other one-act plays* und ihre Verarbeitung in den späteren Werken O'Neills
pp.170                                  L
Munich: Max Hueber                      1969

**6805** GOYAL, BHAGWAT S. O'Neill and his plays
pp.288 DL★
New Delhi: Aarti Book Centre 1970

**6806** HAMBRIGHT, JEANNE K. The playwright as revolutionary: a comparative study of the uses of dramatic expression in the social protest plays of Frank Wedekind and Eugene O'Neill
Medford MA: Tufts U. (PhD) 1970

**6807** SCHEIBLER, ROLF. The late plays of Eugene O'Neill
pp.222 L
Berne: Francke 1970

**6808** BRYER, JACKSON R. (Ed.). The Merrill checklist of Eugene O'Neill
pp.iv, 43 DL★
Columbus OH: Charles E. Merrill 1971

**6809** CHAXEL, FRANÇOISE DU. Eugene O'Neill: textes...points de vue critiques...
pp.188 ★
Paris: Seghers 1971

**6810** FRENZ, HORST. Eugene O'Neill
pp.v, 121 MH
NY: Frederick Ungar 1971
First published Berlin, 1965. Here enlarged and revised. Includes a chapter on performances in Germany.

**6811** LEVITT, HAROLD. Comedy in the plays of Eugene O'Neill
NY: City U. (PhD) 1971

**6812** SVENSSON, BO. Eugene O'Neill's scenanvisningar [stage directions]
DL★
Lund: U. P. 1971
Swedish text with summary in English.

**6813** WALLIS, J. V. Experiment and self in the plays of Eugene O'Neill
Birmingham: U. (MA) 1971

**6814** ATKINSON, JENNIFER M. (Ed.). *Children of the sea* and three other unpublished plays by Eugene O'Neill
pp.xix, 214 L
Washington DC: National Cash Register 1972
*Bread and Butter*, *Now I ask You*, *Shell Shock*. All early works, here transposed from typescript, with introduction, notes and emendations.

**6815** CAMPNETT, A. L. Eugene O'Neill and the search for a classical form
London: U. Royal Holloway College (M.Phil.) 1972

**6816** DAVIDSON, IVAN H. *Long Day's Journey into Night* by Eugene O'Neill: a structural analysis
Iowa City: U. of Iowa (PhD) 1972

**6817** BRIE, FRIEDRICH. Eugene O'Neill als Nachfolger der Griechen
pp.46-59 MH
Heidelberg: Carl Winter [1973]
Reprinted from *Sonderabdruck ans dem Jahrgang XXI der Germanisch-Romanischen Monatsschrift*. A study founded on *Mourning becomes Electra*.

**6818** FLECKENSTEIN, JOAN P. Eugene O'Neill's theatre of Dionysus: the Nietzchean influence upon selected plays
Madison: U. of Wisconsin (PhD) 1973

**6819** MILLER, JORDAN Y. Eugene O'Neill and the American critic: a bibliographical checklist
pp.xi, 553 M
Hamden CT: Shoe String P. 1973
Second edition, revised. First published 1962.

**6820** ATKINSON, JENNIFER M. Eugene O'Neill: a descriptive bibliography
pp.xxiii, 410 DL★
Pittsburgh: U. P. 1974

**6821** FRAZER, WINIFRED L. E.G. and E.G.O.: Emma Goldman and *The Iceman Cometh*
pp.vi, 105; ill. in text O
Gainesville: U. P. of Florida 1974
Combines biography with a critical examination of the play. Goldman was the inspiration for the character Rosa Porritt and the betrayer sub-plot.

**6822** SHEAFFER, LOUIS. O'Neill: son and artist
pp.xviii, 750; ill. in text M
London: Paul Elek 1974
A continuation of the author's *O'Neill: son and playwright*.

**6823** SWEET, HARVEY. Eugene O'Neill and Robert Edmond Jones: text into scene
Madison: U. of Wisconsin (PhD) 1974

**6824** COSENTINO, GIACOMO. L'idea di tragedia nei drammi di Eugene O'Neill
pp.105 MH
Catania: Gianotta 1975
Errata slip. •

**6825** FILIPOWICZ-FINDLAY, HALINA. Eugene O'Neill
pp.295; ill. DL★
Warsaw: Wiedza Powszechna 1975
Text in Polish.

**6826** GOYAL, BHAGWAT S. The strategy of survival: human significance of O'Neill's plays
pp.viii, 244 DL★
Ghaziabad: Vimal Prakashan 1975

**6827** LEWTON, E. P. Form and content in the last plays of Eugene O'Neill
Warwick: U. (M.Phil.) 1975

**6828** NASH, WILLIAM A. The homecoming motif in selected works of Eugene O'Neill
Salt Lake City: U. of Utah (PhD) 1975

**6829** RATCLIFF, GERALD L. An examination of the parabolic nature of 'suffering' in selected plays by Eugene O'Neill, 1913-1923
Bowling Green: State U. (PhD) 1975

**6830** CHABROWE, LEONARD. Ritual and pathos: the theater of O'Neill
pp.xxviii, 226; ill. in text O
Lewisburg PA: Bucknell U. P. 1976

**6831** CHOTHIA, JEAN. Dramatic language and dramatic form: a study of the development of Eugene O'Neill
Cambridge UK: U. (PhD) 1976

**6832** CRONIN, HARRY. Eugene O'Neill, Irish and American: a study in cultural context
pp.iv, 146 MH
NY: Arno P. 1976

**6833** GRIFFIN, ERNEST G. (Ed.). Eugene O'Neill: a collection of criticism
pp.viii. 151 L
NY: McGraw-Hill 1976
Edwin A. Engel: *Ideas in the plays of O'Neill*; Frederick I. Carpenter: *O'Neill, the orient, and American transcendentalism*; Peter J. Gillett: *O'Neill and the racial myth*; Roger Asselineau: *'Desire Under the Elms', a phase of O'Neill's philosophy*; Otis W. Winchester: *O'Neill's 'Strange Interlude' as a transcript of America in the 1920s*; John H. Raleigh: *'Mourning becomes Electra' and 'A Touch of the Poet'*; Elder Olson: *Modern drama and tragedy, a view of 'Mourning becomes Electra'*; Travis Bogard: *'The Iceman Cometh'*; Robert J. Andreach: *O'Neill's women in 'The Iceman Cometh'*; Timo Tiusanen: *Through the fog into the monologue, 'Long Day's Journey...'*; Egil Törnqvist: *Parallel characters and situations in 'Long Day's Journey...'*; Eric Bentley: *O'Neill's pietá*.

**6834** RICH, J. DENNIS. Eugene O'Neill: visions of the absurd
Madison: U. of Wisconsin (PhD) 1976

**6835** OLSSON, TOM J. O'Neill och dramaten: en studie kring arbetet med och mottagundet av fjorton olika O'Neill uppsättrungar på Dramatiska Teatern åren 1923-1962
pp.272; ill. in text MH
Stockholm: Akademilitteratur 1977
Errata slip.

**6836** PHILLIPS, JULIEN L. The mask: theory and practical use in the plays of Eugene O'Neill
Minneapolis: U. of Minnesota (PhD) 1977

**6837** AHRENDS, GÜNTER. Traumwelt und Wirklichkeit im Spätwerk Eugene O'Neill
pp.286 O
Heidelberg: Carl Winter 1978

**6838** JOSEPHSON, LENNART. A role: O'Neill's Cornelius Melody
pp.ii, 166 MH
Atlantic Highlands: Humanities P. 1978
First published Stockholm: Almqvist & Wiksell, 1977. A study of *A Touch of the Poet* focused on the genesis of a character.

**6839** WILLIAMS, JUDITH W. Eugene O'Neill: the philos-aphilos of a mother's eternal son
Ann Arbor: U. of Michigan (PhD) 1978

**6840** CARPENTER, FREDERICK I. Eugene O'Neill
pp.192; ill. in text MH
Boston: Twayne 1979

**6841** CHOTHIA, JEAN. Forging a language: a study of the plays of Eugene O'Neill
pp.x, 243 O
NY: Cambridge U. P. 1979

**6842** FLOYD, VIRGINIA (Ed.). Eugene O'Neill: a world view
pp.ix, 309 O
NY: Frederick Ungar 1979

**6843** LICHTMAN, MYLA R. Mythic plot and character development in Euripides' *Hippolytus* and Eugene O'Neill's *Desire Under the Elms*: a Jungian analysis
Los Angeles: U. of Southern California (PhD) 1979

**6844** PIKE, FRANK. Confession as an implicit structuring device in the late plays of Eugene O'Neill
Minneapolis: U. of Minnesota (PhD) 1980

**6845** WATKINSON, SHARON A. An analysis of characters in selected plays of Eugene O'Neill according to Erik H. Erikson's identity theory
NY: U. (PhD) 1980

**6846** FLOYD, VIRGINIA (Ed.). Eugene O'Neill at work: newly released ideas for plays: edited and annotated...
pp.xl, 407; ill. in text O
NY: Frederick Ungar 1981
O'Neill's notebooks, including his scene designs.

**6847** OSWALD, JOSEF. The discordant, broken, faithless rhythm of our time: eine Analyse der späten Dramen Eugene O'Neills
pp.viii, 208 MH
Frankfurt: Peter D. Lang 1981

**6848** SINHA, C. P. Eugene O'Neill's tragic vision
pp.xi, 176 L
New Delhi: New Statesman 1981
An unexamined revised edition was published 1983.

**6849** BERLIN, NORMAND. Eugene O'Neill
pp.xiii, 178; pl. 4 L
London: Macmillan 1982
Published NY: Grove P. Critical study.

**6850** BRYER, JACKSON R. & ALVAREZ, RUTH M. (Eds). 'The theatre we worked for': the letters of Eugene O'Neill to Kenneth MacGowan...with introductory essays by Travis Bogard
pp.xiii, 274; ill. in text M
New Haven: Yale U. P. 1982

**6851** FALK, DORIS V. Eugene O'Neill and the tragic tension: an interpretive study of the plays
pp.xi, 223 MH
NY: Gordian P. 1982
Second edition, revised. First published New Brunswick: Rutgers U. P., 1958.

**6852** HART, DORIS. An historical analysis of three New York productions of Eugene O'Neill's *Long Day's Journey into Night*
NY: U. (PhD) 1982

**6853** MANNHEIM, MICHAEL. Eugene O'Neill's new language of kinship
pp.xii, 240 MH★
NY: Syracuse U. P. 1982

**6854** ORLANDELLO, JOHN. O'Neill on film
pp.182; ill. in text MH
Rutherford NJ: Fairleigh Dickinson U. P. 1982

**6855** ROBINSON, JAMES A. Eugene O'Neill and oriental thought: a divided vision
pp.ix, 201 MH
Carbondale: Southern Illinois U. P. 1982

## 16. DRAMATIC BIOGRAPHY AND CRITICISM

**6856** HAYASHI, TETSUMARO (Ed.). Eugene O'Neill: research opportunities and dissertation abstracts
pp.x, 155   M
Jefferson NC: McFarland   1983

**6857** AHUJA, CHAMAN. Tragedy, modern temper and O'Neill
pp.viii, 207   L
Delhi: Macmillan India   1984

**6858** FRENZ, HORST & TUCK, SUSAN (Eds). Eugene O'Neill's critics: voices from abroad
pp.xxi, 225   L
Carbondale: Southern Illinois U. P.   1984

Rudolf Haas: *A literary historical assessment*; Alexander Anikst: *Preface to Russian translated works*; Catherine Mounier: *Notes on the 1967 production of 'The Iceman...'*; Hugo von Hofmannsthal: *The beggar and 'The Hairy Ape'*; Lennox Robinson: *'Beyond the Horizon' v. 'Gold'*; Frank Tetauer: *Raw brutal visions; the tragic wanderings of a great dramatist*; Richard Jennings: *Dramatist of monomania*; Erik Reger: *The Georg Kaiser of America*; Alexander Tairov: *Director's notes; creative work of O'Neill*; Sean O'Casey: *Three tributes...*; Frederick Schyberg: *American tragedy of fate*; Dorothy Macardle: *The dual nature of man*; Per Hallstrom: *Nobel prize presentation*; Maurice Le Breton: *O'Neill and the American theatre*; Eugenio Montale: *O'Neill and the future of the theatre*; Gabriel Marcel: *Interpretations by a philosopher*; St. John Ervine: *Counsels of despair*; Toshia Kimura: *O'Neill's 'whited sepulchre'*; Alfonso Sastre: *On the death of O'Neill*; Leon Mirlas: *The scope of O'Neill's drama*; Kenneth Tynan: *The heights and the depths*; Wojciech Natansan: *O'Neill's comeback*; B. Nagy Laszlo: *The O'Neill legend*; Oscar Fritz Schah: *O'Neill's dramatic work: his image of humanity*; An Min Hsia: *Cycle of return: O'Neill and the tao*; Timo Tiusanen: *O'Neill and Wuolijoki: a counter-sketch to 'Electra'*.

**6859** MARTINE, JAMES J. (Ed.). Critical essays on Eugene O'Neill
  DL★
Boston: G. K. Hall   1984

**6860** RANALD, MARGARET L. The Eugene O'Neill companion
pp.xiv, 827; ill. in text   MH
Westport CT: Greenwood P.   1984

**6861** SEIDEL, MARGOT. Aberglaube bei O'Neill
pp.155   L
Frankfurt: Peter Lang   1984

**6862** SEIDEL, MARGOT. Bibel und Christentum im dramatischen Werk Eugene O'Neills
pp.339   L
Frankfurt: Peter Lang   1984

**6863** ALY, A. M. The tragic vision in the major plays of Eugene O'Neill from 1920 to 1941
Dundee: U. (M.Phil.)   1985

**6864** BARLOW, JUDITH E. Final acts: the creation of three late O'Neill plays
pp.vii, 215   MESM
Athens: U. of Georgia P.   1985

*The Iceman Cometh, Long Day's Journey into Night, Moon for the Misbegotten.*

**6865** FLOYD, VIRGINIA. The plays of Eugene O'Neill. A new assessment
pp.xxx, 605; pl. 8   O
NY: Frederick Ungar   1985

**6866** SCHMITT, PATRICK E. *The Fountain, Marco Millions* and *Lazarus Laughed*: O'Neill's 'exotics' as history plays
Madison: U. of Wisconsin (PhD)   1985

**6867** WHITE, LESLIE. Eugene O'Neill and the Federal Theatre Project
NY: U. (PhD)   1985

**6868** ÉGRI, PETER. Chekhov and O'Neill: the uses of the short story in Chekhov's and O'Neill's plays
pp.183   L
Budapest: Akademiai Kiadó   1986

**6869** COMMINS, DOROTHY (Ed.). 'Love and admiration and respect': the O'Neill-Commins correspondence...
pp.xxi, 248   MH
Durham NC: Duke U. P.   1986

**6870** HIRSCH, FOSTER. Eugene O'Neill: life, work, and criticism
pp.48   ★
Fredericton NB: York P.   1986

**6871** McDONOUGH, EDWIN J. Quintero directs O'Neill: an examination of eleven plays of Eugene O'Neill staged by José Quintero in New York City, 1956-1981
NY: U. (PhD)   1986

**6872** PORTER, E. S. The influence of Nietzsche on the plays of Eugene O'Neill
London: U. Royal Holloway College (PhD)   1986

**6873** BLOOM, HAROLD (Ed.). Modern critical views: Eugene O'Neill
pp.viii, 183   MH
NY: Chelsea House   1987

**6874** GARDNER, M. C. The early plays of Eugene O'Neill
Sheffield: U. (M.Phil.)   1987

**6875** GELB, ARTHUR & GELB, BARBARA. O'Neill
pp.xxi, 990; pl. 12   MH
NY: Harper & Row   1987

Reprint of the 1962 edition with some minor amendments and the addition of an epilogue concerning Carlotta Monterey, O'Neill's wife.

**6876** HALFMANN, ULRICH (Ed.). Eugene O'Neill: comments on the drama and the theater, a source book. Collected and edited, with critical and bibliographical notes...
pp.xxxvi, 255; ill. in text   MH
Tübingen: Gunter Narr   1987

**6877** PRASAD, HARI M. Dramatic art of Eugene O'Neill
pp.ix, 113   L
New Delhi: Associated Publishing House   1987

**6878** ROBERTS, NANCY L. & ROBERTS, ARTHUR W. (Eds). 'As ever, Gene': the letters of Eugene O'Neill to George Jean Nathan. Transcribed and edited, with introductory essays...
pp.248; ill. in text   M
Rutherford: Fairleigh Dickinson U. P.   1987

**6879** BAGCHEE, SHYAMAL (Ed.). Perspectives on O'Neill: new essays
pp.112　　　　　　　　　　　　　　　　　　M
Victoria BC: U.P.　　　　　　　　　　　　1988

Judith E. Barlow: *O'Neill's many mothers, Mary Tyrone, Josie Hogan, and their antecedents*; Stephen A. Black: *Tragic anagnorisis in 'The Iceman Cometh'*; Michael Manheim: *The transcendency of melodrama in 'Long Day's Journey...'*; Peter Egri: *The Electra complex of puritan morality and the epic ambition of O'Neillian tragedy*; James A. Robinson: *The metatheatrics of 'A Moon for the Misbegotten'*: Shyamal Bagchee: *Reading O'Neill's poetry*; Marcia Blumberg: *Eloquent stammering in the fog, O'Neill's heritage in Mamet*.

**6880** BOGARD, TRAVIS & BRYER, JACKSON R. (Eds). Selected letters of Eugene O'Neill
pp.xi, 602; ill. in text　　　　　　　　　　MH
New Haven: Yale U. P.　　　　　　　　　1988

**6881** BOGARD, TRAVIS. Contour in time: the plays of Eugene O'Neill
pp.xx, 507; ill. in text　　　　　　　　　　M
NY: Oxford U. P.　　　　　　　　　　　　1988

Revised edition. A critical biography.

**6882** BOGARD, TRAVIS (Ed.). The unknown O'Neill: unpublished or unfamiliar writings of Eugene O'Neill. Edited with commentaries by Travis Bogard
pp.ix, 434　　　　　　　　　　　　　　　L
New Haven: Yale U. P.　　　　　　　　　1988

Includes *The Personal Equation*; an early scenario, *The Reckoning*, turned into a play, *The Guilty One*, by O'Neill's wife; act IV of *The Ole Davil*, a dramatic arrangement of *The Ancient Mariner*; and *Marco's Millions*.

**6883** FLOYD, VIRGINIA (Ed.). Eugene O'Neill: the unfinished plays - notes for *The Visit of Malatesta*, *The Last Conquest*, *Blind Alley Guy*
pp.213　　　　　　　　　　　　　　　　　DL★
NY: Continuum　　　　　　　　　　　　1988

**6884** GALLUP, DONALD C. Pigeons on the granite: memoirs of a Yale librarian
　　　　　　　　　　　　　　　　　　　　DL★
New Haven: Yale U. P.　　　　　　　　　1988

Includes reference to Carlotta Monterey.

**6885** O'NEILL, EUGENE. More Stately Mansions: the unexpurgated edition edited by Martha Gilman Bower
pp.xi, 313;　　　　　　　　　　　　　　MH
NY: Oxford U. P.　　　　　　　　　　　　1988

Based on a typed version of Eugene O'Neill's third long-hand draft, finished 20 January, 1939. Substantial introduction.

**6886** PORTER, LAURIN. The banished prince: time, memory and ritual in the late plays of Eugene O'Neill
pp.ix, 129　　　　　　　　　　　　　　　DL★
Ann Arbor: UMI Research P.　　　　　　1988

**6887** SHAUGHNESSY, EDWARD L. Eugene O'Neill in Ireland: the critical reception
pp.xviii, 221; ill. in text　　　　　　　　　MH
NY: Greenwood P.　　　　　　　　　　　1988

**6888** SMITH, MADELINE & EATON, RICHARD. Eugene O'Neill: an annotated bibliography, 1973-1985
pp.336　　　　　　　　　　　　　　　　　DL★
NY: Garland　　　　　　　　　　　　　　1988

**6889** STROUPE, JOHN H. (Ed.). Critical approaches to O'Neill
pp.x, 220　　　　　　　　　　　　　　　MH
NY: AMS P.　　　　　　　　　　　　　　1988

Twelve essays, eleven of them reprinted from *Comparative Drama*, issued on the occasion of the O'Neill centennial.

**6890** VENA, GARY. O'Neill's *The Iceman Cometh*: reconstructing the première
pp.xiv, 251; ill. in text　　　　　　　　　M
Ann Arbor: UMI Research P.　　　　　　1988

**6891** WAINSCOTT, RONALD H. Staging O'Neill. The experimental years, 1920-1934
pp.xviii, 337; pl. 6　　　　　　　　　　　M
New Haven: Yale U. P.　　　　　　　　　1988

**6892** KOBERNICK, MARK. Semiotics of the drama and the style of Eugene O'Neill
pp.xiii, 159　　　　　　　　　　　　　　L
Amsterdam: John Benjamin　　　　　　1989

An attempt to develop and apply a semiotic analysis to six plays with particular emphasis on *Anna Christie*, *Desire Under the Elms* and *A Long Day's Journey into Night*.

**6893** MAUFORT, MARC (Ed.). Eugene O'Neill and the emergence of American drama
pp.viii, 207　　　　　　　　　　　　　　L
Atlanta GA: Rodopi　　　　　　　　　　1989

Frederick C. Wilkins: *O'Neill's debut*; Paul Voelker: *O'Neill and George Pierce Baker*; Jean Chothia: *Theatre language...in 'The Hairy Ape'*; Michael Manheim: *O'Neill and the founders of modern drama*; John H. Raleigh: *Strindberg and O'Neill*; M. C. Pasquier: *O'Neill's Russianness*; Marc Maufort: *'Mourning becomes Electra' and Melville*; Egil Törnqvist: *O'Neill's play-titles*; Ulrich Halfmann: *The 'clenched fist' motif*; Judith E. Barlow: *Carlotta in 'Long Day's Journey'*; Jackson R. Bryer: *Letters to Donald Pace*; James A. Robinson: *Fathers and sons in O'Neill and Sam Shepard*; Susan H. Smith: *'Hughie's post modern aura*; Mel Cobb: a play, *O'Neill or sunny days and starry nights*.

**6894** ENGLUND, CLAES & BERGSTRÖM, GUNNEL (Eds). Strindberg, O'Neill and the modern theatre: addresses and discussions at a Nobel symposium at the Royal Dramatic Theatre, Stockholm
pp.79　　　　　　　　　　　　　　　　　M
[Stockholm]: [Nobel Foundation/Riksteatern]　1990

Egil Törnqvist: *Strindberg and O'Neill, and their impact on the dramatists of today*; Harry G. Carlson: *In search of the Dionysian actor*; Robert Wilson: *See the text and hear the pictures*.

**6895** ENGLUND, CLAES & BERGSTRÖM, GUNNEL. Strindberg, O'Neill, and the modern theatre; addresses and discussions at a Nobel Symposium at the Royal Dramatic Theatre
pp.79　　　　　　　　　　　　　　　　　M
Stockholm: entré Riksteatern　　　　　　1990

**6896** ESTRIN, MARK W. Conversations with Eugene O'Neill
pp.xxx, 242　　　　　　　　　　　　　　DL★
Jackson: Mississippi U. P.　　　　　　　　1990

**6897** HALFMANN, ULRICH. Eugene O'Neill 1988: deutsche Beiträge zum 100. Geburtstag des amerikanischen Dramatikers
pp.273; ill. in text　　　　　　　　　　　L
Tübingen: Gunter Narr　　　　　　　　1990

**6898** HINDEN, MICHAEL. *Long Day's Journey into Night*: native eloquence
pp.xiii, 129; ill. in text  MH
Boston: Twayne  1990

### Odets, Clifford
### (1906-1963)

**6899** SHUMAN, R. B. Clifford Odets
pp.160  L
NY: Twayne  1962

**6900** KURYK, DAVID. Love's thin awkward plant. A study of the work of Clifford Odets in regard to the individual and his relationship to society
Madison: U. of Wisconsin (PhD)  1964

**6901** MURRAY, EDWARD. Clifford Odets: the thirties and after
pp.ix, 229  L
NY: Frederick Ungar  1968

**6902** MENDELSOHN, MICHAEL J. Clifford Odets, humane dramatist
pp.xviii, 138  DL★
Deland FL: Everett/Edwards  1969
Introduction by Morris Freedman.

**6903** WARSHOW, ROBERT. The immediate experience: movies, comics, theatre & other aspects of popular culture
pp.282  MH
NY: Atheneum  1975
First published Garden City: Doubleday, 1961. Articles reprinted from *Commentary*, the *Partisan Review* and *American Mercury*. Includes material on Clifford Odets.

**6904** CANTOR, HAROLD. Clifford Odets, playwright-poet
pp.viii, 235  O
Metuchen NJ: Scarecrow P.  1978

**6905** BRENMAN-GIBSON, MARGARET. Clifford Odets – American playwright: the years from 1906 to 1940
pp.xiv, 749; pl.8  O
NY: Atheneum  1981

**6906** WEALES, GERALD. Odets the playwright
pp.205  M
London: Methuen  1985
Revised edition. First published NY: Bobbs-Merrill, 1971.

**6907** ODETS, CLIFFORD. The time is ripe: the 1940 journal
  DL★
NY: Grove P.  1988

**6908** COOPERMAN, ROBERT. Clifford Odets. An annotated bibliography of criticism
  DL★
Westport CT: Meckler  1990

### Osborn, Paul
### (1901-1988)

**6909** LAMMEL, EARL C. Paul Osborn: a professional biography
Columbus: Ohio State U. (PhD)  1973

### Paulding, James Kirk
### (1778-1860)

**6910** PAULDING, WILLIAM I. (Ed.). Literary life of James Kirk Paulding
pp.397; front.  L
NY: Charles Scribner  1867

**6911** HEROLD, AMOS L. James Kirk Paulding: versatile American
pp.xiii, 167; front., pl. 3  L
NY: Columbia U. P.  1926

**6912** WATKINS, FLOYD C. James Kirk Paulding. Humorist and critic of American life
Nashville: Vanderbilt U. (PhD)  1951

**6913** PAULDING, JAMES K. *The Lion of the West* retitled *The Kentuckian, or a trip to New York*: a farce in two acts...revised by John Augustus Stone and William Bayle Bernard. Edited and with an introduction by James N. Tidwell
pp.64; ill. in text  L
Stanford: U. P.  1954
From MSS in the British Library. The unamended *Text A* is printed; *Text B* variants are given in an appendix. Introduction offers useful background information. Illustrations comprise playbills and a portrait of J. H. Hackett as Nimrod Wildfire.

### Peabody, Josephine Preston
### (1874-1922)

**6914** BAKER, CHRISTINA H. (Ed.). Diary and letters of Josephine Preston Peabody
pp.ix, 346; pl. 7  L
Boston: Houghton Mifflin  1925

### Perelman, Sidney Joseph
### (1904-1979)

**6915** GALE, STEVEN H. S. J. Perelman: an annotated bibliography
pp.xxviii, 162; front.  L
NY: Garland  1985

**6916** NOT USED

### Pollock, Channing
### (1880-1946)

**6917** POLLOCK, CHANNING. The footlights fore and aft
pp.436; ill. in text  M
Boston: Richard G. Badger  1911
Reprinted articles.

**6918** POLLOCK, CHANNING. The adventures of a happy man
pp.xiv, 206  M
NY: Thomas Y. Crowell  1939
A mosaic of musings on his views on life.

**6919** POLLOCK, CHANNING. Harvest of my years: an autobiography
pp.395; pl. 16  M
Indianapolis: Bobbs-Merrill  1943

### Purdy, James
### (1923-)

**6920** ADAMS, STEPHEN D. James Purdy
pp.166  O
London: Vision  1976

## 16.2. INDIVIDUAL DRAMATISTS

### Rabe, David
### (1940-)

**6921** KOLIN, PHILIP C. David Rabe. A stage history and a primary and secondary bibliography
pp.xii, 273 M
NY: Garland 1988

### Resnik, Muriel

**6922** RESNIK, MURIEL. *Son of any Wednesday*
pp.237; ill. in text M
NY: Stein and Day 1965

A production history. Play opened February 18, 1964 at the Music Box Theatre NY.

### Rice, Cale Young
### (1872-1943)

**6923** BERRY, C. CORNELIUS. A comparative study of the revised poetic dramas of Cale Young Rice with other outstanding American poetic dramas
Jamaica NY: St John's College (PhD) 1949

### Rice, Elmer
### [Reizenstein, Elmer Leopold]
### (1892-1967)

**6924** BROWN, JARED A. The theatrical development of social themes in selected plays by Elmer Rice
Minneapolis: U. of Minnesota (PhD) 1867

**6925** RICE, ELMER. The supreme freedom
pp.32; ill. DL★
NY: Graphics Group 1949

Originally prepared for the Institute for Social and Religious Studies. Concerns freedom of information.

**6926** RICE, ELMER. The show must go on
pp.v, 472 M
London: Gollancz 1950

A novel, dedicated to Sidney Howard and the Playwrights Company, and informed by the author's knowledge of the processes of stage production.

**6927** RICE, ELMER. The living theatre
pp.xiii, 306 M
London: Heinemann 1960

A wide-ranging discussion of theatre topics derived from a course for post-graduates conducted by Rice at NYU.

**6928** RICE, ELMER. Minority report: an autobiography
pp.474 M
London: Heinemann 1963

Published NY: Simon & Schuster.

**6929** HOGAN, ROBERT. The independence of Elmer Rice with a preface by Harry T. Moore
pp.xi, 164 M
Carbondale: Southern Illinois U. P. 1965

**6930** RONEY, EDMUND B. The effect of directing and producing on the playwriting of Elmer Rice
Stanford: U. (PhD) 1968

**6931** DURHAM, FRANK. Elmer Rice
pp.161 L
NY: Twayne 1970

**6932** WEAVER, RICHARD A. The dramaturgy of Elmer Rice
Columbia: U. of Missouri (PhD) 1973

**6933** GRAVES, RICHARD C. The critical response to the produced full-length plays of Elmer Rice
Denver: U. (PhD) 1975

**6934** BEHRINGER, FRED D. The political theatre of Elmer Rice, 1930-1943
Austin: U. of Texas (PhD) 1980

**6935** PALMIERI, ANTHONY F. Elmer Rice: a playwright's vision of America
pp.xiv, 226 DL★
Rutherford NJ: Fairleigh Dickinson U. P. 1980

**6936** BRISTOW, DONALD G. A descriptive catalogue of the Elmer Rice collection at the University of Texas
Lubbock: Texas Tech U. (PhD) 1984

### Riggs, Lynn
### (1899-1954)

**6937** WILSON, ELOISE. Lynn Riggs, Oklahoma dramatist
Philadelphia: U. of Pennsylvania (PhD) 1957

**6938** AUGHTRY, CHARLES E. Lynn Riggs, dramatist. A critical biography
Iowa City: U. of Iowa (PhD) 1959

**6939** ERHARD, THOMAS A. Lynn Riggs: southwest playwright
pp.ii, 44 DL★
Austin TX: Steck Vaughn 1970

**6940** BRAUNLICH, PHYLLIS C. Haunted by home: the life and letters of Lynn Riggs
pp.xiv, 233; ill. in text L
Norman: U. of Oklahoma P. 1988

### Rinehart, Mary Roberts
### (1876-1958)

**6941** RINEHART, MARY R. My story [autobiography]
pp.432; front. L
London: Cassell 1932

Revised edition (not seen) published 1948.

### Robinson, Edwin Arlington
### (1869-1935)

**6942** FRYXELL, LUCY D. Edwin Arlington Robinson as a dramatist and dramatic poet
Lexington: U. of Kentucky (PhD) 1955

### Rodrigues, Nelson

**6943** NUNES, LUIZ. The conflict between the real and the ideal: a study of the elements of naturalism and melodrama in the dramatic works of Nelson Rodrigues
NY: City U. (PhD) 1987

### Rumbold, Zoe Akins
### (1886-1958)

**6944** MIELECH, RONALD A. The plays of Zoe Akins Rumbold
Columbus: Ohio State U. (PhD) 1974

## Saroyan, William
## (1908-1981)

**6945** MORRIS, DAVID W. A critical analysis of the plays of William Saroyan
Denver: U. (PhD)     1961

**6946** SAROYAN, WILLIAM. Here comes there goes you know who: an autobiography
pp.v, 273     L
London: Peter Davis     1962

**6947** SAROYAN, WILLIAM. Not dying [autobiography]
pp.ix, 244; ill. in text     L
NY: Harcourt, Brace & World     1963
Illustrated by the author. Includes memoirs of Paris.

**6948** KHERDIAN, DAVID. A bibliography of William Saroyan
pp.xvi, 204; facsimile titlepages in text     L
San Francisco: Beacham     1965

**6949** FLOAN, HOWARD R. William Saroyan
pp.176     L
NY: Twayne     1966

**6950** SAROYAN, WILLIAM. Days of life and death and escape to the moon
pp.ix, 139     L
London: Michael Joseph     1971
Published NY: Dial P., 1970. Memoirs of Paris and Fresno, 1967-68.

**6951** SAROYAN, WILLIAM. Places where I've done time
pp.182; ill. in text     L
NY: Praeger     1972
Memoirs, including reference to Broadway and theatre in Fresno.

**6952** EVERDING, ROBERT G. The dissolution process in the early plays of William Saroyan
Stanford: U. (PhD)     1976

**6953** SAROYAN, WILLIAM. Sons come and go, mothers hang in forever
pp.211     MH
NY: McGraw-Hill     1976
Includes short pieces on theatre and show-business. A limited edition was also issued.

**6954** FITTS, KENNETH L. The comic vision in the published plays of William Saroyan
Carbondale: Southern Illinois U. (PhD)     1978

**6955** SAROYAN, WILLIAM. Obituaries
pp.ix, 354; pl.1     MH
Berkeley CA: Creative Arts     1979
Stimulated by the author's perusal of *Variety*'s necrology for 1976.

**6956** FOARD, ELISABETH C. William Saroyan: a reference guide
pp.xix, 193     *
Boston: G. K. Hall     1988

**6957** KIM, KI-AE. Theatricalism in the plays of William Saroyan
Honolulu: U. of Hawaii (PhD)     1990

## Sawyer, Lemuel
## (1777-1852)

**6958** SAWYER, LEMUEL. Autobiography of Lemuel Sawyer, formerly Member of Congress from North Carolina
pp.48     MH★
NY: [For the author]     1844

## Schary, Dore
## (1905-1980)
### Playwright, director

**6959** SCHARY, DORE. Heyday: an autobiography
pp.x, 389; ill. in text     L
Boston: Little. Brown     1979

## Shaw, Irwin
## (1913-1984)

**6960** SHAW, IRWIN. The Assassin: a play in 3 acts
pp.xxx, 158     DL★
NY: Random House     1946
Playtext preceded by substantial discussion of the status and nature of the dramatist in the US, of Union rules and of the NY critics.

**6961** GOLDSTEIN, SAMUEL J. A critical analysis of Irwin Shaw's major plays
Columbia: U. of Missouri (PhD)     1977

## Sheldon, Edward B.
## (1886-1946)

**6962** BARNES, ERIC W. The man who lived twice: the biography of Edward Sheldon...with an introductory chapter by Anne Morrow Lindbergh
pp.xi, 367; pl. 5     M
NY: Charles Scribner's Sons     1956
UK edition (London: W. H. Allen, 1957; pl.1) entitled *The high room, a biography...*

**6963** RUFF, LOREN K. Edward Sheldon: theatrical spokesman for the progressive era
Bloomington: Indiana U. (PhD)     1974

**6964** RUFF, LOREN K. Edward Sheldon
pp.196; front.     L
Boston: Twayne     1982

## Shepard, Sam
## [Rogers, Samuel Shepard]
## (1943-)

**6965** O'TOOLE, MAUREEN A. Sam Shepard's plays: an investigation of heroic motifs
Los Angeles: U. of California (PhD)     1971

**6966** FENNELL, PATRICK J. Sam Shepard: the flesh and blood of theatre
Santa Barbara: U. of California (PhD)     1977

**6967** SHEPARD, SAM. Motel chronicles
    L★
San Francisco: City Lights     1982

**6968** COTTON, JERRY D. Sam Shepard's theatre of fragmentation: a performance theory
Lubbock: Texas Tech U. (PhD)     1983

**6969** GRANT, GARY M. A theatre of action images: Sam Shepard and the American avant-garde theatre
Pittsburgh: U. (PhD)     1983

**6970** McGHEE, JAMES H. The architecture of the fantastic in the plays of Sam Shepard
Bowling Green OH: State U. (PhD) 1983

**6971** MOTTRAM, RON. Inner landscapes: the theater of Sam Shepard
pp.ix, 172 L
Columbia: U. of Missouri P. 1984

**6972** DEROSE, DAVID J. Lobster in the living-room: the theatricality of Sam Shepard
Berkeley: U. of California (PhD) 1985

**6973** BURK, ROBERT E. Reading Lacan and Shepard: a dramaturgy of the subject
Seattle: U. of Washington (PhD) 1986

**6974** SHEWEY, DON. Sam Shepard: the life, the loves, behind the legend of a true American original
pp.191 ★
NY: Dell Publications 1986

**6975** HART, LYNDA. Sam Shepard's metaphorical stages
pp.xi, 157; ill. in text L
NY: Greenwood P. 1987

**6976** OUMANO, ELLEN. Sam Shepard: the life and work of an American dreamer
pp.xiii, 174; pl. 4 L
London: Virgin 1987
First published NY: St Martin's P., 1986.

**6977** DICKEY, JOHANNA S. Strategies of menace in plays of John Whiting, Harold Pinter and Sam Shepard
Stanford: U. (PhD) 1988

**6978** MURRAY, FRANK J. Speaking the unspeakable: theatrical language in the plays of Samuel Beckett and Sam Shepard
Stanford: U. (PhD) 1988

**6979** STUCKY, NATHAN P. Conversation analysis and performance: an examination of selected plays by Sam Shepard
Austin: U. of Texas (PhD) 1988

**6980** DANIELS, BARRY (Ed.). Joseph Chaikin and Sam Shepard: letters and texts 1972-1984
pp.252 DL★
NY: New American Library 1989

**6981** DUGDALE, JOHN (Ed.). File on Shepard
pp.69 O
London: Macmillan 1989

### Sherwood, Robert Emmet (1896-1955)

**6982** HARRIS, PAUL C. The relation of dramatic structure to the ideas in Robert E. Sherwood's dramatic works
Stanford: U. (PhD) 1960

**6983** SHUMAN, R. B. Robert Emmet Sherwood
pp.160 L
New Haven: Yale U. P. 1964

**6984** BROWN, JOHN M. The worlds of Robert E. Sherwood
pp.xix, 411; pl. 8 M
NY: Harper & Row 1965

**6985** BROWN, JOHN M. The ordeal of a playwright: Robert E. Sherwood and the challenge of war. Edited and with an introduction by Norman Cousins
pp.320 M
NY: Harper & Row 1968
Includes Sherwood's *There Shall be no Night*.

**6986** MESERVE, WALTER J. Robert E. Sherwood: reluctant moralist
pp.231 MH
NY: Pegasus 1970

**6987** WATTENBERG, RICHARD J. The sense of history in the plays of Robert E. Sherwood
Madison: U. of Wisconsin (PhD) 1979

### Shipman, Louis Evan (1869-1933)

**6988** SHIPMAN, LOUIS E. The true adventures of a play
pp.182; ill. in text, pl. 8 M
NY: Mitchell Kennerley 1914
The genesis and production of Shipman's play *D'Arcy of the Guard*.

### Simms, William Gilmore (1806-1870)

**6989** SIMMS, WILLIAM G. Border Beagles
pp.495; front. L
NY: W. J. Middleton 1855
A new and revised edition in one volume. First published 1840. A novel with Southern rural theatre content, claimed by the author to be drawn from life.

**6990** TRENT, W. P. William Gilmore Simms
pp.ix,351 L
Boston: Houghton Mifflin 1892

**6991** OLIPHANT, MARY C.; ODELL, ALFRED T. & EAVES, T.C. (Eds). The letters of William Gilmore Simms
pp.av. 560; pl. 5 in each vol. L
Columbia: U. of South Carolina P. 1953-1956
Five volumes. Introduction by Donald Davidson. Biographical sketch by Alexander S. Solley.

**6992** PARKS, EDD W. William Gilmore Simms as literary critic
pp.viii, 152 L
Athens: U. of Georgia P. 1961
Chapter IV: *on drama and dramatists*.

**6993** RIDGELY, JOSEPH V. William Gilmore Simms
pp.144 L
NY: Twayne 1962

**6994** WIMSATT, MARY A. The comic sense of William Gilmore Simms. A study of the humor in his fiction and drama
Durham NC: Duke U. (PhD) 1964

**6995** DEWSNAP, JAMES W. William Gilmore Simms as playwright
Athens: U. of Georgia (PhD) 1971

**6996** KIBLER, JAMES E. Pseudonymous publications of William Gilmore Simms
pp.ix, 102 L
Athens: U. of Georgia P. 1976
With some reference to Simms's comments on drama.

### Simon, Neil
### (1927-)

**6997** BERNARDI, JAMES A. The plays of Neil Simon: the first decade of dramatic development
Denver: U. (PhD) 1976

**6998** McGOVERN, EDYTHE M. Neil Simon: a critical study
pp.x, 294 ★
NY: Frederick Ungar 1979

**6999** JOHNSON, ROBERT K. Neil Simon
pp.xiv, 154; ill. in text M
Boston: Twayne 1983

**7000** KOVACS, GEORGE. The stage plays of Neil Simon: the struggle for personal power as contemporary comedy
NY: City U. (PhD) 1986

### Sinclair, Upton Beall
### (1878-1968)

**7001** HEIMERDINGER, CHARLES C. Propagandist in the theatre: the career of Upton Sinclair as an American dramatist
Bloomington: Indiana U. (PhD) 1968

### Sklar, George
### (1908-)

**7002** SEGAL, ERROL. George Sklar: playwright for a socially committed theatre
Ann Arbor: U. of Michigan (PhD) 1986

### Smith, Harry James
### (1880-1918)

**7003** SMITH, HARRY J. Letters of Harry James Smith: with an introduction by Juliet Wilbor Tompkins
pp.xiv, 184 M
Boston: Houghton Mifflin 1919
Biologist turned playwright, best remembered for *A Tailor Made Man* (1917) and *The Little Teacher* (1918)

### Smith, Richard Penn
### (1799-1854)

**7004** McCULLOUGH, BRUCE W. Life and writings of Richard Penn Smith with reprint of his play *The Deformed* (1830)
Philadelphia: U. of Pennsylvania (PhD) 1917

**7005** MABBOTT, THOMAS O. Richard Penn Smith's tragedy of *Caius Marius*
pp.141-156 L
[NY]: [For the author?] 1930
An account of Smith's lost play, with a fragment of the text (Act V, scene V), reprinted from *American Literature* Volume 2, No. 2, May, 1930.

### Stallings, Laurence
### (1894-1968)

**7006** BRITTAIN, JOAN T. Laurence Stallings
pp.128; front. L
NY: Twayne 1975
Chapter three considers the plays and the collaboration with Maxwell Anderson.

### Stavis, Barrie
### (1906-)

**7007** SHAW, IRVING. An analysis of the the techniques of playwriting used by Barrie Stavis in his tetralogy
Provo: Brigham Young U. (PhD) 1974

### Stein, Gertrude
### (1874-1946)

**7008** SAWYER, JULIAN. Gertrude Stein, a bibliography
pp.162 L
NY: Arrow 1940

**7009** HAAS, ROBERT & GALLUP, DONALD C. (Eds). A catalog of the published and unpublished writings of Gertrude Stein exhibited in the Yale University Library
pp.64 L
New Haven: Yale U. 1941

**7010** GARVIN, HARRY R. Gertrude Stein. A study of her theory and practice
Ann Arbor: U. of Michigan (PhD) 1950

**7011** LEACH, WITFORD. Gertrude Stein and the modern theatre
Urbana: U. of Illinois (PhD) 1956

**7012** SPRIGGE, ELIZABETH. Gertrude Stein: her life and her work
pp.xv, 277; pl. 8 MH
London: Hamish Hamilton 1957

**7013** BRIDGMAN, RICHARD. Gertrude Stein in pieces
pp.xvi, 411 O
NY: Oxford U. P. 1970
Critical study. Makes reference to *Four Saints* and other dramatic pieces.

**7014** STEIN, GERTRUDE. Selected operas and plays. Edited and with an introduction by John M. Brennin
pp.xvii,325 L
Pittsburg: U. P. 1970

**7015** WEINSTEIN, NORMAN. Gertrude Stein and the literature of the modern consciousness
pp.150 DL★
NY: Frederick Ungar 1970
Includes material on *Four Saints*.

**7016** ARMATAGE, ELIZABETH. The mother in us all: the woman in the writings of Gertrude Stein
Toronto: U. (PhD) 1974

**7017** FIRMAGE, GEORGE J. A check-list of the published writings of Gertrude Stein
ll.8 L
[Folcroft PA]: Folcroft Library 1974
A reproduction of work first published Amherst: U. Mass., 1954.

**7018** LISTON, MAUREEN R. Gertrude Stein: an annotated critical bibliography
pp.230 ★
Kent OH: State U. P. 1979

**7019** BAINUM, MARY I. Gertrude Stein's theatre
Madison: U. of Wisconsin (PhD) 1981

**7020** RYAN, BETSY. Gertrude Stein's theatre of the absolute
pp.xiv, 232; ill. in text MH
Ann Arbor: UMI Research P. 1984
An examination of Stein's literary and playwriting aesthetic and her dramatic technique and achievement.

**7021** STEIN, GERTRUDE. Look at me now and here I am: writings and lectures
pp.446 L
Harmondsworth: Penguin 1984
Edited by Patricia Meyerowitz. Introduction by Elizabeth Sprigge. Part one includes a section 'Plays'. First published London: Peter Owen, 1967.

**7022** HOBHOUSE, JANET. Everybody who was anybody: a biography of Gertrude Stein
pp.x, 180; pl. 8 L
London: Arena 1986
First published London: Weidenfeld & Nicolson, 1975.

### Steinbeck, John E.
### (1902-1968)

**7023** FRENCH, WARREN. John Steinbeck
pp.190 L
NY: Twayne 1961

**7024** ASTRO, RICHARD & HAYASHI, TETSUMARO (Eds). Steinbeck: the man and his work. Proceedings of the 1970 Steinbeck Conference sponsored by Oregon State and Ball State Universities
pp.ix, 183 O
Corvallis: Oregon State U. P. 1971
Twelve papers. Reference to dramatic work in John Ditsky: *Faulkner land and Steinbeck country*.

**7025** DAVIS, ROBERT M. (Ed.). Steinbeck: a collection of critical essays
pp.vii, 183 O
Englewood Cliffs NJ: Prentice-Hall 1972

**7026** HAYASHI, TETSUMARO. A new John Steinbeck bibliography
pp.xix, 225 DL*
Metuchen NJ: Scarecrow P. 1973
Second edition, revised. First published 1967 as *...A concise bibliography 1930-1965*.

**7027** WHITEBROOK, PETER. Staging Steinbeck: dramatising *The Grapes of Wrath*
pp.157; pl.4 M
London: Cassell 1988

### Tarkington, Newton Booth
### (1869-1946)

**7028** CURRIE, BARTON. Booth Tarkington, a bibliography
pp.vii, 154; front., ill. in text L
NY: Doubleday, Doran 1932

**7029** RUSSO, DOROTHY R. & SULLIVAN, THELMA L. A bibliography of Booth Tarkington, 1869-1946
pp.xix, 303; pl. 13 L
Indianapolis: Indiana Historical Society 1949

**7030** VAN NOSTRAND, ALBERT D. The novels and plays of Booth Tarkington. A critical appraisal
Cambridge MA: Harvard U. (PhD) 1951

**7031** WOODRESS, JAMES. Booth Tarkington: gentleman from Indiana
pp.350; ill. in text, pl. 4 MH
Philadelphia: J. B. Lippincott 1955

**7032** McNALLY, MARY A. Critical appraisal of the leading dramas of Booth Tarkington
Jamaica NY: St. John's U. (PhD) 1957

**7033** DOWNER, ALAN S. (Ed.). On plays, playwrights, and playgoers: selections from the letters of Booth Tarkington to George C. Tyler and John Peter Toohey, 1918-25
pp.vii, 100; pl. 6 M
Princeton: U. Library 1959

**7034** FENNIMORE, KEITH J. Booth Tarkington
pp.167 L
Boston: Twayne 1974

**7035** TORRENTS, JOHN E. Booth Tarkington: a man of the theatre
Bloomington: Indiana U. (PhD) 1974

### Taylor, Charles A.
### (1864?-1942)

**7036** TAYLOR, DWIGHT. Blood and thunder
pp.199 M
London: Michael Joseph 1963
A biography. Taylor wrote and directed melodramas, many of them performed by his wife Laurette Taylor

### Terry, Megan
### (1932-)

**7037** WAGNER, PHYLLIS J. Megan Terry: political playwright
Denver: U. of Colorado (PhD) 1972

**7038** BARRON, ELIZABETH A. A structural analysis of representative plays of Megan Terry
Louisville: U. (PhD) 1983

**7039** LARSEN, JAMES W. Public dreams: a critical investigation of the plays of Megan Terry, 1955-1986
Lawrence: U. of Kansas (PhD) 1988

### Thomas, Augustus
### (1857-1934)

**7040** THOMAS, AUGUSTUS. The print of my remembrance. Illustrated with photographs and... drawings by the author [autobiography]
pp.ix, 477; pl. 16 M
NY: Charles Scribner's Sons 1922

**7041** BERGMAN, HERBERT. Augustus Thomas, dramatist of his age
Madison: U. of Wisconsin (PhD) 1953

**7042** BYNUM, LUCY S. The economic and political ideas of Augustus Thomas
Chapel Hill: U. of North Carolina (PhD) 1954

**7043** KERRICK, GEORGE E. The literary theory and practice of Augustus Thomas
Chapel Hill: U. of North Carolina (PhD) 1971

**7044** DAVIS, RONALD J. Augustus Thomas
pp.xi, 148    L
Boston: Twayne    1984

### Thurber, James
### (1894-1961)

**7045** MORSBERGER, ROBERT E. James Thurber
pp.224    L
NY: Twayne    1964

**7046** BOWDEN, EDWIN T. James Thurber: a bibliography
pp.xii, 353; ill. in text    L
Columbus: Ohio State U. P.    1968

**7047** TOBIAS, RICHARD C. The art of James Thurber
pp.x, 196    L
Athens: Ohio U. P.    1969
Includes an account of *The Male Animal*.

**7048** BLACK, STEPHEN A. James Thurber: his masquerades. A critical study
pp.126    MH
The Hague: Mouton    1970

**7049** HOLMES, CHARLES S. (Ed.). Thurber: a collection of critical essays
pp.xi, 180; ill. in text    L
Englewood Cliggs NJ: Prentice-Hall    1974
Includes Robert E. Morsberger: 'The Male Animal' and the political animal.

### Torrence, Ridgely
### (1875-1950)

**7050** CLUM, JOHN M. Ridgely Torrence
pp.178    L
NY: Twayne    1972

### Treadwell, Sophie
### (1890-1970)

**7051** HECK-RABI, LOUISE. Sophie Treadwell: subjects and structures in 20th century American drama
Detroit: Wayne State U. (PhD)    1976

**7052** WYNN, NANCY E. Sophie Treadwell: the career of a twentieth-century American feminist playwright
NY: City U. (PhD)    1982

### Twain, Mark
### [Clemens, Samuel Langhorne]
### (1835-1910)

**7053** GOLDMAN, R.L. Mark Twain: playwright
London: U. King's College (PhD)    1981

### Tyler, Royall
### (1757-1826)

**7054** TYLER, ROYALL. *The Contrast*. With an introduction by Thomas J. McKee
pp.xii; xxxx, 197; pl. 1    MH
NY: Dunlap Society    1887
Text of play claimed as the first written by an American to be performed by a professional American company. Introduction, with notes, precedes a facsimile reprint of the first edition, Philadelphia: Prichard & Hall, 1790.

**7055** TYLER, ROYALL. The Contrast: a comedy in five acts...with a *History of George Washington's Copy* by James Benjamin Wilbur
pp.xxviii, 120; pl. 4    M
Boston: Houghton Mifflin    1920
Introduction by Helen T. Brown provides a biographical account of Tyler and his play's provenance. Wilbur's account describes his search for the copy presented to George Washington by Thomas Wignell. List of subscribers. 275 copies.

**7056** TUPPER, FREDERICK & BROWN, HELEN T. (Eds). Grandmother Tyler's book: the recollections of Mary Palmer Tyler...1775-1866
pp.xxv, 366; pl. 9, folding tables    L
NY: G. P. Putnam's Sons    1925
The wife of Royall Tyler. Only fleeting mention of theatre and the plays.

**7057** TANSELLE, G. THOMAS. Royall Tyler
pp.xvii, 281    M
Cambridge MA: Harvard U. P.    1967

**7058** BLANDFORD, LUCY. The production history of Royall Tyler's *The Contrast*
Charlottesville: U. of Virginia (MA)    1970

**7059** CARSON, ADA L. & CARSON, HERBERT L. Royall Tyler
pp.172; front.    L
Boston: Twayne    1979

### Updike, John Hoyer
### (1932-)

**7060** GREINER, DONALD J. The other John Updike
pp.xxi, 297    O
Athens: Ohio U. P..    1981
Includes an appreciation of *Buchanan Dying*.

### Van Druten, John
### (1901-1957)

**7061** VAN DRUTEN, JOHN. The way to the present: a personal record [autobiography]
pp.282    M
London: Michael Joseph    1938

**7062** VAN DRUTEN, JOHN. The widening circle [autobiography]
pp.ii, 229    M
London: Heinemann    1957
Published NY: Charles Scribner.

### Van Itallie, Jean-Claude
### (1936-)

**7063** RICHTER, GEORGE R. Jean-Claude Van Itallie, improvisational playwright: a study of his plays
Boulder: U. of Colorado (MA)    1969

### Veiller, Bayard
### (1869-1943)

**7064** VEILLER, BAYARD. The fun I've had [autobiography]
pp.iii, 373; pl. 13    M
NY: Reynal & Hitchcock    1941

### Vidal, Gore
### (1925-)

**7065** VIDAL, GORE. Rocking the boat
pp.xiv, 300    L
London: Heinemann    1963

Articles and essays, many reprinted, including material on Eugene O'Neill, Doré Schary, Paddy Chayefsky. A 'personal section' contains an account of the production of *Visit to a Small Planet* (Booth Theatre, February 7, 1957).

**7066** DICK, BERNARD F. The apostate angel: a critical study of Gore Vidal
pp.xi, 203 (2)   O
NY: Random P.   1974

Chapter six addresses the plays.

**7067** STANTON, ROBERT J. Gore Vidal: a primary and secondary bibliography
pp.xxi, 226   L
Boston: G. K. Hall   1978

### Vonnegut, Kurt
### (1922-)

**7068** HUDGENS, BETTY L. (Ed.). Kurt Vonnegut Jr: a checklist
pp.xvi, 67; ill.   DL★
Detroit: Gale Research   1972

Primary source material. Introduction by Vance Bourjaily.

**7069** KLINKOWITZ, JEROME & SOMER, JOHN (Eds). The Vonnegut statement
pp.271   L
NY: Delacorte P.   1973

Original essays on the life and work of Kurt Vonnegut, with some reference to the plays.

**7070** PIERRAT, ASA B. & KLINKOWITZ, JEROME (Eds). Kurt Vonnegut Jr.: a descriptive bibliography and annotated checklist
pp.xix, 138; ill.   DL★
Hamden CT: Archon   1974

**7071** SCHATT, STANLEY. Kurt Vonnegut Jr
pp.174; front.   L
Boston: Twayne   1976

### Wallace, Lewis
### (1827-1905)

**7072** WALLACE, LEW. The Player's edition [of] *Ben-Hur: a Tale of Christ*. Illustrated with scenes and characters from the play
pp.xi, 555; pl. 48   M
NY: Harper   1904

### Walter, Eugene
### (1874-1941)

**7073** EHRET, DONALD M. A critical study of selected plays by Eugene Walter (1874-1941)
Columbus: Ohio State U. (PhD)   1980

### Warren, Mercy Otis
### (1728-1814)

**7074** BROWN, ALICE. Mercy Warren [biography]
pp.xi, 317; front.   L
London: John Murray   1896

Also published NY: Charles Scribner.

**7075** HUTCHESON, MAUD M. Mercy Otis Warren: a study of her life and works
Washington DC: The American U. (PhD)   1951

**7076** ANTHONY, KATHARINE. First lady of the revolution: the life of Mercy Otis Warren
pp.258   O
Garden City: Doubleday   1958

### Warren, Robert Penn
### (1905-1989)

**7077** BOHNER, CHARLES H. Robert Penn Warren
pp.175   L
NY: Twayne   1964

**7078** WEST, PAUL. Robert Penn Warren
pp.48   L
Minneapolis: U. of Minnesota P.   1964

**7079** HUFF, MARY N. Robert Penn Warren: a bibliography
pp.xi, 171   L
NY: David Lewis   1968

### White, John Blake
### (1781-1859)

**7080** PARTRIDGE, PAUL W. John Blake White: Southern romantic painter and playwright
Philadelphia: U. of Pennsylvania (PhD)   1951

### Wilder, Thornton Niven
### (1897-1975)

**7081** EDELSTEIN, J. M. (Ed.). A bibliographical check-list of the writings of Thornton Wilder
pp.v, 62   O
New Haven: Yale U. P.   1959

**7082** PAPAJEWSKI, HELMUT. Thornton Wilder
pp.166   L
Frankfurt: Athenäum   1961

English translation NY: Frederick Ungar, 1968.

**7083** HABERMAN, DONALD. Thornton Wilder: a study of his theatrical style
New Haven: Yale U. (PhD)   1962

**7084** GREBANIER, BERNARD. Thornton Wilder
pp.48   O
Minneapolis: U. of Minnesota P.   1964

**7085** GOLDSTEIN, MALCOLM. The art of Thornton Wilder
pp.xi, 179   L
Lincoln: U. of Nebraska P.   1965

**7086** BECKMAN, HEINZ. Thornton Wilder
pp.137; ill.   DL★
Velber bei Hanover: Friedrich   1966

**7087** HÄBERLE, ERWIN. Das szenische Werk Thornton Wilders
pp.150   L
Heidelberg: Carl Winter   1967

**7088** HABERMAN, DONALD. The plays of Thornton Wilder
pp.xii, 162   M
Middletown: Wesleyan U. P.   1967

**7089** BLANK, MARTIN J. Thornton Wilder: a study of his dramatic and theatrical ideas, the writing and production of his plays, and the critical response to them
NY: U. (PhD)   1969

**7090** STRESAU, HERMANN. Thornton Wilder
pp.v, 130 L
NY: Frederick Ungar 1971
First published Berlin: Colloquium, 1963.

**7091** KUNER, MILDRED C. Thornton Wilder: the bright and the dark
pp.226 DL★
NY: Thomas Y. Crowell 1972

**7092** GOLDSTONE, RICHARD H. Thornton Wilder: an intimate portrait
pp.xx, 299; front., pl. 4 L
NY: Saturday Review P./E. P. Dutton 1975

**7093** HALBRITTER, RUDOLF. Konzeptionsformen des modernen angloamerikanischen Kurzdramas. Dargestellt an Stücken von W. B. Yeats, Th. Wilder und H. Pinter
pp.250 L
Göttingen: Vandenhoek & Ruprecht 1975

**7094** BURBANK, REX. Thornton Wilder
pp.156 L
NY: Twayne 1978
The second edition. First published 1961.

**7095** CLÜVER, CLAUS VON. Thornton Wilder and André Obey: Untersuchung zum modernen epischen Theater
pp.xii, 374 L
Bonn: Herbert Grundmann 1978

**7096** SIMON, LINDA. Thornton Wilder: his world
pp.xiii, 298; pl. 8 L
Garden City: Doubleday 1979

**7097** WILDER, THORNTON. American characteristics and other essays. Edited by Donald Gallup
pp.xviii, 298 L
NY: Harper & Row 1979
Includes section *On drama and the theater* (pp.75-134).

**7098** CONTA, FLORIA & TORELLI, MARIA. Invito alla lettura di Thornton Wilder
pp.136 DL★
Milan: Mursia 1980

**7099** WILDER, AMOS N. Thornton Wilder and his public
pp.102 DL★
Philadelphia: Fortress P. 1980

**7100** GOLDSTONE, RICHARD H. & ANDERSON, GARY. Thornton Wilder: an annotated bibliography of works by and about...
pp.xii, 104 O
NY: AMS P. 1982

**7101** SNIDER, GERALD E. *Our Town* by Thornton Wilder: a descriptive study of its production modes
East Lansing: Michigan State U. (PhD) 1983

**7102** RICHARDS, W. A. Thornton Wilder: an American dramatist
Bristol: U. (M.Litt.) 1984

**7103** GALLUP, DONALD (Ed.). The journals of Thornton Wilder 1939-1961...with two scenes of an uncompleted play, *The Emporium*. Foreword by Isabel Wilder
pp.xxviii, 354 M
New Haven: Yale U. P. 1985

**7104** LIFTON, PAUL S. Thornton Wilder and 'world theatre'
Berkeley: U. of California (PhD) 1985

**7105** CASTRONOVO, DAVID. Thornton Wilder
pp.xi, 174 M
NY: Frederick Ungar 1986

**7106** [WILDER, THORNTON]. *Our Town* on stage. The original promptbook in facsimile
pp.96 DL★
Cambridge MA: Harvard U. P. 1988
Introduction by Jeanne Newlin.

**7107** HABERMAN, DONALD. *Our Town*: an American play
pp.xiv, 117 DL★
Boston: Twayne 1989

## Williams, Carlos William
### (1883-1963)

**7108** KOCH, VIVIENNE. William Carlos Williams
pp.x, 278 L
Norfolk CT: New Directions 1950

**7109** WHITAKER, THOMAS R. William Carlos Williams
pp.183 MH
NY: Twayne 1968

**7110** FEDO, DAVID A. William Carlos Williams. A poet in the American theatre
pp.x, 203 M
Ann Arbor: UMI Research P. 1983

**7111** LOEVY, STEVEN R. William Carlos Williams's *A Dream of Love*
pp.82 L
Ann Arbor: UMI Research P. 1983

## Williams, Tennessee
### [Williams, Thomas Lanier]
### (1911-1983)

**7112** JACKSON, ESTHER M. The emergence of a characteristic contemporary form in the American drama of Tennessee Williams
Columbus: Ohio State U. (PhD) 1959

**7113** CLAYTON, JOHN S. Themes of Tennessee Williams
New Haven: Yale U. (PhD) 1960

**7114** ASRAL, ERTEM. Tennessee Williams on stage and screen
Philadelphia: U. of Pennsylvania (PhD) 1961

**7115** GOODMAN, RANDOLPH. Drama on stage
pp.xi, 475; pl. 8 MH
NY: Holt, Rinehart & Winston 1961
Playtexts, each preceded by an introductory analysis and other commentary, including interviews with performers and director. Includes Tennessee Williams: *Streetcar named Desire*.

**7116** NELSON, BENJAMIN. Tennessee Williams: his life and work
pp.262; front., pl. 4 L
London: Peter Owen 1961

## 16.2. INDIVIDUAL DRAMATISTS

Published NY: Obolensky

**7117** VAN DORNUM, JACK H. The major plays of Tennessee Williams, 1940 to 1960
Los Angeles: U. of Southern California (PhD) 1962

**7118** HURLEY, PAUL J. Tennessee Williams, critic of American society
Durham NC: Duke U. (PhD) 1963

**7119** WILLIAMS, EDWINA D. Remember me to Tom. As told to Lucy Freeman
pp.255; ill. DL★
NY: G. P. Putnam 1963
Anecdotal reminiscences of Tennessee Williams and others in the family, by his mother. The UK edition, London: Cassell, 1964, has ...the memoirs of Tennessee Williams's mother added to the title.

**7120** DONAHUE, FRANCIS. The dramatic world of Tennessee Williams
pp.ix, 243 L
NY: Frederick Ungar 1964

**7121** QUIRINO, LEONARD S. The darkest celebrations of Tennessee Williams. A study of *Battle of Angels*, *Orpheus Descending*, *A Streetcar named Desire*, *Camino Real*, *Cat on a Hot Tin Roof* and *Suddenly Last Summer*
Providence RI: Brown U. (PhD) 1964

**7122** DILLARD, ROBERT L. The Tennessee Williams hero: an analytical study
Columbia: U. of Missouri (PhD) 1965

**7123** HASHIM, JAMES E. Tennessee Williams and the southern myth
New Haven: Yale U. (PhD) 1965

**7124** JACKSON, ESTHER M. The broken world of Tennessee Williams
pp.xxiv, 179; pl. 2 L
Madison: U. of Wisconson P. 1965

**7125** MAXWELL, GILBERT. Tennessee Williams and friends
pp.xv, 333; pl. 4 MH
Cleveland OH: World 1965

**7126** STARNES, R. LELAND. Comedy and Tennessee Williams
New Haven: Yale U. (DFA) 1965

**7127** WEALES, GERALD. Tennessee Williams
pp.48 O
Minneapolis: U. of Minnesota P. 1965

**7128** FEDDER, NORMAN J. The influence of D. H. Lawrence on Tennessee Williams
pp.131 O
The Hague: Mouton 1966

**7129** PEBWORTH, TED L. & SUMMERS, JAY C. Williams's *The Glass Menagerie*: a critical analysis in depth
pp.124 DL★
NY: Barrister 1966

**7130** MRAZ, DOYNE. The changing image of female characters in the works of Tennessee Williams
Los Angeles: U. of Southern California (PhD) 1967

**7131** BERKMAN, LEONARD. Intimate relationships in Tennessee Williams's plays
New Haven: Yale U. (PhD) 1969

**7132** JAUSLIN, CHRISTIAN M. Tennessee Williams
pp.154; ill. in text MH
Velber bei Hannover: Friedrich 1969

**7133** STEEN, MIKE. A look at Tennessee Williams
pp.xvii, 318; ill. in text MH
NY: Hawthorn 1969
Based on interviews with colleagues and acquaintances of Williams, including Karl Malden, William Inge, Hume Cronyn, Jessica Tandy, Hermione Baddeley, Anaïs Nin.

**7134** SPERO, RICHARD H. The Jungian world of Tennessee Williams
Madison: U. of Wisconsin (PhD) 1970

**7135** MILLER, JORDAN Y. (Ed.). Twentieth century interpretations of *A Streetcar named Desire*: a collection of critical essays
pp.vii, 119 L
Englewood Cliffs NJ: Prentice-Hall 1971

**7136** PERRIER, RONALD G. A study of the dramatic works of Tennessee Williams from 1963 to 1971
Minneapolis: U. of Minnesota (PhD) 1971

**7137** FAYARD, JEANNE. Tennessee Williams
pp.189; ill. DL★
Paris: Seghers 1972

**7138** KOEPSAL, JÜRGEN. Der amerikanische Süden und sein Funktionen im dramatischen Werk von Tennessee Williams
pp.xi, 263 DL★
Berne: Peter Lang 1974

**7139** LINK, FRANZ H. Tennessee Williams Dramen: Einsamkeit und Liebe
pp.144 L
Darmstadt: Thesen 1974

**7140** INGLIS, WILLIAM H. Strindberg and Williams: a study in affinities
Seattle: U. of Washington (PhD) 1975

**7141** PETERSON, CAROL. Tennessee Williams
pp.95 MH
Berlin: Colloquium 1975

**7142** WILLIAMS, TENNESSEE. Memoirs 1939-1975
pp.xxi, 264; pl. 32 MH
Garden City: Doubleday 1975

**7143** ROGERS, INGRID. Tennessee Williams: a moralists's answers to the perils of life
pp.ix, 267 MH
Frankfurt: Peter Lang 1976

**7144** VAHLAND, BARBARA. Der Held als Opfer: Aspekte des melodramatischen bei Tennessee Williams
pp.188 MH
Berne: Herbert Lang 1976

**7145** WINDHAM, DONALD (Ed.). Tennessee Williams' letters to Donald Windham 1940-1965 edited and with comments...
pp.xiii, 333 MH
Verona: Sandy Campbell 1976

# 16. DRAMATIC BIOGRAPHY AND CRITICISM

500 copies.

**7146** AL-KHAYER, M. Tennessee Williams: the search for survival
Exeter: U. (PhD) 1977

**7147** McGEOCH, R. A. The functions of Southern iconography in the work of Tennessee Williams
Bristol: U. (M.Litt.) 1977

**7148** STANTON, STEPHEN S. (Ed.). Tennessee Williams: a collection of critical essays
pp.x, 194 L
Englewood Cliffs NJ: Prentice-Hall 1977
Robert B. Heilman: *TW's approach to tragedy*; R. B. Stein: *'The Glass Menagerie' revisited*; Ruby Cohn: *Garrulous grotesques of TW*; Gerald Weales: *TW's achievement in the 60s*; Harold Clurman: *New note in TW*; Thomas Adler: *Language in TW's later plays, Search for God in the plays of TW*; Esther M. Jackson: *Anti-hero in the plays of TW*; L. Blackwell: *TW and the predicament of women*; D. P. Costello: *TW's fugitive kind*; Arthur Ganz: *TW, a desperate mortality*; Gilbert Debusscher: *TW's lives of the saints*; Nancy Tischler: *TW's self portraits*; Catharine Hughes: *TW - 'What's left?. Work in progress*: S. M. Kahn : *The red devil battery sign*; J. H. Clark: *'This is' (an entertainment)*.

**7149** THARPE, JAC (Ed.). Tennessee Williams: a tribute
pp.xv, 896 L
Jackson: U.P. of Mississippi 1977
Peggy W. Prenshaw: *Paradoxical southern world of TW*; Jacob H. Adler: *TW's south, the culture & the power*; Esther M. Jackson: *TW's poetic consciousness in crisis*; Leonard S. Quirino et al on *Streetcar...*; David C. Mathew on *Battle of Angels* and *Orpheus Descending*; Joseph K. Davis and Thomas E. Schrye on *Glass Menagerie*; Philip C. Kolin on *Rose Tattoo*; James Coakley et al on *Camino Real*; Charles E. May on *Cat...*; Sy Kahn on *Baby Doll*; Alvin Goldfarb on *Period of Adjustment*; Charles Moorman on *Night of the Iguana*; Mary McBride on *Milktrain...*; Rexford Stamper: *the 2-character play*; Sy Kahn: *The Red Devil Battery Sign*; Mary Ann Corrigan: *Echoes of expressionism in the plays...*; June Bennet Larsen: *TW, optimistic symbolist*; Beate Hein Bennet: *TW and European drama*; George Niesen: *Artist against reality...*; Nancy Tischler: *A gallery of witches*; Jeanne M. McGlinn: *TW's women, illusion & reality, sexuality and love*; Leonard Casper: *Triangles of transaction...*; James Haffley: *Abstraction and order in the language of TW*; William J. Scheich: *...talk and touch in the plays of TW*; Albert E. Kalson: *TW at the Delta Brilliant*; Norman J. Fedder: *TW's dramatic techniques*; William J. Free: *TW in the 70s, directions & discontents*; Donald Pease: *Reflections on Moonlake, the presences of the playwright*; S. Alan Chester: *TW, reassessment and assessment*; Edward A. Sklepowich: *Image of the homosexual in TW's prose fiction*; Robert Emmet Jones: *Sexual roles in the works of TW*; Philip M. Armoto: *Meditations on life and death in...*; Delma E. Presley: *Little acts of faith*; John MacNicholas: *TW's power of the keys*; John Ower: *Erotic mythology in poetry of TW*; William E. Taylor: *TW, playwright as poet*; Thomas R. Richardson: *New Orleans and the exotic unreality of TW*; Ren Draya: *Fiction of TW*; Victor A. Kramer: *Memoirs of self-indictment, solitude of TW*; Judith J. Thompson: *Symbol myth & ritual in...*; Gerald M. Berkowitz: *TW's 'other places', a theatrical metaphor in the plays*; Charles B. Brooks: *TW's comedy*.

**7150** YACOWAR, MAURICE. Tennessee Williams and film
pp.viii. 168; ill. in text L
NY: Frederick Ungar 1977
Substantial incidental discussion of Williams's dramatic technique.

**7151** FALK, SIGNI L. Tennessee Williams
pp.194 L
Boston: Twayne 1978
The second edition. First published 1961.

**7152** FLEIT, MURIEL. The application of interaction process analysis to selected plays of Tennessee Williams
NY: U. (PhD) 1978

**7153** LEAVITT, RICHARD F. (Ed.). The world of Tennessee Williams...with an introduction by Tennessee Williams
pp.169; ill. in text M
London: W. H. Allen 1978
Pictorial biography.

**7154** WILLIAMS, TENNESSEE. Where I live: selected essays. Edited by Christine Day and Bob Woods with an introduction by Christine A. Day
pp.xv, 171 MH
NY: New Directions 1978
Reflections on his plays and poems, and on some writers and performers. Also some ocasional writings.

**7155** CHOUKRI, MOHAMED. Tennessee Williams in Tangier
pp.85 ★
Santa Barbara: Cadmus 1979
Translated from the Arabic by Paul Bowles, with a note by Williams.

**7156** HIRSCH, FOSTER. A portrait of the artist. The plays of Tennessee Williams
pp.vi, 121 L
Port Washington NY: Kennikat P. 1979

**7157** LONDRÉ, FELICIA H. Tennessee Williams
pp.vi, 213; pl. 4 L
NY: Frederick Ungar 1979

**7158** McHUGHES, WILLIAM F. A psychological script analysis of the later plays of Tennessee Williams: 1960-1980
Carbondale: Southern Illinois U. (PhD) 1979

**7159** GUNN, DREWEY W. Tennessee Williams: a bibliography
pp.xiii, 255 L
Metuchen NJ: Scarecrow P. 1980

**7160** TISCHLER, NANCY. Tennessee Williams: rebellious Puritan
pp.319 MH
NY: Citadel P. 1981

**7161** CAIN, VERNICE P. The fugitive pattern in selected plays by Tennessee Williams
Bowling Green: State U. (PhD) 1983

**7162** KINNEY, HARRY A. Tennessee Williams and the fugitive kind
Berkeley: U. of California (PhD) 1983

**7163** McCANN, JOHN S. The critical reputation of Tennessee Williams: a reference guide
pp.xxix, 430 DL★
Boston: G. K. Hall 1983

**7164** WILLIAMS, DAKIN & MEAD, SHEPHERD. Tennessee Williams: an intimate portrait
pp.352 DL★
NY: Arbor House 1983

**7165** VAN ANTWERP, MARGARET A. & JOHNS, SALLY (Eds). Dictionary of literary biography, documentary series, an illustrated chronicle, Vol 4: Tennessee Williams
pp.436 DL★
Detroit: Gale Research 1984

**7166** ARNOTT, CATHERINE M. (Ed.). Tennessee Williams on file
pp.80 M
London: Methuen 1985

**7167** RADER, DOTSON. Tennessee Williams: cry of the heart
pp.ix, 348; pl. 4 MH
Garden City: Doubleday 1985
UK edition, London: Grafton, under title *Tennessee Williams: an intimate memoir.*

**7168** SPOTO, DONALD. The kindness of strangers. The life of Tennessee Williams
pp.xix, 409; pl. 8 L
London: Bodley Head 1985

**7169** TENNESSEE WILLIAMS [cover title]
pp.101 MH
Dijon: Siège Social du RADAC 1985

**7170** DEVLIN, ALBERT J. (Ed.). Conversation with Tennessee Williams
pp.xx, 369 L
Jackson: U. P. of Mississippi 1986
Thirty-five interviews. Interviewers include William Inge, Arthur Gelb, Jeanne Fayard, Dotson Rader, Lewis Funke, William Burroughs.

**7171** [SAROTTE, GEORGES-M. et al]. Album masques. Tennessee Williams [cover title]
pp.159; ill. in text MH
Paris: L'Association Masques 1986
Critical essays. Contributors include Cecil Brown, Marie-Claire Pasquier, Gore Vidal.

**7172** BOXILL, ROGER. Tennessee Williams
pp.xv, 186; pl. 4 L
London: Macmillan 1987

**7173** JOHNSTONE, MONICA C. Tennessee Williams and American realism
Berkeley: U. of California (PhD) 1987

**7174** Al-NAMER, A-S. The drama and fiction of Tennessee Williams
Manchester: U. (M.Phil.) 1988

**7175** PETTINELLI, FRANCES. Tennessee Williams: a study of the dramaturgical evolution of the three later plays, 1969-1978
NY: City U. (PhD) 1988

**7176** THOMPSON, JUDITH J. Tennessee Williams's plays: memory, myth and symbol
pp.xi, 253 DL★
NY: Peter Lang 1988

**7177** LONDRÉ, FELICIA H. Tennessee Williams: life, work, and criticism
pp.42 L
Fredericton NB: York P. 1989

**7178** ADLER, THOMAS. *A Streetcar named Desire*: the moth and the lantern
pp.xvii, 99 DL★
Boston: Twayne 1990

**7179** PRESLEY, DELMA E. *The Glass Menagerie*: an American memory
DL★
Boston: Twayne 1990

**7180** SMITH, BRUCE. Costly performances. Tennessee Williams: the last stage
pp.261 DL★
NY: Paragon House 1990

### Willis, Nathaniel Parker
### (1806-1867)

**7181** BEERS, HENRY A. Nathaniel Parker Willis
pp.viii, 365; front. O
Boston: Houghton Mifflin 1885

**7182** DAUGHRITY, KENNETH L. The life and work of Nathaniel Parker Willis
Charlottesville: U. of Virginia (PhD) 1934

**7183** AUSER, COURTLAND P. Nathaniel Parker Willis
pp.175 DL★
NY: Twayne 1969

### Wilson, Edmund
### (1895-1972)

**7184** BERTHOFF, WARNER B. Edmund Wilson
pp.47 O
Minneapolis: U. of Minnesota P. 1968

**7185** FRANK, CHARLES P. Edmund Wilson
pp.213 MH
NY: Twayne 1970
Chapter three addresses the plays. Erratum slip.

**7186** RAMSEY, RICHARD D. Edmund Wilson: a bibliography
pp.ix, 345 L
NY: David Lewis 1971
Section IV: *Plays and dialogues.*

### Wilson, Lanford
### (1937-)

**7187** LELAND, NICHOLAS F. A critical analysis of the major plays of Lanford Wilson
Santa Barbara: U. of California (PhD) 1984

**7188** MYERS, LAURENCE D. Characterization in Lanford Wilson's plays
Kent OH: State U. (PhD) 1984

**7189** CAMERON, JOHN C. Isolation as strategy for characterization in the family dramas of Lanford Wilson
Kent OH: State U. (PhD) 1986

**7190** PAUWELS, GERARD W. A critical analysis of the plays of Lanford Wilson
Bloomington: Indiana U. (PhD) 1986

**7191** BARNETT, GENE A. Lanford Wilson
pp.170 DL★
Boston: G. K. Hall 1987

**7192** GARRISON, GARY W.  Lanford Wilson's use of comedy and humor
Ann Arbor: U. of Michigan (PhD)     1987

**7193** WILLIAMS, PHILIP M.  'A comfortable house': the collaboration of Lanford Wilson and Marshall W. Mason on *Fifth of July*, *Talley's Folly*, and *Talley & Son*
Boulder: U. of Colorado (PhD)     1988

## Wolfe, Thomas C.
### (1800-1938)

**7194** LA SALLE, CLAUDE W.  Thomas Wolfe: the dramatic apprenticeship
Philadelphia: U. of Pennsylvania (PhD)     1964

**7195** GROTH, MELVIN F.  Thomas Wolfe and the Koch idea
Bloomington: Indiana U. (PhD)     1975

**7196** PHILLIPSON, JOHN S.  Thomas Wolfe: a reference guide
pp.xiii, 218     MH
Boston: G. K. Hall     1977

## Woodworth, Samuel
### (1785-1842)

**7197** TAFT, KENDALL B.  Samuel Woodworth
Chicago: U. (PhD)     1936

**7198** WEGELIN, OSCAR.  A bibliographical list of the literary and dramatic productions and periodicals written and compiled by Samuel Woodworth, author of *The [old oaken] Bucket*
pp.19     DL★
New Orleans: [Heartman]     1953
200 copies.

## Wright, Frances
### (1795-1852)

**7199** WRIGHT, FRANCES.  Views of society and manners in America: in a series of letters from that country to a friend in England, during the years 1818, 1819 and 1820
pp.xii, 387     DL★
NY: E. Bliss & F. White     1821

**7200** WRIGHT, FRANCES.  Biography and notes
pp.48     DL★
Boston: [For the author]     1849
Her play *Altorf* was produced in New York in February 1819.

## Wright, Richard
### (1908-1960)

**7201** WRIGHT, RICHARD.  Black boy: a record of childhood and youth [autobiography]
pp.vii, 228     MH
NY: Harper & Brothers     1945

# C. MUSIC

## 17. THE MUSICAL

### 17.1 GENERAL

**7202** TROTTER, JAMES M. Music and some highly musical people: containing brief chapters on I, a description of music. II, the music of nature. III, a glance at the history of music. IV, the power, beauty and uses of music. Following which are given sketches of the lives of remarkable musicians of the colored race. With portraits, and an appendix containing copies of music composed by colored men
pp.353, 152; ill. DL★
Boston: Lee and Shepherd 1881

**7203** WHITTON, JOSEPH. 'The naked truth !' An inside history of *The Black Crook*
pp.32 DL★
Philadelphia: H. W. Shaw 1897

**7204** SMITH, HARRY B. Stage lyrics...
pp.158; ill. in text MB
NY: R. H. Russell 1900

Verses from light and comic operas and musical comedies. Included are 41 character portraits of stage favorites, by Archie Gunn, Ray Brown and E. W. Kemble.

**7205** STRANG, LEWIS C. Prima donnas and soubrettes of light opera and musical comedy in America
pp.xiv, 270; pl. 25 M
Boston: L. C. Page 1900

Alice Nielsen, Virginia Earle, Lillian Russell, Josephine Hall, Mabelle Gilman, Fay Templton, Madge Lessing, Jessie Bartlett Davis, Edna Wallace Hopper, Paula Edwards, Lulu Glaser, Minnie Ashley, Edna May, Marie Celeste, Christie Macdonald, Marie Dressler, Della Fox, Camille D'Arville, Marie Tempest, Maud Raymond, Pauline Hall, Hilda Clark.

**7206** STRANG, LEWIS C. Celebrated comedians of light opera and musical comedy in America
pp.293; pl. 25 M
Boston: L. C. Page 1901

Francis Wilson, James T. Powers, Walter Jones, De Wolf Hopper, Richard Golden, Thomas Q. Seabrooke, Frank Daniels, Jerome Sykes, Dan Daly, Henry Clay Barnabee, Henry E. Dixey, Otis Harlan, Richard Carle, Digby Bell, Jefferson De Angelis, Peter F. Dailey. In addition there are two chapters, *Dutch comedy and its delineators* and *Light comedy in opera and its exponents*.

**7207** LAIT, JACK. The Broadway Melody: novelized from the scenario by Edmund Goulding
pp.ii, 242; pl. 8 L
NY: Grosset & Dunlap 1929

Thinly disguised use of Florenz Ziegfeld and the Follies as models. Illustrated with film stills.

**7208** MARKS, EDWARD B. & LIEBLING, ABBOTT J. They all sang: from Tony Pastor to Rudy Vallee
pp.xi, 321; pl. 33 M
NY: Viking P. 1935

Reminiscences; vocalist entertainers.

**7209** GILBERT, DOUGLAS. Lost chords: the diverting story of American popular songs
xii, 377; ill. in text DL★
Garden City: Doubleday, Doran 1942

**7210** McSPADDEN, JOSEPH W. Operas and musical comedies
pp.xxvi, 607; ill. DL★
NY: Thomas Y. Crowell 1946.

A revised edition in one volume of *Opera Synopses* and *Light Opera and Musical Comedy*

**7211** CHASE, GILBERT. America's music from the Pilgrims to the present
pp.xxiii, 733 DL★
NY: McGraw-Hill 1955

Second edition, revised.

**7212** CROOKER, EARLE T. The American musical play
Philadelphia: U. of Pennsylvania (PhD) 1957

**7213** ENGEL, LEHMAN. Planning and producing the musical show
pp.159; ill. DL★
NY: Crown 1957

**7214** EWEN, DAVID. American musical theatre...a guide to more than 300 productions...with plot, production history, stars, songs, composers, librettists, and lyricists
pp.xxvii, 447; pl. 16 M
NY: Henry Holt 1958

**7215** EWEN, DAVID. The story of America's musical theater
pp.vii, 278 O
NY: Holt, Rinehart and Winston 1959

**7216** KENVIN, ROGER L. Theme and attitude in the American musical
New Haven: Yale U. (PhD) 1961

**7217** KLEIN, ELAINE S. The development of the leading feminine character in selected librettos of American musicals from 1900 to 1960
NY: Columbia U. (EdD) 1962

**7218** MATES, JULIAN. The American musical stage before 1800
pp.xi, 331; pl. 2 L
New Brunswick NJ: Rutgers U. P. 1962

A history from the beginnings to the 1796 production of *The Archers*.

**7219** DUKE, VERNON. Listen here ! A critical essay on music depreciation
pp.vii, 406 O
NY: Ivan Obolensky 1963

A critically disapproving survey of 'modern' trends in music. Includes chapters, *The American musical here and abroad* and *Opera and ballet US style*. Composer of many songs and scores for musicals including the *Ziegfeld Follies 1936* for which he wrote *Can't get started*, and *Cabin in the Sky* (1940).

**7220** SHERR, PAUL C. Political satire in the American musical theatre of the 1930s
Philadelphia: U. of Pennsylvania (PhD) 1964

**7221** O'HARA, MARY. A musical in the making
pp.260 DL★
Chevy Chase MD: Markane 1966

Quasi-fictional account of the progress through to presentation of the author's musical *The Catch Colt*.

**7222** [PARKS, MELVIN]. Musicals of the 1930s: a special exhibition of the Museum of the City of New York
pp.[60] inc. wrappers; ill. in text      M
NY: [For the Friends of the Collection]      [1966]

**7223** ENGEL, LEHMAN. The American musical theatre: a consideration...
pp.236; ill. in text      M
NY: Macmillan      1967
Introduction by Brooks Atkinson.

**7224** WELSH, JOHN D. From play to musical: comparative studies of Ferenc Molnar's *Liliom* with Richard Rodgers' and Oscar Hammerstein II's *Carousel*; and Sidney Howard's *They Knew What they Wanted* with Frank Loesser's *The Most Happy Fella*
New Orleans: Tulane U. (PhD)      1967

**7225** EWEN, DAVID. Composers for the American musical theatre
pp.x, 270; ill.      DL★
NY: Dodd, Mead      1968
First published NY: H. W. Wilson, 1949 as *American composers today*....

**7226** GREEN, STANLEY. The world of musical comedy
pp.xvii, 541; ill. in text      L
South Brunswick: A. S. Barnes      1968
Revised and enlarged edition. First published NY: Ziff-Davis, 1960. A study of the *genre* undertaken through biographical accounts of major composers and lyricists, with full production credits.

**7227** BURTON, JACK. The blue book of Broadway musicals with additions by Larry Freeman
pp.328; ill. in text      L
Watkins Glen NY: Century House      1969
Listed by decades from pre-1900, with credits.

**7228** LAUFE, ABE. Broadway's greatest musicals
pp.xiv, 465      M
NY: Funk & Wagnalls      1969
Wide-ranging and substantial record. Includes an appendix, *The long-running musicals*.

**7229** LERCHE, FRANK M. The growth and development of scenic design for the professional musical comedy stage in New York from 1866 to 1920
NY: U. (PhD)      1969

**7230** MANDER, RAYMOND & MITCHENSON, JOE. Musical comedy: a story in pictures. Foreword by Noël Coward
pp.64; ill. in text      M
London: Peter Davies      1969

**7231** RUMLEY, JERRY B. An analysis of the adaptation of selected plays into musical form from 1943-1963
Minneapolis: U. of Minnesota (PhD)      1969
*Green Grow the Lilacs/Oklahoma!*; *Street Scene*; *My Sister Eileen/Wonderful Town*; *The Rainmaker/110 in the Shade*.

**7232** EWEN, DAVID. New complete book of the American musical
pp.xxv, 800; pl. 24      M
NY: Holt, Rinehart and Winston      1970
Alphabetical listing of musicals with credits, brief production histories and descriptions; librettists, lyricists and composers, with brief biographies. An appendix provides a chronology. Intended to supersede *Story of America's musical theater* (q.v.) but revised format and new material render it effectively a separate work.

**7233** KEMMETMÜLLER, KLAUS. Das amerikanische Musical als Unterhaltungsphänomen
Vienna: U. (PhD)      1970

**7234** MITCHELL, RONALD E. Opera, dead or alive: production, performance, and enjoyment of musical theatre
pp.xii, 322; pl. 8      L
Madison: U. of Wisconsin P.      1970
Includes reference to the US musical, particularly to *Oklahoma!* and *Kiss me, Kate*.

**7235** TUMBUSCH, TOM. Complete production guide to modern musical theatre
pp.187; ill.      DL★
NY: Richards Rosen P.      1970

**7236** ALTMAN, RICHARD & KAUFMAN, MERVYN. The making of a musical: *Fiddler on the Roof*
pp.ix, 214; ill. in text      MH
NY: Crown      1971
Genesis of the Broadway production (Imperial Theatre, September 22, 1964), with accounts also of subsequent tours and of the movie.

**7237** BLAU, ERIC. Jacques Brel is alive and well and living in Paris
pp.191; ill.      DL★
NY: E. P. Dutton      1971
An account by its producer of the off-Broadway hit musical. Lyrics in French and English.

**7238** GREEN, STANLEY. Ring bells! Sing Songs! Broadway's musicals of the 1930s... Introduction by Brooks Atkinson
pp.385; ill. in text      M
New Rochelle NJ: Arlington House      1971
General survey, followed by chronological listing with title, cast, credits, musical numbers, theatre, number of performances. Discography.

**7239** HOCH, IVAN S. A study of the adaptive process in off-Broadway musical comedy
Ithaca: Cornell U. (PhD)      1971

**7240** ROME, FLORENCE. The Scarlett letters
pp.x, 209, 4; pl. 8      M
NY: Random House      1971
Account, with associated correspondence, of the transformation, with the collaboration of Harold Rome, of *Gone With the Wind* into a Japanese musical.

**7241** ALKIRE, STEPHEN R. The development and treatment of the negro character as presented in American musical theatre, 1927-1968
East Lansing: Michigan State U. (PhD)      1972

**7242** DUNN, DON. The making of *No, No Nanette*
pp.335; pl. 8      M
Secaucus NJ: Citadel P.      1972

## 17.1. GENERAL

Detailed chronicle of the Broadway revival, 1972, with substantial reference to Ruby Keeler, Busby Berkeley, Al Jolson, Irving Caesar.

**7243** TUMBUSCH, TOM. Guide to Broadway musical theatre: with additional research and compilation by Marty Tumbusch. Foreword by Richard Rodgers
pp.224; ill. DL*
NY: Richards Rosen P. 1972

114 musicals; plot summaries and requirements for amateur production. A revised edition (unexamined) was published in 1983.

**7244** WILDER, ALEC. American popular song: the great innovators, 1900-1950
pp.544 DL*
NY: Oxford U. P. 1972

Edited and with introduction by James T. Maher. Foreword by Gene Lees.

**7245** DAVIS, LORRIE & GALLAGHER, RACHEL. Letting down my hair
pp.279; pl. 4 M
NY: Arthur Fields 1973

Production history of *Hair* (Rado, J., Ragni, G., MacDermott, G.).

**7246** SHELTON, LYNN M. Modern American musical theatre form: an expressive development of Adolphe Appia's theories of theatre synthesis
Madison: U. of Wisconsin (PhD) 1973

**7247** DRINKROW, JOHN. The vintage musical comedy book illustrated from the Raymond Mander and Joe Mitchenson theatre collection
pp.146; pl. 8 HW
Reading: Osprey 1974

**7248** KINKLE, ROGER D. The complete encyclopedia of popular music and jazz, 1900-1950
pp.various HW
New Rochelle NY: Arlington House 1974

Four volumes. Includes a yearly listing of Broadway musicals with details of cast, book, lyrics and music.

**7249** LANE, RICHARD A. A critical analysis of the treatment of selected American drama in musical adaptation
Pullman: Washington State U. (PhD) 1974

**7250** MADSEN, PATRICIA D. The artistic development of the American musical
Los Angeles: U. of California (PhD) 1974

**7251** PANOWSKI, JAMES A. A critical analysis of the librettos and musical elements of selected musical failures on the Broadway stage: 1964/65-1968/69
Bowling Green: State U. (PhD) 1974

**7252** HALL, ROGER A. Nate Salsbury and his troubadors: popular American farce and musical comedy, 1875-1887
Columbus: Ohio State U. (PhD) 1975

**7253** PARKER, DEREK & PARKER, JULIET. The natural history of the chorus girl
pp.192; ill. in text, some col. M
Newton Abbott: David & Charles 1975

**7254** ALMAGUER, THOMAS M. A historical and critical analysis of selected twentieth century American libretti
Bowling Green: State U. (PhD) 1976

**7255** GLANN, JANICE G. An assessment of the function of dance in the Broadway musical: 1940/41–1968/69
Bowling Green: State U. (PhD) 1976

**7256** MORDDEN, ETHAN. Better foot forward: the history of American musical theatre
pp.xii, 369; ill. in text L
NY: Grossman 1976

**7257** SUMMERS, LOUIS J. The rise of the director/choreographer in the American musical theatre
Columbia: U. of Missouri (PhD) 1976

**7258** ENGEL, LEHMAN. The making of a musical
pp.xvii, 157 MB
NY: Macmillan 1977

Based on the curriculum developed in the musical theatre workshops organized under the aegis of Broadcast Music Inc.

**7259** FRANKEL, AARON. Writing the Broadway musical
pp.x, 182 *
NY: DBS 1977

**7260** GREEN, STANLEY. Encyclopedia of the musical
pp.vii, 488 M
London: Cassell 1977

**7261** GREEN, STANLEY. The Broadway musical: a picture quiz book
Unpaged; ill. in text O
NY: Dover 1977

224 items. Much incidental information.

**7262** JACKSON, ARTHUR. The book of musicals: from *Show Boat* to *A Chorus Line*
pp.208; ill. in text, some col. M
London: Mitchell Beazley 1977

Published NY: Crown, as *The best musicals from...*

**7263** BORDMAN, GERALD. American musical theatre: a chronicle
pp.ix, 749 M
NY: Oxford U. P. 1978

A revised and expanded version (not seen) was published in 1986.

**7264** CRAIG, WARREN. Sweet and lowdown: America's popular song writers
pp.xi, 645 HW
Metuchen NJ: Scarecrow P. 1978

Inludes a listing of theatrical production titles. Foreword by Milton Ager.

**7265** DENNHARDT, GREGORY C. The director-choreographer in the American musical theatre
Urbana-Champaign: U. of Illinois (PhD) 1978

**7266** CIOFFI, ROBERT J. Al Carmines and the Judson Poets' Theater musicals
NY: U. (PhD) 1979

**7267** COMER, IRENE F. *Little Nell and the Marchioness*: milestone in the development of American musical comedy
Medford MA: Tufts U. (PhD) 1979

## 17. THE MUSICAL

**7268** GOTTFRIED, MARTIN. Broadway musicals
pp.353; ill. in text, some col.　　　　　M
NY: Harry N. Abrams　　　　　　　　1979

**7269** OLIN, REUEL K. A history and interpretation of the Princess Theatre [NY] musical plays: 1915-1919
NY: U. (PhD)　　　　　　　　　　　1979
Standard-setting Jerome Kern musicals, including *Oh, Boy!* and *O, Lady!, Lady!!*.

**7270** SCHOETTLER, EUGENIA V. From a chorus line to *A Chorus Line*: the emergence of dance in the American musical theatre
Kent OH: State U. (PhD)　　　　　　1979

**7271** SPURRIER, JAMES J. The integration of music and lyrics with the book in the American musical
Carbondale: Southern Illinois U. (PhD)　1979

**7272** APPELBAUM, STANLEY & CAMNER, JAMES. Stars of the American musical theater in historic photographs: 361 portraits from the 1860s to 1950
pp.vi, 170; ill. in text　　　　　　　　M
NY: Dover　　　　　　　　　　　　1981

**7273** BORDMAN, GERALD. American operetta from *H. M. S. Pinafore* to *Sweeney Todd*
pp.viii, 206; pl. 8　　　　　　　　　M
NY: Oxford U. P.　　　　　　　　　1981

**7274** ENGEL, LEHMAN. Words with music: the Broadway musical libretto
pp.x, 358　　　　　　　　　　　　L
NY: Schirmer　　　　　　　　　　1981
Second edition, revised. First published 1972. Analyses music, plot, character and situation.

**7275** GRAVES, JAMES B. A theory of musical comedy based on the concepts of Susanne K. Langer
Lawrence: U. of Kansas (PhD)　　　　1981

**7276** SMITH, CECIL M. & LITTON, GLENN. Musical comedy in America. From *The Black Crook* to *South Pacific* by Cecil Smith. From *The King and I* to *Sweeney Todd* by Glenn Litton
pp.xv, 367; ill. in text, pl. 8　　　　　MH
NY: Theatre Arts Books　　　　　　1981
Reprinting of Cecil M Smith: *Musical Comedy in America* (1950) updated by additional chapters by Glenn Litton.

**7277** FRASER, BARBARA M. A structural analysis of the American musical theatre between 1955 and 1965: a cultural perspective
Eugene: U. of Oregon (PhD)　　　　1982

**7278** HORN, BARBARA L. *Hair*: changing versions
NY: City U. (PhD)　　　　　　　　1982

**7279** KING, LARRY L. The whorehouse papers
pp.xiii, 283　　　　　　　　　　　DL★
NY: Viking P.　　　　　　　　　　1982
A production history of *The Best Little Whorehouse in Texas* (Entermedia Theatre, April 17, 1978).

**7280** RINALDI, NICHOLAS G. Music as mediator: a description of the process of concept development in the musical *Cabaret*
Columbus: Ohio State U. (PhD)　　　1982

**7281** ENGEL, LEHMAN. Getting the show on: the complete guidebook for producing a musical in your theater
pp.xiii, 226　　　　　　　　　　　M
NY: Schirmer/Macmillan　　　　　　1983
Appendixes list, with brief cast, plot and score analysis, popular musicals available for production, and less frequently seen musicals.

**7282** McKAY, MARILYN L. The relationship between the female performer and the female character in the American musical: 1920-1974
Athens: U. of Georgia (PhD)　　　　1983

**7283** MORDDEN, ETHAN. Broadway babies: the people who made the American musical
pp.ix, 244　　　　　　　　　　　M
NY: Oxford U. P.　　　　　　　　1983
In effect, a history of Broadway stardom from 1900. Includes a substantial discography.

**7284** WHITE, MARK. *You must remember this...*: popular songwriters, 1900-1980
pp.x, 304　　　　　　　　　　　HW
London: Frederick Warne　　　　　1983
Brief biographies. Foreword by David Jacobs.

**7285** BRAHMS, CARYL & SHERRIN, NED. Song by song: the lives and work of 14 great lyric writers
pp.xvi, 282; ill. in text　　　　　　　M
Bolton: Ross Anderson　　　　　　1984
Irving Berlin, Cole Porter, Ira Gershwin, Lorenz Hart, Oscar Hammerstein II, Dorothy Fields, Howard Dietz, E. Y. Harburg, Noel Coward, Johnny Mercer, Frank Loesser, Alan Jay Lerner, Sheldon Harnick, Stephen Sondheim

**7286** GARDINER, N. J. The European background to the American musical
Exeter: U. (MA)　　　　　　　　　1984

**7287** LEWINE, RICHARD & SIMON, ALFRED. Songs of the theater: a definitive index of the songs of the musical stage
pp.xi, 897　　　　　　　　　　　HW
NY: H. W. Wilson　　　　　　　　1984
Indexes 17,000 songs from 1200 Broadway shows, giving composer, lyricist, show and date. First published 1961 as *An encyclopedia of theatre music* and in 1973 as *Songs of the American theatre*, with an introduction by Stephen Sondheim.

**7288** LONEY, GLENN (Ed.). Musical theatre in America: papers and proceedings of the conference... [Long Island U., 1981]
pp.xxi, 441; ill. in text　　　　　　　M
Westport CT: Greenwood P.　　　　1984

**7289** MILLER, RAPHAEL F. The contribution of selected Broadway musical theatre choreographers: Connolly, Rasch, Balanchine, Holm, and Alton
Eugene: U. of Oregon (PhD)　　　　1984

**7290** WHITE, RICHARD K. Historic festivals and the nature of American musical comedy
Eugene: U. of Oregon (PhD)　　　　1984

**7291** BLOOM, KEN. American song: complete music theatre companion, 1900-84
pp.xii, 824; xi, 616　　　　　　　　L
NY: Facts on File　　　　　　　　1985

Two volumes. Substantial data and commentary on approximately 3300 musicals, including all Broadway, off Broadway, and off-off Broadway shows, 1900 to Summer, 1984. Vol 1 comprises an alphabetical list of shows, Vol 2, an index to songs and personnel.

**7292** DELORENZO, JOSEPH P. The chorus in American musical theater: emphasis on choral performance
NY: U. (PhD)   1985

**7293** HUMMEL, DAVID (Ed.). Collectors' guide to the American musical theatre
pp.iv, 669; (ii), 231   MH
Metuchen NJ: Scarecrow P.   1985
Second printing with additions and corrections. Two volumes. Alphabetical listing by title, providing production histories, credits, musical numbers, performers and recordings. A xeroxed supplement was issued in 1988 (ll. 33), adding shows and personalities up to the Winter of 1988.

**7294** MATES, JULIAN. America's musical stage: two hundred years of musical theatre
  DL★
Westport CT: Greenwood P.   1985

**7295** ARCHER, ROBYN & SIMMONDS, DIANA. A star is torn
pp.viii, 208; ill. in text   M
London: Virago P.   1986
A study of women singers and performers, including Bessie Smith, Helen Morgan, Jane Froman, Carmen Miranda, Billie Holliday, Judy Garland, Dinah Washington, Marilyn Monroe, Patsy Cline, Janis Joplin.

**7296** CHALLENDER, JAMES W. The function of the choreographer in the development of the conceptual musical: an examination of the work of Jerome Robbins, Bob Fosse, and Michael Bennett on Broadway
Tallahassee: Florida State U. (PhD)   1986

**7297** GÄNZL, KURT. The British musical theatre. Volume I: 1865-1914 [Volume II: 1915-1984]
pp.x, 1196; ix, 1258   M
Basingstoke: Macmillan   1986
An essay on each year's activity in musical comedy and operetta, with playbills and production history for all works.

**7298** LERNER, ALAN JAY. The musical theatre: a celebration
pp.240; ill. in text, pl. col. 12   M
London: Collins   1986
Popular historical survey, emphasizing the Broadway musical.

**7299** LOWE, LESLIE. Directory of popular music, 1900-1980
pp.1440   HW
Droitwich: Peterson   1986
Second edition. First published 1975. Section three lists over 700 stage shows with details including theatre and opening performance.

**7300** RAMCZYK, SUZANNE M. A performance demands analysis of six major female roles of the American musical theatre
Eugene: U. of Oregon (PhD)   1986

**7301** SUSKIN, STEVEN. Show tunes 1905-1985: the songs, shows and careers of Broadway's major composers
pp.xxii, 728   HW
NY: Dodd, Mead   1986

In three generation groupings. Includes scores by other composers, a chronology of productions, and a list of collaborators.

**7302** WILDBIHLER, HUBERT & VÖLKLEIN, SONJA. The musical: an international annotated bibliography
pp.xxv, 320   M
Munich: K. G. Saur   1986

**7303** ADLER, REBA A. The dance direction of Seymour Felix on Broadway and in Hollywood from 1918 through 1953
NY: U. (PhD)   1987

**7304** EWEN, DAVID. American songwriters...a biographical dictionary
pp.xi, 489; ill. in text   HW
NY: H. W. Wilson   1987

**7305** GREEN, STANLEY. Broadway musicals show by show
pp.xix, 361; ill. in text   L
London: Faber   1987
Published Milwaukee WI: Hal Leonard, 1987. Period 1866-1985. Synopses and full credits.

**7306** SIMAS, RICK. Musicals no one came to see: a guidebook to four decades of musical-comedy casualties on Broadway, off-Broadway, and in out-of-town tryout, 1943-1983
pp.xiii, 639   L
NY: Garland   1987

**7307** STRASSER-VILL, SUSANNE & WEISS, GUNTHER (Eds). Musiktheater-ausbildung: Oper, Musical, Tanz, Technik
pp.244   M
Regensburg: Gustav Bosse   1987

**7308** WOLL, ALLEN. Black musical theatre from *Coontown* to *Dreamgirls*
pp.xix, 301; ill. in text   DL★
Baton Rouge: Louisiana State U. P.   1987

**7309** COHEN-STRATYNER, BARBARA N. Popular music, 1900-1919
  DL★
Detroit MI: Gale Research   1988

**7310** GÄNZL, KURT & LAMB, ANDREW. Gänzl's book of the musical theatre
pp.xv, 1353; pl. 16   M
London: The Bodley Head   1988
European and US. Alphabetical listing under country; production histories, characters, synopses. Indexed by title, author, composer, lyricist, song-title.

**7311** SADIE, STANLEY (Ed.). Twentieth century American masters
pp.xv, 312; ill. in text   P
London: Macmillan   1988

Revised biographical articles from Sadie, S. & Hitchcock, H. W. (Eds): *The New Grove dictionary of American music* (NY, 1986). Includes Richard Crawford & Wayne Schneider: *George Gershwin*; Joan Peyser: *Leonard Bernstein*.

**7312** SLONIMSKY, NICOLAS (Ed.). The concise Baker's biographical dictionary of composers and musicians
pp.xi, 1407 HW
NY: Simon & Schuster 1988

An abridged seventh edition. *Baker's Biographical Dictionary...* was first published in 1900 and republished six times between then and 1984.

**7313** MENDENHALL, CHRISTIAN. American musical comedy from 1943-1964: a theoretical investigation of its ritual function
Evanston: Northwestern U. (PhD) 1989

**7314** RIIS, THOMAS L. Just before jazz: black musical theatre in New York, 1890-1915
pp.xxiv, 309; ill. in text M
Washington DC: Smithsonian Institute P. 1989

**7315** BERKSON, ROBERT. Musical theater choreography
DL★
NY: Back-Stage Books 1990

**7316** CITRON, STEPHEN. The musical: from the inside out
pp.336; pl. 4 L
London: Hodder & Stoughton 1990

The process from conception to first performance.

**7317** CRAIG, DAVID. On singing onstage. The new and completely revised edition
pp.xiv, 209 M
NY: Applause 1990

First published NY: Schirmer, 1978.

**7318** SUSKIN, STEVEN. Berlin, Kern, Rodgers, Hart and Hammerstein: a complete song catalogue
pp.xxiv, 312 L
Jefferson NC: McFarland 1990

Catalogued by title, author, production if any, date, additional publication information. Foreword by Theodore S. Chapin.

## 17.2 BIOGRAPHIES

### Anderson, John Murray
### (1886-1954)
### Director

**7319** ANDERSON, J. MURRAY. Out without my rubbers. The memoirs...as told to and written by Hugh Abercrombie
pp.x, 253; pl. 5 L
NY: Library Publishers 1954

### Arlen, Harold
### [Arluck, Hyman]
### (1905-1986)
### Composer

**7320** JABLONSKI, EDWARD. Harold Arlen: happy with the blues
pp.286; pl. 16 L
Garden City: Doubleday 1961

Biography. Remembered for such songs as *I gotta right to sing the blues*, included in *Earl Carroll Vanities* 1932.

### Astaire, Fred
### (1899-1987)
### Dancer, actor

**7321** ASTAIRE, FRED. Steps in time [autobiography]
pp.xi, 338; pl.12 O
London: Heinemann 1960

**7322** GREEN, STANLEY & GOLDBLATT, BURT. Starring Fred Astaire
pp.x, 501; ill. in text L
NY: Dodd, Mead 1973

Biography, with substantial account of early stage career.

**7323** FREEDLAND, MICHAEL. Fred Astaire
pp.ii, 188; ill. in text L
London: W. H. Allen 1984

Revised edition. First published 1976.

**7324** PICKARD, ROY. Fred Astaire
pp.192; ill. in text, some col. P
London: Hamlyn 1985

**7325** GILES, SARAH (Ed.). Fred Astaire: his friends talk
pp.xiv, 210; ill. in text P
NY: Doubleday 1988

A collection of brief reminiscences.

### Barnet, Robert Ayres
### (1853-1933)
### Playwright, lyricist

**7326** ZUKERMAN, ROBERT S. Robert Ayres Barnet: American playwright and lyricist
NY: City U. (PhD) 1981

### Bennett, Michael
### [Di Figlia, Michael]
### (1943-)
### Choreographer, director

**7327** FLINN, DENNY M. What they did for love: the untold story behind the making of *A Chorus Line*
pp.213 DL★
NY: Bantam 1989

**7328** MANDELBAUM, KEN. *A Chorus Line* and the musicals of Michael Bennett
pp.352; ill. ★
NY: St Martin's P. 1989

**7329** KELLY, KEVIN. One singular sensation: the Michael Bennett story
pp.352; ill. DL★
NY: Doubleday 1990

**7330** VIAGAS, ROBERT; WALSH, THOMMIE & BAAYROK, LEE. On the line: the creation of *A Chorus Line*
pp.366 DL★
NY: William Morrow 1990

## Berkeley, Busby
### [Enos, William Berkeley]
### (1895-1976)
### Choreographer, producer

**7331** PIKE, BOB & MARTIN, DAVID. The genius of Busby Berkeley
pp.194; ill.      DL★
Reseda CA: CFS      1973

**7332** THOMAS, TONY & TERRY, JIM. The Busby Berkeley book. Foreword by Ruby Keeler
pp.192; ill. in text      MH
Greenwich CT: NY Graphic Society      1973

## Berlin, Irving
### [Baline, Israel]
### (1888-1989)

**7333** WOOLLCOTT, ALEXANDER. The story of Irving Berlin
pp.viii, 237; pl. 16      M
NY: G. P. Putnam's Sons      1925

**7334** EWEN, DAVID. The story of Irving Berlin
pp.viii, 179; ill. in text      MB
NY: Henry Holt      1950
Illustrated by Jane Castle.

**7335** FARBERMAN, BORIS. Irving Berlin
pp.32; front.      L
Buenos Aires: Congreso Judío Mundial      1969

**7336** SALSINI, BARBARA. Irving Berlin, master composer of twentieth century songs
pp.32      DL★
Charlotteville NY: SamHar P.      1972

**7337** FREEDLAND, MICHAEL. A salute to Irving Berlin
pp.ix, 316; pl. 8      L
London: W. H. Allen      1986
Biography. Second edition, enlarged. First published 1974 as *Irving Berlin*.

**7338** BERGREEN, LAURENCE. As thousands cheer: the life of Irving Berlin
pp.xiv, 658; front., pl. 16      M
London: Hodder & Stoughton      1990

## Bernstein, Leonard
### (1918-1990)
### Composer

**7339** EWEN, DAVID. Leonard Bernstein
pp.175; pl.2      O
London: W. H. Allen      1967
Published US, Radnor PA: Chilton, 1960.

**7340** GRUEN, JOHN. The private world of Leonard Bernstein
pp.191; ill. in text      L
NY: Viking P.      1968

## Bland, James
### (1854-1911)
### Songwriter

**7341** DALY, JOHN J. A song in his heart
pp.ix, 102; ill. in text      L
Philadelphia: John C. Winston      1951

Biography. Introduction by Harry F. Byrd.

## Blitzstein, Marc
### (1905-1964)
### Composer

**7342** TALLEY, PAUL M. Social criticism in the original theatre librettos of Marc Blitzstein
Madison: U. of Wisconsin (PhD)      1965

**7343** THE WISCONSIN CENTER for Theatre Research of the University of Wisconsin presents an exhibition of the Marc Blitzstein papers [cover title]
pp.[20]      M
[Madison]: U. of Wisconsin      1965
Catalogue. Preface by Aaron Copland. Includes inventory of the Blitzstein archive.

## Bock, Jerrold Lewis 'Jerry'
### (1928-)
### Composer

**7344** KELLY, FRANCIS P. The musical plays of Jerry Bock and Sheldon Harnick
Lawrence: U. of Kansas (PhD)      1978

## Brice, Fanny
### [Borach, Fanny]
### (1891-1951)
### Singer, comedienne

**7345** KATKOV, NORMAN. The fabulous Fanny: the story of Fanny Brice
pp.xiii, 337; pl. 4      M
NY: Alfred A. Knopf      1953

**7346** GROSSMAN, BARBARA. Fanny Brice
Medford MA: Tufts U. (PhD)      1985

## Burrows, Abe
### [Borowitz, Abram Solman]
### (1910-)
### Librettist, director

**7347** BURROWS, ABE. Honest Abe. Is there really no business like show business? [autobiography]
pp.vii, 369; pl. 12      L
Boston: Little, Brown      1980
Librettist and/or co-author of, e.g., *Guys and Dolls* (1950), *Silk Stockings* (1955), *Can-Can* (1953), *How to Succeed in Business without really Trying* (1961), *Cactus Flower* (1965).

## Cahn, Sammy
### (1913-1993)
### Songwriter

**7348** CAHN, SAMMY. I should care: the Sammy Cahn story [autobiography]
pp.xii, 253; pl. 8      L
London: W. H.Allen      1975

## Calloway, Cab
### (1907-)
### Musician, singer

**7349** CALLOWAY, CAB & ROLLINS, BRYANT. Of Minnie the Moocher and me [autobiography]
pp.282; ill.      DL★
NY: Thomas Y. Crowell      1976

## Champion, Gower
### (1920-1980)
### Dancer, director, choreographer

**7350** PAYNE-CARTER, DAVID. Gower Champion and the American musical theatre
NY: U. (PhD)     1987

## Cohan, George Michael
### (1878-1942)
### Producer, director, actor, playwright, song-writer

**7351** COHAN, GEORGE M. Twenty years on Broadway and the years it took to get there. The true story of a trouper's life from the cradle to the 'closed shop'
pp.vii, 264; pl. 8     M
NY: Harper     1925

**7352** MOREHOUSE, WARD. George M. Cohan: prince of the American theater
pp.240; pl. 8     M
Philadelphia: J. B. Lippincott     1942

**7353** MARTIN, CAROL L. A historical study of George M. Cohan and his contribution to American musical theatre
Los Angeles: U. of Southern California (PhD)     1964

**7354** WINDERS, GERTRUDE. George M. Cohan: boy theater genius
pp.200; col. pls.     DL★
Indianapolis: Bobbs-Merrill     1968
Intended for children.

**7355** McCABE, JOHN H. George M. Cohan: the man who owned Broadway
pp.xii, 296; pl. 12     M
Garden City NY: Doubleday     1973
Biography, with a chronology of Cohan's plays and productions.

**7356** GLANN, FRANK W. An historical and critical evaluation of the plays of George M. Cohan, 1901-1920
Bowling Green: State U. (PhD)     1976

**7357** VALLILLO, STEPHEN M. George M. Cohan, director
NY: U. (PhD)     1987

## De Koven, Reginald
### [De Koven, Henry Louis]
### (1859-1920)
### Composer

**7358** DE KOVEN, ANNA F. A musician and his wife [biography]
pp.viii, 259; pl.24     O
NY: Harper     1926

## Dietz, Howard
### (1898-1983)
### Lyricist, librettist

**7359** DIETZ, HOWARD. Dancing in the dark. Words by Howard Dietz [autobiography]
pp.xiii, 370; ill. in text     L
NY: Quadrangle     1974
Foreword by Alan Jay Lerner.

## Duke, Vernon
### [Dukelsky, Vladimir]
### (1903-1969)
### Composer

**7360** DUKE, VERNON. Passport to Paris [autobiography]
pp.502; ill.     DL★
Boston: Little, Brown     1955

## Dunbar, Paul Laurence
### (1872-1906)
### Librettist, lyricist, poet

**7361** METCALF, E. W. Paul Laurence Dunbar: a bibliography
pp.ix, 193     DL★
Metuchen NJ: Scarecrow P.     1975

**7362** REVELL, PETER. Paul Laurence Dunbar
pp.197; ill. in text     MH
Boston: Twayne     1979

## Duncan, Robert Todd
### (1903-)
### Singer

**7363** JOHNSON, MARK. Robert Duncan
    DL★
NY: Twayne     1988
Created the role of Porgy (1935) under his stage name Todd Duncan.

## Engel, Lehman
### (1910-1982)
### Composer, critic

**7364** ENGEL, LEHMAN. This bright day: an autobiography
pp.xv, 366; ill. in text     M
NY: Macmillan     1974

**7365** COCCHI, JEANETTE F. Lehman Engel's criteria for libretti as applied to four musical adaptations of Shakespeare's plays on the Broadway stage
NY: U. (PhD)     1983

**7366** KENNEDY, WILLIAM B. Rhyme and reason: an evaluation of Lehman Engel's contribution to the criticism of musical theatre
Kent OH: State U. (PhD)     1987

## Fosse, Robert Louis (Bob)
### (1927-1987)
### Choreographer, director

**7367** GARGARO, KENNETH V. The work of Bob Fosse and the choreographer-directors in the translation of musicals to the screen
Pittsburgh: U. (PhD)     1979

**7368** SLOAN, RONNA E. Bob Fosse: an analytic critical study
NY: City U. (PhD)     1982

**7369** GRUBB, KEVIN. Razzle dazzle: the life and work of Bob Fosse
pp.292     DL★
NY: St Martin's P.     1989

**7370** GOTTFRIED, MARTIN. All his jazz: the life and death of Bob Fosse
pp.496; ill.     ★
NY: Bantam Books     1990

## Gershwin, George
## [Gershvin, Jacob]
## (1898-1937)
## Composer

## Gershwin, Ira
## [Gershvin, Israel]
## (1896-1983)
## Lyricist

**7371** GOLDBERG, ISAAC. George Gershwin: a study in American music
pp.xi, 305; front., pl. 8      L
NY: Simon & Schuster      1931

**7372** ARMITAGE, MERLE (Ed.). George Gershwin
pp.x, 252; ill. in text      MB
NY: Longmans, Green      1938
A *collage* of memoirs, tributes and assessments by 37 contributors.

**7373** EWEN, DAVID. A journey to greatness: the life and music of George Gershwin
pp.255; pl. 6      MB
London: W. H. Allen      1956
A revised version (not seen) was published NY: 1970 under the title: *George Gershwin: his journey to greatness*.

**7374** JABLONSKI, EDWARD & STEWART, LAWRENCE D. The Gershwin years
pp.313; ill. in text      M
Garden City: Doubleday      1958
Introduction by Carl Van Vechten. A revised edition (not seen) was published London: Robson, 1974.

**7375** GERSHWIN, IRA. Lyrics on several occasions: a selection of stage and screen lyrics to which have been added many informative disquisitions on their why and wherefore...and matters associative
pp.xvi, 362, ix      L
NY: Alfred A. Knopf      1959

**7376** A CATALOGUE of the exhibition *Gershwin George the music/Ira the words*
pp.ii, 30; ill. in text      M
NY: Museum of the City of New York      1968

**7377** GERSHWIN on film: a retrospective of eleven motion pictures featuring the music of America's beloved composer
pp.[23] inc. wrappers; ill. in text      M
NY: Playbill Magazine      1973
An issue of *Playbill* devoted to the screening sponsored by New York Cultural Center and the I. A. M.

**7378** KIMBALL, ROBERT & SIMON, ALFRED. The Gershwins
pp.xliii, 292; ill. in text      L
London: Jonathan Cape      1974
Brief biographical introduction. Chronology of shows, with songs. Alphabetical listing of songs. Discography of original and re-created recordings. Piano rollography.

**7379** SCHWARTZ, CHARLES. Gershwin: his life and music
pp.xiv, 427; ill. in text      L
NY: DaCapo P.      1979
First published NY: Bobbs Merrill. 1973.

**7380** JABLONSKI, EDWARD. Gershwin
pp.xvii, 436; pl. 20      M
NY: Simon & Schuster      1987

**7381** KENDALL, ALAN. George Gershwin: a biography
pp.192; pl 16      L
London: Harrap      1987

## Hammerstein II, Oscar
## (1895-1960)
## Lyricist

**7382** SALUTE to a cockeyed optimist: Oscar Hammerstein II. University of Southern California 4 April 1971
pp.23; front.      M
Los Angeles: Friends of the U.S.C. Libraries      1972
Script of a televised tribute.

**7383** FORDIN, HUGH. Getting to know him: a biography of Oscar Hammerstein II
pp.395      ★
NY: Random House      1977
Introduction by Stephen Sondheim.

## Harris, Charles K.
## (1865-1930)
## Composer

**7384** HARRIS, CHARLES K. After the ball: forty years of melody. An autobiography
pp.376; ill.      DL★
NY: Frank Maurice      1926

## Hart, Lorenz Milton
## (1895-1943)
## Lyricist

**7385** THE HART of the matter: a celebration of Lorenz Hart: Honorary Chairman, Mr Richard Rodgers, September 30, 1973
pp.ii, 44; front.      MH
Los Angeles: U. of South California      1973
A transcription of the evening's tributes. Participants included Henry Fonda, Adolph Green, Gene Kelly, Donald O'Connor.

**7386** HART, DOROTHY. Thou swell, thou witty: the life and lyrics of Lorenz Hart
pp.xi, 254      M
London: Elm Tree      1978

## Herbert, Victor
## (1859-1924)
## Composer

**7387** WATERS, EDWARD N. Victor Herbert: a life in music
pp.xvii, 653; front.      M
NY: Macmillan      1955

## Hopper, De Wolf
## [Hopper, William D'Wolf]
## (1858-1935)
## Singer

**7388** HOPPER, DeWOLF & STOUT, WESLEY W. Once a clown, always a clown: reminiscences...
pp.x, 238; pl. 16      M
Boston: Little, Brown      1927

### Johnson, James Weldon
### (1871-1938)
### Johnson, John Rosamond
### (1873-1954)
### Songwriters

7389  JOHNSON, JAMES W.  Along this way: the autobiography
pp.ix, 418; front., pl 15                L
NY: Viking P.                1933

Substantial contributor to the black musical theatre in the first decade of the twentieth century, initially in a songwriting collaboration with his brother, John. He later abandoned the theatre for a career as a poet, essayist and diplomat.

### Jolson, Al
### [Yoelson, Asa]
### (1886-1950)
### Singer, entertainer

7390  JOLSON, HARRY.  Mistah Johnson...as told to Alban Emley
pp.257; pl. 7                MH
Hollywood: House-Warven           1951

Biography by Al Jolson's brother.

7391  FREEDLAND, MICHAEL.  Al Jolson
pp.318; pl. 8                O
London: W. H. Allen             1972

Published NY: Stein and Day, 1972. Biography.

7392  GOLDMAN, HERBERT G.  Jolson: the legend comes to life
pp.xii, 411; pl. 8             M
NY: Oxford U. P.            1988

### Kern, Jerome David
### (1885-1945)
### Composer

7393  EWEN, DAVID.  The world of Jerome Kern: a biography. Illustrated with photographs
pp.xiii, 178; pl. 8            L
NY: Holt, Rinehart & Winston      1960

Revised edition. First published NY: Henry Holt, 1953 as *The Story of Jerome Kern*.

7394  FREEDLAND, MICHAEL.  Jerome Kern
pp.v, 182; pl. 4             M
London: Robson             1978

7395  BORDMAN, GERALD.  Jerome Kern: his life and music
pp.ix, 438; ill. in text, pl. 8      M
NY: Oxford U. P.           1980

7396  LAMB, ANDREW.  Jerome Kern in Edwardian London
pp.x, 86; pl.6              M
NY: Brooklyn College, Conservatory of Music   1985

Second, revised edition. First published by the author, 1981.

### Kitt, Eartha
### (1930-)
### Singer

7397  KITT, EARTHA.  I'm still here [autobiography]
pp.viii, 280; pl. 12          L
London: Sidgwick & Jackson      1989

### Lerner, Alan Jay
### (1918-1986)
### Lyricist, librettist

7398  LERNER, ALAN JAY.  *My Fair Lady*.  A musical play in two acts, based on *Pygmalion* by Bernard Shaw. Adaptation and lyrics by Alan Jay Lerner. Illustrated by Cecil Beaton
pp.ix, 156; ill. in text        M
London: Max Reinhardt/ Constable   1958

Thirteen full page drawings of the cast.

7399  LERNER, ALAN JAY.  The street where I live: the story of *My Fair Lady*, *Gigi* and *Camelot*.
pp.303; pl. 16              M
London: Hodder & Stoughton    1978

### Levant, Oscar
### (1906-1972)
### Musician, actor

7400  LEVANT, OSCAR.  A smattering of ignorance
189                      DL★
Garden City: Doubleday        1959

Reminiscences. Includes reference to Harpo Marx, George Gershwin.

7401  LEVANT, OSCAR.  The memoirs of an amnesiac
pp.320                 MH
NY: G. P. Putnam's Sons        1965

### Loesser, Frank Henry
### (1910-1969)
### Composer

7402  MANN, MARTIN A.  The musicals of Frank Loesser
NY: City U. (PhD)            1974

### Martin, Mary Virginia
### (1913-1990)
### Singer, actress

7403  NEWMAN, SHIRLEE P.  Mary Martin on stage
pp.126; ill. in text            MH
Philadelphia: Westminster P.    1969

Intended for children.

7404  MARTIN, MARY.  My heart belongs [autobiography]
pp.320; ill. in text           M
London: W. H. Allen          1977

### Merman, Ethel
### [Zimmerman, Ethel]
### (1908-1984)
### Singer

7405  MERMAN, ETHEL.  Don't call me madam [autobiography]
pp.vii, 215; ill. in text, pl. 4     L
London: W. H. Allen          1955

7406  MERMAN, ETHEL & MARTIN, PETE.  Who could ask for anything more [autobiography]
pp.252                  L
Garden City: Doubleday        1955

## 17.2. BIOGRAPHIES

**7407** MERMAN, ETHEL & EELLS, GEORGE. Merman [autobiography]
pp.320; pl. 8 M
NY: Simon & Schuster 1978

**7408** THOMAS, BOB. I've got rhythm: the Ethel Merman story
pp.239 L
NY: G. P. Putnam's Sons 1985

**7409** DIENSTFREY, SHERRI R. Ethel Merman: queen of musical comedy
Kent OH: State U. (PhD) 1986

### Morgan, Helen
### (1900-1941)
### Actress, singer

**7410** MAXWELL, GILBERT. Helen Morgan: her life and legend
pp.192; pl. 9 DL★
NY: Hawthorn 1975

### Nielson, Alice
### (1876-1943)
### Singer

**7411** MISS ALICE NIELSEN in *The Fortune Teller* and *The Singing Girl*. Edition de luxe. Souvenir published by arrangement with Mr Frank L. Perley
pp.13; ill. in text DL★
Washington DC: R. G. Graerin 1899

### Porter, Cole Albert
### (1891-1964)
### Songwriter

**7412** EWEN, DAVID. The Cole Porter story
pp.192; front. DL★
NY: Holt, Rinehart & Winston 1965

**7413** EELLS, GEORGE. The life that late he led: a biography of Cole Porter
pp.383; pl. 8 M
London: W. H. Allen 1967

**7414** THE LIFE THAT HE LED
pp.43 ★
Los Angeles: U. of California, Friends of the Libraries 1967
Commemorative program for Cole Porter, 12 Feb.

**7415** KIMBALL, ROBERT (Ed.). Cole: a biographical essay by Brendan Gill
pp.xix, 283; ill. in text L
London: Michael Joseph 1971
Introductory biographical sketch precedes a 'scrapbook' coverage of songs, shows and events arranged by decades.

**7416** SCHWARTZ, CHARLES. Cole Porter: a biography
pp.xvii, 365; pl. 8 L
London: W. H. Allen 1978

**7417** SMITH, CAROLINE J. Cole Porter's ironic vision: a study of the lyrics, 1909-1958
Berkeley: U. of California (PhD) 1984

### Powers, James T.
### [McGovern, James T.]
### (1862-1943)
### Comedian

**7418** POWERS, JAMES T. Twinkle little star: sparkling memories of seventy years. With a foreword by Charles H. Towne
pp.379; col. front., pl. 31 M
NY: G. P. Putnam's Sons 1939
After experience in vaudeville and broad comedy, particularly with the Casino Theatre, became associated in the 1890s with the US staging of the English Gaiety musicals.

### Prince, Harold Smith
### (1928-)
### Director, producer

**7419** HIRSCH, FOSTER. Harold Prince and the American musical theatre
pp.xvii, 187; ill. in text M
Cambridge: U. P. 1989
Forewords by Harold Prince and Stephen Sondheim.

**7420** ILSON, CAROL. Harold Prince: from *Pajama Game* to *Phantom of the Opera*
DL★
Ann Arbor: UMI Research P. 1989

### Rice, Edward Everett
### (1848-1924)
### Producer

**7421** EDWARD E. RICE'S testimonial in celebration of his forty years in management tendered by members of his companies and other friends Sunday October 28, 1917. 1877-1917. Raymond Hitchcock's 44th Street Theatre.
pp.[36]; ill. in text MB
NY: Kane P. [1917]
Comprises a biographical sketch, a list of artistes associated with Rice over the years, an alphabetical list of Rice productions with details, and illustrations of the testimonial performance, itself a retrospective.

### Rodgers, Richard Charles
### (1902-1979)
### Composer

**7422** TAYLOR, DEEMS. Some enchanted evenings: the story of Rodgers and Hammerstein
pp.195; pl. 24 L
NY: Harper & Brothers 1953

**7423** GREEN, STANLEY. The Rodgers and Hammerstein story
pp.188; pl. 4 L
NY: John Day 1963

**7424** KISLAN, RICHARD J. Nine musical plays of Rodgers and Hammerstein: a critical study in content and form
NY: U (PhD) 1969

**7425** RODGERS, RICHARD. Musical stages: an autobiography
pp.vii, 341; ill. in text, pl. 8 M
NY: Random House 1975

**7426** A CATALOG of theatrical properties offered to professional and amateur production groups by the Rodgers and Hammerstein Library
pp.31; ill. in text M
NY: Rodgers & Hammerstein Library 1976
A list of 'dramatico-musical' works available for performance.

**7427** MARX, SAMUEL & CLAYTON, JAN. Rodgers and Hart: bewitched, bothered and bedevilled
pp.287; pl. 8     M
London: W. H. Allen     1977
Biography of the partnership.

**7428** RODGERS, DOROTHY. A personal book [autobiography]
pp.xvi, 189; ill. in text     M
NY: Harper & Row     1977

**7429** NOLAN, FREDERICK. The sound of their music: the story of Rodgers and Hammerstein
pp.272; ill. in text     M
London: J. M. Dent     1978

**7430** GREEN, STANLEY (Ed.). Rodgers and Hammerstein: fact book. A record of their works together and with other collaborators
pp.x, 772, 32; ill. in text     M
NY: Lynn Farnol     1980
Chronology of shows, with credits, stage and film histories, and a selection of critical reviews. Bibliography amd listing of songs. Revised and enlarged edition of *Richard Rodgers fact book*, NY: Lynn Farnol, 1968.

**7431** RICHARD RODGERS: a checklist of his published songs
pp.25; ill. in text     L
NY: Public Library at Lincoln Center     1984
Catalogue of exhibition *Music by Richard Rodgers*.

**7432** TAYLOR, BETTY S,. An analysis of the script and score of *Oklahoma!*: a prototypical musical play
NY: City U. (PhD)     1985

**7433** RODGERS, RICHARD. Letters to Dorothy. Excerpts edited by William W. Appleton, with a foreword by Dorothy Rodgers
pp.xiii, 253; ill. in text     P
NY: Public Library     1988
276 numbered copies, 26 signed by Dorothy Rodgers.

**7434** EVANS, LAURIE J. Rodgers and Hammerstein's *Oklahoma!*: the development of the 'integrated musical'
Los Angeles: U. of California (PhD)     1990

### Russell, Lillian
### [Leonard, Helen Louise]
### (1861-1922)
### Singer

**7435** MORELL, PARKER. Lillian Russell: the era of plush
pp.xii, 319; pl. 9     M
NY: Random House     1940
Compare Lillian Russell's reminiscences, published in *Cosmopolitan* magazine, February - September, 1922.

**7436** BURKE, JOHN [= O'Connor, Richard]. Duet in diamonds: the flamboyant saga of Lillian Russell and Diamond Jim Brady in America's gilded age
pp.286; pl. 4     M
NY: G. P. Putnam's Sons     1972

**7437** RATHER, LOIS. Two lillies in America: Lillian Russell and Lillie Langtry
pp.87; ill.
Oakland CA: Rather P.     DL★     1973

### Short, Hubert Hassard
### (1877-1956)
### Director, designer

**7438** SEDERHOLM, JACK P. The musical directing career and stagecraft contributions of Hassard Short, 1919-1952
Detroit: Wayne State U. (PhD)     1974

### Sissle, Noble
### (1889-1975)
### Blake, James Hubert ('Eubie')
### (1883-1983)
### Composers, songwriters

**7439** ROSE, AL. Eubie Blake
    DL★
NY: Schirmer Books     1979

**7440** KIMBALL, ROBERT & BALCOM, WILLIAM. Reminiscing with Sissle and Blake
pp.256; ill. in text     L
NY: Viking     1973
Memoir of the musical partnership that created, e.g., *Shuffle Along* (1921).

### Smith, Harry Bache
### (1860-1936)
### Lyricist, librettist

**7441** SMITH, HARRY B. First nights and first editions [autobiography]
pp.x,325; pl 22     M
Boston: Little, Brown     1931
Foreword by William L. Phelps.

**7442** FRIEDMAN, ROBERT. The contributions of Harry Bache Smith to American musical theatre
NY: U. (PhD)     1976

### Sondheim, Stephen Joshua
### (1930-)
### Composer-lyricist

**7443** ADAMS, MICHAEL C. The lyrics of Stephen Sondheim: form and function
Evanston: Northwestern U. (PhD)     1980

**7444** CARTMELL, DAN J. Stephen Sondheim and the concept musical
Santa Barbara: U. of California (PhD)     1983

**7445** ORCHARD, LEE F. Stephen Sondheim and the disintegration of the American Dream: a study of the work of Stephen Sondheim from *Company* to *Sunday in the Park with George*
Eugene: U. of Oregon (PhD)     1988

**7446** GORDON, JOANNE. Art isn't easy: the achievement of Stephen Sondheim
pp.336; ill.     DL★
Carbondale: Southern Illinois U. P.     1990

**7447** ZADAN, CRAIG. Sondheim and co.
pp.viii, 454; ill. in text     L
London: Nick Hern     1990
Third edition, revised and enlarged. First published NY: Macmillan, 1974.

### Sousa, John Philip
### (1854-1932)
### Composer

7448 SOUSA, JOHN P. Marching along: recollections of men, women and music [autobiography]
pp.xv, 384; front., pl. 35     L
Boston: Hale, Cushman & Flint     1928

### Styne, Jule
### [Stein, Julius Kerwin]
### (1905-)
### Composer

7449 TAYLOR, THEODORE. Jule: the story of composer Jule Styne
pp.ix, 293; front., pl.4     L
NY: Random House     1979

### Tucker, Sophie
### [Kalish, Sonia]
### (1884-1966)
### Singer

7450 TUCKER, SOPHIE. Some of these days: an autobiography
pp.293; front.     M
London: Hammond     1951

First published Garden City: Doubleday, 1945.

### Vallee, Rudy
### (1901-1986)
### Singer, actor

7451 VALLEE, RUDY & McKEAN, GIL. My time is your time: the story of Rudy Vallee
pp.viii, 244     MH★
NY: Obolensky     1962

7452 VALLEE, RUDY & with McKEAN, GIL. Let the chips fall [autobiography]
pp.320; ill.     DL★
Harrisburg PA: Stackpole Books     1975

### Weber, Joseph Morris
### (1867-1942)
### Fields, Lew
### [Shanfield, Lewis Maurice]
### (1867-1941)
### Producers

7453 ISMAN, FELIX. Weber and Fields: their tribulations, triumphs and their associates
pp.345; pl. 32     M
NY: Boni & Liveright     1924

Includes music and lyrics of a selection of their songs.

### Wilbur, Richard
### Librettist

7454 FIELD, JOHN P. Richard Wilbur: a bibliographical checklist
pp.x, 85     O
Kent OH: Kent State U. P.     1971

Lyricist for Leonard Bernstein's *Candide* (1956); adaptations include Molière's *Le Misanthrope* and *Tartuffe*. Wilbur himself contributes a note.

### Willson, Meredith
### [Reiniger, Robert Meredith]
### (1902-1984)
### Composer, musician

7455 WILLSON, MEREDITH. 'But he doesn't know the territory'
pp.190     L
NY: G. P. Putnam's Sons     1959

A production history by the author/composer of *The Music Man* (Majestic Theatre, December 19, 1957).

### Wodehouse, Pelham Grenville
### (1881-1975)
### Novelist, lyricist

7456 WODEHOUSE, P. G. & BOLTON, GUY. Bring on the girls: the improbable story of our life in musical comedy, with pictures to prove it
pp.248; pl. 8     M
London: Herbert Jenkins     1954

Respectively lyricist and librettist, collaborating with Jerome Kern to produce a string of successful musicals.

7457 JASEN, DAVID A. The theatre of P. G. Wodehouse
pp.120; ill. in text     M
London: Batsford     1979

A listing, with credits and including revivals.

### Youmans, Vincent Millie
### (1898-1946)
### Composer

7458 BORDMAN, GERALD. Days to be happy, years to be sad: the life and works of Vincent Youmans
pp.xii, 266; pl. 8     L
NY: Oxford U. P.     1982

## 18. MUSIC IN THEATRE

7459 VERNON, GRENVILLE (Ed.). Yankee doodle-do: a collection of songs of the early American stage
pp.165; ill.     DL★
NY: Payson & Clarke     [1927]

7460 ALBRIGHT, HARRY D. The theory and staging of musical drama
Ithaca: Cornell U. (PhD)     1936

7461 BURTON, MAY E. A study of music as an integral part of the spoken drama in the American professional theatre, 1930-1955
Gainesville: U. of Florida (PhD)     1957

7462 MOLNAR, JOHN W. (Ed.). Songs from the Williamsburg Theatre. A selection of fifty songs performed on the stage in Williamsburg in the eighteenth century arranged for voice and keyboard and with introduction and historical commentaries...
pp.xix, 226     M
Williamsburg: Colonial Williamsburg Foundation     1972

Foreword by Carleton Sprague Smith.

7463 ROOTE, DEANE L. American popular stage music, 1860-1880
pp.x, 284; ill. in text     L
Ann Arbor: UMI Research P.     1981

Describes children's operettas, plays with music, spectacles, US operettas, foreign operettas in the US.

7464 FREZZA, CHRISTINE A. Music as an integral design element of theatrical production
Pittsburgh: U. (PhD)     1982

# D. INDEXES
## SUBJECT INDEX

Abbey, Henry E. 3259–3260
Abbott, George 6145–6146
Actor families 3015, 3043
Actor's Workshop 2813
Actors Equity Association 2814
Actors' Equity 216, 1085, 2816, 3808
Actors' Equity Association 2815
Actors Fund 236
Actors' Fund of America 2820–2822
Actors' Laboratory Theatre 2823
Actors Protective Union 2817
Actors Studio 2818–2819
Actors Theatre of Louisville 2000
Actors theatre of Louisville 6116
Adams, Edwin 3025, 3159
Adams, Maude 1445, 2994, 2996, 3001, 3007, 3011–3012, 3021, 3023–3024, 3261–3266
Addams, Jane 3269
Ade, George 1445, 3182, 6147–6152
Adler, Dankmar 3270–3272
Adler, Stella 3273
Aiken, George L. 1475
Albaugh, John W. 2294
Albee, E. F. 2503
Albee, Edward 1646, 3235, 4676, 4690, 5392, 5620, 5684, 5694, 5698, 5700, 5915, 5917, 5919, 5931, 5934, 5939, 5950, 5979, 5989, 6073, 6079–6083, 6085, 6089, 6099, 6101–6102, 6107, 6111, 6125, 6128, 6153–6185, 6187–6193
Alexander technique 943, 994, 998, 1051
Alexander, F. M. 943
Alexander, Jane 1036
Alger, William Rouseville [Rounseville] 126
Allan, Alexander 2970
Allen, Alfred R. 2596
Allen, Andrew Jackson 717
Allen, Fred 3048
Allen, Gracie 4819
Allen, Viola 2994, 3005, 3007, 3012, 3277
Alton, Robert 7289
Amateur Comedy Club 2824
Amateur Players of New York 3200
Amend, Karle O. 3278
American civil war drama 82
American College Theatre Festival 1319, 5061
American Company 1407
American company 6411
American Conservatory Theatre 2825, 6116
American Dramatic Fund 2826
American Dramatists Club 174, 2827
American Laboratory Theatre 2828, 5588
American National Theatre and Academy 2829–2830

American Opera Company 4041
American Place Theatre 2831
American Repertory Theatre 2131, 2832
American Shakespeare Festival Theatre 1852
American Theater Wing 1524, 1622
American Theatre Association 5081
Amerindian drama 7, 40, 695, 699, 1029, 1268, 1330, 1340, 1361, 1377, 1417, 1664, 1666, 1671, 1674, 1680, 1916, 2481, 2726, 5698
Ames, A. D. 5445
Ames, Winthrop 3024, 3279
Anderson, Eleanor Copenhaver 6226
Anderson, John Murray 4809
Anderson, Mary 2321, 2502, 2507, 2975, 2978, 2989, 3010, 3280–3282, 3286
Anderson, Maxwell 4676, 5834, 5852, 5919, 5939, 6060, 6064, 6074, 6079–6080, 6195–6197, 6199–6207, 6209–6218, 7006
Anderson, Robert 5979, 6219–6221
Anderson, Sherwood 6099, 6222–6223, 6225–6226, 6452
Andreini, J. M. 4521
Andrews, George H. 3127
Andrews, Regina M. 6100
Anglin, Margaret 2098, 2994, 3007, 3012, 3179, 3192, 3287–3288, 4045
Anisfeld, Boris 3289–3292
Anouilh, Jean 6046
Appia, Adolphe 7246
Arbuckle, Maclyn 3006
Ardrey, Robert 6227
Arena stage 6116
Arena Stage, Washington 440
Arlen, Harold 7320
Arliss, George 4415
Armbruster Scenic Studios 2545
Armstrong, Will Steven 632
Aronson, Boris 3296–3298
Arthur, Julia 2994
Artists' Theatre of New York 2453
Ashley, Minnie 7205
Asolo Theatre 1869
Association of Producing Artists 2390
Astaire, Fred 853, 3050, 7322–7325
Atkins, Zoe 5357
Atkinson, Brooks 3301
Atkinson, Fred. W. 140
Austin, Mary Hunter 6228
Autonomous theater 1367
Ayers, Lemuel 3302

Bacall, Lauren 3122
Bacon, Frank 3304
Baddeley, Hermione 7133

Baker, Alexina Fisher 2970
Baker, George L. 3308
Baker, George Pierce 3310–3313, 4960, 6893
Baker, Josephine 4810, 4812–4814
Balanchine, George 7289
Baldwin, James 5694, 5915, 5936, 5950, 5955, 6082, 6087, 6092, 6099, 6105, 6108, 6229–6241
Ball, Lucille 3314
Ball, William 3316
Ballard, Lucinda 3317
Bancroft, Anne 893
Bankhead, Tallulah 3048, 3051, 3320–3325
Bannard, John 2970
Baraka, Imamu Amiri 1373, 5392, 5518, 5700, 5705, 5915, 5923, 5936, 5950, 5955–5956, 6082, 6087, 6089, 6092–6093, 6099, 6105, 6108, 6111–6112, 6115, 6117, 6242–6255
Barker, J. N. 5359
Barker, James Nelson 6256–6258
Barnabee, Henry Clay 3326, 7206
Barnes, Djuna 6260–6262
Barnes, John 3127, 3147
Barnet, Robert Ayres 7326
Barras, Charles 3009
Barrett, Lawrence 2502, 2980, 2982, 3010, 3021, 3327–3331, 3445, 4517, 5314
Barrett, Mrs George 2989
Barrett, Wilson 2928
Barry, Eleanor 119
Barry, Philip 5359, 6060, 6080, 6110, 6132, 6263–6269
Barry, Thomas 3147
Barry, William 3159
Barrymore, Ethel 1490, 2507, 2996, 3012, 3032, 3058, 3335, 3342, 3347, 6050
Barrymore, Georgia Drew 2981
Barrymore, John 1268, 3035, 3066–3067, 3094, 3209, 3214, 3230, 3335–3337, 3341, 3343–3346, 3348, 3350, 3929, 3952, 6391
Barrymore, Lionel 3254
Barrymore, Maurice 2987, 3349
Barrymore, Mrs John 3256
Barton Opera House 1787
Barton, Andrew 5736
Barton, Lucy 3352
Basshe, Em Jo 5851
Bateman, Ellen 3353
Bates Theatre 3979
Bates, Blanche 2994, 3021
Bates, Marie 3005
Bay, Howard 3354
Beatty, Lambert F. 1700
Beaudet, Louise 2981
Beck, Julian 2895, 6112
Becks, George 127, 130–131, 3355
Behrman, S. N. 3989, 5847, 5852, 6060, 6110, 6132, 6209, 6271–6272, 6274, 6276–6281

Bel Geddes, Norman 396, 636, 665, 713, 3357, 3359–3364
Belafonte, Harry 3365
Belasco Theatre 1786
Belasco, David 519, 1078, 1378, 1448, 1744, 2507, 3040, 3366–3368, 3370–3378, 3557, 3952, 4625, 4676, 4886, 5317, 5590, 6118, 6491
Belasco, Frederick 3379
Bell, Digby 7206
Bellew, Kyrle 2987, 2996, 4310
Bellow, Saul 374, 6282–6288
Bellows, Henry W. 278, 282, 3153
Bellows, Walter C. 116
Benchley, Robert 3221, 3237, 3381–3382
Bennett, Michael 7296, 7328–7329
Bennett, Richard 3383
Benny, Jack 3048, 3051, 3088, 4819
Bentley, Eric 3385, 4612
Bentley, Walter E. 3386
Berezin, Tanya 2466
Berger, William 2908
Bergere, Valerie 3007
Bergman, Robert 641
Berkeley, Busby 7242, 7331–7332
Berlin, Irving 1523, 4794, 7285, 7318, 7333–7338
Berman, Eugene 3388–3398
Berman, Max 157
Bernard, John 2295, 3399, 3401
Berne, Eric 1007
Bernhardt, Sarah 3104, 4418
Bernstein, Aline 713, 3403–3405
Bernstein, Leonard 7311, 7340, 7454
Bidwell, David 2048
Bidwell, Dollie 4086
Bieber, Albert A. 5370
Biencourt, Jean de 5713
Bingham, Amelia 3005, 3007
Bird, Robert Montgomery 5359, 6289, 6291–6294
Bishop, Anna 2970
Bispham, David 3004
Björnson, Björnstjerne 6000
Black Theatre Alliance 2833–2834
Blair, John 3006
Blake, Eubie 7439
Blake, William Rufus 3002
Blinn, Holbrook 3407
Blisset, Francis 3127
Blitzstein, Marc 7342–7343
Bloomgarten, Kermit 3409
Blum, Daniel 148
Bock, Jerry 7344
Bodenheim, Maxwell 6295–6296, 6452
Boesing, Martha 6297
Bohemian Club 2835–2836
Boker, G. H. 5359
Boker, George Henry 6298–6299
Boleslavsky, Richard 3411–3412
Bonstelle, Jessie 3413
Bontemps, Arna 6543
bookplates 102
Booth, Agnes 2981
Booth, Edwin 82, 807, 1737, 1740, 1744, 2340, 2928, 2937, 2967, 2975, 2980, 2982, 2987, 2991–2992, 3008, 3010, 3025, 3063, 3066–3067, 3076, 3079, 3130, 3153, 3166, 3180, 3183, 3195, 3201, 3414–3447, 3449, 3575, 3700, 3907, 5757
Booth, John Wilkes 3180, 3450–3487, 3578
Booth, Jr., Junius Brutus 1737, 3488
Booth, Junius Brutus 1397, 1737, 2094, 2975, 2998, 3009, 3164–3165, 3455, 3489–3508
Booth, Mary Devlin 3448
Boothbay Theatre Museum 165
Boston Museum 2976, 3575, 4459
Boucicault, Dion 4514, 6300–6315
Bowers, Mrs D. P. 2981
Bowman, Laura 3509
Brackenridge, Hugh Henry 6316–6319
Brady, Alice 3510
Brady, Jim 7436
Brady, William A. 3513–3514
Bragdon, Claude 3518
Bragg, Bernard 5299
Brando, Marlon 3089, 3519–3525
Brann, William Cooper 6320
Bread and Puppet Theatre 1626, 1649, 1656, 2837–2841
Brecht, Bertolt 3384, 6019, 6039
Breuer, Lee 5698, 6112, 6127, 6136
Brice, Fanny 374, 3113, 7345–7346
Broad Alley Theatre 255
Broadhurst, Miss 3145
Brooklyn Academy of Music, the 2468
Brooks, Joseph 4312
Brougham, John 1269, 2976, 2992, 3002, 3009, 3021, 3158, 3165, 4517, 6321–6323
Broun, Heywood 3237, 3526–3528
Brown Potter, Mrs 2981
Brown, Allen A. 3
Brown, Gilmor 3530–3531
Brown, James H. 117
Brown, John Mason 3534–3535
Brown, Kenneth 6082
Brown, William Wells 6324
Browne, Maurice 3538–3539
Browning, Robert 821, 6012
Bruce, Lenny 3102, 4817–4818
Bryant, Dan 2992
Brynner, Yul 3541
Bullins, Ed 1368, 1373, 5392, 5918, 5950, 5979, 5981, 6093, 6108, 6111–6112, 6115, 6326
Bullough, Edward 1193
Burbank Stock Company 4160
Burk, John Daly 6327–6329
Burk, John Junius 6327
Burke, Charles 3127
Burke, Joseph 3544
Burke, Kenneth 4579, 5557
Burns, George 4819
Burroughs, Marie 2994
Burroughs, William 7170
Burton, William E. 2301, 2961, 2975, 2998, 3546–3549

Caesar, Irving 7242
Café la Mama 1626
Caldwell, Ben 6108
Caldwell, James H. 2010, 3550
Caldwell, Zoe 3116
Callahan, Chas. E. 3716
Callahan, Chuck 82
Calvert, Louis 1445
Cameron, Beatrice 4049
Campbell, Bartley 6330
Campbell, Dick 6100
Canby, A. H. 4504
Capote, Truman 6331
Carle, Richard 7206
Carmines, Al 7266
Carnovsky, Morris 893, 3555
Carr, Dabney 3151
Carroll, Earl 4828
Carroll, Vinette 6100
Carter, Mrs Leslie 2994, 3007, 3012, 3021, 3557–3558
Cassidy, Claudia 3559–3560
Cather, Willa 3562
Cavendish, Ada 4518
Cayvan, Georgia 2981
Celeste, Marie 7205
censorship 2103
Chaikin, Joseph 1571, 2919–2920, 2922, 3564–3565, 6260, 6980
Chamber theatre 965, 5525
Chamberlain, Richard 3566
Champion, Gower 7350
Chanfrau, Frank 2961, 2992
Chapman, Caroline 3567
Chapman, William B. 3053
Charles, James S. 3568
Chase, Mary Coyle 6332
Chautauqua 1375, 5270, 5277–5279, 5284, 5286, 5289, 5293–5296, 6402
Chayefsky, Paddy 374, 5926, 6333, 7065
Chekhov, Anton 6010, 6024, 6032, 6868
Chekhov, Michael 1040, 3572–3573
Cheney, Sheldon 3574
Chicago Little Theatre, the 3539
Chicago Theatre Society 3194
Childress, Alice 5979, 6106, 6140
Chorpenning, Charlotte B. 5223, 5247–5248, 5264
Christian College Consortium 322
Churchill, Caryl 5988
Circle stock repertoire theatre 1500
Claire, Ina 853, 3038
Clapp, Henry Austin 3228, 3576, 4607
Clare, Ada 1738, 3222, 3228
Clark, Bobby 3113, 3212
Clark, Hilda 7205
Clark, Marguerite 3577
Clarke, John S. 2975, 3021, 3578–3580
Clemens, Samuel Langhorn 2928
Clift, Montgomery 3102, 3581
Cline, Patsy 7295
Clurman, Harold 3582, 3584
Coburn, Charles 3585
Coghlan, Charles 3021

Coghlan, Rose 2981, 2994, 3011, 3175
Cohan, George M. 1442, 3024, 4415, 4625, 5586, 7352–7357
College Station Tx 406
Columbia University 139
Compass Players 1942
Comstock, Anthony 307
Conduit, Mrs 4528
Congdon, Constance 5979
Connelly, Marc 6335
Conner, Edmond S. 2970
Connolly, Robert 7289
Conquest, Ida 2994, 3007
Conried, Henry 3586
Cook, George C. 3228, 3587–3589, 5869
Cook, Joe 3113
Cooke, G. F. 6362
Cooper Union Museum 613
Cooper, Lizzie 4086
Cooper, Thomas Abthorpe 3127, 3590–3591, 4438
Corbin, John 3592
Cornell, Katharine 853, 893, 3038, 3050, 3199, 3226, 3593–3594, 3596–3597, 4078
Coward, Noel 7285
Cowell, Anna 286
Crabtree, Lotta 1378, 1737, 1744, 1749, 2981, 3115, 3604–3607
Crafton, Allen 3608
Craig, Edward Gordon 4435
Craig, John 2130
Crane, William H. 3000, 3005–3006, 3130, 4312, 4314
Crawford, Cheryl 3610
Crawford, J. W. 6336
Crisp, William Henry 3611–3612
Critics' Circle 5366
Cronin, David E. 123
Cronyn, Hume 7133
Crosman, Henrietta 3007–3008
Crothers, Rachel 5954, 6060, 6337–6340
Crouse, Russel 5655, 6080, 6600
Cukor, George 3613
Cullen, Countee 6087, 6098, 6341
Cummings, Constance 1036
Cummings, E. E. 5606, 5897, 6099, 6342–6346
Curry, Samuel S. 881
Cushman, Charlotte 2300, 2962, 2967, 2975–2976, 2982, 2989, 2999, 3008, 3010, 3021, 3058, 3104, 3115, 3126, 3153, 3160, 3166–3167, 3178, 3183, 3201, 3614–3624, 4517, 4627
Cypher Code 751

D'Arville, Camille 7205
Dahl, Roald 4193
Dailey, Peter F. 7206
Dale, Alan 3625
Dallas Little Theatre 755, 4920
Dallas Theatre Center 6116
Daly, Arnold 3638–3639, 4045
Daly, Augustin 2982, 3021, 3025, 3074, 3191, 3627–3637, 3640, 4277, 5359, 6118
Daly, Dan 2997, 7206

Daly, W. H. 2502
Dandridge, Dorothy 3641
Daniels, Frank 7206
Davenport, Edward Loomis 2975, 3642–3643
Davenport, Fanny 2321, 2340, 2978, 2981, 3642, 3644
Davidson, Jo 4325
Davies, Phoebe 3007
Davis, Bette 3646, 3648
Davis, Fay 2994
Davis, Harry 2631, 2633
Davis, Jessie Bartlett 7205
Davis, Ossie 1368
Davis, Owen 5359, 6350–6352
Davis, Richard Harding 6354
Dawison, Bogumil 3021
Day, Clarence 3208, 6599
De Angelis, Jefferson 7206
De Bar, Benedict 2976, 3651–3652
De Marcos, The 3042
De Mille, Agnes 3655
De Mille, Cecil B. 3654–3655
De Wolfe, Elsie 2994, 3005
Dean, Julia 3658
Decker, John 3214
Dee, Ruby 6100
Deering, Nathaniel 6356
Deeter, Jasper 2601
Delacorte Mobile Theater 4223
Deland, Lorin 3659
Dell, Floyd 3587, 6058
Delsarte 805–806, 808, 811, 813–815, 818, 837, 854, 925, 1000
Dennie, Joseph 5708
Dern, Bruce 978
Dickens, Charles 5995, 6018
Dickinson, Anna 3662
Dies Committee 1525
Dietz, Howard 7285
Dine, Jim 1102
Dithmar, Edward A. 3663
Dixey, Henry E. 7206
Dodge, Mabel 3228
Dodson, J. E. 3000
Donahue, John 5258
Donald Oenslager 4207
Donaldson, W. H. 4781
Dos Passos, John 5851, 6357
Douglass, David 2572, 3189, 6411
Drake, Mrs Alexander 3665
Drake, Samuel 3053
Drama League 2, 212, 2842–2843, 5581
Dramatists Guild 222, 6656
Dramatists' Alliance 1739
Draper, Ruth 3109, 3666–3667, 4639
Dreiser, Theodore 3244, 6056, 6359–6361
Dressler, Marie 3035, 3670, 7205
Drew, John 2928, 2977, 2997, 3000–3001, 3006, 3009, 3013, 3032, 3035, 3074, 3671, 3673, 3677, 3907, 6491
Drew, Louisa Lane 3676
Drew, Mrs John 3126, 3675
Drew, Philip Yale 3677
Drexler, Rosalyn 6106
Drummond, Alexander M. 5643
Duay, Grant 1591

Duff, Mary Ann 2975, 2982, 3021, 3115, 3678–3679
Duffy, Henry 1778, 3680
Duffy, William 2293
Dunbar, Paul Laurence 6098, 7361–7362
Duncan, Robert 7363
Dunlap Society 2844–2845
Dunlap, William 1322, 3248, 3873, 4517, 5359, 6365–6366, 6368, 6370–6373
Duport, Louis 3227
Durang, Christopher 6136
Durang, John 2574, 3681–3682
Durante, Jimmy 3048, 3051, 3113, 4831–4832

Eagels, Jeanne 3683
Earle, Virginia 7205
Eaton, Walter Prichard 3684–3685
Eberhart, Richard 5897, 6260, 6374–6375
Eberson, John 471
Ebert, Joyce 1036
Edeson, Robert 3005
Edmonds, Randolph 1373, 5158
Edwards, Henry 4080
Edwards, Paula 7205
Eichenberg, Ethyl 1654
Eikenberry, Franklin James 1178
El Teatro Campesino 1656, 5698, 5988
Eliot, T. S. 3729
Elkins, Hillard 3686
Elliott, Maxine 2994, 3007, 3012
Ellison, Ralph 6092
Ellsler, Effie 2981
Elssler, Fanny 3185
Ely, Herbert C. 5362
Emerson Minstrels 1756
Emmett, Dan 1397, 4834
Engel, Lehman 7365–7366
Englander, Ludwig 4504
Enters, Angna 3109, 3691
Equity strike 3952
Erikson, Erik H. 6845
Eugene O'Neill Memorial Theatre Center 6116
Evans, Maurice 3692
Everett, William 3029
Eytinge, Rose 3694

Fairbanks, Douglas 3695, 3697–3698
Faragoh, Francis Edward 5851
Farrar, Geraldine 4418
Farren, William 2586
Faulkner, William 6376
Faversham, William 3000, 3006, 3080
Fawcett, Owen 3175
Fay, Frank 3048
Fayard, Jeanne 7170
Faye, Joey 4835
Federal Theatre 82, 203, 220, 1368, 1451, 1520, 1525–1526, 1540, 1542, 1546, 1552, 1562, 1736, 1747, 1909, 2771, 2846–2875, 3101, 3726–3728, 3732, 4486, 5264, 5698, 5821, 5852, 5880, 6867

Felix, Seymour 7303
Fennell, James 3703
Ferber, Edna 6379
Fergusson, Francis 3704
Ferlinghetti, Lawrence 6104
Ferrer, Jose 893
Field, Joseph M. 3706
Fields, Dorothy 7285
Fields, W. C. 3113, 3214, 3707–3708, 3711–3712
Finn, Henry James 3713
Fisher, Charles 2977, 2982, 3002
Fisher, Clara 3147, 4039–4040
Fisher, Jules 4105
Fiske, Harrison Grey 3714–3715
Fiske, Minnie Maddern 2994, 2996, 3005, 3007–3008, 3011, 3021, 3023, 3058, 3126, 3208, 3431, 3716–3724, 6050
Fiske, Stephen Ryder 4607
Fitch, Clyde 2928, 3008, 3194, 5586, 5590, 6054, 6382–6386
Fitzgerald, F. Scott 6387–6388, 6390
Flagg, James Montgomery 6391
Flanagan, Hallie 3730–3733
Florence, W. J. 2975, 2982, 2992, 3008–3009
Florence, William J. 3021
Florida State U. Theatre 406
Flush 3199
Fogg Art Museum 584
Folger Shakespeare Library 35, 156, 159, 162
Fonda, Henry 3111, 3735, 3737, 7385
Fonda, Jane 3089, 6050
Fontanne, Lynn 853, 893, 4025, 4027
Forbes, James 6392
Forbes-Robertson, J. 3282
Ford's Theatre 2782, 3463
Ford, John T. 3738
Foreman, Richard 1628, 5698, 6123, 6127, 6136, 6393, 6395
Fornés, Maria Irene 1591, 5979, 5988, 6136
Forrest, Edwin 807–808, 1502, 1737, 2283, 2301, 2340, 2961, 2976, 2991–2992, 2998, 3008–3010, 3021, 3059, 3063, 3066, 3079, 3127, 3153, 3160, 3739, 3741, 3744–3763, 3765–3767, 4390, 4501–4502, 4627, 5750
Fosse, Bob 7296, 7367–7370
Fowler, Gene 3224, 3230, 3254, 6452
Fox, Della 7205
Fox, George L. 2992, 4836–4837
Fox, George Washington Lafayette 3043
Francis, William 3127
Frank, Laurence 1043
Frank, Waldo 6397–6398
Frankau, Joseph 3402
Frederic, Harold 6400
Frederick, Pauline 3771–3772
Fredericks, John 3042
Free Southern Theatre 2876–2878, 6108
French, Frederick W. 122

Friedman, Bruce Jay 6401
Frohman, Charles 706, 1893, 3773–3774
Frohman, Daniel 3776, 3778
Froman, Jane 7295
Frontier theatre 3029, 5653
Fry, Emma 327
Fuller, Charles 5979, 5984, 6133, 6136
Fuller, Loie 3780–3782
Fullerton, John 256
Funke, Lewis 7170

Gable, Clark 3783–3785
Gale, Zona 3197, 6055, 6403
Games, Ernest 5936
Garden, Mary 3061
Garfield, John 3788
Garland, Judy 7295
Garson, Barbara 5926, 5950
Gassner, John 3790, 4933
Gayler, Charles 2982
Geer, Ellen 1036
Geer, Will 3791
Gelb, Arthur 7170
Gelber, Jack 3235, 5392, 5939, 5950, 6082, 6112, 6117
Gems, Pam 5988
George, Grace 3007
Gershwin, George 4794, 7311, 7371–7374, 7376–7381, 7400
Gershwin, Ira 7285
Gest, Morris 3792
Gibbs, Wolcott 3793
Gielgud, John 879
Gilbert, John 2974, 3008, 3021, 3794
Gilbert, Mrs 3021, 3795
Gilbert, Mrs G. H. 2977, 2982, 3074
Gilder, Rosamund 3796
Gilfert, Charles 3797
Gill, Brendan 3081
Gillette, William 2996, 3000–3001, 3006, 3008, 3013, 3197, 3798–3799, 3801–3807
Gillmore, Frank 3808
Gilman, Mabelle 7205
Gish, Dorothy 3809
Gish, Lillian 3810–3811
Glaser, Lulu 7205
Glaspell, Susan 1448, 2120, 3247, 3587, 5583, 5585, 5954, 6080, 6407–6409
Gleason, Jackie 3813
Godfrey, Thomas 5371
Gogol, Nikolai V. 6008
Gold, Michael 5851, 6412
Golden, John 3815
Golden, Richard 7206
Goldman, Emma 6821
Goodale, George P. 2158
Goodman Theatre Company 3952
Goodman Theatre 6116
Goodman, Paul 2909, 6124
Goodwin, George K. 3817
Goodwin, Nat C. 1269, 2502, 3000, 3005–3006, 3130, 3561, 3819
Goodwin, Thomas 3160
Gordon, Max 3042

Gordone, Charles 5939, 5979
Gorelik, Mordecai 3824
Gottschalk, Louis Moreau 3222
Gourlay, Jennie 4086
Grand Union 2879
Grant, Lee 1036
Green Room Club 2880
Green, Adolph 7385
Green, Paul 2478, 2486, 5359, 5590, 6079, 6413–6414, 6417–6418, 6421, 6423, 6425–6428
Greene, Clay Meredith 6429
Greene, Mrs John 3825
Greenleaf Theatre 830
Greenwall, Henry 3826
Gregory, Paul 3827
Grillparzer, Franz 6017
Grooms, Red 1102
Gropius 406
Group Theatre 1346, 1487, 1518, 2881–2886, 5698, 5852, 6398, 6421–6422
Guare, John 6112, 6136
Guber, Peter 781
Guthrie Theatre 2201, 2203, 6116
Guthrie, Tyrone 2196, 4477

Hackett, J. H. 2975–2976, 3829, 6913
Hackett, James K. 3000, 3005
Hackett, James H. 3021
Haddaway, Thomas H. 2970
Hagen, Uta 1036, 3830
Haines, W. W. 5847
Hair 5950, 7245
Hale, Nathan 4961
Hall, Adrian 3832
Hall, Josephine 7205
Hall, Pauline 2981, 7205
Hallam, Lewis 1085, 2572, 2757, 3248, 3873, 6411
Halprin, Ann 1602
Hamblin, Thomas S. 3833
Hamilton, Clayton 4577
Hammerstein II, Oscar 3042, 7224, 7285, 7318, 7382–7383, 7424
Hammett, Dashiell 6467
Hammond, Percy 3834
Hampden, Walter 3032, 3066, 3516, 3835–3836, 4155
Hansberry, Lorraine 5705, 5915, 5923, 5950, 5954, 6079, 6111, 6115, 6140, 6432–6434
Happenings 1102, 1571, 1602, 1628, 1649
Harburg, E. Y. 7285
Harby, Isaac 6436
Harlan, Otis 7206
Harlem Black Arts Theater 1584
Harned, Virginia 2994, 3012
Harnick, Sheldon 7285, 7344
Harrigan, Edward 3005, 6438–6441
Harris, Aurand 5240, 5264
Harris, C. Fiske 5341
Harris, Cyril 428
Harris, Jed 3048, 3811, 3838, 3840
Harris, Julie 3059, 6050
Harris, Rosemary 3116
Harris, Thomas 3493
Harrison, Carter 5918

358

Harrison, Richard B. 3841
Hart, Bob 4838
Hart, Lorenz 3042, 7285, 7318, 7385–7386
Hart, Moss 3042, 6080, 6443–6444
Hart, Tony 6438
Hart, William S. 4510
Hartman Stock Company 2535
Hartman, Sadakichi 3214
Hartmann, Louis 507, 527
Harvard College 103
Harvard theatre collection 144
Harvard University 6512
Haskin, Byron 3843
Haswell, Anthony 4346
Hatfield, R. M. 286
Hauptmann, Gerhart 6011
Haverly, John H. 4713
Haverstock family 1699
Hawes, A. Eugene 2777
Hawkes, John 6445–6448
Haworth, Joseph 3000
Hawthorne, Nathaniel 5793
Hay, Richard L. 664
Hayes, Helen 853, 893, 3042, 3062, 3072, 3256, 3846–3848, 4027, 4253, 5810, 6614
Hayes, Rutherford Birchard 5291
Hayward, Leland 3042, 3854–3855
Hecht, Ben 6449, 6453
Heffner, Hubert C. 1322
Held, Anna 3007
Hellinger, Mark 3858
Hellman, Lillian 374, 1711, 3042, 5698, 5788, 5847, 5939, 5954, 6080, 6085, 6099, 6123, 6125, 6454–6460, 6462–6466, 6468–6469, 6471–6487
Hemingway, Ernest 6488–6489
Hemple, Samuel 3009
Henley, Beth 5979, 5984, 5988
Henry, Martha 3116
Henry, O. 2703
Hepburn, Katharine 3256, 3859–3865, 4430
Herbert, Victor 7387
Herford, Beatrice 3106
Herne, James A. 3000, 3006, 3008, 3195, 4619, 5700, 6118, 6490–6494
Heron, Matilda 1740, 2975–2976, 3025, 3866
Heyward, Dubose 5847, 6496
Hill, Abram 6100
Hill, George H. 3160, 3868
Hill, W. E. 143
Hillhouse, James A. 6498
Hills, Harry 2305
Hilson, Thomas 3127, 3147
Hirschfeld, Al 3533
Hitchcock, Raymond 7421
Hoblitzelle, Karl 5021
Hochuth, Rolf 6023
Hodgkinson, John 3248, 3874–3875
Hoffman, Dustin 3122, 3876
Holbrook, Hal 3878
Holden, Joan 6136
Holland, E. M. 3000
Holland, George 1423, 2301, 2334, 3002, 3021, 3879–3880, 4391

Holland, Joseph Jefferson 3881
Holliday, Billie 7295
Holliday, Judy 3882
Holm, Hanya 7289
Holman, Joseph George 2646
Holman, Libby 3883
Holtzmann, Fanny 3042
Homan, Gertie 2981
Hope, Bob 3088, 3889–3891
Hopkins, Arthur 1448, 3094, 3894–3895
Hopkinson, Francis 3189
Hopper, De Wolf 7206
Hopper, Edna Wallace 7205
Hopwood, Avery 3179, 6499
Horn, Kate 2961
Horne, Lena 4839
Horney, Karen 908
Horton, Mary Ann 2970
Hosmer, Harriet 3621
House Committee on Un-American Activities 202, 1542, 1546, 1549–1550
House of Witmark 4738
Houseman, John 3898
Howard, Bronson 2928, 3008, 5359, 5586, 6500, 6502
Howard, George C. 1475
Howard, Sidney 5788, 5818, 6060, 6066, 6503–6506, 7224
Howard, Willie 3113
Howe, Frank 2581
Howe, Tina 5979, 5988, 6106
Howells, William Dean 6099, 6507–6518, 6520–6528
Hoyt, Charles H. 6529–6531
Hoyt, Harlowe Randall 3901
Hughes, Glenn 147, 5077, 6064
Hughes, Langston 1368, 1373, 2404, 5705, 6082, 6087, 6092, 6098–6099, 6115, 6534–6545
Hull House 3267–3269
Hull House Players 1900
Hull, Josephine 3903
Hume, Samuel 3904
Huneker, James Gibbons 3905–3906
Hunter, Eddie 6100
Hunter, Robert 6546
Hurlstone, William Y. 3211
Huston, Walter 3911–3912
Hutton, Laurence 3913
Hwang, David 6136
Hyland, Frances 3116

Ibsen, Henrik 5628, 5998, 6000, 6029, 6035, 6041, 6050
Iden, Rosalind 4231
Ingarden, Roman 1191
Inge, William 5694, 5850, 5917, 5979, 6079–6081, 6083, 6102, 6547–6555, 7133, 7170
Innaurato, Albert 5979
International Children's Theatre Association 5243
International Theatre Institute 1228
Ionesco, Eugene 6155
Irving, Henry 1487, 2928
Irving, Isabel 2994

Irving, Washington 4523, 6556–6557
Irwin, May 2994
Isaacs, Edith J. R. 1298, 3914

Jackson, J. A. 4708
James, Louis 2987, 3226
James, William 3916
Jamieson, George W. 3021
Janauschek, Fanny 3917
Janis, Elsie 4842
Jansen, Marie 2981
Jaques-Dalcroze, Emile 918
Jarrett, Henry C. 1474
Javitch, Gregory 40
Jeffers, Robinson 5863, 6079, 6099, 6559–6563, 6565–6568
Jefferson, Joseph 1423, 2928, 2974–2975, 2980, 2982, 3000, 3005, 3008, 3010, 3035, 3167, 3175, 3183, 3419, 3919–3924, 3926, 4516–4517, 5314
Jefferson, Thomas 3063
Jeffrey, Alix 152
Jewett, Henry 3000, 3006
Jimmy Durante 4833
Jo Mielziner 4104
Jolson, Al 7242, 7390–7392
Jonathan character 5654
Jones, George 3601
Jones, James Earl 3932
Jones, Margo 1487, 3082, 3934–3936
Jones, Preston 6569
Jones, Robert Edmond 584, 611, 632, 636, 665, 713, 1507, 1700, 3094, 3190, 3937, 3939, 3941–3947, 4894, 6823
Jones, Walter 7206
Joplin, Janis 7295
Juch, Emma 2981
Judah, Mrs 1737
Judson Poets' Theater 7266
Julia Marlowe 2978, 3061, 4066

Kabuki 1019
Kahn, Otto H. 3950–3951
Kanriye Fujima 1052
Kaprow, Allan 1102, 1602
Karamu House 2518, 2533, 5252
Karloff, Boris 3953
Kauffman, Stanley 3955
Kaufman, George S. 3237, 6060, 6063, 6080, 6377, 6570–6574, 6576–6578
Kaye, Danny 3088, 3122, 3956–3957
Kazan, Elia 1094, 3958–3959, 3961–3967
Kean, Edmund 3080
Keaton, Buster 4843–4845
Keeler, Ruby 7242
Keene, Laura 2340, 2976, 3025, 3115, 3126, 3178, 3968–3969, 4405
Keene, Thomas W. 1487, 3970
Keith, Benjamin Franklin 2113, 4846
Kelcey, Herbert 3000
Kellar, Harry 3004
Kellerd, John E. 3971

Kelly, Gene 7385
Kelly, George 5818, 6060, 6579–6582
Kemble, Fanny 3126
Kennedy, Adrienne 5918, 5979, 6112
Kennedy, Charles Rann 6584
Kennedy, Laurie 1036
Kent State U. Center 410
Kenton, Edna 3587
Kenyon, Elmer Bernard 779
Kern, Jerome 7269, 7318, 7393–7396, 7456
Kerr, Walter 3972, 3974
Kesselman, Wendy 5988
Kidder, Kathryn 2994
Kiesler, Frederick 670
King-Coit school 5250
Kingsley, Sidney 6587
Kinnaird, Douglas 3493
Kinsey, Madge 2550
Kiralfy brothers 3043
Kiralfy, Bolossy 3975
Kiralfy, Imre 3976
Koch, Frederick H. 2476, 2478, 2480, 3977–3978, 7195
Kohm Group 428
Kook, Edward F. 532
Kopit, Arthur 5392, 5934, 5950, 6102, 6111–6112, 6117, 6119
Kotzebue, August von 4221, 6001, 6033
Kraken Group 1151
Krause, Alvina 931
Kreymborg, Alfred 6590
Krutch, Joseph Wood 3981, 3983–3985
Kummer, Clare 6591
Kyle, Howard 2928

La Mama 1605, 2887–2889
Laboratory Theatre 1518
Lackaye, Wilton 3000
Lafayette Stock Company, the 2408
Lahr, Bert 893, 3113, 3986
Lambs 2890–2891
Lanchester, Elsa 3256
Lander, Jean Davenport 2982
Lander, Mrs 3021
Langdon, Harry 4848
Langer, Susanne 5551, 5557, 7275
Langner, Lawrence 3989
Langrishe and Glenn 1700
Larkin, Peter 3990
Latrobe, Benjamin Henry 3991
Lauder, Mrs 2976
Laughton, Marie Ware 5090
Laurents, Arthur 1578
Lawrence, D. H. 7128
Lawrence, Lillian 2994
Lawson, John Howard 3217, 5851–5852, 5869, 6060, 6079, 6593–6596
Le Compte, Elizabeth 6127
Le Doux, Gaston 814
Le Gallienne, Eva 2340, 3082, 3104, 3207, 3994–3996
Le Moyne, William J. 129
Le Noire, Rosetta 3997
League of Resident Theatres 790

Leavitt, M. B. 1737
LeClerq, Carlotta 4639
Lee, Ming Cho 632, 4109
Leiber, Fritz 3999
Lemon, Jack 3122
Lemoyne, Sarah Cowell 2994, 3007
Lennox, Charlotte 6597
Lerner, Alan Jay 7285
Leslie, Elsie 4002
Lessing, Madge 7205
Levant, Oscar 3048, 3051
Lewis, Charles 'Chick' 763
Lewis, Gladys Adelina 6739
Lewis, James 1423, 2977, 2982, 3021, 3074
Lewis, Joe E. 4851
Lewis, Robert 4003
Lewis, Theophilus 2404
Lewisohn, Ludwig 4005
Lewys, Georges 6739
Liebler Company 4437
Liebler, Theodore 4310
Lincoln Center 440
Lincoln dramas 5725
Lincoln, Abraham 1388
Lincoln, Mary Todd 5530
Lind, Jenny 3152
Lindsay, Howard 5655, 6080, 6600
Linney, Romulus 5979
Lipmann, Clara 3004
Lissim, Simon 4006–4011
Living Theatre 726, 1113, 1252, 1571, 1605, 1626, 1649, 2405, 2892–2911, 4687, 4690–4691, 5698, 5915
Lobravico, Carl 2908
Locke, Robinson 141
Loesser, Frank 7224, 7285, 7402
Loew, Marcus 4747
Loftus, Cissie 3106
Logan, Cornelius A. 4017
Logan, Joshua 3735, 4014
Logan, Olive 4019
Long, Mary E. 4020
Longfellow, Henry Wadsworth 6603–6604
Longworth, David and Thomas 5383
Loos, Anita 4022
Lord, Pauline 3190
Losey, Joseph 4023
Lotos Club 2912–2913
Lowell, Robert 6605–6610
Luce, Clare Boothe 6063, 6612–6613
Ludlam, Charles 2451
Ludlow, Noah 2231
Lunt, Alfred 853, 893, 4025–4028
Lust, Geraldine 1580
Lyceum 3775, 5288

MacArthur, Charles 3848, 6452, 6614–6615
Macdonald, Christie 7205
MacDowell, Melbourne 3000
MacGowan, Kenneth 4030, 6850
Mackay, F. F. 2928
MacKaye, Marion Morse 6621
MacKaye, Percy 5585–5586, 6618–6620, 6622, 6713

MacKaye, Steele 854, 1078, 3040, 4031–4037, 4081
Mackey, William W. 5918
Maclaine, Shirley 3089
MacLeish, Archibald 1540, 5897, 6079, 6099, 6623–6629
Maclow, Jackson 6124
Macready, Mrs 4038
Macready, William Charles 3761
Madison, Kitty 4852
Mae Desmond Players 2627
Maguire, Tom 422, 1737, 1740
Mailer, Norman 6631–6634
Major, Clara Tree 5245
Malden, Karl 7133
Malina, Judith 2895
Maltz, Albert 6635
Mamet, David 5392, 5698, 5979, 5981, 5984, 6111–6112, 6133, 6136, 6636, 6638, 6640, 6879
Mamoulian, Rouben 4041–4044
Manhattan Project 2914
Mann, Emily 5979, 6136
Mann, Louis 3006
Mann, Theodore 2392
Mannering, Mary 2994, 3001, 3007, 3012
Manola, Marion 2981
Mansfield, Richard 119, 1445, 2507, 2581, 2928, 2982, 2987, 2991, 2997, 3000, 3005–3006, 3013, 3063, 3175, 3191, 3561, 3907, 4045–4052
Mantell, Robert B. 3000, 4053–4054
Maranca, Bonnie 6127
Marble, Danforth 3150, 4056–4057
March, Fredric 4059–4060
Mark Taper Forum 6116
Marlowe, Julia 1893, 2507, 2989, 2994, 2996–2997, 3001, 3005, 3007, 3012, 3021, 3023, 3025, 3192, 3226, 4062–4065, 4067–4069, 4398
Marquis, Don 6058
Marsh, Norma 5979
Marshall, Mrs 4517
Martin, Mary 7403
Martinot, Sadie 2981
Marx Brothers 4639, 4853–4854, 4858, 4864, 7400
Mason, John B. 3000, 3006
Mason, Marshall W. 2466, 7193
Massachusetts Institute of Technology 406
Massett, Stephen 1737, 1740, 4070
Masterworks Laboratory Theatre 2915
Mathews, Cornelius 2970
Matthau, Walter 3122, 4072
Matthews, Brander 834, 2928, 4075–4076, 5354
Maude, Cyril 6558
May, Edna 7205
May, Rollo 5964
Mayo, Frank 4077
*Mazeppa* 6027
McClintic, Guthrie 4079
McClure, Michael 6104, 6643
McCourt, Peter 1476

McCullers, Carson 5847, 6099, 6644–6648
McCullough, John 1737, 2502, 2975, 2982, 2991, 3010, 3021, 3130, 4080–4083, 4517
McCutcheon, George Barr 6650
McElfratrick, J. B. 421
McHenry, James 6649
McHenry, Nellie 2981
McIntosh, Burr 3005
McKinley, Myrtle 4865
McNally, Terence 6112, 6651
McVicker's Theatre 1902, 1919
McVicker, Mary 3180
Medina, Louisa 3833
Medwick, Murray 1591
Melby, John 6486
melodrama 5734, 5743, 5747, 5801
Melville, Herman 5793
Mencken, H. L. 6452, 6652–6655
Menken, Adah Isaacs 1737–1738, 1740, 1744, 1749, 2267, 3043, 3115, 3188, 4085–4086, 4088–4092–4097
Mercer, Johnny 7285
Mercury Theatre 2916, 4486
Meredith, Burgess 853, 856
Merleau-Ponty, Maurice 2922
Merman, Ethel 3048, 7408–7409
Merrick, David 781
Merry, Anne 3248, 4099
Metcalfe, James Stetson 4100
Midler, Bette 3089
Mielziner, Jo 428, 4101, 4103, 4105
Millay, Edna St. Vincent 6099, 6657–6661
Miller, Arthur 374, 1113, 1305, 1542, 3122, 3955, 4676, 4690, 5484, 5540, 5655, 5680, 5682, 5684, 5698, 5788, 5834, 5847, 5901, 5915, 5917, 5919, 5926, 5928, 5939, 5950, 5958, 5979, 5989, 6067, 6071, 6074–6076, 6079–6083, 6085–6086, 6088, 6099, 6102, 6107, 6111, 6125, 6129, 6662–6663, 6665–6677, 6679–6685, 6687–6692, 6694–6697, 6700–6703
Miller, Gilbert 3042
Miller, Henry 3000, 3006, 4107
Miller, James 4106
Miller, James Hull 418, 615
Miller, Jason 6102
Miller, Joaquin 5359, 6705–6706
Mills, Steve 4866
Miner, Worthington 4108
Minnelli, Liza 3089, 3122
Minstrelsy 1444, 1737, 1740, 1744, 3575
Miranda, Carmen 7295
Mitchell, Langdon 5359, 6707
Mitchell, Loften 1368, 5700, 6708
Mitchell, Maggie 5314
Mitchell, William 2460
Mizner, Addison 6709
Modjeska, Helena 2981–2982, 2989, 2994, 3021, 3023, 3194, 3842, 4111–4112, 4115, 4117–4124, 4126

Moeller, Philip 146, 3179, 4129–4130, 5359
Molière, J. P. 6021
Molnar, Ferenc 7224
Monk, Meredith 1628, 4131
Monroe, Marilyn 3061, 7295
Montague, Henry J. 3025
Montego Bay 1396
Monterey, Carlotta 6875, 6884
Montez, Lola 1737, 1740, 2962, 3043, 3188, 4133, 4136–4151
Montgomery David G. 4406
Moody, William Vaughn 5585, 5590, 6710–6711, 6713, 6715–6720
Moore, Victor 3113
Moorehead, Agnes 4152
Moreau, Charles C. 138
Morehouse, Ward 4154
Morgan, Helen 7295, 7410
Morlacchi, Mlle 3215
Morley, Christopher 6055
Morosco, Oliver 4158–4160
Morrell, T. H. 114
Morris, Clara 2340, 2502, 2975, 2981–2982, 3008, 3021, 4164
Morrison, Hobe 4166
Morrissey, James 2987
Morse, Salmi 6721
Moses, Montrose Jonas 4167
Moses, Robert 4227
Mostel, Zero 3085, 4169
Mowatt, Anna Cora 2975, 3115, 3126, 3178, 4172–4175, 5359, 6118
Mulholland, John 3050
mummers 2607, 2609
Munford, Robert 6722–6723
Muni, Paul 893, 4176–4178
Murdoch, James E. 2502, 2976, 4179–4181
Murrin, Tom 1654
Musical Academy of the West 1799

Nathan, George Jean 3182, 4183, 4185–4191, 6801, 6878
National Art Theatre 1437
National Black Theatre 1368
National Project for the Performing Arts 249
National Theatre Conference 2917
National Theatre of the Deaf 5313
Nature theatre 3955
Nazi character, the 5874
Nazimova, Alla 853, 4192, 4418
Neal, Patricia 4193
Nebe, Henry 123
Negro Ensemble Company 1368, 2918
Neill, James F. 4195
Neilson, Adelaide 2975, 2982, 3021, 4310, 4517
Nelson, Richard 6136
Nesbit, Evelyn 4198
Nethersole, Olga 2994, 3021, 4199
New Chestnut Street Opera House 3817
New Dramatists Committee 5448
New Playwrights' Theatre 5851, 5869

New York Artists' Theatre 2464
*New York Dramatic Mirror* 201
New York school poets 5883, 6137
New York Shakespeare Festival 1596, 4224, 4226, 4228
*New York Times* 4594
Newman, Paul 3085
Niblo's Theatre 3148
Niblo, William 3160
Nichols, Guy 2928
Nielsen, Alice 7205, 7411
Nietzsche, Friedrich 6872
Nin, Anaïs 7133
Nisbet-Snyder Drama Collection 5380
Noah, Mordecai Manuel 6725–6727
Nordica, Lillian 3004
Norman, Marsha 5979, 5984, 5988, 6133, 6136
Norton, Elliot 4201
Nugent, Elliott 4202, 5847, 6080
Nye, Simeon Nash 1841

O'Brien, Fitz-James 6729
O'Brien, Pat 4203
O'Connor, Donald 7385
O'Hara, John 6730–6733
O'Neal, Frederick 6100
O'Neal, John 6108
O'Neil, Nance 6050
O'Neill, Annie 3005
O'Neill, Eugene 1113, 1305, 1507, 1534, 3190, 4676, 4690, 5359, 5468, 5481, 5484, 5518, 5583, 5585–5586, 5590, 5614, 5633, 5680, 5682, 5684, 5698, 5700, 5788, 5818, 5847, 5850, 5863, 5869, 5896, 5902, 5908, 5915, 5919, 5928, 5939, 5958, 5989, 6060, 6065, 6071, 6073–6074, 6076–6080, 6088, 6099, 6107, 6122, 6125, 6129, 6734–6765, 6767–6778, 6780–6794, 6796–6849, 6851–6875, 6877–6881, 6883, 6885–6898, 7065
O'Neill, James 1502, 1737, 3000, 3006, 3079, 3226, 4204
O. L. Story Scenic Co. 547
Odets, Clifford 374, 4676, 5698, 5852, 5919, 5939, 5979, 6060, 6063, 6065, 6075, 6080, 6099, 6107, 6125, 6899–6906, 6908
Oenslager, Donald 428, 584, 4206, 4208–4210
*Oh ! Calcutta !* 4770
Olcott, Chauncey 3005, 4214
Old American company 2572
Oldenburg, Claes 1102, 1602
Oldmixon, Mrs 3145
Olsen, Moroni 4216
Olson, Elder 4589
Omohundro, C. B. 3215
one night-stand theatres 212
Open Theatre 726, 1113, 2919–2922, 3563, 5698
open-air theatre 1205
Orange Coast College 406
Osborn, Paul 6909

Owens, John E. 2992, 3008, 3021, 4217–4218
Owens, John Edmond 2982
Owens, Rachelle 1591

Pace, Donald 6893
Pacino, Al 3085
Packer, Tina 4219
Page, Geraldine 978
Paine, Robert Treat 4220–4221
Paley, W. S. 781
Palmer, Albert M. 133, 1474, 4222
Palmer, Minnie 2981
Palo Alto theatre 5114
Pantages, Alexander 4868
Papp, Joseph 1546, 1594, 2405, 4223, 4225–4228
Paramount Theatre 392
Park Theatre 3716
Parker, Henry Taylor 4230
Parsons, Estelle 978
Pasadena Playhouse 82
Pastor, Tony 2992, 3208, 4869, 7208
Paton, Miss 4528
Patrick, Robert 6124
Paul Green 5633
Paulding, James K. 5359
Paulding, James Kirk 6910–6912
Payne, Ben Iden 3952, 4232
Payne, John Howard 2975, 4234–4246, 6118
Payton, Corse 4247
Peabody collection 82
Peabody, Josephine Preston 6713, 6914
Peck, Gregory 3122
Pelby, William 3127
Pemberton, Brock 4248
Penn State archives 82
Performance Group 726, 1571, 2923–2925, 5698
Phelps, Pauline 3367
physically disabled characters 5885
Pickford, Mary 3042, 4251
Pilgrim, James 4086
Piot, René 4254
Pirandello, Luigi 6031
Piscator, Erwin 6028, 6044
Placide, Alexandre 2648, 3227
Placide, Henry 2975, 3002, 3147, 4255
Placide, Jane 4256
Players Club 2926–2937, 3194
Playwrights' Producing Company 2938–2941, 6218
pleasure gardens 2421
Plummer, Christopher 3067
Poe, Edgar Allan 4257–4262
Poe, Eliza 4263
Poitier, Sidney 893, 4264
Poole, Lucius 128
Porter, Cole 3042, 4794, 7285, 7412–7417
Porterfield, Robert 2754
Post, Lilly 2981
postage stamps 104
Potter, Mrs Brown 2987, 3004, 3200
Povey, John 4448
Power, Tyrone 3011

Power, Tyrone Jr 4266, 4268–4269
Powers, James T. 7206
Price, Stephen 3076
Prince, Harold 7419–7420
Princeton Triangle Club 2942
Proctor, F. F. 4870
Prolet Buehne 2943–2944
Provincetown Players 1534, 1564, 3589, 5869, 6049, 6409, 6658
Provincetown Playhouse 5588
Purdy, James 6089, 6920
*Purlie Victorious* 6347

Quinn, Elizabeth 4272
Quintero, José 4275, 6871

Rabb, Ellis 4276
Rabe, David 5392, 5623, 5964, 5981, 5984, 6102, 6106, 6111–6112, 6136, 6921
Rader, Dotson 7170
Rankin, Arthur McKee 6706
Ranous, Dora Knowlton 4278
Ransom, John Crowe 5532
Rapson, Ralph 458
Rasch, Albertina 7289
Rascoe, Burton 4279
Rathbone, Basil 4281, 5810
Raymond, John 3021
Raymond, John T. 1269, 2975, 2982, 4282
Raymond, Maud 7205
Readers' Theatre 928, 954, 1126, 1180, 5196
Redpath, James 5269
Reed, John 3228
Reed, Roland 3000
Rehan, Ada 2977–2978, 2981, 2989, 2994, 3007, 3021, 3023, 3074, 4284–4287
Reinagle, Alexander 3227
Reinhardt, Max 3811, 6040
Rhéa, Mlle 2502
Ribman, Ronald 5979, 6111
Riccardo, Corona 2994
Rice, Cale Young 6923
Rice, Dan 4871–4877
Rice, Edward E. 7421
Rice, Elmer 374, 5869, 5939, 6063, 6079–6080, 6107, 6924, 6929–6936
Rice, T. D. 1397, 2961, 3160, 4721
Richardson, Jack 6082
Richardson, Willis 1368, 1373, 6115
Richings, Peter 3147
Richman, Charles J. 3006
Richmond theatre 257, 260–261, 274, 284
Riggs, Lynn 6937–6940
Robbins, Jerome 7296
Robbins, Phyllis 860
Robert F. Wagner labor archives 82
Robertson, Agnes 2976
Robeson, Paul 1509, 1546, 3190, 3217, 4290–4292, 4294–4307, 6100
Robinson, D. G. 1737, 4308

Robinson, Edwin Arlington 6713, 6942
Robson, Eleanor 4310
Robson, May 2994, 3005
Robson, Stuart 3000, 3006, 4312, 4314
Rockwell, Kitty 4315
Rodgers and Hammerstein 109, 7422–7423, 7426, 7429–7430, 7434
Rodgers and Hart 7427
Rodgers, Jimmy 4879
Rodgers, Richard 3042, 7224, 7318, 7385, 7424, 7431
Rodrigues, Nelson 6943
Rogers, Ginger 3122
Rogers, John 3236
Rogers, Will 4316–4332, 4334–4335, 4823
Rome, Harold 7240
Rooney, Mickey 3122
Rose, Billy 4337–4339
Rosenthal, Jean 4341
Rosier, Fitz William 2970
Rossi, Ernesto 1487
Rowe, Joseph A. 1737
Rowson, Susannah 1397, 3126, 4345–4348
Rumbold, Zoe Akins 6944
Runyon, Damon 2429, 3229, 4349
Rush, Dr James 802
Russell, Annie 2994, 3001, 3005, 3007, 3012
Russell, Edmund 808
Russell, Lillian 1490, 2981, 7205, 7435–7437
Russell, Sol Smith 2284, 3000, 4352
Ryan, Robert 3735

Sackler, Howard 5923
Sadler, Harley 2709, 2714
*Saint Joan* 1036
Salsbury, Nate 7252
Salter, James 3491
Saltzstein, Joan W. 3272
Salvini, Tommaso 3419, 6042
Sanford, Samuel S. 4881
Sanders, Mary 3007
Sands, Dorothy 3106
San Francisco archives 82
San Francisco Mime Troupe 1649, 1656, 1804, 2945–2947, 5698
San Quentin drama workshop 1806
Sarah Lawrence College 406
Sardou, Victorien 5999
Sargent, Epes Winthrop 4353
Sarony, Napoleon 4354
Saroyan, William 6067, 6101, 6945, 6948–6949, 6952, 6954, 6956–6957
Schaffner, Caroline 4358
Schaffner, Neil 4357–4358
Schary, Doré 7065
Schattner, Gert 5310
Schechner, Richard 668, 944, 1252, 1571, 1605, 2925, 4691
Schenkar, Joan 5979, 5988
Schiller, Friedrich 5993
Schisgal, Murray 6082

Schneider, Alan 4359, 6163
Schuman, Peter 2838–2839
Scott, George C. 3085, 3089
Scott, Sir Walter 6003
Seabrooke, Thomas Q. 7206
Sears, Zelda 4361
Seguin, Anne 2970
Seguin, E. 2961
Selden, Samuel 5149
Serban, André 1628
Sereno and Bodaken trans-per model 6691
Serlin, Oscar 6598
Seymour, William 4364
Shakespeare 426, 807, 988, 1049, 1143, 1148, 1171, 1284, 1343, 1372, 1388, 1401, 1412, 1439, 1474, 1499, 1546, 1606, 1688, 1698, 1713, 1733, 1845–1846, 1848, 1854, 1908, 2346, 2507, 2564, 2566, 2590, 2716, 2729, 2757, 2870, 3066, 3114, 3414, 3438, 3440, 3634, 3636, 3692, 3971, 3999, 4155, 4219, 4223, 4225, 4227, 4312, 4435, 4453, 4467, 4469, 4525, 4571–4572, 4761, 5002, 5082, 5098, 5182, 5524, 5529, 5676, 5996, 6051, 7365
Shange, Ntozake 5979, 5988, 6106, 6140
Shannon, Effie 2994
Sharaff, Irene 4366
Shaw, G. B. 2376, 2952, 3639, 4132, 6671, 7398
Shaw, Irwin 6067, 6961
Shaw, Mary 1490, 2994, 3007, 4367
Shaw, Robert Gould 2107, 2109
Shawn, Wallace 6136
Sheen, Martin 6406
Sheldon, Edward 5586, 6066, 6962–6964
Shepard, Sam 1191, 1591, 5392, 5622–5623, 5696, 5698, 5964, 5979, 5981, 5984, 5989, 6102, 6111–6112, 6119, 6122–6123, 6127, 6133, 6893, 6965–6966, 6968–6981
Sherin, Edwin 4368
Sherwood, Robert E. 5872, 6060, 6080, 6273, 6982–6987
Short, Hassard 7438
Short, Marion 3367
Shotlander, Sandra 5988
Show business awards 1358, 1567, 1622, 5374, 5439, 5456, 5877, 5889, 5978
Show Printing 773
Shubert archive 82
Shubert Brothers 4369–4371
Shumlin, Herman 4372
Silvers, Phil 4374
Simms, William Gilmore 6990–6996
Simon, Neil 374, 5392, 6102, 6112, 6997–7000
Simonson, Lee 584, 611, 665, 713, 4377
Simpson, Edward 4378
Sinclair, Catherine 1737

Sinclair, Upton 7001
Singer, Isaac Bashevis 374
Sissle and Blake 7440
Skinner, Cornelia Otis 4383
Skinner, Otis 2928, 3000, 3005, 3032, 3035, 4386
Sklar, George 7002
Skouras Brothers 466
Sloman, Jane 3148
Small, Ambrose 1487
Smith, Bessie 7295
Smith, Harry Bache 4504, 7442
Smith, Jack 1654
Smith, John 357
Smith, Mark 3025
Smith, Oliver 604, 4388
Smith, Richard Penn 7004–7005
Smith, Russell 4389
Smith, Sol 1385, 2231, 3150, 4392
Smyth, Thomas 266
Sobotka, Ruth 4395
Society of Stage Directors and Choreographers 1149, 2948
Sondheim, Stephen 3122, 6122, 6136, 7285, 7443–7447
Sothern Edward H. 3192
Sothern, Edward H. 4064
Sothern, E. A. 2976
Sothern, E. H. 3000, 3006, 3009, 3021
Sothern, Edward H. 3005, 3025, 3197, 4063, 4398
Southwest Theatre Association 1697
Soyinka, Wole 6246
Spalding and Rogers floating palace 4784
Spencer, Sara 5264
Spencer, William Vaughan 2136
Spewack, Sam and Bella 6080
Split Britches Company 1654
Spolin, Viola 973, 5169
Spong, Hilda 3007
St Ann's Center for Restoration and the Arts, Inc. 2468
Stage fright 864, 984, 1025
Stage Manager's Guide 757
Stallings, Laurence 7006
Stanford Music Centre 410
Stanislavsky, Constantin 878, 881, 887, 889–890, 904, 906–909, 914–915, 924, 935–936, 963, 969, 973–974, 988, 995, 1007, 1040, 1595, 2915, 3965, 5128, 5643
Stapleton, Maureen 893, 4399
Stark, Sarah Kirby 4400
Stavis, Barrie 7007
Stearns, Charles 5264
Stein, Gertrude 6099, 6225, 7008–7013, 7015–7020, 7022
Stein, Jules 781
Steinbeck, John 3735, 6064, 7023–7027
Stempel, Frederick William 2055
Stephens, H. P. 4073
Stevens, Thomas Wood 4401–4403
Stevens, Wallace 5897
Stewart, Ellen 2889
Stewart, James 3050, 3122
Stigwood, Robert 781

Stover, Frederick 3692
Strasberg, Lee 4407–4410, 4526
Streep, Meryl 3122, 4412
Street performers 4790
Streisand, Barbra 3089, 4413
Strindberg, August 6005, 6014, 6078, 6166, 6770, 6894, 7140
Strooker, Shireen 1016
Styne, Jule 7449
Sullivan, Louis 1922, 3270
Summer, Mark R. 4933
Suny-Binghamton collections 628
Sykes, Jerome 7206

Tableaux vivants 2439
Tandy, Jessica 7133
Tannenbaum, Jacob 1712
Tarkington, Booth 3191, 5586, 6055–6056, 7028–7035
Tavel, Ronald 1179, 1591
Tayleure, C. W. 4086
Taylor, Douglas 137
Taylor, Joe 4414
Taylor, Laurette 3058, 4416, 7036
Taylor, Mary 2961
Taylor, Oliver 4417
Tefft, W. Erasmus 125
Tempest, Marie 7205
Terry, Megan 1595, 5979, 5988, 6112, 6136, 7037–7039
Terry, William H. 132
Thaw, Harry 4197
The Berkshire Playhouse 2117
The fairy-tale 5543
The Lafayette Players 1368
*The Orphan* 1394
The Rosier Players 2170
*The School for Scandal* 2455
Theater of All Possibilities 2955
Theatre Architecture Commission 445
Theatre Arts Magazine 1296, 1464
Theatre Guild 643, 1448, 1507, 2949–2954, 3857, 3949, 3952, 3988, 4041, 4129–4130, 4309, 4351, 5698, 6049, 6116, 6280, 6739, 6764
*Theatre Magazine* 23
Theatre Of Arts and Letters 2956
Theatre Research Institution 82
Theatre Union 1518, 2957–2958, 5852
Theatrical Syndicate 1452
Thirkield, Robert 2466
Thomas, Augustus 1711, 3008, 3021, 5585–5586, 7041–7044
Thompson, Alfred 4312
Thompson, Denman 4420–4422
Thompson, Lydia 4061, 4884
Thompson, Woodman 4423
Thorne Jr., Charles Robert 4424
Thorne, Charles R. 2970, 4424
Throckmorton, Cleon 4425
Thurber, James 6080, 6099, 7045–7049
Thurman, Wallace 2404
Tiffany, Annie Ward 3005
Tilden, Harriet Converse 6712
Timm, Henry C. 2970
Tobin, Robert L. B. 164, 663
Todd, Mike 4426

363

Toedteberg, Augustus 136
Toohey, John Peter 7033
Toole, J. L. 2928
Torrence, Ridgely 6713, 7050
Towse, John Ranken 4428
Tracy, Spencer 4429–4430
Trained animals 3223
Traisdale Brothers, the 1456
Treadwell, Sophie 7051–7052
Tree, H. B. 6558
Tremont Theatre 2070
Trevor, Leo 3001
Tucker, Lorenzo 4433
Tucker, Sophie 374
Tucker, St George 5736
Turner, Sophia 3126
Twain, Mark 1269, 3877–3878, 6722, 7053
Tyler, George C. 4310, 4435–4437, 7033
Tyler, Odette 2994
Tyler, Priscilla C. 4438
Tyler, Royall 1397, 5359, 5708, 7056–7059
Tyree, Elizabeth 3007
Tyrone Guthrie Theatre 410, 440, 455

U. of Arkansas Theatre 406
U. of Illinois Theatre, Urbana 440
U. of Miami Theatre 406
*Uncle Tom's Cabin* 1454, 1462, 1470, 1475, 1492
United Scenic Artists Union 2959
Updike, John 7060
Urban, Joseph 4439–4440, 4563, 4894
Urquhart, Isabelle 2981
USO 1523–1524

Vaccaro, John 6127
Vakhtangov 1040
Valdez, Luis 6136
Vallee, Rudy 7208
Vallejo, Antonio Buero 6690
Van Itallie, Jean-Claude 1591, 5950, 5979, 6102, 6112, 6117, 6124, 7063
Vance, Nina 2717
Vandenhoff, George 4442
variety theatre 1444
vaudeville 1268
Verdon, Gwen 3085
Verplanck, G. C. 1388
Vidal, Gore 7066–7067
Viertel, Berthold 3241
Vietnam 3888, 5948, 5952, 5985
Vincent, Mrs James R. 4443–4444
Vokes family 2987
Vokes, Rosina 2981
Vonnegut, Kurt 6099, 7068–7071

Wage-earners Theatre League 3659
Wainright, Marie 2981
Waite, James R. 4445
Walker, Stuart 4446
Wallace, William 4086
Wallack Sr., J. W. 3127, 4447
Wallack Theatres 1466
Wallack, J. L. 2975, 2998
Wallack, J. W. 2975, 3025

Wallack, Lester 2301, 2320, 2987, 2992, 3025, 4448
Waller, Emma 3021
Waller, Lewis 2928
Walsh, Blanche 2994
Walsh, James Edward 5395
Walter, Eugene 1442, 5586, 7073
Walton, Lester 4450
Wandor, Micheline 5988
Ward, Artemus 4518
Ward, Douglas Turner 1368, 4452, 5918
Ward, Theodore 1094, 6115
Ward, Winifred 5264
Warde, Frederick 3226
Warfield, David 3005, 3011, 3021, 3024, 4456
Warhol, Andy 3240
Warner, H. B. 4415
Warren Sr., William 3127, 4457–4458
Warren, Mercy Otis 7074–7076
Warren, Robert Penn 6099, 7077–7079
Warren, William 3008, 3010, 3025, 3157, 3183, 4086, 4459–4462
Washington Square Players 643
Washington Square players 1507
Washington Square Players 6049
Washington, Dinah 7295
Washington, George 1392
Waterston, Sam 978
Watkins, H. 4465
Watts, Richard 4466
Webb, Clifton 1544
Webb, Margot 4885
Weber and Fields 3029, 7453
Webster, Margaret 3082, 4469, 4472–4474
Wedekind, Frank 6806
Weidenthal, Leo 155
Weller, Michael 6136
Welles, Orson 856, 3072, 4475–4487
Wendell, E. J. 2928
Wendell, Evert Jansen 1394, 2928
Wenger, John 4489
West, Lillie 4001
West, Mae 3111, 4492–4494
Western Springs Theatre Il 410
Wheatley, Mrs Sarah 3147
Wheatley, William 2982, 2992, 3009, 3021, 4495
Wheeler, Andrew Carpenter 4496, 4607
White Rats of America 4717
White, Charles 2992
White, John Blake 7080
White, Miles 4498
White, Stanford 2928, 4197–4198
Whitman, Robert 1102
Wignell, Thomas 4500, 7055
Wikoff, Henry 4499, 4502
Wilbur, Richard 7454
Wilder, Thornton 927, 1107, 1339, 5595, 5684, 5698, 5788, 5896, 5908, 5917, 5939, 6071, 6073–6074, 6079–6080, 6099, 6101, 6125, 7081–7096, 7098–7105

Wilfred, Thomas 633
Williams, Barney 1322
Williams, Bert 1509, 4886–4887
Williams, Edward G. P. 4607
Williams, Fritz 3006
Williams, Tennessee 1107, 3072, 3111, 3962, 4103, 4416, 4676, 4690, 5484, 5540, 5604, 5655, 5680, 5684, 5694, 5698, 5834, 5847, 5850, 5863, 5896, 5902, 5908, 5919, 5928, 5931, 5939, 5958, 5979, 5989, 6067, 6071, 6074, 6076, 6078–6080, 6082–6083, 6086, 6099, 6102, 6107, 6111, 6125, 6128–6129, 7112–7134, 7136–7141, 7143–7153, 7155–7177, 7180
Williams, William Carlos 7108–7111
Willis, Eola 3227
Willis, N. P. 5359
Willis, Nathaniel Parker 7181–7183
Wilson, August 6136
Wilson, Edmund 7184–7186
Wilson, Francis 2928, 3005, 3013, 3035, 4504, 4508, 7206
Wilson, George W. 4509
Wilson, Lanford 2466, 5392, 5950, 5979, 6102, 6111–6112, 6117, 6127, 6133, 6136, 7187–7193
Wilson, Robert 1113, 1626, 1628, 2420, 4511–4513, 5698, 6123, 6127
Wilson, Woodrow 4519
Winchell, Walter 2429
Winter, William 3167, 3417, 3444, 3636, 4519–4520, 4522–4525, 4607
Winters, Shelley 893
Wirt, William 3151
Witcover, Walt 2915
Witty, May 4470
Wodehouse, P. G. 7457
Wolfe, Thomas 3405, 5700, 5850, 7194–7196
Wolfson, Susan 3272
Wood, Joseph 4528
Wood, Mrs John 2976
Wood, Peggy 4533
Wood, William Burke 2586
Woodberry, George E. 3419
Woodhull, J. 3147
Woodworth, Samuel 7197–7198
Woollcott, Alexander 3237, 4536, 4538–4539, 4541
Wooster Group 2960
Worth, Irene 3116
Worthing, Frank 3021
Wright, Frank Lloyd 437
Wright, John B. 2128
Wright, Richard 6092
Wynn, Ed. 3113

Yale Repertory Theatre 3540
Youmans, Vincent 7458
Young, Brigham 2720, 2736
Young, Mary 2130
Young, Stark 4544–4550
Yurka, Blanche 6050

Ziegfeld Follies 4823
Ziegfeld Theatre 392

# AUTHOR INDEX

Aaron, Daniel 6072
Aaron, Jules C. 5925
Aaron, Stephen 1025
Aaronson, Boris 645
Abbe, Charles S. 2980
Abbott, Anthony 5572
Abbott, Billy M. 4979
Abbott, George 2336, 6144
Abbott, Lyman [=Brown, Ira V.] 3427
Abdul, Raoul 3083
Abel, Lionel 5492
Abel, Samuel D. 5551
Abercrombie, Hugh 7319
Abookiri, Noereena 5252, 5264
Abrahamson, Irving 6337
Abrahamson, Kenneth Z. 2800
Abrams, Dolores 1759, 5133
Abramson, Doris E. 5862
Acker, Lulu M. 2679
Acker, Will 4993
Ackley, Meredith 6459
Adair, Alan H. 2500
Adams, Agatha B. 6418
Adams, Allen J. 1476, 1836
Adams, Annie C. 2325
Adams, Cindy 4409
Adams, Florence A. [= Fowle, Florence] 809
Adams, Franklin P. 3834
Adams, Hazard 5563
Adams, Henry V. 1707
Adams, Joey 3137–3138, 4748, 4754
Adams, Laura 6632–6634
Adams, Maude 860
Adams, Michael C. 7443
Adams, Samuel H. 4416, 4538
Adams, Stephen D. 6920
Adams, W. Davenport 69
Adams, William J. 6758
Adamson, J. 3843
Adamson, Joe 4859
Addams, Jane 3267–3268
Ade, George 4847
Adelman, Irving 5790
Adelugba, Dapo 1325
Adix, Vernon 595
Adler, Irene 4833
Adler, Jacob H. 6460, 7149
Adler, Reba A. 7303
Adler, Stella 1038
Adler, Thomas 5889, 6221, 7148, 7178
Adolphe, Jules W. 5102
Adubato, Robert A. 2856
Agan, Patrick 3876
Ager, Milton 7264
Agnew, D. Hayes 278
Agnew, Jean-Christophe 1422
Aherne, Brian 3274
Ahrends, Günter 6837
Ahuja, Chaman 6857
Aiken, Samuel C. 265
Akin, H. F. 2559
Al-Khayer, M. 7146
Al-Namer, A-S 7174
Albee, E. F. 4886
Albee, Edward 4360, 5533, 5788, 5875, 5917, 6094

Alberti, Eva 869
Albright, A. 982
Albright, Hardie 1120
Albright, Harry D. 620, 870, 5643, 7460
Aldrich, Mrs Thomas B. [= Woodman, Lilian] 3180
Aldridge, Henry B. 2175
Aldridge, Robert E. 6428
Aleandri, Emelise 1693
Alexander, A [= Tuke, Ann] 257
Alexander, B. Shirley 2797
Alexander, Darrel E. 2556
Alexander, Doris 6769
Alexander, Margaret Walker 6140
Alexander, R. E. 609
Alger, Horatio 3758
Alkire, Stephen R. 7241
Allain, Mathé 1693
Allen, Charles A. 1453
Allen, Fred 3275–3276
Allen, Ralph G. 1226, 1319
Allen, Reynolds K. 1971
Allen, Steve 4808
Allen, Virginia 621
Allensworth, Carl 4953
Allison, Tempe E. 5097
Allison, William 82
Allison, William H. 492
Allman, William A. 2516
Almaguer, Thomas M. 7254
Almaraz, Felix D. 2695
Aloi, Roberto 406, 440
Alpert, Hollis 3867, 6497
Alpert, Horace 3332
Altemus, Jameson T. 4111
Altenberg, Roger M. 3531
Alter, Jean 5576
Altman, George 1218
Altman, Richard 7236
Altshuler, Thelma 5499
Alvarez, Ruth M. 6850
Alvis, Arthur 534
Aly, A. M. 6863
Amacher, Richard 6168, 6183
Amberg, George 582, 3389
Ambler, Mary E. 8
Amiard-Chevrel, Claudine 1566
Amory, Cleveland 1544
Andersen, Christopher 3864
Anderson De Navarro, Mary 3285
Anderson, Annette 5998
Anderson, Bo 5689
Anderson, Brenda J. 1417
Anderson, David J. 4614
Anderson, Deborah D. 999
Anderson, Earl 1746
Anderson, Evelyn C. 2185
Anderson, Gary 7100
Anderson, J. Murray. 7319
Anderson, Jervis 2430
Anderson, Jesse M. 6301
Anderson, John 215, 567, 1282
Anderson, John Q. 51
Anderson, Joyce M. 3950
Anderson, Malcolm C. 2534
Anderson, Marilyn J. 5742
Anderson, Mary 3283–3284

Anderson, Maxwell 5472, 5788, 6198, 6208
Anderson, Michael 5608
Anderson, Robert 5533
Anderson, Sherwood 6224
Andreach, Robert J. 6833
Andrew, Richard H. 3074
Andrews, Bart 3315
Andrews, Charles W. 290
Andrews, Charlton 5405, 5580
Andrews, Gertrude 4247
Andrews, Jack E. 2750
Andrews, Mary L. 5762
Andrews, Rusalyn H. 5311
Andrews, W. D. 5949
Andrus, Thomas O. 2190
Angermeier, Carol 6463
Angoff, Charles 1317, 4188
Angotti, Vincent L. 4583
Anikst, Aleksandr A. 5666, 6858
Ann-Ayya Gauda, Hennur H. 5514
Anobile, Richard J. 4861
Anthony, Katharine 7076
Antoine, Le Roi 3509
Appelbaum, Stanley 1483, 2416, 3107, 7272
Appia, Adolphe 556
Appleton, William W. 7433
Apter, Andrew W. 5797
Arai, Anuar M. 5548
Arant, F. Fairlie 3591
Arata, Esther S. 43–44
Arbenz, Mary H. 6764
Arbus, Doon 2914
Arce, Hector 4110, 4268, 4862–4863
Archer, Leonard C. 1294, 1326
Archer, Robyn 7295
Archer, Stephen M. 1152, 3108, 5145, 6022
Archer, William 1428
Ardmore, Jane K. 3856, 4825
Argelander, Ronald J. 1972
Arliss, George 3800
Armatage, Elizabeth 7016
Armfield, Maxwell 550
Armitage, Merle 1799, 3293–3294, 7372
Armoto, Philip M. 7149
Arms, George 6510
Armstrong, W. G. 2577
Arnavon, C. 5896
Arndt, Xavia D. 5051
Arnold, Edward 3295
Arnold, John C. 1994
Arnold, Richard 606, 677
Arnold, Stephanie 5988
Arnott, Catherine M. 7166
Arnott, James F. 32
Aronson, Arnold 668, 678, 1350
Aronson, Lisa 3297
Aronson, Rudolph 3299
Arthur, Kay 6217
Arvold, Alfred G. 2493
Asahina, Roberta R. 1700, 2736
Asermely, Albert A. 3635
Ashby, Clifford 2714
Asher, Don 6277
Ashley, Elizabeth 3300

Ashton, De Witt C. 1060, 4911
Ashworth, Bradford 588
Asp, Bjorne M. 2499
Asral, Ertem 7114
Asselineau, Roger 5896, 6833
Astaire, Fred 7321
Aston, Anthony 1380
Astro, Richard 7024
Athanasopulos, Christos G. 462
Atkins, Alma N. 331
Atkinson, Brooks 434, 1593, 2339, 2394–2395, 3048, 3056, 3062, 3336, 3834, 4416, 4552, 4670, 4677, 4694, 5810, 6600, 7223, 7238
Atkinson, Frank H. 554
Atkinson, George 2777
Atkinson, Jennifer M. 6387, 6814, 6820
Auerbach, Doris 6119
Aufdemberge, Leon M. 6116
Aughtry, Charles E. 6938
Augustin-Thierry, A. 4142
Ausburn, Lynne J. 1783
Auser, Courtland P. 7183
Auslander, Philip 5883, 6137
Austell, Jan 1107
Auster, Albert 1490
Austin, Addell O. 5886
Austin, F. A. 3014
Austin, Gayle 5982, 5988
Austin, John 3931
Avedisian, Louise J. 4148
Averett, Richard A. 1885
Avery, Laurence G. 6207, 6213
Averyt, William B. 513
Ayck, Thomas 6233
Ayers, David H. 6219
Ayers, Stephen M. 1370
Ayres, Alfred [= Osmun, Thomas E.] 817, 4618
Aysom, Richard H. 6037

Baayrok, Lee 7330
Babcock, Dennis 5332
Babcock, Mrs Bernie 3460
Babnich, Judith M. 2259
Bacall. Lauren 3303
Bach, Earl C. 4980
Bach, Gerhard 6409
Backalenick, Irene 2462
Backes, Nancy 5988
Badal, Robert S. 3353
Badeau, Adam 3153
Bader, A. L. 5443
Badrig, Robert 4557
Baer, Warren 1734
Bagchee, Shyamal 6879
Bagley, Mary 2242
Bagley, Russell E. 1861
Bahou, Victor S. 5843
Bailey, Christine E. 1357
Bailey, Claudia J. 61
Bailey, Frances M. 1701
Bailey, Howard 1084
Bailey, Leon E. 3911
Bailey, Mabel D. 6201
Bailey, Mark 3330
Bailey, Pearl 3305–3307, 4802
Baillou, Clemens De 4246
Bain, Helen P. 2661

Bain, Reginald F. 203
Baine, Rodney M. 6723
Baines, Jimmy D. 4881
Bainum, Mary I. 7019
Baird, C. 5085
Baird, John F. 739
Baisch, Jon E. 977
Bakeless, Katherine L. 3050
Baker, Blanch M. 5, 13
Baker, Christina H. 6914
Baker, Donald G. 5676
Baker, Elmer E. 20
Baker, George P. 1513, 4959, 5408
Baker, James W. 659
Baker, John 6243
Baker, Josephine 4811
Baker, Kitty 5228
Baker, Louis C. 5994
Baker, Paul 399, 3054
Baker, R. 4131
Baker, Robert O. 218
Balch, Marston 1589
Balcom, William 7440
Baldwin, James 4682, 6430
Baldwin, John J. 5022
Baldwin, Leland D. 2591
Baldwin, Raymond P. 3607
Baldwin, Stephen C. 5313
Baleanu, Andrei 5600
Balio, Tino 2917
Ball, Robert H. 75
Ball, W. W. 4459
Ball, William 1156
Ball, William T. 2105, 4460
Ball, Zachary [= Masters, Kelly] 1675
Ballinger, Richard H. 6512
Bamburg, William C. 2929
Bander, Robert G. 6070
Bandmann, Daniel E. 3318
Bangs, John K. 3177
Banham, Martin J. 1576
Bank, Rosemarie K. 1700, 5081, 5767
Bankhead, Tallulah 3055, 3319
Banks, Ann 1562
Banks, Carol P. 5464
Baraka, Imamu Amiri 4682
Baral, Robert 2377, 4753
Barber, Philip 572, 1077
Barber, Rowland 4749, 4856
Barber, Rupert T. 2487
Barclay, George L. 4086
Barello, Rudolph V. 2046
Barer, Bertram 1532
Barker, Barbara M. 3975
Barlow, Judith E. 5805, 5979, 6138, 6864, 6879, 6893
Barlow, Wilfred 943
Barnabee, Henry C. 3326
Barnard, Floy M. 339
Barnay, Ludwig 2326
Barnes, Clive 1593, 4594, 4691
Barnes, Djuna 6259
Barnes, Eric W. 4174, 6962
Barnes, Jack D. 1841
Barnes, Noreen 82, 3676
Barnet, Sylvan 5490
Barnett, Gene A. 7191
Barnett, Martha I. 1729
Barr-Sharrar, Beryl 3394

Barranger, Milly S. 3124
Barratt, Louise B. 4902
Barrett, Lawrence 3619, 3759
Barrett, Raina 4770
Barrie, James M. 3773
Barron, Elizabeth A. 7038
Barron, Elwyn A. 3329
Barrows, Alice 397
Barrows, Sarah T. 829
Barry, Jackson G. 5507
Barry, John D. 4062
Barry, Mary D. 3767
Barrymore, Diana 3340
Barrymore, Elaine 3341
Barrymore, Ethel 3055, 3339
Barrymore, John 3333–3334
Barrymore, Lionel 857, 3338
Barsness, Lawrence 487
Bartholomeusz, Dennis 1345
Barto, Dan 6352
Bartolucci, Giuseppe 2903, 5859
Barton, Henry W. 2676
Barton, Margaret 4145
Barton, Mike A. 3403
Bartow, Arthur 1164
Bass, Robert D. 2639
Bassage, Harold E. 5894
Bassett, Clyde H. 2938
Bassham, Ben L. 4354
Batcheller, David R. 5222
Batcheller, Joseph D. 3040, 3372
Batchelor, Ronald 5303
Bateman, Victory 2325
Bates, Alfred 5630
Bates, Brian 1026
Bates, Esther C. 328
Bates, Esther W. 1061, 4889, 4904
Bates, Finis L. 3459
Bates, Helen M. 3605
Bateson, G. A. 5527
Battye, Marguerite 902
Bauer, Mary V. 475
Bauland, Peter 5875, 6030
Baum, Marlyn V. 2435
Baumol, Hilda 251
Baumol, William J. 229, 251
Bautista, Michael P. 2427
Baxter, Marilyn 6278
Bay, Howard 644–645, 5085
Bayer, Paul S. 3078
Baygan, Lee 747–748
Bazaldua, Charles 4352
Bazarini, Ron 1763
Bazin, Andre 4480
Beach, Claudia A. 3826
Beach, Lewis 2332
Beacham, Richard C. 5517
Beagle, T. A. 519
Beaman, Fred J. 3034
Bean, Lisa K. 4368
Beard, Bill L. 1968
Beath, Robert P. 1145
Beaton, Cecil 7398
Beatty, Jerome 4316
Beck, Julian 1578, 2894, 2896–2897, 2901, 2904, 2906
Beck, Martha R. 3437
Beck, Roy A. 653, 5189
Beck-Horn, Debrah A. 6478
Becker, Albert J. 2492
Becker, Ralph E. 2790

Becker, Samuel L. 21
Beckerman, Bernard 1200, 1319, 4695, 5085, 5508
Beckerman, Gloria Brim 1200
Beckman, Heinz 7086
Becvar, William J. 4042
Bedard, Roger L. 5248, 5264
Beebe, Lucius 2266
Beegle, Joanne P. 2612
Beegle, Mary P. 4892
Beer, Arthur J. 5052
Beers, Henry A. 7181
Beger, Lois L. 5258
Behringer, Clara M. 2151
Behringer, Fred D. 6934
Behrman, Samuel N. 4670, 6270, 6273, 6275
Beil, Norman 171
Bel Geddes, Norman 550, 3356, 3358
Belasco, David 479, 1513, 3369
Belcher, Fannis S. 1398
Belknap, Sarah Y. 17
Bell, Archie 2503, 6382
Bell, Charles H. 2550
Bell, William C. 1825, 2809
Bellamy, Ralph 3380
Belli, Angela 5604
Bellinghiere, Joseph J. 4593
Bellman, Willard F. 528, 654, 673
Bellow, Saul 2407, 5443
Bellows, Henry W. 279
Bellville, Cheryl W. 5259
Belmont, Eleanor R. 4311
Beman, Lamar T. 185
Bemelmans, Ludwig 3657
Ben Avram, Rachmael 927
Ben-Zvi, L. 6138
Benardete, Doris F. 2351
Benchley, Robert 4676
Bender, Jack E. 4075
Bender, Lorelle C. 2015
Benedetti, Robert L. 1110, 1360, 5085
Benedict, E. C. 3425
Benedict, Stephen 1138
Benes, Peter 5699
Bennet, Beate Hein 7149
Bennett, Benjamin 5990
Bennett, Estelline 2649
Bennett, George N. 6516
Bennett, Joan 3383
Bennett, Marilyn D. 5077
Bennett, Melba B. 6563
Bennett, Susan 1201
Benny, Jack 4815
Bensman, Joseph 5549
Benson, Kathleen 4839
Benson, Ray 2396
Benson, Richard L. 1474
Benson, Wilbur T. 1932
Benston, Alice N. 5491
Benston, Kimberly W. 1368, 6249–6250
Bentley, Eric 1368, 1546, 2896, 3384, 4662–4663, 4667, 4676, 4692, 5476, 5496, 5501–5502, 5568, 6023, 6776, 6833
Bentley, Gerald E. 5591
Bentley, Joanne 3733
Bentley, Marion J. 923

Bercowitz, Larry 2896
Berezniak, Leon A. 754
Berg, Aubrey 3094
Berg, Cherney 3387
Berger, Jere S. 6169
Berger, Maurice A. 6332
Berger, Phil 4796
Berger, Spencer M. 3345–3346
Bergfald, Milburn J. 1908
Bergman, Herbert 7041
Bergquist, G. William 5369
Bergreen, Laurence 7338
Bergström, Gunnel 6894
Bergstrom, Lois M. 1902
Berkhofer, Robert F. 1337
Berkman, Leonard 7131
Berkowitz, Gerald M. 1634, 7149
Berkson, Michael A. 3555
Berkson, Robert 7315
Berlin, Michael 3955
Berlin, Normand 5538, 6849
Berlin, Richard M. 1144
Berliner, Rudolf 613
Berlogea, Ileana 1691
Berman, Morton 5490
Berman, Sonia 3855
Bermel, Albert 5518
Bernard, John 3399–3400
Bernard, Karl [= Duke of Saxe-Weimar Eisenach] 1383
Bernard, Mrs Bayle 3400
Bernard, William Bayle 3399, 6913
Bernardi, James A. 6997
Bernardin, Charles W. 6357
Bernhard, Randall L. 5072
Bernheim, Alfred L. 217
Bernstein, Aline 3402
Bernstein, Samuel J. 5533, 6774
Berry, C. Cornelius 6923
Berry, Faith 6544
Berry, Melvin H. 2051
Berthoff, Warner B. 7184
Bertin, Michael 4612
Bertram-Cox, Jean De S. 6021
Best, A. Starr 2842
Best, Katharine 2265–2266
Besterman, Theodore 34
Bestor, Arthur E. 5271
Bethune, Robert W. 1019
Betsko, Kathleen 6130
Bettendorf, Frank B. 1772
Bettisworth, Denny 4361
Betts, B. F. 391
Bianco, Patricia S. 1007
Bibee, Jack L. 4051
Bickford, Charles 3406
Biddle, Edmund R. 6359
Biddle, Stephen P. 6095
Biddulph, Helen R. 4936
Bieber, Albert A. 5370
Bier, Jessa. 3257
Bigelow, Edwin L. 2494
Bigsby, C. W. 1368, 5677, 5698, 5915, 5960, 5979, 6156, 6172, 6636, 6702–6703
Bilgray, Ruth 6006
Billeter, Erika 2893
Billings, Alan G. 2851
Billington, Michael 6608
Bills, Steven H. 6474
Biner, Pierre. 2899

Bing, Sir Rudolf 1138
Binns, Archie 3719
Bird, Mary M. 6291
Bird, Robert M. 6290
Birdman, Jerome M. 6031
Birdoff, Harry 1454
Birdsall, Elizabeth 1573
Birdwell, Christine R. 1694
Birkenhead, Thomas B. 224
Birkmire, William H. 383
Birner, Mona 1978
Birtwistle, Michael D. 615
Bishop, Cynthia A. 1039
Bishop, Emily M. 811
Bishop, George V. 4875
Bishop, James A. 3813
Bishop, Jim 3469, 3858
Bitz, Nellie E. 2286
Bizardel, Yvon 4009
Bjorksten, Ingmar 1583
Black, Eugene 3941
Black, George W. 6622
Black, Lendley C. 3573
Black, Malcolm 1133
Black, Stephen A. 6879, 7048
Blackburn, Clara B. 6002
Blackburn, Joyce 4464
Blackburn, Margaret 2213
Blackie, Pamela 5155
Blackwell, L. 7148
Blackwood, Byrne D. 421
Bladel, Roderick 3973
Blain, Lynda C. 2716
Blair, John P. 2431
Blake, Ben 1518
Blake, Betty 880
Blake, Charles 2634–2635
Blake, Gary 980, 4372
Blake, Peter H. 2160
Blakely, Don 3582
Blakely, Sidney H. 4244
Blanc, Robert E. 6649
Blanchard, Dagny 5126
Blanchard, Fred C. 6196
Blandford, Lucy 7058
Blank, Earl 5117
Blank, Martin J. 7089
Blasingame, D. M. 1976
Blau, Eric 7237
Blau, Herbert 1151, 1188, 1202, 5980, 6676, 6684
Blaugher, Kurt C. 2553
Bledsoe, Jerry H. 432
Blesh, Rudi 4843
Blesi, Marius 4173
Blitgen, Carol 2079, 6465
Bloch, Beverle R. 6596
Block, Anita 1520
Block, Maxine 3041
Blom, Harold 6238
Blom, Thomas A. 4030
Blondell, John 6640
Bloom, Arthur W. 1850
Bloom, Gilbert L. 3793
Bloom, Harold 6873
Bloom, Ken 7291
Bloom, Sol 3408
Bloomfield, Arthur J. 1768
Bloomquist, Jane McC. 5312
Bloore, J. S. 340
Blum, Daniel 1334, 1570, 3049

Blum, Richard 963, 1043
Blumberg, Marcia 6879
Blumenthal, Arthur R. 682
Blumenthal, Eileen 2921, 3564
Blumenthal, George 3410
Blumenthal, Oscar 3416
Blunt, Jerry 911, 983
Blymer, Louise A. 4570
Boardman, Abigail C. 2345
Boatright, Joel 651
Bock, Frank G. 1680
Bock, Fred C. 616
Bock, Hedwig 6111
Bode, Carl 5283, 6655
Bodeen, DeWitt. 3039
Bodman, James E. 366
Boeker, Thomas W. 6104
Bogar, Thomas A. 4218
Bogard, Morris R. 2843
Bogard, Travis 4342, 5110, 5140, 5692, 5788, 5908, 5917, 6776, 6833, 6850, 6880–6882
Bogen, Mel 5235
Boggs, Nancy 246
Bogle, Donald 3097
Bogusch, George 3362
Bohner, Charles H. 7077
Bokar, Camille N. 1796
Boleslavsky, Richard 842, 4959
Bolin, John S. 3904
Bolton, Guy 7456
Bolton, Randy 2839
Bonawitz, Dorothy M. 2116
Bond, Frederick W. 5642
Bond, Roger B. 1857
Bongar, Emmet W. 518
Bongas, Pamela J. 1563
Bonin, Jane F. 5378, 5382
Bonner, T. 5979
Bontemps, Arna 2404
Booth, Edwin 3507
Booth, John E. 893
Booth, John N. 3484
Borchardt, Donald D. 5007
Bordman, Gerald 93, 4797, 7263, 7273, 7395, 7458
Boretz, N. M. 1163
Borgers, Edward W. 2273
Boroff, Phil D. 4014
Borreson, Ralph 3473
Borum, May R. 1728
Bossone, Richard M. 5660
Bost, James S. 1415, 6310
Bosworth, Halliam 833
Bosworth, Patricia 3581
Botto, Louis 2440
Boucher, John N. 2583
Boucicault, Dion 834
Boughton, Donald J. 6210
Bouillon, Jo 4811
Boulanger, Norman 791
Boulton, Agnes 6759
Bourdet, Edouard 5810
Bourjaily, Vance 7068
Bousliman, Charles W. 2544
Boustkeon, Lindy 2811
Bowden, Edwin T. 7046
Bowen, Croswell 6761
Bowen, Elbert R. 2224
Bowen, Roy H. 586
Bowen, William G. 229

Bower, Homer T. 1773
Bower, Martha Gilman 6885
Bowker, Richard R. 179
Bowles, James B. 6610
Bowles, Paul 7155
Bowman, Ned A. 407, 412, 420, 743, 1319, 2568
Bowman, Walter P. 75
Bowman, Wayne 498
Bowmer, Angus L. 2566
Bowyer, Frances E. 4179
Boxandall, Lee 5917
Boxill, Roger 7172
Boyadzhev, G. 5666
Boyar, Burt 4829
Boyd, Alice K. 2347
Boyd, Charles A. 329
Boyd, Theodore E. 2040
Boyden, Walter E. 372
Boyer, Robert 2786
Boyers, Robert 6606
Boyle, Walter P. 404
Boynton, Percy H. 6056
Bracewell, John L. 5046
Brackett, J. Albert 167
Brackin, Edward G. 2608
Bradby, David 2944, 4947
Braden, Edwina C. 2702
Bradfield, Raymond A. 4151
Bradford, Arthur L. 5106
Bradford, Clinton W. 2021
Bradford, Gamaliel 3430, 3924
Bradlee, Frederick. 1544
Bradley, Edward S. 6298
Bradley, Lawrence 1922
Bradley, Mark J. 6346
Bradley, Robert H. 1468
Bradshaw, John 3883
Bradsher, Eviola 2012
Brady, Barbara. 3059
Brady, Donald V. 2696
Brady, Frank 4485
Brady, James J. 4420
Brady, Owen E. 6250
Brady, William A. 3511–3512
Brady, William H. 5023
Braem, Helmut M. 6154, 6777
Bragdon, Claude 3515–3517
Bragg, Lillian C. 1873
Brahms, Caryl 7285
Brainard, Charles H. 4236
Brainerd, Thomas 271
Brandes, K. K. 2555
Brandt, Alvin G. 348
Branen, Jeff 4729
Brastov, Virginia 1732
Brater, Enoch 374, 6138
Braun, Thomas C. 1121
Braunlich, Phyllis C. 6940
Brawley, Benjamin 1280
Brazee, Annie L. 4988
Brazier, Marian H. 2112
Brecht, Stefan 1612, 2420, 2841
Brede, Charles F. 2584
Brede, Regine 6170
Breed, Paul F. 6096
Breen, Robert S. 6560
Breitman, Ellen 161
Breneman, Lucille N. 1881
Brenman-Gibson, Margaret 5531, 6905

Brennan, Jane N. 3767
Brenner, Walter C. 2775
Brenni, Vita J. 6525
Brennin, John M. 7014
Brereton, Austin 2985, 4063
Breslauer, Jan 5988
Brewer, Courtney H. 2733
Brian, Dennis 3320
Brian, George 2022, 2041
Bricker, Herschel L. 766
Bridenbaugh, Carl 2611
Bridge, William H. 850
Bridgeman, Frieda E. 437
Bridgman, Richard 7013
Brie, Friedrich 6817
Briggs, John 2389
Brink, Alice M. 2148
Brinton, Christian 3289
Briscoe, Adelaide M. 5008
Briscoe, Johnson 1441, 3016
Bristol, Michael D. 6051
Bristow, Donald G. 6936
Bristow, Eugene K. 2666
Brittain, Joan T. 7006
Brittin, Norman A. 6658
Bro, Marguerite H. 1215
Brock, Richard B. 1948
Brockett, Lenyth S. 1083
Brockett, Oscar G. 21, 1233, 1239, 1241, 1257, 1322, 4705, 5085
Brockington, John 6454
Brockman, C. Lance 2205
Brodin, Pierre 6089
Brogna, John J. 6412
Brokaw, John W. 1693
Bronner, Edwin 87
Brook, Peter 542
Brooks, Alfred G. 946
Brooks, Charles B. 7149
Brooks, Gwendolyn 6542
Brooks, Mona R. 1419
Brooks, Noah 6321
Brooks, Van W. 1397, 4523, 6517
Broom, Leonard 2481
Broomall, Will 858
Broomfield, William C. 2154
Brophy, Robert J. 6567
Brough, James 4542
Broun, Daniel 2397
Broun, Heywood 180, 307, 3527, 3529, 4886
Broussard, Louis 5902
Brown, Alice 7074
Brown, Benjamin W. 219, 1075
Brown, Betty J. 2686
Brown, Catherine H. 3846
Brown, Cecil 7171
Brown, Edward D. 1706, 2033
Brown, Firman M. 2248
Brown, Frank C. 2
Brown, Gilmor 705, 1066, 3054
Brown, Helen T. 7055–7056
Brown, Henry 301
Brown, Irving M. 2531
Brown, James L. 5033
Brown, Janet 6106
Brown, Jared 4027
Brown, Jared A. 6924
Brown, Joe E. 3532
Brown, John H. 2995

Brown, John M. 567, 3038, 3310, 3533, 3834, 3940, 3942, 4467, 4569, 4640, 4645, 4647, 4649, 4655–4656, 4659–4660, 4665, 4671, 5815, 6984–6985
Brown, John R. 1305
Brown, Joseph Lee 1073
Brown, Kenneth H. 2894
Brown, L. E. 4923
Brown, Laurence R. 4573
Brown, Lloyd L. 4298
Brown, Lloyd W. 6253
Brown, Lorraine 2858
Brown, Maria W. 4872
Brown, Mary 1487
Brown, Maurice F. 6718
Brown, R. M. 6770
Brown, Ray 7204
Brown, Richard P. 944, 6593
Brown, Sterling A. 5639
Brown, T. Allston 2327, 2965, 4712
Brown, Thelma 1880
Brown, William L. 2294
Brown-Guillory, Elizabeth 6140
Browne, Maurice 3536–3537
Browne, Walter 3014
Browning, Beth 2723
Browning, Richard J. 2495
Brownlee, Mary A. 2157
Brownstein, Oscar L. 5539
Broxam, Pearl B. 3035
Bruccoli, Matthew J. 6387, 6732–6733
Bruce, Kitty 4818
Bruce, Lenny 4816
Bruch, Debra L. 5569
Bruck, Peter 6232
Bruder, Karl C. 587, 624
Brumm, Beverly M. 2409
Brüning, Eberhard 5857, 5953
Brustein, Robert 1600, 2896, 3540, 4513, 4612, 4676, 4678, 4686, 4702, 4709, 5597, 5788, 5914, 5917, 5944, 6172, 6606
Bryan, George 63
Bryan, George S. 3467
Bryant, Arthur 4294
Bryant, Billy 4736
Bryant, Donald C. 21
Bryant, Hazel 2833
Bryant, Ruth M. 1963
Bryer, Jackson R. 5979, 6090, 6480, 6808, 6850, 6880, 6893
Brynner, Rock 3541
Brynner, Yul 882
Bryson, John 3865
Bryson, Nicholas L. 634
Buch, Arthur T. 358
Buchanan, Randall J. 6203
Buchloh, Paul G. 5875
Buchman, Herman 744
Buchwald, Art 6325
Buckley, J. M. 291
Bucks, Dorothy S. 5763
Buckstone, J. B. 279
Budke, Timothy D. 211
Buell, William A. 3066
Buerki, F. A. 635
Bulliet, Clarence J. 1886, 4053
Bullins, Ed 5533, 5675, 5920

Bullough, Bess 5155
Bundick, Theresa J. 2203
Bunn, Alfred 1658
Bunnell, Peter 4691
Bunner, H. C. 2977
Bunnett, Rex 112
Burack, A. S. 5454
Buratti, David 4601
Burbank, Rex 7094
Burbick, William G. 2536
Burch, Roger B. 520
Burdick, Elizabeth B. 86, 645
Burdick, Jacques 1242
Burge, James C. 1423
Burger, Isabel B. 5113
Burgess, Frank G. 1777
Burggraaff, Winfield 3386
Burgh, James 793
Burk, Robert E. 6973
Burke, Billie 3542–3543, 4555
Burke, John [= O'Connor, Richard] 7436
Burke, John J. 5178
Burke, William M. 5866
Burkhard, Arthur 6017
Burleigh, Louise 4896
Burley, Gertrude S. 4930
Burman, Ben L. 4739
Burman, Howard V. 5448
Burns, Elizabeth 5515, 5519
Burns, George 4819–4822
Burns, Glen 5875
Burns, Mary W. 2517
Burns, Morris U. 4541
Burns, Tom 5519
Burns, Warren T. 6439
Burr, David H. 4050
Burr, James G. 2469
Burris-Meyer, Harold 83, 405, 444, 501, 576
Burroughs, Marie 2986
Burroughs, Patricia 3838, 4256
Burroughs, Robert C. 18, 694
Burrows, Abe 7347
Burrows, J. L. 284
Burrows, Michael B. 4059
Burto, William 5490
Burton, Chester J. 449
Burton, Clarence M. 2147
Burton, Guthrie 3802
Burton, Jack 4757, 7227
Burton, May E. 7461
Burton, Philip 3545
Burton, Richard 4566, 5753, 6381
Busch, Estelle 1805
Busch, Frederick M. 6445
Busfield, Roger M. 22
Bush, Joan D. 4981
Buss, Stephen R. 1486
Butcher, Margaret J. 1323
Butler, D. E. 593
Butler, Ignatius W. 313
Butler, James H. 1319
Butt, William G. 4972
Buttitta, Tony 2864
Butts, Hugh F. 1368
Buxton, Amity L. 1848
Byers, Jack A. 711
Byers, Ruth 5141
Bynum, Lucy S. 7042
Byrd, Harry F. 7341

Cadby, Louise K. 1679
Cade, Toni 5920
Cady, Edwin H. 6514–6515, 6520, 6526, 6528
Caffaro, Father 264
Caffin, Caroline 4723
Caffin, Charles H. 4564
Cahalan, Thomas L. 5898
Cahill, Thomas H. 2083
Cahn, Dudley D. 984
Cahn, Julius 1662
Cahn, Sammy 7348
Cahn, William 3071, 4832
Cain, Vernice P. 7161
Caldwell, Carolyn E. 3610
Caldwell, George R. 1182
Calhoun, John T. 5929
Calkins, Earnest Elmo 2338
Callahan, John M. 2238
Calloway, Cab 7349
Calvery, Catherine A. 6076
Calvin, Judith S. 4750
Cameron, James 6470
Cameron, John C. 7189
Cameron, Kenneth M. 1259, 5058
Cameron, N. 1374
Camner, James 7272
Campbell, C. Jean 957
Campbell, Charles 6327
Campbell, Douglas 1315
Campbell, Johnstone 6039
Campbell, Kenneth 5027
Campbell, Patricia J. 4790
Campbell, Paul N. 1250
Campbell, Sandy 3324
Campbell, Wayne 841
Campnett, A. L. 6815
Canaday, N. 5979
Canary, Robert H. 6371
Candler, Martha [= Cheney, Martha S.] 326
Canfield, Curtis 1097
Canfield, Mary C. 1544, 4636
Canning, Beverly E. 4230
Cannon, Fanny 5406, 5409
Cantlin, John R. 2578
Cantor, Arthur 772
Cantor, Eddie 3552–3554, 3928, 4553, 4823–4827
Cantor, Harold 6904
Capasso, Maddalena R. 6127
Capbern, A. Martial 5230
Capote, Truman 6495
Cappel, Edith 6011
Capriole, Ettore 2882
Card, James 3346
Cardell, Victor T. 82
Cardullo, Bert 3955
Carey, Gary 3519, 3861, 3882, 4022
Carey, Mathew 256
Carey, William 1390
Cargill, Oscar 6765–6766
Carlson, Eugene T. 6469
Carlson, Harry G. 5808, 6894
Carlson, Marvin 469, 1263, 5552, 5577
Carlson, Susan 5988
Carmichael, Herbert K. 5360
Carne-Ross, D. S. 6608
Carnes, Edwin H. 610

Carney, Benjamin F. 2069
Carney, Saraleigh 2417
Carnine, Dennis 510
Carnovsky, Morris 1008, 1225
Caro, Robert A. 4227
Caro, Warren 1138
Carpenter, Barbara L. 5041
Carpenter, Bruce 5469
Carpenter, Charles A. 64
Carpenter, Dana 5065
Carpenter, Frederick I. 5927, 6562, 6752, 6833, 6840
Carr, Carmelia 3621
Carr, Michael C. 550
Carr, Virginia S. 6646, 6648
Carra, Lawrence 1170, 1319
Carrington, Richard H. 6624
Carroll, David. 3080
Carroll, Dennis 6638
Carroll, Howard. 2974
Carroll, Janet 4473
Carroll, Renee 3198
Carroll, Vernon H. 2706
Carrow, Catherine I. 2680
Carruth, Gorton 6121
Carson, Ada L. 7059
Carson, Neil 6696
Carson, William G. 2217–2218, 2230, 3903
Carter, Everett 6513
Carter, Jean 4916
Carter, Kathryn E. 5555
Carter, Leslie H. 737
Carter, Paul J. 6398
Carter, Randolph 4563
Cartmell, Dan J. 7444
Cartmell, Van H. 851, 892
Carvajal, Christa 1693
Case, Robert O. 5277
Case, Sue-Ellen 1258, 5578, 5988, 6138
Case, Victoria 5277
Casey, J. C. 3560
Cashin, Charles M. 2087
Cashin, Fergus 4492
Casper, Leonard 7149
Cass, Carl B. 5321
Cassady, Marshall 1033, 1253, 2546
Cassady, Pat 1253
Castle, Jane 7334
Castronovo, David 7105
Castronovo, Frank A. 2551
Cather, Willa 3561
Catron, Louis E. 1169, 5462
Cauble, J. R. 225
Caughey, Mary B. 1283
Cavanagh, John 66
Cavanaugh, Jim 776
Cavett, Dick 6575
Celada, A. Rodriguez 6690
Celant, Germano 4131
Centeno, Augusto 5422
Centola, S. R. 5979
Cermele, Dominick J. 5066
Chabrowe, Leonard 6830
Chach, Maryann 82
Chagy, Gideon 237
Chaikin, Joseph 2896, 3563
Chaim, Daphna B. 1194
Challender, James W. 7296

Chalmers, Helena 738, 839
Chametzky, Jules 374, 6239
Champagne, Lenora 6141
Champine, Gemma E. 2452
Champion, Larry S. 1350
Chance, Thomas E. 1855
Chandler, Charlotte. 3111
Chandler, Laura 5979
Chapel, Robert C. 5059
Chapin, Robert F. 1735
Chapin, Theodore S. 7318
Chaplin, Leola B. 6356
Chapman, Frederick L. 2049
Chapman, John 1505, 1531
Charters, Ann 4887
Chase, Chris 4351
Chase, Gilbert 7211
Chase, Ilka 3569–3571
Chase, Mary C. 5847
Chavane, J. Paul 2143
Chaxel, Françoise Du 6809
Cheek, Leslie 3054
Cheifetz, Dan 5147
Chekhov, Michael 882, 1020, 1098
Cheney, Ann 6432
Cheney, Sheldon 551, 555, 1204–1205, 1207, 1235
Chenoweth, Eugene C. 4969
Chesley, Gene 98
Chester, Giraud 3662
Chester, S. Alan 7149
Chester, Violet L. 1730
Chesterton, G. K. 6302
Chestnut, Glenn F. 2687
Chicorel, Marietta 5238, 5375, 5379
Chifre, Joseph S. 2143
Childs, George W. 3163
Chiles, Rosa P. 4241
Chiles, Ruth 1702
Chinoy, Helen K. 875, 1123, 1319, 1467, 1487, 3119
Chisman, Margaret S. 2659
Chmel, Patrick J. 1553
Chopcian, Kendra A. 3539
Chorba, Albert Von 5364
Chorpenning, Charlotte B. 5216
Chothia, Jean 6831, 6841, 6893
Choudhuri, A. D. 6107
Choukri, Mohamed 7155
Chreist, Frederick M. 1945
Christovich, David P. 4154
Chubb, Percival 5087–5088
Chung, F. K. 6682
Churchill, Allen 1534, 1554, 2364
Cicdurel, Aron V. 888
Ciment, Michael 3959, 3966
Cioffi, Robert J. 7266
Cirker, Blanche. 774
Citron, S. J. 5122
Citron, Stephen 7316
Claeren, Wayne H. 6330
Clapp, Henry A. 3575
Clapp, John B. 2108, 2993, 4620
Clapp, William W. 2079
Clark, Barrett H. 183, 310, 558, 766, 1062, 1276, 1826, 5319, 5417–5418, 5494, 5586–5587, 5593, 5640, 5755, 6066, 6195, 6355, 6413–6414, 6740, 6746
Clark, Davis M. 3592

Clark, Edwin L. 1174
Clark, Eleanor 3889
Clark, J. H. 7148
Clark, John L. 4998
Clark, Larry D. 4355
Clark, Leroy W. 3963
Clark, Linda K. 2707
Clark, Samuel S. 4722
Clark, Sidney M. 6587
Clark, Susan F. 6262
Clark, Susie C. 4082
Clark, Walter L. 2117
Clark, William B. 2539
Clarke, Asia B. 3465, 3502, 3505
Clarke, Janis D. 1000
Clarke, Joseph I. 3187
Clarke, M[ARY] 3833
Clarke, Mitchell 1989
Clarke, Norman 2385
Clarke, Shareen M. 3075
Clarkson, Philip B. 6547
Clay, James H. 1106
Clay, Lucille N. 1986
Clayton, Jan 7427
Clayton, John J. 6283
Clayton, John S. 7113
Cleaver, Eldridge 3243
Clement, Clara E. 3618
Cleveland, Charles 288
Clevinger, Donna L. 2180
Clifford, Charles V. 2233
Clifford, John 5236, 6426
Cline, Jay J. 5107
Clinger, Morris M. 5019
Clithero, Edith P. 5003
Clough, 'Goldie' Stanton 6380
Clum, John M. 6333, 7050
Clurman, Harold 1077, 1122, 1579, 1593, 2886, 3583, 4664, 4667, 4679, 4697, 5788, 6083, 6094, 6172, 6676, 7148
Clüver, Claus Von 5665, 7095
Coad, Oral S. 1274, 6368
Coakley, James 7149
Cobb, Mel 6893
Cobbett, William 4345
Cobin, Martin T. 899, 5832
Coburn, Charles 1873
Coburn, Frank W. 4509
Cocchi, Jeanette F. 7365
Cochran, James P. 1088
Cocke, Inez 3784
Coco, William 1200
Cocroft, Thoda. 3204
Cocuzza, Ginnine 3691
Cocuzzo, Giannine 82
Coder, William D. 2589
Coe, Kathryn C. 5357
Coffin, Arthur B. 6565
Coffman, Victoria M. 5302
Cogdill, John C. 1292
Coger, Leslie 881, 898, 920
Cogniat, Raymond 4007
Cogswell, Margaret 413
Cohan, George M. 4107, 4886, 7351
Cohen, Alexander H. 1138
Cohen, Edward M. 1165
Cohen, Hilary U. 1629
Cohen, John 4817
Cohen, Micky 3250

Cohen, Robert 970, 1049, 1130, 1371, 5340
Cohen, Sarah B. 374, 5956
Cohen-Stratyner, Barbara N. 82, 163, 7309
Cohn, Art 4426, 4851
Cohn, Ruby 4612, 5605, 5680, 5701, 5875, 5956, 6112, 6134, 6138, 6157, 7148
Coigne, Frank B. 826
Coigney, Martha W. 1593
Colby, Elbridge 5710
Cole, David 1134
Cole, Edward C. 401, 444, 576, 762
Cole, John R. 958
Cole, Marion 2528
Cole, Toby 875, 936, 1123, 6071
Cole, Wendell 589, 1700
Coleman, Arthur P. 4121
Coleman, Arthur 4680
Coleman, Edwin L. 6537
Coleman, Elizabeth T. 4438
Coleman, J. 5979
Coleman, J. Winston 1998
Coleman, John W. 3476
Coleman, Marion M. 4121–4122, 4124–4125, 6027
Coles, Elizabeth E. 5718
Colin, Paul 4810
Colley, Thomas 2948
Collier, Gaylan 886
Collier, William. 3132
Collinge, Patricia 1524
Collins, Betty J. 4974
Collins, John D. 3259, 5731
Collins, Leslie M. 3044
Collins, Mabel 4112
Collom, Jeffrey R. 646
Colvan, Ezekiel B. 861
Colyer, Carlton 1044
Combs, Charles E. 5264
Combs, Don W. 2001
Comer, Irene F. 7267
Commeret, Lorraine M. 3446
Commins, Dorothy 6869
Comtois, M. E. 4700
Condee, William F. 2458
Conger, Col. E. J. 3471
Conlin, Kathleen A. 1354
Conn, Arthur L. 1784
Connell, Brian 3695
Connelly, Marc 3939, 6334
Conner, Laurence M. 5159
Conner, Patricia S. 4866
Connington, Bill 1051
Connolly, Mike 4343
Connor, Billy M. 5398
Connors, Timothy D. 4791
Conolly, L. W. 1487
Conrad, Earl 4337
Conrad, Edna 5148
Constantinidis, Stratos E. 1157
Conta, Floria 7098
Conway, M. D. 280
Cook, Albert 5478
Cook, David B. 4275
Cook, Doris E. 3804
Cook, Gary D. 4456
Cook, Thomas E. 6772
Cook, William 1368

Cooke, Delmar G. 6507
Cooke, Thomas P. 1116
Cooley, Edna H. 1496
Coolidge, Olivia 6787
Cooper, Allen R. 1933
Cooper, Charles W. 5655
Cooper, Janet L. 5190
Cooper, Paul R. 3994
Cooper, Philip 6605
Cooper, Roberta K. 1854
Cooper, T. G. 1365
Cooperman, Robert 6908
Coote, Albert W. 1851
Cope, Garrett L. 4982
Copeland, Bob H. 2617
Copeland, Charles T. 3423
Copland, Aaron 7343
Copley, Deana K. 5249
Copp, Karen H. 252
Corbin, Germaine 4386
Corbin, John 5788
Cordell, Richard A. 2357
Cordell, William H. 5357
Cordray, Laurie A. 523
Corey, Irene 709, 749
Corio, Anne 4763
Cornberg, Sol 597
Cornelison, Gayle L. 5241
Cornell, Katharine 884, 3595
Cornell, Ted 4224
Cornish, Roger N. 5926
Cornyn, Stan 23
Correll, Laraine 82
Corrigan, Marie 155
Corrigan, Mary Ann 7149
Corrigan, Robert W. 1225, 1247, 1251, 1613, 5669, 6676
Corsaro, Frank 3598
Corsini, B. Andrew 465
Corson, Richard 742
Cortez, Jerry V. 3917
Corvey, Lane 1923
Cosentino, Giacomo 6824
Cosgrave, Luke 3599
Cosgrove, James D. 5983
Cosgrove, Stuart 1495, 2944, 5880
Costello, D. P. 7148
Costigan, Daniel M. 2276
Costopoulos, John 5887
Costy, James O. 6503
Cotten, Joseph 3600
Cotton, Jerry D. 6968
Cottrell, John 3475
Couch, Nena 82
Couch, William 5918
Coughenour, Kay L. 641
Coulson, James P. 1301
Counts, Michael L. 5891
Courtney, Marguerite 4416
Cousins, Norman 6985
Covarrubias, Miguel. 3031
Coven, Brenda 4228, 6120
Covey, Liz 725
Cowan, J. M. 846
Cowan, Robert A. 2369
Coward, Noël 7230
Cowell, Joe 3602
Cowell, W. 286
Cowley, Malcolm 1540, 6077
Cox, Charles W. 1089
Cox, James R. 2645

Cox, Kenneth D. 3819
Cox, Martha 6199, 6202
Cox, Paul R. 5794
Cox, Wallace 3603
Cox, William 3147
Coy, Javier 6081, 6173
Coy, Juan J. 6081, 6173
Coyle, Lee 6151
Coyne, Bernard A. 2767
Crafton, Allen 838, 868, 1057, 1070
Craig, Anna A. 5088
Craig, David 7317
Craig, E. Quita 2860
Craig, Hardin 1667
Craig, Warren 7264
Craig, William S. 1916, 4392
Craig, Wolf R. 680
Crain, Harold C. 5826
Crain, William H. 3790
Crane, Joshua 1180
Crane, Walter 808
Crane, William H. 4313
Crawford, Cheryl 3609
Crawford, Jack R. 4892
Crawford, Jerry L. 985
Crawford, Mary C. 1270, 2101, 2104, 2106
Crawford, Ray S. 1050
Crawford, Richard 7311
Crawford, Robert W. 782
Crawford, Robert A. 2264
Creahan, John 3968
Cressy, Will M. 4724
Crichton, Kyrle 4853
Crick, J. F. 6609
Criswell, Jeron 5418
Crocker, Charlotte 858
Croghan, Leland A. 2386
Cronin, Harry 6832
Cronin, James E.(Ed.) 3248
Crooker, Earle T. 7212
Crosby, Robert L. 6604
Crosscup, Richard 5136
Crossett, David A. 2625
Crothers, Rachel 5413
Crouch, Paul H. 1146
Crow, Duncan. 4502
Crow, Porter J. 5667
Crowe, Rachael M. 5080
Crowley, Alice L. 2358
Crowley, Elmer S. 1824
Crowther, Bosley 465, 4747
Croy, Homer 4329
Croyden, Margaret 1571
Cruikshank, Alfred B. 4155
Cruise, Boyd 2055
Cruise, William 644
Crum, Mabel I. 1995
Cruse, Harold 1584
Csida, Joseph 4781
Cullen, Rosemary L. 82
Cullman, Marguerite 768
Culp, Ralph B. 1117, 5723
Culver, Max K. 535
Cumming, Marsue 78
Cummings-Wing, Julia 1009
Cummins, Douglas M. 4950
Cunningham, Donald H. 3385
Curb, Rosemary 5988
Currey, William L. 196

Currie, Barton 7028
Curry, Richard J. 5309
Curry, Samuel S. 810, 816, 821
Curry, Wade C. 4033
Curtin, Kaier 1366
Curtis, Mary J. 2643
Curtis, P. 6684
Curtis, Thomas Q. 4666
Curvin, J. W. 5643
Cushman, Henry W. 3614
Cutler, Jean V. 3633
Czechowski, Jan 1937

D'Amico, Victor E. 562
D'Angelo, Aristide 859
D'Auvergne, Edmund B. 4138
D'Essen, Lorrain 3223
Dabney, Edith 697
Dace, Letitia 1324, 6243
Dace, Wallace 1324, 1625
Dackslager, Earl D. 1350
Dahl, Curtis 6293
Dahl, Mary K. 5625
Dailey, Irene 946
Dale, Alan [= Cohen, Alfred J.] 1430, 2981
Daley, Elizabeth M. 4588
Daley, Mary P. 4597
Dali, Salvador 4336
Dalrymple, Jean 2413, 3626, 5329
Dalton, Donald B. 2490
Dalva, Harry O. 2518
Daly, Augustin 3417
Daly, Charles P. 299, 1391
Daly, John J. 7341
Daly, Joseph F. 3630
Dameron, Louise 573
Damon, Ruth A. 4994
Daniel, Walter C. 3841
Daniels, Barry 6980
Daniels, Jonathan 3977
Darling, Amanda 4149
Dasgupta, Gautam 1246, 3955, 6117
Dashiell, George 258
Dauber, Max 5099
Daubert, Darlene M. 1185, 5539
Daughrity, Kenneth L. 7182
Davee, Paul W. 4983
Davenport, Allen 1438–1439
Davenport, F. Garvin 2656
Davey, Kate 6394
Davidge, William 283, 3645
Davidson, Donald 6991
Davidson, Frank C. 4744
Davidson, Ivan H. 6816
Davies, Acton 3262
Davis, Ariel R. 499
Davis, Bette 3647
Davis, Blanche E. 5649
Davis, Charles T. 6715
Davis, Christopher 3686
Davis, David F. 3067
Davis, J. M. 5979
Davis, Jackson 2692
Davis, Jed H. 598, 5197, 5227, 5231, 5253, 5329
Davis, Jerry L. 3354
Davis, John P. 1303
Davis, Joseph K. 5875, 7149
Davis, Ken 1197

Davis, Lenwood G. 4303
Davis, Lorrie 7245
Davis, Michael M. 2329
Davis, Ossie 5410
Davis, Owen 5788, 6348–6349
Davis, Peter A. 6546
Davis, R. G. 2945
Davis, Richard B. 2751
Davis, Richard H. 4725, 6353
Davis, Robert M. 7025
Davis, Ronald J. 7044
Davis, Ronald L. 1677
Davis, Ronald O. 5976
Davis, Sammy 4829
Davis, Susan 2632, 6116
Davis, Thadious M. 6126
Davis, Tracy C. 1261
Davy, Kate 6395
Dawson, Mary E. 5474
Dawson, William M. 6078
Day, Charles H. 3649, 4712
Day, Christine 7154
Day, Clarence 6598
Day, Cyrus 6776
Day, Donald 4328, 4330
Day, Myrle 1910
Day, Roy 2930
Day, Susan S. 4495
Dayton, Abram C. 2323
Dayton, Helena S. 4902
Dazey, Charles T. 6355
De Angelis, Jefferson 3650
De Chaine, Faber B. 933
De Goveia, Clarence J. 4903
De Hart, Stanley C. 5179
De Koven, Anna F. 7358
De Metz, Ouida K. 2054
de Mille, Agnes 3545
De Neuf, Richard 4194
De Rohan, Pierre 2846–2847
De Voe, E. T. 6295
De Vries, Jenny B. 6033
De Wolf, Richard C. 182
De Wolfe, Elsie 3656
De Zayas, Marius 4723
Deam, William L. 3413
Dean, Alexander 1170, 4905
Dean, Anne 6641
Debus, Allen G. 107
Debusscher, Gilbert 5979, 6153, 6172, 7148
Dechaine, Faber B. 1832
Decker, Philip H. 5599
Dee, Elaine Evans 4011
Defoe, Louis V. 3369
DeGaetani, Thomas 410
Degitz, Dorothy M. 1821
Deisler, Faith 194
Del Vecchio, Ann 5304
Deland, Margaret 3659
Delarue, Allison 4499
Delgado, Ramon 1027
Dell, Floyd 3660, 5470
Dell, Robert 5783
Delorenzo, Joseph P. 7292
Delsarte, François 803, 812
Demastes, William W. 5984
DeMille, Cecil B. 3653
Demostes, W. W. 5979
Dempsey, David 3607
Denis, Paul 5322

Dennhardt, Gregory C. 7265
Denning, Denis 5853
Denson, Wilbur T. 1934
Dent, Alan. 3213
Dent, Thomas 1368, 2876
Denvir, Arthur 4725
Derlmuth, August 6403
Derose, David J. 6972
Derwent, Clarence 3661
Desai, Rupin 5529
Deshazer, Mary K. 5988
Detzer, Karl 5285
Deuel, Pauline B. 1769
Deutsch, Helen 2114
Devere, Paul 3450
Devin, Ronald B. 2560
Devine, Philip P. 1812
Devlin, Albert J. 7170
Devlin, Diana 1315
Dewberry, Jonathan 253
Dewey, Walter S. 493
Dewsnap, James W. 6995
Dezseran, Catherine A. 5337
Diamond, Elin 5979, 5988, 6138
Diamond, Gladys 2023
Dick, Bernard F. 7066
Dickey, Johanna S. 6977
Dickinson, Donald C. 6540
Dickinson, Hugh 5863
Dickinson, Thomas H. 1212, 4897, 5756, 5813–5814
Dickson, Samuel 1744, 1764
Dienstfrey, Sherri R. 7409
Dier, Caroline L. 4020
Dierolf, Claude E. 1460
Diers, Herman H. 3999
Dietmeyer, Catol W. 5198
Dietrich, John E. 1153
Dietz, Howard 7359
Dietz, Mary M. 1985
Diguentani, J. 5979
Dilker, Barbara 784
Dillard, Robert L. 7122
Dillingham, Charles B. 756
Dillon, J. 5979
Dillon, Josephine [= Gable, Josephine] 862
Dillon, William A. 4830
Dilweg, Joan K. 5076
Dilworth, Mary L. 6713
DiMeglio, John E. 4771
Dimmick, Ruth C. 2331
Dimona, Joseph 4763
Dine, Jim 621
Dini, Massimo 1626
Dippold, Diane 6243
Distler, Paul A. 4755
Dithmar, Edward A. 3637, 3671
Ditsky, John 368, 7024
Dix, William S. 2537
Dixon, Harold W. 1690
Dixon-Stowell, Brenda M. 4885
Dobkin, William E. 4057
Dodd, Dorothy V. 5298
Dodd, Lee W. 4960
Dodge, Caroline 3796
Dodrill, Charles W. 769, 5028
Dody, Sandford 3256, 3341, 3850
Doggett, Frank A. 6619
Doherty, Edward 3683
Doherty, Lynn 3409

Doherty, Mary L. 1647
Dolan, Jill 1198, 4705, 5988
Dolbier, Maurice 3140
Dolch, Catherine 478
Dole, Nathan H. 3921
Dolkey, Matthew 5687
Doll, John L. 201
Dolman, John 876, 1124
Domey, Richard L. 5180
Dommergues, Pierre 6082
Donahoe, Ned 1915
Donahue, Francis 7120
Donegan, Billie D. 1842
Donkin, Ellen 3722
Donnelly, John E. 1765
Donoghue, Denis 5897
Donohue, Joseph W. 3076
Dooling, A. J. 6692
Doran, Philip C. 1810
Dormon, James H. 1659
Dorn, Knut 6792
Dorrell, Robert E. 2540
Dorst, Kenneth R. 422
Dos Passos, John R. 6358
Doty, Gresdna A. 4099
Dougherty, Edward B. 2030
Douglass, Jane 4002
Douty, John T. 590
Dow, Lorenzo 3154
Dowell, George 5004
Dowell, Richard W. 6361
Downer, Alan S. 1306, 1319, 1585–1586, 3682, 4676, 5110, 5770, 5900, 7033
Downey, Fairfax 4067, 6354
Downey, June E. 5470
Downs, Lenthiel H. 4586
Doxtator, Robert L. 4100
Doyen, Peggy J. 1980
Doyle, Esther M. 6625
Doyle, Mary 3664
Doyle, Mary P. 4964
Doyle, Paul A. 5898
Drake, Edwina B. 1148
Drake, Francis 4976
Drake, James A. 4792
Drake, Samuel A. 2094
Drakeford, Vere N. 5260
Draper, Benjamin P. 1838
Draper, Walter H. 4836
Draya, Ren 7149
Drennan, Robert E. 3237
Dreser, James W. 3361
Dressler, Marie 3668–3669
Drew, Elizabeth A. 5415
Drew, John 3672, 3674
Drexler, Malcolm B. 4548
Drexler, Ralph D. 1924
Drinkrow, John 7247
Driver, Tom F. 1232, 4676, 5788, 5917, 6676, 6776
Drummond, A. M. 1068
Drury, Francis K. 5352, 5387
Drutman, Irving 3251
Druxman, Michael B. 4281
Dryden, Deborah M. 720
Dryden, Wilma J. 1921
Du Prey, Deirdre H. 1020
Dube, Anthony 6522
Duberman, Martin B. 4307
Dubin, Karen E. Van L. 351

Dubler, Walter 6073
Dubois, William R. 5380
Duckwall, Ralph W. 1153
Duerr, Edwin 895, 5643
Duffus, Robert L. 1278, 1545
Duffy, Susan 779
Dugdale, John 6981
Duggar, Mary M. 1703
Dugger, Leonard P. 4158
Duke, Charles R. 5162
Duke, Vernon 7219, 7360
Dukore, Bernard F. 24, 3538, 5521, 5606, 5681, 5884
Dulles, Foster R. 1297
Dumais, Alfred 5530
Dumas, Bethany K. 6345
Dumont, Frank 4715
Dunbar, Olivia H. 6714
Dunlap, James F. 2522
Dunlap, William 1264, 1392, 6362–6364, 6367, 6369
Dunlop, John T. 235
Dunn, Don 7242
Dunn, Emma 871
Dunn, Esther C. 1284
Dunnie, Philip 2336
Dunning, Glenda 459
Dunnington, Hazel B. 5129
Dunsany, Lord 5413
Dupler, Dorothy 2776
Duprey, Richard A. 4668
Durang, Charles 2574, 3825
Durham, Frank 6496, 6931
Durham, Weldon B. 1424, 1478, 1498
Durland, Frances C. 5115
Dusenbury, Delwin B. 5764
Dusenbury, Winifred L. 5485
Dutton, Robert R. 6284
Duval, Elaine I. 6255
Duyckinck, Evert A. 2967
Dwerlkotte, Carolyn R. 3724
Dwight, Timothy 262
Dworkin, Rita 5790
Dycke, Marjorie L. P. 1526
Dye, Ottis D. 5044
Dykema, Peter W. 5088
Dymkowski, Christine 6410
Dyson, Jane A. 4584

Eady, Fred A. 6427
Eaker, Sherry 1045
Earley, Michael 5459
Earnest, Sue W. 1745
East, Napoleon B. 3401
Eastman, Fred 309, 336–337
Eastman, James E. 207
Easty, Edward D. 912
Eatman, Rodney H. 3316
Eaton, Quaintance 2387
Eaton, Richard 6888
Eaton, Walter P. 1440, 2332, 2950, 3024, 3029, 4676, 4905, 4959, 5590
Eaves, T. C. 6991
Eberson, Drew 2414
Eble, Kenneth E. 6388
Eckard, Bonnie J. 6043
Eckley, Don M. 1771
Eckman, Fern M. 6229
Eddleman, Floyd E. 4584, 4603

Eddy, Junius 2796, 4923
Edel, Leon 1564
Edelson, Mary E. 2946
Edelstein, J. M. 7081
Edge, Turner W. 4180
Edgecombe, David P. 5082
Edgett, Edwin F. 2993, 3642, 4620
Edmonds, Ralph 1319
Edwards, Anne 3655, 3863
Edwards, Christopher 57
Edwards, Christine 906
Edwards, Flora M. 5618
Edwards, Henry. 3159
Edwards, Herbert J. 6491
Edwards, John 259
Edwards, John C. 414
Edwards, Mary 4080
Edwards, Paul A. 6048
Edwards, Richard H. 304–306
Edwards, Samuel 4096
Edyvean, Alfred R. 343
Eek, Nathaniel S. 5221
Eells, George 4493, 7407, 7413
Effrat, John 1673
Egan, Frank 1789
Egan, Jaqueline E. 2150
Egan, Jenny 618
Egan, P. 5979
Eggers, Robert F. 1884
Egri, Lajos 5429
Egri, Peter 6879
Ehret, Donald M. 7073
Ehrlich, Eugene 6121
Eichelberger, Clayton L. 6527
Eifert, Eunice R. 1195
Einsel, Alan D. 375
Eisenhour, Jerry D. 5881
Eisinger, Chester E. 5927
Elam, Harry J. 1565
Elam, Keir 1166
Elberson, Stanley D. 2766
Elder, Eldon 454, 645
Elderkin, John 2912–2913
Elfenbein, Josef A. 5724
Elias, S. P. 176
Elkind, Samuel 5134
Elleman, Joseph 402
Elliot, Emory 5701
Elliot, Paula 58
Elliot, Walter G. 2319
Elliott, Estelle C. 2749
Elliott, Eugene C. 2762
Elliott, Karin 5594
Elliott, Robert F. 6314
Ellis, Elizabeth 4995
Ellis, Harold M. 5708
Ellis, Leslie E. 1868
Ellis, Morris R. 164
Ellis, Roger 1028
Ellis, W. Harvey 3739
Ellison, Earl J. 361
Ellison, Rhoda C. 1704
Elliston, Stephen F. 5844
Ellsler, John A. 3688
Elrod, James F. 6762
Elson, Charles 645
Elwood, George M. 2285
Elwood, Muriel 3772
Elzey, John M. 2197
Emanuel, James A. 6242, 6534
Embler, Jeffrey 1111

Emery, Gilbert 5413
Emery, Joy S. 721
Emmes, David M. 1797
Endrey, Eugene 3232
Engar, Keith M. 4975, 5831
Engdahl, Eric L. 4877
Engel, Bernard B. 2615
Engel, Bernard F. 6374
Engel, Edwin A. 6749–6750, 6833
Engel, Lehman 4598, 5331, 7213, 7223, 7258, 7274, 7281, 7364
England, Theora C. 5024
Engle, Gary D. 4782
English, Emma J. 6158
Englund, Claes 6894
Enser, A. G. 5396
Enterline, Mildred H. 345
Enters, Angna 3689–3690, 5394
Epolito, Joseph M. 6549
Epperson, James R. 2491
Epstein, Edward Z. 3520, 3889
Epstein, Helen 4219
Epstein, Lawrence 96
Epstein, Leslie 1179
Epstein, Sabin R. 1001
Epton, Anli 78
Erben, R. 5979
Erenberg, Lewis 1485
Erhard, Thomas A. 5386, 6939
Ericson, Robert E. 2269
Ernst, Alice H. 1671, 2561
Ernst, Morris L. 184, 190, 200
Ervine, St. John 3952, 6858
Esser, Grace D. 1799
Esslin, Martin 5506, 6172
Estes, Maxie C. 1864
Estrin, Mark W. 5793, 6476, 6484, 6896
Euba, Femi 5705
Eubanks, Marjorie H. 5288
Eustis, Morton 760, 853
Evans, Betty E. 3377
Evans, Chad 1716
Evans, Dina R. 5100
Evans, Edmund E. 335
Evans, Henry Ridgely 545
Evans, James W. 1447
Evans, Laurie J. 7434
Evans, Mary J. 5253
Evans, Maurice 3693
Evans, Oliver 6645
Evans, Richard I. 6677
Evans, Thomas G. 6028
Everding, Robert G. 6952
Everett, Marshall 1895
Everson, William 1700
Everson, William K. 3708
Ewen, David 7214–7215, 7225, 7232, 7304, 7334, 7339, 7373, 7393, 7412
Ewing, Robert W. 4616
Exton, M. A. 4304
Eysselinck, Walter 5909
Eyssen, D. C. 2509
Eytinge, Rose 3694
Ezekiel, Margaret U. 2541
Ezell, John D. 1339

Fabian, Monroe H. 3077, 3098
Fabre, Genevieve 45, 1566, 1638
Fagin, N. B. 6765

Fagin, Nathan B. 4258
Fairbanks, Charles B. 2080
Fairbanks, Douglas 3696
Fairbanks, Letitia 3697
Faith, William R. 3890
Falge, Francis M. 483
Fallows, Bishop 1895
Falk, Armand E. 4585
Falk, Bernard 4092
Falk, Doris V. 6473, 6851
Falk, Florence A. 6393
Falk, Robert F. 2390
Falk, Robert P. 4571
Falk, Signi L. 4667, 6626, 7151
Fancher, Edwin. 1578
Fanders, Reuben 2257
Farber, Donald C. 771, 778, 937
Farberman, Boris 4176, 7335
Farjeon, Eleanor 3465, 3925
Farmer, Patrick A. 6444
Farnsworth, Marjorie 4555
Farrar, C. A. J. 3699
Farrar, J. Maurice 3280
Farrell, Barry 4193
Farrell, Kenneth L. 2653
Farrell, Robert D. 1926
Farrison, William E. 6324
Fasnaugh, Charles W. 2526
Faulkender, Robert E. 2814
Faulkner, Seldon 2668
Fauset, Jessie 1509, 5920
Faust, Richard 4223
Faversham, William 3700
Favorini, Attilio A. 4054
Fawkes, Richard 1559, 6312
Faxon, Frederick W. 25
Fay, Barbara C. 1964
Fay, Frank 3701
Fay, Theodore S. 4235
Fayard, Jeanne 7137
Fearnow, Mark 1568
Fedder, Norman J. 7128, 7149
Feder, Abe H. 401, 1077
Feder, Sid 3218
Fedo, David A. 7110
Fehl, Fred 2424, 2437
Feibelman, Peter 6482
Feinsod, Arthur B. 683
Feldhaus, Eugene C. 6264
Feldman, Donna R. 4401
Feldman, Jack 6688
Feldman, Lee G. 1588
Felheim, Marvin 3631
Feller, John H. 4870
Fellner, Harriet 6489
Fellom, Martie 4798
Felnagle, Richard H. 1034
Fenaughty, Thomas J. 903
Fenn, Jeffrey W. 5985
Fennell, James 3702
Fennell, Patrick J. 6966
Fennema, Davis H. 6042
Fennimore, Keith J. 7034
Fenton, Elaine R. 6268
Fenton, Frank L. 1749, 1753
Ferber, Edna 6377
Ferguson, Blanche E. 6341
Ferguson, Burnett B. 2727
Ferguson, Phyllis 6069
Ferguson, W. J. 3463
Ferguson, William C. 2596

Fergusson, Francis 4676, 5479, 5595, 5917
Ferlita, Ernest 362
Fernandez, Doreen G. 1642
Ferrar, Eleanor B. 206
Ferres, John H. 6684, 6694
Ferris, Anita B. 327
Ferris, Lesley 1378
Fertik, Marian I. 5181
Fest, Thorrel B. 899
Fetherling, Doug 6453
Ficca, John 6771
Fichandler, Zelda 1138
Fidell, E. A. 5365
Field, Edwin A. 1433
Field, John P. 7454
Field, Joseph M. 1385
Field, Julian 4089
Field, Leslie 374
Fielder, Mari K. 2627
Fields, Mrs James T. 3183
Fields, Victor 858
Fields, W. C. 3709–3710, 4886
Fiet, Lowell A. 1693, 3985
Fife, Iline 1457
Fike, Duane J. 4077
Filipowicz-Findlay, Halina 6825
Filippo, Ivan J. 170
Finch, Robert 5426
Findlay, Robert R. 1239
Finizio, V. L. 6591
Fink, Joel G. 986
Finney, Gail 5626
Finney, James R. 1161
Finsel, Tamara J. 5060
Fiore, Carlo 3524
Firestone, Ross 3300
Firkins, Ina T. 5358, 6381
Firkins, Oscar W. 4643, 6381, 6508
Firmage, George J. 7017
Fisch, Mortimer L. 5780
Fischer-Seidel, Therese 6128
Fischli, Ronald D. 6550
Fisher, Caroline E. 5114
Fisher, Edward J. 6254
Fisher, Irving 6617
Fisher, John. 3088
Fisher, Judith L. 1502
Fisher, Lawrence F. 4204
Fisher, Rhoda L. 992
Fisher, W. J. 6765
Fisher, William A. 2111
Fisher, William J. 6067
Fiske, Harrison G. 68, 3161, 4618
Fiske, John 6053
Fiske, Mary H. 3161
Fiskinn, Abram M. 6775
Fitch, Polly M. 6778
Fitts, Kenneth L. 6954
Fitzgerald, F. Scott 6389
Fitzgerald, Gerald 2463
Fitzgerald, S. J. Adair 6558
Fitzkee, Dariel 546
Fjelster, Stan 1342
Flagg, James M. 3209, 3701
Flanagan, Hallie 3725–3729, 5394
Flanagan, James K. 6701
Flanders, Robert 2243
Flaten, David 4109
Fleche-Salgues, S. 5896

Fleckenstein, Joan P. 6818
Fleischer, Nat 4094
Fleischman, Earl E. 840
Fleit, Muriel 7152
Fleming, Carol A. 5083
Fleming, Martha 5094
Fleshman, Bib 1029
Fletcher, Edward G. 2585, 2677, 6320
Fletcher, James E. 82
Fletcher, Tom 3734
Fletcher, Winona B. 717
Flexner, Eleanor 6060
Fliehr, Kay 2195
Flinn, Denny M. 7327
Flint, Janet A. 3291
Flint, Martha M. 4991
Flint, Richard W. 4780
Floan, Howard R. 6949
Flory, Julia M. 2538
Flowers, H. D. 5067
Floyd, Virginia 5916, 6842, 6846, 6865, 6883
Fluharty, George W. 2127
Flynn, Joyce A. 6045
Flynn, Meredith 1010
Foard, Elisabeth C. 6956
Fogelberg, Donald D. 455
Foley, Doris 4147
Folland, Harold 6303
Fonda, Henry 3736
Foner, Philip S. 4299
Foote, Ronald C. 6200
Forbes-Robertson, Diana 3687
Ford, George D. 3053
Ford, James L. 3181, 3366
Ford, Paul L. 1392, 5706
Ford, Tom 2078
Forde, Gladys I. 3374
Fordin, Hugh 7383
Fordyce, Rachel 5165, 5264
Foreman, Ellen 1368
Foreman, Grant 4242
Foreman, Larry M. 2202
Foreman, Richard 5696, 6394, 6396
Forkert, Otto M. 5223
Fornaro, Carlo De 4489
Forrest, Edwin 3740
Forrest, Sam 3768
Forrester, Izola 3464
Forsyth, Michael 463
Fort, Timothy W. 541
Forte, Jeanie K. 1645
Foster, George G. 2299-2300
Foster, J. Edgar 818-819, 823
Foster, J. F. 1080
Foster, Jacob F. 5823
Foster, Lois M. 5097
Foster, Robert B. 5191
Foster, William T. 2558
Foust, Clement E. 6289
Fowler, C. H. 287
Fowler, Frank C. 5895
Fowler, Gene 3214, 3229, 3337, 4746, 4831
Fowler, Keith F. 2813
Fowler, Larry 1981
Fowler, Robert H. 3474
Fowler, Roy A. 4475
Fowler, S. 6793

Fowler, Will. 3230
Fowles, Anthony 4413
Fox, Beavois. 3801
Fox, Howard L. 408
Fox, Josef 6751
Fox, Mary V. 3347
Fox, Ted 2445
Foy, Eddie 3769
France, Anatole 3779
France, Richard 4479, 4486
Francis, Arlene 3770
Francis, John W. 2302
Francis, Mark S. 2200
Francisco, Charles 2425
Franck, Timothy D. 5291
Frank, Charles P. 7185
Frank, Felicia N. 1557
Frank, Gerald 4343
Frank, Waldo D. 5631
Frankel, Aaron 7259
Frankel, Haskel 945
Franken, Rose 6399
Franklin, Joe 4787
Franklin, Miriam A. 1003
Franklin, William G. 2532
Frantz, Alice H. 1186
Franz, Arthur 4612
Franzblau, Abraham N. 6172
Fraser, Barbara M. 7277
Fraser, John H. 583
Frasher, James E. 3809
Frazer, Fred 5318
Frazer, Winifred L. 6821
Frazier, David L. 6520
Frebault, Hubert J. 2520
Free, Joseph M. 2207
Free, William 4932
Free, William J. 7149
Freedland, Michael 3112, 7323, 7337, 7391, 7394
Freedley, George 70, 74, 399, 1236, 2370, 3090, 4008, 4028, 5593
Freedman, Ann C. 1528
Freedman, David 3554, 4553
Freedman, Morris 5601, 5682, 5906, 6902
Freeman, Benjamin P. 3585
Freeman, John R. 384
Freeman, Larry 7227
Freeman, Lucy 7119
Freeman, Sidney L. 403
Freiberger, Edward 1894
French, Alice M. 2940
French, Charles E. 2092, 2097
French, Warren 1555, 6131, 7023
French, William P. 45, 5622
Frenz, Horst 5665, 6079, 6810, 6858
Frerer, Lloyd A. 6502
Freud, Ralph 1218
Frey, Carroll 6653
Frezza, Christine A. 7464
Frick, Constance 4187
Frick, John W. 98, 2446
Friede, Donald 3210
Friede, Eleanor 3244
Friederich, Willard J. 583
Friedl, Bettina 5807, 5890
Friedman, Arthur B. 5297
Friedman, Daniel H. 1421, 2943

Friedman, Martin E. 2870
Friedman, Michael B. 1035
Friedman, Norman 6342, 6344
Friedman, Robert 7442
Friedman, Sharon 5954
Friedman, Sidney J. 4581
Frink, Peter H. 445
Frobisher, Joseph E. 734, 799, 801
Fröhlich, P. 1601, 4944
Frohman, Daniel 3773, 3775-3777
Frost, David P. 3072
Frost, Jonathan B. 3971
Frost, Warren L. 5450
Frowe, Margaret M. 1879
Frueh, Alfred J. 3026, 3081
Fry, Emma S. 5089
Fryxell, Lucy D. 6942
Fuchs, Theodore 401, 476
Fuente, Patricia De La 6179
Fuerst, Walter R. 556
Fugate, Liz 82
Fuhrich-Leisler, Edda 6040
Fuller, Charles F. 2752
Fuller, Edmund 1214
Fuller, Edward 1428
Fuller, Loie 3779
Fuller, Michael W. 5246
Fullerton, Mary E. 1361
Fülöp-Miller, Rene 1277, 1282
Funk, Nancy L. 1970
Funke, Lewis 893, 3820, 3849
Furber, Mary Hall 3942
Furlong, James 1149
Furman, Evelyn E. 1840
Furnas, J. C. 4434
Furnas, Joseph C. 1462
Furness, Horace H. 3428
Fyles, Franklin 750

Gabor, Eva 3786
Gaer, Joseph 1785
Gaffney, Paul J. 3608
Gafford, Lucille 2005, 2010
Gagen, Jean 5979
Gagey, Edmond M. 1747, 5827
Gagnon, Pauline D. 2889
Gaige, Crosby 3787
Gaines, Frederick E. 1346
Gaines, Robert A. 6269
Gaisford, John 2003
Gale, Cedric 1399
Gale, Steven H. 6915
Gale, Zona 6402
Galizia, Luiz R. 4511
Gall, Ellen M. 737
Gallada, Robert A. 6753
Gallagher, Kent G. 5733
Gallagher, Rachel 7245
Gallaway, Marian 1099, 5430
Gallegly, Joseph 2693, 2703
Gallup, Donald 7097, 7103
Gallup, Donald C. 6884, 7009
Galyean, John G. 5532
Gamble, Michael W. 5245
Gamble, William B. 549, 557
Ganz, Arthur 4676, 5540, 6684, 7148
Gänzl, Kurt 113, 7297, 7310
Garceau, Jean 3784
Garcia, Antonina C. 993
Garcia, R. 5455

Gard, Robert E. 1589, 3054, 3064, 4923, 4928, 4930
Gardiner, John 166
Gardiner, N. J. 7286
Gardner, Bonnie M. 1158
Gardner, Dorothea B. 2605
Gardner, M. C. 6874
Gardner, Martin A. 4858
Gardner, R. H. 1581
Gardner, Robert M. 6595
Garfield, David 2818
Gargan, William 3789
Gargaro, Kenneth V. 7367
Garland, Hamlin 3194–3195, 3197, 5628
Garner, Madelyn L. 1668
Garner, Nathan C. 2789
Garner, Stanton B. 5574
Garness, Jon M. 508
Garnett, Porter 2835–2836
Garrett, Kurt L. 323
Garrett, Michael D. 5068
Garrett, Thomas M. 2421
Garrison, Gary W. 7192
Gartner, David 2281
Garvey, Sheila H. 2441
Garvin, Harry R. 7010
Garwood, Alice 1066
Gasper, Raymond D. 2881
Gassner, John 1077, 1220, 1225–1227, 1305, 1537, 1574, 4683, 5020, 5417, 5443, 5592, 5607, 5611, 5899, 5908, 6060, 6071, 6684, 6776, 6779
Gaston, Edwin W. 51
Gates, Robert A. 6373
Gaver, Jack 4658, 4681, 5366
Gawlik, Jan P. 4115
Gay, Elisabeth F. 5310
Gaye, Freda 3019
Gayle, Addison 5920, 5930
Gaylord, Karen 5549
Gebauer, Emanuel L. 597
Gebbie, George. 2988
Geddes, Virgil 1514–1517, 5816, 6741
Gee, Robert F. 4977
Gehman, Richard 4878
Gehring, Wes D. 3712, 4864
Geier, Woodrow A. 346
Geis, Deborah R. 5986, 6138
Geisinger, Marion 1234
Gelatt, Richard H. 1897
Gelb, Arthur 6875
Gelb, Michael 994
Geller, James J. 5759
Geltner, Frank J. 5074
Gemme, Leila B. 3089
Gemmill, Paul F. 214
Gentile, Gerald G. 401
Gentile, John S. 1375
George, Kathleen 5534
George, Waldemar 3296
Georges, Corwin A. 3634
Gergely, Emro J. 6009
Gerhard, William P. 381–382
Gerlach, Michael C. 4177
Gern, Jesse W. 1829
Gerold, Frank 3340
Gerould, Daniel C. 5606, 5696, 5804

Geroux, Charles L. 1983
Gersh, Ellyn M. 1815
Gershwin, George 1513
Gershwin, Ira 7375
Gerson, Lydia 5991
Gerson, Virginia. 6383
Gerstenberg, Alice 2332
Gerstenberger, Donna 5788
Gervinus, Georg Gottfried 3414
Giantvalley, S. 6189
Gibbs, David A. 456
Gibbs, Wollcott 3221
Gibson, Arrell M. 4334
Gibson, Donald B. 6092
Gibson, W. M. 6510
Gibson, William 6404–6405
Gibson, William H. 6523
Gierow, Karl R. 6760
Giglio, Mary E. 1957
Gilbert, Creighton 1863
Gilbert, Douglas 4740, 7209
Gilbert, Harold J. 168
Gilbert, Julie G. 6379
Gilbert, Robert L. 6205
Gild, David C. 6267
Gilder, Rosamon 4
Gilder, Rosamond 12, 70, 645, 1527, 1573, 1593
Gildzen, Alex 2920, 6260
Giles, Sarah 7325
Gilford, Madeline 4170
Gill, Brendan 2787, 3322, 7415
Gill, Glenda E. 2874, 3101
Gillespie, Patti P. 1259
Gillespie, Richard H. 1504
Gillett, Peter J. 6833
Gillette, A. S. 619, 1319
Gillette, Arnold S. 5210
Gillette, Don C. 4874
Gillette, Henry C. 820
Gillette, J. Michael 543, 685
Gillette, William 3800
Gilliam, Theodore E. 5674
Gillmore, Margalo 1524, 3808
Gilman, Richard 4687–4688, 5616, 5917, 6608
Gilmore, Robert K. 2243
Gilroy, Frank 6406
Gilroy, M. N. 5865
Gilvary, Patrick S. 4776
Gingrich, Arnold 234
Gipson, Rosemary P. 1720
Giraudet, A. 814
Gish, Lillian 3812
Gladding, W. J. 2992
Gladstone, Mark 82
Glann, Frank W. 7356
Glann, Janice G. 7255
Glase, Paul E. 2595
Glaspell, Susan 3587–3588, 5394, 6410
Glasrud, Clarence A. 6317
Glassberg, David 1503
Glazer, Irvin R. 2628–2629
Gledhill, Preston R. 341
Glenn, Stanley L. 964, 1125, 5656
Glerum, Jay O. 464
Glick, Carl 4918
Glover, J. Garrett 1254
Glover, Lyman B. 1892
Gluckman, Emanuel M. 758

Glyer, Richard T. 3304
Gnuse, William J. 2255
Goates, Wallace A. 855
Goatley, Cynthia A. 1189
Gober, Ruth B. 2554
Gobrecht, Eleanor A. 5850
Godfrey, Arthur 4741
Godfrey, Thomas 6411
Godley, Margaret W. 1873
Godwin, Parke 3419
Goetsch, Paul 5528, 5875, 5939
Goff, Lewin A. 5765
Goffman, E. 5527
Gohdes, Clarence 28, 5652
Going, William T. 1711
Gold, Ronald L. 6691
Goldberg, Isaac 4143, 4183, 4185, 4738, 5583, 6727, 7371
Goldberg, Moses 5187, 5239
Goldberg, Roselee 1484
Goldblatt, Burt 7322
Golden, Edwin J. 4462
Golden, George F. 4717
Golden, John 2777, 3814
Golden, Joseph 1291, 1541
Goldfarb, Alvin 1255, 7149
Goldman, Emma 5394, 5808
Goldman, Herbert G. 7392
Goldman, Michael 950
Goldman, R. L. 7053
Goldman, William 2391
Goldsmith, Berthold H. 3638
Goldstein, Malcolm 1552, 4676, 6574, 7085
Goldstein, Norm 3737
Goldstein, Richard M. 3382
Goldstein, Samuel J. 6961
Goldstone, Richard H. 7092, 7100
Goltry, Thomas S. 515
Gonsher, Debra 5961
González, Yolanda Broyles 5988
Gooch, D. H. 1944
Gooch, Donald B. 415
Goodale, Jane M. 2152
Goodale, Katherine [= Molony, Kitty] 3431
Goode, James 6664
Goode, Ruth 3910
Goodefellowe, Robin 6313
Goodfriend, Lewis S. 405
Goodhue, Mary L. 836
Goodman, Edward 884, 2332
Goodman, Gerald T. 1328
Goodman, Paul 208
Goodman, Philip 3816
Goodman, Randolph 6116, 7115
Goodman, Walter 1542
Goodrich, Anne 1684
Goodwin, George K. 3817
Goodwin, Nat C. 3818
Gordon, Albert C. 2939
Gordon, Barbara E. 1708
Gordon, Gale 3315
Gordon, George N. 1464
Gordon, Joanne 7446
Gordon, Max 3820
Gordon, Mel 1040
Gordon, Ruth 2822, 3055, 3821–3823
Gore, John H. 2168
Gorelik, Mordecai 400, 1077

Gorokhov, V. 4292
Gossage, Forest D. 2256
Gossett, Thomas F. 1492
Got, Jerzy 4118, 4123
Gottfried, Martin 1587, 3840, 4684, 4799, 7268, 7370
Gottlieb, Lois C. 6339
Gottlieb, Morton 1138
Gottlieb, Polly R. 4338
Gottlieb, Saul. 2892
Gould, Arthur J. 5828
Gould, Eleanor Cody 1091
Gould, Harold V. 5118
Gould, Jack 6598
Gould, Jean 6080, 6660
Gould, Joseph E. 5287
Gould, Thomas R. 3503
Goulding, Edmund 7207
Gouran, Patrick D. 5945
Gourd, E. W. 1849
Goyal, Bhagwat S. 6805, 6826
Grabes, Herbert 5875, 5950
Grabhorn, Jane Bissell 1734
Grabish, Richard F. 4167
Grady, Billy 3246
Graff, Stephen J. 5744
Graham, Donald L. 5279
Graham, Martha 3597
Graham, Philip 4742
Graham, Philip B. 5212
Graham, Shirley 4291
Grahame, Shirley 3239
Grain, Amelia 560
Grandel, Hartmut 5875
Grandgent, Charles H. 2115
Grandgeorge, William N. 1920
Grandstaff, Russell J. 951, 2536A
Granlund, Nils T. 3218
Grant, Ethel A. 2760
Grant, Gary M. 6969
Grant, Howard F. 2760
Granville, Taylor 4725
Grau, Robert 3173–3174, 3176
Grauch, Arlene E. 4366
Graves, James B. 7275
Graves, Richard C. 6933
Gray, Clayton 3470
Gray, Isabel McReynolds 5097
Gray, James 6659
Gray, John 67
Gray, Paula G. 5300
Gray, Simon 1650
Gray, Virginia P. 2756
Gray, Wallace A. 2024
Graydon, Alexander 2572
Grebanier, Bernard 3084, 5457, 7084
Grebstein, Sheldon N. 6730
Greeley, Lynne 6297
Green, Abel 4743, 4745, 4753
Green, Carol H. 3100
Green, Charles L. 6180
Green, Elizabeth L. 5633
Green, Elvera M. 1877
Green, G. E. 2418
Green, Gordon C. 3981
Green, Harriet L. 1735, 3530
Green, John H. 594
Green, Joseph G. 3983

Green, Paul 1322, 1513, 3054, 4932, 5020, 6415–6416, 6419–6420, 6422, 6424
Green, Richard L. 3766
Green, Stanley 3113, 7226, 7238, 7260–7261, 7305, 7322, 7423, 7430
Green, William 1319
Greenberg, Jan W. 5339
Greenberger, Howard 2400
Greenblatt, Fred S. 5308
Greene, Alexis 1648, 5979
Greenfield, Thomas A. 5882
Greenhall, Margaret P. 1535
Greer, Louise 6012
Gregersen, Charles E. 3272
Gregor, Joseph 1277
Gregoric, Michael T. 4578
Gregory, B. E. 3976
Gregory, Dick 3828
Gregory, James 3314
Gregory, Montgomery 1509, 5920
Gregory, William A. 1108
Greiner, Donald J. 7060
Greiner, Tyler L. 2623
Gremore, Constance F. 5257
Gress, Elsa (Ed.?). 2887
Gressler, Thomas H. 4809
Griffin, Ernest G. 6833
Griffin, Evelyn 1819
Griffith, Frank C. 3717
Griffith, Max E. 2542
Griffiths, Philip R. 1756
Grillo, Jean B. 4253
Grimball, E. B. 696
Grimsley, Charles E. 3271
Grimsted, David 1406
Grinchuk, Robert A. 6372
Grisvard, Larry E. 2231
Grobel, Lawrence 3912
Groetzinger, Richard A. 1011
Gronowicz, Antoni 4116
Grose, Burl D. 5748
Gross, Brenda 2464
Gross, Edwin A. 5214
Gross, Lorraine H. 426
Gross, Nathalie 5214
Gross, Roger D. 1112
Gross, Theodore L. 6242
Grossman, A. M. 2188
Grossman, Barbara 7346
Grossman, Edwina B. 3420
Grossman, Samuel L. 1614
Groth, Melvin F. 7195
Grotowski, J. 5527
Grove, Edwin M. 470
Grover, Charles A. 6392
Grover, Edwin O. 6620
Groves, William McD. 2710
Grubb, Kevin 7369
Gruber, William E. 5564
Gruen, John 3234–3235, 7340
Grunes, D. 5979
Grupenhoff, David G. 4433
Gruver, Bert 775
Gryphon, Gregory 1382
Guare, John 5533
Guernsey, Otis L. 1505, 2459, 5940
Guerra, Jonnie 5988
Guiles, Fred L. 4269

Guillemard, Mary F. 4045
Guinness, Alec 842, 3122
Gundelfinger, George F. 3225
Gunn, Archie 4504, 7204
Gunn, Donald L. 321
Gunn, Drewey W. 7159
Gustafson, Antoinette McC. 5702
Gustafson, R. Eric 82
Guthke, Karl S. 5497
Guthrie, Favid G. 4036
Guthrie, Tyrone 2192, 2195, 5917
Gutman, Kellie O. 3482
Gutting, John G. 5535
Guttmann, Allen 5875

Haaga, Agnes 5085, 5187
Haarbauer, Don W. 1710
Haas, Robert 7009
Haas, Rudolf 1338, 6858
Habecker, Thomas J. 2959
Häberle, Erwin 7087
Haberman, Donald 7083, 7088, 7107
Haberman, Leroy D. 5781
Hackett, James H. 1388
Hackett, Joan 5224
Hackett, Norman H. 3226
Haco, Dion 3451, 3456
Hadley, Charles O. 4201
Hadley, Dorothy S. 5284
Hadley, Richard H. 2746
Haffley, James 7149
Hagan, J. S. G. 3628
Hagan, John P. 3978
Hagen, Uta 945, 3831
Hagler, Nevis E. 3514
Hagnell, Viveka 6247
Hahn, Vera T. 6745
Hailey, Robert C. 2383
Haines, Peggy A. 2171
Hake, Robert 599
Halbritter, Rudolf 7093
Hale, David 2070
Hale, Edward E. 281, 5579
Haley, Elsie G. 6093
Haley, Whitney W. 4220
Halfmann, Ulrich 6797, 6876, 6893, 6897
Haliburton, William 255
Hall, 'Biff' [= Hall, William T.] 3130
Hall, Adrian 1138
Hall, Ben M. 465
Hall, Lillian A. 103
Hall, Roger A. 7252
Hallauer, John W. 5435
Haller, Charles D. 6456
Halline, Alan G. 5359, 5636
Hallowell, Alfred I. 1664
Hallowell, John. 3240
Hallquist, Teryl W. 3116
Hallstrom, Per 6858
Halperin, Ellen I. 1041
Halpern, Martin 6717
Halstead, John S. 1367
Halstead, William P. 620, 765
Halttunen, Karen 1420
Halverson, Bruce A. 3895
Hamar, Clifford E. 4989, 5110
Hambright, Jeanne K. 6806
Hamil, Linda V. 2211

Hamilton, Clayton 3801, 4626, 5407, 5473, 5754, 5812
Hamilton, Frank 775
Hamilton, John L. 485
Hamilton, Mary L. 2019
Hamilton, Milton W. 2595
Hamilton, Robert T. 1967
Hamilton, Robert C. 2838
Hamilton, Stanley K. 5772
Hamilton, William T. 273
Hamm, Gerald 6263
Hamm, Margherita A. 3005, 4455
Hammack, Henry E. 2697
Hammack, J. Alan 579
Hammack, James A. 2031
Hammerstein, Arthur 1513
Hammond, Bryan 4813
Hammond, Percy 4637, 4650
Hammouda, Abdul-Aziz A-S. 2852
Hanau, Stella 2114
Hancock, R. 3697
Hancock, Ralph 3218, 3532
Handel, Beatrice 99
Handley, John G. 1296
Haney, John L. 2590
Haney, Lynn 4812
Hanff, Helene 3231
Hanley, Kathryn T. 2016
Hanlon, R. Brendon 248
Hannaford, Harry P. 3022
Hanners, John 1955
Hannon, Daniel L. 4035
Hannum, Charles R. 4026
Hansberry, Lorraine 1578, 5394, 6430–6431
Hanscom, Warren D. 5292
Hansen, Al 1101
Hansen, Delmar J. 3894
Hansen, Harold I. 338
Hansen, Harry 6449
Hansen, Peggy C. 645
Hanson, Patricia K. 100
Hanson, Willis T. 4240
Hapgood, Elizabeth Reynolds 890
Hapgood, Hutchins 3247
Hapgood, Norman 1435, 3193
Harap, Louis 377
Harbin, Billy J. 3875
Harbin, Shirley M. 2179
Harby, Isaac 6435
Harder, Daniel 6319
Hardin, Wylie A. 2704
Harding, Alfred 216
Harding, Gardner L. 1447
Harding, Sara 217
Hardwick, Mary R. 5791
Hardy, Camille C. 5149
Hardy, Michael C. 3411
Hare, Walter B. 4730
Hargett, Sheila 2050
Harken, Anne H. 191
Harlow, Alvin F. 3650, 3769
Harmon, Charlotte 1844, 5324
Harnish, Frank J. 2650
Harper, Charles H. 3558, 3562
Harper, H. H. 4239
Harper, Henry R. 6437
Harper, Robert D. 5768
Harrigan, Rita K. 2123
Harrigan, W. Patrick 1681
Harriman, Margaret C. 3042

Harrington, Donal F. 1733
Harrington, Mildred 3669
Harriott, Esther 6133
Harris, Albert J. 6116
Harris, Andrew B. 6182
Harris, Aurand 5187
Harris, Bernard. 1305
Harris, Charles K. 7384
Harris, Gayle 3487
Harris, Geraldine 2510
Harris, Jed 3837, 3839
Harris, Jessica B. 1368
Harris, Judy 504
Harris, Julie 732, 938, 4002
Harris, Kenneth 4437
Harris, Paul C. 6982
Harris, Richard H. 5391
Harris, Richard A. 6294
Harris, T. M. 3457
Harris, Trudier. 6126
Harrison, Alan 1737
Harrison, Allie C. 6309
Harrison, Eelin S. 710
Harrison, Gabriel 2322, 3760, 4237
Harrison, Harry P. 5285
Harrison, Paul C. 5516, 5688
Harrison, Shirley M. 2038
Harrison-Pepper, Sally 2467
Harrity, Richard 4764
Harrop, John 1001, 1130
Hart, Doris 6852
Hart, Dorothy 7386
Hart, F. W. 3461
Hart, Jack L. 6320
Hart, James D. 72
Hart, Jerome A. 3196
Hart, Lynda 5988, 6975
Hart, Moss 6442
Hart, Steven E. 5305
Hart, William S. 3842
Hartigan, Karelisa V. 5622
Hartley, Katherine 17
Hartley, Marsden 1268
Hartman, John G. 5683
Hartmann, Louis 479
Harton, Helen L. 5000
Harton, Merle 2055
Hartt, Rollin L. 4718
Harvey, Anne-Charlotte H. 1693
Harvey, E. T. 2505
Harvey, Geoffrey 145
Harvey, Joel 4852
Hashim, James E. 7123
Hashimoto, Yoko 4225
Haskell, Daniel C. 5347
Haskins, James 4839
Haskins, Jim 1368
Hastings, George E. 3189
Haswell, Charles H. 3164
Hatch, James V. 1261, 1368, 1642, 2860, 5376, 5384
Hatch, Katherine 3852
Hatcher, E. Martin 1839
Hatcher, James 3325
Hatfield, Douglas P. 2194
Hatfield, Robert M. 287
Hatlen, Theodore 5541, 6490
Haugen, Ralph H. 6014
Havens, Daniel F. 5741
Havens, John F. 4939

Haverly, Jack 4716
Havoc, June 3844–3845
Hawes, David S. 6322
Hawkins, John A. 4359
Hawks, Francis L. 4136
Hawley, Charles R. 5163
Hawthorne, Edith G. 3201
Hay, Peter. 3142–3143
Hay, Samuel A. 1368
Hayashi, Tetsumaro 6689, 6856, 7024, 7026
Hayden, Donald E. 1178
Haydon, Larras 852
Hayes, Donald 5972
Hayes, Helen 1334, 2788, 3849–3852
Hayes, Laurice M. 2225
Hayes, Peter L. 3853
Hayes, R. 6684
Hayes, Richard 6776
Hayman, Charles 3238
Hayman, Ronald 6685
Hays, David 542, 601
Hays, Michael 5571
Hays, Peter L. 5931
Hayward, Brooke 3252
Haywood, Charles 4761
Hazelrigg, Charles T. 6498
Hazeltine, Alice I. 5205
Hazzard, Robert T. 1536
Hazzard-Piankhi, Maisha L. 5969
Head, Edith 3856
Head, Sadie F. E. 2036
Heagle, Lawrence 2803
Healy, Mary 3853
Heard, Doreen B. 2867, 5264
Heartman, Charles F. 6316
Hebert, Chautel 4806
Hebron, Mary D. 6003
Hecht, Ben 3057, 6450–6452, 6614
Hecht, Ken 3046
Hecht, Stuart J. 5255
Heck-Rabi, Louise 7051
Hedgbeth, Llewellyn H. 82
Hedges, R. Alan 5293
Heffner, Hubert C. 574, 1322
Heidger, John M. 3705
Heidt, Patsy R. 2025
Heigl, Otto 6108
Heilman, Robert B. 5603, 5615, 5927, 7148
Heilmeyer, Jens 1601
Heimerdinger, Charles C. 7001
Helbing, Terry 5389
Helburn, Theresa 3857
Held, McDonald W. 495
Held, R. L. 670
Helfer, Richard 4494
Helfert, Charles J. 5172
Helgesen, Terry 674, 1798
Helle, Anita Plath 5988
Hellie, Thomas L. 6386
Hellman, Lillian 5432, 6461, 6467, 6470
Helps, Mary 2613
Helvenston, Harold 563
Hemming, Mary R. 2187
Hemsley, Gilbert V. 502
Hendel, Douglas B. 1030

Henderson, Archibald 2478, 2480, 5581, 5584, 6411
Henderson, F. C. 6652
Henderson, Jerry E. 2669
Henderson, Kathy. 3117
Henderson, Mary C. 82, 1362, 1376, 2410
Henderson, Myrtle E. 2721
Henderson, Peter W. 6580
Hendricks, Bill L. 763
Hendricks-Wenck, Aileen A. 4287
Hendrix, Erlene C. 2922
Heniford, Lewis W. 6272
Henke, James S. 2630
Henkel, Donald D. 5138
Henkin, William A. 1179
Henle, Fay 6611
Henneke, Ben G. 1178, 1403
Hennequin, Alfred 5400
Hennessee, Don A. 5385
Hennessey, Joseph 4537
Hennessy, W. J. 3415
Hennigan, Shirlee 1154
Henniker-Heaton, Raymond 3290
Henry, David D. 6711
Henry, Donald R. 1469
Henry, T. Charlton 263
Hensley, Donald M. 4279
Hensley, Jack A. 2373
Hensley, Michael 1831
Herbert, Ian 3019
Herbert, Miranda C. 3103
Herbst, Dorothy M. 2511
Herbstruth, Grant M. 3651
Herget, Patsy J. 5218
Herko, Mark S. 1853
Herlihy, Elisabeth M. 2115
Herman, Lewis H. 872
Herman, Richard J. 3565
Herman, William 5981
Herndon, Geneva 6747
Herndon, Marcia 1029
Herne, James A. 4676, 5788
Herne, Julia A. 6491
Herold, Amos L. 6911
Herr, John H. 4500
Herr, Judith L. 1118
Herron, Clifford D. 1012
Herron, Ima H. 5678
Hersh, Sally S. 5231
Herts, Alice M. [=Heniger, Alice M.] 5202
Hervey, Hubert C. 2675
Hess, Dean W. 6146
Hesse, Richard M. 2219
Hester, Wyoline 1870
Heston, Charlton 3867
Hethmon, Robert H. 4408, 6421
Hetler, Louis 887
Hewes, Henry 1505, 6172
Hewett, Edgar L. 2277
Hewitt, Alan 1319
Hewitt, Barnard 569, 1080, 1295, 1319, 1408, 5643
Hewitt, David D. 2271
Heyen, William 5875
Heys, Sandra 1021
Hezlep, William E. 2176
Hiatt, Richard G. 1700, 2565
Hichens, Hal. 3020
Hickenlooper, George 6274

Hicklin, Fannie E. 5854
Hicks, Ami M. 575
Hicks, J. V. 5254, 5264
Hicks, Lee R. 3943
Hieronymus, Clara 6376
Higham, Charles 3525, 3654, 3860, 4483, 4558
Highlander, James L. 1913, 3778
Highsaw, Carol A. 2872
Hild, Stephen G. 204
Hilker, Gordon 1131
Hill, Anthony D. 4708
Hill, Charles R. 4248
Hill, Edward S. 2918
Hill, Errol 1368, 3114
Hill, Frank P. 5355
Hill, George H. 3869
Hill, Gus 1662
Hill, Holly 1036, 2449
Hill, Lawrence J. 2204–2205
Hill, Lynn S. 5803
Hill, P. G. 6684
Hill, Raymond S. 1966
Hill, Richmond C. 2284
Hill, Ruth K. 333
Hill, West T. 1992, 1999
Hillhouse, James 4961
Hillhouse, James A. 5399
Hillyer, Katharine 2265–2266
Himelstein, Morgan Y. 1537, 5841
Hinden, Michael 6898
Hinderyckx, Leslie A. 622
Hindman, Anne A. 5867
Hindman, James T. 1602
Hindsell, Oliver 755, 833
Hines, Dixie 3022
Hingston, Edward P. 4451
Hinkel, Cecil E. 3313
Hinkel, Edgar J. 1736
Hinson, Glenn 1692
Hinton, M. M. 1665
Hippely, E. C. 617
Hirsch, Foster 2819, 6175, 6582, 6870, 7156, 7419
Hirsch, John 4804
Hirsch, Robin M. 5937
Hirsch, Samuel 1579
Hirschfeld, Al 1593, 2354, 2395, 2459, 3056, 3091, 3275, 3870–3871
Hirschfeld, Albert 4694
Hirschfeld, Burt 5326
Hirsen, Ronald B. 3407
Hitch, Arthur M. 4317
Hitchens, Gordon 6662
Hixon, Don L. 5385
Hixon, Orval 4767
Hoak, Eugene Q. 4996
Hoare, John E. 5427
Hobbs, Gary L. 942
Hobbs, Mabel F. 5086, 5101
Hobbs, Robert L. 2371
Hobgood, Burnet M. 907, 5085
Hobhouse, Janet 7022
Hoch, Ivan S. 7239
Hochman, Shirley 94
Hodgdon, Sam K. 3872
Hodge, Francis 636, 1319, 1404, 4024
Hodge, Francis R. 1119
Hodges, C. Walter 2182, 4786

Hodgins, Gordon W. 108
Hodgkinson, John 3873
Hodgson, Sandra K. 2535
Hoffman, Aaron 4725
Hoffman, Fred J. 1453, 5855
Hoffman, Gerhard 5875
Hoffman, Herbert H. 110
Hoffman, Theodore J. C. 5058
Hoffman, William 4264
Hofmannsthal, Hugo von 6776, 6858
Hogan, Robert 5431, 6311, 6665, 6684, 6929
Hogg, James 2319
Hohenberg, John 5439, 5456
Holbein, Woodrow L. 1350
Holbrook, Hal 3877
Holcomb, Richard 4498
Holden, David F. 5933
Holden, William C. 2673
Holdredge, Helen 4146
Holland, Cecil 736
Holland, Reginald 1287
Hollingsworth, Mary C. 1820
Hollingworth, Harry L. 1172
Holloway, C. L. 514
Holloway, Elizabeth R. 3780
Holman, Edna B. 5713
Holmes, Charles S. 7049
Holmes, Margaret G. 1519
Holmes, Ralph 644
Holmes, Susan C. 3488
Holmin, Lorena R. 6468
Holton, Orley I. 1245
Holzer, Adela 3884
Homan, Sidney 1199
Homburg, R. 186
Homrighous, Mary E. 4978
Honaker, Gerald L. 3438
Hood, Donald F. 4190
Hood, John 509
Hood, W. Edmund 536
Hooker, Edward 3799
Hooks, Eugene J. 2937
Hoole, W. S. 2640
Hooper, James M. 1965
Hope, Bob 3885–3888
Hopkins, Albert A. 545
Hopkins, Arthur 766, 1062, 1513, 3892–3893, 3938
Hopper, Arthur B. 3574
Hopper, DeWolf 7388
Horn, Barbara L. 7278
Hornblow, Arthur 1267, 5317, 5810
Hornby, Richard 1142, 5565
Horner, Charles F. 5269, 5281
Horner, John 1817
Hornmann, Otto 5316
Horowitz, Susan N. 5703
Horton, Joel E. 1335
Horton, William E. 3168, 3170
Hossala, Richard J. 3260
Hostetler, Paul S. 3550
Hostetler, Robert D. 679
Houchen, Russell E. 530
Hough, Robert L. 6518
Houghton, Norris 604, 1138, 1521, 4984, 5609
House, Jane 1651
House, Sandra K. 965

Houseman, John 1008, 1138, 1593, 1845, 2858, 3114, 3896–3897, 3899–3900, 6116
Housman, Alfred L. 6504
Hovar, Linn 5054
Howard, Bronson 6501
Howard, John 505
Howard, John T. 671
Howard, Louis 5418
Howard, Mildred L. 4164
Howard, Vernon 5232
Howe, Julia W. 3166
Howe, M[Ark] A. DeW. 3183
Howell, Herbert A. 192
Howells, Edith 6509
Howells, William Dean 4676, 6519
Hoyt, Edwin P. 4295, 4350, 4539
Hoyt, Harlow R. 1461
Hrkach, John 2297
Hruby, John F. 411
Hruby, Norbert J. 5830
Hryciw, Carol A. 6447
Hryciw-Wing, Carol A. 6448
Hsia, An Min 6858
Hubbard, Elbert 3902
Hubbard, Oliver F. 370
Hubbell, Douglas K. 531
Hubenka, Lloyd J. 5455
Huber, Robert C. 1811
Huberman, Caryn 5262
Hubert, Philip G. 5314
Hudgens, Betty L. 7068
Hudnut, Joseph 401
Hudson, Theodore F. 6248
Hudson, Virginia O. 5995
Huff, Mary N. 7079
Huffington, Dale D. 5921
Hufstetler, Loren R. 450
Huftel, Sheila 6668, 6684
Huggins, Nathan I. 2401
Hughes, Catharine 2422, 5938, 6102, 7148
Hughes, Elinor 2122
Hughes, Glenn 852, 1209, 1288, 2760, 2765, 5417
Hughes, Langston 1303, 1307, 1311, 6532–6533
Huizinga, J. 5527
Hull, Gloria T. 6140
Hull, Raymond 5446
Hulsopple, Bill G. 5009
Humble, Charles L. 3866
Hume, Charles V. 1757
Hume, Samuel J. 556, 5097
Hummel, David 7293
Huneker, James G. 3907, 4676, 4703, 5582
Hunningher, Benjamin 6074
Hunt, Althea 2753
Hunt, Douglas L. 2664, 6529
Hunt, Elizabeth R. 5467
Hunt, Gordon 966
Hunter, Alexander 2773
Hunter, Allan 4072
Hunter, Frederick J. 29, 36, 636, 3363–3364, 4577, 5021
Hunter, Jack W. 6307
Hunter, Ruth 3908–3909
Huntley, Stirling L. 496
Huntsman, Jeffrey F. 1693
Hurlbut, Gladys 1458

Hurley, George O. 1959
Hurley, Paul J. 7118
Hurlstone, Katharine 3211
Hurok, S. 3910
Hurrell, John D. 4667
Hutcheson, Maud M. 7075
Hutchinson, William C. 1090
Hutton, Laurence 1265, 1389–1390, 2307, 2975, 3400, 3418, 4449
Hyams, Frances I. 1266
Hyatt, Aeola L. 5205
Hyde, Clinton M. 1693
Hyde, Stuart W. 5775
Hyman, Colette A. 82
Hyman, Stanley E. 1463

Iles, George. 3027
Ilko, Donald W. 4440
Ilson, Carol 7420
Imhof, Martha 454
Immel, Horst. 5700
Inge, M. Thomas 4783, 6105
Inge, William 6094
Ingersoll, Robert G. 2821
Ingham, Rosemary 725
Inglis, William H. 7140
Innes, Christopher D. 1252
Ireland, Joseph N. 2303, 3590, 3619, 3628, 3678
Ireland, Norma O. 5363, 5367, 5372
Iron, William Z. 423
Irvine, Harry 865
Irvine, John C. 6615
Irving, George W. 417
Irving, John D. 4367
Irving, Pierre M. 6556–6557
Irving, Washington 6558
Isaacs, Edith J. R. 396, 842, 1272, 1285, 4913, 5788
Isman, Felix 7453
Israel, Lee 3321
Israel, Mary C. 1560
Israel, Steve Ben 2896
Issacharoff, Michael 1166
Istel, John 78
Itkin, Bella 6754
Itschert, Hans 5684
Izard, Barbara 6376
Izard, Forrest. 3023

Jablonski, Edward 401, 448, 467, 636, 3054, 7320, 7374, 7380
Jack, William T. 1575
Jackman, Michael C. 5970
Jackson, Allan S. 628, 5037
Jackson, Anne 3915
Jackson, Arthur 7262
Jackson, Esther M. 1339, 7112, 7124, 7148–7149
Jackson, Frank H. 2102
Jackson, Norman L. 3878
Jackson, Oliver 5688
Jackson, Phyllis W. 3606
Jackson, Richard S. 4446
Jacobs, David 7284
Jacobs, Milton C. 205
Jacobs, Robert D. 4261
Jacobs, Susan 2382
Jacobsen, Bruce C. 2250

Jacobson, Pauline 1740
Jacobson, Robert 2447
Jacquot, Jean 1113
Jaegar, William 908
James, Ed 4088, 4711
James, Edward T. 3078
James, Louis 2944
James, Reese D. 2586, 2603
James, Robert 3955
James, Sidney 5503
James, Thurston 690, 731
James, William R. 6429
Janaro, Richard P. 5499
Janis, Elsie 4840–4841
Janke, Robert H. 6651
Jasen, David A. 7457
Jasper, Lawrence G. 2453
Jasspe, Arthur 5438
Jaswal, Alice J. 1590
Jauslin, Christian M. 7132
Jean, T. C. G. 347
Jeffers, Robinson 6564
Jefferson, Eugenie P. 3923
Jefferson, Joseph 3918
Jeffery, Jno. B. 1426
Jeffreys, Harvey E. 5150
Jehlinger, Charles 1091
Jencks, Lance H. 1804
Jendyck, Margaret 5187
Jenkins, David 645
Jenkins, Linda C. 1330
Jenkins, Linda W. 3119
Jenkins, Robert F. 4951
Jenkins, Ron 1652
Jenkins, Stephen 2330
Jennings, Coleman A. 5240
Jennings, John 2352
Jennings, John J. 1203
Jennings, Richard 6858
Jensen, George H. 6116
Jenson, John R. 5289
Jeremy, David J. 1381
Jessel, George 3057, 3927–3931, 4752
Jewett, Frances H. 1506
Jewett, I. A. 5627
Jeyifous, Biodun 1368, 5690
Joels, Merrill E. 5330
John, Mary W. 2830
Johns, Sally. 7165
Johnson, Albert 353, 359, 1114, 5142, 5493
Johnson, Albert E. 5766
Johnson, Annette 6464
Johnson, Bertha 1114, 5142
Johnson, C. Raymond 550
Johnson, Claudia D. 59, 3115, 5701
Johnson, David Ray 4491
Johnson, Evamarii A. 2771
Johnson, Foster M. 1847
Johnson, Frances H. 1843
Johnson, Frederick G. 752, 757, 4729
Johnson, Genevieve G. 1906
Johnson, Gordon 3287
Johnson, Harold E. 1750
Johnson, Helen A. 1347, 1368
Johnson, Herrick 294
Johnson, James L. 3827
Johnson, James W. 2344, 7389

Johnson, Mark 7363
Johnson, Norman W. 1046
Johnson, Oliver 277
Johnson, Raoul F. 511
Johnson, Richard C. 5233
Johnson, Robert G. 6666
Johnson, Robert K. 6999
Johnson, Rossiter 4278
Johnson, Rue C. 2728, 3549
Johnson, Ruth P. 2601
Johnson, Stephen B. 2448
Johnson, Theodore C. 2223
Johnson, Vance 4356
Johnson, Vernon E. 59, 6663
Johnston, Alva 4554, 6709
Johnstone, Monica C. 7173
Jolson, Harry 7390
Jonason, Marvin G. 1982
Jones, Alfred H. 5872
Jones, Betty J. 6494
Jones, Cecil D. 2359
Jones, Charles T. 1058
Jones, Charles V. 5168
Jones, Charles A. 5215
Jones, David 3965
Jones, Eugene H. 1425
Jones, Henry B. 5632
Jones, Idwal 1751
Jones, Jane E. 1988
Jones, Jean B. 5817
Jones, John A. 2726
Jones, Joseph S. 3157
Jones, Kenneth L. 1837
Jones, Leo M. 6531
Jones, Leslie A. 570, 577
Jones, Margo 3054, 3933
Jones, Marion P. 2660
Jones, Martha H. 2226
Jones, May W. 1547
Jones, Robert Edmond 550, 552, 604, 3938, 3940, 4667, 5606
Jones, Robert Emmet 7149
Jones, Robin A. 2791
Jones, Robin E. 1166
Jones, Roy. 3122
Jones, Thomas A. 3458
Jones, Victor H. 6650
Jordan, Chester I. 427, 2758
Jordan, Jan 3477
Jorge, Robert R. 6281
Josal, Wendell J. 603
Joseph, Barbara A. 5833
Joseph, Roger 2262
Josephson, Lennart 6838
Jossic, Yvonne F. 566
Jotterand, Franck 1597
Joy, John F. 1618
Joyce, Peggy H. 3948
Joyce, Robert S. 2545
Jumonville, Mary L. 1754
Juneja, M. M. 6086
Jurgen, K. 4923
Justesen, Joel L. 2432

Kadlec, Anthony L. 625
Kadushin, Charles 4223
Kaes, Anton 6038
Kagan-Moore, Patrick 5542
Kahan, Gerald 6642
Kahan, Stanley 896, 922
Kahn, David M. 2865

Kahn, E. J. 6438
Kahn, Otto H. 1271, 3949, 4959
Kahn, S. M. 7148
Kahn, Sy 7149
Kaiser, Louis H. 2810
Kalez, Jay J. 2769
Kalfin, Robert 1138
Kallop, Edward 613
Kalson, Albert E. 7149
Kalter, Joanmarie 978
Kamerman, Jack B. 5549
Kaminsky, Laura J. 4946
Kandel, Gerald A. 4166
Kane, L. 6138
Kane, Whitford 3952
Kanfer, Stefan 1550
Kanin, Garson 2354, 3141, 3344, 4430
Kanter, David R. 5063
Kaough, Joseph B. 4255
Kaplan, Mike 1358, 3105
Kaplan, Samuel 5348
Kaplan, Zoe 6340
Kaprow, Allan 1104, 5917
Karasz, Lawrence J. 2235
Kardon, Janet 716
Karem, Fred J. 1990
Karioth, Emil J. 5139
Karni, Michael G. 1693
Karr, Harrison M. 864
Karschner, Donald W. 5111
Karter, M. Joshua 1340
Kase, Charles R. 5217
Kase-Polisini, Judith 5575
Kash, Bettye C. 1696
Kassak, Nancy. 249
Katkov, Norman 7345
Katter, Nate E. 1298
Katz, Albert M. 959
Katz, Herbert 149
Katz, Susan G. 360
Kaucher, Dorothy J. 5468
Kauffman, Stanley 1368, 3954, 4699
Kauffman, William C. 1731
Kaufman, Alvin S. 5856
Kaufman, Beatrice 4537
Kaufman, Edward K. 1790
Kaufman, George S. 6575
Kaufman, Julian 1320
Kaufman, Mervyn 7236
Kaufman, Michael W. 1368
Kaufman, Roger 510
Kaufmann, Preston J. 466
Kay, Carol McG. 1350
Kaye, Phyllis J. 6114
Kayman, Eleanor K. 2044
Kazacoff, George 2875
Kazan, Elia 3960, 3967
Kazin, Alfred 6085
Kazmark, Mary E. 1561
Kean, Manuel 2619
Kearns, William G. 1126
Keaton, Buster 4844
Keats, John C. 4229
Kedem, Ari 1013
Keefe, Mary M. 352
Keegan, Marcia 4777
Keeler, Ralph 3156
Keeler, Ruby 7332

Keese, William L. 3002, 3169, 3547–3548
Keeton, Guy H. 2212
Keiser, Albert 5716
Keith, Harold 4323
Keller, A. J. 6455
Keller, Betty 5201
Keller, Dean H. 5388
Kellerhouse, Muriel A. 2295
Kelley, Jonathan F. 4056
Kelley, Paul B. 2624
Kelley, W. 3358
Kelly, Eliza F. 5187
Kelly, Ethel K. 3191
Kelly, Francis P. 7344
Kelly, Frank M. 2997
Kelly, Fred C. 6148
Kelly, Kevin 7329
Kelly, Michael F. 314
Kelly, Walter C. 4847
Kemble, E. W. 7204
Kemmerling, James 1979
Kemmetmüller, Klaus 7233
Kempton, Murray 3217
Kendall, Alan 7381
Kendall, John S. 2027
Kennedy, Adrienne 5980, 6583
Kennedy, Albert J. 1900
Kennedy, Carol J. 5185
Kennedy, John P. 3151
Kennedy, Lucile B. 2678
Kennedy, Mary A. 2774
Kennedy, William B. 7366
Kenney, Janet R. 2878
Kenny, Vincent S. 6425
Kent, Evelyn E. 2011
Kenvin, Roger L. 7216
Kenworthy, O. Franklin 5038
Kepke, Allen N. 900, 2530
Keppel, Frederick P. 1278
Ker, Minette A. 1727
Kerjan, Liliane 6162
Kern, Judy B. 5055
Kernan, Alvin B. 5668, 5917
Kernodle, George R. 1229, 1260
Kerr, James S. 349
Kerr, Jean 6585–6586
Kerr, Walter 197, 1577, 3973, 4669, 4672–4673, 4685, 4689, 4694, 4701, 5437, 5500, 6684
Kerrick, George E. 7043
Kesler, Jackson 718
Kesler, William J. 1475
Kessely, Urs 5934, 6276
Ketchum, Richard M. 4332
Ketels, Arthur O. 5845
Ketterer, David 4262
Key, Nancy M. 2056
Keyssar, Helene 5973, 5988, 6115, 6138
Kgositsite, K. William 5920
Kherdian, David 6948
Kibbee, Lois 3383
Kibler, James E. 6996
Kidd, T. J. 5935
Kienzle, Siegfried 5610
Kiesby, Suzanne B. 5870
Kiesendahl, John K. 2240
Kiesler, Lillian 670
Kilby, Quincy 2100
Kile, Sara A. 2128

Kim, Ki-Ae 6957
Kim, Yun-Cheol 5978
Kimball, Robert 7378, 7415, 7440
Kimbrell, Marketa 1138
Kimes, William H. 3974
Kimmel, Stanley 3439
Kimura, Toshia 6858
Kincaid, Arthur 3487
Kindelan, Nancy A. 3572
King, Christine E. 4228
King, Clyde R. 2699
King, Kimball 5392, 6091
King, Larry L. 7279
King, Nancy 939, 5187
King, William R. 6643
Kingsbury, Barry M. 1336
Kingsley, William H. 5225
Kinkle, Roger D. 7248
Kinnamon, Kenneth 6231
Kinne, Wisner P. 3312
Kinney, Harry A. 7162
Kinsila, Edward B. 387
Kipel, Vitaut 1693
Kiraly, Victor 2777
Kirby, E. T. 1231
Kirby, Michael 1102, 1162, 1603, 1615, 5696
Kirfel-Lenk, Thea 6044
Kirk, Clara M. 6521
Kirk, John M. 1159
Kirk, John W. 4579
Kirk, Rudolph 6521
Kirkland, Audrey S. 4181
Kirkpatrick, D. L. 6131, 6134
Kirschman, Marvin 1786
Kirstein, Lincoln 1627
Kiskadden, Annie 3263
Kiser, Edmond L. 4130
Kislan, Richard J. 7424
Kitchin, Laurence 5788
Kitt, Eartha 7397
Kittle, Russell D. 4357
Kittredge, G. L. 6684
Kjerbuhl-Peterson, Lorenz 829
Klaiber, Roger C. 1833
Klappert, Walter R. 538
Klar, Lawrence R. 5047
Klaus, Carl H. 5510
Klautsch, Richard J. 2184
Klee, Bruce B. 2365
Klein, Carole 3404
Klein, Elaine S. 7217
Klein, Howard K. 243
Klein, Maxine 952, 4948
Klein, Ralph A. 5735
Klein, Robert 6116
Klein, Ruth 1082
Kleiner, Dick 929
Kleinfield, H. L. 3375
Klementowski, Nancy 5979
Kline, Kevin 1051
Kline, Peter 940, 5182, 5449
Kline, Ruth F. 719
Kling, Esther L. 2034
Klink, William 6209
Klinkowitz, Jerome 7069–7070
Klock, Mary E. 5151, 5166
Klussen, Robert D. 2170
Knapp, Margaret M. 2433
Knaub, Richard K. 1124
Knepler, Henry W. 1289, 3068

Knight, Charles 2963
Knight, Virginia D. 1875
Knox, George A. 5851
Knox, Rose B. 4737
Knudsen, Vern O. 448
Knudson, Grace P. 2093
Knutson, Wayne 5482
Kobbé, Gustav 3012–3013
Kobernick, Mark 6892
Kobler, John 3348
Koch, E. de Roy 3014
Koch, Frederick H. 2470–2471, 2473–2475, 2477, 2492, 4893, 4910, 4915
Koch, John C. 2655, 2862
Koch, Vivienne 7108
Koenig, Linda L. 2066, 2068
Koenig, Rachael 6130
Koep, Jeffery P. 5070
Koepsal, Jürgen 7138
Koger, Alicia K. 6441
Kohansky, Mendel 1014
Kohler, Katharine 2287
Köhler, Klaus 5953
Kohut, G. A. 6724
Koischwitz, Otto 6743
Koldenhoven, James J. 6720
Kolin, Philip C. 1350, 5979, 6139, 6192, 6921, 7149
Kolodin, Irving 2378
Konas, Gary 5979
Konow, Gary G. 2183
Kook, Edward F. 428, 506, 660
Kooken, Olive 3719
Koon, Helene W. 1698, 6698
Koontz, John G. 2599
Kopit, Arthur 6094, 6588
Korn, Marjorie S. 2857
Kosberg, Milton L. 4126
Kostelanetz, Richard 1308, 1316, 1341
Koster, Donald N. 5761
Kotsilibas-Davis, James 3349–3350
Kouloumbis, Akila 1138
Kourilsky, Francoise 1309, 2837
Kovacs, George 7000
Kovar, Linn S. 777
Kozelka, Paul 1109
Kozlenko, Vladimir 4186
Kozlenko, William 5417
Kraft, Hy 3244
Kraft, Irma 5588
Kramer, Dale 3216, 3528
Kramer, Magdalene E. 5104
Kramer, Sidney 5420
Kramer, Stanley 1577
Kramer, Victor A. 7149
Kramer, William 1530
Kraus, Joanne H. 5187
Krawitz, Herman E. 243, 1138, 2384
Kreider, Barbara 5237
Kreizenbeck, Alan D. 2859
Krempel, Daniel 1106
Kretzmann, Albert J. 4963
Kreuger, Miles 6378, 6380
Kreymborg, Alfred 6589
Kriley, James D. 930
Krone, Charles A. 3979
Kronenberger, Louis 1505, 3980
Krows, Arthur E. 558, 1054, 5414

Krugh, Arthur N. 48
Kruh, David 2146
Krumm, Walter C. 1770
Krutch, Joseph W. 3982, 4667, 5788, 5834, 5838
Krzys, Katherine 5264
Kubiak, Anthony J. 1042
Kubicki, Jan T. 1132
Kuehl, John 6446
Kuehnl, Eileen K. 3266
Kuemmerle, Clyde V. 629, 2065
Kueppers, Brigitte 163
Kuftinec, Sonja 5979
Kuhlke, William 5662
Kuhn, John G. 6257
Kullman, Colby H. 5979
Kuner, Mildred C. 7091
Kunesh, Gregory D. 5156
Kunzog, John C. 4873
Kuryk, David 6900
Kussrow, Van C. 315
Kut, Inge 6116
Kutrzeba, Joseph S. 1685
Kwal, Teri S. 1184
Kydrynski, Juliusz 4127
Kyle, Howard 3426

La Rue, Grace 4805
La Salle, Claude W. 7194
Laborde, Charles B. 5798
Labrenz, Ernest T. 5903
Lacy, Robin T. 692
Ladd, James W. 2761
Ladwig, Ronald V. 2548
Lafler, Joanne 1700
Laforse, Martin W. 4792
LaHoud, John 246
Lahr, Anthea 6588
Lahr, John 1240, 3986, 4693, 4696, 6122, 6588
Lait, Jack 4318, 4320, 7207
Lamb, Andrew 7310, 7396
Lambert, Gavin 3613
Lambert, Marlene K. 1953
Laming, Dorothy W. 4276
Lamm, Martin 5594
Lammel, Earl C. 6909
Lamont, R. C. 6138
Lamparski, Richard 3242
Lampe, Michael 2234
Land, Robert H. 2745
Landau, Jack 1845
Landau, Penny M. 3679
Landis, Jessie R. 3987
Landry, Robert J. 4753
Landy, Robert J. 5188
Lane, Doris A. 2685
Lane, Le Roi 5121
Lane, Mildred R. 1969
Lane, Morgan J. 1780
Lane, Richard A. 7249
Lane, William A. 3510
Lang, William 2253
Langdon, Harry 2253
Langdon, Harry M. 6159
Lange, Jane W. 6555
Lange, Lawrence L. 374
Langford, Martha F. 4358
Langley, Stephen 792, 1138
Langley, Stephen G. 5670
Langley, William O. 1871

Langner, Lawrence 703, 2952–2953, 3988, 5447
Langworthy, Helen 1672, 2506
Lanier, Henry W. 2933
Lanphier, David N. 5061
Lanterbach, Charles E. 1700
Larimer, Cynthia 6462
Larimer, Michael W. 1781
Larsen, Carl F. 1418
Larsen, James W. 7039
Larsen, June B. 3935, 7149
Larson, Carl F. W. 47
Larson, Orville K. 604, 691
Larson, Patricia M. 2563
Laszlo, B. Nagy 6858
Latchan, Truly T. 1456
Latham, E. 6684
Latshaw, George T. 5229
Laubin, Gladys 1377
Laufe, Abe 210, 2379, 7228
Laughlin, H. T. 5736
Laurel, Brenda K. 5463
Laurence, Gil 1805
Laurent, Eugene M. 3835
Laurie, Joseph 4743, 4746
Laver, James 703
Lawick-Goodall, J. V. 5527
Lawlor, Jo A. 2045
Lawren, Joseph 1508
Lawrence, Happy J. 2873
Lawrence, Jerome 4178
Lawrence, Rita. 3200
Lawson, Evelyn 2135
Lawson, Hilda H. 5641
Lawson, John H. 1548, 4676, 5440, 6592, 6776
Layne, William J. 5143
Lazarovic-Hrebelianovic, Princess [= Calhoun, Eleanor] 3551
Lazarus, Arnold L. 6650
Lazenby, Walter S. 6018
Le Breton, Maurice 6858
Le Gallienne, Eva 1513, 3436, 3992–3993, 5394, 5588
Le Vay, John 3288
Lea, Florence B. 1538
Leach, Joseph 3623
Leach, Shelton B. 4422
Leach, Witford 7011
Leacock, Stephen B. 3135
Leaf, Linaya L. 5183
Leaming, Barbara 4482
Leary, Lewis 6131
Lease, Ruth 5116
Leathem, Barclay 3054
Leathers, Dale G. 5910
Leathes, Edmund 3158
Leavitt, Dinah L. 1630
Leavitt, M. B. 3998
Leavitt, Penelope M. 4784
Leavitt, Richard F. 7153
Lebel, Jean-J. 1105, 2895
LeCasse, Donald E. 3447
Lederer, Katherine 6475
Lee, Amy 3207
Lee, Douglas B. 2788
Lee, Frank 213
Lee, Gypsy R. 4849
Lee, Henry G. 6206
Lee, James W. 51
Lee, Ming Cho 431

Lee, Robert C. 6780
Leech, Clifford 6773
Leech, Margaret 307
Leech, Robert M. 5130
Leecing, Walden A. 1760
Leeds, Josiah W. 297
Lees, Charles L. 863, 5717
Lees, Gene 7244
Lees, Sondra 5010
Lefevre, Carl A. 6008
LeFevre, John J. 4720
Legardeur, Rene J. 2037
Lehmann, Lotte 853
Leibowitz, Judith 1051
Leiter, Samuel L. 2388, 2449, 2454
Leitner, Paul 4423
Leland, Nicholas F. 7187
Leman, Walter M. 4000
Lemay, J. A. Leo 6091
Lembke, Russell W. 6570
Lemmerman, Harold B. 5043
Lenthal, Franklyn 165
Léon, Paul 4007
Leonard, Bob F. 3704
Leonard, Charles 1098
Leonard, Dymphna 5596
Leonard, Eddie 4850
Leonard, James M. 2293
Leonard, William F. 3355
Leonard, William T. 4801, 5390, 5393, 5397
Leonardi, Dell 3479
Leone, L. 2182
Lerche, Frank M. 7229
Lerner, Alan Jay 4110, 7298, 7359, 7398–7399
Lescarbot, Marc 5713
Lescaze, William Howard 396
Leslie, Amy 4001
Leslie, Peter 4802
Lesnick, Henry 1607
Lessac, Arthur 946, 971
Lesser, Allen 4093, 4095
Lesser, Joseph L. 4835
Lessley, Merrill 539
Lester, Elenore 5917
Lester, Julius 6431
Lester, N. A. 5979
Lestrud, Vernon A. 317
Leuchs, Fritz A. 5997
Leure, Jeane 5979
Levant, Oscar 7400–7401
Leverett, James 5696
Leverton, Garrett H. 1067
Levey, Andrew 3282
Levi-Strauss, C. 5527
Levin, Harry 5570
Levin, M. H. 6798
Levin, Milton 6271
Levin, Richard L. 5486
Levine, Ira A. 5556
Levine, Lawrence W. 1372
Levine, Samuel P. 3255
Levitt, Bruce 5169
Levitt, Harold 6811
Levy, Edwin L. 1830
Levy, Jonathan 82, 5264
Levy, Julien 3390
Levy, Newman. 3136
Lewandowski, Raymond J. 2164, 2557

Lewine, Richard 7287
Lewis, Allan 5611, 5911
Lewis, David L. 2428
Lewis, Emory 1543
Lewis, Harrison 866
Lewis, Jac 732
Lewis, Jim G. 3612
Lewis, John L. 3526
Lewis, Judith A. 5078
Lewis, Miriam 732
Lewis, Oscar 4144
Lewis, Philip C. 1683
Lewis, Robert 889, 906, 987, 4004
Lewis, Stanley T. 2353
Lewis, Virginia E. 4389
Lewis, William R. 4606
Lewisohn, Lewis 1448
Lewison, Agnes O. 1960
Lewton, E. P. 6827
Lewy, Thomas 1181
Libby, Charles T. 3771
Libin, Paul 1138
Lichtenstein, Hyman 6716
Lichti, Esther S. 2925
Lichtman, Myla R. 6843
Lieberman, Herman 6738
Lieberman, Joseph A. 5878
Liebling, Abbott J. 7208
Lifson, David S. 1693, 6025
Lifton, Paul S. 7104
Limpus, Robert M. 1904
Lincoln, C. Eric 1311
Lincoln, Robert 3425
Lindberg, John 6244, 6250
Lindbergh, Anne Morrow 6962
Lindblom, Ernst 4139
Lindenberger, H. 1261
Lindenberger, Herbert S. 5527
Lindey, Alexander 190
Lindsay, Cynthia H. 4819
Lindsay, Howard 865
Lindsay, John 2718
Lindsey, Henry C. 2026
Link, Franz H. 6790, 7139
Link, James O. 4546
Linnehan, Edward 5647
Linskie, Margaret 2681
Lion, Paul D. 1331
Lippman, Monroe 1452
Lipschutz, Mark 640
Lipsitz, George 2205
Lipsyte, Robert 3828
Lister, Raymond 4009
Liston, Maureen R. 7018
Litchfield, Hope P. 5445
Littell, John Stockton 2572
Little, Paul V. 320
Little, Stewart W. 1619, 4226
Little, Stuart W. 772, 2405
Little, Thomas J. 5743
Littlefield, Daniel 54
Littlefield, Harold 843
Littleford, Roger S. 4781
Littlejohn, David 5912
Litto, Fredric M. 30, 4378
Litton, Glenn 7276
Litwack, Sydney Z. 592
Livermore, Mary E. 2983
Livingstone, Belle 4012–4013
Lizst, Rudolph G. 746
Llovet, Enrique 6081

Lloyd, David D. 4282
Lloyd, Harold 3071
Lloyd, Herbert 4727
Locke, Alain 1323, 1509, 4765, 5920, 5930
Lockridge, Richard 3432
Lockwood, Patton 6548
Loeffler, Donald L. 5946
Loevy, Steven R. 7111
Logan, Herschel C. 3215
Logan, Joshua 877, 2942, 4015–4016
Logan, Nedda Harrigan 2822
Logan, Olive 4017–4018
Logan, Rhea D. 5637
Logan, Winford B. 5785
Loganbill, Bruce 4383
Logasa, Hannah 5351
Loggie, Jean 2822
Loggins, Vernon 3222
Lohner, Edgar 1338
Lomas, John 4448
Lominac, Harry G. 2484
London, Jack 6602
London, Michael 6606
London, Todd 788
Londré, Felicia H. 5039, 5979, 7157, 7177
Loney, Glenn 1171, 1351, 1688, 4683, 5776, 7288
Long, Chester C. 6794
Long, Deborah M. 6129
Long, Eugene H. 5679
Long, Linda S. 3106
Long, Will W. 2481
Longman, Stanley V. 6116
Loos, Anita 3851, 4021
Lord, Everett W. 178
Lord, William J. 5441
Loring, Janet 706
Loudin, Joanne M. 5796
Loudon, George W. 3663
Lounsbury, Althea 867
Lounsbury, Warren 791
Lovell, John 5368
Lowe, Claudia 61
Lowe, Leslie 7299
Lowenthal, Lawrence D. 5922
Lower, Charles B. 1350, 4932
Lown, Charles R. 5727
Lowrie, James A. 2593
Lowry, W. M. 223, 1627
Lübbren, Rainer 6670
Lubell, Albert J. 4259
Lucas, Thomas E. 4589
Lucia, Ellis 4315
Lucid, R. F. 6632
Luckiesh, M. 472–473
Ludes, Francis J. 168
Ludlow, Noah M. 4024
Ludwig, Jay F. 1919
Ludwig, Richard M. 4524
Lumianski, Robert M. 4545
Lummis, Eliza O'B. 302
Lundrigan, Paul J. 1031
Lunt, Alfred 1513
Luter, Gary S. 5802
Luttrell, Wanda M. 2662
Lyle, Beverly B. 2013
Lyman, George D. 2267
Lyman, Kenneth C. 6015

Lyman, Stanford M. 5524
Lynch, Arthur. 4284
Lynch, Edmund 507
Lynch, Richard C. 111
Lynch, Twink 4952
Lynd, Robert S. 1511
Lynes, Russell 1493
Lynn, Kenneth S. 6722
Lyons, Bonnie 374
Lyons, Eugene 1522
Lyons, Jake G. 4322

Mabbott, Thomas O. 7005
Mabley, Edward 5453
Macadam, George 2334
Macaloon, John J. 5553
Macardle, Dorothy 6858
Macarthur, Charlotte W. 3109
MacArthur, Charles 3846
Macarthur, David E. 3279
Macclennan, Robert W. 6145
MacColl, Ewan 1495
MacDermott, G. 7245
MacDonald, Dwight 4675
Macdonald, Robert J. 4985
Macebuh, Stanley 6230
MacGhee, Mildred M. 4286
MacGowan, Kenneth 401, 404, 550, 552, 695, 1206, 1218, 1221, 2114, 3942, 4029, 4908, 5432, 5606
Macheski, Cecilia. 1379
Machlin, Evangeline 913
Machlin, Milt 4867
Mackay, Alice 2227
Mackay, Alice B. 844
Mackay, Constance D. 698, 4891, 4898, 4900, 5203–5204
Mackay, Edward J. 844
Mackay, F. F. 824, 844
Mackaye, Percy 3937, 4031, 4890, 4894, 4896, 4899, 6616–6617, 6621, 6712
Mackeever, Samuel A. 2317
Mackey, Louis J. 3468
MacLaren, Gay 5273
MacLeish, Archibald 5443
MacMinn, George R. 1741
MacNicholas, John 6116, 7149
Macy, Gertrude 3597
Madden, David 5927
Madden, Patricia A. 1350
Madison, James 4725
Madsen, John A. 2804
Madsen, Patricia D. 7250
Magarshack, David 878
Magnuson, Landis F. 1500
Magonigle, J. H. 3880
Magriel, Paul D. 7
Magruder, Henry P. 5011
Mahard, Martha 82
Maher, Dennis M. 2241
Maher, James T. 7244
Mahfouz, Nazih H. 686
Mahon, Thomas A. 5012
Mahoney, Ella V. 3429
Mahovlick, Frank 490
Maiden, Lewis S. 2665, 2671
Mailer, Julia H. 4936
Mailer, Norman 1578, 6630
Mailman, Bruce. 2406

Mainiero, Lisa 6109
Makover, Abraham B. 6726
Malec, Andrew 3807
Malevinsky, Moses L. 5410
Malin, Irving 6286
Malina, Judith 1578, 2894, 2896–2897, 2901, 2904, 2907, 2911, 5394
Malkin, Jeanette R. 5987
Malkin, Michael R. 5175
Mallory, Vincent 501
Maloff, Saul 1529
Malone, John 5345
Malpede, Karen 2920, 5394
Malvern, Gladys 3593
Mamet, David 6637, 6639, 6641
Mammen, Edward W. 2121
Mance, William R. 1631
Mandelbaum, Ken 7328
Mander, Raymond 7230
Manderson, M. Sandra 5295
Maney, Richard 3219
Manfull, Helen A. 5848
Mangum, Valerie B. 5645
Manheim, Michael 6879, 6893
Mankowitz, Wolf 4097
Mann, Martin A. 7402
Mann, Mary 1805
Mann, Theodore 1138
Manners, J. Hartley 4415
Mannheim, Michael 6853
Manning, Ferdinand L. 4924
Manry, Joe E. 2712
Mantegna, Gianfranco 2901
Mantle, Burns 1505, 3834, 5473, 6059, 6061
Mantle, Lydia S. 1505
Mapp, Edward 3093
Mar, Helen 4055
Marble, Annie R. 6365
Marble, Thomas L. 5404
Marbury, Elisabeth 4058
Marcel, Gabriel 6858
Marchand, William M. 5671
Marchetti, Roger 187
Marchiafava, Bruce T. 5737
Marcosson, Isaac F. 3773
Marcuson, Lewis R. 5672
Marder, Carl H. 2968
Marder, Carl J. 2708
Mardis, Robert F. 2855
Maretzek, Max 3238
Margetts, Ralph E. 3658
Margetts, Winifred S. 2725
Margolies, Alan 6390
Margolies, Edward 6087
Marienthal, Harold S. 4034
Marill, Alvin H. 3859
Marinacci, Barbara. 3058
Marine, Don 1930
Marinis, Marco De 1649
Marker, Lise-Lone 3378
Markham, Pauline 4061
Markley, David J. 521
Marks, Edward B. 3043, 7208
Marks, Patricia 4609
Marks, Samuel M. 4439
Markus, Tom 979
Marlor, Clark S. 20
Marlowe, Joan 880
Marowitz, Charles 894, 972

Marquez, Rosa Luisa 1693
Marranca, Bonnie 1246, 6117, 6123
Marre, Diane K. 6434
Marsden, Donald 2942
Marsh, Dorothy D. 4926
Marsh, Florence 914
Marsh, John L. 2620
Marsh, William H. 319
Marsh, William S. 2221
Marshall, A. 2953
Marshall, Alexander C. 5075
Marshall, Brenda K. 1167
Marshall, Eric R. 5750
Marshall, Henry 967
Marshall, Thomas F. 623, 2594
Marshall-Martin, David 369
Marston, William M. 4870
Martin, Boyd. 5824
Martin, Carol L. 7353
Martin, Charlotte M. 3795
Martin, Constance B. 2275
Martin, David 7331
Martin, Frank J. 2504
Martin, James L. 5048
Martin, Jay 6607
Martin, Jerry L. 1695
Martin, Mary 7404
Martin, Pete 7406
Martin, Ralph G. 2402
Martin, Robert C. 5280
Martin, Robert A. 6669, 6693, 6697
Martin, William G. 363
Martine, James J. 6695, 6859
Martorella, Roseanne 5549
Marx, Arthur 4854, 4860
Marx, Groucho 4855, 4857, 4861–4863
Marx, Harpo 4856
Marx, Samuel 7427
Maschio, Geraldine 82, 4561
Mashburn, Robert R. 661
Mashiach, Sellina 5242
Mason, Daniel G. 6710
Mason, Gregory H. 5613
Mason, Hamilton 6004
Mason, Jeffrey D. 6576–6577
Mason, Louise C. 5461
Mason, Raymond M. 1742
Mason, Richard F. 6443
Mason, Rufus O. 3160
Massett, Stephen C. 4071
Masson, Thomas 6147
Masters, Robert W. 6384
Materassi, Mario 5955
Mates, Julian 1319, 7218, 7294
Mather, Charles C. 847, 1063
Mather, Increase 311
Mather, Patricia A. 1975
Matheson, Diana L. 1187
Mathew, David C. 7149
Mathews, Jane D. 2853
Mathews, R. G. 3004
Matlaw, Myron 77, 1502, 4788
Matson, Cecil 2567
Matson, Katinka 3102, 5335
Matson, Lowell. 2357
Mattfeld, Julius 4768
Matthews, Brander 139, 825, 1076, 1269, 1431–1432, 1444, 2975, 3400, 3507, 3800, 4073–4074, 5403, 5629, 5757, 6500
Matthews, Geraldine O. 42
Matthews, J. H. 5617
Matthews, William 39
Matz, Mary J. 3951
Maufort, Marc 6893
Maughan, Ila M. 2730
Maurer, Robert E. 6344
Max Waldman 2920
Maxwell, Bernice J. 5001
Maxwell, Elsa 3233
Maxwell, Everett C. 1735
Maxwell, Gilbert 7125, 7410
Maxwell, William B. 6642
May, Charles E. 7149
May, Robert 274
May, Robin 1551
May, Suzanne D. 2714
Mayberry, Bob 6193
Maychick, Diana 4412
Mayer, Harold F. 4965
Mayer, Martin 433, 2438
Mayne, Ethel C. 3188
Mayo, Margaret 1446
Mayor, A. Hyatt 430, 4208
Mayorga, Margaret G. 5715
Mays, David D. 2035, 6265
Mazzaro, J. 6606, 6608
McAdoo, William 181
McArthur, Benjamin 1491
McBride, Donald M. 5025
McBride, Joseph 4478
McBride, Mary 7149
McBride, Mary M. 3783
McCabe, James D. 2305
McCabe, John H. 7355
McCall, Ellen M. 5186
McCall, John C. 1878
McCalmon, George 4934
McCandless, Stanley R. 474, 500, 509
McCann, John S. 7163
McCarthy, Gerry 6190
McCarthy, Mary 4674, 5490, 5788, 5901
McCarthy, Thomas J. 6026
McCaslin, Nellie 4949, 5187, 5193, 5234, 5263, 5265
McClave, Nancy 2832
McCleery, Albert 4918
McClintic, Guthrie 1077, 4078, 4206, 4431
McCloud, George E. 5525
McClure, Arthur F. 6551
McClure, Stanley W. 2782
McCollum, William G. 5483
McConachie, Bruce A. 1261, 1421, 1502, 5747
McConnell, Frederick 3054
McConnell, Margaret E. 4461
McCormick, John 4947
McCormick, Robert A. 5837
McCormick, Walter J. 4758
McCosker, Susan 1407
McCrary, Margaret M. 1778
McCreath, Harrison W. 6594
McCrindle, Joseph F. 6094
McCrossan, Josephine M. 2280
McCullough, Bruce W. 7004
McCullough, Jack W. 82, 2439
McCurdy, Evelyn M. 1752
McDaniel, Henry A. 1867
McDavitt, Elaine E. 2149, 2793
McDermott, Dana S. 1700, 3946
McDermott, Douglas 1487, 1700, 2850
McDermott, John F. 5470
McDermott, William F. 4665
Mcdonald, Donald 1577
McDonald, Robert A. 5800
McDonald, William F. 2854
McDonough, Edwin J. 6871
McDonough, Patrick D. 2198
McDougald, W. Worth 82
McDowell, John H. 9–11
McDowell, Margaret B. 6647
McDowell, Sara-Jean 2485
McElhaney, John S. 1791
McEntire, Robert M. 2139
McEvoy, Owen 665
McGaw, Charles 11
McGaw, Charles J. 968, 980
McGeever, Charles J. 1135
McGeoch, R. A. 7147
McGhee, James H. 6970
McGill, Earl 1077
McGinnis, William C. 6370
McGlinchee, Claire 2118
McGlinn, Jeanne M. 7149
McGlinn, John 6380
McGovern, Catherine B. 5307
McGovern, Edythe M. 6998
McGraw, Charles J. 4522
McGraw, Rex T. 5734
McGraw, William R. 933
McGrew, Julia H. 5835
McHughes, William F. 7158
McIlrath, Patricia A. 5893
McKay, Frederick E. 2990
McKay, Marilyn L. 7282
McKay, Patricia 1688
McKean, Gil 7451–7452
McKee, Edna H. 2209
McKee, Thomas J. 6363, 7054
McKelvey, Blake 2291
McKenna, Suzanne 5566
McKennon, Joe 1869
McKennon, Marian 1676
McKenzie, Douglas C. 3926
McKenzie, Ruth H. 2600
McKerrow, Margaret 4192
McKinney, Priscilla S. 5979
McLaughlin, Robert G. 238
McLean, Albert F. 4759
McLellan, G. A. 1138
McLennan, Kathleen A. 5806
McMullan, Frank 1096
McMullen, Frank 1079, 1100
McNair, Jennifer S. 5264
McNally, Mary A. 7032
McNally, William 4728
McNamara, Brooks 429, 446, 939, 4131, 4370–4371, 4705
McNeely, Jerry C. 3301
McNeil, Barbara 3103
McNeil, Beatrice H. 5206
McNeir, Waldo F. 1350
McPharlin, Paul 6355
McPherson, James M. 1477
McPherson, Michael L. 6471
McSpadden, Joseph W. 7210

McSpadden, Maurice 4331
McVicker, J. H. 294, 296, 1889
Mead, Shepherd 7164
Meade, Edwards H. 4084
Meadows, Nancy 940
Mecham, E. J. 3360
Meconnahey, Joseph H. 2592
Medley, Mat 1380
Meek, Beryl 1987, 5209
Meerman, Roger 2786, 2788
Meerman, Roger L. 1299
Megarity, Shirley A. 2705
Meinecke, Charlotte D. 2060
Meinken, Ernest F. 1409, 4590
Meister, Charles W. 4611, 6010
Melebeck, Claude B. 2052
Melick, Weldon 1523
Mellinger, M. 480
Melnitz, William W. 16
Melnitz, William 1221
Meloy, Arthur S. 386
Melton, Elston J. 2222
Meltzer, George 1974
Meltzer, Milton 1307, 1311, 6535
Mencken, H. L. 3182, 6099
Mendelsohn, Harold A. 5498
Mendelsohn, Michael J. 6902
Mendenhall, Christian 7313
Mendoza, Barbara M. 3731
Mendoza, George 4169
Meneely, John H. 5707
Menefee, Larry T. 1724
Menken, Adah I. 4087
Menkin, Arthur H. 3410
Mensh, Elaine 247
Merbach, Paul Alfred 567
Mercier, Mary 2382, 2407
Meredith, Burgess 917
Meredith, Scott 6572
Merenda, Marilyn D. 48
Merin, Jennifer 86
Mering, Yolla 4308
Merman, Ethel 7405–7407
Merrell, Helen M. 1511
Merrick, Mary L. 2512
Merrill, Flora 3199
Merrill, John 4098, 5094
Merrill, Lisa 3624
Merrill, Patricia 2237
Mersand, Joseph 334, 1071, 5137, 5208, 5416, 5819, 5822, 5825, 6063
Mertz, Henriette 5349
Merwin, Samuel. 2931
Meserve, Walter J. 52, 1322, 5673, 5692, 5746, 5752, 5788, 6511, 6519, 6986
Meshke, George L. 1604
Messano-Ciesla, Mary A. 3723
Messerli, Douglas 6261
Metcalf, E. W. 7361
Metcalf, William A. 5964
Metizer, Fred W. 2193
Metten, Charles H. 1093
Meyer, Arthur C. 5056
Meyer, Jeanette R. 5220
Meyer, Susan E. 6391
Meyerowitz, Patricia 7021
Mezu, S. Okechukwu 6244
Michael, Mary R. 2119
Michalak, Marion V. 3632

Mickel, Jere C. 1686
Mickle, Alan D. 6737
Middleton, George 222, 6656
Middleton, Herman D. 611
Midyett, Judith A. 6132
Mielech, Ronald A. 6944
Mielziner, Jo 434, 3942, 4102, 5020
Miesle, Frank L. 2514
Mikotowicz, Thomas J. 4388
Millard, David E. 1190
Miller, Adam David 1368
Miller, Anna I. 1210
Miller, Arthur 1225, 1593, 4682, 5432, 5443, 5490, 5538, 5788, 5908, 6678, 6684, 6699, 6704
Miller, Dale 2498
Miller, Ernest C. 3468
Miller, Frank M. 6110
Miller, Fred R. 5135
Miller, Frederick K. 2251
Miller, Gilbert 5429
Miller, James H. 442, 642
Miller, James R. 3331
Miller, Jeanne-Marie A. 5951
Miller, John M. 4547
Miller, Jordan Y. 5847, 6781, 6819, 7135
Miller, Joseph W. 6088
Miller, Karina L. 6034
Miller, Lewis 5266
Miller, Lynn F. 4700
Miller, Michael 2414
Miller, Nellie B. 5585
Miller, Peter R. 1938
Miller, R. Baxter 6542
Miller, Ralph E. 4364
Miller, Raphael F. 7289
Miller, Richard 5694
Miller, Samuel 260–261
Miller, Tice L. 1502
Miller, Thomas C. 3945
Miller, Tice L. 4428, 4607
Miller, William C. 2263
Millett, Fred B. 5591, 6062
Mills, Earl 3641
Mills, Katherine B. 5685
Mills, Kathleen 6186
Milne, Tom 4023, 4041
Milner, Donald 5930
Milsten, David R. 4321
Milton, Paula 1865
Mims, E. 1274
Mincher, John 525
Miner, Harry 1427
Miner, Worthington 1077
Minnelli, Vincente 4110
Minnigerode, Meade 3185
Minor, Charles H. 2360
Minsky, Morton 4867
Minter, Gordon 1073
Miralles, Alberto 1616
Miranne, Joseph J. 5849
Mirecourt, Eugene De 4137
Mirlas, Leon 6744, 6763, 6858
Mishler, John D. 2582
Mitchell, Albert O. 2722, 6197
Mitchell, James W. 2798
Mitchell, Langdon 5413
Mitchell, Lee 401, 620, 1155

Mitchell, Loften 1310, 5920, 5930, 6100
Mitchell, Ronald E. 7234
Mitchell, Roy 1059, 5092
Mitchell, Sallie 4069
Mitchenson, Joe 7230
Mix, Tom 4321
Mizener, Arthur 6623
Mochedlover, Helene G. 5398
Moderwell, Hiram K. 1510
Modisett, Noah F. 3376
Modisette, Eldon L. 5836
Modjeska, Helena 4113
Modlin, Charles E. 6226
Moe, Christian 4934, 5661
Moeller, Philip 2332
Moffitt, Dale E. 973
Mohan, Roberta N. 6573
Moise, Abraham. 6435
Moïse, Lusius C. 6436
Molette, Barbara J. 1363
Molette, Carlton W. 5040, 6234
Molin, Donald C. 1015
Molin, Sven E. 6313
Molnar, John W. 7462
Monaghan, Therese A. 5301
Monck, W. Nugent 145
Monos, James 995
Monroe, John G. 2426
Monson, Leland H. 2729
Monson, William N. 1802
Montalban, Ricardo 4132
Montale, Eugenio 6858
Montano, Severino M. 2829
Montez, Lola 4134–4135
Monti, Carlotta 3711
Montilla, Robert B. 1958
Montley, Patricia A. 365
Moody, Richard 1319, 1322, 1487, 3764–3765, 5373, 5657, 5692, 6440, 6466
Moody, Stanley E. 1175
Moody, William V. 6712
Mooney, Michael 4198
Moore, Dick 5333
Moore, Edward C. 1903
Moore, Harry T. 5682, 5927, 6165, 6342, 6783, 6929
Moore, Henry T. 5869
Moore, Isabel 3913
Moore, Jack B. 6296
Moore, John J. 1191
Moore, Kemper M. 5829
Moore, Lester L. 2274
Moore, Lillian 3227
Moore, Lou 249
Moore, M. Marguerite 2606
Moore, Sonia 909, 924
Moore, Thomas G. 232
Moorman, Charles 7149
Morath, Inge 6678
Moray, John S. 3443
Mordden, Ethan 1344, 7256, 7283
Mordecai, Samuel 2743
Morehouse, Ward 2348, 3202, 4153, 7352
Moreland, James 2058
Morell, Parker 7435
Morella, Joe 3520, 3889
Morgan, Anna 806
Morgan, Floyd T. 5049

Morgan, Geoffrey F. 757
Morgan, John B. 4314
Morgan, John De. 3131
Morgan, Joyce V. 988
Morgan, Kathleen A. 3123
Morgan, Mona 4155
Morgan, Robert L. 5873
Morgan, William 1173
Morgan-Powell, S. 3192
Morison, Bradley G. 2195
Moritz, Charles 3041
Morley, Christopher 2272, 2338, 4156–4157
Morley, Sheridan 3118, 3862, 6575
Morosco, Helen M. 4158
Morosco, Selma P. 867
Morphos, Evangeline 4411
Morrell, Thomas H. 3879, 4447
Morris, Clara 4161–4163
Morris, David W. 6945
Morris, Felix 4165
Morris, Lloyd 1290, 1455
Morris, Mowbray 2972
Morris, William C. 3576
Morrison, A. Craig 2434
Morrison, Andrew C. 2178, 2785
Morrison, Hugh 3270
Morrison, Jack S. 5016
Morrison, Theodore 5290
Morrissey, James W. 3175
Morrissey, Starr 2306
Morrow, Laura 5979
Morrow, Lee A. 1567, 4842
Morrow, Marguerite H. 2006
Morsberger, Katharine M. 6116
Morsberger, Robert E. 7045, 7049
Morse, Frank P. 4107
Morse, William N. 1669
Mosedale, John 2429
Mosel, Tad 3597
Moseley, Florence A. 344
Moses, Gilbert. 2876
Moses, Marilyn 4884
Moses, Montrose J. 3015, 3586, 3763, 4569, 6057, 6383
Moses, William A. 1852
Moskow, Michael H. 235
Moss, Arnold 5057
Moss, Leonard 6672, 6684
Moss, Lynda 3596
Moss, Theodore 3880
Mostel, Kate 4170
Mostel, Zero 4168
Motherwell, Hiram 2949
Motter, Charlotte K. 5194
Mottram, Eric 1305, 6676, 6684
Mottram, Ron 6971
Mould, William A. 6116
Mounier, Catherine 6858
Mouring, Muriel A. 3680
Mowatt, Anna Cora 4171
Mowry, Vera L. 5650
Moyer, Ronald L. 49
Mraz, Doyne 7130
Muchnic, Helen 6776
Mulder, William 2724
Muldrow, Blanche 1402
Mulgrave, Dorothy I. 20
Mulholland, Moira K. 1004
Mullaly, Edward J. 6628

Muller, Herbert J. 6755
Müller, Kurt 1558
Mullin, Donald 435, 3110
Munk, Erica 915, 5808
Munro, Edwin C. 2278
Munson, Gorham B. 6397
Murdoch, James E. 802, 804, 2969
Murphy, Bren A. 1941
Murphy, Brenda 5809
Murphy, D. B. 350
Murphy, Donn B. 2788
Murphy, James R. 5173
Murphy, Maureen 1693
Murphy, Molly 2191
Murphy, Ruby A. 6029
Murray, Clarence 6708
Murray, Donald L. 497, 517
Murray, Edward 6673, 6684, 6901
Murray, Frank J. 6978
Murray, James J. 6385
Murray, Joel K. 5566A
Murray, Ken 4182, 4828
Murray, T. 6138
Musgrove, Stanley 4493
Musser, Paul H. 6256
Myers, Clarence F. 3713
Myers, Denys P. 2808
Myers, Elisabeth 6536
Myers, Henry A. 5481
Myers, Laurence D. 7188
Myers, Norman J. 3684
Myers, Paul 12, 3090
Myler, Charles B. 2701
Myung, Inn S. 3535

Nacarow, David A. 608
Nadel, Ira B. 55
Nadel, Norman 2953
Naeseth, Henriette C. 5999
Nagle, Urban 2350
Nagler, A. D. 430
Nagler, A. M. 448, 895, 1217
Nahas, Rebecca 5336
Naipaul, V. S. 6608
Nalley, Sara 1350
Nance, William L. 6331
Nannes, Caspar H. 5784
Napiecinski, Thomas H. 5842
Nardin, James T. 5769
Nardone, Diane C. 1806
Naremore, James 4481
Nary, Bruce L. 5725
Nash, Doris 5155
Nash, Jay R. 3478
Nash, Ogden 2338
Nash, Rose L. 5795
Nash, William A. 6828
Nassif, Shakeeb J. 2621
Natalle, Elizabeth J. 1256, 1352
Natansan, Wojciech 6858
Nathan, George J. 1317, 1449, 1512, 3134, 3834, 4184, 4622–4625, 4628–4630, 4633, 4635, 4638, 4641–4642, 4644, 4646, 4648, 4652–4653, 4661, 4666–4667, 4676
Nathan, Hans 4834
Nault, Marianne 6287
Naylor, David 2244, 2808
Nazel, Joseph 4301
Neal, Larry 1368, 5930

Neal, Patricia 4194
Nearman, Mark J. 4591
Nederlander, James M. 1138
Needle, Harold F. 6001
Neel, Charles D. 910
Neely, Monty K. 245
Neeson, Jack M. 1856
Neff, Renfreu 2900
Neiheiser, Thomas N. 5971
Neill, Elizabeth 3721
Neiman, Jack 969
Nelms, Henning 578, 630, 1081
Nelson, Benjamin 6667, 6679, 7116
Nelson, Edwin L. 2764
Nelson, Kent E. 5160
Nelson, Robert A. 960
Nelson, Robert M. 2258
Nelson, Stephen 4339
Nelson, Steve 82
Nelson-Cave, W. 6103
Nemchek, Lee R. 82
Nemiroff, Robert 6430–6431
Nesbit, Evelyn 4197
Nettleton, George H. 5722
Neuberger, Richard L. 2267
Neuweiler, Siegfried 5875
Neville, Amelia R. 1732
Newell, James S. 1931
Newhall, Fales H. 285
Newhouse, John W. 1653
Newlin, Claude M. 6318
Newlin, Forrest A. 2205, 3302
Newlin, Jeanne 3317, 7106
Newman, Charles 1179
Newman, Robert B. 448
Newman, Robert P. 6486
Newman, Shirlee P. 3342, 7403
Newquist, Roy 3062
Newton, A. Edward 3762
Newton, William W. 292
Nicely, Tom 2909
Nichols, Charles H. 5956
Nichols, Charles 6543
Nichols, Dean G. 1823
Nichols, Harold J. 5081
Nichols, Kenneth L. 2543
Nicholson, Margaret 195
Nicholson, Retha J. 2210
Nicholson. David B. 5543
Niedeck, Arthur E. 2288
Nielsen, Alan 6721
Nielsen, Mark S. 2757
Nierman, Judith 6661
Niesen, George 7149
Nightingale, Benedict 4706
Nirdlinger, Charles F. 1434
Nixon, Charles E. 1893–1894
Noah, Mordecai M. 6724
Noble, Peter 3646, 4476
Nobles, Milton. 4200
Noe, Marcia 6408
Nolan, Frederick 7429
Nolan, Paul T. 5382, 5792, 6335–6336
Nold, Benjamin M. 1779
Nolte, William H. 6568
Norberg, Janet L. 316
Nordhus, Philip B. 6150
Nordvold, Robert O. 643
Noreen, Robert G. 6288

Norflett, Linda K. 3997
Norkin, Sam 2398
Norman, Charles 6343
Norman, Henry 4956
Norman, Stanley S. 1697
Northall, William K. 2301, 3868
Northcott, Richard 4090
Northhouse, Donna 6116
Northrop, Henry D. 815, 1896
Norton, Albert J. 1899
Norton, Elliot 1319, 1579, 2141
Norton, Sally O. 3791
Norton, Suzanne F. 6719
Norvelle, Lee 2917
Nouryeh, Andrea J. 2916
Novello, Ivor 3542
Novick, Julius 1594, 1627
Nuernberg, Evelyn A. 2795
Nugent, Beatrice 3652
Nugent, Elliott 6728
Nugent, John C. 4202
Nunes, Luiz 6943
Nunn, Curtis 3577
Nunnari, Irene W. 2455

O'Brien, P. J. 1411, 1598, 4319
O'Brien, Pat 4203
O'Brien, Rosary H. 2053
O'Casey, Sean 6858
O'Connel, Mary B. 2392
O'Connor, John 2858
O'Connor, Kathryn K. 2282
O'Connor, Patrick 4813
O'Connor, Richard 1714–1715
O'Daniel, Therman B. 6234, 6538
O'Donnell, Monica M. 95
O'Donnol, Shirley M. 723
O'Hara, Frank H. 1215, 5820
O'Hara, Mary 7221
O'Leary, Ronald T. 4582
O'Malley, Lurana D. 5979
O'Neal, Aaron B. 2042
O'Neill, Eugene 1319, 5432, 5538, 5788, 6779, 6850, 6876, 6882, 6885
O'Neill, R. H. 1163
O'Neill, Rose M. 837
O'Neill, Shane 6761
O'Pool, E. S. 2009
O'Rourke, Joyce W. 6135
O'Shea, Joseph J. 2802
O'Sullivan, Vincent 6652
O'Toole, Maureen A. 6965
Oaks, Harold R. 1470, 2731
Oas, Mabel W. 2159
Obee, Harold B. 1465
Oberstein, Bennett T. 4043
Oblak, John B. 2061
Odell, Alfred T. 6991
Odell, George C. 2337
Odets, Clifford 5531, 6907
Oenslager, Donald 588, 636, 645, 3938, 3942, 4205, 4211–4213
Oettal, Walter 2934
Offer, Ron 3521
Ogden, August R. 1525
Ogden, Dunbar H. 1016, 1700
Ogden, Jess 4916
Ogden-Malouf, Susan M. 371
Oggel, L. Terry 82, 3448
Oggel, Lynwood T. 3440

Oglesby, Catharine 575
Ogunbiyi, Yemi 4599
Ohringer, Frederick. 3095
Okin, Leslie 4005
Olauson, Clarence R. 5017
Olauson, Judith 5879
Olcott, Rita 4214
Olin, Reuel K. 7269
Oliphant, Mary C. 6991
Oliver, Donald 6575
Oliver, George B. 2356
Oliver, William I. 5908
Ollerman, Frederick H. 2807
Olney, Julian 4215
Olson, Elder 6833
Olson, Esther J. 6756
Olson, Ronald C. 532
Olsson, Tom J. 6835
Olszewski, George J. 2781
Olszewski, Joseph F. 5965
Oman, Richard J. 1928
Omanii, Abdullah. 5384
Omans, Stuart E. 1350
Ommanney, Katherine A. 5128
Onyshkevych, Larissa 1693
Opdahl, Keith 374
Oppenheimer, George 3055
Oram, Robert E. 3972
Orange, Linwood E. 1350
Orben, Robert 5327
Orchard, Hugh A. 5268
Orchard, Lee F. 7445
Orlandello, John 6854
Orman, Grace 1670
Ormsbee, Helen 856
Orr, Lynn E. 6305
Orr, William 4889
Ortolani, Benito 62
Osborne, Karin 5127
Oscar 867
Osgood, Chester W. 481
Ostroff, Manning 4824
Oswald, Josef 6847
Otis, John F. 3343
Ott, Pamela W. 1929
Ottemiller, John H. 5398
Otway 266
Oumano, Ellen 6976
Overmyer, Grace 220, 4245
Overstreet, Robert L. 1876
Overton, Grace 5093
Overton, Grant 3186, 6055
Ovington, Adelaide 4068
Owen, Bobbi 729
Owen, Bruce B. 3625
Owen, Michael 3122, 4272
Owens, Henry G. 6417
Owens, Mrs John E. 4217
Owensby, Edward 5651
Ower, John 7149
Oyler, Verne W. 2564

Page, Brett 4725
Page, James A. 3092
Page, Will A. 4731
Pagel, Carol A. 5738
Paine, Albert B. 3811
Paine, Nathaniel 2090
Palkovic, Timothy J. 662
Palmer, A. M. 3417
Palmer, Helen H. 4584

Palmer, James C. 3824
Palmer, Richard H. 540, 1472, 4615
Palmieri, Anthony F. 6935
Pam, Dorothy S. 5801
Panowski, James A. 7251
Paolucci, Anne 5979, 6165, 6172
Papajewski, Helmut 7082
Paparone, Joseph C. 4425
Papp, Joseph 1362, 3095, 4224
Parajón, Maria 6748
Parchem, Georga L. 5256
Parins, James W. 54
Paris, Robert G. 891
Parisi, Barbara 2468
Park, Marie 848
Parker, Brian 6676
Parker, Derek 7253
Parker, Dorothy 1544
Parker, H. T. 4676
Parker, John R. 3145
Parker, John 3019
Parker, Juliet 7253
Parker, Wilfred O. 612, 680
Parks, E. W. 5788
Parks, Edd W. 6992
Parks, Melvin 7222
Parlakian, Nishan 1693
Parnes, Uzi 1654
Parola, Gene J. 3836
Parone, Edward 1582
Parramore, Annie E. 1862
Parrott, Frederick J. 1400
Parry, Albert 3228
Parry, Ellwood C. 5993
Parsons, Billy D. 3568
Parsons, Henry S. 5349
Parsons, T. W. 2927
Partin, Bruce L. 5526
Partridge, Paul W. 7080
Paskman, Dailey 4778
Pasolli, Robert 2919
Pasquier, M. C. 6893
Pasquier, Marie-C. 1628
Pasquier, Marie-Claire 7171
Pastalosky, Rosa 1300
Pasternack, Aron L. 5749
Paterek, Josephine 704, 707
Patraka, Vivian M. 5979, 5988, 6472
Patrick, J. Max 1874
Patterson, Ada 2325, 3263
Patterson, Charlotte A. 5377
Patterson, Lindsay 1313, 1368
Patterson, Perry W. 4760
Pattison, Sheron J. 928
Patton, Eleanor N. 726
Patton, John 6657
Paul, Howard 2988
Paul, John S. 5963
Paulding, James K. 6913
Paulding, William I. 6910
Paulson, Arthur C. 6000
Pauly, Thomas H. 3964
Pauwels, Gerard W. 7190
Pavis, Patrick 1166
Pawley, Eric 410
Pawley, Frederick 395–396
Pawley, Thomas D. 5146
Payne, Ben Iden 4231, 4959
Payne, Darwin R. 669, 681

Payne, John H. 4233
Payne, William H. 4322
Payne-Carter, David 7350
Peake, Dorothy M. 5365
Pearce, T. M. 6228
Pearsall, Robert Brainerd 5875
Pearson, Talbot 4920
Pease, Donald 7149
Peavy, Charles D. 50, 6250
Pebworth, Ted L. 7129
Peck, Ira 4751
Peck, Phoebe 1973
Pecktal, Lynn 647
Pedigo, Frances M. 4576
Peebles, Sheila E. 2622
Peer, Nugent 3250
Peet, Alice L. 605
Peet, Telfair B. 585
Peiss, Kathy 1497
Pelby, William 2072
Peltzer, Otto 295, 298
Peluso, Joseph L. 953, 5144
Pembrook, Carrie D. 5644
Pence, James H. 1
Pender, Thomas M. 6046
Pendleton, Ralph 3942
Pennell, Jane 6258
Pennington, Ron 1805
Penrod, James 949
Penzel, Frederick 533
Peoples, Frank F. 6124
Perdue, Margaret F. 1127
Pereira, John W. 2456
Perelman, S. J. 2407, 3091, 6915
Perkins, J. A. 2007
Perkins, Ulrica B. 2910
Perlett, Robert 5045
Perosa, Sergio 1304, 1348
Perrella, Robert 3249
Perrier, Ronald G. 7136
Perrigo, Lynn 1822
Perrin, Gerry A. 2654
Perry, Clarence A. 4912
Perry, Jeb H. 3099
Perry, John 6493
Perry, Ted 82
Peters, Margot 3351
Peters, Rollo 550
Peters, Steven J. 1032
Peterson, Bernard L. 1368, 3121, 6142
Peterson, Carol 7141
Peterson, Eric E. 989
Peterson, Martin S. 6705
Peterson, Rita 488
Peterson, William A. 2162
Petrie, David T. 2738
Petrova, Olga 3206
Pettinelli, Frances 7175
Pettit, Paul B. 5648
Pevey, Wayne 5029
Pevitts, Beverley B. 5962
Pevitts, Robert 655
Peyrouse, John C. 4417
Peyser, Joan 7311
Pfendler, Robert C. 2521
Phaneuf, Cynthia L. 996
Phelps, Henry P. 807, 2283
Phelps, Laverne P. 2683
Phelps, William L. 1445, 3184, 4249–4250, 5357, 6054, 7441

Philbrick, Norman 1312, 1322
Philippi, Herbert 591
Philistina 4536
Phillips, Elizabeth C. 5913
Phillips, Hazel 5278
Phillips, J. M. 5959
Phillips, Jerrold 648
Phillips, Jerry S. 5071
Phillips, John S. 2932
Phillips, Julien 4559
Phillips, Julien L. 6836
Phillips, Levi D. 6706
Phillipson, John S. 7196
Phister, Montgomerie 2502
Pichel, Irving 389–390, 550
Pickard, Roy 7324
Pickering, Jerry 954
Pickering, Jerry V. 1243
Pickett, Lasalle C. [= Pickett, Mrs General George E.] 3178
Picon, Molly 4252–4253
Pierce, Glenn Q. 3639
Pierce, James F. 486
Pierini, Mary P. 5152
Pierrat, Asa B. 7070
Pietan, Norman 221
Pike, Bob 7331
Pike, Frank 6844
Pike, Morris R. 322
Pildas, Ave 457
Pilkington, John 4549–4550
Pilpel, Harriet F. 198
Pinchot, Ann 3812
Pinciotti, Patricia 5200
Pinckney, Henry L. 6435
Pineault, Wallace 254
Pinkston, Claude A. 4052
Pinnell, William H. 687
Piper, Henry Dan 1540
Piper, Judith A. 1814
Piro, Richard 5153
Pitt, D. K. 6671
Pitts, Ethel L. 1556
Pizer, Donald 6361
Plasters, Warren H. 2684
Plax, Pamela M. 961
Plessow, Gustav L. 5758
Plotkin, Joel A. 240
Plotkins, Marilyn J. 4794
Plotnicki, Rita 3277
Pluggé, Domis E. 4966
Plummer, Gail 767
Plummer, Rick J. 1002
Poag, T. E. 4923
Poe, Harold W. 424
Poggi, Jack 233
Poirier, Richard 6631
Poitier, Sidney 4265
Poland, Albert 2406
Polichak, James W. 48
Polkinhorn, J. H. 2773
Pollack, Rhoda G. 6578
Pollock, Channing 6917–6919
Pollock, Thomas C. 2616
Polsky, Milton E. 1047
Polti, Georg 5421
Pond, J. B. 3167
Poore, Ben P. 3452
Pope, A. Winthrop 102
Popkin, Henry 4676, 5494, 6684
Popovich, James E. 5123

Porter, E. S. 6872
Porter, Esther 2245
Porter, Jack 2367
Porter, Laurin 6886
Porter, Robert E. 1128
Porter, Thomas E. 5864
Postlewait, Thomas 1261
Potts, Edgar L. 2587
Potts, Norman B. 3703
Powell, Alvin L. 482
Powell, Carolyn 2663
Powell, L. Laurence 5974
Powell, Lawrence C. 6559
Powell, Mathew D. 2443
Powell, William S. 2486
Power, Esther P. 2246
Power, Tyrone 4267
Power-Waters, Alma 3336, 3436
Powers, Helen 5299
Powers, James T. 7418
Pradhan, Narindar S. 5529, 5957
Prasad, Hari M. 6877
Pratt, Judith S. 4353
Pratt, Louis H. 6235, 6240
Preddy, Jane 471
Preminger, Marion M. 3220
Prenshaw, Peggy W. 7149
Presley, Delma E. 7179
Press, David R. 931
Pressier, Terra D. 5573
Preuss, R. 6174
Prevots, Naima 4954
Price, David M. 6707
Price, Eugenia 4464
Price, Jonathan 1240
Price, Joyce D. 2700
Price, Julia S. 2368
Price, Vincent 4270
Price, Willard 4756
Price, William T. 3620, 3761, 5401–5402
Prichard, Rosemary F. 974
Pride, Leo B. 79
Prideaux, Tom 1219
Priest, William 3144
Primeaux, Beverly 2032
Primus, Mark 80
Prince, Hal 4271
Prince, Harold 678, 1593
Prince, Jane E. 5693
Prisk, Berneice 711
Pritner, Calvin L. 4458, 5145
Prizeman, Herbert H. 3984
Probst, Leonard. 3085
Probstfield, Evelyn 2496
Proctor, George L. 5619
Proehl, Geoffrey S. 5704
Prosser, William L. 1143
Prossnitz, Gisela 6040
Pryor, William D. 5663
Pufall, Michael E. 2199
Puknat, E. M. 4221
Putnam, Chase 2626
Putnam, George H. 175
Putnam, George P. 180
Pye, Michael 781
Pyper, George D. 2720
Pyros, John A. 3792

Quadri, Franco 4131
Quetz, Jörgen 6160

Quigley, A. E. 6138
Quigley, Austin E. 5624
Quigley, Bernard J. 2597
Quinlan, Michael A. 4565
Quinn, Arthur H. 4257, 5364, 5413, 5652, 5719, 5760, 5788, 6290
Quinn, Edward 5607
Quinn, Elizabeth 4272
Quinn, Germain 4273
Quinn, James J. 5654
Quintero, José 4274
Quirino, Leonard S. 7121, 7149
Quirk, Lawrence J. 4060
Quittner, C. J. 712

Rabb, Norman S. 5030
Rabby, L. B. 419
Rabe, David 5533, 5979
Rabkin, Gerald 5852
Racey, Edgar F. 6776
Rachow, Louis A. 17, 89, 3487
Radel, Nicholas F. 5622
Rader, Dotson 7167
Rado, J. 7245
Radow, Rhoda K. 2792
Rae, Kenneth 73
Raffaniello, William F. 2361
Raghavacharyulu, Dhupaty V. 6782
Ragni, G. 7245
Rahill, Frank 5602
Rahv, Philip 5914
Raider, Roberta 3670
Raines, Lester 849
Raines, Robert A. 5614
Rains, Dale O. 5170
Rainwater, Clarence E. 4901
Rajnath 5529
Raleigh, John H. 5908, 6776, 6783, 6795, 6833, 6893
Rama Murthy, V. 5928
Rambin, William R. 4403
Ramczyk, Suzanne M. 7300
Ramdin, Ron 4306
Ramey, Howard L. 4922
Rampersad, Arnold 6545
Ramsay, Margaret H. 2879
Ramsey, Richard D. 7186
Ramstad, Edith W. 5114
Ranald, Margaret L. 6860
Rang, Jack C. 5932
Rankin, Hugh F. 1405
Ranney, R. H. 3741
Ranous, Dora 4277
Raoul, Rosine 2375
Raphael, Bonnie N. 947
Raphael, D. D. 5487
Raphaelson, Samson 5428
Rapp, Esther J. 6005
Rappel, William J. 4931
Ratcliff, Gerald L. 6829
Rathbone, Basil 4280
Rather, Lois 1803, 7437
Ratliff, Gerald L. 990
Raviv, Zeev 6024
Rawls, Eugenie 3325
Rawson, Clayton 4953
Rawson, Ruth 932
Ray, Helen H. 6784
Ray, Lucille 5421

Rea, Tom P. 1228
Reams, Danny I. 2768
Reardon, John D. 5728
Reardon, William R. 193, 5146
Reaver, Joseph R. 6799
Reck, W. Emerson 3486
Rede, Thomas L. 798
Redford, Hyrum E. 904
Reed, Carole F. 1925
Reed, Charles E. 1722
Reed, Clifford A. 4452
Reed, Duane E. 4785
Reed, Joseph V. 4283
Reed, Kenneth T. 6279
Reed, Perley I. 5709
Reed, Rex 3070
Reed, Roland L. 6245
Reed, Ronald M. 3640
Rees, James 3756, 6052
Reeves, Ann 2694
Reeves, John A. 1236
Regan, Frederick S. 5243
Reger, Erik 6858
Reid, Anthony 1138
Reid, Norman M. 3643
Reidenbaugh, Gerald 916
Reignolds-Winslow, Catherine M. 2976
Reilingh, Maarten A. 1355
Reilly, John E. 4260
Reilly, Joy H. 4199
Reinelt, Janelle 5988
Reiner, Aileen 4968
Reinert, Thomas D. 447
Reines, Philip 2488
Reinhardt, Max 3356
Reiss, Alvin H. 1138
Rella, Ettore 1737
Relph, Patricia C. 962
Renshaw, Edyth 2472
Renton, Edward 4726
Resnik, Muriel 6922
Reston, James 5977
Reuter, William L. 3471
Revell, Peter 7362
Revett, Marion S. 2524
Reyes, Jose Javier 1642
Reynolds, Donald M. 3767
Reynolds, Elwin C. 5015
Reynolds, Ina C. 2039
Reynolds, Nydia J. 5286
Reynolds, R. C. 5888
Reynolds, Robert E. 355
Reynolds, Steven C. 4003
Rezzuto, Tom 637
Rheuban, Joyce 4848
Rhys, Horton 4288
Riach, D. C. 6800
Ricard. Alain 6246
Ricci, Frederick 3962
Rice, Cy 3711
Rice, Edward L. 4719, 4721
Rice, Elmer 5470, 6925–6928
Rice, R. D. 3808
Rice, Wallace 1898
Rich, Frank 3297–3298
Rich, J. Dennis 6834
Richards, Dick 3956
Richards, Lloyd 788
Richards, Sandra L. 6252
Richards, W. A. 7102

Richardson, Genevieve 700
Richardson, Jack 2407
Richardson, James B. 4444
Richardson, Thomas R. 7149
Richey, Michael M. 5167
Richman, Harry 4878
Richmond, Neal(Ed.) 2885
Richmond, Rebecca 5272, 5274, 5276
Richter, George R. 7063
Ricker, Suzanne D. 2709
Rickert, Alfred E. 2292
Rickert, Friedhelm 6125
Ridge, Patricia 2166, 3730
Ridgely, Joseph V. 6993
Ridgeway, Ann N. 6564
Rieser, Judith E. 1635
Rietz, Louis J. 2216
Rife, M. 4923
Rigdon, Walter 3090
Riipa, Timo R. 1693
Riis, Thomas L. 3734, 7314
Riker, Kittie B. 1834
Riley, Carolyn 6097
Riley, Clayton 5930
Rinaldi, Nicholas G. 7280
Rinear, David L. 2460
Rinehart, Mary R. 6941
Riordan, Mary M. 6477
Ripley, John 1343
Risley, Herbert J. 5782
Risvold, Floyd E. 3480
Ritchey, David 2067
Ritchie, Anna C. [= Mowatt, Anna C.] 3128, 4172
Rittenour, Robert G. 1572
Ritter, Carl 1286
Ritter, Charles C. 2667
Ritter, Naomi 1262
Ritter, S. A. 6541
Ritterbush, Alice McC. 231
Rivers, Joan 4289
Rizzo, Raymond 955
Roach, Helen P. 4986
Roach, Joseph R. 1022
Roach, Josh P. 5658
Roache, Joel 6375
Roane, Andrea T. 4772
Robb, John S. 3150
Robbins, J. J. 828
Robbins, Jhan 3848
Robbins, John A. 160
Robbins, Kathleen M. 3947
Robbins, Leonard H. 5975
Robbins, Phyllis 3264–3265
Roberts, Arthur W. 6878
Roberts, J. W. 3412
Roberts, Kenneth H. 2381, 2529
Roberts, Nancy L. 6878
Roberts, Vera M. 1224, 1321, 3124, 5140, 6116
Robertson, Cosby W. 4943
Robertson, Hazel G. 5114
Robertson, Roderick 6801
Robertson, William J. 4580
Robeson, Eslanda G. 4290
Robeson, Paul 4293
Robeson, Susan 4302
Robins, Edward. 2998–2999
Robinson, Alice M. 3124
Robinson, Alice J. 5732

Robinson, David 4845
Robinson, Edward G. 4309
Robinson, Emmett 2642
Robinson, Giles F. 5005
Robinson, Horace W. 438
Robinson, James A. 6855, 6879, 6893
Robinson, John W. 32
Robinson, Kay M. 5751
Robinson, Lennox 6858
Robinson, Marie J. 1533
Robinson, Marion P. 4971
Rockefeller, David 234
Rockey, James R. 1599
Rockwell, Ethel T. 4895, 4909, 5634
Rockwood, Jerome 917, 2815
Rod, David K. 5557
Roden, Robert F. 5344
Roden, Sally A. 2048
Rodgers, Dorothy 7428, 7433
Rodgers, James W. 2169
Rodgers, Mrs J. 4879
Rodgers, R. 482
Rodgers, Richard 1302, 7243, 7425, 7433
Rodman, Ellen R. 5250, 5264
Rodney, Peter M. 6227
Roediger, Virginia M. 699
Rogers, Betty B. 4327
Rogers, Clark McC. 918
Rogers, David 5913
Rogers, Ingrid 7143
Rogers, Priscilla S. 6047
Rogers, Virginia M. 3567
Rogers, Will 3669, 4333
Rogoff, Gordon 4707, 5917
Rohling, Peter. 1342
Rohrer, Mary K. 2763
Rohrig, Gladys M. 6306
Rojo, Jerry 446, 645
Roland, Alan 5531
Rollins, Bryant 7349
Rollins, Charlemae 6539
Rollins, Peter C. 4335
Rollyson, Carl 6483
Roman, Lisbeth J. 628, 3508
Rome, Florence 3770, 7240
Ronen, Dan 1623
Roney, Edmund B. 6930
Roote, Deane L. 7463
Roppolo, Joseph P. 1350, 2020, 6266
Ropsen, Esther M. 4399
Roscoe, Burton 6652
Roscoe, Theodore 3472
Rose, Al 7439
Rose, Billy 4336
Rose, Phyllis 4814
Rose, Rich 693
Rosenberg, Charles G. 3152
Rosenberg, Eth C. 4252
Rosenberg, G. C. 2962
Rosenberg, Helane S. 5200
Rosenberg, James L. 5669
Rosenblatt, Bernard A. 5192
Rosenheim, Richard 5480
Rosenstein, Sophie 852
Rosenthal, Jean 401, 4340
Rosmond, Babette 3381
Ross, Allan S. 2043

Ross, Frances G. 2028
Ross, Frederick G. 4342
Ross, Helen. 3060
Ross, Ishbel 4150
Ross, Laura 78
Ross, Lillian 3060
Ross, Paul L. 3045
Ross, Ralph F. 6552
Ross, Robert T. 5471
Ross, Ronald 1368
Ross, Theophil W. 2863
Rosse, Herman 550, 695
Rossi, Alfred 2196
Rossi, Alfred A. 1977
Rössle, Wolfgang 6680
Rostagno, Aldo 2901
Rostand, Edmond 4045
Roswell, May M. 6019
Roten, Paul 3714
Roth, Emalou 4592
Roth, Lillian 4343–4344
Roth, Moira 1639
Roth, Philip 6172
Rothafel, S. L. 391
Rothgeb, John R. 663, 2205
Rothman, John 4587
Rotoli, Nicholas J. 44
Rotte, Joanna-H. 3273
Roudané, Matthew 5979, 6191, 6194
Rourke, Constance 1397, 1463, 3604
Rousselow, Jesse L. 1632
Rovere, Richard H. 1542
Rovit, Earl 6282, 6286
Rowe, Gabrielle 714
Rowe, Kenneth T. 1094, 5419
Rowland, Lloyd W. 4326
Rowland, Mabel 4886
Rowlands, Walter. 3010
Rowley, Thomas L. 354
Royce, Anya P. 1017
Royer, Jessica 838, 868, 1057
Roylance, Aaron A. 2732
Royle, Edwin M. 3433
Rubenstein, Gilbert M. 4525
Rubin, Benny 4880
Rubin, Janet E. 5247
Rubin, Jerry 3243, 3245
Rubin, Joel E. 410, 503, 512
Rubin, Louis D.(Ed.) 6091
Rubin, Michele McN. 1643
Rubin, Stephen E. 2412
Ruble, Ronald M. 1136
Rucker, Patrick C. 4232
Rude, John A. 1479
Rudel, Julius 3598
Rudick, Lawrence W. 2172
Rudin, Seymour 4189
Rudisill, Amanda 3082
Ruff, Loren K. 1248, 6963–6964
Ruffino, Arthur S. 4191
Ruggles, Eleanor 3435
Ruhl, Arthur B. 1442
Rule, Margaret 6168
Rumley, Jerry B. 7231
Runge, G. 2576
Rupolo-Horhager, Dana J. 6185
Rusch, Frederic E. 6361
Rush, James 795
Rush, Theresa G. 3086

Russell, Benjamin 288
Russell, Charles E. 4065
Russell, Douglas A. 652, 666
Russell, Helen 5664
Russell, Jason A. 5635
Russell, Mary M. 5091
Russell, Rosalind 4351
Russell, Rufus T. 770
Russo, Dorothy R. 6149, 7029
Rust, Brian 107
Rutenberg, Michael E. 6161, 6172
Rutland, James R. 1707
Ryan, Betsy 7020
Ryan, James 2153
Ryan, Kate 2110
Ryan, Owen E. 2780
Ryan, Pat M. 19, 31, 1719, 6323
Ryan, Patricia C. 3815
Ryan, Patrick M. 4222
Ryan, Sheila 82
Ryan, Thomas 3165
Rydahl, Eugene E. 2161
Ryder, Richard D. 1866
Ryder, Sharon L. 454
Ryzuk, Mary S. 2466

Sabin, Joseph 3754
Sabinson, Harvey 3253
Sacks, Benjamin 1808
Saddlemyer, Ann 1487
Sadie, Stanley 7311
Saffron, Robert 4374
Sainer, Arthur 1580, 1620
Sakalauskas, William B. 5874
Salazar, Laura G. 5195, 5264
Salem, James M. 318, 4610, 5387
Salisbury, Harold E. 199
Salmon, Eric 1494
Salsini, Barbara 7336
Salt, Gary M. 5799
Saltzman, Jared 2861
Salvaggio, Odette C. 4604
Salvi, Delia N. 2823
Salzman, Jack 65, 6360, 6635
Samachson, Dorothy 1220, 1222
Samachson, Joseph 1220, 1222
Samples, Gordon 3485, 4600, 5381
Sampson, Henry T. 1501, 4789
Samuel, Raphael 1495
Samuels, Charles 3785, 4463, 4773, 4844
Samuels, Louise 4773
Sanborn, Ralph 6740
Sanburn, Frederick 808
Sander, Peter 1008
Sanders, Joseph E. 5947
Sanders, Leslie C. 1373
Sandford, Carl 3909
Sandle, Floyd L. 5013
Sandmel, Frances F. 2479
Sandrow, Nahma 374, 1237
Sanford, E. S. 756
Sanka, A. H. 4534
Sankus, Patricia H. 2142
Santaniello, A. E. 27, 37
Santino, Jack 1692
Sapoznik, Ran 6101
Saquet, Labeebee J. H. 1230
Saraceni, Eugene A. 6492
Sarlos, Robert K. 1487, 1700, 2132,

Sarotte, Georges-M. 5694, 7171
Saroyan, William 1159, 3927, 3929, 6946–6947, 6950–6951, 6953, 6955
Sastre, Alfonso 6858
Sattler, William M. 14
Saunders, Walter E. 5504
Sauvage, Marcel 4810
Savage, George M. 5638
Savan, Bruce 5325
Savo, Jimmy 2370
Savona, J. L. 6138
Savran, David 2960, 6136
Sawyer, Frederic W. 275
Sawyer, Julian 7008
Sawyer, Lemuel 6958
Sawyer, Raymond C. 3286
Saxon, O. Glenn 2363
Sayler, Oliver M. 142, 567, 1507, 1513
Sayre, Henry M. 1657
Sayward, Samuel 2143
Scales, Robert 516
Scanlan, Tom 5958
Scanlon, Lee E. 2737
Schab, Frederick G. 4254
Schaeffer, Morton H. 2604
Schäfer, Jürgen 5966
Schaffer, Pauline W. 5789
Schaffner, Franklin J. 4108
Schaffner, Neil 4356
Schah, Oscar Fritz 6858
Schall, Celia M. 5923
Schall, David G. 1085
Schanke, R. A. 6050
Schanke, Robert A. 3996
Scharf, J. Thomas 2063
Scharfenberg, Jean 4407
Scharnhorst, Gary 3758
Schary, Dore 6959
Schatt, Stanley 7071
Schaub, Owen W. 1950
Schechner, Richard 446, 1593, 1595, 1608, 1636, 1640, 1655, 2876, 2923, 5527, 5558, 5567
Schechter, Joel 5559
Scheer-Schäzler, Brigitte 6285
Scheibler, Rolf 6807
Scheich, William J. 7149
Scheller, Bernhard 5953
Schenker, Ueli 6785
Scherting, John A. 5739
Schesventer, Robert R. 2525
Schevill, James 1609, 6222
Scheyer, Betty 5436
Schick, Joseph 1962
Schickel, Richard 3698
Schiff, Ellen 373
Schiffman, Jack 2403
Schilling, Katherine T. 5006
Schilling, Lester L. 2562
Schlesinger, Arthur M. 1450
Schlosser, Anatol I. 4296
Schlossmacher, Stephan 4967
Schluesser, Douglas 1951
Schlueter, June 5979, 5989, 5992, 6177, 6701
Schmidt, Inge 1758
Schmitt, Natalie C. 1569
Schmitt, Patrick E. 6866

Schneider, Alan 3054, 4360, 5020, 6094
Schneider, Wayne 7311
Schoberlin, Melvin 1826
Schoell. Edwin R. 4925
Schoen, Leonard 4160
Schoenbaum, S. 2182
Schoenberger, Harold W. 5712
Schoenberger, Mark A. 4466
Schoettler, Eugenia V. 7270
Schofield, Mary A. 1379
Scholes, Robert 5510
Schonberger, Emanuel D. 1072
Schoolcraft, Ralph N. 37
Schooley, Bill J. 4175, 4442
Schopp, Joseph C. 5875
Schraft, Robin J. 688
Schreck, Everett M. [= Morrill, Richard] 933
Schreiber, Lesley C. 991
Schroeder, Patricia R. 5892
Schroeder, Robert J. 1591
Schrye, Thomas E. 7149
Schubert, Hannelore 439
Schubert, Leland 1213
Schueneman, Warren W. 3961
Schulman, Martin 1192
Schulte-Sasse, Jochen 5571
Schultz, Charles A. 5740
Schultz, Jacqueline A. 3379
Schulz, Max F. 6401
Schuman, Mady. 5527
Schuttler, George W. 3806
Schwab, Arnold T. 3905, 4703
Schwartz, Alan U. 200
Schwartz, Charles 7379, 7416
Schwarz, Lyle A. 1689
Schwerin, Arthur M. 741
Schyberg, Frederick 6858
Scott, Charles E. 6505
Scott, Freda 6143
Scott, James B. 6259
Scott, Kathleen S. 1883
Scott, Marion 5275
Scott, Marvin B. 5524
Scribner, Charles 6389
Scroggin, Margaret C. 5214
Sczublewski, Jozef 4118
Seagle, William 184
Searle, Leroy 5563
Seay, Donald W. 626, 5084
Sederholm, Frederick L. 5488
Sederholm, Jack P. 7438
Sedgwick, Ruth W. 3595
See, Earl E. 1480
Seeley, Robert 112
Segal, Errol 7002
Seidel, Margot 6861–6862
Seilhamer, George O. 1312, 2580, 2970, 3504
Selby, David L. 2393
Selden, Samuel 559, 561, 574, 637, 845, 873, 1069, 1074, 1087, 2489, 3977, 4919, 4927, 5020, 5425, 5505
Seldes, G. S. 3834
Seldes, Gilbert V. 1293
Seldes, Marian 4362
Self, Lois S. 5296
Seller, Maxine S. 1693
Sellers, Barbara 1052

Selli, Sergio. 2840
Sellman, Hunton D. 539, 561, 574
Seltsam, William H. 2349
Selznick, Irene M. 4363
Semenza, Edwin S. 2261
Semmes, David. 3064
Semonella, Joan L. 6629
Senelick, Laurence 4837
Sergeant, Elizabeth S. 3190
Sergel, Sherman L. 81
Sesak, Mary M. 4341
Seto, Judith R. 981
Seton, Marie 4294
Setrakian, Edward 3932
Sewell, Bette B. 6569
Sexson, Keith D. 4997
Sexton, R. W. 391
Seymour, George D. 4961
Seymour, Victor 1103
Sgroi, Carol T. 2002
Shadegg, Stephen 6612
Shafer, George W. 5952
Shafer, Yvonne 1263
Shaffer, James F. 1086
Shaffer, Virginia M. 2064
Shaftel, George A. 5423
Shakespeare, William 2963
Shand, P. M. 393
Shandler, Donald D. 1606
Shank, Phillip J. 2711
Shank, Theodore 1637, 1818, 5506
Shannon, Hallie D. 2688
Shanower, Donald T. 2163, 2515
Shapiro, Stephen R. 1617
Sharaff, Irene 4365
Sharp, H. S. 76
Sharp, Kim T. 975
Sharp, M. Z. 76
Sharp, William L. 1115
Sharpe, Robert B. 5484
Sharrar, Jack F. 6499
Sharratt, Bernard. 2944
Shattuck, Charles H. 1412, 1499, 3441, 3449
Shaughnessy, Edward L. 6887
Shaver, Claude L. 854
Shaver, Sara H. 6479
Shaw, Ann M. 5187
Shaw, Arnold 3365
Shaw, Bertha L. 1835
Shaw, Dale. 3079
Shaw, Irving 7007
Shaw, Irwin 6960
Shawn, Edwin C. 925
Shay, Frank 4906, 5350, 5353
Shay, Thomas M. 4987
Shayne, Eddie 4732
Shea, Ann M. 2144
Sheaffer, Louis 6802, 6822
Shechner, Richard 6172
Sheed, Wilfred 4690, 6613
Sheehy, Helen 3936
Sheffey-Stinson, Sandi 1809
Sheldon, Neil 6075
Shelley, Mary W. 4239
Shelton, Lewis E. 6163
Shelton, Lynn M. 7246
Shepard, Sam 5980, 6967
Shephard, William H. 2924
Sheren, Paul 4435
Sheridan, Charles H. 2155

Sheridan, Phil 2549, 2552
Sherk, H. Denis 3803
Sherk, Warren 4152
Sherman, Alfonso 5787
Sherman, John K. 2189
Sherman, Robert L. 1917, 3047, 5361
Sherman, Stuart 6058
Sherman, Susanne K. 2748
Sherr, Paul C. 7220
Sherrin, Ned 7285
Sherwood, Garrison P. 1505
Sherwood, Robert E. 3055, 4882
Shettel, James W. 3681
Shewey, Don 6974
Shields, Shirlee H. 378
Shiff, Cameron 3338
Shiffler, Harold C. 104
Shiffler, Harrold C. 312
Shipley, Joseph 6735
Shipman, David 3523
Shipman, Louis E. 2992, 6988
Shipp, Cameron 3542–3543
Shire, Sanford 4196
Shivers, Alfred S. 6211, 6215–6216
Shockley, Martin S. 2744, 2759
Shoemaker, Alfred L. 2607, 2609
Shoemaker, James H. 219
Shoemaker, Robert W. 6013
Shore, Viola B. 3814
Shorter, Clement 4089
Shoup, Gail L. 1775
Shulim, Joseph I. 6329
Shull, Leo 5424
Shuman, R. B. 374, 6553, 6899, 6983
Shurtleff, Michael 976
Shyer, Laurence 4513
Sicherman, Barbara 3078, 3100
Siebald, Manfred 5700
Siedlecki, Franciszek 4114
Siefkas, James M. 2805
Siegel, Barbara 3566
Siegfried, David A. 3518
Siegman, Howard 4695, 6116
Siena, Marcia A. 2527
Sievers, W. David 4667, 5659
Sievers, Wieder D. 5771
Sigel, David L. 2915
Siks, Geraldine B. 5116, 5129, 5187
Silbiger, Josef 6603
Sillman, Leonard D. 4373
Silver, Reuben 2533
Silverman, Maxwell 3081
Silverman, Ely 4469
Silverman, Kenneth 1413
Silverman, Maxwell 420
Silvers, Phil 4374
Silvestro, Carlo 2905
Simard, Rodney 5623
Simas, Rick 7306
Simmonds, Diana 7295
Simms, William G. 6989
Simon, Alfred 7287, 7378
Simon, Barbara 4533
Simon, Bernard 83
Simon, Henry W. 5098
Simon, John 1621, 4675, 4698
Simon, Linda 7096
Simon, Louis M. 2822

Simon, S. Sylvan 4914
Simond, Ike 4714
Simonson, Lee 396–397, 550, 565, 567, 581, 604, 3942, 4376
Simos, Jack 5125
Simpson, Mary P. 2747
Sinden, Donald 6312
Singer, Kurt 3957
Singer, Norman 1138
Singer, Stanford P. 4803
Singleton, Carole W. 1332
Singleton, Carola 1365
Sinha, C. P. 6848
Sinks, Perry W. 300
Sinnett, Alice R. 2290
Sisson, James E. 6602
Sitton, Fred 5730
Sitwell, Osbert 4145
Skal, David J. 783
Skidmore, Rex A. 342
Skillen, Melita H. 847
Skinner, Cornelia O. 2822, 4379–4382, 6600
Skinner, Donald T. 5721
Skinner, Maud 4465
Skinner, Otis 834, 3434, 3506, 3881, 4384–4385, 4465
Skinner, Richard D. 5818
Skinner, Richard 6742
Sklepowich, Edward A. 7149
Skolsky, Sidney. 3033
Skotheim, Robert A. 3247
Slabaugh, Richard G. 1592
Slattery, Kenneth M. 1956
Slezak, Walter 4387
Slide, Anthony 100, 4704, 4793, 4805
Sloan, J. Blanding 550
Sloan, Ronna E. 7368
Slobin, Mark 374
Slochower, Harry 6065
Slonimsky, Nicolas 7312
Slote, Bernice 3561
Slott, Melvin M. 5031
Slout, William L. 1682, 3825
Sly, Costard 2073
Small, George A. 5779
Small, Harold S. 1740
Small, Miriam 6597
Smalley, Webster L. 5846
Smallwood, James M. 4333
Smedley, Constance 830
Smiley, Sam 1322, 5451, 5868
Smith, Andre 553
Smith, Ardis 2296
Smith, Bill 4779
Smith, Bruce 7180
Smith, C. Ray 434, 715, 745
Smith, Carleton Sprague 7462
Smith, Caroline J. 7417
Smith, Cecil M. 7276
Smith, Dexter 2098
Smith, Edward G. 1693
Smith, Elden T. 3311
Smith, Elihu Hubbard 3248
Smith, Florence C. 82
Smith, Gary L. 244
Smith, Geddeth 4263
Smith, Grover 6627
Smith, Harry A. 3254
Smith, Harry B. 7204, 7441

Smith, Harry J. 7003
Smith, Harry W. 4103
Smith, Harvey 5109
Smith, Harvey K. 680
Smith, Irvine N. 5729
Smith, Joe E. 5174
Smith, John T. 324, 3637
Smith, Kathryn 2296
Smith, Larry A. 1787
Smith, Lucinda 457
Smith, Madeline 6888
Smith, Marjorie M. 602
Smith, Michael 2897
Smith, Milo L. 1314
Smith, Milton 5356
Smith, Milton M. 1076, 5095
Smith, Peter M. 6299
Smith, R. J. 6049
Smith, Robert W. 934
Smith, Rose M. 5213
Smith, Ross D. 5773
Smith, Samuel S. 4567
Smith, Scottie Fitzgerald 6387
Smith, Simeon M. 6644
Smith, Sol 4390–4391, 4393
Smith, Susan H. 5979, 6893
Smith, Susan V. H. 727
Smith, Tallant 1782
Smith, W. 5085
Smith, William F. 1005
Smither, Nelle 2047
Smolian, Steven 105
Smoot, James S. 5282
Smyth, Thomas 267–268
Snider, Gerald E. 7101
Sniderman, Florence M. 6096
Snow, Claude S. 1666
Snow, Stephen E. 2145
Snyder, Frederick E. 4766
Snyder, Robert W. 4807
Snyder, Sherwood 1678
Sobel, Bernard 74, 4394, 4735, 4752
Sobotka, Walter 4395
Soceanu, Marion 2871
Sochen, June 374
Sodders, Richard P. 2648
Sogliuzzo, A. 4398
Solberg, Thorvald 172, 182, 189
Soldo, Betty L. 2270
Soliday, John C. 3445
Soller, Larry S. 6035
Sollers, John F. 3738
Solley, Alexander S. 6991
Sollors, Werner 6251
Solomon, Rakesh H. 6187
Solomon, Theodore O'B. 5184
Somer, John 7069
Somers, John W. 5520
Sommer, Sally 3782
Sommers, John J. 3829
Sondheim, Stephen 5696, 7287, 7383, 7419
Song, Oak 4474
Sontag, Susan 4682
Sorenson, George W. 1416
Sorenson, John 2260
Sorrells, Roy W. 4159
Sothern, Edward H. 4067, 4396–4397
Sothern, Georgia 4883

Soucek, Carol B. 2812
Sousa, John P. 7448
Southern, Eileen 1368
Southern, Richard. 73
Sozen, Joyce L. 1918
Spaeth, Sigmund 4778, 4784
Spargo, John 4346
Sparks, Andrew 1872
Sparrow, Wilbur 852
Spaulding, Alice H. 847
Spaulding, Thelma C. 2883
Spear, Richard D. 2158
Spearman, Walter 2489
Speck, Frank G. 2481
Spector, Susan J. 3830
Speers, Susan D. 3898
Speiser, Maurice J. 186
Spence, George 2483
Spencer, Jenny S. 5988
Sper, Felix 4921
Spergel, Mark 4044
Spero, Richard H. 7134
Sphangos, Mary T. 3977
Spier, Leslie 1674
Spigelglass, Leonard 4309
Spiller, Robert E. 41
Spingarn, Joel E. 4568
Spitzer, Marian 2394
Spolin, Viola 1129, 1160, 5199
Sponsler, W. R. 5124
Sporre, Dennis J. 694
Spoto, Donald 7168
Sprague, Charles 2570
Sprague, Kathleen J. 1699
Sprigge, Elizabeth 7012, 7021
Springer, John 3735, 4751
Springer, Roland A. 5839
Springman, Jay K. 5157
Spritz, Kenneth 1414
Sprunt, James 2469
Spurrier, James J. 7271
Ssutu, Patricia C. 789
St John, James I. 2644
St Martin, Adele C. 1693
Stagg, Jerry 4369
Staggenborg, Robert G. 1353
Stahl, Herbert M. 5851
Stainton, Walter H. 401, 5643
Stallings, Roy 12
Stamper, Rexford 7149
Stanbridge, Alan 250
Standley, Fred L. 6236, 6240
Standley, Nancy V. 6236
Stanislavsky, Constantin 828, 877, 879, 901
Stanistreet, Grace 5187
Stanley, Nina J. 2717
Stanley, William T. 4602
Stanton, Robert J. 7067
Stanton, Stephen S. 7148
Staples, Shirley 4795
Starbuck, James C. 451
Starch, Daniel 761
Stark, Sam 1800
Starkey, Larry 3481
Starnes, R. Leland 7126
Staroba, Frank J. 6423
Starr, Jack D. 5941
Stasio, Marilyn 2407
States, Bert O. 5511, 5560
Statham, Charles M. 4596

Steadman, Daniel L. 5064
Stebbins, Emma 3617
Stebbins, Genevieve 805
Stedman, Edmund C. 3424
Steele, Shelby 1368
Steele, William P. 6310
Steen, Mike 7133
Steene, Kerstin B. 6016
Steenrod, Spencer 2547
Stefano, John P. 997
Stein, Charles W. 4800
Stein, Daniel A. 6788
Stein, Donna M. 633
Stein, Gertrude 7014, 7021
Stein, R. B. 7148
Stein, Rita 6125
Steinberg, M. W. 6676, 6684
Steinberg, Mollie B. 2335, 2340
Steiner, David E. 5860
Steiner, Donald L. 6166
Steiner, George 5489
Steinhardt, Gertrude M. 1827
Stell, W. Joseph 631
Stell, Walter J. 649
Stenz, Anita M. 6176
Stepanian, Laurie A. 2631, 2633
Stephens, Ann B. 2689
Stephens, George D. 6561
Stephens, Henry L. 2961
Stephens, Judith L. 5877
Stephens, Robert N. 2978
Stephens, Robert O. 6488
Stephens, Suzanne S. 6167
Stephenson, Clarence E. 3685
Stephenson, Jim B. 1216, 2156
Stephenson, Nan L. 2646, 3797
Stephenson, Robert R. 1954
Sterling, Wallace S. 2670
Stern, Laurence 787
Stern, Philip Van D. 3466
Stern, Robert I. 2173
Stevens, Ashton 3028, 3032
Stevens, David H.(Ed.) 3054
Stevens, Eva C. 2658
Stevens, Gary L. 1717
Stevens, George 3534
Stevens, Harold K. 4999
Stevens, Katherine B. 2208
Stevens, Thomas W. 1211
Stevenson, Isabelle 1622
Stevenson, Mark P. 5550
Stevenson, Robert L. 5691
Steward, Julian H. 4733
Stewart, Ellen 1138
Stewart, Gary L. 356
Stewart, George R. 1667
Stewart, George W. 2935
Stewart, Lawrence D. 7374
Stewart, R. S. 6172
Stewart, Walter P. 4106
Stickney, Dorothy 865, 4404
Stiles, H. R. 2322
Stillwell, Janet E. 2177
Stine, Lawrence C. 2651
Stine, Richard D. 2598
Stiver, Harry E. 3774, 4990
Stock, Morgan E. 1755
Stock, William H. 926
Stoddard, Richard 452, 656, 2140
Stoddard, Robert 453, 1859

Stoddard, Roger E. 2136, 5355, 5383, 5395, 5445, 5452
Stoddart, Dayton 4375
Stoddart, James H. 4405
Stoehr, Taylor 208
Stoll, Donald R. 6584
Stolp, Dorothy E. 3675
Stolzenbach, Norma F. 2523
Stone, Delza H. 2682
Stone, Ezra C. 1523
Stone, Fred 4406
Stone, Henry D. 2968
Stone, John Augustus 6913
Stone, Mary Isabella 3449
Stone, P. M. 2125–2126, 2130
Stone, Robert B. 998
Stone, Rosaline B. 4562
Stone, Susannah H. 1813
Storms, A. D. 3003
Stott, Jane 2424
Stout, Royal C. 1065
Stout, Wesley W. 7388
Stowell, Donald 713
Stoyle, Judith 2816
Strang, Lewis C. 1436, 2994, 3000, 3006–3008, 7205–7206
Strange, Michael [= Oelrichs, Blanche] 3335
Stransky, Judith 998
Strasberg, Lee 936, 1077, 3598, 4411
Strasberg, Susan 4410
Strasser-Vill, Susanne 7307
Stratman, Carl J. 26, 33
Straton, John R. 308
Stratton, Clarence 1056, 4907
Straumanis, Alfreds 1693
Straus, Stefan 4117
Straus, Todd T. 4605
Strauss, Mary 2244
Strenkovsky, Serge 740
Stresau, Hermann 7090
Strickland, Francis C. 885
Strogoff, Gordon 4612
Strong, Eve E. 2289
Strong, Harry H. 398
Stroupe, John H. 6889
Struck, James A. 5050
Stuart, Donald C. 5589
Stuart, William 3579
Stucky, Nathan P. 6979
Stump, Walter R. 1248
Sturcken, Francis 2641
Sturgis, Granville F. 303
Sturtevant, Catherine 1905
Stutman, Suzanne 3405
Sucke, Greer W. 5251
Sullivan, Claudia N. 1037, 1053
Sullivan, Gerald E. 3559
Sullivan, Leo E. 2778
Sullivan, Thelma L. 7029
Sullivan, William G. 1947
Summers, Jay C. 7129
Summers, Louis J. 7257
Sumner, Mark R. 4935, 4938, 4940–4941
Sumpter, Clyde G. 1318
Suskin, Steven 7301, 7318
Sutherland, J. M. 4838
Sutton, Graham 6734
Suzuki, Tadashi 1023

Svensson, Bo 6812
Swain, James W. 3665
Swan, Mark E. 5412
Swank, Cynthia G. 82
Swanson, Alan M. 6686
Swanson, Alice H. 2236
Sweet, Bruce 3584
Sweet, Harvey 6823
Sweet, Jeffrey 1942
Swerdlove, Dorothy L. 82
Swift, Elliott C. 2902
Swinburne, Algernon C. 4089
Swindell, Larry 3788, 4429
Swinney, Donald H. 1466
Swiss, Cheryl D. 3732, 5053
Switzer, Theodore R. 2652
Swortzell, Lowell 4786, 5187, 5265
Swortzell, Nancy F. 6530
Syle, Louis D. 4619
Sylvander, Carolyn W. 6237
Symons, Arthur. 4064
Sypher, F. J. 85
Szanto, George H. 5621
Szczublewski, Jozef 4119, 4123, 4128
Szeliski, John Von 5512
Szendrey, Thomas 1693
Szilassy, Zoltan 1646
Szondi, Peter 5571
Szydlowski, Roman 1605

Tabbert, Jonathan C. 5176
Taber, Elizabeth S. 740
Tabor, Catherine-A. 3914
Tackel, Martin S. 1488
Tadie, Nancy B. 5073
Taft, Kendall B. 5470, 7197
Tailleur, Roger 3958
Tairov, Alexander 6858
Talarowski, Joseph 5034
Talbott, David S. 2000
Taliaferro, James 5745
Tall, Broughton [= Tall, Stanley B.] 4621
Tallcott, Rollo A. 827
Talley, Paul M. 7342
Tambimutto 2955
Tammany, Jane F. 6041
Tanner, Fran A. 5196
Tanner, Jo 3125
Tanner, Virginia 5187
Tanney, Michael J. 6581
Tanselle, G. Thomas 7057
Taper, Bernard 2137
Tapia, J. E. 5294
Targ, William 5433
Tarkington, Booth 2934, 3672, 4434
Tarrach, Dean A. 4868
Tarshis, Barry 938
Tasistro, Louis F. 3149
Tatar, Ray. 1805
Tate, Hilary 664
Taubman, Howard 1302
Taubman, Joseph 226
Taylor, Betty S, 7432
Taylor, Deems 7422
Taylor, Dorothy J. 3969
Taylor, Douglas 3674, 4040
Taylor, Dwight 7036

Taylor, Emerson G. 1055
Taylor, Guy S. 1196
Taylor, John R. 4484
Taylor, Justus H. 4414
Taylor, Karen M. 1548
Taylor, Laurette 4415
Taylor, Michael M. 3709
Taylor, Robert L. 3212, 3707
Taylor, Robin 6036
Taylor, Rogan P. 5561
Taylor, Rosemary 1844
Taylor, Theodore 7449
Taylor, W. Ellard 2232
Taylor, William E. 5919, 7149
Teague, Anna D. 4402
Teague, Oran B. 2029
Tebbe, Margaret M. 3916
Tedesco, John L. 5942
Tedford, Harold 1723
Teer, Barbara Ann 5394
Tees, Arthur Thomas 4393
Teichmann, Howard 3736, 4540, 6571
Telford, Robert S. 785
Tellegen, Lou 4418
Temkin, Pauline B. 1589
Temple, Laura 2674
Ter-Arutunian, Rouben 4419
Terlecki, Tyman 4120
Terry, Jim 7332
Terry, Megan 2888, 5979
Tessier, André 4006
Tetauer, Frank 6858
Teter, Harry 2788
Thaiss, Christopher J. 1350
Tharpe, Jac 7149
Thatcher, Neil G. 1349
Thiede, Richard W. 5069
This, James L. 1807
Thomas D. Pawley 1368
Thomas, Augustus 6501, 7040
Thomas, Beverly J. 724
Thomas, Bob 3522, 4132, 7408
Thomas, Gladys 4045
Thomas, John Charles 3294
Thomas, Lowell 4319
Thomas, Marjorie 5686
Thomas, Tony 7332
Thomason, D. R. 282
Thompson, Alan R. 5475, 5477
Thompson, David W. 5646
Thompson, E. C. S. 6291
Thompson, Florence L. 2508
Thompson, Isabel C. 2228
Thompson, James R. 600
Thompson, Joseph P. 276
Thompson, Judith J. 7149, 7176
Thompson, M. Francesca 1368
Thompson, Marion S. 3073
Thompson, Mary F. 2408
Thompson, Paula J. 2057
Thompson, Raymond L. 935
Thompson, Robert Farris 1368
Thomson, Ruth G. 5372
Thornburg, Opal 1946
Thorndike, Ashley 5996
Thornton, Helen 71
Thorpe, William H. 325
Thorson, Lillian T. 1911
Throckmorton, Cleon 2338
Thune, Ensof Z. 6020

Thunen, Frances H. 1767, 1776
Thurber, James 5847
Thurman, Bedford 4544
Thurman, William R. 5907
Thurston, Frederick C. 2059
Tichy, Charles A. 2252
Tidwell, James N. 6913
Tift, Thomas N. 5177
Tillinghast, John K. 4079
Tillson, M. W. 5653
Timberlake, Craig 3373
Timpane, J. 5979
Tims, Margaret 3269
Tinapp, A. Richard 1473
Tinsley, James R. 5442
Tischler, Nancy 7148–7149, 7160
Tiusanen, Timo 6796, 6833, 6858
Tobias, Henry. 3138
Tobias, Richard C. 7047
Tobin, Robert L. B. 730
Tobin, Terence 6152
Todd, Harold J. 6068
Todd, Therald F. 2734
Toffler, Alvin 227
Tolan, Robert W. 1952
Tolch, C. J. 5264
Toll, Robert C. 1482, 1489, 4714, 4774
Tollini, Frederick P. 4210
Tolson, Julius H. 6304
Tomasek, Paul 2501
Tompkins, Dorothy L. 607
Tompkins, Eugene 2100
Tompkins, Juliet Wilbor 7003
Toner, J. M. 379
Toner, Marijo C. 458
Toner, Robert L. 6250
Toohey, John L. 5374
Topham, Helen A. 1882
Torelli, Maria 7098
Törnqvist, Egil 6803, 6833, 6893–6894
Torre, Nestor U. 1642
Torrents, John E. 7035
Toscan, Richard E. 2138
Touchet, Gene R. 5943
Toulmin, Mary D. 1350
Towne, Charles H. 2341, 3208, 7418
Towns, Saundra 6487
Townsend, George A. 3453
Townsend, Margaret 2987
Towse, John R. 4427
Towson, John H. 4876
Tozier, Roy B. 5270
Tracy, Virginia. 3133
Tranter, Charles R. 2626
Traoré, Bakory 1325
Trapido, Joel 97
Traube, Shepard 5319
Trauth, Suzanne M. 1183
Traylor, Eleanor W. 1368
Treadwell, Bill 1459
Treib, Manfred 6181
Trent, Spi M. 4324
Trent, W. P. 6990
Trescott, Pamela 3891
Treser, Robert M. 2698
Trewin, J. C. 6668
Triesch, Gisela 6804
Triesch, Manfred 6457

Trilling, Diana 6172
Trilling, Lionel 5788, 6077
Trinka, Zena I. 4243
Triplett, Robert 1006
Tripp, Ellen L. 2877
Tripp, Lloyd M. 2801
Troiani, Elisa A. 1369
Trollope, Frances 3146
Trotter, James M. 7202
Troupe, Quincy 6241
Truax, Sarah 4431
Trulsson, Berton E. 1748
Trumble, Alfred 2971, 2973, 4432
Trussler, Simon 57
Tryon, George W. 293
Tryon, John 4710
Tryon, Virginia V. 3309
Tuck, Susan. 6858
Tucker, Laurence E. 1912
Tucker, Sophie 7450
Tumbleson, Treva R. 3104
Tumbusch, Marty 7243
Tumbusch, Tom 7235, 7243
Tunney, Kieran 3323
Tupper, Frederick 7056
Turbyfill, Subert 5112
Turgeon, Thomas S. 4477
Turnbull, Robert 269
Turner, Darwin T. 1368, 2355, 6234, 6538
Turner, Dennis G. 5536
Turner, Mary M. 3126
Turner, S. H. Regina 5967
Turner, Victor 5544–5545, 5567
Turner, Vivian D. 2008
Turner, Willis L. 5726
Turnipseed, La M. 1705
Turpin, W. E. 6234
Turtledove, Cyndi 1805
Tutor, Richard M. 2174
Tybor, M. Martina 1693
Tyce, Richard 6188
Tyler, Gary R. 4680
Tyler, George C. 4434
Tyler, Henry M. 4957
Tyler, Mary Palmer 7056
Tyler, Moses C. 5695
Tyler, Pamela F. 1743
Tyler, Royall 7054–7055
Tynan, Ken 5917

Ulrich, Carolyn F. 4667, 6858, 1453
Umlas, Rodney J. 5968
Underwood, Peter 3953
Unger, Leonard 6099
Unger, Wilhelm 2905
Unterbrink, Mary. 3120
Urban, Joseph 392, 550, 1513
Utley, Francis L. 4714
Utterback, James 537
Utz, Kathryn E. 2519

Vahland, Barbara 7144
Vail, Robert W. G. 4347
Valgemae, Mardi 5869
Vallee, Rudy 7451–7452
Vallillo, Stephen M. 82, 7357
Van Antwerp, Margaret A. 7165
Van Doren, Mark 6564
Van Dornum, Jack H. 7117

Van Druten, John 5434, 7061–7062
Van Dyke, Leon J. 956
Van Dyke, Mary 5148
Van Erven, Eugene 1656
Van Itallie, Jean-Claude 6094
Van Kirk, Gordon 1907
Van Laan, Thomas F. 5509
Van Lennep, William 144
Van Nostrand, Albert D. 7030
Van Tassel, Wesley 5244
Van Vechten, Carl 1443, 3179, 7374
Van Wyck, Frederick 2342
Van Zanten, John 364
Vance, Mary 461
Vance, Nina 1579
Vandenhoff, George 4441
Vardac, A. Nicholas 1078
Vardamis, Alex A. 6566
Varnado, Alban F. 2018
Varney, George Leon 3326
Vaskelis, Bronius 1693
Vaughan, Stuart 1596
Vaughn, Jack A. 6118
Vaughn, Robert F. 202, 1549
Veiller, Bayard 7064
Velez, Sara 82
Vena, Gary 6890
Ventimiglia, Peter J. 3636
Ver Nooy, Winifred 5351
Vermilye, Jerry 3648
Verne H. Porter 3263
Vernon, Grenville 7459
Viagas, Robert 7330
Vidal, Gore 6094, 7065, 7171
Vidor, King 457
Viertel, Salka 3241
Vigneault, Ronald P. 1137
Vignol, Philippe du 4131
Vilhauer, William W. 2133
Villard, Léonie 1275, 1471, 5896
Vince, R. W. 1261
Vincent, John H. 5266
Vincent, John R. 5267
Vincentini, Claudio 1624
Vineberg, Steve E. 1024
Vineyard, Hazel 2279
Vining, Roscoe H. 5711
Vinson, James 6134
Voelker, Paul 6893
Vogel, Dan 5522
Völklein, Sonja 7302
Volland, Virginia 708
Volz, Jim 1713
Von Szeliski, John J. 5905
Von Tornow, Georgiana J. 5720
Voorhees, Marietta 571
Vorenberg, William 4032
Vorlicky, Robert H. 5697
Vorse, Mary M. 2120
Vos, Nelvin 6155
Vosburgh, David 953
Vreeland, Frank 5323
Vunovich, Nancy 6789

Waack, William L. 5338
Waddell, Richard E. 2755
Waddy, Lawrence 367
Wade, Jere D. 1792
Wade, Leslie 1263

Wagenknecht, Edward 3061, 3063, 3810, 6524
Wager, Walter 6083
Wager, Willis 5206
Wagner, Charles L. 3203
Wagner, Frederick 3059
Wagner, Hilda S. 4992
Wagner, Jean 6098
Wagner, Jearnine 5228
Wagner, Philip 6654
Wagner, Phyllis J. 2888, 7037
Wainscott, Ronald H. 6891
Waite, J. Richard 4445
Walcutt, Charles C. 6731
Waldau, Roy S. 2954
Walden, Daniel 374
Waldera, Jean 2497
Waldman, Max 4168, 4691
Waldo, Arthur L. 1693
Waldo, Lewis P. 6007
Waldo, Paul R. 3944
Waldron, James A. 4618
Walker, Ethel Pitts 1368
Walker, Franklin D. 1738
Walker, J. 5085
Walker, John A. 484, 494
Walker, Mrs D. 3616
Walker, Phillip N. 1793, 4973
Walker, William S. 1887
Walkup, Fairfax P. 705
Wall, Vincent 4676
Wallace, David H. 3236
Wallace, James D. 2201
Wallace, Karl R. 883
Wallace, Lew 7072
Wallace, Raymond V. 4595
Wallace, William J. 786
Wallack, Lester 4449
Waller, Adrian 4945
Wallis, J. V. 6813
Wallis, Severn T. 2062
Waln, Robert 2569
Walser, Richard 6418
Walsh, Alice W. 2690
Walsh, Charles R. 1401
Walsh, Frederick G. 5774
Walsh, James J. 5202
Walsh, Thommie 7330
Walsh, Townsend 6300
Walsh, William H. 4421
Walter, Eugene 5411
Walters, Walter H. 4574
Walton, Elsie M. 1709
Walton, James H. 2254
Wank, Eugene M. 2411
Wann, Jack K. 6351
Wansey, Henry 1381
Ward, Carlton. 98
Ward, Royal A. 3906
Ward, Willie P. 2017
Ward, Winifred 5096, 5108, 5207
Warde, Frederick 4453–4454
Wardrip, Mark A. 5079
Ware, Jno F. W. 289
Ware, Ralph H. 5714
Ware, Robert G. 6178
Warfel, William B. 526, 538
Warfield, David 4455
Warfield, Jack W. 2799
Warford, Aaron A. 800
Warman, Edward B. 813

Warner, Frank L. 5035
Warren, Lisa C. 6315
Warren, Neilla 3667
Warshow, Robert 6676, 6903
Warye, Richard J. 4937
Washburn, Charles 764
Washington, Rhonnie L. 4608
Washington, Von H. 6347
Wasserman, Bruce M. 2770
Wasserman, Julian N. 6184
Wasserman, Nina M. 1193
Wasserman, Steven R. 91
Waterman, Arthur 6407
Watermeier, Daniel J. 3444, 3449
Waters, Clara E. 3618
Waters, Edward N. 7387
Waters, Ethel 4463–4464
Waters, Walter K. 491, 3308
Watkins, Dwight E. 864
Watkins, Floyd C. 6912
Watkinson, Sharon A. 6845
Watson, Charles S. 2647, 6091
Watson, Harmon S. 1359
Watson, Lee 544
Watson, Leland H. 512
Watson, Margaret G. 2268
Watson, Thomas S. 416
Watson, Thomas J. 3315
Watt, Stephen. 1502
Wattenberg, Richard J. 6987
Wattron, Frank J. 5219
Watts, John G. 239
Watts, Stephen 857
Waugh, Frank A. 388
Waugh, Howard 763
Waugh, Jennie 1451
Wayburn, Ned 831
Weales, Gerald 5904, 5924, 5979, 6172, 6633, 6674, 6676, 6683–6684, 6906, 7127, 7148
Weales, Gerald C. 5444
Wear, Elizabeth 5002
Wearing, J. P. 3096
Weaver, Arden W. 3990
Weaver, Richard A. 6932
Webb, Dorothy L. 2618
Webb, J. Edgar 3715
Weber, Alfred 5875
Weber, Brom 6223
Weber, C. 5085
Webster, Glenn R. 568
Webster, Margaret 1077, 4467–4468, 4470–4471
Webster, Mary V. 1801
Wedge, Margaret B. 2165
Wedwick, Daryl M. 522
Weese, Stanley 489
Wegelin, Oscar 4238, 5345, 6364, 6367, 7198
Wegner, Pamela S. 2831
Wehlburg, Albert F. 529, 5161
Wehrum, Victoria 1329
Weichman, Louis J. 3480
Weidenthal, Leo 2507
Weidner, R. W. 527
Weil, Dorothy 4348
Weiland, Richard J. 5513
Weinberg, Mark S. 1364
Weiner, Ed 4349
Weiner, Sydell S. 1816
Weinfeld, Samuel L. 1949

Weingarten, Aaron 6032
Weingarten, Joseph A. 15
Weinman, Richard J. 6204
Weinstein, Norman 7015
Weir, James 2657
Weisert, John J. 1991, 1993, 1996–1997
Weisman, John 1610
Weisman, Martha 5858
Weiss, Burton 2909
Weiss, David W. 4104
Weiss, Elisabeth 6736
Weiss, Gunther 7307
Weissberger, L. Arnold. 3065
Weissman, Philip 5495
Weisstuch, Mark 2957
Weist, Elizabeth M. 6590
Weitz, C. E. 483
Welch, Elizabeth 4813
Welch, Mildred [= Lane, Margaret] 330
Welker, David 627, 657, 1147
Welland, Dennis 6684, 6700
Weller, Betty H. 3357
Weller, Janet H. 2415
Wellman, Paul I. 3215
Wells, Henry W. 3507
Wells, Rhea 696
Wellwarth, George 5598
Welsch, James D. 4970
Welsh, Helen C. 5103
Welsh, John D. 7224
Welsh, Willard 5777
Wemyss, Francis C. 1387, 4488
Wenger, John 550
Wenstrom, David D. 5226
Wente, William C. 1774
Wentworth, Brenda K. 733
Wentz, John C. 2602
Werner, Edgar S. 4618
Wertenbaker, Lael 4340
Wertheim, Albert V. 6111
Weslyn, Louis 4725
West, Constance C. 6675
West, Dorothy H. 5365
West, L. Edna 4575
West, Mae 4490–4491
West, Paul 7078
West, Susan K. 2239
West, William F. 2229
West, William R. 1862A
Westbrook, Virginia 2014
Westerfield, William A. 5171
Westerman, Susan 6171
Westfall, Alfred van R. 4572
Westhafer, Steven J. 5036
Weston, Effie E. 3688
Weston, Pearl O. 1279
Wetzel, Jo Anne 5262
Wetzel, William 568
Weyant, George W. 4076
Whaley, Frank L. 436, 639
Whalon, Marion K. 84
Wharton, John F. 2363, 2941
Wharton, Robert T. 2451
Wheatley, William T. 905
Wheeler, Charles R. 1410
Wheeler, David M. 2457
Wheeler, Hugh 2407
Wheeler, Lucy P. 2434
Wheeler, Roger 759

Wheelwright, J. T. 4962
Whicher, G. F. 5652
Whiffen, Mrs Thomas 4497
Whips, Clara E. 1064
Whitaker, D. 6791
Whitaker, Thomas R. 7109
White, Alice 865
White, Edwin C. 902
White, Irle E. 5018
White, Jean W. 2376
White, Kenneth S. 5620
White, Leslie 6867
White, Mark 7284
White, Melvin R. 920
White, Natalie E. 2346
White, Ray L. 6224–6225
White, Richard K. 7290
White, Sidney H. 6506, 6681
Whitebrook, Peter 7027
Whitehead, Bruce 82
Whitehead, Marjorie 4400
Whiteside, Anna 1166
Whitesides, Glenn 6458
Whitfield, Vantile 1138
Whiting, Frank M. 1223, 2206
Whiting, Lilian 3706
Whitlatch, Michael D. 209
Whitlatch, R. C. 3644
Whitman, Charles W. 357
Whitman, Robert F. 6776
Whitman, Walt 4627
Whitman, Willson 2848
Whitney, Horace G. 2719
Whittington-Egan, Richard 3677
Whitton, Joseph 3009, 7203
Whorf, Richard B. 759
Wikoff, Henry 4501
Wilbur, Cheryl R. 1788
Wilbur, James Benjamin 7055
Wilcox, Robert H. 5546
Wildbihler, Hubert 7302
Wilde, Larry. 3069
Wilder, Alec 7244
Wilder, Amos N. 7099
Wilder, Isabel 7103
Wilder, Marshall P. 3162, 3171
Wilder, Thornton 5422, 7097, 7106
Wiley, Charles 5840
Wiley, David W. 4129
Wilfred, Thomas 614
Wilk, John R. 2825
Wilk, Max 4503, 4527
Wilker, Lawrence J. 3513
Wilkerson, Margaret B. 1368, 1700, 1794, 5988
Wilkins, Frederick C. 6893
Wilkins, Jeanne 6220
Wilkinson, Alfred O. 2215
Wilkinson, Colleen M. 2221A
Willard, Frances 2983
Willard, George O. 2635
Willenbrink, Robert H. 5261
William, Raymond 6676
Williams, Allen 1139, 5158
Williams, Anne St C. 2482, 2754
Williams, Dakin 7164
Williams, Edwina D. 7119
Williams, Elwood P. 2866
Williams, Henry L. 3281
Williams, J. E. 212

Williams, Jay 1481
Williams, Jesse Lynch 5413
Williams, Judith W. 6839
Williams, Kenneth R. 1176
Williams, Mance 1644
Williams, Merrell 6338
Williams, Philip M. 7193
Williams, Richard A. 6212
Williams, Sherley A. 5936
Williams, Stanley T. 6292
Williams, Tennessee 5430, 5788, 7142, 7154
Willis, Eola 2638
Willis, J. Robert 1140
Willis, John 1334, 1570
Willis, R. A. 2828
Willis, Richard 425
Willis, S. A. 6138
Willoughby, Pearl V. 5811
Wills, Arthur 6579
Wills, Garry 6470
Wills, J. Robert 1150, 4019
Willson, Clair E. 1718
Willson, Loretta L. 1961
Willson, Meredith 7455
Wilmeth, Don B. 46, 53, 60, 90, 1487, 3487, 3934, 4783, 5979
Wilshire, Bruce 5547
Wilson, Adrian 1766
Wilson, Arthur H. 2588
Wilson, Bertha A. 2513
Wilson, Crae J. 4216
Wilson, Don 1058
Wilson, Earl 3258, 4741, 4769, 4775
Wilson, Edmund 1564
Wilson, Edwin 1249, 1255
Wilson, Eloise 6937
Wilson, Francis 3462, 3922, 4505–4508
Wilson, Garff B. 919, 1327
Wilson, Glenn 5562
Wilson, Jack A. 2167
Wilson, James G. 6053
Wilson, John M. 948
Wilson, Karen P. 790
Wilson, Louis 336
Wilson, Margery 4510
Wilson, Netta W. 6381
Wilson, Robert 1935, 6894
Wilson, Robert J. 2834
Wilson, Timothy 2908
Wilstach, Paul 4047
Wilt, James N. 1901
Wimsatt, Mary A. 6994
Winbigler, Hugh D. 5105
Winchell, Cedric R. 6164
Winchell, Walter 3834
Winchester, Clarence. 3037
Winchester, Otis R. 6767, 6833
Winchester, S. G. 272
Winchester, Thomas P. 177
Windeler, Robert 4251
Winderl, Ronda R. 376
Winders, Gertrude 7354
Windham, Donald 7145
Winford, Edgar C. 3052
Wingate, Charles E. 2079, 2089, 2989–2991
Winget, Jack B. 3901
Winkelbauer, Stefanie M. 728

Winner, Carole A. 5948
Winnie, John R. 4931
Winship, Frank L. 5119
Winship, Loren 5120
Winsten, Lynne R. 2958
Winter, Jefferson 4520
Winter, Willam. 2982
Winter, William 2977
Winter, William. 2979
Winter, William 3017–3018, 3021, 3025, 3327, 3368, 3421–3422, 3794, 3919, 4048, 4081, 4266, 4285, 4514–4518, 4521, 6321
Winters, Earle 1828
Winters, Shelley 4526
Winther, Sophus K. 6768
Wise, C. M. 697
Wise, Jennings C. 1393
Wismer, Lawrence H. 5786
Witham, Barry 2864
Witham, Barry B. 6350
Withers, Nan W. 3483
Witherspoon, John 261
Witmark, Isidore 4738
Witsen, Leo V. 722
Witt, Daniel M. 1177
Wittenberg, Philip 188
Wittke, Carl 4734
Wittler, Clarence J. 5821
Wodehouse, P. G. 7456
Wohl, Davis 1168
Wolcott, John R. 2614
Wolf, Daniel 1578
Wolf, Laurie J. 82
Wolf, Rennold 4886
Wolf, Simon 6725
Wolfe, Donald H. 2884
Wolfe, Elton C. 6326
Wolfe, Irmgarde H. 5979
Wolfe, Welby B. 658
Wolfert, Wayne R. 2806
Woll, Allen 92, 7308
Wolle, Francis 6729
Wolle, Muriel S. 1080
Wollock, Abe 3991
Wolter, J. C. 5979
Wood, Audrey 4527
Wood, Bret 4487
Wood, Deborah-Jean 6433
Wood, Peggy 3673, 4529–4532
Wood, William B. 4534
Wood, William C. 332
Woodard, Debra J. 4037
Woodbridge, Elisabeth 5466
Woodbury, Lael J. 1141
Woodman, William E. 1846
Woodress, James 7031
Woodruff, Boykin M. 1712
Woodruff, Bruce E. 4083
Woodruff, John R. 2124
Woods, Alan 1244, 1333, 1487
Woods, Alan L. 1795
Woods, Bob 7154
Woods, Donald Z. 2186
Woods, Jeanne 3832
Woods, Porter 1356
Woods, Porter S. 1539
Woods, Robert A. 1900
Woodward, Robert H. 6400
Woolf, Allan 4725
Woolf, S. J. 3205

Woollcott, Alexander 180, 3055, 3718, 4535, 4537, 4540, 4631, 4634, 4639, 4654, 7333
Woolsey, Theodore S. 6366
Wooten, Denham L. 1721
Workman, John P. 4436
Workman, Thelma 1984
Works, Bernhard R. 3359
Worsley, Ronald 4472
Worth, Katharine 6138
Worthen, William B. 1018
Worthon, W. B. 6138
Wraith, Eugene M. 6776
Wright, Charles H. 4297
Wright, Darlene Van B. 2220
Wright, Edward A. 1238, 4586
Wright, Frances 7199–7200
Wright, Jack B. 2898
Wright, James C. 1687
Wright, James W. 1927
Wright, Lin 5154
Wright, Richardson 1395–1396
Wright, Richard 7201
Wright, Thomas K. 4496
Wright, William 6481
Wyatt, Edward A. 6328
Wyndham, Donald. 3139
Wyndham, Horace 4091, 4140–4141
Wynn [pseud.] 6599
Wynn, Keenan 4542
Wynn, Nancy E. 7052

Yaakov, Juliette 5365
Yacowar, Maurice 7150
Yanosky, Sabrina K. 4613
Yarcho, Yvonne V. 5014
Yeater, James W. 3622
Yeomans, Gordon A. 3611
Yocum, Jack H. 2691
Yonick, Cora J. 1914
York, Phil. 4911
York, Zack L. 4377
Young, Artee F. 4450
Young, Barrie J. 5164
Young, James 735
Young, John R. 2580
Young, John W. 1092, 1095, 4929, 4942
Young, Jordan R. 1048
Young, Margaret M. 1095
Young, Miriam 4865
Young, Roland. 3032
Young, Stark 832, 835, 1273, 1544, 3942, 4543, 4632, 4657, 4676, 6776
Young, Toni 1858
Young, William C. 158, 441, 3087
Youngerman, Henry C. 2794

Zabel, Morton D. 4551–3666
Zacek, Dennis C. 3442
Zachary, Samuel J. 5554
Zadan, Craig 7447
Zahlwer, William P. 5871
Zalk, Mark 941
Zanger, Brenda 645
Zapell, Alice L. 5861
Zastrow, Sylvia 5876
Zavin, Theodore S. 198
Zec, Donald 4413

Zeidman, Irving 4762
Zeigler, Joseph W. 1611
Zeisler, Peter 788, 1138
Zellers, Parker 4869
Zelver, Leslie H. 1762
Zeraffa, Michel 6757
Ziegfeld, Patricia 4556
Zif, Yael L. 5306
Zimand, Gertrude 191
Zimbaido, Rose A. 6172
Zimmerman, Leland L. 2849
Zinder, David G. 5537
Zingale, Jeanne W. 5885
Zinsmaster, W. M. 5132
Ziprodt, Patricia 645
Zirner, Laura 702
Zivanovic, Judith K. 468
Zolotow, Maurice 3051, 4025
Zolotow, Michael 3048
Zucchero, William H. 4195
Zukerman, Robert S. 7326
Zukor, Adolph 3216
Zurcher, Carl D. 6687
Zvonchenko, Walter 2461